Psychological Testing and Assessment

Psychological Testing and Assessment

An Introduction to Tests and Measurement

THIRD EDITION

Ronald Jay Cohen

ST. JOHN'S UNIVERSITY

Mark E. Swerdlik

ILLINOIS STATE UNIVERSITY

Suzanne M. Phillips

UNIVERSITY OF PITTSBURGH—JOHNSTOWN

MAYFIELD PUBLISHING COMPANY

Mountain View, California

London • Toronto

Copyright 1996, 1992, 1988 by Mayfield Publishing Company

All rights reserved. No portion of this book may be reproduced in any form or by any means without written permission of the publisher.

Library of Congress Cataloging-in-Publication Data

Cohen, Ronald Jay.
    Psychological testing and assessment : an introduction to tests and measurement / Ronald Jay Cohen, Mark E. Swerdlik, Suzanne M. Phillips. — 3rd ed.
       p. cm.
    Includes bibliographical references and index.
    ISBN 1-55934-427-X
    1. Psychological tests.   I. Swerdlik, Mark E.   II. Phillips, Suzanne M.   III. Title.
BF176.C63   1995
150'.28'7—dc20
                                              95-16822
                                            CIP

Manufactured in the United States of America
10 9 8 7 6 5

Mayfield Publishing Company
1280 Villa Street
Mountain View, California 94041

Sponsoring editor, Franklin C. Graham; production editor, April Wells-Hayes; manuscript editor, Carol Crouse; text designer, Cloyce J. Wall; cover image, Glenn Mitsui; illustrator, Judith Ogus; art editor, Susan Breitbard; art director and cover designer, Jeanne M. Schreiber; manufacturing manager, Amy Folden. The text was set in 10/12 Palatino by G&S Typesetters, Inc., and printed on 45# Glatfelter Restorecote by R. R. Donnelley & Sons Co.

Acknowledgments and copyrights continue on pages C1–C2, which constitute an extension of the copyright page.

 This book is printed on recycled paper.

Contents

Contents

2   Historical, Cultural, and Legal/Ethical Considerations   41

PART **2** *The Science of Psychological Measurement*   *8 3*

7   Test Development   218

PART **4** *Personality Assessment*   *381*

11 Personality Assessment: Overview and Objective Methods   **382**

13 Other Personality and Behavioral Measures 464

PART 5 *Testing and Assessment in Action*   *511*

14 Clinical and Counseling Assessment   **512**

17 Industrial/Organizational Assessment   633

18 Consumer Assessment   672

Preface

In the years since the first edition of this book was published, interest in the field of psychological testing and assessment has been expanding dramatically. Evidence of this renewed interest can be seen in the form of new assessment-related journals, as well as a growing array of assessment-related books, articles, and computer accessories. We are proud of the part we have played, however large or small, in stimulating student interest in this field through the creation of a user-friendly teaching system that helps make learning about—and teaching—measurement an enjoyable and intellectually stimulating task. With this third edition, the tradition continues in the form of a teaching system that consists of this textbook, an instructor's manual (Swerdlik & Phillips, 1996), a test bank (Swerdlik, Cohen & Phillips, 1996), and a companion student workbook and study guide entitled *101 Exercises in Psychological Testing and Assessment* (Cohen, 1996).

Before the publication of the first edition of this book, a tacit assumption about measurement textbooks seemed to prevail. Probably dating back to the mid-1950s, the assumption was that a comprehensive measurement textbook was of necessity challenging for students to get through. Given such a widely held expectation, it is hardly surprising that psychological testing textbooks have been jokingly characterized as rites of passage. Knowing the reputation of the textbooks, students became more and more reluctant to take psychological testing courses. For that reason, and considering other factors, including academic battles about the existence of psychological traits, many psychology departments changed the status of the testing course from mandatory to optional for psychology and education majors. In deference to the complaints of students, and perhaps even the concerns of some faculty members about teaching psychological testing from the available textbooks, the testing course was offered only infrequently at some universities, if not dropped altogether. Thus, even though psychological testing was unquestionably a core subject within psychology in the eyes of many, school after school did not find it desirable to offer the course on a regular basis.

Even as enrollments in psychological testing courses dwindled, most instructors through the 1970s and much of the 1980s continued to rely on 1950s-vintage psychological testing texts. Clearly, such textbooks continued to offer the only available authoritative and comprehensive treatment of the subject; whether they were user-friendly was a secondary or tertiary consideration. Another (more emotional than rational) reason to use such books was that they were the very same books from which the instructors themselves had learned about psychological testing.

By the late 1980s, change was long overdue. Many instructors were using the same psychological testing material for undergraduate and graduate courses, and not finding it entirely satisfactory for either audience. Also, as I reflected in the first edition of the present work, existing texts had other problems:

> As I look back on my own experience with psychological testing textbooks through undergraduate, master's-, and doctoral level training, I remember being keenly aware of lack of a hands-on "feel" in the writing; while comprehensive and technically sound, these textbooks were written, to put it charitably, very, very dryly. . . . In fact, some colleagues half-jokingly advised, "If you're going to write a measurement text, make sure it's not very clear." Asked why, they responded, "Because if the writing's clear, few measurement experts and statisticians will think it's very good." (Cohen et al., 1988, p. xx)

Contrary to such well-intentioned advice, the writing in our book was designed to be clear and engaging. Pedagogical aids, including "Close-up" features, photos, and brief biographies of luminaries in testing and assessment, were included. The "feel" of the book with reference to the tests discussed was decidedly hands-on. In my capacity as a clinical psychology intern and then Senior Psychologist at Bellevue Hospital in Manhattan, I had actually administered and supervised the administration of many of the psychological tests discussed. Authors of competing books did not have that same kind of hands-on experience with tests, and that void was apparent in their writing, most noticeably in chapters having to do with clinical and educational testing.

In 1988, the first edition of our book was published. And just as many consumers understandably stuck with the "safe" choice of IBM or AT&T in the face of the introduction of competitors such as Apple or MCI, so many instructors stuck with a more traditional choice of measurement textbook. Still, some instructors were intent on using the best possible textbook for a new generation of students, even if that meant venturing forward with something brand new. For those instructors, time-worn teaching notes (keyed to a text first introduced 34 years before our first edition was published!) had to be traded in. What they were traded-in for, however, was not just a textbook but an integrated teaching system. Beyond the fresh and contemporary perspective of a new and comprehensive textbook, we developed an instructor's manual for the measurement course that was truly an instructor's manual and not just a test-item bank. Another key element of the teaching package was a student's workbook replete with innovative exercises designed to foster active learning of the subject matter, not merely student playback of the textbook's content.

Research conducted by our publisher has since confirmed that few, if any, of the instructors who switched to our book from whatever they were using before have switched again to any other textbook; with every successive year, the base of instructors using our book has grown. Why?

Instructors have found our textbook to be reasonably comprehensive, and yet different from other comprehensive measurement textbooks in several key ways. Perhaps most important, our book strives to create a dialogue with students, speaking to them and encouraging them to think about and cognitively process the material. We genuinely care about communicating with students. Each page has been written and rewritten with the intention of fostering student understanding of the material. We believe that the care and concern invested in the writing of each page comes through to students. Technical material is presented with sensitivity to the student's understanding. New terms are introduced gradually, laying the proper groundwork for the introduction of more new terms. Throughout, we have tried to keep the tone of our work scholarly yet conversational—even when discussing topics so technical that only psychometricians would raise them in conversation.

Over the years, we have also tried to be responsive to the needs of users of this text. We have replied to every letter sent to us by instructors and students. We keep records of letter writers' suggestions and possible modifications in the text for future editions. And even when instructors do not take the initiative to write to us, we have taken the initiative to reach out to them. In fact, one routine mailing seeking response from a sampling of instructors using our second edition yielded rather momentous results. . . .

A letter requesting instructor reaction to our second edition was sent to Professor Peter Peregoy who, according to our publisher's records, taught the measurement course at the University of Pittsburgh, Johnstown. Professor Peregoy forwarded our letter to his colleague, Professor Suzanne M. Phillips, who taught the course more regularly than he did. Professor Phillips wrote us a thoughtful and thought-provoking letter that said, in part, "I think that the text is probably among the best for the students which I teach, but I believe that it has a basic flaw which most texts in this area seem to share. . . . The problem is that parts of the text which focus on the specific tests are too encyclopedic to serve as a teaching tool. . . ."

By way of background, one of our criticisms of many existing texts was that they tended to bear too much resemblance to *Tests in Print* in some sections. In contrast, our own objective in discussing psychometric aspects of various kinds of tests had been to illustrate how those tests meet or fail to meet certain psychometric criteria. Specific tests were discussed for the purpose of integrating facts about their structure, scoring, and interpretation into a more global understanding of general measurement theory, practice, and issues. Still, Professor Phillips's concerns—presumably representative of some segment of the instructor population using our book—had to be addressed. In response to her letter and subsequent correspondence, we began charting a course that would provide for more "anchoring" of discussion of various tests to psychometric principles. This would be accomplished by weaving more psychometric-related material throughout the text and the *Close-up*s and by creating a new feature, *Everyday Psychometrics,* designed to elaborate on such issues in professional and everyday life. Who better to assist us with all of this rewriting than Suzanne M. Phillips? The correspondence between us caused us to take note not only of Professor Phillips's ideas but also of her writing style, which we believed students would find as accessible and "friendly" as our own. Hence, what started as a query addressed to one instructor resulted in a writing collaboration with another. We welcome Suzanne's contribution to this third edition and look forward to working with her in subsequent editions.

In addition to being a bit more focused on the application of psychometric principles than previous editions, this third edition of our text responds to the needs expressed by other instructors who have written to us asking for more discussion of topics such as (1) culture-related issues in test development and test use; (2) fairness and bias in testing; (3) assumptions inherent in the assessment enterprise; (4) qualitative item analysis; and (5) portfolio and "authentic" assessment. If you are one of the instructors who wrote to us about one of these issues (or any other), we hope that this edition demonstrates to you that we took your suggestions to heart.

This textbook is designed to be a tool for instructors who teach a course, and the students who take a course, variously called "Psychological Testing," "Psychological Assessment," "Psychological Measurement," "Testing and Assessment in Education," and so forth. Two lessons we have learned since the publication of our first edition are that (1) as a group, the instructors who use our book do so with a very wide range of objectives regarding technical aspects of psychological testing and assessment and (2) it is impossible to please all of the instructors all of the time. Consider, for example, that we have on file requests from instructors variously asking for more or less coverage of relatively technical material such as the multitrait-multimethod matrix and the kappa statistic. How could such requests be fielded in the best interest of all concerned?

The second edition of our text ran a total of 886 pages. Although that was only about 70 pages more than the comparable edition of a competitive text, we still believed that the book had to be edited down to a more manageable length for use in a one-semester or one-quarter course. Hence, on the criterion of length alone, the discussion of a technique such as the multitrait-multimethod matrix, which already occupied some half-dozen pages in the second edition, could not be lengthened. In an effort to reduce the overall length of the book, and still be at liberty to add new material and updating where necessary, we shifted some of the material that we believed was not being used by many instructors to the student workbook. Thus, for example, instructors who would like to cover the multitrait-multimethod matrix in detail will find detailed coverage and useful exercises on pages 82–87 in the companion student workbook (Cohen, 1996). Instructors familiar with previous editions of this text will find some features of the main text now transferred to the student workbook.

The seven objectives outlined in the first edition and carried through in the second edition remain unchanged in this third edition. It remains our intention to

1. Provide a thorough, state-of-the-art, and readable description of basic measurement concepts at a level of technical complexity sufficient to equip students to understand technical terms in professional journals, test manuals, and test reports

2. Present up-to-date, reasonably detailed, and well-balanced discussion of various issues in measurement ranging from the issue of heritability in intelligence, to general legal/ethical issues, to administration, scoring, and interpretation concerns with respect to computer-assisted psychological assessment

3. Blend theoretical and applied material in a way so as to provide the student with both a rationale for, and a hands-on feel of, the assessment process

4. Provide ample case illustrations of the wide range of "real world" contexts in which psychological testing and assessment occurs, including clinical,

counseling, neuropsychological, educational, industrial/organizational, and consumer contexts

5. Provide a historical perspective on measurement complete with biographical material on many important contributors such as Alfred Binet, David Wechsler, Hermann Rorschach, Henry Murray, David Rappaport, and Lauretta Bender

6. To excite genuine interest in the field of testing and assessment by writing with warmth, even occasional humor, and liberally illustrating with relevant material

7. To impart a sense of the authors' belief in and respect for the psychological assessment enterprise balanced by a healthy and realistic degree of self-criticism and an eye toward the challenges that still lie ahead.

Previous editions of this text have been praised by many reviewers for the extent to which we have met the objectives we set for ourselves. Every effort has been made in this third edition to maintain that tradition. In the interest of engaging and stimulating student interest, some of the contexts used to illustrate measurement principles are quite varied. Discussion ranges, for example, from psychometric issues in the interpretation of breathalyzer data, to estimating risk of child abuse from test data, to "confessions" of a staff behavior rater in an inpatient institution that maintains a 24-hour behavioral observation and rating program. Closer to home, students will be exposed to some intriguing facts about tests such as the Graduate Record Examination (GRE). In Chapter 7, the *Everyday Psychometrics* feature contains a guide for "translating" student complaints about examination into psychometric parlance. For example, "I spent all last night studying Chapter 3, and there wasn't one item on that test from that chapter!" is translated as "I question the examination's content validity!"

In each chapter of this book, students are invited to think critically and generatively about numerous measurement-related issues ranging from the workplace use of a test that purports to be a measure of personality type (the Myers-Briggs Type Indicator) to the psychometric pros and cons of a widely used neuropsychological test battery (the Luria-Nebraska). Additionally, students are encouraged to understand the complexity of, and form their own opinions about, some of the controversial issues of the day. These range from questions debated in the professional literature (e.g., "Are unisex norms needed for the MMPI?") to assessment-related issues discussed extensively in the popular media, including affirmative action and the assertions of Herrnstein and Murray (1994) in *The Bell Curve.*

As in previous editions, students are provided early on with a firm grounding in areas such as norms, reliability, validity, and test development. We depart from previous editions, however, in the extent to which we demand that students keep applying their knowledge of such areas to specific tests. In this text as well as in its companion study guide and workbook (Cohen, 1996), the student is repeatedly challenged to apply learned templates and models to new instruments. For example, students may be asked to consider issues of reliability in relation to an infant ability measure (the Bayley Scales for Infant Development, Second Edition) or challenged to apply Cronbach's generalizability theory to a measure of field independence (the Group Embedded Figures Test).

Instructors who have used previous editions of this text will find a great deal of new material in the present revision. Chapter 1 has been revised to provide a much broader overview of the field in general, including various psychometric and cultural issues, as well as issues related to the growing use of computers in the assessment enterprise. Discussion of issues related to society at large in the context of assessment has been greatly expanded. We have added material related to the use of tests in self-help publications and the popular media. Perhaps the greatest change in the first chapter is the addition of a discussion concerning assumptions that underlie testing and assessment. Our combined classroom experience suggested that such a discussion of fundamental assumptions was useful in preparing students for and orienting them to the discussion of theory, application, and issues to come.

Some of the other many changes in this edition include an integration of culture-related issues throughout, a presentation of the five-factor model of personality assessment, and greater reliance on and citation of meta-analytic studies reported in the professional literature. When a particular test is focused on, we have generally devoted most or all of the space in a discussion of it to its most current version. Thus for example, the reader will find ample discussion of the MMPI-2, but coverage of the MMPI is somewhat curtailed relative to the second edition. Another change from the second edition entailed the integration of key material from the former "Preschool Assessment" chapter into the third edition's Chapter 10 (Educational Assessment).

We would like to express our appreciation to Louis H. Primavera and Bernard S. Gorman for their joint contribution to this work in the form of the *Close-up* in Chapter 6 on factor analysis, and for their readiness to supply helpful comments and suggestions. Thanks also to Kevin L. Moreland for his assistance in the material in this book on computer-related assessment, and for his co-authorship of a previous version of Chapter 19. Thanks to David W. Stewart for his assistance in the preparation of an earlier version of the chapter on consumer assessment. Thanks to Patricia M. Greene, administrative assistant to John E. Exner, Jr., who prepared for us biographical material on Dr. Exner from which we drew liberally. We would also like to express our appreciation to Stephen A. Karp, George Washington University; Karl Kuhnert, University of Georgia; Chris Piotrowski, University of West Florida; Michael F. Shaughnessy, Eastern New Mexico University; and Terry A. Stinnett, Eastern Illinois University, who served as reviewers for this third edition. Thanks also to Frank Graham at Mayfield Publishing, who pioneered both the use of the term "sponsoring editor" and the best traditions of what it means to be one.

In the pages that follow, one of the concepts to be discussed in the psychometric sense is that of error. But here we make reference to that concept in its nonpsychometric, everyday meaning when we note that the responsibility for any error in this book rests with the authors and not with any of the people who were kind enough to provide us with assistance.

July, 1995

Ronald Jay Cohen
Pawling, New York

To our families

P A R T **1**

An Overview

1

Psychological Testing and Assessment

All fields of human endeavor use measurement in some form, and each field has its own set of measuring tools and measuring units. If you're recently engaged or thinking about becoming engaged, you may have obtained an education on a unit of measure called the *carat*. If you've been shopping for a computer, you may have learned something about a unit of measurement called a *byte*. And if you're in need of an air conditioner, you'll no doubt want to know about the Btu (British thermal unit). Other units of measurement you may or may not be familiar with include a mile (land), a mile (nautical), a ton (long), a ton (short), a hertz, a henry, miles per hour, cycles per second, and candela per square meter. Professionals in the fields that employ these units (as well as various tools to obtain measurements) know the potential uses, benefits, and limitations of the measuring tools they use and the measurements they make. So, too, it is incumbent upon the user or potential user of psychological measurements to have a working familiarity with the tools used in such measurement and the theoretical underpinnings of the enterprise.

Testing and Assessment

The roots of contemporary psychological testing and assessment can be found in turn-of-the-century France. In 1905, Alfred Binet and a colleague had published a test that was designed to help place Paris schoolchildren in appropriate classes. As history records, however, Binet's test would have consequences well beyond the Paris school district. Binet's test would serve as a catalyst to the field of psychological measurement as no test had before it. Within a decade, an English-language version of Binet's test had been prepared for use in schools in the United States. About the same time, psychological testing in the military was either first being contemplated or actually being conducted. In 1917, the

United States declared war on Germany and entered World War I. The military needed a way to quickly screen large numbers of recruits for intellectual as well as emotional problems, and psychological testing provided the methodology. During the Second World War, the military would depend even more on psychological tests to screen recruits for service. The government's large-scale reliance on psychological tests served as a great impetus to the psychological testing enterprise. Following the war, an expanding number of tests purporting to measure a wide array of psychological variables burst onto the American scene.

The heyday of psychological testing was the 1950s and early 1960s. At many mental health facilities, both public and private, clients were administered groups of tests that typically included an intelligence test, a personality test, and a test to screen for neurological impairment. In the schools, the role of various psychological and educational tests in making placement and other decisions broadened. Corporate America, as well as many government agencies, also embraced psychological testing. A wide assortment of tests was being used to make critical decisions about the hiring, firing, and general utilization of personnel.

Paralleling greater reliance on data derived from psychological tests was greater public concern about such data. From the perspective of the public, psychological tests were suspect because they were so shrouded in mystery. Individuals compelled by an employer or a prospective employer to sit for a psychological test were understandably apprehensive. On the basis of data derived from the test, and for reasons not at all clear to the examinee, the testing might result in the denial of a desirable transfer or promotion, even the denial of employment. Examinees were not guaranteed any information about how well they did on the test, and they were seldom informed about the criteria on which their performance was being judged. Before long, the courts, even the Congress, would be grappling with a number of thorny questions and issues. Do psychological tests violate one's constitutional right of privacy? Do the tests really measure what they purport to measure? What kinds of decisions can and cannot be made on the basis of test data, and how should those decisions be made? What credentials, if any, are necessary to administer and interpret psychological tests? What rights do examinees undergoing psychological evaluation have?

Public scrutiny of psychological testing reached its zenith in 1965 with a series of probing and unprecedented congressional hearings (see Amrine, 1965). Against a backdrop of mounting public concern about—as well as legal challenges to—psychological testing, many psychologists in the 1960s began to look anew at the testing enterprise. Beyond being a mere instrument of measurement, a psychological test was conceptualized by many as a tool of a highly trained examiner. The value of a particular test was intimately and irrevocably linked to the expertise of the user of that test. As Sundberg and Tyler (1962) cautioned, "*Tests are tools.* In the hands of a capable and creative person they can be used with remarkable outcomes. In the hands of a fool or an unscrupulous person they become pseudoscientific perversion" (p. 131, emphasis in the original). With the recognition that a test is one tool in a larger, more

Figure 1–1
Cramming for a Performance Test

Would you spend over $1,000 for a private course to prepare you for a test for military service? With hopes of being accepted to an elite combat unit, thousands of high school students in Israel, such as the one pictured here, are doing just that. Military service is highly valued in Israeli culture, and members of elite units enjoy high status among their peers. Taking a prep course to prepare for a test that only 1 in 60 recruits will pass has become increasingly popular, even for teenagers "with jeweled studs glittering from their pierced ears and noses" (Hedges, 1994, p. 4).

multifaceted process of psychological evaluation, the stage was set for a differentiation between the terms *psychological testing* and *psychological assessment.*

Testing and Assessment Defined

Through the 1960s, the term *psychological testing* was used by many to loosely refer to the process of administering and interpreting one or more psychological tests. By the 1970s, many psychologists appreciated the need for a refinement in the use of that term. A more precise use of the term *psychological testing* would distinguish the tool in the evaluative process (that is, a test) from the evaluative process itself. In a textbook entitled *Psychological Assessment*, Maloney and Ward (1976) argued that "assessment" was preferable to "testing" when referring to the thoughtful, problem-solving process of psychological evaluation. Maloney and Ward conceived of this problem-solving process as ever variable in nature and the result of many different factors, beginning with the reason the assessment is being undertaken. Different tools of evaluation—psychological tests among them—might be marshaled in the process of assessment depending on the particular objectives, people, and circumstances involved, as well as other variables unique to the particular situation. By contrast *psychological testing* was seen as much narrower in scope, referring only to "the process of administering, scoring, and interpreting psychological tests" (Maloney & Ward, 1976, p. 9). Testing was also seen as differing from assessment because the process is "test-controlled"; decisions and/or predictions are made solely or largely on the basis of test scores. The examiner is more key to the process of assessment, in which decisions and/or predictions are made on the basis of many possible sources of data (including tests). Maloney and Ward also distinguished "testing" from "assessment" in regard to their respective objectives. In testing, a typical objective is to measure the magnitude of some psychological trait. For example, one might speak of "intelligence testing" if the purpose of administering a test was confined to obtaining a numerical gauge of the examinee's intelligence. In assessment, by contrast, the objective more typically extends beyond obtaining a number to reflect the strength or absence of some psychological trait. According to this view, "assessment" would be preferable to "testing" if an evaluation of a student's intelligence was undertaken, for example, to answer a referral question about the student's ability to function in a regular classroom. Such an evaluation might explore the student's intellectual strengths and weaknesses. Further, the assessment would likely integrate the clinician's findings during the course of the intellectual evaluation that pertain to the student's social skills and judgment. Maloney and Ward (1976) further distinguished testing from assessment by noting that testing

> could take place without being directed at answering a specific referral question and even without the tester actually seeing the client or testee. For example, tests could be (and often are) administered in groups and then scored and interpreted for a variety of purposes. (p. 9)

> . . . while psychometric tests usually just add up the number of correct answers or the number of certain types of responses or performances with little if any regard for the how or mechanics of such content, clinical assessment is often far more interested in *how* the individual processes rather than the results of what he processes. The two operations, in fact, serve very different goals and purposes. (p. 39)

Regarding the collection of psychological assessment data, Maloney and Ward (1976) urged that far beyond the use of psychological tests alone, "literally, any method the examiner can use to make relevant observations is appropriate" (p. 7). Years later, Roberts and Magrab (1991) argued that assessment was not an activity to be confined to the consulting room. In presenting their community-based, interdisciplinary model for the assessment of children, they envisioned a place for traditional testing but viewed more global assessment as key to meaningful evaluation:

> Assessment in this model does not emphasize stable traits but attempts to understand a problem in the larger ecological framework in which it occurs. For assessment to be ecologically valid, a broad range of information must be collected and new methods may be required to obtain the necessary information. These methods could include routine visits to the home and the community or naturalistic observations. (p. 145) . . .

Although standardized assessment procedures are very valuable in gaining insight into the developmental status of a child, they may not provide all the answers. Seeing the child in his or her natural environment may give valuable clues into styles of learning, additional skills, and interactional patterns in the family. (p. 146)

Although discussion of the distinction between testing and assessment has typically been confined to clinical contexts (see, for example, Matarazzo, 1990), a precedent exists for expanding this distinction to all settings in which evaluations of a psychological nature are made. During World War II, the United States Office of Strategic Services (OSS) employed a variety of procedures and measurement tools—psychological tests among them—for the purpose of selecting military personnel for highly specialized positions involving spying, espionage, intelligence gathering, and the like. As summarized in *Assessment of Men* (OSS, 1948) and elsewhere (Murray & MacKinnon, 1946), the assessment data generated were subjected to thoughtful integration and evaluation by the highly trained assessment center staff. The OSS model of using an innovative variety of evaluative tools, with the data derived from the evaluations analyzed by highly trained assessors, would later inspire what is now referred to as the "assessment center" approach to personnel evaluation (Bray, 1982).

The semantic distinction that many have proposed between the terms *psychological testing* and *psychological assessment* has, like many semantic changes, been relatively slow in becoming integrated into everyday parlance. Admittedly, the line between what constitutes "testing" and what constitutes "assessment" is not always as straightforward as we might like it to be. However, by acknowledging that such ambiguity exists, we can work toward sharpening our definition and use of these terms; denying or ignoring their distinctiveness provides no hope of a satisfactory remedy. For our purposes, we will define *psychological assessment* as "the gathering and integration of psychology-related data for the purpose of making a psychological evaluation, accomplished through the use of tools such as tests, interviews, case studies, behavioral observation, and specially designed apparatuses and measurement procedures." We will define *psychological testing* as the process of measuring psychology-related variables by means of devices or procedures designed to obtain a sample of behavior.

The Tools of Psychological Assessment

The test A *test* may be defined simply as a measuring device or procedure. When the word *test* is prefaced with a modifier, what is being referred to is a measuring device or procedure designed to measure a variable related to that modifier. Consider, for example, the term *medical test,* which refers to a measuring device or procedure designed to measure some variable related to the practice of medicine (including a wide range of tools and procedures such as X rays, blood tests, and testing of reflexes). In a like manner, the term *psychological test* refers to a measuring device or procedure designed to measure variables related to psychology (for example, intelligence, personality, aptitude, interests, attitudes, and values). And whereas a medical test might involve the analysis of a sample of blood, of tissue, or the like, a psychological test almost always involves the analysis of a sample of behavior. The behavior sample could range from responses to a pencil-and-paper questionnaire to oral responses to questions to performance of some task. The behavior sample could be elicited by the stimulus of the test itself or could be naturally occurring behavior (under observation).

Psychological tests may differ on a number of variables such as content, format, administration procedures, scoring and interpretation procedures, and psychometric or technical quality. The *content* of the test will, of course, vary with the focus of the particular test. But even two psychological tests purporting to measure the same construct—for example, "personality"—may differ widely in item content because of factors such as the test developer's definition of personality and the theoretical orientation of the test. For example, items on a psychoanalytically oriented personality test may have little resemblance to those on an existentially oriented personality test, yet both are "personality tests." The term *format* pertains to the form, plan, structure, arrangement, and layout of test items as well as to related considerations such as time limits. "Format" is also used to refer to the form in which a test is administered—computerized, pencil-and-paper, or some other form. When making specific reference to a computerized test, "format" also refers to the form of the software—IBM- or Apple-compatible. Because of the unique advantages of computerized testing, many different types of tests, ranging from achievement tests to personality tests to taste tests, are now available in a computerized format (see *Close-up*).

Psychological tests differ widely in *scoring and interpretation guidelines*. Some tests are designed to be scored by testtakers themselves, others are designed to be scored only by a trained examiner, and still others may be scored only by a computer. Some tests, such as most tests of intelligence, come complete with test manuals that are very explicit not only about scoring criteria but also about the nature of the interpretations that can be made from the calculated score. Other tests, such as the Rorschach Inkblot Test (discussed in Chapter 12), are sold with no manual; the purchaser buys the stimulus materials and then selects and uses one of many available guides for administration, scoring, and interpretation.

Tests differ with respect to their *technical or psychometric quality.* At this point, suffice it to say that a good test measures what it purports to measure in a consistent way and that if two tests purport to measure the exact same (identically defined) construct, the test that measures the construct better is the better (that is, the technically superior or more psychometrically sound) instrument. We have more to say about what constitutes a "good test" later in this chapter, and all of Part 2 is concerned with issues related to the psychometric quality of a test. Let's also note here that it is easier to identify a "good test" than to identify a "good assessment process." A developing body of knowledge and a proving ground of experience have yielded methodologies with which tests can be evaluated for psychometric soundness. However, it is generally more difficult to evaluate the soundness of an assessment procedure because there are

Computer-Assisted Psychological Assessment

Computers as Administrators

Computers as administrators, scorers, and interpreters of test and other assessment-related data, have the potential of being a boon to the field of psychological testing. Computers don't come in to work irritable because they stayed out too late the night before. Nothing is dull, monotonous, boring, routine, or too mundane for computers. They wouldn't rather be out jogging, they don't wonder whether they're getting enough fiber or where their kids are, and they couldn't care less about the price of oil; in short, *nothing* distracts them. Minute after minute, hour after hour, day after day, week after week they rigorously pay close attention to detail, adhering to the finest points of a standardized testing procedure—all of this with a cordial if not pleasing "voice," a letter-perfect "penmanship," and an enviable capacity for creating, modifying, and reproducing artwork. Computers are exemplary in their "understanding" of the term *service*. They can be loyal, friendly, and understanding. They thrive on processing data from multitudes of testtakers, on multiple dates—ever ready to remember and compare findings within or between testtakers. Computers have nothing, after all, if they don't have great memory. They don't see the world through rose-colored glasses or prejudicial blinders. They are as patient and as nonbiased as they are programmed to be and have outrageous organizational and planning abilities. They are capable of recording to the milli-second testtakers' response time to an item. They can be programmed to interact with testtakers in any language—even sign language for the deaf or hearing-impaired. They can dispense praise or rewards if so programmed. And they'll even turn themselves off on cue.

Traditionally, the key advantage of automated techniques has been the economy of assessors' time afforded in test administration, scoring, and interpretation. In interpreting test data, the ability of computers to analyze voluminous amounts of data while simultaneously comparing such data with other data in memory is especially advantageous. Related advantages of using computers in assessment include:

- *Automatic tailoring of a test's content and length for each testtaker.* Depending upon their response to initial items, the content of the items testtakers are presented with may vary for each testtaker. In addition, the actual length of the test for different testtakers may also vary. The objective of this "computer adaptive testing" is to tailor tests to the ability (or to the strength of some other trait) that the testtaker is presumed to possess (Weiss, 1985).

- *Measurement of traits or abilities by techniques that could not be measured by more traditional methods.* For example, researchers employing computerized assessment methods to study dyslexia (a learning disability characterized primarily by reading difficulties) reported that the disorder may have a basis in a particular brain

typically many more variables involved. Unlike a test, which may be designed to measure a particular trait, psychological assessment is undertaken in an effort to provide more information relevant to specific questions or issues, and the nature of the tools used and the procedures followed will vary accordingly. Because of the diversity of assessors' backgrounds, it is conceivable that two assessors might use entirely different sets of tools and procedures to answer any given assessment question. Can one approach to assessment be more valid than the other? Yes. But determining the answer to that question with a fair amount

Researchers at Nabisco (National Biscuit Company) employ computers to assess consumers' judgments about taste and related variables regarding their products. From the perspective of these research subjects, it would appear to be good work if you can get it!

circuit that processes rapid sounds (Katz et al., 1992). Should such findings be confirmed by other researchers, equipment similar to the computerized audio equipment that the researchers used may become a standard component of a comprehensive evaluation for dyslexia.

■ *Financial savings.* In cost-conscious times, computer-assisted psychological assessment's (CAPA) promise of significant savings over time has enticed many large corporations to invest in it. For example, IBM developed a multimedia computerized test used to screen and select new manufacturing employees. The test exposes prospective employees to a wide range of manufacturing problems to solve. Developed by psychologist Patricia Dyer and her colleagues at IBM's Testing and Assess-

ment unit, the test also taps an applicant's ability to perform various tasks after having been taught how to perform them. Dyer (1994) believes the test will save her company between three and four million dollars annually because of its effectiveness in screening out unsuitable candidates.

Because of the great proliferation of computerized testing, discussion of CAPA will be integrated throughout this book. It is important to note, however, that although CAPA has the potential to be a great boon to the enterprise of psychological assessment, many unresolved issues related to it persist. In Chapter 19, we will take a close look at those issues.

of certainty can sometimes be an ambitious undertaking. As Maloney and Ward (1976, p. 4) put it: "We do have ways of assessing test-as-tools efficiently. On the other hand, it is much more difficult to determine the efficiency of the process of psychological assessment, primarily because there is much less agreement on what this process is or what it entails."

The interview   Another widely used tool in the process of psychological assessment is the *interview*—a word that may conjure images of face-to-face talk. But an interview as a tool of psychological assessment involves more than talk. If the interview is being conducted face to face, the interviewer will probably be noting nonverbal as well as verbal behavior. For example, the interviewer may make notations regarding the interviewee's dress, manner, or eye contact. A face-to-face interview need not necessarily even involve any speech if the interviewee is deaf or suffering from a hearing impairment; the entire interview might be conducted in sign language. An interview can be conducted over the telephone, in which case the interviewer might make inferences regarding the content of what is said as a function of changes in the interviewee's voice quality. An interview of sorts could also conceivably be conducted by means of other electronic media, with an interviewer at one computer terminal and an interviewee at another terminal. In its broadest sense, then, we can define an *interview* as a method of gathering information through direct, reciprocal communication.

The interview is a very popular information-gathering tool not only in psychology but in virtually all other fields as well. To appreciate just how widespread interviewing is, try to recall the last time you went through a day without being exposed to an interview on television, radio, in the print media, or somewhere else. In psychology as in other professions, there are different types of interviews. For example, in Chapter 14 you will be introduced to one specialized type of clinical interview called the *mental status examination*. Another variety of interview is one that is conducted while the interviewee is in an altered state of consciousness. For example, interviews conducted under hypnosis (Hoffman, 1985) or while the interviewee is under the influence of a drug such as sodium amytal (Pellegrini & Putman, 1984) are sometimes undertaken in an effort to obtain more information than might otherwise be obtained.

A stress interview, as its name implies, is one in which the interviewee is purposely placed in some stressful situation. The stress might take almost any form: seating the interviewee on a wobbly chair, repeatedly interrupting the interviewee, encouraging the interviewee to partake of greasy "finger food" without providing napkins, or giving the interviewee instructions that are impossible to execute. Rarely used, stress interviews may have application in specialized employment settings where it is critical to sample and evaluate a candidate's effectiveness in dealing with stress. During World War II, stress interviews were employed to help select intelligence agents.

The form any interview takes depends on many factors, including the purpose and objectives of the interview (clinical evaluation? evaluation for employment? evaluation for admission to some specialized program?), time or other limitations or restrictions, and the anticipated ability (or willingness) of the interviewee to respond. Interviewers themselves vary widely with respect to variables such as their pacing of interviews, the extent to which they develop a rapport with their interviewees, and the extent to which they convey genuineness, empathy, and a sense of humor (see Figure 1–2).

The portfolio In recent years, the popularity of portfolio assessment in many fields, including education, has been rising. Some have argued, for example, that an evaluation of a student's writing skills can best be accomplished not by

Figure 1–2
On Interviewing and Being Interviewed

Different interviewers have different styles of interviewing and these styles may range widely on numerous variables. Interview styles differ, for example, in the extent to which they are crass versus sophisticated, juvenile versus adult, and dull versus sharp. Interviewers vary in terms of how willing they are to let their interviewee speak versus how eager they are to hear themselves speak. In what other specific ways might interview styles vary? How would you characterize the interview style of Howard Stern versus that of Jay Leno? What types of interviewing skills do you think are necessary for a talk show host? How do these skills differ from those that you think are necessary for a professional in the field of psychological assessment?

the administration of a test but by asking the student to compile a selection of writing samples. From the perspective of education administrators, portfolio assessment would seem to also have distinct advantages in assessing the effectiveness of teachers. By examining teachers' portfolios, and seeing how teachers approach their coverage of various topics, educational evaluators have another tool that can help anchor judgments to work samples.

The case study Also referred to as a *case history,* the case study is a compilation of biographical data from varied sources, including government, medical, and other records; employers; teachers; family; and friends. The focus of the case study will vary as a function of the purpose of the assessment. If a job applicant is being evaluated, the case study will focus on aspects of the applicant's previous employment such as duties and responsibilities, level of performance, inter-personal relations skills, and salary history. Perhaps most typically, the case history is a tool used in clinical settings as an aid in developing a treatment plan. Here the case-study data may include, at a minimum, synopses of available reports by doctors and hospitals and information concerning the patient's early as well as current adjustment. Case history data provide a framework for integrating new information about the person being evaluated.

Behavioral observation   "To the extent that it is practically feasible, direct observation of behavior frequently proves the most clinically useful of all assessment procedures" (Goldfried & Davison, 1976, p. 44). Behavioral observation has indeed proved to be a very useful assessment procedure, particularly in institutional settings such as schools, hospitals, prisons, and group homes. Using published or self-constructed lists of targeted behaviors, staff can observe first-hand the behavior of the person under observation and design interventions accordingly. In a school situation, for example, behavioral observation on the playground of a culturally different child suspected of having linguistic problems might reveal that the child does have English language skills but is unwilling—for reasons of shyness, cultural upbringing, or whatever—to demonstrate those abilities to an adult.

Despite the potential usefulness of behavioral observation in settings ranging from the private practitioner's consulting room to the interior of a manned rock on a space mission, it tends to be used infrequently outside institutional settings. For private practitioners, it is typically not economically feasible to spend hours out of the consulting room engaged in behavioral observation.

Other tools   Varied instruments of measurement can be used in psychological assessment. In addition to video monitors wired to multimedia-equipped computers, video monitors wired to simple videocassette players have become more widespread as a tool of assessment. Specially created videos are used not only in job training, for example, but also in evaluating the learning and competencies of personnel. Although many math- or language-related skills can be reasonably assessed by paper-and-pencil tests, assessment by means of video adds a component of realism and "attention to detail" (Outtz, 1994) that is desirable in many personnel-assessment situations. Corporate managers can be asked to respond to a variety of incidents of sexual harassment in the workplace. Police personnel can be asked about how they would respond to various types of emergencies either reenacted for the assessment video or actually recorded on tape as they happened. Psychotherapists can be asked to respond with a diagnosis and a treatment plan for each of several patients presented to them on videotape. The list of potential applications for video assessment is virtually endless.

Psychologists and others who devise tools to assess the handicapped or people from other special populations have been most innovative. For example, Wilson, Thompson, and Wylie (1982) described a dental plate activated by the tongue as a mechanism for test response to be used by testtakers who lack the capacity for speech or control of their hands or limbs. The device permits five kinds of response, depending on the area of the plate depressed by the tongue.

As researchers learn more about various psychology-related matters, new tools will be pressed into service to measure relevant variables. A new tool, for example, in diagnosing dyslexia may be a multimedia computer device that assesses one's ability to process rapid sounds (Katz et al., 1992). Old tools can also be put to new uses based on new information. For example, ordinary blood pressure or body temperature readings may become tools of assessment in a psychological study, especially if analyzed with measures of stress or other psychological variables (see, for example, McCubbin et al., 1991; Ussher & Wilding, 1991). Biofeedback equipment is useful in obtaining measures of bodily reactions (such as muscular tension or galvanic skin response) to various sorts of stimuli. An instrument called a penile plethysmograph, which gauges male sexual arousal, has found application in sexual therapy programs with normal males experiencing sexual difficulties as well as in the treatment of sexual offenders. Impaired ability to identify odors is not uncommon in disorders such as Alzheimer's disease and Down's syndrome, in which the central nervous system (CNS) may be affected. Tests such as the University of Pennsylvania Smell Identification Test (UPSIT) have been helpful in assessing the extent of olfactory deficit in these and other diseases where there is suspected CNS involvement, such as acquired immunodeficiency syndrome (AIDS) (Brody et al., 1991). The UPSIT testtaker is sequentially exposed to 40 scratch-and-sniff odors and asked to identify each odor from a four-item word list.

There has been no shortage of innovation on the part of psychologists in devising measurement tools, or adapting existing tools, for use in psychological measurement. In any additional courses in psychology you may take—abnormal, social, developmental, experimental, or whatever—you may marvel at the many ingenious ways psychologists have devised to measure variables of interest. Consider, for example, the apparatus illustrated in Figure 1–3.

12 Assumptions in Psychological Testing and Assessment

Our overview of the assessment enterprise continues with a brief look at some of the assumptions that are basic to that enterprise. Be forewarned that these assumptions are deceptively simple. One can state, for example, that "psychologists who use tests to measure psychological traits assume that such traits (1) exist, (2) can be quantified, and (3) can be measured."[1] Yet it is also true that psychologists who use tests to measure psychological traits have engaged in intense debate about the nature of the existence of psychological traits, as well as how—even if—psychological traits can be meaningfully quantified and

---

1. Unless stated otherwise, "test" is used in this context and elsewhere throughout this book to refer not only to tests per se but also to other types of measurement techniques. Consider, for example, that tests for leadership ability can take many different forms, from the paper-and-pencil variety to performance tasks involving groups of people.

Figure 1–3
Measuring Body Image Distortion in Persons
with Eating Disorders

People with eating disorders such as anorexia nervosa *(characterized by maintenance of below-average body weight and a preoccupation with remaining very thin) and* bulimia nervosa *(also known as "binge-purge syndrome") frequently exhibit evidence of body image distortion when interviewed; they tend to see themselves as heavier than they really are (Bruch, 1962; Cash & Brown, 1987; Garner et al., 1976; Slade, 1985). But just how distorted is one's image of one's own body? To address that question a number of measuring devices and procedures have been devised, ranging from paper-and-pencil questionnaires to adjustable calipers to imaging techniques that employ photographs, mirrors, or video recorders (Garner & Garfinkel, 1981; Gleghorn et al., 1987; Lindholm & Wilson, 1988; Ruff & Barrios, 1986). An apparatus called the adjustable light beam apparatus (ALBA), developed by Thompson and Thompson (1986) and described in a number of studies by J. Kevin Thompson and his associates (Penner et al., 1991; Thompson, 1990; Thompson & Spana, 1988), is one of the tools that have been developed as aids to assess body image distortion. The procedure entails the removal of any bulky clothing, so that the assessee is in usual street clothes when the measurements are taken. The use of the ALBA is explained and, after practice with it, assessees adjust four beams of light to reflect what they believe to be the width of their cheeks, waist, hips, and thighs. A measure of the accuracy—or the distortion— of the estimate is obtained by dividing the estimated width by the actual width. The resulting ratio is then multiplied by 100 to yield a percentage of over- or underestimation of body size.*

measured. Indeed, controversy surrounds some of the most basic assumptions about psychological testing and assessment. As you read on, and with every successive chapter in this book, your appreciation for the complexity of the issues involved will deepen.

Assumption 1: Psychological traits and states exist.   A *trait* has been defined as "any distinguishable, relatively enduring way in which one individual varies from another" (Guilford, 1959, p. 6). *States* also distinguish one person from another but are relatively less enduring (Chaplin et al., 1988).

The word *distinguishable* conveys the idea that behavior labeled with one trait term can be differentiated from behavior that is labeled with another trait term. Thus, for example, behavior within a certain context that might be viewed as "religious" should ideally be distinguishable from behavior within the same or another context that might be viewed as "deviant." Note here that it is important to be aware of the *context* or situation in which a particular behavior is displayed when distinguishing between trait terms that may be applicable: A person who is kneeling and talking to God inside a church may be described as "religious," whereas another person engaged in the exact same behavior in a public restroom might more readily be viewed as "deviant." The trait term that an observer applies, as well as the strength or magnitude of the trait presumed to be present, is based on an observation of a sample of behavior. The observed sample of behavior may be obtained in a number of ways, ranging from direct observation of the assessee (such as by actually watching the individual going to church regularly and praying) to the analysis of the assessee's statements on a self-report, pencil-and-paper personality test (on which, for example, the individual may have provided an indication of great frequency in church attendance).

The term *relatively enduring way* in the definition serves as a reminder that a trait cannot be expected to be manifest in an individual 100% of the time. Whether a trait manifests itself, and to what degree, is presumed to depend not only on the strength of the trait in the individual but also on the nature of the situation an individual is in. Stated another way, exactly how a particular trait manifests itself is, at least to some extent, situation-dependent. For example, a "violent" parolee may generally be prone to behave in a rather subdued way with her parole officer and much more violently in the presence of her family and friends. John may be viewed as "dull" and "cheap" by his wife but as "charming" and "extravagant" by his secretary, business associates, and others he is keenly interested in impressing.

The definitions of "trait" and "state" we are using also refer to a *way in which one individual varies from another.* This phrase should serve to emphasize that the attribution of a trait or state term is always a relative phenomenon. For example, in describing one person as "shy," or even in using terms such as "very shy" or "not shy," most people are typically making an unstated comparison with the degree of shyness that could reasonably be expected to be emitted by the average person under the same or similar circumstances. In psychological testing and assessment, assessors may also make such comparisons with respect to the hypothetical "average person." Alternatively, assessors may make comparisons between and among people who, because of their membership in some group or for any number of other reasons, are decidedly not average. As you might expect, the reference group with which comparisons are made can greatly influence one's conclusions or judgments. For example, suppose a psychologist administers a test of shyness to a 22-year-old male who earns his living as an erotic dancer. The interpretation of the test data will almost surely differ as a function of whether the reference group with which the testtaker is compared is other males in his age group or other male erotic dancers in his age group.

The term *psychological trait,* much like the term *trait* itself, covers a very wide range of possible characteristics. Thousands of psychological trait terms can be found in the English language (Allport & Odbert, 1936). Among them are psychological traits that relate to intelligence, specific intellectual abilities, cognitive style, adjustment, interests, attitudes, sexual orientation and preferences, psychopathology, personality in general, and specific personality traits. New concepts or discoveries in research may bring new trait terms to the fore. For example, a trait term seen with increasing frequency in the professional literature in the area of human sexuality is *androgynous* (referring to a lack of primacy of male or female characteristics). Cultural evolution may bring new trait terms into common usage as it did in the 1960s when people began speaking of the degree to which women were *liberated* (or freed from the constraints of gender-dependent social expectations). A more recent example is the trait term *new age,* used in the popular culture to refer to a spiritual, almost mystical orientation.

Few people deny that psychological traits exist. Yet there has been a fair amount of controversy regarding just *how* they exist. For example, do traits have a physical existence, much as we could envision a circuit in the brain has? Although there are those who have argued in favor of such a conception of psychological traits (Allport, 1937; Holt, 1971), compelling evidence to support such a view has been difficult to obtain. For our purposes, a psychological trait exists only as a *construct*—an informed, scientific idea developed or constructed to describe or explain behavior. We can't see, hear, or touch constructs, but we can infer their existence from overt behavior. In this context, "overt behavior" refers to an observable action or the product of an observable action, including test- or assessment-related responses. A challenge facing test developers is to construct tests that are at least as telling and as meaningful as behavior like that illustrated in Figure 1–4.

Assumption 2: Psychological traits and states can be quantified and measured. Amy scored 36 on a test of marital adjustment, and her husband, Zeke, scored 41 on the same test. *Question:* What does this information tell us about Amy, Zeke, and their adjustment to married life? *Answer:* Virtually nothing. To respond professionally to this question, we would need to know much more about (1) Amy; (2) Zeke; (3) how the construct *marital adjustment* was defined on the marital adjustment test they took; (4) the meaning of the test scores according to the test's author; and (5) research relevant to substantiating the test's guidelines for scoring and interpretation.

Test authors, much like people in general, can evidence many different ways of looking at and defining the same phenomenon. Just think, for example, of the wide range of ways a term such as *aggressive* is used. We speak of an

Figure 1–4
Measuring Sensation-Seeking

The psychological trait of sensation-seeking has been defined as "the need for varied, novel, and complex sensations and experiences and the willingness to take physical and social risks for the sake of such experiences" (Zuckerman, 1979, p. 10). A 22-item Sensation Seeking Scale (SSS) seeks to identify people who are high or low on this trait. Assuming the SSS actually measures what it purports to measure, how would you expect a random sample of people lining up to bungee-jump to score on the test, as compared with another age-matched sample of people shopping at the local mall? What are the comparative advantages of using paper-and-pencil measures, such as the SSS, and using more performance-based measures, such as the one pictured here?

"aggressive salesperson," an "aggressive killer," and an "aggressive dancer," and in each of those different contexts *aggressive* carries with it a different meaning. If a personality test yields a score purporting to provide information about how aggressive a testtaker is, a first step in understanding the meaning of that score is understanding how "aggressive" was defined by the test developer. More specifically, what types of behaviors are presumed to be indicative of someone who is "aggressive" as defined by the test?

From a world of behaviors presumed to be indicative of the targeted trait, a test developer has a world of possible items that can be written to gauge the strength of that trait in testtakers.[2] For example, if the test developer deems knowledge of American history to be one component of adult intelligence, then an item that asks "Who was the second president of the United States?" may

---

2. In the language of psychological testing and assessment, the word *domain* is substituted for *world* in this context. As we will see subsequently, assessment professionals speak, for example, of "domain sampling," which may refer to either (1) a sample of behaviors from all possible behaviors that could conceivably be indicative of a particular construct, or (2) a sample of test items from all possible items that could conceivably be used to measure a particular construct.

appear on the test. Similarly, if social judgment is deemed to be indicative of adult intelligence, then it would be legitimate to include an item that asks "Why should guns in the home always be inaccessible to children?" Such items having been included on an adult test of intelligence, one of the many complex issues the test developer will have to deal with is the comparative weight such items are given. Perhaps, correct responses to the social judgment questions should earn more credit than correct responses to the American history questions. Perhaps, for example, a correct response to a social judgment question should be assigned a numerical value of 2 or 3 points toward the overall point total, and each correct response to the American history questions should be assigned a numerical value of 1 point. Weighting the comparative value of a test's items comes about as the result of a complex interplay among many factors, including technical considerations, the way a construct has been defined for the purposes of the test, and the value society attaches to the behaviors being evaluated.

Measurement is the act of assigning numbers or symbols to characteristics of objects (people, events—whatever) according to rules. An example of a measurement rule, this one for scoring each item on a spelling test, is "Assign the number 1 for each correct answer according to the answer key, and 0 for each incorrect answer." Another example of a measurement rule, this one for each item on a test designed to measure depression, is "Using the test's answer key as a guide, assign the number 1 for each response that indicates that the assessee is depressed, 0 for all other responses." For many varieties of psychological tests, some number representing the score on the test is derived from the examinee's responses. The test score, presumed to represent the strength of the targeted ability or trait or state, is frequently based on a *cumulative model* of scoring.[3] Inherent in cumulative scoring models is the assumption that the more the testtaker responds in a particular direction as keyed by the test manual as correct or consistent with a particular trait, the higher that testtaker is presumed to be on the targeted ability or trait. The rules for assigning all numbers have typically been published in the test's manual. Ideally, academically acceptable evidence to support the test's measurement rules, as well as all other related claims of the test author, are also included in the test's manual.

A *scale* is a set of numbers (or other symbols) whose properties model empirical properties of the objects or traits to which numbers are assigned. As we will see in Chapter 3 and again in Chapter 7, different types of scales exist, each with its own assumptions and limitations. *Scaling* may be defined as assigning numbers in accordance with empirical properties of objects or traits. Entire volumes have been written on scaling (see, for example, Gulliksen & Messick, 1960, or Torgerson, 1958), and many different strategies of scaling can be applied in the development of a new test. An underlying assumption in all scaling efforts is that traits and abilities can be meaningfully quantified and measured. The body of professional literature on scaling provides theoretical rationales and mathematical techniques helpful in deciding how such quantification and measurement can best proceed (Maranell, 1974).

---

3. Other, less widely used models of scoring are discussed in Chapter 7.

Assumption 3: Various approaches to measuring aspects of the same thing can be useful. A number of different tests and measurement techniques may exist to measure the same trait, state, interest, ability, attitude, or other construct, or some aspect of same. Some tests are better than others in various ways, such as the extent to which meaningful predictions can be made on the basis of the scores derived. In fact, tests can differ in a great many ways. Let us count them.

Tests vary in the extent to which they are linked to a theory. For example, the items for a personality test called the MMPI-2 were not developed in conformity to any one theory of personality. By contrast, the items for another test, the Myers-Briggs Type Indicator, were developed on the basis of Carl Jung's theory of personality types.

Test items may also differ according to whether they were derived on a rational or an empirical basis. As its name implies, a rational basis for a particular test item exists when the item logically taps what is known about the targeted trait. Logically, for example, we would expect people in a state of severe depression to report that they feel sad much of the time. On a rational basis, then, a test for severe depression might include a true-false item such as "I feel sad much of the time." However, test items can also be developed empirically—that is, on the basis of experience. For example, suppose researchers discovered that severely depressed people tend to agree with the following statement: "The best part of waking up is coffee in my cup." If that were the case—it is not—such a statement could be included on a strictly empirical, not rational, basis as a test item. When tests are developed empirically, the items may or may not seem to belong on the test from the standpoint of reason or logic.

There is a wide array of ways in which test items can be presented. Most familiar to you, perhaps, are items structured in a true-false, a multiple-choice, or an essay form. However, test items may be structured in other ways, so that, for example, the examinee's task is to manipulate stimulus materials by reordering or rearranging them, substituting or correcting them, or presenting them in some new form or way. A test of creative musical ability, for example, might explore the examinee's facility in manipulating a given series of musical notes.

Tests differ in their administration, scoring, and interpretation procedures. Some tests are individually administered; others are designed for group administration. Some tests have strict time limits; others are not timed. Some tests can be scored and interpreted by machines or computers; other tests are designed for submission to a committee of experts who must apply their expertise in the process of scoring and interpreting the test data.

Tests differ in the extent to which their stimulus materials are verbal or nonverbal. Tests differ in the way that they compel examinees to think and reason; success on various tests may require anything from factual recall to social judgment to great creativity—or some combination of those or other skills. Tests differ with respect to their application. One test of depression might be developed for use in an acute-care setting to identify severely depressed individuals. Another test of depression might have been developed to evaluate the effectiveness of a new drug in treating depression. In general, the utility of tests must be proven for the settings in which they were originally designed to be used, and then proven again for any additional settings in which their use is contemplated.

Assumption 4: Assessment can provide answers to some of life's most momentous questions. Every day, throughout the world, momentous questions are addressed on the basis of some type of assessment process. Is this person competent to stand trial? Who should be hired, transferred, promoted, or fired? Who should gain entry to this special program or be awarded a scholarship? Which parent shall have custody of the children? The answers to these kinds of questions are likely to have a significant impact on many lives. If they are to sleep comfortably at night, users of tests and other assessment techniques must believe that the process of assessment employed to answer such questions is fully up to the task.

Assumption 5: Assessment can pinpoint phenomena that require further attention or study. In addition to their function in evaluation for the purpose of making sometimes momentous judgments, an assumption in measurement is that tools of assessment can be used for diagnostic purposes. *Diagnosis* may be defined broadly as a conclusion reached on the basis of evidence and opinion through a process of distinguishing the nature of something and ruling out alternative conclusions. Terms such as *diagnostic test* and *diagnostic method* refer to tools or techniques used to make diagnoses.

In the field of medicine, a diagnosis is perhaps best associated with a name of some illness. A medical diagnosis may be arrived at on the basis of a physical examination, medical test data, and knowledge of the patient's medical history. In the field of education, similar tools may contribute to a comprehensive assessment. For example, a child with a reading problem may be given a thorough optometric examination and a diagnostic reading test. The resulting data will be interpreted in the context of the child's educational history. A precise statement regarding the specifics of the child's reading problem—a diagnosis—will be made.

In psychology, as in medicine, diagnosis is perhaps best associated in the public mind with the names of various illnesses, albeit mental illnesses. For example, one speaks of a diagnosis of depression or schizophrenia. In reality, however, the term *diagnosis* is used in a much broader sense, one that in general has to do with pinpointing psychological or behavioral phenomena, usually for further study. For example, a psychologist specializing in measurement might use diagnostic techniques to analyze how behavior and thinking involved in taking a test administered by computer differs from behavior and thinking involved in taking that same test administered in a paper-and-pencil format. A psychologist specializing in jury research might use diagnostic techniques to analyze what is and is not compelling to a jury about various arguments. A psychologist specializing in engineering psychology might use diagnostic techniques to analyze the pros and cons of different positionings of a new control on an automobile's dashboard.

Assumption 6: Various sources of data enrich and are part of the assessment process. To understand a student, a convict, an employee, a therapy client, or any person in any role or capacity, data from a test can be helpful. However, testing and assessment professionals understand that decisions that are likely to significantly influence the course of an examinee's life are ideally made not on the basis of a single test score but, rather, from data from many different sources. Exactly what type of additional information is needed will, of course, vary with the questions the assessment procedure was initiated to answer. A partial listing of some other types of data that may be relevant to the decision-making process would include information about the examinee's current as well as past physical/mental health and academic and occupational status. Relevant family history and current family status may also make important contributions to the decision-making process, as may knowledge of the examinee's values, aspirations, and motivation.

Assumption 7: Various sources of error are part of the assessment process. In everyday conversation, we use the word "error" to refer to mistakes, miscalculations, and the like. In the context of the assessment enterprise, "error" need not refer to a deviation, an oversight, or something that otherwise violates what might have been expected. To the contrary, "error" in the context of psychological testing and assessment traditionally refers to something that is not only expected but also considered a component of the measurement process. In this context, *error* refers to a long-standing assumption that factors other than what a test purports to measure will influence performance on the test. Because error is a variable in any psychological assessment process, we often speak of *error variance.* Test scores earned by examinees are typically subject to questions concerning the degree to which the test score reflects error variance. For example, a score on an intelligence test could be subject to debate concerning the degree to which the obtained score truly reflects the examinee's IQ, and the degree to which it reflects error variance.

Potential sources of error are legion. An examinee's having the flu or not having the flu when taking a test is one source of error variance. In a more general sense, then, examinees are sources of error variance. Examiners, too, are sources of error variance. For example, some examiners are more professional than others in the extent to which they follow the instructions governing how and under what conditions a test should be administered. Tests themselves are another source of error variance; some tests are simply better than others in measuring what they purport to measure. There are other sources of error variance and we will discuss them in greater detail in Chapter 5.

Instructors who teach the undergraduate measurement course will, on occasion, hear a student refer to error as "creeping into" or "contaminating" the measurement process. Yet measurement professionals tend to view error as simply an element in the process of measurement, one for which any theory of measurement must surely account.

Assumption 8: Tests and other measurement techniques have strengths and weaknesses. Competent test users understand a great deal about the tests they use. They understand, among other things, how a test they use was developed, the circumstances under which it is appropriate to administer the test, how the test should be administered and to whom, how the test results should be interpreted and to whom, and what the meaning of the test score is. Competent test users understand and appreciate the limitations of the tests they use, as well as how those limitations might be compensated for by data from other sources. All of this may sound quite commonsensical. It probably is. Yet this deceptively simple assumption—that test users know the tests they use and are aware of the tests' limitations—is emphasized repeatedly in the codes of ethics of associations of assessment professionals.

Assumption 9: Test-related behavior predicts non-test-related behavior. Many tests involve tasks such as blackening little grids with a number 2 pencil or simply pressing keys on a computer keyboard. The objective of such tests typically has little to do with predicting future grid-blackening or key-pressing behavior. Rather, the objective of the test is more typically to provide some indication of other aspects of the examinee's behavior. For example, patterns of answers to true-false questions on the MMPI are used as indicators of the presence of mental disorders. The tasks in some tests mimic the actual behaviors that the test user is attempting to understand. By their nature, however, such tests yield only a sample of the behavior that can be expected to be emitted under nontest conditions. And in general, testing and assessment are conducted with the presumption that meaningful generalizations can be made from test data to behavior outside the testing situation.

Assumption 10: Present-day behavior sampling predicts future behavior. Tests sample what a person does on the day the test is administered. The obtained sample of behavior is typically used to make predictions about future behavior, such as predicted work performance of a job applicant. A rare exception to this assumption occurs in some forensic (legal) matters, where psychological tests may be used not to predict behavior but to postdict it—that is, to aid understanding of behavior that has already taken place. For example, there may be a need to understand a criminal defendant's state of mind at the time of the commission of a crime. Although it is beyond the capability of any known testing or assessment procedure to reconstruct one's state of mind, behavior samples taken at one point may be useful under certain circumstances in shedding light on the nature of one's state of mind at some point in the past. Additionally, other tools of assessment, such as case history data or the defendant's personal diary during the period in question, might all be of great value in such an evaluation.

Assumption 11: Testing and assessment can be conducted in a fair and unbiased manner. If we had to pick the one of these twelve assumptions that is more controversial than the remaining eleven, this one is it. Decades of court challenges to various tests and testing programs have sensitized test developers and users to the societal demand that tests be developed so as to be fair and that tests be used in a fair manner. Today, all major test publishers strive to develop instruments that, when used in strict accordance with guidelines in the test manual, are fair. One source of fairness-related problems is the test user who attempts to

Table 1-1
SAT Scores in 1987 and 1994 by Group Membership

Data such as these from the testing professionals who developed the SAT stimulate discussion regarding how fair tests actually are. Why, for example, should males consistently do better than females on the Mathematics portion of the test? To what extent can such differences be explained by genetic or environmental factors? To what extent might the test itself account for such differences? Is the test measuring skills that males, for whatever reason, excel at?

| | 1987 | | | | 1994 | | | |
| | Verbal | | Mathematics | | Verbal | | Mathematics | |
	Men	Women	Men	Women	Men	Women	Men	Women
American Indian	396	391	452	413	397	395	459	425
Asian Americans	408	403	543	498	417	414	557	514
Black	354	349	391	367	348	354	399	381
Mexican American	387	373	449	402	375	368	448	410
Puerto Rican	366	355	423	380	371	365	432	395
Other Hispanic	393	382	459	408	389	379	462	414
White	452	442	514	466	445	441	519	475
Other	415	396	485	428	426	424	505	459
National Averages	*435*	*425*	*500*	*453*	*425*	*421*	*501*	*460*

Source: College Board

use a particular test with people whose background and experience are different from the background and experience of people for whom the test was intended. In such instances, it is useful to emphasize that tests are tools that, like other, more familiar tools (hammers, ice picks, shovels, etc.), can be used properly or abused.

Some potential problems related to test fairness are more political than psychometric in nature, such as the use of tests in various social programs. For example, heated debate often surrounds affirmative action programs in selection, hiring, and/or access or denial of access to various opportunities. In many cases, the real question to be debated is, "What do we as a society wish to accomplish?" not "Is this test fair?"

How well does the assessment enterprise live up to the assumption that it can be carried out in a fair and unbiased manner? Alternative responses to such a question would make for a very lively debate. On the Scholastic Aptitude Test (SAT), for example, differences have traditionally existed in test scores as a function of gender and cultural group membership (see Table 1–1). On the basis of such data, some have questioned how predictive such tests are of minority students' ability. Others have argued that such tests rightfully reflect expectations of learning of the majority culture and that any deficits in that learning will be reflected in the test scores.

Assumption 12: Testing and assessment benefit society. At first glance, the prospect of a world devoid of testing and assessment might seem very appealing, especially from the perspective of a harried student preparing for a week of midterm examinations. Yet a world without tests would most likely turn out to be more of a nightmare than a dream. In such a world, people could hold themselves out to the public as surgeons, bridge builders, or airline pilots regardless of their background, ability, or professional credentials. In a world without tests, teachers and school administrators could arbitrarily place children in different types of special classes simply because that is where they believed the children belonged. Considering the many critical decisions that are based on testing and assessment procedures, as well as the possible alternatives (including decision making on the basis of human judgment, nepotism, and the like), we can readily appreciate the need for the assessment enterprise and be thankful for its existence.

Who, What, and Why?

Who are the parties in the assessment enterprise? What types of settings are assessments conducted in? Why is assessment conducted? Think about the answer to each of these important questions before reading on. Then, check your own ideas against those that follow.

Who Are the Parties?

The parties to the assessment enterprise are developers and publishers of tests or other methods of assessment; users of tests and other methods of assessment; and people who are evaluated by means of tests and other methods of assessment. A fourth and frequently overlooked party is society at large. Referring to these parties, respectively, as (1) the test developer, (2) the test user, (3) the test-taker, and (4) society at large, let's take a closer look at each in the context of the assessment enterprise.

The test developer Test developers create tests or other types of methods of assessment. The American Psychological Association (APA) estimates that upward of 20,000 new psychological tests are developed each year (APA, 1993). Among these new tests are some that were created for a specific research study, some that were created in the hope that they would be published, and some that represent refinements or modifications of existing tests. Tests strive to yield insights on topics as diverse as art appreciation and zoophobia (fear of animals). But although the content and objectives of the tests may vary greatly, all of them will have—or should have—something in common: adherence to the standards for test development set by an appropriate professional organization.

Recognizing that tests and the decisions made as a result of their administration can have a significant impact on testtakers' lives, a number of professional organizations have published standards of ethical behavior that specifically address aspects of responsible test development and use (for example, American Association for Counseling and Development, 1988; American Psychological Association, 1990; Committee on Ethical Guidelines for Forensic Psychologists, 1991; Committee on Professional Practice and Standards, 1994; National Association of School Psychologists, 1984). Perhaps the most detailed document addressing such issues is one jointly written by the American Educational Research Association, the American Psychological Association, and the National Council on Measurement in Education. Referred to by many psychologists simply as "the *Standards*," *Standards for Educational and Psychological Testing* covers issues related to test construction and evaluation, test administration and use, and special applications of tests, such as special considerations when testing linguistic minorities. Revised periodically, the *Standards* is an indispensable reference work for professional users and developers of psychological and educational tests. It assists professionals in evaluating the instruments available to them by providing a sound frame of reference for addressing all the relevant issues.

The test user   Tests are used by a wide range of professionals, including clinicians, counselors, human resources personnel, and teachers and other school personnel. The *Standards,* as well as the official guidelines of various other professional organizations, have much to impart to test users about how, why, and the conditions under which tests should be used. The principles of professional ethics promulgated by the National Association of School Psychologists (NASP, 1984) stress, for example, that school psychologists should select and use the test or tests that are most appropriate for each individual student. The NASP principles further emphasize that any questions that serve to prompt the psychological assessment of students be answered in as comprehensive manner as possible—that is, with as much background information and other data as possible, including data from behavioral observation.

The test user has ethical obligations that must be fulfilled even before any testtaker is exposed to a test. For example, the test must be stored in a way that reasonably ensures that its specific contents will not be made known in advance—leaving open the possibilities of irregularities later. Note that we used the term *specific contents* in describing what must be secured from testtakers in advance of the test. In the case of some specific types of tests, mostly tests of achievement, acquainting the testtaker with the general type of questions the test will contain helps to lift the veil of mystery that may surround a test and minimize the associated test anxiety (see, for example, the booklets prepared for prospective Scholastic Aptitude Test or Graduate Record Examination examinees). With some types of tests, such as intelligence tests and projective tests of personality, such pretest descriptions of the test materials would not be advisable because they might compromise the resulting data. Another obligation of the test user before the test's administration is to ensure that a prepared and suitably trained person administers the test properly. The test administrator (or examiner) must be familiar with the test materials and procedures and have at the test site all the materials needed to properly administer the test—a sufficient supply of test protocols and other supplies, a stopwatch, if necessary, and so forth.[4] The test examiner must also ensure that the room the test will be conducted in is suitable and conducive to the testing (see Figure 1–5). To the extent that it is possible, distracting conditions such as excessive noise, heat, cold, interruptions, glaring sunlight, crowding, inadequate ventilation, and so forth should be avoided. Even a badly scratched or graffiti-grooved writing surface on a desk can act as a contaminating influence on the test administration; if the writing surface is not reasonably smooth, the written productions made on it may in some instances lead a test scorer to suspect that the examinee had a tremor or some type of perceptual motor deficit. In short, if the test is a standardized one, it is the obligation of the test administrator to see that reasonable testing conditions prevail during the test administration; if for any reason those conditions did not prevail during an administration of the test (for instance, there was a fire drill or a real fire), an accounting of such unusual conditions should be enclosed with the test record.

Especially in one-on-one or small-group testing, rapport between the examiner and examinee is important. In the context of the testing situation, *rapport* may be defined as a working relationship between the examiner and the examinee. Such a working relationship can sometimes be achieved with a few words of "small talk" when examiner and examinee are introduced. If appropriate, some words regarding the nature of the test as well as why it is important for examinees to do their best may also be helpful. In other instances, as with the case of a frightened child, the achievement of rapport might involve more elaborate techniques such as engaging the child in play or some other activity until the child is deemed to have acclimated to the examiner and the surroundings. It is important that attempts to establish rapport with the testtaker not compromise any rules of the test's standardized administration instructions.

Evidence exists to support the view that examiners themselves may have an effect on test results. Whether the examiner is familiar or a stranger (Sacks, 1952; Tsudzuki et al., 1957), whether the examiner is present or absent (Bernstein, 1956), and the general manner of the examiner (Exner, 1966; Masling, 1959; Wickes, 1956) are some factors that may influence performance on ability as well as personality tests (see also Cohen, 1965; Kirchner, 1966; Masling, 1960). In assessing children's abilities, the effect of examiner sex, race, and experience has been examined with a mixed pattern of results (Lutey & Copeland, 1982). Whereas some studies have indicated that students receive higher scores from female than from male examiners (e.g., Back & Dana, 1977; Gillingham, 1970; Samuel, 1977), others have found that the key variable is whether the examiner and student are of the same or opposite sex. For example, Smith, May, and Lebovitz (1966) and Cieutat (1965) found that students perform better with exam-

---

4. *Protocol* in everyday usage refers to diplomatic etiquette. A less common usage of the word is as a synonym for the first copy or rough draft of a treaty or other official document before its ratification. This second meaning comes closer to the way the word is used with reference to psychological tests, as a noun referring to the form or sheet on which the testtaker's responses have been entered.

Figure 1–5
Less-Than-Optimal Testing Conditions

In 1917, new Army recruits sat on the floor as they were administered the first group tests of intelligence—not ideal testing conditions by current standards.

iners of the opposite sex, but Pedersen, Shinedling, and Johnson (1968) found that students perform better with examiners of the same sex. Examiner race and experience have been examined in a number of studies, and reviews of these studies have concluded that these variables have little effect on student performance (Sattler, 1988; Sattler & Gwynne, 1982).

No matter how psychometrically sound a test is, the purpose of the test will be defeated if the test user fails to competently manage all phases of the testing or assessment process. For that reason alone, it is undeniably necessary for all test users, as well as all potential users of tests, to have a working familiarity with principles of measurement.

The testtaker Testtakers approach an assessment situation in different ways, and test users must be sensitive to the diversity of possible responses to a testing situation. On the day of test administration, testtakers may vary on a continuum with respect to numerous variables, including:

- The amount of test anxiety they are experiencing and the degree to which that test anxiety might significantly affect the test results.

- Their capacity and willingness to cooperate with the examiner or to comprehend written test instructions.

- The amount of physical pain or emotional distress being experienced.

- The amount of physical discomfort brought on by not having had enough to eat, having had too much to eat, or other physical conditions.

- The extent to which they are alert and wide awake as opposed to "nodding out."

- The extent to which they are predisposed to agreeing or disagreeing when presented with stimulus statements.

- The extent to which they have received prior coaching.

- The importance they may attribute to portraying themselves in a good—or bad—light.

- The extent to which they are, for lack of a better term, "lucky" and can "beat the odds" on a multiple-choice achievement test (even though they may not have learned the subject matter).

As we will see, testtakers have a number of rights in assessment situations. For example, testtakers have the right to informed consent to testing, the right to have the results of the testing held confidential, and the right to be informed of the findings.

Society at large

> The uniqueness of individuals is one of the most fundamental characteristic facts of life. . . . At all periods of human history men have observed and described differences between individuals. . . . But educators, politicians, and administrators have felt a need for some way of organizing or systematizing the many-faceted complexity of individual differences. (Tyler, 1965, p. 3)

The societal need for "organizing" and "systematizing" has historically manifested itself in such varied questions as "Who is a witch?" "Who is schizophrenic?" and "Who is qualified?" The nature of the specific questions asked has shifted with societal concerns. The methods used to determine the answers have varied throughout history as a function of factors such as intellectual sophistication and religious preoccupation. Palmistry, podoscopy, astrology, and phrenology, among other pursuits, have had proponents who argued that the best means of understanding and predicting human behavior was through the study of the palms, the feet, the stars, bumps on the head, tea leaves, and so on.

Unlike such pursuits, the assessment enterprise has roots in science. Through systematic and replicable means that can produce compelling evidence, the assessment enterprise responds to what Tyler (1965, p. 3) referred to as the societal "need for some way of organizing or systematizing the many-faceted complexity of individual differences."

What Types of Settings Are Assessments Conducted In and Why?

Educational settings From your own experience, you are probably no stranger to the many types of tests administered in the classroom. You have taken achievement tests—some constructed by teachers, others constructed by measurement professionals. You may have taken tests designed to assess your ability, aptitude, and/or interest with respect to a particular occupation or course of study. You may have also taken a group-administered test of intelligence, now also referred to as a *school ability test*. Such tests are frequently administered, in part, to help identify children who may not be achieving at a level commensurate with their capability. In cases where appropriate, further evaluation with more specialized instruments may follow to assess the need for special education intervention. *Public Law 94–142,* now referred to as the *Individuals with Disabilities Education Act* (IDEA), mandates that appropriate educational programs be made available to individuals with disabilities between the ages of 3 and 21 who require special education. *Public Law 99–457* specifies that services be delivered to preschoolers with disabilities (birth to age 2) and encourages services to at-risk infants, toddlers, and their families.

Tests are often used in educational settings to diagnose learning and/or behavior problems and to establish eligibility for special education programs. Individually administered intelligence and achievement measures are most often used for diagnostic purposes and are generally administered by school psychologists, psychoeducational diagnosticians, or similarly trained professionals. Interviews, behavioral observation, self-report scales, and behavior checklists are also widely used in educational settings.

Another variety of assessment that takes place daily throughout the country, in every classroom, and at every educational level is informal assessment. Evidence of such assessment comes not in test scores but in a variety of ways ranging from a sincere, enthusiastic "Good!" verbalized by instructors to nonverbal expressions of disappointment. As complex and interesting as the study of informal assessment may be, this text will limit its scope to testing and assessment of the more formal variety.

In recent years, we have witnessed the birth of a new type of achievement test: a certification of education. Particularly at the high school level, students in some areas of the country are being evaluated at the end of their course of study to determine if they indeed have acquired the minimal knowledge and skills expected of a high school graduate. Students unable to pass this certification test receive a certificate of attendance as opposed to a high school diploma. Needless to say, the cutting score (that is, the dividing line between passing and failing) on such a test is one with momentous consequences, and its determination must be made only by persons with a very sound technical knowledge of tests and measurement.

Another type of test administered in educational settings is that used for educational selection. Many colleges and universities require scores on standardized tests such as the Scholastic Aptitude Test (SAT) or the Graduate

Record Examination (GRE) as part of the undergraduate or graduate school admission process. Foreign applicants to North American universities may be required to take a standardized test of English proficiency as part of their admission application. Few, if any, universities rely solely on standardized test scores in making admissions decisions. Typically, such decisions are based on an assessment of a number of factors ranging from grade-point average to letters of recommendation to written statements by the applicant to extracurricular interests and activities. To fulfill affirmative action requirements, variables such as ethnic background and gender may sometimes enter into the admission decision as well. Chapter 10 covers in detail psychological testing and assessment in educational settings.

Counseling settings   The use of assessment in a counseling context may occur in environments as diverse as a school, a prison, or a government or privately owned institution. Regardless of where it is done, assessment is typically undertaken to identify various strengths or weaknesses, with the ultimate objective being an improvement in the assessee's adjustment, productivity, and/or general quality of life. Measures of social and academic skills or abilities and measures of personality, interest, attitudes, and values are among the many types of tests that a counselor might administer to a client. Objectives in testing for counseling purposes vary with stage of life and particular situation; questions to be answered range from ''How can this child work and play better with other children?'' to ''What career is the client best suited for?'' to ''What activities are recommended for retirement?'' Since the testtaker is in many instances the primary recipient and user of the data from a test administered by a counselor, it is imperative that a well-trained counselor fully explain the test results. Alternatively, the results of the test should be readily interpretable by testtakers themselves through easy-to-follow instructions.

Clinical settings   Tests and other methods of assessment (such as interviews, case studies, and behavioral observation) are widely used in clinical settings such as inpatient and outpatient clinics; public, private, and military hospitals; private-practice consulting rooms; schools; and other institutions to screen for or diagnose behavior problems. Situations that might call for tests and other tools of clinical assessment include the following:

- A private psychotherapy patient wishes to be evaluated to see if the assessment can provide any nonobvious clues regarding his maladjustment.

- A school psychologist clinically evaluates a child experiencing learning difficulties to determine if her problem lies in a deficit of ability, a problem of adjustment, a discrepancy between teaching techniques being employed and the child's favored receptive and expressive modalities, or some combination of such factors.

- A psychotherapy researcher uses assessment procedures to determine if a particular method of psychotherapy is effective in treating a particular problem.

- A psychologist/consultant retained by an insurance company is called on to give an opinion as to the reality of a patient's psychological problems; is the patient really experiencing such problems or malingering?

- A court-appointed psychologist is asked to give an opinion as to a defendant's competency to stand trial.

- A prison psychologist is called on to give an opinion as to how rehabilitated a prisoner convicted for a violent crime is.

The tests employed in clinical settings may be intelligence tests, personality tests, neuropsychological tests, or other specialized instruments, depending on the presenting or suspected problem area. The hallmark of testing in clinical settings is that the test or measurement technique is employed with only one individual at a time; group testing can be used only for screening at best—identifying those individuals who require further diagnostic evaluation. In Chapter 14 and elsewhere, we will look at the nature, uses, and benefits of clinical assessment.

Business settings   In the business world, tests are used in many areas, particularly human resource management. As we will see in Chapter 17, personnel psychologists use tests and measurement procedures to assess whatever knowledge or skills an employer needs to have assessed—be it the ability of a prospective air traffic controller to sustain attention to detail for hours on end or the ability of a prospective military officer to lead others. A wide range of achievement, aptitude, interest, motivational, and other tests may be employed in the decision to hire as well as in related decisions regarding promotions, transfer, performance and/or job satisfaction, and eligibility for further training. Engineering psychologists also employ a variety of existing and specially devised tests to help people at home and in the workplace, in part by designing ergonomically efficient consumer and industrial products—products ranging from office furniture to spaceship cockpit layout.[5]

Consumer psychologists help corporate America in the development, marketing, and sale of products. Using tests as well as other techniques, psychologists who specialize in this area may be involved in "taking the pulse" of the consumers—helping to predict the public's receptivity to a new product, a new brand, or a new advertising or marketing campaign. "What type of advertising will appeal to which type of individual?"—tests of attitudes and values have proved to be one valuable source of information to consumer psychologists and

---

5. "Ergonomically efficient"? An *erg* is a unit of work and *ergonomics* is the study of work; more specifically in the present context, it is the relationship between people and tools of work. Among other endeavors, engineering psychologists are involved in designing things so that we can see, hear, reach, or generally use them better. For example, it was through extensive research by engineering psychologists that the division of letters and numbers that appears on a telephone was derived. Interested in obtaining a firsthand look at the kind of work engineering psychologists do? Take a moment to look through journals like *Ergonomics, Applied Ergonomics,* and *Man-Environment Systems* next time you're in your university library.

marketing professionals who endeavor to answer such questions. Tests and measurement in consumer psychology are the subject of Chapter 18.

Other settings   Testing and assessment procedures are used in many other areas. Credentialing professionals is one such area. Before they are legally entitled to practice medicine, physicians must pass an examination. Law school graduates cannot hold themselves out to the public as attorneys until they pass their state's bar examination. Psychologists, too, must pass an examination entitling them to present themselves to the public as psychologists. And just as physicians can take further training and a test indicating that they are "board-certified" in a particular area, so can psychologists specializing in certain areas be evaluated for a diploma from the American Board of Professional Psychology to recognize excellence in the practice of psychology.

Measurement may play an important part in program evaluation—be it a large-scale governmental program or a small-scale privately funded one. Is the program working? How can the program be improved? Are funds being spent in the areas where they ought to be spent? These are the types of general questions that tests and measurement procedures used in program evaluation are designed to answer.

Psychological assessment plays a valuable role in the process of psychological theory building; tests and measures may be employed in basic research to confirm or disprove hypotheses derived from behavioral theories. Tests, interviews, and other tools of assessment may be used to learn more about the organization of psychological traits and serve as vehicles by which new traits can be identified.

The courts rely on psychological test data and related expert testimony as one source of information to help answer important questions such as "Is this convict competent to be executed?" "Is this parent competent to take custody of the child?" and "Did this defendant know right from wrong at the time the criminal act was committed?" Issues such as these are covered in the forensic psychology section of Chapter 14.

Issues about testing people with disabling conditions have become increasingly prominent in recent years, and our survey of these issues as well as a glimpse at specialized measurement procedures used in this area appears in Chapter 16. In Chapter 15 we detail some of the methods used by neuropsychologists to help in the diagnosis and treatment of neuropsychological deficits.

Evaluating the Quality of Tests

What Is a "Good" Test or Assessment Procedure?

In everyday language, psychologists, other professionals, and laypeople may use words such as "good" and "bad" in describing a test. But what constitutes a good test? Purely from the standpoint of logic, the criteria for a good test would include clear instructions for administration, scoring, and interpretation. It would also seem to be a plus if a test offered economy in the time it takes to administer, score, and interpret it. Most of all, a good test would seem to be one that measures what it purports to measure. Ideally, the results of the assessment procedure lead to an improved quality of life for the testtaker and others.

Beyond simple logic, there are technical criteria that assessment professionals use to evaluate the quality of tests and other measurement procedures. These technical considerations have to do with psychometrics. Synonymous with *psychometry, psychometrics* may be defined as the science of psychological measurement.[6] Although you may not have thought of it before taking this course, aspects of psychometrics affect the daily lives of millions of people. In *Everyday Psychometrics,* a feature that runs through this book, we link some everyday aspect of psychometrics to a topic under discussion. In this chapter, we raise some basic psychometric questions about the tests you see published in popular magazines as well as in other media.

Reliability   A good test or, more generally, a good measuring tool or instrument is *reliable.* As we will explain in Chapter 5, the criterion of reliability has to do with the *consistency* of the measuring tool, the precision with which the test measures. In theory, the perfectly reliable measuring tool consistently measures in the same way. For example, to determine if a digital scale was a reliable measuring tool, we might take repeated measures of the same standard weight, such as a one-pound gold bar. If the scale repeatedly indicated that the gold bar weighed one pound, we would say that the scale was a reliable measuring instrument. If another scale repeatedly indicated that the gold bar weighed exactly 1.3 pounds, we would still say that the scale was reliable, because it provided a consistent result. But suppose we weighed the bar ten times and six of those times the scale registered one pound, on two occasions the bar weighed in at a fraction of an ounce less than a pound, and on two other occasions it weighed in at a fraction of an ounce more than a pound . . . would the scale still be considered a reliable instrument?

Whether we are measuring gold bars, behavior, or anything else, unreliable measurement is a problem to avoid: we want to be reasonably certain that the measuring tool or test we are using will yield the same numerical measurement every time we observe the same thing under the same conditions. Psychological tests, like other tests and instruments, are reliable to varying degrees. Specific procedures for making determinations as to the reliability of an instrument will be introduced in Chapter 5, as will the various types of reliability.

---

6. Variants of these words include the adjective *psychometric* and the nouns *psychometrist* and *psychometrician.* A *psychometrist* holds a master's degree and is qualified to administer specific tests. A *psychometrician* holds a doctoral degree in psychology or some related field (such as education) and specializes in areas such as individual differences, quantitative psychology, or theories of mental testing.

Self-Administered Tests in the Popular Media

Self-administered tests and quizzes have been a part of our popular-media landscape for as long as anyone living can remember. We note with some amusement, for example, tests published in the popular media purporting to measure a wide variety of skills and other characteristics, including the "sex" of one's brain (Moir & Jessel, 1992), children's "emotional IQ" (Barko, 1993), psychic ability (Woolfolk, 1992), communication style (Sandwith, 1994), healthy living habits (Derrow, 1993), "people smarts" and other supposed forms of intelligence (Clifford, 1992; Granat, 1990). But what do such tests actually reveal, if anything? What follows is a test along with excerpts of its accompanying text as published in a *Writer's Digest* article by Robyn Carr (1994) entitled "Do You Have What It Takes?" After you have self-administered it and tallied your score, think about what you have learned as a result of the exercise. And as you make your way through the rest of this book, think again about such self-administered tests in the popular media, and the types of things their creators would have to do to make the test scores derived from them meaningful.

Do you have what it takes? Put away your doubts, your worries, your fears. Take this simple quiz, and find out once and for all if you have the potential to succeed as a writer. . . . Pick the first answer that pops into your mind, and move on to the next question.

1. *I am drawn to writing because:*
   a. *I have an important message to share with the world.*
   b. *I have had many fascinating life experiences.*
   c. *I love to write, and the challenge excites me.*
   d. *I can do it in my underwear.*

2. *I work on my writing:*
   a. *Daily.*
   b. *Most days.*
   c. *Catch as catch can.*
   d. *I rarely have time.*

3. *I am writing:*
   a. *A novel too complex to describe.*
   b. *The kind of novel I love to read.*
   c. *The kind of novel my mother would approve of.*
   d. *A novel that reflects what is most popular in the marketplace.*

4. *I read:*
   a. *Extensively.*
   b. *Occasionally.*
   c. *Rarely.*
   d. *For entertainment.*

5. *In my writing career, I plan to:*
   a. *Work in my underwear.*
   b. *Be isolated and solitary; I enjoy my time alone.*
   c. *Write fabulous stuff, be a great author, a star.*
   d. *Get used to being a glutton for punishment.*

6. *When my work is criticized, I frequently:*
   a. *Have trouble understanding the problem.*
   b. *Become depressed.*
   c. *Really get into finding a solution.*
   d. *Get angry.*

7. *When feedback on my project suggests major changes, I:*
   a. *Write something else and try harder to get it right.*
   b. *Consider the changes and see how they work.*
   c. *Ignore suggestions and keep gathering opinions.*
   d. *Argue and explain.*

8. *When I finally type The End, after much hard work:*
   a. *I send my manuscript by overnight mail to a publisher.*
   b. *I put it aside for a while, then review and revise.*
   c. *I keep working on it; it can never be too good.*
   d. *I stash it in the closet for a year or two.*

9. *When I get a rejection, I:*
   a. *Sink into depression.*
   b. *Contact the editor and ask for "specifics."*
   c. *Shelve the manuscript and move on to the next.*
   d. *Mail the manuscript to another publisher.*

10. After many rejections on a project, I:
    a. Suffer a grave depression.
    b. Keep working on it until I finally get it right.
    c. Put it aside and work on something else.
    d. Take piano lessons.

11. Once I get that first publishing contract, I will:
    a. Drive something younger than I am.
    b. Wave it in a few unsupportive faces around here.
    c. Write what I really want to write.
    d. Already have begun the next project.

12. The best way to achieve a successful writing career is to:
    a. Attend many conferences.
    b. Study many how-to books and magazines.
    c. Write and read compulsively.
    d. Get to know editors personally.

13. I am fascinated by well-known authors':
    a. Income.
    b. Writing style.
    c. Lifestyle.
    d. Work habits.

14. I have to hurry and complete my current manuscript for:
    a. An upcoming contest.
    b. An interested editor.
    c. Extra money for something.
    d. I don't have to hurry for anything.

15. When I'm involved in my writing, I can be stopped by:
    a. A call from my mother.
    b. My spouse's annoyance.
    c. Parental responsibilities.
    d. Blood. Lots of it. And screams. Loud ones. Nearby.

In Carr's (1994) scoring system, five points are awarded for each response keyed as correct, and two points for other responses. The responses keyed correct are as follows:

1 (c), 2 (a or b), 3 (b), 4 (a), 5 (b or c), 6 (c), 7 (b), 8 (b), 9 (d), 10 (c), 11 (d), 12 (c), 13 (a, b, c, or d), 14 (d), 15 (d).

Summing all points yields a total score which, according to Carr (1994) can be interpreted as follows:

65–75 points: You are gutsy, brazen, brave and determined. You put the quality of your work and your learning ahead of everything else and yet are not afraid to dream, and dream big. Nothing can stop you—New York, take notice!

55–64 points: You stand a good chance of pulling it together; perhaps there are areas you need to work on, like saying no or reading with a new mission to learn. You have many of the qualities of successful writers, and such shortcomings as procrastination or rushing can be cured.

45–54 points: Don't worry—many writers have to learn to accept criticism, take rejection in stride, and write that sex scene even though Aunt Gladys will probably have a heart attack. Most writers are afraid of failure; many have trouble protecting their writing time. But if you want to make it as a writer, there are some things you must do; develop those disciplines and work habits required to do the job.

30–44 points: It's possible you want to be a writer more than you want to write, and probable that you have illusions about how writing is done. Maybe you're not willing to take criticism and rejection, not willing to read, study, and write as much as a successful writer has to in order to make it.

Well, what did you think? Would you be in favor of using such a test as a tool in making important decisions about, say, college admission or the award of a scholarship? If you were a publisher seeking to retain authors to write books, do you think you might use such a test as a screening tool? If you, yourself, were contemplating a career as a writer, how much stock would you place in such a test? Why did you answer each of the last three questions the way that you did?

(continued)

Self-Administered Tests in the Popular Media *(continued)*

Perhaps your answers reflected some of the following concerns. This test does not measure the variety of skills that people need to be writers. Is there any reason to believe that this test identifies people who will be good writers? Furthermore, no information is given about how the cutoff scores are established: Why is a score of 65 rated so much more highly than a score of 64? In a related vein, if a person took several of these kinds of tests, would the result be the same each time? Or could a person receive a "Nothing can stop you" rating on some of these kinds of tests, for example, then score low on others?

Finally, some of the questions on this test could be confusing; perhaps some people get lower scores because of confusion about the questions being asked, not because of their interest in writing.

Psychometric techniques provide us with tools to address the practical questions raised above about the quality of tests. As we proceed in our study of psychometrics, we will come to view the tests published in the popular media as thought-provoking at best, but seldom more than a form of entertainment in nature.

Validity   A good test is a *valid* test, and a test is considered to be valid if it in fact measures what it purports to measure. In the gold-bar example given above, the scale indicating the gold bar weighs one pound is a valid scale. Likewise, a test of reaction time is a valid test if it truly measures reaction time. A test of intelligence is a valid test if it truly measures intelligence. A potential problem, however, is that although there is relatively little controversy about the definition of a term such as *reaction time,* a great deal of controversy exists about the definition of *intelligence.* The validity of a particular test might be questioned with regard to the definition of whatever that test purports to measure. A test creator's conception of what constitutes "intelligence" might be different from someone else's, and therein lies the basis for a claim that the test is "invalid."

Questions regarding a test's validity may focus on the items that collectively make up the test. Do the items adequately sample the range of areas that must be sampled to adequately measure the construct? Individual items will also come under scrutiny in an investigation of a test's validity; how do individual items contribute to or take away from the test's validity? The validity of a test may also be questioned in regard to the scores derived from an administration of the test; what do the scores really tell us about the targeted construct? How are high and low scores on the test related to testtakers' behavior? In general, how do scores on this test relate to scores on other tests purporting to measure the same construct? How do scores on this test relate to scores on other tests purporting to measure opposite types of constructs? For example, we might expect one person's score on a valid test of introversion to be inversely related to that same person's score on a valid test of extraversion. That is, the higher the introversion test score, the lower the extraversion test score, and vice versa.

As we will see when we discuss validity in greater detail in Chapter 6, questions concerning the validity of a particular test or assessment procedure extend beyond the specific test or procedure per se. Critical validity-related questions concern the way in which data from a particular test or assessment procedure are used.

Other considerations   If the purpose of a test is to compare the performance of the testtaker with the performance of other testtakers, a good test is one that contains adequate *norms*. Also referred to as *normative data,* norms provide a standard with which the results of measurement can be compared. These types of tests are referred to as *norm-referenced,* and a common goal of such tests is to yield information on the testtaker's standing or ranking relative to some comparison group of testtakers. The SAT and the GRE are two examples of norm-referenced tests; scores reflect the testtaker's standing relative to other testtakers. As an aid to a prospective test user in judging the appropriateness of administering, scoring, and interpreting a norm-referenced test, a complete description of the *norm group* or *normative sample* (the people who were tested with the instrument and with whom current testtakers' performance is being compared) is required. Unfortunately, manuals for norm-referenced tests differ widely in the specificity they employ in describing the norm group. Because of its greater specificity, a description such as "200 male, Black, freshman community college students between the ages of 18 and 20 at New York City Community College" is preferable to one such as "many minority college students from a large community college in the East." In general, the closer the match between the norm group and the examinee(s), the more appropriate the test may be for a given purpose. Some norm-referenced tests are better than others because of the size of the normative sample; all other things being equal, the larger the normative sample, the better.

In contrast to norm-referenced tests, some tests, particularly in the fields of educational and industrial/organizational assessment, are *criterion-referenced.* Whereas norm-referenced tests yield information about a testtaker's relative standing, criterion-referenced tests yield information about an individual's mastery of a particular skill. Has this applicant mastered the skills necessary to be a pilot for this airline? Has this student mastered the ability to spell "sand"? Has this patient mastered the skills necessary for independent living? These are the types of questions criterion-referenced tests may seek to answer. When evaluating a criterion-referenced test, key issues concern the definition of the criterion used by the test developer, the relevance of the test's criterion to the objectives of the current assessment, and the evidence in hand that supports the use of the test for the contemplated purpose.

Must you be an expert in assessment to be able to know a "good" test when you see one? Not necessarily. In some cases, all you need do is locate a review of the test from a reputable source. But where can one find such reviews?

Reference Sources for Test Information

Many reference sources exist for learning more about published tests. These sources vary with respect to detail; some merely provide descriptions of a test, whereas others provide very technical information regarding reliability, validity, norm sample, and other such matters.

Test catalogues   Perhaps one of the most readily accessible sources of information about a test is a catalogue distributed by the publisher of the test. Since most test publishers make available catalogues of their offerings, this source of test information can be tapped by a simple telephone call or note. As you might expect, however, publishers' catalogues usually contain only a brief description of a test and seldom contain the kind of detailed technical information that a prospective user of the test might require. Further, remember that the objective of the catalogue is to sell the test; expect any quotations from reviews critical of a test to be excluded from the description.

An exhaustive list of test publishers and of recently developed or revised psychological tests can be found in the popular reference work *The Eleventh Mental Measurements Yearbook* (Kramer & Conoley, 1992) and in *Test Critiques*, Volumes I–X (Keyser & Sweetland, 1994).

Test manuals   Much more detailed information concerning the development of a particular test, the normative sample, the test's reliability and validity, and other such information should be found in the manual for the test itself. The chances are good that somewhere within your university (be it the library or the counseling center), a collection of popular psychological test manuals is maintained. If not, most test publishers are willing to sell a test manual by itself, sometimes within some sort of "sampler" kit.

Test reviews   Objective reviews of published tests can be found in a number of sources, including professional journals. Perhaps the most comprehensive and authoritative compilation of test reviews is *The Mental Measurements Yearbook (MMY)*, whose first edition was published in 1938. Written by Oscar Krisen Buros, the first *MMY* was approximately four hundred pages in length. As the number of tests made available by commercial publishers has mushroomed, the number of pages in this reference work has grown. Buros died in 1978, but the work he began lives on at the Buros Institute of Mental Measurements at the Department of Educational Psychology of the University of Nebraska—Lincoln. Over one thousand pages long, *The Eleventh Mental Measurements Yearbook* (Kramer & Conoley, 1992) contains information on 477 commercially published tests, with reviews prepared by 412 professional reviewers. Also included is a publishers' directory with a list of test offerings. From test-publisher catalogues, journal articles, and other less formal means (such as tips from a faculty member or reviewer), the staff of the institute monitors the market of commercially available tests and selects certain new and revised tests for review. Between-edition reviews of new and revised tests are accessible through an on-line computer service; as soon as a review received by the institute

Table 1–2
Frequently Used Psychological Tests

Test use varies according to a number of interrelated variables such as setting, population served, and objectives of the testing (see, for example, Lubin et al., 1985; Piotrowski & Lubin, 1990). A school psychologist testing children for classroom ability, a clinical psychologist testing adult outpatients on adjustment-related questions, and a neuropsychologist testing adult inpatients to determine the extent of neurological injury, for example, will all require somewhat different kinds of assessment instruments.

Below we summarize some of the findings from four surveys of psychological test use, each one reporting on the most frequently used psychological test in a particular type of setting. Hutton, Dubes, and Moir (1992) surveyed a national sample of practicing school psychologists, and their findings are reported under School. Under Adolescents are findings from Archer et al.'s (1991) survey of psychologists who specialize in the assessment and treatment of adolescents in private practice, medical, and postsecondary educational settings. The findings under the heading Outpatient are from a study of trends in outpatient testing (Piotrowski & Keller, 1989). Under the heading Inpatient are the findings from a study of psychological testing practices in acute-care inpatient settings (Sweeney et al., 1987). Abbreviations for many of the tests appear within the grid, and a key to the abbreviations appears below it. The tests include intelligence tests (WISC-R, WAIS-R, WPPSI, Stanford-Binet, Shipley Hartford Institute of Living Scale), achievement tests (PIAT, WRAT, Stanford Achievement Test), personality tests (MMPI, Rorschach, TAT, Sentence Completion Test, Goodenough Draw-A-Man, HFD, H-T-P, KFD), specialized ability tests (Wechsler Memory Scale, Bender-Gestalt, Key Math Diagnostic Arithmetic Test), and other tests such as the Vineland Adaptive Behavior Scales and the Beck Depression Inventory. You probably are not familiar with many of these tests right now . . . but you will be.

What are the most popular psychological tests? Keeping in mind that the answer varies by setting, it seems fair to say that, overall, tests such as the MMPI, the Wechsler intelligence scales (for adults and children), the Bender-Gestalt, the Rorschach, and the TAT are among the most widely used.

From a ten-year study on test usage, Piotrowski and Keller (1992) conclude that "psychologists in applied settings rely on traditional tests and assessment approaches" (p. 77). Changes in patterns of test usage tend to be slow. Some relative newcomers that are not yet in the "top 10" but gaining ground include the Millon Clinical Multiaxial Inventory (MCMI), the Profile of Mood States, and the Personality Inventory for Children (Piotrowski & Keller, 1992).

School	Adolescents	Outpatient	Inpatient
1. WISC-R	WISC-R/WAIS-R	MMPI	MMPI
2. Key Math DAT	Rorschach	WAIS-R	Rorschach
3. WRAT/WRAT-R	Bender-Gestalt	Bender-Gestalt	WAIS-R/WISC-R
4. PIAT	TAT	WISC-R/WPPSI	TAT
5. Vineland	Sentence Completion	HFD	Bender-Gestalt
6. SAT	MMPI	Sentence Completion	Figure Drawings
7. Illinois TPA	HFD	H-T-P	Sentence Completion
8. Goodenough Draw-A-Man	H-T-P	Rorschach	Wechsler Memory Scale
9. WAIS-R	WRAT	TAT	Shipley-Hartford
10. WPPSI	KFD	WRAT	Beck Depression Inventory

Abbreviations: DAT: Diagnostic Arithmetic Test; HFD: Human Figure Drawing; H-T-P: House-Tree-Person; KFD: Kinetic Family Drawing; MMPI: Minnesota Multiphasic Personality Inventory; PIAT: Peabody Individual Achievement Test; SAT: Stanford Achievement Test; TAT: Thematic Apperception Test; TPA: Test of Psycholinguistic Abilities; WAIS-R: Wechsler Adult Intelligence Scale–Revised; WISC-R: Wechsler Intelligence Scale for Children–Revised; WPPSI: Wechsler Preschool and Primary Scales of Intelligence; WRAT: Wide Range Achievement Test.

receives its editorial stamp of approval, it is entered into a computer and is available to anyone with access to it. In addition, supplements are published during some intermediate years. *The Supplement to the Eleventh Mental Measurements Yearbook* (Conoley & Impara, 1994), for example, contains 197 test reviews of 101 commercially available instruments.

In addition to the *MMY,* The University of Nebraska Press distributes a number of other publications from the Buros Institute of Mental Measurements, including *Tests in Print II* (Buros, 1974) and *Tests in Print III* (Mitchell, 1983). *Tests in Print* is essentially an index to tests, test reviews, and literature on tests (including cross-references to the *MMY).* Individual monographs containing information from the *MMY* on a specific area such as personality tests, intelligence tests, vocational tests, mathematics tests, social studies tests, science tests, foreign language tests, English tests, and reading tests are also published by the institute. *Test Critiques,* Volumes I–X (Keyser & Sweetland, 1994) reviews approximately 720 tests. Each review is divided into four parts: a description of the test, the practical applications and uses of the test, technical aspects of the test (normative data, reliability and validity information), and the reviewer's critique of the test.

Test reviews can also be found in a number of other reference works. Critical reviews of a select listing of tests can be found in *Measuring Human Behavior* (Lake et al., 1973).

For reviews of measures used in the fields of personality and social psychology, *Measures of Personality and Social Psychological Attitudes* (Robinson et al., 1991) can be most useful. A review and comparison of measures for the workplace is presented in *The Theory and Measurement of Work Commitment* (Morrow, 1993).

Brief and relatively nonevaluative summaries of various tests are contained in *A Sourcebook for Mental Health Measures* (Comrey et al., 1973). *Measures for Psychological Assessment* (Chun et al., 1975) and *Tests and Measurements in Child Development: Handbook II,* Volumes 1 and 2 (Johnson, 1976), are both noteworthy because they contain reviews of many unpublished as well as published tests. Test reviews also appear in various journals and in publications distributed by various special-interest organizations. As an example of the latter, the Washington, D.C.–based organization Teachers of English to Speakers of Other Languages (TESOL) publishes a review of English-language proficiency tests (Alderson et al., 1987).

Although the format of test reviews may vary, certain dimensions are usually addressed: purpose of the test, age range, administration time, number of forms, scores that are produced, adequacy of the normative sample, evidence of reliability, and evidence of validity. Such information should be available in the test's technical manual.

Our overview of psychological testing and assessment continues in the following chapter with a look backward—the better to appreciate this enterprise in its historical and social context. Some of the legal and ethical considerations in testing will also be introduced.

2

Historical, Cultural, and Legal/Ethical Considerations

A Historical Perspective

Antiquity to the Nineteenth Century

A primitive form of proficiency testing existed in China as early as 2200 B.C. (DuBois, 1966, 1970). Little is known about this Chinese testing program other than that it involved some form of examination of public officials by the Chinese emperor every third year. Much more is known about the civil service examinations extant in China beginning during the Chan dynasty in 1115 B.C. and ending in the year 1905, when a reform measure abolished the system. For three thousand years, the open and competitive system of examinations that prevailed in China provided for evaluation of proficiency in areas such as music, archery, horsemanship, writing, and arithmetic. Proficiency was also examined with respect to skill in the rites and ceremonies of public and social life, civil law, military affairs, agriculture, revenue, and geography (see Figure 2–1).

The historical significance of the testing program in ancient China is that thousands of years ago there existed a civilization that evidenced concern for some of the same basic principles of psychometrics that we are concerned with today. Modern readers might note with fascination that activities such as archery and horsemanship were included among the tests, but keep in mind that the test users of the day felt that civil servants should be proficient in those skills; stated another way, the tests were content-valid. In a period of history when nepotism was no doubt rampant, we can look with admiration to a society where employment was based on open competitive examinations.

Some primitive thoughts about the assessment of personality are evident in early Greco-Roman writings. For example, the Greek physician Hippocrates (460–377 B.C.) advanced the notion that individual differences in temperament were due to the balance of four fluids ("humors," as he referred to them) known to be in the body: blood, phlegm, black bile, and yellow bile. Considering that

Figure 2–1
Testing Booths in China

Unlike exams for a position with the U.S. Postal Service, testing in China went on for days, and examinees occasionally died of the strain in these hundreds of civil service examination "cubicles" in Nanking. This photograph was taken about 20 years after the cessation of such testing in 1905.

Hippocrates lived at a time when exorcism was the treatment of choice for aberrant behavior, the humoral theory represented an important first step in drawing attention away from the supernatural and to the body as a point of focus.

In the *Republic,* Plato (427–347 B.C.) suggested that people should work at jobs consistent with their abilities and endowments, a notion perfectly in accord with the philosophy of modern employment testing. Claudius Galenus (A.D. 131–205), commonly known as Galen, designed experiments to prove that it was the brain and not the heart that was the seat of the intellect. Indeed, historians place the beginning of the Middle Ages, or "Dark Ages," in history at about the time of Galen's death. Interest in individual differences, medicine, and philosophy were subjugated to religious beliefs. The reading of the works of philosophers such as Plato was banned.

Christianity was established as the state religion by A.D. 313 and "psychology texts" of the day dutifully reflected church doctrines. For example, in the *Confessions,* St. Augustine (354–430) discussed topics such as perception, creativity, and self-control while making the point that little could be gained by asking questions about these phenomena, since only God could provide such knowledge. By the time of the Middle Ages, "medical practice" was by and large the province of the clergy, and cures were attempted through methods such as prayer, potions, and magic. In 1265, St. Thomas Aquinas (1225–1274) argued that the notion of a thinking/reasoning capacity in people should be replaced with the notion of an immortal soul.

In a religion-dominated society in which all natural catastrophes were viewed as the work of the devil, persons who seemed different from the rest were viewed as being in league with Satan. Had a manual for diagnosing behavior disorders existed at the time, persons "diagnosed" to be "in league with Satan" might have fallen into one of two subdiagnostic types: "voluntary league" or "involuntary league," the former being viewed as the more severe pathology. Included among the many signs and symptoms deemed to betray demonic possession were a kind of squint referred to as the "evil eye," being cross-eyed, and failing to bleed when pricked. The great need for society to answer the question "Who is possessed?" was reflected in the form of a 1484 papal bull asking the clergy's assistance in identifying evil. Two Dominican monks who responded to the bull, Heinrich Kraemer and Johann Sprenger, wrote an influential treatise on how to identify, try, and dispose of those who threatened the Christian way of life (see Figure 2–2). The sixteenth and seventeenth centuries witnessed innumerable witch hunts, witch trials, and witch executions in Europe as well as in the newly colonized America.

The Renaissance witnessed a rebirth of interest in philosophy and the nature of humanity. Some raised their voices against the clergy's view of abnormal behavior even though doing so placed them in jeopardy. By the seventeenth century, some clergymen were beginning to acknowledge the existence of mental disease. The pendulum had begun to swing toward a more philosophical and scientific view of people.

Many philosophers of the seventeenth, eighteenth, and nineteenth centuries touched in their writings on ideas that later behavioral scientists would research or expand on in theoretical formulations. The French philosopher and mathematician René Descartes (1596–1650) grappled with the question of how mental and physical processes are related. The "British empiricists," as they are called, John Locke, George Berkeley, David Hume, and David Hartley, all made important philosophical contributions. In *An Essay Concerning Human Understanding,* Locke (1690) expressed the view that all knowledge comes from experience, a view elaborated on in works such as Berkeley's *A Treatise Concerning the Principles of Human Knowledge* (1710), Hume's *A Treatise on Human Nature* (1739), and Hartley's *Observations on Man, his Frame, his Duty, and his Expectations* (1749). Christian von Wolff published books entitled *Psychologia Empirica* (1732) and *Psychologia Rationalis* (1734), in which he suggested that a subject called "psychology" be conceived. It was also Wolff who first conceived of psychometry as a science.

The Nineteenth Century

In 1859, a book entitled *On the Origin of Species by Means of Natural Selection* by Charles Darwin (1809–1882) was published. In this important, far-reaching

Figure 2–2
Some "Diagnostic" Techniques of a (Thankfully) Bygone Era

In the Middle Ages, a popular "diagnostic manual" of the day was a book called Malleus Mali-
ficarum *(translated* The Hammer of Witches*). The book was divided into three parts. Part I
affirmed the existence of witches and argued that those who did not accept that fact were either
mistaken or heretics. Part II detailed some telltale signs of collusion with the devil. Part III was
replete with suggestions on how to "examine" witches—usually by torturing them until they
confessed. Also in Part III were guidelines on disposing of witches once a confession had been
extracted; setting the individual on fire, hanging, and mutilations were some of the options
discussed.*

*Two "assessment techniques" used to determine whether an individual was in league with
the devil are illustrated by these nineteenth-century engravings. The procedure illustrated at left
entailed stripping the accused, tying her hand-to-foot, and throwing her into the water; if the
woman floated, it constituted "proof" that the accused was indeed a witch. Other such evidence
might come from an "interview" conducted in a manner illustrated by the engraving at right;
the interviewee was in essence tortured into a confession while on a rack.*

work, Darwin argued that chance variation in species would be selected or rejected for survival by Nature according to adaptivity and survival value. The
case was made that humans had descended from the ape as a result of such
chance genetic variations. This revolutionary notion aroused interest, admiration, and a good deal of enmity—the enmity primarily from members of the
religious community who interpreted Darwin's ideas as an affront to the biblical
account of creation as written in Genesis. An account of a debate that took place

at Oxford University between Thomas Huxley and Bishop Wilberforce conveys the strident tone of the controversy:

> Wilberforce asked Huxley whether it was through his grandmother or his grandfather that he claimed descent from an ape, thus phrasing the central issue in terms every man could understand. Huxley replied that an ape would be preferable to the Bishop as an ancestor, and with that the battle began. (Miller, 1962, p. 129)

Of primary importance to the field of psychology is the fact that the notion of an evolutionary link between human beings and animals conferred a new scientific respectability on experimentation with animals. It also raised questions about how animals and humans compare with respect to states of consciousness—questions that would beg for answers in laboratories of future behavioral scientists.[1]

Darwin's work kindled interest in research in heredity in his half cousin, Francis Galton (1822–1911), an extremely influential figure in measurement history (see the box on pages 46–47).[2] Galton's initial work on inheritance was done with sweet peas, in part because there tended to be fewer variations among the peas in a single pod. In this work with peas Galton pioneered the use of a statistical concept central to psychological experimentation and testing: the coefficient of correlation. Although Karl Pearson (1857–1936) developed the product-moment correlation technique, the roots of this technique can be traced directly to the work of Galton (Magnello & Spies, 1984).

From heredity in peas, Galton's interest turned to heredity in humans and various ways of measuring aspects of people and their abilities. At an exhibition in London in 1884, Galton displayed his Anthropometric Laboratory where, for three or four pence, depending on whether you were already registered or not, you could be measured on variables such as height (standing), height (sitting), arm span, weight, breathing capacity, strength of pull, strength of squeeze, swiftness of blow, keenness of sight, memory of form, discrimination of color, and steadiness of hand. Through his own efforts and his urging of educational institutions to keep anthropometric records on their students, Galton excited widespread interest in psychological-assessment-related data.

Assessment was also an important activity at the first experimental psychology laboratory, founded at the University of Leipzig in Germany by Wilhelm Max Wundt (1832–1920), a medical doctor whose title at the university was Professor of Philosophy. Wundt and his students tried to formulate a general description of human abilities with respect to variables such as reaction

---

1. A tangential note: The influence of Darwin's thinking is also apparent in the theory of personality formulated by Sigmund Freud. From a Darwinian perspective, it would be the strongest persons with the most "efficient" sex drives that would have been most responsible for contributing to the human gene pool. In this context, Freud's notion of the primary importance of instinctual sexual and aggressive urges can better be understood.

2. The reader so inclined is urged to read one of the many volumes that have been written on this highly influential, brilliant, and colorful historical figure (such as Forrest, 1974).

Sir Francis Galton (1822–1911)

It is probably not an overstatement to assert that Sir Francis Galton was one of the world's greatest scientists. Although this brilliant man's interests spanned a wide variety of areas (ranging from fashion to fingerprints to an experimental investigation of the efficacy of prayer) and his writings made contributions in many fields of human endeavor, we focus on those contributions that pertain to the field of psychological testing and assessment.

Galton was the ninth and last child in a large, wealthy, and influential British family. Galton's father was a banker and at his insistence young Galton took up the study of medicine—study that Galton abandoned soon after his father's death. After travel, an award from the Royal Geographic Society for his account of his exploration of southern Africa, the publication of a guide for explorers, and the invention of some new instruments, including a teletype printer and instruments for charting weather, Galton's attention turned to the work of his half cousin Charles Darwin. Galton was intrigued with the implications of Darwin's theory of evolution, and he became increasingly intrigued—particularly with the social implications of the theory—as he grew older. Galton's (1869) study of heredity and genius pioneered the use

of the statistical concept of correlation—a concept most integral to testing. Galton's scientific study of genetics led him to formulate various ways of measuring people, and he described these in his 1883 book, *Inquiries into Human Faculty and Its Development.* Some of the measurement techniques devised by Galton to gauge aspects of human perception included a tool to measure visual discrimination ability (referred to as the Galton bar), a whistle designed for use in measuring auditory discrimination of pitch, and a set of blocks that were similar in appearance but varied in weight in order to measure weight discrimination ability. Also included among the assessment instruments was a questionnaire—not a very revolutionary instrument by contemporary standards but certainly among the first formally used in psychological research when Galton introduced it.

At the International Health Exhibition in London (1884–1885) Galton exhibited the laboratory tools designed to measure people—his "anthropometric laboratory." After the Exhibition closed, the laboratory was reconstructed at London's Science Museum in South Kensington where it continued in operation for six years. During its total period of operation, over 9,000 people had measurements taken on 17 vari-

time, perception, and attention span. The focus at Leipzig was not on how individuals differed but on how individuals were the same. In fact, individual differences were viewed by Wundt as a frustrating source of error in experimentation. Wundt attempted to control all extraneous variables in an effort to reduce error to a minimum. As we will see, attempting to control extraneous variables for the purpose of minimizing error is a routine component of modern-day psychological testing: standardized conditions are used to help ensure that differences in scores are the result of true differences among individuals.

ables—leaving a mass of data that was still being analyzed long after Galton's death in 1911.

Much of Galton's work was used in support of the argument that genius ran in families and that the birth of more eminent people should be encouraged whereas the birth of the less eminent (and, in Darwinian terms, "less fit") should be discouraged. Though he did not completely overlook the effect of environment on intelligence, Galton tended to minimize it—perhaps, as Schultz (1969) has suggested, because "he considered his own education for the most part a waste of time" (p. 92).

In general, Galton is perhaps best remembered for his systematic investigation of individual differences between people—an area of inquiry that has been referred to as a glaring "blind spot" in the field of psychology as it existed before Galton (Murphy, 1949). Despite views on the role of heredity and environment that in today's world would at best be highly controversial, we cannot deny that Galton was a great thinker of his day. As others (such as Flugel & West, 1964) have noted, one would be hard put to name another scientist who was so brilliant and versatile.

In spite of the prevailing research orientation that focused on how people tended to be the same, one of Wundt's students at Leipzig, an American named James McKeen Cattell (Figure 2–3), managed to complete a doctoral dissertation that dealt with individual differences, specifically, individual differences in reaction time. After receiving his doctoral degree from Leipzig, Cattell returned to the United States, and taught at Bryn Mawr and then at the University of Pennsylvania before leaving for Europe to teach at Cambridge. At Cambridge, Cattell came in contact with Francis Galton, whom Cattell later described as "the greatest man I have known" (Roback, 1961, p. 96).

Figure 2–3
The Cattells

The psychologist who coined the term mental test, *James McKeen Cattell (1860–1944), has often been mistakenly credited (along with another psychologist, Raymond B. Cattell—no relation) with the authorship of a measure of infant intelligence called the Cattell Infant Intelligence Scale (CIIS). Actually, it was Psyche (1893–1989), the third of seven children of Cattell and his wife, Josephine Owen, who created the CIIS. From 1919 through 1921, Psyche assisted her famous father in statistical analyses for the third edition of* American Men of Science. *In 1927, she earned a doctor of education degree at Harvard. In 1931, she adopted a son, becoming one of the first unmarried women to do so (Sokal, 1991). Later in the decade she adopted a daughter. Her book* The Measurement of Intelligence in Infants and Young Children *was published in 1940, and it was in that book that the CIIS was introduced. Later in her career, she would write a popular book,* Raising Children with Love and Limits, *which represented a reaction against the permissiveness being advocated by child-rearing authorities such as Benjamin Spock.*

Inspired by his contact with Galton, Cattell returned to the University of Pennsylvania in 1888 and coined the term *mental test* in an 1890 publication. Boring (1950, p. 283) has noted that "Cattell more than any other person was in this fashion responsible for getting mental testing underway in America, and it is plain that his motivation was similar to Galton's and that he was influenced, or at least reinforced by Galton." Cattell went on to accept the position as professor and chairman of the psychology department at Columbia University and for the 26 years he was there not only trained many psychologists but also founded a number of publications (such as *Psychological Review, Science,* and *American Men of Science*). In 1921, Cattell was instrumental in founding the Psychological Corporation, which named 20 of the country's leading psychologists as its directors. The goal of the corporation was the "advancement of psychology and the promotion of the useful applications of psychology." Originally, the corporation's stock was held by 170 psychologists. Today the Psychological Corporation is still very active in providing psychological-test-related services to the profession and to the public.

Other students of Wundt at Leipzig included Charles Spearman, Victor Henri, Emil Kraepelin, E. B. Titchener, G. Stanley Hall, and Lightner Witmer. Spearman is credited with being the originator of the psychometric concept of test reliability. Victor Henri is the Frenchman who would collaborate with Alfred Binet on papers suggesting how mental tests could be used to measure higher mental processes (for example, Binet & Henri, 1895a, 1895b, 1895c). Psychiatrist Emil Kraepelin was an early experimenter with the word association technique as a formal test (Kraepelin, 1892, 1895). Lightner Witmer received his Ph.D. from Leipzig and went on to succeed Cattell as director of the psychology laboratory at the University of Pennsylvania. In March 1896, Witmer was challenged by a public school teacher to provide a solution in the case of a "chronic bad speller" (see Brotemarkle, 1947). Later that year, Witmer founded the first psychological clinic in the United States at the University of Pennsylvania. In 1907, Witmer founded the journal *Psychological Clinic* with the first article entitled "Clinical Psychology" (Witmer, 1907). Witmer has been cited as the "little known founder of clinical psychology" (McReynolds, 1987).

The Twentieth Century

The early 1900s witnessed the birth of the first formal tests of intelligence. As such tests were welcomed into various cultures throughout the world, the testing movement began to gain momentum. As we will see in the rest of this section, there was initially great receptivity throughout the world to instruments that could purportedly measure mental characteristics—intelligence at first and other characteristics (such as those related to personality, interests, attitudes, and values) later.

The measurement of intelligence Much of the nineteenth-century testing that could be described as psychological in nature involved the measurement of sensory abilities, reaction time, and the like. One person who had a vision of broadening testing to include the measurement of cognitive abilities was Alfred Binet (1857–1911). As early as 1895, Binet and his colleague Henri would publish several articles in which they argued for the measurement of abilities such as memory and social comprehension. Ten years later, Binet and collaborator Théodore Simon would publish a 30-item "measuring scale of intelligence" designed to help identify mentally retarded Paris schoolchildren (Binet & Simon, 1905). The Binet test would go through many revisions and translations—and in the process launch both the intelligence testing movement and the clinical testing movement. Before long, psychological tests were in use in settings as diverse as juvenile courts, reformatories, prisons, children's homes, and schools (Pintner, 1931).

In 1939, David Wechsler, a clinical psychologist at Bellevue Hospital in New York City, introduced a test designed to measure adult intelligence—defined as "the aggregate or global capacity of the individual to act purposefully, to think rationally, and to deal effectively with his environment" (p. 3). The test, originally called the Wechsler-Bellevue Intelligence Scale, was revised and renamed the Wechsler Adult Intelligence Scale (WAIS). Later, an "R" (for revision) was added to the name of a further revised version of the test, resulting in the present name, the Wechsler Adult Intelligence Scale (WAIS-R). Later, we will examine Wechsler's definition of intelligence as it was reflected in the series of adults', children's, and young children's intelligence tests that bear his name.

A natural outgrowth of the individually administered intelligence test devised by Binet was the *group* intelligence test. Group intelligence tests came into being in the United States in response to the military's need for an efficient method of screening the intellectual ability of World War I recruits. Because of military manpower needs during World War II, psychologists were enlisted into government service to develop, administer, and interpret group psychological test data. Psychologists returning from military service brought back with them a wealth of applied testing skills that would be useful not only in government service but also in settings as diverse as private industry, hospitals, and schools.

The measurement of personality   The general receptivity to tests of intellectual ability spurred the development of a number of other types of tests (Garrett & Schneck, 1933; Pintner, 1931), including tests of personality. Only eight years after the publication of Binet's scale, the field of psychology was being criticized for being too test-oriented (Sylvester, 1913). By the late 1930s, approximately four thousand different psychological tests were in print (Buros, 1938), and "clinical psychology" was synonymous with mental testing (Institute for Juvenile Research, 1937; Tulchin, 1939).

World War I brought with it not only the need to screen the intellectual functioning of recruits but also the need to screen for personality problems. A government Committee on Emotional Fitness chaired by psychologist Robert S. Woodworth was assigned the task of developing a measure of adjustment and emotional stability that could be administered quickly and efficiently to groups of recruits. The committee developed several experimental versions of what in essence were paper-and-pencil psychiatric interviews. To disguise the true purpose of the test, the questionnaire was labeled and referred to as a Personal Data Sheet. Draftees and volunteers were asked to indicate "Yes" or "No" to a series of questions that probed the existence of various kinds of psychopathology. For example, one of the questions on the test was "Are you troubled with the idea that people are watching you on the street?"

The Personal Data Sheet developed by Woodworth and his colleagues never went beyond the experimental stages, for the armistice ending the war preceded the final form of the test. After the war, Woodworth developed a personality test for civilian use that was based on the Personal Data Sheet and called it the

Woodworth Psychoneurotic Inventory. This inventory was the first widely used self-report test of personality—a method of assessment that would soon be employed in a long line of succeeding personality tests. Personality tests that employ self-report methodologies have both advantages and disadvantages. On the one hand, the person answering the question is—assuming sound judgment and insight—arguably the best qualified person to provide answers. On the other hand, the person may possess neither good judgment nor good insight. And regardless of judgment or insight, respondents might be unwilling to reveal anything that could place them in a negative light. Given these shortcomings of personality assessment by self-report, a need existed for alternative types of personality tests.

One type of test that provided a means of drawing inferences about personality without relying on self-report was the projective test. As we will see in Chapter 12, the projective test is one in which an individual is assumed to "project" onto some ambiguous stimulus his or her own unique needs, fears, hopes, and motivation. The ambiguous stimulus might be an inkblot, a drawing, a photograph, or something else. Perhaps the best known of all projective tests is the Rorschach Inkblot developed by the Swiss psychiatrist Hermann Rorschach. The use of pictures as projective stimuli was popularized in the late 1930s by Henry A. Murray and his colleagues at the Harvard Psychological Clinic (see the box on page 52). In addition to projective tests, other alternatives to reliance on self-report for personality assessment have been—and continually are being—developed. A sampling of these instruments, some additional historical observations, and a general discussion of personality assessment appear in Part 4.

Measurement in various settings   Like the development of the parent field of psychology, the development of psychological measurement can be traced along two distinct threads: the academic and the applied. In the tradition of Galton, Wundt, and other scholars, psychological testing and assessment are practiced today in university psychology laboratories as a means of furthering knowledge about the nature of the human experience: knowledge about intelligence, abilities, potential, personality, creativity, interests, attitudes, values, cognitive processes, social processes, neuropsychological processes—the list goes on.

There is also a very strong applied tradition—one that dates back in modern times to the work of people like Binet and in ancient times to China and the administration of competitive civil service examinations. Which child should be placed in which class? Who of these military recruits should be rejected on the basis of intellectual or personality problems? Which person is best suited for the job? Society requires answers to questions such as these, and psychological tests and measures used in a competent manner can help provide answers. However, because we live in a multicultural society, tests must be developed and used with cultural sensitivity.

Henry A. Murray (1893–1988)

Born in New York City, Henry A. Murray had an impressive collection of initials after his name by 1927; he earned an A.B. (with a major in history) from Harvard in 1915, an M.D. from Columbia in 1919, an M.A. in biology from Columbia in 1920, and a Ph.D. from Cambridge in 1927. Murray (1940, pp. 152–153) reminisced about his budding fascination with the mental life of others, including his colleagues and medical patients at Columbia:

> During my fourth year at the College of Physicians and Surgeons, while waiting for calls to deliver babies in Hell's Kitchen, I completed a modest study of 25 of my classmates, in which 40 anthropometric measures were later correlated with 30 traits.
>
> . . . Later, as an interne [sic] in a hospital, I spent more time than was considered proper for a surgeon, inquisitively seeking psychogenic factors in my patients. Whatever I succeeded in doing for them—the dope fiend, the sword-swallower, the prostitute, the gangster—was more than repaid when, after leaving the hospital, they took me through their haunts in the underworld. This was psychology in the rough, but at least it prepared me to recognize the similarity between downtown doings and uptown dreams. . . . But it was Jung's book, *Psychological Types*, which . . . started me off in earnest toward psychology.

In 1925, Murray visited with Carl Jung in Zurich. He wrote that "we talked for hours, sailing down the lake and smoking before the hearth of his Faustian retreat." Murray was profoundly affected by that meeting: he said that he had *experienced* the unconscious and it was then that he decided to pursue depth psychology as a career.

The Harvard Psychological Clinic had been founded by Morton Prince and it was at Prince's invitation that Murray was hired there as an instructor. In 1937, Murray was made the director of the clinic—one that was fast gaining a reputation for being an exciting, stimulating, innovative place to work. In 1938, Murray with collaborators published the now classic *Explorations in Personality,* a work that described, among other techniques, the Thematic Apperception Test (to be discussed subsequently).

In 1943, Murray left Harvard for a position in the Army Medical Corps to help with the war effort. He established and directed the Office of Strategic Services, an agency charged in part with selecting men for James Bond–like tasks during the war (see OSS, *Assessment of Men,* 1948). In 1947, Murray returned to Harvard, where he lectured part-time and helped establish the Psychological Clinic Annex in 1949. In 1962, Murray became emeritus professor at Harvard. He earned the Distinguished Scientific Contribution Award from the American Psychological Association and the Gold Medal Award for lifetime achievement from the American Psychological Foundation. Murray died of pneumonia on June 23, 1988, at the age of 95.

Culture and Assessment

Culture may be defined as "the socially transmitted behavior patterns, beliefs, and products of work of a particular population, community, or group of people" (Cohen, 1994, p. 5). As taught to us by parents, peers, and societal institutions such as schools, culture prescribes many behaviors and ways of thinking. Spoken language, attitudes toward elders, and techniques of child rearing are but a few critical manifestations of culture. Culture teaches specific rituals to be performed at birth, marriage, death, and other momentous occasions. Culture imparts much about what is to be valued or prized, as well as what is to be rejected or despised. Culture teaches a point of view about what it means to be born of one or another gender, race, or ethnic background. Culture teaches us something about what we can expect from other people and what we can expect from ourselves. Indeed, the influence of culture on an individual's thoughts and behavior may be a great deal stronger than most of us would acknowledge at first blush.

Professionals involved in the assessment enterprise have evidenced an increasing sensitivity to the role of culture in many different aspects of measurement. This sensitivity is manifested in greater consideration of cultural issues with respect to every aspect of test development and use, including decision making on the basis of test data. Unfortunately, it was not always that way (see *Close-up*).

On the subject of culture and assessment, there are many fertile areas for exploration. Here we will briefly examine three: verbal communication, nonverbal communication, and standards of evaluation.

Verbal Communication

Language, the means by which information is communicated, is a key, yet sometimes overlooked, variable in the assessment process. Most obviously, the examiner and the examinee must speak the same language if an assessment is to proceed. If a test is in written form complete with written instructions, the testtaker must obviously be able to read and comprehend what is written. When the language in which the assessment is conducted is not the assessee's primary language, questions may arise as to the extent to which the examinee comprehends all that the examiner verbally communicates. Perhaps to a lesser degree, questions about comprehension also remain when an assessment is conducted with the aid of a translator; subtle nuances of meaning and unusual idioms may somehow become "lost in the translation" and affect the test user's conclusions.

In interview or other situations in which an evaluation is made on the basis of an oral exchange between two parties, a trained examiner may detect through verbal or nonverbal means that the examinee's grasp of the language is deficient. Such is not the case with written tests. If anything, there may well be an assumption that everyone being administered a written test is capable of understanding it and responding appropriately. In the case of written tests, then, it is clearly essential that the testtaker be able to read and comprehend

Tests, Assessment, and Culture

Soon after Alfred Binet introduced intelligence testing in France, the United States Public Health Service began using such tests to measure the intelligence of people seeking to immigrate to the United States. Henry Goddard (1913), the chief researcher assigned to the project and a specialist in the field of mental retardation, early raised (and studied) questions about how meaningful such tests are when used with people from various cultural and language backgrounds. Goddard used interpreters in test administration, employed a bilingual psychologist, and administered mental tests to selected immigrants who appeared mentally retarded to trained observers (Goddard, 1917). This last point is the basis of the false (though widely circulated) claim that Goddard estimated over 80% of all immigrants to be mentally retarded. Goddard states accurately that his research could not make such an estimate about immigrants in general because his subjects were selected for low mental ability.

Thus, the impact of language and culture on the results of scores on mental ability tests was recognized by psychologists even in the early 1900s. One way for the early test developers to deal with this psychometric fact of life was to develop culture-specific tests. That is, the test would be designed for use with people from one culture but not from another. Representative of this approach to test development were early versions of some of the best-known tests of intelligence. For example, the 1937 revision of the Stanford-Binet Intelligence Scale, which enjoyed widespread use until it was revised in 1960, included no minority children in its standardization sample. Similarly, the Wechsler-Bellevue Intelligence Scale, a forerunner of a widely used measure of adult intelligence, contained no minority members in its published standardization sample data. The test's author, David Wechsler (1944), noted that "a large number" of Blacks were tested during the standardization trials but that those data were omitted from the final

test manual "because we did not feel that norms derived by mixing the populations could be interpreted without special provisos and reservations." Hence, Wechsler (1944) stated at the outset that the Wechsler-Bellevue norms could not be used for "the colored populations of the United States." Similarly, the inaugural edition of the Wechsler Intelligence Scale for Children (WISC), first published in 1949 and not revised until 1974, contained no minority children in its standardization sample.

Even though many published tests were, in essence, culture-specific, it soon became apparent that the tests were being administered—improperly—to people from different cultures. Perhaps not surprisingly, testtakers from minority cultures tended to score lower as a group than people from the group for whom the test was developed and standardized. As a specific example, consider this item from the 1949 WISC: "If your mother sends you to the store for a loaf of bread and there is none, what do you do?" Do you see any problem with that item? Do you see any way in which that item might be more apt to be answered correctly by people from one ethnic background than from another? In fact, the item could be problematic for children from Hispanic backgrounds, many of whom had routinely been sent to the store for tortillas; whether they would even know the meaning of "a loaf of bread" was open to question.

Translation of test materials for people who speak a language different from the one the test was initially written in typically poses several problems. Some items may be easier or more difficult than originally intended when translated directly into another language. For example, the old Stanford-Binet vocabulary item *skunk* would have to be changed for administration in Puerto Rico, where skunks are nonexistent. Some vocabulary items may change meanings or have dual meanings when translated. For example, a WISC item such as "Why should most government

Psychological Testing at Ellis Island

Immigrants coming to America via Ellis Island were greeted not only by the Statue of Liberty but also by immigration officials ready to evaluate them with respect to physical, mental, and other variables. Here, a block design test, one measure of intelligence, is administered to a would-be American. Immigrants who failed physical, mental, or other tests were returned to their country of origin at the expense of the shipping company that had brought them. Critics would later charge that at least some of the immigrants who had fared poorly on mental tests were sent away from our shores not because they were indeed mentally deficient but simply because they did not understand English well enough to execute instructions. Additionally, the criterion against which these immigrants from many lands were being evaluated was questioned: Who served as the standardization sample, and how appropriate was that sample for this application?

positions be filled through examinations?" might have to be modified to make reference to "civil service examinations" in languages or cultures where *examinations* most typically refers to medical examinations. Indeed, many items require some change or modification to be both meaningful to the testtaker from another culture and psychometrically equivalent to the original item with respect to its overall contribution to

the test score. Verifying that foreign-language translations of standardized tests are indeed equivalent psychometrically to the original requires a large-scale standardization study in its own right.

Today, test developers typically take many steps to ensure that a major test developed for national use is indeed suitable for use nationally. Those steps might

(continued)

Tests, Assessment, and Culture *(continued)*

involve trying out a preliminary version of the test on a "tryout sample" of testtakers. The data from the tryout sample are typically analyzed in many ways. Test items deemed to be biased with regard to race, gender, or other factors will be eliminated. Further, a panel of independent reviewers may be called upon to go through the test items and review them for possible bias. Examiners who administer the test may be called upon to relate their impressions regarding various aspects of the test administration to the test developer. For example, subjective impressions such as the examiner's impressions of the testtaker's reaction to the test materials may be noted, as might opinions regarding the clarity of instructions and the design of the materials. A national standardization of the test may be executed with the sample of participants mirroring the latest U.S. Census data on age groups by sex, geographical region of the United States, race or ethnic group, and socioeconomic status (as gauged by the highest educational attainment of the head-of-household). Again, rigorous analysis of the data from the standardization sample will typically take place to root out any possible sources of bias. More details regarding the contemporary process of test development will be presented in Chapter 7.

what is written lest the exercise be more reflective of language competency than whatever it is the test purports to measure.

When assessing an individual whose proficiency in the English language is limited or nonexistent, a number of questions and issues arise. How proficient is the assessee in his or her primary language? Can a meaningful assessment take place through an interpreter trained for such an eventuality? Can an alternative and more appropriate assessment procedure be devised to meet the objectives of the assessment? These are questions that by and large must be considered on a case-by-case basis.

If a test developed and standardized on English-speaking people is to be translated into another language, precautions must be taken to ensure that the translation is indeed an equivalent form; merely translating word for word is not satisfactory because some words may have very different connotations, difficulty levels, and/or word frequencies in the other language. If the testing is to be conducted in a language other than English, the examiner should ideally have had special training in administering the test in that language. The reliability and validity of a translated test should be established *for the specific group* the test is to be used with. Thus, for example, if an English-language test designed for use in this country is translated into Spanish, its reliability and validity should be established separately with each of the various Spanish-speaking groups of testtakers with whom it might be used (such as Mexicans, Puerto Ricans, and Guatemalans).

Obvious exceptions to these cautions are tests that have been designed expressly to assess proficiency in the English language. However, even here, a word of caution is in order. An orally administered test of English proficiency should not be construed as representative of written proficiency (and vice versa). Additionally, examiners must ideally be knowledgeable about relevant aspects of the culture from which the people they test come. For example, a child may present as noncommunicative and having only minimal language skills when verbally examined; this finding may be due to the fact that the child is from a culture where elders are revered, where children speak to adults only when they are spoken to and then only in as short a phrase as possible.

In addition to linguistic barriers, the contents of tests from a particular culture are typically laden with items and material—some obvious, some very subtle—that draw heavily from that culture; test performance may, at least in part, reflect not only whatever variables the test purports to measure but also one additional variable—the degree to which the testtaker has assimilated the culture.

Less obvious language-related issues may arise when the examiner and the examinee are native to the same country and speak the same language. Even then, language can sometimes play a subtle role in test outcomes. This is especially true when regional differences in familiarity with particular terms contribute to regional differences in test scores. Consider *lavaliere* as it might appear in the context of a vocabulary test. What does that word mean? The chances that you know the meaning of the word vary depending upon the part of the United States you live in. In some areas of the country, particularly the Midwest, a lavaliere, or pendant, is given by the male to the female in a dating couple as a sign of commitment to the relationship. In the East, a parallel custom involves the pinning on of a pin or the giving of a ring. Owing primarily to cultural practices, and not necessarily to major differences in vocabulary ability, people from the East would be far less likely to answer this vocabulary item correctly. As you might imagine, if a vocabulary test had a number of items on it that were more familiar to students from the Midwest than to students from the East, testtakers from the Midwest would tend to score higher on the test than those from the East. However, would it be fair to conclude on the basis of such test results that the vocabulary of students in the Midwest exceeds that of students in the East? Probably not. At best, such a test might have value in highlighting vocabulary differences that exist between people raised in different areas of the United States.

The spoken dialect of a language may also influence test results. Although Standard American English is the established language in the United States, many variants and dialects of Standard American English are routinely spoken in various communities throughout the country. For example, a dialect of Standard American English that has its own rules of structure, meaning, and pronunciation is Black English (Wolfram, 1971). In assessing African Americans from families and communities in which Black English is predominantly spoken, assessors must be sensitive to the differences, if any, between the language familiar to the assessee and the language of the assessment. Additionally, as

Stephens (1992) points out, the assessor should also be sensitive to the degree to which the person speaking Black English has been exposed to the dominant culture or has made a conscious choice not to become assimilated into the dominant culture. Stephens (1992) observed that in some cases, language may be used by the assessee as a defensive tool to maintain distance from the evaluative relationship.

Nonverbal Communication

Humans communicate not only through verbal means but also through nonverbal means. Facial expressions, finger and hand signs, and shifts in one's position in space may all convey messages. Of course, the messages conveyed by such "body language" may be different from culture to culture. For example, in American culture, one who fails to look another person in the eye when speaking may be viewed as being deceitful or having something to hide. However, in other cultures, such failure to make eye contact when speaking may be a sign of respect.

Having gone on or conducted a job interview, you may have developed a firsthand appreciation for the value of nonverbal communication in an evaluative setting. Interviewees who show enthusiasm and interest have the edge over interviewees who appear to be drowsy or bored. In clinical settings, an experienced evaluator may develop hypotheses to be tested in the interview from the nonverbal behavior of the interviewee. For example, a person who is slouching, moving slowly, and exhibiting a sad facial expression may be depressed. Then again, such an individual may be experiencing physical discomfort as a result of a muscle spasm or an arthritis attack. It will remain for the assessor to determine which of those hypotheses, if any, best accounts for the observed behavior.

Certain theories and systems in the mental health field go beyond more traditional interpretations of body language. For example, in psychoanalysis, a theory of personality and psychological treatment developed by Sigmund Freud, symbolic significance is assigned to many nonverbal acts. From a psychoanalytic perspective, an interviewee's fidgeting with a wedding band during an interview may be interpreted as a message regarding an unstable marriage. As evidenced by his thoughts on "the first chance actions" of a patient during a therapy session, Sigmund Freud (1913) believed he could tell much about motivation from nonverbal behavior:

> The first . . . chance actions of the patient . . . will betray one of the governing complexes of the neurosis. . . . A young girl . . . hurriedly pulls the hem of her skirt over her exposed ankle; she has betrayed the kernel of what analysis will discover later; her narcissistic pride in her bodily beauty and her tendencies to exhibitionism. (Freud, 1913/1959, p. 359)

By the way, this quote from Freud is also useful in illustrating the influence of culture on diagnostic and therapeutic views. Freud lived in Victorian Vienna. In that time and in that place, sex was not a subject for public discussion. In many ways, Freud's views regarding a sexual basis for various thoughts and behaviors were a product of the sexually repressed culture in which he lived.

Standards of Evaluation

Suppose that master chefs from over 100 nations entered a contest designed to discover the best chicken soup in the world. Who do you think would win? The answer to that question hinges on the evaluative standard to be employed. If the sole judge of the contest was the owner of a kosher delicatessen on the Lower East Side of Manhattan, the entry that came closest to the "Jewish mother homemade" variety might well be declared the winner. However, other judges might have other standards and preferences. For example, soup connoisseurs from Arabic cultures might well have a preference for a variety of chicken soup that includes fresh lemon juice in the recipe. Judges from India might be inclined to give their vote to a chicken soup flavored with curry and other exotic spices. For other Asian judges, soy sauce might be viewed as an indispensable ingredient, and any chicken soup prepared without it might lose by default. Ultimately, it probably is not the case that one soup is truly better than all the rest; judging which soup is best will be very much a matter of personal preference and the standard of evaluation employed.

In a somewhat analogous way, judgments related to certain psychological traits can also be culturally relative. For example, whether specific patterns of behavior are considered to be male- or female-appropriate will depend on the prevailing societal standards regarding masculinity and femininity. There are some societies, for example, in which it is role-appropriate for women to fight wars and put food on the table while the men are occupied in more domestic activities. Whether specific patterns of behavior are considered to be psychopathological depends in no small way on the prevailing societal standards. In the Sudan, for example, there are tribes that live among cattle because they regard the animals as sacred. Judgments as to who might be the best employee, manager, or leader may differ as a function of culture, as might judgments regarding intelligence, wisdom, courage, and other psychological variables. For example, every three years since 1982, a group of American immigrants from Ghana elect a leader. By day, the "king" is a security official in a hospital. His duties as king include preserving traditions, resolving disputes, and even handling some criminal matters that may arise among the some 50,000 Ghanaians living in the United States. What leadership qualities would you expect this man to possess? In what ways, if any, would you expect those qualities to differ from those of a person elected to the American presidency?

A challenge inherent in the assessment enterprise has to do with tempering test- and assessment-related outcomes with good judgment regarding the cultural relativity of those outcomes. In practice, this means raising questions about the applicability of assessment-related findings to specific individuals. Thus, in addition to attempting to answer questions such as "How intelligent is this person?" or "How assertive is this individual?" by means of psychological testing, some additional questions must also be raised. How appropriate are the norms or other standards that will be used to make the evaluation? To what extent has the individual been assimilated into the culture the test is drawn from, and what influence might such assimilation (or lack of it) have on the test results? What research has been done on the test that bears on its applicability for use in evaluating this particular individual? Increasingly, these questions are being raised not only by careful test users but by the courts as well.

Legal and Ethical Considerations

A society's *laws* are rules that individuals must obey for the good of the society as a whole—or rules thought to be for the good of society as a whole. Some laws are and have been relatively uncontroversial. For example, the law that mandates driving on the right side of the road has been neither a subject of debate, nor a source of emotional soul-searching, nor a stimulus to civil disobedience. For safety and the common good, most people are willing to relinquish their freedom to drive anywhere on the road they might please. But what about laws pertaining to abortion? to busing? to capital punishment? to euthanasia? to "deprogramming" of religious cult members? to affirmative action in employment? Exactly how laws regulating matters such as these should be written and interpreted are issues of heated controversy—as are some of the laws that pertain to psychological measurement.

Whereas a body of laws is a body of rules, a body of *ethics* is a body of principles of "right," "proper," or "good" conduct. Thus, for example, an ethic of the Old West was "Never shoot 'em in the back." Two well-known principles subscribed to by the seafaring set are "Women and children leave first in an emergency" and "A captain goes down with his ship."[3] The ethics of journalism dictate that reporters present all sides of a controversial issue. A research principle is that the scientist should never "fudge" data; all data must be reported accurately. What kinds of ethical guidelines do you think should govern the professional behavior of psychologists involved in psychological testing and assessment? The answer to this question is important; to the extent that a code of ethics is recognized and accepted by members of a profession, it defines the standard of care expected by members of that profession.

Members of the public and members of the profession have at times in recent history been on "different sides of the fence" with respect to issues of ethics and law. We now trace some concerns of the public and the profession.

The Concerns of the Public

The assessment enterprise has never been very well understood by the public. Even today, it is unfortunate that we may hear statements symptomatic of misunderstanding with regard to tests (for example, "The only thing tests measure

---

3. We leave the problem of what to do when the captain of the ship is a woman to a volume dedicated to an in-depth exploration of seafaring ethics.

is the ability to take tests"). Possible consequences of public misunderstanding include fear, anger, legislation, litigation, and administrative regulations.

Perhaps the first time the American public evidenced widespread concern about psychological testing came in the aftermath of World War I. At that time, various professionals (as well as nonprofessionals) sought to adapt group tests developed by the military (such as the Army Alpha and Beta tests) for civilian use in schools and industry. As noted by Haney (1981), many articles in the periodical literature of the early 1920s reflected discomfort with the growing testing industry. Representative of this discomfort were articles by Walter Lippmann in the popular *New Republic* magazine, such as "The Abuse of Tests" in November 1922 and "The Mental Age of Americans" in October 1922. In the latter article, Lippmann asserted, among other things, that an intelligence test amounted to a "vain effort to discount training and knowledge." The renowned Stanford psychologist Lewis Terman attempted to respond to Lippmann's sensational and misleading remarks in the same magazine. However, because the issues were complex and the forum of the debate was a lay magazine, Terman was the loser in the eyes of the readership. As Cronbach (1975, p. 12) observed, Terman had "tried to play the same game and was hopelessly overmatched."

The 1930s witnessed a boom in the number of published standardized tests. Oscar Buros had the idea to publish a bibliography of available tests called *Educational, Psychological and Personality Tests of 1933 and 1934,* and this was the first edition of what later came to be known as the *Mental Measurements Yearbook.* The book contained only 44 pages; the second edition published later in the decade (Buros, 1938) contained nearly ten times as many pages and listed several thousand tests. Haney (1981) observed that the periodical literature in the 1930s was generally "far freer of criticisms of testing" than was that of the 1920s.

The widespread military testing that took place during the 1940s as a result of World War II did not appear to arouse as much popular interest as did the testing that had been undertaken during World War I. The periodical literature was relatively free of articles dealing with psychological testing until the 1960s, when considerable media attention was focused on gifted children. Perhaps the greatest stimulus to that attention was an event that occurred in the Soviet Union on October 4, 1957. On that day, the Russians launched into space a satellite they called Sputnik—and the race to space was on. About a year after the Russian launch, Congress passed the National Defense Education Act, which provided federal money to local schools for the purpose of ability and aptitude testing, this in an effort to identify gifted and academically talented students.

The subsequent proliferation of large-scale testing programs in the schools combined with the increasing use of ability as well as personality tests in government, military, and business employment selection led to renewed widespread public concern about the efficacy of psychological tests. This concern was reflected in magazine articles such as "Testing: Can Everyone be Pigeonholed?" (*Newsweek,* July 20, 1959) and "What the Tests Do Not Test" (*New York Times Magazine,* October 2, 1960) and in books such as *The Brain Watchers* (Gross, 1962), *They Shall Not Pass* (Black, 1963), and *The Tyranny of Testing* (Hoffman,

1962)—books described by one measurement authority of the day as "sensational books . . . [that] have added to the confusion" (Anastasi, 1968, p. 548).[4] The upshot of the heightened public concern was congressional hearings on the subject of testing (Amrine, 1965).

In 1969, widespread media attention was accorded the publication of an article in the prestigious *Harvard Educational Review,* and once again public concerns with respect to testing were aroused. The article was entitled "How Much Can We Boost IQ and Scholastic Achievement?" and its author, Arthur Jensen, argued that "genetic factors are strongly implicated in the average Negro-white intelligence difference" (1969, p. 82). An outpouring of public and professional attention to nature versus nurture issues regarding intelligence served to focus attention on the instruments used to gauge intellectual differences—instruments we commonly refer to as intelligence tests. The United States Select Committee on Equal Education Opportunity, in preparation for hearings on the matter of the relationships between intelligence, genetics, and environment, compiled a document of over 600 pages called *Environment, Intelligence and Scholastic Achievement* (1972). However, according to Haney (1981), the hearings "were canceled because they promised to be too controversial" (p. 1026). More recently, public concern about testing was reinvigorated by heavy media attention given *The Bell Curve* (Herrnstein & Murray, 1994), a book that is essentially an updated and more politicized version of Jensen's work (to be discussed in greater depth in Chapter 8).

The extent of public concern about psychological assessment is reflected in the extensive involvement of the government in many aspects of the assessment process in recent decades. Assessment has been affected in numerous and important ways by activities of the legislative, executive, and judicial branches of federal and state governments, as the following examples illustrate.

During the 1990s, the U.S. Congress has passed or amended a variety of laws that apply to psychological testing. For example, the *Americans with Disabilities Act of 1990* bans discrimination in employment, transportation, public accommodations, and telecommunications on the basis of physical or mental disability. The law defines a disability as a condition that "substantially limits a major life activity." Facilities must be accessible to individuals with disabilities, and employers must make "reasonable accommodation" for disabled workers to perform their duties. Implications of this act for psychological assessment include designing employment testing materials and procedures to measure the

---

4. Hoffman's (1962) book has been cited as raising some important questions regarding the value of standardized, multiple-choice questions in educational settings. Hoffman argued that these tests tap the variable of quickness or facility as it relates to intelligence and might therefore discriminate against the "deep, brooding" thinker. One might wonder how well "deep, brooding" thinkers such as Kant and Spinoza would have performed on a standardized, multiple-choice examination such as the SAT: would they have labored over the meaning of the questions while other test-takers simply took the questions in stride? This particular concern is a legitimate one and one that psychologists as well as educators still debate.

skills essential to the particular job. For example, using paper-and-pencil tests in selecting employees is not appropriate if such skills are not job-related and if the applicant's performance on these measures would reflect his or her handicap. Tests with time limits are considered inappropriate when speed is not essential to the skill being assessed.

The *Civil Rights Act of 1964* was amended in 1991 by the federal legislature. Also known as the *Equal Opportunity Employment Act,* this law provides for nondiscrimination in employment. The 1991 amendment makes explicit the implications for testing: Section 106 states, "It shall be unlawful employment practice . . . to adjust the scores of, use different cutoff scores for, or otherwise alter the results of, employment related tests on the basis of race, religion, sex, or national origin." In light of this law, the American Psychological Association is evaluating the different interpretations commonly used to understand men's and women's scores on a variety of personality and ability tests (Adler, 1993).

The *Education for All Handicapped Children Act (Public Law 94-142)* was first enacted in 1975 and then amended in 1984, twice in 1988, and again in 1990. In Section 612, the law mandates that all children with suspected mental or physical handicaps be identified through the use of screening instruments, "regardless of the severity of their handicap." Section 101 of the 1990 amendment specifies the broad range of conditions covered by the law: "mental retardation, hearing impairments including deafness, speech or language impairments, visual impairments including blindness, serious emotional disturbance, orthopedic impairments, autism, traumatic brain injury, other health impairments, or specific learning disabilities." Once identified, each individual child must be evaluated by a professional team qualified to determine that child's special educational needs, and then periodically reevaluated during the course of an individualized educational program. Psychological assessment is used extensively in the wide range of evaluations associated with this law.

Records generated as a result of testing have also been subject to federal legislation. For example, the *Family Education Rights and Privacy Act* (1974) mandated that parents and eligible students be given access to school records. Additionally, the act formally granted parents and students the right to challenge findings in those records in a hearing.

The making of laws to govern the assessment process has not been limited to the federal legislature. In the 1970s, numerous states enacted *minimum competency testing programs*—formal testing programs designed to be used in decisions regarding various aspects of students' education (such as award of diplomas, grade promotions, and identification of areas in which the student needs remedial instruction). These laws grew out of grassroots support for the idea that high school graduates should have, at the very least, "minimal competencies" in areas such as reading, writing, and arithmetic. In some jurisdictions, laws provide that a student may be denied a high school diploma if such minimal competencies cannot be demonstrated on a test (Lerner, 1991).

Truth-in-testing legislation was also passed at the state level, beginning in the 1980s. The primary objective of these laws is to provide testtakers with a means of learning the criteria by which they are being judged. In reaching that objective, some laws mandate the disclosure of questions and answers of postsecondary and professional school admissions tests within 30 days of the publication of test scores. Some require that information relevant to a test's development and psychometric soundness be kept on file. Some truth-in-testing laws require provision of descriptions of (1) the test's purpose and its subject matter, (2) the knowledge and skills the test purports to measure, (3) procedures for ensuring accuracy in scoring as well as procedures for notifying testtakers of errors in scoring, and (4) procedures for ensuring the testtaker's confidentiality. Truth-in-testing laws create special difficulties for test developers and publishers, who argue that it is essential that they be able to keep the test items secret. They note that there may be a limited item pool for some tests and that the cost of developing an entirely new set of items for each succeeding administration of a test is prohibitive.

To the extent that state and federal legislators respond to the concerns of the people they represent, the legislative acts described above suggest that Americans are concerned about the way in which psychological testing may affect their lives. The laws that grow out of these concerns often mandate the involvement of the executive branch of government in their application. For example, Title VII of the Civil Rights Act of 1964 created the Equal Employment Opportunity Commission (EEOC) to enforce the act. EEOC has published sets of guidelines concerning standards to be met in constructing and using employment tests. In 1978, the EEOC, the Civil Service Commission, the Department of Labor, and the Justice Department jointly published the *Uniform Guidelines on Employee Selection Procedures,* a document that was hailed by the American Psychological Association Testing Committee as "a major step forward" (Novick, 1981). One sample guideline is as follows:

> The use of any test which adversely affects hiring, promotion, transfer or any other employment or membership opportunity of classes protected by Title VII constitutes discrimination unless (a) the test has been validated and evidences a high degree of utility as hereinafter described, and (b) the person giving or acting upon the results of the particular test can demonstrate that alternative suitable hiring, transfer or promotion procedures are unavailable for . . . use.

Further evidence of public concern about psychological testing comes from an examination of the problems brought to the court system. Many court cases involving testing focus specifically on ability and intelligence testing in schools. Cases have been heard in both state and federal courts concerning the use of such tests for the purpose of placing children in classes for the less able, for children with special needs, or for mentally retarded children. The concern has been one of validity: the tests being used are developed on White middle-class children and may not provide accurate information about children who are not White and middle class.

Hobson v. Hansen (1967) raised these issues relative to an ability tracking system in a desegregated school. Children at this school were tracked on the basis of their scores on an ability test, and the result was that the school had effectively become resegregated: Black students were grouped together in lower-track classes. The Supreme Court found that ability tests developed on Whites could not lawfully be used to track Black students within the school system.

Similar concerns were raised in a California case, *Diana v. State Board of Education* (1970). Although children with Spanish surnames constituted only about 18% of the student body, fully 33% of the students in classes for the educable mentally retarded (EMR) had Spanish surnames. All testing had been done in English using intelligence tests developed primarily on White children. When nine Spanish-speaking children were retested in Spanish, eight scored in the nonretarded range. This case resulted in several changes in the California Education Code. Children must be tested in the language in which they are most fluent, and placement in EMR classes must involve a comprehensive developmental and educational assessment of the child, not just the results of an intelligence test.

Another California case, *Larry P. v. Riles* (1979), involved the placement of Black students in EMR classes using intelligence tests. Six such children were retested using the same intelligence test, with some items reworded to reflect the children's cultural background. Intelligence test scores on retesting increased by 17 to 38 points, and all six children scored in the nonretarded range. Also, as with *Diana,* a higher proportion of Black children were in the EMR classes than in the student body. The judge in this case found that the use of intelligence tests to place Black children in EMR classes was unconstitutional, because such tests are "racially and culturally biased" and have a "discriminatory impact on Black children." This decision was appealed but upheld in 1984. The California judge who made the 1979 ruling affirmed it in 1986 by stating "in no uncertain terms . . . that schools in that state may not use IQ tests to assess Black children for placement in special education classes" (Landers, 1986, p. 18). This moratorium on the intelligence testing of Black children leads to some curious situations, like that of a California child who is suspected of having learning problems but cannot be given an IQ test because she is Black; the child's mother is considering having her status changed to "White" so that she can be tested ("Child denied IQ test," 1994).

The minimum competency legislation discussed above has also created some activity in the judicial system. For example, in *Debra P. v. Turlington* (1981), suit was brought against Florida's Commissioner of Education (Turlington) by ten Black students after they had been denied high school diplomas. The students had failed a statewide test of minimum competency, which was essentially a literacy test. The plaintiffs argued that if the minimum competency test were to be sanctioned as a requirement for the reward of a diploma, 20% of the Black high school seniors in Florida would be denied high school diplomas, as compared with only 2% of the White high school seniors. In 1979, a federal judge ruled that the minimum competency testing program in Florida was unconstitutional because it perpetuated the effects of past discrimination. A moratorium on such testing was ordered. In 1981, the United States Court of Appeals affirmed the lower court's ruling, holding that such a program violated the equal protection clause of the Constitution, because it punished Black students for prior discrimination in schooling.

Not all court cases surrounding psychological testing involve education. The use of tests to select or promote employees, and the potential for such practices to result in racial discrimination, has been examined in a series of cases brought under the Civil Rights Act. Through these cases, we see the court struggling with how to apply the act when different groups score differently on employment tests.

In *Griggs v. Duke Power Company* (1971), Black employees brought suit against a private paper company for discriminatory hiring practices. The company used measures of general ability, such as a high school diploma and the Wonderlic Personnel Test, resulting in the hiring of a relatively small number of Blacks. The Supreme Court agreed with the plaintiffs, finding problems with "broad and general testing devices." Instead, the court stated that tests must "fairly measure the knowledge or skills required by a particular job." The court ruled that employment tests must "measure the person for the job and not the person in the abstract."

A similar issue was explored in *Albemarle Paper Company v. Moody* (1976). The paper mill's industrial psychologist had found that scores on a general ability test predicted measures of job performance, such as supervisors' ratings of competence, and so had been using the general ability test to select employees. The complaint was that, as a group, Whites scored better than Blacks on the general ability test and therefore were given preference in hiring decisions. The U.S. District Court found this use of the test to be sufficiently job-related to be valid, but the decision was reversed on appeal with the argument that discrimination had occurred despite the paper mill's "absence of discriminatory intent."

A more recent case of this type is *Allen v. District of Columbia* (1993), in which a test had been developed to assist with promotion decisions in the city's fire department. The promotional test was not one of general ability but drew questions from specific aspects of the job of firefighter. Blacks scored lower on the test than did Whites, with the result that a smaller proportion of Blacks were promoted than there were in the pool of candidates for promotion. As in *Albemarle,* validity information had been collected showing that the test accurately predicted future job success and was related to others' evaluations of the candidate's abilities. However, in this case, the use of the test was supported by the court: "Because the promotional examination . . . was a valid measure of the abilities and probable future success of those individuals taking the test, the exam serves the legitimate employment goals of the department."

Drawing a consistent lesson from the results of court cases in this area is difficult. Courts at various levels have worked toward a description of what constitutes discriminatory use of tests in the employment setting, but a consistent understanding has not yet been reached. Courts disagree about whether validated tests on which there are racial differences can be used to assist with employment-related decisions.

Legal issues surrounding psychological testing also arise in the practice of clinical psychology and psychiatry. In *Arnett v. Ricketts,* Arnett was convicted of murder in Arizona and was sentenced to death. Arnett then brought a suit about the handling of his case. One concern, upheld by the court, was that

Arnett's rights were violated by mental hospital staff. As part of his preparation for the original trial, Arnett had requested a sanity examination. As a result, he was transferred to a mental hospital, where he was interviewed and tested at length, with the conclusion that he was sane at the time of the crime. At Arnett's trial, the hospital psychiatrist testified for the state (against Arnett) concerning Arnett's sanity. At no time during his stay at the mental hospital was Arnett informed of his Miranda rights (notification of the right to remain silent, with a reminder that "whatever you say may be used against you," the right to the presence of counsel). Arnett argued successfully that his rights had been violated by the hospital staff; because of this and other procedural problems with the trial, the United States District Court judge decided in favor of Arnett.

State and federal legislatures, executive bodies, and courts have been involved in many aspects of the psychological assessment process. This involvement demonstrates both the extent and the nature of public concern about testing. Such concerns are not limited to people outside psychology but often come from professionals as well.

The Concerns of the Profession

As early as 1895, the infant American Psychological Association (APA) had formed its first committee on mental measurement, a committee charged with investigating various aspects of the new practice of standardized testing. Another APA committee on measurements was formed in 1906 to further study the issues and problems attendant upon test standardization. In 1916 and again in 1921, symposia dealing with various issues surrounding the expanding uses of tests were sponsored (*Mentality Tests*, 1916; *Intelligence and Its Measurement*, 1921) and in 1923 an APA committee recommended that nonpsychologists' use of tests be monitored. However, that recommendation was voted down by the APA membership. In 1954, the Association published its *Technical Recommendations for Psychological Tests and Diagnostic Tests*, a document that set forth testing standards and technical recommendations. The following year, another professional organization, the National Educational Association (working in collaboration with the National Council on Measurements Used in Education—now known as the National Council on Measurement) published its *Technical Recommendations for Achievement Tests* (see Novick, 1981). Collaboration between these professional organizations led to the development of testing standards.

Paralleling APA's ongoing concerns regarding the ethics of psychological testing were concerns about general ethics in the field of psychology. In 1953, APA published its *Ethical Standards of Psychologists*, a culmination of the work of many APA committees that had been established over the years to study ethical standards and practices for various types of professional and scientific activities. APA published a *Casebook on Ethical Standards of Psychologists* (1967) and a revised edition, *Casebook on Ethical Principles of Psychologists* (1987), to provide examples of the types of cases brought before the APA Ethics Committee. APA periodically updates its *Ethical Principles of Psychologists* (see, for example, APA, 1981a, 1990, 1992).

Through the years, numerous other publications of the American Psychological Association have reflected the organization's deep concern for maintenance of high professional standards and the welfare of people who take psychological tests. Here is a partial listing of some APA publications that reflect this concern and that deal directly or indirectly with the subject of testing.

Some APA Publications Bearing on Psychological Testing and Assessment

Standards for Educational and Psychological Tests and Manuals (1966b)

Automated Test Scoring and Interpretation Practices (1966a)

Standards for Educational and Psychological Tests (1974)

Principles for the Validation and Use of Personnel Selection Procedures (1980)

Speciality Guidelines for the Delivery of Services by Clinical Psychologists (1981b)

Speciality Guidelines for the Delivery of Services by Counseling Psychologists (1981c)

Specialty Guidelines for the Delivery of Services by Industrial/Organizational Psychologists (1981d)

Specialty Guidelines for the Delivery of Services by School Psychologists (1981e)

Ethical Principles of Psychologists (1981a)

Standards for Educational and Psychological Testing (1985)

Guidelines for Computer-Based Tests and Interpretations (1986)

Ethical Principles of Psychologists (1992)

Standards for Educational and Psychological Testing (in press)

The National Association of School Psychologists (NASP) has also established professional standards for its members. Its *Principles for Professional Ethics,* adopted in 1984, provides guidance in the selection, use, and interpretation of psychological tests and assessment procedures.

Who should be privy to psychological test data? Who should be able to purchase psychological test materials? Who is qualified to administer, score, and interpret psychological tests? What level of expertise in psychometrics is required to be qualified to administer which type of test? A consideration of these important questions follows.

Test-user qualifications   Should anyone be allowed to purchase and use psychological test materials? If not, who should be permitted to use psychological tests? Psychologists have a long history of grappling with these most difficult questions. As early as 1950, an APA Committee on Ethical Standards for Psychology published a report called *Ethical Standards for the Distribution of Psychological Tests and Diagnostic Aids.* This report defined three "levels" of tests in terms of the degree to which the test's use required knowledge of testing and the subject matter of psychology:

Level A: Tests or aids that can adequately be administered, scored, and interpreted with the aid of the manual and a general orientation to the kind of institution or organization in which one is working (e.g., achievement or proficiency tests).

Level B: Tests or aids that require some technical knowledge of test construction and use, and of supporting psychological and educational fields such as statistics, individual differences, psychology of adjustment, personnel psychology, and guidance (e.g., aptitude tests, adjustment inventories applicable to normal populations).

Level C: Tests and aids that require substantial understanding of testing and supporting psychological fields, together with supervised experience in the use of these devices (e.g., projective tests, individual mental tests).

The report, which also included descriptions of the general levels of training corresponding to each of the three levels of tests, was reprinted in APA's *Ethical Standards of Psychologists* (1953) and cited in APA's *Standards for Educational and Psychological Tests and Manuals* (1966a), though it was omitted from mention in the two editions of the *Standards* that followed. Although many test publishers continue to use this three-level classification, some do not. In general, "responsibility for test use should be assumed or delegated only to those individuals who have the training and experience necessary to handle this responsibility in a professional and technically adequate manner" (*Standards,* 1985, p. 42). In a similar vein, NASP's *Principles for Professional Ethics* (1992) includes one principle that states that school psychologists "recognize the strengths and limitations of their training and experience, engaging only in practices for which they are competent" (p. 2) and one that emphasizes the use of "valid and reliable instruments and techniques that are applicable and appropriate for the benefit of the student or client" (p. 7).

APA's *Ethical Principles of Psychologists* (1992) provides guidance in the area of test-user qualifications. Principle A states that psychologists "provide only those services and use only those techniques for which they are qualified by education, training, or experience." Ethical standard 2.02 adds that "psychologists refrain from misuse of assessment techniques, interventions, results, and interpretations, and take reasonable steps to prevent others from misusing the information that these techniques provide."

Despite the publication of ethical guidelines and standards, the situation regarding the issue of test-user qualifications might legitimately be described as chaotic. As Moreland (1986, p. 3) observed, "At present, qualification policies are as plentiful as test publishers." Moreland went on to point out that at least part of the problem lies in the fact that "test users" in no way constitute a homogeneous group; "test users can be found in virtually every walk of life. The owner of the clothing store where I buy my suits tests all prospective employees" (p. 3).

In an effort to remedy the situation, the American Psychological Association, the American Educational Research Association, the National Council on Measurement in Education, and two dozen or so test publishers have banded together and established the Joint Committee on Testing Practices (JCTP). In 1988, the *Code of Fair Testing Practices in Education* was developed by the group. The *Code* delineates the obligations of both test developers and test users in four broad areas: (1) developing/selecting tests, (2) interpreting scores, (3) striving for fairness, and (4) informing testtakers. The *Code* is directed primarily at professionally developed tests such as those sold by commercial test publishers or used in formally administered testing programs. The roles of test developers and test users are addressed separately. Test users are defined as those "who select tests, commission test development services, or make decisions on the basis of test scores." Test developers are those "who actually construct tests as well as those who set policies for particular testing programs" (p. 10). The *Code* has been endorsed by a number of test publishers and is designed to be understood by the general public (see the box on pages 72–74).

Testing people with disabilities   Difficulties analogous to those concerning test-takers from linguistic and cultural minorities are present when testing people with disabling conditions. Specifically, these difficulties may include (1) transforming the test into a form that can be taken by the testtaker, (2) transforming the responses of the testtaker so that they are scorable, and (3) meaningfully interpreting the test data.

The nature of the transformation of the test into a form ready for administration to the individual with disabling conditions will, of course, depend on the nature of the disability. If, for example, the testtaker is blind or visually impaired, the test may have to be transformed into braille or large-type print. In turn, the format for responding to test items will have to be appropriately modified. And if the materials of a test to be transformed contain pictures or other artwork, professional judgment and discretion will be necessary in decisions related to the omission of such materials or the development of oral descriptions of them. One question underlying all such decisions is "What effect will such transformations have on the reliability and validity of the findings?"

Answers to questions like this one are simply not known at this time; precious little research designed to answer such questions has been undertaken. Some tests, particularly group-administered tests, may not be amenable at all to administration to people with particular disabilities. In all phases of testing people with disabling conditions, from setting up the location of the testing with special furniture if need be, to test administration, to test interpretation, reasonable decision making for testing is required. The present authors recommend that, in instances where standardized test conditions have been modified, all such modifications be noted in the record of the tests and considered in the interpretation of test results. Chapter 16 deals with the issues involved in testing people with disabling conditions.

Computerized test administration, scoring, and interpretation   The widespread availability of relatively inexpensive computers has had a great impact on the field of psychological testing. An ever growing number of psychological tests can be purchased on disks, and their administration, scoring, and interpretation are as simple as pressing keys on a keyboard. In many respects, the relative simplicity, convenience, and range of potential testing activities that computer technology brings to the testing industry have been a great boon. Test users have under one roof the means by which they can quickly administer, score, and interpret a wide range of tests. Additionally, they own the technology that allows them to administer complex tests of eye-hand coordination, re-action time, and other abilities (McCullough, 1990). However, if the growing computer-assisted testing industry looks rosy at first, a more careful look reveals a welter of thorns.

The availability of psychological tests that can be administered, scored, and interpreted by computer may be a temptation to the public. Employers who currently use personnel psychologists to screen prospective employees, for example, might well believe it to be more efficient and economical to have psychological testing done by computer and supervised by a clerical worker. This raises the question of access to psychological tests—on disk or otherwise. Who should have access? Why?

Another question—this one a step backward from the access question—involves the issue of the soundness of the test software itself. If the test is a computer version of a paper-and-pencil test, how does one know whether the two versions of the test are indeed equivalent? If the test contains a program for providing a narrative interpretation of the test results, how does one know that the interpretation is valid? What other possible "thorns" can you envision around the "rose" of computerized psychological testing? In Chapter 19, we will explore these issues in greater detail.

The Rights of Testtakers

As prescribed by the *Standards* (APA, 1985), some of the rights test users accord to testtakers are as follows: the right of informed consent to testing, the right to be informed of test findings, the right not to have privacy invaded, the right to the least stigmatizing label, and the right to have findings held confidential.

The right of informed consent to testing   Testtakers have a right to know why they are being tested, how the test data will be used, and what, if any, information will be released to whom. The disclosure of such information must, of course, be in language the testtaker can understand. Thus, for a testtaker as young as 2 or 3 years of age or a mentally retarded individual with limited language ability, a disclosure before testing might be worded as follows: "I'm going to ask you to try to do some things so that I can see what you know how to do and what things you could use some more help with" (APA, 1985, p. 85). If a testtaker is incapable of providing an informed consent to testing, such consent may be obtained from a parent or a legal representative. Ideally, the consent should be written rather than oral, and the written form should specify (1) the general purpose of the testing, (2) the specific reason it is being undertaken in the present case, and (3) the general type of instruments to be administered. Many school districts now routinely send home such forms before testing children. Such forms typically include the option to have the child assessed privately if the parent so desires. In instances where testing is legally mandated (as in a court-ordered situation), obtaining informed consent to test may be considered more of a courtesy (undertaken in part for reasons of establishing good rapport) than a necessity.

Code of Fair Testing Practices in Education

A   Developing/Selecting Appropriate Tests*

Test developers should provide the information that test users need to select appropriate tests.

Test Developers Should:

1. Define what each test measures and what the test should be used for. Describe the population(s) for which the test is appropriate.

2. Accurately represent the characteristics, usefulness, and limitations of tests for their intended purposes.

3. Explain relevant measurement concepts as necessary for clarity at the level of detail that is appropriate for the intended audience(s).

4. Describe the process of test development. Explain how the content and skills to be tested were selected.

5. Provide evidence that the test meets its intended purpose(s).

6. Provide either representative samples or complete copies of test questions, directions, answer sheets, manuals, and score reports to qualified users.

7. Indicate the nature of the evidence obtained concerning the appropriateness of each test for groups of different racial, ethnic, or linguistic backgrounds who are likely to be tested.

8. Identify and publish any specialized skills needed to administer each test and to interpret scores correctly.

Test users should select tests that meet the purpose for which they are to be used and that are appropriate for the intended test-taking populations.

*Many of the statements in the Code refer to the selection of existing tests. However, in customized testing programs test developers are engaged to construct new tests. In those situations, the test development process should be designed to help ensure that the completed tests will be in compliance with the Code.

Test Users Should:

1. First define the purpose for testing and the population to be tested. Then, select a test for that purpose and that population based on a thorough review of the available information.

2. Investigate potentially useful sources of information, in addition to test scores, to corroborate the information provided by tests.

3. Read the materials provided by test developers and avoid using tests for which unclear or incomplete information is provided.

4. Become familiar with how and when the test was developed and tried out.

5. Read independent evaluations of a test and of possible alternative measures. Look for evidence required to support the claims of test developers.

6. Examine specimen sets, disclosed tests or samples of questions, directions, answer sheets, manuals, and score reports before selecting a test.

7. Ascertain whether the test content and norms group(s) or comparison group(s) are appropriate for the intended test takers.

8. Select and use only those tests for which the skills needed to administer the test and interpret scores correctly are available.

B   Interpreting Scores

Test developers should help users interpret scores correctly.

Test Developers Should:

9. Provide timely and easily understood score reports that describe test performance clearly and accurately. Also explain the meaning and limitations of reported scores.

10. Describe the population(s) represented by any norms or comparison group(s), the dates the data were gathered, and the process used to select the samples of test takers.

11. Warn users to avoid specific, reasonably anticipated misuses of test scores.

12. Provide information that will help users follow reasonable procedures for setting passing scores when it is appropriate to use such scores with the test.

13. Provide information that will help users gather evidence to show that the test is meeting its intended purpose(s).

Test Users Should:

9. Obtain information about the scale used for reporting scores, the characteristics of any norms or comparison group(s), and the limitations of the scores.

10. Interpret scores taking into account any major differences between the norms or comparison groups and the actual test takers. Also take into account any differences in test administration practices or familiarity with the specific questions in the test.

11. Avoid using tests for purposes not specifically recommended by the test developer unless evidence is obtained to support the intended use.

12. Explain how any passing scores were set and gather evidence to support the appropriateness of the scores.

13. Obtain evidence to help show that the test is meeting its intended purpose(s).

C   Striving for Fairness

Test developers should strive to make tests that are as fair as possible for test takers of different races, gender, ethnic backgrounds, or handicapping conditions.

Test Developers Should:

14. Review and revise test questions and related materials to avoid potentially insensitive content or language.

15. Investigate the performance of test takers of different races, gender, and ethnic backgrounds when samples of sufficient size are available. Enact procedures that help to ensure that differences in performance are related

primarily to the skills under assessment rather than to irrelevant factors.

16. When feasible, make appropriately modified forms of tests or administration procedures available for test takers with handicapping conditions. Warn test users of potential problems in using standard norms with modified tests or administration procedures that result in noncomparable scores.

Test users should select tests that have been developed in ways that attempt to make them as fair as possible for test takers of different races, gender, ethnic backgrounds, or handicapping conditions.

Test Users Should:

14. Evaluate the procedures used by test developers to avoid potentially insensitive content or language.

15. Review the performance of test takers of different races, gender, and ethnic backgrounds when samples of sufficient size are available. Evaluate the extent to which performance differences may have been caused by inappropriate characteristics of the test.

16. When necessary and feasible, use appropriately modified forms of tests or administration procedures for test takers with handicapping conditions. Interpret standard norms with care in the light of the modifications that were made.

D   Informing Test Takers

Under some circumstances, test developers have direct communication with test takers. Under other circumstances, test users communicate directly with test takers. Whichever group communicates directly with test takers should provide the information described below.

Test Developers or Test Users Should:

17. When a test is optional, provide test takers or their parents/guardians with information to help them judge

(continued)

Code of Fair Testing Practices in Education *(continued)*

whether the test should be taken, or if an available alternative to the test should be used.

18. Provide test takers the information they need to be familiar with the coverage of the test, the types of question formats, the directions, and appropriate test-taking strategies. Strive to make such information equally available to all test takers.

Under some circumstances, test developers have direct control of tests and test scores. Under other circumstances test users have such control. Whichever group has direct control of tests and test scores should take the steps described below.

Test Developers or Test Users Should:

19. Provide test takers or their parents/guardians with information about rights test takers may have to obtain copies of tests and completed answer sheets, retake tests, have tests rescored, or cancel scores.

20. Tell test takers or their parents/guardians how long scores will be kept on file and indicate to whom and under what circumstances test scores will or will not be released.

21. Describe the procedures that test takers or their parents/guardians may use to register complaints and have problems resolved.

One "gray area" with respect to the testtaker's right of fully informed consent before testing involves research and experimental situations wherein the examiner's complete disclosure of all facts pertinent to the testing (including the experimenter's hypothesis and so forth) might irrevocably contaminate the test data. In such instances, professional discretion is in order; testtakers might be given a minimum amount of information before the testing (for example, "This testing is being undertaken as part of an experiment on obedience to authority. . . .") with a full and complete disclosure and debriefing made after the testing.

The right to be informed of test findings   In a bygone era, the inclination of many psychological assessors, particularly many clinicians, was to tell testtakers as little as possible about the nature of their performance on a particular test or test battery and in no case to disclose diagnostic conclusions that could arouse anxiety and/or precipitate a crisis. This orientation was reflected in at least one authoritative text where testers were advised to keep information about test results superficial and focus only on "positive" findings so that the examinee would leave the test session feeling "pleased and satisfied" (Klopfer et al., 1954, p. 15). But all of that has changed, and giving realistic information about test performance to examinees is not only ethically and legally mandated, but may be useful from a therapeutic perspective as well (see Berg, 1985).

Testtakers have a right to be informed, in language they can understand, of the nature of the findings with respect to a test that they took. They are also entitled to know what recommendations are being made as a consequence of the test data. If the test results, findings, or recommendations made on the basis of test data are being voided for any reason (such as irregularities in the test administration), testtakers have a right to know that, as well.

Because of the possibility of untoward consequences as a result of providing individuals with information about themselves—their ability, their lack of ability, their personality, their values—the communication of results of a psychological test is a most important part of the evaluation process. With sensitivity to the situation, the test user will inform the testtaker (and/or the parent or the legal representative) of the purpose of the test, the meaning of the score relative to those of other testtakers, and the possible limitations and margins of error of the test. And regardless of whether such reporting is done in person or in writing, a qualified psychologist should ideally be available to answer any further questions testtakers (or their parents) have about the test scores. Further, the resource of counseling should ideally be available for testtakers who became distraught at learning how they scored on a particular test.

The right not to have privacy invaded   The concept of privacy "recognizes the freedom of the individual to pick and choose for himself the time, circumstances, and particularly the extent to which he wishes to share or withhold from others his attitudes, beliefs, behavior, and opinions" (Shah, 1969, p. 57). When people in court proceedings "take the fifth" and refuse to answer a question put to them on the grounds that the answer might be self-incriminating, they are asserting a right of privacy provided by the Fifth Amendment to the Constitution. The information withheld in such a manner is referred to as *privileged;* it is information that is protected by law from disclosure in a legal proceeding. State statutes have extended the concept of privileged information to parties who communicate with each other in the context of certain relationships, including the lawyer-client relationship, the doctor-patient relationship, the priest-penitent relationship, and the husband-wife relationship. In most states, privilege is also accorded to the psychologist-client relationship. Privilege is extended to parties in these relationships because it has been deemed that the parties' right to privacy serves a greater public interest than would be served by having their communications vulnerable to revelation during legal proceedings. Stated another way, it is for society's good if people feel confident that they can talk freely to their attorneys, clergy, physicians, psychologists, and spouses. Professionals such as psychologists who are parties to such special relationships have a legal and ethical duty to keep their clients' communications confidential. Distinguishing the term *confidentiality* from the term *privilege,* Jagim, Wittman, and Noll (1978, p. 459) pointed out that whereas "confidentiality concerns matters of communication outside the courtroom, privilege protects clients from disclosure in judicial proceedings."

Privilege is not absolute; there are occasions when a court can deem the disclosure of certain information necessary and can order the disclosure of that information. Should the psychologist or other professional so ordered refuse to make the ordered disclosure, he or she does so under the threat of going to jail and/or being fined. Note also that the privilege in the psychologist-client relationship belongs to the client; the competent client can direct the psychologist to disclose information to some third party (such as an attorney or an insurance carrier), and the psychologist is obligated to make the disclosure. In some rare instances, the psychologist may be ethically (if not legally) compelled to disclose information if that information will prevent harm to either the client or some endangered third party. An illustrative case would be the situation where a client details a plan to commit suicide or homicide. In such an instance, the psychologist would be legally and ethically compelled to take reasonable action to prevent such an occurrence—the preservation of life being deemed an objective more important than the nonrevelation of privileged and confidential communications. The guiding principle here was set forth in the 1981 revision of APA's *Ethical Principles of Psychologists:*

> Psychologists have a primary obligation to respect the confidentiality of information obtained from persons in the course of their work as psychologists. They reveal such information to others only with the consent of the person or the person's legal representative, except in those unusual circumstances in which not to do so would result in clear danger to the person or to others.

Of course, determining when there exists one of "those unusual circumstances . . . which . . . would result in clear danger to the person or to others" is no easy matter. Further, a wrong judgment on the part of the clinician might lead to premature disclosure of confidential information and untoward consequences for not only the examinee and the examiner but the profession as well. A landmark court case that set forth the principle that "protective privilege ends where the public peril begins" was the 1974 case *Tarasoff v. Regents of University of California.* In that case, a therapy patient had made known to his psychologist his intention to kill an unnamed but readily identifiable girl two months before the murder. The court in *Tarasoff* held that the therapist had a duty to warn the endangered girl of her peril. The *Tarasoff* precedent was expanded upon by the Vermont Supreme Court in *Peck v. the Counseling Service of Addison County, Inc.* (Stone, 1986). A 1983 United States Court of Appeals (9th Circuit) decision in *Jablonski v. United States* placed a burden upon mental health professionals of being able to predict violent behavior even if no threat of violence had been made; key here was the matching of the profile of the intended victim with the profile of prior victims. In the 1987 Washington, D.C., case of *White v. United States,* the United States Court of Appeals (D.C. Circuit) found a hospital negligent for failing to adequately confine a patient to the hospital grounds. Dwayne White, a psychiatric patient who had been found not guilty by reason of insanity in a preceding case, had been granted privileges that permitted him free access to the hospital grounds for 12 hours a day. White left the grounds through one of three open exits and then repeatedly stabbed his wife, Genoa White, with a pair of scissors. Ms. White survived and brought suit against the hospital and its staff. A more complete discussion of the complex issues involved in duty to warn–type cases can be found elsewhere (for example, Cohen, 1979a; Cohen & Mariano, 1982; Meyers, 1986; Smith & Meyer, 1987; Winslade, 1986).

The right to the least stigmatizing label The *Standards* advise that the least stigmatizing labels should always be assigned when reporting test results. To better appreciate the need for this standard, consider the case of Jo Ann Iverson.[5] Jo Ann was 9 years old and suffering from claustrophobia when her mother brought her to a state hospital in Blackfoot, Idaho, for a psychological evaluation. Arden Frandsen, a psychologist employed part-time at the hospital, conducted an evaluation of Jo Ann, during the course of which he administered a Stanford-Binet Intelligence test. In his report, Frandsen classified Jo Ann as "feeble-minded, at the high-grade moron level of general mental ability." Following a request from Jo Ann's school guidance counselor, a copy of the psychological report was forwarded to the school—and embarrassing rumors concerning Jo Ann's mental condition began to circulate.

Jo Ann's mother, Carmel Iverson, brought a libel (defamation) suit against Frandsen on behalf of her daughter.[6] Mrs. Iverson lost the lawsuit, the court ruling in part that the psychological evaluation "was a professional report made by a public servant in good faith, representing his best judgment. . . ." But although Mrs. Iverson did not prevail in her lawsuit, we can certainly sympathize with her anguish at the thought of her daughter going through life with a label such as "high-grade moron"—this despite the fact that the psychologist had probably merely copied that designation from the test manual. We would also add that, in retrospect, it might have been possible to prevail in a suit against the guidance counselor for breach of confidentiality, since there appeared to be uncontested testimony that it was from the guidance counselor's office that rumors concerning Jo Ann first emanated.

The right to have findings held confidential Testtakers have a right to have their test results held confidential and be released only to third parties who have a legitimate need for access to those records—and such release must also be contingent on the informed consent of the testtaker. Whereas the term *confidentiality* was once thought of solely as a matter of professional ethics, it is now true that "case law, statutes, and licensing regulations in many states have given this standard of conduct legal status as well. For example, a practitioner is legally liable for breach of confidentiality" (Swoboda et al., 1978, p. 449).

Test users must take reasonable precautions to safeguard test records. If these data are stored in a filing cabinet, the cabinet should be locked and preferably made of steel. If these data are stored in a computer, electronic safeguards must be taken to ensure only authorized access. We might also mention here that it is not a good idea for individuals and institutions to store records *in*

---

5. See *Iverson v. Frandsen,* 237 F. 2d 898 (Idaho, 1956) or consult Cohen (1979a, pp. 149–150).

6. An interesting though tangential aspect of this case was the argument advanced by Iverson that she had brought her child in for claustrophobia and, given that fact, the administration of an intelligence test was unauthorized and beyond the scope of the consultation. However, the defendant proved to the satisfaction of the court that the administration of the Stanford-Binet was necessary to determine if Jo Ann had the mental capacity to respond to psychotherapy.

. . . the Ancients measured facial beauty by the **millihelen,** *a unit equal to that necessary to launch one ship . . .*

perpetuity. Rather, the test-using individual or institution should have a reasonable policy covering (1) the storage of test data—when, if at any time, these records will be deemed to be outdated, invalid, and/or useful only from an academic perspective, and (2) the conditions under which requests for release of records to a third party would be entertained.

Psychological Tests in the Courtroom

Increasingly, psychologists are finding themselves in court in various professional capacities. In one such capacity, the psychologist is an expert witness providing the court with expert testimony. The expertise provided may concern any of a number different areas, such as a defendant's competency to stand trial, the legitimacy of a defendant's insanity defense, the award of child custody to one or both parents in a divorce proceeding, the denial of employment, the violation of one's civil rights, a petition of release from a mental institution, the validation of a will—the list goes on. In most of such cases, if not in all, psychologists typically rely on one or more psychological tests to justify their opinions.

In some cases, psychologists are experts debating the merits of using a particular test with a particular population of testtakers. As we have seen, school districts, employers, and other direct or indirect consumers of test data are not immune from lawsuits alleging that the use of a particular test with a particular population of testtakers is discriminatory or otherwise unlawful.

Yet another capacity in which a psychologist or some other user of psychological tests may be found in the courtroom is as a defendant in a suit that alleges malpractice on the part of the test user. This is so because psychological assessors may have occasion to write a psychological test report that is adverse to the interest of the assessee. Were the report allowed to stand unchallenged, the assessee might be deprived of or denied something he or she wants very dearly (such as custody of a child, release from a mental institution, or the proceeds from a will). One tack that may be taken in challenging the psychologist's findings is a challenge to the psychologist's competency and judgment. Psychologists may be found liable for malpractice if it can be demonstrated that they did not act in their professional capacity in a way that any other person in their profession would have acted under the same or similar circumstances (Cohen, 1979a; Cohen & Mariano, 1982). But whether a psychologist acted properly or improperly under a particular set of circumstances is not always crystal-clear; reasonable psychologists may differ as to what constitutes proper or improper test use. As you will see while reading this chapter's *Everyday Psychometrics* feature, psychological tests can be used in courtrooms to help judges and juries render judgments. Yet exactly how a test is used can be a matter of controversy.

Having explored some of the historical, legal, and ethical considerations of psychological testing and assessment, we now turn our attention to some of the more technical, "nuts and bolts" considerations. Many important questions— such as "Is this a valid test?" "Is this a valid item?" and "How does this test or item compare with that test or item?"—can be answered only with reference to statistical tools. For many students, gaining mastery over statistical tools is viewed as a kind of rite of passage to a satisfactory course grade. If that is the way you regard learning about statistics in psychological measurement, we suggest that you modify your thinking. Read Part 2 of our text with the objective of truly learning and understanding the material presented, and ask a great many questions in class about any of the material you find difficult.

Our study begins with a refresher course in some basic statistical concepts. From there, it's on to an explanation of the term *norms* as it is used in psychological measurement. Correlation, discussed in Chapter 4, is a concept that you will find key to understanding everything from how tests are developed to how tests are interpreted. Professionals who use psychological tests and measurement procedures may speak of how "psychometrically sound" a test or procedure is; by that, they are often referring to reliability or validity in the psychometric sense—terms that you will be well acquainted with after reading Chapters 5 and 6. Finally, in Chapter 7 we describe aspects of the construction of a test, from initial idea to final form; you may be surprised to learn about some of the kinds of steps in between.

Test Use, Base Rates, and Jury Impressions

As psychologists become increasingly involved in various types of legal proceedings, a growing number of tests and other tools of assessment have become available for possible use. In child abuse cases, for example, psychologists have employed anatomically correct dolls as an aid in interviewing.

Another tool of assessment that may have value in child abuse cases is a test called the Child Abuse Potential Inventory (CAP; Milner et al., 1986). Created as a screening device to help identify adults at high risk for physically abusing children (Milner, 1991; Murphy-Berman, 1994), the CAP was designed to function as a first step in the process of identification. A high score on the CAP might prompt the test user to seek other evidence regarding the testtaker's history or future plans of child abuse.

The CAP might also be legitimately employed as an outcome measure in a program designed to prevent physical child abuse (Milner, 1989). In such a study, child abusers might be administered the CAP before and upon completion of the program. Yet another application of the CAP is in the courtroom, where data from it may be used as evidence for or against an accused abuser. Although this might sound like a good idea at first, the potential for misuse of the test is too great to justify its use in such a context (Melton, 1989).

The problem is not any psychometric weakness in the CAP. In fact, when used as intended, the test is psychometrically sound. Stated another way, it consistently and accurately measures the likelihood of physically abusive behaviors (Caliso & Milner, 1994; Hart, 1989; Melton, 1989) with an accuracy rate of 85–90% in distinguishing abusers from nonabusers (Milner, 1991).

The problem arises from the low base rate of child abuse in the general population. In this example, *base*

rate refers to the proportion of people who exhibit physical child abuse. A low base rate of child abuse means that a small proportion of the population physically abuses children. It has been estimated that 2–3% of children are physically abused annually (Finkelhor & Dziuba-Leatherman, 1994), a relatively low base rate.

According to Melton (1989), the CAP was designed for use in a population with a high base rate (around 50%) of child abuse, such as might be found in an institutional setting. To be used as its developers intended, the CAP must be used only in a high base rate environment. For example, Milner, Gold, and Wimberley (1986) studied 220 adults, 110 abusers and 110 nonabusers. All subjects completed the CAP, and the test was scored. Fully 82.7% of the abusers and 88.2% of the nonabusers were correctly classified using the CAP (see Table 1). Working down the columns of Table 1, note that of the 110 known abusers, 19 were incorrectly classified as nonabusers. Of the 110 known nonabusers, 13 were incorrectly identified as abusers. Of course, in most applications of the CAP, one would not know whether the person being tested was a physical child abuser; that would probably be the reason for administering the test. To gain an understanding of the errors that would be made, look at Table 1 again, but this time work across the rows. When the CAP indicates that a person is an abuser, that person is an abuser 87.5% of the time (91 of 104 instances). When the CAP indicates that a person is not an abuser, it is correct 83.6% of the time (97 of 116 instances).

The picture changes dramatically, however, in a low base rate environment. For the purposes of this example, let's say that physical child abuse occurs in 5% of the population. In a hypothetical study, we test 1,000 people using the CAP. Since physical child abuse occurs in 5% of the population, we would expect 50 or so of our testtakers to be abusers. And let's say further that just as in the Milner et al. study, 82.7% of the abusers and 88.2% of the nonabusers are correctly identified in our study (see Table 2). Working down the columns in Table 2, if 82.7% of the abusers are correctly identified, 41 will be identified as abusers, and the remaining 9 will be identified as nonabusers. If the test has an 88.2% accuracy rate for nonabusers, 838 of the nonabusers will be correctly identified, and the remaining 112 will be identified as abusers.

Now look at Table 2 again, this time working across the rows. If the CAP score indicates that the individual is an abuser, it is probably *in*correct. Most of the people (73.2% of them, in this example) with CAP scores indicating that they are abusers are, in reality, not abusers. This large inaccuracy is entirely the product of working with a low base rate sample. Even if the CAP were more accurate, because abuse is a low base rate phenomenon, using test results to identify abusers will still result in many identified abusers being wrongly classified. Stated another way, when the nonabusing population is much larger than the abusing population, the chances are that most of the mistakes will be made in classifying the nonabusing population.

Now place yourself in the seat of the judge or the jury hearing a physical child abuse case. A psychologist testifies that the CAP, which has an accuracy rate of 85–90%, indicates that the defendant is a physical abuser. The psychologist attempts an explanation about population base rates and the possibility of error. Still, what might stick in your mind about the psychologist's testimony? Many people would reason that, if the CAP is right more than 85% of the time, and if the defendant was *identified* as a child abuser,

Table 1
Application of the CAP in a Population with a High Base Rate of Child Abuse

	Actual status		
	Abuser	Nonabuser	Row Totals
CAP results indicate:			
Abuser	91	13	104
Nonabuser	19	97	116
Column totals	*110*	*110*	*220*

Table 2
Application of the CAP in a Population with a Low Base Rate of Child Abuse

	Actual status		
	Abuser	Nonabuser	Row Totals
CAP results indicate:			
Abuser	41	112	153
Nonabuser	9	838	847
Column totals	*50*	*950*	*1000*

there must be at least an 85% chance that the defendant *is* a child abuser. This conclusion, as you know now, would be incorrect and could result in serious harm to (conviction of) the defendant (Melton & Limber, 1989).

This example illustrates that the test developer's intended use of the test must be respected. Lacking any compelling psychometric evidence to deviate from the test developer's intended use of the test, such deviations may result in harm to the testtaker. The example further serves as a reminder that when data about the accuracy and consistency of a test are collected, the data are collected using a sampling of people from a particular population. Conclusions drawn from those psychometric data are applicable only to groups of people from a similar population.

PART 2

The Science of Psychological Measurement

3

A Statistics Refresher

From the red-pencil number circled at the top of your first spelling test to the computer printout of your college entrance examination scores, tests and test scores touch your life. They seem to reach out from the paper and shake your hand when you do well and punch you in the face when you do poorly. They can point you toward or away from a particular school or curriculum. They can help you to identify strengths and weaknesses in your physical and mental abilities. They can accompany you on job interviews and influence a job or career choice. Test scores are indeed a very important part of your life. But what makes those numbers meaningful?

In your role as a student, you have probably found that the nature of your relationship to tests has been primarily that of a testtaker. But as a psychologist, teacher, researcher, or employer, you may well find that the primary nature of your relationship with tests is that of a test user—the person who breathes life and meaning into test scores by applying the knowledge and skill needed to interpret them appropriately. You may also one day create a test (whether in an academic or a business setting) and then have the responsibility for reasonably scoring and interpreting the data derived. An understanding of the theory underlying test use and principles of test score interpretation is essential to the prospective test user.

Test scores are frequently expressed as numbers, and statistical tools are used to describe, make inferences from, and draw conclusions about numbers.[1] In this statistics refresher, we cover scales of measurement, tabular and graphic presentations of data, measures of central tendency, measures of variability, and standard scores. If these statistics-related terms look painfully familiar to you, we ask your indulgence and remind you that overlearning is the key to reten-

---

1. Of course, a test score may be expressed in other forms, such as in a letter grade or a pass/fail designation. Unless stated otherwise, terms such as *test score, test data, test results,* and *test scores* will be used throughout this book in reference to numeric descriptions of test performance.

tion. However, if these terms look painfully unfamiliar, we urge you to get—and spend ample time reviewing—a good elementary statistics text. The brief review of statistical concepts that follows is designed only to supplement an introductory course in statistics.

Scales of Measurement

Measurement is the act of assigning numbers or symbols to characteristics of objects (people, events—whatever) according to rules. The rules used in assigning numbers are guidelines for representing the magnitude (or some other characteristic) of the object being measured. An example of a measurement rule is "Assign the number 12 to all lengths that are exactly the same length as a 12-inch ruler." A *scale* is a set of numbers (or other symbols) whose properties model empirical properties of the objects to which the numbers are assigned. Various types of scales exist. One way of labeling a scale is to label it with reference to the type of variable being measured. Thus a scale used to measure a continuous variable might be referred to as a "continuous scale," whereas a scale used to measure a discrete variable might be referred to as a "discrete scale." If, for example, research subjects were to be categorized as being either female or male, the categorization scale would be said to be discrete in nature because it would not be meaningful to categorize a subject as anything other than a female or a male.[2] By contrast, a continuous scale exists when it is possible theoretically to divide any of the values of the scale. A distinction must be made, however, between what is theoretically possible and what is practically desirable; the units into which a continuous scale will actually be divided may depend on the purpose of the measurement. Thus, although it may be theoretically possible to divide measurements of length into millimeters or even micrometers, it may be impractical to do so if the purpose of the measurement is to install venetian blinds.

Measurement using continuous scales always involves some error. For example, the length of the window you measured to be 35.5 inches could, in reality, be 35.7 inches; it's just that your measuring scale is conveniently marked off in more gross gradations of measurement. Most scales used in psychological testing are continuous in nature and can therefore be expected to contain error. A consideration of sources of error in testing appears in the *Close-up* (see page 88) as well as elsewhere in this book. Error will arise from the mere use of a continuous scale; the number or score used to characterize the trait being measured on a continuous scale should be thought of as an approximation of the "real" number. Thus, for example, a score of 25 on some test of anxiety should not be thought of as a precise measure of anxiety but rather as an approximation

---

2. The authors acknowledge that if all females were labeled "1" and all males were labeled "2," some people, most visibly individuals born with a gender-related genetic abnormality might seem to qualify as a 1.5. Such exceptions aside, however, all cases on a discrete scale must lie on a point on the scale, and it is theoretically impossible for a case to lie between two points on the scale.

of the "real" anxiety score had the measuring instrument been calibrated to yield such a score. In such a case, perhaps the score of 25 is an approximation of a "real" score of 24.7 or 25.44. In contrast to numbers or scores used to characterize traits in continuous scales, the numbers or scores used in discrete scales are presumed to be exact.

Measurement can be further categorized with respect to the amount of quantitative information the assigned numbers possess. It is generally agreed that there are four different levels or scales of measurement. Numbers at different levels or scales of measurement convey different kinds of information. In testing and in research in general, it is important to know which scales of measurement are being employed, for the kind of scale will be one factor in determining which statistical manipulations of the data would or would not be appropriate.[3]

The French word for black is *noir* (pronounced "n'wăre"). We bring this up here only to call attention to the fact that this French word is a useful acronym for remembering the four levels or scales of measurement; each letter in *noir* is the first letter of each of the succeedingly more rigorous levels. *N* stands for "nominal," *o* for "ordinal," *i* for "interval," and *r* for "ratio scales."

Nominal Scales

Nominal scales are the simplest form of measurement. These scales involve classification or categorization based on one or more distinguishing characteristics where all objects must be placed into mutually exclusive and exhaustive categories. For example, people may be characterized by gender in a study designed to compare performance of men and women on some test. In such a study, all males might be labeled "Men," "1," "B," or some other symbol, and all females might be labeled "Women," "2," or "A." In the specialty area of clinical psychology, one often-used nominal scale is the American Psychiatric Association's *Diagnostic and Statistical Manual of Mental Disorders IV (DSM-IV)*. Each disorder listed in the manual is assigned its own number. Thus, for example, the number 303.00 identifies alcohol intoxication and the number 307.00 identifies stuttering. But these numbers are used exclusively for classification purposes and cannot be meaningfully added, subtracted, ranked, or averaged (the number 305 does *not* equal an intoxicated stutterer).

Individual test items, such as the following examples from a hypothetical TRW employment application (refer to this chapter's *Close-up*), may also employ nominal scaling.

---

3. For the purposes of our statistics refresher, we present what Nunnally (1978) called the "fundamentalist" view of measurement scales—a view that "holds that 1. there are distinct types of measurement scales into which all possible measures of attributes can be classified, 2. each measure has some 'real' characteristics that permit its proper classification, and 3. once a measure is classified, the classification specifies the types of mathematical analyses that can be employed with the measure" (p. 24). Yet Nunnally (Chapter 1) and others have argued that alternatives to the "fundamentalist" view may also be viable.

Instructions: Answer either Yes or No.

Are you actively contemplating suicide?

Are you currently under professional care for a psychiatric disorder?

Have you ever been convicted of a felony crime?

In each case, a yes or no response results in the placement into one of a set of mutually exclusive groups: suicidal or not, under care for psychiatric disorder or not, and felon or not. Arithmetic operations that can legitimately be performed with nominal data include counting for the purpose of determining how many cases fall into each category and some consequential determination of proportion or percentages.[4]

Ordinal Scales

Like nominal scales, ordinal scales permit classification. However, in addition to classification, rank-ordering on some characteristic is also permissible with ordinal scales. In the industrial/organizational setting, job applicants may be rank-ordered according to their desirability for a position. In the clinical setting, people on a waiting list for psychotherapy may be rank-ordered according to their need for treatment. In these examples, individuals are compared with others and assigned a rank (perhaps "1" to the best applicant or the most needy wait-listed client, "2" to the next, and so forth).

Assessment instruments applied to the individual subject may also use an ordinal form of measurement. The Rokeach Value Survey, presented in Chapter 14, uses such an approach, with testtakers putting a list of personal values (like freedom, happiness, and wisdom) in order according to their perceived importance to the testtaker (Rokeach, 1973). If a set of ten values is rank-ordered, the testtaker may assign a value of "1" to the most important and "10" to the least important.

Ordinal scales imply nothing about how much greater one ranking is than another. Even though ordinal scales typically employ numbers to represent the rank ordering, the numbers do not indicate units of measurement: the difference between the best and the second-best job applicants may be very small, but there may be a large difference between them and the third-best applicant. Likewise, a person completing the Rokeach Value Survey may be able to identify easily the characteristic ranked "1" as the most important value but might struggle with the ordering of the next three items, suggesting that the strength of these values is similar. Furthermore, ordinal scales have no absolute zero point; without units, zero is without meaning. In the case of values, for example, each item on the test is assumed to be of some value to the testtaker.

Because unequal units of measurement may exist in ordinal scales, and because there is no zero point, the ways in which data from such scales can be

---

4. Nominal data may also be analyzed by means of nonparametric statistical techniques, log linear modeling, and other techniques (see Gokhale & Kullback, 1978).

Error of Measurement and the True Score Model

Kathy applies for a job as a word processor at The Rochester Wrenchworks (TRW). To be hired, Kathy must be able to word-process accurately at the rate of 50 words per minute. The personnel office administers a total of seven brief word processing tests to Kathy over the course of seven business days. In words per minute, Kathy's scores on each of the seven tests are as follows:

52   55   39   56   35   50   54

If you were in charge of hiring at TRW and you looked at these seven scores, you might logically ask, "Which of these scores is the best measure of Kathy's 'true' word processing ability?" or, stated more succinctly, "Which is her 'true' score?"

The "true" answer to the question posed above is that we cannot say with absolute certainty from the data we have exactly what Kathy's true word processing ability is—*but,* we can make an educated guess. Our educated guess would be that her true word processing ability is equal to the mean of the distribution of her word processing scores plus or minus a number of points accounted for by *error* in the measurement process. "Error" in the measurement process can be thought of as any factor entering into the process that is not directly relevant to whatever it is that is being measured. If Kathy had the misfortune on one occasion of drawing a word processor that had not been properly serviced and was of lesser quality than the other word processors she had been tested on, that is an example of "error" entering into the testing

process. If there was excessive noise in the room on a testing occasion, if Kathy wasn't feeling well, if light bulbs blew . . . the list could go on, but the point is that any number of factors other than an individual's ability can enter into the process of measuring that ability. We can try to reduce error in a testing situation such as Kathy's by making certain, to the extent that it is possible, that all word processing equipment is functioning equally well, that the test room is free of excessive noise and has adequate lighting, and so forth. However, we can never entirely eliminate "error." The best we can do is estimate how much error entered into a particular test score and then intelligently interpret the score with that information.

The tool used to estimate or infer how far observed scores deviate from "true" scores is a statistic called the *standard error of measurement*. In the case of Kathy and her TRW word processing scores, the standard error of measurement would be equal to the standard deviation of the observed scores. In practice, few developers of tests designed for use on a widespread basis would investigate the magnitude of error with respect to a single testtaker; more typically, an average standard error of measurement is calculated for a sample of the population on which the test is designed for use. More detailed information on the nature and computation of the standard error of measurement will be presented in Chapter 5. As we will see, measures of reliability assist us in making inferences about the proportion of the total variance of test scores attributable to error variance.

treated statistically is limited. One cannot average the qualifications of the first- and third-ranked job applicants, for example, and expect to come out with the qualifications of the second-ranked applicant.

Interval Scales

In addition to the features of nominal and ordinal scales, interval scales contain equal intervals between numbers; each unit on the scale is exactly equal to any other unit on the scale. But, like ordinal scales, interval scales contain no absolute zero point. With interval scales, we have reached a level of measurement at which it *is* possible to take the average of a set of measurements and get a meaningful result.

Intelligence scale scores are often taken to be at an interval level of measurement. The difference in intellectual ability represented by IQs of 80 and 100, for example, is thought to be similar to that existing between IQs of 100 and 120. However, if an individual were to achieve an IQ of 0 (something that is not even possible on many intelligence scales), that would not mean an absence of intelligence.

Ratio Scales

In addition to having all the properties of nominal, ordinal, and interval measurement, a ratio scale has a true zero point. All mathematical operations can meaningfully be performed on ratio scales because there exist equal intervals between the numbers on the scale as well as a true or absolute zero point.[5]

In psychology, ratio-level measurement is used on some items assessing the functioning of the nervous system. An example would be the amount of pressure one can exert with one's grip: someone who can exert 20 pounds of pressure is exerting twice as much as one who can exert 10, and a meaningful zero point exists, representing individuals incapable of squeezing at all, perhaps because of paralysis in the hand. Some intelligence test items use ratio-level measurement: the time taken to complete a puzzle is an example, with 30 seconds being half the time taken to complete the puzzle in 60 seconds, and one can meaningfully talk about a zero point in theory, though in reality no subject will complete the puzzle that quickly.

Measurement Scales in Psychology

The ordinal level of measurement is most frequently used in psychology. As Kerlinger (1973, p. 439) put it, "Intelligence, aptitude, and personality test

---

5. Note that the distinction between ordinal scales and interval scales is the result of the empirical observations on which numerical assignments are based. The difference between interval and ratio scales seems more closely related to theoretical considerations related to the attribute being measured. It has been suggested that another useful scale of measurement lies between the interval and ratio level of measurement (Narens & Luce, 1986).

scores are, *basically and strictly speaking,* ordinal. They indicate with more or less accuracy not the amount of intelligence, aptitude, and personality traits of individuals, but rather the rank-order positions of the individuals." Kerlinger allowed that "most psychological and educational scales approximate interval equality fairly well," though he cautioned that if ordinal measurements were treated as if they were interval measurements, the test user must "be constantly alert to the possibility of *gross* inequality of intervals" (pp. 440–441).

Why would psychologists want to treat their assessment data as interval when those data would be better described as ordinal? Why not just say that they are ordinal? The attraction of interval measurement for users of psychological tests is in the flexibility with which such data can be manipulated statistically, a flexibility that is not available with ordinal data. What kinds of manipulation are we talking about? The remainder of this statistics refresher reviews ways in which test data can be described in a manageable, interpretable form, using computations like the mean, or average, and employing tables and graphs. Some of these techniques can be used if data are interval but not if they are ordinal. Our statistics refresher continues with a review of the various ways test data can be described.

Table 3–1
Data from Your Measurement
Course Test

Student	Score (number correct)
Judy	78
Joe	67
David	69
Miriam	63
Valerie	85
Diane	72
Henry	92
Gertrude	67
Paula	94
Martha	62
Bill	61
Homer	44
Robert	66
Michael	87
Brandon	76
Mary	83
"Mousey"	42
Barbara	82
John	84
Donna	51
Uriah	69
Leroy	61
Ronald	96
Vinnie	73
Patty	79

Describing Data

Suppose you have magically changed places with the professor teaching this course and you have just administered an examination that consists of 100 multiple-choice items (where one point is awarded for each correct answer). The scores for the 25 students enrolled in your class could theoretically range from 0 (none correct) to 100 (all correct). Assume it is the day after the examination and you are sitting in your office with the data listed in Table 3–1. One task at hand is to communicate the test results to your class in a way that will best assist each individual student in understanding how he or she performed on the test in comparison with all the other testtakers in the class. How do you accomplish this objective?

Frequency Distributions

You might begin by setting up a distribution of the raw scores; rather than a helter-skelter listing of all the raw data, a distribution will help you compare the performance of one student with that of another. One way the scores could be distributed is by the frequency with which they occur. In a *frequency distribution,* all scores are listed alongside the number of times each score occurred. The scores might be listed in tabular or graphic form. Table 3–2 lists the frequency of occurrence of each score in one column and the score itself in the other column.

Table 3–2
Frequency Distribution of Scores from Your Test

Score	f (frequency)
96	1
94	1
92	1
87	1
85	1
84	1
83	1
82	1
79	1
78	1
76	1
73	1
72	1
69	2
67	2
66	1
63	1
62	1
61	2
51	1
44	1
42	1

Table 3–3	Class interval	f (frequency)
A Grouped Frequency Distribution	95–99	1
	90–94	2
	85–89	2
	80–84	3
	75–79	3
	70–74	2
	65–69	5
	60–64	4
	55–59	0
	50–54	1
	45–49	0
	40–44	2

Before we see how these data would look in graphic form, we should note that there exists another kind of frequency distribution, a *grouped frequency distribution,* which further summarizes the data. In a grouped frequency distribution, test-score intervals, also called "class intervals," replace the actual test scores. The number of class intervals used and the size or "width" of each class interval (that is, the range of test scores contained in each class interval) will be a matter left for you to decide as regards the data in need of summarizing; the width that most conveniently summarizes the data will be best. But how do you decide?

In *Exploratory Data Analysis,* Tukey (1977) introduced one type of data analysis technique called *stem-and-leaf display,* which may be a useful reference for persons seeking a set of formal ground rules by which to set class intervals. This technique can get quite complicated, especially when there are a great many "stems" or "leaves" (see Tukey, 1977). In most instances, a decision as to the size of a class interval in a grouped frequency distribution is made on the basis of convenience and with the knowledge that virtually any decision will represent a trade-off; a convenient, easy-to-read summary of the data is the trade-off for the loss of detail. To what extent must the data be summarized? How important is detail? These types of questions must be reckoned with in arriving at a determination as to the size of the class interval. In the grouped frequency distribution in Table 3–3, the test scores have been grouped—simply on the basis of a judgment concerning the need for convenience in reading the data as opposed to the need for detail—into 12 class intervals with each class interval being equal to 5 points.[6] The highest class interval (95 to 99) and the lowest class interval (40 to 44) are referred to respectively as the upper and lower limits of the distribution.

---

6. Technically, each number on such a scale would be viewed as ranging from as much as 0.5 below it, to as much as 0.5 above it. For example, the "true" but hypothetical width of the class interval ranging from 95 to 99 would be the difference between 99.5 and 94.5, or 5. The true upper and lower limits of the class intervals presented in the table would respectively be 99.5 and 39.5.

Frequency distributions of test scores can also be illustrated graphically. A *graph* is a diagram or chart composed of lines, points, bars, or other symbols that describe the data being measured. With a good graph, the place of a single score in relation to a distribution of test scores can easily be grasped by a casual "eyeballing" of the data. Three kinds of graphs used to illustrate frequency distributions are the *histogram,* the *frequency polygon,* and the *bar graph* (see Figure 3–1). A histogram is a graph with vertical lines drawn at the true limits of each test score (or class interval) forming a series of contiguous rectangles. It is customary for the test scores (either the single scores or the midpoints of the class intervals) to be placed along the graph's horizontal axis (also referred to as the abscissa or *X*-axis), and numbers indicative of the frequency of occurrence are placed along the graph's vertical axis (also referred to as the ordinate or *Y*-axis). In a bar graph, numbers indicative of frequency also appear on the *Y*-axis, and reference to some categorization (such as Yes/No/Maybe, Male/Female, and so forth) appears on the *X*-axis; here the rectangular bars typically are not contiguous. Data illustrated in a frequency polygon are expressed by a continuous line connecting the points where test scores or class intervals (as indicated on the *X*-axis) meet frequencies (as indicated on the *Y*-axis). As illustrated in the box on page 98, graphs may obscure or distort information as well as convey it.

Frequency distributions of test scores may assume any of a number of different shapes (see Figure 3–2)—this because of a variety of factors, including the variable(s) being researched, the measurement technique(s), and the sampling procedures. The "normal" or "bell-shaped" curve is of particular interest to us, and it is discussed in greater detail later in this chapter. Distributions are also described according to characteristics such as their central tendency, variability, skewness, and kurtosis.

Measures of Central Tendency

Measures of central tendency are indices of the central value or location of a frequency distribution. The center of a distribution can be defined in different ways. Perhaps the most commonly used measure of central tendency is the *arithmetic mean,* referred to in everyday language as the "average." The mean takes into account the actual mathematical size of every score. In special instances, such as when there are only a few scores and one or two of the scores are extreme in relation to the remaining ones, a measure of central tendency other than the mean may be desirable. Other measures of central tendency we review include the *median* and the *mode.* Note that in the formulas that follow, the standard statistical shorthand called "summation notation" (*summation* meaning "the sum of") is used. The Greek uppercase letter *sigma,* Σ, is the symbol used to signify "sum"; if X represents a test score, then the symbol $\Sigma\ X$ means "add all the test scores."

The arithmetic mean The *arithmetic mean,* denoted by the symbol $\bar{X}$ (pronounced "X bar") is equal to the sum of the observations (or test scores in this case) divided by the number of observations. Symbolically written, the formula

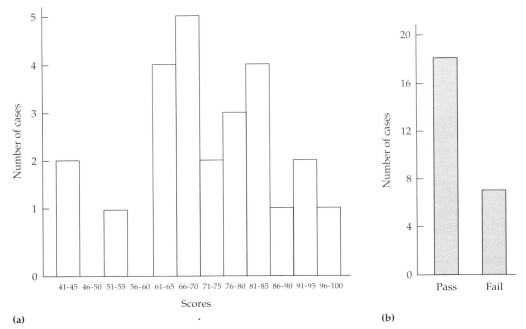

(a)

(b)

Figure 3–1
Graphic Illustrations of Data from Table 3–3

A histogram (a), a bar graph (b), and a frequency polygon (c) all may be used to graphically convey information about test performance. Of course, the labeling of the bar graph and the specific nature of the data conveyed by it depend on the variables of interest; in (b) the variable of interest is the number of students who passed the test (assuming for the purpose of this illustration that a raw score of 65 or higher had been arbitrarily designated in advance to be a passing grade).

for the arithmetic mean is $\bar{X} = \Sigma\ X/n$, where n equals the number of observations or test scores. The arithmetic mean is typically the most appropriate measure of central tendency for interval or ratio data when the distributions are believed to be approximately normal. An arithmetic mean can also be computed from a frequency distribution. The formula for doing this is

$$\bar{X} = \frac{\Sigma\ fX}{n}$$

where $\Sigma\ fX$ means "multiply the frequency of each score by its corresponding score and sum."

As we explain certain concepts, we will urge you to get involved with the subject matter by doing more than merely reading. Your learning of this subject matter may be facilitated if you transcend the role of "observer" and become more of a "participant/observer." Take a few minutes now to use the two arithmetic mean formulas we've just discussed to compute the arithmetic mean for

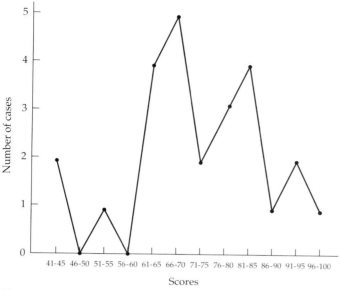

(c)

Returning to the question posed earlier—the one in which you are playing the role of instructor and must communicate the test results to your students—which type of graph would best serve your purpose? Why?

As we continue our review of descriptive statistics, you may wish to return to your role of professor and formulate your response to challenging related questions such as "Which measure(s) of central tendency shall I use to convey this information?" and "Which measure(s) of variability would convey the information best?"

your examination data (contained in Table 3–1 and Table 3–2). As a check on your understanding of how to apply the formulas, note that you should get the same answer using either one.

The median   The *median,* defined as the middle score in a distribution, is another commonly used measure of central tendency. As an example, you can determine the median of a distribution of scores by ordering the scores in a list by magnitude—in either ascending or descending order. When the total number of scores ordered is an odd number, the median will be the score that is exactly in the middle, with one-half of the remaining scores lying above it and the other half of the remaining scores lying below it. When the total number of scores ordered is an even number, the median can be calculated by determining the arithmetic mean of the two middle scores. For example, suppose that ten people took a preemployment word processing test at The Rochester Wrenchworks (TRW) Corporation and obtained the following scores, presented here in descending order:

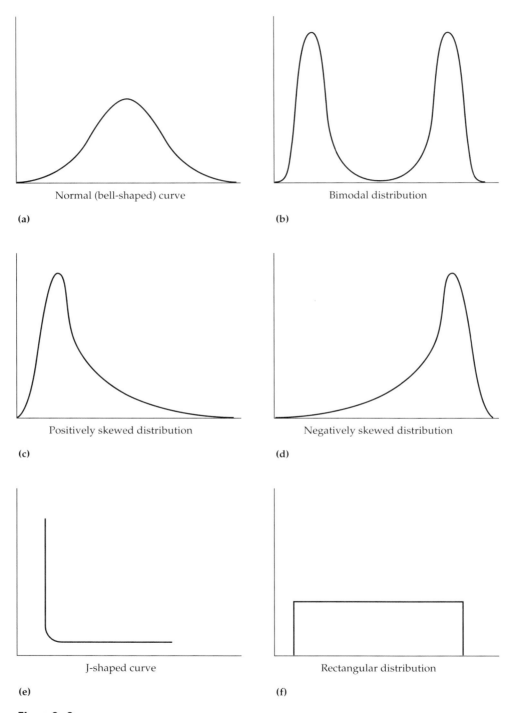

Figure 3–2
Shapes Frequency Distributions Can Take

66
65
61
59
53
52
41
36
35
32

The median in these data would be computed by obtaining the average (that is, the arithmetic mean) of the two middle scores, 53 and 52 (which would be equal to 52.5). The median is an appropriate measure of central tendency for ordinal, interval, and ratio data, especially if data are highly skewed.

Remember Kathy from this chapter's *Close-up* on page 88? You may recall that she applied for a job at TRW and was administered seven word processing tests over the course of seven business days. TRW's policy is not to hire word processors unless they can accurately word-process 50 words per minute. Kathy's word processing scores in words per minute are reprinted below. Should she be hired?

52   55   39   56   35   50   54

If you were to obtain the arithmetic mean for this distribution of scores, the resulting figure is below 50. Thus, if the company's policy was to routinely take an average of word processing test scores and reject people whose average score did not meet the minimum of 50 words per minute, Kathy would have to be dismissed from further consideration. However, if you as the personnel officer had some discretion, you might have used the median and not the mean as the preferred measure of central tendency in this situation. You would have then grouped these scores from highest to lowest and located the middle score in the distribution:[7]

56
55
54
52   (the middle score)
50
39
35

If Kathy's resume looked good in all respects, if the company needed to hire clerks immediately, or for any other good reason, a decision to hire Kathy could

_____

7. Consult an appropriate statistics text for specialized formulas used to calculate the median of (a) a large, unwieldy group of scores (that is, a group of scores so large it would be impractical merely to order them in ascending order and locate the middle score), (b) a grouped frequency distribution, or (c) a distribution where various scores are identical.

Consumer (of Graphed Data) Beware!

"One picture is worth a thousand words" and one purpose of representing data in graphic form is to convey information at a glance. However, although two graphs may be accurate with respect to the data they represent, their pictures—and the impression drawn from a glance at them—may be vastly different. As an example, consider the following hypothetical scenario involving a hamburger restaurant chain we'll call "The Charred House."

The Charred House chain serves very charbroiled, microscopically thin hamburgers formed in the shape of little, triangular houses. In the ten-year period since its founding in 1986, the company has sold on average, 100 million burgers per year. On the chain's tenth anniversary, The Charred House distributes a press release proudly announcing "Over a Billion Served."

Reporters from two business-type publications set out to research and write a feature article on this hamburger restaurant chain. Working solely from sales figures as compiled from annual reports to the shareholders, Reporter 1 focuses her story on the differences in yearly sales. Her article is titled "A Billion Served—But Charred House Sales Fluctuate From Year to Year," and its graphic illustration is reprinted here.

Quite a different picture of the company emerges from Reporter 2's story, titled "A Billion Served—And Charred House Sales Are as Steady as Ever," and its accompanying graph. The latter story is based on a diligent analysis of comparable data for the same number of hamburger chains in the same areas of the country over the same time period. While researching the story, Reporter 2 learned that yearly fluctuations in sales is common to the entire industry and that the annual fluctuations observed in the Charred House figures were—relative to other chains—insignificant.

Compare the frequency polygons that accompanied each story. Although both are accurate insofar as they are based on the correct numbers, the impression they are likely to leave is quite different.

Incidentally, custom dictates that the intersection of the two axes of a frequency polygon be at 0; the fact that this custom is violated in the graph accompanying Reporter 1's story should serve as a warning to evaluate the pictorial representation of the data all the more critically.

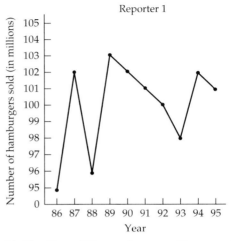

(a) The Charred House sales over a 10-year period

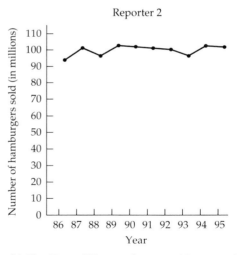

(b) The Charred House sales over a 10-year period

be justified by the use of the median as the measure of central tendency—in this case, as a measure of Kathy's word processing ability. The median may well be the most appropriate measure to use with such a distribution of scores. On the days when Kathy's score was in the thirties, she may not have been feeling well, the word processor used for the test may not have been operating properly, or other factors could have influenced the score. Whereas the mean is the preferred measure of central tendency for symmetrical distributions, the median is the preferred measure for skewed distributions like this.

The mode The most frequently occurring score in a distribution of scores is the *mode.*[8] As an example, determine the mode for the following scores obtained on the TRW test by another applicant for a word processing position, Bruce:

43   46   45   51   42   44   51

The most frequently occurring score in this distribution of scores is 51. Again, place yourself in the role of the corporate personnel officer. Would you hire Bruce? If your hiring guideline dictated that you use the arithmetic mean, you would not hire him, since his mean performance falls below 50 words per minute. But even if you had the leeway to use another measure of central tendency, you still might not hire him; even a casual look at these data indicates that Bruce's typical performance would fall below the level required by the company.

Distributions that contain a tie for the designation as "most frequently occurring score" can have more than one mode. Consider the following scores—arranged in no particular order—obtained by 20 students on the final exam of a new trade school called the "Home Study School of Elvis Presley Impersonators":

51	49	51	50	66	52	53	38	17	66
33	44	73	13	21	91	87	92	47	3

The distribution of these scores is said to be "bimodal" because it contains two scores (51 and 66) that occur with the highest frequency (a frequency of two). Except for use with nominal data, the mode tends not to be a very commonly used measure of central tendency. Unlike the arithmetic mean, which has to be calculated, the value of the modal score is not calculated—one simply counts and determines which score occurs most frequently. Because the mode is arrived at in this manner, the modal score may be a totally atypical score—one at an extreme end of the distribution—but nonetheless one that occurs with the greatest frequency. In fact, it is theoretically possible for a bimodal distribution to have two modes that each fall at the high or the low end of the distribution—thus violating our expectation that a measure of central tendency should be indicative of a point at the middle of the distribution.

---

8. If adjacent scores occur equally often and more often than other scores, custom dictates that the mode be referred to as the "average."

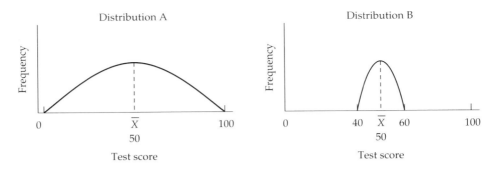

Figure 3–3
Two Distributions with Differences in Variability

Even though the mode is not calculated and even though the mode is not necessarily a unique point in a distribution (a distribution can have two, three, or even more modes), the mode can be useful in conveying certain types of information. For example, suppose you wanted an estimate of the number of journal articles published by clinical psychologists in the United States in the last year. To arrive at this figure, you might total the number of journal articles accepted for publication by each clinical psychologist in the United States, divide by the number of psychologists, and arrive at the arithmetic mean—an indication of the average number of journal articles published. Whatever that number would be, we can say with certainty that it would be more than the mode: it is well known that most clinical psychologists do not write journal articles; therefore, the mode for publications by clinical psychologists in any given year is zero. The mode in this instance provides useful information in addition to the mean because it tells us that no matter what the figure is for the average number of publications, most clinicians do not publish.

Because the mode is not in a true sense calculated, it is a nominal statistic and could not legitimately be used in further calculations. The median is a statistic that takes into account the order of scores and is, itself, ordinal in nature. The mean is the most stable and generally the most useful measure of central tendency, and it is an interval statistic.

Measures of Variability

Variability is an indication of how scores in a distribution are scattered or dispersed. As Figure 3–3 illustrates, two or more distributions of test scores can have the same mean, though differences in the scatter or dispersion of scores around the mean can be wide. In both distributions A and B, test scores could range from 0 to 100. In distribution A, we see that the mean score was 50 and the remaining scores were widely distributed around the mean. In distribution

B, the mean was also 50, though few if any people scored higher than 60 or lower than 40.

Statistics that describe the amount of variation in a distribution include the range, the interquartile range, the semi-interquartile range, the average deviation, the standard deviation, and the variance.

The range The *range* of a distribution is equal to the difference between the highest and the lowest scores. We could describe distribution B of Figure 3–3, for example, as having a range of 20 if we knew that the highest score in this distribution was 60 and the lowest score was 40 (60 − 40 = 20). With respect to distribution A, if we knew that the lowest score was 0 and the highest score was 100, the range would be equal to 100 − 0, or 100. The range is the simplest measure of variability to compute, but it is also of limited use; one extreme score can radically alter the value of the range, since the range is based entirely on the value of the two extreme scores. Suppose, for example, that there was one score in distribution B equal to 90. The range of this distribution would now be equal to 90 − 40, or 50. Yet in looking at the data in the graph for distribution B, it is clear that the vast majority of scores tend to be between 40 and 60.

As a descriptive statistic of variation, the range provides a quick but gross description of the spread of scores. Better measures include the *interquartile range* and the *semi-interquartile range*.

The interquartile and the semi-interquartile range A distribution of test scores (or any other data for that matter) can be divided into four parts such that 25 percent of the test scores occur in each quarter. As illustrated in Figure 3–4, the dividing points between the four quarters in the distribution are referred to as the *quartiles*; there are three of them and they are respectively labeled "Q_1," "Q_2," and "Q_3." Note that "quartile" refers to a specific point, whereas "quarter" refers to an interval; an individual score may, for example, fall *at* the third quartile or *in* the third quarter (but *not* "in" the third quartile or "at" the third quarter). It should not come as a surprise to you that Q_2 and the median are exactly the same. And just as the median is the midpoint in a distribution of scores, so quartiles Q_1 and Q_3 are "quarter-points" in a distribution of scores. Formulas may be employed to determine the exact value of these points. The *interquartile range* is equal to the difference between Q_3 and Q_1 and, like the median, it is an ordinal statistic. A related measure of variability is the *semi-interquartile range*, which is equal to the interquartile range divided by two. Knowledge of the relative distances of Q_1 and Q_3 from Q_2 (the median) provides the seasoned test interpreter with immediate information as to the shape of the distribution of scores. In a perfectly symmetrical distribution, Q_1 and Q_3 will be exactly the same distance from the median. If these distances are unequal, there will be a lack of symmetry, referred to as "skewness" and discussed later in this chapter.

The average deviation Another tool that could conceivably be used to describe the amount of variability that exists in a distribution is the *average deviation*, or *AD* for short. Its formula is

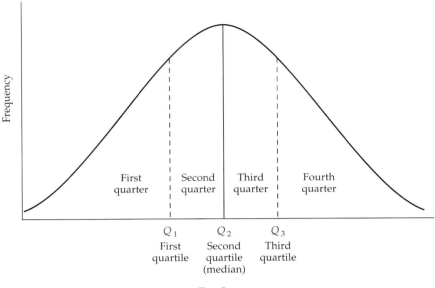

Figure 3–4
A Quartered Distribution

$$AD = \frac{\Sigma \, |x|}{n}$$

The lowercase, italicized "x" in the formula signifies a score's deviation from the mean; it is obtained by subtracting the mean from the score $(X - \text{mean}) = x$. The bars on each side of x indicate that you must use the absolute value of the deviation score (ignoring the positive or negative sign and treating all deviation scores as positive). All the deviation scores are then summed and divided by the total number of scores (n) to arrive at the average deviation. As an exercise, compute the average deviation for the following distribution of test scores:

85   100   90   95   80

Begin by calculating the arithmetic mean. Next obtain the absolute value of each of the five deviation scores and sum them (and note what would happen if you did not ignore algebraic signs—all the deviation scores would sum to 0). Divide the sum of the deviation scores by the number of measurements (5). Did you obtain an AD of 6? The AD tells us that the five scores in this distribution varied, on average, 6 points from the mean.

The AD is a very rarely used statistic, since the arbitrary discarding of algebraic signs renders it a useless measure with respect to any further operations. An understanding of how the *AD* is arrived at, however, is useful in understanding another much more widely used statistic, the standard deviation.

The standard deviation and variance   The *standard deviation* is a measure of variability that is equal to the square root of the average squared deviations about the mean. We could define a standard deviation more succinctly by saying simply that it is equal to the square root of the variance. The *variance* is equal to the arithmetic mean of the squares of the differences between the scores in a distribution and their mean.

In computing the average deviation, the problem of the sum of all deviation scores around the mean equaling zero was solved by employing only the absolute value of the deviation scores. In computing the standard deviation, the same problem is dealt with in a different way; instead of using the absolute value of each of the deviation scores, each score is squared; thus, the sign of the negative deviations becomes positive. Since all the deviation scores are squared, we know that before we are finished with our calculations, we must go back and obtain the square root of whatever number we reach. The formula used to calculate the variance (s^2) using deviation scores is

$$s^2 = \frac{\Sigma\ x^2}{n}$$

Simply stated, the variance is calculated by squaring and summing all the deviation scores and dividing by the total number of scores. The variance can also be computed from raw scores by first calculating the summation of the raw scores squared, dividing by the number of scores, and then subtracting the mean squared:

$$s^2 = \frac{\Sigma\ X^2}{n} - \bar{X}^2$$

The variance is a widely used measure in psychological research. To make meaningful interpretations, the test-score distribution should be approximately normal, which means that the greatest frequency of scores occurs near the arithmetic mean and correspondingly fewer and fewer scores relative to the mean occur on both sides of it as scores differ from the mean.

For some "hands-on" experience with—as well as a sense of mastery of— the concepts of variance and standard deviation, why not allot the next 10 or 15 minutes or so to computing the standard deviation for the test scores originally contained in Table 3–1? Use both formulas to verify that they produce the same results.

Using deviation scores, your calculations should look similar to these:

$$s^2 = \frac{\Sigma\ x^2}{n}$$

$$s^2 = \frac{\Sigma\ (X\ -\ \text{mean})^2}{n}$$

$$s^2 = \frac{[(78 - 72.12)^2 + (67 - 72.12)^2 + \cdots (79 - 72.12)^2]}{25}$$

$$s^2 = \frac{4972.64}{25}$$

$$s^2 = 198.91$$

Using the raw-scores formula, your calculations should look similar to these:

$$s^2 = \frac{\Sigma X^2}{n} - \bar{X}^2$$

$$s^2 = \frac{[(78)^2 + (67)^2 + \cdots (79)^2]}{25} - 5201.29$$

$$s^2 = \frac{135005}{25} - 5201.29$$

$$s^2 = 5400.20 - 5201.29$$

$$s^2 = 198.91$$

In both cases, the standard deviation is the square root of the variance (s^2). According to our calculations, the standard deviation of the test scores is 14.10. If $s = 14.10$, 1 standard deviation unit is approximately equal to 14 units of measurement, or with reference to our example and rounded to a whole number, 14 test-score points. The test data did not provide a good normal curve approximation; rather, they were positively "skewed," a concept we will review shortly. Some things you need to know about test-score interpretation when the scores are *not* skewed—that is, when the test scores are approximately normal in distribution—are presented later in the section Area Under the Normal Curve.

The symbol for standard deviation has variously been represented as *s*, *S*, SD, and the lowercase Greek letter sigma (σ). One custom—the one we adhere to—has it that *s* refers to the sample standard deviation and σ refers to the population standard deviation. The number of observations in the sample is *n* and the denominator $n - 1$ is sometimes used to calculate what is referred to as an "unbiased estimate" of the population value—it's actually only *less* biased (see Hopkins & Glass, 1978). Unless *n* is 10 or less, the use of *n* or $n - 1$ tends not to make a meaningful difference.

But whether the denominator is more properly *n* or $n - 1$ has been something of a matter of debate. Lindgren (1983) has argued for the use of $n - 1$, in part because this denominator tends to make correlation formulas simpler. By contrast, most texts recommend the use of $n - 1$ only when the data constitute a sample; *n* is preferable when the data constitute a population. For Lindgren (1983), it matters not whether the data are from a sample or a population. Perhaps the most reasonable convention—and the one we will follow—is to use *n* when either the population has been assessed (as we might legitimately assume it has when dealing with the examination scores of one class of students—including all the people about whom we're going to make inferences) or no inferences to the population are intended. $\bar{X}$ represents a sample mean, M (mu) a population mean. The formula for the population standard deviation is

$$\sigma = \sqrt{\frac{\Sigma (X - M)^2}{n}}$$

The standard deviation is a very useful measure of variation, since each individual score's distance from the mean of the distribution is employed in its computation. You will come across it frequently in the study of measurement.

Skewness

Distributions can be characterized by their *skewness*, or the nature and extent to which symmetry is absent. Skewness is an indication of how the measurements in a distribution are distributed. A distribution is said to be skewed positively when relatively few of the scores fall at the positive end of the distribution. Results from an examination that are positively skewed may indicate that the test was too difficult; more items that were easier would have been desirable to discriminate better at the lower end of the distribution of test scores. A distribution is said to be skewed negatively when relatively few of the scores fall at the negative end of the distribution. Results from an examination that are negatively skewed may indicate that the test was too easy; in such an instance, more items of a higher level of difficulty would have been desirable so that better discrimination between scores could have been made with respect to the upper end of the distribution of scores. (See Figure 3–2 on page 96 for examples of skewed distributions.)

Experience in teaching measurement courses has indicated to the authors that the term *skewed* carries with it negative implications for many students, perhaps because of an association with abnormality—given that a skewed distribution deviates from a "normal" distribution. However, the presence or absence of symmetry in a distribution (skewness) is simply one characteristic by which a distribution can be described, and skewness is not in and of itself bad (or good). We might expect a distribution of household income in dollars to be skewed negatively if samples such as Beverly Hills residents or Harvard Law School graduates were employed—because of the clustering that could be expected at the higher end of possible household incomes. A hypothetical "Marine Corps Endurance Test" used to screen male applicants might consistently yield positively skewed distributions; its built-in difficulty level would be designed to guarantee that only a few would "pass"—consistent with the advertised objective that the Corps isn't seeking "a lot of good men" but rather only "a few good men." A test purporting to measure abilities that are assumed to be normally distributed in the population would be expected to yield distributions that are also approximately normal in distribution. If testing with such an instrument using samples from the general population repeatedly yielded skewed distributions, the assumptions made by such a test would have to be reconsidered.

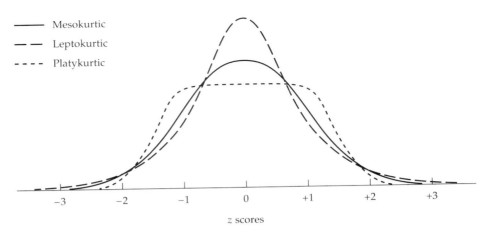

Figure 3-5
The Kurtosis of Curves

Various formulas exist for measuring skewness. One way of gauging the skewness of a distribution is through examination of the relative distances of quartiles from the median. In a positively skewed distribution, $Q_3 - Q_2$ will be greater than the distance of $Q_2 - Q_1$. In a negatively skewed distribution, $Q_3 - Q_2$ will be less than the distance of $Q_2 - Q_1$. In a distribution that is symmetrical, the distances from Q_1 and Q_3 to the median are the same.

Kurtosis

The term testing professionals use to refer to the steepness of a distribution in its center is *kurtosis*, and the descriptive suffix *kurtic* is added to either *platy*, *lepto*, or *meso* to describe the peakedness/flatness of three general types of curves (see Figure 3-5). Distributions are generally described as being either "platykurtic" (relatively flat), "leptokurtic" (relatively peaked), or—somewhere in the middle—"mesokurtic." Although many methods exist for measuring kurtosis, the subject of kurtosis—including technical matters related to its measurement and interpretation—is still a matter of controversy among measurement specialists.

The Normal Curve

Development of the concept of a normal curve began in the middle of the eighteenth century with the work of Abraham DeMoivre and, later, Pierre Simon de Laplace. At the beginning of the nineteenth century, Karl Friedrich Gauss made some substantial contributions to the normal curve concept with his work on his "theory of errors" (work that resulted in a statistical technique known as the method of least squares). In the early nineteenth century, the normal curve was referred to as the Laplace–Gaussian curve. It was Karl Pearson who first referred to this curve as the "normal curve," perhaps in an effort to be diplomatic. Diplomacy aside, referring to the curve as "normal" instead of assigning someone's name to it created some confusion at the time, especially since many wondered aloud whether all other curves should be thought of as "abnormal." Somehow, the name "normal curve" stuck—but don't be surprised if you're sitting at some scientific meeting one day and you hear this distribution or curve referred to as "Gaussian" in nature.

Theoretically, the normal curve is a bell-shaped, smooth, mathematically defined curve highest at the center and then gradually tapered on both sides approaching the X-axis *asymptotically* (meaning that it approaches, but never touches, the axis). In theory, the distribution of the normal curve ranges from negative infinity to positive infinity. The curve is perfectly symmetrical, with no skewness, so if you "folded" it in half at the mean, one side would lie exactly on top of the other. Because it is symmetrical, the mean, the median, and the mode all have the same exact value.

Why is the normal curve important in understanding the characteristics of psychological tests? See this chapter's *Everyday Psychometrics* feature (pages 110–111).

Area Under the Normal Curve

The normal curve can be conveniently divided into areas defined in standard deviation units. A hypothetical distribution of "National Spelling Test" scores with a mean of 50 and a standard deviation of 15 is illustrated in Figure 3–6. In this example, a score equal to 1 standard deviation above the mean would be equal to 65 ($\bar{X} + 1 s = 50 + 15 = 65$). Before reading on, take a minute or two to calculate what a score exactly at 3 standard deviations below the mean would be equal to. How about a score exactly at 3 standard deviations above the mean? Were your answers 5 and 95, respectively? The graph tells us that 99.74% of all scores in these normally distributed spelling tests data lie between ± 3 standard deviations. Stated another way, 99.74% of all spelling test scores lie between 5 and 95. This graph also illustrates other characteristics true of all normal distributions:

- 50% of the scores occur above the mean, and 50% of the scores occur below the mean.

- Approximately 34% of all scores occur between the mean and 1 standard deviation above the mean.

- Approximately 34% of all scores occur between the mean and 1 standard deviation below the mean.

- Approximately 68% of all scores occur between the mean and ± 1 standard deviation.

- Approximately 95% of all scores occur between the mean and ± 2 standard deviations.

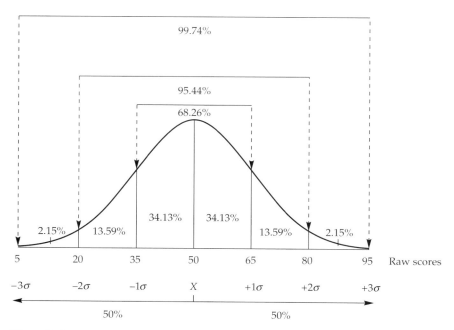

Figure 3–6
Area Under the Normal Curve

Knowledge of the areas under the normal curve can be quite useful to the interpreter of test data. If, for example, you know that some high school student's score on a national, well-reputed spelling test was more than 3 standard deviations above the mean, it's a good bet that the student would know how to spell words like "asymptotic" and "leptokurtic."

Standard Scores

Simply stated, a *standard score* is a raw score that has been converted from one scale into another scale—the latter typically being one that is more widely used and interpretable—that has some arbitrarily set mean and standard deviation. Raw scores may be converted to standard scores because standard scores are more readily interpretable than raw scores. With a standard score, the position of a testtaker's performance relative to other testtakers is readily apparent. Different types of systems for standard scores exist, each unique as regards its respective mean and standard deviations. One type of standard score scale has been referred to as the "zero plus or minus one" scale because it has a mean set at zero and a standard deviation set at one. Raw scores converted into standard scores on the "zero plus or minus one scale" are more popularly referred to as z scores.

z Scores

A z score is equal to the difference between a particular raw score and the mean divided by the standard deviation. In essence, a z score expresses a score in terms of the number of standard deviation units the raw score is below or above the mean of the distribution. Using an example from the normally distributed "National Spelling Test" data in Figure 3–6, we can convert a raw score of 65 to a z score using the following formula:

$$z = \frac{X - \bar{X}}{s} = \frac{65 - 50}{15} = \frac{15}{15} = 1$$

In this test a raw score of 65 is equal to a z score of +1. Knowing simply that someone obtained a raw score of 65 on a spelling test conveys virtually no usable information because information about the context of this score is lacking. However, knowing that someone obtained a z score of 1 on a spelling test provides context and meaning to the score; drawing on our knowledge of areas under the normal curve, for example, we would know that only about 16% of the other testtakers obtained higher scores.

Standard scores provide a convenient way to compare raw scores within and between tests. It helps us little to know, for example, that Crystal's raw score on the "Main Street Reading Test" was 24 and that her raw score on the "Main Street Arithmetic Test" was 42. Knowing Crystal's z scores on the two tests would be more informative. If we were to compute z scores based on the performance of other students in Crystal's class, we might find that her z score on the reading test was 1.32 and her z score on the arithmetic test was −0.75. Thus, although her raw score in arithmetic was higher than in reading, the z scores tell us that Crystal performed above average on the reading test and below average on the arithmetic test, relative to the other students in her class. An interpretation of exactly how much better she performed could be obtained by reference to tables detailing distances under the normal curve (and the resulting percentage of cases that could be expected to fall above or below a particular standard deviation point, or z score).

Of course, to make meaningful comparison of z scores on different tests, the groups on which the z score calculations are based should be similar. For example, it would be pointless to compute Crystal's z score on the reading test relative to non−English speaking children and then compare that with her z score on the arithmetic test computed relative to college mathematics majors; at

The Normal Curve and Psychological Tests

Scores on many psychological tests are often approximately normally distributed, particularly when the tests are administered to large numbers of subjects. Few, if any, psychological tests yield precisely normal distributions of test scores (Micceri, 1989). As a general rule, with ample exceptions, the larger the sample size and the wider the range of abilities measured by a particular test, the more the graph of the test scores will approximate the normal curve. A classic illustration of this was provided by E. L. Thorndike and his colleagues (1927). Thorndike et al. compiled intelligence test scores from several large samples of students. As you can see in Figure 1, the distribution of scores closely approximated the normal curve.

The following sample gives more recent and varied examples of the wide range of characteristics that psychologists have found to be approximately normal in distribution:

- The strength of handedness in right-handed individuals, as measured by the Waterloo Handedness Questionnaire (Tan, 1993).

- Scores on the Women's Health Questionnaire, a scale measuring a variety of health problems in women across a wide age range (Hunter, 1992).

- Responses of both college students and working adults to a measure of intrinsic and extrinsic work motivation (Amabile et al., 1994).

- The intelligence scale scores of eating-disordered girls and women, as measured by the Wechsler Adult Intelli-

gence Scale–Revised and the Wechsler Intelligence Scale for Children–Revised (Ranseen & Humphries, 1992).

- The intellectual functioning of children and adolescents with cystic fibrosis (Thompson et al., 1992).

- Decline in cognitive abilities over a one-year period in people with Alzheimer's disease (Burns et al., 1991).

- The rate of motor-skill development in developmentally delayed preschoolers, as measured by the Vineland Adaptive Behavior Scale (Davies & Gavin, 1994).

- Scores on the Swedish translation of the Positive and Negative Syndrome Scale, which assesses the presence of positive and negative symptoms in people with schizophrenia (von Knorring & Lindstrom, 1992).

- The scores of psychiatrists on The Scale for Treatment Integration of the Dually Diagnosed (those with both a drug problem and another mental disorder). The scale examines opinions about drug treatment for this group of patients (Adelman et al., 1991).

- Responses to the Tridimensional Personality Questionnaire, a measure of three distinct personality features (Cloninger et al., 1991).

- Scores on a self-esteem measure among undergraduates (Addeo et al., 1994).

In each case, the researchers made a special point of stating that the scale under investigation yielded something close to a normal distribution of scores. Why?

best, such a comparison might allow us to conclude that Crystal's reading skills are better relative to non–English speakers than her arithmetic skills are relative to college math majors. If the previous statement seemed like nonsense to you, that's because it described the nonsensical situation of comparing z scores using different comparison groups. Meaningful comparison of any standard scores requires similarity between the comparison groups on which the standard scores are computed.

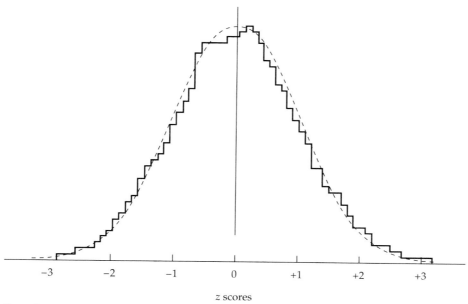

z scores

Figure 1
Graphic Representation of Thorndike et al. Data

The solid line outlines the distribution of intelligence test scores of sixth-grade students (N = 15,138). The dotted line is the theoretical normal curve (Thorndike et al., 1927).

One benefit of a normal distribution of scores is that it simplifies the interpretation of individual scores on the test. In a normal distribution, the mean, the median, and the mode take on the same value. For example, if we know that the average score for intellectual ability of children with cystic fibrosis is a particular value, and that the scores are normally distributed, we know quite a bit more. We know that the average is the most common score and the score below and above which half of all the scores fall. Knowing the mean and the standard deviation of a scale, and knowing that it is approximately normally distributed, tells us that approximately two-thirds of all test-takers' scores are within a standard deviation of the mean. Approximately 95% of the scores fall within 2 standard deviations of the mean.

The characteristics of the normal curve provide a ready model for score interpretation that can be applied to a wide range of test results.

T Scores

If the scale used in the computation of *z* scores is called a "zero plus or minus one" scale, then the scale used in the computation of *T* scores is called a "fifty plus or minus ten" scale: a scale that has a mean set at 50 and a standard deviation set at 10. Devised by W. A. McCall (1922, 1939) and named a *T* score in honor of his professor E. L. Thorndike, this standard score system is composed of a scale that ranges from 5 standard deviations below the mean to 5 standard deviations above the mean. Thus, for example, a raw score that fell exactly at 5 standard deviations below the mean would be equal to a *T* score of 0, a raw score that fell at the mean would be equal to a *T* of 50, and a raw score that fell at a point that was 5 standard deviations above the mean would be equal to a *T* of 100. An advantage in using *T* scores is that none of the scores is negative. By contrast, in a *z* score distribution, scores can be positive and negative, making further computation cumbersome in some instances.

Other Standard Scores

Numerous other standard scoring systems exist. Researchers during World War II developed a standard score with a mean of 5 and a standard deviation of approximately 2. Divided into nine units, the scale was christened a *stanine*, deriving from a contraction of the words "*sta*ndard" and "*nine*." This scale was subsequently refined statistically (see Kaiser, 1958).

Stanine scoring may be familiar to many students from achievement tests administered in elementary and secondary school, where test scores are often represented as stanines. Stanines are different from other standard scores in that they take on whole values from 1 to 9, which represent a range of performance that is 1/2 a standard deviation in width. (See Figure 3–7.) The 5th stanine indicates performance in the average range, from 1/4 standard deviation below the mean to 1/4 standard deviation above the mean, capturing the middle 20% of the scores in a normal distribution. The 4th and 6th stanines are also 1/2 standard deviation wide, and capture the 17% of cases below and above the 5th stanine, respectively. One attraction of the stanine scale is that its whole-number, single-digit values can be readily manipulated computationally.

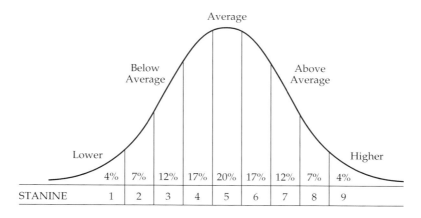

Figure 3–7
Stanines and the Normal Curve

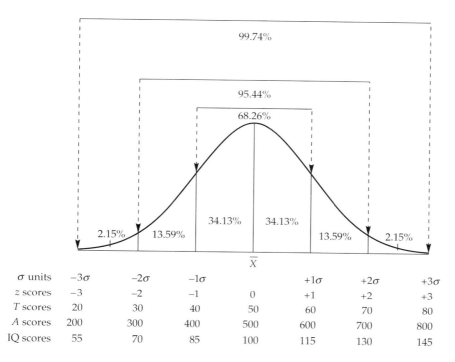

σ units	-3σ	-2σ	-1σ		$+1\sigma$	$+2\sigma$	$+3\sigma$
z scores	-3	-2	-1	0	$+1$	$+2$	$+3$
T scores	20	30	40	50	60	70	80
A scores	200	300	400	500	600	700	800
IQ scores	55	70	85	100	115	130	145

Figure 3–8
Some Standard Score Equivalents

Raw scores on tests such as the Scholastic Aptitude Test (SAT) and the Graduate Record Examination (GRE) are converted to standard scores such that the resulting distribution has a mean of 500 and a standard deviation of 100. If the letter A is used to represent a standard score from a college or graduate school admissions test whose distribution has a mean of 500 and a standard deviation of 100, then the following is true:

$$(A = 600) = (z = 1) = (T = 60)$$

The relationship of z, T, and A scores to each other in a normal distribution is illustrated in Figure 3–8.

Another kind of standard score that you may be familiar with is the "deviation intelligence quotient," or "deviation IQ" or simply "IQ" for short. If you are not familiar with this type of score, rest assured that after studying Part 3 of this text you will be. For most IQ tests, the distribution of raw scores is converted to IQ scores, whose distribution typically has a mean set at 100 and a standard deviation set at 15 (note that we say "typically" because there is some variation in standard scoring systems depending on the test used). The typical mean and standard deviation for IQ tests results in approximately 95% of deviation IQs ranging from 70 to 130—that is, 2 standard deviations below and above the mean, respectively (see Figure 3–8). We will have much more to say about deviation IQs in Part 3. We will also see that each of the individual sub-tests of the Wechsler set of intelligence tests is a standard score itself, with a mean set at 10 and a standard deviation set at 3.

Standard scores converted from raw scores may involve either *linear* or *nonlinear transformations*. A standard score obtained by a linear transformation is one that retains a direct numerical relationship to the original raw score, and the magnitude of differences between such standard scores exactly parallels the differences between corresponding raw scores. Sometimes scores may undergo more than one transformation; for example, the creators of the SAT did a second linear transformation on their data to convert z scores into a new scale that has a mean of 500 and a standard deviation of 100. A *nonlinear* transformation may be required when the data under consideration are not normally distributed and comparisons with normal distributions need to be made. When such a nonlinear transformation is done, the original distribution is said to have been "normalized."

Normalized standard scores   A test developer interested in developing an instrument that yields a normal distribution of scores may find that, even after very large samples have been tested with the instrument, skewed distributions result. If the test developer is intent on having scores on this test be distributed normally, the distribution can be normalized. Conceptually, normalizing a distribution involves "stretching" the skewed curve into a shape of a normal curve and creating a corresponding scale of standard scores—a scale that is technically referred to as a *normalized standard score scale*.

Normalization of a skewed distribution of scores may also be desirable for purposes of comparability. One of the primary advantages of a standard score on one test is that it can readily be compared with a standard score on another test. However, comparison of standard scores is appropriate only when the distributions from which they derived are the same—and in most instances they are the same because the two distributions are approximately normal. But if, for example, distribution A was normal and distribution B was highly skewed, z scores in these respective distributions would represent different amounts of area subsumed under the curve. A z score of -1 with respect to normally distributed data tells us, among other things, that about 84% of the scores in this distribution were higher than this score. A z score of -1 with respect to data that were very positively skewed might mean, for example, that only 62% of the scores were higher.

For test developers intent on creating tests that yield normally distributed measurements, it is generally preferable to "fine-tune" the test according to difficulty and/or other relevant variables so that the resulting distribution will approximate the normal curve—as opposed to trying to normalize skewed distributions. This is so because there are technical cautions to be observed before attempting normalization. Transformations should be made only when there is good reason to believe that the test sample was large and representative enough and the failure to obtain normally distributed scores was due to the measuring instrument. In situations where the distribution is not perfectly normal but closely approximates normal, normalization is not typically conducted, since the normalized standard score (derived from a nonlinear transformation) will closely approximate the standard score (derived from a linear transformation). Further, the score derived from a nonlinear transformation will be limited with respect to additional computations that can legitimately be performed with it, while the score derived from the linear transformation will not.

And speaking of transformations, it's about time to make one to Chapter 4. It may be helpful at this time to review this statistics refresher to make certain that you indeed feel "refreshed." Apply what you have learned about frequency distributions, graphing frequency distributions, measures of central tendency, measures of variability, and the normal curve and standard scores to the question posed on page 91. . . . How would you communicate the data from Table 3–1 to the class? Which type of frequency distribution might you use? Which type of graph? Which measure of central tendency? Which measure of variability? Might reference to a normal curve or to standard scores be helpful? Why or why not?[9]

Come to the next class session prepared with your thoughts on the answers to these questions—as well as your own questions regarding any of the material that could still stand a bit more explanation. We will be building on your knowledge of basic statistical principles in the chapters to come, and it is important that such building be on a rock-solid foundation.

---

9. A detailed, step-by-step illustration of the computation of each of various statistics for these data appears in Cohen (1996), the companion study guide to this text.

4

Norms, Correlation, and Regression

Apopularly held notion is that "the crazies come out of the woodwork when the moon is full." Is there really a correlation between the occurrence of a full moon and "lunacy"? Although the popular belief that such a correlation exists finds support in some published studies, scrutiny of the methods used to analyze and interpret the data has raised a number of questions. Rotton and Kelly (1985) carefully reviewed over three dozen published studies addressed to the "lunacy" question and concluded that phases of the moon could account for no more than 1 percent of the variance in "lunatic"-related behavior such as homicides and other criminal offenses, crisis calls, and mental hospital admissions. Rotton and Kelly suggested that alleged relations between the moon and lunacy found to exist by other researchers were due at least in part to inappropriate statistical analyses.

An understanding of the concept of correlation is basic to the study of psychology and essential in the study of psychological testing. Our statistics refresher continues with a review of correlation and regression, preceded by discussion of another essential subject area in psychological testing: norms.

Norms

Each year, thousands of college-bound students, with number 2 pencil firmly in hand, blacken thousands of little grids on college entrance examination answer forms. After months of anticipation, the mail brings a computer-generated statement with the test scores. Typically enclosed with the scores is a booklet or leaflet explaining how the scores should be interpreted. Students are advised to judge their own individual performance in comparison with the performance of some other group of students that took the test—a *normative sample* (also variously referred to as a *norm group,* a *reference group,* or a *standardization sample*).

Like the tests used to aid colleges in making entry decisions, many other carefully researched tests have been administered to people who are typical with respect to some characteristic(s) of the people for whom the particular test was designed. A test administration to this representative sample of testtakers yields a distribution (or distributions) of scores. This distribution of scores, in raw or more typically in converted score form, is referred to as the *norms* for the test: data that will be used to place into context the score of any individual test-taker relative to the scores of the standardization sample.

Norm in the singular is frequently used in practice to refer to some measure of central tendency with respect to the standardization sample. For example, "Sylvester scored 600 on the quantitative portion of the SAT and the norm is 500." Knowing that the standard deviation for this particular test is equal to 100 and armed with a little knowledge about areas under the normal curve, we would know that Sylvester outperformed approximately 84% of the standardization sample on the quantitative portion of the SAT.

The Normative or Standardization Sample

The process of administering a test to a representative sample of testtakers for the purpose of establishing norms is referred to as "standardizing a test." A test is said to be *standardized* when it has clearly specified procedures for administration and scoring—including normative data. But how are norms obtained? In the process of developing a test, a test developer has targeted some defined group as the "population" for which the test is designed for use. This population is the complete universe or set of individuals with at least one common, observable characteristic. The common observable characteristic(s) might range from "high school seniors who aspire to go to college" to "the 16 boys and girls in Mrs. Smith's day care center," to "all housewives with primary responsibility for household shopping who have purchased over-the-counter headache remedies within the last two months." To obtain a distribution of scores, the test developer could have the test administered to every person in the targeted population; and if the total targeted population consists of something like "the 16 boys and girls in Mrs. Smith's day care center," there would be no problem. However, with tests developed for use with large or wide-ranging populations, it is usually impossible, impractical, or simply too expensive to administer the test to everyone, nor is it necessary.

The test developer can obtain a distribution of test responses by administering the test to a *sample* of the population—a portion of the universe of people deemed to be representative of the whole population. The size of the sample could be as small as one person, though as the size of the sample approaches the size of the population, possible sources of error as a result of insufficient sample size diminish.

Subgroups within a defined population may differ with respect to some characteristics, and it is sometimes essential to have these differences proportionately represented in the sample. Thus, for example, if you devised a "Public Opinion Test" and you wanted to sample the opinions of Manhattan residents with this instrument, it would be desirable to include in your sample people representing different subgroups (or "strata") of the population, such as Blacks, Whites, Asians, other non-Whites, males, females, the poor, the middle class, the rich, professional people, business people, office workers, skilled and unskilled laborers, the unemployed, homemakers, Catholics, Jews, members of other religions, and so forth—all in proportion to the occurrence of these strata in the population of people who reside on the island of Manhattan. Such sampling, referred to as *stratified sampling*, would help prevent sampling bias and ultimately aid in the interpretation of the findings. If such sampling were *random* in nature (that is, if every member of the population had the same chance of being included in the sample), then the procedure would be referred to as *stratified-random sampling*.

Two other types of sampling procedures are *purposive sampling* and *incidental sampling*. If we arbitrarily select some sample because we believe it to be representative of the population, the sample we have selected is referred to as "purposive." Manufacturers of products frequently use purposive sampling when they test the appeal of a new product in one city or market and then make assumptions about how that product would sell nationally. For example, the manufacturer might test a product in a market such as Cleveland because, on the basis of experience with this particular product, "how goes Cleveland goes the nation." The danger in using such a purposive sample is that the sample, in this case Cleveland residents, may no longer be representative of the nation or may simply not be representative of national preferences with regard to the particular product being test-marketed.

Another type of sample, and an all-too-frequently used type, is called an *incidental sample*. When the authors think of this type of sample, we think of the old joke about the drunk searching for some money he lost under the lamppost; he may not have lost it there, but he's searching for it there simply because that's where the light is. Like the drunk searching for money under the lamppost, a researcher may sometimes employ a sample that is not necessarily the most appropriate but, rather, the most convenient. Unlike the drunk, the researcher employing this type of sample is not doing it as a result of poor judgment but because of budgetary limitations or other situational constraints. An incidental sample (also referred to as a *convenience sample*) is one that is convenient or available for use. You may have personally been a party to incidental sampling if you have ever been placed in a subject pool for experimentation with introductory psychology students. It's not that the students in such subject pools are necessarily the most appropriate subjects for the experiments—it's just that they are the most available. Generalization of findings made with respect to incidental samples must be made with caution.

Having obtained a sample, the test developer administers the test according to the standard set of instructions that will be used with the test. The test developer also provides a setting for the testtakers that will be the recommended setting in which the test be given. This may be as simple as making sure that the room is quiet and well lit, or as complex as providing a specific set of toys that will be used to test the cognitive skills of an infant. Establishing a standard set of instructions and conditions under which the test is given makes the test scores of the normative sample more comparable with the scores of testtakers who will later be compared with the normative sample. For example, if a test of concentration ability is given to a normative sample in the summer with the windows open and people mowing the grass and arguing about whether the hedges need trimming, the normative sample probably won't concentrate well. If a testtaker then completes the concentration test under quiet, comfortable conditions, that person will probably do much better than the normative group, resulting in a high standard score. That high score would not be very helpful in understanding the testtaker's concentration abilities because it would reflect the differing conditions under which the test had been taken. This example illustrates how important it is that the normative group take the test under a standard set of conditions, which are then repeated as closely as possible each time the test is given.

After the normative sample is tested, the test developer describes the resulting data using descriptive statistics that include measures of central tendency and variability. The statistical findings for the standardization sample, as well as a precise description of the standardization sample itself, are essential. As stated in the *Standards for Educational and Psychological Testing,* "Norms that are presented should refer to clearly described groups. These groups should be the ones with whom users of the test will ordinarily wish to compare the people who are tested" (1985, p. 33). This standard (number 4.3) continues: "Test publishers should also encourage the development of local norms by test users when the published norms are insufficient for particular test users."[1] In a similar vein, the *Code of Fair Testing Practices in Education* (1988, p. 3) encourages test developers to "describe the population(s) represented by any norms or comparison group(s), the dates the data were gathered, and the process used to select the samples of testtakers."

In practice, descriptions of standardization samples vary widely in precision. Not surprisingly, test authors wish to present their tests in the most favorable light possible, and shortcomings in the standardization procedure (or elsewhere in the process of the test's development) may be given short shrift or be totally overlooked in a test's manual. Sometimes the sample may be scrupulously defined, but the generalizability of the norms to a particular group or individual is questionable. For example, a test carefully normed on school-age children who reside within the Los Angeles school district may be relevant only to some lesser degree to school-age children who reside within the Dubuque, Iowa, school district. How many children in the standardization sample were English speaking? How many were of Hispanic origin? How does the elementary school curriculum in Los Angeles differ from the curriculum in Dubuque? These are the types of questions that must be raised before the Los Angeles norms are judged to be generalizable to the children of Dubuque. Test manuals sometimes supply prospective test users with guidelines for establishing local norms—one of many different ways norms can be categorized.

---

1. "Local norms" will be discussed later in this chapter.

Types of Norms

Some of the many different ways we can classify norms are as follows: age norms, grade norms, national norms, national anchor norms, local norms, norms from a fixed reference group, subgroup norms, and percentile norms. We begin with a detailed explanation of the term *percentile* because the norms for many tests are expressed as *percentile norms.* Percentile norms are the raw data from a test's standardization sample converted to percentile form.

Percentiles   In our discussion of the median, we saw that a distribution could be divided into quartiles where the median was the second quartile (Q_2), the point at which 50% of the scores fell at or below and the remaining 50% fell above. Instead of dividing a distribution of scores into quartiles, we might wish to divide the distribution into *deciles,* or 10 equal parts. Alternatively, we could divide a distribution into 100 equal parts—100 *percentiles.* In such a distribution, the xth percentile is equal to the score at or below which x% of scores fall. Thus, the 15th percentile is the score at or below which 15% of the scores in the distribution fall; the 99th percentile is the score at or below which 99% of the scores in the distribution fall. If 99% of a particular standardization sample answered fewer than 47 questions on a test correctly, then we could say that a raw score of 47 corresponds to the 99th percentile on this test. It can be seen that a percentile is a ranking that conveys information about the relative position of a score within a distribution of scores.

A *percentile* is a raw score that has been converted into something else—an expression of the percentage of people whose score falls below a particular raw score. A more familiar description of test performance, the concept of *percentage* correct, must be distinguished from the concept of a percentile. A percentile is a converted score that refers to a percentage of testtakers. "Percentage correct" refers to the distribution of raw scores—specifically, the number of items that were answered correctly multiplied by 100 and divided by the total number of items.

Because percentiles are easily calculated, they are a popular way of organizing test data—be they data from the standardization sample or otherwise. Additionally, percentiles are very adaptable for use with a wide range of tests. A problem with using percentiles with normally distributed scores is that real differences between raw scores may be minimized near the ends of the distribution and exaggerated in the middle of the distribution. This distortion problem may even be worse with highly skewed data. In the normal distribution, the highest frequency of raw scores occurs in the middle. That being the case, the differences between all those scores that cluster in the middle might in reality be quite small, yet even the smallest difference will appear as differences in percentiles. The reverse is true at the extremes of the distributions, where differences between raw scores may be great, though we would have no way of knowing that from the relatively small differences in percentiles.

Age norms   Also referred to as *age-equivalent scores, age norms* indicate the average performance of different samples of testtakers who were at various ages at the time the test was administered. If the measurement under consideration is height in inches, for example, we know that children's "scores" (that is, heights) will gradually increase at various rates as a function of age up to their middle to late teens.

Carefully constructed age norm tables for physical characteristics such as height enjoy widespread acceptance and are virtually noncontroversial. This is not the case, however, with respect to age norm tables for psychological characteristics such as intelligence. Suppose you created the "National Intelligence Test" (NIT) and designed it for use with children between the ages of 5 and 14. And let's say that you obtained NIT norms using large, nationally representative, random samples of 5-year-olds, 6-year-olds—all the way through to 14-year-olds. Your standardization sample data tell you the average 6-year-old obtains a raw score of, say, 30 on your test, and the average 12-year-old obtains a raw score of 60. In the course of examining your data, you note that one 12-year-old, Adolf, scored 30 on your test. You also find that one 6-year-old, Anna, obtained a raw score of 60. Is it legitimate for you to make statements like "Adolf has a mental age of 6 and Anna has a mental age of 12"?

For many years psychologists have made statements like those referring to "mental ages" of testtakers. The child of any chronological age whose performance on a valid test of intellectual ability indicated that he or she had intellectual ability similar to that of the average child of some other age was said to have the "mental age" of the norm group in which his or her test score fell. The reasoning here was that irrespective of chronological age, children with the same "mental age" could be expected to read the same level of material, solve the same kinds of math problems, reason with a similar level of judgment, and so forth. But some have complained that the concept of "mental age" is too broad and that although a 6-year-old might, for example, perform intellectually like a 12-year-old, the 6-year-old might not be very similar at all to the average 12-year-old socially, psychologically, and otherwise. In addition to such intuitive considerations, the "mental age" concept has also been criticized on technical grounds.[2]

Grade norms   Designed to indicate the average test performance of testtakers in a given grade, *grade norms* are developed by administering the test to representative samples of children over a range of consecutive grade levels (such as first through sixth grade). Next, the mean or median score for children at each grade level is computed. Because the school year typically runs from September to June—ten months—fractions in the mean or median are easily expressed as

---

2. For many years, IQ (intelligence quotient) scores on tests such as the Stanford-Binet were calculated by dividing "mental age" (as indicated by the test) by chronological age. The quotient would then be multiplied by 100 to eliminate the fraction. The distribution of IQ scores had a mean set at 100 and a standard deviation of approximately 16. A child of 12 with a "mental age" of 12 had an IQ of 100 ($12/12 \times 100 = 100$). The technical problem here is that IQ standard deviations were not constant with age; at one age, an IQ of 116 might be indicative of performance at 1 standard deviation above the mean, whereas at another age an IQ of 121 might be indicative of performance at 1 standard deviation above the mean.

decimals. Thus, for example, a sixth-grader performing exactly at the average on a grade-normed test administered during the fourth month of the school year (December) would achieve a grade-equivalent score of 6.4. Like age norms, grade norms have widespread application with children of elementary school age, the thought here being that children learn and develop at varying rates but in ways that are in some aspects predictable.

Suppose Raoul is in grade 12 but his score on a grade-normed spelling test is 6. Does this mean that Raoul has the same spelling abilities as the average sixth-grader? The answer is no: accurately interpreted, all this finding means is that Raoul and a hypothetically average sixth-grader answered the same fraction of items correctly on that test. Grade norms do not provide information as to the content or type of items that a student could or could not answer correctly. Perhaps the primary use of grade norms is as a convenient, readily understandable gauge of how one student's performance compares with that of fellow students in the same grade.

Some experts in testing have called for a moratorium on the use of grade-equivalent as well as age-equivalent scores because such scores may so easily be misinterpreted. Cronbach (1970, p. 98) described age and grade norms as "archaic." He argued that "grade conversions should never be used in reporting on a pupil or a class, or in research. Standard scores or percentiles or raw scores serve better. Age conversions are also likely to be misinterpreted." Another—most obvious—drawback to using grade norms is that they are useful only with respect to years and months of schooling completed. They have little or no applicability to children who are not yet in school or who are out of school. Age norms are also limited in this regard, since, for many tests, the value of such norms is limited with an adult population.[3]

National norms   As the name implies, a *national norm* is derived from a standardization sample that was nationally representative of the population. In the fields of psychology and education, for example, national norms may be obtained through the testing of large numbers of students representative of different variables of interest such as socioeconomic strata, geographical location (such as North, East, South, West, Midwest), and different types of communities within the various parts of the country (such as rural, urban, suburban). Norms would typically be obtained for every grade to which the test sought to be applicable, and other factors related to the representativeness of the school itself might be criteria for inclusion in or exclusion from the standardization sample. For example, is the school the student attends publicly funded, privately funded, religiously oriented, military-oriented, or something else? How representative are the pupil-teacher ratios in the schools under consideration? Does the school have a library and, if so, how many books are in it? These are

---

3. But use of age norms in tests standardized with adult populations can be expected to rise in future years. With the "graying of America," there is increased interest in performance on various types of psychological tests as a function of advancing age. Already, we are beginning to see more and more age-specific norms in the adult age range in the area of neuropsychological assessment.

only a sample of the types of questions that could be raised in assembling a standardization sample to be used in the establishment of national norms. The precise nature of the questions asked will depend on whom the test is designed for and what it is designed to do. Since norms from different tests all represented as "national" in nature may have "nationally representative" standardization samples that differ in many important respects, it is always a good idea to check the manual of the tests under consideration to see exactly how comparable the tests are. The greater the differences in standardization sample among such tests, the less the comparability of students' scores.

National anchor norms   Even the most casual survey of catalogues from various test publishers will reveal that, with respect to almost any human characteristic or ability, there exist many different tests purporting to measure the characteristic or ability. There exist dozens of tests, for example, that purport to measure reading. Suppose we select a reading test designed for use in grades 3 to 6, which—for the purposes of this hypothetical example—we call "The Best Reading Test" (BRT). Suppose further that we now want to be able to compare findings obtained on another national reading test designed for use with grades 3 to 6, the "XYZ Reading Test," with the BRT. An equivalency table for scores on the two tests or *national anchor norms* could provide the tool for such a comparison. Just as an anchor provides some stability to a vessel, so "national anchor norms" provide some stability to test scores by "anchoring" them to other test scores.

The method by which such equivalency tables or national anchor norms are established typically begins with the computation of percentile norms for each of the tests to be compared. Using what has been referred to as the *equipercentile method,* the equivalency of scores on different tests is calculated with reference to corresponding percentile scores. Thus, if the 96th percentile corresponds to a score of 69 on the BRT, and if the 96th percentile corresponds to a score of 14 on the XYZ, we can say that a BRT score of 69 is equivalent to an XYZ score of 14. We should note that the national anchor norms for our hypothetical BRT and XYZ tests must have been obtained on the same sample—each member of the sample took both tests and the equivalency tables were then calculated on the basis of these data. Although national anchor norms provide an indication of the equivalency of scores on various tests, it would be a mistake, because of technical considerations, to treat these equivalencies as precise equalities (Angoff, 1964, 1966, 1971).

Subgroup norms   A standardization sample can be segmented by any of the criteria initially used in selecting subjects for the sample, and *subgroup norms* for any of these more narrowly defined groups can be developed. Thus, for example, suppose criteria used in selecting children for inclusion in the "XYZ Reading Test" standardization sample were age, educational level, socioeconomic level, geographic region, community type, and "handedness" (whether the child was right-handed or left-handed). The test manual or a supplement to it might report normative information by each of these subgroups. A community school board member might find the regional norms to be most useful, whereas a psychologist doing exploratory research in the area of brain lateralization and reading scores might find the handedness norms most useful.

Local norms   Typically developed by test users themselves, *local norms* provide normative information with respect to the local population's performance on some test. A local company personnel director might find some nationally standardized test useful in making selection decisions but might deem the norms published in the test manual to be far afield from local job applicants' score distributions. Individual high schools may wish to develop their own school norms (local norms) for student scores on some examination that is administered statewide. A school guidance center may find that locally derived norms for a particular test—say, a survey of personal values—are more useful in counseling students than the national norms printed in the manual.

Fixed Reference Group Scoring Systems

Norms provide a context for interpreting the meaning of a test score. Another type of aid in providing a context for interpretation is what has been called a *fixed reference group scoring system.* Here, the distribution of scores obtained on the test from one group of testtakers—referred to as the "fixed reference group"—is used as the basis for the calculation of test scores for future administrations of the test. Perhaps the test most familiar to college students that exemplifies the use of a fixed reference group scoring system is the SAT. This test was first administered in 1926. Its norms were then based on the mean and standard deviation of the people who took the test at the time. With passing years, more colleges—as well as a variety of different kinds of colleges—became members of the College Board, the sponsoring organization for the test. It soon became evident that SAT scores tended to vary somewhat as a function of the time of year the test was administered. In an effort to ensure perpetual comparability and continuity of scores, the custom of norming the SAT with respect to the group of testtakers who had taken a given administration of the test was abandoned in 1941.

The distribution of scores from the 11,000 people who took the SAT in 1941 was immortalized as a standard to be used in the conversion of raw scores on future administrations of the test. The scores obtained by this "fixed reference group" of 1941 paralleled successive administrations of the test. A new fixed reference group, the more than 2 million testtakers who completed the SAT in 1990, began to be used in 1995. A score of 500 on the SAT corresponds to the mean obtained by the 1990 sample, a score of 400 corresponds to a score that is 1 standard deviation below the 1990 mean, and so forth. As an example, suppose John took the SAT in 1995 and answered 50 items correctly on a particular scale. And let's say Mary took the test in 1996 and, just like John, answered 50 items correctly. Although John and Mary may have achieved the same raw score, they would not necessarily achieve the same scaled score. If, for example, the 1996 version of the test under discussion was judged to be somewhat easier than the 1995 version, scaled scores for the 1996 testtakers would be calibrated downward so that scores achieved in 1996 would be comparable to scores earned in 1995. The statistical procedures used to equate scores from one administration to the next are technically sophisticated; see Donlon (1984) for a readable description of the process.

Test items common to each new version of the SAT and each previous version of it are employed in a procedure (called *anchoring*) that permits the conversion of raw scores on the new version of the test into what are technically referred to as "fixed reference group scores." Like other fixed reference group scores, including Graduate Record Examination scores (see *Everyday Psychometrics*), SAT scores are most typically interpreted with respect to local norms. Thus, for example, admissions offices of colleges typically rely on their own independently collected norms to make selection decisions. Judgments may, in part, be based on SAT scores for those who successfully completed their program as opposed to scores for dropouts. Conceptually, the idea of a "fixed reference group" seems analogous to the idea of a "fixed reference foot"—the foot of the English king that also became immortalized as a measurement standard (Angoff, 1962).

Norm-Referenced Versus Criterion-Referenced Interpretation

As we have seen, one way to derive meaning from test scores is to evaluate the test score in relation to other scores on the same test. This approach to testing is referred to as *norm-referenced*; test scores are understood relative to other test scores on the same test. Terms such as *norm group* and *normative group* may be used to describe the body of scores with which an individual testtaker's performance is being compared.

Unlike norm-referenced approaches to testing, a *criterion-referenced* approach does not describe test performance in terms of the testtaker's relative standing among others; rather, test scores are interpreted with regard to some standard or criterion. Examples of the criterion-referenced approach to measurement abound. A community might legislate as a standard that students must demonstrate at least a sixth-grade reading level as one requirement for the award of a high school diploma. An airline might require that all its pilots meet a certain set level of proficiency on a battery of tests. The professional community may decide that a particular level of performance on a licensing examination is necessary to demonstrate competence to practice as a psychologist.

The criterion in criterion-referenced assessments typically derives from the values or standards of an individual or organization. An airline, for example, may have little interest in how a particular pilot performs on a flight simulator relative to other pilots taking the same test on the same day. Rather, the airline requires assurance that the pilot demonstrates a reasonable level of proficiency—regardless of how well or how poorly all the other pilots performed.

What we are referring to as "criterion-referenced" tests have been variously called "domain-" or "content-referenced" tests because the focus of interest is

Good Ol' Norms and the GRE

Some time before or after you graduate from college, the Graduate Record Exam (GRE) may be on your "to do" list. If you take the traditional paper-and-pencil version of the test, you will receive a report of your test results about six weeks later in the mail. Like more and more testtakers, you might take a computerized version of the test instead. In that case, you would receive your scores immediately. Knowing that the GRE test scores will influence the choices you have in graduate schools and, by extension, your graduate career and your life in general, you are likely to read the test results eagerly but a bit fearfully as well. Assuming you have taken the GRE General Test, you will have three scores, one each for verbal ability, quantitative ability, and analytical ability. How do you understand those scores?

Knowing what you do about norms, and knowing that the GRE has a mean of 500 and a standard deviation of 100, you might feel confident about making certain interpretations about a given set of scores. However, what you also need to know is that the mean of 500 and the standard deviation of 100 apply to scores obtained by people who took the GRE in 1952; their scores were immortalized as a normative or fixed reference group. To know the meaning of a score earned today requires current normative tables supplied by the Educational Testing Service (ETS).

By way of explanation, consider the plight of Dexter, an English literature major. Dexter has just received the following GRE scores: 640 on verbal ability, 700 on quantitative ability, and 520 on analytical ability. Knowing that the GRE has a mean of 500 and a standard deviation of 100, and not taking the time to learn much more about the actual meaning of the scores, Dexter comes to some immediate conclusions about his abilities.

Dexter concludes that quantitative ability is his strong suit. After all, his quantitative score was 2 standard deviations above the mean—a score that exceeded the scores of over 97% of his fellow testtakers.

"Perhaps English literature was the wrong major," he thinks aloud. He then goes on to analyze his analytic ability score. "Average to slightly above average compared with those I will be competing with for entrance to graduate school," Dexter thinks. So far, is Dexter's analysis accurate?

In a word, no. Dexter is wrongly assuming that the GRE among current testtakers has a mean of 500 and a standard deviation of 100. But the GRE uses a fixed reference group scoring system. The reference group for the verbal and quantitative portions of the test comprised people who took the GRE in 1952. On that occasion, the mean score of the people who took the test was set at 500, with a standard deviation at 100. In the 40-plus years since the fixed reference group was tested, there have been significant changes in the population taking the GRE. These changes in the population of testtakers have necessitated changes in the way a contemporary GRE score report is interpreted.

ETS makes available the current norms of the GRE to individual students and institutions. The information is presented in terms of percentiles, with the percentage of examinees scoring below a particular score reported across the distribution of GRE scores. The report of scores sent to testtakers includes such percentile information for the scores earned by that testtaker. Had Dexter taken the time to read this information, he could have more accurately interpreted his scores relative to the half-million college seniors and college graduates who took the test between October 1, 1989, and September 30, 1992. These data are presented in the *GRE 1993–1994 Guide to the Use of the Graduate Record Examinations Program* (1993).

According to Table 1B in the *Guide,* verbal ability scores of 640 are at the 87th percentile, quantitative ability scores of 700 are at the 79th percentile, and analytical ability scores of 520 are at the 35th percentile. With that information, a different picture of Dexter and his abilities emerges.

Relative to the 1989–1992 testtakers, Dexter does best in the verbal ability area, scoring better than 87% of other testtakers. His quantitative ability performance, better than 79% of others, is clearly above the median but not as outstanding as his verbal performance. Dexter's analytical performance is actually below the median, with only 35% of testtakers scoring lower than he did. After reviewing his score report with a staff member in his school's counseling center, Dexter is reassured that English literature was a good choice of major after all.

Learning about the derivation and interpretation of GRE scores, you may wonder about the benefits of perpetuating what may seem to be a needlessly complicated and outdated system. Why retain 40-year-old data as a fixed reference norm group? Why the necessity for changing percentile values corresponding to specific GRE scores? Why hasn't ETS reset the GRE mean at 500 and its standard deviation at 100 for each new year, if not for each administration of the test? Certainly such a resetting would simplify interpretation of individual scores.

According to Rob Durso,[1] a staff member at ETS, frequent renorming of the GRE would make meaningful comparisons between people who sat for the examination at different times extremely difficult, if not impossible. By contrast, the system that is in place guarantees that meaningful comparisons between people and across time can be made. Indeed, the GRE exists for the purpose of assisting institutions in making decisions about matters such as graduate school admission and the award of scholarships. The test's ability to make meaningful comparisons is retained under the current system. A GRE score of 500 on the quantitative (or verbal) test means that the testtaker has performed at the average level of people who took the GRE in 1952. For this or any other specific score,

the score represents a set level of performance regardless of when the test was taken.

When members of the fixed reference group took the test in 1952, the GRE scores were set with a mean of 500 and a standard deviation of 100. Assuming a normal distribution of scores, percentile values for a sampling of specific scores would be as follows:

GRE Score	Percentile Value in 1952
700	98
600	84
500	50
400	16
300	2

As evidenced in Table 1B of the *GRE 1993–1994 Guide,* current patterns of test scores are somewhat different:

GRE Score	Percentile Value in 1952	Percentile value in 1989–1992	
		Verbal	Quantitative
700	98	95	79
600	84	79	56
500	50	51	31
400	16	19	11
300	2	3	2

As compared with 1952, the distribution of scores on the verbal ability test is not vastly different. Although the scores seem to have spread out a bit more in recent years, the median is essentially the same. A slightly larger proportion of people score both at the lower and at the higher ends of the scale. For example, 16% of students scored over 600 in 1952, and 21% of students scored over 600 in 1989–1992.

The distribution of scores on the quantitative ability test is considerably different for the two time periods. In this case, a greater proportion of people

1. Personal communication, July 6, 1994.

(continued)

Good Ol' Norms and the GRE *(continued)*

are getting higher scores than was the case in 1952. In 1952, students scoring over 700 constituted only about 2% of the population of testtakers. In the 1989–1992 sample, such students constituted fully 21% of the group.

According to Durso, a significant factor contributing to the change in the distribution of quantitative scores is that more foreign students now take the GRE than in 1952. Many of these students have better math ability than do U.S. students, causing a rise in the median ability level among all testtakers.

Returning to the issue of renorming the GRE more frequently, can you imagine how things would be different if that were the case? If the level of ability being tested in the population were to change, as it seems to have done for quantitative ability, then the meaning of specific scores would also change. This can be illustrated by the case of two students taking the GRE five years apart. The two students are applying for admission to the same competitive graduate program. During the five-year period separating the testings, an increasing proportion of people with good quantitative ability entered the population and took the GRE. The first student took the GRE with relatively few highly quantitatively skilled people and got a score of 660 on

the quantitative test. The second student took the GRE with many highly quantitatively skilled people and also got a score of 660 on the quantitative test.

Under the current system, in which the test is not renormed annually, we would conclude that two students with similar scores have similar levels of quantitative performance; a direct comparison would be valid. However, if the test were renormed annually, the second student's score described above would actually represent better quantitative skill because that student was compared with more quantitatively skilled people. Clearly, renorming would diminish comparability of scores across different testings.

In this discussion, we have touched on issues related to the GRE verbal and quantitative test scores. As you might suspect, there are additional issues related to norms concerning the analytical ability scores (a relatively recent innovation), and Subject Test scores. A consideration of these more complex norm-related issues awaits you after you have taken the GRE and earned a place in a graduate psychometrics program. Alternatively, you can write to Educational Testing Service, P.O. Box 6000, Princeton, New Jersey, 08541-6000, for more information about the GRE or any of its other tests.

not on individual scores in relation to other people's scores but on scores in relation to a particular content area or domain.[4] Generally speaking, it can be said that criterion-referenced interpretations provide information about what people can do, whereas norm-referenced interpretations provide information about how people have done in relation to other people. Criterion-referenced

---

4. Although acknowledging that "content-referenced" interpretations can be referred to as "criterion-referenced" interpretations, the 1974 edition of *Standards* also noted a technical distinction between interpretations referred to as "criterion-" and "content-referenced": "*Content-referenced* interpretations are those where the score is directly interpreted in terms of performance at each point on the achievement continuum being measured. *Criterion-referenced* interpretations are those where the score is directly interpreted in terms of performance at any given point on the continuum of an *external* variable. An external criterion variable might be grade averages or levels of job performance" (p. 19; footnote in original omitted).

tests are frequently used to gauge achievement or mastery (and are sometimes referred to as *mastery tests* in this context). "Has this flight trainee mastered the material she needs to be an airline pilot?" This is the type of question that an airline personnel office might have to address with a test of mastery (that is, a criterion-referenced test). If a standard, or criterion, for passing on a hypothetical "Airline Pilot Test" (APT) has been set at 85% correct, then trainees who score 84% correct or less will not pass; it matters not whether they scored 84% or 42%. Conversely, trainees who score 85% or better on the test will pass whether or not they scored 85% or 100%; all who score 85% or better are said to have mastered the skills and knowledge necessary to be an airline pilot. Taking this example one step further, another airline might find it useful to set up three categories of findings based on criterion-referenced interpretation of test scores:

85% or better correct = pass

75% to 84% correct = retest after two-month refresher course

74% or less = fail

How should cutoff scores in mastery testing be determined? How many test items and what kinds of test items are needed to demonstrate mastery in a given field? The answers to these and related questions could be the subject of a text in itself; they have been tackled in such diverse ways as empirical analyses (for example, Panell & Laabs, 1979) and applications of decision theory (Glaser & Nitko, 1971) and other prediction techniques (Ferguson & Novick, 1973).

The criterion-referenced approach has enjoyed widespread acceptance in the field of computer-assisted education programs where mastery of segments of materials is assessed before the program user can proceed to the next level of material. This approach is also utilized in educational assessment to determine if students have mastered basic academic skills, including reading and arithmetic. The criterion-referenced approach is the basis for curriculum-based assessment. Critics of the criterion-referenced approach argue that if it is strictly followed, potentially important information about an individual's performance relative to other testtakers is lost. Another criticism is that although this approach may have value with respect to the assessment of mastery of basic knowledge and/or skills, it has little or no meaningful application at the upper end of the knowledge/skill continuum. Although it might be meaningful to use criterion-oriented tests to see if pupils have mastered basic reading, writing, and arithmetic, the value of such tests would be at best questionable in gauging the progress of an advanced doctoral-level student in his or her area of specialization; stand-alone originality and brilliant analytic ability are not the stuff of which criterion-oriented tests are made. By contrast, brilliance and superior abilities are recognizable in tests that employ norm-referenced interpretations; they're the scores you see all the way to the right, near the third standard deviation, or the tenth decile or the one-hundredth percentile.

Before leaving our comparison of norm- and criterion-referenced testing, let's note that all testing is in reality normative—even if the scores are as seemingly criterion-referenced as "pass/fail" in nature. Even in a pass/fail score, there is an inherent acknowledgment that a continuum of abilities exists—it's just that some dichotomizing cutoff point has been applied.

We now proceed to a discussion of another one of those words that—along with "impeach" and "percentile"—would easily make a national list of "Frequently Used but Little Understood Terminology." The word is *correlation*—a word that enjoys widespread confusion with the concept of causation. Let's state at the outset that correlation is *not* synonymous with causation. But what does correlation mean? Read on.

Correlation

Central to psychological testing and assessment is finding out how some things (such as traits, abilities, or interests) are related to other things (such as behavior). A *coefficient of correlation* is the number that provides us with an index of the strength of the relationship between two things. An understanding of the concept of correlation and an ability to compute a coefficient of correlation is therefore central to the study of tests and measurement.

The Concept of Correlation

Simply stated, *correlation* is an expression of the degree and direction of correspondence between two things; a coefficient of correlation (r) expresses a linear relationship between two (and only two) variables. It reflects the degree of concomitant variation between variable X and variable Y. The *coefficient of correlation* is the numerical index that expresses this relationship; it tells us the extent to which X and Y are "co-related."

The meaning of a correlation coefficient is interpreted by its sign (positive or negative—indicative of a positive or a negative correlation) and by its magnitude (the greater its absolute value, the greater the degree of relatedness). A correlation coefficient can range in value from $+1$ to -1. If a correlation coefficient is $+1$ or -1, this means that the relationship between the two variables is perfect—without "error" in the statistical sense. Here, "error" refers to variability or imprecision of measurement and not to a mistake. Perfect correlations in psychological work—or other work for that matter—are difficult to find (just as perfection in almost anything tends to be difficult if not impossible to find). If a correlation is zero, then no relationship exists between the two variables. If two variables simultaneously increase or simultaneously decrease, then those two variables are said to be *positively* (or "directly") correlated. The height and weight of normal, healthy children ranging in age from birth to 10 years tends to be positively or directly correlated; as children get older, their height and their weight generally increase simultaneously. A positive correlation also exists when two variables simultaneously decrease (for example, the less preparation a student does for an examination, the lower the score on the examination). A *negative* (or "inverse") correlation occurs when one variable increases while the other variable decreases. For example, there tends to be an inverse relationship between the number of miles on your car's odometer (mileage indicator) and the number of dollars a used-car dealer is willing to give you on a trade-in allowance; all other things being equal, as the mileage increases, the number of dollars offered as a trade-in decreases.

As we stated in our introduction to this topic, "correlation" is often confused with "causation." It must be emphasized that a correlation coefficient is merely an index of the relationship between two variables, *not* an index of the causal relationship between two variables. If you were told, for example, that from birth to age 5 there is a high positive correlation between hat size and measurable intelligence, would it be appropriate to conclude that hat size causes intelligence? Of course not; this is a time of maturation in *all* areas, including development in cognitive and motor abilities as well as growth in physical size. Thus, although intellectual development parallels physical development in these years and although it is true that a relationship clearly exists between physical and mental growth, it is not necessarily a causal relationship.

Although correlation does not imply causation, there *is* an implication of prediction. Stated another way, if we know that there is a high correlation between X and Y, we should be able to predict—with various degrees of accuracy, depending on other factors—the value of one of these variables if we know the value of the other.

The Pearson r

The *Pearson product-moment correlation*, also referred to as the *Pearson correlation coefficient* and simply as the "Pearson r," is the most widely used of several alternative measures of correlation (see *Close-up*). It can be the statistical tool of choice when the relationship between the variables is linear and when the two variables being correlated are continuous (that is, they can theoretically take any value). Other correlational techniques can be employed with data that are discontinuous and where the relationship is nonlinear. The formula for the Pearson r takes into account the relativity of each test score's position (or, stated more broadly, each measurement's position) with respect to the mean of its distribution of scores (see box on page 134).

A number of formulas can be used to calculate a Pearson r. One formula necessitates converting each raw score to a standard score and then multiplying each pair of standard scores. A mean for the sum of the products is calculated, and that mean is the value of the Pearson r. Even from this simple verbal conceptualization of what a Pearson r is, it can be seen that the sign of the resulting r would be a function of the sign and the magnitude of the standard scores being used; if, for example, negative standard score values for measurements of X always corresponded with negative standard score values for Y scores, the resulting r would be positive (since the product of two negative values is positive). Similarly, if positive standard score values on X always corresponded with positive standard score values on Y, the resulting correlation would also be positive. However, if positive standard score values for X corresponded with negative standard score values for Y and vice versa, an inverse relationship would exist and a negative correlation would result. A zero or near-zero correlation could result when some products are positive and some are negative.

Pearson, Galton, Correlation, and Regression

Why is the correlation coefficient abbreviated as *r*? If Galton is credited with developing correlation, why do they call it a Pearson *r*?

Investigating the role of genetics with respect to physical characteristics, Galton developed several statistical techniques. His interest in being able to describe the rank of each subject in contrast to the rank of every other subject led him to the development of the concept of a median—the point at which 50% of the sample falls above and below. Because physical measurements from generation to generation in humans had not been made, much of Galton's initial experimentation involved work with plants. Galton examined the diameter and weight of mother and daughter sweet pea seeds and through tables and graphs constructed ways of examining their relationship. Karl Pearson later recollected that these tables and graphs were the early precursors to more familiar correlation tables and scatterplots.

In an 1877 paper, "Typical Laws of Heredity," Galton presented his findings with formulas for a phenomenon he labeled "reversion"—and abbreviated by reference to the first initial *r*. The *r* used today to denote "correlation" is a statistical descendant of the *r* Sir Francis Galton used to describe what he called "reversion" (which has subsequently come to be referred to as "regression"). Galton had observed that the mother pea's magnitude of deviation from the population mean differed from the daughter pea's magnitude of deviation from the population mean. Although it was generally true that the larger the mother sweet pea, the larger the daughter, there was also some "reversion" in size toward the average ancestral type.

In 1884 Galton fulfilled a dream by setting up his "Anthropometric Laboratory" at the International Health Exhibition in South Kensington, England. One of the traits Galton was interested in measuring was "stature" (that is, height), specifically the stature of fathers and sons. During the course of the one-year Exhibition, approximately nine thousand people went through the doors of Galton's Laboratory. Even at that

Karl Pearson and His Daughter

time, Galton was aware that the father did not contribute solely to that characteristic in his son; Galton described the contribution of the father to the son's height as a "partial" contribution—other ancestral or genetic factors were operative as well. In a paper read by Galton at a scientific meeting on December 5, 1888, he discussed his findings, and promised that "it will be shown how the closeness of co-relation in any particular case admits of being expressed by a single number" (cited in Magnello & Spies, 1984).

Galton felt that a numerical index of the strength of the reversion or regression phenomenon could be obtained by calculating the slope for the *regression line*—the line of best fit through all the points in the scatterplot. The numerical index of the strength of the reversion or regression is the "coefficient of regression" (symbolized by the letter *r*). But as a result of the work of Galton's contemporary, Karl Pearson, we have now come to view what Galton labeled *r* to be a measure of the slope (*b*) of a regression line. Pearson developed an alternative formula for Galton's *r*, and it is the latter *r* (the Pearson *r*) that has become the most-used measure of correlation.

The formula used to calculate a Pearson r from raw scores is as follows:

$$r = \frac{\Sigma\ (X - \bar{X})\ (Y - \bar{Y})}{\sqrt{[\Sigma\ (X - \bar{X})^2]\ [\Sigma\ (Y - \bar{Y})^2]}}$$

This formula can and has been simplified for "shortcut" purposes. One such shortcut formula is a deviation formula employing "little x," or x in place of $X - \bar{X}$, and "little y," or y in place of $Y - \bar{Y}$:

$$r = \frac{\Sigma\ xy}{\sqrt{(\Sigma\ x^2)\ (\Sigma\ y^2)}}$$

Another formula for calculating a Pearson r is as follows:

$$r = \frac{N\ \Sigma\ XY - (\Sigma\ X)\ (\Sigma\ Y)}{\sqrt{N\ \Sigma\ X^2 - (\Sigma\ X)^2}\ \sqrt{N\ \Sigma\ Y^2 - (\Sigma\ Y)^2}}$$

Although this formula looks more complicated than the previous deviation formula, it is easier to use. N represents the number of paired scores; $\Sigma\ XY$ is the sum of the product of the paired X and Y scores; $\Sigma\ X$ is the sum of the X scores; $\Sigma\ Y$ is the sum of the Y scores; $\Sigma\ X^2$ is the sum of the squared X scores and $\Sigma\ Y^2$ is the sum of the squared Y scores. Similar results are obtained with the use of each formula.

The next logical question concerns what to do with the number obtained for the value of r. The answer is that you ask even more questions, such as "Is this number statistically significant given the size and nature of the sample?" or "Could this result have occurred by chance?" At this point, you will need to consult tables of significance for Pearson r—tables that are probably in the back of your old statistics textbook. In those tables you will find, for example, that a Pearson r of .899 with an $N = 10$ is significant at the .01 level. You will recall from your statistics course that "significant at the .01 level" tells you, with reference to these data, that a correlation such as this could have been expected to occur by chance alone one time or less in a hundred if X and Y are not correlated in the population. You will also recall that significance at either the .01 level or the (somewhat less rigorous) .05 level—meaning that result could have been expected to occur by chance alone five times or less in a hundred—provides a basis to conclude with confidence that a correlation does indeed exist.

The value obtained for the coefficient of correlation can be further interpreted by deriving from it what is called a *coefficient of determination* or r^2. The coefficient of determination is an indication of how much variance is shared by the X and the Y variable. The calculation of r^2 is quite easy; simply square the correlation coefficient, multiply by 100, and express the result equal to the percentage of the variance accounted for. If, for example, you calculated an r to be .9, then r^2 would be equal to .81; the remaining variance, equal to 100 $(1 - r^2)$, or 19%, could presumably be accounted for by chance, error, or otherwise unmeasured or unexplainable factors. In an interesting but somewhat technical article, Ozer (1985) cautioned that the actual estimation of a coefficient of determination must be made with scrupulous regard to the assumptions operative

Why *r* Is Referred to as "Product-Moment Correlation"

A *moment* is a relatively brief, indefinite, time interval—according to one usage of that word. In psychometric parlance, the word *moment* is used to describe a deviation about a mean of a distribution.

Now consider the word *deviate*. Individual deviations about the mean of a distribution are referred to as *deviates*. In psychometric parlance, deviates are referred to as the "first moments" of the distribution. The "second moments" of the distribution are the moments squared. The "third moments" of the distribution are the moments cubed, and so forth.

The computation of the Pearson *r* in one of its many formulas entails multiplying corresponding standard scores on two measures. One way of conceptualizing standard scores is as "the first moments of a distribution"—this because standard scores are deviates about a mean of zero. A formula that entails the multiplication of two corresponding standard scores can therefore be conceptualized as one that entails the computation of the *product* of corresponding *moments*. Because *r* is the average product of the first moments of two distributions, it may well have been referred to in terms such as "product-of-moments correlation," "average-product-of-first-moments correlation," or "average-product-of-corresponding-moments correlation." The simpler *product-moment correlation* is the term commonly used to refer to *r*.

YOU STANDARD SCORES ARE A BUNCH OF DEVIATES ABOUT A MEAN OF ZERO!

in the particular case; evaluating a coefficient of determination solely in terms of variance accounted for may lead to interpretations that underestimate the magnitude of a relation.

The Spearman rho

The Pearson *r* enjoys such widespread use and acceptance as an index of correlation that if, for some reason, it is not used to compute a correlation coeffi-

Charles Spearman (1863–1945)

Charles Spearman developed the Spearman *rho* statistic and the "Spearman-Brown prophecy formula," and earned the distinction of being the "father of factor analysis." You might conclude that, with all of these accomplishments in the field of statistics, numbers were his first love—a reasonable but incorrect conclusion. Spearman loved most of the philosophical aspects of psychology, and his chief research work was in the area of intelligence.

Spearman received his doctorate at Leipzig and went on to obtain an instructorship—there called a "readership"—in experimental psychology at the University of London. He worked at that institution until his retirement, when he was succeeded as Grote Professor of Philosophy by Professor of Psychology Cyril Burt (a now controversial figure in the history of psychology since the veracity of his data was called into question). Spearman was fairly moderate when it came to statistical as opposed to more intuitive approaches to the subject matter of psychology. He summed up the psychology of his day in the following way: "At one extreme, statistical zealots have accumu-

lated masses of figures that remain psychologically senseless. At the other extreme, no less ardent typologists have been evolving an abundance of psychological ideas with little or no genuine evidence as to their truth" (Spearman, 1930–1936, Vol. 2).

cient, mention is made of the statistic that was used. One commonly used alternative statistic is variously called a "rank-order correlation coefficient," a "rank-difference correlation coefficient," or, simply, Spearman's rho. Developed by Charles Spearman, a British psychologist (see the box above), this coefficient of correlation is frequently used when the sample size is small (fewer than 30 pairs of measurements) and especially when both sets of measurements are in ordinal (or rank-order) form. Special tables are used to determine if an obtained rho coefficient is or is not significant.[5]

---

5. Another ranking method of correlation is embodied in a correlation coefficient with another Greek letter name: the *tau* (τ). It is also referred to as "Kendall's tau" and use of this coefficient rests on no special assumptions. Interested readers are invited to consult Kendall (1948) for a detailed discussion of its development and applications.

Graphic Representations of Correlation

One type of graphic description of correlation is called a *scatterplot* or *scatter diagram*. A scatterplot is a simple graphing of the coordinate points for values of the X variable (placed along the graph's horizontal axis) and the Y variable (placed along the graph's vertical axis). Scatterplots are useful because they provide a quick indication of the direction and magnitude of the relationship, if any, between the two variables. Figures 4–1 and 4–2 offer a quick course in "eyeballing" the nature and degree of correlation by means of scatterplots. In distinguishing positive from negative correlations, note the direction of the curve. And in estimating the strength of magnitude of the correlation, note the degree to which the points form a straight line.

Scatterplots are useful in revealing the presence of curvilinearity in a relationship. Remember that a Pearson r should be used only if the relationship between the variables is linear; if the graph does not appear to take the form of a straight line, the chances are good that the relationship is not linear (see Figure 4–3). When the relationship is nonlinear, other statistical tools and techniques may be employed.[6]

A graph also makes the spotting of outliers relatively easy. An *outlier* is an extremely atypical point located at a relatively long distance—an "outlying" distance—from the rest of the coordinate points in a scatterplot (Figure 4–4). Outliers stimulate interpreters of test data to speculate about the reason for the atypical score. For example, the professor interpreting midterm examination data correlated with study time might wonder about Curly's performance on the test; Curly studied for ten hours and achieved a score of only 57. Was this "outlier" due to some situational emotional strain? Poor learning skills or study habits? Or was it simply reflective of using a very small sample? If the sample size were larger, perhaps more low-scorers who put in large amounts of study time would have been identified. Sometimes an outlier can provide a hint regarding some deficiency in the testing or scoring procedures.

Before leaving the subject of graphic representations of correlation, we should point out that the interpreter of such data needs to know, among other things, if the range of scores has been restricted in any way. To understand why this is the case, look at Figure 4–5. Let's say that graph A describes the relationship between Public University entrance test scores for 600 applicants (all of whom were later admitted) and their grade-point averages at the end of the first semester. The scatterplot indicates that the relationship between entrance test scores and grade-point average is both linear and positive. But what if the admissions officer had accepted only the applications of the students who scored within the top half or so on the entrance exam? To a trained eye, this scatter-

---

6. The specific statistic to be employed will depend at least in part on the suspected reason for the nonlinearity. For example, if it is believed that the nonlinearity is due to one distribution being highly skewed because of a poor measuring instrument, the skewed distribution may be statistically normalized and the result may be a correction of the curvilinearity. If even after graphing the data a question remains concerning the linearity of the correlation, a statistic called *eta squared* (η^2) can be used to compute the exact degree of curvilinearity.

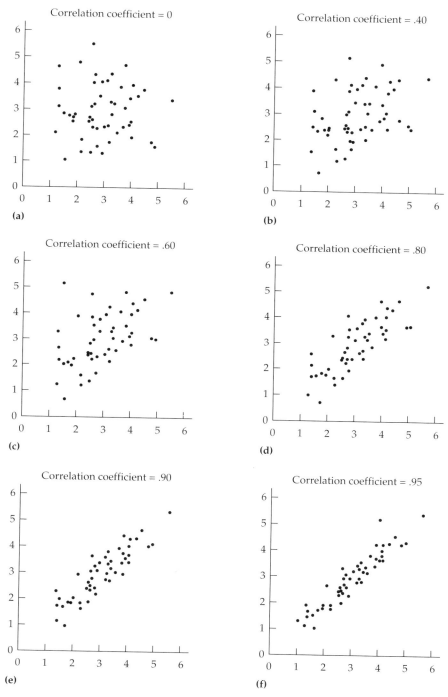

Figure 4–1
Scatterplots and Correlations for Positive Values of _r_

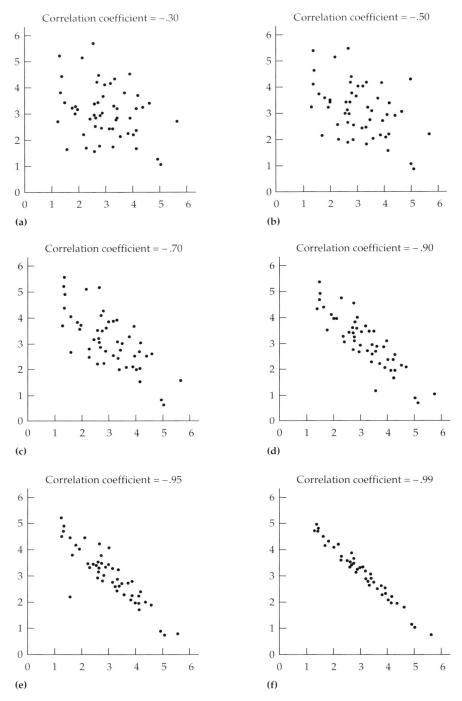

Figure 4–2
Scatterplots and Correlations for Negative Values of _r_

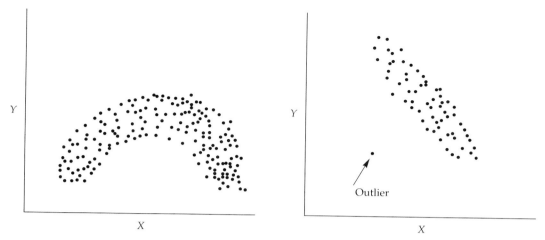

Figure 4–3
A Scatterplot Showing a Nonlinear Correlation

Figure 4–4
Scatterplot Showing an Outlier

plot (graph B) appears to indicate a weaker correlation than that indicated in graph A—an effect attributable exclusively to the restriction of range. Graph B is less of a straight line than graph A, and its direction is not as obvious.

Regression

In everyday language, the word *regression* is synonymous with "reversion to some previous state." In the language of statistics, *regression* also describes a kind of reversion—a reversion to the mean.

Defined broadly, *regression* is the analysis of relationships among variables. *Simple regression* involves one independent variable (X) and one dependent variable (Y). Simple regression analysis results in an equation for a regression line. The *regression line* is the "line of best fit," the straight line that, in one sense, comes closest to the greatest number of points on the scatterplot of X and Y.

Does the following equation look familiar?

$$Y = a + bX$$

In high school algebra, you were probably taught that this is the equation for a straight line. It's also the equation for a regression line. In the formula, a and b are *regression coefficients*; b is equal to the slope of the line, and a is the *intercept*, a constant indicating where the line crosses the Y-axis. The regression line represented by specific values of a and b is fitted precisely to the points on the scatterplot, such that the sum of the squared vertical distances from the points to the line will be smaller than for any other line that could be drawn through

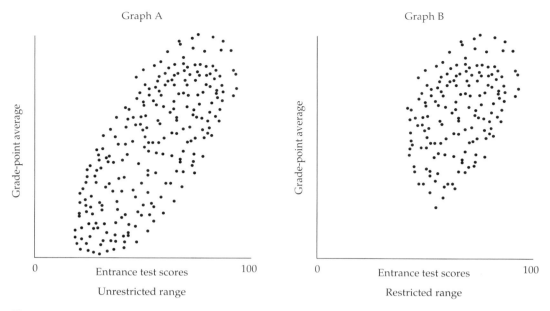

Figure 4–5
Two Scatterplots Illustrating Unrestricted and Restricted Ranges

the same scatterplot. Although finding the equation for the regression line might seem difficult, the values of *a* and *b* can be determined through simple algebraic calculations.

The primary use of a regression equation in testing is to predict one score or variable from another. For example, suppose a dean at the "De Sade School of Dentistry" wishes to predict what grade-point average (GPA) an applicant might have after the first year at De Sade. The dean would accumulate data about current students' scores on the dental college entrance examination and end-of-the-first-year GPA. These data would then be used to help predict the GPA (*Y*) from the score on the dental college admissions test (*X*). Individual dental students are represented by points in the scatterplot in Figure 4–6. The equation for the regression line is computed from these data. This means that the values of *a* and *b* are calculated. In this hypothetical case:

$$GPA = 0.82 + 0.03 \text{ (entrance exam)}$$

This line has been drawn onto the scatterplot in Figure 4–6.

Using the regression line, the likely value of *Y* (the GPA) can be predicted based on specific values of *X* (the entrance exam), by plugging the *X*-value into the equation. A student with an entrance exam score of 50 would be expected to have a GPA of 2.3. A student with an entrance exam score of 85 would be expected to earn a GPA of 3.7. This prediction could also be done graphically by tracing a particular value on the *X*-axis (the entrance exam score) up to the regression line, then straight across to the *Y*-axis, reading off the predicted GPA.

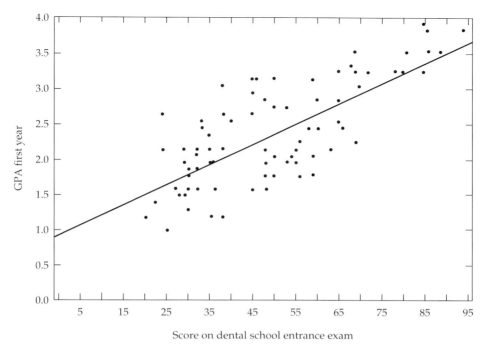

Figure 4–6
Graphic Representation of Regression Line

The correlation between X *and* Y *is 0.76. The equation for this regression line is* Y = 0.82 + *0.03(X); for each unit increase on* X *(the dental school entrance examination score), the predicted value of* Y *(the first-year grade-point average), is expected to increase by .03 unit. The standard error of the estimate for this prediction is 0.49.*

Of course, all students who get an entrance exam score of 50 do not earn the same GPA. This can be seen in Figure 4–6 by tracing from any specific entrance exam score on the X-axis up to the cloud of points surrounding the regression line. This is what is meant by error in prediction: each of these students would be predicted to get the same GPA based on the entrance exam, but in fact they earned different GPAs. This error in the prediction of Y from X is represented by the *standard error of the estimate*. As you might expect, the higher the correlation between X and Y, the greater the accuracy of the prediction, and the smaller the standard error of the estimate.

Multiple Regression

Suppose that the dean suspects that the prediction of GPA will be enhanced if another test score—say, a score on a test of fine motor skills—is also used as a predictor. The use of more than one score to predict Y requires the use of a *multiple regression* equation.

The multiple regression equation takes into account the correlations among all the variables involved. The correlation between each of the predictor scores and what is being predicted (in this case, the correlation of the entrance exam and the fine motor skills test with the GPA in the first year of dental school) is reflected in the weight given to each predictor. Predictors that correlate highly with the predicted variable are generally given more weight, meaning that their regression coefficients (referred to as b-values) are larger. This is logical, since one would want to pay the most attention to predictors that predict Y best.

The multiple regression equation also takes into account the correlations among the predictor scores. In this case, it takes into account the correlation between the dental college admissions test scores and scores on the fine motor skills test. If many predictors are used, and one is not correlated with any of the other predictors but is correlated with the predicted score, then that predictor may be given relatively more weight because it is providing unique information. In contrast, if two predictor scores are highly correlated with each other, they could be providing redundant information. If both were kept in the regression equation, each might get less weight, so that they would "share" the prediction of Y.

More predictors are not necessarily better. If two predictors are providing the same information, the person using the regression equation may decide to use only one of them for the sake of efficiency. If the De Sade dean observed that dental school admission test scores and scores on the test of the fine motor skills were highly correlated with each other and that each of these scores correlated about the same with GPA, the dean might decide to use only one predictor because nothing was gained by the addition of the second predictor.

Meta-analysis

No single research study can precisely determine the correlation between two variables or the exact coefficients for a regression equation.[7] For example, in a study of height and weight, we would not expect the correlation to be exactly the same each time the study is repeated. The relationship between height and weight will probably be at least slightly different for each group of people studied. To most accurately estimate the correlation between height and weight, we might want to include data from all available studies. However, using information from several studies creates a problem, because the correlation (or the mean, or the regression coefficients) will differ from study to study. How is this diverse information understood? One option is to present the range of statistical values that appear in various studies: "The correlation between variable X and variable Y ranges from .73 to .91." Another option is to combine statistically the

---

7. This is true unless all members of the population of interest are included in the study, something that almost never occurs.

information across the various studies. This statistical combination of information across studies is called *meta-analysis*. Meta-analysis produces a single estimate of the statistic being studied: for example, "Meta-analysis estimates the correlation between variable X and variable Y at .81." Meta-analysis gives more weight to studies that have larger numbers of subjects, information that is not readily available when ranges are used to describe the data. This weighting process results in more accurate estimates (Hunter & Schmidt, 1990).

In the remainder of Part 2, we build on your knowledge of correlation and regression as we see how these statistical techniques are integrally involved in the computation of coefficients of reliability and validity as well as methods of test development and item analysis. Data from studies using meta-analysis will be presented in the context of our discussion of the reliability and validity of various tests.

Reliability

In everyday conversation, *reliability* is a synonym for dependability or consistency—as in "the reliable train that you can set your watch by" or "the reliable friend who is always there if you are in need." In the language of psychometrics, reliability refers, broadly speaking, to the attribute of consistency in measurement. And whereas in everyday conversation "reliability" always connotes something that is positively valued, "reliability" in the psychometric sense merely connotes something that is consistent—not necessarily consistently good or bad, but simply consistent.

It is important for us as users of tests and consumers of information about tests to know how reliable tests and other measurement procedures are. But reliability is seldom an all-or-none matter; there are different types and degrees of reliability. A *reliability coefficient* is an index of reliability. More technically, it is a proportion that indicates the ratio between the "true" score variance on a test and the total variance. In this chapter, we explore different kinds of reliability coefficients, including those for measuring test-retest reliability, alternate-forms reliability, split-half reliability, and inter-scorer reliability.

The Concept of Reliability

Why might test scores vary? We know from our discussion of the true score model in Chapter 3 that an ability test score may vary because of (1) the true ability of the testtaker or (2) other factors ranging from unwanted influences on the test situation (such as noise from a construction site outside) to chance.[1] If

---

1. For illustration purposes, ability as a trait being measured is frequently used. However, unless stated otherwise, the principles to which we refer with respect to ability tests also hold true with respect to other types of tests, such as tests for personality. Thus, according to the true score

we use X to represent an observed score, E to represent an error score (a score resulting from random, irrelevant influences on the test—anything except what the test is measuring), and T to represent a true score (part of the observed score not affected by error), then the observed score equals the true score plus the error score, or

$$X = T + E$$

A statistic useful in describing sources of test score variability is the variance (σ^2)—the standard deviation squared. This statistic is useful because it can be broken into components. Variance from true differences is called *true variance,* and variance from irrelevant, random sources is called *error variance.* If σ^2 represents the total variance, σ^2_{tr} represents the true variance, and σ^2_e represents error variance, then the relationship of the variances can be expressed as

$$\sigma^2 = \sigma^2_{tr} + \sigma^2_e$$

In this equation, the total variance in an observed distribution of test scores (σ^2) equals the sum of the true variance (σ^2_{tr}) plus the error variance (σ^2_e). The term *reliability* refers to the proportion of the total variance attributed to true variance. The greater the proportion of the total variance attributed to true variance, the more reliable the test. Since true differences are assumed to be stable, they are presumed to yield consistent scores on repeated administrations of the same test as well as on equivalent forms of tests. Because error variance may increase or decrease a test score by varying amounts, consistency of the test score—and thus the reliability—would be affected. Note that a systematic source of error would *not* affect score consistency. If a measuring instrument, such as a weight scale, consistently underweighed everyone who stepped on it by five pounds, then the relative standings of the people would remain unchanged (even though the weights themselves would consistently vary from the true weight by five pounds). A scale underweighing all comers by five pounds is analogous to a constant being subtracted from (or added to) every test score. It is a systematic error source that does not change the variability of the distribution or affect reliability.

Sources of Error Variance

As we have intimated, error variance is everything in addition to true variance that makes up a test score. Error variance can come "from anywhere," but in the following discussion we limit our focus to sources of error variance during the development of a test and selection of items, test administration, and test scoring and interpretation.

Test construction   One source of variance during test construction is called *item sampling* or *content sampling,* a term that refers to variation among items within

---

model, it is also true that the magnitude of the presence of a certain psychological trait (such as extraversion) as measured by testing with a test of extraversion will be due to (1) the "true" amount of extraversion and (2) other factors.

a test, as well as to variation among items between tests. Consider two or more tests designed to measure a specific skill, personality attribute, or body of knowledge. Differences in the way the items are worded and differences in the exact content sampled are sure to be found. Each of us has probably walked into an achievement test setting, thinking "I hope they ask this question" or "I hope they don't ask that question." With luck, only the questions we wanted to be asked appeared on the examination. In such situations, some testtakers achieve higher scores on one test than they would on another test purporting to measure the same thing, simply because of the specific content sampled on the first test, the way the items were worded, and so on. The extent to which a testtaker's score is affected solely by the content sampled on the test as well as the way the content is sampled (that is, the way in which the item is constructed) is a source of error variance.

Test administration Sources of error variance that occur during test administration may influence the testtaker's attention or motivation; thus, the testtaker's reactions to those influences are the source of one kind of error variance. Examples of untoward influences operative during administration of a test include factors related to the test environment: the room temperature, the level of lighting, and the amount of ventilation and noise, for instance. A relentless fly may develop a tenacious attraction to an examinee's face. A wad of gum on the seat of the chair makes itself known only after the testtaker sits down on it; the list goes on. Other environment-related variables include the instrument used to enter responses (such as a pencil with a broken point or a pen that has dried up) and the writing surface (which may be riddled with hearts carved into it—the legacy of past years' students who felt compelled to express their lifelong devotion to someone whom they by now have probably long forgotten).

Other potential sources of error variance during test administration include testtaker variables such as degree of physical discomfort, amount of sleep the night before, the degree of test anxiety present, the extent of pressing emotional problems, or the effects of drugs. A testtaker may, for whatever reason, make a mistake in entering a test response. For example, the examinee may blacken a "b" grid when he or she had meant to blacken the "d" grid. An examinee might look at a test question such as "Which is not a factor that prevents measurements from being exactly replicable?" and mistakenly read, "Which is a factor that prevents measurements from being exactly replicable?" One carelessly skipped question on a long list of multiple-choice grid-type questions could result in subsequent test responses being "out of sync"; thus, for example, the testtaker might respond to the eighteenth item but blacken the grid for the seventeenth item—this because the twelfth item was inadvertently skipped. Formal learning experiences, casual life experiences, therapy, illness, and other such events that may have occurred in the period between administrations of parallel forms of a test will also be sources of examinee-related error variance.

Examiner-related variables that are potential sources of error variance include the presence or absence of an examiner, the examiner's physical appearance and demeanor, and the professionalism the examiner brings to the test situation. Some examiners in some testing situations may knowingly or unwittingly depart from the procedure prescribed for a particular test. On an oral examination, some examiners might unwittingly provide clues by posing questions that emphasize various words, or they may unwittingly convey information about the correctness of a response through head-nodding, eye movements, or other nonverbal gestures.

Test scoring and interpretation   The advent of computer scoring and the growing reliance on objective, computer-scorable items have virtually eliminated error variance caused by scorer differences in many tests. However, not all tests can be scored from grids blackened by number 2 pencils. Individually administered intelligence tests, some tests of personality, tests of creativity, various behavioral measures, and countless other tests still require hand scoring by trained personnel. Manuals for individual intelligence tests tend to be very explicit about scoring criteria lest examinees' IQs vary as a function of who is doing the testing and scoring. In some tests of personality, examinees are asked to supply open-ended responses to stimuli such as pictures, words, sentences, and inkblots, and it is the examiner who must then "score" (or perhaps more appropriately, "assess") the responses. In one test of creativity, examinees might be given the task of creating as many things as they can out of a set of blocks. For a behavioral measure of social skills in an inpatient psychiatric service, the scorers or raters might be asked to rate patients with respect to the variable of "social-relatedness." Such a behavioral measure might require the rater to check "Yes" or "No" to items like "Patient says 'Good morning' to at least two staff members."

You can appreciate that as soon as a psychological measure uses anything but objective-type items amenable to reliable computer scoring, the scorer or the scoring system becomes a source of error variance. If subjectivity is involved in scoring, the scorer (or rater) can be a source of error variance. Indeed, despite very rigorous scoring criteria set forth in many of the better-known tests of intelligence, examiner/scorers will occasionally still be confronted by situations where an examinee's response lies in a "gray area." The element of subjectivity in scoring may be present to a much greater degree in the administration of certain non-objective-type personality tests and certain academic tests (such as essay examinations) and even in behavioral observation. Consider the case of two observers given the task of rating one psychiatric inpatient on the variable of social-relatedness. On an item that asks simply whether two staff members were greeted in the morning, one rater might judge the patient's eye contact and mumbling of something to two staff members to qualify as a "Yes" response, whereas another observer might feel strongly that a "No" response to the item is appropriate. Such problems in scoring agreement can be addressed through rigorous training designed to make the consistency—or reliability—of various scorers as near perfect as can be.

Given the numerous and varied sources of error inherent in a testing situation, there is good news and bad news. The bad news is that even with the greatest minds and the highest-speed computers, we will never be able to know what the "true" value of a given reliability coefficient is.[2] The good news is that we have ways of estimating the value of reliability coefficients.

Types of Reliability Estimates

Test-Retest Reliability Estimates

A ruler made from the highest-quality steel can be a very reliable instrument of measurement; every time you measure something that is exactly 12 inches in length, for example, your ruler will tell you that what you are measuring is exactly 12 inches in length. The reliability of this instrument of measurement may also be said to be stable over time; whether you measure the 12 inches today, tomorrow, or next year, the ruler is still going to measure 12 inches as 12 inches. By contrast, a ruler constructed of putty might be a very unreliable instrument of measurement. One minute it could measure some known 12-inch standard as 12 inches, the next minute it could measure it as 14 inches, and a week later it could measure it as 18 inches. One way of estimating the reliability of a measuring instrument is by using the same instrument to measure the same thing at two points in time. In psychometric parlance, this approach to reliability evaluation is called the "test-retest method," and the result of such an evaluation is an estimate of "test-retest reliability."

Test-retest reliability is an estimate of reliability obtained by correlating pairs of scores from the same people on two different administrations of the same test. The test-retest measure is appropriate when evaluating the reliability of a test that purports to measure something that is relatively stable over time, such as a personality trait. If the characteristic being measured is assumed to fluctuate over time, there would be little sense in assessing the reliability of the test using the test-retest method; insignificant correlations between scores obtained on the two administrations of the test would be found. Such insignificant correlations would be due to real changes in whatever is being measured rather than to factors inherent in the measuring instrument.

As time passes, people change; they may, for example, learn new things, forget some things, and acquire new skills. It is generally the case—though there are exceptions—that as the time interval between administrations of the same test increases, the correlation between the scores obtained on each testing decreases. The passage of time can be a source of error variance. The longer the time that passes, the more likely the reliability coefficient will be lower. When the interval between testing is greater than six months, the estimate of test-retest reliability is often referred to as the *coefficient of stability*. An estimate of test-retest reliability from a math test might be low if the testtakers took a math tutorial before the second test was administered. An estimate of test-retest reli-

---

2. In this context, Stanley's (1971) classic caution that a *true score* is "not the ultimate fact in the book of the recording angel" (p. 361) seems relevant.

ability from a personality profile might be low if the testtaker either suffered some emotional trauma or received counseling during the intervening period. A low estimate of test-retest reliability may be found even when the interval between testings is relatively brief—this if the tests happen to be conducted during a time of great developmental change with respect to the variables the test was designed to assess. An evaluation of a test-retest reliability coefficient must therefore extend beyond the significance of the obtained coefficient; it must extend to a consideration of possible intervening factors between test administrations if proper conclusions about the reliability of the measuring instrument are to be made.

An estimate of test-retest reliability may be most appropriate in gauging the reliability of tests that employ as outcome measures reaction time or perceptual judgments (such as discriminations of brightness, loudness, or taste). However, even in measuring variables such as these and even when the time period between the two administrations of the test is relatively small, note that various factors (such as experience, practice, memory, fatigue, and motivation) may be operative and render confounded an obtained measure of reliability.[3]

Parallel-Forms and Alternate-Forms Reliability Estimates

If you have ever taken a makeup examination in which the questions on the makeup were not all the same as on the test initially given, you have had experience with different forms of a test. And if you have ever wondered whether the two forms of the test were really equivalent, you have wondered about the *alternate-forms* reliability of the test. The degree of the relationship between various forms of a test can be evaluated by means of an *alternate-forms* or *parallel-forms* coefficient of reliability, which is often referred to as the *coefficient of equivalence.*

"Alternate" forms and "parallel" forms are terms sometimes used interchangeably, though there is a technical difference between them. *Parallel forms* of a test exist when for each form of the test, the means and the variances of observed test scores are equal. In theory, the means of scores obtained on parallel forms correlate equally with the "true score." More practically, scores obtained on parallel tests correlate equally with other measures. *Alternate forms* are simply different versions of a test that have been constructed so as to be parallel. Although they do not meet the requirements for the legitimate designation of "parallel," alternate forms of a test are typically designed to be equivalent with respect to variables such as content and level of difficulty.

Estimates of alternate- and parallel-forms reliability are similar to an estimate of test-retest reliability in two ways: (1) two test administrations with the same group are required, and (2) test scores may be affected by factors such as

---

3. Although we may make reference to a number as the summary statement of the reliability of individual tools of measurement, any such index of reliability can meaningfully be interpreted only in the context of the process of measurement—the unique circumstances surrounding the use of the ruler, the test, or some other measuring instrument in a particular application or situation.

motivation, fatigue, or intervening events such as practice, learning, or therapy. However, an additional source of error variance—item sampling—is inherent in the computation of an alternate- or parallel-forms reliability coefficient; test-takers may do better or worse on a specific form of the test, not as a function of their "true" ability, but simply because of the particular items that were selected for inclusion in the test.[4] Another potential disadvantage of an alternate test form is financial in nature; it is typically time-consuming and expensive to develop alternate or parallel test forms—just think of all that might be involved in getting the same people to sit for repeated administrations of an experimental test! A primary advantage of using an alternate or parallel form of a test is that the effect of memory for the content of a previously administered form of the test is minimized.

Certain traits are presumed to be relatively stable in people over time, and we would expect tests measuring those traits—alternate forms, parallel forms, or otherwise—to reflect that stability. As an example, we expect that there will be—and in fact there is—a reasonable degree of stability in scores on intelligence tests. Conversely, we might expect there to be relatively little stability in scores obtained on a measure of state anxiety (anxiety felt at the moment); the level of anxiety experienced by the testtaker could be expected to vary from hour to hour—let alone day to day, week to week, or month to month.

An estimate of the reliability of a test can be obtained without developing an alternate form of the test and without having to administer the test twice to the same people. Such an assessment entails the scrutiny of the individual items that make up the test and their relation to each other. Because this type of reliability estimate is obtained not through comparison with data from an alternate form and not through a test-retest procedure but, rather, through an examination of the items of the test, it is referred to as an "internal-consistency" estimate of reliability or as an estimate of "inter-item consistency." Our focus now shifts to such types of reliability estimates, beginning with the "split-half" estimate.

Split-Half Reliability Estimates

An estimate of *split-half reliability* is obtained by correlating two pairs of scores obtained from equivalent halves of a single test administered once. It is a useful measure of reliability when it is impractical or undesirable to assess reliability with two tests or to have two test administrations (because of factors such as time or expense). The computation of a coefficient of split-half reliability generally entails three steps, each listed below and then explained further.

Step 1. Divide the test into equivalent halves.

Step 2. Compute a Pearson r between scores on the two halves of the test.

Step 3. Adjust the half-test reliability using the Spearman-Brown formula.

---

4. According to the classical true score model, the effect of such factors on test scores is indeed presumed to be measurement error. There are alternative models in which the effect of such factors on fluctuating test scores would not be considered error (Atkinson, 1981).

You may have heard the saying that "there's more than one way to skin a cat." A corollary to that bit of wisdom could be that "there are some ways you should never skin a cat." An analogous bit of wisdom when it comes to calculating split-half reliability coefficients is: "there's more than one way to split a test," or "there are some ways you should never split a test." Simply dividing the test in the middle is not recommended, since this procedure would probably spuriously raise or lower the reliability coefficient (because of factors such as differential fatigue for the first as opposed to the second part of the test, differential amounts of test anxiety operative, and differences in item difficulty as a function of placement in the test). One acceptable way to split a test is to randomly assign items to one or the other half of the test. A second acceptable way is to assign odd-numbered items to one half of the test and even-numbered items to the other half (yielding an estimate that is also referred to as "odd-even reliability").[5] A third way is to divide the test by content so that each half of the test contains items equivalent with respect to content and difficulty. In general, a primary objective in splitting a test in half for the purpose of obtaining a split-half reliability estimate is to create what might be termed "mini-parallel-forms," with each half equal to the other—or as nearly equal as humanly possible—in format, stylistic, statistical, and related aspects.

Step 2 in the procedure entails the computation of a Pearson r, which requires little explanation at this point. However, the third step requires the use of the Spearman-Brown formula.

The Spearman-Brown formula   Use of the Spearman-Brown formula to estimate internal consistency reliability from a correlation of two halves of a test is a specific application of a more general formula that allows a test developer or user to estimate the reliability of a test that is lengthened or shortened by any number of items. Because the reliability of a test is affected by its length, a formula is necessary for estimating the reliability of a test that has been shortened or lengthened. The general Spearman-Brown (r_{SB}) formula is

$$r_{SB} = \frac{nr_{xy}}{1 + (n - 1)r_{xy}}$$

where r_{SB} is equal to the reliability adjusted by the Spearman-Brown formula, r_{xy} is equal to the Pearson r in the original-length test, and n is equal to the number of items in the revised version divided by the number of items in the original version.

By determining the reliability of one-half of a test, a test developer can then use the Spearman-Brown formula to estimate the reliability of a whole test. Because a whole test is two times longer than half the test, n becomes 2 in the

---

5. One precaution here: with respect to a group of items on an achievement test that deals with a single problem, it is usually desirable to assign the whole group of items to one half of the test. Otherwise—if part of the group were in one half and another part in the other half—the similarity of the half scores would be spuriously inflated; a single error in understanding, for example, might affect items in both halves of the test.

Spearman-Brown formula for the adjustment of split-half reliability. The symbol r_{hh} stands for the Pearson r of scores in the two half tests:

$$r_{SB} = \frac{2r_{hh}}{1 + r_{hh}}$$

It is generally—though not always—true that reliability increases as test length increases, providing that the additional items are equivalent with respect to the content and the range of difficulty of the original items. Estimates of reliability based on consideration of the entire test will therefore tend to be higher than those based on half of a test. Table 5–1 shows half-test correlations presented alongside adjusted reliability estimates for the whole test. You can see that all the adjusted correlations are higher than the unadjusted correlations—this because Spearman-Brown estimates are based on a test that is twice as long as the original half-test. For the data from the kindergarten pupils, for example, a half-test reliability of .718 can be estimated to be equivalent to a whole-test reliability of .836.

If test developers or users wish to shorten a test, the Spearman-Brown formula may be used to estimate the effect of the shortening on the test's reliability. Reduction in test size for the purpose of reducing test administration time is a common practice in situations where the test administrator may have only limited time with the testtaker or in situations where boredom or fatigue could produce responses of questionable meaningfulness.

A Spearman-Brown formula could also be used to determine the number of items needed to attain a desired level of reliability. In adding items to increase test reliability to a desired level, the rule is that the new items must be equivalent in content and difficulty so that the longer test still measures what the original test measured. If the reliability of the original test is relatively low, it may be impractical to increase the number of items to reach an acceptable level of reliability. Another alternative would be to abandon this relatively unreliable instrument and locate—or develop—a suitable alternative. The reliability of the instrument could also be raised in some way—for example, by creating new items, clarifying the test's instructions, or simplifying the scoring rules.

Internal-consistency estimates of reliability, such as that obtained by use of the Spearman-Brown formula, are inappropriate for measuring the reliability of heterogeneous tests and speed tests. The impact of test characteristics on reliability is discussed in detail later in this chapter.

Table 5–1
Odd-Even Reliability Coefficients Before and After the Spearman-Brown Adjustment*

Grade	Half-Test Correlation (unadjusted r)	Whole-Test Estimate (r_{SB})
K	.718	.836
1	.807	.893
2	.777	.875

*for scores on a test of mental ability

Other Methods of Estimating Internal Consistency

In addition to the Spearman-Brown formula, other methods in wide use to estimate internal consistency reliability include formulas developed by Kuder and Richardson (1937) and Cronbach (1951). *Inter-item consistency* is a term that refers to the degree of correlation between all the items on a scale. A measure of inter-item consistency is calculated from a single administration of a single form of a test. An index of inter-item consistency is, in turn, useful in assessing the *homogeneity* of the test. Tests are said to be *homogeneous* if they contain items that measure a single trait. As an adjective used to describe test items, *homogeneity* (derived from the Greek words *homos,* meaning "same," and *genous,* meaning "kind") refers to the degree to which a test measures a single factor, the extent to which items in a scale are unifactorial.

In contrast to test homogeneity is the concept of test *heterogeneity,* a term that refers to the degree to which a test measures different factors. A *nonhomogeneous* or *heterogeneous* test is composed of items that measure more than one trait. A test that assesses knowledge of only color television repair skills could be expected to be more homogeneous in content than a test of electronic repair. The former test assesses only one area and the latter assesses several, such as knowledge not only of television but also of radios, videorecorders, compact disc players, and so forth. The more homogeneous a test is, the more it will have inter-item consistency. Since the test would be sampling a relatively narrow content area, it would contain more inter-item consistency. A person who is skilled in color television repair might be somewhat familiar with the repair of other electronic devices such as radios and stereo systems, but would probably know virtually nothing about videorecorders or compact disc players. Thus, there would be less inter-item consistency in this test of general repair ability than in a test designed to assess only color television repair knowledge and skills.

Test homogeneity is desirable because it allows relatively straightforward test-score interpretation. Testtakers with the same score on a homogeneous test probably have similar abilities in the area tested. Testtakers with the same score on a more heterogeneous test may have quite different abilities. But although a homogeneous test is desirable because it so readily lends itself to clear interpretation, it is often an insufficient tool for measuring multifaceted psychological variables such as intelligence or personality. One way to circumvent this potential source of difficulty has been to administer a series of homogeneous tests, each designed to measure some component of a heterogeneous variable.[6] In addition to some of the random influences that can affect reliability measures, error variance in a measure of inter-item consistency comes from two sources:

---

6. As we will see elsewhere throughout this text, important decisions are seldom made on the basis of one test only. Psychologists frequently rely on what is called a *test battery*—a selected assortment of tests and assessment procedures in the process of evaluation. A test battery may or may not be composed of homogeneous tests.

(1) item sampling and (2) the heterogeneity of the content area. The more heterogeneous the content area sampled, the lower the inter-item consistency will be.

The Kuder-Richardson formulas   Dissatisfaction with existing split-half methods of estimating reliability compelled G. Frederic Kuder and M. W. Richardson (1937; Richardson & Kuder, 1939) to develop their own measures for estimating reliability. The most widely known of the many formulas they collaborated on is their Kuder-Richardson formula 20 or "KR-20" (so named because it was the twentieth formula developed in a series). In the instance where test items are highly homogeneous, KR-20 and split-half reliability estimates will be similar. However, KR-20 is the statistic of choice for determining the inter-item consistency of dichotomous items, primarily those items that can be scored right or wrong (such as multiple-choice items). If test items are more heterogeneous, KR-20 will yield lower reliability estimates than the split-half method. Table 5–2 summarizes items on a sample heterogeneous test. Assuming the difficulty level of all the items on the test to be about the same, would you expect a split-half (odd-even) estimate of reliability to be fairly high or low? How might you suspect the KR-20 reliability estimate to compare with the odd-even estimate of reliability—would it be higher or lower?

We might guess that since the content areas sampled for the 18 items from this "Hypothetical Electronics Repair Test" are ordered in a manner whereby odd and even items tap the same content area, the odd-even reliability estimate will probably be quite high. With respect to a reasonable guess concerning the KR-20 reliability estimate, because of the great heterogeneity of content areas when taken as a whole, it could reasonably be predicted that the KR-20 estimate

	Item Number	Content Area
Table 5–2 **Content Areas Sampled for** **18 Items of the "Hypothetical** **Electronics Repair Test" (HERT)**	1	Color television
	2	Color television
	3	Black-and-white television
	4	Black-and-white television
	5	Radio
	6	Radio
	7	Videorecorder
	8	Videorecorder
	9	Typewriter
	10	Typewriter
	11	Compact disc player
	12	Compact disc player
	13	Stereo receiver
	14	Stereo receiver
	15	Turntable
	16	Turntable
	17	Microwave
	18	Microwave

of reliability will be lower than the odd-even one. How can KR-20 be computed? The following formula may be used:

$$r_{\text{KR20}} = \left(\frac{k}{k-1}\right)\left(1 - \frac{\Sigma\,pq}{\sigma^2}\right)$$

where r_{KR20} stands for the Kuder-Richardson formula 20 reliability coefficient, k is the number of test items, σ^2 is the variance of total test scores, p is the proportion of testtakers who pass the item, q is the proportion of people who fail the item, and $\Sigma\,pq$ is the sum of the pq products over all items. For this particular example, k equals 18. Based on the data in Table 5–3, $\Sigma\,pq$ can be computed to be 3.975. The variance of total test scores is 5.26. Thus, $r_{\text{KR20}} = .259$.

An approximation of KR-20 can be obtained by the use of the twenty-first formula in the series developed by Kuder and Richardson, a formula known— you guessed it—as "KR-21." KR-21 may be used if there is reason to believe that all the test items have approximately the same degree of difficulty—an assumption, we should add, that is seldom justified. Formula KR-21 tends to be outdated in an era of calculators and computers, since it was used as an approximation of KR-20 that required less computation. Another formula once used in the measurement of internal-consistency reliability and now for the most part outdated was a statistic referred to as the Rulon formula (Rulon, 1939).

Though numerous modifications of Kuder-Richardson formulas have been proposed through the years (for example, Horst, 1953; Cliff, 1984), perhaps the one variant of the KR-20 formula that has received the most acceptance to date is a statistic called "coefficient alpha," sometimes referred to as *coefficient α-20* (*α* being the Greek letter *alpha* and "20" referring to KR-20).

Coefficient alpha   Developed by Cronbach (1951) and subsequently elaborated on by others (such as Kaiser & Michael, 1975; Novick & Lewis, 1967), *coefficient*

	Item Number	Number of Testtakers Correct
Table 5–3 **"HERT" Performance by** **Item for 20 Testtakers**	1	14
	2	12
	3	9
	4	18
	5	8
	6	5
	7	6
	8	9
	9	10
	10	10
	11	8
	12	6
	13	15
	14	9
	15	12
	16	12
	17	14
	18	7

alpha may be thought of as the mean of all possible—the "good" along with the "bad"—split-half correlations, corrected by the Spearman-Brown formula. As we have noted above, KR-20 is appropriately used on tests with dichotomous items. Coefficient alpha may also be used on tests with dichotomous items. Additionally, coefficient alpha is appropriate for use on tests containing nondichotomous items: items that can individually be scored along a range of values. Examples of such tests include opinion and attitude polls, where a range of possible alternatives are presented; essay tests; and short-answer tests, where partial credit can be given. The formula for coefficient alpha is

$$r_\alpha = \left(\frac{k}{k-1} \right) \left(1 - \frac{\Sigma \, \sigma_i^2}{\sigma^2} \right)$$

where r_α is coefficient alpha, k is the number of items, σ_i^2 is the variance of one item, $\Sigma \, \sigma_i^2$ is the sum of variances of each item, and σ^2 is the variance of the total test scores. In the age of computers and programmable calculators, few of the people who would have occasion to calculate this statistic would undertake the rather laborious calculations by hand—and the number of people who would prefer "the old-fashioned way" could reasonably be presumed to dwindle as the number of items on the test rises. Today, perhaps because of the ready availability of computers (mainframe to laptop), coefficient alpha is the preferred statistic for obtaining an estimate of internal consistency reliability (Keith & Reynolds, 1990).

Measures of Inter-Scorer Reliability

For many, if not all, situations in which we are in some way being evaluated, we usually would like to believe that no matter who is doing the evaluating, we would be evaluated in the same way.[7] For example, if the instructor of this course were to evaluate your knowledge of the subject matter by means of an essay test, you would like to think that the grade you would receive on the essay test would be the same whether it was graded by your professor or any other professor who teaches this course. If you take a road test for a driver's license, you would like to believe that whether you pass or fail is solely a matter of your performance behind the wheel and not a function of who is sitting in the passenger's seat. Unfortunately, in some types of tests under some conditions, the score is sometimes more a function of the scorer than anything else. This was demonstrated back in 1912 when researchers presented one pupil's English composition to a convention of teachers, and volunteers graded the papers—with grades that ranged from a low of 50% to a high of 98% (Starch & Elliott, 1912).

---

7. We say "usually" because exceptions in real-life situations do exist. Thus, for example, if you go on a job interview and the employer/interviewer is your father, you might reasonably expect that the nature of the evaluation you receive would *not* be the same were the evaluator to be someone else.

Variously referred to as "scorer reliability," "judge reliability," "observer reliability," and "inter-rater reliability," *inter-scorer reliability* refers to the degree of agreement or consistency that exists between two or more "scorers" (or "judges" or "raters"). Reference to levels of inter-scorer reliability for a particular test may be published (either in the test's manual or elsewhere) and if the reliability coefficient is very high, the prospective test user knows that test scores can be derived in a systematic, consistent way by various scorers with sufficient training. A responsible test developer who is unable to create a test that can be scored with a reasonable degree of consistency by trained scorers will go "back to the drawing board" to discover the reason for this problem. If, for example, the problem is a lack of clarity in scoring criteria, then the remedy might be to rewrite the scoring criteria section of the manual to include clearly written scoring rules. One review of the literature on training raters to make performance ratings suggests that lectures to raters on scoring rules are not as effective in promoting inter-rater consistency as is providing raters with the opportunity for group discussion along with practice exercises and information on rater accuracy (Smith, 1986).

Perhaps the simplest way of determining the degree of consistency that exists between scorers in the scoring of a test is to calculate a coefficient of correlation, a coefficient of inter-scorer reliability. Assuming, for example, that a 30-item test of reaction time was administered to one subject and scored by two scorers, the inter-scorer reliability would be equal to the value of the Spearman-Brown corrected correlation coefficient obtained with respect to 30 pairs of scores. If the reliability coefficient were found to be, say, .90, this would mean that 90% of the variance in the scores assigned by the raters stemmed from true differences in the subject's reaction time, whereas 10% could be attributed to factors other than the subject's reaction time (that is, error). In many cases, more than two scorers are used in such reliability studies. In such instances, scores obtained by the two scorers would be correlated, using Pearson *r* or Spearman *rho,* depending on the scale of measurement of the test score.

The kappa statistic   A statistic called *kappa* was initially designed for use in the case where scorers make ratings using nominal scales of measurement (Cohen, 1960). The kappa statistic was subsequently modified by Fliess (1971) for use with multiple scorers. The kappa statistic has generally been received quite well as a measure of inter-scorer reliability (Hartmann, 1977), though there are special instances where it may be appropriate to use kappa in a modified form (Conger, 1985) or to use another measure, such as Yule's *Y* (Spitznagel & Helzer, 1985).

Using and Interpreting a Coefficient of Reliability

We have seen that with respect to the test itself, there are basically three approaches to the estimation of reliability: (1) test-retest, (2) alternate or parallel forms, and (3) internal or inter-item consistency. The method or methods

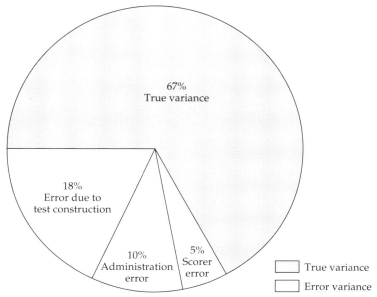

Figure 5–1
Sources of Variance in a Hypothetical Test

employed will depend on a number of factors—primary among them the purpose of obtaining a measure of reliability and the way that measure will be used.

The Purpose of the Reliability Coefficient

How repeatable are repeated measurements—with the same form of a test or alternate forms of a test—over short intervals of time? over long intervals? These are some of the types of questions we seek to answer with reference to a coefficient of reliability. If a specific test of employee performance is designed for use at various times over the course of the employment period, it would be reasonable to expect the test to demonstrate reliability across time—in which case knowledge of the instrument's test-retest reliability would be essential. For a test designed for a single administration only, an estimate of internal consistency would be the coefficient computed. If the purpose of determining reliability is to analyze the error variance into its parts, as has been done for the illustration in Figure 5–1, then a number of reliability coefficients will have to be computed.

Note that the various reliability coefficients do not all reflect the same sources of error variance. Thus, an individual reliability coefficient may provide an index of error from test construction, test administration, or test scoring and interpretation. A coefficient of inter-rater reliability, for example, provides information about error as a result of test scoring. Specifically, it can be used to answer questions about how consistently two scorers score the same test items.

Table 5-4
Summary of Reliability Types

Type of Reliability	Number of Testing Sessions	Number of Test Forms	Source(s) of Error Variance	Statistical Procedures
Test-retest	2	1	Administration	Pearson *r* or Spearman *rho*
Alternate forms	1 or 2	2	Test construction Administration	Pearson *r* or Spearman *rho*
Internal consistency	1	1	Test construction	Pearson *r* between equivalent test halves with Spearman-Brown correction, or Kuder-Richardson for dichotomous items, or Coefficient alpha for multipoint items
Inter-scorer	1	1	Scoring and interpretation	Pearson *r*, or Spearman *rho*, or kappa coefficient

For response to questions such as "How did illness affect this testtaker's score?" a different reliability coefficient would have to be calculated. Table 5–4 summarizes the different kinds of error variance that are reflected in different reliability coefficients.

The Nature of the Test

Closely related to considerations concerning the purpose and use of a reliability coefficient are considerations concerning the nature of the test itself. Included here are considerations such as whether (1) the test items are homogeneous or heterogeneous in nature; (2) the characteristic, ability, or trait being measured by the test is presumed to be dynamic or static; (3) the range of test scores is or is not restricted; (4) the test is a speed or a power test; and (5) the test is or is not criterion-referenced. Some tests present special problems regarding the measurement of their reliability (see this chapter's *Close-up*).

Homogeneity versus heterogeneity of test items If the test is homogeneous in items (that is, if it is functionally uniform throughout because it is designed to measure one factor, such as one ability or one trait), it would be reasonable to expect a high degree of internal consistency. If the test is heterogeneous in items, an estimate of internal consistency might be low relative to a more appropriate estimate of test-retest reliability.

Dynamic versus static characteristics Whether what is being measured by the test is *dynamic* or *static* is also a consideration in obtaining an estimate of reliability. Dynamic characteristics are presumed to be ever changing as a function of situational and cognitive experiences. If, for example, one were to take hourly measurements of the dynamic characteristic of anxiety as manifested in a stockbroker throughout a business day, one might find the measured level of this characteristic to change from hour to hour. Such changes might even be related

The Reliability of the Bayley Scales for Infant Development

The Bayley Scales for Infant Development, Second Edition (BSID-II; Bayley, 1993) is a test designed to assess the developmental level of children between 1 month and 3½ years old. It is used primarily to help identify children who are developing slowly and might benefit from cognitive intervention (Bayley, 1993). The BSID-II includes three scales. Items on the Motor Scale focus on the control and skill employed in bodily movements. Items on the Mental Scale focus on cognitive abilities. The Behavior Rating Scale assesses behavior problems, such as lack of attention.

Is the BSID-II a reliable measure? The way in which reliability of the BSID-II is assessed depends in part on the nature of the test itself. For example, because the Mental, Motor, and Behavior Rating Scales are each expected to measure a homogeneous set of abilities, internal consistency reliability is an appropriate measure of reliability for the scales. Note that internal consistency reliability is not calculated across all three BSID-II scales at once, because the test as a whole is not assumed to be homogeneous. Rather, each of these three scales is expected to measure a somewhat different set of skills from those measured by the others. Other characteristics of the BSID-II also justify the evaluation of internal consistency reliability. The abilities measured are not expected to change during the course of the testing session (about 30 to 60 minutes). Further, the BSID-II is norm-referenced and is a power test. As noted later in this section, all of these characteristics are consistent with examining the test's internal consistency reliability.

Bayley (1993) reported coefficient alphas ranging from .78 to .93 for the Mental Scale (variations exist across the age groups), .75 to .91 for the Motor Scale, and .64 to .92 for the Behavior Rating Scale. From these reliability studies, Bayley (1993) concluded that the BSID-II is internally consistent.

Examining the test-retest reliability of the BSID-II poses a problem unique to instruments that undertake the assessment of infants. We know that cognitive development during the first months and years of life is uneven and fast. Children often grow in spurts, changing dramatically over a few days (Hetherington & Parke, 1993). The child tested just before and again just after a developmental advance may perform very differently on the BSID-II at the two testings. In such cases, a change in test score would not be the result of error in the test itself or in test administration. Instead, such changes in the test score could reflect an actual change in the child's skills. Still, of course, not all differences between the child's test performance at two test administrations need to result from changes in skills. The challenge in gauging the test-retest reliability of the BSID-II is to do it in such a way that it is not spuriously lowered by the testtaker's actual developmental changes between testings.

Bayley's solution to this dilemma entailed examining test-retest reliability over short periods of time. The median interval between testings was just four days. Correlations between the results of the two testing sessions were strong for both the Mental (.83 to .91) and the Motor (.77 to .79) Scales. The Behavior Rating Scale demonstrated lower test-retest reliability: .48 to .70 at 1 month of age, .57 to .90 at 12 months of age, and .60 to .71 at 24 to 36 months of age (Bayley, 1993).

Inter-scorer reliability is an important concern for the BSID-II, because many items require judgment on the part of the examiner. The test manual provides clear criteria for scoring the infant's performance, but by their nature many tasks involve some subjectivity in scoring. For example, one of the Motor Scale items is "Keeps hands open . . . Scoring: Give credit if the child holds his hands open most of the time when he is free to follow his own interests" (Bayley, 1993, p. 147). Sources of examiner error on this item can arise from a variety of sources: different examiners may note the position of the child's hands at different times. Examiners may define differently when the child is "free to follow his own interests." And examiners may disagree about what constitutes "most of the time." As a second example, one of the Mental Scale items is "Attends to story . . . Scoring: Give credit if the child attends to the entire story. Attending includes decreasing motor activity and looking at the pictures, listening to the words, or talking to you about the pictures as you read" (Bayley, 1993, p. 114). Examiners may differ in noticing lapses of attention or in their strictness about attention to the whole story. Is a single distraction enough for the child to lose credit on this item?

Correlations between the scores assigned by the examiner and an observer sitting unobtrusively nearby during the same testing session were as follows: .96 for the Mental Scale, .75 for the Motor Scale, .57 to .82 for the different factors of the Behavior Rating Scale, and .88 for the total Behavior Rating Scale (Bayley, 1993).

An alternate or parallel form of the BSID-II does not exist, so *alternate-forms reliability* cannot be assessed. An alternate form of the test would be useful to have, especially in cases in which the examiner makes a mistake in administering the first version of it. Still, the creation of an alternate form of this test would almost surely entail a great investment of time, money, and effort. If you were the test's publisher, would you make that investment? In considering the answer to that question, don't forget that the ability level of the testtaker is changing rapidly.

In reviewing the BSID-II, Nellis and Gridley (1994) note that a primary goal in the revision was to

Nancy Bayley

strengthen the test psychometrically. Based on the data provided in the test manual, which has been summarized in this Close-up, Nellis and Gridley conclude that this goal was accomplished: the BSID-II does seem to be more reliable than the original Bayley Scales. However, there are still some important weaknesses. For example, the manual focuses on the psychometric quality of the BSID-II as administered to children without significant developmental problems; whether the same levels of reliability would be obtained with developmentally delayed children is unknown (Nellis & Gridley, 1994). Because the original Bayley Scales were so widely used, Nellis and Gridley predict that interested professionals will speedily conduct and publish research to answer questions about the reliability of the revised test. They, like the authors of your textbook, are eager to see the results of such studies to better understand the psychometric quality of the BSID-II.

to the magnitude of the Dow Jones index. Since the "true" amount of anxiety presumed to exist would vary with each assessment, a test-retest measure would be of little help in gauging the reliability of the measuring instrument. The best estimate of reliability could be obtained from an internal-consistency measure. Contrast this situation to one in which hourly assessments of this same stockbroker are made on a characteristic that is not dynamic in nature but presumed to be relatively unchanging or static (such as intelligence). In this instance, obtained measurement would not be expected to vary significantly as a function of time, and either the test-retest or the alternate-forms method would be appropriate.

Restriction or inflation of range   In using and interpreting a coefficient of reliability, the issue variously referred to as "restriction of range" or "restriction of variance" (or, conversely, as "inflation of range" or "inflation of variance") is important. If the variance of either variable in a correlational analysis is restricted by the sampling procedure used, then the resulting correlation coefficient tends to be lower. If the variance of either variable in a correlational analysis is inflated by the sampling procedure, then the resulting correlation coefficient tends to be higher. Also of critical importance is whether the range of variances employed is appropriate to the objective of the correlational analysis. Consider in the latter context, for example, a published educational test designed for use with children in grades 1 through 6. Ideally, the manual for this test should contain not one reliability value covering all the testtakers in grades 1 through 6, but reliability values for testtakers at each grade level. A corporate personnel officer who employs a certain screening test in the hiring process must maintain reliability data with respect to scores achieved by job applicants—as opposed to hired employees—if the range of measurements is not to be restricted (this because the people that were hired typically scored higher on the test than any comparable group of applicants).

Speed versus power tests   When a time limit is long enough to allow testtakers to attempt all items and if some items are so difficult that no testtaker is able to obtain a perfect score, then the test is referred to as a *power* test. By contrast, a *speed* test generally contains items of uniform level of difficulty (typically uniformly low) so that when given generous time limits, all testtakers should be able to complete all the test items correctly. In practice, however, the time limit on a speed test is established so that few if any of the testtakers will be able to complete the entire test. Score differences on a speed test are therefore based on performance speed, since items attempted tend to be correct. A reliability estimate of a speed test should be based on performance from two independent testing periods using one of the following: (1) test-retest reliability, (2) alternate-forms reliability, or (3) split-half reliability from two, separately timed half tests. If a split-half procedure is used, the obtained reliability coefficient is for a half test and should be adjusted using the Spearman-Brown formula.

Because a measure of the reliability of a speed test should reflect the consistency of response speed, the reliability of a speed test should not be computed from a single administration of the test with a single time limit. If a speed test is administered once and some measure of internal consistency is computed, like the Kuder-Richardson or a split-half correlation, the result will be a spuriously high reliability coefficient. A couple of examples illustrate how this occurs. When a group of testtakers completes a speed test, almost all the items completed will be correct. If reliability is examined using an odd-even split, and if the testtakers completed the items in order, testtakers will get close to the same number of odd as even items correct. A testtaker completing 82 items will probably get 41 odd and 41 even items correct. A testtaker completing 61 items will probably get 31 odd and 30 even items correct. When the number of odd and even items correct are correlated across a group of testtakers, the correlation will be close to 1.00—an impressive-looking value that tells us nothing about response consistency. A Kuder-Richardson reliability coefficient would yield a similar coefficient. Recall that KR-20 reliability is based on the proportion of testtakers correct (p) and the proportion of testtakers incorrect (q) on each item. In the case of a speed test, it is conceivable that p would equal 1.0 and q would equal 0 for many of the items. Toward the end of the test—when many items would not even be attempted because of the time limit being imposed—p might equal 0 and q might equal 1.0. For many, if not a majority, of the items, then, the product of pq would equal or approximate 0. When 0 is substituted in the KR-20 formula for $\Sigma\ pq$, the reliability coefficient is 1.0 (a meaningless coefficient in this instance).

Criterion-referenced tests   In Chapter 4, we presented the differences between norm-referenced and criterion-referenced testing and noted that the latter is designed to provide an indication of where a testtaker stands with respect to some criterion such as an educational or a vocational objective. Unlike norm-referenced tests, criterion-referenced tests tend to contain material that has been mastered in hierarchical fashion; the would-be pilot masters on-ground skills before attempting to master in-flight skills. Scores on criterion-referenced tests tend to be interpreted in "pass/fail" (or, perhaps more accurately, "master/failed-to-master") terms, and any scrutiny of performance on individual items tends to be for diagnostic (and remedial) purposes. Traditional techniques of estimating reliability employ measures based on total test scores. In test-retest reliability, a reliability estimate is based on the correlation between the total scores on two administrations of the same test. In alternate-forms reliability, a reliability estimate is based on the correlation between the two total scores on the two forms. In split-half reliability, a reliability estimate is based on the correlation between scores on two halves of the test and then adjusted using the Spearman-Brown formula to obtain a reliability estimate of the whole test. These traditional procedures of estimating reliability are inappropriate for use with criterion-referenced tests. To understand why, recall that reliability is defined as the proportion of total variance (σ^2) attributable to true variance (σ^2_{tr}). Total variance in a test score distribution equals the sum of the true variance plus the error variance (σ^2_e):

$$\sigma^2 = \sigma^2_{tr} + \sigma^2_e$$

A measure of reliability, therefore, depends on the variability of the test scores: how different the scores are from one another. In criterion-referenced testing and particularly in mastery testing, individual differences between examinees on total test scores may be minimal; the key issue is not the test scores in comparison with the other test scores but simply if a certain criterion score has been obtained. As individual differences (and the variability) decrease, a traditional measure of reliability would also decrease (regardless of the stability of individual performance). Traditional ways of estimating reliability are therefore not always appropriate for criterion-referenced tests, though there may be instances in which traditional estimates can be adopted (such as the case where the same test is used at different stages in some program—training, therapy, or the like—and variability in scores could reasonably be expected; see Ebel, 1973).[8]

Before proceeding to the discussion of alternatives to the true score model, read about a "real-life" application of the types of reliability coefficients we have discussed to this point in this chapter's *Everyday Psychometrics*.

Alternatives to the True Score Model

Thus far, and throughout this book unless specifically stated otherwise, the model we have assumed to be operative is the "true score" or "classical" model—the most widely used and accepted model in the psychometric literature today. Historically, the true score model of the reliability of measurement enjoyed a virtually unchallenged reign of acceptance from the early 1900s through the 1940s. The 1950s saw the development of an alternative theoretical model, one referred to as the *domain sampling theory* originally and as *generalizability theory* in one of its many modified forms. As set forth by Tryon (1957), the theory of domain sampling rebels against the concept of a "true" score existing with respect to the measurement of psychological constructs (in the same way that a "true" score might exist with respect to measurement in the physical sciences). Whereas those who subscribe to true score theory seek to estimate the portion of a test score that is attributable to "error," proponents of domain sampling theory seek to estimate the extent to which specific sources of variation under defined conditions are contributing to the test score. In the latter model, a test's reliability is conceived of as an objective measure of how precisely the test score assesses the domain from which the test draws a sample (Thorndike, 1985). A *domain* of behavior—or the universe of items that could conceivably measure that behavior—can be thought of as a hypothetical construct: one that shares certain characteristics with (and is measured by) the sample of items that make up the test. In theory, the items in the domain are thought to have the same means and variances of those in the test that samples from the domain. Of the three types of estimates of reliability, measures of internal consistency are perhaps the most compatible with domain sampling theory.

Generalizability theory may be viewed as an extension of true score theory wherein the concept of a universe score replaces that of a true score (Shavelson

---

8. Statistical techniques applicable to the assessment of the reliability of criterion-referenced tests are discussed in detail elsewhere (e.g., Hambleton & Jurgensen, 1990; Hambleton & Novick, 1973; Lord, 1978; Millman, 1974, 1979; Panell & Laabs, 1979; Subkoviak, 1980).

et al., 1989). Developed by Lee J. Cronbach (1970) and his colleagues (Cronbach et al., 1972), this theory is based on the idea that a person's test scores vary from testing to testing because of variables in the testing situation. Instead of conceiving of all variability between a person's scores as error, Cronbach encourages test developers and researchers to describe the details of the particular test situation or *universe* leading to a specific test score. This universe is described in terms of its *facets,* which include things like the number of items in the test, the amount of training the test scorers have had, and the purpose of the test administration. According to generalizability theory, given the exact same conditions of all the facets in the universe, the exact same test score should be obtained. This test score is the *universe score,* and it is analogous to a true score in the true score model.

"What is Mary's typing ability?" This must be interpreted as, "What would Mary's score be if a large number of measurements were collected and averaged?" The particular test score Mary earned is just one out of a *universe* of possible observations, any of which the investigator would be willing to base his conclusion or decision on. If one of these scores is as acceptable as the next, then the mean, called the *universe score* and symbolized here by M_p (mean for person *p*), would be the most appropriate statement of Mary's performance in the type of situation the test represents.

The universe is a collection of possible measures "of the same kind," but the limits of the collection are determined by the investigator's purpose. If he needs to know Mary's typing ability on May 5 (for example, so that he can plot a learning curve that includes one point for that day), the universe would include observations on that day and on that day only. He probably does want to generalize over passages, testers, and scorers—that is to say, he would like to know Mary's ability on May 5 without reference to any particular passage, tester, or scorer. . . .

The person will ordinarily have a different universe score for each universe. Mary's universe score covering tests on May 5 will not agree perfectly with her universe score for the whole month of May. . . . Some testers call the average over a large number of comparable observations a "true score"; e.g., "Mary's true typing rate on 3-minute tests." Instead, we speak of a "universe score" to emphasize that what score is desired depends on the universe being considered. For any measure there are many "true scores," each corresponding to a different universe.

When we use a single observation as if it represented the universe, we are generalizing. We generalize over scorers, over selections typed, perhaps over days. If the observed scores from a procedure agree closely with the universe score, we can say that the observation is "accurate," or "reliable," or "generalizable." And since the observations then also agree with each other, we say that they are "consistent" and "have little error variance." To have so many terms is confusing, but not seriously so. The term most often used in the literature is "reliability." The author prefers "generalizability" because that term immediately implies "generalization to what?" . . . There is a different degree of generalizability for each universe. The older methods of analysis do not separate the sources of variation. They deal with a single source of variance, or leave two or more sources entangled. (Cronbach, 1970, pp. 153–154)

The Reliability Defense and the Breathalyzer Test

Breathalyzer is the generic name for a number of different types of instruments used by law enforcement agencies to determine if a suspect, most typically the operator of a motor vehicle, is legally drunk. The driver is required to blow into a tube that is attached to the breathalyzer. The breath sample then mixes with a chemical that is added to the machine for each new test. The resulting mixture is automatically analyzed for alcohol content in the breath. The value for the alcohol content in the breath is then converted to a value for blood alcohol level. Whether the testtaker is deemed to be legally drunk will vary from state to state as a function of the specific legislation on the books regarding the blood alcohol level necessary to be declared intoxicated.

In the state of New Jersey, the blood alcohol level required to be declared legally drunk is one-tenth of one percent (.10%). Drivers in New Jersey found guilty for a first drunk-driving offense face fines and surcharges amounting to about $3,500, mandatory detainment in an Intoxicated Driver Resource Center, suspension of driving privileges for a minimum of six months, and a maximum of 30 days' imprisonment. Two models of a breathalyzer (model 900 and 900A made by National Draeger Inc.) have been used

in New Jersey since the 1950s. Well-documented test-retest reliability regarding the 900 and 900A breathalyzers indicate that the instruments have a margin of error of about one one-hundredth of a percentage point. This means that an administration of the test to a testtaker who in reality has a blood alcohol level of .10% (a "true score," if you will) might yield a test score of anywhere from a low of .09% to a high of .11%.

A driver in the state of New Jersey who was convicted of driving drunk appealed the decision on grounds relating to the test-retest reliability of the breathalyzer. The breathalyzer had indicated that the driver's blood alcohol level was .10%. The driver argued that the law did not take into account the margin of error inherent in the measuring instrument. However, the State Supreme Court ruled against the driver, finding that the legislature must have taken into consideration such error when it wrote the law. As a footnote, a New Jersey legislator has proposed legislation to lower the blood alcohol necessary to be deemed legally drunk to .08% (Romano, 1994).

Another issue related to the use of breathalyzers has to do with where and when they are administered. In some states, the test is most typically administered

How can these ideas be applied? Cronbach et al. suggested that tests be developed with the aid of a *generalizability study* followed by a *decision study*. A generalizability study examines how generalizable scores from a particular test are if the test is administered in different situations. Stated in the language of generalizability theory, a generalizability study examines how much of an impact different facets of the universe have on the test score. Is the test score affected by group as opposed to individual administration? Is the test score affected by the time of day in which the test is administered? The influence of particular facets on the test score is represented by *coefficients of generalizability*. These coefficients are similar to reliability coefficients under the true score model.

at police headquarters, not at the scene of the arrest. Expert witnesses were once retained on behalf of defendants to calculate what the defendant's blood alcohol was at the actual time of the arrest. Working backward from the time the test was administered, and figuring in values for variables such as what the defendant had to drink and when, as well as the defendant's weight, they could calculate a blood alcohol level at the time of arrest. If that level was lower than the level required to be declared legally drunk, the case might be dismissed. However, in some states, such as New Jersey, such a defense would not be entertained. In such states, higher courts have ruled that since it was aware that breathalyzer tests would not be administered at the arrest scene, the legislature had intended the measured blood alcohol level to apply at the time of its administration at police headquarters.

One final reliability-related issue relevant to the use of breathalyzers has to do with inter-scorer reliability. When using the 900 and 900A models, the police officer who conducted the arrest also records the measured blood alcohol level. Although the vast majority of police officers are honest when it comes to such recording, there is potential for abuse. A police officer who wished to "save face" on a drunk-driving arrest,

A suspect being administered a breathalyzer test

or even a police officer who simply wanted to add to a record of drunk-driving arrests, could record an incorrect breathalyzer value to ensure a conviction. In 1993, one police officer in Camden County, New Jersey, was convicted of and sent to prison for recording incorrect breathalyzer readings (Romano, 1994).

After the generalizability study is done, Cronbach et al. recommended that test developers do a decision study, which involves the application of information from the generalizability study. In the decision study, the usefulness of test scores in helping the test user make decisions is examined. In practice, test scores are used to guide a variety of decisions, from placing a child in special education to hiring new employees and discharging mental patients from the hospital. The decision study is designed to tell the test user how test scores should be used and how dependable those scores are as a basis for decisions, depending on the context of their use. Why is this so important? Cronbach (1970) outlines the effects of errors in decisions guided by test results:

The decision that a student has completed a course or that a patient is ready for termination of therapy must not be seriously influenced by chance errors, temporary variations in performance, or the tester's choice of questions. An erroneous favorable decision may be irreversible and may harm the person or the community. Even when reversible, an erroneous unfavorable decision is unjust, disrupts the person's morale, and perhaps retards his development. Research, too, requires dependable measurement. An experiment is not very informative if an observed difference could be accounted for by chance variation. Large error variance is likely to mask a scientifically important outcome. Taking a better measure improves the sensitivity of an experiment in the same way that increasing the number of subjects does. (p. 152)

Generalizability has not replaced the true score model. Still, its appeal remains strong, as evidenced by a recent book for neophytes (Shavelson & Webb, 1991) and by a variety of research articles employing generalizability techniques (Marcoulides, 1994; McKenzie et al., 1993; Shrout, 1993; Suen et al., 1993). Inherent in its appeal is its message that a test's reliability does not reside within the test itself. Rather, a test's reliability is very much a function of the circumstances under which the test is developed, administered, and interpreted.

Reliability and Individual Scores

The reliability coefficient helps the test developer build an adequate measuring instrument, and it helps the test user select a suitable test. However, the usefulness of the reliability coefficient does not end with test construction and selection. By employing the reliability coefficient in the formula for the standard error of measurement, the test user now has another descriptive statistic relevant to test interpretation, this one useful in describing the amount of error in a test or a measure.

The Standard Error of Measurement

The standard deviation of a theoretically normal distribution of test scores obtained by one person on equivalent tests is called the *standard error of measurement*, abbreviated SEM or SEm. Also referred to as the *standard error of a score* and denoted by the symbol σ_{meas}, the standard error of measurement is an index of the extent to which one individual's scores vary over tests presumed to be parallel. In accordance with the true score model, an obtained test score represents one point in the theoretical distribution of scores the testtaker could have obtained. Further, the test user has no way of knowing the testtaker's "true score." However, if the standard deviation for the distribution of test scores is known (or can be calculated) and if an estimate of the reliability of the test is known (or can be calculated), an estimate of the standard error of a particular score (that is, the standard error of measurement) can be determined through the use of the following formula:

$$\sigma_{meas} = \sigma\sqrt{1 - r}$$

where σ_{meas} is equal to the standard error of measurement, σ is equal to the standard deviation of test scores by the group of testtakers, and r is equal to the reliability coefficient of the test. The standard error of measurement allows us to estimate the range in which the true score is likely to exist, with a specific level of confidence.

If, for example, a spelling test has a reliability coefficient of .84 and a standard deviation of 10, then:

$$\sigma_{meas} = 10\sqrt{1 - .84} = 4$$

To use the standard error of measurement to estimate the value of the true score, we make an assumption: if the individual were to take a large number of equivalent tests, scores on those tests would tend to be normally distributed with the individual's true score as the mean. Because the standard error of measurement functions like a standard deviation in this context, we can use it to predict what would happen if an individual took additional equivalent tests:

- 68% of the scores would be expected to occur within $\pm 1 \sigma_{meas}$ of the true score.
- 95% of the scores would be expected to occur within $\pm 2 \sigma_{meas}$ of the true score.
- 99.7% of the scores would be expected to occur within $\pm 3 \sigma_{meas}$ of the true score.

Of course, we don't know the true score for any individual testtaker, and so we must estimate it. The best estimate available about the individual's true score on the test is the test score already obtained. Thus, if a student achieved a score of 50 on one spelling test, and if that test had a standard error of measurement of 4, as per the example above, then we could state the following about the student's future performance on equivalent tests:

- 68% of the scores would be expected to occur within $50 \pm \sigma_{meas}$, or 50 ± 4, or between 46 and 54.
- 95% of the scores would be expected to occur within $50 \pm 2 \sigma_{meas}$, or 50 ± 8, or between 42 and 58.
- 99.7% of the scores would be expected to occur within $50 \pm 3 \sigma_{meas}$, or 50 ± 12, or between 38 and 62.

When applied to the prediction of future test performance, these ranges are known as *confidence intervals*. As per the above computations, we can predict with 95% confidence that a person who scored 50 on a test with a standard error of measurement of 4 would go on to score between 42 and 58 on an equivalent test in the future. Confidence intervals also provide a way for us to return to an issue raised at the beginning of this section concerning estimation of the true score. Although our best guess as to the true score is the obtained test score, no test is so completely reliable that we can translate the obtained test score into a true score with perfect confidence. If we wish to estimate the value of the true score with some level of confidence, we can use the standard error of measurement. We can be

- 68% confident that a true score falls within $\pm 1 \sigma_{meas}$ of the obtained score.
- 95% confident that a true score falls within $\pm 2 \sigma_{meas}$ of the obtained score.
- 99.7% confident that a true score falls within $\pm 3 \sigma_{meas}$ of the obtained score.

Continuing with the previous example, if a person scores 50 on a test that has a standard error of measurement of 4, we can be 95% confident that the true score is between 42 and 58.

The standard error of measurement, like the reliability coefficient, is one way of expressing test reliability. If the standard deviation of a test is held constant, the smaller the σ_{meas}, the more reliable the test will be; as r increases, the σ_{meas} decreases. For example, when a reliability coefficient equals .64 and σ equals 15, the standard error of measurement equals 9:

$$\sigma_{meas} = 15\sqrt{1 - .64} = 9$$

With a reliability coefficient equal to .96 and σ still equal to 15, the standard error of measurement decreases to 3:

$$\sigma_{meas} = 15\sqrt{1 - .96} = 3$$

In practice, the standard error of measurement is most frequently used in the interpretation of individual test scores. For example, intelligence tests are given as part of the assessment of individuals for mental retardation. One of the criteria for mental retardation is an IQ score of 70 or below (when the mean is 100 and the standard deviation is 15) on an individually administered intelligence test (American Psychiatric Association, 1994). One question that could be asked about these tests is how scores that are close to the cutoff value of 70 should be treated. Specifically, how high above 70 must a score be to conclude confidently that the individual is unlikely to be retarded? Is 72 clearly above the retarded range, so that if the person were to take a parallel form of the test, we could be confident that the second score would be above 70? What about a score of 75? A score of 79?

The answer to these questions entails an application of the standard error of measurement. The WAIS-R is a commonly used intelligence test and thus might be used to determine IQ for an assessment of retardation. The standard error of measurement for the WAIS-R is based on the standard deviation, which is 15, and the reliability, which averages approximately .97 (Wechsler, 1981). Applying the formula results in a standard error of measurement of 2.53, as is reported in the manual of the WAIS-R (Wechsler, 1981).

Now we can answer the questions posed previously about how far above 70 test scores must be for us to be confident that a repeated testing would also be above 70. Two standard errors of measurement above 70, or a score of 75.06 (70 + 2(2.53)), would be high enough for one to conclude that there is only a 2.5% chance of another testing resulting in a score of 70 or less. (Only 2.5%, rather than 5%, because we are considering only the original test score dropping—someone obtaining the score of 75 would also have just a 2.5% chance of scoring above 80 on repeated testing, resulting in a 95% confidence interval of 70–80 for the score of 75.) Thus, one could say that, with an obtained score of 75 on the WAIS-R, one would have 97.5% confidence that a repeated testing would not result in a score in the retarded range.

The standard error of measurement can be used to set the confidence interval for a particular score or to determine whether a score is significantly different from a criterion (such as the cutoff score of 70 described above). The standard error of measurement cannot be used to compare scores. To accomplish those kinds of comparisons, read on.

The Standard Error of the Difference Between Two Scores

Error related to any of the number of possible variables operative in a testing situation (such as item sampling, testtaker's physical or mental state, and the test environment) can contribute to a change in a score achieved on the same test (or a parallel test) from one administration of the test to the next. The amount of error in a specific test score is embodied in the standard error of measurement. But scores can change from one testing to the next for reasons other than error.

True differences in the characteristic being measured can also affect test scores. These differences may be of great interest, as in the case of a personnel officer who must decide which of many applicants to hire. Indeed, such differences may be hoped for, as in the case of a psychotherapy researcher who hopes to prove the effectiveness of a particular approach to therapy. Comparisons between scores are made using the *standard error of the difference,* a statistical measure that can aid a test user in determining how large a difference should be before it is considered statistically significant. As you are probably aware from your course in statistics, custom in the field of psychology dictates that if the probability is more than 5% that the difference occurred by chance, then for all intents and purposes it is presumed that there was no difference. A more rigorous standard is the 1% standard; by this criterion, no statistically significant difference would be deemed to exist unless the observed difference could have occurred by chance alone less than one time in a hundred.

The standard error of the difference between two scores can be the appropriate statistical tool to address three types of questions:

1. How did this individual's performance on test 1 compare with his or her performance on test 2?

2. How did this individual's performance on test 1 compare with someone else's performance on test 1?

3. How did this individual's performance on test 1 compare with someone else's performance on test 2?

As you might have expected, when comparing scores achieved on the different tests, it is essential that the scores be converted to the same scale. The formula for the standard error of the difference between two scores is

$$\sigma_{\text{diff}} = \sqrt{\sigma_{\text{meas 1}}^2 + \sigma_{\text{meas 2}}^2}$$

where σ_{diff} is the standard error of the difference between two scores, $\sigma_{\text{meas 1}}^2$ is the squared standard error of measurement for test 1, and $\sigma_{\text{meas 2}}^2$ is the squared standard error of measurement for test 2. If we substitute reliability coefficients for the standard errors of measurement of the separate scores, the formula becomes

$$\sigma_{\text{diff}} = \sigma\sqrt{2 - r_1 - r_2}$$

where r_1 is the reliability coefficient of test 1, r_2 is the reliability coefficient of test 2, and σ is the standard deviation—both tests having the same standard deviation, since they would have had to have been on the same scale (or converted to the same scale) before a comparison could be made.

The standard error of the difference between two scores will be larger than the standard error of measurement for either score alone because the former is affected by measurement error in both scores. This also makes good sense: if two scores *each* contain error, such that in each case the true score could be higher or lower, we would want the two scores to be further apart before we conclude that there is a significant difference between them.

The value obtained when the standard error of the difference is calculated is used in much the same way as the standard error of the mean. If we wish to be 95% confident that the two scores are different, we would want them to be separated by two standard errors of the difference. A separation of only one standard error of the difference would give us 68% confidence that the two true scores are different.

As an illustration of the use of the standard error of the difference between two scores, consider the situation of a corporate personnel manager who is seeking a highly responsible person for the position of vice president of safety. The personnel officer in this hypothetical situation decides to use a new published test called the "Safety-Mindedness Test" (S-MT) to screen applicants for the position. After placing an ad in the employment section of the local newspaper, the personnel officer tests 100 applicants for the position, using the S-MT. The personnel officer narrows the search for the vice president to the two highest scorers on the S-MT: Moe, who scored 125, and Larry, who scored 134. Assuming the measured reliability of this test to be .92 and its standard deviation to be 14, should the personnel officer conclude that Larry performed significantly better than Moe? To answer this question, first compute the standard error of the difference:

$$\sigma_{\text{diff}} = 14\sqrt{2 - .92 - .92} = 14\sqrt{.16} = 5.6$$

Note that in this application of the formula, the two test reliability coefficients are the same because the two scores being compared are derived from the same test.

What does this standard error of the difference mean? For any standard error of the difference, we can be

■ 68% confident that two scores differing by one σ_{diff} represent true score differences.

- 95% confident that two scores differing by two σ_{diff} represent true score differences.
- 99.7% confident that two scores differing by three σ_{diff} represent true score differences.

Applying this information to the standard error of the difference just computed for the "Safety-Mindedness Test," we see that the personnel officer can be

- 68% confident that two scores differing by 5.6 represent true score differences.
- 95% confident that two scores differing by 11.2 represent true score differences.
- 99.7% confident that two scores differing by 16.8 represent true score differences.

The difference between Larry's and Moe's scores is only 9 points, not a large enough difference for the personnel officer to conclude with 95% confidence that the two individuals actually have true scores that differ on this test. Stated another way, if Larry and Moe were to take a parallel form of the "Safety-Mindedness Test," the personnel officer could not be 95% confident that, at the next testing, Larry would again outperform Moe. The personnel officer in this example would have to resort to other means to decide whether Moe, Larry, or someone else would be the best candidate for the position.

As a postscript to the preceding example, suppose Larry got the job primarily on the basis of data from our hypothetical S-MT. And let's further suppose that it soon became all too clear that Larry turned out to be the hands-down, absolute worst vice president of safety that the company had ever seen. Larry spent much of his time playing practical jokes on fellow corporate officers, and he spent many of his off-hours engaged in his favorite pastime: flagpole sitting. The personnel officer might then have very good reason to question how well the instrument called the "Safety-Mindedness Test" truly measured "safety-mindedness." Or, to put it another way, the personnel officer might question the *validity* of the test. Not coincidentally, the subject of test *validity* is taken up in the next chapter.

6

Validity

In everyday language, we say that something is *valid* if it is sound, meaningful, or well grounded on principles or evidence. For example, we speak of a valid theory, a valid argument, or a valid reason. In legal terminology, lawyers say that something is valid if it is "executed with the proper formalities" (Black, 1979), such as a valid contract and a valid will. In each of these instances, someone makes a judgment based on evidence of the meaningfulness or the veracity of something. Similarly, in the language of psychological assessment, *validity* is a term used in conjunction with the meaningfulness of a test score—what the test score truly means.

The Concept of Validity

Stated succinctly, the word *validity* as applied to a test refers to a judgment concerning how well a test does in fact measure what it purports to measure. More specifically, it is a judgment based on evidence about the appropriateness of inferences drawn from test scores.[1] An *inference* is a logical result or deduction in a reasoning process. Characterizations of the validity of tests and test scores are frequently phrased in terms such as "acceptable" or "weak"—such terms reflecting a judgment about how adequately the attribute the test was designed to measure is actually measured. Inherent in a judgment of validity is a judgment of usefulness. One respected psychometrician even defined validity as how "useful scientifically" an instrument of measurement is (Nunnally, 1978, p. 86).

---

1. The word *test* is used in this chapter and throughout the book in the broadest possible sense; it may therefore also apply to measurement procedures and processes that would not, strictly speaking, colloquially be referred to as "tests."

Validation is the process of gathering and evaluating validity evidence. Both the test developer and the test user may play a role in the validation of a test for a specific purpose. It is the test developer's responsibility to supply validity evidence in the test manual. It may sometimes be appropriate for test users to conduct their own validation studies with their own groups of testtakers. Such "local" validation studies are a necessity in instances where the test user plans to alter in some way the format, instructions, language, or content of the test (such as changing the test from written form to braille form). Local validation studies would also be appropriate when the test will be used with a population of testtakers that differs in some significant way from the population on which the test was standardized.

How does one go about evaluating the validity of a test? A prerequisite to addressing this question is the development of a more precise conceptualization of validity. One way of conceptualizing validity has been with respect to the following three-category taxonomy:

Content validity

Criterion-related validity

Construct validity

This view of validity—referred to by Guion (1980) as the *trinitarian* view—is clearly the prevailing one in the field of psychology today and has been at least since the 1950s. Accordingly, answers to questions about methods for determining the validity of a test tend to be couched in terms such as content validation strategies, criterion-related validation strategies, and construct validation strategies. There are also references to other categories, such as predictive validity and concurrent validity, but these two terms tend to be collapsed under the more general category of criterion-related validity.

Within the context of the three-category taxonomy, the validity of a test may be evaluated by (1) scrutinizing its content, (2) relating scores obtained on the test to other test scores or other measures, and (3) executing a comprehensive analysis of not only how scores on the test relate to other test scores and measures but also how they can be understood within some theoretical framework for understanding the construct the test was designed to measure. These three approaches to validity assessment are not mutually exclusive; each should be thought of as one type of evidence that, with others, contributes to a judgment concerning the validity of the test. All three types of validity evidence contribute to a unified picture of a test's validity, though a test user may not need to know about all three types of validity evidence. Depending on the use to which a test is being put, one or another of these three types of validity evidence may not be as relevant as the next. For example, a personnel officer using a particular test in an applicant selection process might be very interested in content and criterion-related validity but not be particularly interested in construct validity. Let us also note at the outset that although the three-category taxonomy of validity is widely accepted, it is not "gospel" and has its critics (see, for example, Landy, 1986). We will return to this point in the section on validity in employment testing in Chapter 17.

Face Validity

The concept of *face validity* relates more to what a test appears to measure than to what the test actually measures. Face validity is a judgment concerning how relevant the test items appear to be. Stated another way, if a test definitely appears to measure what it purports to measure "on the face of it," it could be said to be high in face validity. A paper-and-pencil personality test labeled "The Introversion/Extraversion Test" with items that ask respondents whether they have acted in an introverted or an extraverted way in particular situations will be perceived as a highly *face-valid* test by the respondents. On the other hand, a personality test in which respondents are asked about a variety of inkblots may generally be perceived as a test with low face validity; no doubt many respondents would wonder how on earth what they said they saw in the inkblots really had anything at all to do with personality.

In contrast to judgments concerning the reliability of a test and in contrast to judgments concerning the content, construct, or criterion-related validity of a test, judgments concerning the face validity of a test are frequently thought of from the perspective of the testtaker as opposed to that of the test user. It is conceivable that the lack of face validity could contribute to a lack of confidence with respect to the perceived effectiveness of the test—with a consequential decrease in the testtaker's motivation to do his or her best. Also, parents may object to having their children tested with such an instrument. Their concern might stem from a belief that such testing will result in invalid conclusions. A test may in reality be very relevant and useful in a particular context, but if it is not perceived as such by examinees, negative consequences (ranging all the way from a negative test-taking attitude to a lawsuit) may result. From the perspective of the test user, face validity may also be important as it contributes (or fails to contribute) to users' confidence in the test. It can therefore be concluded that face validity may have "p.r. (public relations) value" for both testtakers and test users. However, the face validity of a test—the mere appearance of validity—is not an acceptable basis for interpretive inferences from test scores (APA, 1974, p. 26).

Content Validity

Content validity refers to a judgment concerning how adequately a test samples behavior representative of the universe of behavior the test was designed to sample. For example, the universe of behavior referred to as "assertive" is very wide-ranging. A content-valid paper-and-pencil test of assertiveness would be one that is adequately representative of these wide-ranging situations. We might expect that such a test would contain items sampling from hypothetical situations at home (such as whether the respondent has difficulty in making her or his views known to fellow family members), on the job (such as whether the respondent has difficulty in asking subordinates to do what is required of them), and in social situations (such as whether the respondent would send back a steak not done to order in a fancy restaurant).

With respect to educational achievement tests, it is customary to consider a test a content-valid measure when the proportion of material covered by the test approximates the proportion of material covered in the course. A cumulative final exam in introductory statistics would be considered content-valid if the proportion and type of introductory statistics problems on the test approximated the proportion and type of introductory statistics problems presented in the course.

The early stages of a test being developed for use in the classroom—be it one classroom or those throughout the state or the nation—typically entail research exploring the universe of possible instructional objectives for the course. Included among the many possible sources of information on such objectives are course syllabi, course texts, and teachers who teach the course, specialists who develop curricula, and professors and supervisors who train teachers in the particular subject area. From the pooled information (along with the judgment of the test developer), a blueprint for the structure of the test will emerge—a blueprint representing the culmination of efforts designed to adequately sample the universe of content areas that could conceivably be sampled in such a test.[2]

For an employment test to be content-valid, the content of the test must be a representative sample of the job-related skills required for employment. One technique frequently used in "blueprinting" the content areas to be covered in certain types of employment tests is observation: the test developer will observe successful veterans on that job, note the behaviors necessary for success on the job, and design the test to include a representative sample of those behaviors. Those same workers (as well as their supervisors and others) may subsequently be called on to act as experts or judges in rating the degree to which the content of the test is a representative sample of the required job-related skills. What follows is one method for quantifying the degree of agreement between such raters.

The Quantification of Content Validity

The measurement of content validity is important in employment settings, where tests used to hire and promote people are carefully scrutinized for their relevance to the job. Recall from Chapter 2 that courts often require evidence that employment tests are work-related. Probably partly in response to this legal pressure, and doubtless also out of a concern for the quality of employment tests, methods for quantifying content validity have been created. One such method was developed by Lawshe (1975), who proposed a simple formula for

---

2. The application of the concept of "blueprint" and of "blueprinting" is, of course, not limited to achievement tests. Blueprinting may be used in the design of a personality test, an attitude measure, or any other test, sometimes employing the judgments of experts in the field.

quantifying the degree of consensus by asking a panel of experts to determine the content validity of an employment test. This method has been used to assess many employment-related tests, as diverse as police training evaluations (Ford & Wroten, 1984) and measures of the work behavior of psychiatric aides (Distefano et al., 1983). The method can also be applied to other situations requiring a panel of experts to render some judgment, as in the examination of the content validity of mathematics achievement tests (Crocker et al., 1988).

Irrespective of the specific application, Lawshe's (1975) approach to the quantification of content validity involves a panel of judges. Each panel member responds to the following question for each of several items: "Is the skill or knowledge measured by this item

- essential
- useful but not essential
- not necessary

to the performance of the job?" (p. 567). For each item, the number of panelists stating that the item is essential is noted. According to Lawshe, if more than half the panelists indicate that an item is essential, that item has at least some content validity. Greater levels of content validity exist as larger numbers of panelists agree that a particular item is essential. Using these assumptions, Lawshe developed a formula called the *content validity ratio*:

$$CVR = \frac{n_e - N/2}{N/2}$$

where CVR = content validity ratio, n_e = number of panelists indicating "essential," and N = total number of panelists. Assuming a panel consists of ten experts, the following three examples illustrate the meaning of the CVR when it is negative, zero, and positive.

1. *Negative CVR:* When fewer than half the panelists indicate "essential," the CVR is negative. Assume four of ten panelists indicated "essential":

$$CVR = \frac{4 - (10/2)}{10/2} = -0.2$$

2. *Zero CVR:* When exactly half the panelists indicate "essential," the CVR is zero:

$$CVR = \frac{5 - (10/2)}{10/2} = .00$$

3. *Positive CVR:* When more than half but not all the panelists indicate "essential," the CVR ranges between .00 and .99. Assume nine of ten indicated "essential":

$$CVR = \frac{9 - (10/2)}{10/2} = .80$$

In validating a test, the content validity ratio is calculated for each item. Lawshe (1975) recommends that if the amount of agreement observed has more than a 5% chance of occurring by chance, the item should be eliminated. The minimal *CVR* values corresponding to this 5% level are presented in Table 6–1. In the case where there are ten panelists, an item would need a minimum *CVR* of .62. In our third example (the one in which nine of ten panelists agreed), the *CVR* of .80 is significant; the item could therefore be retained. We now turn our attention from an index of validity derived from looking at the test itself to an index of validity derived from an examination of how scores on the test are related to some criterion.

Criterion-Related Validity

Criterion-related validity is a judgment regarding how adequately a test score can be used to infer an individual's most probable standing on some measure of interest—the measure of interest being the criterion. Two types of validity evidence are subsumed under the heading "criterion-related validity." *Concurrent validity* refers to the form of criterion-related validity that is an index of the degree to which a test score is related to some criterion measure obtained at the same time (concurrently). *Predictive validity* refers to the form of criterion-related validity that is an index of the degree to which a test score predicts some criterion measure. Before we discuss each of these types of validity evidence in detail, it seems appropriate to raise (and answer) an important question.

Table 6–1
Minimum Values of the Content Validity Ratio to Ensure That Agreement Is Unlikely To Be Due to Chance

Number of Panelists	Minimum Value
5	.99
6	.99
7	.99
8	.75
9	.78
10	.62
11	.59
12	.56
13	.54
14	.51
15	.49
20	.42
25	.37
30	.33
35	.31
40	.29

Source: Lawshe (1975)

What Is a Criterion?

A *criterion* may be broadly defined as the standard against which a test or a test score is evaluated. Operationally, a criterion can be most anything: "pilot performance in flying a Boeing 767," "grade on examination in Advanced Hair-weaving," "number of days spent in psychiatric hospitalization." In short, there are no hard-and-fast rules for what constitutes a criterion; it can be a specific behavior or group of behaviors, a test score, an amount of time, a rating, a psychiatric diagnosis, a training cost, an index of absenteeism, an index of alcohol intoxication, and so on. But although a criterion can be almost anything, it ideally is reliable, relevant, valid, and uncontaminated.

Characteristics of a criterion   Like test scores, the criterion scores should be reliable. The reliability of the criterion and the reliability of the test each limit the magnitude of the validity coefficient according to the following theoretical relationship:

$$r_{xy} \leq \sqrt{(r_{xx})(r_{yy})}$$

Here, r_{xy} is the validity coefficient (the correlation between the test and the criterion), r_{xx} is the test reliability, and r_{yy} is the criterion reliability. The formula is read as follows: The validity coefficient is less than or equal to the square root of the test's reliability coefficient multiplied by the criterion's reliability coefficient.

An adequate criterion is also relevant. We would expect, for example, that a test purporting to tell us something about an individual's aptitude for a career in psychology had been validated using some sort of criterion involving data obtained from psychologists.

An adequate criterion measure must also be valid for the purpose for which it is being used. If one test (X) is being used as the criterion to validate a second test (Y), then evidence should exist that test X is valid. If the criterion used is a rating made by a judge or a panel, then evidence should exist that the rating is valid. If, for example, a test manual for a diagnostic test of personality reported that the test had been validated using a criterion of "diagnoses made by a blue ribbon panel of psychodiagnosticians," the test user might wish to probe further—either by reading on in the manual or by writing the test publisher—regarding variables such as (1) the specific definitions of diagnostic terms and categories, (2) the precise nature of the background, training, and experience of the "blue ribbon panel," and (3) the nature and extent of panel members' extra-test contact with the diagnosed subjects.

Ideally, a criterion is also uncontaminated. *Criterion contamination* is the term applied to a situation where the criterion measure itself has been based, at least in part, on predictor measures. Suppose that we just completed a study of how accurately a test called the MMPI predicted psychiatric diagnosis in the psychiatric population of the Minnesota state hospital system. In this study, the predictor is the MMPI, and the criterion is the psychiatric diagnosis that exists in the patient's record. Let's suppose further that, while we are in the process of analyzing our data, someone informs us that the diagnosis for every patient in the Minnesota state hospital system was determined, at least in part, by an MMPI test score. Should we still proceed with our analysis? The answer, of course, is no; since the predictor measure has "contaminated" the criterion measure, it would be of little value to find, in essence, that the predictor can indeed predict itself.

Concurrent Validity

If test scores are obtained at about the same time that the criterion measures are obtained, measures of the relationship between the test scores and the criterion provide evidence of *concurrent validity*. Statements of concurrent validity indicate the extent to which test scores may be used to estimate an individual's present standing on a criterion. If, for example, scores (or classifications) made on the basis of a psychodiagnostic test were to be validated against a criterion of already diagnosed psychiatric patients, the process would be one of concurrent validation. In general, once the validity of the inference from the test scores is established, the test may provide a faster, less expensive way to offer a diagnosis or a classification decision. A test with satisfactorily demonstrated concurrent validity may therefore be very appealing to prospective users, since it holds out the potential of savings of money and professional time; what administrator, for example, wouldn't prefer to use an inexpensive paper-and-pencil test if he or she could obtain the same results with this test as through the use of highly trained mental health personnel (who might more efficiently and valuably be spending their time doing other things, such as conducting research or therapy)?

Sometimes the concurrent validity of a particular test (we'll call it "Test A" for the purposes of this example) is explored with respect to how it compares with another test (one we'll call "Test B"). In such studies, prior research has satisfactorily demonstrated the validity of Test B, and the question of interest becomes "How well does Test A compare with Test B?" Here, Test B is used as what is referred to as the "validating criterion." In some studies, Test A is either a brand new test or a test being used for some new purpose, perhaps with a new population. In the example of a concurrent validity study that follows, a group of researchers explored whether a test that had been validated for use with adults could be used with adolescents.

The Beck Depression Inventory (BDI; Beck et al., 1979) is a 21-item, self-report measure that is widely used by clinicians and researchers as an aid to quantifying the severity of depressive symptoms. First introduced in 1961 and subsequently revised, the BDI has undergone extensive study of its validity in numerous investigations using adult subjects. But is the BDI valid for use with outpatient adolescents? And more specifically, can the BDI successfully differentiate depressed from nondepressed patients in a population of adolescent outpatients? These were the questions for which Ambrosini, Metz, Bianchi, Rabinovich, and Undie (1991) sought answers. Diagnoses generated from the concurrent administration of an instrument previously validated for use with adolescents (the Kiddie-Schedule for Affective Disorders and Schizophrenia) were used as the criterion validators. The findings suggested that the BDI is valid for use with adolescents.

We now turn our attention to another form of criterion validity, one in which the criterion measure is obtained not concurrently but at some future time.

Predictive Validity

Test scores may be obtained at one time and the criterion measures obtained at a future time—after some intervening event has taken place (such as training, experience, therapy, medication, or simply the passage of time). Measures of the relationship between the test scores and a criterion measure obtained at a future time provide an indication of the *predictive validity* of the test (that is, how accurately scores on the test predict to some criterion measure). Measures of the relationship between college admissions tests and freshman grade-point average, for example, provide evidence of the predictive validity of the admissions tests.

In settings where tests might be employed, such as a personnel agency, a college admissions office, or a warden's office, a test's high predictive validity can be a very useful aid to decision makers who must select successful students, productive workers, or convicts who are good parole risks. Whether a test result is valuable in making a decision depends on how well the test results improve selection decisions over those decisions made without knowledge of test results. In an industrial setting where volume turnout is important, if the use of a personnel selection test can have the effect of enhancing productivity to even a small degree, the enhanced productivity will pay off year after year and may translate into millions of dollars of increased revenue. And in a clinical context, no price could be placed on a test that has the effect of saving more lives from suicide or homicide if the test could provide predictive accuracy over and above existing tests with respect to such acts. Unfortunately, the difficulties inherent in developing such tests are numerous and multifaceted (see Mulvey & Lidz, 1984; Murphy, 1984; Petrie & Chamberlain, 1985).

Judgments of criterion-related validity, whether concurrent or predictive, are based on two types of statistical evidence: the validity coefficient and expectancy data.

The validity coefficient   The *validity coefficient* is a correlation coefficient that provides a measure of the relationship between test scores and scores on the criterion measure. The correlation coefficient computed from a score (or classification) on a psychodiagnostic test and the criterion score (or classification) assigned by psychodiagnosticians is one example of a validity coefficient. Typically, the Pearson correlation coefficient is used to determine the validity between the two measures. However, depending on variables such as the type of data, the sample size, and the shape of the distribution, other correlation coefficients could be used. For example, in examining self-rankings of performance on some job with rankings made by job supervisors, the formula for the Spearman *rho* rank-order correlation would be employed.

Like the reliability coefficient and other correlational measures, the validity coefficient is affected by restriction or inflation of range. And as in other correlational studies, a key issue is whether the range of scores employed is appropriate to the objective of the correlational analysis. In situations where, for example, attrition in the number of subjects has occurred over the course of the study, the validity coefficient may be adversely affected. To illustrate, suppose that a clinical psychologist working in the psychiatric emergency room of a municipal hospital has developed a new test called "The Very Brief Psychodiagnostic Classification Inventory" (VBPCI). The psychologist hypothesizes that a patient's score or classification on this (hypothetical) test will be predictive of the diagnosis on the patient's chart seven days from the day it was administered. Since the test takes only a minute or two to administer—it is indeed *very* brief—all people who present themselves at (or who are brought to) the psychiatric emergency room are administered the test as part of a validation study. The study runs for one month, at the end of which time a statistically significant validity coefficient describing the relationship between VBPCI score and the criterion diagnosis is computed. Should the psychologist immediately proceed to a test publisher's office, VBPCI in hand?

Not necessarily—at least not until the effects of attrition, if any, in the sample have been analyzed. The impressive VBPCI findings might well be an artifact of such attrition, and the findings might more accurately be interpreted as reflecting the fact that the VBPCI is an accurate predictor of psychiatric diagnosis for conditions in the middle range of psychopathology only; one may not be able to tell from the design of this study how well a predictor the VBPCI is at extreme ranges. Here's why: if the municipal hospital psychiatric emergency room the study was conducted in is typical of others, the least disordered patients will have been discharged after a day or two—and they therefore will be eliminated from the sample. Attrition of the sample can be expected to occur not only with respect to the least disordered patients but at the other extreme as well; many of the severely disordered patients will have been transferred to a state hospital before seven days from the time of their initial admission. Because the data for the remaining subjects represent only the middle range of the wide range of psychodiagnostic types that could be encountered in a psychiatric emergency room, the reported measure of the VBPCI's validity would likely be deflated.[3]

The problem of restricted range can occur through a self-selection process in the sample employed for the validation study. Thus, for example, if the test purports to measure something as technical and/or dangerous as "oil barge fire-fighting aptitude," it may well be that the only people who reply to an ad for the position of oil barge firefighter are people who actually are highly qualified for the position; hence, you would expect the range of the distribution of

---

3. A more detailed discussion of the influence on correlation coefficients of (1) restriction of range and (2) combining data from different groups can be found in Allen and Yen (1979, pp. 34–36).

scores on some test of "oil barge fire-fighting aptitude" to be restricted. For less technical or dangerous positions, a self-selection factor might be operative if the test developer selects a group of newly hired employees to test (with the expectation that criterion measures will be available for this group at some subsequent date). However, because the newly hired employees have probably already passed some formal or informal evaluation in the process of being hired, there is a good chance that ability to do the job among this group will be higher than ability to do the job among a random sample of ordinary job applicants. Consequently, scores on the criterion measure that is later administered will tend to be higher than scores on the criterion measure obtained from a random sample of ordinary job applicants; stated another way, the scores will be restricted in range.

Whereas it is the responsibility of the test developer to report validation data in the test manual, it is the responsibility of test users to carefully read the description of the validation study and evaluate the suitability of the test for their specific purposes. What were the characteristics of the sample used in the validation study? How matched are those characteristics to the people for whom an administration of the test is being contemplated? Are some subtests of a test more appropriate for a specific test purpose than the entire test is?

How high should a validity coefficient be for a user or a test developer to infer that the test is valid? There are no rules for determining the minimum acceptable size of a validity coefficient. In fact, Cronbach and Gleser (1965) cautioned against the establishment of such rules. They argued that validity coefficients need to be large enough to enable the test user to make accurate decisions within the unique context in which a test is being used. Essentially, the validity coefficient should be high enough to result in the identification and differentiation of testtakers with respect to target attribute(s), such as employees who are likely to be more productive, police officers who are less likely to misuse their weapons, and students who are more likely to be successful in a particular course of study.

Incremental validity   Test users involved in predicting some criterion from test scores are often interested in the utility of multiple predictors. The value of including more than one predictor depends upon a couple of factors. First, of course, each measure being used as a predictor should have criterion-related predictive validity. Second, additional predictors should possess *incremental validity,* defined as the degree to which an additional predictor explains something about the criterion measure not explained by predictors already in use.

Incremental validity may be used when predicting something like academic success in college. Grade-point average (GPA) at the end of the first year may be used as a measure of academic success. A study of potential predictors of GPA may reveal that time spent in the library and time spent studying are highly correlated with GPA, and how much sleep one's roommate allows one to have during exam periods correlates with GPA to a smaller extent. What is the most accurate but most efficient way to predict GPA? One approach, employing the principles of incremental validity, is to start with the best predictor, the predictor that is most highly correlated with GPA. This may be time spent studying. Then, using multiple regression techniques, one would examine the usefulness of the other predictors. Even though time in the library is highly correlated with GPA, it may not possess incremental validity if it overlaps too much with the first predictor, time spent studying. Said another way, if time spent studying and time in the library are so highly correlated with each other that they reflect essentially the same thing, then only one of them needs to be included as a predictor: including both will provide little new information over one alone. In contrast, one may find that the amount of sleep one's roommate permits one to have during exams has good incremental validity because it reflects a different aspect of preparing for exams (resting) from the first predictor (studying). Incremental validity has been used to improve the prediction of job performance for Marine Corps mechanics (Carey, 1994) and the prediction of child abuse (Murphy-Berman, 1994). In both instances, predictor measures were included only if they demonstrated that they could explain something about the criterion measure that was not already known from the other predictors.

Expectancy data Expectancy data provide a source of information that can be used in evaluating the criterion-related validity of a test. Using a score obtained on some test(s) or measure(s), expectancy tables illustrate the likelihood that the testtaker will score within some interval of scores on a criterion measure—an interval that may be seen as "passing," "acceptable," and so on. An expectancy table shows the percentage of people within specified test-score intervals who subsequently were placed in various categories of the criterion (for example, placed in "passed" category or "failed" category). An expectancy table may be created from a scatterplot according to the steps listed in Figure 6–1. An expectancy table showing the relationship between scores on a subtest of the Differential Aptitude Test (DAT) and course grades in American history for eleventh-grade boys is presented in Table 6–2. You can see that of the students who scored between 40 and 60, 83% scored 80 or above in their American history course.

To illustrate how an expectancy table might be used by a corporate personnel office, suppose that on the basis of various test scores and personal interviews, personnel experts rated all applicants for a manual-labor position that entailed piecework as "excellent," "very good," "average," "below average," and "poor." In this example, then, the "test score" is actually a rating made by personnel experts on the basis of a number of test scores and a personal interview. Let's further suppose that because of a severe labor scarcity at the time, all the applicants were hired (a dream-come-true for a researcher interested in conducting a validation study with respect to the validity of the assessment procedure). Floor supervisors who were blind with respect to the composite score obtained by the newly hired workers provided the criterion measure in this validation study; specifically, they provided ratings of each employee's performance—"satisfactory" or "unsatisfactory." Figure 6–2 is the resulting *expectancy chart* (or graphic representation of an expectancy table). It can be seen that of all applicants originally rated "excellent," 94% were rated "satisfactory" on

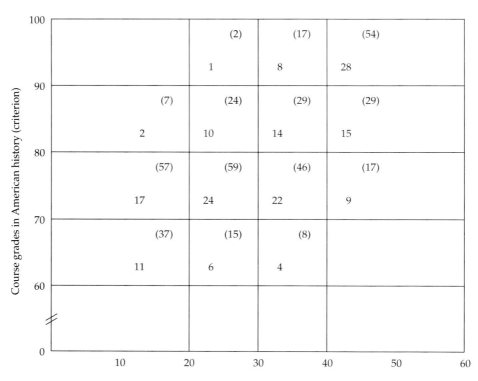

Language usage raw scores from the Differential Aptitude Tests
( ) percentage of points per cell

Figure 6–1
Seven Steps to an Expectancy Table

1. *Draw a scatterplot such that each point in the plot represents a particular test score–criterion score combination. The criterion should be on the Y-axis.*

2. *Draw grid lines in such a way as to summarize the number of people who scored within a particular interval.*

3. *Count the number of points in each cell (n_i) as shown in the figure.*

4. *Count the total number of points within each vertical interval (N_v). This number represents the number of people scoring within a particular test score interval.*

5. *Convert each cell frequency to a percentage (n_i / N_v). This represents the percentage of people obtaining a particular test score–criterion score combination. Write the percentages in the cells. Enclose the percentages in parentheses to distinguish them from the frequencies.*

6. *On a separate sheet, create table headings and subheadings and copy the percentages into the appropriate cell tables as shown in Table 6–2. Be careful to put the percentages in the correct cell tables. (Note that it's easy to make a mistake at this stage because the percentages of people within particular score intervals are written horizontally in the table and vertically in the scatterplot.)*

7. *If desired, write the number and percentage of cases per test-score interval. If the number of cases in any one cell is very small, it is more likely to fluctuate in subsequent charts. If cell sizes are small, the user could create fewer cells or accumulate data over several years.*

Table 6-2

DAT Language Usage Subtest Scores and American History Grade for 171 Eleventh-Grade Boys (Showing Percentage of Students Obtaining Course Grades in the Interval Shown)

Test Score	Course grade interval				Cases per test-score interval	
	0–69	70–79	80–89	90–100	N_v	%
40 and above		17	29	54	52	100
30–39	8	46	29	17	48	100
20–29	15	59	24	2	41	100
below 20	37	57	7		30	101*

*Total sums to more than 100% because of rounding.

the job. By contrast, among applicants originally rated "poor," only 17% were rated "satisfactory" on the job. In general, this expectancy chart tells us that the higher the initial rating, the greater the probability of job success. Stated another way, it tells us that the lower the initial rating, the greater the probability of job failure. The company experimenting with such a rating system could reasonably expect to improve its productivity by using this rating system. Specifically, job applicants who obtained ratings of "average" or higher would be the only applicants hired.

Tables that could be used as an aid for personnel directors in their decision-making chores were published by H. C. Taylor and J. T. Russell in the *Journal of Applied Psychology* in 1939. Referred to by the names of their authors, the Taylor-Russell tables provide an estimate of the extent to which inclusion of a particular test in the selection system will actually improve selection. More specifically, the tables provide an estimate of the percentage of employees hired by the use

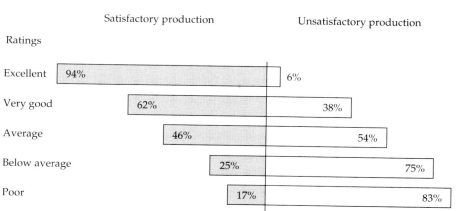

Figure 6-2
Test Ratings and Job Performance
(Source: The Psychological Corporation)

of a particular test who will be successful at their jobs, given different combinations of three variables: the test's validity, the selection ratio used, and the base rate, or the proportion of people currently employed in positions similar to the vacant position who are considered successful. The value assigned for the test's validity is the computed validity coefficient. The selection ratio is a numerical value that reflects the relationship between the number of people to be hired and the number of people available to be hired. For instance, if there are 50 positions and 100 applicants, the selection ratio is 50/100, or .50. The base rate is an indication of the personnel office's current "batting average" using whatever techniques it is currently using. If, for example, a firm employs 25 computer programmers and 20 are considered successful, the base rate would be .80. With knowledge of the validity coefficient of a particular test along with the selection ratio, reference to the Taylor-Russell tables would provide the personnel officer with an estimate of how much using the test would improve selection over existing methods.

A Taylor-Russell table is presented in Table 6–3. This table is for the base rate of .60, meaning that 60% of those hired under the existing system are suc-

Table 6–3
Taylor-Russell Table for a Base Rate of .60

Validity (ρ_{xy})	Selection ratio										
	.05	.10	.20	.30	.40	.50	.60	.70	.80	.90	.95
.00	.60	.60	.60	.60	.60	.60	.60	.60	.60	.60	.60
.05	.64	.63	.63	.62	.62	.62	.61	.61	.61	.60	.60
.10	.68	.67	.65	.64	.64	.63	.63	.62	.61	.61	.60
.15	.71	.70	.68	.67	.66	.65	.64	.63	.62	.61	.61
.20	.75	.73	.71	.69	.67	.66	.65	.64	.63	.62	.61
.25	.78	.76	.73	.71	.69	.68	.66	.65	.63	.62	.61
.30	.82	.79	.76	.73	.71	.69	.68	.66	.64	.62	.61
.35	.85	.82	.78	.75	.73	.71	.69	.67	.65	.63	.62
.40	.88	.85	.81	.78	.75	.73	.70	.68	.66	.63	.62
.45	.90	.87	.83	.80	.77	.74	.72	.69	.66	.64	.62
.50	.93	.90	.86	.82	.79	.76	.73	.70	.67	.64	.62
.55	.95	.92	.88	.84	.81	.78	.75	.71	.68	.64	.62
.60	.96	.94	.90	.87	.83	.80	.76	.73	.69	.65	.63
.65	.98	.96	.92	.89	.85	.82	.78	.74	.70	.65	.63
.70	.99	.97	.94	.91	.87	.84	.80	.75	.71	.66	.63
.75	.99	.99	.96	.93	.90	.86	.81	.77	.71	.66	.63
.80	1.00	.99	.98	.95	.92	.88	.83	.78	.72	.66	.63
.85	1.00	1.00	.99	.97	.95	.91	.86	.80	.73	.66	.63
.90	1.00	1.00	1.00	.99	.97	.94	.88	.82	.74	.67	.63
.95	1.00	1.00	1.00	1.00	.99	.97	.92	.84	.75	.67	.63
1.00	1.00	1.00	1.00	1.00	1.00	1.00	1.00	.86	.75	.67	.63

Source: Taylor and Russell (1939)

cessful in their work. Down the left-hand side are validity coefficients for a test that could be used to help select employees. Across the top are the various selection ratios. They reflect the proportion of the people applying for the jobs who will be hired. If a new test is introduced to help select employees in a situation with a selection ratio of .20, and if the new test has a predictive validity coefficient of .55, the table shows the base rate will increase to .88. This means that, rather than 60% of the hired employees being expected to perform successfully, a full 88% can be expected to do so. When selection ratios are low, as when only 5% of the applicants will be hired, even tests with low validity coefficients, such as .15, can result in improved base rates.

One limitation inherent in the use of the Taylor-Russell tables is that the relationship between the predictor (the test) and the criterion (rating of performance on the job) must be linear. If, for example, there is some point at which job performance levels off, no matter how high the score on the test gets, use of the Taylor-Russell tables would be inappropriate. Another limitation inherent in the use of the Taylor-Russell tables is the potential problem of having to identify a criterion score that separates "successful" from "unsuccessful" employees. This problem was avoided in an alternative set of tables (Naylor & Shine, 1965) that provide an indication of the difference in average criterion scores for the selected as compared with the original group. Use of the Naylor-Shine tables entails obtaining the difference between the means of the selected and unselected groups to obtain an index of what the test (or some other tool of assessment) is adding to already established procedures. Both the Taylor-Russell and the Naylor-Shine tables can assist in judging the utility of a particular test, the former by determining the increase over current procedures and the latter by determining the increase in average score on some criterion measure. With both tables, the validity coefficient used must be one obtained by concurrent validation procedures—a fact that should not be surprising, since it is obtained with respect to current employees hired by the selection process in effect at the time of the study.

If hiring decisions were made solely on the basis of variables such as the validity of an employment test and the prevailing selection ratio, then tables such as those offered by Taylor and Russell and Naylor and Shine would be in wide use today. The fact is that many other kinds of variables might well enter into hiring decisions (for example, minority status, general physical and/or mental health of applicant, or drug use by applicant). Given that many variables may enter into a hiring—or some other—decision, of what use is a given test in the decision process? After publication of the Taylor-Russell tables, a number of articles probing ways to determine how appropriate the use of a given test is with respect to different types of assessment procedures began to appear (Brogden, 1946, 1949; Smith, 1948), and a literature dealing with "test utility theory" began to grow. Also during this period, statisticians such as Wald (1947, 1950) were involved in identifying statistical rules for developing a sequential analysis of a problem that would lead to an optimal decision; "decision theory" had been born, and it would be applied to answering questions about the utility of psychological tests.

Decision theory and test utility Perhaps the most oft-cited application of statistical decision theory to the field of psychological testing is Cronbach and Gleser's *Psychological Tests and Personnel Decisions,* though other work in this area (not so comprehensive as Cronbach and Gleser's) was published subsequently (for example, Darlington & Stauffer, 1966; Dunnette, 1963; Mahoney & England, 1965; Rorer et al., 1966). The idea of applying statistical decision theory to questions of test utility was conceptually appealing and promising, and an authoritative textbook of the day reflects the great enthusiasm with which this marriage of enterprises was greeted:

> The basic decision-theory approach to selection and placement . . . has a number of advantages over the more classical approach based upon the correlation model. . . . There is no question but that it is a more general and better model for handling this kind of decision task, and we predict that in the future problems of selection and placement will be treated in this context more frequently—perhaps to eventual exclusion of the more stereotyped correlational model. (Blum & Naylor, 1968, p. 58)

Stated generally, Cronbach and Gleser (1965) presented (1) a classification of decision problems (for an example of their work in this area, see the box on the opposite page), (2) various selection strategies ranging from single-stage processes to sequential analyses, (3) a quantitative analysis of the relationship between test utility, the selection ratio, cost of the testing program, and expected value of the outcome, and (4) a recommendation that in some instances job requirements be tailored to the applicant's ability instead of the other way around (a concept they refer to as "adaptive treatment").

Before we illustrate decision theory in action, let us briefly—and somewhat loosely—define five terms frequently encountered in discussions of decision theory as applied to psychological testing and measurement: base rate, hit rate, miss rate, false positive, and false negative.

A *base rate* may be defined as the extent to which a particular characteristic or attribute exists in the population (expressed as a proportion). A *hit rate* may be defined as the proportion of people a test accurately identifies as possessing a particular characteristic or attribute (for example, the proportion of people accurately predicted to be able to perform graduate-school-level work or the number of patients accurately diagnosed as having a brain tumor). A *miss rate* may be defined as the proportion of people the test fails to identify as having— or not having—a particular characteristic or attribute; a *miss* amounts to an inaccurate prediction. The category of "misses" may be further subdivided. A *false positive* is a miss wherein the test predicted that the testtaker did possess the particular characteristic or attribute being measured. A *false negative* is a miss wherein the test predicted that the testtaker did not possess the particular characteristic or attribute being measured.

Suppose you developed a measurement procedure you called the "Vapor Test" (VT), which was designed to determine if alive-and-well subjects are indeed breathing. The procedure for the VT entails having the examiner hold a mirror under the subject's nose and mouth for a minute or so and observing if

Addressing a Personnel Decision Problem

If you had a personnel decision problem, you might begin by asking yourself the following questions. Your answer to each of these six pairs of questions will result in the identification of the specific type of personnel decision problem with which you are dealing—one of 64 (or 2 to the sixth power) possible types of personnel decision problems identified by the authors of these questions, Cronbach and Gleser (1965):

1. (a) Are the benefits obtained from a decision evaluated in the same way for each person? (or)
   (b) Are different values used in deciding about each person?
2. (a) Is the decision about each person made independently? (or)
   (b) Are decisions about various persons interrelated?

3. (a) Is each individual assigned to just one of the available treatments [jobs]? (or)
   (b) May each individual be assigned to multiple treatments?
4. (a) Is one of the allowable treatments "reject" [that is, is this a selection situation]? (or)
   (b) Are all persons retained in the institution [a placement decision]?
5. (a) Is the information used in univariate form? (or)
   (b) Is it in multivariate form?
6. (a) Are decisions final? (or)
   (b) May one decide to obtain further information prior to final decisions?

---

the subject's breath fogs the mirror. Let's say that 100 introductory psychology students are administered the VT and it is concluded that 89 were, in fact, breathing (while 11 are deemed, on the basis of the VT, not to be breathing). Is the VT a good test? Obviously not. Since the base rate is 100% of the (alive and well) population, we really don't even need a test to measure the characteristic "breathing"—and if for some reason we did need a measurement procedure, we probably wouldn't use one that was inaccurate in approximately 11% of the cases. A test is obviously of no value if the hit rate is higher *without* using it; one measure of the value of a test lies in the extent to which its use improves on the hit rate that exists without its use.

As a simple illustration of decision theory applied to testing, suppose a test is administered to a group of 100 job applicants and some cutoff score is applied to distinguish applicants who will be hired (applicants judged to have "passed" the test) from applicants whose employment application will be rejected (applicants judged to have "failed" the test). And let's further suppose that some criterion measure will be applied some time later to ascertain whether the newly hired person worked out—whether the newly hired person was considered a success or a failure at the job. In such a situation, if the test is a perfect predictor (if its validity coefficient is equal to 1), two distinct types of outcomes can be identified: (1) some applicants will score at or above the cutoff score on the test and be successful at the job, and (2) some applicants will score below the cutoff score and would not have been successful at the job. But since few, if any, employment tests are perfect predictors, two other types of outcomes are also possible: (3) some applicants will score at or above the cutoff score, be hired, and fail at the job (the criterion), and (4) some applicants who scored below the cutoff score and were not hired could have been successful at the job. People who fall into group 3 could be categorized as "false positives," and those who fall into group 4 could be categorized as "false negatives."

We don't need to resort to any formulas or tables—logic alone tells us that if the selection ratio is, say, 90% (nine out of ten applicants will be hired), the cutting score will probably be set lower than if the selection ratio if 5% (only five of the 100 applicants will be hired). Further, if the selection ratio is 90%, it is a good bet that the number of "false positives" (people hired who will fail on the criterion measure) will be greater than in a case where the selection ratio is 5%. Conversely, if the selection ratio is only 5%, it is a good bet that the number of "false negatives" (people not hired who could have succeeded on the criterion measure) will be greater than in a case where the selection ratio is 90%. Decision theory provides guidelines for setting optimal cutting scores. In setting such scores, the relative seriousness of making false-positive or false-negative selection decisions is frequently taken into account. Thus, for example, it is a prudent policy for an airline personnel office to set cutoff scores on tests for pilots that might result in a false negative (a pilot who is truly qualified being rejected) as opposed to a cutoff score that would allow a false positive (the hiring of a pilot who is, in reality, unqualified).

In the hands of highly skilled researchers, principles of decision theory applied to problems of test utility have led to some enlightening and impressive findings. For example, Schmidt, Hunter, McKenzie, and Muldrow (1979) demonstrated in dollars and cents how the utility of a company's selection program (and the validity coefficient of the tests used in that program) can play a critical role in the profitability of the company. Focusing on one employer's population of computer programmers, these researchers asked supervisors to rate, in dollars, the value of "good," "average," and "poor" programmers. This information was used in conjunction with other information, including these facts: (1) each year the employer hired 600 new programmers, (2) the average programmer remained on the job for about ten years, (3) the Programmer Aptitude Test currently in use as part of the hiring process had a validity coefficient of .76, (4) it cost about $10 per applicant to administer the test, and (5) the employer currently had in excess of 4,000 programmers in its employ.

Schmidt et al. (1979) made a number of calculations using different values for some of the variables. For example, knowing that some of the tests previously used in the hiring process had validity coefficients ranging from .00 to .50, they varied the value of the test's validity coefficient (along with other factors such as different selection ratios that had been in effect) and examined the relative efficiency of the various conditions. Among their findings was the fact that the existing selection ratio and selection process provided a great gain in efficiency over a previous situation (when the selection ratio was 5% and the validity coefficient of the test used in hiring was equal to .50)—a gain equal to almost $6 million per year. Multiplied over, say, ten years, that's $60 million. The existing selection ratio and selection process provided an even greater gain in efficiency over a previously existing situation in which the test had no validity at all and the selection ratio was .80; here, in one year, the gain in efficiency was estimated to be equal to over $97 million.

By the way, the employer in the study above was the United States government. Hunter and Schmidt (1981) applied the same type of analysis to the national workforce and made a compelling argument with respect to the critical relationship between valid tests and measurement procedures and our national productivity. In a subsequent study, Schmidt, Hunter, and their colleagues found that substantial increases in work output or reductions in payroll costs would result from using valid measures of cognitive ability as opposed to nontest procedures (Schmidt et al., 1986).

Employers are reluctant to use decision theory–based strategies in their hiring practices because of the complexity of their application and the threat of legal challenges (Algera et al., 1984; Dunnette & Borman, 1979; Guion, 1967; Wiggins, 1973). Thus, although decision theory approaches to assessment hold great promise, their promise has yet to be fulfilled.

Construct Validity

Construct validity refers to a judgment about the appropriateness of inferences drawn from test scores regarding individual standings on a variable called a construct. A *construct* is an informed, scientific idea developed or "constructed" to describe or explain behavior. "Intelligence" is a construct that may be invoked to describe why a student performs well in school. "Anxiety" is a construct that may be invoked to describe why a psychiatric patient paces the floor. Other examples of constructs are "job satisfaction," "personality," "bigotry," "clerical aptitude," "depression," "motivation," "self-esteem," "emotional adjustment," "potential dangerousness," "creativity," and "mechanical comprehension." Constructs are unobservable, presupposed (underlying) traits that a test developer may invoke to describe test behavior or criterion performance. The researcher investigating a test's construct validity must formulate hypotheses about the expected behavior of high scorers and low scorers on the test. From these hypotheses arises a tentative theory about the nature of the construct the test was designed to measure. If the test is a valid measure of the construct, the high scorers and the low scorers will behave as predicted by the theory. If high scorers and low scorers on the test do not behave as predicted, the investigator will need to reexamine hypotheses made about the construct (and/or reexamine the nature of the construct itself). One possible reason for obtaining results contrary to those that would have been predicted by the theory is that the test simply is not a valid measure of the construct. An alternative explanation could lie in the theory that generated hypotheses about the construct—perhaps that theory needs to be reexamined. Perhaps the reason for the contrary finding can be traced to the incorrect inclusion in the experimental design of a particular statistical procedure or the incorrect execution of the procedure. Thus, although confirming evidence contributes to a judgment that the test is indeed a valid measure of some construct, contrary evidence—on the bright side—provides a stimulus for the discovery of new facets of the construct and/or alternative ways to measure it.

Increasingly, construct validity has been viewed as the unifying concept for all validity evidence; all types of validity evidence, including the content and criterion-related varieties, are forms of construct validity. A group of validity coefficients for a given test when considered individually can be interpreted with respect to the test's criterion-related validity; collectively, however, these coefficients have bearing on the construct validity of the test (Guion, 1980).

Evidence of Construct Validity

A number of procedures may be used to provide different kinds of evidence that a test has construct validity. The various techniques of construct validation may provide evidence, for example, that

- The test is homogeneous, measuring a single construct.

- Test scores correlate with scores on other tests in accordance with what would be predicted from a theory that covers the manifestation of the construct in question.

- Test scores increase or decrease as a function of age or the passage of time as theoretically predicted.

- Test scores obtained subsequent to some event or to the mere passage of time (that is, posttest scores) differ from pretest scores as theoretically predicted.

- Test scores obtained by people from distinct groups vary as predicted by theory.

A brief discussion of each type of construct validity evidence and the procedures used to obtain it follows.

Evidence of homogeneity *Homogeneity,* also called *internal consistency,* generally refers to how well a test measures a single concept. A test developer can increase the homogeneity of an instrument in several ways. Consider, for example, a test of academic achievement that contains subtests in areas such as mathematics, spelling, and reading comprehension. The Pearson *r* could be used to correlate average subtest scores with average total test score. Subtests that in the test developer's judgment do not correlate very well with the test as a whole might have to be reconstructed (or eliminated) lest the test not measure the construct "academic achievement." Correlations between subtest scores and total test score are generally reported in the test manual as evidence of homogeneity.

One way a test developer can improve the homogeneity of a test containing items that are scored dichotomously (for example, "right" or "wrong") is by eliminating those items that do not show significant correlation coefficients with total test scores. If all test items show significant, positive correlations with total test scores, and high scorers on the test tend to pass each item more than low scorers, then each item is probably measuring the same construct as the total test, thereby contributing to test homogeneity.

The homogeneity of a test in which items are scored on a multipoint scale can also be improved. For example, some attitude and opinion questionnaires require respondents to indicate level of agreement with specific statements by responding, for example, "Strongly agree," "Agree," "Disagree," or "Strongly disagree." Each response is then assigned a numerical score, and items that do not show significant Spearman rank-order correlation coefficients are eliminated. If all test items show significant, positive correlations with total test scores, then each item is most likely measuring the same construct that the test as a whole is measuring (and thereby contributing to the test's homogeneity). Coefficient alpha may also be used in estimating the homogeneity of a test composed of multiple-choice items (Novick & Lewis, 1967).

As a case study illustrating how a test's homogeneity can be improved, consider the Marital Satisfaction Scale (MSS; Roach et al., 1981). Designed to assess various aspects of married people's attitudes toward their marital relationship, the MSS contains an approximately equal number of items expressing positive and negative sentiments with respect to marriage (for example, "My life would seem empty without my marriage" and "My marriage has 'smothered' my personality"). In one stage of the development of this test, subjects indicated how much they agreed or disagreed with the various sentiments in each of 73 items by marking a five-point scale that ranged from "Strongly agree" to "Strongly disagree." Based on the correlations between item scores and total score, the test developers elected to retain 48 items with correlation coefficients greater than .50, thus creating a more homogeneous instrument.

In addition to correlational measures of test homogeneity, let us also mention an item-analysis procedure that entails focusing on the relationship between testtakers' scores on individual items and their score on the entire test. Each item is examined with respect to how high scorers as opposed to low scorers on the test responded to it. If it is an academic test and high scorers on the entire test for some reason tended to get that particular item wrong and low scorers on the test as a whole tended to get the item right, the item is obviously not a good one. In fact, such an item should be eliminated in the interest of test homogeneity, among other considerations. If the test is one of, say, marital satisfaction and individuals who score high on the test as a whole respond to a particular item in a way that would indicate that they are not satisfied, whereas people who tend not to be satisfied respond to the item in a way that would indicate that they are satisfied, then again the item should probably be eliminated or at least reexamined for its clarity.

Although test homogeneity is desirable because it assures us that all the items on the test tend to be measuring the same thing, it is not the "be-all and end-all" with respect to construct validity. Knowing that a test is homogeneous contributes no information about how the construct being measured relates to other constructs. It is therefore important that evidence of a test's homogeneity be reported along with other evidence of construct validity.

Evidence of changes with age   The nature of some constructs is such that changes in them would be expected to occur over time. "Reading ability," for example, tends to increase dramatically year by year from age 6 to the early teens. If a test score purports to be a measure of a construct that could be expected to change over time, it too should show the same progressive changes with age if the test score is to be considered a valid measure of the construct. We would expect, for example, that if children in grades 6, 7, 8, and 9 sat for a test of eighth-grade reading skills, the total number of items scored as correct from all the test protocols would increase as a function of the higher grade level of the testtakers.

Some constructs lend themselves more readily to predictions concerning changes over time than other constructs do. Thus, although we may be able to predict, for example, that a gifted child's scores on a test of reading skills will increase over the course of the testtaker's years of elementary and secondary education, we may not be able to predict with such confidence how a newlywed couple will score through the years on a test of marital satisfaction. This fact does not relegate a construct such as "marital satisfaction" to any less stature than "reading ability"; rather, it simply means that measures of "marital satisfaction" may be less stable over time and/or more vulnerable to situational events (such as in-laws coming to visit and refusing to leave for three months) than is "reading ability" in specific instances. It must also be kept in mind that evidence of change over time, like evidence of test homogeneity, does not in itself provide information about how the construct relates to other constructs.

Evidence of pretest/posttest changes   Evidence showing that test scores change as a result of some experience between a pretest and a posttest can be evidence of construct validity. Some of the more typical intervening experiences responsible for changes in test scores are formal education, a course of therapy or medication, and on-the-job experience. Of course, depending on the construct being measured, almost any intervening life experience could be predicted to yield changes in score from pretest to posttest. Reading an inspirational book, watching a TV talk show, undergoing surgery, serving a prison sentence, or the mere passage of time may each prove to be a potent intervening variable.

Returning to our example regarding the use of the Marital Satisfaction Scale, one investigator cited in Roach et al. (1981) compared scores on that instrument before and after a sex therapy treatment program. Scores showed a significant change between pretest and posttest. A second posttest given eight weeks later showed that scores remained stable (suggesting the instrument was reliable) while the pretest/posttest measures were still significantly different. Such changes in scores in the predicted direction after the treatment program contribute to evidence of the construct validity for this test. Conversely, we would expect a decline in marital satisfaction scores if a pretest were administered to a sample of couples shortly after they took their nuptial vows and a posttest was administered shortly after members of the couples first consulted their respective divorce attorneys (employing for the purposes of the experimental group in this study only couples who consulted divorce attorneys). The design of such pretest/posttest research should ideally include a control group as a way of ruling out alternative explanations of the findings. Thus, with reference to the two examples above, simultaneous testing of a matched group of couples who did not undergo sex therapy and simultaneous testing of a matched group of couples who did not consult divorce attorneys would be advisable. In both instances, there would presumably be no reason to expect any significant changes in the test scores of these two control groups.

Evidence from distinct groups   Also referred to as the method of contrasted groups, one way of providing evidence for the validity of a test is to demonstrate that scores on the test vary in a predictable way as a function of membership in some group. The rationale here is that if a test is a valid measure of a particular construct, then test scores from groups of people who would be presumed to differ with respect to that construct should have correspondingly different test scores. It would be reasonable to expect that on a test designed to measure depression (wherein the higher the test score, the more depressed the testtaker is presumed to be), individuals psychiatrically hospitalized for depression should score higher than a random sample of fans at the local baseball stadium. Suppose it was your intention to provide construct validity evidence for the Marital Satisfaction Scale by means of showing differences in scores between distinct groups; how might you go about doing that?

Roach et al. (1981) proceeded by identifying two groups of married couples, one relatively satisfied in their marriage, the other not so satisfied. The groups were identified by means of ratings by peers and by professional marriage counselors. A t-test on the difference between mean score on the test was significant ($p < .01$)—evidence to support the notion that the Marital Satisfaction Scale is indeed a valid measure of the construct "marital satisfaction."

In a bygone era, the tool many test developers used to create distinct groups was deception. For example, if it had been predicted that more of the construct would be exhibited on the test in question if the subject was made to feel highly anxious, an experimental situation might be designed to make the subject feel highly anxious. Virtually any feeling state (such as low self-esteem or impotence) the theory called for could be induced by an experimental scenario that typically involved giving the research subject some misinformation. However, given the ethical constraints of contemporary psychologists combined with the fact that academic institutions and other sponsors of research tend not to condone deception in human research, the method of obtaining distinct groups by creating them through the dissemination of deceptive information is seldom employed.

Convergent evidence   Evidence for the construct validity of a particular test may "converge" from a number of sources, such as other tests or measures designed to assess the same (or a similar) construct. Thus, if scores on the test undergoing construct validation tend to correlate highly in the predicted direction with scores on older, more established, and already validated tests designed to measure the same (or a similar) construct, this would be an example of convergent evidence.[4]

Convergent evidence for validity may come not only from correlations with tests purporting to measure an identical construct but also from correlations with measures purporting to measure related constructs. Consider, for example, a new test designed to measure the construct "test anxiety." Generally speaking, we might expect high positive correlations between this new test and older, more established measures of test anxiety. However, we might also expect more moderate correlations between this new test and measures of general anxiety.

Roach et al. (1981) provided convergent evidence of the construct validity of the Marital Satisfaction Scale by computing a validity coefficient between scores on it and scores on the Marital Adjustment Test (Locke & Wallace, 1959). The validity coefficient of .79 provided additional evidence of the construct validity of the instrument.

Discriminant evidence   A validity coefficient showing little (that is, a statistically insignificant) relationship between test scores and/or other variables with which scores on the test being construct-validated should *not* theoretically be correlated provides *discriminant evidence* of construct validity (also referred to as *discriminant validity*). In the course of developing the Marital Satisfaction Scale (MSS), its authors correlated scores on that instrument with scores on the Marlowe-Crowne Social Desirability Scale (Crowne & Marlowe, 1964). Roach et al. (1981) hypothesized that high correlations between these two instruments would suggest that respondents were probably not answering entirely honestly to items on the MSS but were instead responding in socially desirable ways. But the correlation between the MSS and the social desirability measure did not prove to be significant, and the test developers concluded that social desirability could be ruled out as a primary factor in explaining the meaning of MSS test scores.

In 1959, an experimental technique useful for examining both convergent and discriminant validity evidence was presented in the pages of *Psychological Bulletin*. This rather technical technique, called the multitrait-multimethod matrix, is presented in Cohen (1996), the companion study guide to this text. Here, let's simply point out that "multitrait" means "two or more traits" and "multimethod" means "two or more methods." The multitrait-multimethod matrix (Campbell & Fiske, 1959) is the matrix or table that results from correlating variables (traits) within and between methods. Values for any number of traits (such as aggressiveness or extraversion) as obtained by various methods (such as behavioral observation or a projective test) are inserted into the table, and the

---

4. Data indicating that a test measures the same construct as other tests purporting to measure the same construct are also referred to as *convergent validity*. One question that may be raised at this juncture concerns the necessity for the new test if it simply duplicates existing tests that measure the same construct. The answer, generally speaking, is a claim that the new test has some advantage over the more established test. For example, the new test may be shorter and capable of administration in less time without significant loss in reliability or validity.

resulting matrix of correlations provides insight with respect to both the convergent and the discriminant validity of the methods used.[5]

Factor analysis Both convergent and discriminant evidence of construct validity can be obtained by the use of *factor analysis*. "Factor analysis" is a term used to describe a class of mathematical procedures designed to identify *factors* or—in the case of psychological test data—to identify the specific variables that are presumed to influence or explain test performance. It is, in essence, a data reduction method in which several sets of scores and the correlations between them are mathematically considered; its purpose is to identify the factor or factors that are presumed to cause the test scores to correlate.

A new test purporting to measure bulimia, for example, can be factor-analyzed with other known measures of bulimia, as well as with other kinds of measures (such as measures of intelligence, self-esteem, general anxiety, anorexia, or perfectionism). High factor loadings by the new test on a "bulimia factor" would provide convergent evidence of construct validity. Moderate to low factor loadings by the new test with respect to measures of other eating disorders such as anorexia would provide discriminant evidence of construct validity. A *factor loading* has been explained by Tyler (1965, p. 44) as "a sort of metaphor. Each test is thought of as a vehicle carrying a certain amount of one or more of the abilities. Another way of explaining it is that the loading of a certain factor in a certain test shows us the extent to which this factor determines the scores individuals make on the test."

Factor-analytic procedures may involve technical procedures so complex that few contemporary researchers would attempt to routinely conduct one without the aid of a prepackaged computer program. But although the actual data analysis has become work for computers, humans still tend to be very much involved in the *naming* of factors once the computer has identified them. Thus, for example, if a factor analysis identified a common factor being measured by two hypothetical instruments, a "Bulimia Test" and an "Anorexia Test," a question concerning what to name this factor would arise. One factor analyst looking at the data and the items of each test might christen the common factor an "Eating Disorder Factor." Another factor analyst examining exactly the same materials might label the common factor a "Body Weight Preoccupation Factor." A third analyst might name the factor a "Self-Perception Disorder Factor," and so forth. The point here is that the naming of factors that emerge from a factor analysis tends not to be a matter of mathematical skill; it has more to do with variables such as knowledge, judgment, and verbal, abstraction ability.[6]

---

5. For an interesting, "real-life" application of the multitrait-multimethod technique, see Meier's (1984) examination of the validity of the construct "burnout." In a subsequent construct validity study, Meier (1991) used an alternative to the multitrait-multimethod matrix to examine another construct: "occupational stress."

6. No specific rules for labeling factors exist; factor analysts can be expected only to make their best judgment concerning what name accurately communicates the meaning of the factor.

Factor analysis is a widely used tool, and many references to it can be found in the current scholarly literature. Recently, for example, Sodowsky et al. (1994) used factor analysis to help understand the dimensions underlying a new measure of skill in multicultural counseling. Eisen et al. (1994) factor-analyzed questions on an interview for psychiatric hospital admissions. Stone et al. (1994) examined the factors underlying a measure of benefits from group psychotherapy. Hackett et al. (1994) factor-analyzed a measure of worker commitment to an organization. McGuire (1994) used factor-analytic methods to explore the dimensions underlying helping behavior. Church and Burke (1994) used factor analysis to explore questions related to an ongoing debate about the number of factors in personality. White et al. (1994) used factor analysis to study the construct validity of various measures of impulsivity, and whether some tests were more related to delinquency than others.[7] In this chapter's *Close-up*, we focus on providing a basic understanding of factor analysis. A more extended discussion can be found in volumes devoted to this statistical tool's more technical aspects (e.g., Comrey, 1992; Gorsuch, 1974).

Validity and Test Bias

Our discussion of test validity would be incomplete without mention of the topic of test bias. In the eyes of many laypeople, questions concerning the validity of a test are intimately tied to questions concerning the fair use of a test and the issue of test bias. Let us hasten to point out that validity, fairness in the use of a test, and test bias are three separate issues. It is possible for a valid test to be used fairly or unfairly. It is even possible for a test that is biased to be used fairly or unfairly. Furthermore, people can disagree about whether a test is biased, depending on the definition of bias being used. To see why, you must have an understanding of test bias and related terminology.

The Definition of "Test Bias"

The term *bias* as applied to tests may be defined as a factor inherent within a test that systematically prevents accurate, impartial measurement. If the test in question were a "flip-coin test" (FCT), the FCT would be considered to be biased if the "instrument" (the coin) were weighted so that either heads or tails would appear more frequently than it would by chance alone. If the test in question were an intelligence test, the test would be considered to be biased if it were constructed so that people who had brown eyes consistently and systematically obtained higher scores than people with green eyes—assuming, of course, that in reality people with brown eyes are not generally more intelligent than people with green eyes. "Systematic" is a key word in our definition of test bias. We

---

7. The last study formed the basis for one of the exercises in the companion study guide to this text. See Exercise 34 in Cohen (1996).

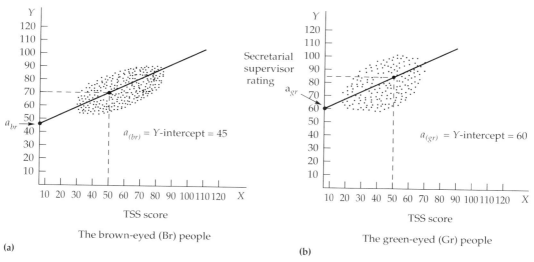

Figure 6–3
TSS Scores and Supervisor Ratings for Two Groups

Note the different points of the Y-intercept corresponding to a TSS score of 50 for the green-eyed and brown-eyed testtakers. If the TSS were an unbiased test, any given score on it would correspond to exactly the same criterion score for the two groups.

have previously looked at sources of *random* or chance variation in test scores. *Bias* implies *systematic* variation.

To illustrate, let's suppose we need to hire 50 secretaries, and so we place an ad in the newspaper. In response to the ad, 200 people reply, including 100 people who happen to have brown eyes and 100 people who happen to have green eyes. Each of the 200 applicants is individually administered a hypothetical test we will call the "Test of Secretarial Skills" (TSS). Logic tells us that eye color is probably not a relevant variable with respect to performing the duties of a secretary; we would therefore have no reason to believe that green-eyed people are better secretaries than brown-eyed people or vice versa. We therefore might reasonably expect that after the tests have been scored and the selection process has been completed, an approximately equivalent amount of brown-eyed and green-eyed people would have been hired (that is, approximately 25 brown-eyed people and 25 green-eyed people). But what if, in the end, it turned out that 48 green-eyed people were hired and only 2 brown-eyed people were hired? Is this evidence that the TSS is a biased test?

Although the answer to this question seems simple on the face of it—"Yes the test is biased because they should have hired 25 and 25!"—a truly responsible answer to this question would entail statistically "troubleshooting" the test and the entire selection procedure (see Berk, 1982). To begin with, the following three characteristics of the regression lines (see Figure 6–3) used to

Factor Analysis: What It Is,
How It's Done, and What to Do with It*

All scientists attempt to identify the basic underlying dimensions that can be used to account for the phenomena they study. For example, physicists refer to inferred dimensions or constructs such as "force" or "energy" in their attempt to identify and account for a large number of physical phenomena that occur in the universe. Behavioral scientists speak of other dimensions, constructs, or factors in their own attempt to identify, label, and understand behavioral phenomena.

Consider the case of a psychologist involved in personality research who has accumulated data on hundreds of testtakers who each sat for a dozen personality tests—personality tests that are supposed to measure about six dozen personality dimensions (also called "traits"). After analyzing the data, the psychologist may come to the conclusion that only three or four dimensions of personality are being measured by all those tests. Or, how about a hypothetical instrument we'll call the "Test of Executive Potential" (TEP)—a test that claims to provide scores on 21 dimensions or factors related to managerial success. After extensive research and experience with the TEP, an industrial/organizational psychologist might conclude that the TEP actually measures only 10 dimensions or factors related to managerial success. In each of these cases, the behavioral scientist began with measurements on several variables, analyzed the data, and concluded as a result of data analyses that some basic dimensions or factors could more efficiently account for the observed data. Several different, related procedures may be used to analyze data for the purpose of identifying basic dimensions or factors. Collectively, these techniques are known as *factor analysis*.[1]

*Prepared by Louis H. Primavera and Bernard S. Gorman.

1. Keep in mind, however, that although for our purposes we speak of "factor analysis" in the singular sense—as if it were one technique, like "simple addition"—there are many different ways of factor-analyzing data, and some may yield results that differ from others.

What Is Factor Analysis?

We will define *factor analysis* as "a set of mathematical techniques used to identify dimensions underlying a set of empirical measurements." To examine the process, let's do an informal kind of factor analysis. Imagine that you are a clinical psychologist and a new patient, a 45-year-old woman whom you refer to as "Annette O.," has just entered your office for her first consultation. Days before, when she had made the appointment, this woman would not explain over the phone why she sought therapy. In fact, she wouldn't even tell you her last name! After a brief exchange of pleasantries you say, "How may I be of help to you?" And then it all comes out.

Annette tells you how unhappy and miserable she is; a long-term relationship ended abruptly three months before this consultation when the man she was seeing suddenly decided that he wanted to go to school full-time to become a court reporter. Since that day she's been experiencing headaches, stomach pains, poor appetite, an inability to get a good night's sleep (or even feel very calm anytime during the day), a reluctance to get out of bed in the morning, a general and overwhelming feeling of dread, and an outbreak of acne—the likes of which she hadn't seen since adolescence.

During the course of this initial session with Annette, you are not only an "active listener" but an "active watcher" as well. You pay close attention not only to her verbal behavior but also to her nonverbal behavior. You note the generally sad expression on her face, the nonstop hand-wringing behavior, the plaintive cry in her voice, and the fact that you're almost completely out of tissues.

As your clock signals the end of the session, two words—neither one of them uttered among the hundreds of words spoken during the course of the session—seem to summarize much of the information you obtained in this first session with Annette: "depression" and "anxiety."

Turning the pages in your calendar with one hand while you try gracefully to fumble for your pen (which during the course of the session fell between the cracks of your leather chair) with the other, your mind races to thoughts of alternative therapy plans. You are too preoccupied to reflect on the elements of the process that has just transpired. One way of looking at that process is to think of it as data reduction. You have mentally reduced mounds of data to a more manageable and workable amount. More specifically, there were five steps in that process. Step 1 involved your observation of the person's behavior during the therapy session. In Step 2, you tried to understand how the themes that you observed went together—that is, what observations were similar to one another. Step 3 involved decisions regarding what everything you saw and heard had in common—that is, what the processes or underlying dimensions were. Step 4 involved a decision on your part regarding the relative weights or importance of each of the dimensions; depression and anxiety were the dimensions that struck you as most prominent. Step 5 involved your formulation of a plan of therapeutic intervention—a plan for using the data in a way that you deem will best help Annette.

As we shall soon see, the five-step process described above in many ways parallels the five-step description of factor analysis that follows. A major difference, of course, is that factor analysis, as it is typically used in psychology, is based on the administration of a number of measures to a scientifically selected sample of people—not one person's subjective observations and judgments about another person. Also, before moving on from the question "What is factor analysis?" we might make note of what factor analysis is *not*. The process of factor analysis is sometimes confused with the process of *cluster analysis*—a set of methods for grouping similar measures without necessarily searching for underlying, quantifiable dimensions.

How Is Factor Analysis Done?

Our goal here is to convey a general understanding of the process of factor analysis, as used in psychological measurement, not a "nuts-and-bolts" primer on how to do it. The mathematical procedures used in factor analysis are very complex. The reader who is interested in a more mathematically detailed, how-to-do-it presentation is referred to other sources, such as Gorsuch (1983).

Step 1
The first step in doing a factor analysis involves choosing a set of tests or measures. These measures or variables could be items on one test or two or more complete tests. For the purpose of this discussion, we will refer to these variables—either test items or whole tests—simply as "measures." Once you choose the measures that you wish to use, you administer them to a sample of testtakers. This sample is selected—as in all good empirical research—to represent the population to which you wish to generalize your results. This first step is similar to the initial step in the therapy session described above: careful observation of the patient's behavior.

Step 2
The second step in factor analysis is to compute all correlations among the set of measures that you have chosen to represent the construct or constructs. Recall that in Step 2 in Annette's initial therapy session, you decided, through some subjective process, which of the patient's behaviors were similar to each other. The second step in a factor analysis may also be thought of as a process of distilling relationships, though here, the method is not so subjective. Instead, mathematically computed coefficients of correlation are used.

Correlation coefficients provide a gauge of the degree of similarity that exists between measures.

(continued)

Factor Analysis: What It Is,
How It's Done, and What to Do with It *(continued)*

Correlations quantify the degree to which two variables have something in common. The squared value of the correlation coefficient, called the *coefficient of determination,* is interpreted as the proportion of variance shared by two variables. It provides a quantitative index of how much two measures have in common. For example, if we found that a test of anxiety correlated .60 with a test of neuroticism, then we could conclude that they had .36, or 36 percent, shared variance; that is, 36 percent of what was being measured by the anxiety test was also measured by the neuroticism test. The correlations are arranged into a matrix of intercorrelations, and this matrix is used in the next step of the process.

Step 3

The third step in a factor analysis is to factor the matrix of intercorrelations among a set of measures. This step is similar to the third step in the therapy session; there decisions were made regarding what the major underlying dimensions of the patient's behaviors were. The matrix of intercorrelation is factored using one or more mathematical procedures.

Factoring is a term that you may already have some familiarity with. You probably remember hearing a grade-school teacher use the term to describe a method in algebra by which a large, unwieldy expression was made more manageable by division of common factors. In modern factor-analysis methods, computer programs analyze the matrix of intercorrelations into a smaller matrix of a few common factors.

Most of the factoring procedures used in factor analysis produce a set of independent, uncorrelated factors. Most of them also can produce as many factors as there are variables. Some of these factors are thought to be *common factors,* and others are thought to be *specific factors* and *error factors.* Common factors represent the dimensions that all the measures have in common. They are the underlying, basic dimensions that scientists seek to identify—the

basic taxonomies of fields of scientific endeavor. Specific factors are simply those factors that are related to some specific aspect of the measuring procedure but are not common to any of the other measures in the analysis. Error factors refer to error of measurement or unreliability, which is always a part of any measuring process.

It is up to the researcher to decide which of the factors produced by the factor analysis are the common factors, since that is usually the purpose for doing factor analysis. The problem of identifying which of the factors are the common factors has occupied a great deal of the factor analysis literature and will not be covered here. Most factor analysts agree that this identification process is complex and difficult. A great deal of converging evidence is needed to make the decision as to which factors are the common factors. However, as we shall see shortly, common factors usually "stand out" in an understandable pattern.

Now, let's see how the first three steps of a factor analysis might work.

An Example of Steps 1–3 in Practice

Suppose that an educational psychologist wants to study both mathematics and verbal ability. She researches the literature and comes up with a test plan from which she constructs the five items that she believes will measure both these abilities. It's a good bet that, in practice, many more than five items would be needed to adequately represent the two factors of interest, but for now, five items provide a manageable example. Item 1 is a vocabulary item and item 3 is a word analogy problem. Item 2 tests a basic algebra concept and item 4 tests a basic geometry concept. Item 5 is an algebra word problem.

The researcher uses a standard factor-analysis computer program, which first computes the matrix of intercorrelations among the measures. The matrix of intercorrelations for the five items is presented in Table 1. Each entry in the matrix is a correlation co-

Table 1
The Matrix of Intercorrelations Among the Five Items

	Item				
	1	2	3	4	5
1 Vocabulary	1.00	.22	.77	.20	.50
2 Algebra	.22	1.00	.21	.65	.48
3 Analogy	.77	.21	1.00	.19	.52
4 Geometry	.20	.65	.19	1.00	.47
5 Algebra-Word	.50	.48	.52	.47	1.00

efficient between two of the items. Note in Table 1 that the correlation between the vocabulary item and the algebra concept item is .22 and that the correlation between the geometry item and the algebra word problem is .47. Now, examine the rest of this matrix of intercorrelations. Is any particular pattern present?

The vocabulary and the word analogy items have a high correlation, but each has low correlations with the algebra concept and geometry concept items. The algebra concept and geometry items have a high correlation, but each has a low correlation with the vocabulary and word analogy items. The algebra word problem has a moderate correlation with the other four items. These results suggest that there are two factors underlying these five items, with the vocabulary and word analogy items being most associated with one factor and the algebra and geometry concept items being associated with the second factor. It also seems that the algebra word problem may be associated with both factors.

In the present example, it's relatively easy to see that the patterns of correlations suggest what the two underlying factors might be for this set of five items. However, finding common factors would be an overwhelming task if you had a large number of items (for example, 100 or more). For this reason, you would probably need a method that would find these under-

lying dimensions in an objective way. Mathematical factoring is just such a method.

After the computer program computes the matrix of intercorrelations among all the measures, it next factors that matrix. Using the results from the computer program and several converging criteria that include some mathematical indices as well as interpretability, the educational researcher decides that there are two common factors underlying these five items.[2]

The entries in Table 2 are called "factor loadings" and can be treated like correlations between the measure and the underlying factors. Item 1, a vocabulary item, "loads" or correlates very highly with Factor I and very low with Factor II. Item 2, an algebra problem, correlates very low with Factor I and very highly with Factor II. In interpreting this factor matrix, it is necessary to decide what size or magnitude a factor loading should have before we can consider it to have a meaningful or important contribution to a factor. There is no agreed-upon significance test for factor loadings and, therefore, it is necessary to specify some value that indicates that a factor loading is meaningful or important. Cattell (1978) proposed a concept he called *salience*—a concept analogous to another concept that is no doubt more familiar to you, that of *significance*. Cattell proposed that, as a rule, a factor loading might be considered salient if it is greater than either .30 or .40. The choice of the value for salience is dependent on the size of the sample of subjects. If the sample is small (say, less than 100), factor loadings of .40 or greater may be thought to be

(continued)

2. To make the factors most interpretable, it is often necessary to use another mathematical procedure, called "rotation." *Rotation* is a mathematical procedure that adjusts the results of factor analysis so that it will be more interpretable without distorting the relationship of the factors to the original data. The interested reader is again directed to Gorsuch (1983) for a more detailed explanation.

Factor Analysis: What It Is,
How It's Done, and What to Do with It *(continued)*

salient. If the sample is large, a value of .30 or greater may be used as the cutoff for salience. For the present example, we chose a value of .30 as the cutoff because we know—since we made up the example—that the educational psychologist used a very large sample of subjects for her study.

The salient factor loadings have been underlined in Table 2. Using this criterion for salience or meaningfulness, you can see that the vocabulary and word analogy items load saliently on Factor I and that the algebra concept and geometry concept items load saliently on Factor II. These items are called *factorially simple* items because they load saliently on only one factor. It can be seen that these factorially simple items reflect only one dimension or factor. The algebra word problem loads saliently on both Factors I and II. A variable that loads saliently on more than one factor is called *factorially complex* because it reflects more than one dimension.

Nowhere in the statistical procedure of factor analysis is it written, or even suggested, how the names for common factors should be derived. That is a task left to the factor analyst and, sometimes, there is a great deal of subjectivity when naming them. Common factors may be named anything from "Factor I" to "Introversion" to "Belief in an Afterlife" to . . . whatever seems reasonable on the basis of the data at hand. With respect to factorially simple measures, the investigator typically makes some decision on the name of the factor based on the dimension the factors seem to have in common. The factorially complex items are, it is hoped, interpretable and understandable through the names given the factors. Before reading on, what names would *you* give the factors in Table 2?

We named Factor I "Verbal Ability" because we judged verbal ability to be a primary dimension or ability for completing vocabulary and analogy problems. We named Factor II "Mathematical Ability" because we judged this ability to be the primary

Table 2
The Results of the Factor Analysis of the Five Items

	Factors		
	I	II	Communality
Vocabulary	.917	.101	.851
Algebra	.113	.885	.796
Analogy	.925	.094	.864
Geometry	.086	.891	.801
Algebra-Word	.594	.573	.681
Eigenvalue	2.700	1.30	
Percent of Total Variance	54.000	26.000	

dimension or ability used for solving algebra and geometry problems. Through the names that we gave to the two factors, the algebra word problem can be interpreted as a measure of *both* mathematical and verbal abilities.

You may have chosen different names for the factors from the names we chose. Similar problems—those related to different names for observations—often arise in factor-analytic research and may even be responsible for theoretical debates about what the underlying dimensions for a given set of behaviors really are. For one example, the interested reader is referred to the debate over how many factors there *really* are in the factor analytically derived 16PF (Personality Factors) test (see Cattell & Krug, 1986; Comrey & Duffy, 1968; Eysenck, 1972; Guilford, 1975; and Howarth & Browne, 1971).

Step 4
Getting back to Annette O.'s therapy session and, more specifically, the fourth step in the model presented above, recall that the psychologist decided that Annette's behavior was symptomatic of depression and, secondarily, of anxiety. In making that judgment, the psychologist assigned relative importance to each of the factors or dimensions. Similarly, the results of

a factor analysis provide a numerical index called an *eigenvalue,* or characteristic root. An eigenvalue is a number that indicates the relative strength or importance of each of the factors. Eigenvalues from most factor analyses will vary from a value of 0.0 to that equal to the number of measures that are being factored. Divide the eigenvalue by the number of variables in the analysis and multiply the result by 100, and you will obtain the percent of total variance accounted for by a given factor. The eigenvalues and the total percent of variance associated with each of the two factors for the five items are given at the bottom of Table 2. Note that for these five items, the Verbal Ability Factor (54%) is more than twice as strong as the Mathematical Ability Factor (26%). The results of a factor analysis will allow us to estimate not only how many factors or dimensions there are for a set of measures but also the relative importance or strength of each of these factors.

Step 5
The final step in the therapy session scenario described above entailed your planning of a therapeutic intervention, perhaps with regard to your judgment concerning the relative importance of the observed symptomatology. Analogously, once factor analysts decide on the number of factors in a factor analysis, they can compute an index called *communality.* Communality assesses how well each measure is explained by the common factors. You will recall that the square of a correlation can be interpreted as the proportion of variance that two measures have in common. The square of a factor loading provides an indication of how much a factor and a measure have in common. Square each factor loading for a measure and then add the sum of the squares; the sum will be equal to the total proportion of variance of all of the common factors that is accounted for by that measure. The communality for the algebra concept item was computed by squaring its factor loadings, .113

and .885, and adding them together. Since communalities can vary between 0.0 and 1.0, we can see that all the measures in this analysis have a moderate to strong communality. Try computing the communalities for the other four items yourself.

What Does One Do with a Factor Analysis?
Over the last 20 years, a great increase in the use of factor analysis in many areas of psychological research has occurred. This increase is partially due to the availability of high-speed computers and relatively easy-to-use computer programs. Factor analysis is used in numerous ways, such as:

- Finding underlying factors of ability tests
- Identifying personality dimensions
- Identifying clinical syndromes
- Finding dimensions of worker satisfaction
- Finding the dimensions that people use when judging social behaviors

One way that factor analysis should *never* be used is as a haphazard method to attempt to make order from chaos; *it is totally inappropriate to factor-analyze just any set of measures with the hope of finding meaningful common factors.* A factor analysis should be planned as a tool that will be used at some appropriate point in a study. Do I understand the problem thoroughly? Do I understand the phenomena for which I am attempting to identify common factors? Are the measures I've chosen the best available ones with respect to the phenomena I'm investigating? These are only some of the questions that must be raised (and satisfactorily answered) before the execution of a factor analysis.

Suppose you were interested in identifying the dimensions of the construct "anxiety." Ideally, you would need to choose the test(s) or test items that most clearly represented what is known about anxiety. To accomplish this, you would read as much of the

(continued)

Factor Analysis: What It Is, How It's Done, and What to Do with It *(continued)*

psychological literature about anxiety as possible and choose the measure(s) that you thought best represented the domain of anxiety. Again, the measuring tool you ultimately select must ideally be one about which a good deal is known—one with demonstrated reliability and validity. To do otherwise would be to impair your ability to identify—and jeopardize the likelihood of identifying—meaningful factors. Further, poor "up-front" homework will lessen the likelihood that your work will be replicable; the factors you iden-

tify will probably not be found in subsequent studies by other researchers. In this context, a modern saying springs to mind: "Garbage in, Garbage out."

There are many technical issues in conducting a factor analysis that are beyond the scope of this introductory presentation. Our main goal was to introduce you to some of the basics. More in-depth approaches to this very important technique of data analysis are as far away as your campus library!

predict success on the criterion would have to be scrutinized: (1) the slope, (2) the intercept, (3) the error of estimate. And because these three factors of regression are functions of two other statistics (the validity coefficient and the reliability coefficient for both the test and the criterion) that could vary with respect to the two groups in question, a total of five characteristics must be statistically examined. A test of significance could indicate that our brown-eyed and green-eyed groups are the same or different with respect to any of these five characteristics. This binary choice (that is, same or different) taken to the fifth power (meaning that there are five ways that the two groups could conceivably differ) means that a comprehensive "troubleshooting" would entail examination of a total of 32 ($2^5 = 32$) possible ways the test could be found to be biased.

If, for example, a test systematically underpredicts or overpredicts the performance of members of a particular group (such as people with green eyes) with respect to a criterion (such as supervisory rating), there exists what is referred to as *intercept bias*—a term taken from the point where the regression line intersects the *Y*-axis. If a test systematically yields significantly different validity coefficients for members of different groups, there exists what is referred to as *slope bias*—so named since the slope of one group's regression line is different in a statistically significant way from the regression line of another group.

Stone (1992) identified slope and intercept bias on the Differential Abilities Scale (DAS; Elliot, 1990a, 1990b). The DAS is designed to measure school-related ability and achievement in children and adolescents. The test yields a General Conceptual Ability score, which is a measure of general ability, and achievement scores in a variety of areas, including Basic Number Skills and Word Reading. Stone (1992) computed regression lines for two racial groups: Whites and Asian Americans. When Word Reading scores were predicted from General Conceptual Ability, the regression lines for the two races had different slopes, indicating slope bias. When Basic Number Skills were predicted from General Conceptual Ability, the regression lines for the two races crossed the Y-axis at different places, indicating intercept bias.

The presence of slope and intercept bias on the DAS has important practical implications for testtakers. We will look specifically at the slope bias that Stone found in relation to the Word Reading achievement test. To understand the impact of that bias, draw a graph, using Figure 6–3 as a guide. Place General Conceptual Ability on the X-axis and Word Reading on the Y-axis. Then draw two regression lines with different slopes. Both lines should have a positive slope and should cross the Y-axis in the same place. The line with the steeper slope represents the Asian American children, and the other line represents the White children.

On your drawing, examine the relative position of the regression lines on each graph for X-axis values that are in the intermediate range, representing realistic test scores. You should find that the regression line for the Asian American children is higher than the regression line for the White children. This means that Asian American children at a particular level of achievement generally have lower ability scores than White students achieving at the same level. To see how this is so, pick a point relatively high on the Y-axis, representing a high level of achievement. Then draw a horizontal line across to the two regression lines, and drop a vertical line down to the X-axis from where you cross each regression line (as was done in Figure 6–3). The resulting points on the X-axis represent the average ability levels for the level of reading achievement selected on the Y-axis. You should cross the line for the Asian American students first, meaning that those students have a lower X-value, corresponding to a lower ability level than the White students at the same level of performance.

Now let's assume that teachers nominate students to a program for gifted individuals based on classroom achievement. However, entry to the gifted program is based on ability. This is the approach that is taken in many programs for gifted students. Nominated students are given an ability test, and those above a specific score are admitted. The exercise you just completed indicates that a smaller percentage of nominated Asian American students would be accepted into the gifted program. The Asian American students may well feel discriminated against—they were doing as well in the classroom as their White counterparts but were denied a place in a special program in which they might receive extra attention and more challenging work. Note further that, because of the nonparallel nature of the lines, this will become a greater problem at higher levels of achievement. This is just one of several results of slope and intercept bias explored by Stone (1992). The interested student is referred to the original article for a more detailed discussion.

One reason some tests have been found to be biased has more to do with the design of the research study than the design of the test; if there are too few testtakers in one of the groups (such as the minority group—literally), this methodological problem will make it appear as if the test is biased when in fact it may not be. A situation in which a test may justifiably be deemed biased is one in which some portion of its variance stems from some factor(s) irrelevant to performance on the criterion measure; as a consequence, one group of test-takers will systematically perform differently from another. Prevention (during test development) is the best cure for test bias, though a procedure called "esti-mated true score transformations" represents one of many available *post hoc* remedies (Mueller, 1949; see also Reynolds & Brown, 1984).[8]

Rating error   A *rating* is a numerical or verbal judgment (or both) that places a person or an attribute along a continuum identified by a scale of numerical and/or word descriptors called a *rating scale.* Simply stated, a *rating error* is a judgment resulting from the intentional or unintentional misuse of a rating scale. Thus, for example, a *leniency error* (also referred to as a *generosity error*) is, as its name implies, an error in rating that arises from the tendency on the part of the rater to be lenient in marking. From your own experience during course registration, you might be aware that a section of a particular course will fill very quickly if the section is being taught by a professor who has a reputation for committing leniency errors when it comes to end-of-term grading. At the other extreme from a leniency error in rating is a *severity error.* Movie critics who pan just about everything they review may be guilty of severity errors (assum-ing that these critics review a wide range of movies that might consensually be viewed as good and bad). Another type of error might be referred to as a *central tendency error.* Here, the rater, for whatever reason, exhibits a general and sys-tematic reluctance to giving ratings at either the positive or the negative ex-treme, and so all ratings tend to cluster in the middle of the rating continuum. One way to overcome what might be called "restriction of range rating errors" (central tendency, leniency, severity errors) is to use *rankings,* a procedure that requires the rater to measure individuals against one another instead of against an absolute scale. Now the rater is forced to select first, second, third choices and so forth.

A *halo effect* refers to the fact that, for some raters, some ratees can do no wrong. More specifically, a halo effect may also be defined as a tendency to give a particular ratee a higher rating than he or she objectively deserves because of the rater's failure to discriminate among conceptually distinct and potentially independent aspects of a ratee's behavior. To give a (very) hypothetical ex-ample, suppose Mel Gibson consented to write and deliver a speech on multi-variate analysis. His speech would probably earn much higher all-round ratings if given before the founding chapter of the Mel Gibson Fan Club than if deliv-ered before and rated by the membership of, say, the Royal Statistical Society

---

8. Lest the student think that there is something not quite right about transforming data under such circumstances, we would add that even though "transformation" is synonymous with "change," the change referred to here is merely a change in form—not meaning. Data may be transformed to place them in a more useful form, not to change their meaning.

(even in the unlikely event that the members of each group were equally savvy with respect to multivariate analysis).

Criterion data may also be influenced by the rater's knowledge of the ratee's race or sex (Landy & Farr, 1980). Males have been shown to receive more favorable evaluations than females in traditionally masculine occupations. Except in highly integrated situations, ratees tend to receive higher ratings from raters of the same race (Landy & Farr, 1980). Returning to our TSS situation, a particular rater may have had particularly great—or particularly distressing—prior experiences with green-eyed (or brown-eyed) people and be making extraordinarily high (or low) ratings on that irrational basis.

Training programs to familiarize raters with common rating errors and sources of rater bias have shown promise in reducing rating errors and increasing measures of reliability and validity. Lecture, role playing, discussion, watching oneself on videotape, and computer simulation of different situations are some of the many techniques that could be brought to bear in such training programs.

Test bias and the federal courts "How good are federal judges in detecting differences in item difficulty on intelligence tests for ethnic groups?" This was the intriguing question raised by Sattler (1991) in an article titled with this same question. Sattler's inquiry was spurred by two conflicting judgments made in two different federal courts regarding allegations of bias in individually administered intelligence tests. In the 1979 California case of *Larry P. et al. v. Wilson Riles et al.,* individual intelligence tests were found to be biased against Black children. In the 1980 Illinois case of *Parents in Action on Special Education (PASE) v. Joseph P. Hannon,* individual intelligence tests were not found to be culturally biased. Both judges had reached their decisions regarding the weight of the evidence on the basis of personal inspection of test items and on the testimony of expert witnesses. Although their final judgments differed, both judges had expressed the opinion that certain items on the Wechsler Intelligence Scale for Children (WISC), and on a revised version of this test, the WISC-R, were biased. According to Sattler (1991, p. 125), "A reading of the two judges' opinion briefs suggests that the term 'biased' was used in the sense of 'too difficult' or 'too hard,' and thus these items were biased from the judges' point of view." Sattler (1991) reviewed the literature on the issue of bias in WISC and WISC-R items, and reported on his investigation of the comparative difficulty of 25 selected items from these tests. Twelve of the 25 items were found to be significantly more difficult for the Black children than for the White children. Of these 12 items, six had been cited by the two judges—yielding an accuracy hit rate that was no better than chance for the judges attempting to judge the comparative difficulty of intelligence-test items.

One question that consideration of these cases brings to the fore is: "If members of one ethnic group consistently score significantly lower than members of another ethnic group on a particular test, is the test necessarily biased?"

For members of the lay public—and perhaps some federal judges as well— the answer to the latter question is yes (Reschley & Grimes, 1990; Reynolds &

Kaiser, 1990a, 1990b). Underlying the opinion that differences among groups on ability tests represent bias in the test is the assumption that there is no reason to expect differences in level of performance on various tasks by various groups of people. Accordingly, any test demonstrating such differences is deemed to be biased. But just as there is no reason to believe that differences in performance exist between groups, there is no reason for deciding in advance that no differences exist (Reynolds & Kaiser, 1990a, 1990b).

Fairness as Applied to Tests

As difficult and complex as it is to define *bias*, it is a "piece of cake" when compared with the difficulty encountered in searching for a definition of *fairness*. Though the definition of "bias" in the statistical sense may be technically complex, it is after all a definable mathematical entity as applied to a test. By contrast, issues of fairness tend to be rooted in moral/philosophical questions regarding the use of test data—questions that cannot be answered with mathematical preciseness or conceptualized in terms of statistical probabilities. Apart from the patently obvious unfair use of tests—situations that any reasonable person would consider unfair (for instance, the misuse of psychological tests in some countries to detain, even imprison)—what constitutes a "fair" and an "unfair" use of tests is a matter left to parties such as the test developer (in the test manual's usage guidelines), the test user (in the way the test is actually used in practice), and society (in the form of legislation, judicial decisions, and administrative regulations).[9] Although a definition of fairness as applied to testing eludes any simple definition, Ghiselli, Campbell, and Zedeck (1981) offered the following: "In general fairness refers to whether a difference in mean predictor scores between two groups represents a useful distinction for society, relative to a decision that must be made, or whether the difference represents a bias that is irrelevant to the objectives at hand" (p. 320).

Although fairness as applied to tests is at best difficult to address, it is possible to address some rather common misunderstandings regarding what are sometimes perceived as "unfair" or even "biased" tests. Some tests, for example, have been termed "unfair" because they discriminate between groups of people;[10] the reasoning here goes that although differences may exist between individuals, all people are created equal and any differences found between groups of people on any psychological trait must be an artifact of the "unfair" or "biased" test. Because this position is so rooted in faith as opposed to scien-

---

9. In the context of society, you may wish to consult an interesting review article by Russell (1984) that provides an overview of federal fair-employment legislation, administrative guidelines, and court cases that relate to issues such as the "fairness" of personnel selection practices involving the use of training as a criterion.

10. The verb *discriminate* here is used in the psychometric sense, meaning, "to show a statistically significant difference between individuals or groups with respect to measurement." The great difference between this statistical, scientific definition and other colloquial definitions (such as "to treat differently and/or unfairly because of group membership") must be kept firmly in mind in discussions of bias and fairness.

tific evidence—it in fact flies in the face of scientific evidence—it is virtually impossible to refute; one either believes it or doesn't. We would all like to believe that people are equal in every way and are capable of rising to the same heights given equal opportunity, but a more realistic view would appear to be that each person is capable of fulfilling a personal potential. Because people differ so obviously with respect to physical traits, one would be hard put to believe that psychological differences found to exist between individuals—and groups of individuals—are purely a function of inadequate tests. Again, although a test is not inherently unfair or biased simply because it is a tool by which group differences are found, the *use* of the test data can, like the use of any data, be unfair.

Another misunderstanding of what constitutes an unfair or biased test is that it is unfair to administer to a particular population a standardized test that did not include members of that population in the standardization sample. In fact, it may well be biased, but that must be determined by statistical or other means; the sheer fact that no members of a particular group were included in the standardization sample does *not*, in and of itself, invalidate the test for use with that group. Consider in this context a test we will call "The 7-Year Itch Test" (7-YIT). Initially designed to explore whether husbands really do become "itchy" (read "restless") after seven years of marriage, this hypothetical test of marital restlessness was originally standardized in the 1960s on a large sample of men who had been married for seven years. But in the 1990s, the test is being used to assess how "itchy" not only men but also women get after seven years of marriage. Suppose that a couple married seven years, Bob and Carole, take the 7-YIT and are informed that they each scored at the 95th percentile in marital "itchiness." We can conclude that their 7-YIT scores are higher than 95% of the men who take the test. We would have no basis on these data alone, however, to draw any comparisons between Bob and Carole and other couples with respect to 7-YIT performance, nor any basis for conclusions about Carole's "itchiness" relative to other women who have also been married seven years.

A final source of misunderstanding is the complex problem of remedying situations where bias or unfair test usage has been found to occur. In the area of selection for jobs, positions in universities and professional schools, and the like, a number of different preventive measures and remedies have been attempted. As you read about the tools used in these attempts in this chapter's *Everyday Psychometrics*, form your own opinions regarding what constitutes a fair use of employment and other tests in a selection process.

If performance differences between identified groups of people on a valid and reliable test used for selection purposes are found, some "hard" questions may have to be dealt with if the test is to continue to be used. Is the problem due to some technical deficiency in the test, or is the test, in reality, "too good" at identifying people of different levels of ability? Regardless, is the test being used fairly? If so, what might society at large do about remedying the skill disparity between different groups as reflected on the test?

The current controversy that exists over the ethics and legality of test-score adjustment calls to mind words written by John Dewey nearly a century ago:

Psychology will never tell us just what to do ethically, nor just how to do it. But it will afford us insight into the conditions which control the formation and execution of aims, and thus enable human effort to expend itself sanely, rationally, and with assurance. (p. 124)

Our discussion of issues of test fairness and test bias may seem to have brought us far afield of the seemingly cut-and-dried, relatively nonemotional subject of test validity. However, the complex issues accompanying discussions of test validity, including issues of fairness and bias, must be wrestled with by us all. For further consideration of the philosophical issues involved, the interested student is referred to the solitude of his or her own thought and the "reading" of his or her own conscience.

Adjustment of Test Scores by Group Membership: Fairness in Testing or Foul Play?

Any test, regardless of its psychometric soundness, may be knowingly or unwittingly used in a way that has an adverse impact on one or another group. If such adverse impact is found to exist, and if social policy demands some remedy and/or an affirmative action program, then psychometricians have a number of techniques at their disposal to create change. The table on pages 216–217 lists some of these techniques.

Although psychometricians have the tools at their disposal to institute special policies through manipulations in test development, scoring, and interpretation, there are few clear guidelines in this controversial area (Brown, 1994; Gottfredson, 1994; Sackett & Wilk, 1994). The waters are further muddied by the fact that some of the guidelines seem to have contradictory implications. For example, although racial imbalance in employee selection (disparate impact) is unlawful, the use of valid and unbiased selection procedures virtually guarantees disparate impact. This state of affairs will change only when racial disparities in job-related skills and abilities are minimized (Gottfredson, 1994).

In 1991, Congress enacted legislation that would effectively bar employers from adjusting testtakers' test scores for the purpose of making hiring or promotion decisions. Section 106 of the Civil Rights Act of 1991 made it illegal for employers "in connection with the selection or referral of applicants or candidates for employment or promotion to adjust the scores of, use different cutoffs for, or otherwise alter the results of employment related tests on the basis of race, color, religion, sex, or national origin."

The law prompted concern on the part of many psychologists who believed it would adversely affect various societal groups, and may reverse social gains made. Brown (1994, p. 927) forecasted that "the ramifications of the Act are more far-reaching than Congress envisioned when it considered the amendment

and could mean that many personality tests and physical ability tests that rely on separate scoring for men and women are outlawed in employment selection." Arguments in favor of group-related test-score adjustment have been made on philosophical as well as technical grounds. From a philosophical perspective, increased minority representation is socially valued to the point that minority preference in test scoring is warranted. In the same vein, minority preference is viewed both as a remedy to past societal wrongs and as a contemporary guarantee of proportional workplace representation among various groups. From a more technical perspective, it is argued that some tests require adjustment in scores because (1) the tests are biased and a given score on them does not necessarily carry the same meaning for all testtakers, and/or (2) "a particular way of using a test is at odds with an espoused position as to what constitutes fair use" (Sackett & Wilk, 1994, p. 931).

In contrast to advocates of test-score adjustment are those who view such adjustments in the context of a social agenda for preferential treatment of certain groups. These opponents of test-score adjustment reject the subservience of individual effort and ability to group membership as criteria in the assignment of test scores (Gottfredson, 1988). Hunter and Schmidt (1976, p. 1069) described the unfortunate consequences to all parties involved in a college selection situation wherein poor-risk applicants were accepted on the basis of score adjustments or quotas. With reference to the employment setting, Hunter and Schmidt (1976) described one case in which entrance standards were reduced so as to hire more members of a particular group. However, many of these new-hires did not pass promotion tests—with the result that the company was sued for discriminatory promotion practice. Yet another consideration has to do with the feelings of "minority applicants who are selected

(continued)

Adjustment of Test Scores by Group Membership: Fairness in Testing or Foul Play? (continued)

under a quota system but who also would have been selected under unqualified individualism and must therefore pay the price, in lowered prestige and self-esteem" (Jensen, 1980, p. 398).

A number of psychometric models of fairness in testing have been presented and debated in the scholarly literature (Hunter & Schmidt, 1976; Petersen & Novick, 1976; Schmidt & Hunter, 1974; Thorndike, 1971). Despite a wealth of research and debate, a long-standing question in the field of personnel psychology remains, "How can group differences on cognitive ability tests be reduced while existing high levels of reliability and criterion-related validity can be retained?" According to Gottfredson (1994), the answer probably will not come from measurement-related research because differences in scores on many of the tests in question arise principally from differences in job-related abilities. For Gottfredson (1994, p. 963), "the biggest contribution personnel psychologists can make in the long run may be to insist collectively and candidly that their measurement tools are neither the cause of nor the cure for racial differences in job skills and consequent inequalities in employment." Do you agree? What is your opinion about the use of procedures to adjust test scores on the basis of group membership? Do you agree with Section 106 of the Civil Rights Act of 1991? Why? More on this controversial issue is presented in Chapter 17.

Psychometric Techniques for Preventing or Remedying Adverse Impact and/or Instituting an Affirmative Action Program

Some of these techniques may be preventive if employed in the test development process, and others may be employed with already established tests. Some of these techniques entail direct score manipulation; others, such as banding, do not. Preparation of this table benefited from Sackett and Wilk (1994), and their work should be consulted for more detailed consideration of the complex issues involved.

Technique	Description
Addition of Points	A constant number of points is added to the test score of members of a particular group. The purpose of the point addition is to reduce or eliminate observed differences between groups.
Differential Scoring of Items	This technique incorporates group membership information, not in adjusting a raw score on a test, but in deriving the score in the first place. The application of the technique may involve the scoring of some test items for members of one group but not scoring the same test items for members of another group. This technique is also referred to as *empirical keying by group.*
Elimination of Items Based on Differential Item Functioning	This procedure entails removing from a test any items found to inappropriately favor one group's test performance over another's. Ideally, the intent of the elimination of certain test items is not to make the test easier for any group but simply to make the test fairer. Sackett and Wilk (1994) put it this way: "Conceptually, rather than asking 'Is this item harder for members of Group X than it is for Group Y?' these approaches ask 'Is this item harder for members of Group X with true score Z than it is for members of Group Y with true score Z?'"

Technique	Description	Technique	Description
Differential Cutoffs	Different cutoffs are set for members of different groups. For example, a passing score for members of one group is 65, whereas a passing score for members of another group is 70. As with the addition of points, the purpose of differential cutoffs is to reduce or eliminate observed differences between groups.	Banding	The effect of banding of test scores is to make equivalent all scores that fall within a particular range or band. For example, thousands of raw scores on a test may be transformed to a stanine having a value of 1 to 9. All scores that fall within each of the stanine boundaries will be treated by the test user as either equivalent or subject to some additional selection criteria. A *sliding band* (Cascio et al., 1991) is a modified banding procedure wherein a band is adjusted (or "slid") to permit the selection of more members of some group than would otherwise be selected.
Separate Lists	Different lists of testtaker scores are established by group membership. For each list, test performance of testtakers is ranked in top-down fashion. Users of the test scores for selection purposes may alternate selections from the different lists. Depending on factors such as the allocation rules in effect and the equivalency of the standard deviation within the groups, the separate-lists technique may yield effects similar to those of other techniques, such as the addition of points and differential cutoffs. In practice, the separate list is popular in affirmative action programs where the intent is to overselect from previously excluded groups.	Preference Policies	In the interest of affirmative action, reverse discrimination, or some other policy deemed to be in the interest of society at large, a test user might establish a policy of preference based on group membership. For example, if a municipal fire department sought to increase the representation of female personnel in its ranks, it might institute a test-related policy designed to do just that. A key provision in this policy might be that when a male and a female earn equal scores on the test used for hiring, the female will be hired.
Within-Group Norming	Used as a remedy for adverse impact if members of different groups tend to perform differentially on a particular test, within-group norming entails the conversion of all raw scores into percentile scores or standard scores based on the test performance of one's own group. In essence, an individual testtaker is being compared only with other members of his or her own group. When race is the primary criterion of group membership and separate norms are established by race, this technique has been referred to as *race-norming*.		

7

Test Development

All tests are not created equal. The creation of a "good test" is not a matter of chance; it is the product of the thoughtful and sound application of established principles of test construction. In this chapter, we explore the basics of test development and examine in detail the processes by which tests are constructed. Although we focus on tests of the published, standardized variety, much of what we have to say also applies to "custom-made" tests such as those created by teachers, researchers, and employers.

The process of developing a test occurs in five stages:

Test conceptualization

Test construction

Test tryout

Item analysis

Test revision

Briefly, once the idea for a test is conceived (test conceptualization), items for the test are drafted (test construction). This "first draft" of the test is then tried out on a group of sample testtakers (test tryout). Once the data from the tryout are in, testtakers' performance on the test as a whole and on each of the test's items will be analyzed. Statistical procedures collectively referred to as *item analysis* will be employed to assist in making judgments about which items are good as they are, which items may need to be revised, and which items should be discarded. The analysis of the test's items may include analyses of item reliability, item validity, item discrimination, and—depending on the type of test it is—item-difficulty level. On the basis of the item analysis and related considerations, a revision or "second draft" of the test will be created. This revised version of the test will now be tried out on a new sample of testtakers, the results will be analyzed, the test further revised if necessary—and so it goes (Figure 7–1).

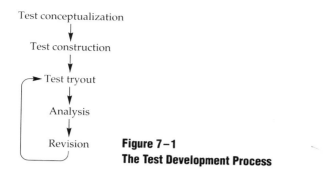

Figure 7–1
The Test Development Process

Test Conceptualization

The beginnings of any published test can probably be traced to thoughts—"self-talk," in behavioral terms. The test developer says to himself or herself something like: "There ought to be a test designed to measure [fill in the blank] in [such and such] way." The stimulus for such a thought could be almost anything. A review of the available literature on existing tests designed to measure a particular construct might indicate that such tests leave much to be desired in psychometric soundness—and the would-be test developer thinks he or she can do better. The emergence to prominence of some social phenomenon or pattern of behavior might serve as the stimulus for the development of a new test. If, for example, celibacy were to become a widely practiced lifestyle, we might witness the development of "celibacy tests," tests that might measure variables like reasons for adopting a celibate lifestyle, commitment to a celibate lifestyle, and degree of celibacy by specific behaviors. The analogy in medicine is straightforward. Once a new disease (such as acquired immune deficiency syndrome [AIDS], Legionnaire's disease, or toxic shock syndrome) comes to the attention of medical researchers, they attempt to develop diagnostic tests to assess its presence or absence as well as the severity of its manifestations in the body. The development of a new test may be in response to a need to assess level of mastery in relatively new professions (such as financial planning).

Regardless of the stimulus for developing the new test, the prospective test developer must at some point confront a number of important questions if the test is to be published by a reputable publisher and taken seriously by potential test users. A partial listing of the questions to be dealt with includes:

- *What is the objective of the test?* How is this objective the same as or different from existing tests designed to measure the same thing? How will the objective(s) be met?

- *Is there really a need for this test?* Are there other tests that purport to measure the same thing? In what ways will the proposed test be better than existing tests? Will it be more reliable? More valid? More comprehensive? Take less time to administer? How might this not be better than other tests? Who would use this test and why?

- *Who would need to take this test?* Who would need the data derived from an administration of it? Why?

- *What content area should the test cover?* How and why is this different from the content of existing similar tests?

- *How will the test be administered?* Will the test be individually administered or group-administered, or should it be amenable to both individual and group administration? What differences will exist between the individually administered version and the group-administered version? Will the test be designed for computer administration? How might differences between different versions of the test be reflected in test scores?

- *What is the ideal item format for this test?* Why?

- *Should more than one form of the test be developed?* Why?

- *What special training will be required of test users for administering or interpreting the test?* What background and qualifications will a prospective user of data derived from an administration of this test need to have? What restrictions, if any, should be placed on distributors of the test and on the test's usage?

- *What types of responses will be required by testtakers?* What "real world" behaviors would be anticipated to correlate with these responses? Why will scores on this test be important?

Depending on the nature of the test and the specific questions asked, the task of answering such questions may require activity ranging from simple logic, to literature reviews, to experimentation, to "soul-searching." Some tests are designed to measure hypothetical constructs (such as anxiety, intelligence, introversion) that are measurable only to the extent that they are linked to observable behavior. Here, "observable behavior" is very broadly defined, running the gamut from sweaty palms to grids blackened with a number 2 pencil on an answer sheet. In planning to develop the test, the test creator will strive to detail as thoroughly as possible the nature of the relationship between the construct being measured and behaviors related to it. What types of behavior will confirm the existence of the construct? What types of behavior may be taken as evidence against the existence of the construct? What type of testing situation will provide the best forum for the elicitation of behaviors related to this construct? These are the types of questions that will be raised.

Preliminary or *pilot* work on a new test may entail research designed to explore the feasibility of a particular approach to measurement. For example, as background for the development of a new test of introversion-extraversion, a test developer might conduct interviews with people believed for some reason (perhaps on the basis of some existing test) to be introverted or extraverted. Additionally, interviews with parents, teachers, friends, and others who know the subject might be arranged. The subjects could be placed in some experimental situation, for the purpose of observing and measuring their reactions. Yet another type of pilot study might entail physiological monitoring of the subjects (such as monitoring of heart rate) as a function of exposure to different types of visual, auditory, or other stimuli.

Once all pilot studies have been completed and the test has been conceived, the process of test construction begins.

Test Construction

Scaling

We have previously defined *measurement* as "the assignment of numbers according to rules" and noted that *scales* are the rules of measurement. *Scaling* may be defined as the process of setting rules for assigning numbers in measurement. Stated another way, scaling refers to the process by which a measuring device is designed and "calibrated," the way numbers (or other indices)—scale values—are assigned to different amounts of the trait, attribute, or characteristic being measured.

The prolific L. L. Thurstone is historically credited for being at the forefront of efforts to develop methodologically sound scaling methods. He adapted psychophysical scaling methods to the study of psychological variables such as attitudes and values (Bock & Jones, 1968; Thurstone, 1959; Thurstone & Chave, 1929). Thurstone's (1925) article "A Method of Scaling Psychological and Educational Tests" introduced, among other things, the notion of *absolute scaling*—a procedure for obtaining a measure of item difficulty across samples of testtakers who vary in ability. Two years later came his influential paper on the "law of comparative judgment" (Thurstone, 1927). Thurstone once told his students that this law was his proudest achievement (Nunnally, 1978, pp. 60–61).

Types of scales In common parlance, *scales* are instruments used to measure something. These instruments may be categorized by typologies as a function of different characteristics. For example, we may refer to a scale used for weighing variously as a "type of instrument used to measure weight," or "a type of tool used to convert the pressure a stimulus exerts into a number representing ounces (pounds, tons—whatever)," or "an instrument of the variety that yields ratio-level measurement." Of course, such typologies are not mutually exclusive; a weight scale is a ratio-level instrument of measurement that converts a stimulus of pressure into a number representing units of weight.

In psychometrics, *scales* may also be conceived of as "instruments used to measure something"—that "something" typically being a psychological trait, characteristic, or attribute. Further, it is meaningful to speak of different types of scales as a function of various characteristics. We have seen, for example, that scales can be meaningfully categorized along a continuum of level of measurement and referred to as nominal, ordinal, interval, or ratio in nature. But we might also characterize scales in other ways. If the testtaker's performance on a test as a function of age is of critical interest, then the test might be referred to as an "age scale." If the testtaker's performance on a test as a function of grade is of critical interest, then the test might be referred to as a "grade scale." If all raw scores on the test are to be transformed into scores that can range from 1 to 9, then the test might be referred to as a "stanine scale." A scale might be referred to in other ways, such as unidimensional as opposed to multidimensional, and comparative as opposed to categorical.

Test developers design a measurement method (that is, scale a test) in the manner they believe is optimally suited to the way they have conceptualized measurement of the target trait(s). There is no one method of scaling; scaling may be accomplished in various ways. There is also no best type of scale; whether a scale to be developed should be nominal, ordinal, interval, or ratio in nature will depend in part on variables such as the objectives of the scale and the mathematical legitimacy of the manipulations and transformations of the resulting data.[1]

Scaling methods   Speaking generally, a testtaker is presumed to have more or less of the characteristic measured by a (valid) test as a function of the test score; the higher or lower the score, the more or less of the characteristic he or she presumably possesses. But how are numbers assigned to responses so that a test score can be calculated? This is done through scaling the test items, using any one of several available methods.

For example, consider a moral issues opinion measure called the Morally Debatable Behaviors Scale—Revised (MDBS-R; Katz et al., 1994). Developed to be "a practical means of assessing what people believe, the strength of their convictions, as well as individual differences in moral tolerance" (p. 15), the MDBS-R contains 30 items. Each item contains a brief description of a moral issue or behavior on which testtakers express their opinion by means of a ten-point scale that ranges from "never justified" to "always justified." Here is a sample:

Cheating on taxes if you have a chance is:

1	2	3	4	5	6	7	8	9	10
never justified									always justified

This is an example of a *rating scale,* which can be defined as a grouping of words, statements, or symbols on which judgments concerning the strength of a particular trait, attitude, or emotion are indicated by the testtaker. Rating scales can be used to record judgments of oneself, others, experiences, or objects, and may take several forms (see Figure 7–2).

On the MDBS-R, the ratings that the testtaker makes for each of the 30 test items are added together to obtain a final score. Scores range from a low of 30 (if the testtaker indicates that all 30 behaviors are never justified) to a high of 300 (if the testtaker indicates that all 30 situations are always justified). Because the final test score is obtained by summing the ratings across all the items, it is called a *summative scale.*

---

1. Many scholarly volumes have been written on the subject of scaling alone (e.g., Gulliksen & Messick, 1960; Maranell, 1974; Torgerson, 1958), and our treatment should be thought of as only a brief overview of some general principles. More detailed and technical expositions of this topic can be found not only in the books devoted specifically to it but in others as well (such as Chapter 8 in Allen & Yen, 1979; Chapters 2 and 10 in Guilford, 1954a; Chapter 2 in Nunnally, 1978).

Rating Scale Item A
I believe I would like the work of a lighthouse keeper.
True   False   (circle one)

Rating Scale Item B
Please rate the employee on ability to cooperate and get along with fellow employees:
Excellent _____ /_____ /_____ /_____ /_____ /_____ /_____ / Unsatisfactory

Rating Scale Item C
How did you feel about what you saw on television?

Figure 7–2
The Many Faces of Rating Scales

Rating scales can take many forms. "Smiley" faces, such as those illustrated here as Item C, have been used in social-psychological research with young children and adults with limited language skills. The faces are used in lieu of words such as "positive," "neutral," and "negative."

One type of summative rating scale, the Likert scale (Likert, 1932), is used extensively within psychology, usually to scale attitudes. Likert scales are relatively easy to construct. Each item presents the testtaker with five alternative responses, usually on an agree/disagree or approve/disapprove type of continuum. If Katz et al. had used a Likert scale, an item on their test might have looked like this:

"Cheating on taxes if you have a chance"
      This is (check one):

| _____ | _____ | _____ | _____ | _____ |
| never justified | rarely justified | sometimes justified | usually justified | always justified |

Likert scales are usually reliable, which may account for their widespread popularity. Likert (1932) experimented with different weightings of the five categories but concluded that assigning weights of 1, for endorsement of items at one extreme, through 5, for endorsement of items at the other extreme, generally worked best.

The use of rating scales of any type results in ordinal-level data. With reference to the Likert scale item, for example, if the response "never justified" is assigned the value 1, "rarely justified" the value of 2, and so on, the higher the score, the more the response is indicative of permissiveness with regard to cheating on taxes. Respondents could even be ranked with regard to such permissiveness. However, the difference in permissiveness between the opinions of a pair of people who scored 2 and 3 on this scale is not necessarily the same as the difference between the opinions of a pair of people who scored 3 and 4.

Rating scales differ in the number of dimensions underlying the ratings being made. Some rating scales are unidimensional, meaning that only one dimension is presumed to underlie the ratings. Other rating scales are multidimensional, meaning that more than one dimension is thought to guide the testtaker's responses. Consider in this context an item from the MDBS-R regarding marijuana use. Responses to this item, particularly responses in the low to middle range, may be interpreted in many different ways. Such responses may reflect the view that people should not engage in illegal activities, or that people should not take risks with their health, or that people should avoid activities that could lead to contact with a "bad crowd." Responses to this item may reflect other attitudes and beliefs, such as those related to the beneficial use of marijuana as an adjunct to chemotherapy for cancer patients. When more than one dimension is being tapped by an item, multidimensional scaling techniques are used to identify the dimensions (see Green et al., 1989; Kruskal & Wish, 1978).

Another scaling method that produces ordinal data is the method of paired comparisons. Testtakers are presented with pairs of stimuli (two photographs, two objects, two statements), which they are asked to compare. They then must select one of the stimuli as per some rule (they agree more with one statement, they find one stimulus more appealing than the other, etc.). Had Katz et al. used the method of paired comparisons, an item on their scale might have looked like this:

> Select the behavior that you think would be more justified:
> a. Cheating on taxes if you have a chance
> b. Someone accepting a bribe in the course of his or her duties

For each pair of options, testtakers would receive a higher score if they selected the option that was deemed more justifiable by the majority of a group of judges. The judges would have been asked to rate the pairs of options before the distribution of the test, and a list of the options selected by the judges would be provided along with the scoring instructions as an answer key. The test score would reflect the number of times the choices of a testtaker agreed with those of the judges. If we use Katz et al.'s (1994) standardization sample as the judges, the more justifiable option is cheating on taxes. A testtaker who selected that option might receive a point toward the total exam score if option *a* was selected, but no points if option *b* was selected. An advantage of the method of paired comparisons is that it forces testtakers to choose between items.

Another way of deriving ordinal information through a scaling system entails sorting tasks. In these approaches, printed cards, drawings, photographs, objects, or other such stimuli are typically presented to testtakers for evaluation. One method of sorting, called *comparative scaling,* entails judgments of a stimulus in comparison with every other stimulus on the scale. A version of the

MDBS-R that employs comparative scaling might feature each of the 30 items printed on a separate index card. Testtakers would be asked to sort the cards from most to least justifiable. Comparative scaling could also be accomplished by providing testtakers with a list of 30 items on a sheet of paper and asking them to rank the justifiability of the items from 1 to 30.

Another scaling system that relies on sorting is called *categorical scaling*. Stimuli are placed into one of two or more alternative categories that differ quantitatively with respect to some continuum. In our running MDBS-R example, testtakers might be given 30 index cards on which are printed the 30 items. They would then be asked to sort the cards into three piles: one pile of those behaviors that are never justified, one pile that are sometimes justified, and one pile that are always justified.

A Guttman (1944, 1947) scale is yet another scaling method that yields ordinal-level measures. Items on it range sequentially from weaker to stronger expressions of the attitude, belief, or feeling being measured. A feature of Guttman scales is that they are designed so that all respondents who agree with the stronger statements of the attitude will also agree with milder statements. Using the MDBS-R scale as an example, consider the following statements that reflect attitudes toward suicide.

> Do you agree or disagree with each of the following:
> A. All people should have the right to decide whether they wish to end their lives.
> B. People who are terminally ill and in pain should have the option of having a doctor assist them in ending their lives.
> C. People should have the option of signing away the use of artificial life-support equipment before they become seriously ill.
> D. People have the right to a comfortable life.

If this were a perfect Guttman scale, all respondents who agree with *A* (the most extreme position) should also agree with *B, C,* and *D.* All respondents who disagree with *A* but agree with *B* should also agree with *C* and *D,* and so forth. Guttman scales are developed through the administration of a number of items to a target group. The resulting data are then analyzed by means of a procedure called scalogram analysis. The objective is to obtain an arrangement of items wherein endorsement of one item automatically connotes endorsement of less extreme positions.

All the foregoing methods yield ordinal data. The method of equal-appearing intervals, first described by Thurstone (1929), is one scaling method used to obtain data that are presumed to be interval. Again using the example of attitudes about the justifiability of suicide, let's outline the steps that would be involved in creating a scale using Thurstone's equal-appearing intervals method.

1. A reasonably large number of statements reflecting positive and negative attitudes toward suicide are collected, such as "Life is sacred, so people should never take their own lives," and "A person in a great deal of physical or emotional pain may rationally decide that suicide is the best option available to him or her."

2. Judges (or experts in some cases) judge each statement as to how much it indicates that suicide is justified. Each judge is instructed to rate each statement on a scale *as if* the scale were interval in nature. For example, the scale might range from 1 (the statement indicates that suicide is never justified) to 9 (the statement indicates that suicide is always justified). Judges are instructed that the 1-to-9 scale is being used *as if* there is equal distance between each of the values; that is, as if it were an interval scale. Judges are cautioned to focus their ratings on the statements, and not their own views on the matter.

3. A mean and a standard deviation of the judges' ratings are calculated for each statement. For example, if 15 judges rated 100 statements on a scale from 1 to 9, then for each of these 100 statements, the 15 judges' ratings would be averaged together. Suppose five of the judges rated a particular item as a 1. Five other judges rated it as a 2, and the remaining five judges rated it as a 3. The average rating would be 2 (with a standard deviation of 0.816).

4. Items are selected for inclusion in the final scale based on several criteria, including the degree to which the item contributes to a comprehensive measurement of the variable in question and the degree of confidence the test developer has that the items have indeed been sorted into equal intervals. Item means and standard deviations are also considered. Items should represent a wide range of attitudes reflected in a variety of means. A low standard deviation is indicative of a good item; the judges agreed about the meaning of the item with respect to how it reflected attitudes toward suicide.

5. The scale is now ready for administration. The way the scale is used depends on the objectives of the test situation. Typically, respondents are asked to select those statements that most accurately reflect their own attitudes. The values of the items that the respondent selects (based on the judges' ratings) are averaged together, producing a score on the test.

The method of equal-appearing intervals is an example of a scaling method of the direct estimation variety. In contrast to other methods that involve indirect estimation, there is no need to transform the testtaker's responses into some other scale.

The particular scaling method employed in the development of a new test will depend on many factors, including the variables being measured, the group for whom the test is intended (children may require a less complicated scaling method than adults, for example), and the preferences of the test developer.

Writing Items

In the grand scheme of test construction, considerations related to the actual writing of the test's items go hand in hand with scaling considerations. Three questions that the prospective test developer/item writer faces immediately are:

- What range of content should the items cover?
- Which of the many different types of item formats should be employed?
- How many items should be written?

When devising a standardized test using a multiple-choice-item format, it is usually advisable that the number of items for the "first draft" of a standardized test contain approximately twice the number of items that the final version of the test will contain.[2] If, for example, a test called "American History: 1940 to 1990" was to have 30 questions in its final version, it would be useful to have as many as 60 items—items that comprehensively sample the domain of the test—in the "item pool." An *item pool* is the "reservoir" or "well" from which items on the final version of the test will be drawn or discarded. A comprehensive sampling provides a basis for content validity of the final version of the test. Because approximately half of these items will be eliminated in the test's final version, the test developer needs to ensure that the final version of the test also contains items that adequately sample the domain. Thus, if all the questions on the Persian Gulf War from the original 60 items were determined to be poorly written items, it would be incumbent on the test developer to either rewrite items sampling this period or create new items—and then subject the rewritten or new items to tryout as well. If this were not done, the content validity of the test would be jeopardized because some aspects of the test domain would not be represented in the final version of the test. Of course, the number of planned forms of the test is another consideration here; multiply the number of items required in the pool for one form of the test by the number of forms planned.

How does one develop items to place into the item pool? The test developer may write a large number of items from personal experience or academic acquaintance with the subject matter. Help may also be sought from others, including experts. For psychological tests designed for use in clinical settings, clinicians, patients, patients' family members, clinical staff, and others may be interviewed for insights that could assist in the item writing. For psychological tests designed for use by personnel psychologists, interviews with members of a targeted industry or organization will likely be of great value. For psychological tests designed for use by school psychologists, interviews with teachers, administrative staff, educational psychologists, and others may be invaluable. Searches through the research literature may be fruitful sources of inquiry, as might searches through nonresearch literature.

Considerations related to variables such as the purpose of the test and the number of examinees to be tested at one time enter into decisions regarding the

---

2. Common sense and the practical demands of the situation may dictate that fewer items be written for the first draft of a test. If, for example, the final draft were to contain 1,000 items, it could be an undue burden to attempt to create an item pool of 2,000 items. Further, if the test developer was a very knowledgeable and capable item writer, it might be necessary to create only about 1,200 items for the item pool.

format of the test. Thus, for example, if the purpose of a test is to screen large numbers of military recruits for minimal intellectual ability, a constructed-response format, such as one including essay items, would be impractical. Preferable would be a test format wherein an examinee must select one of many alternative answers—a selected-response format. Selected-response formats facilitate automated scoring and can readily accommodate a large number of examinees.

Both selected- and constructed-response formats are described in the following section.

Item formats As noted, the *selected-response item format* presents the examinee with a choice of answers and requires selection of one alternative. If the test is one of achievement, the examinee's task is to select the correct (that is, the "keyed") answer. If the test is one designed to measure the strength of a particular trait, the examinee's task may be to select the alternative that best answers the question with respect to themselves. For the sake of simplicity, we'll confine our examples to achievement tests. The reader may wish to mentally substitute other appropriate terms for words such as "correct" because such substitutions might apply to personality or other types of tests that are not achievement tests.

Three types of selected-response item formats are multiple-choice, matching, and true-false items. As illustrated by Item A in the following example, a multiple-choice item has three elements: (1) a stem, (2) a correct alternative or option, and (3) several incorrect alternatives or options variously referred to as "distractors" or "foils":

Item A

Stem $\longrightarrow$ A psychological test, an interview, and a case study are:

Correct alt. $\longrightarrow$ (a) psychological assessment tools

(b) standardized behavioral samples

Distractors $\longrightarrow$ (c) reliable assessment instruments

(d) theory-linked measures

Now consider Item B:

Item B

A good multiple-choice item in an achievement test:

(a) has one correct alternative
(b) has alternatives that are grammatically parallel
(c) has alternatives of similar length
(d) has alternatives that fit grammatically with the stem
(e) includes as much as possible of the item in the stem to avoid unnecessary repetition
(f) avoids ridiculous distractors
(g) is not excessively long
(h) all of the above
(i) none of the above

If you answered "h" to Item B, you are correct. In the process of going through the list of alternatives, it may have occurred to you that Item B violated many of the rules it set forth!

A matching item is a variant of a multiple-choice item. The examinee is presented with two columns of responses and the task is to determine which response from one column "goes with" which response from the other. An example follows:

Match the following actors' names with their roles by writing the appropriate number next to the letter.[3]

____	A.	Sylvester Stallone	1.	Ace Ventura
____	B.	Jim Carrey	2.	Victor
____	C.	Johnny Depp	3.	Arthur
____	D.	Cliff Robertson	4.	Rocky
____	E.	Dustin Hoffman	5.	Charly
____	F.	Christopher Reeve	6.	Ed Wood
____	G.	Barbra Streisand	7.	Luke
____	H.	Robin Williams	8.	Superman
____	I.	Julie Andrews	9.	Mrs. Doubtfire
____	J.	Paul Newman	10.	Tootsie
____	K.	Dudley Moore	11.	Yentl
			12.	Bugsy

You may have noticed that there are different numbers of items in the two columns. If the number of items in the two columns were the same, then a person unsure about one of the actor's roles could deduce it by matching all the other options first. A perfect score would then result even though the testtaker did not actually know all of the material. Providing more options than are needed is designed to eliminate such a possibility.

A true-false item is another of the selected-response variety, this one in the form of a sentence that requires the examinee to indicate whether the statement is or is not a fact. A good true-false item contains a single idea, is not excessively long, and is not subject to debate; that is, it is indeed either true or false.

Like multiple-choice items, true-false items have the advantage of being readily applicable to a wide range of subject areas. Also like the multiple-choice items, acceptable levels of item reliability can be achieved with true-false items. True-false items need not contain a list of distractor alternatives. Therefore, true-false items tend to be easier to write than multiple-choice items. A disadvantage of true-false items is that the probability of obtaining a correct

---

3. For the record, the answers to this matching question are as follows: A-4, B-1, C-6, D-5, E-10, F-8, G-11, H-9, I-2, J-7, and K-3. In case you are wondering, Julie Andrews played Victor (as well as Victoria) in *Victor/Victoria*. Paul Newman played Luke in *Cool Hand Luke*.

response purely on the basis of chance (guessing) on any one item is .5, or 50%.[4] By contrast, the probability of obtaining a correct response by guessing on a four-alternative multiple-choice question is .25, or 25%.

An alternative to a selected-response format is a *constructed-response format*—one that requires the examinee to supply or to create the correct answer, as opposed to merely selecting it. Three types of constructed-response items are the completion item, the short answer, and the essay. A completion item requires the examinee to provide a word or phrase that completes a sentence, as in the following example.

> The standard deviation is generally considered the most useful measure of _____ .

A good completion item should be worded so that the correct answer is specific. Completion items that can be correctly answered in many ways can lead to scoring problems. The correct completion for the item above is *variability*. An alternative way of writing this item would be as a short-answer item:

> What descriptive statistic is generally considered the most useful measure of variability? _____

A good short-answer item is written clearly enough that the testtaker can indeed respond succinctly—with a "short answer." There are no hard-and-fast rules specifying how short an answer must be to be considered a "short answer"; a word, a term, a sentence, or a paragraph may suffice. Beyond a paragraph or two, the item might more properly be referred to as an *essay item*. Here is an example of an essay item:

> Compare and contrast definitions and techniques of classical and operant conditioning. Include examples of how principles of each have been applied in clinical as well as educational settings.

An essay is a useful type of item when the test developer wants the examinee to demonstrate a depth of knowledge about a single topic. In contrast to selected-response items and constructed-response items such as the short answer and the completion items, the essay question not only permits the restating of learned material but also allows for the creative integration and expression of the material in the testtaker's own words. It can also be appreciated that the skills tapped by essay-type items are different from those tapped by items of the true-false and matching genres. Whereas an essay requires recall, organization, planning, and writing ability, the other types of items require

---

4. We note in passing, however, that although the probability of guessing correctly on an individual true-false item on the basis of chance alone may be .5, the probability of guessing correctly on a *sequence* of true-false items decreases as the number of items increases. The probability of guessing correctly on two such items is equal to $.5^2$, or 25%. The probability of guessing correctly on ten such items is equal to $.5^{10}$, or .001; there is therefore a one-in-a-thousand chance that a testtaker would guess correctly on ten true-false items on the basis of chance alone.

only recognition. Drawbacks to essay items as compared with short-answer items may include a more limited area of coverage relative to the amount of testing time and a degree of subjectivity in the scoring.

Scoring of Items

Many different test-scoring models have been devised. In psychological testing, the *cumulative* model is the most common, perhaps because of its sheer simplicity and logic. Typically, the rule in a cumulatively scored test is that the higher the score on the test, the higher the testtaker is on the ability, the trait, or some other characteristic the test purports to measure. For each testtaker response to targeted items made in a particular way, the testtaker earns cumulative credit with regard to a particular construct.

In tests that employ a *class* or category approach to scoring, testtaker responses earn credit toward placement in a particular class or category with other testtakers whose pattern of responses is presumably similar in some way. This approach is used in some diagnostic systems, wherein individuals must exhibit a certain number of symptoms to qualify for a specific diagnosis. A third scoring model, *ipsative* scoring, departs radically in rationale from either cumulative or class models. A typical objective in ipsative scoring is the comparison of a testtaker's score on one scale within a test with another scale within that same test. Consider, for example, a personality test called the Edwards Personal Preference Schedule (EPPS), which is designed to measure the relative strength of different psychological needs. The EPPS ipsative scoring system yields information on the strength of various needs in relation to the strength of other of the testtaker's needs. The test does not yield information on the strength of a testtaker's need relative to the presumed strength of that need in the general population.

Once all of the groundwork for a test has been laid and a draft of the test is ready for administration, the next step is, logically enough, test tryout.

Test Tryout

Having created a pool of items from which the final version of the test will be developed, the test developer will next try out the test. The test should be tried out on people similar in critical respects to the people for whom the test was designed. Thus, for example, if a test is designed to aid in decisions regarding the selection of corporate employees with management potential at a certain level, it would be appropriate to try out the test on corporate employees at the targeted level—and inappropriate to try out the test on introductory psychology students.

Equally important as questions concerning *whom* the test should be tried out on are questions regarding *how many* people the test should be tried out on. There are no hard-and-fast rules here, but some have recommended that there be no fewer than five subjects, and preferably as many as ten subjects, for every one item on the test. In general, the more subjects in the tryout the better; all other things being equal, ten subjects per test item is better than five because of the lessening of the role of chance in subsequent analyses of the data, particularly in factor analysis. A definite risk in using too few subjects during test tryout comes during factor analysis of the findings, when what we might call "phantom factors"—nonexistent factors that are actually artifacts of the small sample size—may emerge.

The test tryout should be executed under conditions that are as identical as possible to the conditions under which the standardized test will be administered. This means that all instructions, and everything from the time limits allotted for completing the test to the "atmosphere" at the test site, should be as similar as possible. As Nunnally (1978, p. 279) so aptly phrased it, "If items for a personality inventory are being administered in an atmosphere that encourages frankness and the eventual test is to be administered in an atmosphere where subjects will be reluctant to say bad things about themselves, the item analysis will tell a faulty story." In general, the test developer endeavors to ensure that differences in response to the test's items are due in fact to the items, not to extraneous factors.

What Is a "Good" Item?

Before reading on, pick up a piece of paper and just jot down—using logic and common sense—what you believe the criteria of a good test item are. After you've done that, compare what you've written with the following discussion.

In the same sense that we can speak of a good test as being reliable and valid, we can speak of a good test item as being reliable and valid. Further, a good test item helps to discriminate testtakers; a good test item is one that high scorers on the test as a whole get right. An item that high scorers on the test as a whole do not get right is probably not a good item. We may also describe a good test item as one that low scorers on the test as a whole get wrong; an item that low scorers on the test as a whole get right may not be a good item.

How does a test developer identify "good" items? After the first draft of the test has been administered to a representative group of examinees, it remains for the test developer to analyze test scores and responses to individual items. The different types of statistical scrutiny that the test data can potentially undergo at this point are referred to collectively as "item analysis." Note that although item analysis tends to be regarded as a quantitative endeavor, it may be, as we shall see, qualitative as well.

Item Analysis

Statistical procedures used to analyze items may become quite complex, and our treatment of this subject should be thought of only as introductory. We briefly survey some procedures typically used by test developers in their efforts to select the best items from a pool of tryout items. The student should understand that the criteria for the "best" items may differ as a function of the test developer's objectives. Thus, for example, one test developer might deem the "best" items to be those that optimally contribute to the internal reliability of the test. Another test developer might wish to design a test with the highest possible criterion-related validity—and select items accordingly. Among the tools test developers might employ to analyze and select items will be an index of an item's difficulty, an item-validity index, an item-reliability index, and an index of the item's discrimination. Brief coverage of each of these statistics appears in this section. For a more in-depth treatment, the interested reader is referred to Gulliksen (1950).

In the interest of simplifying our discussion and clearly illustrating the concepts presented, assume that you are the author of 100 items for a ninth-grade-level American History Test (AHT) and that this 100-item (draft) test has been administered to 100 ninth-graders. Hoping in the long run to standardize the test and have it distributed by a commercial test publisher, you have a more immediate, short-term goal: to select the 50 best of the 100 items you originally created. How might that short-term goal be achieved? As we will see, the answer lies in item-analysis procedures. Before elaborating on those procedures, however, we once again remind and invite students to apply the following material—making "translations" in phraseology when appropriate—to tests other than achievement tests, such as tests of personality.

Item-Difficulty Index

Suppose every examinee got item 1 of the test correct. Can we say that item 1 is a good item? What if no one got item 1 correct? In either case, item 1 is not a good item. If everyone gets the item right, the item is too easy. If everyone gets the item wrong, the item is too difficult. Just as the test as a whole is designed to provide an index of degree of knowledge about American history, so each individual item on the test should be "passed" (scored as correct) or "failed" (scored as incorrect) on the basis of testtakers' differential knowledge of American history.[5]

An index of an item's difficulty is obtained by calculating the proportion of the total number of testtakers who got the item right. A lowercase, italicized p (p) is used to denote item difficulty, and a subscript refers to the item number (p_1 is read "item-difficulty index for item 1"). The value of an item-difficulty index can theoretically range from 0 (if no one got the item right) to 1 (if everyone got the item right). If 50 of the 100 examinees got item 2 right, then the item-difficulty index for this item would be equal to 50 divided by 100, or .5 ($p_2 = .5$). If 75 of the examinees got item 3 right, p_3 would be equal to .75, and we could say that item 3 was easier than item 2. Note that the larger the

---

5. An exception here may be a "giveaway" item. Such an item might be inserted near the beginning of a test to spur motivation and a positive test-taking attitude and lessen testtakers' test-related anxiety. In general, however, if an item analysis suggests that a particular item is too easy or too difficult, the item must be either rewritten or discarded.

item-difficulty index, the easier the item. Since p refers to the percent of people passing an item, the higher the p for an item, the easier the item. The statistic referred to as an item-difficulty index in the context of achievement testing may be referred to as an item-endorsement index in other contexts, such as personality testing. Here, the statistic provides not a measure of the percent of people passing the item but a measure of the percent of people who said "yes" to, agreed with, or otherwise "endorsed" the item.

An index of the difficulty of the "average" test item for a particular test can be calculated by averaging the item-difficulty indices for all the test's items. This is accomplished by summing the item-difficulty indices for all test items and dividing by the total number of items on the test. For maximum discrimination among the abilities of the testtakers, the optimal average item difficulty is approximately .5, with individual items on the test ranging in difficulty from about .3 to .8. Note, however, that the possible effect of guessing must be taken into account when considering items of the selected-response variety. With this type of item, the optimal average item difficulty is usually the midpoint between 1.00 and the chance success proportion, defined as the probability of answering correctly by random guessing. In a true-false item, the probability of guessing correctly on the basis of chance alone is 1/2, or .50. Therefore, the optimal item difficulty is halfway between .50 and 1.00, or .75. In general, the midpoint representing the optimal item difficulty is obtained by summing the chance success proportion and 1.00 and then dividing the sum by 2, or:

$$.50 + 1.00 = 1.5$$
$$\frac{1.5}{2} = .75$$

For a five-option multiple-choice item, the probability of guessing correctly on any one item on the basis of chance alone is equal to 1/5, or .20. The optimal item difficulty is therefore .60:

$$.20 + 1.00 = 1.20$$
$$\frac{1.20}{2} = .60$$

Item-Validity Index

The item-validity index can be calculated once the following two statistics are known:

- The item-score standard deviation
- The correlation between the item score and the criterion score

The item-score standard deviation of item 1 (denoted by the symbol s_1) can be calculated using the index of the item's difficulty (p_1) in the following formula:

$$s_1 = \sqrt{p_1(1 - p_1)}$$

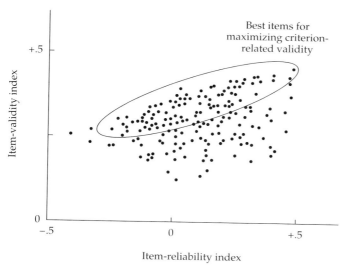

Figure 7–3
Maximizing Criterion-Related Validity
(Source: Allen & Yen, 1979)

The correlation between the score on item 1 and a score on the criterion measure (denoted by the symbol r_{1C}) is multiplied by item 1's item-score standard deviation (s_1), and the product is equal to an index of an item's validity ($s_1 r_{1C}$). The calculation of the item-validity index will be important when the test developer's goal is to maximize the criterion-related validity of the test. A visual representation of the best items on a test (if the objective is to maximize criterion-related validity) can be achieved by a plotting of each item's item-validity index and item-reliability index (see Figure 7–3).

Item-Reliability Index

The item-reliability index provides an indication of the internal consistency of a test (Figure 7–4); the higher this index, the greater the test's internal consistency. This index is equal to the product of the item-score standard deviation (s) and the correlation (r) between the item score and the total test score.

Factor analysis and inter-item consistency A statistical tool useful in determining whether items on a test appear to be measuring the same thing(s) is the technique of factor analysis (discussed in Chapter 6). Through the judicious use of factor analysis, items that do not "load on" the factor that they were written to tap (that is, items that do not appear to be measuring what they were designed to measure) can be revised or eliminated. If too many items appear to be tapping a particular area, the weakest of such items can be eliminated. Additionally, factor analysis can be useful in the test interpretation process, especially

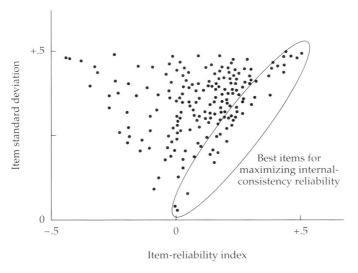

Figure 7–4
Maximizing Internal-Consistency Reliability
(Source: Allen & Yen, 1979)

when comparing the constellation of responses to the items from two or more groups. Thus, for example, if a particular personality test is administered to two groups of hospitalized psychiatric patients, each group with a different diagnosis, the same items may be found to load on different factors in the two groups. Such information will compel the responsible test developer to revise or eliminate certain items from the test or to describe the differential findings in the test manual.

Item-Discrimination Index

Measures of item discrimination indicate how adequately an item separates or discriminates between high scorers and low scorers on an entire test. In this context, a multiple-choice item on an achievement test is a good item if most of the high scorers answer correctly and most of the low scorers answer incorrectly. If most of the high scorers fail a particular item, then it is possible that these testtakers may be making an alternative interpretation of a response intended to serve as a distractor. In such a case, the test developer would do well to interview the examinees to understand better the basis for the choice and then appropriately revise (or eliminate) the item. Common sense dictates that an item on an achievement test is not doing its job if it is answered correctly by respondents who understand the subject matter least. Similarly, an item on a test purporting to measure a particular personality trait is not doing its job if responses to it indicate that people who, for example, score very low on the test

Table 7–1
Item-Discrimination Indices for Five Hypothetical Items

Item	U	L	U − L	n	d [(U − L)/n]
1	20	16	4	32	.13
2	30	10	20	32	.63
3	32	0	32	32	1.00
4	20	20	0	32	0.00
5	0	32	− 32	32	− 1.00

as a whole (indicating the absence or low level of the trait in question) tend to score very high on the item (indicating that they are very high on the trait in question—contrary to what the test as a whole indicates).

The *item-discrimination index* is a measure of item discrimination symbolized by a lowercase, italicized letter d (*d*). This estimate of item discrimination, in essence, compares performance on a particular item with performance in the upper and lower regions of a distribution of continuous test scores. The optimal boundary lines to demarcate what we are referring to as the "upper" and "lower" areas of a distribution of scores are scores within the upper and lower 27% of the distribution of scores—provided the distribution is normal (Kelley, 1939). As the distribution of test scores becomes more platykurtic (flat), the optimal boundary line for defining "upper" and "lower" gets larger and approaches 33% (Cureton, 1957). Allen and Yen (1979, p. 122) assure us that "for most applications, any percentage between 25 and 33 will yield similar estimates."

The item-discrimination index is a measure of the difference between the proportion of high scorers answering an item correctly and the proportion of low scorers answering the item correctly; the higher the value of *d*, the greater the number of high scorers answering the item correctly. A negative *d* value on a particular item is a "red flag" because it indicates a situation where low-scoring examinees are more likely to answer the item correctly than high-scoring examinees. This situation calls for some action such as revision or elimination of the item.

Assume a teacher gave a test to 119 people and isolated the upper (*U*) and lower (*L*) 27% of the test papers with a total of 32 papers in each group. Data and item-discrimination indices for items 1 through 5 are presented in Table 7–1. Note that 20 testtakers in the *U* group answered item 1 correctly and 16 testtakers in the *L* group answered item 1 correctly. With an item-discrimination index equal to .13, item 1 is probably a reasonable item because more members of the *U* than of the *L* group answered it correctly. The higher the value of *d*, the more adequately the item discriminates the higher-scoring from the lower-scoring testtakers. For this reason, item 2 is a better item than item 1; its item-discrimination index is .63. The highest possible value of *d* is +1.00—this in the case where all members of the *U* group answer the item correctly and all members of the *L* group answer the item incorrectly. In a situation where the same proportion of members of the U and L group pass the item, the item is not discriminating between testtakers at all, and d, appropriately enough, would be equal to 0. The lowest value that an index of item discrimination can take is -1. A d equal to -1 is a test developer's nightmare; it indicates a situation where all the members of the U group fail the item and all the members of the L group pass it. On the face of it, such an item is the worst possible type of item and is in dire need of revision or elimination. However, the test developer might learn or discover something new about the construct being measured if he or she takes the time to try to uncover the reason for this unanticipated finding.

Analysis of item alternatives   The quality of each alternative within a multiple-choice item can be readily assessed with reference to the comparative performance of upper and lower scorers. No formulas or statistics are really necessary here; by charting the number of testtakers in the U and L groups who chose each alternative, the test developer can get an idea of the effectiveness of a distractor by means of a simple "eyeball test." For purposes of illustration, let's analyze responses to five items on a hypothetical test, assuming that there were 32 scores in the upper level (U) of the distribution and 32 scores in the lower level (L) of the distribution. Let's begin by looking at the pattern of responses to item 1. In each case ★ denotes the correct alternative.

Alternatives

Item 1		★a	b	c	d	e
	U	24	3	2	0	3
	L	10	5	6	6	5

The response pattern to item 1 indicates that the item is a good one. More members of the U than of the L group answered the item correctly, and each of the distractors attracted some testtakers.

Item 2		a	b	c	d	★e
	U	2	13	3	2	12
	L	6	7	5	7	7

Item 2 signals a situation in which a relatively large number of members of the U group chose a particular distractor choice (in this case, "b"). This item could probably be improved upon revision, preferably one made after an interview with some or all of the U students who chose "b."

Item 3		a	b	★c	d	e
	U	0	0	32	0	0
	L	3	2	22	2	3

Item 3 indicates a most desirable pattern of testtaker response. All members of the U group answered the item correctly, and each distractor attracted one or more members of the L group.

Item 4		a	★b	c	d	e
U		5	15	0	5	7
L		4	5	4	4	15

Item 4 is more difficult than item 3—fewer examinees answered it correctly. Still, this item provides useful information about discrimination because it effectively discriminates higher-scoring from lower-scoring examinees. For some reason, one of the alternatives ("e") was particularly effective—perhaps too effective—as a distractor to students in the low-scoring group. The test developer may wish to further explore why this was the case.

Item 5		a	b	c	★d	e
U		14	0	0	5	13
L		7	0	0	16	9

Item 5 is a poor item because more members of the L than of the U group answered the item correctly. Furthermore, none of the examinees chose the "b" or "c" distractors.

Item-Characteristic Curves

A graphic representation of item difficulty and discrimination can be made in an *item-characteristic curve* (ICC). As shown in Figure 7–5, an ICC is a graph on which ability is plotted on the horizontal axis and probability of correct response is plotted on the vertical axis. Note that the extent to which an item discriminates high- from low-scoring examinees is apparent from the slope of the curve; the steeper the slope, the greater the item discrimination. Also note that if the slope is positive, more high scorers are getting the item correct than low scorers; if the slope is negative, the reverse is true. Now focus on the item-characteristic curve for item A; do you think this is a good item? The answer is that it is not a good item; the probability of a testtaker's responding correctly is high for testtakers of low ability and low for testtakers of high ability. What about item B; is that a good item? Again, the answer is no. The curve tells us that testtakers of moderate ability have the highest probability of answering this item correctly; testtakers with the greatest amount of ability—as well as their counterparts at the other end of the ability spectrum—are unlikely to respond correctly to this item. Item B may be one of those items to which people who "know too much" or "think too much" are likely to respond incorrectly.

Item C is a good item; the probability of responding correctly to it increases with ability. What about item D? This item-characteristic curve profiles an item that discriminates at only one point on the continuum of ability; the probability is very high that all testtakers at or above this point will respond correctly to the item. We can also say that the probability of an incorrect response is very high for testtakers who fall below that particular point in ability. An item such as D has excellent discriminative ability and would be useful in a test designed, for example, to select applicants on the basis of some cutting score. However, such an item might not be desirable in a test designed to provide

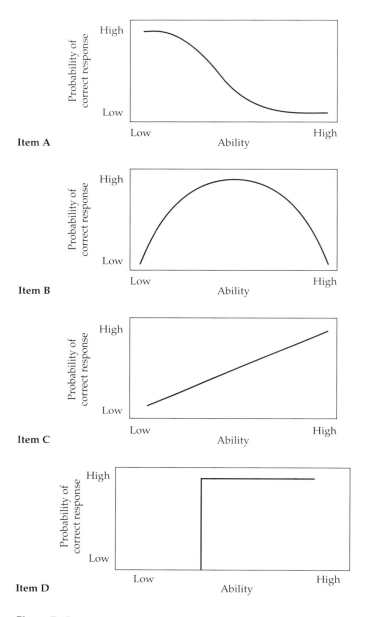

Figure 7–5
Some Sample Item-Characteristic Curves
(Source: Ghiselli et al., 1981)

In the interest of simplicity, we have omitted scale values for the axes. The vertical axis in such a graph lists probability of correct response in values ranging from 0 to 1. Values for the horizontal axis, which we have simply labeled "ability," are total scores on the test. In other sources you may find the vertical axis of an item-characteristic curve labeled something like "proportion of examinees who respond correctly to the item" and the horizontal axis labeled "total test score."

detailed information on testtaker ability across all ability levels—as might be the case, for example, in a diagnostic reading or arithmetic test.

Latent-trait models A test is typically designed to provide an estimate of the amount of knowledge or ability (or strength of a particular trait) possessed by the testtaker. The variable on which performance on the test is presumed to depend—be it knowledge, ability, a personality trait, or something else—is never directly measurable itself; an estimate of the amount of the variable is obtained through the test. In this way, latent traits are like the factors in factor analysis, which are not directly measured but are reflected in the test items. According to the latent-trait model of measurement, this underlying, unobservable variable—this latent trait—is unidimensional. Presumably, all the items on a test are measuring this trait. An application of the latent-trait model can be found in the Illness Causality Scale, a measure of children's understanding of illness (Sayer et al., 1993). Researching the validity of the test, the authors expected that three latent traits would be found: an understanding of illness, level of cognitive development of the child, and verbal intelligence. They demonstrated the likely presence of these latent traits by correlating the Illness Causality Scale with other scales, each of which was designed to reflect one of the latent traits. For example, the authors found that the Illness Causality Scale was moderately correlated with a scale measuring verbal intelligence, presumably because the two scales share the latent trait of verbal intelligence.

Latent-trait models differ in some important ways from classical "true score" test theory. For example, in contrast to classical "true score" test theory, in which no assumptions are made about the frequency distribution of test scores, inherent in latent-trait models are assumptions regarding the probability of the occurrence of a particular observed score in testtakers with a particular true score. As Allen and Yen (1979, p. 240) put it, "Latent-trait theories propose models that describe how the latent trait influences performance on each test item. Unlike test scores or true scores, latent traits theoretically can take on values from $-\infty$ to $+\infty$ [minus to plus infinity]."

The applicability of latent-trait models to psychological tests has been questioned by some theoreticians. It has been argued, for example, that the assumption of test unidimensionality is violated when many psychological tests are considered. It has been further argued that even the same item on a psychological test may be tapping different abilities from the same testtaker, depending on the life experiences of the testtaker. Despite lingering theoretical questions, latent-trait models appear to be playing an increasingly dominant role in the design and development of new tests and testing programs.[6]

---

6. More detailed discussion of the various types of latent-trait models (also referred to as *item-response theory* in some of the literature) can be found in various sources (such as Hambleton, 1979, 1988; Hambleton & Cook, 1977; Lord, 1980; Lord & Novick, 1968; Weiss & Davison, 1981; Wright & Stone, 1979). One effort to bring the various latent-trait models together under a single theory culminated in the development of generalized linear item-response theory (Mellenbergh, 1994).

Other Considerations in Item Analysis

Guessing   In achievement testing, the problem of how to handle testtaker guessing is one that has eluded any universally acceptable solution. It is true that a number of different procedures purporting to be corrections for guessing have been published, but none has proven to be entirely satisfactory. The reason is that the problem of guessing is more complex than it first appears. To understand why, consider the following three criteria that any correction for guessing must meet as well as the interacting problems that must be addressed.

1. A correction for guessing must recognize that when a respondent guesses at an answer on an achievement test, the guess is not typically made on a totally random basis. It is more reasonable to assume that the testtaker's guess is based on some knowledge of the subject matter and the ability to rule out one or more of the distractor alternatives. However, the individual testtaker's amount of knowledge of the subject matter will vary from one item to the next.

2. A correction for guessing must also deal with the problem of omitted items. Sometimes, instead of guessing, the testtaker will simply omit a response to an item. Should the omitted item be scored "wrong"? Should the omitted item be excluded from the item analysis? Should the omitted item be scored as if the testtaker had made a random guess? Exactly how should the omitted item be handled?

3. Just as some people may be luckier than others in front of a Las Vegas slot machine, so some testtakers may be luckier than others in guessing the choices that are keyed correct. Any correction for guessing may seriously underestimate or overestimate the effects of guessing for "lucky" and "unlucky" testtakers.

A number of different solutions to the problem of guessing have been proposed. In addition to proposed interventions at the level of test scoring through the use of corrections for guessing (referred to as *formula scores*), intervention has also been proposed at the level of test instructions. Testtakers may be instructed to provide an answer only when they are certain (no guessing) or to complete all items and guess when in doubt. Individual differences in testtakers' willingness to take risks result in problems for this approach to guessing (Slakter et al., 1975). Some people who don't mind taking risks may guess even when instructed not to do so. Others, who tend to be reluctant to take risks, refuse to guess under any circumstances. This creates a situation in which one's predisposition to take risks can affect one's test score.

To date, no solution to the problem of guessing has been deemed to be entirely satisfactory. The responsible test developer addresses the problem of guessing by including in the test manual (1) explicit instructions regarding this point for the examiner to convey to the examinees, and (2) specific instructions for scoring and interpreting omitted items.

Guessing on responses to personality and related psychological tests is not thought of as a great problem; although it may sometimes be difficult to choose the most appropriate alternative on a selected-response format personality test (particularly one with forced-choice items), the presumption is that the testtaker does indeed make the best choice.

Item fairness   Item-characteristic curves provide one tool for identifying which items are to be considered fair and which may be biased. Specific items are identified as biased in a statistical sense if they exhibit differential item functioning. Differential item functioning is exemplified by different shapes of item-characteristic curves for different groups (say, men and women) even though the two groups do not differ in total test score (Mellenbergh, 1994). Conversely, if an item is to be considered fair to different groups of testtakers, the item-characteristic curves for the different groups should not be significantly different:

> The essential rationale of this ICC criterion of item bias is that any persons showing the same ability as measured by the whole test should have the same probability of passing any given item that measures that ability, regardless of the person's race, social class, sex, or any other background characteristics. In other words, the same proportion of persons from each group should pass any given item of the test, provided that the persons all earned the same total score on the test. (Jensen, 1980, p. 444)

A determination of the presence of differential item functioning requires a statistical test of the null hypothesis of no difference between the item-characteristic curves of the two groups. Advantages and problems of different statistical tests for detecting differential item functioning continue to be debated (e.g., Raju et al., 1993). Items that show significant difference in item-characteristic curves should either be revised or be eliminated from the test. If a relatively large number of items biased in favor of one group coexist with approximately the same number of items biased in favor of another group, it cannot be claimed that the test measures the same abilities in the two groups—this although overall test scores between the individuals in the two groups may not be significantly different (Jensen, 1980).

Analysis of item-characteristic curves represents only one way of detecting item bias. Ironson and Subkoviak (1979) evaluated different methods for detecting item bias across different groups, including differences in item difficulty, item discrimination, item-characteristic curves, and the distribution of incorrect responses. These investigators concluded that the choice of item-analysis method does indeed affect determinations of item bias. Camilli and Shepard (1985) reported on the development of a computer program to aid in the detection of biased items on ability tests; a "biased item" was defined in the program as an item that favors one particular group of examinees in relation to another when differences in group ability are controlled.

Speeded tests   Item analyses of tests taken under speeded conditions yield misleading or uninterpretable results; the more toward the end of the test an item is, the more difficult it may appear to be—this simply because a testtaker may not have reached it! Similarly, measures of item discrimination may be artificially high for late-appearing items because examinees who know the material better may work faster and would be more likely to answer the later items. Thus, items appearing late in a speeded test are more likely to show positive item-total correlations because of the select group of examinees reaching those items. One obvious solution to the problem is to restrict the item analysis of items on a speeded test only to the items completed by the testtaker. However, this solution is *not* recommended for at least three reasons: (1) item analyses of the later items would be based on a progressively smaller number of testtakers, yielding progressively more unreliable results; (2) if the more knowledgeable examinees reach the later items, part of the analysis is based on all testtakers and part of the analysis is based on a selected sample; and (3) because the more knowledgeable testtakers are more likely to score correctly, their performance will make items occurring toward the end of the test appear easier than they might in reality be.

An example drawn from the research literature serves to illustrate the effects of a speeded test on item score–total score correlations. Wesman (1949) administered the same test to comparable groups of female nursing school applicants. One group took the test under speeded conditions, and the other group took the same test with generous time limits (power condition). The results showed that for items appearing toward the beginning of the test, there were no real differences under speed and power conditions. For items appearing late in the test, the item-total correlations were lower under the speed condition.

If speed is not an important element of the ability being measured by the test and because speed produces misleading information about item performance, the test developer should ideally administer the test to be item-analyzed with generous time limits to complete the test. Once the item analysis is completed, norms should be established using the speed conditions intended when the test is used in actual practice.

Qualitative Item Analysis

Test users have had a long-standing interest in understanding testtakers' test performance (Fiske, 1967; Mosier, 1947), and many different approaches to achieving such an understanding exist. To this point, we have focused on quantitative methods. However, *qualitative techniques* or nonquantitative methods that emphasize verbal rather than mathematical techniques may also be of great value. Through the use of simple questionnaires and/or individual or group discussions with testtakers, any test user—be it a classroom teacher, an individual researcher, or a large test publisher—can obtain valuable information on how the test could be improved. Some of the topics test users may wish to explore by the use of such methods are summarized in Table 7–2.

On a cautionary note, it is true that in some instances, providing testtakers with the opportunity to describe a test parallels providing students with the opportunity to describe their instructors. In both cases, there is a potential abuse of the process, especially by respondents who have extra-test (or extra-

Table 7–2
Potential Areas of Exploration by Means of Qualitative Item Analysis

This table lists sample topics and questions of possible interest to test users. The questions could be raised either orally or in writing shortly after a test's administration. Additionally, depending upon the objectives of the test user, the questions could be placed into other formats, such as true-false or multiple-choice. Depending upon the specific questions to be asked and the number of test-takers being sampled, the test user may wish to guarantee the anonymity of the respondents.

Topic	Sample Question
Cultural Sensitivity	Did you feel that any item or aspect of this test was discriminatory with respect to any group of people? If so, why?
Face Validity	Did the test appear to measure what you expected it would measure? If not, what about this test was contrary to your expectations?
Test Administrator	Did the behavior of the test administrator affect your performance on this test in any way? If so, how?
Test Environment	Did any conditions in the room affect your performance on this test in any way? If so, how?
Test Fairness	Do you think the test was a fair test of what it sought to measure? Why or why not?
Test Language	Were there any instructions or other written aspects of the test that you had difficulty understanding?
Test Length	How did you feel about the length of the test with respect to (a) the time it took to complete, and (b) the number of items?
Testtaker's Guessing	Did you guess on any of the test items? About what percentage of the items would you estimate you guessed on? Did you employ any particular strategy for guessing, or was it basically random guessing?
Testtaker's Integrity	Do you think that there was any cheating during this test? If so, please describe the methods you think may have been used.
Testtaker's Mental/Physical State upon Entry	How would you describe your mental state going into this test? Do you think that your mental state in any way affected the test outcome? If so, how? How would you describe your physical state going into this test? Do you think that your physical state in any way affected the test outcome? If so, how?
Testtaker's Mental/Physical State During the Test	How would you describe your mental state as you took this test? Do you think that your mental state in any way affected the test outcome? If so, how? How would you describe your physical state as you took this test? Do you think that your physical state in any way affected the test outcome? If so, how?
Testtaker's Overall Impressions	How would you describe your overall impression of this test? What suggestions would you offer the test developer for improvement?
Testtaker's Preferences	Was there any part of the test that you found educational, entertaining, or otherwise rewarding? What specifically did you like or dislike about the test? Was there any part of the test that you found anxiety-provoking, condescending, or otherwise upsetting? Why?
Testtaker's Preparation	How did you prepare for this test? If you were going to advise others as to how to prepare for it, what would you tell them?

instructor) axes to grind. Respondents may be disgruntled for any number of reasons, ranging from a failure to prepare adequately for the test to disappointment in their test performance. In such cases, the opportunity to evaluate the test is tantamount to an opportunity to lash out. The test, the test administrator, and the institution, agency, or corporation responsible for the test administration may all become objects of criticism. For this reason, testtaker questionnaires, much like other qualitative research tools, if they are to be interpreted properly, must be interpreted "with a grain of salt." At the very least, the fact that the testtaker is asked for an evaluation bespeaks sincere concern for the testtaker's test-taking experience.

The "think aloud" test administration   First introduced in the late 1980s by Cohen et al. (1988), the "think aloud" test administration is a qualitative research tool designed to shed light on the testtaker's thought processes during the administration of a test. On a one-to-one basis with an examiner, examinees are asked to take a test, thinking aloud as they respond to each item. If the test is designed to measure achievement, such verbalizations may be useful in assessing not only if certain students (such as low or high scorers on previous examinations) are misinterpreting a particular item, but also why and how they are misinterpreting the item. If the test is designed to measure personality or some aspect of it, the think aloud technique may also yield valuable insights regarding the way individuals perceive, interpret, and respond to the items.

Expert panels   In addition to the interviewing of testtakers individually or in groups, experts may also be used to provide qualitative analyses of test items. Perhaps most typically, test publishers employ panels of experts to screen test materials for possible sources of bias. For example, in an effort to root out any possible bias in the Stanford Achievement Test Series (Eighth Edition), the test publisher formed an advisory panel of twelve minority group members, each a prominent member of the educational community. Panel members met with the publisher to obtain an understanding of the history and philosophy of the test battery, and to discuss and define the problem of bias (Stanford Special Report, 1992). Some of the possible forms of content bias that may find their way into any achievement test were identified as follows:

> *Status:* Are the members of a particular group shown in situations that do not involve authority or leadership?
> *Stereotype:* Are the members of a particular group portrayed as uniformly having certain: 1) aptitudes, 2) interests, 3) occupations, or 4) personality characteristics?
> *Familiarity:* Is there greater opportunity on the part of one group to: 1) be acquainted with the vocabulary, or 2) experience the situation presented by an item?
> *Offensive Choice of Words:* 1) Has a demeaning label been applied, or 2) has a male term been used where a neutral term could be substituted?
> *Other:* Panel members were asked to be specific regarding any other indication of bias they detected. (Stanford Special Report, 1992, pp. 3–4)

On the basis of qualitative information from an expert panel or testtakers themselves, a test user or developer may elect to modify a test. Modification might take many different forms, including the deletion of existing items and the addition of acceptable ones.

Test Revision

A tremendous amount of information is generated at the item-analysis stage, particularly given that a developing test may have hundreds of items. On the basis of that information, some items from the original item pool will be eliminated and others will be rewritten. How is information about the difficulty, validity, reliability, discrimination, and bias of test items, along with information from the item-characteristic curves, integrated and used to revise the test? There are probably as many ways of approaching test revision as there are test developers. One approach would be to characterize each item according to its strengths and weaknesses: some items may be highly reliable but lack criterion validity, whereas other items may be purely unbiased but too easy. Some items will be found to have many weaknesses, making them prime candidates for deletion or revision. For example, very difficult items have a restricted range (all or almost all testtakers get them wrong), which lowers correlation coefficients, as you may remember from Chapter 4. Because many reliability and validity coefficients are based on correlations, very difficult items will tend to lack reliability and validity because of their restricted range. The same is true of very easy items. Furthermore, test developers may find they must balance various strengths and weaknesses across items. For example, if many otherwise good items tend to be somewhat easy, the test developer may purposefully include some more difficult items even if they have other problems; those more difficult items may be specifically targeted for rewriting. The purpose of the test also influences the way the revision is done. If the test will be used to influence major decisions concerning educational placement or employment, the test developer will want to be scrupulously concerned with issues of item bias. If there is a need to identify the most highly skilled individuals among those being tested, items demonstrating excellent item discrimination, leading to the best possible test discrimination, will be emphasized.

As the test is being revised, the advantage of writing a large item pool become obvious: poor items can be eliminated in favor of those that were shown on the test tryout to be good items. Even when working with a large item pool, the test developer engaged in test revision must be aware of the domain from which the test should sample. Some aspects of the domain may be particularly difficult to write good items for, and blind deletion of all poorly functioning items could cause those aspects of the domain to remain untested.

Having balanced all these concerns, the test developer comes out of the revision stage with a test of improved quality. The next step will be an administration of the revised test under standardized conditions to a second appropriate sample of examinees. On the basis of an item analysis of data derived from this administration of the second draft of the test, the test developer may deem the test to be in its finished form—in which case the test's norms may be developed from the data, and the test will be said to have been "standardized" on this (second) sample.

Standardization can be viewed as "the process employed to introduce objectivity and uniformity into test administration, scoring and interpretation" (Robertson, 1990, p. 75). The standardization sample represents the groups of individuals with whom examinees' performance will be compared. For norm-referenced tests, it is important that this sample be representative of the population on those variables that might affect performance. Ability tests, for example, are developed so that the standardization group is representative of the population on such characteristics as age, gender, geographic region, type of community, ethnic group, and parent education. The latest census data are usually utilized to ensure that the standardization sample closely matches the population on these demographic characteristics.

In those instances in which the item analysis of the data for a test administration indicates that the test is not yet in finished form, the steps of revision, tryout, and item analysis are repeated until the test is satisfactory and standardization can occur. Once the items of the test have been finalized, professional test development procedures dictate that conclusions about the test's validity await what is called a *cross-validation* of findings.

Cross-Validation

The term *cross-validation* refers to a revalidation of a test on a sample of testtakers other than the ones on whom test performance was originally found to be a valid predictor of some criterion. It is to be expected that items selected for the final version of the test (in part because of their high correlations with a criterion measure) will have smaller item validities when administered to a second sample of testtakers—this because of the operation of chance factors. The decrease in item validities that inevitably occurs after cross-validation of findings is referred to as *validity shrinkage.* Such shrinkage is to be expected and is viewed as integral to the test development process. Further, such shrinkage is infinitely preferable to a scenario wherein (spuriously) high item validities are published in a test manual as a result of the inappropriate use of the identical sample of testtakers for test standardization and cross-validation of findings; users will in all likelihood be let down by the lower-than-expected validity of such a test. The test manual accompanying commercially prepared tests should outline the test development procedures used. Reliability information, including test-retest reliability and internal consistency estimates, should be reported along with evidence of the test's validity (Robertson, 1990).

Before we finish describing the test development process, you may want to consider the development of a "real-life" personality test, as presented in the *Close-up.* As you read about this test, try to apply the steps of test development as presented in this chapter.

Our discussion of test development now comes to a close—but not before we touch on a topic near, though maybe not dear, to the heart of every college student: instructor-prepared examinations. Have you ever thought about the psychometric rigor of such tests? As you will see in *Everyday Psychometrics,* these tests tend to be evaluated more informally than formally.

Anatomy of the Development of a Test: The Personality Research Form

Test author Douglas N. Jackson afforded readers an "inside look" at the way his test, the Personality Research Form (PRF), was created in his detailed account of the sequential system used. According to Jackson (1970), the PRF was developed in the hope that "by a careful application of modern conceptions of personality and of psychometric theory and computer technology more rigorous and more valid assessment of important personality characteristics would result" (p. 62). More specifically, Jackson viewed four interrelated principles as essential to the development of the PRF (as well as other tests of personality). He described them as follows:

1. The importance of psychological theory (see Cronbach & Meehl, 1955; Loevinger, 1957)

2. The necessity for suppressing response style (for example, suppressing the tendency to respond in socially desirable ways or the tendency to respond nonpurposively or randomly) (see Jackson & Messick, 1958)

3. The importance of scale homogeneity and scale generalizability

4. The importance of fostering convergent and discriminant validity

Jackson (1970) labeled four major stages in the development of the PRF as follows:

I. The substantive definition of personality scale content

II. A sequential strategy in scale construction

III. The appraisal of the structural component of validity

IV. Evaluation of the external component of validity.

In abbreviated, simplified fashion, each stage is described following.

I: The Substantive Definition of Personality Scale Content

A. The Choice of Appropriate Constructs
Jackson (1970) advises that "the first step in constructing a personality test is to decide what to mea-

sure" (p. 66). If, for example, a test or a scale within a test is to measure "aggressiveness," a clear definition of this construct must be arrived at; do we mean physical aggression? verbal aggression? overt aggression? covert aggression? all of these? The answers to these and related questions will depend on variables such as the objectives of the test and the "costs" involved—the latter term referring to factors such as the length of the test and time it will take to administer the test (see Cronbach & Gleser, 1965). An additional consideration in selecting a construct for measurement concerns how much is already known about it: "It is easier to prepare large numbers of items for dimensions whose correlates are well established" (Jackson, 1970, p. 67). The PRF was based on personality variables conceptualized and defined by Henry Murray and his colleagues (Murray, 1938). To help lay the foundation for items to be written that will be high in validity, mutually exclusive definitions of each personality variable had to be derived if they did not already exist (for example, "exhibition" had to be distinguished from "need for social recognition").

B. The Development of Substantively Defined Item Sets
Jackson (1970, p. 67) described this step as "the most difficult of all—the creation and editing of the item pool of some three thousand items, comprising the set from which PRF scales were finally developed." He went on to describe the evaluation and editing of each item with respect to the following criteria:

- their conformity to the definition of the scale for which they were written

- the adequacy of the negative instances of the trait

- their clarity and freedom from ambiguity

- their judged freedom from extreme levels of desirability bias

- their judged discriminating power and popularity levels when administered to appropriate populations

(continued)

Anatomy of the Development of a Test:
The Personality Research Form *(continued)*

- their judged freedom from various forms of content bias and their representativeness as a set

- the degree to which they conformed to the definition of the scale for which they were written as well as their "fortuitous convergence with irrelevant constructs, particularly those which were to be included in the PRF" (p. 68).

C. A Multidimensional Scaling Evaluation of Substantive Item Selection

The empirical value of rational judgment methods used in item selection was demonstrated by means of a technique called "multidimensional successive intervals scaling" (see Torgerson, 1958). Through the use of judges' ratings of descriptions of hypothetical people, information was obtained with respect to (1) the number of dimensions along which items were perceived to differ and (2) the scale value of each stimulus on each of the dimensions.

D. Empirical Evaluation of Homogeneity of Postulated Item Content

An empirical evaluation of the structured properties of the set of theoretically defined items was undertaken by means of the administration of provisional scales to an approximately equal number of male and female university students. Estimates of item reliability were obtained through the use of the KR-20 formula; the median reliability was found to be .925 with the highest reliability estimate being .94 for six of the scales: Aggression, Endurance, Exhibition, Harmavoidance, Order, and Social Recognition. Interestingly, the lowest reliability estimate (.80) was obtained for the scale called "Defendence." Of this finding, Jackson (1970, pp. 71–72) wrote: "This is not at all surprising, since defensive people might be less willing to admit defensiveness consistently."

II. A Sequential Strategy in Scale Construction

Responses to each of the items on the provisional PRF underwent a computerized item analysis to determine if the item would be retained or rejected. Some of the criteria employed at this stage of the test development process follow:

- Infrequently endorsed items—or items that almost everyone would endorse—were to be eliminated, since they reveal little about respondents. Stated a bit more technically, they will fail to appreciably add to the reliability and validity of the test because of their small variances. Further, such items have been found to elicit stylistic tendencies to respond deviantly or nonpurposively. For these reasons, items with a *p* value of either below .05 or above .95 were eliminated. An obvious exception to this rule would be items deliberately selected for use in the "Infrequency" scale—a scale designed to detect nonpurposive or random responding and related response styles. A sample item on this scale might be one like "I have visited the Republic of Samoa during the past year."

- If an item correlated higher with any content-scale total score other than the one it was written for, the item was eliminated—a method of helping to ensure convergent and discriminant validity.

- An evaluation was made as to the degree to which the item elicited tendencies to respond desirably. This was accomplished, at least in part, by evaluating each item's correlation with a desirability scale.

- An evaluation was made of the item's saturation as indicated by the magnitude of its correlation with the total scale.

- An evaluation was made of the item's content saturation in relation to its desirability bias as indicated by a specially devised Differential Reliability Index.

- Items were assigned to parallel forms of the test on the basis of item and scale statistical properties. The rigor with which this process was executed can be seen graphically in Figure 1.

- Each item was subjected to a final substantive review designed to evaluate its generalizability and its representativeness with respect to scale content.

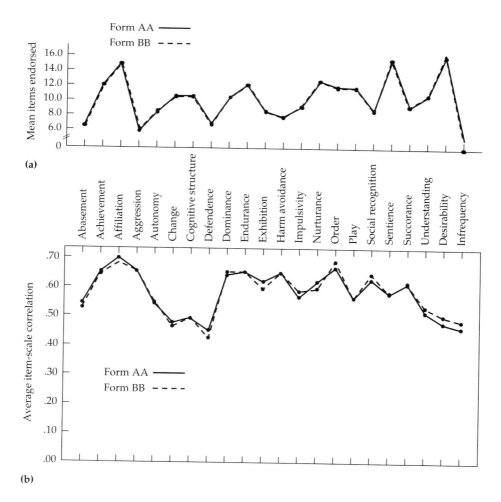

Figure 1
Comparison of Parallel Forms
(Source: Jackson, 1970)

(continued)

Anatomy of the Development of a Test:
The Personality Research Form *(continued)*

III. The Appraisal of the Structural Component of Validity

Steps were taken to ensure that optimal levels of homogeneity existed—homogeneity attributable to the test's content as opposed to response style or other variables.

IV. Evaluation of the External Component of Validity

Paid volunteers who lived in Stanford University housing and who were all "well acquainted with one another" served as the sample for the validity study. Jackson (1970, p. 88) informs us that each subject sat for a four-hour assessment battery including two forms of the PRF, a set of behavior ratings of 20 variables relevant to the 20 PRF content scales, and 600 adjectives measuring the same 20 traits relevant to each of the 20 scales. Subjects responded true or false to each of the 600 adjectives as self-descriptive, and later judged the desirability of each of them in other people. This latter task was included to appraise the hypothesis that a person's point of view about the desirability of a trait would tell us something valid about his own personality (Jackson, 1964; Stricker et al., 1968).

An examination of correlations between PRF scales and appropriate criterion measures revealed that there was substantial convergent and discriminant validity associated with PRF scales.

Psychometrics in the Classroom

Many concerns that professors and students have about testing are psychometric in nature. Professors want to give, and students want to take, reliable and valid measures of student knowledge. Even students who have not taken a course in psychological testing and assessment seem to understand psychometric issues regarding the tests they are administered in the classroom. As an illustration, consider each of the following pairs of statements. The first is a criticism of a classroom test you may have heard (or said yourself). The second statement is that criticism "translated" into the language of psychometrics.

"I spent all last night studying Chapter 3, and there wasn't one item on that test from that chapter!"
Translation: "I question the examination's content validity!"

"The instructions on that essay test weren't clear, and I think it affected my grade."
Translation: "There was excessive error variance related to the test administration procedures."

"I wrote the same thing for this short-answer question as my friend did—how come she got full credit and the professor took three points off my answer?"
Translation: "I have grave concerns about rater error affecting reliability."

"I didn't have enough time to finish; this test didn't measure what I know—only how fast I could write!"
Translation: "I wish the person who wrote this test had paid more attention to issues related to criterion-related validity and the comparative efficacy of speed as opposed to power tests!"

Like their students, professors have concerns about the tests they administer. They want their examination questions to be clear, relevant, and representative of the material covered. They sometimes wonder about the length of their examinations. Their concern is to cover sometimes voluminous amounts of material while still providing enough time for stu-

dents to give thoughtful consideration to their answers.

For most published psychological tests, these types of psychometric concerns would be addressed in a formal way during the test development process. In the classroom, however, rigorous psychometric evaluation of the dozen or so tests that any one instructor may administer during the course of a semester is impractical. Classroom tests are typically created for the purpose of testing just one group of students during one semester. In the classroom, tests change to reflect changes in lectures and readings as courses evolve. Also, if tests are reused, they are in danger of becoming measures of who has seen or heard about the examination previously, rather than measures of how well the students know the course material. Of course, although formal psychometric evaluation of classroom tests may be impractical, informal methods are frequently used.

Concerns about content validity are routinely addressed, usually informally, by professors in the test development process. For example, suppose an examination containing 50 multiple-choice questions and five short essays is to cover the reading and lecture material on four broad topics. The professor might systematically include 12 or 13 multiple-choice questions, and at least one short essay from each topic area. The professor might also draw a certain percentage of the questions from the readings and a certain percentage from lecture. Such a deliberate approach to content coverage may well boost the test's content validity—although no formal evaluation of the test's content validity will be made. The professor may also make an effort to inform the testtakers that all textbook boxes and appendices and all instructional media presented in class (such as videotapes) are "fair game" for evaluation (if that is indeed the case).

Criterion-related validity is difficult to establish on many classroom tests because no obvious criterion

(continued)

Psychometrics in the Classroom *(continued)*

reflects the level of the students' knowledge of the material. Exceptions may exist for students in a technical or applied program who take an examination for licensure or certification. Informal assessment of something akin to criterion validity may occur on an individual basis in a student-professor chat; a student who obtained the lowest score in the class may demonstrate to the professor an unambiguous lack of understanding of the material. It is also true that by the same method, the criterion validity of the test may be called into question. For example, a chat with the student who scored the highest might also reveal that the student has not a clue about the material the test was designed to tap. Such a finding would give the professor pause.

The construct validity of classroom tests is often assessed informally as well, as when an anomaly in test performance may call attention to construct validity-related issues. For example, consider a group of students who have a history of performing at an above-average level on exams. Now suppose that on one exam, all students in this group perform poorly. If all these students report not having studied for the test, or just not having understood the text material, then there is an adequate explanation for their low scores. However, if the students report that they studied and understood the material, as usual, then one might question the construct validity of the test as an explanation of the outcome.

Aspects of a classroom test's reliability can also be informally assessed. For example, a discussion with students can shed light on the internal consistency of the test. Then again, if the test was designed to be heterogeneous in nature, low internal consistency ratings might be desirable. On essay tests, inter-rater reliability can be explored by providing a group of volunteers with the criteria used in grading the essays and letting them grade some. Such an exercise might shed light on the clarity of the scoring criteria. In the rare instance when the same classroom test, for some reason, is given twice or in an alternate form, a discussion of the test's test-retest or alternate-forms reliability can be conducted. In practice, however, it is rare that classroom tests are administered twice or in alternate forms.

Have you ever taken an exam in which one student quietly asks for clarification about a specific question, and the professor then announces to the entire class the response to the student's question? This professor is attempting to reduce administration error (and increase reliability) by providing the same experience for all testtakers. When grading short-answer or essay questions, professors may try to reduce rater error by several techniques. For example, they may ask a colleague to decipher a student's poor handwriting or re-grade a set of essays (blind to the original grades). Professors also try to reduce administration error, and increase reliability, when they eliminate items that many students misunderstand.

Tests developed for classroom use may not be perfect; few if any tests for any purpose are. Still, most professors are always on the lookout for ways—formal and informal—to make the tests they administer as psychometrically sound as possible.

PART 3

The Assessment of Intelligence

8

Intelligence and Its Measurement

In this chapter, we will examine some of the general ways intelligence has been defined and measured. For example, you will see that the intelligence of infants is, of necessity, measured quite differently from the intelligence of adults. In Chapter 9, we will focus on psychometric and other attributes of specific intelligence tests. The measurement of intelligence and other constructs in preschool and educational settings is the subject of Chapter 10. We begin, however, by raising a question that must precede consideration of measurement-related issues.

What Is Intelligence?

Before reading on, take a piece of scrap paper and jot down your own definition of the word *intelligence.* How does your definition compare with those written by the experts we cite? In comparing your definition with the many different ones that follow, you may come to the conclusion, as did Neisser (1979), that because of its nature, "intelligence" cannot be explicitly defined. Drawing on the work of Rosch (1978) and Wittgenstein (1953) in the area of concept formation and categorization, Neisser noted that for certain categories of things, no single prototype exists. As an example, consider the word *game;* no sharp boundary separates games from nongames, many categories of "game" exist, and there is no single feature that all games have in common. According to Neisser, concept formation and categorization are organized around prototypes, and it is possible to imagine prototypes that we have not in reality encountered. Neisser argues further that "the ideally intelligent person is one such imaginary prototype" (p. 220). Neisser's description of the intelligent person as an "imaginary prototype" does *not* imply that intelligence does not exist or that the concept lacks utility. It does not even imply that intelligence cannot be measured. Rather, Neisser's essay spoke only to the difficulty in defining a multi-faceted construct.

Research conducted by Robert Sternberg and his associates at Yale University (Sternberg, 1981, 1982; Sternberg et al., 1981) was designed to shed light on questions such as "What does 'intelligence' mean to laypeople?" and "How does the layperson's definition differ from that of the research psychologist?" The researchers asked a total of 476 people from the New Haven, Connecticut, area to respond to a questionnaire or participate in a personal interview. Students, commuters, supermarket shoppers, people who answered newspaper advertisements, and people randomly selected from the phone book were asked for their views of intelligence. They were asked to list the behaviors considered to be characteristic of "intelligence," "academic intelligence," "everyday intelligence," and "unintelligence." After a list of various behaviors characterizing intelligence was generated, 28 nonpsychologists in the New Haven area were asked to rate on a scale of 1 (low) to 9 (high) how characteristic each of the behaviors was for the ideal "intelligent" person, the ideal "academically intelligent" person, and the ideal "everyday intelligent" person. The views of 140 doctoral-level research psychologists who were experts in the area of intelligence were also solicited. These experts were themselves involved in research on intelligence in major university and research centers around the United States.

All people polled in Sternberg's study had definite ideas about what intelligence, or the lack of it, was. For the nonpsychologists, the behaviors most commonly associated with intelligence were "reasons logically and well," "reads widely," "displays common sense," "keeps an open mind," and "reads with high comprehension." Leading the list of most frequently mentioned behaviors associated with "unintelligence" were "does not tolerate diversity of views," "does not display curiosity," and "behaves with insufficient consideration of others."

Sternberg and his colleagues grouped the list of 250 behaviors characterizing intelligence and unintelligence into subsets that were most strongly related to each other. The analysis indicated that the nonpsychologists and the experts conceived of intelligence in general as practical problem-solving ability (such as "listens to all sides of an argument"), verbal ability ("displays a good vocabulary"), and social competence ("is on time for appointments"). Each specific type of intelligence was characterized by various descriptors. "Academic intelligence" included verbal ability, problem-solving ability, and social competence, as well as specific behaviors associated with acquiring academic skills (such as "studying hard"). "Everyday intelligence" included practical problem-solving ability, social competence, character, and interest in learning and culture. In general, the researchers found a surprising degree of similarity between the experts' and laypeople's conceptions of intelligence. With respect to academic intelligence, however, the experts tended to stress motivation ("is persistent," "highly dedicated and motivated in chosen pursuits"), whereas laypeople stressed the interpersonal and social aspects of intelligence ("sensitivity to other people's needs and desires," "is frank and honest with self and others").

In another study (Siegler & Richards, 1980), students enrolled in college developmental psychology classes were asked to list behaviors associated with intelligence in infancy, childhood, and adulthood. Perhaps not surprisingly, different conceptions of intelligence as a function of developmental stage were noted. In infancy, intelligence was associated with physical coordination, awareness of people, verbal output, and attachment. In childhood, verbal facility, understanding, and characteristics of learning were most often listed. Verbal facility, use of logic, and problem solving were most frequently associated with adult intelligence.

A study conducted with first-, third-, and sixth-graders (Yussen & Kane, 1980) suggested that children as young as first grade also have notions about intelligence. Younger children's conceptions tended to emphasize interpersonal skills (acting nice, being helpful, being polite), whereas older children emphasized academic skills (being good at reading).

The 1921 Symposium

In a symposium published in the *Journal of Educational Psychology* in 1921, seventeen of the country's leading psychologists addressed the following questions: (1) What is intelligence? (2) How can it best be measured in group tests? and (3) What should the next steps in the research be? No two psychologists agreed (see Thorndike et al., 1921). Six years later, Spearman (1927, p. 14) would observe, "In truth, intelligence has become . . . a word with so many meanings that finally it has none." And decades after the symposium was first held, Wesman (1968, p. 267) concluded that there appeared to be "no more general agreement as to the nature of intelligence or the most valid means of measuring intelligence today than was the case 50 years ago."

As Neisser (1979) observed, although the *Journal* felt that the symposium would generate vigorous discussion, it generated more heat than light and led to a general increase in exasperation with discussion on the subject. Symptomatic of that exasperation was an unfortunate statement by a historian of psychology and—nonpsychometrician—experimental psychologist, Edwin G. Boring. Boring (1923, p. 5) attempted to quell the argument by pronouncing that "intelligence is what the tests test." Although such a view is not entirely devoid of merit (see Neisser, 1979, p. 225), it is an unsatisfactory, incomplete, and circular definition. The thoughts of some other behavioral scientists throughout history, as well as more contemporary views, follow.

Francis Galton

Sir Francis Galton advanced the intuitively appealing hypothesis that the most intelligent persons were those equipped with the best sensory abilities, for it is through the senses that one comes to know the world. In his book *Inquiries into Human Faculty and Development*, Galton (1883, p. 27) wrote, "The only information that reaches us concerning outward events appears to pass through the avenues of our senses; and the more perceptive the senses are of difference, the larger is the field upon which our judgment and intelligence can act." Following this logic, tests of visual acuity or hearing ability were generally thought of as tests of "intelligence." If we view them in that context, we can appreciate the great efforts Galton expended in obtaining measurements of these and related variables.

Not all scientists of the day agreed with Galton's views. Among the dissenters was the Frenchman Alfred Binet.

Alfred Binet

Although Alfred Binet (see page 260) never provided an explicit definition of intelligence, as early as 1890, he wrote that the components of intelligence included reasoning, judgment, memory, and the power of abstraction (Varon, 1936). In a paper critical of Galton's approach to intellectual assessment, Binet and a colleague called for more complex measurements of intellectual ability (Binet & Henri, 1895). Unlike Galton, Binet was motivated by the very demanding and challenging task of developing and recommending a procedure for identifying intellectually limited Parisian schoolchildren who could not benefit from a regular instructional program and required special educational experiences. Galton viewed intelligence as a number of distinct processes or abilities that could be assessed only by separate tests. By contrast, Binet argued that when one solves a particular problem, the distinct abilities used cannot be separated but, rather, interact to produce the solution. For example, memory and concentration interact when a subject is asked to reiterate digits presented orally. When analyzing a subject's response to such a task, it is difficult to determine the relative contribution of memory and concentration to the successful solution. This difficulty is the reason that Binet called for more-complex measurements of intellectual ability. Binet sought to measure "general mental ability," the pervasive component of intelligence that plays a role in all intelligent behavior.

Consistent with present-day beliefs concerning the assessment of intelligence, Binet also acknowledged that an intelligence test could provide only a *sample* of all of an individual's intelligent behaviors. Further, Binet wrote that the purpose of an intelligence test was to classify, not to measure:

> I have not sought in the above lines to sketch a method of measuring, in the physical sense of the word, but only a method of classification of individuals. The procedures which I have indicated will, if perfected, come to classify a person before or after such another person, or such another series of persons; but I do not believe that one may measure one of the intellectual aptitudes in the sense that one measures a length or a capacity. Thus, when a person studied can retain seven figures after a single audition, one can class him, from the point of his memory for figures, after the individual who retains eight figures under the same conditions, and before those who retain six. It is a classification, not a measurement . . . we do not measure, we classify. (Binet, quoted in Varon, 1936, p. 41)

In Chapter 9, we examine in detail the test that is a direct descendant of Binet's early work in the area of intelligence testing. We also examine in detail

Alfred Binet (1857–1911)

Born in Nice, France, to a family in which both his father and his grandfather were physicians, young Alfred was also expected to take up medicine as his calling. It is believed, however, that a childhood exposure to a cadaver by his father pushed the young Binet away from medicine and into law school instead. Binet was a lawyer by age 21 but because of his family's wealth felt no necessity to practice law. Binet spent much of his time in the library, reading psychology books, among other things. In 1880, Binet himself published a psychology-related article, though it was subsequently criticized as having been plagiarized. Binet's interest was caught for a while by the subject of "animal magnetism"—hypnosis—and he published numerous papers detailing how magnets could change emotions, influence perceptions, and accomplish all sorts of other things—things that hypnosis is known to be able to accomplish. To Binet's embarrassment, his findings would be shown to have been an artifact of poor experimental methodology.

In 1894, Binet earned a doctorate in natural science from the Sorbonne. His doctoral dissertation concerned the correlation between insects' physiology and behavior. In 1899, while he was director of the physiological psychology laboratory at the Sorbonne, Binet took into his employ a 26-year-old physician

Alfred Binet with his two daughters

named Théodore Simon. The association was to be of historic significance. Given impetus by Binet's growing dedication to finding a way of identifying and then properly educating the slow child, the Binet-Simon test of intelligence would be published in 1905—a test that most historians view as the launching stimulus for the testing movement.

the work of David Wechsler, another renowned psychologist whose name is closely identified with intelligence testing.

David Wechsler

David Wechsler's conceptualization of "intelligence" can perhaps best be summed up in his own words:

> Intelligence, operationally defined, is the aggregate or global capacity of the individual to act purposefully, to think rationally and to deal effectively with his environment. It is aggregate or global because it is composed of elements or

abilities which, though not entirely independent, are qualitatively differentiable. By measurement of these abilities, we ultimately evaluate intelligence. But intelligence is not identical with the mere sum of these abilities, however inclusive. . . . The only way we can evaluate it quantitatively is by the measurement of the various aspects of these abilities. (Wechsler, 1958, p. 7)

Elsewhere, Wechsler added that there are nonintellective factors that must be taken into account when assessing intelligence (Kaufman, 1990). Included among those factors are "capabilities more of the nature of connative, affective, or personality traits (which) include such traits as drive, persistence, and goal awareness (as well as) an individual's potential to perceive and respond to social, moral and aesthetic values" (Wechsler, 1975, p. 136). Binet also had observed that a comprehensive study of intelligence involved the study of personality as well.

Jean Piaget

Since the early 1960s, the theoretical research of the Swiss developmental psychologist Jean Piaget (1954, 1971) has received increasing attention. Piaget's research focused on the development of cognition in children: how children think, how they understand themselves and the world around them, and how they reason and solve problems. For Piaget, intelligence may be conceived of as a kind of evolving biological adaptation to the outside world; as cognitive skills are gained, adaptation (at a symbolic level) increases and mental trial and error replaces actual physical trial and error. Yet, according to Piaget, the process of cognitive development is thought to occur neither solely through maturation nor solely through learning. He believed that as a consequence of interaction with the environment, psychological structures become reorganized. Piaget carefully described four stages of cognitive development through which, he theorized, all of us pass during our lifetimes. Although individuals can move through these stages at different rates and ages, he believed that their order was unchangeable. Piaget viewed the unfolding of these stages of cognitive development as the result of the interaction of biological factors and learning.

According to this theory, biological aspects of mental development are governed by inherent maturational mechanisms. As individual stages are reached and passed through, the child is also having experiences within the environment. Each new experience, according to Piaget, requires some form of cognitive organization or reorganization in a mental structure called a *schema*. More specifically, Piaget used the term *schema* to refer to an organized action or mental structure that, when applied to the world, leads to knowing or understanding. Infants are born with several simple *schemata* (the plural of schema), including sucking and grasping. Learning initially by grasping and by putting almost anything in their mouths, infants use these schemata to understand and appreciate their world. As the infant grows older, schemata become more complicated and are tied less to overt action than to mental transformations. For example, when you add a series of numbers, you are transforming numbers mentally to reach your answer. Infants, children, and adults continue to apply schemata to objects and events to achieve understanding, and these schemata are constantly being adjusted.

Piaget hypothesized that the individual learns through the two basic mental operations of *assimilation* (actively organizing new information so that it fits in with what already is perceived and thought) and *accommodation* (changing what is already perceived or thought to fit in with new information). For example, a child who sees a butterfly and calls it a bird has *assimilated* the idea of butterfly into an already-existing mental structure, bird. However, when the new concept of "butterfly," separate from "bird," has additionally been formed, the mental operation of *accommodation* has been employed. Piaget also stressed the importance of physical activities and social peer interaction in promoting a disequilibrium that represents the process by which mental structures change. Disequilibrium causes the individual to discover new information, perceptions, and communication skills.

The four periods of cognitive development, each representing a more complex form of cognitive organization, are outlined in Table 8–1. The stages range from the sensorimotor period, wherein infants' thoughts are dominated by their

Table 8–1
Piaget's Stages of Cognitive Development

Stage	Age Span	Characteristics of Thought
Sensorimotor period	Birth–2 years of age	Child develops ability to exhibit goal-directed, intentional behavior; develops the capacity to coordinate and integrate input from the five senses; acquires the capacity to recognize the world and its objects as permanent entities (that is, the infant develops "object permanence").
Preoperational period	2–6 years of age	Child's understanding of concepts is based largely on what is seen; the child's comprehension of a situation, an event, or an object is typically based on a single, usually the most obvious, perceptual aspect of the stimulus; thought is irreversible (child focuses on static states of reality and cannot understand relations between states; for example, child believes the quantities of a set of beads change if the beads are pushed together or spread apart); animistic thinking (attributing human qualities to nonhuman objects and events).
Concrete operations period	7–12 years of age	Reversibility of thought now appears; conservation of thought (certain attributes of the world remain stable despite some modification in appearance); part-whole problems and serial ordering tasks can now be solved (able to put ideas in rank order); can deal only with relationships and things with which he or she has direct experience; able to look at more than one aspect of a problem and able to clearly differentiate between present and historical time.
Formal operations period	12 years of age and older	Increased capacity for abstraction and to deal with ideas independent of his or her own experience; greater capacity to generate hypotheses and test them in a systematic fashion ("if-then" statements, more alternatives); able to think about several variables acting together and their combined effects; can evaluate own thought; applies learning to new problems in a deductive way.

perceptions, to the formal operations period, wherein an individual has the ability to construct theories and make logical deductions without the need for direct experience.

A major thread running through the theories of Binet, Wechsler, and Piaget is the concept of *interactionism*. Interactionism refers to the complex concept by which heredity and environment are presumed to interact to influence the development of one's intelligence. Tackling the nature of intelligence from a somewhat different perspective is a group of theorists we will refer to collectively as "the factor analysts."

The Factor Analysts

As we have already seen, factor analysis refers to a group of statistical techniques designed to determine if underlying relationships between sets of variables (including test scores) exist. Factor-analytic theories of intelligence tend to fall into two main schools of thought that can be categorized as a "general" school and a "multiple-factor" school. The general theory of intelligence postulates the existence of a general intellectual ability that is partially tapped by all intellectual activities and numerous specific aptitudes. According to the multiple-factor viewpoint, an individual's intellect is composed of many independent abilities or faculties such as verbal, mechanical, artistic, and mathematical faculties.

As early as 1904, the influential British psychologist Charles Spearman (see p. 135) proposed a theory of the "universal unity of the intellective function," which was based on the observation that all intelligence tests correlated to a greater or lesser degree with each other. Spearman (1927) hypothesized that the proportion of the variance that the tests had in common accounted for a general (or g) factor of intelligence. The remaining portions of the variance were accounted for either by some specific (s) component of this general factor or by error (e). This "two-factor theory of intelligence," as it was later called, is graphically illustrated in Figure 8–1. Tests that correlated highly with other intelligence tests were thought to be highly saturated with the g factor. Those tests with no g factor were not considered to assess intelligence or cognition but, rather, were viewed as tests of pure sensory, motor, or personality traits.

Spearman (1927) conceived of the basis of the g factor as some type of general electrochemical mental energy available to the brain for problem solving. In addition, it was associated with facility in thinking of one's own experience and in making observations and extracting principles. It was g rather than s that was assumed to afford the best prediction of overall intelligence. Abstract-reasoning problems were thought to be the best measures of g in formal tests. As Spearman and his students continued their research, they acknowledged the existence of an "intermediate" class of factors common to a group of activities but not to all. This class of factors, called *group factors*, is neither so general as g nor so specific as s. Examples of these broad group factors include linguistic, mechanical, and arithmetical abilities.

E. L. Thorndike (1874–1949), a pioneer in the area of psychometrics, conceived of intelligence as a large number of interconnected intellectual elements,

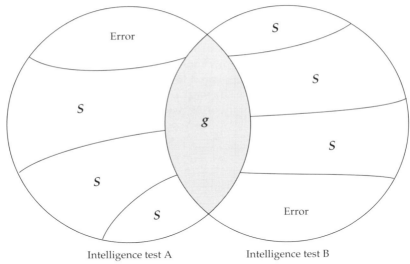

Figure 8–1
Spearman's Two-Factor Theory of Intelligence

Here, g *stands for a general intelligence factor and* s *stands for a specific factor of intelligence (specific to a single intellectual activity only).*

each representing a distinct ability. He advanced a theory that is known today as the "multifactor theory of intelligence" (Thorndike et al., 1909; Thorndike et al., 1921), in which he identified three clusters of intelligence, including social intelligence (dealing with people), concrete intelligence (dealing with objects), and abstract intelligence (dealing with verbal and mathematical symbols). In addition, Thorndike incorporated a general (g) mental ability factor as part of his theory. He defined g as the total number of modifiable neural connections available in the brain, which he called "bonds." A person's ability to learn, according to Thorndike, is determined by the number and speed of the "bonds" that are brought to bear on a problem.

Louis L. Thurstone, another pioneer in the development of factor analysis, conceived of intelligence as being composed of distinct abilities called primary mental abilities (PMAs): verbal meaning, perceptual speed, reasoning, number facility, rote memory, word fluency, and spatial relations. Thurstone (1938) developed and published the Primary Mental Abilities Test, which consisted of separate tests—each designed to measure only one PMA. Although Thurstone's original theory did not include a general mental ability factor (g), he found that his primary mental abilities correlated moderately with each other. This finding led Thurstone to acknowledge the existence of second-order factors that are fewer in number than primary factors. These factors were labeled by Vernon (1950) as "V:ed," representing verbal-educational aptitudes, and K:m, representing spatial, mechanical, and "practical" aptitudes. Thurstone subsequently came to believe that it is impossible to develop a test in the cognitive domain if it does not at least partially tap *g*.

Raymond B. Cattell proposed an innovative theory of the structure of intelligence that has special significance and application to the issue of cultural bias in mental testing (Cattell, 1971). Cattell's major contribution has been his two-factor theory of intelligence, the two factors being "fluid intelligence" and "crystallized intelligence." The abilities that make up *fluid intelligence* are non-verbal, relatively culture-free, and independent of specific instruction (such as memory for digits). *Crystallized intelligence* includes acquired skills and knowledge that are very much dependent on exposure to a particular culture as well as formal and informal education (vocabulary, for example). Retrieval of information and application of general knowledge are frequently tapped as part of crystallized intelligence. Cattell's theory of the structure of intelligence stresses that crystallized intelligence develops through the use of fluid intelligence and that the two are highly correlated—and very highly correlated among school-age children who share similar experiences such as a common culture, language, and schooling.

Unlike the other theorists discussed, the American theoretician and factor analyst J. P. Guilford has argued that there exists no general mental ability factor (*g*) in intelligence. Guilford (1967) proposed as an alternative a "three-dimensional structure of intellect model" whereby all mental activities could be classified and explained. According to this model, a mental activity can be classified according to (1) its operation (cognition, memory, divergent thinking, convergent thinking, and evaluation), (2) its content (figural, symbolic, semantic, and behavioral), and (3) the product resulting from the mental operation (units, classes, relations, systems, transformations, and implications). This leads to 120 possible separate ability factors (5 operations $\times$ 4 content $\times$ 6 products; see Figure 8–2). Thus, for example, a word fluency task (e.g., "name all the words that have the letter *a* in them") would be classified as a divergent thinking (operation), symbolic (content) unit (product).

Guilford has attempted to develop tests that can be used to individually measure the separate ability factors; the tests are expressly designed to minimize factors from correlating (and hence are designed to prevent *g* from occurring). Some have criticized this approach for its lack of a central factor (Eysenck, 1967; McNemar, 1964), and others have sought to shift focus to the "process of intelligent thinking" (Lohman, 1989, p. 535). Despite efforts to minimize the saturation of *g* in specific tests of mental ability, individual tests tapping each of the 120 separate ability factors have not yet been developed.

A de-emphasis, if not elimination, of the concept of *g* can also be found in the writing of others. Concluding a study of highly talented individuals, Commons (1985) wondered aloud whether there might not exist 800,000 or more intellectual abilities. And likening human abilities to the free-floating swarms of clouds of the Milky Way on a clear night, Horn (1988) asked, "Is there genuine order in this throng, or can one at least impose an order that will not do great injustice to the complexity and still enable one to organize thinking and talking about it?" (p. 645). Citing the Commons estimate regarding the number of different human abilities that may exist, Horn further speculated:

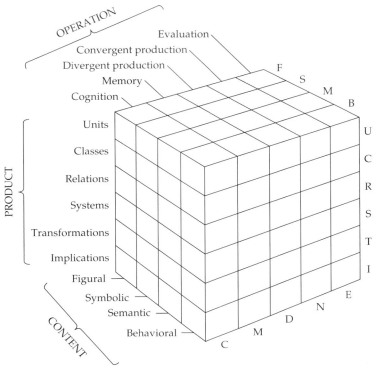

Figure 8–2
Guilford's Model of the Structure of Intellect

when one realizes that humans develop new abilities as circumstances change (as when printing, the slide rule, video games, and other such inventions enter a culture), it is not difficult to see that humans do indeed display a myriad of abilities. When one realizes, also, that every human possesses billions of neurons that can be arranged in other billions of ways, and each arrangement can support a different pattern of abilities, then again it is not difficult to suppose that 800,000 abilities could be an underestimate of the number of different specific abilities humans possess. (p. 646)

If we, in fact, conceptualize the range of human abilities as a kind of Milky Way, an intriguing problem arises for the factor analyst: where and how to draw the lines of commonality (see the box opposite). Acknowledging that "a small number of common-factor concepts can help describe and understand this Milky Way," Horn (1988) grappled with the many alternative means by which that feat could be accomplished.

The Information-Processing View

Another approach to conceptualizing intelligence derives from the work of the Russian neuropsychologist Aleksandr Luria (1966a, 1966b, 1970, 1973, 1980). This approach focuses on the mechanisms by which information is processed—

Where to Draw the Lines?

As Horn (1988) has observed, some might look at the welter of stars in the galaxy—each representing a human ability for the sake of this example—and say there is no possible way to draw order. Others may impose order only with respect to relatively few of the many potential "lines" of abilities that could be drawn (such as the lines A, D, E, and J), concluding, as Carroll (1985, p. 9) did, that "there exist only a relatively small number of identifiable, replicable abilities." Other people may draw the lines elsewhere, using any of the several available systems of factor analysis—statistical tools used to identify, describe, and understand common factors. Yet factor-analytic techniques will not fully take into account all available information about the data (Thurstone, 1947), such as how human abilities are unique, yet different from each other.

The concept of "general intelligence," usually abbreviated as *g*, is thought to cut across many, if not all, of the lines of common factors between abilities. But a problem arises when one contemplates where and how the "*g*-line" should be drawn. And as we will see in our study of various tests, general intelligence not only is referred to in different tests by different terms (such as "IQ," "general conceptual ability," and "general cognitive ability"), but also is conceived of as being composed of different abilities. Because different tests of intelligence conceive of *g* differently, the question arises, "Does a true *g* exist?" Though the concept of *g* is very much alive and well in mainstream psychology, voices of discontent have been heard. Horn (1988, p. 680), for example, has argued that "different intelligences can be distinguished even in early childhood, partly because they stem from separate genetic determiners and partly because they stem from separate environmental determiners" and that "the trend of the future is away from further study of very broad concepts of intelligence and toward the study of somewhat less broad abilities—separate intelligences."

how information is processed, rather than *what* is processed. Two basic types of information-processing styles, "simultaneous" and "successive," have been distinguished (Das et al., 1975; Luria, 1966a, 1966b). In *simultaneous* (also referred to as *parallel*) *processing,* information is integrated all at one time. In *successive* (also referred to as *sequential*) *processing,* each bit of information is individually processed in sequential fashion. As its name implies, sequential processing is logical and analytic in nature; piece-by-piece and one-piece-after-the-other, information is arranged and rearranged so that it makes sense. When you try to anticipate who the murderer is while watching a mystery movie, your thinking could be characterized as sequential in nature; you are constantly integrating bits of information that will lead you to a solution of the problem of "Whodunnit?" Memorizing a telephone number or learning the spelling of a new word is typical of the types of tasks that involve acquisition of information through successive processing.

By contrast, simultaneous processing may be described as synthesized in nature; information is integrated and synthesized at once and as a whole. As you stand before and appreciate a painting in an art museum, the "information" conveyed by the painting is processed in a manner that, at least for most of us, could reasonably be described as simultaneous—art critics and connoisseurs may be exceptions to this general rule. Tasks that involve the simultaneous mental representations of images or information, as is typical in map reading and in thinking about relationships between things, involve simultaneous processing.

Some tests, such as the Kaufman Assessment Battery for Children (Kaufman & Kaufman, 1983), which will be discussed in Chapter 10, rely heavily on this concept of a distinction between successive and simultaneous information processing. The strong influence of an information-processing perspective is also evident in the work of others (Das, 1972; Das et al., 1975; Naglieri, 1989, 1990; Naglieri & Das, 1988) who have developed a "PASS" model of intellectual functioning—"PASS" being an acronym for Planning, Attention, Simultaneous, and Successive. Within this model, *planning* refers to strategy development for problem solving, *attention* (also referred to as *arousal*) refers to receptivity to information, and *simultaneous* and *successive* refer to the type of information processing employed. Proponents of the PASS model have argued that existing tests of intelligence do not adequately assess planning. In general, research has supported the utility of the PASS model. One PASS-based intelligence test battery was deemed more sensitive to learning disabilities deficits than more traditional tests (Naglieri & Reardon, 1993). A factor analysis of tasks completed by children in kindergarten yielded factors consistent with the PASS model (Naglieri et al., 1993).

Robert Sternberg (1986) proposed another information-processing approach to intelligence, arguing that "the essence of intelligence is that it provides a means to govern ourselves so that our thoughts and actions are organized, coherent, and responsive to both our internally driven needs and to the needs of the environment" (Sternberg, 1986, p. 141). He proposed a triarchic theory of intelligence with three principal elements: metacomponents, performance components, and knowledge-acquisition components. Metacomponents are involved in planning what one is going to do, monitoring what one is doing, and evaluating what one has done upon completion. Performance components administer the instructions of metacomponents. Knowledge-acquisition components are involved in "learning how to do something in the first place" (Sternberg, 1994, p. 221).

The 1921 Symposium Revisited

Sixty-five years after the publication of the 1921 Symposium, an updated version raising many of the same questions with contemporary scholars was published (Sternberg & Detterman, 1986). The volume contained 24 essays representing a wide range of modern perspectives on the nature of intelligence. Has anything changed?

Definitions of intelligence have changed; contemporary experts seem more sensitive to "real world" as opposed to theoretical aspects of intelligence. Although the individual's abilities to adapt to the environment, to reason, and to solve problems are emphasized in both collections, the 1986 readings take more account of the importance of the context in which intelligence is exercised. There is also greater interest in metacognition (being able to think about and guide one's thought processes), which is a contribution of information-processing and computer models. Detterman (1986) notes that the more recent definitions of intelligence are more detailed and elaborate than the 1921 definitions. However, one constant across the years is disagreement over "the issue of the one versus the many" (Sternberg & Berg, 1986, p. 157)—that is, the issue of whether intelligence is a unitary phenomenon or many different things. Should personality and motivation be included in definitions of intelligence? Is intelligence more a biological or a cognitive construct? These are the types of questions that scholars continue to debate.

Judging from the affiliations of the invited participants, it is reasonable to conclude that the topic of intelligence has broader-based appeal today than it did in 1921; people who hold themselves out to the public as experts in intelligence come from a very wide variety of backgrounds. By contrast, most contributors to the 1921 symposium were educational psychologists. The 1921 contributors were concerned primarily with the use of intelligence tests in the schools. The 1986 contributors discussed applications of intelligence that went far afield of the classroom. The contributors included experts in cognitive psychology, developmental psychology, cognitive science, behavior genetics, mental retardation research, psychometrics, and social psychology (Sternberg & Berg, 1986), in addition to educational psychology.

In contrast to their 1921 counterparts, the 1986 contributors were less interested in future research designed to detail statistical aspects of various intelligence tests, and the relation of the tests to one another. Rather, the class of '86 placed greater emphasis on future research on understanding how intelligence guides behavior within the context of the environment (Sternberg & Berg, 1986) and the "real world" (Detterman, 1986).

Our consideration of the nature of intelligence continues with a brief overview of the ways intelligence is measured at various developmental stages.

Measuring Intelligence

The measurement of intelligence entails sampling an examinee's performance on different types of tests and tasks as a function of developmental level. At all developmental levels, the intellectual assessment process also provides a standardized situation from which the examinee's approach to the various tasks can be closely observed: an opportunity for assessment in itself, and one that can have great clinical utility. Using data from the administration of an intelligence test and other tests, behavioral observation during testing, and other sources, the clinician can obtain a well-rounded picture of the problem areas as well as the strengths of the examinee.

Measuring Intelligence in Infancy

In infancy (the period from birth through 18 months), intellectual assessment consists primarily of measurement of sensory-motor development. This includes, for example, the measurement of nonverbal, motor responses such as turning over, lifting of the head, sitting up, following a moving object with the eyes, gestural imitation, and reaching for a group of objects. (See Figure 8–3.) The examiner who attempts to assess the intellectual and related abilities of infants must be skillful in establishing and maintaining rapport with examinees who do not yet know the meaning of words like "cooperation" and "patience." Typically, measures of infant intelligence rely to a great degree on information obtained from a structured interview with the examinee's parents, guardians, or other caretakers.

Measuring the Intelligence of Children

Whereas the assessment of intelligence in infancy primarily involves evaluation of sensory-motor development, the focus of evaluation in the older child shifts to verbal and performance abilities. More specifically, the child may be called on during the course of a test to perform tasks designed to yield a measure of general fund of information, vocabulary, social judgment, language, reasoning, numerical concepts, auditory and visual memory, attention, concentration, and spatial visualization. The administration of many of the items may be preceded, as prescribed by the test manual, with "teaching items" designed to provide the examinee with practice in what is required by a particular item. In a bygone era, many intelligence tests were scored and interpreted with reference to the concept of "mental age."[1]

Especially when individually administered by a trained professional, the tests afford the examiner a unique opportunity to observe the child's reactions to success, failure, and frustration, and his or her general approach to problem

---

1. A detailed discussion of the concept of mental age is presented in Cohen (1996).

270   Part 3: The Assessment of Intelligence

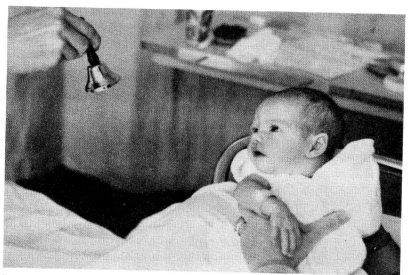

Figure 8–3
Testing the "Alerting" Response

One assessment technique common to infant development tests is a test of the "alerting" response. An alerting response *is indicative of an infant's capacity for responsiveness and it is deemed to be present when the infant's eyes brighten and widen—this in contrast to the term* orientation, *which is used to define the response of turning in the direction of a stimulus (Erickson, 1976). Here the child is exhibiting an alerting response to the sound of the bell.*

solving and the test situation. Keen observation of the child's verbal and non-verbal behavior during the testing can yield a wealth of insights that in many cases will help to clarify ambiguities that arise in the test data. The tests may be extremely useful in bringing to light hitherto unidentified assets or deficits and may have value not only in general class placement but also in individual tailoring of teaching agendas.

A list of the most frequently administered children's intelligence tests would include individually administered tests such as the Wechsler Intelligence Scale for Children—III, the Wechsler Preschool and Primary Scale of Intelligence—Revised, the Kaufman Assessment Battery for Children, the Stanford-Binet Intelligence Scale: Fourth Edition, and a group test called the Otis-Lennon School Ability Test. All these tests will be discussed in the coming chapters. In Chapter 10, we will look at a "new breed" of intelligence test for children, the psychoeducational test battery. Integrated into such tests is not only coverage of many of the abilities tapped in more traditional intelligence tests, but measures of more school-related ability and achievement as well.

Measuring the Intelligence of Adults

According to Wechsler (1958, p. 7), adult intelligence scales should assess the individual's global capacity "to act purposefully, think rationally, and deal effectively with [the] environment." The tests should tap such abilities as retention of general information, social judgment, quantitative reasoning, and expressive language and memory. The specific types of tasks used to reach these objectives on the Wechsler scale for adults are the same as many of the tasks used with children.

During childhood and adolescence, intelligence is considered in the context of skill acquisition and learning potential (such as the learning of reading, writing, and arithmetic), whereas during adulthood a more relevant area of focus might be skill application. Wesman (1968) argued that the areas in which adults have learned are not tapped on conventional intelligence tests. Some have also questioned the extent to which some of the tasks used in the assessment of adult intelligence engage the motivation of adults in the same way that they engage the motivation of children (Marquette, 1976). Schaie (1978) has pointed out that although novelty in a task may be important as a motivator for the young child, this may not be the case for adults.

The purpose of intelligence testing with adults differs in some respects from the purpose of intelligence testing with children. Tests of intelligence are seldom administered to adults for purposes of educational placement. Rather, they are generally administered to obtain some measure of potential along with clinically relevant information (Harrison et al., 1988).

Publishers of intelligence tests have made available series of tests that can be used through a period that not quite—but almost—spans "cradle to grave." The Wechsler series of tests, for example, includes a preschool measure, a children's measure, and an adult measure. The current edition of the Stanford-Binet has an age range of 2 years to adulthood. The current revision of the Woodcock-Johnson Psychoeducational Battery has an age range of 2½ years to 84 years. The Kaufman Assessment Battery for Children, combined with its sister test, the Kaufman Adolescent and Adult Intelligence Scale, has an age range of 2½ years through 75 years.

Measuring the Intelligence of Special Populations

Measuring the intelligence of disabled or exceptional individuals is an important part of evaluating their overall strengths and deficits to provide a basis for designing intervention. When administering and interpreting tests of cognitive functioning as part of a full evaluation, the examiner attempts to explain the effects of the individual's ability on all aspects of his or her growth and development and to design an intervention strategy that will enhance the examinee's growth and development.

People with disabilities   When assessing people with disabilities, it is often important to include in a full evaluation tests designed specifically for and standardized on a particular special population. This is necessary because of the comparatively lower performance and decreased validity of tests developed for the nondisabled when used with an individual with a particular disabling condition. These lower scores are due to a variety of factors, including the differences in the life experiences of the two groups and the fact that the tests often require skills (motor, visual, auditory, or language) that the disabled individual may lack.

Although it is important to be sensitive to the effects of a test designed for and standardized on the nondisabled on the performance of the disabled, as part of a full evaluation it is often important to also compare the performance of exceptional individuals with that of their nondisabled peers. It is the nondisabled who set the standards in the world at large and into whose social group the exceptional individual may want to move as a functioning member. More specifically, how the disabled individual compares with nondisabled peers may be critical in determining whether the exceptional individual can compete in a particular educational, recreational, or work setting. To meet this critical aspect of the evaluation, test developers and users have modified standardized tests in a number of ways to meet the needs of exceptional individuals. These modifications include adapting test stimuli and mode of responding to make the tests more response-fair and, therefore, more valid.

Hearing-impaired individuals often cannot respond to the verbal directions included as part of most conventional tests and/or cannot respond verbally because of the severe language deficits that often accompany hearing loss. For the hearing-impaired, directions, test stimuli, and the subject's responses are often pantomimed. The visually impaired often require modifications such as enlarged test stimuli (enlarged print, for example) or the presentation of test stimuli by tactile-kinesthetic perception. There are also a number of specifically designed intelligence tests for the visually impaired and the hearing-impaired. Individuals with motor impairments reflected in their speech or body movement resulting from stroke, cerebral palsy, or other disease may require modification such as using their eye movements for indicating responses, modifying written tasks to require an oral response, or presenting test items in an oral multiple-choice format. In the assessment of developmental disabilities, state and federal law dictate the use of supplementary adaptive behavior measures or measures of social competency assessment techniques (measures that we cover in Chapter 16). Items on these scales might assess adaptive behavior in a number of areas, including self-help eating (skills such as drinking from a cup, using a spoon to eat), locomotion (walking, going about town), self-direction (use of money, looking after one's own health), and communication (comprehension of instructions, use of telephone, use of mail, enjoyment of reading).

People with psychological disorders   Various psychological disorders affect cognitive functioning and performance on intelligence tests. For example, dementias such as those associated with strokes, Alzheimer's disease, alcoholism, and head injury may dramatically affect memory and the ability to engage in abstract thought (American Psychological Association, 1994). Also, as a group, people with schizophrenia tend to score lower on intelligence tests than people in general. People with schizophrenia also score lower than people with other major mental disorders, such as depression and manic-depressive disorder (Goldberg et al., 1993). These findings hold true even with regard to people diagnosed as having the paranoid type of schizophrenia, the type with the latest onset and best prognosis (American Psychiatric Association, 1994).

Inappropriate levels of abstraction, as well as other cognitive deficits, are hallmarks of schizophrenia (Weiner, 1966). When asked, for example, how wood and bricks are alike, someone with schizophrenia may offer a reply that reflects too little abstraction ("both are hard" or "both are made of elements") or excessive abstraction ("they are the building blocks of civilization"). A correct response demands an intermediate level of abstraction ("both are used to build houses"). When asked what is missing in a picture, people with schizophrenia often name nonessential objects. For example, when shown a picture of a calculator without any buttons, the person with schizophrenia might respond that a pencil (to record the results of the calculation) is missing.

Interestingly, people with schizophrenia sometimes produce an inconsistent pattern of correct answers on intelligence tests. Several of the most difficult vocabulary or arithmetic items may be answered correctly after some of the easier items were missed (Weiner, 1966). Such inconsistency extends to the general level of intellectual ability in the schizophrenic population; although as a group they score below average on intelligence tests, there are also exceptional individuals who score significantly above average.

A general caution exists with respect to interpreting the test scores of people with psychological disorders like schizophrenia: understand the respondent's history and current situation. To ignore this caveat is to risk mistaking low intellectual functioning for psychological disorder.

In some instances, psychological tests are employed to help answer questions about an individual's *premorbid level* of intellectual ability—that is, the individual's level of ability before the onset of the disorder or the disease. In some instances, a test of reading skills may be used for such purposes, although this practice is not without its critics (Jones & Rodgers, 1993). Perhaps the surest premorbid measure, if available, is psychological test data gathered before the onset of the disorder.

Researchers are interested in the specific difficulties that people with schizophrenia have on intelligence tests as a means of better understanding the disorder. Estimates of premorbid intelligence are helpful because they provide an understanding, sometimes quantitative in nature, of the degree of cognitive impairment that has actually taken place. All such information may be applied in treatment programs.

The gifted   Tests of intelligence are widely used as an aid in the identification of members of special populations at all points in the possible range of human abilities—including that group of exceptional people we collectively refer to as "the gifted." But who are these people and how do psychological tests help us to identify them?

Gifted people have been described in many ways. Witty (1940, p. 516) succinctly described the gifted individual as "one whose performance is consistently remarkable in any positively valued area." Public Law 95-561 defined

Table 8–2
"Giftedness" as Defined by Public Law 95-561

Intellectual Ability—The child possessing general intellectual ability is consistently superior to other children in the school to the extent that he or she needs and can profit from specially planned educational services beyond those normally provided by the standard school program.

Creative Thinking—The creative thinking child is that child who consistently engages in divergent thinking that results in unconventional responses to conventional tasks to the extent that he or she needs and can profit from specially planned educational services beyond those normally provided by the standard school program.

Leadership Ability—The child possessing leadership ability is that child who not only assumes leadership roles, but also is accepted by others as a leader to the extent that he or she needs and can profit from specially planned educational services beyond those normally provided by the standard school program.

Visual and Performing Arts Ability—The child possessing visual and performing arts ability is that child who, by virtue of consistently outstanding aesthetic production in graphic arts, sculpture, music, or dance, needs and can profit from specially planned educational services beyond those normally provided by the standard school program.

Specific Ability Aptitude—The child possessing a specific ability aptitude is that child who has an aptitude in a specific area such as mechanical aptitude or psychomotor ability that is consistently superior to the aptitudes of other children in the school to the extent that he or she needs and can profit from specially planned educational services beyond those normally provided by the standard school program.

giftedness a little less broadly and with reference to specific areas such as intellectual ability, creative thinking, leadership ability, and visual and performing arts (see Table 8–2).

Studies of gifted children have yielded a number of findings, many of which are summarized in Table 8–3. The most extensive study of the gifted was undertaken in 1921 by Lewis M. Terman at Stanford University. Using the 1916 edition of the Stanford-Binet, Terman and colleagues began the longitudinal research project by identifying 1,528 children (with an average age of 11) whose IQ of 140 or over placed them within the top 1 percent in the country in intellectual functioning. Terman followed these gifted children for the remainder of his own life, taking measures of physical and social development, achievement, character traits, books read, and recreational interests. Also included were interviews with parents, teachers, and the subjects themselves. Terman first published some of his findings four years after the study had begun (Terman et al., 1925), though others have continued to collect data and analyze them (for example, Sears, 1977). The early results from the study served to dispel many of the myths and stereotypes that existed with respect to the gifted—myths such as "early ripe, early rot" and "genius and insanity go hand in hand." In general, the gifted tended to maintain their superior intellectual ability. Further, they tended to have lower mortality rates and were in general in better physical and mental health than were their nongifted counterparts. They tended to hold moderate political and social views, were successful in educational and vocational pursuits, and committed less crime than did the nongifted.

How are gifted people identified? Intelligence tests are widely used for this purpose, though as you might expect from what you have read so far in this chapter, the definition of "gifted" may change as a function of the

Table 8–3
Characteristics of Gifted Children

1. Superior physique as demonstrated by above-average height, weight, coordination, endurance, and general health.
2. Longer attention span.
3. Learns rapidly, easily, and with less repetition.
4. Learns to read sooner and continues to read at a consistently more advanced level.
5. More mature in the ability to express himself or herself through the various communicative skills.
6. Reaches higher levels of attentiveness to his or her environment.
7. Asks more questions and really wants to know the causes and reasons for things.
8. Likes to study some subjects that are difficult because he or she enjoys the learning.
9. Spends time beyond the ordinary assignments or schedule on things that are of interest to him or her.
10. Knows about many things of which other children are unaware.
11. Is able to adapt learning to various situations somewhat unrelated in orientation.
12. Reasons out more problems since he or she recognizes relationships and comprehends meanings.
13. Analyzes quickly mechanical problems, puzzles, and trick questions.
14. Shows a high degree of originality and often uses good but unusual methods or ideas.
15. Possesses one or more special talents.
16. Is more adept in analyzing his or her own abilities, limitations, and problems.
17. Performs with more poise and can take charge of the situation.
18. Evaluates facts and arguments critically.
19. Has more emotional stability.
20. Can judge the abilities of others.
21. Has diverse, spontaneous, and frequently self-directed interests.

Source: French (1964)

particular test used. Models of intelligence range from the unidimensional, as in Spearman's (1927) g, to the multidimensional—3 dimensions according to Sternberg's (1985) triarchic theory, and 120 according to Guilford (1967; Comrey et al., 1988; Meeker & Meeker, 1973). Tests in the Wechsler series of tests (as well as other intelligence tests) yield two primary factors: a verbal factor and a performance factor. The verbal and performance scores taken together yield what is known as a full scale score—interpreted by professionals to reflect g, and colloquially referred to as "IQ." In some programs designed to identify gifted children, a cutoff point for a (high) IQ on a Wechsler test is established for the criterion used to define giftedness. This practice is questionable because it obscures (1) superior performance on individual subtests if the record as a whole is not superior, (2) a significant discrepancy, if one exists between the verbal and performance scores, and (3) the fact that each of the subtests administered does not contribute equally to g; stating this third point in the language of factor analysis, the various subtests "load" differentially on g. In one study that employed gifted students as subjects, Malone, Brownstein, von Brock, and Shaywitz (1991) cautioned that their findings might be colored by what is called a *ceiling effect*. Some of the subtests apparently had "too low a ceiling" to accurately gauge the gifted student's ability and a greater range of items at the high end of the difficulty continuum would have been preferable. One practical implication of Malone et al.'s (1991) findings was that "the use of the overall IQ score to classify students as gifted, or as a criterion for acceptance into special advanced programs, may contribute to the lack of recognition of the ability of some students" (p. 26).

Identification of the gifted should ideally be made not simply on the basis of an intelligence test but also on the basis of the goals of the program for which the test for giftedness is being conducted. Thus, for example, if an assessment program is undertaken to identify gifted writers, common sense indicates that a component of that assessment program should be a writing sample taken from the examinee and evaluated by an authority in the area. It is true, however, that the most effective—and most frequently used—instrument for identifying gifted children is an intelligence test. School systems screening for candidates for gifted programs might employ a group test for the sake of economy. A group test frequently employed for this purpose is the Otis-Lennon School Ability Test. To screen for social abilities or aptitudes, tests such as the Differential Aptitude Test or Guilford et al.'s (1974) Structure of Intellect (SOI) test may be administered. Creativity might be assessed through the use of the SOI, through personality and biographical inventories (Davis, 1989), or through other measures of creative thinking.

Numerous other assessment tools may be pressed into use to identify gifted people. Nominating techniques whereby people such as parents, teachers, and peers answer questions such as "Who has the most leadership ability?" "Who has the most original ideas?" and "Who would you most like to help you with this project?" may be employed. Although teacher nomination is a widely used method of identifying gifted children, it is not necessarily the most reliable one (French, 1964; Gallagher, 1966; Jacobs, 1970; Tuttle & Becker, 1980). The gifted child may be a misbehaving child in the classroom, and this misbehavior may be due to boredom with the low level of the material being presented. The gifted child may ask questions of or make comments to the teacher that the teacher either doesn't understand or misconstrues as "smart alec" in nature. Clark (1988) outlines specific behaviors that gifted children may display in the classroom (see Table 8–4). Parents are probably better judges than are teachers; however, there is some evidence suggesting that parents tend to be quite conservative when assessing their children's abilities (Mandell & Fiscus, 1981).

Behavior rating scales such as Clark's (1979) Rating Scale for the Identification of Gifted Children may provide a useful adjunct to instruments used in identifying gifted children (see Figure 8–4). Some behavior rating scales designed for use with children who have emotional difficulties may also have application in the evaluation of giftedness (Landrum & Ward, 1993). The case-study method in which information from home, school, and other sources is collected and integrated provides an excellent basis on which to make a determination of giftedness. Included in the case study are not only formal psychological test data but also the results of sociometric techniques (such as nominating techniques), if available, and any autobiographical material that is available—statements of interests and aspirations that have been recorded. A complete assessment of the gifted child will contain not only adequate documentation of the giftedness but also a report on any "islets of difficulty" that may exist with respect to physical, psychological, social, or academic functioning.

Table 8–4
Classroom Behaviors That May Indicate Giftedness

Cognitive Giftedness
   Asks a lot of questions
   Has lots of information on many things
   Becomes unusually upset at injustices
   Seems interested in and concerned about social or political problems
   Refuses to drill on spelling, math facts, flash cards, or handwriting
   Criticizes others for dumb ideas
   Becomes impatient if work is not "perfect"
   Completes only part of an assignment or project and then takes off in a new direction
   Sticks to a subject long after the class has gone on to other things
   Daydreams
   Likes solving puzzles and problems
   Loves metaphors and abstract ideas
   Loves debating issues

Academic Giftedness
   Shows unusual ability in some areas
   Enjoys meeting or talking with experts in the fields
   Gets math answers correct but finds it difficult to tell you how
   Invents new, obscure systems and codes

Creative Giftedness
   Tries to do things in different, unusual, and imaginative ways
   Enjoys new routines or spontaneous activities
   Loves variety and novelty
   Loves controversial and unusual questions
   Seems never to proceed sequentially

Giftedness in Leadership Ability
   Organizes and leads group activities
   Enjoys taking risks
   Seems cocky, self-assured
   Enjoys decision making
   Synthesizes ideas and information from a lot of different sources

Giftedness in Performing Arts
   Seems to pick up skills in the arts without instruction
   Invents new techniques
   Sees minute detail in products or performances
   Has high sensory sensitivity

Source: Clark (1988)

Issues in the Measurement of Intelligence

Do you believe that intellectual ability is innate and that it simply "unfolds" from birth onward? How stable are IQ scores over time? What factors influence measured intelligence? These are some of the many questions and issues that have been raised with respect to intelligence and its measurement. Before read-

Check the column that best describes this child's emotional development. Please note that a high score may not be desirable on all of the items that follow.

	Little		Moderate		Much
	1	2	3	4	5
42. *Emotional Stability.* Is able to cope with normal frustrations of living; adjusts to change with minimum of difficulty.					
43. *Emotional Control.* Expresses and displays emotions appropriately; emotional outbursts rarely occur.					
44. *Openness to Experience.* Appears to be receptive to new tasks or experiences; seems able to take reasonable risks; can respond naturally to unusual or unexpected stimuli.					
45. *Enthusiasm.* Enters into most activities with eagerness and whole-hearted participation; maintains enthusiasm for duration of activity.					
46. *Self-Acceptance.* Seems to understand and accept self; able to view self in terms of both limitations and abilities.					
47. *Independence.* Behavior usually is dictated by his or her own set of values; is concerned with the freedom to express ideas and feelings.					

Figure 8–4

Excerpt from a Rating Scale for the Identification of Gifted Students (Clark, 1979)

Teachers using this rating scale would be asked to evaluate individual children on the items shown.

ing on, make a note of your own answers to these questions—and then see if (and if so, how) your answers have changed when you reach the end of the chapter.

Nature Versus Nurture

Although most behavioral scientists today believe that measured intellectual ability represents an interaction between (1) innate ability and (2) environmental influences, such a belief was not always popular.

The doctrines of preformationism and predeterminism hold that intelligence is genetically encoded and will "unfold" with maturation. The roots of

Figure 8–5
A Human Sperm Cell According to a Preformationist

This is how one scientist drew a human sperm cell as he saw it through a microscope—dramatic testimony to the way in which one's beliefs can affect perception. (From Hartsoeker, 1694, cited in Needham, 1959, p. 20)

these doctrines go at least as far back as 1672, when one scientist reported that butterflies were preformed inside their cocoons and that their maturation was a result of an "unfolding." In that same year, another scientist, this one studying chick embryos, generalized from his studies to draw a similar conclusion about humans (Malphigi, *De Formatione Pulli in Ovo,* 1672; cited in Needham, 1959, p. 167).

The invention of the compound microscope in the late seventeenth century provided a new tool with which preformationists could attempt to gather supportive evidence. Scientists confirmed their expectations by observing semen under the microscope. Various investigators "claimed to have seen a microscopic horse in the semen of a horse, an animalcule with very large ears in the semen of a donkey, and minute roosters in the semen of a rooster" (Hunt, 1961, p. 38; see Figure 8–5).

The influence of preformationist theory waned slowly as evidence inconsistent with it was brought forth. For example, the theory could not explain the regeneration of limbs by crayfish and other organisms. With the progression of work in the area of genetics, preformationism, as the dominant theory of development, was slowly replaced by *predeterminism*—the belief that behavior "unfolds" as a result of genetic inheritance. Experimental work with animals was often cited in support of the predeterminist position. For example, a study by Carmichael (1927) showed that newly born salamanders and frogs that were anesthetized and deprived of an opportunity to swim, swam at about the same time as unanesthetized controls. Carmichael's work did not take into consideration the influence of the environment in the swimming behavior of salamanders and frogs. In parallel studies with humans, Dennis and Dennis (1940) observed the development of walking behavior in Hopi Indian children. Comparisons were made between children who spent much of their first year of life bound to a cradle board and children who had spent no such time constricted. Their conclusion was that there was no significant difference between the two groups of children at time of onset of walking and that walking was not a skill that could be enhanced by practice. Walking had been "proved" to be a human activity that unfolded with maturation.

Another proponent of the determinist view was Arnold Gesell. Generalizing from early twin studies that showed that practice had little effect on tasks such as climbing stairs, cutting with scissors, building with cubes, and buttoning buttons, Gesell (with Helen Thompson, 1929) concluded that "training does not transcend maturation." For Gesell, it was primarily the maturation of neural mechanisms and not learning or experience that was most important in the development of what might be referred to as intelligence. Gesell described mental development as a "progressive morphogenesis of patterns of behavior" (Gesell et al., 1940, p. 7) and argued that behavior patterns are determined by "innate processes of growth" that he viewed as synonymous with maturation (Gesell, 1945). Gesell (1954, p. 335) described infancy as "the period in which the individual realizes his racial inheritance" and has argued that this inheritance "is the end product of evolutionary processes that trace back to an extremely remote antiquity."

Is intelligence genetically encoded and something that unfolds with maturation? Or does the learning environment account for our intelligence? Nature / nurture questions like these have been raised for as long as there have been concepts of intelligence and tests to measure those concepts—sometimes amid great publicity and controversy (see *Everyday Psychometrics*). Galton firmly believed that genius was hereditary, a belief that was expressed in works such as *Hereditary Genius* (1869) and *English Men of Science* (1874). Richard Dugdale, another predeterminist, argued that degeneracy, like genius, was also inherited. Dugdale (1877) traced the immoral, lecherous lineage of the infamous Jukes family and hypothesized that the observed trail of poverty, harlotry, and laziness was a matter of heredity. Complementing the work of Dugdale was Henry Goddard's book, *The Kallikak Family* (1912). Goddard traced the family lineage resulting from the legitimate and illegitimate unions of a man given the pseudonym "Martin Kallikak" (the last name was a combination of the Greek words for "good" and "bad"). Kallikak had fathered children with a mentally defective waitress and with the reportedly normal woman he married. Goddard documented how Kallikak's illegitimate descendants were far less socially desirable than the legitimate ones.

Based on his testing of a sample of Mexican and Native American children, the father of the American version of Binet's test, Lewis M. Terman, concluded that people from these cultures were genetically inferior. The noted English statistician Karl Pearson wrote that as compared with the native Britishers, immigrating Jews were "somewhat inferior physiologically and mentally" (Pearson & Moul, 1925, p. 126). Although such observations seem flawed, even prejudiced—if not racist—by current standards, we should remember that they tended to reflect the prevailing truisms of the day.

Although a scholarly consideration of the role of environmental and cultural factors (not to mention language barriers) is not evident in the writings of behavioral scientists such as Dugdale, Terman, and Pearson, a research literature that shed light on the environment side of the hereditary / environment issue subsequently began to mount. It was found, for example, that when identical twins are reared apart, they still show remarkably similar intelligence test scores, though not so similar as if they had been reared together (Johnson,

The Bell Curve Controversy

In 1994, a book entitled *The Bell Curve: Intelligence and Class Structure in American Life* by Richard Herrnstein and Charles Murray became a stimulus for widespread public debate on the nature of intelligence, as well as the implications of group differences in measured intelligence. Although the book was given extraordinary attention in the print and electronic media, many people aware of a similar spectacle in the late 1960s had a sense of déjà vu about it all. To place discussion of *The Bell Curve* in proper historical perspective, then, let's begin with a brief look backward.

In a *Harvard Educational Review* article entitled "How Much Can We Boost IQ and Scholastic Achievement?" Arthur R. Jensen (1969) presented evidence that Blacks score lower on average than Whites on standardized intelligence tests. Jensen argued that this difference was due primarily to genetic rather than environmental influences. His analysis of the available data suggested to him that the frequency of genes carrying higher intelligence is lower in the Black population as a whole than in the White population. He estimated that the variability in measured intelligence was about 20% due to heredity. The article touched off a storm of public controversy about intelligence tests. Few people seemed to be without a strong opinion about the value of intelligence tests, what group differences in intelligence really meant, and what the government should or should not do as a result of such differences.

Citing many of the same studies and data that Jensen (1969) had used to make his case, Herrnstein and Murray (1994) also noted racial and ethnic differences in intelligence, which they presumed to be partly the result of genetics. Herrnstein and Murray went further, however, speculating on the meaning such group differences might have for the future of the United States. These authors envision a future wherein differences in measured intelligence divide society into a cognitive elite, fiercely defensive of its material possessions, and a cognitive underclass, more disposed to making ends meet through crime and/or dependency on social programs. To slow society's march to the apocalypse they envision, Herrnstein and Murray make a number of recommendations including (1) the cessation of affirmative action programs (such programs are viewed as having a negative effect on race relations, since the unqualified are unfairly promoted); (2) the cessation of remedial education programs (the effects of such efforts have been questionable, and the dollars could be better spent on further developing talent in the talented); and (3) the cessation of welfare and other such programs, which, according to Herrnstein and Murray, encourage young, unwed mothers—usually with low intelligence—to reproduce. The message of *The Bell Curve* is that society should stop trying to eradicate differences between groups. Because differences between groups cannot be changed by any known means, society would do better to try to find ways for people with different intellectual levels to live together with dignity for all.

From this account of *The Bell Curve* and from what you might know of the book from other sources, what do you think of its thesis? Commit your thoughts to writing before reading our comments, which follow.

Some Thoughts on *The Bell Curve*

- Because of complex methodological difficulties in conducting such research, it is difficult to estimate with any real accuracy the respective contributions of heredity and environment to measured intelligence.

- Because of complex methodological difficulties in conducting research on social programs, it is difficult to estimate the true impact of such environmental interventions. For example, most studies show that the beneficial effects of Head Start programs erode over time. Critics of such studies argue that such erosion is due not to genes but to the return of children to environments where the learning that has taken place will not be reinforced.

- Even Richard Herrnstein (1982) acknowledged that measured intelligence could be raised, although he wrote that "raising it much is hard, given existing methods of teaching and measurement" (p. 74).

- Many of Herrnstein and Murray's conclusions and recommendations have more to do with political opinion than scientific findings. For example, political opinion about the role of government in providing aid to the poor—irrespective of measured IQ—varies considerably.

- Although group differences in measured intelligence do exist, no such thing as "group intelligence" exists. Thus, intelligence is ultimately an individual, one-by-one matter. Further, the personal and social value of measured intelligence is tempered by a number of other factors, such as one's values and motivation.

- According to Herbert (1994), Catholics have a legacy of discrimination in Northern Ireland, where they tend to test about 15 points lower than Protestants on intelligence tests. Because both groups are White, Herbert (1994) construes such evidence as having a lesson for Herrnstein and Murray with regard to the influence of heredity as opposed to environment in measured intelligence.

- As Sternberg (1986) has argued, there are alternatives to intelligence as measured by intelligence tests, such as a streetwise type of intelligence that Sternberg calls "practical intelligence." Because ways of measuring practical intelligence have not been established, it is impossible to tell what, if any, differences among groups exist with respect to this form of intelligence, and what the implications of such differences might be.

- Arthur Jensen, whose research called attention to differences in measured intelligence among groups, is among those who have advocated equal education opportunities for all. Further, Jensen (1980, pp. 737–738) has argued that differences in measured intelligence between the races "should not be permitted to influence the treatment accorded to *individuals* of any race—in education, employment, legal justice, and political and civil rights. The well-established finding of a wide range of individual differences in IQ and other abilities within all major-racial populations and the great amount of overlap of their frequency distributions, absolutely contradicts the racist philosophy that persons of different races should be treated differently, one and all, only by reasons of their racial origins. Those who would accord any treatment to individuals solely by virtue of their race will find no rational support in any of the scientific findings from psychological testing or present day theories of differential psychology."

1963; Newman et al., 1937). Children born to poverty-stricken parents, but adopted at an early age by better-educated, middle-class families, tend to have higher intelligence test scores than do their counterparts who are not adopted by families of higher socioeconomic status—though the natural mothers with the higher IQs tend to have the children with the higher IQs irrespective of the family in which the adopted child is raised (Leahy, 1932, 1935).

In general, proponents of the "nurture" side of the nature/nurture controversy emphasize the crucial importance of factors such as prenatal and postnatal environment, socioeconomic status, educational opportunities, and parental modeling with respect to intellectual development. Proponents of this view characteristically suspect that opposing arguments that champion the role of nature in the controversy are based more on factors such as political leanings than on sound and impartial scientific inquiry and analysis.

Somewhere between the rhetoric arguing that heredity plays *no* part in intelligence (Kamin, 1974) and assertions such as "Nature has color coded groups of individuals so that statistically reliable predictions of their adaptability to intellectually rewarding and effective lives can easily be made and profitably be used by the pragmatic man-in-the-street" (Shockley, 1971, p. 375) lies the middle ground of the interactionist position: the position that intelligence, as measured by intelligence tests, is the result of the interaction between heredity and environment.

Inheritance and interactionism   People differ in intelligence levels just as they differ in blood pressure levels, cerebrospinal fluid levels, and many other ways. Once that is understood, it is natural to wonder *why* people differ in intellectual abilities, to wonder what accounts for the variability. According to the interactionist view, people inherit a certain intellectual potential and exactly how much of that genetic potential is realized depends partially on the nature of the environment in which it is nurtured. No one to date has inherited the ability to fly or to have "X-ray vision." You might spend your entire life in libraries or on mountaintops visiting gurus, but all your studies cannot result in your acquiring the ability to fly or to see through things, since those abilities have not been encoded in your genetic makeup. As a psychologist, you may one day administer an intelligence test to a mentally deficient adult who does not have the ability required to reiterate five digits or to tell you how a ball and an apple are similar. You may wonder to yourself, as you administer that test, whether the deficiency was inherited, whether it was the result of some environmental insult (anything from improper prenatal nutrition on the part of the mother to inferior educational opportunities), or whether it was the result of a combination of the two. Remember that the intelligence test data you obtain will indicate predefined strengths or weaknesses in various subject areas, but the data will not necessarily tell you why that deficiency exists.

The interactionist perspective on intellectual development tends to be a very optimistic one; according to it, we are free to become all that we can be. The notion that we can use the environment to push our genetic potential to the limit can be illustrated most graphically by reference to the honing of physical abilities by dedicated sports people. In the 1980 Olympic winter games in Lake

Placid, New York, Eric Heiden won five gold medals for the United States in speed-skating events ranging from the 500-meter sprint to the grueling 10,000-meter. He broke Olympic marks in each. It can be presumed that Heiden had fulfilled (or had come very close to fulfilling) the full extent of his genetic ability with respect to his ice-skating ability.

How many of us come that close to fulfilling our genetic potential with respect to our physical abilities? our mental abilities? Probably not very many of us. Environmental conditions have to be conducive to allow us to pursue such a course. We also have to have other needs satisfied first, such as the need for financial or other security. Also entering into the equation are personality factors such as the degree to which we are motivated to achieve. Finally, we have to be fortunate enough to be born in the right place at the right time. Would Eric Heiden have been a world-renowned Olympic ice-skater had he been born in Appalachia? had he been training in Bosnia-Herzogovina in the 1990s? had he been born to royalty? Born at some other time or in some other place, might he have achieved greatness by some other route, or, alternatively, would he have faded into obscurity? Although such rhetorical questions defy any simple answer, they provide useful points of departure in considering the nature/nurture controversy.

The Stability of Intelligence

Longitudinal research studies have in general suggested that above the age of 7, IQs tend to remain relatively stable over time. Below the age of 7 and particularly below the age of 5, measured IQs have not generally been shown to be very stable, although evidence to the contrary may also be found (see Lamp & Krohn, 1990; and Smith, Bolin, & Stovall, 1988). A lack of stability in measured intelligence in very young children is understandable in light of the fact that there is typically a great amount of intellectual growth during the early childhood years. There is little reason to have great confidence that the measured intelligence of infants and preschool children would correlate highly with measures of intelligence obtained in later years (Wesman, 1968). This is so because the types of measures used in infant and preschool tests differ so markedly from those used to measure intelligence in school-age, adolescent, and adult individuals.

The correlation coefficient referred to as a *stability coefficient* is used to express the degree of the relationship that exists between scores on the same test (or parallel forms of the same test) observed at two points in time. The stability coefficient does not necessarily represent the degree of consistency between the measurements but, rather, the degree of consistency in the person's relative standing among others on the same test. If all the subjects in the longitudinal research study improved or lowered their scores by approximately the same magnitude and a particular individual's relative standing in the group remained the same, the stability coefficient would be high.

We mention in passing that the responsible test user would, if possible, look to more than a test's stability coefficient in determining the degree of confidence with which projections could be made about a particular examinee's future intellectual ability; generalizations about data obtained in the course of longitudinal research with a group of subjects may not hold true for any one individual in the group. Especially with young children, any predictions about future intellectual ability must be considered tenuous and should ideally be made not only on the basis of measured IQ with a valid test but also on the basis of an assessment of the child's personality and the environmental resources available at home, school, and elsewhere to foster intellectual growth.

The rise and fall of IQ   Since the early 1900s, it has been widely held that intellectual growth begins to decline at about age 20. If that is true and you are at about that age, then you're at the height of your intellectual powers right now—you've "peaked" and it's all downhill from here.

The conclusion that an intellectual decline occurs at about age 20 or so was based on cross-sectional research studies in which people of different ages were examined and compared at the same time. Results of those studies did, in fact, suggest that mean IQ scores declined after around age 20. However, several factors were overlooked by the interpreters of the data; most important, decrements in measured intelligence as a result of age appeared to be confounded with decrements in measured intelligence as a function of cultural changes between the younger and older subjects. In a cross-sectional research study that compares a group of, say, 20-year-olds with a group of, say, 70-year-olds, it cannot be overlooked that the experiential background of members of these two groups is quite different; perhaps it was the experiential background and exposure to society at two different points in time that was primarily responsible for the differences in measured intelligence. Additionally, it should be noted that educational opportunities for the younger group may have been much greater than those available to the older subjects. Further, the younger group may have also had a wider range of potential learning experiences because of the widespread accessibility of radio and television. Indirect benefits were also accorded the younger group from variables related to improvements in nutrition, medical care, and general quality of life.

Contrary to what turn-of-the-century behavioral scientists believed, it may well be that intellectual ability continues to increase as one gets older. In one longitudinal study, a mean increase of 11.13 IQ points from age 13 to age 29 and a mean increase of 6 IQ points between the ages of 29 and 42 were reported (Bradway & Thompson, 1962). On average, significant intellectual decrements do not begin to appear until people get into their sixties; and even at that point, it appears that a decline in general intellectual functioning may be related to overall level of health as opposed to age per se (Birren, 1968; Palmore, 1970). When intellectual decrements do occur, they are more likely to occur in fluid rather than crystallized abilities (see page 265). Exactly how, and if, such intellectual decline affects an individual may be based on numerous factors, such as whether education is continued in later life (Kaufman, 1990).

Other Issues

Beyond the respective contributions of heredity and environment to measured intelligence, a number of issues have been topics for debate. For example, the process of measurement itself has been deemed by some to play a large part in the outcome of the measurement process. Here we briefly review some issues regarding the measurement of intelligence.

The process of measurement   Measured intelligence may vary as a result of factors related to the measurement process, such as the instrument used to measure intelligence, including the test author's definition of intelligence, the standardization sample employed, the competency of the test administrator, and the accuracy of the scoring. Other factors related to the measurement process itself include the amount of testtaking experience and/or prior coaching on the part of the examinee and numerous personality and situational factors (such as the examinee's level of anxiety or fatigue and the extent to which the conditions of the test's administration conform to the requirements of the test manual).

Personality factors   Sensitive to the manifestations of intelligence in *all* human behavior, Alfred Binet had conceived of the study of intelligence as being synonymous with the study of personality. David Wechsler (1958) also believed that all tests of intelligence measure traits of temperament and personality, such as drive, energy level, impulsiveness, persistence, and goal awareness.

Longitudinal and cross-sectional studies of children have explored the relationship between various personality characteristics and measured intelligence. Aggressiveness with peers, initiative, high need for achievement, competitive striving, curiosity, self-confidence, and emotional stability are some personality factors that are associated with gains in measured intelligence over time. Passivity, dependence, and maladjustment are some of the factors present in children whose measured intellectual ability has not increased over time.

In discussions of the role of personality in the measured intelligence of infants, the term *temperament* (rather than *personality*) is typically employed. There is evidence to suggest that infants differ quite markedly in temperament with respect to a number of dimensions, including vigor of responding, general activity rate, restlessness during sleep, irritability, and "cuddliness" (Chess & Thomas, 1973). An infant's temperament can affect his or her measured intellectual ability in that irritable, restless children who do not enjoy being held have a negative reciprocal influence on their parents—perhaps even on test administrators as well. Parents are less likely to want to pick such children up and spend more time with them engaging in activities that are known to stimulate intellectual development, such as talking to them (White, 1971).

Gender   It is generally believed that the sexes do not differ significantly in general intelligence as measured by the most widely used standardized intelligence tests. Although differences in some specific abilities have been observed, these differences tend to be insignificant statistically (Maccoby & Jacklin, 1974). Thus, for example, it has been found that females as a group tend to score slightly higher than males as a group in tasks involving verbal ability, whereas males tend to outscore females in tasks involving quantitative or mathematical ability (Maccoby & Jacklin, 1974; Silverstein & Fisher, 1960; Terman & Tyler, 1954).

Family environment Environmental factors such as parental ability and parental concern regarding the child's achievement have been shown to correlate positively with the child's measured intelligence (Honzik, 1967). High measured intelligence in children has also been associated with warm democratic homes in which there are explanations for discipline policies (Baldwin et al., 1945; Kent & Davis, 1957; Sontag et al., 1958).

The relationship of maternal age to measured IQ has also been studied. Generally, children of older mothers have higher mean IQ scores (Davis et al., 1972; Record et al., 1969). The effect of maternal age on measured intelligence is often attributed to social class, because younger mothers often tend to be of lower socioeconomic status. However, this positive relationship between maternal age and measured intelligence has also been reported after social class, birth order, and family size were controlled (Davis et al., 1972; Zybert et al., 1978).

Culture As a group, members of some minority groups, including Blacks (Baughman & Dahlstrom, 1968; Dreger & Miller, 1960; Lesser et al., 1965; Shuey, 1966), Hispanics (Gerry, 1973; Holland, 1960; Lesser et al., 1965; Mercer, 1976; Simpson, 1970), and Native American Indians (Cundick, 1976), score lower on average on intelligence tests than do those who are not members of a minority group. In one sense, such findings are not surprising. A culture provides specific models for ways of thinking, acting, and feeling; it enables people to survive both physically and socially and to master and control the world around them (Chinoy, 1967). Items on tests of intelligence tend to reflect the culture of the society where such tests are employed; to the extent that a score on such a test reflects the degree to which testtakers have been integrated into the society and the culture, it would be expected that members of subcultures (as well as others who for whatever reason choose not to perceive themselves as identified with mainstream society) would score lower. Zuckerman (1990), however, cautions that there is much more variation within racial groups than between racial groups on such variables as temperament and basic personality traits. It is therefore possible that studies purporting to show differences between various minority groups may reflect sampling differences and not "true" group differences.

At one time in the history of intelligence testing, developers of intelligence tests sought to develop "pure" measures of intelligence that would be "culture-free." The assumption was that if cultural factors could be controlled, scores of average measured intelligence for minority and majority group members should not significantly differ. One way that the effect of culture could be controlled was through the elimination of verbal items and exclusive reliance on nonverbal, performance items. Researchers thought that the nonverbal items represented the best available means for determining the cognitive ability of minority group children and adults. On the face of it, such an assumption seemed reasonable. However, the presumption that the use of nonverbal test items would eliminate the differences between minority and majority groups in measured intelligence was not found to be true for native-born, English-speaking minority groups. For example, on the average, Blacks tended to score as low on performance as on verbal tests (Cole & Hunter, 1971; McGurk, 1975).

Superior performance on these nonlanguage tests as compared with more conventional IQ tests administered in English has been observed with non-English-speaking or bilingual groups such as Mexican Americans, Puerto Ricans, Chinese, Japanese, and Native American Indians (Jensen, 1980). This difference in performance on the two types of tests (verbal and performance) is attributed more to language effects than to intellectual abilities. It may be speculated that Blacks tend to score low on nonverbal tests for the same reasons that account for lower performance on verbal tests (for example, cultural deprivation). Another problem with exclusive reliance on nonverbal or nonlanguage tests was that they did not have the same high level of predictive validity as did the more verbally loaded tests, primarily because these items do not sample the same psychological processes as do the more verbally loaded, conventional tests of intelligence. Further, most academic courses and business and industrial jobs require at least some verbal facility. It should therefore come as no surprise to find that the nonverbal (performance) items have a low relation to success in the setting the tests were intended to predict for. The idea of developing a truly culture-free test has had great intuitive appeal but has proven to be a practical impossibility. All tests of intelligence, to a greater or lesser degree, reflect the culture in which they were devised and will be used.

The concept of *cultural loading* is used in discussions regarding the magnitude with which cultural influence is reflected in the measured intelligence. For example, a test item such as ''Name three words for snow'' is a highly cultural-loaded item—one that draws heavily from the Eskimo culture where many words exist for snow. By contrast, people from Brooklyn would be hard put to come up with more than one word for snow (well, maybe two, if you count *slush*). Soon after it became evident that no test could legitimately be called ''culture-free,'' a number of tests referred to as ''culture-fair'' began to be published. Some of the ways in which items for such tests were developed are presented in Table 8–5.

In general, the rationale behind culture-fair test items was to include only those tasks that seemed to reflect experiences, knowledge, and skills common to all different cultures. In addition, all the tasks were designed to be motivating to all groups (Samuda, 1982). An attempt was made to minimize the importance of factors such as verbal skills thought to be responsible for the lower mean scores of various minority groups. Therefore, the culture-fair tests tended to be nonverbal in nature, with directions that were simple, clear, and administered orally by the examiner. The nonverbal tasks typically consisted of assembling, classifying, selecting, or manipulating objects, and drawing or identifying geometric designs. Some sample items from the Cattell Culture Fair Test are illustrated in this chapter's *Close-up.* In general, although the culture loading of culture-fair intelligence tests has been reduced, so has their value as tests of intelligence. Culture-fair tests were found to lack what has been the hallmark of traditional tests of intelligence: predictive validity. And still, minority group members tended to score lower on these tests than did majority group members. Various subcultural characteristics have been presumed to penalize unfairly some minority group members who take intelligence tests that are culturally loaded with American White, middle-class values. Some have argued, for

Table 8-5
Ways of Reducing the Cultural Loading of Tests

Culturally Loaded	Cultural Loading Reduced
Paper-and-pencil tasks	Performance tests
Printed instructions	Oral instructions
Oral instructions	Pantomime instructions
No preliminary practice	Preliminary practice items
Reading required	Purely pictorial
Pictorial (objects)	Abstract figural
Written response	Oral response
Separate answer sheet	Answers written on test itself
Language	Nonlanguage
Speed tests	Power tests
Verbal content	Nonverbal content
Specific factual knowledge	Abstract reasoning
Scholastic skills	Nonscholastic skills
Recall of past-learned information	Solving novel problems
Content graded from familiar to rote	All item content highly familiar
Difficulty based on rarity of content	Difficulty based on complexity of relation education

Source: Jensen (1980)

example, that Americans living in urban ghettos share common beliefs and values that are quite different from those of mainstream America. Included among these common beliefs and values, for example, are an inability to delay gratification, a "live for today" orientation, and a reliance on slang in verbal communication. Native American Indians also share a common subculture with core values that may negatively influence their measured intelligence. Central to these values is the belief that individuals should be judged with respect to their relative contribution to the group rather than individual accomplishments. Native Americans also value their relatively unhurried and present-time-oriented lifestyle (Foerster & Little Soldier, 1974).

Frustrated by their seeming inability to develop culture-fair equivalents of traditional intelligence tests, some test developers attempted to develop equivalents of traditional intelligence tests that were culture-specific. Expressly developed for members of a particular cultural group or subculture, such tests were thought to be able to yield a more valid measure of mental development. One culture-specific intelligence test developed expressly for use with Blacks was the Black Intelligence Test of Cultural Homogeneity (Williams, 1975), a 100-item multiple-choice test containing items such as the following:[2]

1. *Mother's Day* means
   a. Black independence day
   b. a day when mothers are honored
   c. a day the welfare checks come in
   d. every first Sunday in church

---

2. The answers keyed correct are as follows: 1(c), 2(d), and 3(d).

2. *Blood* means
   a. a vampire
   b. a dependent individual
   c. an injured person
   d. a brother of color

3. The following are popular brand names. Which one does not belong?
   a. Murray's
   b. Dixie Peach
   c. Royal Crown
   d. Preparation H

As you read the items above, you may be smiling and asking yourself questions like "Is this really an intelligence test?" or "Should I be taking this seriously?" If you were thinking such questions, you are in good company; many psychologists probably asked themselves the same questions. In fact, a kind of parody of the BITCH (the acronym for the test) was published in the May 1974 issue of *Psychology Today* (p. 101) and it was called the "S.O.B. (Son of the Original BITCH) Test." However, the Williams (1975) test was purported to be a genuine culture-specific test of intelligence, one that was standardized on 100 Black high school students in the St. Louis area. Williams was awarded $153,000 by the National Institute of Mental Health to develop the BITCH.

In what was probably one of the few published studies designed to explore the test's validity, the Wechsler Adult Intelligence Scale (WAIS) and the BITCH were both administered to Black ($n = 17$) and White ($n = 116$) applicants for a job with the Portland, Oregon, police department. The Black subjects performed much better on the test than did the White subjects with a mean score that exceeded the White mean score by 2.83 standard deviations. The White mean IQ as measured by the WAIS exceeded the Black mean IQ by about 1.5 standard deviations. None of the correlations between the BITCH score and any of the following variables for either the Black or the White testtakers differed significantly from zero: WAIS Verbal IQ, WAIS Performance IQ, WAIS Full Scale IQ, and years of education. It was also noteworthy that even though the Black sample in this study had an average of more than 2½ years of college education, and even though their overall mean on the WAIS was about 20 points higher than Blacks in general, their scores on the BITCH fell below the average of the standardization sample (high school pupils ranging in age from 16 to 18). What, then, is the BITCH measuring? The study authors, Matarazzo and Wiens (1977) concluded that the test was measuring "street wiseness," though Jensen (1980, p. 681) questioned whether it is even a psychometrically good test of Black slang and "street wiseness."

Although many of the culture-specific tests did yield higher mean scores for the minority group they were specifically designed for use with, they lacked predictive validity and provided little useful and practical information.[3] The

---

3. Perhaps the most psychometrically sound of the instruments designed especially for use with Black subjects was the Listening Comprehension Test (Carver, 1968–1969, 1969; Orr & Graham, 1968). On this test, however, Blacks tended to score lower than Whites even when the groups were matched with respect to socioeconomic status.

Culture-Fair/Culture-Loaded

W hat types of test items are thought to be "culture-fair"—or at least more culture-fair than other, more culturally loaded items? The items reprinted below

from the Culture Fair Test of Intelligence (Cattell, 1940) provide a sample. As you look at them, think about how culture-fair they really are.

Mazes

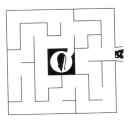

Classification
Pick out the two odd items in each row of figures.

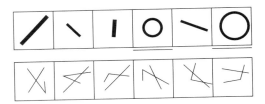

Figure Matrices
Choose from among the six alternatives, the one that most logically completes the matrix pattern above it.

Series
Choose one figure from the six on the right that logically continues the series of three figures at the left.

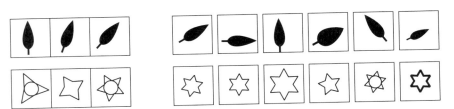

Sample Items from the Culture Fair Test of Intelligence (Cattell, 1940)

In contrast to items designed to be culture-fair, consider the items on the Cultural/Regional Upper-crust Savvy Test (CRUST; Herlihy, 1977). This tongue-in-cheek test of intelligence was intentionally designed for illustrative purposes to be culture-loaded. Members of society's "upper crust" should have no problem at all achieving a perfect score.

1. When you are "posted" at the country club, (a) you ride horses with skill, (b) you are elected to the governance board, (c) you are publicly announced as not having paid your dues, (d) a table is reserved for you in the dining room, whether you use it or not.

2. An arabesque in ballet is (a) an intricate leap, (b) a posture in which the dancer stands on one leg, the other extended backward, (c) a series of steps performed by a male and a female dancer, (d) a bow similar to a curtsy.

3. The Blue Book is (a) the income tax guidelines, (b) a guide to pricing used cars, (c) a booklet used for writing essay exams, (d) a social register listing 400 prominent families.

4. Brookline is located (a) in suburban Boston, (b) on Cape Cod, (c) between Miami Beach and Fort Lauderdale, (d) on the north shore of Chicago.

5. Beef Wellington is (a) the king's cut of roast beef, (b) tenderloin in a pastry crust lined with pâté, (c) a hors d'oeuvre flavored with sherry, (d) roast beef with béarnaise sauce.

6. Choate is (a) a gelded colt used in fox hunts, (b) a prep school, (c) an imported brandy, (d) the curator of the Metropolitan Museum of Art.

7. The most formal dress for men is (a) white tie, (b) black tie, (c) tuxedo, (d) décolletage.

8. *The Stranger* is (a) the . . . family who moved into the neighborhood, (b) Howard Hughes, (c) a book by Camus, (d) an elegant restaurant in San Francisco.

9. Waterford is (a) a health spa for the hep set, (b) a "fat farm," (c) hand-cut crystal from Ireland, (d) the Rockefeller family estate in upper New York.

10. Dining "alfresco" means (a) by candlelight, (b) a buffet supper, (c) at a sidewalk cafe, (d) outdoors.

According to Herlihy (1977), the answers keyed correct are 1(c), 2(b), 3(d), 4(a), 5(b), 6(b), 7(a), 8(c), 9(c), 10(d).

knowledge that is required to score high on all of the culture-specific and culture-reduced tests has not been seen as relevant for educational purposes within our pluralistic society. Such tests have low predictive validity for the criterion of success in academic as well as vocational settings.

At various phases in the "life history" of an intelligence test—including its development, administration, and interpretation—a number of approaches to reduce cultural bias may be employed. Panels of experts may evaluate the potential bias inherent in a newly developed test, and those items judged to be biased are eliminated. The test may be devised so that relatively few verbal instructions are needed to administer it, and/or provide for demonstrations of how to respond to what is required—all in an effort to minimize any possible language bias. A tryout or pilot testing with ethnically mixed samples of test-takers may be undertaken. If differences in scores emerge solely as a function of ethnic group membership, the individual items can be studied further for possible bias.

Major tests of intelligence have undergone a great deal of scrutiny for bias in many investigations—ranging from study of individual items to study of the validity of the predictions that can be made from their administration—and it has generally been concluded that these tests are relatively free of any systematic bias. However, even if an individual test is free of bias, it is important to remember that there are other potential sources of bias ranging from the criterion for referral for assessment, to the conduct of the assessment, to the scoring of items (particularly those items that are somewhat subjective), and, finally, to the interpretation of the findings.

A Perspective on Intelligence

Variously referred to by a dozen or so other designations, such as "mental ability," "learning potential," and "cognitive ability," *intelligence* is an abstract, multifaceted construct that defies simple definition; subsumed in this global and broad term are numerous special abilities and talents such as the ability to reason, judge, remember, understand, calculate, hypothesize, think abstractly, visualize spatially, and learn quickly. Intelligence sometimes overlaps (and sometimes does not overlap) with other abilities, such as creativity, and with various personality traits, such as curiosity, persistence, and goal awareness. People who have high measured intelligence typically earn high grades in school and then go on to succeed in many varied vocational settings.

The construct of intelligence has value to psychologists in their efforts to understand and predict human behavior. Intelligence tests have proved to be of great value not only in basic research but also in applied settings where they may be used as an aid in selection, classification, placement, and diagnostic decisions.

Questions concerning the role of nature versus nurture in measured intelligence have not gone away (Reschly, 1981). Some (such as Burt, 1958; Herrnstein, 1971) have argued that the preponderance of the evidence points to the conclusion that differences in measured intelligence are due primarily to heredity. Others have argued that this position has been used to foster racist ideology and amounts, in essence, to a political tool to oppress many of society's religious, ethnic, and racial minorities.

It is likely that the nature/nurture dichotomy is too simplistic; it is impossible to separate out the confounding influences of personal, family, socioeconomic, and cultural variables associated with racial and ethnic group memberships. Although human beings do certainly differ in size, shape, and color—and it is therefore reasonable to consider that there is also a physical base for differences in intellectual ability—researchers have found it impossible to develop a pure measure of innate genetic potential. And though few would deny that genetic factors influence measured intelligence, a problem that defies solution is the determination of the amount of the variance in intellectual ability that can reasonably be attributed to genetics (not to mention the difficulty in determining which abilities are indeed hereditary). It is quite likely that nature as opposed to nurture is responsible for at least some of the variance for some abilities. But notwithstanding genetic technology, we have control only over the environmental factors that play a part in intellectual development; and it is those (environmental) factors that will play a great role in determining whether the genetic potential—or more likely, a portion of that potential—will ever indeed be realized. It would therefore seem incumbent on future researchers in this area to identify and develop a taxonomy of the essential environmental factors responsible in intellectual development. Some of these factors may be found to be "direct" in that once they are introduced to a group of subjects, the measured intelligence of that group rises. Other factors may be found to be "indirect" in that they do not directly affect measured intelligence but act as a catalyst to some preexisting genetic potential that had been dormant.

As our overview of intelligence and its measurement draws to a close, let's return for a moment to a question raised near the beginning of this chapter. *What is intelligence?* Any new thoughts on the matter? If so, what kinds of items would be on a test of intelligence based on those thoughts? In the following chapter, we will see how various models of intelligence have been incorporated into tests of intelligence.

9

Tests of Intelligence

Charged with the task of developing a test to screen for developmentally disabled children in Paris schools, Alfred Binet collaborated with Théodore Simon to create the world's first formal test of intelligence in 1905. Adaptations and translations of Binet's work soon appeared in many countries throughout the world. The original Binet-Simon Scale was in use in the United States at a training school in New Jersey as early as 1908 (Goddard, 1908, 1910), and by 1912 a modified version of the scale that extended the range of the test downward to 3 months had been published (Kuhlmann, 1912). However, it was the work of Lewis Madison Terman at Stanford University that culminated in what would become the most-used and most-researched offspring of the Binet-Simon Scale, the Stanford-Binet Intelligence Scale.

Although the first edition of the Stanford-Binet was certainly not without major flaws (such as the lack of representativeness of the standardization sample), it also contained some important innovations. It was the first published intelligence test to provide organized and detailed administration and scoring instructions. Another milestone was that it was the first American test to employ the concept of "IQ." And it was also the first test to introduce the concept of an "alternate item": an item to be used only under certain conditions, for instance, if the regular item had not been administered properly by the examiner.

In 1926, Terman began a collaboration with a Stanford colleague, Maude Merrill, in a project to revise the test—a project that would take 11 years to complete. Innovations in the 1937 scale included the development of two equivalent forms, labeled "L" and "M," and new types of tasks for use with preschool-level and adult-level testtakers.[1] In addition, the manual for this test

---

1. Why the letters *L* and *M* for the two forms of the Stanford-Binet? What do these letters stand for? They are the first letters in the first names of the test's authors, Lewis and Maude. L. M. Terman left no clue as to what initials would have been used if his coauthor's name had not begun with the letter *M*.

contained many scoring examples to aid the examiner. Although the test authors went to then-unprecedented lengths in attempting to achieve an adequate standardization sample (Flanagan, 1938) and the test was praised for its technical achievement in the areas of validity and especially reliability, a serious criticism of the test was, again, the lack of representativeness of the sample.

Another revision of the Stanford-Binet was well under way at the time of Terman's death at age 79 in 1956. The third edition of the Stanford-Binet, published in 1960, consisted of only a single form (labeled "L-M") composed of the items considered to be the best from the two forms of the 1937 test with no new items added to the test. A major innovation, however, in the 1960 test manual was the use of the deviation IQ tables in place of the ratio IQ tables. Earlier versions of the Stanford-Binet had employed the ratio IQ. The ratio IQ uses the concept of the *mental age*, which is the age level at which an individual appears to be functioning intellectually. The *ratio IQ* is the ratio of the testtaker's mental age divided by his or her chronological age, multiplied by 100 to eliminate decimals:

$$\text{ratio IQ} = \frac{\text{mental age}}{\text{chronological age}} \times 100$$

If the child's mental age was equal to his or her chronological age, the IQ would equal 100. In place of the ratio IQ, the deviation IQ was used beginning with the third edition of the Stanford-Binet. The *deviation IQ* reflects a comparison of the performance of the individual with the performance of others of the same age in the standardization sample. Essentially, test performance is converted into a standard score with a mean of 100 and a standard deviation of 16. If an individual performs at the same level as the average person of the same age, the deviation IQ is 100. If performance is a standard deviation above the mean for the examinee's age group, the deviation IQ is 116.

The Stanford-Binet was revised again in 1972, and, as with previous revisions, the quality of the standardization sample was criticized. Specifically, the manual was vague about the number of minority individuals in the standardization sample, stating only that a "substantial portion" of Black and Spanish-surnamed individuals was included. The 1972 norms may also have overrepresented the West and large, urban communities (Waddell, 1980).

In this chapter, we review the Stanford-Binet in its most current incarnation, as well as a sampling of the many other individual and group intelligence tests currently on the market. We also look at some tests designed to assess specific abilities associated with intelligence. As you read about these tests, contemplate how the types of tasks on them fit into your own conception of what intelligence is and how you believe intelligence as you conceive it could best be measured.

The Stanford Binet: Fourth Edition

The fourth edition of the Stanford-Binet Intelligence Scale (SB:FE; Thorndike et al., 1986) represents a significant departure from previous versions of the Stanford-Binet in theoretical organization, test organization, test adminis-

Table 9–1
The Subtests of the Stanford-Binet Intelligence Scale: Fourth Edition (SB:FE)

Subtest	Description
Verbal Reasoning	
Vocabulary	Consists of 14 picture vocabulary items (in which the subject's task is to identify the pictured object) and 32 items that are words the subject defines—words that may be presented visually as well as orally.
Comprehension	Items range in difficulty from identifying parts of the body to questions regarding social judgment, reasoning, and evaluation (such as "Why should people be quiet in a hospital?"). Again, items may be both read to the examinee and presented visually.
Absurdities	The examinee's task on these items is to identify what is wrong or silly about a picture. This type of item taps the subject's visual-analysis skills.
Verbal Relations	Each of these items presents the examinee with four words, and it is the examinee's task to state what it is that is similar about the first three things but different about the fourth. An example: "Newspaper. Magazine. Book. But not television." A correct response here would indicate that newspapers, magazines, and books are all read but television is not.
Abstract/Visual Reasoning	
Pattern Analysis	Exactly which items will be administered from this subtest will vary with the entry level of the examinee; the timed tasks range from placing cutout forms into a form-board to reproducing complex designs with blocks.
Copying	The examinee's task here is to copy a design. At the earliest level, the design is made from blocks. Subsequently, the designs are copied directly into a record booklet.
Matrices	Here the examinee's task is to solve increasingly difficult matrices that use geometric symbols, letters, and common objects as stimuli. Items on this nonverbal test are presented in a multiple-choice format, and the items are deemed to be especially useful in gauging the general mental ability of non-English-speaking people.
Paper Folding and Cutting	These multiple-choice-type items present the examinee with the task of identifying how a folded and cut piece of paper will look when unfolded.

tration, test scoring, and test interpretation. Previously, different items were grouped by age and the test was referred to as an age scale. By contrast, the SB:FE is a point scale containing 15 separate subtests yielding scores in the following four areas of cognitive ability: "Verbal Reasoning," "Abstract/Visual Reasoning," "Quantitative Reasoning," and "Short-Term Memory" (see Table 9–1). The rationale for the change was that clinically useful diagnostic information could more easily be obtained from such a format. Nine of the subtests were based on the types of items that appeared in previous versions of the test, and six of the subtests are new. In addition to scores in the four general areas listed, a *test composite*—formerly referred to as a deviation IQ score—may also be obtained.

Also new to the SB:FE is an explicit exposition by the test's authors of the theoretical model of intelligence that guided the revision. Briefly, the model is a hierarchical one with general intelligence, or *g*, at the top of the hierarchy. The term *general mental ability* is wide-ranging but encompasses, among other

Subtest	Description
Quantitative Reasoning	
Quantitative Subtest	Items on this subtest range from simple counting to knowledge of various arithmetic concepts and operations.
Number Series	The examinee's task is to complete a number sentence with the next logical number in the sequence. For example, consider the following sequence of numbers and determine which two numbers should come next: 1 2 4 ___ ___. The answer is 8 and 16 and the reasoning is that each number in the sequence has been added to itself to yield the next number ($1 + 1 = 2$; $2 + 2 = 4$; $4 + 4 = 8$; $8 + 8 = 16$; and so on).
Equation Building	The examinee's task here is to rearrange a scrambled arithmetic equation so that it makes sense. As an example, rearrange the numbers and/or signs in the following equation to make a true number sentence: $5 + 12 = 7$. An acceptable rearrangement would be: $5 + 7 = 12$.
Short-Term Memory	
Bead Memory	Examinees study a picture of a bead sequence for five seconds and then must replicate the sequence using actual beads. The beads come in three different colors and four different shapes.
Memory for Sentences	The examiner orally presents a sentence and the examinee's task is to repeat it. The length of the sentence may vary from 2 to 22 words depending on the level of the examinee.
Memory for Digits	The examiner orally presents sequences of digits, forward and backward, and it is the examinee's task to repeat the digits presented in the same order.
Memory for Objects	Familiar objects are presented at one-second intervals and the examinee's task is to recall the presentation in the correct order.

things, (1) information-processing abilities, (2) planning and organizing abilities, and (3) reasoning and adaptation skills. Included in the second level of the theoretical hierarchy are (1) crystallized abilities (also referred to as scholastic or academic abilities), (2) fluid-analytic abilities (that is, nonlanguage abilities that relate to variables such as spatial skills and originality in problem solving), and (3) short-term memory. At the third level are included the following areas: verbal reasoning, abstract/visual reasoning, and quantitative reasoning. These three areas, along with short-term memory at the second level of the hierarchy, make up what are called the "area scores" of the test. This theoretical model is based on Horn and Cattell's (1966) model of intelligence.

Items from the previous edition of the test that were deemed to be outdated or biased or weakly correlated with a particular area of ability the item was supposed to tap were dropped. Items were balanced for gender, ethnic, racial, and disabled representation. Pictures of children representing various ethnic appearances, a child in a wheelchair, and related modifications were made in the test materials. The test's authors were assisted in the editorial process by a panel of minority-member psychologists who reviewed the materials and oversaw revisions where necessary. The word *brunette,* for example, was eliminated from the vocabulary test because of its lack of saliency to Black children.

The Standardization Sample

The standardization sample consisted of 5,013 subjects ranging in age from 2 years through 23 years, 11 months. The sample was stratified with respect to the following variables based on the 1980 U.S. census data: geographical region, community size, race/ethnic group, gender, parental occupation, and parental education. In approximating the population of the United States in the sample, Blacks were somewhat overrepresented and Whites were somewhat underrepresented. There was also an overrepresentation of families from higher-socioeconomic-status homes (43.1% of the sample versus 19.0% of the United States population). As a correction, the norms were weighted. This meant, for example, that a subject from a more advantaged background was counted as a fraction of a case in the construction of the norms but a subject from a less advantaged background was counted as more than one case. An assumption inherent in such a weighting process is that the examinees in the sample are indeed representative of the entire population (Glutting, 1989).

Treating the 18- to 23-year age range as a single group, rather than developing separate norms for different ages within this range, is another norm-related concern (Kaufman, 1990). Test performance may change enough between 18 and 23 years of age to warrant different norms for different ages within this range (Wechsler, 1981).

Psychometric Properties

Thorndike, Hagen, and Sattler (1986b) reported Kuder-Richardson (KR-20) internal consistency measures of reliability, and test-retest measures of stability. The median reliabilities for all the tests with the exception of the Memory for Objects subtests were in the .80s to .90s range. The test composite has an internal consistency reliability of .95 to .99. No inter-scorer reliability estimates were reported.

A number of studies have examined the criterion validity of the SB:FE when used with "normal" subjects (Thorndike & Scott, 1986), and the validity coefficients have generally been acceptable. Criterion validity for the test when used with exceptional testtakers has also been established (Thorndike et al., 1986b). One independent study of developmentally delayed children found that SB:FE scores correlated well with measures of adaptive behavior (.67) and nonverbal intelligence (.78) that are frequently used with exceptional children (Atkinson et al., 1992). Reviewing the literature on the SB:FE's criterion-related validity, Laurent, Swerdlik, and Ryburn (1992) reported a median validity coefficient of .70, with a range from .21 to .91, depending on the range of abilities represented in the specific study and the criterion instrument used for comparison. The correlation of .21 was from a gifted sample, which would have a restricted range of intelligence test scores, thus lowering the correlation.

The construct validity of the SB:FE has been explored by means of factor analysis (Keith et al., 1988; Kline, 1989; Sattler, 1988; Thorndike et al., 1986b). Construct validity is supported by the identification of factors reflecting the hierarchical model of intelligence the test was designed to reflect. Consistent with the theoretical model, factor analyses of data for all age groups indicate that a general cognitive ability factor, or *g*, underlies test scores. A verbal factor, variously labeled "verbal comprehension," "verbal reasoning," or simply "verbal," has been identified by all researchers at all age levels. Factor structures that most clearly support the hierarchical model of intelligence were those obtained for the older age groups by Thorndike et al. (1986b) and Keith et al. (1988). With some exceptions, then, the research seems to support the SB:FE's four-factor model of intelligence, though not for testtakers under 6 years of age.

Test Administration

Developers of intelligence tests, and particularly developers of intelligence tests designed for use with children, have traditionally been sensitive to the need for adaptive testing. *Adaptive testing* refers to testing that is individually tailored to the testtaker. Other terms used to refer to adaptive testing include *tailored testing, sequential testing, branched testing,* and *response-contingent testing.* As employed in intelligence tests, adaptive testing might pose to a testtaker a question in the middle range of difficulty. If the testtaker responds correctly to the item, an item of greater difficulty is posed next. If the testtaker responds incorrectly to the item, an item of lesser difficulty is posed. Adaptive testing is in essence designed "to mimic automatically what a wise examiner would do" (Wainer, 1990, p. 10). Adaptive testing helps ensure that the early test or subtest items will not be so difficult as to frustrate the testtaker, and not be so easy as to lull the testtaker into a false sense of security or a state of mind in which the task will not be taken seriously enough. Three other advantages of beginning an intelligence test or subtest at an optimal level of difficulty are these: (1) it allows the test user to collect the maximum amount of information in the minimum amount of time, (2) it facilitates rapport, and (3) it minimizes the potential for examinee fatigue as a result of being administered an overabundance of items.

After the examiner has established a rapport with the testtaker, the examination formally begins with an item from the Vocabulary subtest. The level of the item employed at the outset is determined by the examinee's chronological age, though the level of subsequent items will be based on the testtaker's performance; the highest level of the Vocabulary subtest wherein the examinee passes two consecutive items is the level at which further testing will begin. In this context, the Vocabulary subtest is referred to as the *routing test,* since it is used to direct or route the examinee to a particular level of questions. A purpose of the routing test, then, is to route the child to test items that have a high probability of being at an optimal level of difficulty. Vocabulary was selected as the routing test primarily because general word knowledge is highly correlated with overall intellectual ability.

Once the examinee has passed four items at two consecutive levels, a *basal* (base) level is said to have been established. After the examinee has failed three out of four or four out of four items at two consecutive levels, a *ceiling* level is said to have been reached and testing is discontinued. *The Examiner's Handbook: An Expanded Guide for Fourth Edition Users* (Delaney & Hopkins, 1987) elaborates on the administration and scoring procedures for each subtest and provides suggestions for administering the subtests to special populations.

Scoring and Interpretation

A *Guide for Administering and Scoring the Fourth Edition* (Thorndike et al., 1986a) contains explicit directions for administering, scoring, and interpreting the test, as well as numerous examples of correct and incorrect responses useful in the scoring of individual items. Each item is scored either correct (1 point) or incorrect (0 points). Scores on the individual items of the various subtests are tallied to yield raw scores on each of the various subtests. The scorer then employs tables found in the manual to convert each of the subtest scores into a standard score. From these standard scores, a composite score as well as scores in each of the four general areas tested may be derived.

In addition to formal scoring, the occasion of an individually administered test affords the examiner an opportunity for behavioral observation; the way the examinee copes with frustration, how the examinee reacts to items considered very easy, the amount of support the examinee seems to require, the general approach to the task, how anxious, fatigued, cooperative, distractable, or compulsive the examinee appears to be—these are the types of behavioral observations that will supplement formal scores.

Information on test interpretation can be found in the test manual as well as in supplementary sources such as Delaney and Hopkins (1987), Sattler (1988), and Swerdlik and Dornback (1988). Delaney and Hopkins (1987) focus on the abilities presumed to underlie test performance. They point out, for example, that verbal expression underlies performance on the Vocabulary, Comprehension, Absurdities, and Verbal Relations subtests. Swerdlik and Dornback (1988) provide specific strategies for using SB:FE data in the classroom. On the basis of his own factor-analytic research, Sattler (1988) offered an alternative method of combining subtest data to yield composite test scores.

An Evaluation

The SB:FE is a reliable and valid measure of overall general ability, including general reasoning and social judgment skills (Laurent et al., 1992). Strengths of the test include the large size of its standardization sample and the efforts of the publisher to eliminate problems of bias and discrimination in test items. The adaptive testing format is another plus, since it tends to minimize the number of test items that must be administered.

Although undeniably a strength of the test because of its sheer size, the sample used for standardization purposes may also be criticized. Children from the upper social class were overrepresented, as were children with college-educated parents. Norms were weighted in an effort to correct for the over-representations, but the full effect of the imbalance on scoring and interpreting data is open to question. Factor-analytic studies have not supported the hypothesized hierarchical factor structure of the test across all age levels. No inter-scorer reliability estimates are provided in the manual. KR-20 estimates of inter-item consistency are provided, but those estimates may be inflated. The estimates are based on the assumption that all items more difficult than a series of items failed by the testtaker would also be failed.[2] Another problem has to do with the test kit, which now contains only pictures of certain objects (such as a spoon or a thimble) instead of, as in previous editions, the actual objects. This economy may diminish the utility of the test for examinees who lack satisfactory visual representation skills and examinees of limited intellectual ability.

The Stanford-Binet has been a mainstay of assessors for decades, with traditionally good prediction rates of academic success at early age levels (Kaufman, 1973b) and psychometrically sound estimates of adult reasoning and judgment (Janzen, 1981). Yet recent years have witnessed a decline in the test's usage, and it is no longer in psychology's "top 10" list of tests in use (Archer et al., 1991; Hutton et al., 1992). One possible reason concerns administration. Another valid and reliable series of tests, the Wechsler tests, are a bit easier to learn to administer. We now turn our attention to that series.

The Wechsler Tests

David Wechsler (see the box on page 304) designed a series of individually administered intelligence tests to assess the intellectual abilities of people from preschool through adulthood. In their current revisions, the three Wechsler intelligence tests are the Wechsler Adult Intelligence Scale—Revised (WAIS-R), for ages 16 and up; the Wechsler Intelligence Scale for Children—Third Edition (WISC-III), for ages 6 through 16; and the Wechsler Preschool and Primary Scale of Intelligence—Revised (WPPSI-R), for ages 3 years to 7 years, 3 months.

Each of the Wechsler tests was designed to assess an individual's "overall capacity to understand and cope with the world around him" (Wechsler, 1974, p. 5). Because the tests share this common theoretical foundation, they are also similar in structure. Each test contains a Verbal Scale and a Performance Scale, each of which is, in turn, made up of subtests. As you can see from Table 9–2 (page 305), similar subtests are found on the three Wechsler tests. Some subtests are common to all three Wechsler tests, such as Vocabulary and Block Design. Others are unique to particular tests, such as Geometric Design on the WPPSI-R and Symbol Search on the WISC-III. The subtest that is most highly correlated with the overall intelligence test score on the WISC-III and the WAIS-R (though not on the WPPSI-R) is Vocabulary. (A brief description of the subtests appears in Table 9–3 on pages 306–307.)

---

2. Experienced examiners who have had occasion to "test the limits" of an examinee will tell you that this assumption is not always correct. *Testing the limits* is a procedure that entails the administration of test items beyond the level at which the test manual dictates discontinuance. The procedure may be employed when an examiner has reason to believe that an examinee can respond correctly to items at the higher level.

David Wechsler (1896–1981)

Born in Romania in 1896, David Wechsler came to New York City six years later with his parents and six older siblings. He completed his bachelor's degree in 1916 at City College (New York) and obtained a master's degree at Columbia University the following year. While awaiting induction into the Army at a base in Long Island, Wechsler came in contact with the renowned historian of psychology, E. G. Boring. Wechsler assisted Boring by evaluating the data from one of the first large-scale administrations of a group intelligence test (the Army Alpha test) as the nation geared up for World War I. Wechsler was subsequently assigned to an Army base in Fort Logan, Texas, where his primary duty was administering individual intelligence tests such as the newly published Stanford-Binet Intelligence Scale. Discharged from the Army in 1919, Wechsler spent two years studying in Europe, where he had the opportunity to study with Charles Spearman and Karl Pearson, two brilliant English statisticians known primarily for their work in the area of correlation. Upon his return to New York City, he took a position as a staff psychologist with the Bureau of Child Guidance. In 1935, Wechsler earned a Ph.D. from Columbia University. His dissertation was entitled "The Measurement of Emotional Reactions." By 1932, Wechsler was appointed Chief Psychologist at Bellevue Psychiatric Hospital. Seven years later, the individually administered test Wechsler had designed to measure an adult's intelligence in adult terms, the Wechsler-Bellevue Intelligence Scale, was a reality. Three years later, in 1942, came a revision of that test referred to variously as the Wechsler-Bellevue II and as the Army Wechsler. In 1949, Wechsler published the Wechsler Intelligence Scale for Children (WISC). This was followed in 1955 by a revision of the Wechsler-Bellevue II that was named the Wechsler Adult Intelligence Scale (WAIS). The Wechsler Preschool and Primary Scale of Intelligence (WPPSI) was published in 1967, and in 1974 a revision of the WISC, the Wechsler Intelligence Scale for Children—Revised (WISC-R), was published. Wechsler's revision of the WAIS, the Wechsler Adult Intelligence Scale—Revised (WAIS-R), was published in 1981, the same year that this prolific and internationally respected psychologist died.

The tests in the Wechsler series are relatively easy to administer. Because there is so much overlap across different tests in the specific subtests included, the examiner trained to administer one Wechsler test can easily master another. In the administering of Wechsler tests, each subtest has its own beginning point, usually determined by the testtaker's age. In testing a younger individual in the designated age range, the examiner might begin, for example, with the first item

Table 9-2
The Composition of the Wechsler Tests

	WPPSI-R	WISC-III	WAIS-R
Verbal Scales			
Information	X	X	X
Comprehension	X	X	X
Similarities	X	X	X
Arithmetic	X	X	X
Vocabulary	X	X	X
Digit Span[2]	—	X [1]	X
Sentences	X	—	—
Performance Scales			
Picture Completion	X	X	X
Picture Arrangement	—	X	X
Block Design	X	X	X
Object Assembly	X	X	X
Coding[3]	—	X	X
Animal Pegs	X	—	—
Mazes	X	X [1]	—
Geometric Design	X	—	—
Symbol Search	—	X [1]	—

[1] Optional supplementary subtest that is not included to determine IQ Score.
[2] The WPPSI-R equivalent of Digit Span is called Sentences.
[3] This subtest is Digit Symbol on the WAIS-R; its equivalent on the WPPSI-R is Animal Pegs.

in the Information subtest, whereas in testing an older person, the examiner might begin with the fourth. The stopping point in a subtest occurs where the testtaker has failed a certain prescribed number of items in a row or has passed every item for that subtest. Many of the items, especially for the younger test-takers, call for demonstrations of what is required before the actual testing. The manual contains explicit directions for administering the subtests as well as a number of standard prompts for dealing with virtually any contingency, question, or comment that might arise during the test session. The administration of Verbal and Performance subtests are alternated; first a Verbal subtest might be given, followed by a Performance subtest, followed by a Verbal subtest, and so forth.

Our emphasis on the ease with which these tests may be administered does not mean that examiners cannot err. In fact, examiner errors may be very common. Slate et al. (1993) found errors on each WAIS-R test record they studied. For over half of these test records, the errors were significant enough to produce a change in the final IQ scores. These findings underscore the importance of thorough training for examiners who will give tests in the Wechsler series (see Figure 9-1 on page 308).

The fact that the Wechsler tests are relatively easy to administer probably partly explains their great popularity among examiners. Another factor making the Wechsler intelligence tests popular is their psychometric soundness. In

Table 9–3
A Brief Description of the Wechsler Subtests

Subtest	Description
Information	"In what continent is Brazil?" This is the type of question on the Wechsler Information subtests. In general, the questions tap general knowledge and in part assess learning and memory. Interests, education, cultural background, and reading skills are some influencing factors in the Information subtest score.
Comprehension	In general, these questions tap social comprehension, the ability to organize and apply knowledge, and what is colloquially referred to as "common sense." An illustrative question is "Why should children be cautious in speaking to strangers?"
Similarities	"How are a pen and a pencil alike?" This is illustrative of the general type of question that appears in this subtest; pairs of words are presented to the examinee and the task is to determine how they are alike. The ability to analyze relationships and engage in logical, abstract thinking are two of the intellectual functions tapped by this type of test.
Arithmetic	Arithmetic problems, presented and solved entirely verbally for older testtakers, are presented (at the lowest levels, this subtest may involve simple counting). Learning of arithmetic, alertness and concentration, and short-term auditory memory are some of the intellectual functions tapped by this test.
Vocabulary	The testtaker is called on to define words in this subtest that is generally viewed as the best measure of general intelligence, although education and cultural opportunity greatly influence scores on vocabulary tests as well.
Digit Span/Sentences	Digit Span, a subtest on the WAIS-R and the WISC-III, entails the examiner's verbally presenting a series of numbers, with the examinee's task being to then repeat the numbers in the same sequence. In the WPPSI-R equivalent of this task, Sentences, the examiner verbally presents sentences composed of vocabulary within preschoolers' range (such as "Jane goes to school"), and the child's task is to repeat the sentence verbatim. Both subtests tap attention, concentration, and short-term auditory memory, although Sentences appears to be more dependent on verbal skills.
Picture Completion	The subject's task here is to identify what important part is missing from a picture. For example, the testtaker might be shown a picture of a chair with one leg missing. This subtest draws on visual perception abilities, alertness, memory, concentration, attention to detail, and ability to differentiate essential from nonessential detail. Because respondents may point to the missing part, this test provides a good nonverbal estimate of intelligence. However, successful performance on a test such as this still tends to be highly influenced by cultural factors.
Picture Arrangement	In the genre of a comic strip panel, this subtest requires the testtaker to re-sort a scrambled set of cards with pictures on them into a story that makes sense. Because the testtaker must understand

general, the Wechsler tests have been evaluated favorably from a psychometric standpoint. Although the coefficients of reliability vary as a function of the specific type of reliability assessed, it is fair to say that the Wechsler tests are generally satisfactory with respect to internal consistency and test-retest reliability. Evidence for the criterion-related validity of each Wechsler test can be found in the individual test manuals along with a detailed presentation of the rationale for inclusion of the specific subtests. Factor-analytic studies by a number of independent investigators have tended to provide support for the construct validity of the Wechsler tests, as have studies of (1) correlations between a Wechsler test and other tests purporting to measure intelligence and (2) the intercorrelations of the individual subtests.

Subtest	Description
	the whole story before a successful re-sorting will occur, this subtest is thought to tap the ability to comprehend or "size-up" a whole situation. Additionally, attention, concentration, and ability to see temporal and cause-and-effect relationships are tapped.
Block Design	A design with colored blocks is illustrated either with blocks themselves or with a picture of the finished design, and the examinee's task is to reproduce the design. This test draws on perceptual-motor skills, psychomotor speed, and the ability to analyze and synthesize. Factors that may influence performance on this test include the examinee's color vision, frustration tolerance, and flexibility or rigidity in problem solving.
Object Assembly	The task here is to assemble, as quickly as possible, a cut-up picture of a familiar object. Some of the abilities called on here include pattern recognition, assembly skills, and psychomotor speed. Useful qualitative information pertinent to the examinee's work habits may also be obtained here by careful observation of the approach to the task (for example, does the examinee give up easily or persist in the face of difficulty?).
Coding	On the Digit Symbol subtest on the WAIS-R, the Coding subtest on the WISC-III, and the Animal Pegs subtest on the WPPSI-R, the examinee's task is to follow a code. If you were given the dot and dash equivalents of several letters in Morse code and then had to write out letters in Morse code as quickly as you could, you would be completing a coding task. The codes for the WAIS-R and WISC-III are copied from a printed key. On the WPPSI-R, the task is to place pegs of different colors into an appropriate space based on a color code. This subtest taps learning ability, rote recall ability, psychomotor speed, concentration, and attention.
Mazes	This subtest does not appear on the WAIS-R and is a supplementary test (not included for purposes of calculating IQ) on the WISC-III. On the WPPSI-R, this subtest is composed of paper-and-pencil mazes, some of which are identical to those that appear on the WISC-III. Perceptual-motor skills, psychomotor speed, and visual planning abilities are tapped by this subtest.
Geometric Design	In no other Wechsler test but the WPPSI-R, this subtest consists of geometric designs that the child is required to copy with a pencil. In general, this subtest provides an index of the child's perceptual-motor skills.
Symbol Search	This is a new, optional performance subtest found only on the WISC-III. The child's task is to visually scan two groups of symbols, one search group and one target group, and determine whether the target symbol appears in the search group. The test is presumed to tap cognitive processing speed.

Manuals for the Wechsler tests are clear about the scoring of responses, a fact that accounts for the typically high estimates of inter-rater reliability obtained in research studies. On some items, extra points may be earned depending on the quality of the response. On some Performance subtest items, extra points may be earned as a function of the speed with which the task is completed. Scores on the individual items are tallied to yield raw scores on each of the subtests. Using tables in the manual, the raw scores for each subtest are converted into scaled scores, and all the scaled scores on each subtest have a mean of 10 and a standard deviation of 3. From these scaled scores, a Verbal Scale IQ, a Performance Scale IQ, and a Full Scale IQ (composite) can be derived. On any one of the Wechsler tests, a Full Scale IQ calculated to be 100 will be

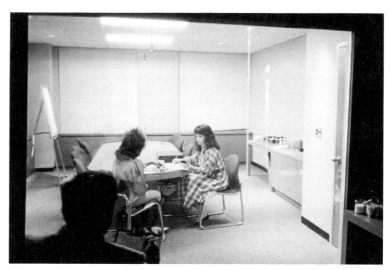

Figure 9–1
Learning to Administer the WAIS-R

It takes a trained examiner to administer an intelligence test such as the Stanford-Binet or any of the Wechsler tests. Fantuzzo and Moon (1984) described a competency-based training model for teaching graduate students how to administer the WAIS-R. The program evaluates competence in test administration by very discrete examiner behaviors and assesses performance of the examiner under conditions that approximate clinical situations. The trainee's administration of the test is observed through a one-way mirror, and the trainee is given detailed information about his or her performance based on a criteria checklist. Also involved in the program is observation by the trainee—and subsequent discussion—of a videotape of a model administering the test. The trainee then administers the WAIS-R, again being observed and obtaining feedback. Fantuzzo and Moon (1984) reported that such a procedure resulted in competent test administration at posttraining.

considered "average." And because the Wechsler tests are all point scales that yield deviation IQs with a mean of 100 (interpreted as "average") and a standard deviation of 15, any Full Scale IQ in the range of 85 to 115 will also be considered "average." On each of the Wechsler tests, a testtaker's performance is compared with scores earned by individuals in his or her own age group.

The manuals for the Wechsler tests tend to contain bare-bones guidelines for the interpretation of the test data. More detailed interpretive information can be obtained from any of a number of publications devoted to the subject.

Kaufman (1979) described what he termed a "successive levels" approach to Wechsler test interpretation, which entails successive evaluation of scale scores for the Verbal Scale, the Performance Scale, and the Full Scale, followed by an analysis and comparison of other data, such as clusters of selected subtests. In practice, a great deal of the data obtained during the testing, including and beyond scores and score clusters (such as the examiner's notes regarding the testtaker's extra-test behavior), may hold great interpretive significance for the capable examiner. Ultimately, test interpretation skills for a Wechsler test—like many other tests—are honed through a combination of activities, such as administering the test and observing firsthand a variety of testtakers as they take it, reading about test interpretation in various sources, and scoring and interpreting a number of test protocols under the tutelage of a skilled, experienced, and knowledgeable supervisor.

The Wechsler Adult Intelligence Scale—Revised (WAIS-R)

The WAIS-R is the latest in a series of instruments designed to measure the intelligence of adults. In the early 1930s, Wechsler's employer, Bellevue Hospital in Manhattan, needed an instrument suitable for evaluating the intellectual capacity of multilingual, multinational, and multicultural clients being referred there. Wechsler was dissatisfied with existing intelligence tests when used with such a population, and he began to experiment with various tests to find one more appropriate for measuring adult intelligence. The eventual result was the Wechsler-Bellevue I (W-B I), published in 1939. This new test borrowed in format, though not in content, from existing tests.

Unlike the most popular individually administered intelligence test of the time, the Stanford-Binet, the W-B I was a *point scale* rather than an age scale; the items were classified by subtests rather than by age. The test was organized into six verbal subtests and five performance subtests, and all the items in each test were arranged in order of increasing difficulty. Another form of the test designed to be an equivalent alternate, the Wechsler-Bellevue II (W-B II), was published in 1942, though it was never thoroughly standardized (Rapaport et al., 1968). Unless a specific reference is made to the W-B II, reference here (and in the literature in general) to "the Wechsler-Bellevue" is to Wechsler-Bellevue I.

Problems identified with the Wechsler-Bellevue eventually led to the development of a new test. Although research had suggested that the W-B was indeed measuring something comparable to what other intelligence tests were measuring, the test had the following problems: (1) the standardization sample was rather restricted, (2) some subtests lacked sufficient inter-item reliability, (3) some of the subtests were made up of items that were too easy, (4) the scoring criteria for certain items were too ambiguous. Sixteen years after publication of Form I of the W-B, a revised form with a new name, the Wechsler Adult Intelligence Scale (Wechsler, 1955), was published.

The WAIS contained 257 items, 147 of which had been retained from the Wechsler-Bellevue. Like its predecessor, the WAIS was organized into six subtests designated as "Verbal" and five subtests designated as "Performance."

Again, scoring yielded a Verbal IQ, a Performance IQ, and a Full Scale IQ. Modifications were made to improve the directions for administering and scoring the subtests. The WAIS was a widely researched test thought by many to be the best available measure of adult intelligence. As one reviewer observed, the WAIS "was carefully constructed and carefully standardized. The norms were intelligently conceived and meticulously developed . . . this test has become the standard against which other adult tests can be compared" (Lyman, 1972, p. 429). Primarily because of the need for a more contemporary norm group, the WAIS was revised and published as the Wechsler Adult Intelligence Scale—Revised (Wechsler, 1981).

Although the WAIS-R was ultimately published after his death, Wechsler assumed a very active role in its development. Approximately 80 percent of the WAIS-R items remained essentially unchanged from the WAIS. The WAIS-R directions for scoring and the record form were changed, as were the administration instructions for the tests. In the older version, verbal subtests were administered before the performance subtests, whereas in the WAIS-R the examiner alternates between administering a verbal and a performance subtest.

The standardization sample   The WAIS-R sample of 1,880 White and non-White Americans was stratified along the variables of age, sex, race, geographic region, occupation, education, and urban-rural residence in a manner representative of the 1970 U.S. census. People whose primary language was not English were included only if they were able to both speak and understand English. Excluded from the sample were institutionalized mental retardates, brain-damaged or severely behaviorally or emotionally disturbed individuals, or subjects physically disabled in some way who would be restricted in their ability to respond to test items. No more than one member of any family was tested.

Psychometric properties   Correlations reported between total WAIS-R IQ score and individual subtest scores ranged from .52 to .82 for the 25- to 34-years age group, indicating good internal consistency of the test as a whole (Kaufman, 1990). The manual reports split-half reliability coefficients for specific subtests for which that statistic is appropriate, to determine the internal consistency of the subtests; these reliability estimates range from .68 (Object Assembly) to .96 (Vocabulary) in the 25- to 34-years age group (Wechsler, 1981). Note that split-half reliability is not appropriate (and was not calculated) for Digit Symbol, which is a speeded test, and Digit Span, which is essentially two different tests. Reliability estimates are similar across the age range for which the WAIS-R is designed. For example, reliability is estimated at .62 (Object Assembly) to .95 (Vocabulary) for people in the 70- to 74-years age group. Test-retest reliability was also reported in the manual for the 25- to 34-years age group over a two- to seven-week retesting period. Reliability was estimated at .94 for Verbal IQ, .89 for Performance IQ, and .95 for Full Scale IQ (Wechsler, 1981). Parker et al. (1988) estimated the reliability of the Full Scale IQ using meta-analysis to combine information across 12 studies. The reliability estimate was .87, with a 95% confidence interval of .86 to .88.

Table 9–4
Some Factor-Analytic Studies Using the WAIS-R Standardization Data

Researcher(s)	Factors Identified
Silverstein (1982)	Verbal (Information, Digit Span, Vocabulary, Arithmetic, Comprehension, Similarities) Performance (Picture Completion, Picture Arrangement, Block Design, Object Assembly, Digit Symbol)
Gutkin, Reynolds, & Galvin (1984)	Verbal Comprehension (Information, Vocabulary, Comprehension, Similarities) Perceptual Organization (Block Design, Object Assembly)
Parker (1983)	Verbal Comprehension (Information, Vocabulary, Comprehension, Similarities)
Ryan & Sattler (1988)	Perceptual Organization (Picture Completion, Block Design, Object Assembly) Freedom from Distractibility (Digit Span, Arithmetic)
Waller & Waldman (1990)	Verbal Comprehension (Information, Vocabulary, Comprehension, Similarities) Perceptual Organization (Picture Completion, Block Design, Object Assembly) Freedom from Distractibility (Digit Span, Arithmetic, Digit Symbol)

One type of construct validity study employs factor analysis to explore whether a test is measuring what it purports to measure. Such factor-analytic procedures have been employed for the standardization sample and a variety of clinical populations, and the number of factors that the test has been deemed to tap has varied by study from one to three. A summary of a sampling of the studies in which the WAIS-R standardization data were used is presented in Table 9–4. The one-, two-, and three-factor structures identified by various researchers for the WAIS-R may all be viable (Fraboni & Saltstone, 1992). Meta-analysis of 26 convergent validity studies yielded an estimate of .62 for the convergent validity of the WAIS-R (Parker et al., 1988).

In Chapter 6, we noted that the validity of a test is limited by its reliability. With that point in mind, consider a criterion-related validity study conducted by Hanson et al. (1988). These researchers studied the criterion validity of the 11 WAIS and WAIS-R subtests along with Verbal IQ, Performance IQ, and Full Scale IQ scores, in relation to criterion variables such as scores on other intelligence tests, brain damage, and educational achievement. They expected that the subtests and other variables with the higher reliability coefficients should also be more highly correlated with the criterion measures—thus indicating higher validity for those subtests. They also hypothesized that Full Scale IQ, because it was the most reliable of the variables under consideration, would demonstrate the highest level of criterion validity (as represented by the highest correlations with the criterion measures).

Information from the test manual provided estimates of reliability. Criterion validity was estimated from a meta-analysis of 36 published criterion-related validity studies, most of which had used another intelligence test, such as the Stanford-Binet, as a criterion. Some of the studies had used other variables, such as educational achievement, or the presence/absence of brain damage as the criterion. Meta-analytic estimates were obtained for the criterion validity of each subtest and for Verbal IQ, Performance IQ, and Full Scale IQ.

The researchers next examined the relationship between the reliability and validity coefficients. The correlation between the reliability and validity estimates of the subtests was found to be .68. Subtests with relatively low reliability (Digit Span at .67, Picture Arrangement at .67, and Object Assembly at .68) had lower criterion validity (.37, .40, and .46, respectively) than subtests with relatively high reliability (Vocabulary at .95, Information at .92, and Digit Symbol at .92), which, in turn, had higher criterion validity (.45, .46, and .52, respectively). As predicted, the test score with the highest reliability, the Full Scale IQ score (.97), also had the highest criterion validity (.65). Verbal IQ, a somewhat more reliable measure than Performance IQ (.96 compared with .93), also yielded a slightly larger criterion validity coefficient (.61 compared with .57).

Hanson et al.'s findings serve as a reminder that the reliability of a test affects its validity. However, it would be a mistake to interpret such findings as meaning that the criterion-related validity of a test is simply a reflection of that test's reliability. To understand why, note the overlapping size of the validity coefficients of the three most reliable and three least reliable subtests. The correlation between reliability and validity coefficients, though impressive at .68, is not a perfect correlation of 1. Obviously, other facets of a subtest affect its validity aside from that subtest's reliability.

An evaluation The WAIS-R is the standard with which other tests of adult intelligence are compared and by which they are judged. The WAIS-R standardization is sound, and a number of studies have shown it to be a reliable and valid measure of adult intelligence.

The Wechsler Intelligence Scale for Children—Third Edition (WISC-III)

The Wechsler Intelligence Scale for Children (WISC) was first published in 1949. It represented a downward extension of another Wechsler test, the Wechsler-Bellevue Scale (W-B I).[3] "A well standardized, stable instrument correlating well with other tests of intelligence" (Burstein, 1972, p. 844) that was welcomed by the professional community, the WISC was not, however, without its flaws. The standardization sample contained only White children, and some of the test items were viewed as perpetuating gender and cultural stereotypes. Further, parts of the test manual were so unclear as to lead to ambiguities in the administration and scoring of the test. A revision of the WISC, called the Wechsler Intelligence Scale for Children—Revised (WISC-R), was published in 1974. The WISC-R included non-Whites in the standardization sample. Test material pictures were also made more culturally balanced. The test's language was modernized and "child-ized." The word "cigars," in an arithmetic item, for example, was replaced with "candy bars." There were also innovations in the ad-

---

3. The W-B I was an adult test and a revision of it had been planned. The revision would be called the Wechsler-Bellevue II (W-B II). Interestingly, many of the items originally planned for use in the W-B II found their way into the downward extension of the test, the WISC.

ministration and scoring of the test. For example, Verbal and Performance tests were now administered in alternating fashion, a practice now common with respect to Wechsler and other tests. The revision of the WISC-R yielded the Wechsler Intelligence Scale for Children—III, published in 1991. According to Sattler (1992), the primary reason for this latest revision was to update the normative data, though over a quarter of the WISC-III's items represent significant alterations from its predecessor.

The WISC-III includes a new subtest called Symbol Search, designed to measure cognitive processing speed. The artwork in the Picture Arrangement, Picture Completion, and Object Assembly subtests was modernized and rendered in color. The Mazes subtest was enlarged, as was the Coding subtest. The Coding key was set at the top of the sheet in the Coding subtest so that it would not be blocked by left-handed testtakers as they write. Other changes were designed to increase the range of possible scores on the subtests. For example, the Coding subtest was lengthened so that fewer testtakers would finish within the allotted time. Easier items were added to the Arithmetic scale to assess counting ability. At the other end of the Arithmetic scale, relatively difficult, multistep word problems were added.

The procedures used to revise the WISC-R and create the WISC-III illustrate many sound principles of test construction and revision. The publisher began the process with an in-house review of the test, including suggestions received from WISC-R users, recommendations solicited by experts, and ongoing correspondence with test users before and during the revision. New items and subtests were piloted, and a "tryout version" of the new test was administered to 500 children nationally. On the basis of the resulting data and in consultation with experts and high-volume users of the WISC-R, the WISC-III was then constructed. As has become standard practice in the development of new tests designed for wide commercial distribution, great pains were taken by the test developer to minimize any potential source of bias in any of the test's items. Using data from the WISC-R normative sample, each item was statistically analyzed with regard to performance as a function of gender, ethnicity, and age. Proposed replacement items underwent the same statistical review for item bias. WISC-R items and draft WISC-III items were reviewed by a panel of experts in an effort to balance references to ethnicity and gender. Items deemed to be outdated were deleted. Color vision experts were consulted to ensure that color-blind testtakers would not be adversely affected by the new color artwork in the test materials.

An attempt was made to make the WISC-III more "user-friendly" to both examiners and examinees than prior versions of this test. In addition to changes in the test itself, improvements were made in the test materials. For example, the cardboard "shield" used by the examiner in administering the Object Assembly subtest was constructed so that it could stand on its own. Previously, this shield had to be held with one hand while the examiner awkwardly tried to arrange pieces of the object to be assembled with the other hand. A computer-based interpretive program called WISC-III Writer was designed to generate numerous interpretive options and statistical indices applicable to a variety of evaluation settings and purposes.

The standardization sample   The norm sample for the WISC-III consisted of 2,200 children between the ages of 6 and 16. There were 200 children in each of 11 age groups, divided equally by gender. Variables in the stratification were closely matched to 1988 U.S. Census data for race/ethnicity, region of the country, and parental education level. Parental education level instead of parental occupation was used because prior research had indicated that parental education level accounts for more variance in test scores than parental occupation. Additional testing was conducted with Black and Hispanic children to ensure accuracy of item bias statistics. Additional testing was also conducted for the purpose of comparing same-subject performance on the WPPSI-R and the WISC-III (the subjects were 200 6-year-olds), the WAIS-R and the WISC-III (the subjects were 200 16-year-olds), and the WISC-R and the WISC-III (the subjects were 200 children across the age range). About 300 children who had taken the WISC-III were re-tested for research purposes within 4 to 8 weeks between test administrations. In all, upward of 4,500 test administrations at various sites around the country were conducted.

Who administered all these tests and how was quality control ensured? Most test publishers do not maintain an in-house staff of trained examiners who can arrange for the administration of, and actually administer, 4,500 tests throughout the country within a reasonable amount of time. Rather, the publisher contracts with experienced examiners throughout the country who may be screened by means of a background questionnaire that solicits information on educational and background experience. This was the case with respect to the standardization of the WISC-III. Additionally, graduate students under the supervision of a qualified professional were employed. The test publisher used several tools of examiner "quality control" throughout the standardization, including

1. The completion and submission of practice protocols before testing
2. Information about the accuracy of administration and scoring of the practice protocol, provided to the examiner by telephone and letter
3. Frequent communication with examiners during the standardization process such as through a "standardization newsletter"
4. Rigorous checking procedures to evaluate each protocol for completeness and accuracy of administration and scoring

The reliability of persons responsible for checking the accuracy of the other examiners' scoring of test protocols was ensured by means such as the use of *anchor protocols*—that is, protocols generated by the test publisher and given to an examiner for scoring for the purpose of checking the accuracy of the examiner's scoring.

Psychometric properties   The WISC-III appears to be a psychometrically sound instrument. Average internal consistency reliability estimates across the various age groups range from .69 (on Object Assembly) to .87 (on Block Design and Vocabulary) as computed by a measure of split-half reliability. Internal consistency reliability is not reported for speeded tests, such as Coding and Symbol

Search; test-retest reliabilities of those subtests yielded coefficients of .79 and .76, respectively. The internal consistency reliability of the test as a whole is estimated at .95 for Verbal IQ, .91 for Performance IQ, and .96 for Full Scale IQ. The test also has good test-retest reliability, with Full Scale IQ scores correlating .92 to .95, depending on the age group, over a three-week median interval between testings. Inter-rater reliability of specific subtest scores was in the .90s, even for subtests that require some judgment in scoring, such as Mazes (.92) and Vocabulary (.98). Such findings suggest that trained raters contribute little error variance to test scores (Wechsler, 1991).

Evidence for the construct validity of the WISC-III comes from many sources, including factor-analytic studies (see *Everyday Psychometrics*). WISC-III scores have been shown to correlate in the expected directions with tests of neurological functioning in a sample of learning-disabled and/or attention-deficit-disordered boys. Measures that suggested the presence of a neuropsychological problem were negatively related to WISC-III scores. School achievement, as measured by the individually administered Wide Range Achievement Test, by group-administered achievement tests, and by school grades, is positively related to WISC-III scores. Children previously identified as gifted or retarded obtain WISC-III scores in the expected ranges (Wechsler, 1991). These relationships all support the construct validity of the WISC-III.

With reference to the test's concurrent criterion validity, the WISC-R and the WISC-III are highly correlated with each other. When children were given both tests over a short (median three-week) interval, correlations between the two tests were found to be: Verbal IQ, .90; Performance IQ, .81; and Full Scale IQ, .89 (Wechsler, 1991). Over a three-year interval between test administrations, correlations between the WISC-R and the WISC-III were .82 for Verbal IQ, .81 for Performance IQ, and .86 for Full Scale IQ (Graf & Hinton, 1994). These results indicate that the two tests are largely measuring the same construct. Because both the WISC-III and the WAIS-R have norms for 16-year-olds, concurrent criterion validity data were also collected by giving a group of 16-year-olds both tests; correlations were .90 for Verbal IQ, .80 for Performance IQ, and .86 for Full Scale IQ. Similarly, both the WISC-III and the WPPSI-R were given to a sample of 6-year-olds, with validity coefficients of .85 for Verbal IQ, .73 for Performance IQ, and .85 for Full Scale IQ. These comparisons with other Wechsler tests suggest that because the WAIS-R and WPPSI-R are considered valid measures of intelligence, the WISC-III is valid as well (Wechsler, 1991).

Outside the realm of other Wechsler tests, evidence of concurrent criterion validity can also be found. The full scales of the WISC-III and the Otis-Lennon School Ability Test (a measure of school-related ability) correlate .73. The verbal scales of the two tests correlate .69, and the nonverbal or performance scales correlate .59. The WISC-III and the Differential Ability Scales, another scale of school-related ability, correlate .92 in their full scales, .87 in their verbal scales, and .78 in their nonverbal scales (Wechsler, 1991).

An evaluation The WISC-III is a well-constructed and well-standardized measure of intelligence in children that is reliable and valid. It has been well received by professional reviewers (Little, 1992).

Construct Validity, Factor Analysis, and the WISC-III

The evaluation of the construct validity of a test proceeds on the assumption that one knows in advance exactly what the test is supposed to measure. For intelligence tests, it is essential to know in advance how the test developer defined intelligence. If in a specific test intelligence was defined as Spearman's *g*, for example, then we would expect a factor analysis of such a test to yield a large, single common factor. The large, single common factor would indicate that the different questions or tasks on the test largely reflected the same underlying characteristic (intelligence or *g*). By contrast, if intelligence was defined by a test developer in accordance with Guilford's theory, no one factor would be expected to dominate. Instead, one would anticipate many different factors reflecting a diverse set of abilities. Recall that from Guilford's perspective, there is no single underlying intelligence for the different test items to reflect. Therefore, there would be no basis for a large common factor.

In a sense, a compromise between Spearman and Guilford is Thorndike. Thorndike's theory of intelligence leads us to look for one central factor, reflecting *g*, along with three additional factors representing social, concrete, and abstract intelligences. In this case, analysis would have to suggest that testtakers' responses to specific items reflected a general intelligence in part, but also different types of intelligence: social, concrete, and abstract.

Wechsler defined intelligence as being general in nature ("the global capacity of the individual") but having origins in distinct components ("composed of . . . abilities which . . . are quantitatively differentiable"). Wechsler (1974) said that there were two such components, "verbal" and "performance." The case for a Wechsler test's construct validity would be helped greatly, therefore, by a demonstration that there indeed exists a general intelligence factor, as well as verbal and performance factors.

Reviewing some of the material on factor analysis presented in Chapter 6, let's see how such an analysis might work in exploring the construct validity of the WISC-III. Step 1 would be to choose and administer the set of measures on which the factor analysis will be conducted. In the present case, these measures are the 13 subtests of the WISC-III, and these 13 subtests would be administered to a group of testtakers. Step 2 would be to create a correlation matrix. In this case, correlations would be computed between all possible pairs of the 13 subtest scores. According to available data (Sattler, 1992; Wechsler, 1991), an examination of this matrix would suggest that the verbal subtests correlate more highly with one another than with the performance subtests. Also, correlations among the performance subtests are higher than those between verbal and performance subtests. These findings support Wechsler's idea that the subtests constitute two distinct groups: performance subtests and verbal subtests.

Step 3 in our factor analysis would be to factor the correlation matrix developed in the previous step. Step 4 would involve gaining an understanding of the factors. At this point we might ask, is there evidence of a general factor? Sattler (1992) argues that there is. The first factor that appears on the WISC-III is large, reflecting 43% of the variance in test scores; stated another way, 43% of the variability in test scores among any very large group of testtakers could be accounted for by a single underlying factor. A sensible name for a single factor that explains so much of the variability in intelligence test scores would seem to be general intelligence.

Additional factors seem to be present when the

WISC-III is factor-analyzed—but just how many additional factors exist is a matter of controversy (Kamphaus et al., 1994). In factor analysis, there are several different criteria that may be used in determining how many factors exist (Gorsuch, 1983). In the case of the WISC-III, the criteria do not all point to the same number of factors (Wechsler, 1991). As different researchers depend to a greater or lesser extent on particular criteria, they will reach different conclusions concerning the number of factors they are willing to acknowledge. For example, some ways of doing the analysis point to a two-factor solution, with the subtests lining up neatly into "verbal" and "performance" camps. Sattler's (1992) analysis points to a three-factor solution, with factors he labeled "verbal comprehension," "perceptual organization," and "processing speed." The verbal comprehension factor includes the same subtests as Wechsler's original verbal factor, but Wechsler's original performance factor is split between perceptual organization and processing speed. This dichotomy reflects two different nonverbal abilities underlying performance on the test. The factor solution endorsed as "best" in the WISC-III manual and elsewhere (Kamphaus et al., 1994; Wechsler, 1991) involves four factors, including two "major" factors ("verbal comprehension" and "perceptual organization") and two "minor" factors ("freedom from distractibility" and "processing speed"). Kamphaus et al. (1994) conceded that none of the factor solutions provided a very good fit with the data. Still, as you have probably noticed yourself, there are commonalities in the names of the factors; different investigators are probably not far apart conceptually.

In a general way, we can conclude that factor analysis supports the construct validity of the WISC-III relative to David Wechsler's definition of intelligence. After all, the WISC-III measures a general intelligence factor in addition to some more-specific factors. Granted that with regard to these specific factors, there may be more than the two (verbal and performance) that Wechsler (1974) posited. We are prepared, however, to "cut some slack" in this regard, since the test has undergone such substantial revision in the decades since Wechsler defined intelligence. We cannot ignore the addition, for example, of a new subtest, Symbol Search, designed to measure cognitive processing speed. Had David Wechsler been around when the decision was made to add this test, "cognitive processing speed" might well have been added to his list of specific factors in intelligence.

"Hard-liners" might hold the publisher of the WISC-III more strictly to the definition of intelligence put forth by Wechsler before deeming the test to be construct-valid. Yet in light of the ongoing debate among professionals about how intelligence shall be defined, Wechsler's pronouncements not only seem to hold up quite well but also continue to be measured by revisions of his test.

When applied appropriately and with reasonable judgment, factor analysis can help provide an understanding of the adequacy with which a test reflects the theory on which it was based. Should the factor analysis indicate an incongruence between the theory and the test, revisions in the theory or the test may be necessary. Taken as a whole, the body of literature of factor-analytic research on the WISC-III leaves us with no compelling need to rewrite Wechsler's thoughts on intelligence or readjust the content of the WISC-III.

The Wechsler Preschool and Primary Scale of Intelligence— Revised (WPPSI-R)

Project Head Start as well as other 1960s programs for preschool children who were culturally different or exceptional (defined in this context as atypical in ability—gifted or retarded) fostered interest in the development of new tests (Zimmerman & Woo-Sam, 1978). The Stanford-Binet had traditionally been the test of choice for use with preschoolers, though test users were open to experimenting with alternative methods. Although some advocated a restandardization of the WISC for children under 6, Wechsler (1967) had decided that a new scale should be developed and standardized especially for children under age 6. The new test was the WPPSI (usually pronounced like "whipsy"), and with its publication in 1967 the Wechsler series of intelligence tests was extended downward in age range to age 4. The WPPSI was the first major intelligence test that "adequately sampled the total population of the United States, including racial minorities" (Zimmerman & Woo-Sam, 1978, p. 10)—a fact that contributed to the success of the WPPSI, especially in an era when standardized tests were under attack for not having adequate minority representation in the standardization sample.

The WPPSI-R was published in 1989 and is designed to assess the intelligence of children from ages 3 years through 7 years 3 months. Major changes from the WPPSI included extension of the age range, addition of the Object Assembly subtest, and the renaming of the Animal Pegs subtest (formerly Animal House). Approximately 48% of the WPPSI items (excluding Animal Pegs) were retained intact or with only slight modifications from the WPPSI. New items were developed for the younger age range and for the older age range. There is a one-year overlap with the WISC-R at ages 6 years 0 months (6–0) through 7 years 3 months (7–3).

The standardization sample   The WPPSI-R was standardized on 1,700 children, including 100 boys and 100 girls in each of eight age groups, ranging in half-year intervals from age 3 years to 7 years, and one age group of 50 boys and 50 girls in the 7 years to 7 years 3 months interval. The sample closely reflects 1986 census estimates on stratification variables such as geographic region, ethnicity, parental education and occupation, and urban-rural residence.

Psychometric properties   Average subtest split-half reliability estimates for internal consistency range from .80 to .86 on the Verbal Scale, and from .63 to .85 on the Performance Scale. Test-retest reliability coefficients for the subtests range from .70 to .81 for the Verbal Scale and from .52 to .82 for the Performance Scale. For the global scales, the split-half reliability coefficients range from .92 (Performance Scale) to .96 (Full Scale), and test-retest reliability coefficients range from .88 (Performance Scale) to .91 (Full Scale). Inter-scorer reliability coefficients for the Comprehension, Vocabulary, Similarities, Mazes, and Geometric Design subtests range from .88 to .96 (Gyurke, 1991).

Factor analyses of the data from the standardization sample yielded findings consistent with two previous studies of the WPPSI; a verbal factor and a performance factor were the two primary factors tapped by the test (Gyurke et al., 1990). Several validity studies, all of which support the validity of the test, are reported in the WPPSI-R manual. A number of other studies also support the test's validity (Faust & Hollingsworth, 1990; Karr et al., 1993). Kaplan (1993) provided evidence for the test's predictive validity in a study that entailed its administration to 50 children before they entered kindergarten. Achievement test scores were evaluated with reference to test scores at the end of the first grade, two years later. Although Performance IQ before kindergarten was not found to be predictive of academic achievement at the end of first grade, Verbal IQ and Full Scale IQ were found to be predictive of academic achievement. Achievement in the four areas covered by the achievement test—Listening, Math, Reading, and Word Analysis—was significantly correlated with Full Scale IQ (correlations ranged from .38 to .65) and with Verbal IQ (correlations ranged from .44 to .71).

An evaluation Standardization procedures for the WPPSI-R can perhaps best be described as, or as nearly, "state-of-the-art," and the psychometric properties of the test are strong. Scoring criteria for the subtests are clear, and as a result, inter-rater reliability in scoring overall tends to be impressive. Bracken (1992) concluded that "the WPPSI-R will likely be the test of choice for psychologists who are willing to expend the time and energy to conduct comprehensive, interactive assessments to obtain thorough understandings of their preschool clients" (p. 1029).

The Wechsler Tests in Perspective

The standardization of all the Wechsler tests closely approximates the highest level of standards advocated by professional groups such as the American Psychological Association. In addition, each test has been thoroughly researched with respect to all facets of reliability and validity and in general has been found to be psychometrically sound.

The organization of the Wechsler Scales into a Verbal and a Performance Scale, with individual subtests constituting each scale, facilitates the interpretation of the test data and the generation of diagnostic hypotheses. Additionally, the identification of areas of the testtaker's strengths and weaknesses can be delineated from analysis of performance on Wechsler subtests.

The clarity of the instructions for administering the Wechsler tests is exemplary when it comes to test-manual writing. For example, if an examiner poses a question that requires the respondent to provide not one but two reasons for something (in order for the examinee to earn full and not partial credit for the item), the administration manual provides not only the "permission" to probe for a second reason if only one is initially given, but also the precise language with which to probe. And while the trained examiner may find the Wechsler tests fairly easy to administer, testtakers generally find the materials "easy to take"—that is, engaging. After one or two items on a particular subtest are failed, it's on to a new subtest and another intellectually challenging task. Preschool children, older children, and adults tend to respond favorably to the Wechsler test materials designed for use with their respective age groups.

One problem an examiner might have with the Wechsler materials may come not while administering the test but while attempting to score it. Wechsler (1955) himself noted that the evaluation of a testtaker's responses to some of the items—perhaps most noticeably on subtests such as Comprehension, Similarities, and Vocabulary—may require subjective judgment on the part of the examiner. For example, the manual can offer only a sampling of the many different definitions a child can give for a word on the Vocabulary subtest—and then it is up to the examiner to determine whether the response should be credited. This element of subjectivity in some of the scoring has been thought to depress correlations observed in some studies of inter-scorer reliability (Sattler et al., 1969; Sattler et al., 1978; Woo-Sam & Zimmerman, 1973), and level of inter-scorer agreement may not be related to amount of examiner experience (Miller et al., 1972).

A second problem involves the interpretation of subtest scores. Scaled scores for the various age ranges and various Wechsler subtests are not uniform; the same number of scaled-score points cannot be earned on all subtests. For example, the highest number of scaled-score points possible on the WISC-III Mazes subtest is 19 points at ages 6 through 10. For ages 11 and 12, the highest number of scaled-score points is 18. For children 13 and older, the highest number of scaled-score points that can be earned is only 17. For the WAIS-R, in the reference group (ages 20–34) that is used to transform raw scores into scaled scores and then into deviation IQs, scaled scores of 19 can be earned on five subtests, a score of 18 on three subtests, and 17 on another three subtests. This lack of conformity among scaled scores may complicate the analysis and interpretation of the test data.

The Wechsler tests of intelligence are among the most-used tests of intelligence. Should you elect to pursue a career in psychology, you will no doubt obtain more detailed training in these tests, and you will observe firsthand how they can provide an index of not only the examinee's intelligence but other factors as well, such as personality and neurological intactness.

Other Tests of Intelligence

Psychologists who have occasion to administer intelligence tests are familiar not only with names such as "Binet" and "Wechsler" but also with names such as "Slosson," "Kaufman," and "Peabody"—to cite but a few. "Slosson" is the name associated with one of a variety of intelligence tests—the variety that is speedily administered and scored.

The Slosson Intelligence Test—Revised (SIT-R)

Also referred to by some practitioners as the "Short Intelligence Test," the Slosson was designed to be a quick, easily administered, yet valid measure of intelligence. The test was originally conceived of as an abbreviated version of the Stanford-Binet (Slosson, 1963). The 1991 revision of the Slosson (SIT-R) contains, in addition, items similar to those found on the Wechsler scales. Intended for use as "a screening test of intelligence specifically measuring the verbal intelligence factor" (Slosson, 1991, p. 2), the SIT-R taps skills in the following domains: vocabulary, general information, similarities and differences, comprehension, auditory memory, and quantitative ability. It was standardized on 1,854 individuals loosely matched to the U.S. population with respect to educational and social characteristics—"loosely" since, for example, 83% of the standardization sample, as compared with 74% of the U.S. population, was White. The members of the standardization sample also tended to be better educated than the general U.S. population.

The SIT-R also has many of the types of items found in infant intelligence scales and does extend downward in range to the infant level (as well as upward to age 27). Above age 7, the test becomes increasingly weighted with verbal items, though items assessing motor, perceptual-motor, and related abilities are also included. The test "kit" contains only two items: the test manual and score sheets. In contrast to the administration of a Binet or a Wechsler test, which may take as much as an hour (or more), the administration of the Slosson seldom takes more than 15 to 20 minutes. Further, the items can be scored quickly, with little room for subjectivity.

As reported in the test manual, the test-retest reliability coefficient for 41 examinees retested after one week was .96. Validity studies with 234 children divided into four groups ranging in age from 6 to 16 compared the Verbal scale scores of the SIT-R with those of the WISC-R and yielded validity coefficients ranging from .83 to .91. When full scale scores of the two tests were compared, correlations ranged from .61 to .92. In another study with adults, correlations between the SIT-R and WAIS-R verbal scales were found to be .88, and the SIT-R/WAIS-R full scale correlation was found to be .82.

In contrast to the Stanford-Binet and the Wechsler scales, the Slosson does not have to be administered by a highly trained examiner. The test has been promoted as one that can be used for screening purposes by personnel who may have had only minimal exposure to principles of psychological testing (such as counselors, special education teachers, reading specialists, and speech therapists). A potential problem, however, is that although such users may appreciate the convenience of the test, they may not appreciate the great limitations of the data derived from it. The Slosson must be viewed as a good test for what it is: a quick screening device that can be used to generate hypotheses about specific problem areas that could then be more fully explored using more comprehensive or specialized measures.

Figure Drawings as Measures of Intelligence

Asking a testtaker to draw a figure is one relatively quick, nonverbal method used by many psychologists to obtain an estimate of intelligence. As we will see in Chapter 12, figure-drawing tasks may also be employed in the assessment of personality. Most typically, examinees are asked to draw a person, although they may be requested to draw a house and/or a tree as well (Buck, 1948). Many published methods exist for analyzing drawings with regard to variables such as detail, position, and proportion. The best known of the systems for estimating intelligence from drawings of people is the Goodenough-Harris scoring system (see Figure 9–2; Harris, 1963). A question of long-standing interest and controversy, however, is whether this scoring system is "good enough."

The scoring of figure drawings tends to be advocated only as a quick way to screen for intellectual level. This means that if a drawing suggests low intellectual functioning, a more formal intellectual assessment is undertaken. Proponents of the use of human figure drawings to estimate intelligence point to various studies that indicate the validity of this practice. As discussed following, estimates of intelligence obtained using figure drawings do correlate with estimates obtained from more elaborate procedures, such as the administration of an intelligence test (Bardos, 1993; Holtzman, 1993; Naglieri, 1993). Furthermore, the scoring of figure drawings using the Goodenough-Harris system is somewhat reliable. Inter-rater reliability estimates range from .81 to .98, and test-retest reliability estimates range from .52 to .87 over a two-week period (Scott, 1981).

Not all research studies support the use of figure drawings to estimate intelligence. In fact, most of the contemporary literature on the topic would probably lead away from this controversial practice. Concerns have centered on the validity of figure drawings as estimates of intelligence. In one study examining the validity of figure drawings, Aikman et al. (1992) administered either the WISC-R or the WAIS-R (depending on the subject's age) to adolescent psychiatric inpatients. Afterward, each subject completed male and female human-figure drawings. Goodenough-Harris scores of the drawings were then correlated with the results of the intelligence test. The correlations were .48 for the male drawing and .49 for the female drawing, both statistically significant. However, calculating the coefficient of determination (by squaring the correlation coefficient) indicates that the figure-drawing score accounted for just under 25% of the variance in intelligence test scores (Aikman et al., 1992). Compare this with criterion validity coefficients based on correlations between the WISC-III and other established intelligence tests, which range from .82 to .90, explaining 67% to 81% of the variance in test scores (Wechsler, 1991). On the basis of their results, Aikman et al. (1992) concluded that, although figure-drawing scores are positively related to intelligence test scores, replacing intelligence tests with figure-drawing tests, even for screening purposes, would be inappropriate. Literature reviews of many studies like the one just described reach similar conclusions. Scott (1981) found that the average criterion validity coefficient across 96 studies was .49. Motta et al.'s (1993) review turned up validity coefficients primarily in the .40s and .50s. Like Aikman et al., these reviewers conclude that the drawings should not be used to estimate intelligence, even in a screening capacity.

Given these research findings, why are figure drawings still used to estimate intelligence? Kamphaus and Pleiss (1993) note that human-figure-drawing scores tend to have good reliability, and they suggest that some users may mistakenly interpret this as evidence of the validity of the assessment method. Another attraction of human-figure drawings as measures of intelligence is perceived efficiency (Motta et al., 1993). A psychologist may administer a human-

Figure 9–2
Goodenough-Harris Scores for Figure Drawings

Two 12½-year-old boys completed these drawings of men, which were scored by Harris (1963) for intellectual level. Drawing (a) is considered to reflect relatively high intelligence, at the 87th percentile. Drawing (b) is considered to reflect lower intelligence, at the 19th percentile. Ways in which drawing (a) is considered to reflect superior intelligence include the quality of the neck, details in the eyes, the presence of hair, correct proportions of the hands, and the relative proportion of the head and the trunk. In all, Harris identified 53 good-quality features in drawing (a) but only 31 such features in drawing (b).

figure drawing to assess personality; if the same drawing can be used to estimate intelligence, then time has been saved.

The value of a quick way to estimate intelligence is not to be disregarded, of course. Quick methods of estimating intelligence can be used to screen large numbers of people, such as all admissions to a psychiatric hospital or all kindergarten students entering a school system. People with low scores on the screening test can then be given a full-length intelligence test. This is more efficient than giving everyone the full-length intelligence test, making time for the psychologist to do other things, such as treatment and research. However, some quick estimates of intelligence have better validity coefficients than human-figure drawings typically yield. For example, one might use a "short form" of a widely accepted intelligence test, as discussed in this chapter's *Close-up*. On the Wechsler scales, scores on the vocabulary subtest correlate reasonably well (.74 on the WISC-III; Sattler, 1992) with the total test score and may function as a kind of short form. The Vocabulary subtest can be administered and scored in an amount of time comparable to that needed for figure drawings. Thus, if one is pressed for time, the Vocabulary subtest would likely provide a more valid index of intelligence than a figure drawing. However, we must emphasize that neither of these quick ways of measuring intelligence should be used for more than screening. The point here is that if one plans to use a screening test, more valid screening measures than human-figure drawings are readily available. Given these considerations, one can understand why Sattler (1992) concluded that the use of figure drawings to estimate intelligence is inadvisable.

Group Intelligence Tests

If you are like many students, reading about intelligence tests may have piqued your curiosity about what your own IQ is. And if you are like many students, if you ever have taken an intelligence test, the chances are good it was a group test, not an individual test. That is probably the case, since out of the many millions of psychological tests administered annually in a variety of settings (Brim et al., 1969; Holmen & Docter, 1972), a relatively small fraction of those tests are individually administered intelligence tests; most people who have taken an intelligence test have taken a group test of intelligence (Hopkins & Bracht, 1975).

Perhaps the most obvious advantage of group tests over individual tests is that they can be administered to large numbers of people at the same time and so are more efficient. Most group tests can be reliably machine- or computer-scored. They are also more economical than individual tests because, in most cases, only a one-page computer answer sheet is used, thus avoiding the necessity for expensive, nonreusable test booklets. Inherent in this efficiency is a lowered "turnaround time" in scoring. A larger and, in some instances, more representative sample of respondents can be tested. The test administrator need not be highly trained, thus further bringing down the cost and ease with which such a test may be administered. One advantage of limiting the role of the test administrator to reading instructions and keeping time is that the test administrator may have less effect on the examinee's score than a test administrator in a one-on-one situation. Because of the general ease of administering and scoring group tests, they often are normed on larger and more representative standardization samples than are many individual tests.

A primary use of group tests of intelligence is screening. Test results can suggest which subjects, students, or clients require more extensive assessment with individually administered tests. In the schools, group intelligence tests may also be helpful in identifying children who require extensive preparation and/or enrichment experience before beginning first grade. In research settings, group intelligence tests may be used, for example, to provide valuable information to an agency or institution (such as a school or the military) for program-planning purposes.

Short Forms: Do They Work?

What do you do when you, as an examiner, want to administer an intelligence test but don't have the time to administer the entire test? Some examiners in this position opt to administer a short form of the test. As the name implies, *short form* refers to a test that has been abbreviated in length, typically to reduce the time needed for test administration, scoring, and interpretation. Sometimes, particularly when the test-taker is believed to have an atypically short attention span or other problems making a full test administration difficult, a sampling of some representative subtests instead of the complete test may be administered. Arguments for the use of a short form of the WAIS-R can be found with reference to testtakers from the general adult population (Kaufman et al., 1991), as well as elderly testtakers (Paolo & Ryan, 1991) and testtakers from psychiatric populations (Benedict et al., 1992; Boone, 1991; Grossman et al., 1993; Randolph et al., 1993; Sweet et al., 1990).

Short forms of intelligence tests are nothing new. In fact, they have been around almost as long as the "long forms." Soon after the Binet-Simon reached the United States, a short form of it was proposed (Doll, 1917). In 1958, Wechsler himself described the use of short forms as appropriate provided they were used only for screening purposes. But years later, perhaps in response to possible abuses of short forms, Wechsler (1967) advised that "reduction in the number of [subtests] as a time-saving device is unjustifiable and not to be encouraged" (p. 37). He further advised those who might claim that they do not have enough time to administer an intelligence test in its entirety to "find the time" (p. 37). Subsequent reviews of the literature on short forms have borne out the wisdom of Wechsler's later advice. Watkins (1986) concluded that short forms may be used for screening purposes only, and that they should not be used to make placement or educational decisions. Silverstein (1990) provided an incisive review of the history of short forms, focusing on four issues: (1) how to abbreviate the original test; (2) how to select subjects; (3) how to estimate scores on the original test; and (4) the criteria to apply when comparing the short form with the original.

To understand why short forms are recommended for screening purposes only, and not to make important decisions that will dramatically affect the life of the testtaker, recall some of the concepts from Chapters 5 and 6. From a psychometric standpoint, it is important to keep in mind that the validity of a test is affected by, and is somewhat dependent on, the test's reliability. Therefore, changes in a test that lessen its reliability may also lessen the test's validity. Reducing the number of items in a test typically reduces the test's reliability and, hence, its validity as well. For that reason, major decisions should not be made on the basis of short forms of intelligence tests (Nagle & Bell, 1993; Wechsler, 1967). Instead, if short forms are used at all, they should be followed by the administration of a full-length intelligence test when the short form indicates the need for intervention or placement.

Lest we paint too rosy a picture in our overview of group tests, let us point out that these tests also carry with them distinct disadvantages. Two assumptions inherent in the use of group tests are that people taking the test understand what is expected of them and that they are motivated to perform on the test. If these assumptions are violated, the results obtained will be invalid. During an individually administered test, the examiner is able to observe the subject's "individual learning style," such as a tendency to solve problems by trial-and-error or in an impulsive rather than a reflective manner. The examiner is also able to observe confusion, anxiety, lack of interest, or other factors that would hinder the examinee's performance; during the group test, the examiner has no such opportunity and not only is the opportunity for observing extra-test behavior lost, but so might be important information bearing on the test score. Group tests are, as their name implies, designed for the masses, and they therefore place the atypical person (for example, the individual with some disability not identified before testing or the individual who "walks to the beat of a different drummer") at a greater risk of obtaining a score on the test that does not accurately approximate that individual's hypothetical "true score."

All examinees taking a group test, regardless of ability, typically start on the same item and frequently end on the last item as well. This state of affairs stands in marked contrast to the more custom-designed individually administered test situation in which all examinees need not start with or end on the same item and need not be exposed to all the items on the test. Most individually administered intelligence tests contain specific rules for beginning the test (such as "begin at the level of the examinee's chronological age provided he or she answers the first two consecutive items correctly; if not, work backward until the first two consecutive items of a level are answered correctly") and for discontinuing the test ("discontinue after four consecutive failures"). Such procedures serve to prevent boredom or a failure to take the test seriously (because of the administration of too many easy items) and feelings of discouragement resulting from a sequence of too-difficult items.

Most group intelligence tests require the testtaker to be able to read. And although the reading level required may be simpler than the cognitive demands of the item, the fact that the item does require reading may confound the value of the score achieved on the test by certain testtakers (Cassel, 1971). In a study conducted with prisoners, a group test of intelligence identified 4% of the subjects as mentally retarded, in contrast to only 1% of the subjects when an individually administered intelligence test was used (Spruill & May, 1988). This pattern of lower scores on group intelligence tests could be the result of reading problems that are common in incarcerated populations. In another study, scores on a group-administered intelligence test predicted the reading achievement of learning-disabled high school students better than scores on an individually administered intelligence test, presumably because of the greater need for reading skills when taking a group test of intelligence (Bracy-Nipper et al., 1987). By the way, the group test was also as good as the individual test in predicting success in other areas of academic achievement.

In addition to reading ability, another skill expected of the testtaker is the ability to manipulate a pencil and to mark an answer sheet—a task with which some normal first- and second-graders may have difficulty even if given prior practice sessions (Ramseyer & Cashen, 1971). Children who have difficulties with eye–hand coordination or concentration will be especially vulnerable to difficulties with a test administered in such a format.

Although the standardization samples for group intelligence tests are often large, they are rarely as representative as they may appear. Group intelligence tests designed for use in the schools, for example, tend to be standardized on school districts rather than on individuals. Although a particular district may be viewed as representative of a state, the particular individuals who make up that district and who participate in the testing are not necessarily representative of the population of individuals the test publisher would like to sample from. This is so because (1) the particular district may have volunteered to take part in the standardization process and (2) testtakers within the district may be required to obtain parental permission to participate. The latter situation will almost certainly bias the composition of the sample, since there is a tendency on the part of better-educated, higher-socioeconomic-status parents to consent to testing, as opposed to parents of lower socioeconomic status with little education. That such subtle biasing factors exist may not be noted in a description of the sample in the test's manual.

The data from group intelligence tests—like the data from any test administration—can be misused. In the schools, for example, it is not unknown for such data to be used to track students into various types of special educational programs—a misuse of the test, since such tracking should ideally be done only on the basis of a comprehensive evaluation that includes an individually administered intelligence test. Data from the administration of a group intelligence test—administered in a school, employment, military, or any other setting—may also be misused when they become the basis for unrealistic academic expectations from children.

Despite our list of limitations and caveats, it cannot be denied that group intelligence tests can be of great value when used as screening instruments. We now briefly discuss the application of such tests in various settings.

Group intelligence tests in the schools   At one time, perhaps no more than a decade or two ago, approximately two-thirds of all school districts in the United States used group intelligence tests on a routine basis to screen 90% of their students; the other 10% were administered individual intelligence tests (Macmillan & Myers, 1980). Litigation and legislation surrounding the routine use of group intelligence tests have altered this picture somewhat (see Chapter 2), though the group intelligence test, now also referred to as a "school ability test," is by no means extinct. In many states, legal mandates exist prohibiting the use of group intelligence data alone for tracking purposes. However, group intelligence test data, combined with other data, can be extremely useful in developing a profile of a child's intellectual assets.

Group intelligence test results provide school personnel with information of value for instruction-related activities and increased understanding of the individual pupil. One primary function of data from a group intelligence test is to alert educators to students who require more extensive assessment with individually administered IQ tests—and possible placement in a special class or program. Group intelligence test data can also help a school district plan educational goals for all children.

Group intelligence tests in the schools are used in special forms as early as the kindergarten level. The tests are administered to groups of 10–15 children, each of whom receives a test booklet that includes printed pictures and diagrams. For the most part, simple motor responses are required to answer items; oversized alternatives in the form of pictures in a multiple-choice test might appear on the pages, and it is the child's job to circle or to place an "X" on the picture that represents the correct answer to the item presented orally by the examiner. In some tests, machine-scorable booklets are used as early as first grade, though reading or writing is not required. During such testing in small groups, the testtakers will be carefully monitored to make certain they are following the directions.

The California Test of Mental Maturity, the Kuhlmann-Anderson Intelligence Tests, the Henmon-Nelson Tests of Mental Ability, and the Cognitive Abilities Test are some of the many group intelligence tests available for use in school settings. The first group intelligence test to be used in American schools—the one we have chosen to acquaint you with in the remainder of this section—is the Otis-Lennon School Ability Test, formerly "The Otis Mental Ability Test."

Designed for use in grades kindergarten through 13, the primary purpose of the current (sixth) edition of the Otis-Lennon School Ability Test (OLSAT) is to assess examinees' "ability to cope with school learning tasks, to suggest their possible placement for school learning functions, and to evaluate their achievement in relation to the talents they bring to school learning situations." From a pool of over 4,000 items submitted by 50 freelance item writers, new items were considered for use in the sixth edition. In 1987, approximately 354,000 students from 65 schools participated in a national tryout of new items. Stratification variables included geographic region, socioeconomic status, and average school district enrollment per grade as per 1980 census data. Both qualitative analysis in the form of editorial examination of items by experts, as well as quantitative methods were used in an effort to eliminate possible item biases. Different levels of items designated as Levels "A" through "G" (replacing confusing terms such as *primary* and *intermediate* in the prior edition of the test) are included in the sixth edition, and there are an equal number of verbal and nonverbal items at each level. In a break with a tradition of this instrument that dates as far back as 1918—that of yielding only a Total Score—the sixth edition of the OLSAT yields both Verbal and Nonverbal part scores. These scores may be expressed in the form of School Ability Indexes or SAIs, which are normalized standard scores with a mean of 100 and a standard deviation of 16. Looking at the Verbal SAI, the Performance SAI, and the Total SAI, the seasoned examiner might experience a sense of déjà vu with respect to the concept of IQ— and exactly how SAI differs from IQ is never quite made clear.

In his *Eleventh Mental Measurements Yearbook* review of the OLSAT, Swerdlik (1992) concluded that although the test was technically adequate, it could be improved if the following problems were addressed:

1. More specific details regarding the procedures used in the standardization process could be provided in the test manual.

2. The brief (one paragraph) account of the theory underlying this test is insufficient and needs to be expanded.

3. The manual requires more detail in helping the test user to make meaningful and actionable interpretations from the test data.

4. Some caveat in the test manual regarding the need for caution in interpreting and acting on group test data would seem desirable.

Group intelligence tests in the military   Group intelligence measures such as the Army Alpha (primarily verbal in nature) and the Army Beta (primarily nonverbal in nature) were first developed in response to manpower problems of the military during World War I. At that time, there was the need to select potential officer candidates and to eliminate draftees who were mentally unfit for military service.

Today, group intelligence tests, as well as more specialized group tests, are still administered to prospective recruits, not only for routine screening purposes, but also as an aid in assigning soldiers to training programs and jobs. Data from group intelligence testing have indicated that there is a downward trend in the mean intelligence level of recruits since the ending of the draft and the inception of an all-volunteer army. In response to such findings, the military has developed new weapons training programs incorporating, for example, lower-level vocabulary in programmed instruction, a strategy designed to provide a better match between the learning ability of the trainee (recruit) and the material to be learned.

Included among many group tests used by the armed forces are the Officer Qualifying Test (a 115-item multiple-choice test used by the Navy as an admissions test to Officer Candidate School), the Airman Qualifying Exam (a 200-item multiple-choice test given to all Air Force volunteers), and the Armed Services Vocational Aptitude Battery (ASVAB). The ASVAB is administered to prospective new recruits in all the armed services. Let's look at it in more detail.

The ASVAB consists of 334 multiple-choice items organized into ten different subtests. A description of the subtests and some sample items are presented in the box on pages 330–331.

A set of 100 selected items included in the subtests of arithmetic reasoning, numerical operations, word knowledge, and paragraph comprehension make up a measure within the ASVAB called the Armed Forces Qualification Test (AFQT). The AFQT is a measure of general ability used in the selection of recruits into the military. The different armed services employ different cutoff scores in making accept/reject determinations for service based on considerations such as their preset quotas for people from a particular demographic group. In addition to the AFQT score, ten aptitude areas are also tapped on the ASVAB, including general technical, general mechanics, electrical, motor-mechanics, science, combat operations, and skill-technical. These are combined to assess aptitude in five separate career areas, including clerical, electronics, mechanics, skill-technical (medical, computers), and combat operations. A form of the test is also available for administration to high school students for counseling purposes.

The Armed Services Vocational Aptitude Battery (ASVAB)

The ASVAB is used by the armed services to determine qualifications for enlistment as well as most suitable job assignment. Testtakers are advised to do their best, since ASVAB scores "will determine which job areas you are qualified to enter. The better your scores are, the more opportunities you will have available to you."

The test is administered in a group setting with a two-hour, 24-minute time limit. All the items on the ASVAB are multiple-choice with four or five possible answers. Score is based on the number right, and testtakers are encouraged to guess if they are unsure of the correct response; there is no penalty for guessing. Testtakers are further advised to "get a good night's rest before taking the test." Sample items from each of the ten subtests follow with the answer key printed at the end. To get a feel for the type of questions asked, why not sample these items yourself—even if you perchance didn't get a good night's rest last night.

I. General Science
Included here are general science questions, including questions from the areas of biology and physics.

1. An eclipse of the sun throws the shadow of the
A moon on the sun
B moon on the earth
C earth on the sun
D earth on the moon

II. Arithmetic Reasoning
The task here is to solve arithmetic problems. Testtakers are permitted to use (government-supplied) scratch paper.

2. It costs $0.50 per square yard to waterproof canvas. What will it cost to waterproof a canvas truck that is 15' × 24'?
A $ 6.67
B $ 18.00
C $ 20.00
D $180.00

III. Word Knowledge
Which of four possible definitions best defines the underlined word?

3. <u>Rudiments</u> most nearly means
A politics
B minute details
C promotion opportunities
D basic methods and procedures

IV. Paragraph Comprehension
A test of reading comprehension and reasoning.

4. Twenty-five percent of all household burglaries can be attributed to unlocked windows or doors. Crime is the result of opportunity plus desire. To prevent crime, it is each individual's responsibility to
A provide the desire
B provide the opportunity
C prevent the desire
D prevent the opportunity

V. Numerical Operations

This speeded test contains simple arithmetic problems that the testtaker must do quickly; it is one of two speeded tests on the ASVAB.

5. $6 - 5 =$
   A 1
   B 4
   C 2
   D 3

VI. Coding Speed

This subtest contains coding items that measure perceptual/motor speed among other factors.

KEY

| green . . . 2715 | man . . . 3451 | salt . . . 4586 |
| hat . . . 1413 | room . . . 2864 | tree . . . 5927 |

	A	B	C	D	E
6. room	1413	2715	2864	3451	4586

VII. Auto and Shop Information

This test assesses knowledge of automobile, shop practice, and the use of tools.

7. What tool is shown above?
   A Hole saw
   B Keyhole saw
   C Counter saw
   D Grinding saw

VIII. Mathematics Knowledge

This is a test of ability to solve problems using high-school-level mathematics. Use of scratch paper is permitted.

8. If $3X = -5$, then $X =$
   A -2
   B $-5/3$
   C $-3/5$
   D $3/5$

IX. Mechanical Comprehension

Knowledge and understanding of general mechanical and physical principles are probed by this test.

9. Liquid is being transferred from the barrel to the bucket by
   A capillary action
   B gravitational forces
   C fluid pressure in the hose
   D water pressure in the barrel

X. Electronics Information

Here, knowledge of electrical, radio, and electronics information is assessed.

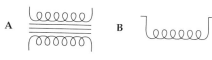

10. Which of the above is the symbol for a transformer?
    A A
    B B
    C C
    D D

Answer Key

1. B	6. C
2. C	7. A
3. D	8. B
4. D	9. B
5. Why are you looking this one up?	10. A

A large-scale study bearing on the validity of the test compared the performance of high- and low-scoring men who were all accepted into the Air Force. It was found that the lower-scoring men were less likely to complete basic training, had more unsuitable discharges, and were less likely to attain the required level of success (Grunzke et al., 1970). The ASVAB has been found to predict success in computer-programming and computer-operating roles (Besetsny et al., 1993) and grades in military technical schools across a variety of fields (Earles & Ree, 1992; Ree & Earles, 1990). A review of validity studies supports the construct, content, and criterion-related validity of the ASVAB as a device to guide training and selection decisions (Welsh et al., 1990). In general, the test has been deemed to be quite useful in making selection and placement decisions in the armed forces.

Measures of Specific Intellectual Abilities

There are certain intellectual abilities and talents that are not—or are only indirectly—assessed by the more widely used measures of intelligence. One such ability is creativity. And although it is true that most tests of intelligence do not measure creativity, the reverse of that statement cannot be stated with equal certainty. To the extent that the components of creativity include numerous variables related to general intellectual ability (such as originality in problem solving, originality in perception, originality in abstraction, ideational fluency, and inductive reasoning abilities), measures of creativity may also be thought of as tools for assessing aspects of intellectual functioning.

Measures of Creativity

A criticism frequently leveled at group standardized intelligence tests (as well as other ability and achievement tests) is that evaluation of test performance is too heavily focused on whether the answer is correct—as opposed to giving more weight to the examinee's thought process in arriving at the answer. On most achievement tests, for example, the skill that is required is called *convergent thinking;* after a consideration of the facts and after a logical series of logical judgments is made, a solution to a problem is arrived at. Convergent thinking is a deductive reasoning process that emphasizes one solution to a problem. In his structure of intellect model discussed in Chapter 8, Guilford (1967) drew a distinction between the intellectual processes of convergent and *divergent* types of thinking. Divergent thinking involves a reasoning process in which thought is permitted the freedom to move in many different directions, making several solutions possible. Divergent thinking requires flexibility of thought, originality, and imagination. There is much less emphasis on recall of facts than in convergent thinking. Guilford's model has served as a stimulus to focus research attention on not only the products of creative thought but the process as well.

A number of tests and test batteries designed to measure creativity in children and adults are available. Guilford (1954) described tasks such as Consequences ("Imagine what would happen if . . . ") and Unusual Uses (for example, "Name as many uses as you can think of for a rubber band") as ways of assessing creativity. Included in Guilford et al.'s (1974) test battery, the Structure-of-Intellect Abilities, are Consequences and Unusual Uses subtests, four Christensen-Guilford Fluency tests (Word Fluency, Ideational Fluency, Expressional Fluency, and Associational Fluency), and other verbally oriented subtests (such as Simile Interpretation) as well as relatively nonverbal subtests (such as Sketches, Making Objects, and Decorations).

Based on the work of Mednick (1962), the Remote Associates Test (RAT) presents the testtaker with three words, and the task is to find a fourth word that is associated with the other three. The Torrance (1966, 1987a, 1987c) Tests of Creative Thinking consist of word-based, as well as picture-based and sound-based, test materials. In a subtest of different sounds administered with the aid of a phonograph record, for example, the examinee's task is to respond with what thoughts each sound conjures. Each subtest is designed to measure some or all of four characteristics deemed to be important in the process of creative thought: flexibility, originality, fluency, and elaboration—and responses are scored in three or more of these four areas. Flexibility refers to the variety of ideas presented and the ability to shift from one approach to another. Fluency involves the number of ideas or total responses actually produced. Elaboration alludes to the richness of detail in a verbal explanation or pictorial display. Originality refers to the ability to produce nonobvious ideas or figures. Test-retest reliability on this battery has not been encouraging, though such findings may be similar with respect to other measures of creativity—an ability that may be highly susceptible to the effect of emotional or physical health, motivation, and related factors. And although a number of studies have explored aspects of the construct validity of this test (see, for example, Lieberman, 1965), many test reviewers (such as Wallach & Kogan, 1965) have remained skeptical, wondering aloud whether the test might more properly be thought of as one of intelligence. One large-scale factor-analytic study did not support the distinction of the fluency, flexibility, originality, and elaboration factors (Yamamoto & Frengel, 1966). A library of over 200 creativity tests exists at the University of Georgia and at the State University College at Buffalo (Haensly & Torrance, 1990).

Other Measures

A number of tests exist to measure specific intellectual abilities ranging from critical thinking (such as the Watson-Glaser Critical Thinking Appraisal) to music listening skills (such as the Seashore Measures of Musical Talents) to art judgment and aesthetic perception (see Figure 9–3).

Creativity. Critical thinking. Music listening ability. Art judgment. As you read about each of these skills and how they all might be related to that intangible construct "intelligence," you may have said to yourself, "Why doesn't anyone create a test that measures all these diverse aspects of intelligence?"

Figure 9–3
A Sample Item from the Meier Art Judgment Test

The Meier Art Tests (including the Meier Art Judgment Test and the Meier Aesthetic Percep-
tion Test) were based on the research of Norman Charles Meier in the area of aesthetic sensi-
tivity. The task in the Aesthetic Perception Test is to rank four versions of the same work of art
in order of perceived aesthetic merit. The Art Judgment Test consists of 100 pairs of paintings or
drawings reproduced in black and white, one rendering of the original altered in some way. Ex-
aminees are informed of the difference between the two pictures (to control for potential problems
in perception) and then asked which of the two versions of the artwork they like best. Here, the
difference between the two pictures has to do with the positioning of the objects on the shelf.

Although no one has undertaken that ambitious project, test packages have
been developed, in recent years, to test not only intelligence but also related
abilities in the context of an educational setting. These test packages, called
"psychoeducational batteries," are discussed in the following chapter, along
with other tests used to measure academic abilities.

10

Educational Assessment

Whated are some of the things you associate with the word *school?* If the word *test* comes to mind, you probably have lots of company. This is so because many different tests are administered in public and private schools: intelligence tests, personality tests, tests of physical and sensory abilities—all kinds of tests. Educators are interested in answers to questions as diverse as "How good is your reading ability?" and "How far can you broad-jump?" In much of this chapter, we consider tests designed to facilitate the process of education. Included here are achievement and aptitude tests, as well as diagnostic tests. We begin, however, with a look at education-related tests that may be administered long before a child sets foot in a classroom.

Preschool Assessment

The first five years of life—the span of time referred to by the term *preschool period*—is a time of profound change. Basic reflexes develop, affording many proud moments for the parents as the child passes through a number of sensory-motor milestones—crawling, sitting, standing, walking, running, grasping an object, and so forth. Usually between 18 and 24 months, the child becomes capable of symbolic thought and develops language skills. By age 2, the average child has a vocabulary of over two hundred words. Of course, all such observations about the development of children are of more than mere academic interest to professionals legally charged with the responsibility of assessment.

In the mid-1970s, Congress enacted Public Law (PL) 94-142, which mandated that children age 3 and up suspected of having physical or mental disabilities be evaluated professionally to determine what their special educational needs might be. The law also provided federal funds to help the states meet those educational needs. In 1986, a set of amendments to PL 94-142, known as

PL 99-457, extended downward to birth the obligation of states toward disabled children. It further mandated that beginning with the school year 1990–1991, all disabled children from ages 3 to 5 be provided with a free, appropriate education.

At the earliest levels, "intelligence" is gauged by infant intelligence scales that, in essence, note the presence or absence of various developmental achievements through means such as observation and parental (or caretaker) interviews. By age 2, the child enters into a challenging period for psychological assessors. Language and conceptual skills are beginning to emerge, yet the kinds of verbal and performance tests traditionally used with older children and adults are inappropriate. The attention span of the preschooler is short. Ideally, test materials are colorful, engaging, and attention-maintaining. Approximately one hour is a good rule-of-thumb limit for an entire test session with a preschooler, and less time is preferable; as testing time increases, so does the possibility of fatigue and distraction—with a resultant underestimation of the examinee's ability. Motivation of the young child may vary from one test session to the next, and this is something that the examiner must be aware of. Most welcomed by examiners who regularly work with preschoolers are tests that are relatively easy to administer, have simple start/discontinue rules, and allow the examiner ample opportunity to make behavioral observations of the examinee. Dual-easel test administration format (see Figure 10–1), sample and teaching items for each subtest, and dichotomous scoring (for example, right/wrong) all serve to facilitate test administration.

Data from infant intelligence tests, especially when combined with other information (such as birth history, emotional and social history, health history, data on the quality of the physical and emotional environment, and measures of adaptive behavior) have proved useful to health professionals when suspicions about developmental disability and related deficits have been raised. The tests have also proved useful in helping to define the abilities, as well as the extent of disability, in older, psychotic children. Furthermore, the tests have been in use for a number of years by many adoption agencies that will disclose and interpret such information to prospective adoptive parents. Infant tests also have wide application in the area of research and can play a part in selecting infants for specialized early educational experiences or measuring the outcome of educational, therapeutic, or prenatal care interventions.

What is the meaning of a score on an infant intelligence test? Whereas some of the developers of infant tests (such as Cattell, 1940; Gesell et al. 1940) claimed that such tests were predictive of future intellectual ability because they measured the developmental precursors to such ability, others have insisted that performance on such tests is at best reflective of the infant's physical and neuropsychological intactness. It would seem that a middle ground between these extreme positions is best supported by the research literature. In general, the tests have not been found to be predictive of performance on child or adult intelligence tests—tests that tap vastly different types of abilities and thought processes (Bayley, 1955, 1959, 1993; Bradway, 1945; Honzik et al., 1948; Welcher et al., 1971). The predictive efficacy of the tests does tend to increase with the extremes of the infant's performance; the test interpreter can say with authority

Figure 10–1
A "Dual-Easel" Format in Test Administration

An "easel format" in the context of test administration refers to test materials, usually some sort of book that contains test-stimulus materials and that can be folded and placed on a desk; pages are turned by the examiner to reveal to the examinee, for example, objects to identify or designs to copy. When corresponding test-administration instructions or notes are printed on the reverse side of the test-stimulus pages for the examiner's convenience during test administration, the format is sometimes referred to as "dual easel."

more about the future performance of an infant whose performance was either profoundly below age expectancy or significantly precocious (Sattler, 1982). Still, infancy is a developmental period of many spurts and lags, and infants who are slow or precocious at this age might catch up or fall back in later years.

Many tests used with preschool children are referred to as screening tests. To better appreciate the concept of a *screening test* in the context of preschool testing, it may be useful to begin by thinking of a somewhat analogous but more familiar type of screening test, a blood test. Human blood is composed of many substances, and after many analyses of what an average blood sample should contain, various levels of these substances have come to be regarded as "within normal limits," or "wnl." Levels of these substances above or below the "wnl" mark, or the presence of some foreign substance, signal the need for further medical testing. In like fashion, psychological testing with a sample of young-sters serves to establish a kind of "wnl" mark for performance on a test. Perfor-mance that falls on the low side of the "wnl" range signals the need for further psychological evaluation.

Many screening tests are designed to identify children who are "at risk." *At risk* has been defined in many ways; for example, it may describe a child who is in danger of not being ready for first grade (Martin, 1981), or it may describe a level of functioning that is not within normal limits (Paget, 1985). States—even individual school districts—have developed their own definitions of the term. From its origins as an alternative to a diagnostic classification that might have detrimental effects on young children (Smith & Knudtson, 1990), the term itself is at high risk for being misinterpreted when it is used.

Some preschool children do very poorly in some or all of the many areas in which they are assessed, including sensory functioning, motor functioning, cognitive skills, communication skills, and behavior (see National Joint Com-mittee on Learning Disabilities, 1985, for an elaboration on these areas of as-sessment). When a child's poor performance in any or all of these areas is significant—say, for the purpose of this example, 1 standard deviation or more below the mean—"at risk" becomes a euphemism in describing a child with a documented problem, developmental lag, or disability that requires remedia-tion. In contrast, many school districts prefer, more appropriately, to apply this term to children who have difficulties but who nonetheless might "fall through the cracks" were it not for routine screening and individualized follow-up as-sessment. In essence, these are children who are at risk for not being identified as having a problem and who therefore would not receive the tailored educa-tional interventions that could make their school years fulfilling.

Preschool Tests

Some tests used for preschool assessment purposes are listed and compared in Table 10–1. In general, the predictive validity of ability tests designed for use with infants and preschoolers within the range of normal functioning tends to be weak. This is partly because many factors aside from the child's cognitive capacity affect later cognitive development. Characteristics of the family envi-ronment and of the parents themselves, differences in temperament that influ-ence how the child approaches opportunities to learn, and the child's health may all play critical roles in future development. Therefore, testing a sampling of a child's abilities at a young age will invariably fail to yield sufficient infor-mation about future performance. Perhaps the great value of preschool tests lies in their ability to help in the identification of children who are in a very low range of functioning and in need of intervention.

A potential area for future research in preschool and infant assessment has emerged from work done by Thompson and Fagan (1991). These researchers reported that infants who prefer novel stimuli tend to demonstrate higher levels of intelligence as young children. On the basis of such research, we may see novelty preference subtests incorporated into new and revised infant tests.

Table 10–1
A Sampling of Tests Used in Preschool Assessment

	BSID-II	BDI	ESP	DIAL-R	IMS	MAP
Administration time	25–60 min.	60–90 min.	15–30 min.	20–30 min.	10–45 min.	20–30 min.
Age range (in years-months)	0–1 to 3–6	0–0 to 8–0	2–0 to 6–11	2–0 to 5–11	0–0 to 3–0	2–9 to 5–8
General area assessed	Current developmental functioning	Developmental strengths and weaknesses	Developmental functioning	Early development	Cognitive and learning skills	Detection of developmental problems
Subtests	Mental Motor Behavioral	Cognitive Communication Motor Personal/social Adaptive	Cognitive/language Motor Self-help/social	Concepts Language Motor	Receptive language Expressive language Gross motor base Receptive visual Expressive visual	Complex tasks Verbal Coordination Nonverbal Foundations
Standardization date(s)	1993	1982–1983	After 1990	1983	1980s	1981
Reliability estimates	.64 to .93	.70 to 1.0	.70 to .90	.70 to .90	.70 to .97	.79 to .98
Validity estimates	Not yet available	.64 to .94	.58	.21 to .55	.78 to .98	.17 to .38

Test Name with Authors (in parentheses) and Information Sources
BSID-II: Bayley Scales for Infant Development, Second Edition (Bayley); Bayley, 1993
BDI: Battelle Developmental Inventory (Newborg et al., 1984); Johnson et al. (1992); Snyder et al. (1993)
ESP: Early Screening Profile (Harrison); Smith, Lasee, & McCloskey (1990); Lasee & Smith (1990)
DIAL-R: Developmental Indicators for the Assessment of Learning, Revised (Mardell-Czudnowski & Goldenberg); Cooper & Shepard (1992)
IMS: Infant Mullen Scales of Early Learning (Mullen); Hart (1992)
MAP: Miller Assessment for Preschoolers (Miller); DeLoria (1985); Schouten & Kirkpatrick (1993)

Achievement Tests

Achievement tests are designed to measure accomplishment. An achievement test for a first-grader might have as its subject matter the English language alphabet, whereas an achievement test for someone such as yourself might contain questions relating to principles of psychological assessment. In short, achievement tests are designed to measure the degree of learning that has taken place as a result of exposure to a relatively defined learning experience. The "relatively defined learning experience" may be something as broad as a sampling of "what you learned from four years of college" or something as narrow as "administering first aid for snake bites." A test of achievement may be standardized nationally, regionally, or locally, or it may not be standardized at all; the "pop quiz" on the anatomy of a frog given by your high school biology teacher qualifies every bit as much for the title "achievement test" as does the statewide biology examination you may have been given at the completion of the school year. Like other tests, achievement tests vary widely with respect to their psychometric soundness. A sound achievement test is one that adequately samples the targeted subject matter and reliably gauges the extent to which all the examinees learned it.

Achievement tests assist school personnel in making decisions concerning a student's advancement to higher levels and the grouping of students for instructional purposes. Achievement tests are sometimes used to screen for difficulties, and in such instances they may precede the administration of diagnostic tests employed to identify areas where remediation will be necessary. Achievement test data can be used to gauge the quality of instruction in regard to one particular teacher, an entire school district, or a state, though such a use of test data presumes that students' abilities and related factors are relatively constant across situations—a tenuous assumption in some situations.

Measures of General Achievement

Measures of general achievement may survey learning in one or more academic areas. Tests that cover a number of academic areas are typically divided into several subtests and are referred to as *achievement batteries.* Such batteries may be individually administered (such as the Peabody Individual Achievement Test) or group-administered (such as the Metropolitan Achievement Test). They may consist of a few subtests, as does the Wide Range Achievement Test—Revised (Jastak & Jastak, 1984) with its measures of reading, spelling, and arithmetic, or be as comprehensive as the STEP Series that includes subtests in reading, vocabulary, mathematics, writing skills, study skills, science, and social studies, a behavior inventory, an educational environment questionnaire, and an activities inventory. Some batteries, such as the SRA California Achievement Tests, span kindergarten through grade 12, whereas others are grade- or course-specific. Some batteries are constructed to provide both norm-referenced and criterion-referenced analyses. Others are concurrently normed with scholastic aptitude tests to enable a comparison between achievement and aptitude. Some batteries are constructed with practice tests that may be administered several days before actual testing. Such practice tests serve to help students familiarize themselves with testtaking procedures. Other batteries contain "locator" or "routing" tests: pretests administered for purposes of determining the level of the actual test most appropriate for administration.

Of the many available achievement batteries (see Table 10–2), the test that is most appropriate for use is the one most consistent with the educational objectives of the individual teacher or school system. It may be that for a particular purpose, a battery that focuses on achievement in a few select areas is preferable to one that attempts to sample achievement in several areas. On the other hand, a test that samples many areas may be advantageous when an individual comparison of performance across subject areas is desirable. If a school or a local school district undertakes to follow the progress of a group of students as measured by a particular achievement battery, the battery of choice will be one that spans the targeted subject areas in all the grades to be tested. If ability to distinguish individual areas of difficulty is of primary concern, achievement tests with strong diagnostic features will be chosen. Although achievement batteries sampling a wide range of areas, across grades, and standardized on large, national samples of students have much to recommend them, they also have certain drawbacks. For example, such tests usually take years to develop; in the interim the items, especially in fields such as social studies and science, may become outdated. Further, any nationally standardized instrument is only as good as the extent to which it meets the (local) test user's objectives.

Measures of Achievement in Specific Subject Areas

Whereas achievement batteries tend to be standardized instruments, most measures of achievement in specific subject areas are teacher-made tests; every time a teacher gives a quiz, a test, or a final examination in a course, a test in a specific subject area has been created. Still, there are a number of standardized instruments designed to gauge achievement in specific areas.

At the elementary school level, the acquisition of basic skills such as reading, writing, and arithmetic is emphasized. From Table 10–3 (see page 344), you can see that the consumer of reading achievement tests has a great deal of choice with respect to variables such as individual or group administration, silent or oral reading, and type of subtest data provided. In general, the tests present the examinee with words, sentences, or paragraphs to be read silently or aloud, and reading ability is assessed by variables such as comprehension and vocabulary. When the material is read aloud, accuracy and speed will be measured. Tests of reading comprehension also vary with respect to the intellectual demands placed on the examinee over and above mere comprehension of the words read. Thus, some tests might require the examinee to simply recall facts from a passage, whereas others might require interpretation and the formation of inferences.

At the secondary school level, one popular battery is the Cooperative Achievement Test. It consists of a series of separate achievement tests in areas as diverse as English, mathematics, literature, social studies, science, and

Table 10–2
Some Achievement Test Batteries

Test	Subtests	Grade Level	Forms	Normative Data
California Achievement Test	Prereading Reading Spelling Language Mathematics Use of References	K–12 10 overlapping levels	2	Yes
Iowa Tests of Basic Skills	Vocabulary Reading Language Work Study Mathematics	K–9* 10 levels	2	Yes
Metropolitan Achievement Test	Reading Comprehension Mathematics Language Social Studies Science	K–12 8 levels	1 (for pre-primer) 2 at remaining levels	Yes
Peabody Individual Achievement Test—Revised	Mathematics Reading Recognition Reading Comprehension Spelling Written Expression General Information	K–12	1	Yes
SRA Achievement Series	Reading Mathematics Language Arts	K–12 8 levels	2	Yes
Stanford Achievement Test**	Vocabulary Spelling Reading Comprehension Word Study and Skills Language Arts Mathematics Science Social Studies Listening Comprehension	1.5–9.5 6 levels	3	Yes
Wide Range Achievement Test—Revised	Reading Spelling Arithmetic	K–adult 2 levels (1) for those under 12 (2) for those over 12	1	Yes

*The Tests of Achievement and Proficiency (TAP) expand the Iowa through high school levels. Additional subtests included in TAP are Use of Information Sources, Science, and Social Studies.
**The Stanford Early School Achievement Test (SESAT) and the Stanford Test of Academic Skills (TASK) extend the Stanford Series from kindergarten through grade 13.

Criterion-Referenced Data	Concurrent Norming***	Locator Test****	Practice Test	Diagnostic Information	Group/Individual
Yes	ShortForm Test of Academic Aptitude	Yes	No	No	Group
Yes	Cognitive Abilities Test	No	No	No	Group
Yes	Otis-Lennon School Ability Test	No	Yes	Reading Mathematics Language	Group
No	No	No	No	No	Individual
Yes	Educational Ability Series	No	No	No	Group
Yes	Otis-Lennon Mental Ability Test	No	Yes	No	Group
No	No	No	No	No	Individual

***Refers to the fact that the two tests were standardized using the same sample of people.
****A locator test, also known as a routing test, is a test given early on, the results of which guide the order of tests subsequently administered.

Table 10–3
Some Reading Achievement Tests

Test	Group/Individual	Grade	Scores	Forms	Time Required	Description of Subtests
Gray Oral Reading Test	Ind.	1–12	Grade equivalents by sex	4	3–10 min. (untimed)	13 reading passages of varying difficulty: Accuracy, Speed, Comprehension, Error Analysis
Gilmore Oral Reading Test	Ind.	1–8	Stanines, percentiles, grade equivalents	2	15–20 min. (untimed)	10 reading passages: Accuracy, Speed, Comprehension, Error Analysis
Durrel Listening Reading Series	Group	1–9 (3 levels)	Grade and age equivalents, stanines, percentiles, and a score reflecting difference between Listening and Reading achievement	2	140–170 min.	Combination oral/silent reading test. Reading Test assesses Vocabulary Knowledge and Comprehension. Listening Test assesses comprehension of the spoken word.
Iowa Silent Reading Test	Group	Level 1 (6–9) Level 2 (9–14) Level 3 (accelerated high school & college)	Stanines, standard scores, percentiles, Reading Efficiency Index (relating speed with accuracy)	1	60–90 min.	Vocabulary Comprehension Speed Skimming material Use of reference material
Gates-MacGinitie Reading Test	Group	K–12 (7 levels)	Raw scores for 1.0 and 1.9 Other levels: percentiles, stanines, grade equivalent, extended scale scores	2 3 at grades 4–9	55 min.	Vocabulary Comprehension
Nelson Reading Skills Test	Group	3–9 (3 levels)	Stanines, percentile rank, percentile rank band, grade equivalent, normal curve equivalent	2	33 min.	Word Meaning Reading Comprehension Speed Test (optional) Word Parts (optional)

foreign language. Each test was standardized on different populations appropriate to the grade level, and in general the tests tend to be technically sound instruments. For example, the American History component of the Social Studies series was standardized on seventh- and eighth-graders who represented 44 junior and 73 senior high schools. The sample was randomly selected and stratified according to public, parochial, and private schools. Alternate-form reliability for the test was found to be .87 for the junior high school sample and .79 for the senior high school sample. Kuder-Richardson reliability estimates of internal consistency at the junior high school level resulted in reliability coefficients of .88 and .90 for Forms A and B, respectively, and .90 for both forms at the high school level. Assessment of achievement in high school students may involve evaluation of minimum competencies, often as a requirement for a high-school diploma (see *Close-up*, pages 346–347).

At the college level, recent years have witnessed growing interest on the part of state legislatures to mandate end-of-major outcomes assessment in state colleges and universities; apparently, taxpayers are increasingly desirous of some concrete affirmation that their education tax dollars are being well spent. Thus, for example, undergraduate psychology students attending a state-run institution could be required in their senior year to sit for a final—in the literal sense—examination encompassing a range of subject matter that could be described as "everything that an undergraduate psychology major should know." And if that sounds formidable to you, trust us when we advise you that the task of developing such examinations will be all the more formidable.

Another use for achievement tests at the college as well as the adult level is for the purpose of placement. The Advanced Placement Program developed by the College Entrance Examination Board offers high school students the opportunity to achieve college credit for work completed while in high school. Successful completion of the advanced placement test may result in advanced standing and/or advanced course credit, depending on the college policy. Since its inception, the advanced placement program has resulted in advanced credit or standing for over one hundred thousand high school students in approximately two thousand colleges. Another type of test that has application for placement purposes, particularly in areas of the country where English may be spoken as a second language by a relatively large segment of the population (such as parts of California, Florida, and Texas) is a test of English proficiency. A listing of some of the instruments currently available to assess English proficiency appears in Table 10–4 (see pages 348–349). One way in which data from an English proficiency test are currently used is in the placement of applicants to college programs in an appropriate level of an English-as-a-second-language program. However, other uses of data from measures of English proficiency can be foreseen. In an era in which there appear to be growing numbers of native as well as immigrant Americans with limited English proficiency, and in a social climate that has legislators writing bills proclaiming English to be the official language of the state, one can foresee the increasing importance of issues related to the testing of English proficiency.

Tests of Minimum Competency

Soon after the founding of the United States as an independent nation, one citizen commented in a book
entitled *Letters from an American Farmer* that a
"pleasing uniformity of decent competence appears
throughout our habitations" (Crevecoeur, 1782, cited
in Lerner, 1981). Over two hundred years later, widespread dissatisfaction with the *lack* of competence in
this country has become evident. At about the time of
the nation's bicentennial celebration, a grassroots
movement aimed at eradicating illiteracy and anumer-
acy began taking shape. By 1980, 38 states had legis-
lated regulations requiring that the schools administer
a test to determine whether its secondary school
graduates had developed "minimum competence."
Exactly what constituted minimum competence would
vary from one jurisdiction to the next, but it generally
referred to some basic knowledge of reading, writing,
and arithmetic. The movement has gained momentum
with the realization that the illiterate and anumerate often wind up not only unemployed but unemployable
as well. The unfortunate consequence is that too
many of these individuals require public assistance or,
alternatively, turn to crime—some finding their way
to jail.

A minimum competency testing program is designed to ensure that the student given the high
school diploma has at least acquired the minimal
skills to become a productive member of society. Representative of such minimal skills necessary in everyday living are the ability to fill out an employment
application and the ability to write checks, balance
a checkbook, and interpret a bank statement.

As an example of one test for minimal competency, we focus attention on the Alabama High School
Graduation Exam (AHSGE). A publication of the Alabama State Department of Education (Teague, 1983)
sets forth very detailed specifications for items to be
used in the AHSGE. The skills that are tested are
based on ninth-grade minimal competencies in the
areas of Reading, Language, and Mathematics. Some
of the skills listed in the area of Language are:

- *Observe pronoun-antecedent agreement*
  Items for this competency require the student to choose
  the pronoun that agrees with its antecedent.

- *Use correct forms of nouns and verbs*
  Items for this competency require the student to choose
  the correct form of the nouns (singular and/or plural) and
  of verbs (regular and/or irregular) and to select verbs
  that agree with the subjects.

- *Include in a message or request all necessary information (who, what, when, where, how, or why)*
  Items for this competency require the student to demonstrate knowledge about what information is necessary in
  a message or request.

- *Determine what information is missing from a message,
  an announcement, or a process explanation; or what information is irrelevant*

- *Identify the comma to separate works in a series*

- *Identify question marks, periods, and exclamation points
  to punctuate sentences*

- *Identify words frequently used in daily activities*
  Items for this competency require the student to recognize frequently used words that are spelled incorrectly.

- *Complete a common form, such as a driver's license application or change of address form*

- *Identify the proper format of a friendly letter*

- *Identify the proper format of a business letter*
  Items for this competency require the student to demonstrate knowledge of the proper format of a business letter, which includes punctuation and capitalization. Test
  questions refer to business letters reproduced in the test
  booklet. An example appears at the end of this *Close-up.*

Although the idea of "minimum competency" may on
the face of it seem like a good idea, it has not gone
unchallenged in the courts. Who should determine the
skills necessary for "minimum competence" and the
lack of "minimum competence"? What should the
consequence be if an individual is not found to be
"minimally competent"? Will a minimum competence

requirement for a high school diploma act to motivate the academically unmotivated? In 1979, a federal judge in Florida held the scheduled application of that state's minimum competency law to be unconstitutional. Condemning the judge's decision, Lerner (1981) wrote that "disputes over empirical questions cannot be resolved by judicial fiat," and she went on to document that (1) substantial numbers of Americans are failing to master basic skills, such as reading, (2) the consequences of such deficits warrant action, and (3) the actions recommended by minimum competence advocates offer reasonable hope of bringing about the desired change (see also Lerner, 1980). Critics of such programs (such as Airasian et al., 1979; Haney & Madaus, 1978; Tyler, 1978) object primarily on grounds pertaining to the potential for abuse inherent in such programs, though some criticisms regarding the psychometric soundness of the instruments have also been voiced.

---

120 Drewry Road
Monroeville Alabama 36460

Miss Ann Andrews, Director
Parks and Recreation
Monroeville, Alabama 36460

Dear Miss Andrews:

Our class would like to use the Community House for our senior prom. The tentative date for the prom is April 30, 1982. Please let me know if the ballroom is available on this date and the charges for the use of this facility.

yours truly,

Jan Austin

1. What part of the letter is the salutation?

   a. Jan Austin
   *b. Dear Miss Andrews:
   c. yours truly,
   d. Miss Ann Andrews

2. Which part of the letter has an error in punctuation?

   a. The salutation
   b. The closing
   c. The signature
   *d. The heading

3. Which part of the letter has an error in capitalization?

   *a. The closing
   b. The body
   c. The inside address
   d. The heading

4. Which part of this business letter has been omitted?

   *a. The date of the letter
   b. The salutation
   c. The closing
   d. The inside address

Sample Items Designed to Evaluate the Testtaker's Knowledge of the Format for a Business Letter

Table 10–4
Tests of English Proficiency

A brief description of some of the instruments available for measuring proficiency in the English language follows. Critical reviews as well as articles dealing with these or other English-language proficiency tests may be found in specialized publications such as Foreign Language Annals; Journal of Reading; Language Learning; Language, Speech, and Hearing Services in the Schools; Language Testing; Modern Language Journal; NABE Journal; TESOL Quarterly; *and* TESOL Canada Journal *or other compendiums of reviews (such as Alderson et al., 1987, or Mitchell, 1985).*

Test	Description
Basic English Skills Test (BEST) The Psychological Corporation San Antonio, Texas	Although this test of basic language skills was initially intended for use with Southeast Asian refugees in adult education programs, it can be used with any adult with limited proficiency in English. The test contains an individually administered section of items (that employs oral as well as pictorial stimuli that demand oral or written responses) and a section that may be individually or group administered (requiring only writing or marking responses). The test is designed to be useful as a diagnostic as well as a vocational counseling tool.
Basic Inventory of Natural Language (BINL) CHECpoint Systems, Inc. San Bernardino, California	The BINL (usually pronounced like "vinyl" with a *b*) is a test designed for use with children in grades K through 12. Pictures are used to elicit the examinee's natural speech, and the verbal productions are then analyzed with respect to variables such as fluency and syntactic complexity. The test is available in 32 languages, including Chinese, Japanese, Portuguese, and Vietnamese.
Bilingual Vocational Oral Proficiency Test (BVOPT) Resource Development Institute, Inc. Austin, Texas	According to its manual, this test was designed in part to "screen people for enrollment in a bilingual vocational training program" and to "determine the gain in English proficiency achieved during the training period." The test must be administered in the examinee's native tongue (either by an examiner proficient in the language or by a prerecorded tape), and it contains subtests tapping the ability to (1) respond appropriately in an interview, (2) repeat sentences, (3) respond correctly when orally instructed to manipulate an object. The test comes in two forms, one typically administered as a pretest and the other administered after training.
Comprehensive English Language (CELT) McGraw-Hill Book Company New York, New York	The CELT (pronounced like "felt" with a *k*) was designed for use with high school, college, and adult education students for whom English is either a second language or a foreign language. The 1986 revision of this test comes in two forms which may be used as a pre- and postinstruction outcome measure. The three subtests of the CELT are Listening (administered by a prerecorded tape), Structure (in which it is the examinee's task to supply a missing word by choosing from four alternatives), and Vocabulary (containing two parts: one in which a missing word in a sentence must be supplied from four alternatives, and another where the task is to select from four alternatives of the word that is being defined).
Diagnostic Assessment of Basic Skills—Spanish Curriculum Associates North Billerica, Massachusetts	Written by A. H. Brigance and typically referred to as "the Brigance," this test is designed to assess English- and Spanish-language proficiency among other skills (such as math and reading skills). Testing in ten areas (Readiness, Speech, Functional Word Recognition, Oral Reading, Reading Comprehension, Word Analysis, Listening, Writing and Alphabetizing, Numbers and Computation, and Measurement) in levels from prekindergarten through sixth grade is designed to yield diagnostic information, including an assessment of language dominance. Directions to the student are administered mostly in Spanish, though some, for the language dominance assessment, are administered in English. See Swerdlik (1985) for a review of the English-language version of this test.
Dos Amigos Verbal Language Scales Academic Therapy Publications Novato, California	This test is designed to provide a measure of English- or Spanish-language dominance as well as information as to the comparative development of the testtaker's English- or Spanish-language proficiency. Appropriate for use in kindergarten through sixth grade, this individually administered test consists of lists of English and Spanish words that are read to the examinee. The child's task is to supply the antonym to the stimulus word. After five consecutive failures in one language, the test continues with words being read in the alternate language. The test was standardized on 1,224 Mexican American children in Texas whose first language was Spanish.

Test	Description
Ilyin Oral Interview (IOI) Newbury House/HarperCollins Scranton, Pennsylvania	Pictures depicting everyday activities provide the stimuli for this individually administered oral interview. Examinees are instructed to respond with whole sentences and these responses are scored with respect to variables such as appropriateness, intelligibility, and grammatical accuracy. Information on the relationship between IOI test scores and course levels in the San Francisco Community College District is contained in the test manual, though its author cautions that this information "should be used only as tentative until test users can see their own norms and guidelines for their particular programs" (Ilyin, 1976, p. M2).
Michigan Test of English Language Proficiency The University of Michigan Ann Arbor, Michigan	Usually referred to simply as "the Michigan," this test is designed for use as a part of a battery to determine if the examinee, typically a foreign-born applicant to an American university, is proficient enough in the English language to undertake university-level coursework. First published in 1968, this multiple-choice test contains vocabulary, structure, and reading comprehension items that may be administered to groups or individuals.
Secondary Level English Proficiency Test (SLEP) Educational Testing Service Princeton, New Jersey	The SLEP (usually pronounced like "slept" without the *t*) is a group-administered test appropriate for use in grades 7 through 12. The test is designed to be helpful in making various kinds of language-related placement decisions, such as whether a bilingual education program is indicated. The test contains a Listening Comprehension and a Reading Comprehension section, with each of these sections containing four subtests. A criterion-related validity study conducted by the test publisher with 1,239 students in 20 states indicated that statistically significant correlations existed between SLEP test scores, number of years of English study, and number of years the examinee has lived in the United States.
Test of English as a Foreign Language (TOEFL) Jointly sponsored by: The College Board, New York, New York The Graduate Record Examinations Board, Princeton, New Jersey Educational Testing Service, Princeton, New Jersey	Referred to as the TOEFL (pronounced like "toe" and "full" combined), this test is the most widely used instrument for determining if a nonnative English speaker has proficiency in English sufficient to do university-level coursework. The TOEFL is a secure test that is administered only at authorized test centers—approximately a thousand such centers exist in 135 countries. Administered to groups or individuals, the TOEFL consists of multiple-choice items grouped into three separately timed sections: Listening Comprehension (administered by audiotape), Structure and Written Expression (including items that tap knowledge of grammar), and Reading Comprehension and Vocabulary. A new equated form of the test is published monthly, as are statistical reports for each test form. Included among the many supplementary materials made available by the test publisher are publications and a videotape for use in training personnel involved in test administration and bulletins covering various aspects of test administration, scoring, and interpretation.

Achievement tests at the college or adult level may also be of the variety that assess whether college credit should be awarded for learning acquired outside a college classroom. Numerous programs exist that are designed to systematically assess whether sufficient knowledge has been acquired to qualify for course credit. The College Level Examination Program (CLEP) is based on the premise that knowledge may be obtained through independent study and sources other than formal schooling. The program includes exams in subjects ranging from African American History to Tests and Measurement. Participants in programs such as CLEP tend to think very favorably of them (Losak, 1978). The Proficiency Examination Program (PEP) offered by the American College Testing Program is another service designed to assess achievement and skills learned outside the classroom.

The special needs of adults with a wide variety of educational backgrounds are addressed in tests such as the Adult Basic Learning Examination (ABLE), a test intended for use with examinees age 17 and older who did not complete eight years of formalized schooling. The test is designed to assess achievement in the areas of vocabulary, reading, spelling, and arithmetic; it was developed in consultation with experts in the field of adult education.

Achievement tests in nationwide use may test for information or concepts that are not taught within a specific school's curriculum. Some children will do well on such items, anyway, having been exposed to the concepts or information independently. Performance on a school achievement test is therefore not entirely dependent on school achievement. Rather, factors external to the classroom may affect performance. Concern about such issues has led to an interest in "curriculum-based assessment" (CBA), assessment that clearly and faithfully reflects what is being taught in school. CBA tends to be viewed favorably but probably is not used consistently (Shapiro & Eckert, 1993). Additionally, CBA has been criticized for focusing too much on curriculum and not enough on the child's perspective concerning the curriculum (Fredrickson, 1993).

Before leaving the topic of achievement tests, we will briefly point out that there are at least two distinctly different types of achievement test items. One type demands only rote memory. An example of such an item on an examination designed to measure mastery of the material in this chapter might look like this:

1. One type of item that could be used in an achievement test is an item that requires
    a. remote memory
    b. rote memory
    c. memory loss
    d. none of the above

Alternatively, items in achievement tests could require the testtaker not only to know and understand the material but also to be able to apply it. In a test of English proficiency, for example, it might be important for the examinee to know more than vocabulary or rules of grammar; items that gauge the ability of the examinee to understand or speak conversational English might be of far greater importance. (See the box opposite.)

The World (of Test Items) According to Students

Would you study longer for a test composed of fill-in-the-blank items than you would for a test of true-false items? According to Thomas Rocklin, the answer is yes. In a study designed to examine the different ways students perceive different types of items, Rocklin (1987) asked college student subjects ($n = 31$) to make judgments concerning the dissimilarity between each possible pair created from eight item types (true-false, multiple-choice, essay, fill-in-the-blank, matching, short-answer, analogy, and arrangement). Suggestive evidence was found to support the idea that college students discriminate among test items on three dimensions; included here is the degree to which items are perceived as (1) difficult, (2) objective (presumably with respect to scoring), and (3) drawing on reasoning or analytic skills. An interesting finding was that objectivity was negatively correlated with fairness—presumably, Rocklin hypothesizes, "because objective tests either 'don't let you demonstrate what you know' or because they can be 'tricky'" (p. 7). Rocklin writes that "students make important decisions about their study strategies based on expectations about testing" (p. 2) and that "students report that they spend considerably more time reviewing for supply items than for selection items" (p. 8).

Tests of Aptitude

True or false: "Achievement tests measure learned knowledge, whereas aptitude tests measure innate potential." The correct answer to this question is "False." To understand why this is so, consider for a moment how we acquire knowledge. Each of us is born with a mental and a physical apparatus that does have certain limitations—not everyone is born with the same mental and physical gifts as everyone else. Working with the biological equipment we have in conjunction with psychological factors (such as motivation) and environmental factors (such as educational opportunities), we are constantly acquiring information through everyday life experiences and through formal learning experiences such as coursework in school. The primary difference between tests that are referred to as "achievement tests" and those that are referred to as "aptitude tests" is that aptitude tests tend to focus more on informal learning or life experiences as their subject matter, whereas achievement tests tend to focus on the learning that has occurred as a result of relatively structured input. Keeping this distinction in mind, consider the following two items, the first from a hypothetical achievement test and the second from a hypothetical aptitude test.

1. A correlation of .7 between variables X and Y in a predictive validity study accounts for what percentage of the variance?
   a. 7%
   b. 70%
   c. .7%
   d. 49%
   e. 25%

2. o is to O as x is to
   a. /
   b. %
   c. X
   d. Y

At least on the face of it, item 1 appears to be more dependent on formal learning experiences than does item 2. The successful completion of item 1 hinges on familiarity with the concept of correlation and the knowledge that the variance accounted for by a correlation coefficient is equal to the square of the coefficient (in this case, $.7^2$, or .49—choice "d"). The successful completion of item 2 requires experience with the concept of size, as well as the ability to grasp the concept of analogies, two abilities that tend to be gleaned from life experiences (witness how quickly you determined that the correct answer was choice "c"). It must also be kept in mind that the label "achievement" or "aptitude" for a test is very much dependent on the intended use of the test, not just on the type of items contained in it. It is possible for two tests to contain some of the same items and for one of the tests to be called an "aptitude" test, whereas the other is referred to as an "achievement" test. Item 2 in our example was presented as representing an item that might appear on some aptitude test, though it might well appear on an achievement test if the area of learning covered by the latter test encompassed the concept of size and/or analogous thinking. Similarly, item 1, presented as an illustrative achievement test item, might well be used to assess aptitude (in statistics, or psychology, for example) were it to be included in a test that was not expressly designed to measure achievement in this area.

Aptitude tests, also referred to as "prognostic tests," are tests typically used to make predictions. Some aptitude tests have been used to measure readiness for school, aptitude for college-level work or graduate school, and aptitude for work in a particular profession (such as medicine, law, art, or music). Achievement tests may also be used for predictive purposes. Thus, for example, an individual who performs well on a first-semester foreign-language achievement test might be considered a good candidate for the second term's work. The assumption is made that since the individual was able to master certain basic skills, the individual will be able to master more advanced skills—hence, the achievement test has been used as if it were a test of aptitude. Few situations exist where the reverse is true—where a test expressly designed to test for aptitude is used as an achievement test. Note that when achievement tests are used to make predictions, they tend to draw on narrower (more formal) learning experiences and are therefore typically used to make predictions with respect to some equally narrow variable (for example, success in Basic French predicts success in Advanced French). Aptitude tests draw on a broader fund of information and abilities and are typically used to predict to broader variables (just as "general fund of information" might be used to predict to success in higher education). Another hallmark of the aptitude test in contrast to the achievement test is the utilization of tasks that are not formally taught in the schools, such as figural analogies and number series. Such tasks are designed to reduce the likelihood that they had been specifically taught to the examinee.

To summarize the sometimes blurry distinction between achievement and aptitude tests: although both types of tests measure learning to some degree, achievement tests are typically more limited in scope in the learning they assess. Achievement tests reflect learning that has occurred under controlled and definable conditions, usually where there has been specific training. Aptitude tests tap a combination of learning experiences and inborn potential that was obtained under uncontrolled and nondefined conditions. Predictions about future learning and behavior can be made from both kinds of tests, though predictions made on the basis of achievement tests are usually limited to the subject matter of the test.

In the following sections, we survey some aptitude tests used in schools from entry level through graduate and professional institutions. Note that at the entry level an aptitude test is often referred to as a "readiness" test, since its primary purpose is to assess the child's readiness for learning. As the level of education climbs, however, the term *readiness* is dropped in favor of the term *aptitude*, although readiness is very much implied at all levels. The Scholastic Aptitude Test (SAT), given late in high school and widely used as a predictor of ability to do college-level work, might well have been called the "College Readiness Test." Similarly, the Graduate Record Examination (GRE), given in college and used as a predictor of ability to do graduate-level work, might have been christened the "Graduate School Readiness Examination." Both tests can be used effectively to predict aptitude for advanced-level work. For example, the GRE Guide (1993) indicates that correlations between the GRE and grades in the first year of graduate school range from .30 to .37, depending on the field of study. College grades are also predictive of first-year grades in graduate school, with correlations ranging between .35 and .39. Using college grades and GRE scores together results in even more accurate predictions of first-year graduate school grades. Correlations ranging from .44 to .48 indicate that between 19% and 23% of the variance in first-year graduate school grades can be accounted for by college grades and GRE scores together.

Aptitude tests such as the GRE and the SAT provide more than a mere indicator of "readiness." Especially at the upper levels, educational standards vary not only from community to community but also from school to school—even from class to class. Additionally, teacher prejudices as well as a host of other factors may enter into grading procedures. Aptitude tests represent a kind of "equalizer," for they provide a sample of academic performance on a standardized test that can be compared with the performance of all other students taking the test. When used in conjunction with grades and various other criteria, aptitude test data can be a good predictor of future academic success.

The Elementary School Level

The age at which a child is mandated by law to enter school varies from state to state. Yet, individual children of the same chronological age may vary widely in how ready they are to separate from their parents and begin academic learning. Children entering the educational system come from a wide range of backgrounds and experiences, and their rates of physiological, psychological, and social development also vary widely. School readiness tests provide educators with a yardstick by which to assess pupils' abilities in areas as diverse as general information and sensory-motor skills. One of many instruments designed to assess children's readiness and aptitude for formal education is the Metropolitan Readiness Tests (MRT).

The Metropolitan Readiness Tests (MRT)   The MRT is a group-administered battery that assesses the development of reading and mathematics skills important in the early stages of formal, school learning. The test is divided into two levels: Level I, to be used with beginning and middle kindergarteners, and Level II, which spans the end of kindergarten through first grade (see Table 10–5). There are two forms of the test at each level. The tests are orally administered in several sessions and are untimed, though they typically require about 90 minutes to administer. A practice test (especially useful with young children who have had minimal or no prior testtaking experience) may be administered several days before the actual testing to help familiarize students with procedures and the format involved in taking such a test.

Normative data for the 1986 edition of the MRT are based on a national sample of approximately thirty thousand children. The standardization sample was stratified according to geographic regions, socioeconomic factors, prior school experience, and ethnic background. Data were obtained from both public and parochial schools and from both large and small schools. Split-half reliability coefficients for both forms of both levels of the MRT as well as Kuder-Richardson measures of internal consistency were in the acceptably high range. Content validity was developed through an extensive review of the literature,

Table 10-5
The Subtests of the Metropolitan Readiness Tests

Level I

Auditory Memory: Four pictures containing familiar objects are presented. The examiner reads aloud several words. The child must select the picture that corresponds to the same sequence of words that were presented orally.

Rhyming: The examiner supplies the names of each of the pictures presented and then gives a fifth word that rhymes with one of them. The child must select the picture that rhymes with the examiner's word.

Letter Recognition: The examiner names different letters and the child must identify each from the series presented in the test booklet.

Visual Matching: A sample is presented and the child must select the choice that matches the sample.

School Language and Listening: The examiner reads a sentence, and the child is instructed to select the picture that describes what was read. The task involves some inference-making and awareness of relevancy of detail.

Quantitative Language: Comprehension of quantitative terms and knowledge of ordinal numbers and simple mathematical operations are assessed.

Level II

Beginning Consonants: Four pictures representing familiar objects are presented in the test booklet and are named by the examiner. The examiner then supplies a fifth word (not presented), and the child must select the picture that begins with the same sound.

Sound-Letter Correspondence: A picture is presented followed by a series of letters. The examiner names the pictures, and the child selects the choice that corresponds to the beginning sound of the pictured item.

Visual Matching: As in the corresponding subtest at Level I, a model is presented, and the child must select the choice that matches the model.

Finding Patterns: A stimulus consisting of several symbols is presented followed by a series of representative options. The child must select the option that contains the same sequence of symbols, even though presented in a larger grouping with more distractions.

School Language: As in the School Language and Listening Test at Level I, the child must select the picture that corresponds to an orally presented sentence.

Listening: Material is orally presented, and the child must select the picture represented that reflects comprehension of, and the drawing of conclusions from, that material.

Quantitative Concepts ⎫ Both are optional tests that, like the Quantitative Language of Level I, assess comprehension of basic
Quantitative Operations ⎭ mathematical concepts and operations.

---

analysis of the skills involved in the reading process, and the development of test items that reflected those skills. Items were reviewed by minority consultants in an attempt to reduce (if not eliminate) any potential ethnic bias. The predictive validity of MRT scores has been examined with reference to later school achievement indices, and the obtained validity coefficients have been acceptably high.

The Secondary School Level

Perhaps the most obvious example of an aptitude test widely used in the schools at the secondary level is the Scholastic Aptitude Test (SAT). The test has been of value not only in the college selection process but also as an aid to high school guidance and job placement counselors in advising students about what course of action might be best for them. In addition to the SAT, the American College Testing (ACT) programs provide another well-known aptitude test.

How much do colleges really rely on criteria such as SAT scores in making college entrance decisions? Probably less than most people believe. Institutions of higher learning in this country differ widely with respect to their admission criteria. In one large-scale national survey of college admissions officers, it was found that only 48 percent of the responding institutions required SAT or ACT scores of all applicants (Undergraduate Admissions, 1980). Even among the schools that required these test scores, varying weights were accorded to the scores with respect to admission decisions. Highly selective institutions may admit large numbers of students with lower test scores and reject large numbers of students with high test scores (Harnett & Feldmesser, 1980). It has been argued that higher education is available to any American citizen who wants it and that "in no major system of higher education in the world is access to higher education less dependent on the results of a single examination or set of examinations than in the United States" (Hargadon, 1981, p. 1112). With that preface, we briefly describe the SAT—a test with which many of our readers have had some firsthand experience.

The Scholastic Aptitude Test (SAT)   The SAT was first introduced as an objective exam in 1926. Until 1995, the SAT was a three-hour test divided into two parts: Verbal and Mathematics. The Verbal part consisted of sections that included Analogies, Reading Comprehension, Antonyms, and Sentence Completion. The Reading Comprehension section consisted of reading passages containing subject material from a variety of academic areas, such as science, social studies, and the humanities. The Sentence Completion section consisted of single sentences or paragraphs in which one or two words had been omitted, and the examinee's task was to select the choice that best completes the written thought. Vocabulary knowledge was measured by performance on the Antonyms and Analogies items. In 1974, a Test of Standard Written English was introduced for the first time to assess the student's ability to comprehend the type of language utilized in most college textbooks. It consisted of 50 multiple-choice questions and required 30 minutes to complete. A Reading Comprehension score based on the Sentence Completion and Reading Comprehension sections was also computed. The Mathematics part of the SAT assessed the understanding and application of mathematical principles, as well as numerical reasoning ability. The subject matter of the test questions on this section assumed knowledge of the basic arithmetic operations such as addition, subtraction, multiplication, division, averages, percentages, odd-even integers, and geometric and algebraic concepts, including linear and quadratic equations, exponents, and factoring (Braswell, 1978).

Test items for the SAT are constructed by experts in the field and pretested on national samples during the actual examination. The experimental items are placed in separately timed sections of the examination. Such a pretesting procedure on a sample of examinees who are representative of the group that will be taking future forms of the test provides the test constructors with useful information regarding the value of proposed new items. The responses of students are statistically analyzed to determine the percent answering each question correctly, the percent choosing each of the distractor items, and the percent who omit the item; and an index of the response to each item with the total score on the test (that is, a difficulty rating for each item) is computed (Jones et al.,

1977). The test is under continual revision, and the total time to develop an item may be upward of 18 months.

The technical quality of the SAT is good. Reliability of recent forms of the test as measured by internal-consistency estimates have resulted in reliability coefficients in the .90s for both the Verbal and the Mathematics scales. Research concerning the validity of the SAT has focused mostly on correlations between SAT scores and college grades, or on a combination of SAT scores and high school grades with college grades. In general, high school grades have been found to correlate higher with college grades than do SAT scores. When SAT scores and high school grade-point average are combined, the correlation with college performance increases. For example, in one study, grades in the first year of college correlated .200 with SAT scores and .304 with high school class rank. Together, SAT scores and high school class rank correlated .336 with college grades, accounting for 11.3% of the variance in college grades (Baron & Norman, 1992). Correlations between the Verbal and Mathematics parts of the SAT have been in the high .60s, a finding that suggests that overlapping skills, probably verbal in nature, are tapped on both parts of the exam.

The SAT is administered several times a year under carefully controlled conditions in cities throughout the United States and in foreign countries. Foreign-language editions of the test have been made available, as have special editions for students with disabilities. A special form (the Preliminary Scholastic Aptitude Test, or PSAT) is available for administration as a practice exam and as a tool for counselors. An authoritative source for more information, particularly technical information on this test, is *The College Board Technical Handbook for the Scholastic Aptitude Test and Achievement Tests* (Donlon, 1984).

Major changes in the SAT's format and normative base were instituted in the early 1990s. The format changes were designed to make the test more "educationally relevant" with respect to its objective of predicting college performance (Moses, 1991). Essentially, the format change involved dichotomizing the SAT into two major components: Reasoning tests and Subject tests.

The first component is essentially a revised and expanded version of the preexisting SAT. It includes verbal and mathematical tests, and continues to measure ability or aptitude for college-level education. It also features increased emphasis on critical reading in the verbal sections. Some math questions require the student to produce a written answer. Students may use a calculator on math questions. The second SAT component consists of a set of achievement tests in the areas of writing, literature, history, foreign languages, mathematics, and sciences (College Board Review, 1990–1991; Q & A, 1994).

When the SAT was standardized in 1941, the average performance was reflected in a score of 500. In the years since 1941, SAT scores have declined, such that the average testtaker in 1993 received a verbal SAT score of 424 and a mathematics score of 478. Because the norms were anchored, the scores retained the same meaning in 1993 as they had in 1941; a score of 500 in 1993 meant that the testtaker performed at the average level of testtakers in 1941. This made possible the comparison of students taking the test during different years. A similar shift in GRE scores had taken place (see *Everyday Psychometrics* in Chapter 4). As of April 1995, the SAT norms were "recentered" so that a score of 500 indicates average performance among current testtakers. Test users, like college admissions offices, have been provided with tables to convert "old" SAT scores (based on the 1941 norms) to scores based on the 1995 norms for comparison purposes (Q & A, 1994). Unless recentering occurs in the meantime, an SAT score of 500 in the year 2000 or anytime thereafter will be indicative of an average level of performance relative to the "immortalized" performance of people who took the test in 1995.

The College Level and Beyond

If you are a college student planning to pursue further education after graduation, you are probably familiar with acronyms such as GRE, MAT, MCAT, and LSAT. Respectively, these acronyms stand for the Graduate Record Examination, the Miller Analogies Test, the Medical College Admission Test, and the Law School Admission Test. The GRE is widely used as one criterion for admission to many graduate school programs. An important new development in the format of the GRE is discussed in this chapter's *Everyday Psychometrics*. The MAT is a 100-item multiple-choice analogy test that draws not only on the examinee's ability to perceive relationships but also on general intelligence, vocabulary, and academic learning. As an example, complete the following analogy:

Classical conditioning is to *Pavlov,* as *operant conditioning* is to
(a) Freud
(b) Rogers
(c) Skinner
(d) Jung
(e) Westheimer

Successful completion of this item demands not only the ability to understand the relationship between classical conditioning and Pavlov but also the knowledge that it was B. F. Skinner (choice "c") whose name—of the names listed— is best associated with operant conditioning.

Applicants for training in certain professions are required to take specialized examinations. Students applying to medical school are required to take the Medical College Admission Test (MCAT). Offered twice a year, the MCAT is a multiple-choice test divided into four separately timed sections. These include Verbal Ability (comprising 75 items to be completed in 20 minutes), Quantitative Ability (50 items to be completed in 45 minutes), General Information (75 items to be completed in 25 minutes), and Science (86 items to be completed in 60 minutes). Items in the Verbal Ability section consist of analogy items, synonyms, and antonyms. The Quantitative section assesses knowledge and application of algebraic, geometric, and arithmetic principles. The General Information section includes items pertaining to a variety of subject areas such as music and sports; and the Science section, probably the most closely related to the field of medicine, includes test items pertaining to biology, chemistry, and physics. Although the test continues to be used as one criterion in medical school admission, scores on it have not been found to be predictive of class rank in medical school.

Adapting to Adaptive Testing: The Case of the GRE

In 1993, Educational Testing Service introduced the computerized GRE. Among the chief benefits of the computerized version of the GRE is greater flexibility in the date and time of test administration. Instead of reporting to a large auditorium or some other test center along with hundreds of others, students taking the computerized version report to a computer center to take the test on an individual basis—that is, one-on-one with a computer on a preappointed day at a preappointed time.

The computerized version of the GRE features an adaptive format. This means that the first items presented on the subtests will be of medium-level difficulty. Depending on whether one answers correctly or incorrectly, the items will become either progressively easier or progressively more difficult. In theory, the adaptive testing format means that in contrast to paper-and-pencil test administration, fewer items in total will have to be administered to obtain a final score. In addition to the advantages of adaptive testing, the computerized GRE drastically reduces the time it takes to receive a score report. Whereas the more traditional method of testtaking entailed a ritual, anxiety-fraught waiting period of weeks, students taking the computerized GRE receive their score report almost immediately upon completion of the examination.

So far, it would seem as if the transition of the GRE to a computer-administered, adaptive format has resulted in a "win-win" situation for all concerned. Well, not exactly. In fact, both the testtaker and the test administrator have had to make some adjustments or adaptations during the transitional period. For testtakers, the cost of taking the GRE nearly doubles if one chooses to take the computerized version. In 1995, the privilege of sitting at a computer at a preappointed date and time cost $96, as compared with $56 for bringing your number 2 pencils to an auditorium and sitting every-other-seat with a couple of hundred other people.

For the test administrator, Educational Testing Service, a model for what was envisioned as the future of educational testing had to be temporarily put on hold because of the risk of irregularities. For the adaptive testing format to work in a system in which hundreds of thousands of testtakers will be taking the test, some more than once, a very large number of items must be stored in the item bank. If not, it would be possible for a group of people intent on memorizing the test items to do just that. In fact, one company that is in business to coach students in taking the GRE sent three of its employees to take the test with the specific objective of memorizing test items—which is exactly what they did. Afterward, the bogus testtakers reconstructed the test. They claimed that between 70% and 80% of their items matched the real thing (Celis, 1994). Did the coaching company begin coaching their clients using real GRE items? No, such action not only would have been illegal but also might well have eventually put the test coaching company out of business. After all, once word got out that GRE items could be purchased, the test would no longer be administered—and the test coaching company would have "killed the goose that laid the golden egg." Instead, the test coaching company reported their concerns, along with their evidence, directly to Educational Testing Service.

Educational Testing Service acknowledged that it had a problem with which it had to deal. All GRE testing was suspended between December 26, 1994, and January 3, 1995. In the meantime, ETS added more items to its GRE bank and publicized a warning that its test items were copyrighted. Anyone releasing such items without its permission would be subject to charges of copyright infringement. The moral of this story could be stated as follows: "Adapt your test to an adaptive testing format by having sufficient items to make adaptive testing feasible, or risk behavior on the part of some testtakers that could only be described as maladaptive."

Applicants to law school are required to take the Law School Admissions Test (LSAT). The test is presented in two testing sessions, one in the morning and one in the afternoon, and a separate score is obtained for each session. The morning session consists of five separately timed sections: Logical Reasoning, Practical Judgment, Data Interpretation, Quantitative Comparisons, and Principles and Cases. Based on the premise that the legal profession itself relies heavily on verbal skills (both in comprehension and in communication), the LSAT is purposely developed to primarily reflect verbal abilities. The test items themselves are designed to assess comprehension, interpretation, critical analysis, evaluation, and application of information. To that end, each test item presents a body of information followed by multiple-choice items. The Logical Reasoning and Practical Judgment sections present information in the form of reading passages, and the Data Interpretation section employs graphs and tables. Subject matter representative of many different fields of study is included in the test. The only section that contains legally oriented subject material is the Principles and Cases section, which presents hypothetical situations involving legal principles. It is assumed, however, that the testtaker has had no previous legal training and that the answers may be obtained through general reasoning skills. The afternoon session is divided into three sections (Error Recognition, Sentence Correction, and Usage) that together form the Writing Ability Score. Taken together, these sections provide an indication of ability to express oneself in writing. Predictive validity studies examining the relationship between score obtained on the LSAT and grade-point average of first-year law students have yielded relatively low correlations.

Numerous other aptitude tests have been developed to assess specific kinds of academic and/or occupational aptitudes. For example, the Seashore Measures of Musical Talents (Seashore, 1938) is a musical aptitude test administered with the aid of a prerecorded record or tape. The six subtests measure specific aspects of musical talent (for example, comparing different notes and rhythms on variables such as loudness, pitch, time, and timbre). The Horn Art Aptitude Inventory is a measure of art aptitude that is divided into two sections. The Scribbles and Doodles section contains items thought to measure variables such as clarity of thought and originality. Items in the Imagery section contain key lines or "springboards" from art masterpieces to be incorporated in the examinee's artistic production. Scoring categories for the Imagery section include Design, Imagination, and Scope of Interests.

Diagnostic Tests

In medical jargon, the noun *diagnosis* may be defined as "the act or process of identifying or determining the nature of a disease through examination." In the language of educational assessment, a diagnostic test is designed to pinpoint where a student is having difficulty with a particular academic skill. Typically included in such a test will be a number of subtests, each analyzing a specific knowledge or skill required to successfully perform a specific task. Thus, for example, a diagnostic reading test is designed to segment the various components of reading so that the specific problem areas with respect to the skill of reading will be brought into full relief. It is important to emphasize that diagnostic tests do not necessarily provide information that will answer questions concerning *why* the learning difficulty exists; it will remain for other educational, psychological, and perhaps medical examinations to answer the "why" question. In general, diagnostic tests are administered to students who have already demonstrated their problem with a particular subject area through their poor performance either in the classroom or on some achievement test. It is therefore understandable that diagnostic tests tend to contain simpler items than do achievement tests designed for use with members of the same grade.

Reading Tests

The ability to read is integral to virtually all classroom learning, and so it is not surprising that many diagnostic tests are available to help pinpoint difficulties in acquiring this skill (for example, the Stanford Diagnostic Reading Test, the Metropolitan Reading Instructional Tests, the Diagnostic Reading Scales, the Durrell Analysis of Reading Test). For illustrative purposes we briefly describe one such diagnostic battery, the Woodcock Reading Mastery Tests.

The Woodcock Reading Mastery Tests—Revised (WRMT-R) Developed by Richard W. Woodcock and typically referred to as "the Woodcock," the tests were revised in 1987, and are suitable for children age 5 and older, and adults up to age 75—and beyond according to the promotional literature. The subtests include

- *Letter Identification:* This subtest consists of items that measure the ability to name letters presented in different forms. Both cursive/manuscript and uppercase/lowercase letters are presented.

- *Word Identification:* This subtest consists of words in isolation arranged in order of increasing difficulty. The student is asked to read each word aloud.

- *Word Attack:* This subtest consists of nonsense syllables that incorporate phonetic as well as structural analysis skills. The student is asked to pronounce each nonsense syllable.

- *Word Comprehension:* This subtest consists of items that assess word meaning by using a four-part analogy format.

- *Passage Comprehension:* This subtest consists of phrases, sentences, or short paragraphs read silently in which a word is missing. The student must supply the missing word.

The tests are individually administered and are designed to measure skills inherent in reading. The tests come in two forms labeled "G" and "H," and each form contains the five subtests listed above. (Form G also contains a test labeled "Visual Auditory Learning.") A cassette tape is packaged with the tests and serves as a guide to the proper pronunciation of the Word Attack items and the Word Identification items. Test scores may be combined to form what are referred to as "clusters," such as a Readiness cluster (the Visual-Auditory Learning and Letter Identification tests), a Basic Skills cluster (the Word Identification and Word Attack tests), a Reading Comprehension cluster (the Word Comprehension and Passage Comprehension tests), a Total Reading—Full Scale cluster (the Word Identification, Word Attack, Word Comprehension, and Passage Comprehension tests), and a Total Reading—Short Scale (the Word Identification and Passage Comprehension tests). The last scale may be used for quick-screening (about 15 minutes) purposes, although each cluster of tests typically takes between 10 and 30 minutes to administer. An optional microcomputer software program is also available for score conversion and storage of pre- and posttest scores.

Math Tests

The Stanford Diagnostic Mathematics Test, the Metropolitan Mathematics Instructional Tests, the Diagnostic Mathematics Inventory, and the KeyMath Revised: A Diagnostic Inventory of Essential Mathematics exemplify some of the many tests that have been developed to help diagnose difficulties with arithmetic and mathematical concepts. Items on such tests typically analyze the skills and knowledge necessary for segregating the parts of mathematical operations. The KeyMath Revised test, for example, contains 13 subtests designed to assess areas such as basic concepts (including knowledge of symbols, numbers, and fractions), operations (including skill in addition, subtraction, multiplication, division, and mental computation), and applications (numerical problems employing variables such as money and time). Diagnostic information is obtained from an evaluation of the examinee's performance in the various areas, subtests, and items. Total test scores are translated into grade equivalents, area performance may be translated into a general pattern of mathematical functioning, and subtest performance may be translated into a profile illustrating strengths and weaknesses. For each item on the test, the manual lists a description of the skill involved and a corresponding behavior objective—information useful in determining the skills to be included in a remedial program. A computerized scoring program converts raw scores into derived scores, summarizes the examinee's performance, and offers suggestions for remedial instruction.

Other Diagnostic Tests

In addition to individually administered diagnostic tests such as the KeyMath Revised, a number of diagnostic tests designed for group administration have been developed. Two examples of group diagnostic tests are the Stanford Diagnostic Reading Test (SDRT) and the Stanford Diagnostic Mathematics Test (SDMT). Although developed independently and standardized on separate populations, the two instruments share certain characteristics related to test design and format. Both instruments are available in two forms, and both are divided into four overlapping levels that assess performance from grade 1 through high school. The SDRT consists of ten subtests that reflect skills required in three major areas of reading: decoding, vocabulary, and comprehension. The SDMT consists of three subtests administered at all levels. Norm-referenced as well as criterion-referenced information is provided in the test manual for each of these tests. Normative data are presented as percentile ranks, stanines, grade equivalents, and scaled scores. Criterion-referenced information is provided for each skill through the use of a "progress indicator," a cutoff score that shows if the student is sufficiently competent in that skill to progress to the next stage of the instructional program. The manuals for both instruments include an index of behavioral objectives useful in prescriptive teaching strategies.

Learning Disabilities Assessment

Some children do poorly in school even though they are at least in the average range of intellectual ability. When the source of the learning problem is not a physical disability or the result of emotional disturbance, economic deprivation, or mental retardation, the diagnosis "specific learning disability" is applicable. Samuel A. Kirk is credited with coining the term *learning disability* at a conference in support of the Fund for Perceptually Handicapped Children. Kirk suggested that this term be used to describe children with learning problems in language, communication, and reading. As a result of Kirk's efforts, the Association for Children with Learning Disabilities—since renamed the Association for Children and Adults with Learning Disabilities—was formed. But what exactly is a "learning disability"? An answer to this question can be found in the definition published in the *Education for All Handicapped Children Act of 1975* (Public Law 94-142), at Section 5(b)(4):

> Specific learning disability means a disorder in one or more of the basic psychological processes involved in understanding or in using language, spoken or written, which may manifest itself in an imperfect ability to listen, think, speak, read, write, spell, or to do mathematical calculations. The term includes such conditions as perceptual handicaps, brain injury, minimal brain dysfunction, dyslexia, and developmental aphasia. The term does not include children who have learning problems which are primarily the result of visual, hearing, or motor handicaps, or mental retardation, or of environmental, cultural, or economic disadvantages.

Other characteristics often associated with learning disabilities (LD) include hyperactivity, perceptual-motor impairments, emotional disability, general coordination deficits, disorders of attention (such as distractibility or perseveration), impulsivity, disorders of memory and thinking, equivocal neurological signs, language problems, and disorders of speech and hearing. The *Federal Register* dated December 29, 1977, mandated that the diagnosis of specific learning disability be multidisciplinary in nature and be made by three people, including (1) a teacher or another specialist knowledgeable in the field of the suspected handicap, (2) the child's regular teacher, and (3) at least one person qualified to conduct individual diagnostic examinations of children (such as a school psychologist, a speech language pathologist, or a remedial reading teacher). The diagnosis of specific learning disability could be made only if the child demonstrated a discrepancy between ability and achievement in one or more of the following areas: oral expression, listening comprehension, written expression, basic reading skill, reading comprehension, mathematics calculation, or mathematics reasoning. The existence of a discrepancy between the child's achievement and expected level of achievement (the latter criterion based on the child's ability as measured by an intelligence test and the child's age) is emphasized in the federal guidelines partly to emphasize the view that a learning disability is not a minor or temporary condition.

In the years following the federal mandate to identify children with a "severe discrepancy between achievement and intellectual ability" (Procedures for Evaluating Specific Learning Disabilities, 1977, p. 65083), individual states employed a wide array of methods in an attempt to comply (Shepard, 1983). In its general form, the most common solution to the problem has entailed three steps: (1) quantifying achievement, (2) quantifying intellectual ability, and (3) developing some formula for determining when a "severe discrepancy" exists between the two. Existing formulas have employed a number of variables such as grade-level deviation scores or standard scores on ability and achievement tests. Telzrow (1985) presents a highly readable account of some problems inherent in common discrepancy models. One psychometrically sound discrepancy model is the predicted-achievement model. According to it, a regression line predicting scores on an achievement test from an intelligence test is calculated on the basis of testing with a large sample of subjects. In one application of the model, scores on the Wechsler Individual Achievement Test (WIAT; The Psychological Corporation, 1992) are predicted from the Wechsler Intelligence Scale for Children (WISC-III). The resulting regression line is then used to predict the expected WIAT score for an individual child based on that child's WISC-III score. If the child's actual WIAT score is significantly lower than the predicted WIAT score, a learning disability would be suspected (Flanagan & Alfonso, 1993a, 1993b). This is so because the WIAT test results would be interpreted as being indicative of lower-than-expected academic achievement.

As more states have adopted a formula-based method for determining whether a severe discrepancy between achievement and ability exists, computer software has been developed to do the necessary computations. Such software can also be helpful in storing data for later access and in automatically alerting test users to various psychometric issues (Evans, 1993).

Federal legislation has also required schools to address the needs of the learning-disabled after high school. And here again, psychological assessment techniques are used in the ongoing examination of students' educational progress, intellectual skills, and vocational and recreational needs (Spruill, 1993). The Carl D. Perkins Vocational Act of 1984 requires that each learning-disabled individual in a vocational program be assessed relative to the appropriateness of the program for that student. For example, variables related to students' ability to learn within the particular program are considered. More recently, the Individuals with Disabilities Education Act of 1990 mandated that schools plan specifically for learning-disabled students' transition into adult roles. Now, educational programming for learning-disabled students must consider needs after high school. Educational objectives include developing independent living skills, as well as interest in recreational and leisure activities.

Although learning-disabled children are formally classified as those with a severe discrepancy between ability and achievement, some researchers have sought alternative means to identify learning disabilities. Many of these approaches have focused on subtest or scale discrepancies on various intelligence and ability tests (Bain, 1993; Kaufman & Kaufman, 1983; Kline et al., 1993; Wechsler, 1991).

Psychoeducational Test Batteries

Psychoeducational test batteries are test kits that generally contain two types of tests: those that measure abilities related to academic success and those that measure educational achievement in areas such as reading and arithmetic. Data derived from these batteries allow for normative comparisons (how the student compares with other students within the same age group), as well as an evaluation of the testtaker's own strengths and weaknesses—all the better to plan educational interventions. Below, we survey two such batteries.

Kaufman Assessment Battery for Children (K-ABC)

Alan and Nadine Kaufman, a husband/wife team of psychologists, approached the task of test development with some experience; both had previously worked closely with Dorothea McCarthy in the development of the McCarthy Scales of Children's Abilities, and Alan Kaufman had worked with David Wechsler on the development of the WISC-R.

Together, the Kaufmans developed the Kaufman Assessment Battery for Children (K-ABC). The K-ABC is an individually administered test battery that was designed for use with both normal and exceptional children from age 2½ through age 12½. The test battery rests on several theories about intelligence. For instance, the battery includes tests designed to measure both intelligence and achievement. The tests of intelligence focus on what Cattell (1971) called "fluid" abilities, or information-processing skills that are reflective of the child's ability to adapt and learn from the environment in ongoing fashion. The achievement tests measure what Cattell called "crystallized" abilities, or knowledge that the child has gained from past learning.

For the Kaufmans, intelligence is largely a matter of the problem-solving ability and the effectiveness of one's information-processing skills. The K-ABC intelligence subtests are divided into two groups, reflecting the two kinds of information-processing skills identified by Luria and his students (Das et al., 1975; Luria, 1966a, 1966b): simultaneous skills and sequential skills (see pages 266–268). Table 10–6 presents the particular learning and teaching styles that reflect the two types of intelligence measured by the K-ABC. Scores on the simultaneous and sequential subtests are combined into a Mental Processing Composite, which is analogous to the "IQ" measure calculated on other tests.

Table 10–6
Characteristics and Teaching Guidelines for Sequential and Simultaneous Learners

Learner characteristics

The Sequential Learner	The Simultaneous Learner
The sequential learner solves problems best by mentally arranging small amounts of information in consecutive, linear, step-by-step order. He/she is most at home with verbal instructions and cues, because the ability to interpret spoken language depends to a great extent on the sequence of words.	The simultaneous learner solves problems best by mentally integrating and synthesizing many parallel pieces of information at the same time. He/she is most at home with visual instructions and cues, because the ability to interpret the environment visually depends on perceiving and integrating many details at once.
Sequential processing is especially important in:	Simultaneous processing is especially important in:
<ul><li>learning and retaining basic arithmetic facts</li><li>memorizing lists of spelling words</li><li>making associations between letters and their sounds</li><li>learning the rules of grammar, the chronology of historical events</li><li>remembering details</li><li>following a set of rules, directions, steps</li><li>solving problems by breaking them down into their components or steps</li></ul>	<ul><li>recognizing the shape and physical appearance of letters and numbers</li><li>interpreting the overall effect or meaning of pictures and other visual stimuli, such as maps and charts</li><li>understanding the overall meaning of a story or poem</li><li>summarizing, comparing, evaluating</li><li>comprehending mathematical or scientific principles</li><li>solving problems by visualizing them in their entirety</li></ul>
Sequential learners who are weak in simultaneous processing may have difficulty with:	Simultaneous learners who are weak in sequential processing may have difficulty with:
<ul><li>sight word recognition</li><li>reading comprehension</li><li>understanding mathematical or scientific principles</li><li>using concrete, hands-on materials</li><li>using diagrams, charts, maps</li><li>summarizing, comparing, evaluating</li></ul>	<ul><li>word attack, decoding, phonics</li><li>breaking down science or arithmetic problems into parts</li><li>interpreting the parts and features of a design or drawing</li><li>understanding the rules of games</li><li>understanding and following oral instructions</li><li>remembering specific details and sequence of a story</li></ul>

The 16 subtests of the K-ABC are listed and summarized in Table 10–7. Three of the subtests assess the sequential processing type of intelligence, seven assess the simultaneous processing type of intelligence, and six assess achievement. Because some of the subtests are appropriate for limited age ranges, any one child will take no more than 13 of the subtests.

The standardization sample   Two thousand children between the ages of 2½ and 12½ years served as subjects in the standardization sample. The sample was designed to be representative of the population of the United States based on 1980 census data, and it appears to be satisfactory in this regard (Coffman, 1985; Kamphaus & Reynolds, 1984; Merz, 1984). The sample was stratified at each age group by the variables of sex, race, socioeconomic status, geographic region,

Teaching guidelines

For the Sequential Learner	For the Simultaneous Learner
1. Present material step by step, gradually approaching the overall concept or skill. Lead up to the big question with a series of smaller ones. Break the task into parts.	1. Present the overall concept or question before asking the child to solve the problem. Continue to refer back to the task, question, or desired outcome.
2. Get the child to verbalize what is to be learned. When you teach a new word, have the child say it, aloud or silently. Emphasize verbal cues, directions, and memory strategies.	2. Get the child to visualize what is to be learned. When you teach a new word, have the child write it and picture it mentally, see it on the page in the mind's eye. Emphasize visual cues, directions, and memory strategies.
3. Teach and rehearse the steps required to do a problem or complete a task. Continue to refer back to the details or steps already mentioned or mastered. Offer a logical structure or procedure by appealing to the child's verbal/temporal orientation.	3. Make tasks concrete wherever possible by providing manipulative materials, pictures, models, diagrams, graphs. Offer a sense of the whole by appealing to the child's visual/spatial orientation.

For example, the sequential learner may look at one or two details of a picture but miss the visual image as a whole. To help such a student toward an overall appreciation of the picture, start with the parts and work up to the whole. Rather than beginning with "What does the picture show?" or "How does the picture make you feel?" first ask about details:

"What is the little boy in the corner doing?"
"Where is the dog?"
"What expression do you see on the woman's face?"
"What colors are used in the sky?"

Lead up to questions about the overall interpretation or appreciation:

"How do all these details give you clues about what is happening in this picture?"
"How does this picture make you feel?"

The sequential learner prefers a step-by-step teaching approach, one that may emphasize the gradual accumulation of details.

The simultaneous learner may react to a picture as a whole but may miss details. To help such a student notice the parts that contribute to the total visual image, begin by establishing an overall interpretation or reaction:

"What does the picture show?"
"How does the picture make you feel?"

Then consider the details:

"What is the expression on the woman's face?"
"What is the little boy in the corner doing?"
"What colors are used in the sky?"

Relate the details to the student's initial interpretation:

"How do these details explain why the picture made you feel the way it did?"

The simultaneous learner responds best to a holistic teaching approach that focuses on groups of details or images and stresses the overall meaning or configuration of the task.

Source: Kaufman et al. (1984)

and community size. Exceptional children, including children with learning disabilities and children with behavior problems, were included in the standardization sample.

Psychometric properties   In general, satisfactory estimates of test-retest and split-half reliability for the test have been reported by the test's authors. Test-retest reliability coefficients ranged from .77 to .97 for 246 children who spanned the age range of the battery and were tested twice at intervals of two to four weeks.

The manual for the K-ABC presents the results of 43 validity studies conducted before publication of the test. Comparisons were made with other tests of ability and achievement using varied samples of subjects. In these studies,

Table 10–7
A Description of the K-ABC Subtests

Sequential Processing Scale
Hand Movements (ages 2-6 through 12-5)—Performing a series of hand movements in the same sequence performed by the examiner.
Number Recall (ages 2-6 through 12-5)—Repeating a series of digits in the same sequence spoken by the examiner.
Word Order (ages 4-0 through 12-5)—Touching a series of silhouettes of common objects in the same sequence as these objects were named orally by the examiner.

Simultaneous Processing Scale
Magic Window (ages 2-6 through 4-11)—Identifying a picture that the examiner exposes by slowly moving it behind a narrow window; hence, the picture is only partially visible at any one time.
Face Recognition (ages 2-6 through 4-11)—Selecting from a group photograph the one or two faces that were exposed briefly.
Gestalt Closure (ages 2-6 through 12-5)—Naming an object or a scene pictured in a partially completed "inkblot" drawing.
Triangles (ages 4-0 through 12-5)—Assembling several identical triangles into an abstract pattern that matches a model.
Matrix Analogies (ages 5-0 through 12-5)—Selecting the meaningful picture or abstract design that best completes a visual analogy.
Spatial Memory (ages 5-0 through 12-5)—Recalling the placement of pictures on a page that was exposed briefly.
Photo Series (ages 6-0 through 12-5)—Placing photographs of an event in chronological order.

Achievement Scale
Expressive Vocabulary (ages 2-6 through 4-11)—Naming the object pictured in a photograph.
Faces and Places (ages 2-6 through 12-5)—Naming the well-known person, fictional character, or place pictured in a photograph.
Arithmetic (ages 3-0 through 12-5)—Demonstrating knowledge of numbers and mathematical concepts, counting and computational skills, and other school-related arithmetic abilities.
Riddles (ages 3-0 through 12-5)—Inferring the name of a concrete or abstract concept when given a list of its characteristics.
Reading/Decoding (ages 5-0 through 12-5)—Identifying letters and reading words.
Reading/Understanding (ages 7-0 through 12-5)—Demonstrating reading comprehension by following commands given in sentences.

the correlation between K-ABC Mental Processing Composite and the Full Scale IQ on the WISC-R and the WPPSI ranged from .55 to .77. The correlation between the K-ABC Mental Processing Composite and the third edition of the Stanford-Binet ranged from .36 to .74. In general, these and other data have been construed as supportive of the validity of the K-ABC (Bloom et al., 1988; Donders, 1992; Hayden et al., 1988; Klanderman et al., 1985; Krohn & Lamp, 1989; Krohn et al., 1988; Naglieri, 1985a, 1985b; Naglieri & Anderson, 1985; Smith & Lyon, 1987; Smith et al., 1989; Zucker, 1985; Zucker & Copeland, 1987). Noteworthy for its contrary conclusion, however, is research that examined the results of educational decisions based on the child's processing style as defined by the K-ABC. Good et al. (1993) found that using the K-ABC did not improve the quality of these decisions.

A number of studies have examined the factors measured by the K-ABC (Kamphaus et al., 1982; Kaufman, 1993; Kaufman & Kamphaus, 1984; Kaufman & McLean, 1987; Keith, 1985; Keith & Dunbar, 1984; Keith et al., 1985; Naglieri & Jensen, 1987; Willson et al., 1985). Many of the factor analyses suggested that the test was, indeed, tapping three factors—but which three? Although most factor analyses indicate the presence of simultaneous and sequential processing factors, there is some disagreement regarding the factor the K-ABC manual calls "achievement." Although Kaufman (1993) found evidence for the presence of an achievement factor, others have different ideas about the third factor. Good and Lane (1988) identified it as verbal comprehension and reading achievement. Kaufman and McLean (1986) identified it as achievement and reading ability. Keith and Novak (1987) identified it as reading achievement and verbal reasoning. It is also true that although the Kaufmans have made a convincing case for the utility of the distinction between sequential and simultaneous learning, factor-analytic evidence suggests that these two types of learning are not entirely independent (Bracken, 1985; Keith, 1985).

Administering the test Starting and stopping points are based on the child's chronological age. The number of subtests administered varies from 7 at age 2½ years, to 13 at ages 7 years and above. Test items are presented on an easel facing the child, and examiner instructions are printed on the side of the easel facing the examiner.

Oral instructions from the examiner and verbal responses from the examinee are minimal compared with other tests of intelligence, and the manual contains special instructions for test administration to bilingual and hearing-, speech-, or language-disabled testtakers. Some of the mental processing subtests require the examiner to teach or demonstrate what is required, although there are no sample or teaching items on the achievement portion of the test.

Scoring and interpreting the test Subtest items are scored correct (1 point) or incorrect (0 points), and the manual provides explicit directions and criteria for administering and scoring the test. Scores on the individual items are tallied to yield raw scores on each of the subtests. Tables in the manual are then used to convert each of the subtest scores into a standard score. From these standard scores, Sequential Processing, Simultaneous Processing, Mental Processing Composite, and Achievement standard scores are derived. Sociocultural percentile ranks, based on the child's ethnic group and parents' educational level, can also be obtained.

One method of interpreting the K-ABC is the successive levels approach. As applied to the K-ABC, the test user evaluates processing style (simultaneous or sequential), as well as the relationship between ability and achievement as reflected respectively by the Mental Processing Composite and Achievement scores. A subtest-by-subtest evaluation of assets and deficits follows. An alternative to the interpretation of the Achievement score suggested in the manual has been proposed by Kamphaus & Reynolds (1987).

Recommendations for teaching based on Kaufman and Kaufman's (1983) idea of "processing strength" can be derived from the K-ABC test findings. It may be recommended, for example, that a student whose strength is processing sequentially should be taught using the teaching guidelines for sequential learners. Students who do not have any particular processing strength may be taught using methods that employ a combination of methods. This model of test interpretation and consequential intervention has great intuitive appeal. However, research findings related to this approach have been mixed (Ayres & Cooley, 1986; Good et al., 1989; McCloskey, 1989; Salvia & Hritcko, 1984). Until this intervention model is employed in actual classrooms within the context of a regular curriculum over a reasonable period of time (one year or so), it will be impossible to know with any certainty of its effectiveness.

An evaluation   The K-ABC was introduced with extensive reliability and validity data supportive of its psychometric soundness. Factor-analytic studies were used to confirm that the test taps three primary factors, although, as noted earlier, controversy remains regarding the nature and naming of one of them. The well-defined theoretical basis of the test facilitates continuing research into the validity of the instrument from a theoretical perspective. The K-ABC was designed to be as culture-fair as possible, and researchers have found this to be the case (Bracken, 1985; Chattin & Bracken, 1989; Cummings & Merrell, 1993). The use of sample items, teaching items, and the minimal verbal emphasis on the mental processing subtests all contribute to making the test culture-fair.

An unresolved issue for future research concerns the factor structure of the test; exactly what that third factor is measuring remains a nagging question that begs for an answer. The test authors' as yet unvalidated recommendations for teaching based on sequential or simultaneous processing skills is another source of controversy related to the K-ABC.

Woodcock-Johnson Psycho-Educational Battery—Revised (WJ-R)

The WJ-R (Woodcock & Johnson, 1989) was designed to measure cognitive abilities, academic achievement, and scholastic aptitude. How much of a discrepancy is there between the testtaker's ability, as reflected by the test, and his or her achievement or aptitude? What are the testtaker's strengths and weaknesses with respect to her or his achievement and abilities? These are the types of questions that may be addressed using, at least in part, data derived from an administration of the WJ-R.

Developed for use with individuals ranging in age from 2 to 95, the WJ-R has two parts: the Woodcock-Johnson Tests of Cognitive Ability and the Woodcock-Johnson Tests of Achievement. As listed in Table 10–8, a total of 21 tests compose the Cognitive Ability battery (7 standard and 14 supplemental), and a total of 18 tests make up the Achievement battery (9 standard and 9 supplemental). Subtests are organized into clusters, which yield measures such as one of "broad cognitive ability" (similar to a WISC-R Full Scale score), as well as measures of aptitude in various areas. For example, the cluster score for reading aptitude is based on performance on the Memory for Sentences, Visual Matching, Sound Blending, and Oral Vocabulary subtests. Cognitive abilities measured by the cognitive subtests are summarized in Table 10–9. Curriculum areas tapped by the WJ-R achievement tests are summarized in Table 10–10.

The standardization sample   The WJ-R was standardized on 6,359 subjects selected from communities across the country, including 705 preschool children, 3,245 individuals from the kindergarten through twelfth-grade level, 916 college/university students, and 1,493 adults not in school. A stratified sampling based on the 1980 census that controlled for variables such as geographic

Table 10–8
Subtests of the WJ-R

Subtest	Description
Cognitive Ability Subtests	
Memory for Names	Measures the ability to learn associations between unfamiliar auditory and visual stimuli
Memory for Sentences	Measures the ability to remember and repeat phrases and sentences
Visual Matching	Measures the ability to locate and circle the two identical numbers in a row of six numbers
Incomplete Words	Measures auditory closure
Visual Closure	Measures the ability to identify a drawing or picture that is altered in one of several ways
Picture Vocabulary	Measures the ability to name familiar and unfamiliar pictured objects
Analysis-Synthesis	Measures the ability to analyze the presented components of an incomplete logic puzzle and to determine the missing components
Visual-Auditory Learning	Measures the ability to associate new visual symbols with familiar words and to translate a series of symbols into verbal sentences
Memory for Words	Measures the ability to repeat lists of unrelated words in the correct sequence
Cross Out	Measures the ability to scan and compare visual information quickly
Sound Blending	Measures the ability to integrate and then say whole words after hearing parts of the words
Picture Recognition	Measures the ability to recognize a subset of previously presented pictures within a field of distracting pictures
Oral Vocabulary	Measures knowledge of word meanings
Concept Formation	Measures the ability to identify the rules for concepts when shown illustrations of both instances and noninstances of the concepts
Delayed Recall— Memory for Names	Measures the ability to recall (after 1 to 8 days) the space creatures presented in Memory for Names
Delayed Recall— Visual-Auditory Learning	Measures the ability to recall (after 1 to 8 days) the symbols presented in Visual-Auditory Learning
Numbers Reversed	Measures the ability to say a series of random numbers backward
Sound Patterns	Measures the ability to indicate whether pairs of complex sound patterns are the same or different
Spatial Relations	Measures the ability to match shapes visually
Listening Comprehension	Measures the ability to listen to a short tape-recorded passage and supply the single word missing at the end of the passage
Verbal Analogies	Measures the ability to complete phrases with words that indicate appropriate analogies
Achievement Subtests	
Letter-Word Identification	Measures reading identification skills by identifying isolated letters and words
Passage Comprehension	Measures skill in reading a short passage and identifying a missing key word
Calculation	Measures skill in performing mathematical calculation
Applied Problems	Measures skill in analyzing and solving practical mathematical problems
Dictation	Measures prewriting skills and skill in providing written responses to a variety of questions requiring knowledge of letter forms, spelling, punctuation, capitalization, and word usage
Writing Samples	Measures skill in writing responses to a variety of demands
Science	Measures knowledge in the various areas of biological and physical sciences
Social Studies	Measures knowledge of history, geography, government, economics, and other aspects of social studies
Humanities	Measures knowledge in various areas of art, music, and literature
Word Attack	Measures skills in applying phonic and structural analysis skills to the pronunciation of unfamiliar printed words
Reading Vocabulary	Measures skill in reading words and supplying appropriate meanings
Quantitative Concepts	Measures knowledge of mathematical concepts and vocabulary
Proofing	Measures skill in identifying a mistake in a typed passage and indicating how to correct the mistake
Writing Fluency	Measures skill in formulating and writing simple sentences quickly

Source: Adapted from Examiner's Manuals for the WJ-R

Table 10-9
Cognitive Factors Measured by the WJ-R Subtests

Cognitive Factors	Standard Battery	Supplemental Battery
Long-Term Retrieval	Memory for Names	Visual-Auditory Learning Delayed Recall—Memory for Names Delayed Recall—Visual-Auditory Learning
Short-Term Memory	Memory for Sentences*	Memory for Words* Numbers Reversed*
Processing Speed	Visual Matching	Cross Out
Auditory Processing	Incomplete Words*	Sound Blending* Sound Patterns*
Visual Processing	Visual Closure	Picture Recognition Spatial Relations
Comprehension-Knowledge	Picture Vocabulary	Oral Vocabulary Listening Comprehension* Verbal Analogies*
Fluid Reasoning	Analysis-Synthesis	Concept Formation Spatial Relations Verbal Analogies

*Audiotaped subtest

region, community size, race, educational level, and occupation was used. The norms were weighted to approximate the distribution of the United States population (Woodcock & Mather, 1989).

Psychometric properties   As reported in the test manual, internal consistency reliability estimates for the cognitive ability subtests ranged from .62 to .98, with median reliability coefficients of .69 to .93 for the nine age groups (ages 2, 4, 6, 9, 13, 30–39, 50–59, and 70–79 years). Cluster reliabilities range from .73 to .98, with median reliability coefficients of .81 to .97 (Woodcock & Mather, 1989). For the achievement subtests, internal reliability coefficients range from .75 to .98 with median reliability coefficients of .76 to .93 for the nine age groups. Cluster reliabilities range from .85 to .99, with median reliability coefficients of .91 to .96 (Woodcock & Mather, 1989, 1990). Test-retest reliability except for the Writing Fluency subtest was not reported.

Three concurrent validity studies are reported in the test manuals (Woodcock & Mather, 1989, 1990). These studies related the WJ-R performance of individuals with a mean age of 3 years, 9 years, and 17 years to performance on a number of other ability and achievement measures. The age 3 sample was administered the WJ-R, Boehm Tests of Basic Concepts, Bracken Basic Concept Scale, K-ABC, McCarthy Scales of Children's Abilities, Peabody Picture Vocabulary Test—Revised, and SB:FE. The age 9 sample completed the WJ-R, K-ABC, SB:FE, WISC-R, Basic Achievement Skills Individual Screener

Table 10–10

Curriculum Areas Measured by the WJ-R Subtests

Curriculum Areas	Standard Battery	Supplemental Battery
Reading	Letter-Word Identification Passage Comprehension	Word Attack Reading Vocabulary
Mathematics	Calculation Applied Problems	Quantitative Concepts
Written Language	Dictation Writing Samples	Proofing Writing Fluency 　*Punctuation and Capitalization 　*Spelling 　*Usage 　**Handwriting
Knowledge	Science Social Studies Humanities	

*Composed of selected items from the Dictation and Proofing subtests
**Utilizes the examinee's response on Writing Samples subtest

(BASIS), Kaufman Test of Educational Achievement (KTEA), Peabody Individual Achievement Test (PIAT), and the Wide Range Achievement Test—Revised (WRAT-R). The age 17 sample was given the WJ-R, SB:FE, WAIS-R, BASIS, KTEA, PIAT, and WRAT-R. Correlation coefficients between the WJ-R cognitive battery and the other ability measures were in the .60 to .70 range, except for the preschool level, at which the correlation coefficients were lower (ranging from .48 to .69). Correlations between the WJ-R achievement battery and other achievement measures yielded coefficients in the .60 to .70 range at the school-age level. Interpretation of these findings is hampered, however, by the fact that little detail was provided regarding sample selection, test administration procedures, and sample attrition over the course of the studies. Factor-analytic studies as described by Woodcock (1990) were construed as supportive of the theory underlying the cognitive battery. However, an independent factor analysis of the achievement battery suggested that two factors were present, one of which was relatively small (Sinnett et al., 1993).

Administering the test　Starting points based on the examinee's estimated ability level are provided on several subtests. Other subtests begin with the first item regardless of the examinee's age or estimated ability. Three of the subtests are timed (Visual Memory, Cross Out, and Writing Fluency). Several subtests are administered by means of audiocassette to minimize the possibility of examiner error or deviation from the standardization protocol. The estimated administration time is 40 minutes for the standard cognitive battery and 40 minutes for the supplemental cognitive battery. The estimated administration time for the standard achievement battery is 50–60 minutes.

Scoring and interpreting the test   Items are scored correct or incorrect, though there are exceptions to this general rule. Raw scores for each subtest are converted to age-equivalent scores, grade-equivalent scores, and "W" scores—the last being a "special transformation of the Rasch ability scale" (Woodcock & Mather, 1989, p. 66). W scores are converted to standard scores with a mean of 100 and a standard deviation of 15. Cluster scores are calculated from various combinations of subtests, and discrepancies between individual subtests and clusters are analyzed. A computer scoring system is available for calculating cluster and discrepancy scores.

Interpretation of WJ-R data, like that of data from many other tests, may take many different forms. Individual subtest scores, aptitude scores, and cluster scores may be compared with scores of examinees of similar age to determine whether the examinee is at, above, or below average as compared with peers. Alternatively, the data may be used not to compare the examinee with others but to analyze the examinee's performance with respect to her or his own performance; what discrepancy, if any, exists between measured ability and measured achievement? How do aptitude clusters in areas such as reading, mathematics, written language, and oral language compare? What are the examinee's unique strengths and weaknesses? A guide to facilitate WJ-R interpretation is available (Mather, 1991).

An evaluation   The WJ-R is relatively easy to administer; scoring and interpretation are another matter. The conversion of raw scores to standard scores and the calculation of cluster scores can be difficult and time-consuming. And even after scores on the WJ-R are calculated, exactly what these scores mean is open to question. At this writing, reliability and validity data for the WJ-R are lacking, and although an examiner's manual is available, a technical manual is not. Initial factor-analytic studies are supportive of the factor structure of the WJ-R, though Woodcock himself has observed that most of the reading and written language subtests "have not been studied thoroughly" (Woodcock, 1990, p. 235) within the theoretical framework (that of fluid as opposed to crystallized abilities) in which the test is couched (see also Reschly, 1990; and Ysseldyke, 1990). Additionally, there is a dearth of validity studies to satisfactorily relate WJ-R data to those obtained with more proven instruments.

Other Tests Used in Educational Settings

The Peabody Picture Vocabulary Test—Revised (PPVT-R)

Working in the special education department at the George Peabody College for Teachers, Lloyd Dunn (1959) developed the Peabody Picture Vocabulary Test, which was subsequently revised (Dunn & Dunn, 1981) and is now simply referred to as the PPVT-R. The test consists of pictures that are exposed to the testtaker four at a time. The examiner reads a word, and the testtaker points to (or otherwise indicates by head-nodding, blinking—whatever) the picture that best describes that word.[1] The two parallel forms of the test employ the identical sets of pictures but different stimulus words. The test is most frequently administered individually, though it can be adapted for group administration.

The entire test typically takes less than 15 minutes to administer and can be scored quickly. Raw scores are converted to age equivalents and/or standard scores that have a mean of 100 and a standard deviation of 15. In the older version of the test, raw scores were converted into "mental age" or "IQ" scores, though this practice has been recognized as misleading; the PPVT-R is not an intelligence test but, rather, a test that measures one facet of cognitive ability—receptive (hearing) vocabulary for standard American English. It is also useful as a language assessment tool for people who have expressive language disorders (Maxwell & Wise, 1984) and as a rough measure of scholastic aptitude for individuals with multiple disabilities (Umberger, 1985). The test enjoys rather wide usage, particularly by school psychologists who employ it for screening purposes (Levy, 1982).

The PPVT-R was standardized on a sample of 4,200 children between the ages of 2½ and 18 years. The sample was designed to be nationally representative of geographic location, community size, age, sex, race, and occupation of the primary wage earner according to 1970 U.S. Census data. A second sample of 828 adults (defined here as age 19 or over) was also tested; however, this sample was representative of the U.S. population only with respect to the variables of geographic location, age, sex, and occupation—not race or community size. The standardization sample for the original PPVT had been limited to whites residing in the Nashville, Tennessee, area.

Satisfactory reliability evidence has been reported for the PPVT-R (Bracken et al., 1984; McCallum & Bracken, 1981). A number of studies examining the relationship between the PPVT-R and traditional measures of intelligence such as the Stanford-Binet (Form L-M) and the WISC-R have yielded low to moderate correlation coefficients (Bracken & McCallum, 1981; Bracken & Prasse, 1982; Breen, 1981; Naglieri, 1981; Naglieri & Naglieri, 1981; Prasse & Bracken, 1981; Pound & McChesney, 1982). These types of correlations should be expected once it is acknowledged that, unlike some of the tests with which it has been compared, the PPVT-R is not a test of general intelligence.

Peer Appraisal Techniques

One method of obtaining information about an individual is by asking that individual's peer group to make the evaluation. Techniques employed to obtain such information are referred to as *peer appraisal* methods. A teacher, a supervisor, or some other group leader may be interested in peer appraisals for a variety of reasons. Peer appraisals can help call needed attention to an individual

---

1. The 300 stimulus pictures included in the older version were criticized as being sex-role- and racially stereotyped. Women were depicted only in domestic activities and only one minority member, a black train porter, was included. Dunn and Dunn (1981) attempted to remedy this problem in the revision of the test.

who is experiencing academic, personal, social, or work-related difficulties—difficulties that for whatever reason have not come to the attention of the person in charge. Peer appraisals allow the individual in charge to view individuals in a group from a different perspective, the perspective of people who work, play, socialize, eat lunch, and walk home with the individual being evaluated. In addition to providing information about behavior that is rarely observable, peer appraisals supply information about the group's dynamics: who takes which roles under what conditions. Knowledge of an individual's place within the group is an important aid in guiding the group to optimal efficiency.

Peer appraisal techniques may be used in university settings (Klockars, 1978) as well as in grade school, industrial, and military settings. Such techniques tend to be most useful in settings where the individuals doing the rating have functioned as a group long enough to be able to evaluate each other on specific variables. The nature of peer appraisals may change as a function of changes in the assessment situation and the membership of the group (Veldman & Sheffield, 1979); thus, for example, an individual who is rated as the "shiest" in the classroom can theoretically be quite gregarious—and perhaps even be rated "the rowdiest"—in a peer appraisal undertaken at an after-school center.

One method of peer appraisal that can be employed in elementary school (as well as other) settings is called the "Guess Who?" technique. Brief descriptive sentences (such as "This person is the most friendly") are read or handed out in the form of questionnaires to the class and the children are instructed to "guess who?" Whether negative attributes should be included in the peer appraisal (for example, "This person is the least friendly") must be decided on an individual basis in consideration of the potential negative consequences such an appraisal could have on one member of the group.

The *nominating technique* is a method of peer appraisal in which individuals are asked to select or "nominate" other individuals for various types of activities. A child being interviewed in a psychiatric clinic may be asked, "Who would you most like to go to the Moon with?" as a means of determining which parent or other individual is most important to the child. Members of a police department might be asked, "Who would you most like as your partner for your next tour of duty and why?" as a means of finding out which police officers are seen by their peers as being especially competent or incompetent.

The results of a peer appraisal can be graphically illustrated. One graphic method of organizing such data is called the *sociogram*. Here figures such as circles or squares are drawn to represent different individuals, and lines and arrows are drawn to indicate various types of interaction. At a glance, the sociogram can provide information such as who is popular in the group, who tends to be rejected by the group, and who is relatively "neutral" in the opinion of the group. Nominating techniques have been the most widely researched of the peer appraisal techniques, and they have generally been found to be highly reliable and valid (Kane & Lawler, 1978, 1980). Still, the careful users of such techniques must be aware that an individual's perceptions within a group are constantly changing. As some members leave the group and others join it, the positions and roles the members hold within the group change; new alliances form, and members may be looked at in a new light. It is therefore important to update periodically information obtained from peer appraisal methods so that accurate, up-to-date information is maintained.

Performance, Portfolio, and Authentic Assessment

For many years, "performance assessment" has served as a very broadly defined term that has vaguely referred to any type of assessment that requires the examinee to do more than choose the correct response from a small group of alternatives. Thus, for example, essay questions and the development of an art project would be examples of performance tasks. By contrast, true-false questions and multiple-choice test items would not be considered performance tasks.

Among testing and assessment professionals, contemporary usage of performance-related terms focuses less on the type of item or task involved, and more on the knowledge, skills, and values that the examinee must marshall and exhibit. Additionally, there is a growing tendency to speak of performance tasks and performance assessment in the context of a particular domain of study, with experts in that particular domain of study typically being required to set the evaluation standards. For example, a performance task for an architecture student might be to construct a blueprint for a contemporary home. The overall quality of the student's work, as well as the knowledge, skill, and values inherent in that work, will be judged according to standards set by architects acknowledged by the community of architects to have expertise in the construction of contemporary homes. In keeping with contemporary trends, particularly in educational and work settings, we will define a *performance task* as a work sample designed to elicit representative knowledge, skills, and values from a particular domain of study. *Performance assessment* will be defined as an evaluation of performance tasks according to criteria developed by experts from the domain of study tapped by those tasks.

One of many possible types of performance assessment is portfolio assessment. "Portfolio" is a word with many meanings in different contexts. It may refer to a portable carrying case, most typically used to carry artworks, drawings, maps, and the like. Bankers and investors use it as a shorthand reference to one's financial holdings. In the language of psychological and educational assessment, *portfolio* is synonymous with "work sample." *Portfolio assessment* refers to the evaluation of one's work samples. In many educational settings, dissatisfaction with some more traditional methods of assessment has led to calls for more performance-based evaluations. "Authentic assessment" (discussed following) is one name given to this trend toward more performance-based assessment. When used in the context of like-minded educational programs, portfolio assessment and authentic assessment are techniques designed to target academic teachings to "real world" settings, external to the classroom.

As an example of portfolio assessment, consider how it might be implemented to gauge student progress in a high school algebra course. Students might be instructed to devise their own personal portfolios to illustrate all they have learned about algebra. An important aspect of portfolio assessment is the freedom of the person being evaluated to select the content of the portfolio.

Some students might include narrative accounts of their understanding of various algebraic principles. Other students might reflect in writing on the ways algebra can be used in daily life. Still other students might attempt to make a convincing case that they can do some types of algebra problems that they could not do before taking the course. Throughout, the portfolio may be illustrated with items such as gas receipts (complete with algebraic formulas for calculating mileage), paychecks (complete with formulas used to calculate an hourly wage and taxes), and other items limited only by the individual student's imagination. The illustrations might go from simple to increasingly complex—providing compelling evidence regarding the student's grasp of the material.

The portfolio method has been used to assess giftedness (Hadaway & Marek-Schroer, 1992) and reading (Henk, 1993), among many other characteristics. Portfolios have also been applied at the college and graduate level as devices to assist students with career decisions (Bernhardt et al., 1993). Benefits of the portfolio approach include engaging students in the assessment process, giving them the opportunity to think generatively, and encouraging them to think about learning as an ongoing and integrated process. A key drawback, however, is the penalty such a technique may levy on the noncreative student. Exceptional portfolios are typically creative efforts; a person whose strengths do not lie in creativity may have learned the course material but be unable to adequately demonstrate that learning in such a medium. Another drawback, this one from the other side of the instructor's desk, concerns the evaluation of portfolios. Typically, a great deal of time and thoughtfulness must be devoted to their evaluation; in a lecture class of 300 people, for example, portfolio assessment would be impractical. Also, it is difficult to develop reliable criteria for portfolio assessment given the great diversity of work products. Hence, inter-rater reliability in portfolio assessment can become a problem.

A related form of assessment is authentic assessment, also known as "performance-based assessment" (Baker et al., 1993) and by other names. Christenson (1991, p. 294) views authentic assessment in educational contexts as focusing on the measurement of "students' performance on meaningful tasks [including] tasks that enhance student engagement in schoolwork and are relevant or 'transfer' to intelligent functioning in non-school, real world activities." Authentic assessment of students' writing skills would therefore be based on writing samples rather than on responses to multiple-choice tests (Popham, 1993). Authentic assessment of students' reading would be based on tasks that have to do with reading—preferably "authentic" reading, such as an article in a local newspaper as opposed to a piece contrived especially for the purposes of assessment (Henk, 1993). Students in a college-level psychopathology course might be asked to identify patients' psychiatric diagnoses on the basis of videotaped interviews with the patients.

Authentic assessment is thought to increase student interest and the transfer of knowledge to settings outside the classroom. A drawback is that the assessment might assess prior knowledge and experience, not simply what was learned in the classroom (Henk, 1993). For example, students from homes where there has been a long-standing interest in legislative activities may well do better on an authentic assessment of reading skills using an article on legislative activity. Additionally, authentic skill may inadvertently entail the assessment of some skills that have little to do with classroom learning. For example, authentic assessment of learning a cooking school lesson on fileting fish may be confounded with an assessment of the would-be chef's perceptual-motor skills.

Study Habits, Interests, and Attitudes

Academic performance is the result of a complex interplay of a number of factors. Ability and motivation are inseparable partners in the pursuit of academic success. A number of instruments designed to look beyond ability and toward factors such as study habits, interests, and attitudes have been published. For example, the Study Habits Checklist, designed for use with students in grades 9 through 14, consists of 37 items that assess study habits with respect to note taking, reading material, and general study practices. In the development of the test, potential items were presented for screening to 136 Phi Beta Kappa members at three colleges. This procedure was based on the premise that good students are the best judges of important and effective study techniques (Preston, 1961). The judges were asked to evaluate the items according to their usefulness to students having difficulty with college course material. Although the judges conceded that they did not always engage in these practices themselves, they identified the techniques they deemed to be the most useful in study activities. Standardization for the Checklist took place in 1966, and percentile norms were based on a sample of several thousand high school and college students residing in Pennsylvania. In one validity study, 302 college freshmen who had demonstrated learning difficulties and had been referred to a learning skills center were evaluated with the Checklist. As predicted, it was found that these students demonstrated poor study practices, particularly in the areas of note taking and proper use of study time (Bucofsky, 1971).

If a teacher knows what a child's areas of interest are, instructional activities engaging those interests can be employed. The What I Like to Do Interest Inventory (Meyers, 1975) consists of 150 forced-choice items that assess four areas of interests: academic interests, artistic interests, occupational interests, and interests in leisure time (play) activities. Included in the test materials are suggestions for designing instructional activities that are consonant with the designated areas of interest.

Attitude inventories used in educational settings assess student attitudes toward a variety of school-related factors. Interest in student attitudes is based on the premise that "positive reactions to school may increase the likelihood that students will stay in school, develop a lasting commitment to learning, and use the school setting to advantage" (Epstein & McPartland, 1978, p. 2). Instruments have been developed that assess attitudes in one specific subject area, such as reading (Engin et al., 1976; Heathington & Alexander, 1978; Wallbrown et al., 1978), as well as in several other areas (for example, the Survey of School Attitudes, the Quality of School Life Scales). Other instruments, such as the Survey of Study Habits and Attitudes (SSHA) and the Study Attitudes and Methods Survey, combine an attitude assessment with the assessment of study methods. The SSHA, intended for use in grades 7 through college, consists of

100 items tapping poor study skills and attitudes that could affect academic performance. Two forms, Form H for grades 7–12 and Form C for college, are available, each requiring 20–25 minutes to complete. Students respond to items on the following five-point scale: "Rarely," "Sometimes," "Frequently," "Generally," or "Almost Always." Test items are divided into six areas, which include Delay Avoidance, Work Methods, Study Habits, Teacher Approval, Education Acceptance, and Study Attitudes. The test yields a study skills score, an attitude score, and a total orientation score.

While we are on the subject of study habits, skills, and attitudes, perhaps a self-assessment as we end this chapter will prove useful. How have your own study habits, skills, and attitudes been? Might they be improved in any way? Experiment with your answer to the latter question by employing what you believe to be a more effective approach as you read the next chapter.

PART 4

Personality Assessment

11

Personality Assessment:
Overview and Objective Methods

In a 1950s-vintage oldie-but-goodie rock 'n' roll tune called "Personality," singer Lloyd Price described the subject of his song with the words walk, talk, smile, and charm. In so doing, Price used the term *personality* the way most people tend to use it. For laypeople, "personality" refers to components of an individual's makeup that can elicit positive or negative reactions from others. The individual who consistently tends to elicit positive reactions from others is thought to have a "good" personality. The individual who consistently tends to elicit not-so-good reactions from others is thought to have a "bad" personality or, perhaps worse yet, "no personality." Descriptive epithets such as "aggressive personality," "cold personality," and "warm personality" also enjoy widespread usage.

When behavioral scientists seek to define and describe personality, the terms they use are more rigorous than those describing simple social skills and are more precise than all-encompassing adjectives. The search has led to the serious study of constructs such as personality traits, personality types, and personality states.

Defining and Measuring "Personality"

Dozens of different definitions of "personality" exist in the psychology literature (Allport, 1937). Some definitions appear to be all-inclusive in nature. For example, McClelland (1951, p. 69) defined personality as "the most adequate conceptualization of a person's behavior in all its detail." Menninger (1953, p. 23) defined it as "the individual as a whole, his height and weight and love and hates and blood pressure and reflexes; his smiles and hopes and bowed legs and enlarged tonsils. It means all that anyone is and that he is trying to become."

Some definitions rely heavily on a particular aspect of the person, such as the individual's phenomenal field (Goldstein, 1963) or the individual as a social being (Sullivan, 1953). At an extreme end of the spectrum of definitions are those proposed by theorists who have scrupulously avoided definition. For example, Byrne (1974, p. 26) characterized the entire area of personality psychology as "psychology's garbage bin in that any research which doesn't fit other existing categories can be labeled 'personality.'" Deploring personality theorists who avoid defining their subject matter, Dahlstrom (1970) observed that

> Some sidestep the issue, apparently to satisfy a demand for ostensive definitions. Thus, Sarason states, "We shall consider personality as an area of investigation rather than as an entity, real or hypothetical" (1966, p. 15). While such a definition makes it easy to point to the definienda ("I am studying what the personologist over there is doing"), it obviously leaves the central definition itself unformulated. (p. 2)

In their widely read and authoritative textbook *Theories of Personality*, Hall and Lindzey (1970, p. 9) wrote that "it is our conviction that *no substantive definition of personality can be applied with any generality*" and that "*personality is defined by the particular empirical concepts which are a part of the theory of personality employed by the observer*" [emphasis in the original]. They went on, "If this seems an unsatisfactory definition to the reader, let him take consolation in the thought that in the pages to follow he will encounter a number of specific definitions any one of which will become his if he chooses to adopt that particular theory" (p. 9).[1]

Traits, Types, and States

At this point, you might well ask, "If venerable authorities like Hall and Lindzey aren't going to define personality, who are Cohen, Swerdlik, and Phillips to think that they can do it?" Our response is to formulate a middle-of-the-road definition: one that represents a middle ground between the all-inclusive "whole person" types of definitions and the nondefinition types of definitions. We define *personality* as *an individual's unique constellation of psychological traits and states.* Accordingly, *personality assessment* entails the measurement of traits and states.

Personality traits   The vocabulary of personality assessment relies heavily on trait terms (such as "warm," "reserved," "trusting," and "imaginative"). If you have taken a course in personality theory you are probably aware that just as there is no consensus about the definition of personality, no consensus exists regarding the word *trait*. Theorists such as Gordon Allport (1937) have tended

---

1. Hall and Lindzey (1970) did point out that important theoretical differences underlie the various different types of definitions of "personality" that exist. After Allport (1937), Hall and Lindzey (1970, p. 8) noted, for example, that a distinction can be made between *biosocial* and *biophysical* types of definitions. *Biosocial* definitions equate personality with the social stimulus value of the individual. *Biophysical* definitions do not take account of the social stimulus value of the individual but are solely rooted within the individual.

to view personality traits as real physical entities that are "bona fide mental structures in each personality" (p. 289). For Allport, a trait is a "generalized and focalized neuropsychic system (peculiar to the individual) with the capacity to render many stimuli functionally equivalent, and to initiate and guide consistent (equivalent) forms of adaptive and expressive behavior" (p. 295). Robert Holt (1971) noted that there "*are* real structures inside people that determine their behavior in lawful ways" (p. 6), and he went on to conceptualize these structures as changes in brain chemistry that might occur as a result of learning: "learning causes submicroscopic structural changes in the brain, probably in the organization of its biochemical substance" (p. 7). Raymond Cattell (1950) also conceptualized traits as "mental structures," but for him "structure" did not necessarily imply actual physical status.

Our own preference is to shy away from definitions that elevate *trait* to the status of physical existence. We view psychological traits as attributions made in an effort to identify threads of consistency in behavioral patterns. In this context, a definition of *trait* offered by Guilford (1959, p. 6) has great appeal: "any distinguishable, relatively enduring way in which one individual varies from another."

Inherent in this relatively simple definition are commonalities with the writings of other personality theorists such as Allport (1937), Cattell (1950, 1965), and Eysenck (1961). The word *distinguishable* indicates that behaviors labeled with different trait terms are actually different from one another. For example, a behavior labeled "friendly" should be distinguishable from a behavior labeled "rude." The *context,* the situation in which the behavior is displayed, is important in applying trait terms to behaviors. A behavior present in one context may be labeled with one trait term, but the same behavior exhibited in another context may be better described using another trait term. For example, if we observe someone involved in a lengthy, apparently interesting conversation, we would observe the context before drawing any conclusions about the person's traits. A person talking with a friend over lunch may be demonstrating friendliness, whereas a person talking during a wedding may be considered rude. Thus, the trait term selected by an observer is dependent both on the behavior itself and on the context in which that behavior appears. Behavior and its context may be observed using a wide variety of methods, from direct observation (watching the person with a variety of peers, hearing the person express attitudes about others, watching the person at work or at school) to an analysis of responses on a self-report questionnaire (on which the individual may describe relationships and interactions with others).

In his definition of trait, Guilford did not assert that traits represent enduring ways in which individuals vary from one another; rather, he used the term *relatively enduring way.* The modifier "relatively" serves to emphasize that exactly how a particular trait manifests itself is, at least to some extent, situation-dependent. For example, a "violent" parolee may generally be prone to behave in a rather subdued way with her parole officer and much more violently in the presence of her family and friends. John may be viewed as "dull" and "cheap" by his wife but as "charming" and "extravagant" by his secretary, business associates, and others he is keenly interested in impressing. Allport (1937) addressed the issue of cross-situational consistency of traits—or lack of it—as follows:

> Perfect consistency will never be found and must not be expected. . . . People may be ascendant and submissive, perhaps submissive only towards those individuals bearing traditional symbols of authority and prestige; and towards everyone else aggressive and domineering. . . . The ever changing environment raises now one trait and now another to a state of active tension. (p. 330)

Returning to our elaboration of Guilford's definition, note that *trait* is described as a *way in which one individual varies from another*. Here it is important to emphasize that the attribution of a trait term is always a *relative* phenomenon. For instance, some behavior described as "patriotic" may differ greatly from other behavior also described as "patriotic." There are no absolute standards. In describing an individual as "patriotic," we are, in essence, making an unstated comparison with the degree of patriotic behavior that could reasonably be expected to be emitted by the average person.

Research demonstrating a lack of cross-situational consistency in traits such as honesty (Hartshorne & May, 1928), punctuality (Dudycha, 1936), conformity (Hollander & Willis, 1967), attitude toward authority (Burwen & Campbell, 1957), and introversion/extraversion (Newcomb, 1929) are the types of studies typically cited by Mischel (1968, 1973, 1977, 1979) and others who have been critical of the predominant role of the concept of traits in personality theory. Such critics may also allude to the fact that some undetermined portion of behavior exhibited in public may be governed more by societal expectations and cultural role restrictions than by an individual's personality traits (see Barker, 1963; Goffman, 1963). Research designed to shed light on the primacy of individual differences as opposed to situational factors in behavior is methodologically complex (see Golding, 1975), and the verdict as to the primacy of the trait or the situation is far from being in (see Moskowitz & Schwartz, 1982).

Personality types   Having defined personality as a unique constellation of traits and states, we might define a personality *type* as a constellation of traits and states that is similar in pattern to one identified category of personality within a taxonomy of personalities. For assistance in elaborating on this definition of type, we can look to the work of Isabel Briggs Myers and Katharine C. Briggs, authors of the Myers-Briggs Type Indicator (Myers & Briggs, 1943/1962), a test inspired by the theoretical typology of Carl Jung (1923). An assumption guiding the development of this test was that people exhibit definite preferences in the way that they perceive or become aware of, and judge or arrive at conclusions about, people, events, situations, and ideas. According to Myers (1962, p. 1), these differences in perception and judging result in "corresponding differences in their reactions, in their interests, values, needs, and motivations, in what they do best, and in what they like to do." For example, in one study designed to better understand the personality of chess players, the Myers-Briggs Type Indicator was administered to 2,165 chess players (including masters and senior masters). The chess players were found to be significantly more introverted, intuitive, and thinking (as opposed to feeling) than members of the general

Table 11-1
Two Typologies: Adler and Hippocrates

Adlerian Type	Corresponding Type of Hippocrates
Ruling type: This type of person exhibits high activity but in an asocial way; typical of "bossy" people and, in the extreme, homicidal people.	Choleric type
Getting type: This type of person has low social interest and a moderate activity level; typical of people who are constantly depending on others for support.	Phlegmatic or sluggish type
Avoiding type: This type of person has very low social interest combined with a very low activity level; method of coping is primarily avoidance.	Melancholic type
Good Man type: This type of person has high social interest combined with a high activity level; she or he lives life to the fullest and is very much concerned with the well-being of her or his fellow human beings.	Sanguine type

Source: Adler (1927/1965)

population. The investigator also found masters to be more judging than would be expected in the general population (Kelly, 1985).

Whereas traits are frequently discussed as if they were something individuals possess, types are more clearly only descriptions of people—not something presumed to be inherent in them. Hypotheses and notions about various *types* of people have appeared in the literature through the ages. Perhaps the most primitive personality typology was the humoral theory of Hippocrates (see Chapter 2). Centuries later, the personality theorist Alfred Adler would differentiate personality types in a way that was somewhat reminiscent of Hippocrates (Table 11–1). Adler's personality types represented different combinations of social interests and varying degrees of vigor with which they attacked life's problems. Adler (1933/1964, p. 127) never developed a formal system to measure these types, since he realized that they were generalizations, useful primarily for teaching.

Personality states The word *state* has been used in at least two distinctly different ways in the personality assessment literature. In one usage, a personality state is an inferred psychodynamic disposition designed to convey the dynamic quality of id, ego, and superego in perpetual conflict. Assessment of these psychodynamic dispositions may be made through the use of various psychoanalytic techniques such as free association, word association, symbolic analysis of interview material, dream analysis, and analysis of slips of the tongue, accidents, jokes, and forgetting.

Presently, a more popular usage of the word *state*—and the one to which we make reference in the discussion that follows—refers to the transitory exhibition of some personality trait. Put another way, the use of the word *trait* presupposes a relatively enduring behavioral predisposition, whereas the term *state* is indicative of a relatively temporary predisposition (Chaplin et al., 1988). Thus, for example, Sally may be described as being "in an anxious state" before her midterms, though no one who knows Sally well would describe her as "an anxious person."

Measuring personality states amounts, in essence, to a search for and an assessment of the strength of traits that are relatively transitory in nature and/or fairly situation-specific. Relatively few existing personality tests seek to distinguish traits from states. Seminal work in this area was done by Charles D. Spielberger and his associates. These researchers developed a number of personality inventories designed to distinguish various states from traits. Included here are the State-Trait Anxiety Inventory (Spielberger et al., 1970), the State-Trait Anxiety Inventory for Children (Spielberger et al., 1973), the State-Trait Anger Scale (Spielberger et al., 1980a), and the Test Anxiety Inventory, Research Edition (Spielberger et al., 1980b).

In the manual for the State-Trait Anxiety Inventory (STAI), for example, we find that *state anxiety* refers to a transitory experience of tension because of a particular situation. By contrast, *trait anxiety* or "anxiety proneness" refers to a relatively stable or enduring personality characteristic. The STAI test items consist of short descriptive statements, and subjects are instructed to indicate either (1) how they feel "right now" or "at this moment" (and to indicate the intensity of the feeling), or (2) how they "generally feel" (and to record the frequency of the feeling). The test-retest reliability coefficients reported in the manual are consistent with the theoretical premise that trait anxiety is the more enduring characteristic, whereas state anxiety is transitory; test-retest reliability coefficients for the *state*-anxiety measure over a one-hour interval were .33 and .16 for males and females, respectively, and the test-retest reliability coefficients for the *trait*-anxiety measure for males and females were .84 and .76, respectively. Similar trends were observed in the test-retest reliability coefficients over longer intervals.

Measuring Personality

Why measure personality? Clinicians and counselors seeking to identify their clients' problem areas and/or to confirm their own clinical hunches may use a test of personality to supplement interviews and other assessment tools. The test results not only may prove insightful as stand-alone data but also may be useful as a stimulus to further investigation of previously unexplored or under-explored areas. The test data may also prove useful in identifying strengths that can be drawn on and weaknesses that may be remediable within the context of a planned psychotherapeutic or behavioral intervention. In school situations, personality test data can point the way to nonacademic factors that may be acting to impede academic performance. In a private practice situation, personality test data may prove useful with respect to decisions regarding specific modes of intervention. For example, if there are strong indications that the assessee is a social isolate, these as well as other data should factor into a decision regarding the timing and appropriateness of group treatment.

Beyond the clinical arena, personality tests are widely used in occupational contexts. Vocational counselors administer such tests and on the basis of the resulting profile, advise examinees as to the lines of work in which they might best find their "niche." Depending on the entire record as well as other factors, a vocational counselor might advise a client with a decided preference for social isolation against going into a career that entails daily interpersonal contact (such as sales or tending bar) and urge the individual instead to consider occupations more along the lines of computer programming or copy editing.

Psychological research is another major area in which tests of personality are used. Here there are many possible subcategorizations, but for our purposes, we will dichotomize all such applications into (1) studies of individual psychological variables and (2) studies of psychological theories. The researcher intent on learning about every possible facet and correlate of social isolationism through the use of personality tests exemplifies how personality tests might be used to study individual psychological variables. A researcher who has developed an "interpersonal theory of personality" might also use personality tests to test hypotheses derived from that theory. Hypotheses might concern the number of postulated primary, secondary, and tertiary personality dimensions there are, whether these personality dimensions are hierarchical in nature, and so forth. Personality test data may be used to research individual variables and to develop theory in many different ways. For example, suppose you subscribed to a theory that predicted that social isolates—let's refer to them as "introverts"—learned certain types of tasks more quickly than more socially oriented, gregarious people—let's refer to the latter group as "extraverts." Your classmate subscribes to another theory, which has it that the key to learning is not social isolationism or introversion-extraversion but, rather, drive level; according to the latter view, people with higher drive level learn more quickly. One way you might go about settling your dispute is to administer a test of drive level, a test of introversion/extraversion, and a learning task. Analysis of the learning curves for the subjects should provide insight into the question—provided, as Burisch (1984a) reminds us, the instruments used to gauge introversion/extraversion and drive level are satisfactory:

> I recall trying to make sense out of the controversy between Hans Eysenck and Kenneth Spence during much of the 1960s on the question of whether "drive level" or "introversion-extraversion" governs speed of conditioning in human subjects. Drive level was almost always operationalized by Taylor's Manifest Anxiety Scale, introversion-extraversion by one scale of the Maudsley Personality Inventory. Even to a neophyte such as myself, it seemed that the two instruments were much too fragile a basis for carrying much weight in the argument. (p. 216)

Burisch's concerns about instruments of personality assessment being "too fragile" for carrying much weight in an argument raise another important question: What makes a "good" personality test? You know from your reading of previous chapters that at least a partial answer to this question is going to have to do with the psychometric concepts of reliability and validity. But let's take the answer "validity" one step further and ask in this context, "Validity with respect to what?" What do we need to know, for example, about a hypothetical personality test, one we'll call the "Unresolved Oedipal Conflict Scale" (UnOCS); against what criterion or criteria should we judge scores on the UnOCS? And since the notion of an "unresolved Oedipal conflict" is unique to psychoanalytic theory and not a universally accepted reality, must we also require evidence of its existence before entertaining notions about the validity of the UnOCS? These types of issues, among others (such as the use to which the test will be put), must be raised in the context of the evaluation of any test.

Methods of personality assessment   Take a moment at this juncture to think about how you might go about developing and validating a paper-and-pencil test of personality. Jot down those ideas before continuing to read.

- What is the purpose of the personality test you've developed? What is it designed to do?

- Is it to be used to measure traits, types, states, or some combination thereof?

- Is it to be used to gauge the relative strength of various traits? If so, which traits are to be measured?

- Is it to be used to distinguish people on the basis of the healthiness of their personality? Is it to be used to distinguish people on the basis of the suitability of their personalities for a particular kind of work? Is it to be used in general research on personality?

- What kinds of items would your test contain? How would you decide on the content and wording of these items? Would you, for example, rely on a particular theory of personality in devising these items? Or would you rely on no particular theory but, rather, on your own life experiences?

- In writing your test items, did you use a true-false format or some other format? Will the items of your test be grouped in any particular order?

- How might you convincingly demonstrate that your test measures what it purports to measure?

Like you, would-be authors of personality tests have had to struggle with these questions and dozens more like them. Some test authors have relied on theories of personality in constructing their test items, whereas others have steered clear of personality theory and have used more empirical methods. Some test authors have devised forms designed to take a general "inventory" of personality, and others have devised forms to measure specific aspects of it, such as the strength of a particular trait. Paper-and-pencil measures of personality differ with respect to the rationale of the measurement model that underlies the test construction. Measures of personality can have their bases in self-report, behavioral observation, or some other variety of response, including verbal, nonverbal, and physiological responses. Items or tasks on paper-and-pencil-type tests to measure personality can be objective (in which the testtaker must typically select one answer from two or more provided) and/or projective (a term that is explained below and taken up in detail in the following chapter). You know from your experience with ability tests what an objective-type item is (true-false, multiple-choice, etc.), as compared with, say, an essay item. Objective measures of personality employ item formats that are identical or similar to those found in many objective ability tests (true-false, multiple-choice, etc.). The difference, of course, is that whereas a "True" response on an ability test with a true-false format is scored as correct or incorrect, a "True" response on a personality test is scored with regard to the personality characteristics the test is designed to measure and/or related variables (such as whether the testtaker is responding in a purposeful way to the test items). Similar to their use in ability tests, the use of objective items in personality measures carries with it many advantages: (1) the items can be answered fairly quickly, so testtakers can be administered many items, covering varied aspects of the trait or traits the test was designed to assess, in a relatively short period of time; (2) the items, if well written, require little explanation, making them suitable for group administration or for independent computer-assisted administration; and (3) objective items are amenable to quick and reliable scoring by machine, by hand (usually with the aid of a template held over the scoring sheet), or by computer.

Most objective tests of personality rely on the testtaker's own self-report about what he or she likes or dislikes, does or doesn't do, thinks or doesn't think, and so forth. Assuming testtakers have reasonably accurate insight into their own thinking and behavior, and assuming they are motivated to respond to test items honestly, self-report measures can prove to be extremely valuable in learning about the people being evaluated; after all, under ideal circumstances, who knows testtakers better than testtakers themselves? Further, self-report under such circumstances takes the burden of making huge inferences about the testtaker off the test user. Still, as we point out in this chapter's *Close-up* (see pages 392–393), self-report measures also have their share of limitations.

To avoid some of the pitfalls of self-report measures, evaluators and researchers use other types of measures, including situational performance measures, behavioral assessment by trained observers, and rating scales completed by friends, family, employers, teachers, or other people who know or have contact with the person being evaluated. Another alternative or adjunct to self-report measures are methods designed to measure personality indirectly. One such group of measures relies on bodily indices (such as heart rate, electrical conductivity of the skin, and so forth) to make inferences about the mental state of the person being evaluated. Thus, a person might respond to test questions wired to a device that is constantly recording one or more types of bodily activity, much like an examination conducted with the aid of a so-called lie detector. Inferences are then made about psychological variables on the basis of patterns of bodily response to the test items. Personality assessment by means of situational performance tests, behavioral observation, rating scales, physiological means, and other methods are discussed in Chapter 13.

Other techniques that avoid many of the measurement-related problems associated with self-report—but have no shortage of their own measurement-related problems—are called projective methods. As we will see in Chapter 12, the testtaker's task when administered a projective test is to respond in some fashion to some ambiguous stimulus (such as an inkblot, a picture, a word, or an incomplete sentence). Because there are typically few, if any, limits set on the nature of the testtaker's response, the response is thought to be indicative of the testtaker's unique personality structure. The pattern of responses to the test may then be used to formulate a picture or profile of the testtaker's personality.

We focus now on objective measures of personality and the four general ways such measures have been developed. Be forewarned that these four general approaches go by different names in different sources and that there is even some question as to the number of distinctly different test development models or strategies that exist (Gynter & Gynter, 1976). We refer to the four approaches as (1) logical or content test construction, (2) factor-analytic test construction, (3) test construction by empirical criterion keying, and (4) the theoretical approach to test construction. As you will see, these approaches are not necessarily mutually exclusive. Different aspects of a test's development may contain features of each. Prospective items for a test could be selected, for example, on a rational/logical basis and/or a theoretical basis. The selected items could then be arranged into scales on the basis of factor analysis.

Logical or Content Test Construction

One strategy of personality-test construction has been variously referred to as the "logical," "content," "intuitive," or "rational" approach. Here the personality inventory comprises items that logically, intuitively, or rationally seem to belong in the test. Inherent in the logical approach to personality-test construction is the assumption that the test constructor has indeed been logical in the selection of test items. As an adjunct to his or her own logic or intuition, the test developer frequently employs aids such as textbooks, clinical records, experimental data, and conversations with colleagues or experts.

The first formal efforts to measure personality employed the logical approach to test construction. The Personal Data Sheet (Woodworth, 1917), later known as the Woodworth Psychoneurotic Inventory, was an early test of personality designed to screen World War I recruits for personality and adjustment problems. The test items tapped self-report of fears, sleep disorders, and other problems deemed to be symptomatic of a trait called psychoneuroticism; the greater the number of such problems, the more psychoneurotic the respondent was presumed to be.

In general, the logically constructed test has a certain appeal to testtakers, since the content is so straightforward and so directly related to the objective of the test. The respondent typically feels more in control of the information he or she is revealing in a content-constructed device than, for example, on an indirect measure of personality such as the Rorschach Inkblot Test. Logically constructed tests have all the drawbacks previously discussed of self-report measures in general. A classic example of a content-constructed instrument—one that is still in use more than 40 years after its development—is the Mooney Problem Checklist (Mooney & Gordon, 1950).

The Mooney Problem Checklist

Items on this checklist were developed after evaluating statements of problems obtained from approximately four thousand high school students, as well as on the basis of counseling interviews and a review of clinical records. The Checklist

Limitations of Self-Report

Many personality inventories rely on the self-report of the testtaker. Asking testtakers about themselves can produce insightful information about the individual's thought processes, including motives and feelings. But the self-report approach to personality assessment is not without its limitations. Consider what would happen if employers were to rely on job applicants' representations concerning their personality and their suitability for a particular job. They might well receive universally glowing references—and still not hire the most suitable personnel. This is so because many job applicants, as well as other people in a wide variety of other contexts—contexts as diverse as singles bars, custody hearings, and high school reunions—attempt to "fake good" in their presentation of themselves to other people. The other side of the "faking good" coin is, as you might expect, "faking bad." Litigants in civil actions who claim injury may seek high awards to compensate them for their alleged pain, suffering, and emotional distress—all of which may be exaggerated and dramatized for the benefit of a judge and jury. The accused in a criminal action may view time in a mental institution as preferable to time in prison (or capital punishment) and strategically choose an insanity defense—with accompanying behavior and claims to make such a defense as believable as possible. A homeless person who prefers the environs of a mental hospital to that of the street may attempt to "fake bad" on tests and in interviews if failure to do so will result in discharge. In the days when a military draft existed, it was not uncommon for draft resisters to attempt to be deferred from their obligation to serve on psychiatric grounds—and many such people went to great lengths to "fake bad" when assessed.

Consideration of situations such as those described above can help you to appreciate that a problem inherent in personality testing and assessment—one that is particularly acute with respect to self-report methods—is the problem of "seeing through" assessees' attempts to present themselves in a favorable or an unfavorable light. *Impression management* is a term social psychologists use to describe the behavior of attempting to manipulate others' impressions through "the selective exposure of some information (it may be false information) . . . coupled with suppression of [other] information" (Braginsky et al., 1969, p. 51).

In the process of personality assessment, it is possible for examinees to employ any number of impression management strategies for any number of reasons. Del Paulhus (1984, 1986, 1990; Paulhus & Levitt, 1987) and his colleagues have explored impression management in testtaking as well as the related phenomena of *enhancement* (the claiming of positive attributes), *denial* (the repudiation of negative attributes), and *self-deception*—"the tendency to give favorably biased but honestly held self-descriptions" (Paulhus & Reid, 1991, p. 307; see also Flett et al., 1988, and Gur & Sackheim, 1979). Testtakers who consistently engage in impression management are exhibiting, in the broadest sense of the term, a "response style" (Jackson & Messick, 1962).

Also known as "response set," *response style* refers to the tendency to respond to a question in some characteristic manner regardless of the content of the question. For example, some individuals are more apt to answer "Yes" or "True" than "No" or "False" on short-answer tests. Although there are those who consider the notion of a response style to be a myth (Rorer, 1965), the vast amount of research done in this area suggests it is a reality. The following table contains a sampling of some of the different response styles psychologists have distinguished. Nunnally (1978) made the point that response styles may themselves be important personality measures:

A Sampling of Response Styles

Response style name	Explanation: A tendency to respond on a test . . .
Socially desirable responding	to present oneself in a favorable (read "socially acceptable" or "socially desirable") light
Acquiescence	to agree with whatever is presented
Nonacquiescence	to disagree with whatever is presented
Deviance	to make unusual or uncommon responses
Extreme	to make extreme, as opposed to middle, ratings on a rating scale
Gambling/cautiousness	to guess—or not guess—when in doubt

Some of the response styles that have been catalogued sound like important personality traits, e.g., cautiousness, acquiescence, and extremeness. To the extent that such stylistic variables can be measured independently of content relating to nonstylistic variables or to the extent that they can somehow be separated from the variance of other traits, they might prove useful as measures of personality traits. (p. 660)

Some personality tests contain items that are part of the test for the express purpose of identifying the respondent who has a tendency to give unusual or uncommon responses. Thus, for example, a "True" response to an item like "I recently vacationed in downtown Baghdad" might lead the test scorer/interpreter to raise some questions about the findings: Did the testtaker understand the instructions? Did the testtaker take the test seriously? Did the testtaker respond "True" to all the items on the test? Did the testtaker respond randomly to items on the test? Analysis of the entire protocol might help to provide additional answers.

Ultimately, a response to a single item on an objective personality measure can be interpreted in many different ways, and is most typically interpreted according to the pattern of testtaker responses to the test as a whole. Thus, for example, a response of "True" to a true-false item such as "I tend to enjoy meeting new people" may, at best, tell us that the testtaker would have us believe that she or he tends to enjoy meeting new people. In truth, we do not know whether the testtaker (a) veritably does enjoy meeting new people, (b) honestly believes that he or she enjoys meeting new people but in reality does not enjoy meeting new people (i.e., the testtaker has poor insight), (c) does not enjoy meeting new people but would have us believe that she or he does, or (d) did not even really read the item, is not taking the test seriously, and is randomly marking items either true or false.

Some testtakers, because of prevailing medical or psychological conditions at the time of testing, simply do not have sufficient insight into their own thinking to answer self-report questions in a way that will be most beneficial to them. The other side of the coin is the testtaker who has a great deal of self-insight and conveys it quite expertly on the self-report measure. For such testtakers, on the basis of self-report measure alone, Burisch (1984a) argued that "clinicians cannot tell patients anything they do not already know" (p. 225). Well, Burisch may be overstating the case. Clinicians may well be able to accomplish that feat by looking at various patterns or clusters of response. The more compelling question for us is "How much can the clinician tell about the patient on the basis of self-ratings alone?" And in the context of our discussion of impression management strategies, we might rephrase that question: "How much can the clinician *really* tell about the patient on the basis of self-rating alone?"

items relate to emotional functioning in areas such as home and family; boy / girl relations; courtship and marriage; morals and religion; school / occupation; economic security; social skills and recreation; and health and physical development. Respondents are instructed to underline all problems that are of concern to them and to circle those items that "are of most concern."

There are four forms of the instrument, each appropriate for administration to a different age group from junior high school through adult. The test may be administered individually or in groups. Test-retest reliability coefficients for the various forms of the Mooney Checklist have been found to be relatively high, suggesting consistency in the way that testtakers perceive their problems over time. The test results have been found to be especially useful in counseling situations, where they may be used as a kind of catalyst to treatment and as a pre- and postmeasure of the effectiveness of treatment.

Factor-Analytic Test Construction

Recall from our discussion in Chapter 6 that factor analysis is a data-reduction method. It has been used as an aid in personality research designed to identify major traits, cognitive styles, and other factors in personality. Factor analysis has also been used to create tests to measure personality factors. Here we focus on the use of this statistical technique to identify the minimum number of variables or "factors" that account for the intercorrelations in a number of observed phenomena. To illustrate, let's use an example in which the "number of observed phenomena" are a multitude of colors. Let's suppose that you want to paint your apartment but have no idea what color would go best with your "early undergraduate" decor. You go to the local paint stores in your area and obtain free card samples of every shade of color paint known to humanity—thousands of color samples. Let's further suppose you undertook a "factor analysis" of these thousands of color samples—that is, you attempted to identify the minimum number of variables or factors that account for the intercorrelations between all of these colors. You would discover that, accounting for the intercorrelations, there existed three factors (which might be labeled "primary" factors) and four more factors (which might be labeled "secondary" or "second-order" factors), the latter set of factors being combinations of the first set of factors. Since all colors can be reduced to three primary colors and their combinations, the three primary factors would correspond to the three primary colors, red, yellow, and blue (which you might christen factor R, factor Y, and factor B), and the four secondary or second-order factors would correspond to all the possible combinations that could be made from the primary factors (factors RY, RB, YB, and RYB).

The paint-sample illustration might be helpful to keep in mind as we review how factor analysis is used in test construction and personality assessment. In a way analogous to the factoring of all those shades of paint into three primary colors, think of all personality traits being factored into what one psychologist referred to as "the most important individual differences in human transactions" (Goldberg, 1993, p. 26). After all of the factoring is over and the dust has settled, how many personality-related terms do you think would remain? Scholars disagree on the answer to that question. To highlight some of the relevant issues, let's briefly look at two tests that were developed on the basis of factor-analytic strategies.

The 16 PF

Just as you might have an idea that you wish to analyze all colors into their primary factors, so the notion Raymond Bernard Cattell had when he set out to construct a personality test was the analysis of all personality traits into what might be called primary or "source" traits. Construction of the test items began with a look at the previous research by Allport and Odbert (1936), which suggested that there were more than 18,000 personality trait names and terms in the English language. Of these, however, only about a quarter were "real traits of personality" or words and terms that designated "generalized and personalized determining tendencies—consistent and stable modes of an individual's adjustment to his environment . . . not . . . merely temporary and specific behavior" (Allport, 1937, p. 306). Cattell added to this list some trait names and terms employed in the professional psychology and psychiatric literature and then had judges rate "just distinguishable" differences between all the words (Cattell, 1957). The result was a reduction in the size of the list to 171 trait names and terms. College students were asked to rate their friends with respect to these trait names and terms, and the factor-analyzed results of that rating further reduced the number of names and terms to 36, which Cattell referred to as "surface traits." Still more research indicated that 16 basic dimensions or "source traits" could be distilled (Table 11–2).

The culmination of this pioneering research program that had begun in the mid-1940s (Cattell, 1946, 1947, 1948a, 1948b) was the publication of the Sixteen Personality Factor (16 PF) Questionnaire in 1949. Revisions of the test were published in 1956, 1962, 1968, and 1993.[2]

The most recent revision of the 16 PF, the fifth edition (Cattell, Cattell, & Cattell, 1993), contains updated language, items that were reviewed for potential bias, and new normative data based on over 2,500 testtakers selected to reflect the 1990 U.S. Census. The fifth edition of the test contains 185 items and is designed for use with people at least 16 years old who can read at a fifth-grade level. Special forms of the 16 PF for use with exceptional testtakers (including people with limited reading skills or visual handicaps) and children

---

2. The astute reader will quickly notice that much of the discussion of the 16 PF is based on sources that predate the 1993 revision of the test. Revisions to the 16 PF have not been directed at the basic structure of the test but, rather, have focused on clarification of items and the reduction of bias. Furthermore, earlier editions of the test continue to be actively marketed. Thus, we follow the approach taken in the 16 PF literature in considering pre-1993 sources to be of continued relevance in discussing the 1993 revision of the test. Still, because fully 24% of the items in the fifth edition are new (Russell & Karol, 1994), we eagerly look forward to the collection and publication of data specific to this revision of the 16 PF.

Table 11-2
Factors of the 16 PF

Factor	Low Score	High Score
Warmth	Reserved	Warm, cooperative
Reasoning	Dull	Bright
Emotional stability	Affected by feelings, undemonstrative	Emotionally stable, calm
Dominance	Obedient, submissive	Assertive
Liveliness	Sober, serious	Enthusiastic
Rule-consciousness	Disregards rules, undependable	Conscientious
Social boldness	Shy	Venturesome
Sensitivity	Tough-minded, realistic, vigorous	Tender-minded, sensitive
Vigilance	Trusting	Suspicious
Abstractedness	Practical, conventional	Imaginative
Privateness	Forthright, naive	Sophisticated, shrewd
Apprehension	Self-assured	Guilt-prone, timid
Openness to change	Conservative, traditional	Experimenting
Self-reliance	Group-dependent	Self-sufficient, resourceful
Perfectionism	Uncontrolled	Controlled
Tension	Relaxed	Tense

and adolescents have also been developed (Porter et al., 1992), as have translations into German, Spanish, and Japanese.

One goal of the most recent revision of the 16 PF was to improve the psychometric quality of the test. One meta-analysis of published research on prior versions of the test estimated internal consistency to be .52, which was considered acceptable given that the test's factor scales contained only 12 items each on average (Schuerger et al., 1989); the new edition has a somewhat higher level of average internal consistency, at .74 (Russell & Karol, 1994). The test-retest reliability of older versions of the test over periods of one to five years was estimated to be .63 using meta-analysis (Schuerger et al., 1989). The fifth edition has average test-retest reliability of .80 over a two-week period and .70 over two months (Russell & Karol, 1994).

Over the years, perhaps the most controversial aspect of the 16 PF is its construct validity, and more specifically, the factor structure of the test. Studies with large numbers of subjects of different ages and nationalities, with various forms of the test, suggest that the 16 PF is indeed measuring 16 factors—give or take a factor or two; studies may find 14, 15, or 17 factors with a particular sample (Cattell, 1986; Cattell & Krug, 1986; Lichtenstein et al., 1986).

Cattell's assumption that his test, as well as any other broad-spectrum test of personality, measures 16 factors has not gone unchallenged (Cattell & Krug, 1986; Eysenck, 1985, 1991; Goldberg, 1993). Some have argued that the 16 PF may be measuring somewhat fewer than 16 factors, because several of the factors are substantially intercorrelated (Bloxom, 1978). Eysenck (1947, 1991) has argued that as few as three factors are sufficient to describe personality. Other theorists have variously argued that three, four, five, or six factors can best describe personality (Church & Burke, 1994). At least four different five-factor models exist (Johnson & Ostendorf, 1993; Costa & McCrae, 1992a), and Waller and Zavala (1993) argued for a seven-factor model. In general, the trend among personality theorists has been toward what one might call "an economy of factors" when describing the factors that purportedly describe personality.

How and why can such extensive disagreement about the number of factors in personality exist? The variables entered into the factor analysis, and the range of personality attributes tapped by a test's items, will, of course, affect the factors that will be identified; what comes out of the factor analysis is very much a consequence of what went into it in the first place. According to Cattell (1986), the 16 PF carefully sampled from a very broad range of personality traits (Cattell, 1986), whereas many other researchers incorporated a more limited range of personality features in their measures. Because fewer aspects of personality were reflected in test items, fewer factors are needed to represent them (Cattell & Krug, 1986).

It is also true, however, that even when working with the same variables, such as all the items on the 16 PF, factor analysts other than Cattell have reached different conclusions as to the number of common factors. These disagreements may be based upon differences in the criteria used to decide upon the number of factors (Cattell & Krug, 1986). Disagreements about the number of common factors may also reflect differences in the type of factor analysis used (H. E. P. Cattell, 1993; Eysenck, 1991; Russell & Karol, 1994). Some researchers, such as Cattell (1986), emphasize first-order or "primary" factors as having the greatest utility in explaining behavior; these are the factors derived from a factor analysis of the scale items themselves (Cattell & Krug, 1986). The scales derived from factor analysis may be somewhat intercorrelated, as they are on the 16 PF, and a factor analysis of those scales results in second-order factors (Comrey, 1992). By contrast, other researchers emphasize these second-order factors (Guastello, 1993). Second-order factor analyses of the 16 PF by Cattell and others reveal approximately five second-order factors (Cattell & Krug, 1986; Guastello, 1993; Russell & Karol, 1994; see also Terpylak & Schuerger, 1994). Still, Cattell has argued that the second-order factors are not the true "source" factors in personality and that they lack the predictive value of the first-order factors scored on the 16 PF (Cattell & Krug, 1986).

Controversy aside, the 16 PF remains among the most widely used of objective personality tests (Karson & O'Dell, 1989). As the first major personality test to use factor analysis extensively, the 16 PF has demonstrated the viability of the factor-analytic approach to test development and has served as a model for others. Indeed, the current "electrifying burst of interest" (Goldberg, 1993, p. 26) in personality factors can probably be traced back to the innovative efforts of Raymond Cattell (Digman, 1990). A brief discussion of one product of that burst of interest, a test called the NEO-PI—dubbed playfully by some the "5 PF"—follows.

The NEO-PI and the NEO-PI-R

Through the years, a number of researchers have concluded that personality can be described adequately by five major factors (Amelang & Borkenau, 1982;

Digman & Takemoto-Chock, 1981; Goldberg, 1981; Norman, 1963; Tupes & Christal, 1961), although these researchers have not always agreed on exactly which five factors those might be. Most recently, a five-factor theory of personality developed by Paul T. Costa, Jr., and Robert R. McCrae (1985, 1988, 1989; Costa, 1991; McCrae, 1991; McCrae & Costa, 1987, 1991; Piedmont et al., 1991) has been received enthusiastically by the professional community (Digman, 1990; Miller, 1991; Ozer & Reise, 1994; Piedmont & Weinstein, 1993). Cohen (1994, pp. 29–30) summarized the five factors in this model as follows:

Neuroticism, including dimensions such as worrying versus calm, and even-tempered versus temperamental

Extraversion, including dimensions such as loner versus joiner, and sober versus fun-loving

Openness to Experience, including dimensions such as original versus conventional, and preference for routine versus preference for variety

Conscientiousness, including dimensions such as laziness versus hardworking, and punctual versus late

Agreeableness, including dimensions such as lenient versus critical, and good-natured versus irritable

The NEO-Personality Inventory (NEO-PI; Costa & McCrae, 1985) is a factor-analytically derived self-report scale designed to test for these five personality factors, often called the "big five." In the acronym NEO-PI, "NEO" stands for the factors Neuroticism, Extraversion, and Openness to Experience. "PI" stands for personality inventory. Neuroticism, Extraversion, and Openness to Experience are included in the acronym because they are explored in great depth through the use of *facets,* or subfactors in the 1985 version of the test. For example, Neuroticism comprises the following six facets: anxiety, hostility, depression, self-consciousness, impulsiveness, and vulnerability to stress. A revised version of the NEO-PI, the NEO-PI-R (Costa et al., 1991), expanded to include facet scales for the Agreeableness and Conscientiousness factors as well. In the NEO-PI-R, each of the five factors comprises six facets. Each facet is measured with eight items, resulting in a total of 240 items on the test.

Normative data for the NEO-PI-R come from 526 college students and 983 adults. Because the people in the normative sample were better educated than the general population, questions have been raised about the representativeness of the normative sample (Widiger, 1992).

Internal consistency estimates for the self-report form of the test range from .56 to .81 for the facets, and from .86 to .92 for the factors (Costa & McCrae, 1992c). Test-retest reliabilities for the factors range from .86 to .91 over a six-month period, and exceed .80 over a six-year interval, reflecting considerable stability (Hess, 1992; Widiger, 1992).

Studies of the way children (Donahue, 1994), workers (Mount et al., 1994), and spouses (Hess, 1992) evaluate people have been interpreted as suggesting that the "big five" are in use in everyday descriptions of personality. Also offered in support of the NEO-PI and the NEO-PI-R is the fact that most five-factor models, and even some models with fewer factors (e.g., Eysenck, 1991), reach consensus on at least two of the five factors: N (also called anxiety and emotional stability) and E (also called sociability and surgency; Goldberg, 1993; Zuckerman et al., 1993). The nature and appropriate names of the remaining three factors remain a matter of controversy. Costa and McCrae (1992a) attribute the controversy to selection of the most appropriate name for the same or similar factors. However, others have found more serious and fundamental differences between the various five-factor models (Zuckerman, 1992).

An evaluation of the construct validity of the NEO-PI and the NEO-PI-R, like that of the 16 PF, cannot be divorced from debates concerning the number of factors there are in personality, and technical aspects of conducting factor-analytic research with the test. Differences exist in factor-analytic methods, as well as the criteria applied in determining how many factors exist. Thus, two researchers can reach different conclusions about the number of factors present when using factor analysis on data derived from an administration of one test to one group of testtakers. Because the naming of factors is to some extent subjective, even the identical factors identified independently in two different research laboratories may be given two different names. For example, one of the "big five" personality factors, "openness to experience" (McCrae & Costa, 1991), has been labeled "receptivity" (Cattell, 1986), "intellect" (Goldberg, 1992; Hogan, 1986), and "culture" (Tupes & Christal, 1961).

A general criticism of the factor-analytic approach to test construction concerns its lack of theoretical grounding (Eysenck, 1993; Kroger & Wood, 1993; Merenda & Fava, 1994). That is, the tests are built not on the basis of any particular theory of personality but, rather, on a *lexical,* or language-related, basis—more specifically, the language of psychological trait terms. The lexical foundation on which factor-analytic development of personality tests has been built is questionable (Eysenck, 1993). The limits of our trait-related vocabulary may not do justice to the potential richness and diversity of behavior (Zuckerman, 1992).

Although the five-factor theory of personality and its corresponding tools of measurement have strong advocates (Digman, 1990; Ozer & Reise, 1994), the controversy about which factor-analytic approach to personality measurement is best remains lively. For example, in bemoaning the status of the study of personality, Eysenck (1985) wrote that "Cattell's work [on the 16 PF] falls far short of acceptable standards of scientific criticism" (p. 8). This article prompted a number of retorts, including one from Cattell (1986), to which Eysenck (1986) in turn replied. A similar scenario developed as a result of the publication of Costa and McCrae's (1992a) ideas about how to determine which personality factors are basic ones (see, for example, Eysenck, 1992a, 1992b; Costa & McCrae, 1992b; Zuckerman, 1992).

Test Construction by Empirical Criterion Keying

Personality-test construction by the strategy of empirical criterion keying may be summed up in the following simplified way:

1. Create a number of test items that presume to measure one or more traits.
2. Administer the test items to at least two groups of people:
   a. a "criterion group" composed of people you know to possess the trait being measured, and
   b. a control group of people who are presumed not to possess the trait in question
3. Items that discriminate in a statistically significant way with respect to the criterion and control groups are retained, whereas those items that do not discriminate between the two groups are discarded.

This method of test construction is referred to as "empirical" because only those items that demonstrate an actual (empirical) relationship between the test item and the trait in question are retained. It is called "criterion keying" because each item of the test is keyed to a criterion, the criterion being related to the particular trait in question. Burisch (1984a) characterized the essence of this approach by saying, "If shoe size as a predictor improves your ability to predict performance as an airplane pilot, use it" (p. 218). He offered this tongue-in-cheek description of how a test developer might develop an "M-F" test—a test to differentiate males from females—by means of empirical criterion keying:

> Allegedly not knowing where the differences were, he or she would never dream of using an item such as "I can grow a beard if I want to" or "In a restaurant I tend to prefer the ladies' room to the men's room." Rather, a heterogeneous pool of items would be assembled and administered to a sample of men and women. Next, samples would be compared item by item. Any item discriminating sufficiently well would qualify for inclusion in the M-F test. (p. 214)

Since test construction by means of empirical criterion keying always involves the comparison of at least two groups of people (one group possessing the trait, the other not), this approach to test construction has also been referred to as the method of "contrasted groups." Perhaps the best known and most widely used of the personality tests developed by this method is the Minnesota Multiphasic Personality Inventory (MMPI), as well as its revision, the MMPI-2.

The MMPI

Conceived in the 1930s by psychologist Starke R. Hathaway and psychiatrist/neurologist John C. McKinley as an aid in assessing the mental health of patients seen in medical practice, a test first called the "Medical & Psychiatric Inventory" was renamed when published by the University of Minnesota Press in 1941 as the "Minnesota Multiphasic Personality Inventory" (MMPI). Hathaway (see box on pages 402–403) reminisced that "it was difficult to persuade a publisher to accept the MMPI" (Dahlstrom & Welsh, 1960, p. vii), though the test quickly gained popularity among psychologists.

The MMPI consists of 550 statements to which the examinee responds "True" or "False." In one form of the test, statements are printed on cards, which the examinee sorts into "True," "False," and "Cannot Say" piles (Dahlstrom et al., 1972). For the group-administered version of the test, all unan-

Table 11–3
The Clinical Criterion Groups for MMPI Scales

Scale	Criterion Group
1. Hypochondriasis (Hs)	Patients who showed exaggerated concerns about their physical health
2. Depression (D)	Clinically depressed patients; unhappy and pessimistic about their future
3. Hysteria (Hy)	Patients with conversion reactions
4. Psychopathic deviate (Pd)	Patients who had had histories of delinquency and other antisocial behavior
5. Masculinity-femininity (Mf)	Minnesota draftees, airline stewardesses, and male homosexual college students from the University of Minnesota campus community
6. Paranoia (Pa)	Patients who exhibited paranoid symptomatology such as ideas of reference, suspiciousness, delusions of persecution, and delusions of grandeur
7. Psychasthenia (Pt)	Anxious, obsessive-compulsive, guilt-ridden, and self-doubting patients
8. Schizophrenia (Sc)	Patients who were diagnosed as schizophrenic (various subtypes)
9. Hypomania (Ma)	Patients, most diagnosed as manic-depressive, who exhibited manic symptomatology such as elevated mood, excessive activity, and easy distractibility
10. Social introversion (Si)	College students who had scored at the extremes on a test of introversion-extraversion

swered items in the test booklet are scored in the "Cannot Say" category. The MMPI may be used with persons 16 or older who have at least a sixth-grade education (or an IQ of 80). Most testtakers complete the group-administered form of the MMPI in 45 to 75 minutes. Tape-recorded and foreign-language versions of the inventory have also been constructed.

As reported by the test authors (Hathaway & McKinley, 1940, 1951), research preceding the final selection of items involved the study of psychiatric textbooks, psychiatric reports, and previously published personality-test items. The test items that were ultimately selected reflected 26 content categories, including general health, family issues, religious attitudes, sexual identification, and psychiatric symptomatology (Hathaway & McKinley, 1951). These items were then presented to both criterion groups and a control group. Lanyon and Goodstein (1971, p. 76) described the normal control group as follows: "1500 control subjects were drawn from hospital visitors, normal clients at the University of Minnesota Testing Bureau, local WPA workers, and general medical patients." Eight clinical groups of psychiatric inpatients from the University of Minnesota hospital made up the criterion groups. Those items to which a particular clinical criterion group responded differently from the control subjects were placed on scales corresponding to the disorder of the clinical criterion group. For example, if the response of depressed subjects to an item was different from the control group's response, that item was placed on a depression scale. Eight clinical scales were developed in this fashion (Scales 1 through 4 and Scales 6 through 9). Two additional clinical scales, Masculinity-Femininity (Scale 5) and Social Introversion-Extraversion (Scale 0), were developed using nonpsychiatric criterion groups. A brief description of each criterion group used in the development of the ten clinical scales appears in Table 11–3. More detailed information concerning the construction and validation of the MMPI can be found in Welsh and Dahlstrom (1956).

Starke Rosecrans Hathaway (1903–1984)

"**W**ith his consistent emphasis on objectivity and eclecticism, his insistence on data in preference to inference, his commitment to collegiality and scientific openness, and his scholarly respect for both the biological and psychological dimensions of human personality, Starke Hathaway has an assured place as one of the founders of modern clinical psychology"—so read the obituary for the co-developer of the MMPI, a test that in "its many versions and in nearly 50 languages . . . has been employed in hundreds of different research uses and practical applications for nearly five decades" (Dahlstrom, Meehl, & Schofield, 1986).

Born in Michigan, Hathaway spent much of his youth in Marysville, Ohio. He earned his bachelor's and master's degree at Ohio University in Athens and his Ph.D. at the University of Minnesota. Through the efforts of a psychiatrist at the University Medical School, J. Charnley McKinley, Hathaway was granted a position in the neuropsychiatry division. The two men would subsequently collaborate in the development of the Minnesota Multiphasic Personality Inventory (MMPI) (Hathaway & McKinley, 1940).

Dahlstrom, Meehl, and Schofield (1986, p. 835) remind us that

> Hathaway's identification with the MMPI overshadowed his equally important contributions as a teacher and

therapist. He was a master clinician to whom medical colleagues frequently referred puzzling or difficult patients for diagnosis or treatment. The more difficult and challenging the case was, the more intense, persistent, and innovative were Hathaway's efforts. He rarely failed to achieve a significant result. . . . Many of Hathaway's treatment methods anticipated the behavioral interventions of today, including such methods as mild aversive shock, suggestion and hypnosis, modeling, and habit retraining.

Hathaway's long list of lifetime achievements includes being recipient of the American Psychological Association's award for Distinguished Contributions for Applications in Psychology. Hathaway retired from the University of Minnesota in 1971, and he died in his home in Minneapolis on July 4, 1984.

> "When I came to the University hospitals in about 1937 and began to work with patients, I started to change from a physiological psychologist toward becoming a clinical psychologist. As we went on grand rounds, I with my white coat and newly developing sense of role, expected that the medical staff would want the data and insights of a psychologist. I still remember one day when I was thinking this and suddenly asked myself, suppose they *did* turn to me for aid in understanding the patients'

In addition to ten clinical scales, the MMPI contains three "validity scales" that were designed to serve as indicators of factors such as the operation of response sets, attitudinal factors, and misunderstandings of directions that may influence test results. These include the L scale (sometimes referred to as the "Lie" scale), the F scale (sometimes referred to as the "Infrequency" scale), and the K (correction) scale. The L scale contains 15 items that are somewhat negative but that apply to most people, such as "I do not always tell the truth" or "I gossip a little at times" (Dahlstrom et al., 1972, p. 109). The preparedness of the examinee to reveal *anything* negative about himself or herself will be called into question if the score on the L scale does not fall within certain limits.

data that would go deeper or be more analytically complex than what would suggest general statements, such as that the patient was maladjusted. . . . [As] I then perceived [personality inventories, the] variables and interpretation were not in current jargon nor did they develop suggestions that would be of value to a staff required to make routine diagnostic, prognostic, and treatment decisions.

"The real impetus for the MMPI came from reports of results with insulin shock treatment of schizophrenia. The early statistics on treatment outcomes, as is characteristic of new treatment ideas, promised everything from 100% cure to no effect and no value. It occurred to me that the enormous variance in effectiveness as reported from hospital to hospital depended partly upon the unreliability of the validity criterion—the diagnostic statements. If there were some way in which we could pick experimental groups of patients using objective methods, then outcome tests for treatment efficacy should be more uniform and meaningful. I did not have any objective personality instrument that was adaptable to such a design; and, thinking about the needs, I got the idea of an empirically developed inventory that could be extended indefinitely by development of new scales." (S. R. Hathaway, quoted in Mednick et al., 1975, pp. 350–351)

psychology; what substantive information did I have that wasn't obvious on the face of the case or that represented psychology rather than what the psychiatrist had already said. I could, perhaps, say that the patient was neurotic or an introvert or other such items suggested from my available tests. I had intelligence tests, . . . and a few other inventories. I didn't have any objective personality

The 64 items on the F scale (1) are infrequently endorsed by members of non-psychiatric populations (that is, normal people) and (2) do not fit into any known pattern of deviance. A response of "True" to an item such as the following would be scored on the F scale: "It would be better if almost all laws were thrown away" (Dahlstrom et al., 1972, p. 115). An elevated F score may mean that the respondent did not take the test seriously and was just responding to items randomly. Alternatively, the individual with a high F score may be a very eccentric individual or someone who was attempting to "fake bad." Malingerers in the armed services, people intent on committing fraud with respect to health insurance, and criminals attempting to "cop a psychiatric plea" are some of the groups of people who might be expected to have elevated F scores on their profiles.

Like the L score and the F score, the K score is a reflection of the frankness of the testtaker's self-report. An elevated K score is associated with defensiveness and the desire to present a favorable impression. A low K score is associated with excessive self-criticism, desire to detail deviance, and/or desire to fake bad. A "True" response to the item "I certainly feel useless at times" and a "False" response to "At times I am all full of energy" (Dahlstrom et al., 1972, p. 125) would be scored on the K scale. The K scale is sometimes used to "correct" scores on five of the clinical scales; the scores are statistically corrected for an individual's overwillingness or unwillingness to admit deviancy.

Another scale that bears on the validity of a test administration is the "Cannot Say" scale, also referred to as the question mark ("?") scale. This scale is a simple frequency count of the number of items to which the examinee responded "Cannot Say" or failed to mark any response. Items may be omitted or marked "Cannot Say" for many reasons, including respondent indecisiveness, defensiveness, carelessness, and lack of experience relevant to the item (Graham, 1977). Traditionally, the validity of an answer sheet with a Cannot Say count of 30 is called into question and is deemed uninterpretable (Dahlstrom et al., 1972). Even for tests with a Cannot Say score of 10, caution has been urged in test interpretation. High Cannot Say scores may be avoided by a proctor's emphasis in the initial instructions to answer all items and by the proctor's scanning of answer sheets for omitted items before the testtaker leaves the examination room.

The MMPI may be computer-scored and computer-interpreted. Computerized reports range in detail from simply a numerical score for each scale to long and detailed narrative reports. Whether computer-scored or hand-scored, the raw test scores are converted to T-scores, standard scores that have a mean of 50 and a standard deviation of 10. Standard scores of 70 or greater on the clinical scales indicate a problem for more in-depth study. For example, a T-score of 88 on the Depression scale would suggest an extremely depressed and pessimistic individual. Interpretations are generally made, however, on the basis of the entire test pattern or profile, not on the basis of a score on any one scale.

In contemporary usage, MMPI scales are referred to by number rather than their original name. This is so because literal interpretation of the names of the scales would be inaccurate. A high score on the Schizophrenia (Sc) scale does not necessarily mean that the testtaker would be diagnosed as schizophrenic; the testtaker might well be diagnosed as suffering from some other form of psychosis. It might even be possible for an individual with an elevated Sc scale to be diagnosed as normal. In practical usage, the scales are viewed as continuums with respect to particular personality traits associated with the criterion group the scale was based on. For example, a person scoring high on the Paranoia scale would be regarded as high in suspiciousness, feelings of persecution, and distrust. Note that this use is inconsistent with its original objective, that of being an instrument used for classification and differential diagnosis.

One consequence of decades of research on this test has been a proliferation of new MMPI scales based on the test patterns of various populations. Over 400 new MMPI scales have been devised since the test's publication. Recently, for example, MMPI scales for possible use or research were reported on for identifying adolescents with overcontrolled hostility (Truscott, 1990), as well as people with panic disorders (Lewis et al., 1990), drug misuse habits (Lavelle et al., 1991), and memory and concentration difficulties due to closed-head trauma (Gass et al., 1990). In addition to creating new scales, researchers frequently reevaluated, and suggested new uses for, existing scales. For example, in their reevaluation of the MMPI Masculinity-Femininity scale, Ward and Dillon (1990) reported that male and female patients who scored high on femininity were rated higher on anxiety, depressed mood, guilt feelings, and tension than were low-scorers. Researchers have examined and compared not only the MMPI responses of normals and persons with various psychiatric diagnoses, but also the test protocols of members of more offbeat populations as well. Included in the latter category is research with members of groups as diverse as a serpent-handling religious cult (Tellegen et al., 1969), castrated males (Yamamoto & Seeman, 1960), submarine school dropouts (King, 1959), and civilians selected for isolated northern stations (Wright et al., 1963). Several encyclopedias of MMPI profiles—referred to in the profession as "cookbooks"—are available for use by clinicians (for example, Dahlstrom et al., 1972; Hathaway & Meehl, 1951; see also, Butcher, 1979; Dahlstrom et al., 1986; Swenson et al., 1973).

Critics of the MMPI have cited limitations relating to its construction and use. In light of the widespread use of this instrument, the original normative sample has been criticized as being deficient in size and in the representativeness of the general population. Other criticism has been leveled at the sheer age of the norms; as Dahlstrom et al. pointed out (1972, p. 8): "Each subject taking the MMPI, therefore, is being compared to the way a typical man or woman endorsed those items. In 1940, such a Minnesota normal adult was about thirty-five years old, was married, lived in a small town or rural area, had had eight years of general schooling, and worked at a skilled or semiskilled trade (or was married to a man with such an occupational level)."

In October 1983, a new set of MMPI norms for normal adults was published. The norms were developed by a group of researchers from the Mayo Clinic of Rochester, Minnesota (Colligan et al., 1983), and included MMPI responses from 1,408 normal subjects (people who were not under the care of any health care professional), ranging in age from 18 through 99 years and living in the same general geographic area as the sample used by Hathaway and McKinley (1940). The results indicated that people living in the 1980s tended to have elevated MMPI profiles in contrast to a comparable sample of people living in the 1940s (and the increases tended to be greater for men than for women). Colligan, Osborne, Swenson, and Offord (1984) offered two alternative (though not mutually exclusive) explanations for this finding: (1) people in the 1980s may be under more psychological and physical stress than were people in the 1940s, and (2) changes in response patterns may be due to changes in societal mores and perceptions. Colligan et al. (1984) interpreted their findings as being of practical as well as statistical significance, and they cautioned that "clinicians take a somewhat more conservative approach to profile interpretation with more careful consideration of the impact of age and sex on profile configuration.'' The lack of comparability between the two sets of norms has prompted caution when using the newer norms and the recommendation that the newer norms not be used independently but in conjunction with the original norms (Greene, 1985; Miller & Streiner, 1986).

Whether the new or the original norms are employed, it has always been important for the test user to temper interpretations made from the test data with reference to the limitations of the population used as a normative sample. Thus, for example, Colligan et al. (1983) pointed out that their norms would not be appropriate for use with ethnic minority groups, and they encouraged the development of norms expressly designed for such use. In this vein, it would also be important to learn more about the applicability of the new norms to other geographic areas and groups (Miller & Streiner, 1986).

From the standpoint of test construction, the MMPI has been criticized for using some of the same items in the different scales. The result of this structural redundancy is that some of the scales are highly correlated with one another. If the instrument is to be used as a tool of differential diagnosis, it would be preferable for the scales not to correlate with one another. There also exists some confusion as to the meaning of a low score on the clinical scales; although the meaning of an elevated score on a clinical scale may be clear, Wiggins (1973) has pointed out that given the way the MMPI was constructed, the meaning of a significantly low score is unclear. Other frequently cited limitations of the MMPI have to do with the ready availability of its computerized scoring and the possible misuses inherent in any computer-generated test reports (more on that subject in Chapter 19); the offensiveness of some of the questions to some testtakers (Butcher & Tellegen, 1966; Gallucci, 1986), particularly questions related to sex, religion, bladder and bowel functions; and the length of the test (which has been viewed by some as excessive). One attempted remedy for the last criticism has been the development of short forms of the test—forms that contain only a sampling of items from each of the scales and a fraction of the original total of items (Stevens & Reilley, 1980). In general, however, the short form of the MMPI seems not to have lived up to its promise regarding psychometric soundness or clinical utility (Hart et al., 1986; Helmes & McLaughlin, 1983).

Many of the MMPI's shortcomings could be addressed with a revision and restandardization of the test. The sample on which the MMPI had been standardized was limited and unrepresentative of the United States population. Some of the items had language or content that was either not contemporary or sexist. There was also concern that ''the original MMPI item pool was not broad enough to permit assessment of many characteristics judged important by many test users'' (Graham, 1990a, p. 9). These were the types of issues that were addressed in the development of the MMPI-2.

The MMPI-2

In August of 1989, a revision of the MMPI, known as the MMPI-2, was published. The revision authors (Butcher, Dahlstrom, Graham, & Tellegen, 1989; see the box opposite) rewrote approximately 14% of the original items to correct

Authors of the MMPI-2

 (a)

 (b)

 (c)

James Butcher, pictured in photo (a), was born in Bergoo, West Virginia, in 1933. He was orphaned when he was about ten years old, and he and his four siblings raised themselves without adults in the home. After graduation from high school, he served in a combat infantry unit during the Korean War. He then worked as a private detective for two years before beginning college. In college, his first psychology course convinced him that he should pursue a career in psychology. He completed a B.A. in psychology at Guilford College in 1960 and then received two graduate degrees from the University of North Carolina at Chapel Hill: an M.A. in experimental psychology in 1962 and a Ph.D. in clinical psychology in 1964. He then began an academic career at the University of Minnesota, where he continues to teach and do research. In addition to his work on the MMPI and the MMPI-2, Professor Butcher has been actively involved in research in cross-cultural personality studies, computer-based personality assessment, and abnormal psychology. His contributions have been considered so significant that he was awarded an honorary doctorate from the Free University of Brussels in 1990.

Pictured in photo (b) is W. Grant Dahlstrom. He was born in Minneapolis in 1922. As a child, he lived in a variety of places, including Montana, where he attended a racially integrated school on an Indian reservation, and Pennsylvania, where he attended a racially mixed high school. He returned to Minneapolis for college and graduate school. From the University of Minnesota he received his B.A. in 1944 and his Ph.D. in 1949 with Starke Hathaway as his mentor. He took teaching positions at Ohio Wesleyan University and the University of Iowa before joining the faculty at the University of North Carolina at Chapel Hill in 1952, where he remained until retirement. Professor Dahlstrom is well known for his reference works on the MMPI published in the 1950s. He has also completed research on achievement and ability in Black and White students in segregated schools and on the health sequelae of personality characteristics in

undergraduates. He was honored with the American Psychological Association Award for Distinguished Contribution to Knowledge in 1991 and with the Bruno Klopfer Distinguished Contribution Award from the Society for Personality Assessment in 1994. Although retired from the university since 1993, Professor Dahlstrom continues research in the areas of personality and health.

John R. Graham, pictured in photo (c), is professor of psychology at Kent State University. He wrote the widely used text *The MMPI: A Practical Guide* in 1977, and in 1990 completed *MMPI-2: Assessing Personality and Psychopathology,* an authoritative guide to the revised test. Much of his published research has focused on specific issues surrounding the MMPI and the MMPI-2, including ethnic differences in response to the tests and personality profiles of pathological gamblers.

Auke Tellegen (not shown) is at the University of Minnesota and has published extensively, not only on the MMPI and the MMPI-2, but also on topics including the measurement of personality, personality and stress in children and in adults, and genetics.

grammatical errors and to make the language more contemporary, nonsexist, and readable. Items from the original scale judged to have been objectionable because they contained references to religion, sex, or bodily functions were eliminated. Added were items addressing topics such as drug abuse, suicide potential, "Type A" behavior patterns, marital adjustment, and attitudes toward work.[3] In all, the MMPI-2 contains 394 items identical with the original MMPI, 66 items that were modified or rewritten, and 107 new items (Archer, 1992). A comparison of the MMPI-2 with the original MMPI is presented in Table 11–4, and a listing of the MMPI-2 scales is presented in Table 11–5.

The MMPI-2 still contains its original validity scales, although three new validity scales—Back-Page Infrequency (Fb), True Response Inconsistency (TRIN), and Variable Response Inconsistency (VRIN) have been added. Some testtakers' diligence in testtaking wanes as the test wears on, so that by the "back pages," a random and/or an inconsistent pattern of responses is evident. The Fb scale contains seldom-endorsed items and is designed to detect such a pattern. The TRIN scale consists of 23 pairs of items worded as opposites; that is, consistency would dictate a "True" response to one form of the item, and a "False" response to its opposite wording. Similar to the TRIN scale, the VRIN scale also yields a measure of consistency; it contains item pairs worded either as opposites or as similar statements.

The original ten clinical scales from the MMPI are also on the MMPI-2. The practice of referring to the clinical scales by number, and only secondarily by name, has been continued. The items on the various clinical scales have also been grouped into subscales by content. Recall here that the empirical criterion approach tends to de-emphasize the importance of item content; how keyed the item is to the criterion is what is important. For that reason, the items that make up a scale of any empirically keyed test may be quite heterogeneous in content. Yet some users of the original MMPI, such as Harris and Lingoes (1955, 1968, cited in Graham, 1990a), and others (e.g., Comrey & Marggraff, 1958) developed numerous MMPI subscales by grouping items of similar content that seemed to be measuring the same trait or attitude. For example, Harris and Lingoes (1968, cited in Graham, 1990a) divided the items in MMPI Scale 2 into five subscales: Subjective Depression, Psychomotor Retardation, Physical Malfunctioning, Mental Dullness, and Brooding. The idea was to maximize the clinician's interpretive ability with regard to the data accumulated from an MMPI administration. Now referred to as "Harris-Lingoes subscales" or simply "Harris subscales," scores on these and other subscales are reported in MMPI-2 profiles (Ben-Porath et al., 1989). Also derived from the MMPI clinical scales, the Wiener-Harmon Subtle-Obvious subscales organize items according to the ex-

---

3. First described by cardiologists Meyer Friedman and Ray Rosenman (1974; Rosenman et al., 1975), the "Type A" personality is characterized by competitiveness, haste, restlessness, impatience, feelings of being time-pressured, and strong needs for achievement and dominance. In contrast, "Type B" behavior is more mellow and "laid-back." A 52-item, self-report inventory called the Jenkins Activity Survey (Jenkins et al., 1979) has been widely used to measure the degree to which a respondent is Type A or Type B.

Table 11–4
A Comparison of the MMPI and the MMPI-2

MMPI	MMPI-2
566 items, including 16 repeated items	567 items with no repeated items
Includes nonworking, nonscored items	No nonworking, nonscored items
4 validity scales (?, L, F, K)	7 validity scales (?, L, F, K, Fb, VRIN, TRIN)
10 clinical scales (Hs, D, Hy, Pd, Mf, Pa, Pt, Sc, Ma, Si)	10 clinical scales (1, 2, 3, 4, 5, 6, 7, 8, 9, 10), with objectionable content eliminated from F, 1, 2, 5, and 10 scales
Standardized on 724 individuals with mean educational level of eighth grade from rural, white Minnesota	Standardized on 2,600 individuals with mean educational level of 13 years and representative of 1980 U.S. Census on gender, ethnicity, and socioeconomic level
Can be hand-scored or computer-scored	Can be hand-scored or computer-scored

Adapted from Butcher and Graham (1989)

tent that they are obvious or subtle from the perspective of the testtaker with regard to tapping psychopathological behavior. The idea here is that people who have a particular disorder but are unwilling to admit it may avoid responding in the keyed direction to items that are obviously indicative of the disorder. However, they might respond in the keyed direction to items that are more subtle indicators of the disorder. The subtle-obvious dimension has had great appeal to MMPI users and was incorporated into the MMPI-2—this although research has questioned whether the information it provides surpasses what is already available in the validity scales (Graham, 1990a; Timbrook et al., 1993).

A new set of content scales designed to assess personality factors such as anxiety, fears, obsessiveness, depression, health concerns, anger, cynicism, antisocial practices, self-esteem, social discomfort, family problems, and work interference was developed for the MMPI-2 by Butcher, Graham, Williams, and Ben-Porath (1989). These scales were developed using "both rational and statistical procedures to assure rational content relevance and strong statistical properties" (Butcher & Pope, 1990, p. 37). MMPI-2 supplementary scales (refer to Table 11–5) were developed by many different researchers, usually by the method of empirical criterion keying. Typically, these independent researchers sought to determine the utility of the MMPI in detecting certain conditions or varieties of pathological behavior. For example, the Ego Strength scale includes those items that distinguished between people who improved and who did not improve after six months of psychotherapy. The MacAndrew Alcoholism scale includes those items that distinguished between psychiatric patients who did and did not have a history of serious problems with alcohol. Using a somewhat different technique, the supplementary Anxiety and Repression scales are based on a factor analysis of the MMPI clinical scales (Welsh, 1956). The inclusion and standardization of various supplementary and content scales has been favorably received by the professional community (Archer, 1992).

Table 11-5
MMPI-2 Scales

Scale Name	Scale Type	Number of Items	Some Possible Interpretations of High Scale Scores
?	V	Omitted items	Profile may be invalid; testtaker may have been careless, or unwilling to respond to items.
L	V	15	Trying to create a favorable impression.
F	V	60	Trying to create a negative impression or severe psychological distress.
K	V	30	Trying to appear in control, effective.
Fb	V	40	If F is valid, respondent stopped paying attention later in the test.
TRIN	V	46	Give true responses indiscriminately.
VRIN	V	134	Inconsistent responses to similar items.
Scale 1—Hs	CI	32	Excessive bodily concerns.
Scale 2—D	CI	57	Display depressive symptoms.
Scale 3—Hy	CI	60	React to stress and avoid responsibility through development of physical symptoms.
Scale 4—Pd	CI	50	Have difficulty incorporating values and standards of society.
Scale 5—Mf	CI	56	Men: may have sexual problems or concerns. Women: reject traditional female role.
Scale 6—Pa	CI	40	Have a paranoid predisposition.
Scale 7—Pt	CI	48	Experience psychological turmoil.
Scale 8—Sc	CI	78	Have a psychotic disorder.
Scale 9—Ma	CI	46	Exhibit symptoms of a manic episode.
Scale 0—Si	CI	69	Are socially introverted.
Anxiety (A)	S	39	General maladjustment; uncomfortable.
Repression (R)	S	37	Submissive, unexcitable, formal.
Ego Strength (Es)	S	52	Stable, reliable, responsible.
MacAndrew (MAC-R)	S	49	Possibility of substance abuse.

The standardization sample   The 2,600 individuals (1,462 females, 1,138 males) from seven states who made up the MMPI-2 standardization sample had been matched to 1980 United States Census data on the variables of age, gender, minority status, social class, and education (Butcher, 1990). Whereas the original MMPI did not contain any non-Whites in the standardization sample, the MMPI-2 sample was 81% White and 19% non-White. Age of subjects in the sample ranged from 18 years to 85 years. Formal education ranged from 3 years to 20+ years, with more highly educated people and people working in the professions overrepresented in the sample (Archer, 1992; Graham, 1990a). Median annual family income for females in the sample was $25,000 to $30,000. Median annual family income for males in the sample was $30,000 to $35,000.

Standardization sample data provide the basis for transforming the raw

Scale Name	Scale Type	Number of Items	Some Possible Interpretations of High Scale Scores
Overcontrolled-Hostility	S	28	Impunitive, report few angry feelings.
Dominance (DO)	S	25	Appear poised and self-assured.
Social Responsibility	S	30	Deep concern over moral/ethical problems.
College Maladjustment	S	41	Ineffectual, pessimistic, procrastinate.
Masculine Gender Role	S	47	Self-confident, free from worries.
Feminine Gender Role	S	46	Religiosity, abuse of alcohol.
Post-Traumatic Stress Disorder Scale (PK)	S	46	Post-traumatic stress disorder.
Post-Traumatic Stress Disorder Scale (PS)	S	60	Post-traumatic stress disorder.
Anxiety	C	23	Feel anxious, nervous, worried.
Fears	C	23	Feel fearful and uneasy.
Obsessiveness	C	16	Have great difficulty making decisions.
Depression	C	33	Feel depressed, sad, blue, or despondent.
Health Concerns	C	36	Deny good physical health.
Bizarre Mentation	C	24	Have psychotic thought processes.
Anger	C	16	Feel angry and hostile much of the time.
Cynicism	C	23	See others as dishonest, selfish, uncaring.
Antisocial Practices	C	22	Likely to have been in trouble in school or with the law.
Type A	C	19	Hard-driving, fast-moving, work-oriented.
Low Self-Esteem	C	24	Have very poor self-concepts.
Social Discomfort	C	24	Are shy and socially introverted.
Family Problems	C	25	Describe considerable discord in family.
Work Interference	C	33	Attitudes . . . likely to contribute to poor work performance.
Negative Treatment Indicators	C	26	Have negative attitudes toward doctors and mental health treatment.

Key for Scale Type abbreviations: C = content; Cl = clinical; S = supplementary; V = validity.

Source: Graham (1990a). Interpretations are all quotations from Graham (1990a).

scores obtained by respondents into *T*-scores. Because the distribution of responses obtained from the standardization sample was positively skewed for most of the clinical and content scales, these distributions were normalized, or molded into a normal distribution (Nichols, 1992). The decision to use normalized standard scores on the MMPI-2, rather than the standard scores used on the MMPI, rested on an interest in making *T*-scores more comparable across the different scales (Graham, 1990a). As a result of the normalization, a *T*-score of 60, for example, represents someone at the 84th percentile relative to the people in the standardization sample—whether that *T*-score was obtained on Scale 4, the K scale, or any other scale. MMPI-2 norms are computed separately for men and women. Some have asked whether unisex norms for the MMPI-2 are needed, and the issue is taken up in this chapter's *Everyday Psychometrics*.

Are Unisex Norms for the MMPI-2 Needed? Would They Work?*

Traditionally, MMPI scales have been normed separately for men and women, in large part because McKinley and Hathaway (1940) found a somewhat different distribution of scores for men and women on some scales. They observed:

> Likewise, the scores for females are, without exception, higher than for the corresponding males. One might indulge in considerable speculation on these findings, but since the validity of the test within the normal group is at present in process of study, and the differences themselves are slight, we are not prepared to draw any conclusions as to the meaning of such differences. (p. 266)

However, some scales, notably Si, were based on a single norm for men and women. Observed gender differences in personality scale responding even prompted some authors to recommend different items (in separate booklets) for men and women in order to refine interpretation on certain personality scales (Block, 1965). For a current evaluation of gender differences, see recent discussions by Deaux (1985) and Deaux and Major (1987).

Recent civil rights legislation (Adler, 1993) has called into question the use of separate norms for men and women, especially when employers use the tests in employment selection situations. The implications of changing the basic normative approach on which more than fifty years of research has accumulated could be great and need to be examined. Consequently, Tellegen, Butcher, and Hoeglund initiated a first study to evaluate the potential impact of employing "unisex" norms for the MMPI-2 clinical scales.

Results

First, Tellegen, Butcher, and Hoeglund evaluated possible differences between men and women in their responses to the items on MMPI-2 by examining the endorsement percentages for each item by men and

women. They found that most MMPI-2 items are endorsed by similar percentages of men and women. Furthermore, most items that did show substantial differences belonged to the Mf scale, not to items reflecting psychopathology.

Next, to evaluate the impact of different norming procedures on the MMPI-2 scales, Tellegen et al. (1993) developed a set of "unisex norms" for the MMPI-2 clinical scales. Using a combined sample of 1,138 men and to avoid confusion, 1,139 women from the MMPI-2 restandardization sample, they computed uniform T scores following the same procedures employed in the development of the MMPI-2 norms (Butcher, Dahlstrom, Graham, Tellegen, & Kaemmer, 1989). They found that the frequency distributions for the MMPI-2 clinical scales for the combined (unisex) sample closely resembled the frequency distributions of the separate gender norms. As a result, the unisex norms appeared to operate in a manner similar to the correct gender-specific MMPI-2 norms. Relatively small T score changes occur for either men or women when unisex norms were employed instead of gender-specific norms. The effect of unisex norms on MMPI-2 using scores of two forensic cases is illustrated in Figure 1. Their scores for the cases have been plotted on both the MMPI-2 gender-specific and unisex norms. It is apparent that interpretations of the profiles would be the same, regardless of which set of norms were used.

Such differences as do occur between the MMPI-2 clinical scale distributions tend to be small and differ somewhat at different ages. That is, for some age groups the differences are greater than for others.

*By Auke Tellegen, James Butcher, and Tawni Hoeglund (1993).

Figure 1

The MMPI-2 scores for the two forensic cases are plotted ▶
on both the "unisex norms" and the standard MMPI-2 norm

(a)

MMPI-2 S.R. Hathaway and J.C. McKinley
Minnesota Multiphasic Personality Inventory-2

Profile for Basic Scales

Minnesota Multiphasic Personality Inventory-2
Copyright © by THE REGENTS OF THE UNIVERSITY OF MINNESOTA
1942, 1943 (renewed 1970). 1989. This Profile Form 1989.
All rights reserved. Distributed exclusively by NATIONAL COMPUTER SYSTEMS, INC.
under license from The University of Minnesota.

"MMPI-2" and "Minnesota Multiphasic Personality Inventory-2" are trademarks owned by
The University of Minnesota. Printed in the United States of America

Name _____
Address _____
Occupation _Sales_____ Date Tested _/ /_
Education _13_ Age _42_ Marital Status _D_
Referred By _Court_
MMPI-2 Code _____
Scorer's Initials _____

MALE

- - - - Unisex Norms
——— Male Norms

Raw Score: 5 12 16   7 20 25 26 25 13 14 15 25 25
K to be Added: 8   6   16 16 3
Raw Score with K: 15   32   30 31 28

NATIONAL COMPUTER SYSTEMS (NCS)
24001

(b)

MMPI-2 S.R. Hathaway and J.C. McKinley
Minnesota Multiphasic Personality Inventory-2

Profile for Basic Scales

Minnesota Multiphasic Personality Inventory-2
Copyright © by THE REGENTS OF THE UNIVERSITY OF MINNESOTA
1942, 1943 (renewed 1970). 1989. This Profile Form 1989.
All rights reserved. Distributed exclusively by NATIONAL COMPUTER SYSTEMS, INC.
under license from The University of Minnesota.

"MMPI-2" and "Minnesota Multiphasic Personality Inventory-2" are trademarks owned by
The University of Minnesota. Printed in the United States of America

Name _____
Address _____
Occupation _____ Date Tested _/ /_
Education _14_ Age _39_ Marital Status _M_
Referred By _attorney_
MMPI-2 Code _____
Scorer's Initials _____

FEMALE

——— Female MMPI-2 Norms
- - - Unisex Norms

Raw Score: 6 3 23   13 26 34 21 40 14 10 10 15 30
K to be Added: 12   9   23 25 5
Raw Score with K: 25   30   35 35 20

NATIONAL COMPUTER SYSTEMS (NCS)
24001

(continued)

Are Unisex Norms for the MMPI-2 Needed? Would They Work? *(continued)*

Conclusions

■ Item response differences between men and women were relatively small for most items. The Mf scale accounted for most of the items that showed substantial differences between men and women.

■ Applying the MMPI-2 normative data to the clinical scales, unisex norms appear to operate in a manner similar to that of traditional gender-specific norms. Unisex norms do not appear to "disadvantage" either gender. On the other hand, the traditional normative approach initiated by Hathaway and McKinley, which is represented by MMPI-2 T scores (based on gender-specific distributions), likewise does not appear to "disadvantage" either gender. Similar distributions and T scores are ob-

tained irrespective of which normative procedure is followed.

■ Relatively small differences were found on a few scales in some elevation ranges. The differences appeared to be somewhat influenced by age. That is, at some age levels the normative gender differences are larger than at others, but no extreme differences were found.

■ This study did not examine the relative validities of one set of norms over another. An important next step would be for interested researchers to evaluate the extent to which either unisex norms or traditional gender-specific norms actually perform better in the prediction of behavior.

MMPI-2 test data were also collected for research purposes from samples of various populations such as airline pilot applicants, people in chronic pain, college students, psychiatric inpatients, and couples in marital counseling. Research with this instrument in its finished or pilot form has been reported regarding its utility in areas as diverse as chemical dependency evaluation (McKenna & Butcher, 1987), marital counseling and assessment (Hjemboe & Butcher, 1990), psychiatric evaluation in inpatient settings (Graham & Butcher, 1988), and evaluation of patients with chronic pain (Keller & Butcher, 1989).

Psychometric properties In considering the application of the types of reliability discussed in Chapter 5, keep in mind that no alternate form of the MMPI-2 is available. The objective scoring of the test minimizes the impact of error variance due to rater differences, so inter-rater reliability is not a concern. The types of reliability of primary interest to evaluators of the test, then, are test-retest reliability and internal consistency reliability.

The utility of many of the MMPI-2 scales rests on their stability over time. Whether the MMPI-2 is used as an instrument to assist with diagnosis, to explore aspects of personality, or to gather information about the concerns a person brings to psychotherapy, consistency, at least over the short term, is expected on most scales. Such consistency is reflected in estimates of the MMPI-2's test-retest reliability.

For the validity and clinical scales, test-retest reliability over a one-week period ranges from .58 (Scale 6) to .92 (Scale 0), with a median value of .81. Similar levels of test-retest reliability exist for the content scales over a nine-day interval. Coefficients range from .78 (Bizarre Mentation) to .91 (Social Discomfort and Work Interference), with a median value of .85. The test-retest reliability of the supplementary scales has been assessed over periods ranging from three days to four months, with most coefficients in the .80s (Dominance ranged from .83 to .86, Social Responsibility ranged from .74 to .88, and College Maladjustment ranged from .86 to .90). Among the supplementary scales, the lowest estimates were for the Overcontrolled-Hostility scale (.56 to .72). Most of the MMPI-2 scales have test-retest reliability estimates in acceptable ranges (Graham, 1990a).

Internal consistency reliability was not something the original developers of the MMPI attempted to build into the test. Rather, items were placed on scales if they distinguished between criterion groups—irrespective of their relationship to other items on the same scale. In this tradition of empiricism, internal consistency of MMPI-2 clinical and validity scales tends to be low, with a median internal consistency reliability estimate of .63, encompassing a range that goes from a low of .34 on Scale 6 to a high of .87 on Scale 7.

The Harris-Lingoes subscales were designed to enhance clinical interpretations that could be made from MMPI data, by grouping items of similar content together. Therefore, a by-product of grouping homogeneous items should be subscales that each are more internally consistent than the umbrella scale from which the subscales were derived. In fact, this is true for some but not all of the Harris-Lingoes subscales. For example, Scale 2 (Depression) has an internal consistency reliability of .59 for male respondents. Internal consistency reliability estimates for the Harris-Lingoes subscales of Scale 2 with male respondents are .56 (Psychomotor Retardation), .61 (Physical Malfunctioning), .81 (Subjective Depression), .85 (Mental Dullness), and .91 (Brooding).

Items for the various content scales were selected on a rational basis; that is, the test developers sought out items that appeared to go together on particular scales. Further, the content scales were subjected to a test tryout, after which items with low item–total correlations were eliminated (Graham, 1990a). As a result of such attention to homogeneity in the scales' development, internal consistency reliability for the content scales tends to be higher than that for the clinical scales. Internal consistency estimates of the content scales range from a low of .68 on the Type A scale to a high of .86 on both the Depression and the Cynicism scales. The median value for all the content scales is .78.

The supplementary scales vary widely in internal consistency. Recall that the supplementary scales were devised by many different researchers, so the approach used in their development, as well as the amount of attention paid to homogeneity, varies across the scales. Some internal consistency values are relatively low. The internal consistency of the MacAndrew scale, for example, ranges from .45 to .56, and that of the Overcontrolled-Hostility scale ranges from .24 to .56. The most internally consistent supplementary scales include the Anxiety scale (with coefficients ranging from .88 to .94), the College Maladjustment scale (.85 to .94), and the two post-traumatic stress disorder scales (.85 to .94). Among all the supplementary scales, the median internal consistency reliability is approximately .75 (Graham, 1990a).

Relevant to a psychometric evaluation of the validity of MMPI-2 is a consideration of the test's content validity, criterion validity, and construct validity. With regard to content validity, the method used to construct the clinical scales—empirical criterion keying—largely ignores content validity issues. Thus, for example, if responses to a hypothetical item such as "I just had my hairstyle changed dramatically" demonstrated ability to discriminate between depressed and nondepressed people, the item might be included on the test's depression scale—even though there is no obvious relation between the content of this test item and depression. Indeed, the conceptual link to depression of many of the items that are actually on the MMPI-2's Depression scale is elusive.

In contrast to content validity, one would expect acceptably high criterion validity coefficients from scales developed by means of empirical criterion keying. The essence of the empirical criterion approach, after all, is to develop scales on which people from different known groups will score differently from a control group. However, changes in diagnostic categories since the development of the original MMPI, and other technical modifications needed to maintain continuity of the test, made difficult the systematic evaluation of the criterion-related validity of the MMPI-2 through the usual means (Archer, 1992). Alternatively, one strategy for establishing the criterion-related validity of the MMPI-2 has involved first establishing the criterion-related validity of the original test, and then arguing that the revision is sufficiently similar to the original test to warrant that such validity evidence is generalizable to the MMPI-2 (Graham, 1990a).

The abundant amount of criterion-related validity evidence that exists for the original MMPI has been grouped by Graham (1990a) into studies that show that (1) people with different diagnoses have different patterns of clinical scale scores on the MMPI; (2) MMPI scores correlate with various aspects of behavior in a predicted way; and (3) clinical judgment is improved by inclusion of MMPI data. Arguing the case for criterion-related validity of the MMPI-2 based on the criterion-related validity of the original MMPI, Graham (1990a) notes that exceptionally high correlation coefficients (.98 and higher) have been found between the MMPI-2 clinical scales and the corresponding original MMPI clinical scales. Others (e.g., Hargrave et al., 1994) have taken issue with these numbers, as well as with the logic of the argument. Using other methods of comparing the two MMPIs (see, for example, Archer, 1992, and Nichols, 1992), some have asked exactly how similar the MMPI and the MMPI-2 are (Adler, 1990). Archer (1992) cites this equivalence issue as "the major area of controversy" (p. 560) surrounding the MMPI-2.

Criterion-related validity data for the MMPI-2 must be gathered to convince those unwilling to generalize findings related to the original MMPI to its revisions. Indeed, such studies have been under way since the test's publication. One of the few such studies that has been published supports the criterion validity of the Anger content scale but raises questions about whether the Cynicism content scale is valid (Clark, 1994).

One study examining the criterion validity of the MMPI-2 compared clinical scale scores for normal subjects with the results of a rating scale completed by the subject's spouse. The various clinical scales were related to the ratings in ways that would be expected given interpretations of the scales. For example, people scoring high on Scale 2 (Depression) were rated by their spouses as lacking energy and interest, worrying, feeling sad, and not being self-confident. People scoring high on Scale 7 (Psychasthenia) were rated by their spouses as having bad dreams and many fears, being indecisive, and not being self-confident. Similar results were obtained by comparing the MMPI-2 scores of psychiatric patients with ratings by treatment professionals (Graham, 1990a).

A common type of criterion validity study with a test such as the MMPI-2 entails asking people without mental disorders to respond to the test as though they had mental disorders (Bagby et al., 1994; Sivec et al., 1994; Wetter et al., 1994). The goal of such studies is to determine whether the validity scales on the MMPI-2 are sensitive to attempts to "faking bad," or presenting oneself as psychologically disordered. This is an important practical question relative to the use of the test, since individuals may try to fake bad for many reasons, such as to qualify for or maintain current disability benefits. Lamb et al. (1994) asked some of the college students in their study to complete the MMPI-2 without any special instructions (the "control" subjects). Other students were asked to respond as though they were experiencing psychological symptoms as the result of a closed head injury. The researchers encouraged students to make their responses believable, and they even offered monetary incentives for the most convincing test results. The validity scales "did their stuff" in this experiment. The profiles for the students attempting to appear disordered were less valid than those completed by the control subjects. Specifically, the profiles for the students who were faking bad had higher scores on the F and Fb scales, and lower scores on the K scale, than did the control students. This was true even of students who were given information about the symptoms of closed head injury and about the MMPI-2 validity scales. The results suggest that the MMPI-2 validity scales may successfully identify people who have been coached about how to respond dishonestly on the MMPI-2. A meta-analysis (Rogers et al., 1994) of this literature also concludes that the MMPI-2 validity scales are effective in this way.

Relationships between the content scales and the clinical scales have been explored to provide information about the construct validity of the content scales. Understanding the ways the content scales relate to the clinical scales helps the MMPI-2 user, already familiar with the clinical scales, to better understand what the content scales are measuring. For example, the Health Concerns content scale is correlated .89 to .91 with Scale 1, and the Social Discomfort content scale is correlated .84 to .85 with Scale 0. These correlations demonstrate convergent validity for the two content scales, and indicate that the content scales can be interpreted like the clinical scales with similar labels. By contrast, the Depression content scale and Scale 2 correlate only .52 to .63 (Graham, 1990a). This suggests that elevations on the Depression content scale should not be interpreted like Scale 2 elevations. The difference between Scale 2 and the Depression content scale is also reflected in their relationships with other measures of depression: correlations with other scales ranged from .55 to .83 (median = .69) for the Depression content scale, but only .35 to .55 (median = .48) for Scale 2. Thus, the Depression content scale seems to be tapping the same construct that other depression scales reflect (Boone, 1994).

Nichols (1992) notes that evidence of discriminative validity is lacking for several of the supplementary scales, including the two posttraumatic stress disorder scales, and the College Maladjustment, Type A, and Negative Treatment Indicators scales. Many of the people who score high on either of the posttraumatic stress disorder scales may not actually meet the criteria for being diagnosed with posttraumatic stress disorder (Nichols, 1992).

An evaluation   The reliability of the MMPI-2 is acceptable for the majority of the scales. The evidence for the validity of the original MMPI is impressive, and to the extent that such evidence is generalizable to the MMPI-2, there is reason to believe that the MMPI-2 may well be as valid as its predecessor. Still, much remains to be done to demonstrate the specific merits of the MMPI-2 with regard to its criterion-related and construct validity.

Although research studies with the original MMPI explored the test's efficacy with regard to populations at both ends of the normal–abnormal continuum, the trend in MMPI-2 research, with some exceptions, seems more focused on the abnormal end of the spectrum. This trend may be due, at least in part, to the proliferation of many tests designed to assess the "normal personality" (Ozer & Reise, 1994).[4]

The usefulness of the MMPI-2 for non-Caucasian populations has received much attention since the test's publication. The original MMPI was standardized on Caucasians, but the MMPI-2 used a broader normative sample. Research has supported the adequacy of the MMPI-2 and its new norms for African American (Timbrook & Graham, 1994) and Hispanic American individuals (Whitworth & Unterbrink, 1994). Work has also begun on translating the test for use among Spanish-speaking Mexicans, with encouraging initial results (Lucio et al., 1994).

Certainly the MMPI-2 is not without its critics. The comparability of MMPI and MMPI-2 scores, the validity of the new content scales, and the utility of treatment recommendations made on the basis of MMPI-2 scores have all been questioned (Adler, 1990). Heterogeneity of item content within the scales remains a problem, as does overlapping items across the different scales (Helmes & Reddon, 1993). The MMPI-2 has also been criticized for the atheoretical nature of its development and its continued use of scales keyed to diagnostic categories that no longer exist (Helmes & Reddon, 1993). Still, if only on the strength of the popularity of its predecessor, there is reason to expect that the MMPI-2

---

4. The California Psychological Inventory (CPI) is one such test designed to assess the "normal personality," and it is discussed in detail in Cohen (1996), the companion study guide to this text.

will continue the tradition of being one of the world's most widely used and widely researched psychological tests.

The MMPI-A

Issues related to the use of the MMPI with adolescents have also been of long-standing interest to the test's users. Separate adolescent norms for the original MMPI had been developed, and the developers of the MMPI-2 would have had to gather normative data on adolescents for the revision as well. Instead of doing that, they seized the opportunity to develop a new version of the MMPI for adolescents. This new test, the MMPI-A ("A" for Adolescent), was published in 1992. Developed to apply to individuals 14 to 18 years of age who can read at the sixth-grade level, the MMPI-A contains 478 true-false items, making it somewhat shorter than the MMPI and the MMPI-2. Although no attempt was made to select the standardization sample on the basis of census data, the normative data are based on 1,620 adolescents in several geographic regions, selected specifically to include ethnically diverse areas.

The MMPI-A contains all of the same clinical and validity scales as the MMPI-2. Although there is some overlap in the content and supplementary scales that can be scored, other content and supplementary scales bear a distinctly adolescent "stamp." For example, there are content scales for Conduct Problems, Social Discomfort, and School Problems. In addition to the Mac-Andrew Alcoholism scale, which appears on both the adolescent and the adult forms of the test, the MMPI-A includes supplementary scales entitled Alcohol/Drug Problem Acknowledgement and Alcohol/Drug Problem Proneness. For many long-term users of the original MMPI, much of what they are seeing in the research literature is a repeat of themes such as the development of supplementary scales (e.g., an Immaturity Scale by Archer et al., 1994), and the identification of so-called critical items, the endorsement of which signals a particular problem, such as suicide risk or predisposition toward violence (Archer & Jacobson, 1993).

The Theoretical Approach to Test Construction

Perhaps in reaction to the widespread popularity of computerized personality testing, complete with neatly printed narrative interpretations, at least a few voices have begun to call for more clinical and more theoretically based approaches to personality assessment. In the latter camp, we can include Sugarman (1991), who has argued that personality theory as applied in personality assessment serves an organizing function and an integrative function, clarifies gaps in test data, and better allows for prediction. Using an article entitled "Psychiatric Diagnosis: Are Clinicians Still Necessary?" (Spitzer, 1983) as their point of departure, Pilkonis, Heape, Ruddy, and Serrao (1991) explored how multifaceted assessments employing multiple sources of data could be brought to bear to enhance the validity of diagnoses of personality disorder.

Instruments used in personality testing and assessment range from what we might term "theory-saturated" to relatively atheoretical—allowing for the test users, should they so desire, to impose their own theoretical preferences on the interpretation of the findings. An example of a theory-saturated instrument is "The Blacky Pictures Test" (Blum, 1950). This test, now seldom if ever used, consists of pictures of Blacky, a dog, in various situations, each image designed to elicit fantasies associated with various psychoanalytic themes. For example, one card depicts Blacky with a knife hovering over his tail, a scene, according to the test's author, designed to elicit material related to the psychoanalytic concept of castration anxiety. The respondent's task is to make up stories in response to such cards, and the stories are then analyzed according to the guidelines set forth by Blum (1950).[5] More contemporary psychoanalytically based assessment efforts can be found in other sources, such as the writings of Robert Plutchik, Hope Conte, and their associates (Conte & Plutchik, 1981; Conte et al., 1991; Plutchik & Conte, 1989).

One widely used, theoretically based personality test is the Myers-Briggs Type Indicator. This test is based on the personality typology of Carl Jung (see Briggs et al., 1987; Myers & Briggs, 1943/1962; and Myers & McCaulley, 1985). Other personality tests, such as the Personality Research Form (Jackson, 1984a; see the *Close-up* in Chapter 7) and the Edwards Personal Preference Schedule (described below), are based on the theory of personality developed by Henry Murray.

The Edwards Personal Preference Schedule (EPPS)

The EPPS (Edwards, 1953) is a personality inventory based on the theory of personality presented by Henry Murray in *Explorations in Personality* (1938). *Explorations* presented a complex but academically elegant theory of personality that not only introduced new concepts (such as "press," "regnancy," and "serial programs") but also provided the impetus for renewed study of more traditional concepts.[6] In the latter context, for example, Murray explored the facets of the word *need*, defining it, writing about its consequences, and detailing how various needs could be inferred. According to Murray, needs could be either primary or secondary, overt or covert, focal or diffuse, proactive (determined from within) or reactive (occurring in response to or as a result of some environmental event), and modal (done for the sheer pleasure of doing) or effect (done to effect some result). The list of needs originally published in *Explorations* is presented in Table 11–6.

---

5. This brief description of a test that employs pictures used as a stimulus for story telling will serve as a preview of things to come in the following chapter on projective instruments.

6. "Press" is a construct Murray used to refer to significant determinants of behavior that lie outside the person. It is a term used in contrast to the construct "need," which refers to the significant determinants of behavior from *within*. "Regnancy" is a concept Murray used to link physiological (brain) processes to psychological processes (see Murray, 1938, p. 45). "Serial program" is used to refer to a set of subgoals that must be reached before some final goal can be attained.

Table 11–6
List of Needs Presented in Murray (1938)*

Need	Definition (the need to . . .)
Abasement	submit passively
	accept blame, injury, criticism, or punishment
	admit inferiority, error, wrongdoing, or defeat
Achievement	accomplish and excel
	rival and surpass others
Affiliation	please, win affection of, and remain loyal to a friend
	draw near others
Autonomy	be independent, unattached, and defy convention
	resist restrictions
Counteraction	make up for failure with renewed efforts
	overcome a weakness or a fear
Defendance	protect or shield from blame, criticism, assault, and humiliation
Dominance	influence or direct others by authority or force
Exhibition	influence others by entertaining, shocking, exciting, or enticing them
Harmavoidance	avoid physical injury, pain, illness, and death
Infavoidance	avoid embarrassment and humiliation
Nurturance	help, support, protect, comfort, nurse, heal, and give sympathy
Order	achieve balance, precision, and organization
Play	participate in games, sports, other pleasurable activities
	act sheerly for "fun"
Rejection	separate or snub a person deemed to be inferior in some way
Sentience	seek and enjoy sensuous activities
Sex	have erotic relationships and sexual outlets
Succorance	be nursed, supported, sustained, protected, advised, forgiven, consoled
	have a steadfast, sympathetic supporter
Understanding	question, theorize, analyze, speculate, generalize

*We have abbreviated the definitions of these needs for the purposes of this tabular presentation. Consult Murray (1938, pp. 152–226) for complete definitions.

Edwards selected 15 of the needs listed by Murray and constructed items designed to assess each of those needs. He next conducted research designed to assess the social desirability of each of the items he wrote. Items assessing different needs that were found to be generally equivalent with respect to social desirability were then placed into pairs (Edwards, 1957a, 1957b, 1966). For example, a pair of statements deemed to be approximately equivalent with respect to social desirability might be

I feel depressed when I fail at something.

I feel nervous when giving a talk before a group.

Edwards constructed his test of 210 pairs of statements in a way such that respondents were "forced" to answer "True" or "False" or "Yes" or "No" to one of two statements that were equivalent in social desirability. This "forced-choice" technique represented an attempt to control for respondents' attempts to fake good or fake bad. Note also that each of the two statements above, like each of the statements in every pair of EPPS statements, is keyed to a different need in Murray's system. Endorsement of an item keyed to one scale in essence serves to reject an item keyed to an alternative scale. The score that is computed for each of the EPPS needs or scales thus represents the intensity of a particular need *in relation* to the intensity of the individual respondent's other needs. EPPS scores are, in psychometric jargon, *ipsative* in nature (see Chapter 7); the scores do not represent the strength of the need in absolute terms but, rather, the strength of the need in relation to the individual respondent's other needs. To elaborate, ipsative scoring allows for comparison of personality characteristics exhibited by an individual examinee with respect only to that examinee and does now allow for comparison between examinees. Such scoring is useful in *intra*-individual comparison and not in *inter*-individual comparison. For example, on the basis of personality inventory data derived by means of ipsative scoring, it might be appropriate to make a statement like "John's need for achievement is higher than his need for succorance." However, it would be inappropriate on the basis of such data to compare any of John's needs with those of another person as in a statement like "John's need for achievement is higher than Jane's need for achievement."

In addition to the use of the forced-choice format, Edwards built other precautionary measures into the EPPS in an effort to detect and/or minimize the effects of faking, response sets, and other factors that would threaten the validity of the obtained scores. A Consistency scale is designed to check on the consistency of the examinee's responses. This scale consists of 15 identical items that are repeated in various places throughout the inventory.

As a further measure of consistency, a "stability" score may be obtained; this score is equal to the correlation coefficient that describes the relationship between two halves of the test (odd and even scores in the 15 scales).

Normative data for the EPPS were initially gathered on a sample of 760 male and 749 female college students from 29 campuses throughout the country and approximately 9,000 men and women from the general adult population. Subsequently, data based on the test results for 559 male and 986 female high school students were added. Test-retest reliability coefficients for the 15 scales based on one-week intervals were found to range between .74 and .87. Internal-consistency measures resulted in split-half reliability coefficients ranging from .60 to .87 with a median of .78. Interpretation of these findings is complicated because the test contains repeated items. In general, the test is viewed as being within acceptable standards of test-retest and inter-item reliability; the objection many reviewers have raised concerns the lack of compelling validity data (Heilbrun, 1972). Additionally, questions have been raised concerning the extent to which the forced-choice format of the test does indeed eliminate the effect of the social desirability response set on scores (Heilbrun & Goodstein, 1961a, 1961b; Rorer, 1965; Wiggins, 1966). Validity of the test has been supported in research that has found meaningful relationships between the EPPS and the five-factor model of personality embodied in the NEO-PI (Piedmont et al., 1992). Reviewers have also questioned the appropriateness of converting ipsative scores into normative percentiles and the representativeness of the normative sample. The test was originally designed for use with college students and adults and is often used for research, teaching, and counseling purposes (Drummond, 1984).

Clinical Versus Actuarial Prediction

Data derived from psychological tests, sometimes in combination with data derived from other tools of assessment (such as information gathered from case history and interview files) will ultimately be used to formulate a description of, predict something about, or take some action regarding the assessee. There are two different general approaches to interpreting data derived from personality tests and related sources. An *actuarial* approach (also referred to as a *statistical* approach) entails evaluation of test data, and in some cases other data as well, according to preset rules. The actuarial approach is distinguished by its reliance on statistical and empirical procedures, and normative data (Meehl, 1954). By contrast, in the *clinical* approach to assessment, interpretation of assessment data is made not on the basis of preset and uniformly applied rules but on the basis of the evaluator's judgment. Underlying the clinical approach is a reliance on the individual evaluator's experience, intuition, and judgment.

In general, research employing assessment data from various sources including test scores, interviews, and case histories has suggested that the actuarial or statistical approach tends to be superior to the clinical approach in prediction (Meehl, 1954, 1959, 1965). However, few if any of these studies have focused on the role of the clinician in the data-gathering process. In practice, clinicians seldom gather data using any rigorous set of rules. Rather, they gather data in a manner consistent with their own perception of the particular situation and with the dictates of their own background, training, and clinical experience. It is certainly possible that in some types of situations, the clinical data-gathering process employed by some clinicians—as well as the subsequent predictions made as a result of that process—may prove superior to any comparable actuarial process. The clinical interpretation process does have advantages over the actuarial process in those interpretation situations wherein there are insufficient data to formulate reliable and valid statistical rules.

Most contemporary objective tests of personality published by major test publishers come complete with mounds of normative data, which presumably will be put to use in some actuarial fashion. By contrast, a whole class of other psychological tests have traditionally not been norm-based with regard to test interpretation. Rather, this whole class of other psychological tests has traditionally relied more on the judgment and expertise of the clinician administrator/test interpreter. These traditionally more clinical tools of assessment are referred to as projective methods. Projective methods have been used by psychologists for a very long time, although interest in them has waxed and waned. Still, they are very much a part of the current scene in psychological testing and assessment. The following chapter will introduce you both to the great appeal of projective methods and to the reasons some psychologists believe these tests are of limited utility.

12

Projective Methods

Suppose the lights in your classroom were dimmed and everyone was told to stare at the clean chalkboard for a minute or so. And suppose everyone was then asked to take out some paper and write down what he or she thought he or she could "see" on the chalkboard—other than the chalkboard itself. If you examined what each of your fellow students wrote, you would probably find as many different things "seen" on that blank chalkboard as there are students responding. You might even assume that the students "saw" on the chalk-board—or, more accurately, *projected* onto the chalkboard—something that was not really on the chalkboard but, rather, in (or on) their own minds. You might further assume that each student's response to the blank chalkboard reflected something very telling about the student's personality structure.

The *projective hypothesis* holds that an individual supplies structure to un-structured stimuli in a manner consistent with the individual's own unique pat-tern of conscious and unconscious needs, fears, desires, impulses, conflicts, and ways of perceiving and responding. In the chalkboard exercise described, a blank chalkboard served as the unstructured stimulus upon which respondents projected. However, any relatively unstructured stimulus will do. In a scene in Shakespeare's play *Hamlet,* Polonius and Hamlet discuss what can be seen in clouds. Indeed, clouds could be used as a projective stimulus.[1] But psycholo-gists, slaves to practicality (and scientific methods) as they are, have developed projective measures of personality that are more reliable than clouds and more portable than chalkboards. In the sampling of tests to be discussed in this chap-ter, inkblots, pictures, words, drawings, and other things have been used as projective stimuli.

Unlike self-report methods, projective tests are *indirect* methods of person-

---

1. In fact, clouds *have* been used as projective stimuli. Wilhelm Stern's Cloud Picture Test, in which subjects were asked to tell what they saw in pictures of clouds, was one of the earliest projective measures.

ality assessment; the examinee's task is to talk about something or someone other than herself or himself, and inferences about the examinee's personality will be made from the response. On such a task, the ability—and presumably the inclination—of examinees to fake is greatly minimized. Also somewhat minimized is the testtaker's need for great proficiency in the English language; minimal language skills are required to respond to—or create—a drawing. For that reason, and because some projective methods may be less culture-linked than other measures of personality, proponents of projective testing believe that there is a promise of cross-cultural utility with these tests that has yet to be fulfilled. Proponents of projective measures also argue that a major advantage of such measures is that they tap unconscious as well as conscious material. And in the words of the man who coined the term *projective techniques*, "the most important things about an individual are what he cannot or will not say" (Frank, 1939, p. 395).[2]

Projective tests were born in the spirit of rebellion against normative data and through attempts by personality researchers to break down the study of personality into the study of specific traits of varying strengths. This orientation is exemplified in the following excerpts from Frank (1939):

> It is interesting to see how the students of personality have attempted to meet the problem of individuality with methods and procedures designed for study of uniformities and norms that ignore or subordinate individuality, treating it as a troublesome deviation which derogates from the real, the superior, and only important central tendency, mode, average, etc. (pp. 392–393)

> . . . physicists are using such devices as the Wilson Cloud Chamber and the Geiger Counter to obtain data on the *individual* electrical particle, which reveals its presence and energy by the path traced in water vapor, or by activation of the Counter, although never itself observable or directly measurable.

> These methodological procedures are being refined and extended because they offer possibilities for ascertaining what is either unknowable by other means or is undeterminable because the older analytic methods destroyed part or all of that which was to be studied. (pp. 398–399) [emphasis in the original]

Thus, in contrast to methods of personality assessment that focused on the individual from a statistics-based, normative perspective, projective techniques were at one time viewed as the technique of choice for focusing on the individual from a purely clinical perspective—a perspective that examined the unique way an individual projects onto an ambiguous stimulus "his way of seeing life, his meanings, significances, patterns, and especially his feelings" (Frank, 1939, p. 403). As we will see, however, years of clinical experience with these tests and a growing volume of research data have led interpretation of responses to projective stimuli to become increasingly norm-referenced in nature.

---

2. The first published use of the term *projective methods* that we are aware of was in an article entitled "Projective Methods in the Psychological Study of Children," by Ruth Horowitz and Lois Barclay Murphy (1938). However, these authors had read Lawrence K. Frank's (1939) as-yet-unpublished manuscript and had credited him for having "applied the term 'projective methods.'"

Figure 12–1
A Rorschach-like Inkblot

Inkblots as Projective Stimuli

In the film *Take the Money and Run,* Woody Allen, as Virgil Starkwell, a confirmed sociopath, responds to an inkblot similar to that presented in Figure 12–1 with: "It looks like two elephants making love to a men's glee club."

The public has become familiar with inkblot measures of personality through many such media gags. However, as is the case with much mass media psychology, many misconceptions attend the publicity. For example, one misconception concerning inkblot tests pertains to the importance of *what* an individual sees. In actuality, what an individual sees in the inkblots is important, but it is only one facet of a multifaceted task; factors related to *how* the individual sees the blot (that is, does he or she respond to large or small parts of it? to primarily the white or black area? to shading or color?) are all important in the interpretation process. Here we review the major test of this type, the Rorschach Inkblot Test.

The Rorschach

Developed by the Swiss psychiatrist Hermann Rorschach (1921/1942), the Rorschach Inkblot Test consists of ten bilaterally symmetrical—mirror-imaged if folded in half—inkblots that are printed on separate cards (see the box opposite). Five inkblots are achromatic (meaning "without color," or black-and-white); two are black, white, and red; and three are multicolored. The test comes with the cards only: no test manual, nor any administration, scoring, or interpretation instructions, nor any rationale for why some of the inkblots are achromatic and others are chromatic (with color). Filling the need for a test manual and administration, scoring, and interpretation instructions have been a number of manuals and handbooks that set forth a variety of methods (such as Beck, 1944, 1945, 1952, 1960; Exner, 1974, 1978, 1986; Exner & Weiner, 1982; Klopfer & Davidson, 1962; Piotrowski, 1957). Although there are differences among the systems in administration, scoring, and interpretation instructions, what follows is a description of the process in very general terms.

Hermann Rorschach (1884–1922)

Over a hundred years ago on November 8, Hermann Rorschach was born in Zurich, Switzerland. Hermann studied medicine in Zurich, Nuremberg, Bern, and Berlin and by 1909 had earned his license to practice medicine in Switzerland. Specializing in psychiatry, Rorschach came into contact with members of the psychoanalytic community in Zurich and himself employed psychoanalytic procedures with some of his patients. During his studies, he met a Russian female colleague, whom he married. At the end of 1913, Rorschach left his position in a Swiss mental asylum and moved with his wife to Russia, where he worked in a private clinic. But by July 1914, Rorschach had returned to Switzerland, where he served as an assistant director at a regional asylum. Rorschach's wife was detained from leaving the country by a declaration of war and did not rejoin him in Switzerland until the spring of 1915. Mrs. Rorschach's explanation for her husband's return to Switzerland was that "in spite of his interest in Russia and the Russians, he remained a true Swiss, attached to his native land. . . . He was European and intended to remain so at any price" (cited in Pichot, 1984, p. 591).

Complementing Rorschach's interest in psychoanalysis was an interest in art and drawing—an interest that perhaps stemmed from the fact that his father had been a teacher of art and drawing. By 1913, Rorschach had published papers on analyzing mental patients' artwork as a means of learning more about the personality. Among the more specific influences that may have contributed to Rorschach's development of his now-famous test were his familiarity with the work of his contemporary, Carl Jung. Jung was a pioneer in the area of word association testing—an assessment technique that employed a stimulus (a word) as an aid in bringing unconscious material to light. The published use of inkblots as a stimulus for association had appeared as early as 1857:

> The utilization of forms obtained "through chance" by folding over a piece of paper into the center of which some ink had been dropped had a long history. In 1857 Justinus Kerner had published a collection of poems entitled "Kleksographien." Kerner, who belonged to the so-called romantic school of German psychiatry, had been at one and the same time both a physician and a painter of repute. . . . In "Kleksographien" he had published a series of "chance inkblots" for each of which he had composed a poem. . . . In the collection of the "Kleksographien," each page showed, in justaposition [sic], an inkblot form and the poem it had evoked. It was a very successful book in German-speaking countries. Later it was republished and was thus known to Rorschach. (Pichot, 1984, pp. 594–595)

In turn-of-the-century France, Alfred Binet had experimented with inkblots as a test of imaginative ability. As Pichot (1984) says, the contribution of Hermann Rorschach lies not only in his development of the test but also in his "viewing the responses as determined by the *peculiarities of perception* which, in turn, were dependent upon the underlying structure of the personality" (p. 595, emphasis added). Rorschach's test was published in 1921 and was not an immediate success. He died the following year from appendicular peritonitis at the age of 38, unaware of the great legacy he was to leave.

The cards are presented to the subject one at a time in a prescribed sequence. The subject is instructed to tell what is on each of the cards with a question such as "What might this be?" from the examiner. The examiner records the subject's responses verbatim as well as the length of time required before the first response to each card. Other factors, such as the position of the card, spontaneous statements that the subject makes, and noteworthy nonverbal gestures or body movements, are also recorded. The examiner does not engage in any discussion concerning the subject's responses during the initial administration of the cards. Every effort is made to provide the subject with the opportunity to "project," free from any outside distractions.

After the entire set of cards has been administered once, a second administration, referred to as the "inquiry," is conducted. During the inquiry, the examiner attempts to determine what features of the inkblot played a role in formulating the subject's perceptions. Questions such as "What made it look like _____?" and "How do you see _____?" are asked in an attempt to clarify what was seen and which aspects of the inkblot were most influential in forming these percepts. The inquiry provides information that is useful in scoring and interpreting the responses. Also learned in the inquiry is whether the examinee remembers earlier responses, whether the original percept is still seen, and whether any new responses are now perceived.

A third component of the administration, referred to as "testing the limits," may also be included. This procedure enables the examiner to restructure the situation for the subject by asking specific questions that provide additional information concerning personality functioning.

If, for example, the subject has utilized the entire inkblot when forming percepts throughout the test, the examiner might want to determine if the subject would be able to respond to details within the inkblot. Under those conditions, the examiner might say, "Sometimes people use a part of the blot to see something." Alternatively, the examiner might point to a specific area of the card and ask the subject, "What does this look like?" A limit-testing procedure may also be undertaken, the objective being (1) to identify any confusion or misunderstanding concerning the task, (2) to aid the examiner in determining if the subject is able to refocus his or her percepts given a new frame of reference, and (3) to see if a subject made anxious by the ambiguous nature of the task is better able to perform given this added structure. At least one Rorschach researcher has advocated the technique of trying to elicit "one last response" from test-takers who think they have already given as many responses as they are going to give; the rationale is that "endings have many meanings," and the one last response may provide a source of questions and inferences applicable to treatment considerations (Cerney, 1984).

Hypotheses concerning personality functioning will be formed on the basis of all the variables we have outlined (such as the content of the response, the location of the response, the length of time to respond) plus many additional ones. In general, Rorschach protocols are scored according to several categories, including location, determinants, content, popularity, and form. *Location* refers to the part of the inkblot that was utilized in forming the percept. Individuals may use the entire inkblot, a large section, a small section, a minute detail, or white spaces. *Determinants* refers to the qualities of the inkblot that determine what the individual perceives: the form, color, shading, and/or movement that the individual attributes to the inkblot. *Content* refers to the content category of the response; although different scoring systems vary in some of the categories scored, certain general content areas such as human figures, animal figures, anatomical parts, blood, clouds, X rays, and sexual responses are usually included. *Popularity* refers to the frequency with which a certain response has been found to correspond with a particular inkblot or section of an inkblot. A popular response is one that has frequently been obtained from the general population. A rare response is one that has been perceived infrequently by the general population. The *form* of a response refers to how accurately the individual's perception matches or fits the corresponding part of the inkblot. Form level may be evaluated as being adequate or inadequate, or good or poor.

The scoring categories are considered to correspond to various aspects of personality functioning, and hypotheses concerning aspects of personality are based both on the number of responses that fall within each category and on the interrelationships among the categories. For example, the number of Whole responses (using the entire inkblot) in a Rorschach record is thought to be associated with conceptual thought processes. Form level is associated with reality testing, human movement with imagination, and color responses with emotional reactivity. Patterns of response, recurrent themes, and the interrelationships among the different scoring categories are all considered in arriving at a final description of the individual from a Rorschach protocol. Data concerning the responses of various clinical and nonclinical groups of adults, adolescents, and children have been compiled and are available for comparisons (see Ames et al., 1971; Ames et al., 1974; Exner, 1978, 1986; Exner & Weiner, 1982; Goldfried et al., 1971).

Psychometric properties   Assessing the reliability of the Rorschach test—regardless of the particular scoring system employed—presents difficulties, because traditional methods for assessing reliability have not proved feasible for this test (or other projective tests; see McClelland, 1980). It would be inappropriate, for example, to assess reliability by means of the split-half method, since each inkblot is considered to have a unique stimulus quality and is not comparable to any other inkblot on the test. In a study involving 67 emotionally disturbed children who were in residential treatment, Hayden (1981) found certain cards to be associated with parental figures. When asked to select the card "which in some way makes you think of your mother/father" (p. 227), two cards (IV and VII) were selected significantly more often than chance would allow. We should note that a subsequent analysis of the literature on the Rorschach cards that have come to be known as the "Mother" (card VII) and "Father" (card IV) cards has called into question the practice of evaluating parental relationships based on responses to those cards (Liaboe & Guy, 1985). However, if we concede that each card does have a unique stimulus quality, then we must also accept that a procedure such as the split-half method for evaluating the reliability of the test would be inappropriate.

The test-retest procedure for determining reliability has similarly been found to be lacking as a measure of reliability because responses to the stimulus cards are the result of many factors (needs, conflicts, concerns) occurring within the individual at the time of administration. Although certain themes may persist, the extent to which these factors are operative varies from administration to administration and with any changes that occur in the subject. Even the subject's familiarity with the test may influence the responses obtained. The difficulties inherent in devising an alternate form equivalent to the Rorschach were exemplified in the work of Behn, who, under Sigmund Freud's direction, was able to develop a similar but not alternate form of the test called the Behn-Rorschach (Buckle & Holt, 1951; Eichler, 1951; Swift, 1944).

With respect to inter-scorer reliability, a distinction must be made between (1) inter-scorer agreement on the basic scoring categories for a given system of scoring the Rorschach and (2) inter-scorer agreement on interpretations made from Rorschach protocols. In general, studies have shown acceptable levels of inter-scorer reliability with respect to basic scoring categories among trained scorers for a given scoring system. In an early study of the degree of inter-scorer agreement, 90% agreement was found for the location category; 83% agreement was found for the determinants of form and movement; and 75% agreement was found for the color and shade determinants (Remzy & Pickard, 1949). The highest degree of agreement was found to exist for the category of content (99%). These findings are similar to those obtained by Ames and her associates, who reported product-moment correlation coefficients of .92 (location), .90 (form and movement), .80 (color and shading), and .97 (content) among different scorers (Ames et al., 1952). Exner (1986) reported inter-rater agreement ranging from 87% to 99% for form, movement, color, and shading determinants. DeCato (1994) reported inter-rater reliabilities averaging .90 for simple responses and .81 for complex responses. One meta-analytic study of the Rorschach estimates reliability to be .86, with a 95% confidence interval of .82 to .90 (Parker et al., 1988). As illustrated in the box opposite, one journal that publishes a number of Rorschach studies, the *Journal of Personality Assessment*, began in 1991 to require evidence of at least 80% inter-scorer agreement with respect to ''variables central to the particular study'' (Weiner, 1991, p. 1).

Studies of inter-scorer reliability with respect to interpretations made from Rorschach protocols have not been nearly so encouraging. A study done as a doctoral dissertation at Yale University by Lisansky (1956) is noteworthy on two counts. First, the six Rorschach experts who participated in the study were polled in advance of the experiment to list the kinds of items they would feel confident in predicting from the Rorschach. The evolved list contained nine items (such as intellectual capacity, rigidity, and ambition) to be checked off on as many as five adjectives ranging from ''very superior'' to ''dull'' and a tenth item that asked for outstanding symptoms or diagnostic features. Second, the study represented an early sensitivity to the problems inherent in attempts to simulate clinical conditions. Thus, the study was responsive to the most frequently cited criticism of experimental work on personality tests:

The Agreement Requirement

Satisfied that adequately trained examiners can agree on the scoring of the variables of interest in a Rorschach study, the *Journal of Personality Assessment* published this notice in its first issue of 1991. Note that agreement with respect to how specific responses should be scored according to a particular scoring system does not necessarily imply agreement with respect to the interpretation of the scoring; interpretation is another matter entirely.

Editor's Note:
Inter-Scorer Agreement in
Rorschach Research

Ample evidence indicates that adequately trained examiners can agree reasonably well in their scoring of Rorschach variables for which clearly defined scoring criteria have been explicated. Although these data demonstrate the potential reliability of Rorschach scoring, they do not assure that Rorschach protocols will be reliably scored in each instance. The potential for reliable scoring is sometimes taken by researchers as sufficient basis for assuming scorer reliability of the protocols used in their studies. Such assumptions are unwarranted.

Accordingly, in keeping with sound psychometric practice, the *Journal of Personality Assessment* will now routinely require evidence of interscorer agreement in articles reporting Rorschach research. Investigators unfamiliar with methodology for examining scoring reliability on the Rorschach should follow the following procedures.

At least 20 protocols in a study should be scored by two or more examiners to monitor scoring reliability. For the purposes of this reliability check, the scores should be partitioned into such categories as location, determinants, form level, contents, and so on. For each category, a percentage tally should be made of the agreement between examiners on that category. For example, 20 protocols with a mean of 20 responses will yield 400 location scores. Of these 400 location scores, on what percentage were the scorers in agreement? Likewise, on what percentage of the 400 responses were the examiners in agreement concerning what the determinants should be, the form level, the content categories, and so on? Instances in which a researcher's examiners are unable to reach at least 80% agreement on a category indicate a need for revised scoring prior to any attempts to relate the Rorschach variables to other test or behavioral variables.

Reports of Rorschach research that do not include information on scoring reliability or indicate less than 80% agreement on variables central to the particular study will be returned for further work before being accepted for publication.

Irving B. Weiner

Blind interpretations are considered to be parlor tricks by most competent Rorschach interpreters. On the other hand, a history including description of the patient's symptoms and a psychiatric evaluation undoubtedly influences interpretation so that we are no longer dealing with the reliability of the Rorschach test alone as a clinical instrument. The aim of the study was to simulate clinic conditions but to minimize cues other than the Rorschach test. Each Rorschach protocol was therefore accompanied by an abstract of the patient's life history containing some facts of his life but no information about the patient's personality traits, emotional reactions or the opinions of others about him. The life history abstract included the patient's age and sex and the most important facts of his family, educational, occupational, marital, religious, military and medical history. (Lisansky, 1956, pp. 311–312)

A total of 40 Rorschach protocols chosen so that there were at least 15 and not more than 60 responses were given to two groups of three Rorschach experts to score on the prearranged checklist. The experts had an average of 10.5 years of experience in clinical psychology and at least 8 years' experience with the Rorschach. All had published on the Rorschach and all had taught the Rorschach. As a control group, six other clinicians who averaged 7½ years of experience were given only the abstracts and asked to complete the same checklist. The degree of agreement among the clinicians in the control group was only .32, poor reliability by any standard. The degree of agreement among the expert Rorschach users—who not only had the case history and Rorschach to judge with but also were using an outcome measure that they had devised— was only .33 (virtually the same low degree of reliability as that of the controls). The finding is particularly compelling because the questionnaire had been specifically designed to tap question areas that the Rorschach (and not the life history abstract) was supposed to be able to answer.

In another inter-scorer reliability study (Korner & Westwood, 1955), degree of agreement among three trained Rorschach users was only .31. Even two researchers who were clearly sympathetic to the use of this test were compelled to conclude from their data that "a substantial majority of Rorschach reports have very little communication value" (Datel & Gengerelli, 1955, p. 380).

Efforts to improve inter-rater agreement with respect to interpretation have involved developing clear criteria for particular interpretations. For example, Coleman et al. (1993) examined the degree to which raters would agree concerning the presence of thought disorder in Rorschach records using a measure called the Thought Disorder Index (Solovay et al., 1986). Thought disorder is a classic characteristic of schizophrenia that includes a wide range of irregularities in thinking, such as incoherence and loose associations between ideas. The ambiguity of an inkblot or some other projective stimulus is thought by many advocates of projective methods to be a favorable medium for eliciting evidence of thought disorder. The Thought Disorder Index, developed for use with Rorschach protocols, was designed to be an aid in identifying and estimating the severity of thought disorder. In the Coleman et al. study, teams of raters applied the Thought Disorder Index to 20 Rorschach protocols. Inter-rater reliability ranged from .80 to .90 for the total Index score, and from .52 to .93 (median .75) for specific aspects of thought disorder. Coleman et al. concluded that raters can agree on their conclusion about thought disorder in Rorschach protocols when using the Thought Disorder Index as an interpretive guide. Other researchers exploring the inter-rater reliability of the Rorschach in similar contexts have arrived at similar conclusions (e.g., Stricker & Healey, 1990).

Answers to questions concerning the validity of the Rorschach test, regardless of the scoring system employed, have been matters of heated controversy; academicians have traditionally claimed that experimental data, primarily from the large number of studies executed in the 1950s, provide no evidence or justification for the widespread use of this test, whereas clinicians have retorted that the Rorschach is a rich source of valuable clinical data. Studies such as those indicating that the Rorschach test is ineffective in differentiating between clinical groups (for example, Guilford, 1948; Wittenborn & Holzberg, 1951) or is not predictive of psychotherapy outcome (Rogers et al., 1951) have been cited frequently. Further, clinical experience with the test was *not* shown to enhance accuracy of interpretation. In one study (Turner, 1966), four groups of 25 judges ($n = 100$) were asked to score Rorschach protocols and then to predict statements pertaining to the patient that had previously been made by the hospital staff. The members of the four groups were varied in their familiarity with the Rorschach and in their knowledge of the Rorschach scoring system. In one group were 25 Fellows of the Society for Projective Techniques who were considered experts in the use of the Rorschach. The other three groups consisted of recently graduated clinical psychologists, graduate students in clinical psychology, and undergraduates who had little or no familiarity with the Rorschach. The results were that all of the four groups were right in about 65 percent of their predictions.

A meta-analysis compared the convergent validity of the Rorschach, the WAIS, and the MMPI. The WAIS was found to have the highest levels of convergent validity (estimated to be .62). Interestingly, the estimate for the Rorschach was .41, which was not significantly different from the convergent validity estimate of .46 for the MMPI (Parker et al., 1988). Such findings reflect positively on the validity of the Rorschach, especially given the wide esteem in which the MMPI is held.

Goldfried, Stricker, and Reiner (1971) suggested that interpretation based on the Rorschach is most justified in those situations where the test is viewed as a structured interview, the results of which are analyzed by skilled clinicians. In a similar vein, Korchin and Schuldberg (1981) took note of a trend to regard the Rorschach as "less of a test" and more as "an open and flexible arena for studying interpersonal transactions" (p. 1151). Commenting on that trend, Berg (1984) wrote, "This shift in perspective opens the door to a range of useful interventions and ways of understanding test data not otherwise available to the examiner" (p. 11). One such new way of understanding Rorschach data—indeed, a relatively new way of administering, scoring, and interpreting the test—is the "consensus method of administration," described and illustrated with case material on two couples (Klopfer, 1984).

It has been argued that even if the validity of the Rorschach has not been satisfactorily demonstrated for clinical use, it is still useful as a research instrument. In fact, the Rorschach has been utilized extensively for research purposes (see the box on pages 435–437). A perusal of any relatively recent edition in the *Mental Measurements Yearbook* series will list not dozens of references, not hundreds of references, but thousands of references to this test. And regardless of the question of its validity, the Rorschach remains a widely used clinical tool (Howes, 1981). In a survey of 194 members of the Society for Personality Assessment that included a checklist for reporting frequency of usage of 18 popular psychological tests, it was found that "the Rorschach was by far the most frequently utilized projective technique" (Piotrowski et al., 1985, p. 117). A survey of universities in the United States offering graduate-level training in clinical psychology indicated that "the greatest proportion of required diagnostic training is allocated to projective testing" (Kolbe et al., 1985, p. 60), followed by training in intelligence testing. When members of the Division of Clinical Psychology of the American Psychological Association were asked which tests they would advise graduate students to learn, the Rorschach was at the top of the list. The survey authors hypothesized that clinicians were probably unaffected by negative research, in part because they accord greater weight to personal clinical experience than to experimental evidence (Wade & Baker, 1977). The Rorschach is the most frequently taught projective technique in counseling psychology programs (Watkins et al., 1990) and is widely used at practicum sites (Craig, 1990).

Exner's Comprehensive System   By the mid-1950s, no fewer than five systems for administering and scoring the Rorschach test were in use—systems developed by Samuel J. Beck, Marguerite R. Hertz, Bruno Klopfer, Zygmund Piotrowski, and David Rapaport with Roy Schafer. Despite differences among the systems and even though many clinicians might "pick and choose" elements from each of the different systems to employ in their own administrations of the test, general usage of the test by clinicians flourished, and it tended to be referred to as *the* Rorschach—as if it were a standardized test.[3]

Which of the five existing Rorschach systems had the greatest clinical utility? That was the question John E. Exner, Jr. (see the box on page 439), tackled in a study designed to compare the empirical strengths of each existing system. Exner's (1969) work highlighted the differences among the existing systems and served as a stimulus to the establishment of a Rorschach Research Foundation, with an objective of surveying practitioners and reviewing and cross-referencing the scholarly literature on the test. Using the findings and experimentally exploring the efficacy of a sixth system that integrated into it the best features of the five existing systems, Exner (1974) published what he called a "Comprehensive System" for administering, scoring, and interpreting the

---

3. An example of "picking and choosing" in the context of interpretive criteria can be found in a recent article having to do with Rorschach indicators of child abuse. Describing the measures she used in her study, Saunders (1991, p. 55) writes: "Rorschach protocols were scored using Rapaport et al.'s (1945–46) system as the basic framework, but special scores of four different types were added. I borrowed two of these additional measures from other researchers (Holt, 1977; Wilson, 1985) and developed the other two specifically for this study."

The Computerized Rorschach

Computer-assisted scoring and interpretation of the Rorschach can be accomplished in the clinician's office with specially developed software, or through centralized scoring services where protocol data are processed. In both cases, the trained clinician administers the test and then prepares the raw data for computer scoring and interpretation. The computer may be programmed with any one of a variety of existing Rorschach scoring systems—each with its own rules for scoring and interpreting individual responses and combinations of responses. All the findings may be integrated in narrative summaries that deal with cognitive, emotional, and other aspects of the testtaker's functioning.

To illustrate the type of information obtained from such an administration of the Rorschach, consider the case of Hermann Goering (1893–1946), a high-ranking official in Germany during Hitler's reign. Born to a distinguished family in Bavaria, Goering distinguished himself as a member of Germany's Air Force during World War I and received the Iron Cross, First Class. After meeting Hitler, he became active in the Nazi party in Germany. He helped organize the secret police as well as the concentration camps and held more than 20 offices in Nazi Germany; among his titles was that of "Chief Liquidator." Goering is also credited—or discredited—with having signed the most drastic of the anti-Semitic decrees issued by the German state. Described as one of the world's most powerful industrialists of the time and as the economic dictator of Germany, Goering had been designated as Hitler's successor. However, Goering was convicted of war crimes at the Nuremberg trials and sentenced to death. Goering committed suicide by taking poison the night before he was to be executed.

Shortly after the German surrender in 1945, while the captured Nazis were awaiting trial, Rorschach tests were administered to them by the prison psychologist, Gustave Gilbert. The Rorschach responses were published in a book entitled *The Nuremberg Mind* (Miale & Selzer, 1975), and these published data served as the raw data by which two Rorschach experts independently scored the test and then fed their findings into a computerized program based on the Klopfer et al. (1954; Klopfer & Davidson, 1962) scoring system (the Century Diagnostics Computer Interpreted Rorschach). What the computer had to say about Hermann Goering on the basis of his Rorschach data follows. Compare these findings with the profile of a typical healthy adult as published in Klopfer and Davidson (1962, pp. 147–148) or as shown in the second profile on page 437.

(continued)

The Computerized Rorschach *(continued)*

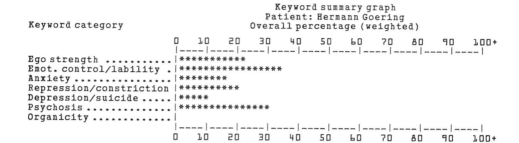

```
                                          Keyword summary graph
                                          Patient: Hermann Goering
          Keyword category               Overall percentage (weighted)

                                   0   10   20   30   40   50   60   70   80   90  100+
                                   |----|----|----|----|----|----|----|----|----|----|
          Ego strength ...........|**********
          Emot. control/lability .|*****************
          Anxiety ...............|********
          Repression/constriction |**********
          Depression/suicide .....|*****
          Psychosis .............|**************
          Organicity ............|
                                   |----|----|----|----|----|----|----|----|----|----|
                                   0   10   20   30   40   50   60   70   80   90  100+
```

Patient ID: Goering   Sex: M
Cognitive function

This individual's ego strength score which represents his overall adaptive capacity for
cognitive processing, reality function and ability to handle stress effectively is POOR.
There will likely be difficulties in coping with stress cognitively. In addition, this
individual may be uncomfortable in new social situations and experience difficulties in
his outward adjustment with others. Because of his limited cognitive resources, his level
of sexual and/or aggressive impulses, although not excessive, may result in disruption of
judgment and intermittent acting out. However, he shows an ability to react to situations
in a calm, dispassionate, and impartial manner when such a response is appropriate. A tendency toward distorted perceptual/thought processes is present, but may or may not be indicative of psychosis.

Emotional function

This individual's emotional control/lability score is ELEVATED. The possibility of emotional lability and subsequent loss of control when placed under stress should be carefully considered. This individual exhibits a definite lack in the ability to meet emotional needs in an adaptive, socially appropriate manner. There are high levels of
emotional lability and impulsivity. There is a strong likelihood of breakdown of emotional
control when placed under stress. This individual is likely to be unable to delay gratification of his immediate emotional needs. Impulsive or explosive behavior and egocentric
personality features are prominent. A MODERATE level of anxiety is indicated.

Interpersonal function

The ability to meet dependency and security needs through socially appropriate interactions with others is very poor. Success in meeting these needs through secondary channels
of gratification, such as recognition, achievement, or adaptive conformity is unlikely.
Overall reduced awareness, repression and/or denial of dependency and security needs may
result in unsuccessful and frustrating interpersonal relationships.

THIS NARRATIVE SUMMARY IS BASED UPON THE PRECEDING RORSCHACH REPORT. IT IS NOT INTENDED AS A
SUBSTITUTE FOR THAT REPORT, WHICH SHOULD BE READ IN ITS ENTIRETY. THIS REPORT IS INTENDED FOR
PROFESSIONAL USE ONLY.

Figure 1
Profile of Hermann Goering

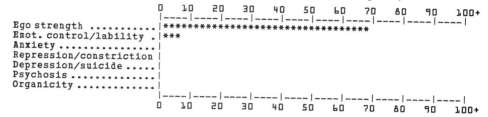

```
                                  Keyword summary graph
                                    Patient ID: NORMAL
 Keyword category                Overall percentage (weighted)

                           0   10   20   30   40   50   60   70   80   90  100+
                           |----|----|----|----|----|----|----|----|----|----|
 Ego strength ...........  |*******************************************
 Emot. control/lability .  |***
 Anxiety ................  |
 Repression/constriction   |
 Depression/suicide .....  |
 Psychosis ..............  |
 Organicity ............   |
                           |----|----|----|----|----|----|----|----|----|----|
                           0   10   20   30   40   50   60   70   80   90  100+
```

Patient ID: Normal   Sex: F   Age: 38

Cognitive function

This individual's ego strength score which represents her overall adaptive capacity for cognitive processing, reality function and ability to handle stress effectively is EXCELLENT. This individual appears capable of taking a balanced intellectual and perceptual approach to problem solving situations. She has the ability to develop an overview of situations while simultaneously dealing with the common sense aspects of a problem. This person is fully able to utilize her adaptive resources in her interaction with others. She has a reasonable acceptance regarding the presence of a sexual and aggressive impulse life. No maladaptive cognitive defensive strategies are noted. She shows an ability to react to situations in a calm, dispassionate, and impartial manner when such a response is appropriate.

Emotional function

This individual's emotional control/lability score is LOW and suggests the possibility of emotional overcontrol. However, this individual is capable of considering others in the expression of her emotions. She has the capacity to delay gratification of her emotional needs in the face of environmental stress. There is a healthy control over emotional impact without loss of flexibility. Responsiveness is appropriately modulated. Overall, this individual shows potential for appropriate emotional spontaneity which is likely to be an asset to her adjustment.

Interpersonal function

This individual appears to have adequate potential for meeting dependency and security needs through socially appropriate interactions with others. She is capable of meeting her needs through derived secondary channels of gratification, such as, recognition, achievement, or adaptive conformity. In addition, there is adequate potential for deeper, more primary affectional responsivity, such as physical contact and closeness. Overall, this person appears to have achieved an appropriate level of socialization, wherein she should be able to meet her needs through socially satisfying interaction with others.

THIS NARRATIVE SUMMARY IS BASED UPON THE PRECEDING RORSCHACH REPORT. IT IS NOT INTENDED AS A SUBSTITUTE FOR THAT REPORT, WHICH SHOULD BE READ IN ITS ENTIRETY. THIS REPORT IS INTENDED FOR PROFESSIONAL USE ONLY.

Figure 2
Profile of a Healthy Adult

Rorschach test. Subsequent volumes (Exner, 1978, 1986; Exner & Weiner, 1982) have elaborated on—and made yet more comprehensive—the comprehensive system. After administration of the ten cards and an inquiry, responses to each card are scored or, to use Exner's preferred term, "coded." The coding process is too complicated to detail in its entirety here. In general, each response is coded with reference to the following seven categories: Location, Determinant(s), Form Quality, Content(s), Popularity, Organizational Activity, and Special Scores. Using the category scores, interpretive scores and indices such as an obsessive style index, a depression index, a coping deficit index, and a schizophrenia index may be derived. Exner and associates (for example, Exner et al., 1978) have reported impressive test-retest reliability coefficients for the system. However, as Exner (1983) has pointed out, some scoring categories are, of necessity, unreliable, since they are sensitive to the present state of the testtaker:

> The psychological state of the subject at the time of testing is one variable that potentially affects a test's psychometric properties. Using the Comprehensive System, this variable does not effect [sic] the entire Rorschach test or many of the scoring variables. There are, however, some variables that are *state* related. For example, the scores for inanimate movement (m) and diffuse shading (Y) are very unstable over short periods and longer intervals of time. Yet, their interpretive significance seems unquestionable; both are clearly correlated with external variables which indicate the presence of situational stress (Exner, 1978; Exner & Weiner, 1982). Thus, some Comprehensive System scores defy the axiom that something cannot be valid unless it is also reliable. (pp. 410–411)

Normative findings that employed a sample of more than 2,500 subjects were reported by Exner (1978, 1986), and findings with respect to 1,970 nonpatient children were reported by Exner and Weiner (1982). The most recent set of norms (Exner, 1993) included 700 "normal" adults who produced protocols with more than 14 responses. Interpretation of a properly coded test protocol with reference to this normative base of data can lead, according to Exner (1990, 1993) and others, to interpretive statements that are sound from a psychometric viewpoint.

When assessing personality in children, many psychologists find projective devices such as the Rorschach attractive. Most projective tests don't require the testtaker to read or write. The instructions, to tell a story or to explain what one sees in an inkblot, are clear and appealing even to young children. Indeed, Exner (1990) indicates that the Rorschach can be used with children as young as age 5.

Do children's Rorschach responses actually indicate anything about their personalities? Exner (1990) notes that young children often give a smaller number of responses than needed for his scoring system, and that little can be learned from such a child's Rorschach responses. Even if we assume that the child does produce a sufficient number of responses, some researchers would still question the validity of conclusions drawn from the Rorschach. For example, measures of depression derived from the Rorschach seem to be unrelated to objective measures of depression in children (Ball et al., 1991; Belter

John E. Exner, Jr.

John E. Exner, Jr., was born in 1928 in Syracuse, New York. His postsecondary education was delayed and then significantly molded by his military service. He served in the Army Air Corps from 1945 to 1949. He had completed just three semesters of pre-law college courses at the University of Buffalo after he was recalled to military service in 1950, just before the Korean War began. He returned from Korea in 1951, and while still on active duty, took courses at Trinity University in San Antonio, Texas. From Trinity he earned both B.S. (1953) and M.S. (1955) degrees. The Air Force then offered to transfer him to a base close to a graduate school. Exner was admitted to Cornell University and transferred to Sampson Air Force Base, about 30 miles from the Cornell campus. The Air Force arranged his schedule so that he could fulfill both his academic and his military commitments. He completed the Ph.D. in clinical psychology at Cornell in 1958.

Exner became interested in the Rorschach at Cornell, while studying with Frank S. Freeman, a specialist in psychological testing. Freeman arranged for Exner to spend the summers of 1954 and 1955 with two of the most prominent figures of Rorschach history, Samuel Beck at the University of Chicago and Bruno Klopfer at the University of California—Los Angeles. Exner was struck by the fact that although both Beck and Klopfer received him warmly, they disliked each other so much that they had not spoken to one another since 1939. Their impact on Exner was considerable. Their encouragement, coupled with Freeman's, caused Exner to concentrate on Rorschach research and to complete a Rorschach study for his doctoral dissertation in 1958.

Exner's curiosity about the reasons for the extensive disagreements between Beck and Klopfer led to a lifelong interest in the Rorschach. Exner also became interested in the ideas of other well-known Rorschach figures, including David Rapaport, Marguerite Hertz, and Zygmund Piotrowski. He studied their ideas as he taught psychology at DePauw University (1957–1962), Bowling Green State University (1962–1969), and Long Island University (1969–1984). Exner attempted to resolve the disagreements among the various Rorschach figures by taking from each those ideas that had the strongest research support. He integrated these into a single approach, which was first published in 1974 as *The Rorschach: A Comprehensive System. Volume 1.* It has been revised twice (1986, 1993), and Volumes 2 (1978, 1991) and 3 (1982, 1994) were written to expand the information concerning research about the test and its clinical applications. Exner has also published over 60 articles and book chapters related to personality assessment in general and the Rorschach in particular. Exner's work has been recognized by the Society for Personality Assessment, which honored him in 1990 with the Walter Klopfer Award for Contribution to the Literature, and again in 1993 with the Marguerite Hertz Memorial Lecture Series Award.

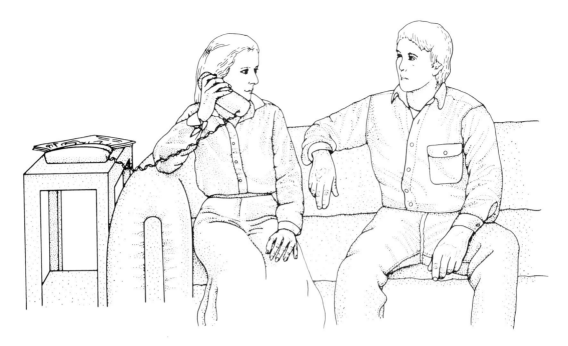

Figure 12–2
A TAT-like Picture

et al., 1989), and little relationship is found between Rorschach and pencil-and-paper measures of children's self-concept (Belter et al., 1989). Other studies support the Rorschach's validity with children. Test scores differ in expected ways between children with and without gender disturbance (Lerner, 1990) and from before to after treatment (Gerstle et al., 1988). Ridley (1987) found that Rorschach indices of cognitive development are associated with WISC-R intelligence test scores, and Wenar and Curtis (1991) note that the age-related changes in Rorschach responses reflected in Exner's age norms are consistent with cognitive developmental theories. Clearly much more research is needed before firm conclusions can be drawn that the Rorschach is (or is not) an effective means of assessing personality in children.

As the use of Exner's scoring system grows in popularity, we can look forward to the publication of more studies by independent investigators with respect to the psychometric soundness of the system. As we saw previously, however, studies of the psychometric soundness of the Rorschach test that employed a variety of systems other than the Comprehensive System have tended to reinforce the image of the test as a tool that may be clinically useful but unable to pass muster under rigorous scrutiny from a psychometric perspective.

Pictures as Projective Stimuli

Look at Figure 12-2. Having looked at it, make up a story about it. Your story should have a beginning, a middle, and an end. Write it down, using as much paper as you need. Bring the story to class with you and compare it with some other student's story.[4] What does the story reveal about your needs, fears, desires, impulse control, ways of viewing the world—your personality? What does the story written by your classmate reveal about her or him?

This exercise introduces you to the use of pictures as projective stimuli. Pictures used as projective stimuli may be photos of real persons, of animals, of objects, or of anything; they may be paintings, drawings, etchings, or any other variety of picture. One of the earliest uses of pictures as projective stimuli came at the turn of the century. An article by Brittain (1907) in a journal called *The Pedagogical Seminary* reported sex differences in stories that children gave in response to nine pictures. The author reported that the girls were more interested in religious and moral themes than were the boys. The next year, another experimenter used pictures and a story-telling technique to investigate the imagination of children, and differences in themes as a function of age were observed (Libby, 1908). In 1932, a psychiatrist working at the Clinic for Juvenile Research in Detroit developed the Social Situation Picture Test (Schwartz, 1932), a projective instrument that contained pictures relevant to juvenile delinquents. Working at the Harvard Psychological Clinic in 1935, Christiana D. Morgan and Henry Murray published the Thematic Apperception Test (TAT)—pronounced by saying the letters and not by rhyming with "cat"—the instrument that has come to be the most widely used of all of the picture/story-telling projective tests. We discuss the TAT as well as some related instruments.

The Thematic Apperception Test (TAT)

The TAT was originally designed as an aid to eliciting fantasy material from patients in psychoanalysis (Morgan & Murray, 1935). The stimulus materials consist of 31 cards, of which one is blank. The 30 picture cards, all black-and-white, contain a variety of scenes that were designed to present the testtaker with "certain classical human situations" (Murray, 1943). Some of the pictures contain a lone individual, some contain a group of people, and some contain no people. Some of the pictures appear to be as real as a photo, and others are surrealistic drawings. Examinees are introduced to the examination with the "cover story" that it is a "test of imagination" in which it is their task to tell what events led up to the scene in the picture, what is happening at that moment, and what the outcome will be. Examinees are also asked to tell what the people depicted in the cards are thinking and feeling. In the TAT *Manual*, Murray (1943) also advised that the examiners attempt to find out what the

---

4. Do it! At the very least, it's a good way of introducing yourself to someone in the class whom you haven't yet met.

source of the story was; in this context, it is noteworthy that the noun *apperception* is derived from the verb *apperceive,* which is defined as "to perceive in terms of past perceptions." The source of a story could be anything—a personal experience, a dream, an imagined event, a book, an episode of *Roseanne,* and so on. If the blank card is administered, examinees are instructed to imagine that there is a picture on the card and then proceed to tell a story about it.

In clinical practice, examiners tend to take liberties with various elements pertaining to the administration, scoring, and interpretation of the TAT. For example, although 20 cards is the recommended number for presentation, in practice an examiner might administer as few as one or two cards or as many as all 31. If a clinician is assessing a patient who has a penchant for telling stories that fill reams of the clinician's notepad, it's a good bet that fewer cards will be administered. If, on the other hand, a patient tells brief, one- or two-sentence stories, more cards may be administered in an attempt to collect more raw data with which to work. Some of the cards are suggested for use with adult males, adult females, or both, and some are suggested for use with children. This is so because certain pictorial representations lend themselves more than others to identification and projection by members of these groups. In one study involving 75 males (25 each of 11- , 14- , and 17-year-olds), Cooper (1981) identified the ten most productive cards for use with adolescent males. *In practice,* however, any card—be it one recommended for use with males, with females, or with children—may be administered to any subject; the clinician administering selects the cards that he or she believes will elicit responses pertinent to the objective of the testing.

The raw material used in drawing conclusions about the individual examined with the TAT are (1) the stories as they were told by the examinee, (2) the clinician's notes about the way or the manner in which the examinee responded to the cards, and (3) the clinician's notes about extra-test behavior and verbalizations. The last two categories of raw data (test and extra-test behavior) are sources of clinical interpretations for almost any individually administered test. Analysis of the story content requires special training. One illustration of how a testtaker's behavior during testing may influence the examiner's interpretations of the findings was provided by Sugarman (1991, p. 140), who told of a "highly narcissistic patient [who] demonstrated contempt and devaluation of the examiner (and presumably others) by dictating TAT stories complete with spelling and punctuation as though the examiner was a stenographer."

A number of systems for interpreting TAT data exist, though all are based to a greater or lesser degree in Henry Murray's influential theory of personality, excellent summaries of which are available (in, for example, Hall & Lindzey, 1970; Murray, 1959; Murray & Kluckhohn, 1953). In particular, interpretive systems for the TAT tend to incorporate the Murrayan concepts of *need* (determinants of behavior arising from within the individual), *press* (determinants of behavior arising from within the environment), and *thema* (a unit of interaction between needs and press). In general, the guiding principle in interpreting TAT stories is that the testtaker is identifying with someone (the protagonist) in the story and that the needs, environmental demands, and conflicts of the protagonist in the story are in some way related to the concerns, hopes, fears, or desires

Table 12–1
A Description of the Sample TAT-like Picture

Author's Description

A male and a female are seated in close proximity on a sofa. The female is talking on the phone. There is an end table with a magazine on it next to the sofa.

Manifest Stimulus Demand

Some explanation of the nature of the relationship between these two persons and some reason the woman is on the phone are required. Less frequently noted is the magazine on the table and its role in this scene.

Form Demand

Two large details, the woman and the man, must be integrated. Small details include the magazine and the telephone.

Latent Stimulus Demand

This picture is likely to elicit attitudes toward heterosexuality and, within that context, material relevant to the examinee's "place" on optimism-pessimism, security-insecurity, dependence-independence, passivity-assertiveness, and related continuums. Alternatively, attitudes toward family and friends may be elicited with the two primary figures being viewed as brother and sister, the female talking on the phone to a family member, etc.

Frequent Plots

We haven't administered this card to enough people to make judgments about what constitutes "frequent plots." We have, however, provided a sampling of plots (Table 12–2).

Significant Variations

Just as we cannot provide information on frequent plots, we cannot report data on significant variations. We would guess, however, that most college students viewing this picture would perceive the two individuals in it as being involved in a heterosexual relationship. Were that to be the case, a significant variation would be a story in which the characters are not involved in a heterosexual relationship (for example, they are employer/employee). Close clinical attention will also be paid to the nature of the relationship of the characters to any "introduced figures" (persons not pictured in the card but introduced into the story by the examinee). The "pull" of this card is to introduce the figure to whom the woman is speaking. What is the phone call about? How will the story be resolved?

---

of the examinee. In his discussion of the TAT from the perspective of a clinician, William Henry (1956) examined each of the cards in the test with regard to such variables as "manifest stimulus demand," "form demand," "latent stimulus demand," frequent plots, and significant variations. To get an idea of how some of these terms are used, look again at Figure 12–2—a picture that is *not* a TAT card—and then read Tables 12–1 and 12–2, which are descriptions of the card and some responses to the card from college-age respondents. Although a clinician may obtain bits of information from the stories told about every individual card, the clinician's final impressions will usually derive from a consideration of the overall patterns of themes that emerge.

TAT scoring and interpretation systems based on the work of personality theorists other than Henry Murray may also be found. For example, an "Affect Maturity Scale" that has its basis in Anna Freud's notion of affect development and maturation has been described by Thompson (1986). Westen and his colleagues (Westen et al., 1985; Westen et al., 1988) have reported on the develop-

Table 12-2
Some Responses to the Sample Picture

Respondent	Story
1. (Male)	This guy has been involved with this girl for a few months. Things haven't been going all that well. He's suspected that she's been seeing a lot of guys. This is just one scene in a whole evening where the phone hasn't stopped ringing. Pretty soon he is just going to get up and leave.
2. (Female)	This couple is dating. They haven't made any plans for the evening and they are wondering what they should do. She is calling up another couple to ask if they want to get together. They will go out with the other couple and have a good time.
3. (Male)	This girl thinks she is pregnant and is calling the doctor for the results of her test. This guy is pretty worried because he has plans to finish college and go to graduate school. He is afraid she will want to get married, and he doesn't want to get trapped into anything. The doctor will tell her she isn't pregnant, and he'll be really relieved.
4. (Female)	This couple has been dating for about two years and they're very much in love. She's on the phone firming up plans for a down-payment on a hall that's going to cater the wedding. That's a bridal magazine on the table over there. They look like they're really in love. I think things will work out for them even though the odds are against it—the divorce rates and all.
5. (Male)	These are two very close friends. The guy has a real problem and needs to talk to someone. He is feeling really depressed and that he is all alone in the world. Every time he starts to tell her how he feels, the phone rings. Pretty soon he will leave feeling like no one has time for him and even more alone. I don't know what will happen to him, but it doesn't look good.

ment of the Object Relations and Social Cognition Scale (ORSCS), a measure used in conjunction with the TAT and based in object relations theory as well as social-cognitive psychology.

Reliability   Inter-scorer reliability for trained examiners using the same scoring methods can be acceptably high. For evaluations of complexity in TAT protocols, inter-rater reliability coefficients ranging from .89 to .93 have been reported (Leigh et al., 1992). For evaluations of affective content on the TAT, Thomas and Dudek (1985) reported inter-rater reliability coefficients ranging from .93 to .97. For a TAT coding system designed to tap several psychodynamic personality characteristics, inter-rater reliabilities ranging from .75 to .95 have been reported (Stricker & Healey, 1990; for comparison, see also Sivik & Hosterey, 1992). However, although scorers can be trained to agree with respect to specific scoring criteria, the reliability of interpretations made from TAT data is not readily amenable to assessment by the usual means of determining reliability (such as split-half, test-retest, alternate-form) because of the nature of the task (see McClelland, 1980) and the susceptibility of responses on the test to various factors, including those discussed in the following paragraphs.

Situational factors can affect TAT responses. Variables such as the examiner, experiences just before test administration, and even the manner in which instructions and/or comments are given during the test administration all have an effect on TAT responses. In a study that examined the effect of the age of the examiner on TAT performance (Mussen & Scodel, 1955), two groups of male college students were shown slides of nude females and were instructed to rate their attractiveness. One group had the slides presented by a "stern man" in his sixties; the other by a "young, informal" graduate student. TAT's were then administered and scored for expressed sexual themes. The scores from the group with the "informal" presenter were higher than those of the other group, suggesting that the aroused need was inhibited to a greater degree in the presence of a presenter viewed as an authority figure. Significant differences in TAT scores as a function of the examiner's presence or absence have also been found to occur (Bernstein, 1956). In examining the way experiences just before TAT administration may affect performance, Lindzey (1950) found that exposing subjects to socially frustrating situations just before TAT administration resulted in a greater incidence of aggressive acts carried out by the hero of the stories, and Feshback (1961) found that subjects insulted before TAT administration exhibited more aggression in their stories than did a noninsulted group. Bellak (1944) was able to demonstrate that subjects criticized *during* TAT administration increased their use of aggressive words on the remaining cards. Although the variables in these studies cited were carefully manipulated and controlled, in most cases the extent to which situational factors are operative and affect performance is unknown, making measurement of the test's reliability difficult.

Transient internal-need states can affect TAT responses. Need states such as hunger, thirst, fatigue, and higher-than-ordinary levels of sexual tension experienced by the subject during a particular administration of a picture-story task can affect the subject's responses on that occasion. For example, the effect of food deprivation on TAT protocols has been investigated (McClelland & Atkinson, 1948; Sanford, 1936), with the findings indicating that food responses were found to vary as a function of the degree of food deprivation experienced (that is, the greater the deprivation, the higher the number of food responses). Investigations of the effect of sleep deprivation and other variables on TAT protocols have also been conducted (see Atkinson, 1958). To the extent that responses on the TAT are subject to temporary states, determination of the more enduring personality characteristics becomes difficult, and the accuracy of reliability estimates becomes questionable.

The TAT cards themselves have different stimulus "pulls." Some of the TAT pictures are more likely than others to elicit stories with themes of depression or despair, for example, than are other cards (see Goldfried & Zax, 1965). Some cards are more apt to elicit stories that deal with such needs as the need for achievement, for example, than are other cards. Given that the cards themselves have different stimulus "pulls" or, more technically stated, different "latent stimulus demands," it would become difficult for a psychometrist to determine the inter-item reliability of the test; card 1 might reliably elicit need achievement themes, whereas card 16, for example, might not usually elicit any such themes.

The open-ended nature of the task contributes to methodological difficulties in determining psychometric soundness. One can readily appreciate the methodological difficulties in determining the inter-item reliability inherent in a test where one item may elicit only one or two sentences in response and another item might elicit one or two pages. The open-ended nature of the TAT enables highly individualistic responses, but it also creates numerous possibilities for response patterns. Variations occur not only in length of response but in content, story themes, and levels of abstraction as well. Although it may be established that certain factors affect these variables, such as intelligence contributing to number of story themes (Rubin, 1964) and length of response (Webb & Hilden, 1953), developing a psychometrically rigorous procedure to account for all these variables would be an unenviably complex task.

Intentional desire to fake good or to fake bad can affect TAT response. One of the assumptions inherent in the TAT and in projective measures in general is that the examinee is unaware of the significance of his or her responses. This point has been made by the author of the TAT: "Whatever peculiar virtue the TAT may have, if any, it will be found to reside not as some have assumed in its power to mirror overt behavior or to communicate what the patient knows and is willing to tell, but rather in its capacity to reveal things that the patient is unwilling to tell because he is unconscious of them" (Murray, 1951, p. 577). But research designed to explore this assumption has questioned its validity. Weisskopf and Dieppa (1951) instructed a group of subjects to produce stories that would create the best impression of themselves possible, and another group was instructed to produce stories that would create the worst impression possible. Not only were the subjects successful in conveying the desired impression, but also judges were able to correctly identify only 58 percent of those who had faked good impressions. The ability of subjects to fake a need for achievement was demonstrated in a study by Holmes (1974). In another study (Hamsher & Farina, 1967), subjects who were playing the roles of people attending a psychological clinic were able to successfully present the impression of being "open" or "guarded," depending on what they had been instructed to convey. The extent to which the TAT may be sensitive to faking must be considered by test users in assessing reliability.

Validity   In general, validity research on the TAT has focused on questions like "What is the relationship between expressions of fantasy stories and real-life behavior?" A sampling of some of the research that has been conducted with respect to one variable, aggressive behavior, follows. One study addressing this question focused on the relationship between aggression expressed in fantasy and overt aggression (Mussen & Naylor, 1954). These researchers observed that need for aggression expressed on the TAT was predictive of overt aggressive behavior and that a low expectation of punishment for aggression led to an even stronger likelihood that aggression would be expressed. The subjects in this study were 29 adolescent delinquent males (between the ages of 9 and 16) from lower-class environments. Kagan (1956) examined the relationship between TAT-expressed aggression in 118 middle-class boys in grades 1 through 3 (mean age of 7.9) and teacher ratings of the subjects with respect to their tendency to express or inhibit feelings of anger. Although Kagan noted a positive relationship between fantasy aggression and ratings of overt aggression, the relationship was not significant. In a study on hostility involving 51 neuropsychiatric patients in an army hospital, Gluck (1955) hypothesized that the greater the hostility expressed on the TAT, the greater the hostile behavior that would be exhibited when presented with a frustrating situation. The results did not, however, support that hypothesis. Barends, Westen, Leigh, Silbert, and Byers (1990) found a significant correlation between TAT and interview measures with respect to the psychoanalytic concept of "affect tone"—the extent to which people and relationships tend to be seen as enriching as opposed to hostile and malevolent.

Conflicting opinions and questioning appear in the literature not only with respect to validity of the assumptions of the test but also with respect to the validity of diagnostic inferences. Some have concluded that the validity of the interpretation of the data derived from a TAT administration is based more on the clinician's skills than on the psychometric properties of the test (Worchel & Dupree, 1990). With so many questions about the psychometric soundness of the TAT, the student might well ask why this test remains one of the most popular in clinical assessment.[5] Among the possible reasons that could be cited is the test's longevity; like the Rorschach test, the TAT is a test that many practicing clinicians were taught when they were in graduate school, and it is a projective test with which they are very familiar. Another reason is the great intuitive appeal of the projective hypothesis as applied to this test; it makes sense that people would project their own motivation when asked to construct a story about ambiguous scenes. Because many of the pictures with figures in them contain more than one figure, the instrument is particularly well suited to uncovering information related to those needs, desires, and conflicts that are related to social, interpersonal, and familial relationships. Unlike personality inventories with items that are set and administration procedures that are rigorously standardized, the TAT not only allows the examiner to select the particular cards to be used for a given testing but also gives a fair amount of leeway with respect to the type of probing during the test. Such "hands-on" involvement in preparing for the testing and in administering the test—not to mention scoring and interpreting the test—may have great appeal to a clinician; the opportunity to take an active and vital role in the assessment is becoming harder and harder to come by in an age when "testing" is almost always tantamount to handing the testtaker an answer sheet, an answer book, and a number 2 pencil—and then waiting for the narrative summary and profile to come back from the computer.

Other Picture-Story Tests

Since the publication of the TAT in the mid-1930s, many adaptations of it have appeared. For example, the Thompson (1949) modification of the TAT was

---

5. But although the TAT remains a popular clinical tool, it has not, in recent years, served as a great stimulus for research. Polyson, Norris, and Ott (1985) counted TAT references in *Psychological Abstracts* and in the Buros series of yearbooks for the years 1970 to 1983 and found that research with the TAT had declined substantially.

expressly designed for administration to Black subjects, and pictures contained both Black and White protagonists. The Children's Apperception Test (CAT), written by Leopold Bellak and first published in 1949, was designed specifically for use with children ages 3 to 10 and featured animals instead of humans in the pictures. However, in response to research indicating that children might produce more clinically valuable material when cards featured humans in the pictures (see Murstein, 1963, for example), an alternative version of the CAT called the CAT-H ("H" standing for the use of human figures in the pictures) was published (Bellak & Bellak, 1965). The clinician's choice of either the CAT or the CAT-H was to be influenced by his or her judgment concerning the mental age and personality of the child subject (Bellak & Hurvich, 1966). Subsequently, Bellak developed a TAT-like test for the elderly and christened it the Senior Apperception Technique (Bellak & Bellak, 1973). Some of the other published modifications of the original TAT include tests designed for American Indians, South Africans, and South Micronesians (Bellak, 1971). The Blacky Pictures Test (Blum, 1950) was a psychoanalytically based TAT-like projective test for children that employed "Blacky" the dog as well as his family and friends. Phillipson (1955) devised a measure containing more diffuse, less differentiated pictures than the TAT. The test, described as "a cross between the TAT and the Rorschach," is reportedly "more widely used in Great Britain, but gaining in popularity here" (Stricker & Healey, 1990, p. 226).

Numerous other picture-story instruments have been published, and we will briefly describe a sampling of them. In general, the tests are designed to elicit information from respondents in a particular age group and/or in a particular situation (such as school) or diagnostic category. Like the TAT, the picture-story tests tend not to offer strong evidence for their psychometric soundness; to a greater degree than most objective personality tests, the validity of such instruments is often limited by the skill, ability, and clinical acumen of the test user.

The Picture Story Test (Symonds, 1949) was designed expressly for use with adolescents, and the 20 pictures contained in it were designed to elicit stories pertinent to those years (for example, coming home late, leaving home, and planning for the future). The Education Apperception Test (Thompson & Sones, 1973) and the School Apperception Method (Solomon & Starr, 1968) are two picture-story instruments designed to tap children's attitudes toward school and learning. The Michigan Picture Test was developed for use with children between the ages of 8 and 14, and it contains 16 pictures designed to elicit various responses, ranging from conflicts with authority figures to feelings of personal inadequacy (Andrew, 1953). A thematic apperception technique designed for use with urban Hispanic children called TEMAS depicts Hispanic characters in urban settings (Costantino et al., 1988; Malgady et al., 1984). The Roberts Apperception Test for Children (RATC; McArthur & Roberts, 1982) contains cards depicting a variety of situations, including family confrontation, parental conflict, parental affection, attitudes toward school, and peer action. It was developed with one objective being a standardized scoring system. Reviews of this instrument to date can at best be described as mixed (Obrzut & Bolick, 1986; Sines, 1985). The Children's Apperceptive Story-Telling Test (CAST; Schneider,

1989; Schneider & Perney, 1990) has its basis in Adlerian theory, contains color cards, and was designed to reflect "contemporary figures in contexts of modern problems while retaining stimulus ambiguity" (Schneider, 1989, p. 9).

In one projective test, testtakers construct their own pictures and then tell a story. Designed for use with individuals 6 years of age or older, the Make A Picture Story Method (Shneidman, 1952) consists of 67 cut-up figures of people and animals that may be presented on any of 22 pictorial backgrounds. The figures (which vary in posture and position) represent males, females, children, nudes, minority groups (such as Blacks, Mexicans, and Orientals), legendary characters, and well-known fictitious characters (such as Superman). A number of figures with blank faces are also included. The backgrounds represent diverse settings (for example, a living room, street, nursery, stage, schoolroom, bathroom, bridge, dream, camp, cave, raft, cemetery, cellar), and there is also one blank background, onto which the testtaker may assign any background. Examinees are instructed to arrange the figures on the backgrounds "as they might be in real life" (Shneidman, 1952, p. 7). The subject is then instructed to construct a story pertinent to their creation and indicate who the characters are, what they are doing, what they are thinking, how they are feeling, and what the outcome of the story will be.

A relatively new variation of the picture-story method may prove to have appeal to both "old school" clinicians and the more actuarily inclined. The Apperceptive Personality Test (APT; Karp et al., 1990) represents an attempt to address some long-standing criticisms of the TAT as a projective instrument while introducing objectivity into the scoring system. The test consists of eight stimulus cards "depicting recognizable people in everyday settings" (Holmstrom et al., 1990, p. 252), including males and females of different ages, as well as minority group members. This, by the way, is in contrast to the TAT stimulus cards, some of which depict fantastic or unreal types of scenes.[6] As summarized in Table 12–3, another difference between the APT and the TAT is the emotional "tone" and "draw" of the stimulus cards. A long-standing criticism of the TAT cards has been their "negative" or "gloomy" tone, which might work to restrict the range of affect projected by a testtaker (Garfield & Eron, 1948; Ritzler et al., 1980). After telling a story about each of the pictures either orally or in writing, testtakers respond to a series of multiple-choice questions. In addition to supplying quantitative information, the questionnaire segment of the test was designed to fill in any information gaps from stories that would be too brief or cryptic to otherwise score. Responses are thus subjected to both clinical and actuarial interpretation and may, in fact, be scored and interpreted with the aid of available computer software. If the norm base of the test is extended and made representative of census data, and if the test is found to be psychometrically sound on the basis of independent research with acceptably large samples of subjects, the APT is apt to become much more widely known in the years to come.

---

6. Murray et al. (1938) believed that fantastic or unreal types of stimuli might be particularly effective in tapping unconscious processes.

Table 12–3
A Comparison of the TAT and the APT *

	TAT	APT
Total number of cards	31	8
Recommended number of cards to administer according to test author	A total of 20 over the course of 2 administrations.	8 in one session.
Number of cards administered in everyday practice	Varies according to test user's judgment; usually only 1 session.	8
Description of stimulus cards	Varied scenes; of wide-ranging ambiguity; with/without people; some "everyday," others fantastic. No racial minority group members depicted.	Pen-and-ink drawings of everyday people in familiar settings designed to evoke a consistently moderate level of ambiguity. Minority group members depicted.
Emotional "tone"	Variously described as "negative" and "gloomy."	Wide-ranging.
Scoring system	Many available, each having in common a set of rules for judges to assign numbers on the basis of elements of testtaker's stories.	One scoring system that allows for both clinical judgment and quantitative analysis of questionnaire responses.
Norms	No formal normative data are packaged with the test, nor has the publisher attempted to provide any; some normative data are available from various published studies.	Normative data are available for college undergraduates (517 males and 689 females), adolescents (60 males and 71 females), and a geriatric group (20 males and 45 females).
Administration time	Varies by the number of cards administered and related variables idiosyncratic to the examiner.	About 40–50 min.

*Source of information on the APT was Karp et al. (1990).

Words as Projective Stimuli

Although many projective techniques involve the use of verbalizations either in providing directions or in obtaining responses, there are those instruments that use words as the projective stimulus material. Projective techniques that employ open-ended words, phrases, and sentences are referred to as semistructured techniques because, although they are open-ended and allow for a variety of responses, they still provide a framework within which the subject must operate. The two best-known examples of verbal projective techniques are word association and sentence completion tests.

Word Association Tests

The first attempt at investigating word association was made by Galton (1879). Galton's method consisted of presenting a series of unrelated stimulus words and instructing the subject to respond with the first word that came to mind. Continued interest in the phenomenon of word association resulted in additional studies being conducted. Precise methods for recording the responses given and the length of time elapsed before obtaining a response were developed (Cattell, 1887; Trautscholdt, 1883). Cattell and Bryant (1889) were the first to use cards with stimulus words printed on them, and Kraepelin's (1896) investigations studied the effect of physical states such as hunger and fatigue as well as the effect of practice on word association. Mounting experimental evidence led psychologists to believe that the associations individuals made to words were not chance happenings but, rather, the resultant interplay of the individual's life experiences, attitudes, and unique personality characteristics.

Jung (1910) maintained that by selecting certain key words that represented possible areas of conflict, word association techniques could be employed for psychodiagnostic purposes. Jung's experiments served as an inspiration to developers of such tests as the Word Association Test developed by Rapaport, Gill, and Schafer (1946) at the Menninger Clinic. This test consists of three parts. In the first part, each stimulus word is administered to the examinee, who has been instructed to respond quickly with the first word that comes to mind. The examiner records the length of time it takes the subject to respond to each item. In the second part of the test, each stimulus word is again presented to the examinee. Here the examinee is instructed to reproduce the original responses. Any deviation between the original and this second response is recorded, as is the length of time before reacting. The third part of the test is the inquiry. Here the examiner asks questions to try to clarify the relationship that exists between the stimulus word and the response (for example, "What were you thinking about?" or "What was going through your mind?"). In some cases, the relationship may be obvious, but in others the relationship between the two words may be idiosyncratic or even bizarre.

The test consists of sixty words, some considered neutral by the test authors (for example, *chair, book, water, dance, taxi*) and some termed "traumatic." In the latter category are "words that are likely to touch upon sensitive personal material according to clinical experience, and also words that attract associative disturbances" (Rapaport et al., 1968, p. 257). Examples of words designated as "traumatic" are *love, girlfriend, boyfriend, mother, father, suicide, fire, breast,* and *masturbation.*

Responses on the Word Association Test are evaluated with respect to variables such as popularity, reaction time, content, and test-retest responses. Normative data are provided on the percentage of occurrence of certain responses for college students and schizophrenic groups. For example, to the word *stomach*, 21% of the college group responded with "ache"; 13% with "ulcer." Ten percent of the schizophrenic group responded with "ulcer." To the word *mouth*, 20% of the college sample responded with "kiss"; 13% with "nose"; 11% with "tongue"; 11% with "lips"; and 11% with "eat." In the schizophrenic group, 19% responded with "teeth," and 10% responded with "eat."

The Kent-Rosanoff Free Association Test[7]   The Kent-Rosanoff Free Association Test (1910) represents an attempt at standardizing the response of individuals to specific words. The test consists of 100 stimulus words, all commonly used and believed to be neutral with respect to emotional impact. The standardization sample consisted of 1,000 normal adults who varied in geographic location, educational level, occupation, age, and intellectual capacity. Frequency tables based on the responses of these 1,000 cases were developed. These tables were used to evaluate examinees' responses according to the clinical judgment of psychopathology. Psychiatric patients were found to have a lower frequency of popular responses than did the normals in the standardization group. However, as it became apparent that individuality of response may be influenced by many variables other than psychopathology (such as creativity, age, education, and socioeconomic factors), the popularity of the Kent-Rosanoff as a differential diagnostic instrument diminished. Damaging, too, is Ward et al.'s (1991) finding that scores on the Kent-Rosanoff were unrelated to other measures of psychotic thought. Still, the test endures as a standardized instrument of word association responses, and more than 80 years after its publication, it continues to be used in experimental research and clinical practice.

Sentence Completion Tests

Other projective techniques that use verbal material as projective stimuli are sentence completion tests. How might *you* complete the following sentences?

I like to _____

Someday, I will _____

I will always remember the time _____

I worry about _____

I am most frightened when _____

My feelings are hurt _____

My mother _____

I wish my parents _____

Sentence completion tests may contain items that, like the items listed, tend to be quite general in nature and appropriate for administration in a wide variety of settings. Alternatively, sentence completion *stems* (the first part of the item) may be developed for use in very specific types of settings (such as school or business) or for highly specific purposes. Sentence completion tests may be

---

7. The term *free association* refers to the technique of having subjects relate all their thoughts as they are occurring and is most frequently used in psychoanalysis; the only structure imposed is provided by the subjects themselves. The technique employed in the Kent-Rosanoff is that of *word association* (not free association), in which the examinee relates the first word that comes to mind in response to a stimulus word. The term "free association" in the test's title is, therefore, a misnomer.

relatively atheoretical in nature or linked very closely to some theory. As an example of the latter, the Washington University Sentence Completion Test (Loevinger et al., 1970) was based on the writings of Loevinger and her colleagues in the area of ego development. Loevinger (1966; Loevinger & Ossorio, 1958) has argued that with maturity, knowledge, and awareness comes a transformation from a self-image that is essentially stereotypic and socially acceptable to one that is more personalized and realistic. The Washington University Sentence Completion Test was constructed in an attempt to assess self-concept according to Loevinger's theory. Inter-rater reliability for this test has been estimated to range from .74 to .88, internal consistency is in the high .80s, and test-retest reliability ranges from .67 to .76 or from .88 to .92, depending upon how the test is scored (Weiss et al., 1989). Some evidence for the validity of this test comes from its ability to predict social attitudes in a manner consistent with Loevinger's theory (Browning, 1987).

A number of standardized sentence completion tests are available to the clinician. One such test, the Rotter (pronounced like "rote," not "rot," with an "r" added on) Incomplete Sentences Blank (Rotter & Rafferty, 1950) is the most popular of all (Lah, 1989a). Consisting of 40 incomplete sentences, the test was developed for use with populations from grade 9 through adulthood and is available in three levels: high school (grades 9 through 12), college (grades 13 through 16), and adult. Testtakers are instructed to respond to each item in a way that expresses their "real feelings." The manual suggests that responses on the test be interpreted according to several categories: family attitudes, social and sexual attitudes, general attitudes, and character traits. Each response is evaluated on a seven-point scale that ranges from "need for therapy" to "extremely good adjustment." The responses of several subjects on the Rotter, as well as some background information about the subjects, are presented in the test manual to provide illustrations of the different categories. The manual also contains normative data for a sample of 85 female and 214 male college freshmen but no norms for high school and adult populations. Reliability estimates for male and female college students were found to be .84 and .83, respectively. Estimates of inter-scorer reliability with respect to scoring categories were in the .90s. The majority of the validity studies with the Rotter were conducted in the 1950s and 1960s, and they employed "expert judge" and/or "known group" experimental designs. More recently, sociometric techniques have been used to demonstrate the validity of the Rotter as a measure of adjustment (Lah, 1989b).

In general, a sentence completion test may be a useful method for obtaining diverse information relating to an individual's interests, educational aspirations, future goals, fears, conflicts, needs, and so forth. The tests have a high degree of "face validity"; a child having difficulty in school, for example, would consider it appropriate to answer a list of questions or statements concerning feelings toward school. However, with this high degree of face validity comes a certain degree of transparency with respect to the objective of this type of test; for that reason, sentence completion tests are perhaps the most vulnerable of all the projective methods to faking on the part of the examinee intent on making a good—or a bad—impression.

Figure Drawings as a Projective Technique

One relatively quick and easy-to-administer projective technique is the analysis of drawings. Drawings can provide the psychodiagnostician with a wealth of clinical hypotheses to be confirmed or discarded as the result of other findings (see the box opposite). The use of drawings in clinical and research settings has extended beyond the area of personality assessment. Attempts have been made to use artistic productions as a source of information about intelligence, neurological intactness, visual-motor coordination, cognitive development, and even learning disabilities (Neale et al., 1993; Oakland & Dowling, 1983). Figure drawings are an appealing source of diagnostic data, since the instructions for them can be administered individually or in a group by nonclinicians such as teachers and no materials other than a pencil and paper are required.

Machover's Draw-A-Person Test

The classic work on the use of figure drawings as a projective stimulus is a book entitled *Personality Projection in the Drawing of the Human Figure: A Method of Personality Investigation,* by Karen Machover (1949). Machover wrote that "the human figure drawn by an individual who is directed to 'draw a person' related intimately to the impulses, anxieties, conflicts, and compensations characteristic of that individual. In some sense, the figure drawn is the person, and the paper corresponds to the environment" (p. 35).

The instructions for administering the Draw-A-Person (DAP) test are quite simple; the examinee is given a pencil and an 8½-by-11-inch blank sheet of white paper and is told to "Draw a person." Inquiries on the part of the examinee concerning how the picture is to be drawn are met with statements such as "Make it the way you think it should be" or "Do the best you can." Immediately after the first drawing is completed, the examinee is handed a second sheet of paper and instructed to draw a picture of a person of the opposite sex from the person just drawn.[8] Subsequently, many clinicians will ask questions concerning the drawings such as "Tell me a story about that figure," "Tell me about that boy/girl, man/lady," "What is the person doing?" "How is the person feeling?" "What is nice or not nice about the person?" Responses to these questions are used in forming various hypotheses and interpretations concerning personality functioning.

Traditionally, the drawings generated on the DAP have been formally evaluated through analysis of various characteristics of the drawing. Attention has been given to such factors as the length of time required to complete the picture, placement of the figures, the size of the figure, pencil pressure used, symmetry, line quality, shading, the presence of erasures, facial expressions,

---

8. Most people will draw a person of the same sex when instructed to simply "draw a person." It is deemed to be clinically significant if the person draws a person of the opposite sex when given these instructions. Reirdan and Koff (1981) found that in some cases, children are uncertain as to the sex of the figure drawn and hypothesize that in such cases "the child has an indefinite or ill-defined notion of sexual identity" (p. 257).

Some Sample Interpretations Made from Figure Drawings

(Source: Hammer, 1981)

Drawing by a 25-year-old schoolteacher after becoming engaged. Previously, she had entered psychotherapy because of problems relating to men and a block against getting married. The positioning of the hands is indicative of a fear of sexual intercourse that remains.

Drawing by a male with a "Don Juan" complex—a man who pursued one affair after another. The collar pulled up to guard the neck and the excessive shading of the buttocks is suggestive of a fear of being attacked from the rear. It is possible that this man's Don Juanism is an outward defense against the lack of masculinity—even feelings of effeminacy—he may be struggling with within.

Drawing by an authoritarian and sadistic male who had been head disciplinarian of a reformatory for boys before he was suspended for child abuse. His description of this picture was that it "looked like a Prussian or a Nazi General."

The manacled hands, tied feet, exposed buttocks, and large foot drawn to the side of the drawing taken together are reflective, according to Hammer, of masochistic, homosexual, and exhibitionistic needs.

This drawing by an acutely paranoid, psychotic man was described by Hammer (1981, p. 170) as follows: "The savage mouth expresses the rage-filled projections loose within him. The emphasized eyes and ears with the eyes almost emanating magical rays reflect the visual and auditory hallucinations the patient actually experiences. The snake in the stomach points up his delusion of a reptile within, eating away and generating venom and evil."

posture, clothing, and overall appearance. Various hypotheses have been generated based on these factors. For example, the placement of the figure on the paper is seen as representing how the individual functions within the environment; the person who draws a tiny figure at the bottom of the paper might have a poor self-concept or be insecure and/or depressed. The individual who draws a picture that cannot be contained on one sheet of paper and goes off the page is considered to be impulsive. A sampling of some other hypotheses related to various aspects of figure drawings are as follows:

- Unusually light pressure suggests character disturbance (Exner, 1962).

- Placement of drawing on the right of the page suggests orientation to the future; to the left, orientation to the past; upper right suggests desire to suppress an unpleasant past plus excessive optimism about the future; lower left suggests depression with desire to flee into the past (Buck, 1948, 1950).

- Large eyes and/or large ears suggest suspiciousness, ideas of reference, or other paranoid characteristics (Machover, 1949; Shneidman, 1958).

- Unusually large breasts drawn by male suggest unresolved Oedipal problems with maternal dependence (Jolles, 1952).

- Long and conspicuous ties suggest sexual aggressiveness, perhaps overcompensating for fear of impotence (Machover, 1949).

- Button emphasis suggests dependent, infantile, inadequate personality (Halpern, 1958).

For a comprehensive and readable summary of various interpretations of projective drawings, the interested reader is referred to Knoff (1990a).

Other Figure-Drawing Tests

Another projective test employing figure drawings is the House-Tree-Person test (HTP) developed and popularized by Buck (1948). In this procedure, as its name implies, the subject is instructed to draw a picture of a house, a tree, and a person. In much the same way that different aspects of the human figure are presumed to be reflective of psychological functioning, the way in which an individual represents a house and a tree is considered to have symbolic significance. In this context, one might find, for example, an account of how the House-Tree-Person test has been used to identify physically abused children (Blain et al., 1981). A Draw-An-Animal procedure was developed based on the assumption that more projective material may be obtained through representations of animals as opposed to human figures (see Campo & Vilar, 1977, for an example of a study comparing the clinical utility of animal and human figure drawings).

Another projective drawing technique, this one thought to be of particular value in learning about the examinee in relation to her or his family, is the Kinetic Family Drawing (KFD). Derived from Hulse's (1951, 1952) Family Drawing Test, an administration of the KFD (Burns & Kaufman, 1970, 1972) begins with the examinee being given an 8½-by-11-inch piece of paper (which can be positioned any way) and a pencil with an eraser. The examinee, usually though not necessarily a child, is instructed as follows:

> Draw a picture of everyone in your family, included you, DOING something. Try to draw whole people, not cartoons or stick people. Remember, make everyone DOING something—some kind of actions. (Burns & Kaufman, 1972, p. 5)

In addition to yielding graphic representations of each family member for analysis, this procedure may yield a wealth of information in the form of examinee verbalizations while the drawing is being executed. After the examinee has completed the drawing, a rather detailed inquiry follows. The examinee is asked to identify each of the figures, talk about their relationship, and detail what they are doing in the picture and why (see Knoff & Prout, 1985). A number of formal scoring systems for the KFD are available (such as McPhee & Wegner, 1976; Meyers, 1978; Mostkoff & Lazarus, 1983). Related techniques include a school adaptation called the Kinetic School Drawing (KSD; Prout & Phillips, 1974), a test that combines aspects of the KFD and the KSD called the Kinetic Drawing System (KDS; Knoff & Prout, 1985), and the Collaborative Drawing Technique (Smith, 1985), a test that provides an occasion for family members to collaborate on the creation of a drawing—the better to "draw together."

Like other projective techniques, figure-drawing tests, although thought to be clinically useful, have had a rather embattled history when the literature on psychometric soundness is reviewed. Questions have been raised concerning the reliability and validity of the KFD (see, for example, Cummings, 1981; Harris, 1978). No widely accepted reliable scoring system exists for the KFD. Different raters interpreting the same drawings often reach different conclusions about what those drawings mean, even when the raters use the same scoring system (Neale & Rosal, 1993). Given that reliability provides a foundation for validity, it is not surprising that validity studies involving the KFD are often unsupportive. Some specific studies suggest that the KFD may be able to identify those with special problems, such as incest victims and children with low self-esteem. Other studies find no distinctions between the drawings of different groups of children (Neale & Rosal, 1993).

No compelling evidence has been adduced to date to support the claim that human-figure drawings approximate self-representations. Quite the contrary, the literature tends to support the view that there is no relationship between figure drawings and self-representations. In one study, DAP test data from 25 obese and 20 ideal-weight women were matched for age, education, IQ, marital status, and the career/housewife dichotomy. Out of 129 chi-squares run on 43 criteria, only seven of the tests achieved significance, and this result could have occurred by chance. In short, contrary to the body-image hypothesis, there were no differences between the drawings of obese and ideal-weight women (Kotkov & Goodman, 1953). Another study compared the DAP protocols of 49 hemiplegic and 43 normals and found no differences (Prater, 1957). However, body-image *concerns* have been found to be reflected in human-figure drawings by psoriasis (an unattractive skin ailment) patients (Leichtman et al., 1981). In a study that employed DAP and KFD drawings from children ages 9 to 14 (some with diagnosed mood or anxiety disorders and the rest normal controls), quantitative scoring of emotional indicators failed to differentiate the groups (Tharinger & Stark, 1990).

It is somewhat paradoxical that the common lay argument against the DAP ("But I'm not a good artist!") is well founded. Contrary to Hammer's (1958) summary dismissal of this argument, drawing ability *is* a source of variance affecting the quality of drawings (Sherman, 1958; Swensen, 1968). As early as 1953, at least one experimenter concluded that "as judged by the 'average' clinical psychologist today, human figure drawings executed by persons of average or above average intelligence seem to indicate art achievement but do not seem to show any consistent relationship to level of personal adjustment" (Whitmyre, 1953, p. 424).

One tacit assumption is that all other things being equal, the more experience the clinician has with the DAP, the better—the more valid—the clinical interpretations. Yet experimental work with the DAP has yielded the rather unexpected finding that experience and expertise do not necessarily correlate with greater judgmental accuracy as measured by an external criterion. In one study, 25 DAP experts assigned rank-ordered probabilities of diagnosis to pairs of drawings made by patients from five criterion groups. It was found that the experts were able to identify only the drawings of the mental defectives beyond chance—even after being given a second try to make the correct diagnosis (Wanderer, 1967). In another study (Watson, 1967), psychologists of three different levels of familiarity and expertise with the DAP were asked to categorize 48 DAP protocols as organic, paranoid schizophrenic, nonparanoid schizophrenic, or normals. The psychologists in the study included ten psychologists who said they frequently used the DAP, ten who said they did not use it, and four "experts" (defined as such by their extensive writing on projective tests; the author noted that 21 experts had been petitioned to participate but 17 refused). Diagnostic acuity was not found to vary as a function of familiarity or sophistication with the DAP. The author concluded that "the results suggest that reliance on the DAP as a diagnostic indicator is actually detrimental to overall diagnostic acuity, except in those rare settings where the base-rate frequencies of the various nosological categories are essentially equal" (p. 145). Indeed, a psychologist whose name has become virtually synonymous with figure drawings as a means of assessment, Karen Machover, expressed "grave misgivings" about the misuse of the DAP in diagnosis (Machover, cited in Watson, 1967, p. 145).

One way to begin to address problems with reliability and validity of scoring and interpretations is to introduce a formal scoring system. Numerous objective scales reflecting groups of features on the DAP have been developed for the purpose of differential diagnosis. For example, Hozier's (1959) schizophrenic scale was said to differentiate normal from schizophrenic women on the basis of a 15-item DAP checklist that included items related to presence or absence of various features, proportion, flexibility of joint, and clothing transparencies. The Reznikoff-Tomblen (1956) scale differentiated the neurologically impaired from neurotics on the basis of such variables as synthesis, misplacement of parts, emptiness of figures, and various distortions at the extremities. The Baugh-Carpenter (1962) scale differentiated delinquents from nondelinquents on the basis of such factors as presence or absence of parts, nudity, non-stick drawings, and other factors (such as "gangster identification"). A review of such scales did not support their validity (Watson et al., 1967). A study of differential diagnosis (Covetkovic, 1979) involving 70 hospitalized schizophrenic adults and 71 normal subjects sought to determine if differences existed between the two groups' conception and representation of space in human-figure drawings. The results revealed similar tendencies for the two groups, and any differences that did exist were related to sex rather than diagnostic category.

In what might be characterized as a herculean effort to bolster the status of figure drawings as a clinical tool, Naglieri, McNeish, and Bardos (1991) have developed a rigorously standardized version of the DAP, complete with a detailed scoring system (see this chapter's *Close-up*).

A Perspective

Although the Rorschach, story-telling methods, figure drawings, and other projective techniques enjoy widespread use, the psychometric soundness of projective methods seems to be the source of a long-standing, continuing controversy that will not go away. In recent years, efforts to convince psychometric purists of the soundness of projective tests seem to have been invested in the development of alternate versions/scoring systems of more traditional projective methods. Exner's Comprehensive System for scoring the Rorschach, the APT story-telling technique, and the DAP:SPED each represent, in essence, an attempt to sharpen psychometrically a projective method that traditionally has had wide appeal to clinicians. Coefficients of reliability and validity, norms, and other indices of sensitivity to psychometric concerns are increasingly likely to accompany the publication of a new projective technique. Still, many academicians and others tend to remain wary of projective measures. Why? In this chapter's *Everyday Psychometrics* (pages 462–463), we explore some basic concerns about projective methods.

The Draw-A-Person: Screening Procedure for Emotional Disturbance

The Draw-A-Person: Screening Procedure for Emotional Disturbance (DAP:SPED; Naglieri et al., 1991) is a rigorously standardized quantitative scoring system designed to screen testtakers (ages 6 through 17) for emotional problems. The test's rationale is that the rendering of unusual features in figure drawings signals emotional problems. A score on the test is a function of the number of unusual features produced in a figure drawing; one point is awarded for each such feature. Test protocols with high scores are not interpreted in diagnostic terms but as signals that more detailed evaluation for emotional problems is advisable.

The standardized test administration begins with testtakers being asked to draw a man, then a woman, then themselves. The figures are drawn on forms supplied with the test materials, thus ensuring that all testtakers will use the same form. Examiners record the time taken to complete each drawing, and a time limit of five minutes per drawing is imposed.

Standardization of the DAP:SPED employed the drawings of 2260 testtakers, ages 6 through 17 years, who were similar demographically to age-matched groups in the 1980 U.S. Census and who had no history of emotional disturbance. Eight physical measurements of the drawings were taken, including the drawing's height, width, and distance from the bottom and the top of the page. Trained raters also evaluated the drawings with regard to 73 criteria that required some judgment, including unusual treatment of facial features and whether the figure drawn seemed to be acting aggressively. Twenty of these criteria were subsequently eliminated from the scoring system because they were too common to be of discriminative value. For example, omission of the neck, although uncommon in drawings by children over age 8, occurred in over half of the drawings by children ages 6 through 8. Broken lines in the drawings were uncommon in drawings by younger children but were present in 26% of the drawings by 13- to 17-year-olds. Six other criteria were eliminated because they had low or negative item−total correlations and thus reduced the internal consistency of the scoring system. In the end, 47 criteria were selected for use, along with the eight

measurements of the drawing. Raw scores on the test are obtained by scoring one point for each unusual feature, including unusual aspects of the drawing's measurements. As a result, the highest possible raw score for a single drawing is 55.

For each age group, a certain number of unusual features is considered to be within normal limits. For example, across all three drawings (man, woman, self), the average 9- to 12-year-old boy produces 11 unusual features. To facilitate score interpretation, the total number of unusual features in the three drawings is converted into a T-score based on the performance of the standardization sample. Different T-score conversion tables are presented in the test manual for males and females in each of three age groups.

Adequate levels of reliability are reported for the DAP:SPED. Recall that special attention was given to internal consistency reliability in the selection of scoring criteria. This produced good results in the final scoring system: internal consistency reliability of the DAP:SPED, as measured by coefficient alpha, ranged from .67 to .78, with a median value of .74. Other indices of reliability are also at acceptable levels. Total test scores obtained by two raters correlated .84. Test-retest reliability over a one-week interval was .67.

Four validity studies are also reported in the test manual. The focus in each of these studies was on the test's ability to function as a screening device. Specifically, the test's ability to identify emotionally disturbed individuals as such without identifying nonemotionally disturbed individuals as being emotionally disturbed was assessed. The initial validity study involved 162 subjects with an average age of 10.6. Of these, 81 had been identified as emotionally disturbed within the school system. The other 81 were members of the standardization sample matched to the emotionally disturbed group on relevant demographic variables, serving as "normal" controls. As a group, the 81 emotionally disturbed children scored higher (T-score = 55.3) than the normal controls (T-score = 49.5). Using these data, the test developers established the criterion of a T-score of 55 or higher as an indicator of possible emotional disturbance.

The remaining three validity studies reported in the test manual used a similar procedure. The test records of groups of emotionally disturbed children or adolescents were compared with those of demographically similar children without emotional disturbance from the standardization sample. The results of these studies are summarized in the table. Based on these data, the test's authors suggested that the DAP: SPED is a valid predictor of emotional disturbance, although they acknowledged the need for additional research.

Motta et al. (1993a, 1993b) evaluated Naglieri et al.'s validity data and concluded that the DAP:SPED lacked criterion-related validity. Motta et al. did not dispute that testtakers who are emotionally disturbed earn higher scores on the test than normal controls. Rather, they expressed concern that the test might misidentify emotionally disturbed children as normal (called a "false negative" error) and misidentify normal children as emotionally disturbed (called a "false positive" error). To understand why, consider that Naglieri et al. did not present criterion-related validity coefficients but chose instead to present this information in terms of mean *T*-scores and standard deviations. The DAP:SPED manual does contain sufficient information to compute correlations, which function as validity coefficients. The correlation coefficients for the four validity studies are approximately .31, .45, .22, and .27, respectively. By presenting the validity data in this familiar metric, you can quickly see that the validity of the test is not strong. At most, 20% of the variability in classifications of children as emotionally disturbed or not is associated with DAP:SPED test scores.

There is a second way of translating the results of the validity studies into a form that allows us to examine the test's utility as a screening measure. This involves determining how many misclassifications would be made if scores 55 and higher, as suggested by Naglieri and colleagues, are used to identify students as likely to have emotional disturbance. As noted previously, two types of classification errors can occur: people without emotional disturbance may have scores 55 or larger ("false positives"), and people with emotional disturbance may have scores under 55 ("false negatives"). The two types of errors are associated with distinct costs. If people without emotional disturbance score 55 or over, additional evaluation will be done, which should indicate

Mean *T*-Scores (and Standard Deviations) on DAP:SPED

Study (from DAP: SPED manual)	Emotionally disturbed children	"Normal" children from the standardization sample
Validity Study 1	55.3 (10.6)	49.5 (8.6)
Validity Study 2	57.0 (6.4)	49.1 (8.1)
Validity Study 3	54.8 (9.2)	49.7 (9.0)
Validity Study 4	56.6 (10.3)	49.9 (9.0)

that these individuals are not emotionally disturbed. The cost here is the evaluator's time to do the additional testing, and the possibility of anxiety or unwarranted concern on the part of the child's family. If people with emotional disturbance score under 55, they will not be evaluated; their need for special services may be overlooked, leading to a personal cost if they could have benefited from special services.

False-positive and false-negative rates from the first validity study in the manual are presented by McNeish and Naglieri (1993). When a *T*-score of 55 is used to classify children, a false-negative rate of 51% is found: 41 of the 81 emotionally disturbed children, or 51%, are misclassified as not emotionally disturbed. The false-positive rate is 32%: 26 of the 81 controls are misclassified as emotionally disturbed. Overall, 59% of the students are correctly identified, and 41% are misclassified. If we consider that simply classifying the children using some random method, such as flipping a coin, would have resulted in the correct classification of approximately 50% of the children, we can see that the test is improving on chance classifications by only a small amount.

From these considerations, the conclusion drawn by Motta and colleagues seems justified: the DAP: SPED has adequate reliability but questionable criterion validity. This is not surprising, as the authors focused on reliability in test development by dropping unreliable items but did not address item validity. Validity could be addressed with an empirical criterion-keying approach. For instance, the existing DAP:SPED items could be applied to the drawings of emotionally disturbed and "normal" children; those items that distinguished between groups could be retained. If such a scale demonstrated good validity on a different sample of children (cross-validation), the scale might function well as a screening device. However, in its current state, the DAP:SPED does seem to lack the validity necessary for a screening device.

Some Basic Concerns
About Projective Methods

In general, critics have attacked projective methods on grounds related to the assumptions inherent in their use, the situational variables that attend their use, and the paucity of sound psychometric data to support their reliability and validity.

Assumptions

Murstein (1961) examined ten assumptions of projective techniques and argued that none of them was scientifically compelling. Several assumptions concern the stimulus material. For example, it is assumed that the more ambiguous the stimuli, the more subjects reveal about their personality. However, Murstein describes the stimulus material as only one aspect of the "total stimulus situation." Environmental variables, response sets, reactions to the examiner, and related factors all contribute to response patterns. In addition, in situations where the stimulus properties of the projective material were designed to be unclear, or hazy, or are presented with uncompleted lines—thereby increasing ambiguity—projection on the part of the subject was not found to increase. Another assumption concerns the supposedly idiosyncratic nature of the responses evoked by projective stimuli. In fact, similarities in the response themes of different subjects to the same stimulus cards suggest that the stimulus material may not be as ambiguous and as amenable to projection as had been previously assumed. Some consideration of the stimulus properties and the ways in which they affect the subject's responses is therefore indicated. The assumption that projection is greater to stimulus material that is similar to the subject (in physical appearance, gender, occupation, and so on) has also been found to be questionable.

Other assumptions questioned by Murstein concern how responses on projective tests are interpreted. These include the assumption that every response provides meaning for personality analysis; that a relationship exists between the strength of a need and its manifestation on projective instruments;

that subjects are unaware of what they are disclosing about themselves; that a projective protocol reflects sufficient data concerning personality functioning to formulate judgments; and, finally, that there is a parallel between behavior obtained on a projective instrument and behavior displayed in social situations. It is Murstein's contention that these "cherished beliefs have been accepted by some clinical psychologists without the support of sufficient research validation" (p. 343).

Another assumption basic to projective testing is that there is such a thing as an "unconscious." Though the term *unconscious* is used by many psychologists and laypeople as well, some academicians have questioned whether in fact the "unconscious" exists in the same way that the "liver" exists. The scientific studies typically cited to support the existence of the unconscious (or perhaps more accurately, the efficacy of the construct "unconscious") have used a very wide array of methodologies—see, for example, Diven (1937), Erdelyi (1974; Erdelyi & Goldberg, 1979; Erdelyi & Kleinbard, 1978), Greenspoon (1955), McGinnies (1949), and Razran (1961). The conclusions from each of these types of studies are subject to alternative explanations. Additionally, conclusions about the existence of the unconscious based on experimental testing of predictions derived from hypnotic phenomena, from signal detection theory, and from specific personality theories have been, at least, inconclusive (Brody, 1972).

Situational Variables

Proponents of projective techniques have claimed that such tests are capable of illuminating the recesses of the mind in a manner similar to the way that X rays illuminate the body. Frank (1939) conceptualized projective tests as tapping personality patterns without disturbing the pattern being tapped. If that were true, then variables related to the test situation should have no effect on the data obtained. However, as we have seen, the variable of the examiner's being present or absent can significantly affect the responses of experimental subjects. TAT stories written in private are likely to be less guarded, less optimistic, and more affectively involved than those written in the presence of the examiner (Bernstein, 1956). The age of the examiner is likely to affect projective protocols (Mussen & Scodel, 1955), as are the specific instructions (Henry & Rotter, 1956) and the subtle reinforcement cues provided by the examiner (Wickes, 1956).

Masling (1960) reviewed the literature on the influence of situational and interpersonal variables in projective testing and concluded that there was strong evidence for the role of situational and interpersonal influences in projection. Moreover, Masling argued that it was not only the subjects who utilized every available cue in the testing situation (for example, the room or the actions and appearance of the examiner) but also the examiners, who capitalized on cues over and above their training and orientation. Examiners appeared to interpret projective data with regard to their own needs and expectations, their own subjective feelings about the subject being tested, and their own constructions regarding the total test situation. In a later study, Masling (1965) experimentally demonstrated that Rorschach examiners are capable of unwittingly eliciting the responses they expect through postural, gestural, and facial cues.

Even in "nonprojective" situations such as taking a psychiatric history or taking an objective test, the effect of the clinician's training (Chapman & Chapman, 1967; Fitzgibbons & Shearn, 1972) and role perspective (Snyder et al., 1976), the patient's social class (Hollingshead & Redlich, 1958; Lee, 1968; Routh & King, 1972) and motivation to manage a desired impression (Edwards & Walsh, 1964; Wilcox & Krasnoff, 1967) may influence ratings of pathology (Langer & Abelson, 1974) as well as attribution of the locus of the problem (Batson, 1975). These and other variables are given wider latitude in the projective test situation in which the examiner may be at liberty to choose not only the test and extra-test data on which interpretation will be focused, but also the scoring system that will be used to arrive at that interpretation; as we have noted, for many of the projective methods, a number of different alternative scoring systems are available.

Psychometric Considerations

The psychometric soundness of many widely used projective instruments has yet to be demonstrated. Kinslinger (1966) has cited the failure of researchers to cross-validate findings as a source of spurious validity estimates for projective techniques. Others (such as Cronbach, 1949; Vernon, 1964; Zubin et al., 1965) have called attention to variables such as uncontrolled variations in protocol length, inappropriate subject samples, inadequate control groups, and poor external criteria as factors contributing to spuriously increased ratings of validity. Recall that there are very real methodological difficulties in demonstrating the psychometric soundness of *any* instrument, let alone projective instruments where test-retest or split-half methods may be inappropriate. Mention must also be made of the difficulty of designing reliability and validity studies that effectively rule out, limit, or statistically take into account the unique situational variables (such as extra-test cues) that attend the administration of such tests.

The debate between academicians who argue that projective tests are not technically sound instruments and clinicians who find such tests useful has been raging ever since projectives came into widespread use. Frank (1939) responded to those who would reject projective methods because of their lack of technical rigor:

These leads to the study of personality have been rejected by many psychologists because they do not meet psychometric requirements for validity and reliability, but they are being employed in association with clinical and other studies of personality where they are finding increasing validation in the consistency of results for the same subject when independently assayed by each of these procedures. . . .

If we face the problem of personality, in its full complexity, as an active dynamic process to be studied as a *process* rather than as entity or aggregate of traits, factors, or as static organization, then these projective methods offer many advantages for obtaining data on the process of organizing experience which is peculiar to each personality and has a life career. (Frank, 1939, p. 408) [emphasis in the original]

CHAPTER

13

Other Personality and Behavioral Measures

Some people see the world as filled with love and good, where others see hate and evil. Some people equate "living" with behavioral excess, whereas others strive for moderation in all things. Some people have relatively realistic perceptions of themselves and other people, and others labor under grossly distorted self-images and inaccurate perceptions of family, friends, and acquaintances. Many assessment techniques other than those described to this point can be used to shed light on these and other aspects of individuals—their behavior, their thought processes, their attitudes, beliefs, fears, hopes, perceptions, social skills, internal physiological states—all that constitutes the multifaceted construct "personality."

In Chapter 11, we surveyed some empirical and theoretical issues related to personality assessment in general, and we examined some specific approaches to test construction. In Chapter 12, we focused on issues unique to projective methods. In this chapter, we consider other types of personality measures, beginning with a consideration of measures wherein the primary responsibility for assessment is on assessees themselves. As you might expect, these measures have much in common with the self-report measures discussed in Chapter 11. However, in contrast to that discussion of omnibus "inventories" of personality, our coverage here samples self-rating measures that focus on particular aspects of personality. We then proceed to a consideration of measures wherein people other than the assessees themselves have the responsibility for making various kinds of personality or behavioral ratings and evaluations.

Self-Report/Self-Rating Measures

As you have probably begun to appreciate, psychologists have devised many ways to learn about various aspects of an individual's personality. Psychologists can learn about an individual's self-concept, for example, through interviews, case history data, and projective methods. Assuming that assessees have a reasonable amount of insight into themselves—and are willing to freely share that insight in their responses to test questions—an efficient, economical, and effective way of gathering information is a psychometrically sound self-report measure. Let's look at a sampling of instruments and measures devised to assess various aspects of personality through self-report methods.

Self-Concept Measures

Measures of self-concept are self-report measures designed to devise a description of the assessee from the perspective of the assessee. Among other potential uses of such data, self-concept data are thought to be of value in assessing risk for, or severity of, psychological disorders (Ingham et al., 1986). Self-concept data may also hold application in the assessment of a variety of other life difficulties, including marriage and family problems and academic and workplace problems. In addition to methods such as personality inventories and projective tests that are capable of yielding information pertinent to self-concept, other, more specialized techniques have been found to be effective. We present a sampling of such techniques, cautioning, however, that it has not been established that each of the many available tests purporting to measure self-concept is indeed measuring the same thing (Demo, 1985; Robson, 1988; Wylie, 1974, 1979).

The Beck Self-Concept Test   The Beck Self-Concept Test (BST; Beck & Stein, 1961) was initially designed as a method of evaluating the negative view of the self held by depressed patients, as has been observed and described by Aaron T. Beck (1963, 1967, 1976). For Beck, the self-concept construct consists of various characteristics that people can ascribe to themselves (such as interpersonal attractiveness), each of which may be operationally defined by descriptors (such as "attractive"). According to Beck, Steer, Epstein, and Brown (1990):

> The descriptors, in turn, are weighed by an individual with respect to how much they are valued by himself or herself. The overall self-concept thus reflects the summation of an individual's self-evaluations of the set of descriptors and represents how good the person feels about himself or herself. The self-concept is the product of input of self-relevant data and relatively stable structures (self-schemata) that serve as information processors. The stronger a self-schema, the greater its influence on the input of self-relevant information (i.e., data supporting the self-concept will be processed, whereas data not supporting the self-concept will be ignored). For example, in depression, individuals direct their cognitive processing toward critical self-evaluations, and self-schemata assume a crucial role. Data supporting a depressed person's negative self-concept are more readily acceptable to the individual than data fostering positive self-evaluations. (p. 191)

The BST was developed on the basis of personality- and ability-related characteristics that psychiatric patients considered to be important aspects of themselves (for example, looks, knowledge, memory, and telling jokes). Test-takers describe themselves with these 25 traits by selecting the phrase next to the trait that best describes them in comparison with people they know. For example, for the trait "telling jokes," testtakers will indicate whether they are better than nearly anyone they know, better than most people they know, about the same as most people, worse than most people they know, or worse than nearly anyone they know. Scores are calculated by summing the ratings for the 25 traits; the higher the score, the higher the self-concept.

The BST is self-administered and takes only about ten minutes to complete. Beck, Steer, Epstein, and Brown (1990) reviewed research on the psychometric soundness of this instrument and found it to be satisfactory, though they acknowledged the need for more research on it. They suggested that in addition to other possible applications, the test may have value as an indicator of suicidal risk in psychiatric outpatients.

An awareness of the importance of self-concept in childhood with respect to subsequent adjustment has compelled test developers to turn their attention toward the measurement of children's self-concept (see, for example, Coopersmith, 1967; Fitts, 1965). One scale designed to assess children's perceptions of themselves is the Piers-Harris Children's Self Concept Scale (Piers, 1969).

Piers-Harris Children's Self Concept Scale (CSCS)   Appropriate for use with subjects in grades 3 through 12, the CSCS consists of 80 statements about oneself (such as "I like the way I look"; "I don't have any friends"). The subject responds either "yes" or "no" to each item. A factor analysis of the CSCS indicated that the items covered six general areas of self-concept: (1) behavior, (2) intellectual and school status, (3) physical appearance and attributes, (4) anxiety, (5) popularity, and (6) happiness and satisfaction.

The CSCS was standardized on 1,183 children who were enrolled in grades 4 through 12 in one school district in Pennsylvania. Estimates of internal consistency were found to range from .78 to .93, and test-retest reliability coefficients were in the .70s range. The test manual reports moderate correlations of the CSCS with similar instruments. In a study exploring the validity of the test, the CSCS was administered along with another self-concept scale, the Self Esteem Inventory, to 248 fourth-graders from five elementary schools and to 321 seventh-graders from one junior high school. A correlation coefficient of .78 was obtained between scores on the two instruments (Franklin et al., 1981). Saylor (1984) noted a significant relationship between the Piers-Harris and the Children's Depression Inventory. In another study that bears on the validity of this test, the CSCS was administered to 39 mentally retarded and emotionally disturbed children between the ages of 11 and 16. In this study, the test items in many instances had to be read aloud to the testtakers, given their reading difficulties. The responses on the CSCS were compared with the observations of teachers and teachers' aides on two rating scales: the Behavior Problem Checklist (which assesses, among other things, deviant behavior) and the Conners Teacher Rating Scale (which assesses, among other things, activity level). The results indicated that although behavior and activity level were positively correlated (children high in deviant behavior were also high in activity level), self-concept was negatively correlated with activity level and deviant behavior; children with high activity levels who exhibited deviant behaviors expressed negative self-concepts, whereas those with low activity levels and nondeviant behaviors expressed positive self-concepts (Wolf, 1981). For a sampling of various research applications of the CSCS, see Chiu (1989), Gill and Hayes-Butler (1989), and McWatters (1989).

Q-sort techniques   Not all self-report measures are "pencil-and-paper" measures. The term *Q-sort* refers to a method of personality assessment in which the assessee's task is to sort a group of index cards with certain statements printed on them into some kind of rank order, usually ranging from "least descriptive" to "most descriptive." Some sample statements printed on the cards might be "I try hard to please others," "I am sensitive to criticism," "I'm often uncomfortable in social situations," and "If I put my mind to it, I can do anything." The technique was originally developed by Stephenson (1953), though a number of variations on this method—in variables such as the content of the statements on the card and the administration instructions—designed for use in various settings have since appeared in the assessment literature (Stephenson, 1980).

One of the most well known applications of Q-methodology in clinical and counseling settings was the use of the Q-sort as advocated by the personality theorist and psychotherapist Carl Rogers. Rogers (1959) used the Q-sort as a method of determining how much discrepancy there was between how clients saw themselves and how they would like to be, that is, the discrepancy between the actual and the "ideal" self. At the beginning of a course of psychotherapy, clients might be asked to sort cards twice, once according to how they perceived themselves to be and once again according to how they would ultimately like to be. The larger the discrepancy between the sortings, the more work would be needed in therapy. Presumably the retesting of the client who successfully completed a course of psychotherapy would reveal much less discrepancy between the present and idealized self. Beyond the application of the Q-sort technique in initial assessment and reevaluation of a therapy client, the technique has also been used extensively in basic research in the area of personality as well as in other areas. Some of the highly specialized kinds of Q-sorts that have been published include the Leadership Q-Test (Cassel, 1958) and the Tyler Vocational Classification System (Tyler, 1961). The former test was designed for use in military settings and contains cards with statements the subject is instructed to sort with respect to their perceived importance to effective leadership. The Tyler Q-sort contains cards on which occupations are printed, the subject's task being to sort them into piles representing occupations that he or she might choose, would not choose, or have no opinion about. Further sortings help to yield a listing of occupations that are perceived to be most and least desirable. Modifications of these and other Q-sorts may be made as the situation warrants. For example, Williams (1978) expanded the list of occupations represented in the original Tyler cards to include a wider range of occupations.

Q-methodology is a very flexible measurement technique and one that can be adapted to virtually any assessment situation. Insights into self-concept may be obtained by asking testtakers to sort cards not only with respect to how they see themselves in general but also with respect to how they see themselves in specific situations (such as alone at home, in school, in the office, in social/

sexual situations), how they see others (such as family members, friends, instructors, employers, spouse, dates), how they would like to see others—the opportunities are limitless. The California Q-Sort (Block, 1961) was originally designed for sorting by professionally trained observers, though a modified version of it designed for laypeople has since been developed.

The primary advantage in using a Q-sort lies in its versatility and relative ease of application. It is of great utility when the assessor requires relatively precise comparative responses from a large number of stimuli, though, as Nunnally (1978, p. 625) cautioned, "before the Q-sort is employed, it is important to ensure that sensible comparative responses can be made among the stimuli employed in the particular study." Nunnally cited other advantages of the Q-sort related to the versatility with which such data could be analyzed:

> if one elects to use the Q-sort as a rating method, one is not necessarily tied to the use of particular techniques of mathematical analysis rather than others . . . [C]hoices among approaches to mathematical analysis . . . are mainly matters of taste and hunch. In the long run we shall learn which approaches are generally more fruitful, but at this early stage in the growth of science, it is good that all of the research eggs are not being placed in the same methodological basket. (p. 625)

The Q-sort is, of course, subject to all the limitations of any self-report measure regarding the willingness and ability of sorters to make accurate and insightful revelations about themselves. It must be noted, however, that there is a wealth of evidence to support the view that respondents can generally supply meaningful and predictive information about themselves (see Bem & Allen, 1974; Bem & Funder, 1978).

Adjective checklists   Another general approach to measuring self-concept is referred to as the adjective checklist method. The popularity of such techniques derives in no small part from their great intuitive appeal; present examinees with a list of adjectives and then have them check off the ones they deem to be most descriptive of themselves. One such test, the Adjective Check List (ACL), consists of 300 adjectives arranged in alphabetical order. Gough (1960; Gough & Heilbrun, 1980) devised an elaborate scoring system for this test with 37 scales based in part on the personality theory of Henry Murray. The ACL is a popular research instrument and has been used in many different ways, such as in the study of parents' perceptions of their children (Brown, 1972) and clients' perceptions of their therapists (Reinehr, 1969) and therapeutic environment (Sutker et al., 1978). In a study employing middle-level managers as subjects, Hills (1985) found that subjects who had described themselves on the ACL as assertive, competitive, self-confident, and willing to function autonomously were subsequently rated by others as more effective in problem-solving exercises than were subjects who had given relatively higher emphasis to characteristics such as cooperativeness, self-discipline, and tact.

Adjective checklist methodology can be used to obtain a relatively quick assessment of an individual's emotional state. Testtakers consider a wide variety of words or phrases and need only make a brief response—a check—alongside those that apply. The Depression Adjective Checklist (Lubin, 1967, 1981; Lubin & Levitt, 1979) instructs testtakers to indicate which adjectives best describe how they are feeling at that moment. It is, in essence, an instrument designed to measure the state, rather than the trait, of depression.

The Multiple Affect Adjective Check List—Revised (MAACL-R; Zuckerman & Lubin, 1985) consists of 132 adjectives arranged in alphabetical order. The test may be administered under two different types of instructions, both standardized. One set, the "Today" (or state) form, instructs testtakers to select those adjectives that describe how they feel at the time of testing. The "In General" (or trait) form instructs testtakers to select those adjectives that describe how they usually feel. Based on factor-analytic research, the MAACL-R is scored on each of five affective scales (factors) by counting the number of adjectives contributing to the scale. The "In General" form of the MAACL-R was normed on a nationally representative sample of 1,543 people 18 years old and older. Available normative data for the "Today" form included only 538 students. The test has acceptable internal consistency reliability, with coefficients ranging from .50 to .95 (median = .80) for the state form and from .07 to .96 (median = .82) for the trait form, across a variety of samples. Internal consistency for one of the scales (the Sensation Seeking scale) is low (.07 to .63), whereas all other internal consistency reliability coefficients on the trait form are over .73. Test-retest reliability has been examined on college students over periods ranging from two days to eight weeks. As expected, the state form demonstrated lower levels of test-retest reliability (.00 to .48, median = .16) than did the trait form (.10 to .92, median = .60).

The MAACL-R test manual cites studies to support the test's construct and criterion-related validity. For example, there is evidence that students' scores on the Anxiety scale move in the predicted direction before students take examinations; that is, they report greater anxiety. In general, the scales correlate well with self-ratings and with the ratings of observers and peers. Also, people with diagnosed mental disorders tend to score differently on the MAACL-R than do people without mental disorders. Discriminative validity seems to be a major weakness for the MAACL-R. Because the factors overlap to a degree, several different factors may be correlated with a particular validity measure. For example, three of the five MAACL-R scales correlate with Scale 2 (Depression) of the MMPI. Still, the MAACL-R tends to be regarded as a psychometrically sound test of affect.

Self-concept differentiation   Some newer measures of self-concept are based on the notion that states and traits related to self-concept are to a large degree context-dependent—that is, ever changing as a result of the particular situation (Callero, 1992; Donahue et al., 1993). The term *self-concept differentiation* is used to refer to the degree to which a person has different self-concepts in different roles (Donahue et al., 1993). People characterized as "highly differentiated" are likely to perceive themselves quite differently in various roles. For example, a highly differentiated businessman in his forties may perceive himself as motivated and hard-driving in his role at work, conforming and people-pleasing in his role as son, and emotional and passionate in his role as husband. By contrast, people whose concept of self is not very differentiated tend to perceive themselves similarly across their social roles. According to Donahue et al. (1993), people with low levels of self-concept differentiation tend to be healthier psychologically, perhaps because of their more unified and coherent sense of self.

Locus of Control

Much has been written about the construct *locus of control,* and indeed you may already have become acquainted with this term in another psychology course. *Locus*—meaning "place" or "site"—*of control* refers to the perception people have about the source of things that happen to them; do they see themselves as largely responsible for what happens to them in their lives, or do they attribute what happens to them to other factors (such as fate, luck, other forces, or other people)? Rotter first introduced this construct in a 1966 monograph and with it provided an Internal/External (I/E) scale. Other scales designed to measure internal/external orientations or styles (in the broadest sense) have since been published. The following item is representative of the items typically found on such tests; answer it "True" or "False" and, before reading further, "score" your response as to whether you think it places you more on the internal or external end of the locus-of-control continuum:

Sample Item: I believe in the value of seat belts and use them willingly.

True or False

If you answered "True" to this statement, it would indicate an internal rather than an external orientation. People who believe in the value of seat belts perceive themselves as being able to do something to help prevent serious injury in the event of an automobile accident. At the other end of the spectrum are people who do not believe in the value of seat belts and who—sometimes in violation of state safety-belt laws—refuse to buckle them. Among the familiar rationales offered for not using seat belts are some (such as "if it's meant to be, it's meant to be") that exemplify an orientation representative of an external (as opposed to an internal) locus of control.

From a psychometric standpoint, Rotter's (1966) measure of locus of control is reliable, and numerous studies have attested to the validity of the construct. A survey of the recent scholarly literature will reveal hundreds of experimental investigations that relate scores on a measure of internal/external locus of control to numerous variables such as academic achievement, occupational success, psychiatric diagnosis, and marital adjustment.

The theoretical foundation on which Rotter's I/E scale rests suggests that behavior will be affected by one's locus of control differentially as a result of specific activities (Rotter, 1966). Accordingly, a number of situation-specific locus-of-control scales have been developed, such as the Multiple Health Locus of Control Scale (Wallston et al., 1978), which has high predictive validity with regard to health-related behavior.

Learning Styles

Individual differences in learning styles have been a topic of educational research for decades (Newstead, 1992), and the assessment of learning styles may be accomplished in many different ways. Perhaps the most direct method of assessment would be to measure learning across various tasks or situations that differ in the kinds of learning styles they demand or encourage. The particular conditions under which the most and the least learning takes place could then be subject to further study. However, conducting such a research project would be costly and time-consuming. An alternative approach would be to develop a self-report measure of learning style—which is exactly what many researchers have done. For example, Kirby et al. (1988) developed a measure designed to distinguish between visual and verbal learners. Biggs (1987; cited in Kramer & Conoley, 1992) developed a measure that focuses on the assessees' motivation for learning, as well as strategy and approach. Other such measures approach the assessment of learning styles in sundry ways (Entwistle & Ramsden, 1983; Kiewra & McShane, 1992; Lavelle, 1993; Newstead, 1992; Silver & Hanson, 1980, cited in Kramer & Conley, 1992; Torrance, 1987b).

In general, a problem in this area of research is the lack of any consistent theory concerning what learning styles are. Lacking any widely accepted theory, it is difficult to assess the construct validity of these tests. One test may correlate only faintly and insignificantly with another (Newstead, 1992). Even the use of factor-analytic techniques has produced no consistent picture of learning styles (Geiger et al., 1993; Kirby et al., 1988; Newstead, 1992). Should more research be conducted in this area? "Yes," says Robert Sternberg (1992), who views such research as key to understanding practical and applied aspects of intelligence (see Sternberg, 1981, 1985).

Situational Performance Measures

If you have ever applied for a part-time secretarial job and been required to take a typing test, you have had firsthand experience with what we are calling "situational performance measures." Broadly stated, a *situational performance measure* is a procedure that allows for observation and evaluation of an individual under a standard set of circumstances. A situational performance measure typically involves performance of some specific task under actual or simulated conditions. The road test you took to obtain your driver's license was a situational performance measure that entailed an evaluation of your driving skills in a real car, on a real road, in real traffic. On the other hand, situational performance measures used to assess the skills of prospective astronauts are done in rocket simulators in scientific laboratories that are firmly planted on Mother Earth.

The range of variables that may be focused on in situational performance measures is virtually limitless. In addition to evaluating skills such as typing and driving, situational performance measures have been used to assess a wide variety of variables related to personality. For example, the responses of prospective astronauts placed in simulated space conditions are closely observed with respect to such variables as tolerance for weightlessness; irritability; ability to eat, sleep, and exercise routine duties; and ability to get along with others under such conditions for a prolonged time. What all the situational performance measures have in common is that the construct they measure is thought to be more accurately assessed by examining behavior directly than by asking subjects to describe their behavior. In some cases, subjects may be motivated to misrepresent themselves, as when asked about moral behavior. In other situations, subjects may simply not know how they will respond under particular circumstances, as in a stress test.

The Character Education Inquiry

The Character Education Inquiry was the name of a project designed to explore the nature of children's "character," and it represented one of the earliest psychological assessment research projects that employed situational performance measurements (Hartshorne & May, 1928). The behaviors to be observed took place in the context of tasks and activities that regularly occurred during the pupils' day, and none of the research subjects knew that they were being observed and evaluated. The component of "character" that was focused on in most of the tests was honesty, though measures of self-control and altruism were also included. In one measure of honesty, for example, children were presented with the opportunity to cheat on the grading of a test. This measure involved the administration of a test, the collection of the test papers, and, unbeknownst to the students, the scoring of the papers. No marks were actually made on the test papers. The following day, the test papers were returned to the students with instructions to grade their own papers. The grades made by the students were compared with the grades the examiners had obtained before returning the test papers to the students.

Another index of honesty was stealing. A test that provided the opportunity for stealing involved having each child receive a box containing coins that were to be used in playing a game. Upon completion of the game, the children were instructed to place the coins back into the box and return the box to the person in charge. A record of the number of coins in each box was made before the boxes were distributed. The number of coins returned in the different boxes was compared with the original number; thus, it was possible to ascertain if the children did in fact return all the coins or if they kept some for themselves.

The results obtained on the different tests of the Character Education Inquiry indicated that the children's responses varied depending on the situation they were in. Stated another way, the children could not be absolutely classified as "honest" or "dishonest"; their behavior was a function of the circumstances they were in, not of an absolute "character." Low correlations were observed for different measures purporting to measure the same trait (here, honesty). The findings of Hartshorne and May have been cited as evidence for Mischel's (1968) position that a cross-situational trait "honesty" does not exist but, rather, that people are honest in some situations but not in others. To this day, one still occasionally reads of research being conducted with measures very much like those pioneered by Hartshorne and May (for example, Leming, 1978).

Leaderless-Group Situations

The leaderless group is another situational assessment procedure, one in which the subjects being evaluated are usually aware that their behavior is being observed and/or recorded. The procedure typically involves organizing several people into a group for the purpose of carrying out a specific task. Although the group knows the objectives of the exercises, no one is placed in the position of leadership or authority. In addition, purposely vague instructions are typically provided for the group. The group determines how it will accomplish the task and who will be responsible for what duties. An observer monitors the group's progress and evaluates both the group's functioning as a whole and the way in which each individual member functions within the group. The leaderless-group situation provides an opportunity to observe the degree of cooperation exhibited by each individual group member and the extent to which each individual is able to function as part of a team.

The leaderless-group technique has been employed in military and industrial settings. Its use in the military developed out of attempts by the U.S. Office of Strategic Services (OSS, 1948) to assess such characteristics as cooperation, leadership, and initiative. The procedure was designed to aid in the establishment of cohesive military units—cockpit crews, tank crews, and so forth—in which members would work together well and each could make a significant contribution. Assessees might, for example, be assigned the task of transporting equipment over some obstacle-ridden terrain. The way in which the group as a group proceeded through the assignment, as well as how each individual member of the group contributed—or failed to contribute—to the group's process would be carefully noted. From such a sample of behavior, information about an individual's leadership ability, initiative, organization and planning abilities, communication skills, social skills, and related skills and abilities could be obtained.

The use of the leaderless-group procedure in industrial settings has similarly been useful in identifying leaders—persons with managerial or executive potential. Less commonly, the technique has also been employed to identify those combinations of personnel that would have a high probability of functioning well together. Manz and Sims (1984) have called attention to a puzzling paradox that exists in an era when more and more organizations are adopting the self-managed work-group approach: How does one lead those who are supposed to lead themselves? On the basis of their research with 320 employees in a production plant that used a self-managed work system, Manz and Sims identified a unique type of leader required in such a work system—"the unleader." These authors described the effective "unleader" as primarily a facilitator who is able to balance both a "hands-off" and a directive management style in a variety of situations.

Situational Stress Tests

Situational stress tests are measures designed to assess how an individual will react to a specific type of anxiety, frustration, or stress. Most situational stress tests are designed to present a task that must be completed, an activity that must be carried out, or a problem that must be solved. Frustrating obstacles, such as a "helper" who hinders more than helps, are typically an essential part of the exercise. The way in which the examinee responds to this situation provides some indication of the way the examinee tends to respond to frustration in stressful situations.

Situational stress tests were frequently employed by the U.S. Office of Strategic Services (OSS, 1948) during the Second World War in efforts to select candidates for military intelligence and other positions. This technique is still widely used by military organizations for selection as well as research purposes. Tziner and Eden (1985) described the use of such techniques by the Israeli military to determine what the ideal composition of a crew is.

Today, some of the larger corporations have personnel departments that administer measures quite reminiscent of the OSS's situational stress tests. Of course, we are not privy to published descriptions of such tests, which are typically kept confidential. However, it would not be too difficult to conceive, for example, of a "Stockbroker Stress Test" that might proceed as outlined in the box opposite.

Measures of Cognitive Style

Are you reflective or impulsive? Dependent or independent? Flexible or rigid? A "sharpener" or a "leveler"? These are some of the terms used by psychologists to denote *cognitive styles*, the particular thought patterns characteristically used by an individual in problem-solving (in the broadest sense) situations. Although quite similar to the way the term "trait" is used, "cognitive style" implies something more than "trait" about thought processes. The distinction is admittedly fine but one that we hope you will understand after a brief review of some of the instruments that were designed to measure it.

Field Dependence and Independence

Herman Witkin and his associates (Berry, 1976; Witkin & Berry, 1975; Witkin & Goodenough, 1981; Witkin et al., 1954; Witkin et al., 1962) have devoted considerable research energy to investigating a cognitive style related to how much an individual relies on environmental cues in perception. In perceiving an object, people who are highly "field-dependent" rely heavily on the visual field that surrounds that object. On the other hand, people who are highly "field-independent" rely less on the surrounding visual field and are able to focus more on the object itself. As illustrated in Figure 13–1, the tools used by Witkin

A Hypothetical "Stockbroker Stress Test"

It is not inconceivable that some major brokerage houses use performance work samples as one method by which candidates for positions are selected. What might such a stockbroker stress test be like? Using imagination as well as knowledge of the typical components of such procedures, we could envision the following.

Initially, candidates for the position of stockbroker might be told that they will be observed by trained raters in a performance work test that will be one of the criteria used in deciding whether they are given further consideration for the position. They might then be led to the room where the experiment will be conducted, a room designed to look very much like the typical work environment of a broker. And now the "stress test" begins. . . .

Candidates are told that they have just been hired by a hypothetical brokerage house—let's call the firm "Merry Lynch." Next, candidates are given time sufficient to familiarize themselves with a number of written materials, including (1) a listing of various personnel in the firm, (2) information on various (hypothetical) stocks, (3) a listing and description of the personality and holdings of seven of their best clients, and (4) a listing of a hundred or so prospects (potential customers).

After studying these materials, each candidate is placed in an office situation (along with three or four other candidates) where each person has a desktop computer (from which current quotes on the hypothetical stocks may be obtained) and (1) an office assistant (who seldom assists and is more apt to hinder), (2) a phone that seems to keep ringing with clients wishing to place orders or ask advice on certain stocks, (3) a number of pieces of correspondence

and interoffice memos that must be answered, and (4) the delivery of company advisories on various stocks and newly issued stocks. Within a certain time limit, the candidates must deal with all these tasks; how competently and professionally candidates establish priorities and policies, communicate information to clients and fellow employees, and generally deal with the duties and stresses of the "Merry Lynch" situation will in part determine whether they are given further consideration for a position at the firm.

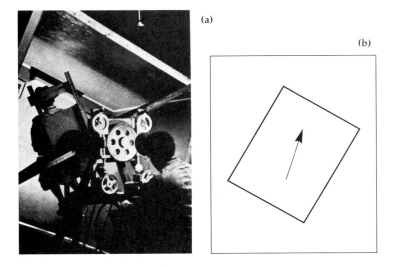

Figure 13–1
Measuring Field Dependence and Independence

If someone asked you, "Which way is up?" you would probably have no difficulty in pointing the right way. But think of the visual cues you rely on to make that judgment: the floor, the ceiling, other objects in your line of vision, and so forth. What if those cues were taken away? Worse yet, what if those cues were purposely distorted? Do you think you would still be able to readily answer the question "Which way is up?"

*Measurement techniques designed to explore questions such as these were devised by Witkin and his associates (1962). In the tilting-room/tilting-chair device (see **a**), the subject sits in a chair that may be tilted and is in a room that may be tilted as well—this can get you dizzy just thinking about it! The subject's task is to identify which way is up after the chair and the room have been set at different angles. On the rod-and-frame test (see **b**), the frame and the rod may be rotated, and—here again—the subject's task is to indicate which direction is true upright with reference to the rod. Both of these techniques are designed to measure the cognitive style of field dependence/independence.*

in his experimental investigations of this cognitive style have been the rod-and-frame-test, the tilting-room/tilting-chair test, and the Embedded Figures Test (Oltman et al., 1971). In general, the person labeled "field-dependent" rather than "field-independent" would be one who was unable to adjust the rod or the chair to a true upright position when a background of confusing environmental cues was present. The field-dependent person may also be identified as such on the basis of a paper-and-pencil measure, the Embedded Figures Test. Low scores on this test reflect difficulty or slowness in separating the targeted figure from the complex background.

What started out as a program of basic research has led to an impressive array of findings with applied value. Primarily through correlational studies, a

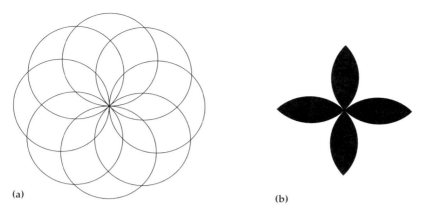

(a)   (b)

Figure 13–2
An Illustration of a Sample Embedded-Figure-Type Item

The examinee's task on one type of embedded-figure item would be to locate the target figure (b) within a stimulus figure (a).

profile of the personality of people with respect to this cognitive style has emerged. In contrast to the field-independent person, a field-dependent person tends to have less self-esteem and tends to be more conforming, more socially oriented, more passive, less creative, less analytic, and less self-aware. The field-independent individual is more independent in social relations and tends to have more initiative than does the field-dependent person (Heesacker, 1981; Witkin & Goodenough, 1977, 1981; Witkin et al., 1954; Witkin et al., 1962). In a study involving 102 suburban Philadelphia students enrolled in grades 2 through 4, the cognitive style of field independence was found to be related to high achievement in mathematics (Vaidya & Chansky, 1980). The field-dependence measure has more recently found application in the study of the reading comprehension processes. Meng and Patty (1991) observed differences in the reading patterns of their elementary school subjects as a function of cognitive style.

Paper-and-pencil measures of field dependence and independence include the Embedded Figures Test (Oltman et al., 1971), the Children's Embedded Figures Test (Karp & Konstadt, 1963/1971), the Preschool Embedded Figures Test (Coates, 1972), and the Group Embedded Figures Test, this last test now described in greater detail.

The Group Embedded Figures Test   The Group Embedded Figures Test, or GEFT (Oltman et al., 1971), was designed for use with subjects 10 and older. It consists of 25 embedded-figure problems printed in a booklet, the subject's task being to identify a simple design from within a more complex one (see Figure 13–2). Normative data for the GEFT are based on a college sample of 155 men and 242 women. Correlations between the GEFT and the Embedded Figures Test were found to be .82 for males and .63 for females, a difference that is unexplained in the test manual. In a study involving 22 sixth-grade students, internal-consistency reliability coefficients were found to range from .83 to .98, and long-term-stability coefficients were found to be .80 for boys and .71 for girls (Lis & Powers, 1979). Issues associated with the GEFT's reliability have also been addressed using generalizability theory (see *Everyday Psychometrics,* pages 480–481).

A study with 88 sixth-grade boys explored the relationship between cognitive style, self-concept, and leadership ability (Hoffman, 1978). Subjects were administered the Group Embedded Figures Test to determine field dependence/independence. The Piers-Harris Children's Self Concept Scales (discussed earlier in this chapter) provided a measure of self-concept. Leadership ability was assessed by assigning the subjects to groups for the purpose of completing an unstructured task and recording the amount of participation and verbalization of each subject. In addition, each member in the group rated the other members on a leadership rating scale. Boys identified as field-independent were more likely to have been evaluated by their peers as demonstrating leadership ability and were more likely to have exhibited a positive self-image as measured by the Piers-Harris.

Other research has raised questions concerning the meaning of performance on the GEFT. Lusk and Wright (1981) have suggested that higher scores obtained on the second half of the GEFT are the result of learning that occurs during the test administration—learning that may influence subsequent performance on the test. In another study, the researchers concluded that when the GEFT is used with an adult alcoholic population, cognitive impairment rather than cognitive style is the dimension assessed (O'Leary et al., 1980). It has also been suggested that the skills involved in tests of field dependence and independence may be confounded with general intelligence (Brody, 1972) or general spatial ability.

Reflective Versus Impulsive Cognitive Style

The *reflective-versus-impulsive* cognitive-style dimension has been described as the "consistent tendency to display slow or fast response times in problem situations with high response uncertainty" (Kagan, 1965, p. 134). Persons exhibiting a reflective style will spend more time examining the problem and considering alternative solutions, and will check for the accuracy and completeness of each hypothesis. The impulsive style is characterized by a tendency to make quick decisions and to respond with what comes to mind rather than with critical examination. Reflective-versus-impulsive style has been shown to be stable over time, though there is a tendency for reflection to increase as the subject gets older (Kagan, 1965).

The theoretical formulation of reflective-versus-impulsive style was an outgrowth of the work of Kagan and his associates (Kagan et al., 1964) at the Fels Institute. Kagan et al. observed that there were differences in the way children approach those "problem situations where many solution hypotheses are available simultaneously, (and where) the child has to evaluate the differential adequacy of each possibility" (p. 13). The Matching Familiar Figures Test (MFFT) was developed as an instrument to research the reflective-impulsive dimension in children. The construct of impulsivity has also been studied by means of situational tests that involve delay of gratification (see Mischel, 1966) and by the use of a combination of procedures such as the MFFT and situational tests (Block et al., 1974).

The MFFT consists of 12 items that represent familiar objects (such as telephone, airplane, and cowboy) and two sample items. The subject is presented with a standard picture and six "strikingly similar" pictures, of which only one is identical to the standard. The subject is instructed to select that picture which is identical to the standard. Scores are based on the length of time required before responding and on the number of errors produced. Respondents with short response times and a high number of errors will earn scores indicative of impulsivity, and respondents with longer response times and a low number of errors will earn scores indicative of being "reflective." It has been demonstrated that high negative correlations exist between response time on the MFFT and the number of errors produced; that is, testtakers who respond quickly tend to make more errors than those who respond more slowly (Kagan, 1965).

In research comparing the performance of 58 11-year-olds on the MFFT with performance on the Wechsler Intelligence Scale for Children—Revised (WISC-R), children designated as reflective based on MFFT performance were found to perform significantly higher on visual organization and attention-concentration subtests of the WISC-R than did children designated as impulsive (Brannigan et al., 1980).

The MFFT has been criticized for a lack of normative data and the lack of an alternate form to reduce practice effects in retesting (Arizmendi et al., 1981). Still, the test has been used in a number of research projects, including studies exploring how impulsivity in children might be modified. Kagan, Pearson, and Welch (1966) were able to lengthen MFFT response times of impulsive first-graders by providing training experiences in visual matching, inductive reasoning, and enforced periods of delay before giving a response. In a study involving 48 impulsive second- and third-graders, Nelson and Birkimer (1978) demonstrated that training in self-reinforcement could lengthen response time on the MFFT and significantly reduce errors. In another study, it was shown that training in verbal self-instruction could result in an increase in MFFT response time and a decrease in MFFT errors for impulsive subjects, as well as improved teacher ratings of classroom behavior (Kendall & Finch, 1978). Although the MFFT is used primarily in research with children, investigations of Kagan's formulations with adult populations have been conducted (for example, Brodzinsky & Dein, 1976; O'Keefe & Argulewicz, 1979).

Leveling Versus Sharpening

A cognitive dimension of leveling/sharpening refers to differences in the way people perceive and recall stimuli. *Levelers* tend to minimize differences in a stimulus field and to organize and recall stimuli in a simple and diffuse manner. *Sharpeners,* on the other hand, tend to maximize differences in stimuli and to prefer complex and detailed organization (Holzman, 1954). The process of leveling and sharpening has been illustrated in experimentation with the

Classical Versus Generalizability Theory in Psychometric Evaluations

According to classical or true score test theory, variability in test scores can be divided into two components: true score variance and error variance. In a psychometric evaluation of the GEFT, the application of classical test theory would entail deriving some measure of how much each testtaker's score approximates the true amount of each testtaker's field independence. Test scores would be expected to differ from whatever the true measure of the testtaker's ability is as a result of error. Although potential sources of error are numerous, they are most typically presumed to be inherent in the test itself, in the test administration, and/or in the test's scoring and interpretation.

You may recall from Chapter 5 that generalizability theory involves conceptualizing variation in test scores somewhat differently than the true score model. Rather than trying to estimate a single "true score," consideration is given to how test scores would be expected to shift across situations as a result of changes in the characteristic being measured (Cronbach, 1984). For example, if a person took the GEFT twice and obtained two different scores, the possibility would be entertained that different levels of field independence existed at the time of two test administrations. Note how this view of the two test scores differs from that of the classical one, wherein some part of the two scores would be attributed to error because the scores differ. In generalizability theory, the emphasis is shifted from a search for possible sources of error to the factors contributing to the achievement of a particular score.

For the purposes of illustration, let's assume that a testtaker was well rested for the first administration of the GEFT but fatigued when taking the second administration of it. Analyzing such data from a classical perspective, one might conclude that testtaker fatigue was a substantial source of error and that the testtaker's "true score" probably is best approximated by the well-rested score. By contrast, from a perspective that relies on generalizability theory, the analysis of the data would in essence entertain the notion that field independence may be to some extent affected by how well rested a person is at the time. Thus, people may have two (or more) "true" levels of field independence: one level when rested, and another when tired.

The practical utility of such relatively subtle distinctions between classical and generalizability theories depends on the use to which test data will be put. As an example, let's say that the GEFT is being used to select people to work as air traffic controllers at one of the world's busiest airports. And let's further suppose for the sake of this example that people who exhibit high levels of field independence are more desirable candidates for air traffic controller positions than people who exhibit low levels of field independence. The GEFT is being administered to screen applicants for an air traffic controller position that frequently will entail erratic scheduling over 24-hour shifts. Given such circumstances, the GEFT will ideally be administered not only when applicants are well rested but also when they are tired. Measured levels of field independence may change over the course of the two administrations. All other things being equal, the employer would be more confident in the abilities of applicants whose scores were consistently high.

Generalizability theory was applied in a study of the reliability of a version of the GEFT that contains 18 embedded-figure items (Thompson & Melancon, 1987). The test was administered to 175 students over the course of two sessions, with nine problems presented in each session. Data analysis was designed to help the researchers understand why a particular student got a specific item right or wrong. Three influences on testtaker response were identified: (1) the students themselves; (2) the specific test item; and (3) the session in which the item was given (that is, the first or second session). It was presumed that each of these three influences (or, more technically stated, sources of variance) could act either alone or in combination with one or more of the other influences to affect the students' responses. Interactions between the different variance components were considered. For example, did some students respond differently to particular items depending on the session in which the items were presented? Did some students perceive a particular item as easier when it was presented in the first session because they were "fresh" to the test and not bored or confused by other items? Did some students find a particular item easier if it was presented in the second session because they benefited from the practice obtained during the first session? The goal of the data analysis was to explore how much variance in responses to test items was explained by three sources of variance as well as the various interactions of these variables.

The researchers concluded that variability associated with the subjects themselves explained the majority of variability in responses to particular items.

Stated another way, the primary reason that different subjects responded differently to particular test items had to do with the subjects themselves—a most desirable feature of a test, according to the study authors (Thompson & Melancon, 1987). Of course, a validity study would be needed to determine whether these differences in responses were indeed related to differential levels of field independence.

Generalizability theory is considered to be helpful in understanding variability in test scores and in responses to test items. Yet if that is indeed the case, why is it used relatively infrequently? Perhaps, as Cronbach (1984) implied, generalizability theory is more applicable to behavioral measures than to personality measures. Behavior obviously changes across situations, making necessary an approach to reliability that can account for those changes. By contrast, personality traits are thought by many to be relatively stable across various types of situations; as such, personality traits may be more amenable to measurement in accordance with classical test theory.

The late 1970s was an era in which many personality researchers and theorists were wondering out loud whether personality traits did indeed exhibit cross-situational consistency. In such an environment, it would not be surprising to read predictions of the demise of true score theory and the complementary rise in applications of generalizability theory (see, for example, Dyer, 1979). Contrary to such predictions, however, classical test theory not only is alive and well but also has remained the dominant force in the study of tests and measurement.

Schematizing Test (Gardner et al., 1959). Described briefly, this procedure has subjects judge the size of 150 squares. The squares vary in size from 1 to 14 inches and are projected onto a screen in groups of five, according to a pre-scribed order. The five smallest squares were presented three times in ascending order, then randomly. Following random presentation, the smallest square was removed and replaced with one slightly larger than any previously shown. In like manner, the new group of squares was presented first in ascending order, then randomly; finally, the substitution of the smallest square with a larger one was made. This procedure continued until all the squares were shown. Con-tinuous substitution of a larger for a smaller square created a gradual shift in the relative position each square held within the group. The way in which the subjects incorporated these changes in their judgments of size was analyzed. Some subjects were alert to differences, able to adapt to changes as new stimuli were introduced, and to adjust their estimations accordingly (sharpeners). Others (levelers) were less attuned to differences, more influenced by the stimuli they had previously observed, and less likely to modify their judg-ments as new stimuli were introduced (Holzman & Klein, 1954; Klein & Holz-man, 1950).

In a separate investigation, the effect leveling and sharpening had on the recall of early experiences was explored (Holzman & Gardner, 1960). The Sche-matizing Test was administered to 41 undergraduate female students of similar socioeconomic background between the ages of 18 and 22. In a separate testing session, the subjects were asked to recount the childhood story of the Pied Piper, which was scored for the presence of eleven thematic elements. The Pied Piper was selected as a tale that most people have been exposed to but are not overly familiar with. In general, sharpeners recalled more of the key elements of the story in a more organized fashion than did levelers. Levelers tended to be vague in their accounts and often supplied only "an indistinct general impression" (Holzman & Gardner, 1960, p. 178). These findings led the authors to conclude that the phenomenon of leveling and sharpening not only operates in the labo-ratory setting but also may be an "enduring aspect of cognitive organization" (p. 179) that may be generalized to a variety of situations.

Behavioral Assessment

An Overview

Traits, states, motives, needs, drives, defenses, and related psychological con-structs have no tangible existence; they are constructs whose existence must be inferred from behavior. In the traditional approach to clinical assessment, tests as well as other tools are employed to gather data; from these data, diagnoses and inferences are made concerning the existence and strength of psychological constructs. The traditional approach to assessment might therefore be termed a "sign" approach, since test responses are deemed to be signs or clues to underlying personality or ability. In contrast to this traditional approach is an alternative philosophy of assessment that may be termed the "sample" approach. This approach focuses on the behavior itself; emitted behavior is not viewed as a sign of something but, rather, as a sample to be interpreted in its own right. The emphasis in behavioral assessment is on "what a person *does* in situations rather than on inferences about what attributes he *has* more globally" (Mischel, 1968, p. 10). Predicting what a person will do is thought to entail an understanding of the assessee with respect to antecedent conditions and consequences for the particular situation in question. Upon close scrutiny, however, the trait concept is still present in many behavioral measures, though more narrowly defined and more closely linked to specific situations (Zuckerman, 1979).

To illustrate behavioral observation as an assessment strategy, consider the plight of the single female client who presents herself at the university counseling center complaining that even though all her friends tell her how attractive she is, she is experiencing great difficulty in meeting men—so much so that she doesn't even want to try anymore. A counselor confronted with such a client might, among other things, (1) interview the client with respect to this problem, (2) administer an appropriate test to the client, (3) ask the client to keep detailed diaries of her thoughts and behaviors with respect to her efforts to meet men, and/or (4) accompany the client to a singles bar and observe her behavior. The latter two strategies come under the heading of behavioral observation; in one situation, the counselor is doing the actual observing, in another it is the client herself.

The administration of a psychological test or test battery to a client such as this single woman might yield signs that then could be inferred to relate to the problem. For example, if a number of the client's TAT stories involved themes of demeaning, hostile, or otherwise unsatisfactory heterosexual encounters as a result of venturing out into the street, the counselor might make an interpretation at a "deeper" or "second" level of inference: the client's expressed fear of going outdoors (and ultimately her fear of meeting men) might in some way be related to an unconscious fear of promiscuity—a fear of becoming a "streetwalker."

In contrast to the sign approach, the clinician employing the sample or behavioral approach to assessment might examine the behavioral diary that the client kept with respect to her problem and design an appropriate therapy program on the basis of those records. Thus, for example, the antecedent conditions under which the client would feel most distraught and unmotivated to do anything about the problem might be delineated and worked on in counseling sessions.

An advantage of the sign as opposed to the sample approach is that in the hands of a skillful, perceptive clinician, the client might be put in touch with feelings that even she was not really aware of before the assessment. The client may have been consciously (or unconsciously) avoiding certain thoughts and images (those attendant on the expression of her sexuality, for example), and this inability to deal with those thoughts and images may indeed have been a factor contributing to her ambivalence with respect to meeting men.

Behavioral assessors seldom make such "deeper level" inferences; and if sexuality is not raised as an area of difficulty by the client (in an interview, on a checklist, or by some other behavioral assessment technique), this problem area may well be ignored or given short shrift. The behavioral assessor does, however, tend to be more comprehensive and systematic in his or her approach to assessing the breadth and magnitude of the client's problem. Instead of searching for signs in Rorschach or other test protocols, the behaviorally oriented counselor or clinician might simply ask such a client a question like "What are some of the reasons you think you are unable to meet men?" and then take it from there. By obtaining a complete self-report either verbally or through a pencil-and-paper behavioral checklist and by obtaining behavioral observation data, the behaviorally oriented assessor will discover specific areas that need to be focused on in therapy. You can see that the behavioral approach does not require as much "clinical creativity" as the sign approach; perhaps for that reason, it is generally considered to be the more scientific of the two approaches to psychological assessment.

Unlike traditional psychological assessors, behaviorally oriented clinicians have characteristically found little use for traditional psychological tests and procedures in their work. This division in the field of clinical psychology was taken note of as early as 1967 by Greenspoon and Gersten, who observed that "psychologists in the practicum agencies contend that tests are the 'bread and butter' of the clinical psychologist and the university personnel contend that if such is the case the clinical psychologist is on an ersatz diet" (p. 849). In their article entitled "A New Look at Psychological Testing: Psychological Testing from the Standpoint of a Behaviorist," they argued that "psychological tests should be able to provide the behavior therapist with information that should be of value in doing behavior therapy. This contention is based on the assumption that the behavior on any psychological test should be lawful" (Greenspoon & Gersten, 1967, p. 849). Accordingly, psychological tests could be useful, for example, in helping the behavior therapist to identify the kinds of contingent stimuli that would be most effective with a given patient. For example, patients with high percentages of Color or Color/Form responses on the Rorschach and with IQs in excess of 90 might be most responsive to positive verbal contingencies (such as "good," "excellent"), whereas patients with high percentages of movement or vista (three-dimensional) responses and IQs in excess of 90 might be most responsive to negative verbal contingencies ("no," "wrong"). Although the ideas expressed by Greenspoon and Gersten seem not to have been greeted with a rush of experimental enthusiasm—perhaps because there exist more direct ways to assess responsiveness to various contingencies—their article did represent a truly innovative attempt to narrow a widening schism in the field of clinical assessment.

Differences between traditional and behavioral approaches to assessment have to do with varying assumptions about the nature of personality and the causes of behavior. The data from traditional assessment are used primarily to describe, classify, or diagnose, whereas the data from a behavioral assessment are typically more directly related to the formulation of a specific treatment program. Some of the other differences between the two approaches are summarized in Table 13–1.

Table 13–1

Differences Between Behavioral and Traditional Approaches to Psychological Assessment

	Behavioral	Traditional
Assumptions		
Conception of personality	Personality constructs mainly employed to summarize specific behavior patterns, if at all	Personality as a reflection of enduring, underlying states or traits
Causes of behavior	Maintaining conditions sought in current environment	Intrapsychic or within the individual
Implications		
Role of behavior	Important as a sample of person's repertoire in specific situation	Behavior assumes importance only insofar as it indexes underlying causes
Role of history	Relatively unimportant, except, for example, to provide a retrospective baseline	Crucial in that present conditions seen as a product of the past
Consistency of behavior	Behavior thought to be specific to the situation	Behavior expected to be consistent across time and settings
Uses of data	To describe target behaviors and maintaining conditions	To describe personality functioning and etiology
	To select the appropriate treatment	To diagnose or classify
	To evaluate and revise treatment	To make prognosis; to predict
Other characteristics		
Level of inferences	Low	Medium to high
Comparisons	More emphasis on intraindividual or idiographic	More emphasis on interindividual or nomothetic
Methods of assessment	More emphasis on direct methods (e.g., observations of behavior in natural environment)	More emphasis on indirect methods (e.g., interviews and self-report)
Timing of assessment	More ongoing; prior, during, and after treatment	Pre- and perhaps posttreatment, or strictly to diagnose
Scope of assessment	Specific measures and of more variables (e.g., of target behaviors in various situations, of side effects, context, strengths as well as deficiencies)	More global measures (e.g., of cure, or improvement) but only of the individual

Source: Hartmann, Roper, and Bradford (1979).

The Who, What, When, Where, and How of It

The name says it all; *behavior* is the focus of assessment in behavioral assessment—not traits, states, or other constructs presumed to be present in various strengths, just behavior. This will become clear as we continue our overview with a look at what we could call the "who, what, where, when, and how" of behavioral assessment.

Who is assessed? Most typically, only one person at a time. Regardless of whether the assessment is for research, clinical, or other purposes, the hallmark of behavioral assessment is intensive study of individuals—this is in contrast to mass testing of groups of people to obtain normative data with respect to some hypothesized trait or state. *Who* is the assessor? Depending on the particular assessment, the assessor may be a highly qualified professional, or a technician/assistant trained to conduct a particular assessment (such as recording the number of times young Johnny leaves his seat during hygiene class).

What is measured in behavioral assessment? Not surprisingly, the behavior or behaviors targeted for assessment will vary as a function of the objectives of the assessment. Whatever behavior or behaviors are being measured, a careful definition of what constitutes a targeted behavior must be drawn. And for the purposes of assessment, the targeted behavior must be measurable—quantifiable in some way. Examples of such measurable behaviors can range from "the number of seconds Johnny spends out of his seat during hygiene class" to "the number of degrees Celsius body temperature is altered"—the latter being an observable event that may be considered "behavior" in its broadest sense. Note that descriptions of targeted behaviors in behavioral assessment typically begin with the phrase "the number of. . . ."

When is an assessment of behavior made? Beyond fairly general answers to this question (such as "during the school day except at lunch"), behavioral assessors may employ any of various schedules or formats of assessment. For example, one schedule of assessment is referred to as *frequency,* or *event recording*. Here, each time the targeted behavior occurs, it is recorded. Another schedule of assessment is referred to as *interval recording*. Assessment according to this schedule occurs only during predefined intervals of time (for example, every other minute, every 48 hours, every third week). Beyond merely tallying the number of times a particular behavior is emitted, the assessor may also maintain a record of the intensity of the behavior as gauged by observable and quantifiable events such as the *duration* of the behavior, stated in number of seconds, minutes, hours, days, weeks, months, or years, or some ratio or percentage of time that the behavior occurs during a specified interval of time.

Where does the assessment take place? Unlike the administration of psychological tests, which are most likely to be administered in a psychologist's office or in some institutional setting such as a hospital or a school, behavioral assessment may take place virtually anywhere—usually preferably in the environment where the targeted behavior is most likely to occur naturally. For example, a behavioral assessor studying the obsessive-compulsive habits of a patient might wish to visit the patient at home to see firsthand the variety and intensity of the compulsive behavior the patient exhibits (for example, whether the patient checks the oven for having left the gas on and, if so, how many times per hour).

How is behavioral assessment conducted? The answer to this question will vary, of course, according to the purpose of the assessment. In some situations, the only special equipment required will be a trained observer with pad and pencil. In other types of situations, highly sophisticated recording equipment may be necessary. As an example of the latter situation, imagine that you were a NASA psychologist studying the psychological and behavioral effects of space travel on astronauts; what types of behavioral measures might you employ, and what special equipment would you need—or design—to obtain those measures?

As you consider this question, our brief overview of behavioral assessment continues with a look at some tools of behavioral assessment.

Behavioral Observation and Behavior Rating Scales

A child psychologist observes a patient in a playroom through a one-way mirror; a family therapist views a videotape of a troubled family attempting to resolve a conflict; a psychologist's assistant accompanies a patient lacking in interpersonal skills to a disco for the purpose of observing her; a school psychologist observes a child interacting with peers in the school cafeteria. These are all examples of the use of an assessment technique called *behavioral observation*. As its name implies, this technique entails watching the activities of targeted clients or research subjects and, typically, maintaining some kind of record of those activities. Researchers, clinicians, or counselors may themselves serve as observers, or they may designate trained assistants or other people (such as parents, siblings, teachers, and supervisors) to be the observers. Even the observed person herself or himself can be the behavior observer, as in the case of the dieter maintaining a diary of food intake and emotional feelings—although in that instance, the term *self-observation* would be more appropriate than *behavioral observation*. In some instances, behavioral observation entails mechanical means, such as a videorecording of an event; this relieves the clinician, the researcher, or any other observer of the necessity to be physically present at the time the behavior occurs and allows him or her to view its occurrence when it is convenient to do so. Regardless of who actually does the observing, and whether the observation is accomplished through a "live" or a recorded viewing, factors noted in behavioral observation will typically include a notation of the presence or absence of specific, targeted behaviors, behavioral excesses, behavioral deficits, behavioral assets, and the situational antecedents and consequences of the emitted behaviors.

The "nuts and bolts" of behavioral observation may take many forms, though underlying watchwords in such endeavors are standardization and reliability; every observer using the technique should be trained to systematically look for and record the same well-defined behavior. In one form of behavioral observation, the observer may, in the tradition of the naturalist, record a running narrative of events, using tools such as pencil and paper, a video, film, or still camera, and/or a cassette recorder. Another form of behavioral observation employs what is called a *behavior rating scale*—a preprinted sheet on which the observer notes the presence and/or intensity of targeted behaviors, usually by checking boxes or by filling in coded terms. For example, if the focus of interest was whether an institutionalized patient took out the garbage on a daily basis, an "Emptying Garbage" behavioral scale or checklist (like the one reprinted in Cohen, 1996) might be employed. Sometimes the user of a behavior rating form writes in coded descriptions of various behaviors; the code is preferable to a running narrative, since it takes far less time to enter the data and frees the observer familiar with the code to enter data relating to any of hundreds of possible behaviors, not just the ones printed on the sheets. For example, a number of coding systems for observing the behavior of couples and families are available. Two such systems are the Marital Interaction Coding System (Weiss & Summers, 1983) and the Couples Interaction Scoring System (Notarius & Markman, 1981). In an attempt to facilitate the work of the observer, Filsinger (1983) describes the use of a handheld data-entry device for the observer to use while entering coded observations made from a combination of the Marital Interaction Coding System, the Couples Interaction Scoring System, and two other systems.

Behavior rating scales and systems, as approaches to behavioral assessment in general, may be categorized in different ways. A categorization of "direct" to "indirect" has to do with the setting in which the observed behavior occurs, and how closely that setting approximates the setting in which the behavior naturally occurs. The more natural the setting, the more "direct" the measure; the more removed from the natural setting, the less direct the measure (Shapiro & Skinner, 1990). According to this categorization, assessing a client's reactions in a real disco would provide a direct measure, whereas assessment of behavior in a simulated or videotaped evening at a disco would provide an indirect behavioral measure. Shapiro and Skinner (1990) also draw a distinction between "broad-band" instruments that seek to measure a wide variety of behaviors, and "narrow-band" instruments that may focus on behaviors related to single, specific constructs such as hyperactivity, shyness, or depression.

A number of behavior rating scales designed to assess various aspects of children's behavior are available, among them the Child Behavior Checklist (Achenbach & Edelbrock, 1983; see also Achenbach & Edelbrock, 1986, 1987; Christenson, 1990; Edelbrock, 1988; Martin, 1988; Martin et al., 1986; McConaughty & Achenbach, 1988; Mooney, 1984), the Behavior Rating Profile (Brown & Hammill, 1978), the Eyberg Child Behavior Inventory (Eyberg & Robinson, 1983; Eyberg & Ross, 1978; Burns & Patterson, 1990), the Revised Behavior Problem Checklist (Quay & Peterson, 1983), the Play Performance Scale for Children (Lansky et al., 1985, 1987), and the Walker Problem Behavior Identification Checklist (Walker, 1983). Below we examine one such checklist, which focuses on social skills assessment. Then we look at an innovative newcomer to the field of behavioral assessment instruments—one designed to gauge tissue damage as a result of self-injurious behavior.

The Social Skills Rating System   The Social Skills Rating System (SSRS; Gresham & Elliott, 1990) was designed to measure social skills in individuals from preschool through high school (ages 3 to 18 years) using Teacher and Parent forms and a Student self-report form (grades 3 through 12). The Social Skills Scale assesses positive social behaviors in five areas (cooperation, assertion, responsibility, empathy, and self-control), and the Problem Behavior Scales measure behavior in three areas referred to as "externalizing" problems (including behaviors with observable impact and consequences, such as delinquent-type behaviors), "internalizing" problems (including problems such as fearfulness and

Table 13–2

Sample Items from the Social Skills Rating System—Elementary Level

Social Skills Subscales	Teacher Form	Parent Form	Student (Self-Rating) Form
Cooperation	Finishes class assignments within time limits.	Completes household tasks within a reasonable time.	I finish classwork on time.
Assertion	Initiates conversations with peers.	Starts conversations rather than waiting for others to talk first.	I start talks with class members.
Responsibility	(Not in this form)	Reports accidents to appropriate persons.	(Not in this form)
Empathy	(Not in this form)	(Not in this form)	I feel sorry for others when bad things happen to them.
Self-Control	Controls temper in conflict situations with peers.	Controls temper when arguing with other children.	I control my temper when people are angry at me.

Problem Behaviors Subscales	Teacher Form	Parent Form	Student (Self-Rating) Form
Externalizing Problems	Gets angry easily.	Gets angry easily.	(Not rated by students)
Internalizing Problems	Appears lonely.	Appears lonely.	(Not rated by students)
Hyperactivity	Is easily distracted.	Is easily distracted.	(Not rated by students)

Adapted from Gresham and Elliott (1990).

inhibitions), and hyperactivity. Items on the Social Skills Scales are rated on the basis of frequency (never, sometimes, or very often) and their importance (not important, important, critical), whereas the Problem Behavior Scales are rated on frequency (never, sometimes, or very often). Sample items from the Social Skills Scales and Problem Behavior Scales are presented in Table 13–2.

The SSRS was standardized on a national sample of 4,170 children during the spring of 1988. An attempt was made to approximate the 1990 U.S. Census estimates for the variables of race or ethnicity, geographic region, and community size. Overall, the standardization sample was 73% White and 27% minority. Southern and North Central states as well as central city, suburban, and small-town communities were somewhat overrepresented in the standardization sample, whereas Western and Northeastern areas along with rural communities were underrepresented. The number of disabled students in the standardization sample was greater than in the United States population (17.3% versus 11.0%). Median internal consistency (coefficient alpha) reliabilities were .90 for the Social Skills Scale and .84 for the Problem Behavior Scale across all forms and levels. Test-retest reliability was assessed, with samples of teachers, parents, and students rating the same students four weeks after the original ratings. Test-retest correlations for Social Skills ranged from .68 (students) to

.85 (teachers) to .87 (parents) and for Problem Behaviors from .65 (parents) to .84 (teachers). Initial validity studies compared the SSRS with similar instruments, including the Child Behavior Checklist, and produced moderate to high correlations. Correlations between the SSRS and the social and communication skills subtests on a measure of adaptive behavior would provide evidence of scale validity. In a sample of primary-grade children with disabilities, these correlations ranged from .38 to .64 (median = .50; Merrell & Popinga, 1994). Evidence of the criterion-related validity comes from research that shows that the SSRS can distinguish between children who do and do not have disabilities or behavioral problems (Bramlett et al., 1994; Stinnett et al., 1989).

The Self-Injury Trauma (SIT) Scale   The Self-Injury Trauma (SIT) Scale provides a method for quantifying surface tissue damage caused by self-injurious behavior. Injuries are categorized according to their location, type, and number, as well as an estimate as to severity (see Figure 13–3). Fifty pairs of independently scored SIT Scale records were subjected to inter-rater reliability analyses, and the percentage of agreement for all the variables measured ranged from a low of 92% agreement for the test's "Severity Index" to a high of 100% agreement for the test's "Estimate of Current Risk" measure (Iwata et al., 1990). Such a scale may have many potential applications, including (1) measuring pre- and post-treatment changes in injuries, (2) assessing the level of risk a patient may be at for evidencing self-injurious behavior, and (3) designing or instituting effective treatments for self-injurious behavior, and monitoring their effectiveness.[1]

Analogue Studies

The behavioral approach to clinical assessment and treatment has been likened to the researcher's approach to experimentation; the behavioral assessor proceeds in many ways like a researcher, with the patient's problem being the dependent variable and the factor(s) responsible for causing and/or maintaining the problem behavior being the independent variable(s). Behavioral assessors will typically use the phrase *functional analysis* of behavior to convey the process of identifying the dependent and independent variables with respect to the presenting problem. However, just as it is true that experimenters must frequently employ independent and dependent variables that imitate how those variables occur in the "real world," so behavioral assessors must, too. This type of study, where a variable or two are similar or analogous to the "real" variable the investigator wishes to examine, is referred to as an *analogue study.* The subjects for most of the analogue research in experimental psychology have been white rats and introductory psychology students. However, as we shall see, real patients with real problems can also be assessed in an analogue study.

Suppose Mr. Johnson, a weekend hunter, presents himself at the office of a behavior therapist to be treated for a fear of snakes (harmless and otherwise)—

---

1. Somewhat related in potential application to the SIT scale are methods of quantifying various effects of medical treatment, such as nausea and vomiting (Morrow, 1984) and pain (Jay et al., 1987).

THE SELF-INJURY TRAUMA (SIT) SCALE

Patient:_____ Examiner:_____ Date:_____

PART I. GENERAL DESCRIPTION AND SUMMARY OF HEALED INJURIES

Check each type of self-injurious behavior exhibited by the patient. Next, note any physical evidence of healed injuries (scars, permanent disfigurement, missing body parts), along with the specific site.

Self-Injurious Behaviors:

___ Forceful contact with head or face

___ Forceful contact with other body part

___ Scratching, picking, rubbing skin

___ Biting

___ Eye gouging

___ Ingestion of inedible materials (pica)

___ Vomiting or rumination

___ Air swallowing (aerophagia)

___ Hair pulling (trichotillomania)

___ Other:_____

Healed Injuries:

1 _____

2 _____

3 _____

4 _____

5 _____

PART II. MEASUREMENT OF SURFACE TRAUMA

For each area of the body containing a current (unhealed) injury, identify the location and number of wounds, and note the type and the severity of the worst wound at that particular location.

Number: Score:
    1)--One wound
    2)--Two-four wounds
    3)--Five or more wounds

Type:
    Abrasion or Laceration (AL): A break in the skin, either superficial or deep, caused by tearing, biting, excessive rubbing, or contact with a sharp object.

    Contusion (CT): A distinct area marked by abnormal discoloration or swelling, with or without tissue rupture, caused by forceful contact.

Severity: Score AL as: 1)--Area is red or irritated, with only spotted breaks in the skin.
    2)--Break in the skin is distinct but superficial; no avulsion.
    3)--Break in the skin is deep or extensive, or avulsion is present.

    Score CT as: 1)--Local swelling only or discoloration without swelling.
    2)--Extensive swelling.
    3)--Disfigurement or tissue rupture.

(scoring chart on next page)

Figure 13–3
A Page from the SIT Scale

The complete scale, as well as a detailed description of its development, use, and potential applications, is provided by its authors, Iwata, Pace, Kissel, Nau, and Farber (1990).

a fear that is seriously interfering with his weekend activities. The therapist, desirous of learning more specific behavioral information about this fear, might arrange to accompany Johnson on one of his forays into the woods. More likely, however, Johnson and his therapist would simply discuss the problem—what types of snakes bother him, to what degree, what effect they have on him, and so forth. Alternatively, the therapist might arrange to perform an analogue study in the office. When Johnson shows up for his appointment the following week, the therapist may present him with a harmless snake, caged or free, at some distance from him. The assessment would then be made according to how close to the snake Johnson could get without self-reported debilitating anxiety. Incidentally, the goal of the therapy would have been reached when Johnson was able to comfortably walk right up to the animal and pet it. This is *analogue research* because an attempt has been made to replicate in the consulting room the conditions that exist in the wild; Johnson's reaction to the snake in the laboratory is analogous to—though not identical to—his reaction to a snake in the wild.

A problem with such an assessment procedure is the problem inherent in all analogue research; that problem may be stated succinctly in the question "How analogous are the findings to the real world?" In the present example, Johnson might feel secure enough to warmly embrace a boa constrictor if the assessment was being executed in the environs of a university psychology laboratory. However, it would remain for a "real world" test to see if Johnson's fear had truly been ameliorated as a result of the laboratory experience.

Self-Monitoring

If you have ever attempted to stop smoking or lose weight, you are probably familiar with the assessment technique of self-monitoring. As its name implies, self-monitoring converts the assessee into an assessor: the assessee carefully records the emission of target behaviors (such as the number of cigarettes smoked per hour or the number of calories consumed in different situations). Self-monitoring-type tasks have also been attempted with other, less overt "behavior" (in the broadest sense of that word), such as thoughts and feelings (Lee & Piersel, 1989). Self-monitoring is different from self-report. In self-report, subjects might be asked, for example, to estimate the number of cigarettes smoked per day during the past week. In self-monitoring, subjects observe and record their behavior, typically as it occurs. The utility of self-monitoring obviously depends almost entirely on factors related to the competence, diligence, and motivation of the assessee. Additionally, there is a problem of reactivity; if you're on a diet and recording everything you eat—as you should be if you're watching your weight (Cohen, 1979a)—perhaps you will forego the blueberry cheesecake if you know you have to write it down and then have your behavioral diary read aloud by the therapist. As we will see, the problem of reactivity in behavioral assessment and research can be circumvented when so-called unobtrusive measures are employed. Self-monitoring has proven its utility as a cost-effective method of ongoing assessment in many different types of behavioral intervention programs (Kratochwill & Sheridan, 1990).

Role Play

The technique of *role play*, or acting a particular part in a simulated situation, can be used in teaching and in therapy. Police departments, for example, routinely prepare rookies for emergencies by having them play roles—such as that of an officer confronted by a criminal holding a hostage at gunpoint. A therapist might use role play to help a feuding couple avoid harmful shouting matches and to learn more effective methods of conflict resolution. Role play may also be used as an assessment technique. For example, part of the prospective police officer's final exam may be successful performance of role-playing tasks. And a couple's successful resolution of role-played issues may be one of a therapist's criteria for terminating therapy.

A large and growing literature exists on role play as a method of assessment (see, for example, Becker & Heimberg, 1988; Bellack, 1983; Bellack et al., 1979; Helzel & Rice, 1985; Higgins et al., 1979; Wessberg et al., 1979). In general, role play can provide a relatively inexpensive and highly adaptable means for assessing various behavior potentials; we say "potentials" because of the uncertainty that role-played behavior will be elicited in a naturalistic situation (Kern et al., 1983; Kolotkin & Wielkiewicz, 1984).

To explore the social skills of psychiatric patients as compared with those of nonpatient controls, for example, Bellack, Morrison, Mueser, Wade, and Sayers (1990) employed a role-play test, videotaped on a living room–type "set." After enacting two practice scenes, the subjects were presented with 12 social encounter–type scenes to which they had to react. The investigators described one such sample scene involving the subject and a "confederate" (in research, someone working with the experimenter):

> in one scene the subject is home watching television and someone walks in and changes the channel, saying "let's watch this instead." If the subject demurred [objected], the confederate said, "You always get to watch your show. Now let's watch mine instead." If the subject complied with the original prompt, the confederate said, "Movies are really much better." (pp. 249–250)

The videotaped interactions were subsequently rated on a number of variables, and the data were analyzed. It was found that role play discriminated not only between patient and nonpatient groups but also between diagnostic groups of patients. The authors acknowledged that "the ultimate validity criterion for any laboratory- or clinic-based assessment is unobtrusive observation of the target behavior in the community" (p. 253). However, the inability, inconvenience, or expense of such observations may lead investigators to role-play techniques in the first place. Bellack et al. (1990) suggest that role play as an assessment technique has diagnostic applications and can be used to identify specific strengths and weaknesses. It may even have application one day as a technique to assess psychiatric patients' readiness for return to the community.

Unobtrusive Measures

A class of measures referred to by Webb et al. (1966) as *unobtrusive measures* are nonreactive and do not require a willing patient or research subject. In the words of Webb et al., these are measures that "do not require the cooperation of a respondent and that do not themselves contaminate a response" (p. 2). The length of a nailbiter's nails might be used by a clinician as an unobtrusive or nonreactive measure of anxiety; the client's verbalizations may express a bright picture and may verbalize that all is well, but the nails may speak to the contrary (allowance must be made for manicures and other possible confounding variables here). In a book that was almost entitled *The Bullfighter's Beard*,[2] Webb et al. (1966, p. 2) listed numerous examples of unobtrusive measures, including the following:

- The degree of fear induced by a ghost-story-telling session can be measured by noting the shrinking diameter of a circle of seated children.

- Popularity of a museum exhibit can be measured by examination of the erosion of the floor around it relative to the erosion of other exhibits.

- Amount of whiskey consumption in a town can be measured by counting the number of empty bottles in ashcans.

- The effect of the introduction of television into a community can, among other ways, be assessed by examining library book withdrawal records.

In general, the case was made that unobtrusive measures such as physical traces and records were underutilized measurement techniques that could usefully complement other research techniques, such as interviews and questionnaires. In at least one research study, referred to by its authors as a "garbology analysis" (Cote et al., 1985), one of the unobtrusive (?!) dependent measures employed was subjects' garbage.

Issues in Behavioral Assessment

One issue, not unique to behavior assessment methods, is what we might term the issue of definition—how to define the targeted behavior well enough so that it is both meaningful and measurable. Suppose, for example, that you wished to behaviorally assess newly released inmates of a juvenile house of detention for aggressive behavior. How would you define *aggression?* Would your definition of and/or criteria for "aggressive behavior" be the same for "aggressive behavior" on the part of the officers and detectives of your municipal police department? the current members of the National Hockey League? the top 1% of life insurance salespeople? the winner and runners-up in the last running of the Indianapolis 500? the pilot with the most "kills" in the Persian Gulf War? United States senators on the Judiciary Committee who interviewed Judge Clarence Thomas, Anita Hill, and other witnesses in the Thomas confirmation hearings? If not, how would it differ? One may speak of aggressive behavior in

---

2. Webb et al. (1966) explained that the provocative, if uncommunicative, title *The Bullfighter's Beard* was a "title drawn from the observation that toreadors' beards are longer on the day of the fight than on any other day. No one seems to know if the toreadors' beard really grows faster that day because of anxiety or if he simply stands further away from the blade, shaking razor in hand. Either way, there were not enough American afficionados to get the point" (p. v). The title they finally settled on was *Unobtrusive Measures: Nonreactive Research in the Social Sciences.*

many contexts, including, for example, criminal, noncriminal, managerial, political, and familial contexts. And as you can begin to see, "aggressive behavior" may have vastly different meanings, depending on the context in which it is considered; an important first step in behavioral assessment, then, is to specify clearly the context, meaning, and method of measurement for whatever behavior is being assessed.

Having developed what you believe is a solid foundation for behavioral assessment—that is, a sound definition of what it is you will be measuring— you next must demonstrate that what you wish to measure can in fact be reliably measured. To do that, you may employ one or more of the techniques described in Chapter 5, such as the split-half method if you have developed a paper-and-pencil behavioral scale, or estimates of inter-rater reliability if you have developed a measure that requires behavioral observation. In the latter situation, many potential pitfalls await. Training behavioral observers so that they can agree, some agreed-on percentage of the time, on what has been observed and how to record it may seem easier to accomplish than it typically is in practice. For example, teaching professionals how to use the behavior observation and coding system of The Marital Interaction Coding System "takes two to three months of weekly instruction and practice to learn how to use its 32 codes" (Fredman & Sherman, 1987, p. 28). Borman and Hallam (1991) studied human observation accuracy using jet-engine mechanics watching a videotape of mechanics installing a jet engine; these investigators concluded, in part, that "even relatively simple human-evaluation tasks have a substantial subjective component" (p. 17). Various strategies for dealing with this "substantial subjective component," that is, for reducing measurement error, have been proposed. For example, Tsujimoto, Hamilton, and Berger (1990) propose that such error could be reduced by the computation of a "composite judge," an averaging of multiple judgments.

The reliability and validity of behavioral observation hinge directly on the accuracy of the report by the behavioral observer and the extent to which observer bias enters into the reporting. There may be one or more observers, each with his or her own biases concerning variables such as the assessee, the purpose of the assessment, and the judgments to be made. Some types of observer bias may be prevented by careful training of observers to the point that they agree on what they are to observe and how they are to go about it. However, other types of bias do not practically or readily lend themselves to remedy. For example, in behavioral observation involving the use of videotape equipment, it would on many occasions be advantageous if multiple cameras and recorders could be used to cover various angles of the ongoing action, to get close-ups, and so forth. The economic practicality of the situation (let alone other factors, such as the limited engineering skills on the part of the clinician using such equipment) is that more than one camera in a fixed position recording the action is seldom feasible. The camera in a sense is "biased" in that one fixed position, because in many instances it is recording information that may be quite different from the information that would have been obtained had it been placed in another position—or if multiple recordings were being made. The practicality of most such situations, however, mandates the use of one recording of the action.

Another factor that must be recognized and dealt with in behavioral measurement has to do with a particular type of rating error behavioral raters can make, one referred to as a "contrast effect." To understand what this is, think of yourself as a behavioral rater of professional performance; during the course of one day of classes, you are going to rate each of the class lectures you are exposed to on a number of variables, such as how informative and how thought-provoking you thought it was. At one point in the day, perhaps it is just after lunch, you sit through what you rate as the world's worst lecture—it took a great deal of effort to stay awake and mark the rating scale! Your next class features a lecture that, under other circumstances, you probably would have rated only "average"; however, in contrast to the previous lecture, this one seems so much better that you rate it "excellent." Here, a contrast effect has occurred.

Stated informally, a contrast effect might be termed an error of "unfair comparison" or "shifting standards." Stated formally, a *contrast effect* occurs when "the magnitude of a rating assigned to behavioral stimuli is contrasted away from the level observed in the same context or a preceding context" (Maurer & Alexander, 1991, p. 3). How important are contrast effects? They can be very important and have a great impact on the findings. They have been observed in interviews (Kopelman, 1975; Schuh, 1978; Wexley et al., 1973), in performance evaluations in laboratory settings (Murphy et al., 1985; Smither et al., 1988), and in field performance evaluations (Grey & Kipnis, 1976; Ivancevich, 1976). In one study, 80% of the total variance could be explained by contrast effects (Wexley et al., 1972).[3]

Reactivity is another possible limitation inherent in behavioral observation techniques. This term refers to the fact that people react differently in experimental as opposed to natural situations; microphones, cameras, and one-way mirrors may themselves alter the observed behavior. Some patients may attempt, for example, to minimize the amount of psychopathology they are willing to record for posterity, whereas others may exaggerate it. Illustrations of reactivity are probably quite familiar to you; even the most unruly child in the classroom can manage to appear angelic when the school principal is seated in the back with a pad and pencil. One possible solution to the problem of reactivity is the use of hidden observers and/or clandestine recording techniques, though such methods raise serious ethical issues. Many a time, all that is required to solve the problem is an adaptation period in which the people being observed are given some time to adjust to the idea of observation. They soon pay little attention to the observer and/or the recording device. Most clinicians are aware from personal experience that a tape recorder in the therapy room might put off some patients at first but in only a matter of minutes, the chances are good that it will be ignored. One form of reactivity that has received relatively little attention in the behavioral literature has to do with the relationship

---

3. Detailed discussion of contrast and related effects, as well as ways to avoid them, may be found in a number of sources (for example, Bernardin & Buckley, 1981; Latham et al., 1975; Maurer & Alexander, 1991; Pulakos, 1986; and Wexley et al., 1973).

between the behavior rater and the person being rated; that is the subject of this chapter's *Close-up* (pages 498–499).

One final issue that we will consider with respect to behavioral measures may be referred to as the issue of *generalizability:* how generalizable are the findings? When we find on the basis of laboratory or field observation of behavior, for example, that a child meets specified criteria for being considered "hyper-active," or that an adolescent's behavior meets our criteria for being termed "aggressive," or that a couple meets our criteria for being termed "argumenta-tive"—how generalizable are such findings to other contexts? This issue is a complicated one and one that mirrors some of the same types of questions raised when we considered the cross-situational application of traits and states. Perhaps it is, as Funder and Colvin (1991) among others have noted, that behaviors elicited or triggered by specific situational stimuli are not likely to occur across a broad range of situations. For example, a sales executive eager to impress a prospective account may welcome the opportunity to engage in the behavior of "picking up the check and paying for the dinner" at a posh restaurant. Yet the executive might dread the thought of engaging in that same behavior when the fellow diners at the table are not prospective accounts but the in-laws along with their nine children.[4]

Psychophysiological Assessment

The search for clues to understanding and predicting human behavior has led researchers to the study of variables such as heart rate, respiration rate, blood pressure, electrical resistance of the skin, brain waves, voice waves, and pupillary response.

Biofeedback

Biofeedback instrumentation provides a vehicle by which individuals can monitor—or obtain feedback from—some of their own biological processes. This monitoring usually takes the form of visual displays, such as lights or scales, or auditory stimuli, such as bells and buzzers. The stage was set for biofeedback technology in the early 1960s when it was reported that animals given rewards (and hence feedback) for the emission of certain involuntary responses (such as heart rate, urine production, and intestinal contraction) could successfully modify such responses in a predictable direction (Miller, 1969). In some of the early studies with humans, Kamiya (1962, 1968) showed that people with attached electrodes from an *electroencephalograph* (a machine that produces a

---

4. More detailed discussion of the generalizability as well as related issues in behavioral assessment can be found in numerous sources, such as Bellack and Hersen (1988), Cone and Hawkins (1977), Goldberg (1978), Hersen and Bellack (1988), Jackson (1982), Kuncel and Fiske (1974), Mash and Terdal (1988), Shapiro and Kratochwill (1988), and Wicklund and Koller (1991).

Confessions of a Behavior Rater

So often in discussions of behavioral assessment, the focus is placed squarely on the individual being evaluated. Only infrequently, if ever, is reference made to the thoughts and feelings of the person who has responsibility for evaluating the behavior of another person. What follows are the hypothetical thoughts of one behavior rater. We say hypothetical because these ideas are not really based on the thinking of one person but on a compilation of thoughts from many people responsible for conducting behavioral evaluations.

The behavior raters interviewed for this *Close-up* were all on the staff at Supervised Lifestyles, Inc., a community-based, inpatient/outpatient facility in Brewster, New York. An objective of this facility is to prepare its adolescent and adult members for a constructive, independent life. Members live in residences with varying degrees of supervision, and their behavior is monitored on a 24-hour basis. Each day, members are issued an eight-page behavior rating sheet referred to as a CDR (clinical data recorder), which is circulated to supervising staff for rating through the course of the day. The staff records behavioral information for variables such as activities, social skills, support needed, and dysfunctional behavior (see Figure 1).

CDR behavioral data is the backbone of an evaluation and treatment system called TEM-2000 (Santoro et al., 1995). Designed for use in psychiatric institutions, community residences, or other group settings, TEM-2000 (pronounced like "team") is a computer program for analyzing behavioral data. It is capable of yielding, among other things, behaviorally specific diagnostic information as well as empirically grounded and individualized treatment planning. On the basis of behavioral data, for example, certain medical or other

types of interventions may be recommended. Because behavioral monitoring is daily and consistent, changes in patient behavior as a function of medication, activities, or other variables are quickly noted and intervention strategies are adjusted. In short, the behavioral data inputted into the TEM-2000 system may significantly affect the course of a patient's institutional stay—everything from amount of daily supervision, to privileges, to date of discharge will be influenced by the behavioral data. Both patients and staff are aware of this fact of institutional life. Therefore, both patients and staff take the completion of the CDR very seriously. With that as background, here now are some private thoughts of a behavior rater:

I record behavioral data in the presence of patients, and the patients are usually keenly aware of what I am doing. After I am through coding patients' CDRs for the time they are with me, other staff members will code them with respect to the time they spend with the patient. And so it goes. It is as if each patient is keeping a detailed diary of their life; only, it is we, the staff, who are keeping that diary for them.

Sometimes, especially for new staff, it feels odd to be rating the behavior of fellow human beings. One morning, perhaps out of empathy for a patient, I tossed a blank CDR to a patient and jokingly offered to let him rate my behavior. By dinner, long after I had forgotten that incident in the morning, I realized the patient was coding me for poor table manners. Outwardly, I laughed. Inwardly, I was really a bit offended. Subsequently, I told a joke to the assembled company that in retrospect probably was not in the best of taste. The patient coded me for being socially offensive. Now, I was genuinely becoming self-conscious. Later that evening, we drove to a local video store to return a tape we had rented, and the patient coded me for reckless driving. My discomfort level rose to the point that I thought it was time to end the joke. In retrospect, I had experienced firsthand the self-consciousness and discomfort some of our patients had experienced as they had their every move monitored on a daily basis by staff members.

Even though patients are not always comfortable having their behavior rated—and indeed many patients have outbursts with staff members that are in one way or another related to the rating system—it is also true that the system seems to work. Sometimes, self-consciousness is what is needed for people to get better. Here, I think of Sandy, a bright young man who gradually became fascinated by the CDR, and soon spent much of the day asking staff members various questions about it. Before long, Sandy asked if he could be allowed to code his own CDR. No one had ever asked to do that before, and a staff meeting was held to mull over the consequences of such an action. As an experiment, it was decided that this patient would be allowed to code his own CDR. The experiment paid off. Sandy's self-coding kept him relatively "on track" with regard to his behavioral goals, and he found himself trying even harder to get better as he showed signs of improvement. Upon discharge, Sandy said he would miss tracking his progress with the CDR.

Instruments such as the CDR can and probably have been used as weapons or rewards by staff. Staff may threaten patients with a poor behavioral evaluation. Overly negative evaluations in response to dysfunctional behavior that is particularly upsetting to the staff is also an ever present possibility. Yet all the time you are keenly aware that the system works best when staff codes patients' behavior consistently and fairly.

Figure 1

A member at Supervised Lifestyles receives training in kitchen skills for independent living as a staff member monitors behavior on the CDR.

continuous written record of brain-wave activity) could learn to produce alpha-type brain waves on command; the subjects were given previous training in identifying alpha waves by the experimenter, who sounded a bell when a subject's brain was emitting such waves. Since that time, two dozen or so American companies have become manufacturers of biofeedback equipment (Schwitzgebel & Rugh, 1975), offering machines that provide feedback not only to alpha waves but to other physiological responses as well—muscle tension, galvanic skin response, and changes in skin temperature, for example.

Biofeedback has been used as a psychotherapeutic technique in alleviating unpleasant or unhealthy physiological conditions (such as high blood pressure) or psychological problems. In the latter context, for instance, it has been used as an aid to relaxation in therapeutic interventions where the patient must be in a relaxed state while mentally creating prescribed imagery. Biofeedback techniques may be employed in conjunction with the monitoring of physiological processes to help the patient learn to control body functioning. Although biofeedback as a psychotherapeutic technique is not without its critics (see Blanchard & Young, 1974), encouraging results have been observed with respect to problems ranging from hyperactivity (Omizo & Williams, 1981) to headaches (Satinsky & Frerotti, 1981). As an adjunct to assessment, biofeedback may be used in various ways—for example, as a tool to reduce initial anxiety (through relaxation) or as an aid in identifying the way that psychological conflicts may be related to physical conditions (Sarnoff, 1982).

The Polygraph

Commonly referred to as a "lie detector," the *polygraph* (literally, "more than one graph") is an apparatus used to provide a written record of selected physiological responses during a specially devised interview by a polygrapher (also referred to as a polygraphist). Proceeding on the theory that certain measurable physiological changes take place when a person lies, polygraphers claim that they can determine whether the subject is lying or telling the truth in response to a question (or, alternatively, declare the testing to be inconclusive). Is that claim true? Is the polygraph really a lie detector? This is an important question, given that an estimated two hundred thousand to a half-million polygraph examinations are administered annually in the private sector alone (Youth, 1986) and given that the consequences of a polygraph examination can be more momentous than the consequences of a Rorschach, an MMPI, or any other psychological test. In his book *A Tremor in the Blood,* Lykken (1981) refers to the lie-detector industry as "one of the most important branches of applied psychology both in dollar volume and, especially, in its social consequences" (p. 4).

Specific instrumentation may vary, but typically polygraphs contain three sensors, which respectively monitor respiration, galvanic skin response, and blood volume/pulse rate. As the subject responds with yes or no answers to a series of questions posed by the polygrapher, a continuous written record (variously referred to as a tracing, a graph, a chart, or a polygram) of physiological response provides the basis for judging the subject's honesty. This judgment might be made informally by "eyeballing" the graphs or more formally by means of a numerical scoring system.

Evaluating deception by means of the polygraph has been criticized on a number of grounds. Different methods of conducting polygraphic examinations exist (Lykken, 1981), and polygraphic equipment itself is not standardized (Abrams, 1977; Skolnick, 1961). Kleinmuntz and Szucko (1984) noted that a problem with polygraph technology is false positives; they asserted that the procedure "may label more than 50% of the innocent subjects as guilty" (p. 774). The ultimate burden for determining where the truth lies is placed not on the machine but on the polygrapher—an individual who may have had as little as six weeks of instruction at polygraph school. In light of all the available psychometric and related data, it seems reasonable to conclude that the promise of a machine capable of detecting dishonesty has gone unfulfilled (Alpher & Blanton, 1985).

Plethysmography

The *plethysmograph* is an instrument that records changes in the volume of a part of the body arising from variations in blood supply. Investigators have been interested in determining any changes that occur in flow of blood as a result of personality factors. Kelly (1966) found significant differences in the blood supply of normal, anxiety-ridden, and psychoneurotic groups (the anxiety group having the highest mean) by using a plethysmograph to measure blood supply in the forearm. In another investigation, changes in finger volume by use of a plethysmograph were compared with results on the "emotional-stability" factor of the Bell Adjustment Inventory (Theron, 1948; Van der Merwe & Theron, 1947); those identified as emotionally labile were found to exhibit greater rates of change in finger volume.

A *penile plethysmograph* is designed to measure changes in penis volume during periods of sexual arousal. Freund (1963) developed one such instrument for use in his research concerning differences in penile volume of homosexual and heterosexual males when shown slides of male nudes. On the basis of summed reactions, Freund was able to correctly identify 48 of the 58 homosexuals who participated in the study, and all of the 65 heterosexual subjects. This type of device in variously modified forms, and the subsequent collection of what is referred to as "phallometric" data, has unique value in the assessment and treatment of male sexual offenders (Abel et al., 1981; Barbaree & Marshall, 1989; Blader & Marshall, 1984; Earls & Marshall, 1983; Earls et al., 1987; Farrall & Card, 1988; Freund et al., 1965; Laws & Osborne, 1983; Marshall et al., 1988; Quinsey et al., 1975). In one such type of application, the offender—a rapist, a child molester, an exhibitionist, or some other sexual offender—is exposed to visual and/or auditory stimuli depicting scenes of normal and deviant behavior while penile tumescence is simultaneously gauged (see, for example, Malcolm et al., 1985). In one study with rapists, the subjects demonstrated more sexual arousal to descriptions of rape, and less arousal to consenting-sex stories, than did control subjects (Quinsey et al., 1984). Offenders who continue to deny deviant sexual object choices may be confronted with the findings from such studies as a means of compelling them to speak more openly about their thoughts and behavior (Abel et al., 1986).

Researchers in this area have cautioned that it may be misleading to rely exclusively on phallometric data for the purposes of understanding sexual preferences; such data must ideally be complemented by other data, such as interviews (Haywood et al., 1990). Legal and ethical issues that attend the use of plethysmography have been discussed by Travin, Cullen, and Melella (1988).

Pupillary Responses

Another involuntary physiological response upon which some researchers have sought to make inferences about psychological functioning is the response of the eye's pupil (the part of the eyeball through which light enters). Referred to as "pupillometrics," the research conducted pertains to changes that occur in the pupil in response to a variety of personality aspects (Goldwater, 1972; Hess, 1972; Janisse, 1973). Among the dimensions found to affect the functioning of the pupil are interests, attitudes, and preferences (Hess, 1965; Hess & Polt, 1960, 1964, 1966). Some investigators have attempted to identify differences in the pupillary responses of different diagnostic groups (Rubin, 1974). Other investigators have applied pupillometrics to psychotherapeutic research. For example, in his work with alcoholics, Kennedy (1971) found that those patients nearing completion of treatment whose pupils dilated in response to their favored alcoholic beverage had a higher rate of recidivism than did those patients who exhibited decreased pupil dilation. Pupillometrics has also been employed to assess consumer preferences—with dubious results (see Chapter 18).

Ratings of Personality and Behavior by Others

In some situations, the best available method for the assessment of personality and/or behavior entails reporting by a third party such as a parent, teacher, peer, supervisor, spouse, or trained observer. Consider, for example, the assessment of a child for emotional difficulties. The child may be unable or unwilling to complete any measure (self-report, performance, or whatever) that will be of value in making a valid determination as to that child's emotional status. Even case history data may be of minimal value, because the problems may be so subtle as to become evident only after careful and sustained observation. In such cases, the use of a test in which the testtaker is an informant and not the subject of study may be valuable. One example of a test in which the testtaker is an informant and not the subject of study is the Personality Inventory for Children. After a brief look at that assessment tool, we survey some potential problems with rating scales in general.

The Personality Inventory for Children

One of the best ways to learn about a child's personality with an economy of time is to talk to the child's parent. Child psychologists and others who work with children know this well, and an interview with a child's parent or guardian has always been standard operating procedure in mental health facilities where children are treated. The Personality Inventory for Children (PIC) is a kind of standardized interview of a child's parent; though the child is the subject of the test, the respondent is the child's parent. In a research program that began at the University of Minnesota, investigators (Wirt et al., 1977/1984) developed the empirical scales of the PIC in the "mold" of the MMPI. The method of contrasting groups that is characteristic of the MMPI was used along with an additional item-analytic procedure described by Darlington and Bishop (1966). The other scales were constructed using a content-oriented strategy or an internal-consistency strategy, or both (Lachar & Gdowski, 1979a).

The original PIC was published in 1958, formalized in 1977 with the publication of a test manual, and revised in 1984. The tests consists of 600 true-false items answered by the parent (usually the mother) or another appropriate adult (such as the child's guardian). The test's items are reportedly free of racial and gender bias (Kline & Lachar, 1992; Kline, Lachar, & Boersma, 1993). The 1984 revision consists of the same 600 items as the original test, but the order of the items is changed to allow test users to adapt the length of the test to their needs. For example, if the test is used as a screening device, parents need complete only the first 131 items. Greater specificity of diagnostic hypotheses is achieved with an administration of the first 420 items. Still more information regarding the child's difficulties becomes available upon completion of all 600 items (Knoff, 1989).

The standardization sample for the PIC included 2,400 normal males and females within the 6- to 16-year-old age range and 200 males and females within the 3- to 5-year-old age range. There are 13 clinical scales, one screening scale (labeled "Adjustment"), and three validity scales (labeled "Lie," "Frequency," and "Defensive"; see Table 13–3). The PIC validity scales closely parallel the validity scales found on the MMPI, while the PIC clinical scales do not. Additionally, there are four broad-band factor-derived scales and a critical-item list that may be useful in the diagnostic process. Empirically derived interpretations have been developed for individual scales (Lachar, 1982; Lachar & Gdowski, 1979b) and for profile types (Lachar et al., 1986).

The PIC has been the subject of numerous studies by many different researchers since its publication in 1977. The application of the PIC to preschool screening issues (Keenan & Lachar, 1988) and to problems such as hyperactivity (Forbes, 1985) and cognitive dysfunction (Kline et al., 1985) only begins to sample the number of published studies with this instrument. According to the test's publisher, over one million children have been assessed with it.

In general the PIC appears to be psychometrically sound. Measures of test-retest reliability over a 15- to 51-day interval yielded coefficients ranging from .46 to .97, with the average coefficient in the high .80s. Test-retest reliability of the Defensiveness scales was consistently low (Knoff, 1989). Internal consistency of the various subscales was found to range from .74 to .86 and has been judged acceptable (Knoff, 1989). Inter-rater reliability assessed by comparing the ratings of the parents ranged from .21 to .79, averaging around .60 (Knoff, 1989).

Table 13-3
The Scales of the Personality Inventory for Children

Validity scales
Lie Scale (L)—designed to detect lying as evidenced by a tendency to ascribe the most virtuous kinds of behaviors to the child while denying minor but fairly common behavior problems.
Frequency Scale (F)—composed of infrequently endorsed items and designed, in part, to identify a deviant or random response set or difficulty in following directions. An elevated F scale may also be indicative of the child's presentation of extreme or delinquent behavior.
Defensiveness Scale (DEF)—designed to detect defensiveness on the part of the respondent.

Screening scale
Adjustment Scale (ADJ)—designed to identify children with problems in need of professional intervention.

Clinical scales
Achievement Scale (ACH)—designed to detect the presence of poor academic achievement independent of cognitive and neurological status.
Intellectual Screening Scale (IS)—designed to detect the need for an intellectual evaluation.
Developmental Scale (DVL)—detects not only cognitive and neurological impairment but impairment in areas of social functioning as well.
Somatic Concern Scale (SOM)—taps the child's expression and exhibition of physical symptoms such as headache and fatigue.
Depression Scale (D)—related to various behavioral indices of depression, including sleep disturbances and social withdrawal.
Family Relations Scale (FAM)—designed to assess family effectiveness and cohesion.
Delinquency Scale (DLQ)—taps dimensions such as compliance, hostility, impulsivity, and antisocial behaviors.
Withdrawal Scale (WDL)—designed to detect withdrawal from social contact.
Anxiety Scale (ANX)—designed to detect anxiety as manifested in behavioral correlates such as sleep disturbances.
Hyperactivity Scale (HPR)—reflects distractibility, overactivity, impulsivity, and the absence of perfectionistic behavior.
Social Skills Scale (SSK)—designed to measure the various characteristics that reflect effective social relations.

Evidence of the validity of the PIC lies in studies such as those which have demonstrated the ability of the test to predict observations of teachers, clinicians, and peers (see Wirt et al., 1977/1984). The test's criterion-related validity in identifying children with developmental disorders (such as autistic disorder and mental retardation) has been shown to be superior to its criterion-related validity in identifying children with behavioral disorders, such as hyperactivity. In general, however, the PIC tends to demonstrate incremental validity over other ratings, such as those provided by teachers and mental health workers (Kline, Lachar, & Boersma, 1993; Kline et al., 1992). Also relevant to the criterion-related validity of the test is the finding that specific factors in the child's history, such as a prior diagnosis of mood disorder or the experience of a trauma, are associated with particular PIC profiles (LaCombe et al., 1991).

Some (such as Achenbach, 1981, and Cornell, 1985) have expressed concern about the reliance on parental report for the derivation of PIC scores. These concerns have persuasively been rebutted with reference to research on the validity of the test (Lachar & Wirt, 1981; Lachar et al., 1985). Recently, a version of the PIC to be completed by adolescents about themselves, called the Personality Inventory for Youth, has been developed (Lachar & Gruber, 1993). Given the conceptual relationship between the PIC and the MMPI, relationships between the Personality Inventory for Youth and the MMPI-A are sure to be examined by researchers interested in the measurement of personality in adolescence.

Potential Limitations of Rating Scales

Some measures involve procedures wherein one individual observes and evaluates someone else. Some of the considerations that need to be kept in mind in such a situation have already been touched on in Chapter 6, in the section on bias. Here we review and expand on that discussion with reference to rating scales and raters.

The rater Mrs. Jones, a third-grade teacher, had Alvin Farkas's brother Fred in her class five years ago. She remembers Fred to be an excellent, all-round student, and he was every bit the "teacher's pet." Will this fact enter into Mrs. Jones's judgment when she evaluates Alvin? Maybe it shouldn't, but few people would be surprised if it did. Teachers are human, too, and experience, attitudes, hopes, and fears are some of the factors that might enter into—and bias—their ratings. In the situation of two brothers, a "halo effect" may be operative with respect to Mrs. Jones's ratings of Alvin; the Farkas name has generated so much goodwill in the mind of Mrs. Jones that Alvin may be perceived as "capable of doing no wrong." More broadly, a *halo effect* is a type of error in rating wherein some single attribute or combination of attributes biases judgments or ratings regarding other attributes.

Many raters have an investment in the people they rate. Thus the school, industrial, or organizational instructor who has spent six months teaching a particular course has a personal investment in the ratings of the students; it doesn't look good for the instructor if too many of the students fail on some final measure of outcome. Thus, situations might exist where the rater's own self-interests are at odds with, and may interfere with, a fair and unbiased rating (Figure 13–4).

Numerous other factors may contribute to bias in a rater's ratings. The rater may feel competitive with, physically attracted to, or physically repulsed by the subject of the ratings. The rater may not have the proper background, experience, and "trained eye" needed for the particular task. The rater's judgments may be limited by his or her general level of conscientiousness and willingness to devote the time and effort required to do the job properly. The rater may harbor biases concerning various stereotypes. The rater may have a tendency to rate highly (a *leniency* or *generosity error*), a tendency to rate harshly (a *severity error*), or a tendency to rate everyone near the midpoint of the rating scale (an *error of central tendency*). Subjectivity based on the rater's own subjective preferences and taste may also enter into judgments. Bo Derek was a perfect "10" for Dudley Moore in the film by the same name, though others may find this woman less than perfect to greater or lesser degrees.

One attempt at controlling for raters' biases involves educating raters as to the types of biases that exist and the ways in which they may interfere with the accuracy of ratings. Another attempt at controlling for raters' biases has been to provide training sessions for raters. Such training sessions afford the opportunity for raters to (1) clarify terminology to increase the reliability of their ratings (for example, terms such as "satisfactory" and "unsatisfactory" may be construed differently by different people), (2) to obtain practice in observing and

Figure 13–4
A Halo Effect

"Monsters and screamers have always worked for me; I give it 'thumbs up,' Roger."

rating others, and (3) to compare their ratings with those of experienced raters. Research has demonstrated the effectiveness of rater-training programs (see Bernardin, 1978).

The instrument   By now you have already acquired much firsthand experience with a small sample of the various rating systems that have an impact on everyone's academic, business, and social life. Some of these familiar rating systems are as follows:

> "NC17" is a rating of a motion picture in which there is rather graphic presentation of sexual and/or violent material. When you were younger, such a rating prohibited you from entering the theater.

> "****" is a rating used in many travel guidebooks to denote the highest quality accommodations and dining.

"√√√" is something your friend Jane uses in her little black book next to the names of men she has dated to distinguish those who have conformed to her highest specifications in terms of mental, physical, and related attributes.

"D" is the rating your instructor gave you as a final grade in your economics course. This is why you decided to shun the business world and become a psychology major.

Rating scales are used to classify, to determine eligibility, and to predict effectiveness. Ratings are also useful in the process of validating a particular test because they provide a convenient criterion against which test scores can be measured. Thus, for example, scores on a paper-and-pencil "Work Effectiveness Test" taken by a worker might be compared with a supervisor-filled-out "Work Effectiveness Rating Scale." Given that rating scales may play a large part in individuals' academic and business futures, a word about the construction of these types of instruments is in order. Rating scales (like tests) with the same name may be focusing on vastly different things. For example, one "Worker Effectiveness Rating Scale" might contain items on it that relate mostly to a worker's creativity and initiative, whereas another "Worker Effectiveness Rating Scale" might contain items that focus more on the worker's ability to cooperate with fellow workers. Thus, a rating scale, like a test, must be judged by its validity for use in a specific context and for a specific purpose, not by its name.

Rating scales come in many varieties. There are rating scales to rate the self and there are rating scales to rate others. Some rating scales require the rater to make careful observations (such as "Does the patient make his bed?"), whereas others require the rater to make evaluations and express opinions (such as "How well does the patient get along with the other patients on the ward?"). Rating scales vary in format; in general, they are alphabetical, numerical, graphic, or of the forced-choice variety. The alphabetical rating scale uses letters keyed to some type of description as the rating system. The letter-grade rating system of A to F (excluding the letter "E") is an example of an alphabetical rating system. A numerical format, as its name implies, employs numbers keyed to descriptions (for example, 0 = the least, 100 = the most). With graphic rating scales, the rater's task is to check off or mark some line, number, letter, or point on a figure. One widely used rating scale of the graphic variety is called the "semantic differential." Developed by Osgood, Suci, and Tannenbaum (1957), the *semantic differential* is a technique that employs bipolar adjectives and a seven-point rating scale (Figure 13–5). The examinee is instructed to respond to the presentation of some idea, concept, or issue by checking off one of the seven spaces between the bipolar adjectives. Forced-choice rating scales contain two or more descriptions from which the rater must select the most appropriate. Forced-choice ratings are useful in self-rating instruments and in other situations where there might exist a special need to minimize errors in ratings as a function of bias or response sets.

One special form of rating is ranking. In essence, ranking entails an ordering of ratings with reference to some bipolar variable (such as highest-lowest, most-least, or strongest-weakest). Like forced-choice procedures, ranking

Warm	____:____:____:____:____:____:____	Cold
Tense	____:____:____:____:____:____:____	Relaxed
Optimisitc	____:____:____:____:____:____:____	Pessimistic
Frugal	____:____:____:____:____:____:____	Extravagant
Weak	____:____:____:____:____:____:____	Strong
Brooks Brothers suit	____:____:____:____:____:____:____	Hawaiian shirt

Figure 13–5
The Semantic Differential

This is a technique that can be applied to the rating of people, products—most anything. Here the rater is being asked to place checkmarks at the point in the continuum that best describes his or her spouse.

procedures may force the rater to make fine distinctions and to identify positive as well as negative choices. The *paired-comparison method* of ranking entails individually comparing every item to be ranked with every other item to be ranked. Another ranking method entails comparing each item or individual to be ranked according to some preestablished standard or criterion. Rankings generally provide little information in and of themselves. For example, what does it mean to be ranked fifth in a class of gifted children? To make such a ranking meaningful, we would have to know more (such as measures of central tendency and variability, and the method by which the ranking was derived).

Inter-rater reliability tends to increase as a function of the clarity and specificity with which terms on a particular rating scale are defined. Thus, all other things being equal, a random group of raters will probably exhibit less agreement on a rating scale that merely has categories such as ''Excellent,'' ''Good,'' ''Fair,'' and ''Poor'' than on one where clear behavioral referents to these terms are specified.

The context of evaluation A parent may indicate on a rating scale that a child is hyperactive, whereas that same child's teacher may indicate on that same rating scale that the child's activity level is within normal limits. Who is right? Can they both be right? And can the information from both informants be integrated into a comprehensive and context-specific treatment plan? As Achenbach et al. (1987) reported on the basis of their meta-analysis of 119 articles in the scholarly literature, different informants may have different perspectives on the subjects of evaluation based on the different contexts in which they interact with the subjects. Interestingly, Achenbach et al. found that raters were more likely to agree about the difficulties of young children (ages 6 to 11) than about those of older children and adolescents. Raters also tended to show more agreement when the child was exhibiting problems of self-control (such as hyperactivity and mistreating other children) than when the child was exhibiting "over-control" problems (such as anxiety or depression). The researchers urged professionals to view the differences in evaluation that arise from different perspectives as something more than error in the evaluation process. In fact, Achenbach et al. (1987) advised professionals to employ these evaluative differences in planning treatment. Many of these ideas regarding context-dependent evaluation have been incorporated into Achenbach's (1993) Multiaxial Empirically Based Assessment system. The system is an approach to the assessment of children and adolescents that incorporates cognitive and physical assessments of the subject, self-report of the subject, and ratings by parents and teachers. Additionally, performance measures of the child alone, with the family, or in the classroom may be included.

Other evidence for the influence of context and immediate prior experience on behavior comes from a study by Thompson and Smith (1991). These researchers chronicled how the mere exposure to people in costume under certain conditions could trigger behavior in some individuals that mimics severe psychiatric symptoms. For example, they described the case of "Mr. P.," who was recuperating in the hospital from pneumonia when, on the afternoon of Halloween, "several ward nurses, medical students, and house staff held a costume party and walked through the ward to 'cheer up the patients'" (p. 2). Because he was in a semidelirious state, Mr. P. believed the costumed figures to be real, causing him to wonder whether he had "died and gone to hell" (p. 2). A psychiatric consultant was called in to see Mr. P. for what was described as a brief reactive psychosis. In reality, what appeared to be severe psychiatric symptoms was simply a product of the unique context of the evaluation.

Now, armed with knowledge about the context of evaluations, as well as other benefits and possible limitations of the assessment enterprise, we proceed in Part 5 to take a detailed look at how test theory has been put into practice in various areas.

Testing and Assessment in Action

14

Clinical and Counseling Assessment

Clinical psychology is that branch of psychology that has as its primary focus the prevention, diagnosis, and treatment of abnormal behavior. Clinical psychologists receive training in psychological assessment and in psychotherapy and are employed in hospitals, public and private mental health centers, independent practice, and academia. Like clinical psychology, counseling psychology is a branch of psychology that is concerned with the prevention, diagnosis, and treatment of abnormal behavior; but its province tends to be the less severe behavior disorders and the "everyday problems in living" (such as marital and family communication problems, career decisions, and difficulties with school study habits). Although counseling psychologists work in a variety of settings, most are employed by schools, colleges, and universities, where they teach and/or work in the school counseling center. The distinction between clinical and counseling psychology is sometimes blurred by the overlap of the domains, but it is fair to say that clinical psychologists are more apt to focus their research and treatment efforts on the more severe forms of behavior pathology; members of the two fields have in common the objective of fostering personal growth. Toward that end, clinical and counseling psychologists may use many of the same tools in the process of assessment—the interview, psychological tests, the case history, and behavioral measures. Counseling psychologists are most apt to employ psychological tests when the presenting problem involves a career-choice decision (Fee et al., 1982; Watkins & Campbell, 1989; Watkins et al., 1988).

You may well appreciate that virtually any of the tests we have covered in this book to this point—tests of intelligence, general measures of personality, measures of self-concept, measures of cognitive style—would be appropriate for coverage in this chapter, for all have potential application in clinical and counseling contexts. Further, other specialized instruments might be appropriate for coverage here as well (such as tests and assessment procedures designed to measure various personal and social problems related to school, family, and employment). In an introductory text such as this, however, choices must be made as to coverage and organization.

In the previous chapter, a variety of behavioral measures were introduced, along with discussion of a sampling of applications in clinical and counseling contexts. In this chapter, we will look at the interview, the case history, and psychological tests in the context of clinical and counseling applications. The chapter concludes with a look at the end product of an assessment undertaken for clinical or counseling purposes—the psychological report.

An Overview

Clinical assessment may be undertaken for various reasons. For the clinical psychologist in a hospital, an independent practice, or some other clinical setting, tools of assessment are frequently used to clarify the nature of the psychological problem, make a diagnosis, or design a treatment plan. Let's review some specific types of assessment questions such a clinician might raise.

"Does this patient have a mental disorder? If so, what is the diagnosis?" In many cases, tools of assessment, including an interview, a test, and case history data can provide an answer. Before or after interviewing a patient, a clinician may administer tests such as the WAIS-R or the MMPI-2 to obtain estimates of the patient's intellectual functioning and level of psychopathology. The data from this testing may provide the clinician with initial hypotheses about the nature of the individual's difficulties, which will then guide the interview. Alternatively, the data from this testing can confirm or refute hypotheses made on the basis of the clinical interview. Interview and test data will be supplemented with case history data, especially when the patient will not or cannot cooperate. The clinician may interview people who know the patient, such as family members, co-workers, and friends, and obtain records relevant to the case.

"What is this person's current level of functioning? How does it compare with that of other people of the same age?" Consider the example of an individual who is suspected to have dementia resulting from Alzheimer's disease. The patient has experienced a steady and progressive loss of cognitive skills over a period of months. A diagnosis of dementia may involve tracking the individual's performance with repeated administrations of tests of cognitive ability, including memory. Periodic testing with various instruments, including tests of adaptive behavior (to be discussed in Chapter 16), may also provide information about the kinds of activities the patient should be advised to pursue, as well as the kinds of activities the patient should be encouraged to curtail or give up entirely.

"What type of treatment shall this patient be offered?" Tools of assessment can help guide decisions relating to treatment. Patients found to be high in intelligence, for example, tend to make good candidates for insight-oriented methods that require high levels of abstract ability. A person who complains of being depressed may be asked periodically to complete a measure of depression. If such a person is an inpatient, trends in the depth of depression as measured by the instrument may contribute to critical decisions regarding level of supervision within the institution, strength of medication administered, and date of discharge.

"How can this person's personality best be described?" Gaining an understanding of the individual need not focus on psychopathology. People who do not have any mental disorder sometimes seek psychotherapy for personal growth or for support in coping with a difficult set of life circumstances. In such instances, interviews and personality tests geared more to the "normal" test-taker might be employed.

Researchers may raise a wide variety of assessment-related questions, including "Which treatment approach is most effective?" or "What kind of client tends to benefit most from a particular kind of treatment?" A researcher may believe, for example, that people with a field-dependent cognitive style would be most likely to benefit from a cognitive-behavioral approach to treatment, and people with a field-independent cognitive style would be most likely to benefit from a humanistic approach to treatment. The researcher would use a variety of assessment tools to combine subjects into treatment groups and then to measure outcome in psychotherapy.

Counseling psychologists who do employment counseling may use a wide variety of assessment tools to help determine not only what kinds of occupations a person might enjoy doing but also which occupations would be sufficiently challenging without being overwhelming. School psychologists and counseling psychologists working in a school setting may be called upon to assist students with a wide variety of problems, including those related to studying. Here, behavioral measures, including self-monitoring, might be employed to better understand exactly how, when, and where the student engages in study behavior. The answer to related questions such as "Why am I not doing well in school?" may in part be found in diagnostic educational tests, such as those designed to identify problem areas in reading and reading comprehension. Another part of the answer may be obtained through other tools of assessment, including the interview, which may focus on aspects of the student's motivation and other life circumstances.

In the remainder of this chapter, we will look more closely at the tools of assessment as they are applied in clinical settings.

The Interview

An interview is a technique for gathering information by means of discussion. Except for rare circumstances (such as an individual known to be totally non-communicative), an interview will be part of every clinician's or counselor's typical individual assessment. In a clinical situation, for example, an interview may be conducted to arrive at a diagnosis, to pinpoint areas that must be addressed in psychotherapy, or to determine whether an individual will be harmful to himself or others. In a typical counseling application, an interview is conducted to assist the interviewee in learning more about himself or herself—the better to make a career or other life choice. Usually face to face in clinical and counseling applications, interviewers learn about interviewees not only from what the interviewees say but also from how they say it and how, in general, they present themselves during the interview.

Often, the interview guides decisions about what else needs to be done to assess the individual. If symptoms or complaints are described by the interviewee in a vague or inconsistent manner, the administration of a test designed to screen in a general way for psychopathology may be indicated. If the interviewee is unable to describe the frequency with which a particular problem occurs, a period of self-monitoring may be requested. If no clear "presenting problem" emerges during the interview, the interview may be used as a forum to solidify what is sometimes referred to as the "therapeutic contract," a clarification and verbalization by both patient and therapist of goals, expectations, and obligations regarding the therapeutic process.

The training of most clinicians and counselors has sensitized them to issues concerning the role of the interviewer in an interview situation. Having been interviewed yourself on any number of occasions, you are probably aware that not only does the content of the interview vary from one situation to the next, but the tone of the interview as set by the interviewer may vary widely as well. Some interviewers, by virtue of their manner and their verbal and nonverbal responses to you and what you say, may make you feel relaxed and responsive, whereas others do not. Some interviewers may convey to you that they are "with you" and understand you, whereas others prompt you to feel that they have no comprehension of you or "where you're at." Some interviewers are warm and accepting; others are cold and aloof. Some interviewers prefer to ask open-ended questions (such as "Could you tell me something about yourself?"), and others prefer to pose closed questions—some posed so sharply as to be reminiscent of the Inquisition (such as "Are you now, or have you ever been, a member of the Communist Party?"). In general, the clinician or the counselor strives to create an atmosphere throughout the interview that will put the interviewees at ease and will motivate them to answer questions to the best of their ability.

An interview may be wide-ranging in subject matter covered or narrowly focused on a particular area—depending on variables such as the nature of the referral question, the nature and quantity of available background information, the demands (with respect to time, the willingness or ability of the interviewee to respond, and so forth) of the particular situation, and the judgment of the clinician or the counselor.

Interviews may also vary with respect to *structure*. A highly structured interview is one in which all the questions that will be asked have been prepared in advance. In an interview with little structure, few or no questions are prepared in advance, and the interviewer is free to enter (or not to enter) into subject areas as his or her judgment dictates. The structured interview represents a cost-efficient, quick, uniform method of interviewing when the objective is to screen large numbers of people. In clinical or counseling research, for example, a structured interview provides a uniform method of gauging subjects' psychopathology at either the pre- or the postintervention stage; thus the effect on interview behavior of counseling, a new psychiatric drug, or some other therapeutic intervention can be assessed.

Areas that may be covered in an initial, exploratory clinical interview include:

- *Demographic data.* Name, age, sex, religion, number of persons in family, race, occupation, marital status, socioeconomic status, address, telephone numbers.

- *Reason for referral.* Why is this individual requesting or being sent for psychological assessment? Who is the referral source?

- *Past medical history.* What significant events are there in this individual's medical history?

- *Present medical condition.* What current medical complaints does this individual have? What medications are currently being used?

- *Familial medical history.* What chronic or familial types of disease are present in the family history?

- *Past psychological history.* What traumatic events has this individual suffered? What psychological problems (such as disorders of mood or disorders of thought content) have troubled this individual?

- *Current psychological conditions.* What psychological problems are currently troubling this person? How long have these problems persisted? What is causing these problems? What are the "psychological strengths" of this individual?

Throughout the interview, the interviewer may be jotting down subjective impressions about the interviewee's general appearance (appropriate?), personality (sociable? suspicious? shy?), mood (elated? depressed?), emotional reactivity (appropriate? blunted?), thought content (hallucinations? delusions? obsessions?), speech (normal conversational? slow and rambling? rhyming? singing? shouting?), and judgment (regarding such matters as prior behavior and plans for the future). During the interview, any chance actions by the patient that may be relevant to the purpose of the assessment are noted.[1]

Seasoned interviewers endeavor to create a positive, accepting climate in which to conduct the interview. They may use open-ended questions initially and then closed questions to obtain specific information. The effective interviewer conveys understanding to the interviewee by verbal or nonverbal means; a statement summarizing what the interviewee is trying to convey and an attentive posture and understanding facial expression are some of the ways by which understanding can be conveyed. Responses conveying that the interviewer is indeed listening attentively include head-nodding behavior and vocalizations such as "um-hmm." However, here the interviewer must exercise caution: such vocalizations and head-nodding have been observed to act as reinforcers that increase the emission of certain interviewee verbalizations (Greenspoon, 1955). For example, if a therapist vocalized an "um-hmm" every

---

1. Tangentially we note the experience of the senior author (RJC) while conducting a clinical interview in the Bellevue Hospital Emergency Psychiatric Service. Throughout the intake interview, the patient sporadically blinked his left eye. At one point in the interview, the interviewer said, "I notice that you keep blinking your left eye"—in response to which the interviewee said, "Oh, this . . ." as he proceeded to remove his (glass) eye. Once he regained his breath, the interviewer noted this vignette on the intake sheet.

time John Smith brought up material related to the subject of "mother," then—other things being equal—it is conceivable that John Smith would spend more time talking about the subject of mother than would other patients not "reinforced" for bringing up that topic. An interview conducted to determine whether a student has the social skills and maturity to function effectively in a particular classroom setting will vary greatly in content from an interview designed to determine if an accused sex offender is competent to stand trial. Clearly, many types of interviews exist. One type commonly used in clinical settings is the "mental status examination."

The Mental Status Examination

A parallel to the general physical examination conducted by a physician is a *mental status examination* conducted by a clinician. This examination, used to screen for intellectual, emotional, and neurological deficits, will typically include provision for questioning or observation with respect to each area discussed in the following list.

- *Appearance.* Are the patient's dress and general appearance appropriate?
- *Behavior.* Is anything remarkably strange about the patient's speech or general behavior during the interview? Does the patient exhibit facial tics, involuntary movements, difficulties in coordination or gait?
- *Orientation.* Is the patient oriented to person; that is, does he know who he is? Is the patient oriented to place; that is, does she know where she is? Is the patient oriented to time; does he or she know the year, the month, and the day?
- *Memory.* How is the patient's memory for recent and long-past events?
- *Sensorium.* Are there any problems related to the five senses?
- *Psychomotor activity.* Does there appear to be any abnormal retardation or quickening of motor activity?
- *State of consciousness.* Does consciousness appear to be clear, or is the patient bewildered, confused, or stuporous?
- *Affect.* Is the patient's emotional expression appropriate? For example, does the patient (inappropriately) laugh while discussing the death of an immediate family member?
- *Mood.* Throughout the interview, has the patient generally been angry? depressed? anxious? apprehensive? what?
- *Personality.* In what terms can the patient best be described? sensitive? stubborn? apprehensive? what?
- *Thought content.* Is the patient hallucinating—seeing, hearing, or otherwise experiencing things that aren't really there? Is the patient delusional—expressing untrue, unfounded beliefs (such as the delusion that someone follows him or her everywhere)? Does the patient appear to be obsessive—does the patient appear to think the same thoughts over and over again?

- *Thought processes.* Is there under- or overproductivity of ideas? Do ideas seem to come to the patient abnormally slowly or quickly? Is there evidence of loosening of associations? Are the patient's verbal productions rambling or disconnected?

- *Intellectual resources.* What is the estimated intelligence of the interviewee?

- *Insight.* Does the patient realistically appreciate his or her situation and the necessity for professional assistance if such assistance is necessary?

- *Judgment.* How appropriate has the patient's decision making been with regard to past events and future plans?

A mental status examination begins at the first moment the interviewee enters the room. The examiner takes note of the examinee's appearance, gait, and so forth. Orientation is assessed by straightforward questions such as "What is your name?" "Where are you now?" and "What is today's date?" If the patient is indeed oriented to person, place, and time, the assessor may note in the record of the assessment "Oriented × 3" (read "oriented times 3"). Different kinds of questions based on the individual examiner's own preferences will typically be employed to assess the other areas in the examination. For example, to assess intellectual resources, a variety of questions may be asked, ranging from those of general information (such as "What is the capital of this state?"), to arithmetic calculations (such as "What is 81 divided by 9?"), to proverb interpretations (such as "What does this saying mean: People who live in glass houses shouldn't throw stones?"). Insight may be assessed, for example, simply by asking the interviewee why he or she is being interviewed; having little or no appreciation of the reason for the interview will indicate little insight (if not malingering). As a result of a mental status examination, a clinician might be better able to diagnose the interviewee, if in fact the purpose of the interview is diagnostic (see the box on pages 520–521). The outcome of such an examination might be, for example, a decision to hospitalize, a decision not to hospitalize, or a request for a more in-depth psychological or neurological examination.

A number of published mental status examinations are available, including the Mini-Mental State Exam (MMS; Folstein et al., 1975)—so called because of its relative ease of administration. Although widely used, especially in the assessment of cognitive impairment in the elderly, the instrument does have its limitations (Anthony et al., 1982). For example, the MMS may lack structure for administration and scoring sufficient for obtaining acceptable inter-rater reliabilities (Molloy et al., 1991). There is also evidence that people tested with it who have an eighth-grade education or less are more apt to be diagnosed as suffering from dementia than people with education beyond eighth grade (Murden et al., 1991). A number of researchers have cited the need for revision of the MMS.

Other Specialized Interviews

Numerous other specialized types of interviews have appeared in the literature, and only a sampling of them can be reviewed here. The Structured Clinical Interview for Dissociative Disorders (SCID-D) is designed to assist clinicians in the diagnosis of DSM-IV dissociative disorders (Steinberg et al., 1993). Dissociative disorders include disorders such as multiple personality, now referred to as Dissociative Identity Disorder (American Psychiatric Association, 1994). The Diagnostic Interview for Borderlines is designed to distinguish people diagnosed with borderline personality disorder from people who fall into other diagnostic categories. Hurt (1986) found this instrument to be useful in distinguishing patients diagnosed as borderline from inpatients diagnosed as psychotic and outpatients diagnosed as personality-disordered, though he questioned the psychometric rationale of the construction of some of the scales. The Schedule for Affective Disorders and Schizophrenia (SADS; Endicott & Spitzer, 1978) is a standardized interview designed to detect schizophrenia and disorders of affect. A study with one form of the SADS suggested that this interview may be of particular value in detecting schizophrenia in mentally retarded adults (Meadows et al., 1991). A number of different approaches have been attempted in long-standing efforts to detect psychologically related malingering—the feigning or deliberate exaggeration of symptoms related to mental disorder (see, for example, Davidson, 1949; Greene, 1988; Lachar & Wrobel, 1979; Resnick, 1988; Ritson & Forrest, 1970; and Wachspress et al., 1953). One instrument in this ongoing field of study is the Structured Interview of Reported Symptoms (SIRS; Rogers, 1986; Rogers et al., 1991). The authors reported that this interview may be useful as an adjunct to tests such as the MMPI or in situations where a suspected malingerer refuses to take the MMPI.

A *stress interview* is the general name applied to any interview where one objective is to place the interviewee in a pressured state for some particular reason. The stress may be induced to test for some aspect of personality (such as aggressiveness or hostility) that might be elicited only under such conditions. Screening for work in the security or intelligence fields might well entail stress interviews if one of the criteria for the job is the ability to remain "cool" under pressure. Exactly what the source of the stress will be varies as a function of the specific purpose of the evaluation, though disapproving facial expressions, critical remarks, condescending reassurances, and relentless probing are among the interviewer behaviors that have been employed. To induce a stressed condition in a neurological examination, the examiner might say something like "You have only 5 seconds in which to complete this task." Then, the interviewer emphasizes the stressful condition by counting the numbers 1 through 5 while the examinee attempts to respond.

Another type of specialized interview is conducted after an altered state of consciousness has been induced in the interviewee by means of hypnosis or a drug such as sodium amytal. In addition to the use of such techniques in clinical assessment, proponents of the amytal interview have claimed that this method has therapeutic value in treating conditions such as amnesia (loss of memory) and posttraumatic stress disorder (Perry & Jacobs, 1982). Claims for the therapeutic value of such interventions continue despite long-standing reservations regarding the efficacy of such procedures (see Dysken, Chang, Cooper, et al., 1979; Dysken, Kooser, Harasziti, et al., 1979). Note that because such a procedure entails injection of a drug, it may be performed only by a physician, most

The DSM-IV

Now in its fourth edition, the *Diagnostic and Statistical Manual of Mental Disorders* (DSM-IV) names and describes all known mental disorders and even includes a category called "conditions not attributable to a mental disorder that are a focus of attention or treatment." A DSM-IV diagnosis immediately conveys a great deal of descriptive information about the nature of the behavioral deviance, deficits, or excesses in the diagnosed person. Whether for treatment or related purposes (such as general record keeping, insurance reimbursement, or research), mental health professionals frequently have occasion to diagnose patients. Psychological tests and measures may be a useful adjunct to other tools of assessment (such as the interview, the case study, or behavioral observation) in arriving at a diagnosis.

Some clinical psychologists, most vocally the behaviorally oriented clinicians, have expressed dissatisfaction with DSM-IV on many grounds, including the fact that it is firmly rooted in the medical model; patterns of behavior are described in DSM-IV in a way akin to diseases as opposed to a scientific description of behavior. This diagnostic system has also been criticized for being relatively unreliable; different clinicians interviewing the same patient may well come up with different diagnoses. An additional criticism is that even if the "right" diagnosis is made, this system of assessment provides no guidance as to what method of treatment will be optimally effective.

Proponents of DSM-IV argue that this diagnostic system is useful because of the wealth of information that is conveyed by a psychiatric diagnosis. They argue that perfect inter-diagnostician reliability cannot be achieved because of the nature of the subject matter. In response to the medical model criticism, DSM-IV supporters maintain that the diagnostic system is useful whether any particular diagnostic category is or is not actually a disease; each of the disorders listed is associated with pain, suffering, or disability. The classification system, it is argued, provides useful subject headings under which practitioners can search for (or add to) the research literature with respect to the different diagnostic categories.

In DSM-IV, diagnoses are coded according to five dimensions or axes. The types of disorders subsumed under each axis are as follows:

Axis I: Disorders of infancy, childhood, and adolescence; dementias such as those caused by Alzheimer's disease; disorders arising out of drug use; mood and anxiety disorders; and schizophrenia. Also included here are conditions that may be the focus of treatment (such as academic or social problems) but not attributable to mental disorder.

Axis II: Mental retardation and personality disorders.

Axis III: Physical conditions that may affect mental functioning—from migraine headaches to allergies—are included here.

---

typically a psychiatrist, competent and legally entitled to engage in such procedures.

Tests are tools of assessment that are routinely evaluated for psychometric soundness. But what about that other tool of assessment, the interview? Can interview techniques be evaluated for psychometric soundness as well? That question is addressed in this chapter's *Everyday Psychometrics* (see pages 522–523).

Axis IV: Different problems or sources of stress may be operative in an individual's life at any given time. Financial, legal, marital, occupational, or other problems may precipitate behavior ranging from starting to smoke after having quit to attempting suicide. The presence of such problems is noted on this axis.

Axis V: This axis calls for a global rating of overall functioning. At the high end of this scale are ratings indicative of no symptoms and just everyday kinds of concerns. At the low end of this scale are ratings indicative of people who are a clear and present danger to themselves or others and must therefore be confined in a secure facility.

DSM-IV diagnoses are descriptive and atheoretical; that is, they merely describe behavior and make no theoretical assumptions regarding its origin. The first two axes contain all the diagnostic categories for mental disorders, and the remaining three axes provide additional information regarding an individual's level of functioning and current life situation. Multiple diagnoses are possible; an individual may be diagnosed, for example, as exhibiting behavior indicative of the disorders listed on both Axis I and Axis II.

Because DSM-IV was published in May 1994, research on psychometric aspects of the diagnostic categories described therein have only recently begun to be published (e.g., Brody et al., 1994). Increased diagnostic reliability over previous versions of the DSM was a key objective in the manual's development (American Psychiatric Association, 1994; Nathan, 1994).

Major Diagnostic Categories in DSM-IV

Disorders of Childhood

Cognitive Disorders

Disorders Due to a General Medical Condition

Substance-Related Disorders

Schizophrenia

Mood Disorders

Anxiety Disorders

Somatoform Disorders

Factitious Disorders

Dissociative Disorders

Sexual and Gender Identity Disorders

Eating Disorders

Sleep Disorders

Impulse-Control Disorders

Adjustment Disorders

Personality Disorders

The Case History

A case history is composed of biographical data about the subject. The data may be obtained by interviewing the patient and/or "significant others" in the patient's life. Additionally, hospital records, school records, employment records, and related documents may be useful in piecing together a picture of subjects

Psychometric Aspects of the Interview

Principles applied to estimate the reliability and validity of tests can also be used to evaluate interviews. After an interview, an interviewer usually reaches some conclusions about the interviewee. Those conclusions, like test scores, can be evaluated for their level of reliability and validity.

If more than one interviewer conducts an interview with the same individual, inter-rater reliability for interview data could be represented by the agreement that exists between the different interviewers' conclusions. In a study that explored the diagnosis of schizophrenia through two different types of interviews, one structured and one unstructured, Lindstrom et al. (1994) found that more structured interviews produced more reliable information, even though the content of the two types of interviews was similar.

Consistent with the findings of Lindstrom et al. (1994), the inter-rater reliability of interview data may be increased when different interviewers consider specific issues systematically. Systematic and specific consideration of various interview issues can be fostered in various ways. One way involves having interviewers complete a scale designed to rate the interviewee on targeted variables at the conclusion of the interview. In one study, family members were interviewed by several psychologists for the purpose of diagnosing depression. The actual content of the interviews was left to the discretion of the interviewers,

although all interviewers completed the same rating scale at the conclusion of the interview. Completion of the postinterview rating scale improved inter-rater reliability (Miller et al., 1994).

In general, when an interview is undertaken for diagnostic purposes, the reliability and validity of the diagnostic conclusions made on the basis of the interview data are likely to increase when the diagnostic criteria are clear and specific. Efforts to increase inter-rater reliability for diagnostic purposes are evident in the third revision of the Diagnostic and Statistical Manual (DSM-III), published in 1980. Although its predecessor, DSM-II (1968), had provided descriptive information about the disorders listed, the descriptions were inconsistent in specific detail, and in some cases could be fairly vague. For example, this is the DSM-II description of paranoid personality:

> This behavioral pattern is characterized by hypersensitivity, rigidity, unwarranted suspicion, jealousy, envy, excessive self-importance, and a tendency to blame others and ascribe evil motives to them. These characteristics often interfere with the patient's ability to maintain satisfactory interpersonal relations. Of course, the presence of suspicion itself does not justify the diagnosis, since suspicion may be warranted in some cases. (American Psychiatric Association, 1968, p. 42)

A description such as this may be helpful in communicating the nature of the disorder, but because of

and at least some of the foundations of their current life circumstances. In the rather unusual circumstance where there exist factual, published accounts of a biographical or autobiographical nature, this material too might be incorporated into the case history.[2]

---

2. For an example of a case study from the psychology literature, the interested reader is referred to "Socially Reinforced Obsessing: Etiology of a Disorder in a Christian Scientist" (Cohen & Smith,

its nonspecificity and openness to interpretation, it is of only minimal value for diagnostic purposes. In an effort to bolster the reliability and validity of psychiatric diagnoses, the DSM-III (American Psychiatric Association, 1980) provided specific diagnostic guidelines, including a specific number of symptoms that had to be present for the diagnosis to be made. The diagnostic criteria for paranoid personality disorder, for example, listed eight ways in which suspicion might be displayed, at least three of which must be present for the diagnosis to be made. It listed four ways in which hypersensitivity might be displayed, two of which had to be present for the diagnosis to be made. It listed four ways in which restricted affect might be displayed, two of which had to be present for the diagnosis to be made (American Psychiatric Association, 1980). This tradition of increased specificity in diagnostic descriptions was evident in an interim revision of DSM-III (published in 1987 and referred to as DSM-III-R) as well as in the more recent revision, DSM-IV (American Psychiatric Association, 1994).

Evaluating the consistency of conclusions drawn from two interviews separated by some period of time produces a coefficient of reliability that conceptually parallels a coefficient of test-retest reliability. As an example, consider a study of the reliability of a semi-structured interview for the diagnosis of alcoholism, as well as commonly co-occurring disorders (such as substance dependence, substance abuse, depression, and antisocial personality disorder). The authors found that some disorders (substance dependence and depression) were diagnosed with greater test-retest reliability than were other disorders (substance abuse and antisocial personality disorder; Bucholz et al., 1994).

Criterion validity of conclusions made on the basis of interviews is of as much concern to psychometricians as the criterion validity of conclusions made on the basis of test data. The degree to which an interviewer's findings or conclusions concur with other test results or other behavioral evidence reflects on the criterion-related validity of the conclusions. Consider in this context a study that compared the accuracy of two different tools of assessment, an objective test and a structured interview, in predicting the behavior of probationers. Harris (1994) concluded that the structured interview was much more accurate in predicting the criterion (later behavior of probationers) than was the test. In another study, this one having as a criterion the accurate reporting of the subject's drug use, a paper-and-pencil test was also pitted against an interview. The written test was found to be more criterion-valid than the interview, perhaps because people may be more disposed to admit to illegal drug use in writing than in a face-to-face interview (McElwrath, 1994).

Case history data may be invaluable in helping a counselor or a clinician gain understanding of an individual, yet as others have noted, "Sources and

---

1976), wherein the authors suggest that a woman's exposure to Christian Science predisposed her to an obsessive disorder. The article stirred some controversy and elicited a number of comments (for example, Coyne, 1976; Halleck, 1976; London, 1976; McLemore & Court, 1977), including one from a representative of the Christian Science church (Stokes, 1977)—all rebutted by Cohen (1977, 1979a, pp. 76–83).

textbooks on psychological assessment have paid little attention to the importance and value of case history data" (Maloney & Ward, 1976, p. 85). The usefulness, meaningfulness, and interpretability of data derived from other sources such as interviews and tests depend to no small degree on the context in which such data are viewed.

Psychological Tests

Virtually any of the tests we have described so far could be used in clinical or counseling assessment; tests such as the MMPI and the Rorschach would certainly be near the top of the list with respect to use by clinicians. However, clinicians and counselors employ a wide range of tests in their work, and each year brings with it the publication of new tests designed to assist in the identification and/or assessment of various conditions. Surveys tell us that psychologists express confidence in the value of testing (Levy & Fox, 1975; Lubin et al., 1983). Despite such confidence, however, questions have emerged over the years regarding the extent to which psychological tests are actually used. According to one survey of clinicians employed in mental health facilities, the amount of professional time devoted to psychological assessment dropped from about 44% in the late 1950s to about 28% in the late 1960s (Lubin & Lubin, 1972). Others (Cleveland, 1976; Glaser, 1981; Korchin & Schuldberg, 1981) have also taken note of what appears to be a trend of declining interest in traditional clinical assessment. Reasons typically cited for this decline include (1) disappointing reliability and validity estimates of many instruments, (2) the amount of time necessary to administer, score, and interpret many traditional tests, and (3) the rise in prominence of behaviorally oriented assessment techniques (Elbert, 1984).

The Psychological Test Battery

Psychologists often use more than one test in assessing an individual. The term used to describe a group of tests used in an assessment is *test battery.* Some of our students have asked what a "battery" is in this context. You are probably aware that the term *batter* refers to a beaten liquid mixture that typically contains a number of ingredients. Somewhat similar in meaning to this definition of *batter* is one definition of the word *battery:* an array or grouping of like things to be used together. When psychological assessors speak of a battery, they are referring to a group of tests administered together for the purpose of gathering information about an individual from a variety of instruments.

A *personality test battery* refers to a group of personality tests. A *projective test battery* also refers to a group of personality tests, though this term is more specific because it additionally tells us that the battery is confined to projective techniques (such as the Rorschach, the TAT, figure drawings, sentence completion, and word association tests). In "shoptalk" among clinicians, if the specific type of battery referred to is left unspecified or if the clinician refers to a battery of tests as a "standard" battery, what is usually being referred to is a group of tests including one intelligence test, at least one personality test, and a test designed to screen for neurological deficit (discussed in the following chapter).

Each test in the standard battery provides the clinician with information that goes beyond the specific area that the test is designed to tap. Thus, for example, a test of intelligence may yield not only information about intelligence but also information about personality and neurological functioning. Conversely, information about intelligence and neurological functioning can be gleaned from personality test data (and here we refer specifically to projective tests rather than personality inventories). The insistence on using a battery of tests and not a single test in evaluating patients was one of the many contributions of David Rapaport (see page 526). At a time when using a battery of tests might mean using more than one projective test, Rapaport (1946/1967) argued that a testing would be incomplete if there weren't "right or wrong answers" to at least one of the tests administered; here he referred to a test of intellectual ability. This orientation is reflected in Rapaport's now-classic work in the area of clinical assessment, *Diagnostic Psychological Testing* (Rapaport et al., 1945–1946). Ogdon (1982) provides a useful sourcebook of studies from the research literature that sample the various interpretations that can be made from some of the tests typically used in a standard battery.

Beyond the small circle of widely used intelligence, personality, and neuropsychological measures lie thousands of other tests, which vary not only with respect to their frequency of use but also with respect to their breadth of applicability to assessment situations. Following is a brief look at one thin slice of the universe of clinical and counseling tests and measures.

Diagnostic Tests

Some tests are designed primarily to be of diagnostic assistance to clinicians and counselors. One such group of tests was developed by Theodore Millon.

The Millon tests   The Millon Clinical Multiaxial Inventory (MCMI; Millon, 1983) consists of 175 true-false items that yield scores related to enduring personality features as well as acute clinical symptoms. The MCMI has been revised twice, resulting in the MCMI-II (Millon, 1987) and the MCMI-III (Millon et al., 1994). The MCMI-III yields scores for 14 personality scales that correspond to the DSM-IV personality disorders. There are also ten clinical scales, including scales to measure anxiety and depression, and four validity indices. Such information may be useful in assisting clinicians to make diagnoses with respect to the "multiaxial" DSM-IV and to assess outcome in psychotherapy. Because the MCMI tests are designed specifically for use with clinical populations, norms were gathered only on mentally disordered people: the standardization sample included 1,000 male and female patients with many different mental disorders.

The Millon Adolescent Personality Inventory (MAPI; Millon et al., 1982) consists of 150 true-false items written at a sixth-grade level, and it yields scores on eight personality scales and three "behavior correlate" scales (referred to as impulse control, societal conformity, and scholastic achievement). Whereas the

David Rapaport (1911–1960)

Born in Budapest, Hungary, David Rapaport specialized in mathematics and physics in college. However, after entering into psychoanalysis, his interest shifted to psychology and philosophy, and he earned a Ph.D. in psychology from the University of Budapest in 1938, the same year he emigrated to the United States. After working for a brief period as a psychologist at Mount Sinai Hospital in New York City, Rapaport moved to Kansas to accept a position as a staff psychologist at the Osawatamie State Hospital. He worked there until 1940, when Karl Menninger offered him a position at the Menninger Clinic in Topeka, Kansas; Rapaport was to be the clinic's first full-time psychologist.

The years 1940 through 1948 witnessed Rapaport's rise to prominence through a number of publications, including his now-classic work, *Diagnostic Psychological Testing* (1945–1946), written with Roy Schafer, B.S. [now, Ph.D.], and Merton Gill, M.D. Although hailed by many clinicians as a milestone in the assessment literature, the work was criticized on many counts, such as its lack of statistical rigor. By 1960, all of the remaining stock from the numerous reprintings of the book had been exhausted, and the plates used for reprinting were no longer usable. Two publishers were prepared to republish the two volumes of *Diagnostic Psychological Testing* in their original form. However, as Holt (1968) tells us:

> David Rapaport had been hurt by the criticisms of the book and had taken them to heart; he realized that many were justified, and he did not feel that he could allow so many undeniable errors to stand in a reissued book; yet he did not have time or inclination to undertake a revision. His own interests and practice had turned toward theory, experimental research, and therapy, and those of Roy Schafer had similarly grown away from testing into psychoanalysis. As for the third member of the original team, though he remained interested in and informed about testing beyond most of his psychiatric and psychoanalytic colleagues, Merton Gill was clearly not the man for the job. (p. 1)

The person who turned out to be "the man for the job" was Robert R. Holt; Rapaport had spent a sabbatical year at New York University between 1959 and 1960 and had met Holt, who had discussed his ideas for revision. Some time later, shortly before Rapaport's death, Rapaport wrote Holt and asked if he would undertake the revision (which he did).

While at Menninger, Rapaport had been head of the psychology department and chairman of research. In 1948, Rapaport left Topeka for Stockbridge, Massachusetts, and a position at the Austen Riggs Foundation there. Unburdened of administrative duties, he immersed himself in the study of psychoanalysis and produced, among other publications, *Organization and Pathology of Thought* and *Structure of Psychoanalytic Theory: A Systematizing Attempt*. At the age of 49 and very much involved in his work, David Rapaport died in Stockbridge, Massachusetts, while dining with friends. He was survived by his two daughters and by his wife, Elvira, whom he had met on a kibbutz in Israel before he emigrated to the United States.

MAPI is appropriate for both normal and mentally disordered adolescents, a newer scale, the Millon Adolescent Clinical Inventory (MACI; Millon, 1993), is specific to adolescents with clinical problems. The MACI contains 160 items requiring sixth-grade reading skills. It produces 12 personality scores, eight scores focusing on the adolescent's concerns (such as sexual discomfort and childhood abuse), and seven clinical scores (including scales assessing suicide risk and eating disorders), along with three validity scores. Like the MCMI scales for adults, the MACI is intended for clinical populations and, therefore, was standardized on over 1,000 adolescents with mental disorders.

All these tests must be computer-scored and cannot be hand-scored. At the foundation of each of these tests is Millon's (1969, 1981, 1986a, 1986b) notion of two primary dimensions of personality. One dimension refers to ways of gaining satisfaction and avoiding stress; the other refers to an overall pattern of coping, which may be described as active or passive. Scores on the Millon tests may be interpreted with respect to these two dimensions of personality, which, in turn, may be interpreted according to DSM-IV categories. For example, the condition of an individual who exhibits, according to Millon's system, a passive-dependent personality style may be diagnosed with "dependent personality disorder" according to DSM-IV.

The Millon tests were constructed and meant to be interpreted from actuarial base-rate data. In practice, this means that raw scores on the scales are transformed into base-rate scores corresponding to known diagnostic prevalence data. A transformed score on any clinical scale of 75 or higher is considered significant and is said to "correspond to the clinically judged prevalence rate for presence of a personality disorder or clinical syndrome's symptom features" (Millon & Green, 1989, p. 10). Suppose, for example, you administered the MCMI to the person who sits next to you in class and that person was found to have scored 75 on the Drug Abuse scale. What would that mean?

The by-the-book (or in this case, the by-the-manual) answer to the question just raised might be something like "I think the person who sits next to me in class is a drug abuser." Such a response would be quite reasonable, especially since Millon (1983) reported that his Drug Abuse scale correctly classified 94% of his sample, with a false-positive rate—that is, a rate of misidentifying non–drug abusers as abusers—of only 4%. Similarly, Millon reported that the MCMI Alcohol Abuse scale correctly classified 88% of his sample with a false-positive rate of 9%.

Researchers who have investigated the validity of the MCMI might answer the same question somewhat differently—perhaps by saying something like, "I'm not really sure what that means." In one study that employed known alcohol and drug abusers, only 49% of the alcoholics and only 43% of the drug abusers scored 75 or higher on the corresponding MCMI scales (Bryer et al., 1990; see also Marsh et al., 1988, whose study yielded similar findings). Rates of false positives—that is, scores of 75 or higher in non–alcohol abusers or non–drug abusers on the corresponding MCMI scales—were 50% for each scale. Moreover, Millon's (1983) claims that the two scales measure independent constructs and correlate insignificantly ($r = -.08$) are at odds with the data from at least two studies, which indicate that a significant positive correlation exists between the MCMI Alcohol Abuse and Drug Abuse scales (Bryer et al., 1990; Jaffe & Archer, 1987). Bryer et al. (1990) noted that the MCMI-II retained most of the items from the MCMI Alcohol Abuse and Drug Abuse scales, and they advised readers that more direct and face-valid measures, such as the Michigan Alcohol Screening Test (Selzer, 1971), might prove a useful alternative to the comparable MCMI scale.

Other independent inquiries into the psychometric soundness and related aspects of the MCMI (Choca et al., 1988; Choca et al., 1990; Dana & Cantrell, 1988; Goldberg et al., 1987; Libb et al., 1990; McCormack et al., 1989; Morey & LeVine, 1988; Overholser, 1990; Wetzler, 1990), the MCMI-II (Libb et al., 1992; McCann, 1990, 1991; Retzlaff et al., 1990; Streiner & Miller, 1989), and the MAPI (Pantle et al., 1990; Reidy & Carstens, 1990; Witt et al., 1990) have yielded findings that, taken as a whole, can best be described as equivocal. For example, McCann (1990) found the MCMI-II to have good convergent validity, as illustrated by correlations like .84 between the MCMI-II anxiety scale and the corresponding MMPI scale in a sample of 85 psychiatric inpatients. However, MCMI-II scales designed to measure different problems often had poor discriminant validity: the MCMI-II anxiety and depression scales correlated .94, for example. Anxiety and depressive disorders are separate diagnoses, and the experience of anxiety and depression are not the same. However, because McCann's subjects with high MCMI-II anxiety scores nearly always had high MCMI-II depression scores, the high anxiety score could indicate anxiety, depression, or both. McCann (1990) provides additional examples that illustrate significant problems with the discriminant validity of the MCMI-II. At this writing, the MCMI-III and the MACI are too new for a research base to have been published, but perhaps they will more effectively distinguish between various clinical problems than does the MCMI-II.

Measures of Depression

Depression is the most common mental health problem and reason for psychiatric hospitalization (Dean, 1985). From 5% to 9% of adult women, from 2% to 3% of adult men (American Psychiatric Association, 1994), and from 18% to 35% of adolescents (Clarizio, 1989) may experience depression at any given time. The DSM-IV criteria for diagnosing depression are presented in Table 14–1. Depression may be diagnosed through an interview alone or through the use of varied other clinical tools (Ponterotto et al., 1989). Here we will briefly survey some of the many instruments that exist to screen for depression and explore the nature of an individual's experience of the disorder.

Beck Depression Inventory Originally published in 1961 (Beck et al., 1961), and twice revised since (Beck & Beamesderfer, 1974; Beck, 1978), the Beck Depression Inventory (BDI) is among the most frequently used measures of depression (Ponterotto et al., 1989). The test manual was first published in 1987 and revised in 1993 (Beck & Steer, 1993). The test consists of 21 items, each tapping a specific symptom or associated attitude. For each item, testtakers circle one of four statements—each reflecting increasing intensity—that best describes how they

Table 14–1

Criteria for Diagnosis of Depression

A. Five (or more) of the following symptoms have been present during the same 2-week period and represent a change from previous functioning; at least one of the symptoms is either depressed mood (1) or loss of interest or pleasure (2).
   Note: Do not include symptoms that are clearly due to a general medical condition; or mood-incongruent delusions or hallucinations.
   1. Depressed mood most of the day, nearly every day, as indicated by either subjective report (e.g., feels sad or empty) or observation made by others (e.g., appears tearful). **Note:** In children and adolescents, can be irritable mood.
   2. Markedly diminished interest or pleasure in all, or almost all, activities most of the day, nearly every day (as indicated by either subjective account or observation made by others)
   3. Significant weight loss when not dieting or weight gain (e.g., a change of more than 5% of body weight in a month), or decrease or increase in appetite nearly every day. **Note:** In children, consider failure to make expected weight gains.
   4. Insomnia or hypersomnia nearly every day
   5. Psychomotor agitation or retardation nearly every day (observable by others, not merely subjective feelings of restlessness or being slowed down)
   6. Fatigue or loss of energy nearly every day
   7. Feelings of worthlessness or excessive or inappropriate guilt (which may be delusional) nearly every day (not merely self-reproach or guilt about being sick)
   8. Diminished ability to think or concentrate, or indecisiveness, nearly every day (either by subjective account or as observed by others)
   9. Recurrent thoughts of death (not just fear of dying), recurrent suicidal ideation without a specific plan, or a suicide attempt or a specific plan for committing suicide
B. The symptoms do not meet criteria for a Mixed Episode.
C. The symptoms cause clinically significant distress or impairment in social, occupational, or other important areas of functioning.
D. The symptoms are not due to the direct physiological effects of a substance (e.g., a drug of abuse, a medication) or a general medical condition (e.g., hypothyroidism).
E. The symptoms are not better accounted for by Bereavement, i.e., after the loss of a loved one, the symptoms persist for longer than 2 months or are characterized by marked functional impairment, morbid preoccupation with worthlessness, suicidal ideation, psychotic symptoms, or psychomotor retardation.

Source: American Psychiatric Association (1994).

have been feeling the past week, "including today." Scoring for each item, done by computer or by hand, is on a 0–3 basis, and a total score of 16 or higher suggests the presence of depression.

Studies of this test's psychometric soundness have been generally favorable. Internal consistency reliability estimates range from .73 to .95, and test-retest reliability has been estimated at .48 to .86 over periods ranging from several hours to four weeks. Concurrent criterion-related validity ranges from .60 to .76 (Sundberg, 1992). Perhaps the greatest drawback of the BDI is its face validity (Stehouwer, 1985). Testtakers can handily fake depression, or its absence, if they so desire. Another problem is that a response set may emerge; that is, a testtaker might simply choose a particular type of response on each item, such as the extreme response indicative of the most or the least depression. Researchers who randomly ordered the alternative statements for each item reported obtaining what they believed to be more accurate scores than when they presented the BDI in its original form (Dahlstrom et al., 1990).

Children's Depression Inventory   Similar to the BDI, the Children's Depression Inventory (CDI; Kovacs, 1977) is a self-report questionnaire containing 27 items, each item consisting of three statements from which one is selected as reflective of how the respondent has felt over the course of the last two weeks. Appropriate for use with children and adolescents, the CDI has been studied extensively (see, for example, Carey et al., 1987; Kavan, 1990; Knoff, 1990b; Mattison et al., 1990; Saylor et al., 1984; Semrud-Clikeman, 1990; Siegel, 1986; Smucker et al., 1986). In general, the test has been shown to be reliable and valid, capable of distinguishing depressed children and adolescents from normal controls. The CDI is less robust in its ability to distinguish children and adolescents diagnosed as depressed from children and adolescents with other psychiatric diagnoses. The factor structure of the test appears to vary as a function of the age of the children and adolescents tested. The CDI appears particularly useful in identifying children and adolescents as depressed when used as part of a multi-instrument battery (Kazdin et al., 1986).

Other measures of depression   Numerous other measures of depression are available to clinicians and counselors. The Center for Epidemiological Studies (CES) at the National Institute of Mental Health developed its own measure of depressive symptoms in adults, a measure commonly referred to as the CES-D (Radloff, 1977). In the context of research with adolescents that compared the CES-D with other instruments, Roberts et al. (1991) explained that because symptoms of depression are highly correlated with numerous other psychiatric and medical conditions, it seems inevitable that almost any instrument designed to screen for depression will pick up many "false positives," meaning that depression will be suggested by the test when it is not actually present. These researchers wondered aloud about the possibility of creating a second screening instrument, designed specifically for use with people who score positive for depression on the first screen.

Among self-report instruments designed to be of value in diagnosing depression and assessing its severity is the Inventory to Diagnose Depression (IDD; Zimmerman et al., 1986). The IDD has shown promise in research use with psychiatric inpatients (Zimmerman et al., 1986), community samples (Zimmerman & Coryell, 1987, 1988), and college subjects (Goldston et al., 1990). A self-report instrument designed only to screen for depression in adolescents is the Reynolds Adolescent Depression Scale (RADS; Reynolds, 1987). Testtakers respond to items such as "I feel happy" or "I feel sad," using the following four-point scale: Almost never, Hardly ever, Sometimes, and Most of the time. Published opinion regarding this test has been mixed. For example, Kaplan (1990) opined that the test adds little to existing measures, but others (for example, Evans, 1988; Kundert, 1990) intimate that the test shows promise as a screening measure.

The primary function of other measures of depression is neither diagnosis nor screening. Rather, these tests focus on one aspect of depression. One such test, called the Automatic Thoughts Questionnaire (ATQ-N; Hollon & Kendall, 1980) focuses only on negative cognitions that may accompany depression. The other side of the coin—that is, positive cognitions that may accompany depression—has been explored in a test called the Positive Automatic Thoughts Questionnaire (ATQ-P; Ingram & Wisnicki, 1988). Both instruments may be of value in exploring changes over time in positive and negative thought in depressed individuals (Ingram et al., 1990).

Measures of Values

A synonym for the word *value* is *worth,* and when we speak of an individual's "values," we are talking about whatever the individual prizes or believes in. Knowledge of an individual's priorities with respect to values can be helpful in counseling that individual about career choice; if, for example, the individual prizes independence above all, he or she is probably not very happy—and probably not optimally productive—punching a time clock on a 9-to-5 job. Knowledge of priorities with respect to values can also be helpful in making myriad other life choices, among them decisions to get married (or get divorced). How well do the values of the two individuals mesh? This is an important question with regard to the choice of a lifetime mate. And although common folklore—mythology—has it that "opposites attract," any psychologist who has done marital or premarital counseling will tell you that when it comes to values of a husband and wife, the more similar the better.

Clinicians may find information on a patient's values useful in understanding factors that contribute to or serve to maintain maladaptive behavior. The management of a company—a multinational corporation or a small business—may have certain values to which they would like their employees to subscribe. Educators, especially educators in the private and parochial sectors, may seek to obtain knowledge of an individual's values as one admission criterion. There are many potential applications—within and beyond counseling settings—of data from a test of values. The classic measurement instrument in this area is the Study of Values, and that is where we begin our review of some of the available tests.

The Study of Values   A book published in 1928 with the title *Types of Men* contained the following six categories of people and what they value:

Theoretical—values discovery of truth through empirical and rational approaches; values attempt at order and systematizing knowledge

Esthetic—values form and harmony

Economic—values the practical and useful

Political—values personal power and influence

Social—values love of people

Religious—values unity of the cosmos as a whole

The categorization of values in *Types of Men* (Spranger, 1928) was a source of inspiration to psychologists Gordon Allport and Phillip Vernon, who used it in constructing a questionnaire they called the Allport-Vernon Study of Values. Since its revision in 1951—a revision Gardner Lindzey collaborated on—this questionnaire has been known as the Allport-Vernon-Lindzey Study of Values (A-V-L).

Designed for use with people at or above the second year of high school, the A-V-L contains 45 items distributed in two parts of the test. Part 1 contains items such as the following, to which examinees indicate their agreement or disagreement: "The main object of scientific research should be the discovery of pure truth rather than its practical applications."

Such an item is designed to tap a theoretical-values orientation, and if the examinee agreed with the statement, he or she would earn points in the theoretical-values category. The second part of the test contains 15 four-choice items. Examinees must rank-order the four alternatives into an order consistent with their values. A sample item follows:

Do you think good government should aim chiefly at:
(a) More aid for the poor, sick, and old.
(b) Development of manufacturing and trade.
(c) Introducing more ethical principles into its policy and diplomacy.
(d) Establishing a position of prestige and respect among nations.

If an examinee's rank-ordering of these alternatives matched the order in which they appear, the examinee would earn four points on the social-values scale, three points on the economics-values scale, two points on the religious (also referred to as the "ethical") scale, and one point on the political-values scale.

Revised again in 1960, the A-V-L test manual contains normative data on more than six thousand high school students and 8,360 college students, as well as normative data on persons from a wide variety of occupational groups. In 1968, additional normative data based on a national sample of 5,320 male and 7,296 female high school students in grades 10 through 12 were obtained and published in a revised test manual. Both split-half and test-retest reliability estimates have been computed for the Study of Values. The median split-half reliability coefficient for the different scales was found to be .82; and the median test-retest reliability coefficients based on one- or two-month intervals were found to be .88 and .89 for the different subscales. The validity data presented in the manual are based on the profiles that were obtained from various educational and occupational groups. These profiles were found to exhibit significant differences in ways that would be predicted by the descriptions of the various value types. For example, theological students were found to obtain their highest score on the religious-value type. Scores on the test are plotted on a profile and indicate the examinee's own position relative to each of the values; the scoring is ipsative.

The Rokeach Value Survey   Suppose you were given two lists of gummed labels with a word or term imprinted on each label. Your task: to detach the labels and readhere them in creating a rank-ordering for two new lists that reflects their importance to you as guiding principles. How would you reorder the following lists?

List 1	List 2
ambitious	a comfortable life
broad-minded	an exciting life
capable	a sense of accomplishment
cheerful	a world at peace
clean	a world of beauty
courageous	equality
forgiving	family security
helpful	freedom
honest	happiness
imaginative	inner harmony
independent	mature love
intellectual	national security
logical	pleasure
loving	salvation
obedient	self-respect
polite	social recognition
responsible	true friendship
self-controlled	wisdom

If you'd like to know more about what Rokeach says your lists reveal about you, consult his (1973) book, *The Nature of Human Values,* the book that is also the manual for the Rokeach Value Survey (RVS). Reprinted from the RVS, list 1 contains values that are modes of conduct designed to help people get to where they would like to be in life. List 2 contains places or end points where one would like to be at some time in the future. In the terminology of the test's developer, Milton Rokeach (1973), list 1 comprises "instrumental" values and list 2 comprises "terminal" values.

Test-retest reliability coefficients with samples of college students over intervals of from three to seven weeks ranged from .70 to .72 for instrumental values and from .78 to .80 for terminal values. Median test-retest reliability coefficients (with a three-week interval) for a younger sample of seventh- and ninth-graders were mostly in the .60s range. No normative data are included in the test's manual; users of this test develop their own (local) norms.

The Work Values Inventory   Would you prefer to work at a job that offers economic rewards, security, or prestige? What would you need to be motivated to work hard and to feel satisfied in a job? The Work Values Inventory (WVI; Super, 1970) was designed to assess the degree to which individuals value different work-related factors, the rationale being that job satisfaction contributes to job success. The test is designed for vocational-guidance use with junior and senior high school students and college and adult populations. The test consists of 45 items arranged to represent 15 areas of values important in determining job satisfaction (such as surroundings, associates, and independence). The items are presented in a Likert-scale format, and testtakers indicate the extent to which the statement presented is important to them. The entire test takes only 15 minutes or so to administer. The test manual contains normative data based on a national sample of close to ten thousand students in grades 7 through 12. Test-retest reliability estimates obtained for the WVI based on a two-week interval were found to range from .74 to .88 with a median reliability coefficient of .83. Also presented in the manual are some suggestive findings with respect to the test's concurrence and construct validity. In a study designed to examine differences in WVI scores as a function of gender and job level, the test was administered to a sample of approximately two hundred males and females between the ages of 18 and 25 (Drummond et al., 1978). These investigators reported that, in contrast to the females, males were more apt to value intellectual stimulation, independence, and creativity. Females were found to value the personal work environment (that is, surroundings and supervisory relations) as more important than did the male group. Differences in values were not found to be related to job level.

Other Tests

Literally thousands of other tests are available for use in clinical and counseling contexts. (For example, see the *Close-up*.) Moreover, as different types of problems in living and psychopathology require greater attention, so different tests and measures can be expected to be created to meet the changing need. Consider in this context, for example, the history of the assessment of posttraumatic stress disorder (PTSD). Although it had long been recognized that war can produce its own brand of emotional distress and behavioral aberrance in prisoners (Bing & Vischer, 1919) as well as veterans and others (Freud et al., 1921; Grinker & Spiegel, 1945), the study of PTSD—one possible consequence of war or other catastrophic stress—did not receive a great deal of attention until the Vietnam era. It has been estimated that the war in Vietnam left in its wake nearly half a million veterans suffering from PTSD and an additional 350,000 veterans with partial PTSD (Kulka et al., 1988). Comparable data addressing PTSD among veterans of World War II and the Korean conflict are hard to come by, although estimates range from 46% (Zeiss & Dickman, 1989) to 90% (Sutker et al., 1990; see also, Sutker et al., 1991). As one group of researchers put it with specific reference to the large number of Vietnam veterans: "Development of reliable and valid diagnostic instruments is essential for identifying these troubled veterans, the majority of whom have not yet received formal psychiatric assistance" (McFall et al., 1990, p. 114).

Techniques developed to assess PTSD in recent years have ranged from elaborate interviews to psychophysiological methods (Blanchard et al., 1991; Lyons et al., 1988; Wolfe et al., 1987). The PTSD scale of the MMPI (Keane et al., 1984) has also been used, although it fails to measure the full domain of symptoms as specified in DSM-IV. Watson (1990) has reviewed the comparative

Marital and Family Assessment

"Are you happily married?" "How does the family get along?" Beyond such general, straightforward questions, how else might you obtain information on the functioning of a married couple or a family? What other questions would you pose? What other methods might you employ?

Stated succinctly, that's the challenge of the would-be constructor of a scale designed to assess aspects of the functioning of a married couple or a family. Through the years, hundreds of researchers have attempted to answer the call to that challenge with sundry different approaches to couple—also referred to in this context as marital—assessment and family assessment.

Marital and Family Assessment Using "Traditional" Tests

With few exceptions, most of the tests discussed in this book to this point have at least some applicability to marital and family assessment and can yield insights into family relationships, insights that other techniques, including interviews, behavioral observation, and other test data, may ultimately corroborate. For example, verbal responses to various subtests of many intelligence tests (even some nonverbal responses on subtests such as a Wechsler Picture Arrangement task) may yield provocative clues with respect to family relationships. Similarly, personality

(continued)

Figure 1

Question: Who says the American family is on the decline? Answer: Popular culture as reflected in the form of television sitcoms. Contrast the contemporary Bundy family (that's Bud, Al, Peg, and Kelly seated on the couch) as depicted in the popular series Married with Children *with the Andersons (that's Kathy, Jim, and Margaret seated, and Betty and Bud standing) of* Father Knows Best *(which was aired nationally from 1954 through 1963). Jim Anderson was a content-enough agent for General Insurance Company, who would typically come home from work, put on his sweater, have dinner with the family, and then proceed to sort out the day's problems. Al Bundy is a horribly frustrated shoe salesman in a mall, who doesn't know from day to day what he will come home to, though no dinner, no respect, and a heavy dose of life's frustrations are a given.*

From what you know of the Bundys, or some other family—even your own—think about the types of responses you would expect to find on the marital and family assessment tools discussed in this Close-up. *The next step would be to think about how such data could be used therapeutically to make each of the family members' lives, as well as the family's life as a whole, more fulfilling.*

Marital and Family Assessment *(continued)*

inventories and other measures of personality may be revealing in this context. One of the scales of the MMPI deals with family conflicts, and the responses to many of the individual items may be further explored for their implications with respect to family issues. Family assessment by means of some situational performance measure is also a possibility. What types of alliances form in the course of solving the problem? How is communication directed? Who is most and least dominant? These are important questions that could be answered in the context of a group exercise and later used as a stimulus to more general discussion and assessment.

Projective measures may provide a wealth of leads to pursue regarding marriage and family assessment. On the TAT, for example, a test administrator interested in focusing on couple or family issues would select cards with a relevant stimulus. For other cards, what would be noteworthy would be the extent to which people designated as family members are introduced into stories, their roles in the stories, and their relationships to the protagonist. The Rorschach, although not typically thought of as the instrument of choice for couple or family assessment, may be adapted for just such purposes (Dudek, 1954; Dudek & Gottlieb, 1954; Levy & Epstein, 1964; Loveland et al., 1963). Projective drawing tests such as the Draw-A-Person and the House-Tree-Person are "naturals" for assessment in a couple or family context, as are kinetic family drawing techniques. Other projective measures, such as word association tests and sentence completion tests, are also capable of yielding valuable insights with respect to marital and family functioning.

Other measures of personality and behavior, such as those discussed in Chapter 13 and elsewhere in this text, may also prove useful in marital or family assessment. For example, a measure of values may yield important clues regarding each family member's worldview. Such an assessment may be particularly important for married couples that do not share the same religion; issues ostensibly related to religion may mask values orientations that typically accompany a particular religious persuasion. A measure of values administered to each member of the couple can help to bring differences to the fore for discussion.

Marital and Family Assessment Using Specialized Tests and Measures

Alongside the more customary measures, increasingly specialized instruments and procedures have been developed to assess marital and family functioning. In the period from 1934 to 1975, over eight hundred marital and/or family measures were in fact produced (Straus & Brown, 1978). In general, the bulk of such measures can be categorized as being paper-and-pencil inventories, structured interviews, behavior observation systems, projective measures, or other techniques—the last category including assessment procedures such as family sociograms and genograms. There are inventories and adjustment methods focused on various aspects of married and family life, including adjustment (Epstein et al., 1983; Spanier, 1976; Spanier & Filsinger, 1983), assets (Olson et al., 1985), communication (Bienvenu, 1978), feelings (Lowman, 1980), satisfaction (Roach et al., 1981; Snyder, 1981), stability (Booth & Edwards, 1983), trust (Larzelere & Huston, 1980), expectancies (Notarius & Vanzetti, 1983), coping strategies (McCubbin, Larsen, & Olson, 1985), strength of family ties (Bardis, 1975), intimacy (Waring & Reddon, 1983), and overall satisfaction with quality of life with respect to financial well-being, neighborhood and community, and other variables (Olson & Barnes, 1985). What follows is a nonevaluative listing and brief description of some of the available instruments and assessment techniques.

Adult-Adolescent Parenting Inventory
(Bavolek, 1984)
Using a five-point scale (Strongly agree, Agree, Uncertain, Disagree, Strongly disagree) with reference to 32 items stating opinions about parenting (for example, "Parents will spoil their children by picking them up and comforting them when they cry"), this test is de-

signed to yield insights about parents' beliefs about child rearing, as well as their expectations and empathy for their children.

Beavers-Timberlawn Family Evaluation Scale (Beavers, 1985)

The test is designed as a structured interview in which a family as a group discuss what they would like to change about the family. The session is videotaped, and the last ten minutes of the discussion is rated on dimensions such as "structure of the family" (encompasses questions of power, coalitions, and closeness) and "family affect" (which includes expression of feelings, mood and tone of communications, and presence or absence of empathy).

Beier-Sternberg Discord Questionnaire (Beier & Sternberg, 1977)

How much agreement exists between marital partners on topics such as money, children, sex, and politics? How much of a problem is the amount of agreement (or disagreement) that exists for each marital partner? These are the types of questions posed directly on this seven-point Agree/Disagree scale and corresponding seven-point Happy/Unhappy scale.

Child's Attitude Toward Mother Scale (Hudson, 1982)
Child's Attitude Toward Father Scale (Hudson, 1982)

Each of these two 25-item tests contains statements about the examinee's mother or father. The wording is virtually identical except for the word *mother* or *father*—for example, "My mother [father] doesn't understand me." For each item, respondents indicate whether what is stated is true on the following five-point scale:

Rarely or none of the time

A little of the time

Some of the time

Good part of the time

Most or all of the time

Each of the tests is designed to yield clinical data about the nature and extent of problems the testtaker expresses having with a parent.

Conflict Tactics Scales (Straus, 1979)

Marital and/or family conflict is inevitable. Given that premise, what tactics or techniques do the parties involved characteristically use to resolve conflict? Are the issues calmly discussed? Is someone else brought in to mediate? Is crying, sulking, or the "silent treatment" used? Is a threat or physical contact made? In this paper-and-pencil inventory, both the husband and the wife respond to items questioning the number of times in the last year various types of conflict-resolution tactics have been used. Different forms of the test are available to assess conflict tactics as seen through the eyes of husbands, wives, parents, and children.

Family Environment Scale (Moos & Moos, 1981)

The "environment" referred to in the name of this scale means social climate—a gauge of various dimensions of relationship and personal growth within the family. How well do family members get along? How expressive can family members be about telling each other problems? How important to family members are recreational pursuits? religion? How much control is exercised over family members? These are the types of issues addressed. The authors have also developed similar scales for measuring social climate in other systems such as school, work, military, and treatment environments.

Family Inventory of Life Events and Changes (McCubbin, Patterson, & Wilson, 1985)

Changes such as a move, loss of employment, a death, an unanticipated pregnancy, or starting a new business may prove disruptive in many ways to a family. This 71-item test in yes/no format surveys such changes over the previous 12-month period and yields a measure of how stressed the family is. The data may be of diagnostic value for use with distressed families.

Family Task Interview (Kinston et al., 1985)

As its name implies, this measurement technique entails observing how a family handles various tasks (such as planning something together, building a

(continued)

Marital and Family Assessment *(continued)*

tower out of blocks, and discussing likes and dislikes), after which family members' observations are
discussed. Ratings are made on a "Family Health
Scale," which covers topics such as "Alliances,"
"Family Competence" (encompassing observations
on areas such as conflict resolution and parental management of children), and "Communication" (encompassing observations on expression and reception of
messages).

Marital Adjustment Test (Locke & Wallace, 1959)
This 15-item paper-and-pencil inventory test may take
only five minutes, give or take a few, to administer.
Respondents are asked to indicate, "everything considered," their degree of happiness with their marriage. They are also asked to indicate how often they
agree with their mate on various matters such as
financial, sexual, and recreation issues. Some of the
other areas tapped by this brief self-report instrument
concern leisure-time pursuits, ways of handling disagreements, and willingness to confide in one's
spouse. The test was originally published with a scoring system based on weighted responses, though a
simplified scoring system was subsequently proposed
by Hunt (1978).

Marital Alternatives Scale (Udry, 1981)
This is a multiple-choice, paper-and-pencil test designed to probe the respondent's feelings regarding
alternatives to being married—remaining single, getting divorced, and marrying someone else. Data from
it may be used to shed light on the question of how
much better off or worse off individuals would be
were they not married.

Marital Comparison Level Index (Sabatelli, 1984)
How do spouses feel about their marital experience
relative to their expectations? Using a scale ranging
in degree from "Worse than I expect," to "About
what I expect" to "Better than I expect," the testtaker
responds to 32 items, which all begin with "The
amount" (such as "The amount your partner is willing to listen to you"). Marital dissatisfaction is presumed to be in evidence where a negative discrepancy
exists between expectations and experience.

*Parent-Adolescent Relationship Questionnaire
(Robin et al., 1990)*
Based on the behavioral family-systems model of
Robin and Foster (1989) that regards "parent-
adolescent conflict as a developmental phenomenon
of families whose functioning has been disrupted by
the biologically driven, culturally mediated striving for
independence of the young adolescent" (Robin et al.,
1990, p. 451), this self-report inventory assesses
problem-solving communication skills, belief systems,
and family structure.

*Productivity Environmental Preference Survey
(Price et al., 1982)*
Individual preferences may play a very important role
in a couple's compatibility. To better appreciate that,
simply take note of some of the many preferences
expressed by people seeking to meet other people
through personal ads in a newspaper: for example,
"nonsmoker preferred," "enjoys dining out, discos,
and long walks on the beach," and "loves quiet evenings at home." This 100-item test surveys preferences
with respect to areas such as the physical environment (addressing factors such as temperature, lighting, and noise level) and the social environment (self-
versus other-oriented). The test has potential application with respect not only to home environments but
to workplace environments as well.

*Self-Report Jealousy Scale—Revised
(Bringle et al., 1979)*
On a five-point scale of "Pleased," "Mildly upset,"
"Upset," "Very upset," and "Extremely upset," how
would you indicate you felt if your partner went to a
bar several evenings without you? Or commented to
you about how attractive another person is? How
would you feel if someone flirted with your partner?
Or your best friend suddenly showed interest in doing
things with someone else? These are some of the
types of items contained in this 25-item test designed
to measure romantic as well as nonromantic aspects
of jealousy. The test has been used as an aid in the
counseling of both heterosexual and homosexual
couples.

merits of a sampling of what he referred to as the "large, rather bewildering assortment of posttraumatic stress disorder (PTSD) measuring instruments" (p. 460).

As you may readily appreciate, there are certain areas of specialization within the general fields of clinical and counseling psychology, in which unique types of assessment tools and approaches may be employed or more traditional techniques used in some not-so-traditional way. We now turn our attention to clinical assessment in special contexts.

Special Applications of Clinical Measures

Forensic Psychological Assessment

The word *forensic* means "pertaining to or employed in legal proceedings," and the term *forensic psychological assessment* can be defined broadly as the theory and application of psychological evaluation and measurement for legal ends. Psychologists, psychiatrists, and other health professionals may be called on by courts, corrections and parole personnel, attorneys, and others involved in the criminal justice system to offer expert opinion on some matter. With respect to criminal proceedings, the opinion may, for example, concern an individual's competency to stand trial or his or her criminal responsibility (that is, "sanity") at the time a crime is committed. With respect to a civil proceeding, the opinion may have to do with issues as diverse as the extent of emotional distress suffered in a personal injury suit, the suitability of one or the other parent in a custody proceeding, or the testamentary capacity (capacity to make a last will and testament) of a person before death.

Before discussing some of the assessment-related aspects in a sampling of the many areas of forensic psychology, it is important to note that there are important differences between forensic and general clinical practice. As noted by Rappeport (1982), the biggest difference is that in the forensic situation, the clinician is not serving the patient but a third party, such as a court or an attorney, and that fact (as well as its implications with respect to issues such as confidentiality) must be made clear to the assessee. Another difference is that the patient is consulting the professional not for therapy but for help in dealing with the third party. There is therefore "a great likelihood that the patient will not be as truthful as he or she would be in other circumstances" (Rappeport, 1982, p. 333). Consequently, it is imperative that the assessor rely not only on the assessee's representations but on all available documentation, such as police reports and interviews with persons who may have pertinent knowledge. The mental health professional who performs forensic work would do well to be educated in the language of the law. As Rappeport put it:

> To go into court and render the opinion that a person is not responsible for a crime because he is psychotic is to say nothing of value to the judge or jury. However, to go into the same court and state that a man is not responsible because as a result of a mental disorder, namely, paranoid schizophrenia, "he

lacked substantial capacity to conform his behavior to the requirements of the law''—because he was hearing voices that told him he must commit the crime to protect his family from future harm—would be of great value to the judge or jury. It is not because the man had a psychosis that he is not responsible; it is how his illness affected his behavior and his ability to form the necessary criminal intent or to have the *mens rea,* or guilty mind, that is important. (p. 333)

The forensic assessor may sometimes be placed in the role of psychohistorian, as in the case in which an individual's testamentary capacity has been called into question. Here the assessor may offer an opinion about an individual he or she may have never personally seen—a situation that seldom if ever arises in nonforensic assessments.

The very appropriateness of mental health professionals as expert witnesses in many situations has been vigorously challenged in recent years. Faust and Ziskin (1988a, 1988b) point to the unreliability of psychiatric diagnoses, the unreliability and invalidity of certain tests for specific purposes, and questionable conclusions reached by mental health professionals on the basis of interviewing, testing, and other methods of assessment. The interested reader is referred to the writings of Faust and Ziskin as well as the response of Matarazzo (1990) for a firsthand look at this spirited debate.

Competency to stand trial   ''Competency'' in the legal sense has many different meanings. One may speak, for example, of competence to make a will, enter into a contract, commit a crime, waive constitutional rights, consent to medical treatment . . . the list goes on. Before convicted murderer Gary Gilmore was executed in Utah, he underwent an examination designed to determine whether or not he was competent to be executed. That is so because the law mandates that a certain propriety exists with respect to state-ordered executions, and it would not be morally proper to execute insane persons. *Competence to stand trial* has largely to do with a defendant's ability to understand the charges against him or her and assist in his or her own defense. As stated in the Supreme Court's ruling in *Dusky v. United States,* a defendant must have ''sufficient present ability to consult with his lawyer with a reasonable degree of rational . . . (and) factual understanding of the proceedings against him.'' This ''understand and assist'' requirement, as it has come to be called, is in effect an extension of the constitutional prohibition against trials *in absentia;* a defendant must be not only physically present during the trial but mentally present as well.

The competency requirement serves to protect an individual's right to choose and assist counsel, the right to act as a witness on one's own behalf, and the right to confront opposing witnesses. The requirement also increases the probability that the truth of the case will be developed, since the competent defendant is able to monitor continuously the testimony of witnesses and help bring discrepancies in testimony to the attention of the court. In general, persons who are mentally retarded, psychotic, or suffering from a debilitating neurological disorder are persons held to be incompetent to stand trial. However, it cannot be overemphasized that any one of these three diagnoses is not sufficient in itself for a person found to be incompetent. Stated another way: it is possible for a person to be mentally retarded, psychotic, or suffering from a

Table 14–2
Georgetown Criteria for
Competency to Stand Trial

Factual Items

Defendant's ability to:
1. understand his [or her] current legal situation
2. understand the charges made against him [or her]
3. understand the legal issues and procedures in the case
4. understand the possible dispositions, pleas, and penalties
5. understand the facts relevant to the case
6. identify and locate witnesses

Inferential Items

Defendant's ability to communicate with counsel and to:
7. comprehend instructions and advice
8. make decisions after advice
9. follow testimony for contradictions or errors
10. maintain a collaborative relationship with his [or her] attorney
11. testify if necessary and be cross-examined
12. tolerate stress at the trial or while awaiting trial
13. refrain from irrational behavior during the trial

Source: Bukatman, Foy, and DeGrazia (1971)

debilitating neurological disorder—or all three—and still be found competent to stand trial. The person will be found to be incompetent if and only if he or she is unable to understand the charges against him or her and is unable to assist in his or her own defense.

To help psychologists and other mental health professionals determine whether a defendant meets the "understand and assist" requirement, a number of test instruments have been developed. For example, researchers at Georgetown University Law School (Bukatman et al., 1971) enumerated 13 criteria of competency to stand trial and specific questions for a competency screening interview (see Tables 14–2 and 14–3).

According to Bukatman et al., a thorough competency evaluation would entail answers to each of the interview questions listed "with sufficient information on each point to indicate whether there is, or might be in the future, a problem in that area" (p. 1226). Lipsitt, Lelos, and McGarry (1971) developed a sentence completion test called the Competency Screening Test (see Table 14–4) that contains 22 items, each of which relates to a legal criterion of competency to stand trial. The test is scored on a three-point scale ranging from 0 to 2, with appropriate responses being scored 2, marginally appropriate responses being scored 1, and clearly inappropriate responses being scored 0. For example, a 2-point response to the item "When I go to court, the lawyer will ____" would be "defend me." Such a response indicates that the assessee has a clear understanding of the lawyer's role. By contrast, a 0-point response might be "have me guillotined," which would be indicative of an inappropriate perception of the lawyer's role. Lipsitt et al. reported the inter-rater reliability among trained scorers of this test to be $r = .93$. They also reported that their test was successful in discriminating seriously disturbed, state-hospitalized men from control groups consisting of students, community adults, club members, and civilly

Table 14–3
Georgetown Screening Interview for Competency to Stand Trial

Understanding of current situation
 Who is your lawyer at this time?
 Have you had other lawyers in this case?
 How did you get them?
 What is your lawyer's job?
 What is the purpose of the judge?
 What does the jury do?
 What will the prosecutor do?
 Since your arrest, have you spent time in jail? If so, how long?
 Have you been questioned by the police? When? Where?
 Did they tell you what rights you have in this case?

 What are the charges against you?
 What do they mean to you?
 Why were they made against you?

 When is your trial going to take place?
 In which court is your trial going to take place?
 Can the judge or prosecutor make you take the witness stand in court and make you answer questions?

 Since your arrest, have you gone before any court or court official? When? Where? What was the reason?
 What kind of official was it?
 What was decided?
 Did you have a lawyer? If so, how did you get him [or her]?

 What is the difference between guilty and not guilty?
 If the court should find you guilty, what are the possible sentences in your case?
 What do you think will happen? Why?
 What does a suspended sentence mean?
 What does probation mean?

Cooperation and participation in own defense
 What is your plea at this time?
 What alibi or defense do you think you have now? Does your lawyer agree with this?
 Why are you going to use this alibi? Defense?
 Have you and your lawyer discussed any other alibi or defense that you could use, but don't plan to use? What
  are they? Why are you not using them?
 What does incompetent to stand trial mean to you?
 Do you think there is any reason why you should be found incompetent?
 Would you like to be found incompetent to stand trial? If so, why?
 Will there be any witnesses against you? Do you think you know what they might say?
 If one of them tells a lie, or makes a mistake, what would you do?
 Will there be any witnesses for you?
 What have you done to contact them and make sure they will be at your trial?
 What have you done to be certain that what they say will help your case?

 Has your lawyer been helpful in letting you know about your rights . . . ?
 Has there been anything you thought your lawyer could do to help your case which you have been reluctant to
  ask him or her to do? If so, what?
 Is there something about your lawyer that makes it difficult for you to work with him [or her]?
 Is your lawyer charging you for his [or her] service in this case?

 Have you ever testified before? When? Describe what happened.
 Do you think you have to testify at your trial? If so, how do you feel about doing so?
 What will you do if you are asked a question you don't want to answer?

Source: Bukatman, Foy, and DeGrazia (1971)

Table 14–4
Competency Screening Test

1. The lawyer told Bill that _____ .
2. When I go to court, the lawyer will _____ .
3. Jack felt that the judge _____ .
4. When Phil was accused of the crime, he _____ .
5. When I prepare to go to court with my lawyer _____ .
6. If the jury finds me guilty, I _____ .
7. The way a court trial is decided _____ .
8. When the evidence in George's case was presented to the jury _____ .
9. When the lawyer questioned his client in court, the client said _____ .
10. If Jack had to try his own case, he _____ .
11. Each time the D.A. asked me a question, I _____ .
12. While listening to the witnesses testify against me, I _____ .
13. When the witness testifying against Harry gave incorrect evidence, he _____ .
14. When Bob disagreed with his lawyer on his defense, he _____ .
15. When I was formally accused of the crime, I thought to myself _____ .
16. If Ed's lawyer suggests that he plead guilty, he _____ .
17. What concerns Fred most about his lawyer _____ .
18. When they say a man is innocent until proven guilty _____ .
19. When I think of being sent to prison, I _____ .
20. When Phil thinks of what he is accused of, he _____ .
21. When the [members of the jury hear] my case, they will _____ .
22. If I had a chance to speak to the judge, I _____ .

Source: Lipsitt, Lelos, and McGarry (1971)

committed hospitalized patients. Subsequent research by independent investigators (Nottingham & Mattson, 1982) further supports the clinical utility of the Competency Screening Test.

Criminal responsibility "Not guilty by reason of insanity" is a plea to a criminal charge that we have all heard about at one time or another. But stop and think about the meaning the legal term *insanity* has to mental health professionals and the evaluation procedures by which psychological assessors could identify the "insane." The insanity defense has its roots in the idea that only blameworthy persons (that is, those with a "criminal mind") should be punished. Possibly exempt from blame, therefore, are children, mental incompetents, and others who may be irresponsible, lack control of their actions, or have no conception that what they are doing may be criminal. As early as the sixteenth century, it was argued in an English court that an offending act should not be considered a felony if the offender had no conception of good and evil. By the eighteenth century, the focus had shifted from good and evil as a criterion for evaluating criminal responsibility to the issue of whether the defendant "doth not know what he is doing no more than . . . a wild beast." Judicial history was made in nineteenth-century England when in 1843 Daniel M'Naghten was found not guilty by reason of insanity after attempting to assassinate the British Prime Minister (and mistakenly shooting and killing the Prime Minister's secretary). In the words of the court that acquitted M'Naghten, exculpation would be made if "at the time of the committing of the act, the party accused was laboring under such a defect of reason from disease of the mind as not to know the nature and quality of the act he was doing, or if he did know it, that he did not know he was doing what was wrong."

The decision in the M'Naghten case has come to be referred to as the "right or wrong test." To the present day, this test of sanity is adhered to in England as well as in a number of jurisdictions in the United States. However, a deficiency in the "right or wrong test" is that it does not allow for the exculpation of persons who might know right from wrong but are unable to control impulses to commit criminal acts. In 1954, an opinion written by the United States Court of Appeal for the District of Columbia in the case of *Durham v. United States* held a defendant not to be culpable for criminal action "if his unlawful act was the product of a mental disease or defect." Still another standard of legal insanity was set forth by the American Law Institute (ALI) in 1956, and this standard has become one of the most widely used throughout the United States (Weiner, 1980). With slight alterations from one jurisdiction to another, this legal test of sanity provides as follows:

> A person is not responsible for criminal conduct i.e., insane if, at the time of such conduct, as a result of a mental disease or defect, he lacks substantial capacity either to appreciate the criminality (wrongfulness) of his conduct, or to conform his conduct to the requirements of the law.
>
> As used in this article, the terms "mental disease or defect" do not include an abnormality manifested only by repeated criminal or otherwise antisocial conduct.

In clinical practice, defendants who are mentally retarded, psychotic, or neurologically impaired are likely to be the ones found to be not guilty by reason of insanity. However, as was the case with considerations of competency to stand trial, the mere fact that a person is judged to be mentally retarded, psychotic, or neurologically impaired is in itself no guarantee that the individual will be found not guilty; other criteria, such as the ALI standards cited, must be met. To help psychological assessors determine if those standards are met, a number of instruments such as the Rogers Criminal Responsibility Assessment Scale (RCRAS) have been developed. Psychologist Richard Rogers and his colleagues (Rogers & Cavanaugh, 1980, 1981; Rogers et al., 1981) designed the RCRAS to be a systematic and empirical approach to insanity evaluations. This instrument consists of 25 items tapping both psychological and situational variables. The items are scored with respect to five scales: reliability (including malingering), organic factors, psychopathology, cognitive control, and behavioral control. After scoring, the examiner employs a hierarchical decision model for the purpose of arriving at a decision concerning the assessee's sanity. Table 14–5 contains a listing of the scales as well as sample items from the RCRAS. Validity studies done with this scale (for example, Rogers et al., 1983; Rogers et al., 1984) have shown it to be useful in discriminating between sane and insane patients/defendants.

Debate about the reasonableness of insanity as a defense has been a fact of life perhaps as long as there has been an insanity defense (Fingarette & Hasse, 1979; Finkel et al., 1985; Goldstein, 1967; Keilitz, 1987; Lanyon, 1986; Morse,

Table 14-5
Scales and Items of the RCRAS

Item Name		Range	Score
Scale 1. Patient's Reliability			
1 Reliability of patient's self-report (voluntary)		1–5	
2 Involuntary interference with patient's self-report		1–5	
Scale 2. Organicity	Summation	(2–10)	_____
3 Intoxication		1–6	
4 Brain damage or disease		1–5	
5 Brain damage and crime		1–5	
6 Mental retardation		1–6	
7 Retardation and the crime		1–5	
Scale 3. Psychopathology	Summation	(5–27)	_____
8 Bizarre behavior		1–5	
9 Anxiety		1–6	
10 Amnesia		1–6	
11 Delusions		1–5	
12 Hallucinations		1–5	
13 Depressed mood		1–6	
14 Elevated or expansive mood		1–6	
15 Verbal coherence		1–5	
16 Affect		1–5	
17 Thought disorder (list)			
Scale 4. Cognitive Control	Summation	(9–49)	_____
18 Planning and preparation		1–6	
19 Awareness of criminality		1–4	
15 Verbal coherence		1–5	
17 Thought disorder (list)			
Scale 5. Behavioral Control	Summation	(3–15)	_____
20 Focus of the crime		1–5	
21 Level of activity		1–6	
22 Responsible social behavior		1–5	
22 Reported self-control		1–6	
24 Estimated self-control		1–6	
25 Control and psychosis		1–4	
8 Bizarre behavior		1–6	
	Summation	(7–38)	_____

Sample Items

10. Amnesia about the alleged crime.
(This refers to the examiner's assessment of amnesia, not necessarily the patient's reported amnesia.)
(0) No information.
(1) None. Remembers the entire event in considerable detail.
(2) Slight; of doubtful significance. The patient forgets a few minor details.
(3) Mild. Patient remembers the substance of what happened but is forgetful of many minor details.
(4) Moderate. The patient has forgotten a major portion of the alleged crime but remembers enough details to believe it happened.
(5) Severe. The patient is amnesic to most of the alleged crime but remembers enough details to believe it happened.

(6) Extreme. Patient is completely amnesic to the whole alleged crime.

11. Delusions at the time of the alleged crime.
(0) No information.
(1) Absent.
(2) Suspected delusions (e.g., supported only by questionable self-report).
(3) Definite delusions but not actually associated with the commission of the alleged crime.
(4) Definite delusions which contributed to, but were not the predominant force in the commission of, the alleged crime.
(5) Definite controlling delusions on the basis of which the alleged crime was committed.

1985; Reynolds, 1984; Simon, 1967; Simon & Aaronson, 1988; Slobogin, 1985). In recent years, the disagreement has become even more heated, however, as attempts have been made at the federal and state level to modify or even abolish existing statutes affecting a defense of insanity. Different insanity defense standards will have differential effects on court findings. Empirical research on how changed standards might affect court findings is currently in an exploratory stage (see, for example, Wettstein et al., 1991).

Readiness for parole or probation   Some people convicted of a crime will "pay their dues" to society and go on to lead fulfilling, productive lives after their incarceration. At the other extreme are career criminals who will violate laws at the first opportunity upon their release—or escape—from prison. Predicting who is ready for parole or probation and what the outcome of such a release might be has proved no easy task, yet this has not deterred psychologists from trying to develop effective measures.

A classic work by Cleckley (1976) provided a detailed profile of *psychopaths*—people with few inhibitions who may pursue pleasure or money with callous disregard for the welfare of others. Based on a factor-analytic study of Cleckley's description, Robert D. Hare (1980) developed a 22-item Psychopathy Checklist (PCL) that reflects personality characteristics as rated by the assessor (such as callousness, impulsiveness, and empathy), as well as prior history as gleaned from the assessee's records (such as "criminal versatility"). In the revised version of the test, the Revised Psychopathy Checklist (PCL-R; Hare, 1985), two items from the original PCL were omitted because of their relatively low correlation with the rest of the scale, and the scoring criteria for some of the remaining items were modified. Hare et al. (1990) report that the two forms are equivalent.

Preliminary findings with the PCL have been impressive. Harris, Rice, and Cormier (1989) report that in a maximum-security psychiatric sample, the PCL correctly identified 80% of the violent recidivists. A study by Hart, Kropp, and Hare (1988) indicates that psychopaths are four times more likely than nonpsychopaths to fail on release. A version of the PCL specially modified for use with young male offenders produced scores that correlated significantly with variables such as number of conduct disorder symptoms, previous violent offenses, violent recidivism, and violent behavior within the maximum security institution in which the study was conducted (Forth et al., 1990). In another study, psychopathy ratings were found to predict outcome for both temporary absence and parole release; psychopaths were recommitted four times more frequently than nonpsychopaths (Serin et al., 1990).

Another line of research in this area has been undertaken by Glenn Walters (1991) at the federal penitentiary in Leavenworth, Kansas. Walters and White (1989) have characterized the criminal lifestyle as one marked by self-indulgence, interpersonal intrusiveness, social rule breaking, and irresponsibility. The 14-item Lifestyle Criminality Screening Form (LCSF; Walters et al., 1991) yields scores on such characteristics based on information from an offender's presentence investigation report. In a study in which the subjects' probation officers served as the raters, offenders obtaining high scores on the LCSF exhibited a higher rate of parole and probation failure than offenders obtaining lower scores (Walters et al., 1990). Walters et al. (1990) caution, however, that additional research is required to explore the generalizability and implications of their findings.

Custody Evaluations

As the number of divorces in this country continues to climb, so does the number of custody proceedings. Before the 1920s, it was fairly commonplace for the father to be granted custody of the children (Lamb, 1981). The pendulum swung, however, with the widespread adoption of what was referred to as the "tender years" doctrine, and the belief that the child's interest would be best served if the mother was granted custody. In recent years, and with the coming of age of the dual-career household, the courts have begun to be more egalitarian in their custody decisions; it is recognized that the best interest of the child may be served by father custody, mother custody, or joint custody (McClure-Butterfield, 1990). Psychological assessors can assist the court in making awards of custody with reports that detail the parental capacity of the parents, and/or the parental preferences of the children (Weithorn, 1987). Ideally, one impartial expert in the mental health field should be responsible for assessing *all* family members and submitting a report to the court (Gardner, 1982). More often than not, however, the husband has his doctor, the wife has hers, and the battle is on.

Evaluation of the parent The evaluation of the parental capacity typically entails a detailed interview that focuses primarily on various aspects of child rearing, though tests of intelligence, personality, and adjustment may be employed if questions remain after the interview. The assessor might begin with open-ended questions designed to let the parent ventilate some of his or her feelings and then proceed to more specific questions tapping a wide variety of areas, including

- the parent's own childhood: how happy? abused?
- the parent's own relationship with parents, siblings, peers
- the circumstances that led up to the marriage and the degree of forethought that went into the decision to have (or adopt) children
- the adequacy of prenatal care and attitudes toward the pregnancy
- the parent's description of the child
- the parent's own evaluation of himself or herself as a parent, including strengths and weaknesses
- the parent's evaluation of his or her spouse regarding strengths and weaknesses as a parent
- the quantity and quality of time spent caring for and playing with children
- the parent's approach to discipline
- the parent's receptivity to the child's peer relationships

During the course of the interview, the assessor may find evidence that the interviewee really does not want custody of the children but is undertaking the custody battle for some other reason. For example, custody may be nothing more than another issue to bargain over with respect to the divorce settlement. Alternatively, a mother might, for example, be embarrassed to admit to herself and to all observers of the proceedings that she really doesn't want custody of the children. Sometimes a parent, emotionally scathed by all that has gone on before the divorce, may be employing the custody battle as a technique of vengeance—to threaten to take away that which is most prized and adored by the spouse. The clinician performing the evaluation must appreciate that such ill-motivated intentions do underlie some custody battles; and, in the best interest of the children, it is the obligation of the clinician to report such findings.

Evaluation of the child   The court will be interested in knowing if the child in a custody proceeding has a preference with respect to future living and visitation arrangements. Toward that end, the psychological assessor can be of assistance with a wide variety of tests and techniques. Most authorities agree that the preferences of children under the age of 5 are too unreliable and too influenced by recent experiences to be accorded much weight. However, if intelligence test data indicate that the child who is chronologically 5 is functioning at a higher level, then his or her preferences may be accorded greater weight. This is particularly true if the Comprehension subtest score on a Wechsler test (such as the Wechsler Preschool and Primary Scale of Intelligence—Revised) is elevated, for, you will recall, the Comprehension subtest requires the child to draw on the knowledge of social situations. Some methods that can be useful in assessing a child's parental preference include structured play exercises with dolls that represent the child and other family members, figure drawings of family members followed by story telling to the drawings, and the use of projective techniques such as the TAT and related tests (see Figure 14–1).

Sometimes impromptu innovation on the part of the examiner is required. In performing a custody evaluation on a 5-year-old child, the senior author of this text (RJC) noted that the child seemed to identify very strongly with the main character in a then-popular film, *E. T., The Extraterrestrial.* The child had seen the film three times, came into the test session carrying two *E. T.* bubble-gum cards, and identified as "E. T." the picture he drew when instructed to draw a person. As a means of obtaining a measure of parental preference, the examiner took four figures and represented them as "E. T.," "E. T.'s mother," "E. T.'s father," and "E. T.'s sister." An empty cardboard box was then labeled a "spaceship," and the child was told that E. T. (stranded on Earth and longing to return to his home planet) had the opportunity to go home but that the spaceship had room for only two other passengers. The child boarded his mother and his sister in addition to "E. T." and told the examiner that E. T.'s father would "wave goodbye."

Specially constructed sentence completion items can also be of value in the assessment of parental preferences. For example, the following items might prove to be useful in examining the differing perceptions of each parent:

Figure 14–1
Projective Techniques Used in Custody Evaluation

The picture on the left is from the Children's Apperception Test—H (Bellak & Bellak, 1965), and the one on the right is from The Boys and Girls Book About Divorce *(Gardner, 1971). These, as well as TAT and other pictures used as projective stimuli, may be useful in evaluating children's parental preferences.*

Mothers _____.
If I do something wrong, my father _____.
It is best for children to live with _____.
Fathers _____.
Mommies are bad when _____.
I like to hug _____.
I don't like to hug _____.
Daddies are bad when _____.
The last time I cried _____.
My friends think that my mother _____.
My friends think that my father _____.

The data-gathering process for the evaluation begins at the moment the child and the parent(s) come into the office. The assessor takes careful note of the quality of the interaction between the parent(s) and the child. The child will then be interviewed alone, and questions about the nature and quality of the relationship will be posed. If the child expresses a strong preference for one parent or the other, it is the burden of the assessor to evaluate how meaningful that preference is. For example, a child who sees his rancher father only every other weekend might have a "good ol' time" on the brief occasions that they are together and express a preference for living there—unaware that life in the country would soon become just as routine as life in the city with Mom. For those children with no expressed preference, insight into their feelings can be obtained by using the tests described earlier, combined with skillful interviewing. Included among the topics for discussion will be the child's physical description of his or her parents as well as his or her living quarters. Questions about the routine aspects of life (such as, "Who makes breakfast for you?") as well as questions about recreation, parental visitation, parental involvement with their education, their general well-being, and their siblings and friends will be asked.

Child Abuse and Neglect

A legal mandate exists in most states for many licensed professionals to report child abuse and child neglect when they have knowledge of it. The legal definitions of "child abuse" and "child neglect" vary from state to state. Typically, definitions of *abuse* refer to the creation of conditions that may give rise to abuse of a child (a person under the state-defined age of majority) by an adult responsible for the care of that person. The abuse may be in the form of (1) the infliction or allowing of infliction of physical injury or emotional impairment that is nonaccidental, (2) the creation or allowing the creation of substantial risk of physical injury or emotional impairment that is nonaccidental, or (3) the committing or allowing of a sexual offense to be committed against a child. Typical definitions of *neglect* refer to a failure on the part of an adult responsible for the care of a child to exercise a minimum degree of care in providing the child with food, clothing, shelter, education, medical care, and supervision.

A number of excellent general sources for the study of child abuse and child neglect are currently available (see, for example, Cicchetti & Carlson, 1989; Ellerstein, 1981; Fontana et al., 1963; Helfer & Kempe, 1988; Kelley, 1988; Reece & Groden, 1985). More specifically, literature is available to assist professionals in recognizing child abuse in the form of head injury (Billmire & Myers, 1985), eye injury (Gammon, 1981), mouth injury (Becker et al., 1978), emotional trauma (Brassard et al., 1986), burns (Alexander et al., 1987; Lung et al., 1977), bites (American Board of Forensic Odontology, 1986), fractures (Worlock et al., 1986), poisoning (Kresel & Lovejoy, 1981), sexual abuse (Adams-Tucker, 1982; Faller, 1988; Friedrich et al., 1986; Sanfillipo et al., 1986; Sebold, 1987), and shaken infant syndrome (Dykes, 1986). What follows are some brief, very general guidelines to the assessment of physical and emotional signs of child abuse.

Physical signs of abuse and neglect Although psychologists and other mental health professionals without medical credentials do not typically have occasion to physically examine children, a knowledge of physical signs of abuse and neglect is important. Obvious physical injuries may be described by abused children or abusing adults as the result of an accident, and it is incumbent on the knowledgeable professional to have a working familiarity with the various kinds of injuries that may signal more ominous causes. For example, in the case of injury to the face, in most veritable accidents, only one side of the face is injured. It may therefore be significant if a child evidences injury on both sides of the face—both eyes and both cheeks. Marks on the skin may be telling—

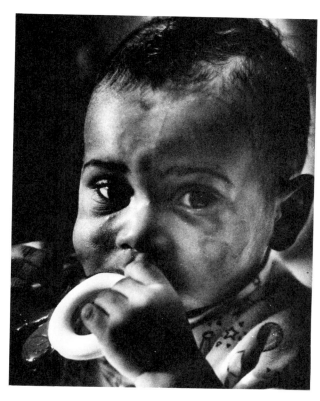

Figure 14–2
Abused and Neglected

This physically abused child (note facial bruises) was abandoned by his parent and left in a shopping cart outside a supermarket on a cold winter night.

"grab" marks made by an adult-size hand, marks that form a recognizable pattern, such as the tines of a fork, a belt buckle, a cord or rope, or human teeth. Burns from a cigarette or lighter may be in evidence as marks on the soles of the feet, the palms of the hands, the back, or the buttocks, and burns from scalding water may be in evidence as a "glovelike" redness on the hands or feet. Any bone fracture or dislocation should be investigated, as should head injuries, particularly when a patch of hair appears to be missing—as would be the case if the child's hair was pulled.

Physical signs that may or may not be indicative of neglect include dress that is inappropriate for the season, poor hygiene, and lagging physical development. Physical signs indicative of sexual abuse are not present in the majority of cases. In many instances, there is no penetration or only partial penetration by the abusing adult and no physical scars. In young children, physical signs that may or may not be indicative of sexual abuse include difficulty in sitting or walking, itching or reported pain or discomfort of genital areas, stained, bloody, or torn underclothing, and foreign bodies in orifices. In older children, the presence of sexually transmitted diseases or a pregnancy may or may not signal child sexual abuse.

Emotional and behavioral signs of abuse and neglect Emotional and behavioral indicators may reflect something other than child abuse and neglect; child abuse or neglect is only one of several possible explanations underlying the appearance of such signs. Fear of going home or fear of adults in general and reluctance to remove outer garments may be signs of abuse. Other emotional and behavioral signs that may be abuse-related include unusual reactions or apprehension in response to other children crying, low self-esteem, extreme or inappropriate moods, aggressiveness, social withdrawal, and nail biting, thumb sucking, or other habit disorders. Frequent lateness to or absence from school, chronic fatigue, chronic hunger, and age-inappropriate behavior (such as that of a child who has taken on the role of an adult because of the absence of a caregiver at home) may be signs of neglect.

In children under 8 years of age, problems such as fear of sleeping alone, eating disorders, enuresis, encopresis, sexual acting out, change in school behavior, tantrums, crying spells, sadness, and suicidal thoughts may or may not be indicative of sexual abuse. In older children, a professional might additionally observe memory problems, emotional numbness, violent fantasies, hyperalertness, self-mutilation, and sexual concerns or preoccupations, which may be accompanied by guilt or shame.

Interviews, behavioral observation, and psychological tests are all used in identifying child abuse. However, professionals disagree about the appropriate tools for such an assessment, particularly when the assessment involves sexual abuse. One technique involves observing children while they play with *anatomically detailed dolls* (ADDs), which are dolls having accurately represented genitalia. Sexually abused children may, on average, engage ADDs in more sexually oriented activities than other children, but differences between groups of abused and nonabused children are not large. Many nonabused children play in a sexually explicit way with ADDs, so such play is not necessarily diagnostic of sexual abuse (Elliott et al., 1993; Wolfner et al., 1993). Human-figure drawings are also used to assess sexual and physical abuse, though their accuracy in distinguishing abused from nonabused children is debated (Burgess et al., 1981; Chantler et al., 1993; Kelley, 1985). Questionnaires designed for administration to a child who may have been abused (Mannarino et al., 1994) or to adults such as teachers or parents, who know that child well (Chantler et al., 1993) have been explored, though no well-developed and thoroughly validated instrument yet exists. In short, no widely accepted, reliable, and valid set of techniques for the assessment of sexual abuse is available (Hysjulien et al., 1994). That may be why Horner et al. (1993) found little consensus among professionals asked to make an evaluation of sexual abuse in a specific case. Lanyon (1993) encourages those doing sexual abuse assessment to integrate information from many assessment methods and sources and to avoid reliance on any single technique. However, selecting techniques to include in such an integrative evaluation is difficult, given the controversies surrounding specific assessment methods.

Issues in reporting child abuse and neglect Child abuse, when it occurs, is a tragedy. A claim of child abuse when in fact there has been no such abuse is also a tragedy—one that can irrevocably scar an accused but innocent individual for life. It is incumbent on professionals who undertake the weighty obligation of assessing a child for potential abuse not to approach their task with any preconceived notions, because such notions can be conveyed to the child and be perceived as the "right answer" to questions that are posed (King & Yuille, 1987; White et al., 1988). Children from the ages of about 2 to 7 are highly suggestible and their memory is not as well developed as that of older children; for that reason, it is possible that events that occur after the alleged incident—including events only referred to in conversations—may be confused with the actual incident (Ceci et al., 1987; Goodman & Reed, 1986; Loftus & Davies, 1984). Other such considerations in the psychological examination of a child for abuse have been discussed in detail by Weissman (1991). Sensitivity to the rights of the accused in a child abuse proceeding are critical to making certain that justice is served (Ackerman, 1987; Besharov, 1985; Coleman, 1989; Corwin et al., 1987; Green, 1986; Jones & McGraw, 1987; Raskin & Yuille, 1987; Wong, 1987).

Risk assessment In an effort to prevent child abuse, test developers have sought to create instruments useful in identifying parents and others who may be at risk for abusing children. The Child Abuse Potential Inventory (CAP; Milner et al., 1986; Milner, 1991), as discussed in Chapter 2, has demonstrated impressive validity in identifying abusers. Another test, the Parenting Stress Index (PSI; Loyd & Abidin, 1985), measures stress associated with the parental role. Parents are asked to reflect on their relationship with one child at a time. Some of the items focus on child characteristics that could engender stress, such as activity level and mood. Other PSI items reflect potentially stressful aspects of the parent's life, such as lack of social support and marital problems (Gresham, 1989). The test's authors report internal consistency reliability coefficients ranging from .89 to .95 for factors and total scores. Test-retest reliability coefficients range from .71 to .82 over three weeks, and .55 to .70 over a one-year interval (Loyd & Abidin, 1985). With respect to the test's validity, parents who physically abuse their children tend to score higher on the PSI than parents who do not (Wantz, 1989).

What are the appropriate uses of measures like the CAP and the PSI? Although positive relationships exist between child abuse and scores on the tests, the tests cannot be used to identify or prosecute child abusers in a legal context (Gresham, 1989). Because child abuse is a low base-rate phenomenon, even the use of highly reliable instruments will produce many false positives; that is, the test will erroneously identify the assessee as an abuser. For some parents, high levels of stress as measured by the PSI may indeed lead to physical abuse. However, for most parents, they will not. Some parent-child relationships, such as those involving children with disabilities, are inherently stressful (Innocenti et al., 1992; Orr et al., 1993). Still, most parents manage to weather the relationship without inflicting any harm. Some parents who experience high levels of stress as a result of their relationship with a child may themselves be harmed— even more stressed—to hear from a mental health official that they are at risk for child abuse. For that reason, great caution is called for in interpreting and acting on the results of a test designed to assess risk for child abuse.

On the other hand, high CAP or PSI scores may well point the way to an abusive situation, and they should alert concerned professionals to be watchful for signs of abuse. A second appropriate use of such scores concerns the allocation of resources designed to reduce parenting stress. Parents who score high on the CAP and the PSI could be given priority for placement in a parenting skills class, individualized parent training, child care assistance, and other such programs. If reducing the stress of the parent will reduce the risk of child abuse, everything that can possibly be done to reduce the parental stress should be attempted.

Assessment in Health Psychology

Clinical tools of assessment, as well as other tools of assessment, enjoy widespread use in the field of health psychology. *Health psychology* is a relatively new but fast-growing specialty that seeks to understand the role of psychological variables in the onset, course, treatment, and/or prevention of illness, disease, and disability (Cohen, 1994). Health psychologists are involved in teaching, research, or direct-service activities designed to promote good health.

Individual interviews, surveys, and paper-and-pencil tests are perhaps among the most frequently used tools of researchers in health psychology. Such instruments may be employed to help assess a current state of affairs with regard to some disease or condition, gauge treatment progress, and/or evaluate outcome of intervention (Brown, 1989). One general research approach entails reporting on the nature of the psychological adjustment of members of a targeted group. In this context, researchers have shown interest in a wide variety of populations. They have studied, for example, the postpartum adjustment of women shortly after childbirth (O'Hara et al., 1992), the postrelease adjustment of former defendants acquitted on an insanity plea (Wiederanders & Choate, 1994), and the health and happiness of the clinically obese (Bray, 1986). There has also been a steady stream of articles focusing on psychological adjustment to a variety of medical conditions, such as cancer (Heidrich et al., 1994; Schag et al., 1990), rheumatoid arthritis (Smith et al., 1995), irritable bowel syndrome (Suls et al., 1994), and adult (Fleishman & Fogel, 1994) or pediatric (Boivin et al., 1995) HIV infection. Closely related variables such as quality of life (Goodwin et al., 1994; Walker & Rosser, 1988), satisfaction with life (Frisch et al., 1992; Huebner, 1994; Pavot & Diener, 1993), and reasons for living (Osman et al., 1993) have also received research attention. How people cope with physical setbacks (Barbarin & Chesler, 1986; Brown, 1984; Brown et al., 1989; Carver et al., 1991; Cohen & Lazarus, 1973; Derogatis et al., 1979; Dunkel-Schetter et al., 1992; Felton & Revenson, 1987; Hamburg & Adams, 1967; McCrae & Costa, 1986) and/or social disadvantage (Parron et al., 1982) is another topic of great interest, as is the assessment of coping behavior itself (Vitaliano et al., 1987).

Many studies in the health psychology literature focus on aspects of personality, behavior, or lifestyle, and their relationship to physical health or longevity (Friedman, 1990). "What personality traits or behavior patterns are predictive of what types of health or disease patterns?" is a question that has taken many different forms in the health psychology literature (a sampling of which follow). What personality attributes are predictors of smoking initiation and cessation

(Lipkus et al., 1994)? What factors are predictive of vigorous physical exercise in women and in men (Sallis et al., 1992)? What are the predictors of survival among hemodialysis patients (Christensen et al., 1994)? What are the predictors of cancer progression in young adult men and women (Epping-Jordan et al., 1994)? What psychological factors may influence one's immune function (Arnetz et al., 1987; Irwin et al., 1990; Keller et al., 1981; Kiecolt-Glaser & Glaser, 1988; McNaughton et al., 1990)? What effect do one's beliefs about health (Bond et al., 1992) and one's general outlook on life (Scheier & Carver, 1987) have on physical health? What are the psychological predictors of heart disease (Booth-Kewley & Friedman, 1987) and myocardial infarction (Connolly, 1976; Theorell et al., 1975)? What changes can be expected in alcoholics as they progress in treatment (DiClemente & Hughes, 1990)? What role might social support play in post-hospitalization recovery (Wilcox et al., 1994), the rehabilitation of burn patients (Davidson et al., 1979), and the mortality rate in the population of an elderly community (Blazer, 1982)?

Another major area of inquiry concerns patients' compliance with doctors' instructions (Dunbar, 1990). What cognitive, behavioral, social, and related factors are critical in this context? Such questions have been studied with regard to conditions such as diabetes (Ary et al., 1986), rheumatoid arthritis (Corish et al., 1989), and alcoholism (Rees, 1985). Indeed, scales to measure degree of patient compliance have been developed (see, for example, DiMatteo et al., 1993; Haynes et al., 1979). In a somewhat related vein, researchers have examined causes of patient dissatisfaction with medical care (Marshall et al., 1993).

Other research questions raised by health psychologists probe areas such as the value of education efforts, skills training, or other such interventions in treatment or prevention (see, for example, Mazzuca, 1982). Gender-related (Cotton, 1992) and cultural (Bachman et al., 1991; Chan, 1994; Strassberg, 1992) factors, as well as relatively universal motivations for engaging in some health- or illness-related behavior (Allison et al., 1992; Cooper, 1994; Nolan et al., 1994; Rakowski et al., 1992; Wright et al., 1992) have all been variables of interest.

In each of these and other areas, the need exists for reliable and valid tools to gauge change with regard to some psychological variable. When existing instruments are inappropriate, new ones have been created. Regardless, the assessment literature in health psychology tends to serve as a reminder that defining and measuring psychological variables is more complex than it may appear to the novice at first glance. For example, *stress* may be studied in the context of being an antecedent or a consequence of something—or both—and researchers have had to take that into account in defining and measuring it (Dohrenwend & Shrout, 1985; Kanner et al., 1981; Whitehead, 1994). The psychological concept of *social support* is ubiquitous in the health psychology literature, yet there is little agreement among researchers about exactly how it should be defined and measured (see, for example, Barrera, 1981; Brandt & Weinert, 1981; Cohen & Syme, 1985; Heitzmann & Kaplan, 1988; Norbeck et al., 1981; Procidano & Heller, 1983; Sallis et al., 1987; Sarason et al., 1983). In somewhat similar fashion, the measurement of variables related to obesity (Foreyt, 1987), alcoholism (Miller et al., 1991), pain (Melzack & Wall, 1982; Mikail et al., 1993; Turk & Rudy, 1986), and arthritis (Liang et al., 1988; Meenan & Pincus, 1987) have also proven a bit more complicated than one might expect.

Many tests useful in health psychology research may also be useful in clinical and counseling contexts. For example, the Cocaine Expectancy Questionnaire (Jaffe & Kilbey, 1994) was developed on the basis of interviews with adult cocaine users and a review of the relevant literature. To the degree that it can yield insights about a testtaker's expectancies associated with cocaine use, it may be useful in helping a therapist influence the client's decisions to initiate use, continue use, or terminate use. Another relatively new instrument, the Condom Attitude Scale—Adolescent Version, is reprinted in Table 14–6. How might you envision that scale being used in clinical or counseling contexts?

The Psychological Report

A critical component of any testing or assessment procedure is the reporting of the findings. The high reliability or validity of a test or assessment procedure may be "cast to the wind" if the assessment report is not written in an organized and readable fashion. Of course, what constitutes an "organized" and "readable" report will vary as a function of the goal of the assessment and the audience for whom the report is intended; a psychoanalyst's report exploring a patient's unresolved Oedipal conflict designed for presentation to the New York Psychoanalytic Society will look and sound very different from a school psychologist's report to a teacher concerning a child's learning disability. Reports differ in the extent to which they rely on one or another assessment procedure. Of course, reports also are written and used in widely different settings; although we will be focusing our attention on the writing of clinical reports, it should be clear that report writing is a skill necessary for educational, industrial/organizational, and other settings where psychological assessment takes place.

Writing the Clinical Report

Because there is no one universally accepted style or form for psychological report writing, most assessors develop a style and form that they believe best suits the goal of the assessment. In their comprehensive review of clinical report-writing styles and forms, Hammond and Allen (1953) noted that reports differ widely in the extent to which they focus on specific referral questions and on the data derived from tests; they also differ in the extent to which they rely on particular theories of personality. Generally, however, most clinical reports of psychological evaluation contain, at a minimum, the following elements: demographic data, reason for referral, findings, recommendations, and summary (see the box on pages 559–560).

Now that we've specified some of the types of material that belong in the clinical report, we proceed to outline some of the types of material that have no place in it. Here we are referring to what psychologists call "the Barnum effect."

Table 14–6
Condom Attitude Scale—Adolescent Version

In an effort to learn more about the attitudes of adolescents toward condoms, Janet St. Lawrence and her colleagues (1994) modified an existing scale (Sacco et al., 1991) to create the scale that follows.

1. Using a condom takes the "wonder" out of sex. (R)
2. I am concerned about catching AIDS or some other sexually transmitted disease.
3. A condom is not necessary when you and your partner agree not to have sex with anyone else. (R)
4. Condoms are messy. (R)
5. A condom is not necessary if you know your partner. (R)
6. Using condoms shows my partner I care about him/her.
7. A condom is not necessary if you're pretty sure the other person doesn't have a sexually transmitted disease. (R)
8. If I'm not careful, I could catch a sexually transmitted disease.
9. I wouldn't use a condom if my partner refused. (R)
10. People who carry condoms would have sex with anyone. (R)
11. I wouldn't mind if my partner brought up the idea of using a condom.
12. Condoms create a sense of safety.
13. People who use condoms sleep around a lot. (R)
14. If I'm not careful, I could catch AIDS.
15. Condoms take away the pleasure of sex. (R)
16. If my partner suggested using a condom, I would respect him or her.
17. Other people should respect my desire to use a condom.
18. I worry that I could catch a sexually transmitted disease.
19. If my partner suggested using a condom, I would feel relieved.
20. People who carry condoms are just looking for sex. (R)
21. A condom is not necessary when you are with the same partner for a long time. (R)
22. If my partner suggested using a condom, I would think he/she was only being cautious.
23. Condoms protect against sexually transmitted diseases.

Note: Items marked with (R) are reverse scored. *Source:* Sacco et al. (1991).

The Barnum Effect

The showman P. T. Barnum is credited with the quote "There's a sucker born every minute." Psychologists, among others, have taken P. T. Barnum's words about the widespread gullibility of people quite seriously. In fact, *Barnum effect* is a term that should be familiar to any psychologist called on to write a psychological report. Before reading on to find out exactly what the Barnum effect is, imagine that you have just completed a computerized personality test and that the printout describing the results reads as follows:

> You have a strong need for other people to like you and for them to admire you. You have a tendency to be critical of yourself. You have a great deal of unused capacity which you have not turned to your advantage. While you have some personality weaknesses, you are generally able to compensate for them. Your

sexual adjustment has presented some problems for you. Disciplined and controlled on the outside, you tend to be worrisome and insecure inside. At times you have serious doubts as to whether you have made the right decision or done the right thing. You prefer a certain amount of change and variety and become dissatisfied when hemmed in by restrictions and limitations. You pride yourself as being an independent thinker and do not accept others' opinions without satisfactory proof. You have found it unwise to be too frank in revealing yourself to others. At times you are extraverted, affable, and sociable while at other times you are introverted, wary, and reserved. Some of your aspirations tend to be pretty unrealistic.

Still imagining that the preceding test results had been formulated specifically for you, please rate the accuracy of the description as it does or does not apply to you personally.

I feel that the interpretation was:
_____ Excellent
_____ Good
_____ Average
_____ Poor
_____ Very Poor

Now that you have completed the exercise we can say, "Welcome to the ranks of those who have been subject to the Barnum effect." This psychological profile is, as you no doubt have noticed, vague and general. The same paragraph (sometimes with slight modifications) has been used in a number of psychological studies (Forer, 1949; Jackson et al., 1982; Merrens & Richards, 1970; Sundberg, 1955; Ulrich et al., 1963), with similar findings: *People tend to accept vague and general personality descriptions as uniquely applicable to themselves without realizing that the same description could be applied to just about anyone.*

The finding that people tend to accept vague personality descriptions as accurate descriptions of themselves came to be known as "The Barnum Effect" after psychologist Paul Meehl's (1956) condemnation of "personality description after the manner of P. T. Barnum."[3] Meehl suggested that the term *Barnum effect* be used "to stigmatize those pseudo-successful clinical procedures in which personality descriptions from tests are made to fit the patient largely or wholly by virtue of their triviality." Tallent (1958) made a related observation. Deploring the generality and vagueness that seemed to plague too many psychological reports, Tallent wrote:

> Quite similar to the Barnum phenomenon is what might be called the *Aunt Fanny description* in clinical reports. Superfluous statements, such as, "This client had difficulty in performing at optimal capacity when under stress," or "The client has unconscious hostile urges" might readily prompt the report reader to think "so has my Aunt Fanny!"

---

3. Meehl credited D. G. Patterson with having first used the term *Barnum effect.*

Elements of a Typical Report of Psychological Assessment

Demographic Data

Included here are all or some of the following: the patient's name, address, telephone number, education, occupation, religion, marital status, date of birth, place of birth, ethnic membership, citizenship, date of testing. The examiner's name must also be considered part of the identifying material in the report.

Reason for Referral

Why was this patient referred for psychological assessment? This section of the report may sometimes be as short as one sentence (for example, "Johnny was referred for evaluation to shed light on the question of whether his inattention in class is due to personality, neurological, or other difficulties"). Alternatively, this section of the report may be extended with all relevant background information (for example, "Johnny complained of hearing difficulties in his fourth-grade class according to a note in his records"). If all relevant background information is not covered in the "Reason for Referral" section of the report, it may be covered in a separate section labeled "Background" or in a section labeled "Findings."

Tests Administered

Here the examiner simply lists the names of the tests that were administered. Thus, for example, this section of the report may be as brief as the following:

Wechsler Intelligence Scale for Children—Revised (1/8/90; 1/12/90)

Bender Visual-Motor Gestalt Test (1/8/90)

Rorschach Test (1/12/90)

Thematic Apperception Test (1/12/90)

Sentence Completion Test (1/8/90)

Figure drawings (1/8/90)

Note that the date of the test administration has been inserted next to the name of each test administered.

This is a good idea under any circumstances and particularly important if testing was executed over the course of a number of days, weeks, or longer. In the sample section above, it will be noted that the WISC-R was administered over the course of two testing sessions on two days (1/8/90 and 1/12/90), that the Bender, the Sentence Completion Test, and figure drawings were administered on 1/8/90, and that the Rorschach and the Thematic Apperception Test were administered on 1/12/90.

Also in this section, the examiner might place the names and the dates of tests known to have been previously administered to the examinee. If the examiner has a record of the findings (or better yet, the original test protocols) from this prior testing, this information may be integrated into the next section of the report, "Findings."

Findings

Here the examiner reports not only findings (for example, "On the WISC-R Johnny achieved a Verbal IQ of 100, a Performance IQ of 110, yielding a full-scale IQ of 106") but also all extra-test considerations, such as observations concerning the examinee's motivation (for instance, "the examinee did/did not appear to be motivated to do well on the tests"), the examinee's level of fatigue, the nature of the relationship and rapport with the examiner, indices of anxiety, and method of approach to the task. The section labeled "Findings" may begin with a description of the examinee that is detailed enough for the reader of the report to almost visualize him or her. For example:

John is a 20-year-old college student with brown, shoulder-length, stringy hair and a full beard. He came to the testing wearing a "psychedelic" shirt, cut-off and ragged shorts, and sandals. He sat slouched in his chair for most of the test session, tended to speak only when spoken to, and spoke in a slow, lethargic manner.

(continued)

Elements of a Typical Report of Psychological Assessment *(continued)*

Also included in this section is mention of any extraneous variables that might in some way have affected the test results. Was testing in a school interrupted by any event such as a fire drill, an earth tremor, or some other disturbance? Did loud or atypical noise in or out of the test site affect the testtaker's concentration? Did the hospitalized patient receive any visitors just before an evaluation, and could such a visit have affected the findings? Answers to these types of questions may prove invaluable in interpreting assessment data.

The "Findings" section of the report is where all the background material, behavioral observations, and test data are integrated to provide an answer to the referral question. Whether or not the examiner makes reference to the actual test data is a matter of personal preference. Thus, for example, one examiner might simply state, "There is evidence of neurological deficit in this record" and stop there. Another examiner would document exactly why this was being asserted: "There is evidence of neurological deficit as indicated by the rotation and preservation errors in the Bender-Gestalt record. Further, on the TAT, this examinee failed to grasp the situation as a whole and simply enumerated single details. Additionally, this examinee had difficulty abstracting—still another index of neu-

rological deficit—as evidenced by the unusually low score on the WAIS Similarities subtest." The findings section should logically lead into the "Recommendations" section.

Recommendations

On the basis of the psychological assessment, with particular attention to factors such as the personal aspects and deficiencies of the examinee, recommendations addressed to ameliorating the presenting problem are given. The recommendation may be for psychotherapy, a consultation with a neurologist, placement in a special class, short-term family therapy addressed to a specific problem—whatever the examiner believes is required to ameliorate the situation is spelled out here.

Summary

The summary section includes in "short form" a statement concerning the reason for referral, the findings, and the recommendation. This section is usually only a paragraph or two, and it should provide a concise and succinct statement of who the examinee is, why the examinee was referred for testing, what was found, and what needs to be done.

The "Barnum" or "Aunt Fanny" effect has been the subject of numerous research studies. In one study conducted by Ulrich, Stachnick, and Stainton (1963), 57 college students were given two personality tests by their psychology instructor, who promised to score the tests and have the results back to each individual student at a later date. One week later, all students were given the identical personality description—the one that appears earlier in this section—though the descriptions were arranged in different orders. The students were asked to rate the interpretations as excellent, good, average, poor, or very poor and to make any additional comments. The ratings were as follows:

Excellent	27
Good	26
Average	3
Poor	1
Very Poor	0

Some of the comments made by the students were:

> I feel that you have done a fine job with the material which you had to work with. I agree with almost all of your statements and think they answer the problems I may have.

> On the nose! Very good. I wish you had said more, all you did mention was all true without a doubt. I wish you could go further into this personality sometime.

> The results have brought out several points which have worried me because I was not sure if I had imagined these to be personality traits of mine. Tests like this could be valuable to an individual in helping him to solve some of his own problems.

In a follow-up study executed by these same researchers, 79 other college students were shown how to administer two personality tests (the same tests that had been administered by the instructor in the first experiment). The students were then asked to play the role of test examiner and to use as an examinee any one available person, such as a roommate or a neighbor. At the completion of the test administration, the student examiner would tell the examinee that the test would be scored and returned with an interpretation. The "interpretation" was the same as in the prior study, and once again the ratings of its applicability were quite high:

Excellent	29
Good	30
Average	15
Poor	5
Very Poor	0

Some of the comments made by the examinees on the accuracy of the student examiners' "results" were as follows:

> I believe this interpretation applied to me individually, as there are too many facets which fit me too well to be a generalization.

> The interpretation is surprisingly accurate and specific in description. I shall take note of many of the things said.

> I feel that the interpretation does apply to me individually. For the first time things I have been vaguely aware of have been put into concise and constructive statements which I would like to use as a plan for improving myself.

> It appears to me that the results of this test are unbelievably close to the truth. For a short test of this type, I was expecting large generalizations for results, but this was not the case; and I give all the credit to the examiner whose conclusions were well calculated.

It can be seen that even in a situation in which nonexperienced, student examiners were involved, 59 of the 79 examinees rated the generalized interpretation as excellent or good. In reviewing the surprising results of their experiments, Ulrich and his collaborators concluded that the persons given the phony test interpretations were not only "taken in" by the interpretations but also "very likely to praise highly the examiner on his conclusions."

Other research serves to underscore just how powerful the Barnum effect can be. In one study, students were unable to select their actual personal description when it was paired with a generalized description (Sundberg, 1955). In another, students preferred a generalized interpretation to an interpretation written on the basis of their actual psychological test scores (Merrens & Richards, 1970). The effect has since been explored with reference to situational variables (Hinrichsen & Bradley, 1974; Snyder & Shenkel, 1976; Snyder et al., 1977) such as the prestige of the diagnostician (Bradley & Bradley, 1977; Dmitruk et al., 1973; Halperin et al., 1976; Snyder & Larson, 1972), the sex of the diagnostician (Zeren & Bradley, 1982), the number of assessees (Snyder & Newburg, 1981), and the type of assessment instrument used (Snyder, 1974; Weinberger & Bradley, 1980). Cognizance of this effect and the factors that may heighten or diminish it is necessary if psychological assessors are to avoid making interpretations "in the manner of P. T. Barnum."

15

Neuropsychological Assessment

Modern-day investigators exploring the link between the brain and the body use a number of varied tools and procedures in their work, including laboratory testing and field observation of head-trauma victims, experimentation involving the electrical or chemical stimulation of various human and animal brain sites, experimental lesioning of the brain of animal subjects, and autopsies of normal and abnormal human and animal subjects.

The branch of medicine that focuses on the nervous system and its disorders is *neurology*. The branch of psychology that focuses on the relationship between brain functioning and behavior is *neuropsychology*. Formerly a specialty area within clinical psychology, neuropsychology has evolved into a specialty in its own right in recent years. Psychologists doing routine clinical evaluations are trained to screen for signs and symptoms of neurological deficit. Such signs or symptoms may present themselves during history taking (for example, the examinee reports a fall in which consciousness was lost for a few minutes), interviewing (the examinee complains of severe, long-lasting headaches), or testtaking (involuntary movements are observed); signs may also be evident in data derived from an intelligence test (such as a large discrepancy between measured verbal and performance IQ) or other tests. If, on the basis of such signs, neurological deficit is suspected, the examinee will be referred to a neurologist or a neuropsychologist for further evaluation. Succinctly put, the objective of the typical neuropsychological evaluation is "to draw inferences about the structural and functional characteristics of a person's brain by evaluating an individual's behavior in defined stimulus-response situations" (Benton, 1994, p. 1).

Research conducted with various tools of neuropsychological assessment is wide-ranging. One active area of study has to do with determining the effects of various medical and environmental conditions on neuropsychological integrity. Representative of research in this area are studies that have explored the neuropsychological consequences of prenatal brain damage (Dennis & Barnes, 1994), diabetes (Diabetes Control and Complications Trial Research Group, 1994), HIV infection (Iragui et al., 1994), Parkinson's disease (Appollonio et al., 1994), and exposure to industrial chemicals (Reidy & Bolter, 1994). Other neuropsychological researchers have used instruments of assessment to investigate questions related to the cognitive skills of older airplane pilots (Salive, 1994), the detection of malingering (Rawling & Coffey, 1994), the prediction of memory loss in response to a traumatic injury (Forrester et al., 1994), and the effect of failing eyesight in the taking of neuropsychological tests (Kempen et al., 1994). Even from this relatively small sampling of research studies, one might correctly conclude that neuropsychological research can be conducted with people at all stages of the lifespan, and in diverse settings and contexts.

In this chapter, we survey some of the tools used by clinicians and neuropsychologists to screen for and diagnose neurological disorders. We begin with a brief introduction to neuroanatomy and brain-behavior relationships. This material is presented to help lay a foundation for appreciating how testtaking (as well as other) behavior can be evaluated to form hypotheses about the level of intactness or functioning in various parts of the brain.

The Nervous System and Behavior

The nervous system is composed of various kinds of *neurons* (nerve cells) and can be divided into the *central* nervous system (consisting of the brain and the spinal cord) and the *peripheral* nervous system (consisting of the neurons that convey messages to and from the rest of the body). Viewed from the top, the large, rounded portion of the brain called the cerebrum can be divided into two sections or hemispheres (see Figure 15–1). This mass appears gray, since mixtures of capillary blood vessels and cell bodies of neurons have a gray brown color. Connecting the left and right hemispheres is a band of nerve fibers called the *corpus callosum.* Much of the surface of the cerebral hemispheres constitutes what is called the cerebral *cortex* (from the Latin meaning "bark, shell, rind," or outer layer). The cortex appears wrinkled because of the many clefts or indentations in its surface. A cleft is technically referred to as a *fissure* or a *sulcus,* depending on its depth (fissures are deeper than sulci), and the ridge between the depression is called a *gyrus* (the plural is *gyri*). Fissures divide each cerebral hemisphere into four areas referred to as *lobes:* the frontal, temporal, occipital, and parietal lobes. Just beneath the corpus callosum, at the approximate center of the brain, lies a group of nuclei called the *thalamus,* and below that lies another group of nuclei called the *hypothalamus* ("hypo" meaning "below"). The thalamus and the hypothalamus are actually part of the structure called the brain stem, which connects the brain to the spinal cord. Also part of the brain stem, just above the spinal cord, is a mass of nuclei and fibers called the *reticular formation.*

Some brain–behavior correlates are summarized in Table 15–1. In Figure 15–2, we see the projection of sensory information onto the somatosensory area

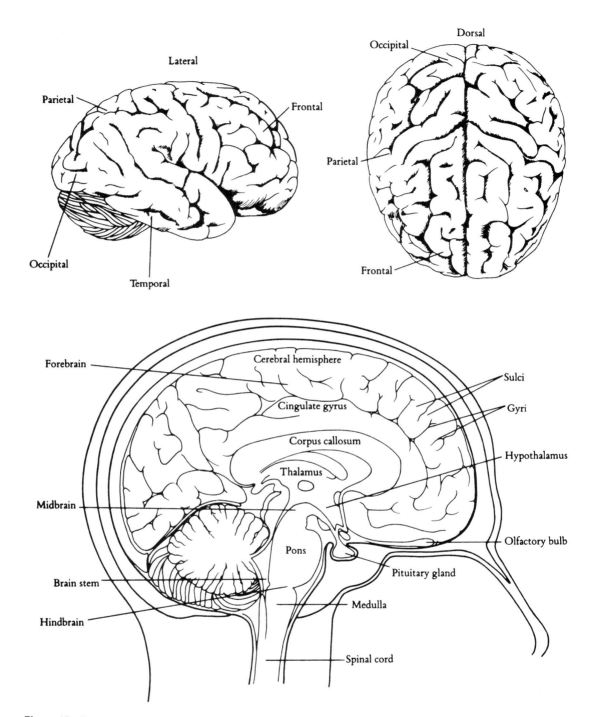

Figure 15–1
The Human Brain from Three Perspectives

Table 15–1
Some Brain–Behavior Characteristics for Selected Nervous System Sites

Site	Characteristic
Temporal lobes	These lobes contain auditory reception areas as well as certain areas for the processing of visual information. Damage to the temporal lobe may affect sound discrimination, recognition, and comprehension; music appreciation; voice recognition; and auditory or visual memory storage.
Occipital lobes	These lobes contain visual reception areas. Damage to this area could result in blindness to all or part of the visual field or deficits in object recognition, visual scanning, visual integration of symbols into wholes, and recall of visual imagery.
Parietal lobes	These lobes contain reception areas for the sense of touch and for the sense of bodily position. Damage to this area may result in deficits in the sense of touch, disorganization, and distorted self-perception.
Frontal lobes	These lobes are integrally involved in ordering information and sorting out stimuli. Concentration and attention, abstract-thinking ability, concept-formation ability, foresight, problem-solving ability, speech, as well as gross and fine motor ability may be affected by damage to the frontal lobes.
Thalamus	The thalamus is a kind of communications relay station for all sensory information being transmitted to the cerebral cortex. Damage to the thalamus may result in altered states of arousal, memory defects, speech deficits, apathy, and disorientation.
Hypothalamus	The hypothalamus is involved in the regulation of bodily functions such as eating, drinking, body temperature, sexual behavior, and emotion. It is sensitive to changes in environment that call for a "fight or flight" response from the organism. Damage to it may elicit a variety of symptoms ranging from uncontrolled eating or drinking to mild alterations of mood states.
Cerebellum	Together with the pons (another brain site in the area of the brain referred to as the hindbrain), the cerebellum is involved in the regulation of balance, breathing, and posture—among other functions. Damage to the cerebellum may manifest itself as problems in fine motor control and coordination.
Reticular formation	In the core of the brain stem, the reticular formation contains fibers en route to and from the cortex. Because stimulation to this area can cause a sleeping organism to awaken and cause an awake organism to become even more alert, it is sometimes referred to as the *reticular activating system*. Damage to this area can cause the organism to sleep for long periods of time.
Limbic system	Composed of the amygdala, the cingulate cortex, the hippocampus, and the septal areas of the brain, the limbic system is integral to the expression of emotions. Damage to this area may profoundly affect emotional behavior.
Spinal cord	Many reflexes necessary for survival (such as withdrawing from a hot surface) are carried out at the level of the spinal cord. In addition to its role in reflex activity, the spinal cord is integral to the coordination of motor movements. Spinal cord injuries may result in various degrees of paralysis or other motor difficulties.

of the brain and the corresponding motor areas. Note that each of the two cerebral hemispheres receives sensory information from the opposite side of the body and also controls motor responses on the opposite side of the body—a phenomenon called *contralateral control*. It is due to the brain's contralateral control of the body that an injury to the right side of the brain may result in sensory and/or motor defects on the left side of the body. The "meeting ground" of the two hemispheres is the corpus callosum, though one hemisphere, most frequently the left one, is dominant. It is because the left hemisphere is most frequently dominant that most people are right-handed. The dominant hemisphere dominates in activities such as reading, writing, arithmetic, and speech, and the nondominant hemisphere has as its forte tasks involving spatial and textural recognition as well as art and music appreciation. In the normal, neurologically intact individual, one hemisphere works to complement the other.

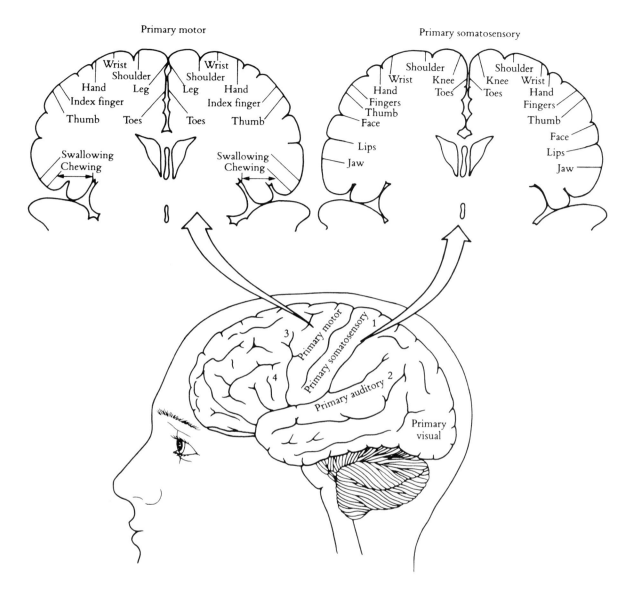

Figure 15–2
Cross-Sections of Two Areas of the Brain

Cross-sections of the primary motor and somatosensory areas of the brain are pictured. Although it is not clear from the illustration, the amount of space that a body area has represented in the cortex is determined by the degree of fine motor control associated with that body area, not by its size. Thus, for example, the fingers have far greater representation on the motor cortex than does the trunk. The lips are given a great amount of representation on the somatosensory cortex.

Neurological Damage and the Concept of "Organicity"

Neurological damage may take the form of a *lesion* in the brain or any other site within the central or peripheral nervous system. A lesion is a pathological alteration of tissue, such as that which could result from injury or infection. Neurological lesions may be physical or chemical in nature, and they may be focal (relatively circumscribed at one site) or diffuse (scattered at various sites). Since different sites of the brain control various functions, focal and diffuse lesions at different sites will manifest themselves in varying behavioral deficits. A partial listing of the technical names for the many varieties of sensory and motor deficits appears in Table 15–2.

Note that a focal lesion may have what could be referred to as diffuse ramifications with regard to behavioral deficits (that is, a circumscribed lesion in one area of the brain may affect many different kinds of behaviors). Conversely, it is possible that a diffuse lesion may affect one or more areas of functioning so severely that it masquerades as a focal lesion. In a sense, the neuropsychologist works backwards—examining behavior by means of a variety of tests and procedures and trying to determine from the pattern of findings where a neurological lesion, if any, exists. Neuropsychological assessment also plays a critical role in determining the extent of behavioral impairment that has occurred or can be expected to occur because of a neurological disorder. Such information is useful not only in designing remediation programs but also in assessing the consequences of drug treatments, physical training, and other therapy.

The terms "brain damage," "neurological damage," and "organicity" have, unfortunately, been used interchangeably in much of the psychological literature. The term *neurological damage* is most all-inclusive, since it covers not only damage to the brain but also damage to the spinal cord and to all the components of the peripheral nervous system. *Organicity*, still a very popular term with clinicians, derives from the post–World War I research of the German neurologist Kurt Goldstein. Studies of brain-injured soldiers led Goldstein to the conclusion that the factors differentiating organically impaired individuals ("organics" for short) from normals included the loss of abstraction ability, deficits in reasoning ability, and inflexibility in problem-solving tasks. Accordingly, Goldstein (1927, 1939, 1963a) and his colleagues developed psychological tests that tapped these factors and were designed to help in the diagnosis of organic brain syndrome, or "organicity" for short. Some of these tests are illustrated in Figure 15–3.

In the tradition of Goldstein and his associates, two German psychologists, Heinz Werner and Alfred Strauss, examined brain–behavior correlates in brain-injured, mentally retarded children (Werner & Strauss, 1941; see also Strauss & Lehtinen, 1947). Like their predecessors who had worked with brain-injured adults, these investigators attempted to delineate characteristics common to *all* brain-injured people, including children. Although such work led to a better understanding of the behavioral consequences of brain injury in children, one unfortunate consequence was that a unitary picture of brain injury emerged; all "organic" children were presumed to share a similar pattern of cognitive, behavioral, sensory, and motor deficits—regardless of the specific nature or site

Table 15–2

Technical Names for Various Kinds of Sensory and Motor Deficits

Name	Description of Deficit
Acalculia	Inability to perform arithmetic calculations
Acopia	Inability to copy geometric designs
Agnosia	Deficit in recognizing sensory stimuli (for example, *auditory agnosia* is a difficulty in recognizing auditory stimuli)
Agraphia	Deficit in writing ability
Akinesia	Deficit in motor movements
Alexia	Inability to read
Amnesia	Loss of memory
Amusia	Deficit in ability to produce or appreciate music
Anomia	Deficit associated with finding words to name things
Anopia	Deficit in sight
Anosmia	Deficit in the sense of smell
Aphasia	Deficit in communication due to impaired speech or writing ability
Apraxia	Voluntary movement disorder in the absence of paralysis
Ataxia	Deficit in motor ability and muscular coordination

of their impairment. The unitary concept of "organicity" prevailed through the 1950s. Toward the end of that time, researchers such as Birch and Diller (1959) began to complain about what they termed the "naivete of the concept of 'organicity'":

> It is abundantly clear that "brain damage" and "organicity" are terms which though overlapping are not identities and serve to designate interdependent events. "Brain-damage" refers to the fact of an anatomical destruction, whereas "organicity" represents one of the varieties of functional consequences which may attend such destruction. (p. 195)

Through the 1960s, a number of researchers echoed the view that "organicity" and "brain damage" should not be viewed as unitary in nature and that no one set of behavioral characteristics can be applied to all brain-injured persons. Thus, for example, Haynes and Sells (1963) observed that "both native practice and the overwhelming bulk of published research appear to accept the term brain damage as a unitary diagnostic entity, although the predominant evidence indicates that it represents a complex and multifaceted category" (p. 316). The conceptualization of "organicity" and "brain damage" as nonunitary in nature was supported by a number of observations, which are summarized in Table 15–3.

The Neuropsychological Examination

The tests and other procedures employed in a neuropsychological examination will vary as a function of several factors—such as the purpose of the examination, the neurological intactness of the examinee, and the thoroughness of the

Figure 15–3
The Goldstein-Scheerer Tests of Abstract and Concrete Thinking

(a) *The Stick Test is a measure of recent memory. The subject's task is to reproduce designs from memory using sticks.* **(b)** *The Cube Test challenges the subject to replicate with blocks a design printed in a booklet. This subtest was the predecessor of the Block Design task on Wechsler intelligence tests. It is used as a measure of nonverbal abstraction ability.* **(c)** *The Color-Form Sorting Test contains 12 objects, including 4 triangles, 4 circles, and 4 squares (each piece in one of four colors). The objects are presented in a random order, and the subject is instructed to sort according to which belong together. Once they are sorted, the subject is next asked to sort the objects a different way. The subject's flexibility in shifting from one sorting principle to another is noted.* **(d)** *The Object Sorting Test consists of 89 objects, which the subject is required to group. Concrete thinking and organic impairment may be inferred if the subject sorts, for example, by color instead of function.* **(e)** *The Color Sorting Test employs several woolen skeins of varying colors. The task here is to sort the skeins according to a sample sketch displayed by the examiner.*

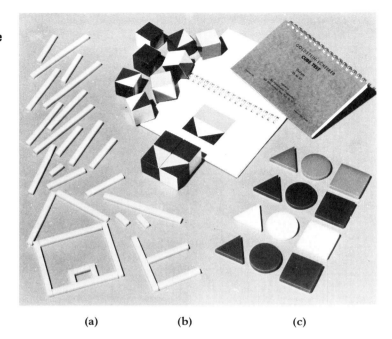

(a)   (b)   (c)

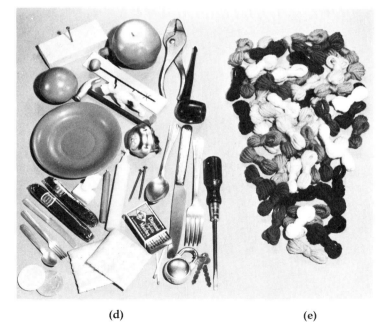

(d)   (e)

Table 15-3
Evidence for the Nonunitary Nature of Organicity

Persons who have identical lesions in the brain may exhibit markedly different symptoms. Reed, Reitan, and Klove (1965) have observed that "behavior deficits associated with cerebral lesions in children may be quite different from the ability losses typically demonstrated by brain-damaged adults" (p. 250). In a similar vein, Pincus and Tucker (1974) noted that "large unilateral injuries in infants . . . tend to produce a more widespread deficit in intellectual abilities than similar injuries in adults" (pp. 123–124).

Many interacting factors such as the patient's premorbid functioning, the site and diffuseness of the lesion, the cause of the lesion and its rate of spread may make one "organic" appear quite dissimilar clinically from another (Goldfried et al., 1971; Reitan & Davison, 1974; Smith, 1962).

Considerable similarity may exist in the symptoms exhibited by persons who have entirely different types of lesions. Further, these different types of lesions may arise from a variety of causes, such as trauma with or without loss of consciousness, infection, nutritional deficiencies, tumor, stroke, neuronal degeneration, toxins, insufficient cardiac output, and a variety of metabolic disturbances. (Many conditions that are not due to brain damage produce symptoms that mimic those produced by brain damage. For example, an individual who is psychotic, depressed, or simply fatigued may produce data on an examination for organic brain damage that is characteristically diagnostic of neuropsychological impairment.)

Factors other than brain damage (such as psychosis, depression, fatigue) influence the responses of brain-damaged persons. Some types of responses are consequences (rather than correlates) of the brain damage. For example, if brain-injured children as a group tend to be described as more "aggressive" than normals, this may reflect more on the way such children have been treated by parents, teachers, and peers than on the effect of any lesions per se. Conversely, persons who are in fact brain-damaged are sometimes able to compensate for their deficits to such an extent that some functions are actually taken over by other, more intact parts of the brain.

---

examination. In a sense, any routine administration of a battery of psychological tests within a clinical setting can also serve the purpose of neuropsychological screening; in the course of intelligence testing, personality testing, or other psychological testing, the clinician may be alerted to suspicious findings signaling that a more in-depth neuropsychological examination should be conducted. Sometimes a patient is referred to a psychologist for screening for neurological problems; in such a case, a battery of tests will be administered—consisting, at a minimum, of an intelligence test, a personality test, and a perceptual-motor/memory test.[1] If neurological signs are discovered in the course of the evaluation, the examinee will be referred for further and more detailed evaluation.

In addition to general screening purposes, an individual might be referred for an in-depth neuropsychological evaluation because of the nature of the presenting problem (such as memory impairment). A neuropsychological examination might be ordered by a neurologist who seeks to find out more about the site of a suspected or known lesion. A neurologist's referral note to a neuropsychologist in such an instance might read:

---

1. We have listed here what we believe to be the minimum amount of testing for an adequate neuropsychological screening. It is, however, not uncommon for some clinicians to administer only a perceptual-motor/memory test such as the Bender Visual Motor Gestalt test as a screening device. In the light of strong cautions against such practices (see, for example, Bigler & Ehrenfurth, 1981), some have stated flatly that the singular use of such a test "could certainly be considered negligent" (Kahn & Taft, 1983, p. 79).

My examination was negative but I feel I might be missing something. This patient did have a head injury about six months ago and he still complains of headaches and slight memory problems for recent events. I found no hard signs, some soft signs such as a right hand tremor (possibly due to anxiety), and a pattern of findings on laboratory tests ranging from negative to equivocal. Please evaluate this patient and let me know whether you find the headaches and other vague complaints to be organic or functional in origin.[2]

In addition to asking whether any observed deficits are organic (physically based) or functional (psychologically based), the referral note might also ask the neuropsychologist other kinds of questions, such as: Is this condition acute or chronic? Is the damage focal (local in one area) or diffuse (present in a number of areas)? Will there be progressive deterioration? Is this individual ready to go back to school or work? What skills require remediation?

The neuropsychological examination will vary widely as a function of the nature of the referral question. In contrast to referral questions concerning the location and nature of suspected lesions, for example, questions concerning the functional or organic origin of observed behavior will require more in-depth examination of personality and psychiatric history.

The content and nature of the examination will also vary as a function of the neurological intactness of the assessee. Neuropsychologists have occasion to assess persons exhibiting a wide range of physical and psychological disabilities. Some, for example, have known visual or auditory deficits, concentration and attention problems, speech and language difficulties, and so forth. Allowance must be made for such deficits and a way must be found to administer the appropriate tests in such a way that meaningful results can be obtained. Frequently, neuropsychologists will administer preliminary visual, auditory, and other such examinations to ascertain the gross intactness of sensory and motor functioning before proceeding with more specialized tests. An olfactory (sense of smell) deficit, for example, may be symptomatic of a great variety of neurological and nonneurological problems as diverse as Alzheimer's disease (Serby et al., 1991), Parkinson's disease (Serby et al., 1985), and AIDS (Brody et al., 1991). The discovery of such a deficit by means of a test such as the University of Pennsylvania Smell Identification Test (Doty et al., 1984) would be a stimulus for continued diagnostic assessment.

Common to all thorough neuropsychological examinations is a history taking, a mental status examination, and the administration of tests and procedures designed to uncover any problems with respect to neuropsychological functioning. Throughout the examination, the neuropsychologist's knowledge of neuroanatomy, neurochemistry, and neurophysiology will be essential for optimal interpretation of the data gathered. In addition to guiding decisions concerning what to test for and how to test for it, such knowledge will also come into play

2. In the jargon of neuropsychological assessment, a *hard sign* may be defined as an indicator of definite neurological deficit (for example, abnormal reflex performance). Hard signs may be contrasted with *soft signs,* which are suggestive of neurological deficit but not necessarily indicative of such deficit (for example, a 15-point discrepancy between the verbal and performance scales on a Wechsler intelligence test).

with respect to the decisions concerning *when* to test. Thus, for example, it would be atypical for a neuropsychologist to psychologically test a stroke victim immediately after the stroke occurred. Because some recovery of function could be expected to spontaneously occur in the weeks and months following the stroke, testing the patient immediately after the stroke would therefore yield an erroneous picture of the extent of the damage.

The History

The typical neuropsychological examination begins with a careful history taking. Areas that will be of interest to the examiner include the following:

- The medical history of the patient.

- The medical history of the patient's immediate family and other relatives. A sample question here might be "Have you or any of your relatives experienced dizziness, fainting, blackouts, or spasms?"

- The presence or absence of certain developmental milestones; a particularly critical part of the history-taking process when examining young children. A listing of some of these milestones appears in Table 15–4.

- Psychosocial history, including level of academic achievement and estimated level of intelligence; an estimated level of adjustment at home and at work or school; observations regarding personality (for example, is this individual hypochondriacal?), thought processes, and motivation (is this person willing and able to respond accurately to these questions?).

- The character, severity, and progress of any history of complaints involving disturbances in sight, hearing, smell, touch, taste, or balance; disturbances in muscle tone, muscle strength, and muscle movement; disturbances in autonomic functions such as breathing, eliminating, and body temperature control; disturbances in speech; disturbances in thought and memory; pain (particularly headache and facial pain); and various types of thought disturbances.

A careful history is critical to the accuracy of the assessment. Consider, for example, a patient who exhibits flat affect, is listless, and seems not even to know what day it is or what time of day it is. Such an individual might be suffering from something neurological in origin (such as a dementia); however, a functional disorder (such as severe depression) might instead be causing the problem. A good history taking will shed light on the answer to the referral question of whether the observed behavior is the result of a genuine dementia or a product of what is referred to as a pseudodementia. History-taking questions might include the following: How long has the patient been in this condition and what emotional or neurological trauma may have precipitated it? Does this patient have a personal or family history of depression or other psychiatric disturbance? What factors appear to be operating to maintain the patient in this state? Whether the disorder is organic or functional in origin, the history will also shed light on questions relative to its progressive or nonprogressive nature.

Table 15–4
Some Developmental Milestones

Age	Development
16 weeks	Gets excited, laughs aloud Spontaneous smile in response to people Anticipates eating at sight of food Sits propped for 10 to 15 minutes
28 weeks	Smiles and vocalizes to a mirror and pats at mirror image Many vowel sounds Sits unsupported for brief period and then leans on hands Takes solids well When lying on back, places feet to mouth Grasps objects and transfers objects from hand to hand When held standing, supports most of weight
12 months	Walks with only one hand held Says "mamma" and "dada" and perhaps two other "words" Gives a toy in response to a request or gesture When being dressed, will cooperate Plays "peek-a-boo" games
18 months	Has a vocabulary of some ten words Walks well, seldom falls, can run stiffly Looks at pictures in a book Feeds self, although spills Can pull a toy or hug a doll Can seat self in a small or adult chair Scribbles spontaneously with a crayon or pencil
24 months	Walks up and down stairs alone Runs well, no falling Can build a tower of six or seven blocks Uses personal pronouns ("I" and "you") and speaks a three-word sentence Identifies simple pictures by name and calls self by name Verbalizes needs fairly consistently May be dry at night Can pull on simple garment
36 months	Alternates feet when climbing stairs and jumps from bottom stair Rides a tricycle Can copy a circle and imitate a cross with a crayon or pencil Comprehends and answers questions Feeds self with little spilling May know and repeat a few simple rhymes
48 months	Can dry and wash hands, brushes teeth Laces shoes, dresses and undresses with supervision Can play cooperatively with other children Can draw figure of a person with at least two clear body parts
60 months	Knows and names colors, counts to 10 Skips on both feet Can print a few letters, can draw identifiable pictures

Source: Gesell and Amatruda (1947)

The Neuropsychological Mental Status Examination

An outline for a general mental status examination was presented in Chapter 14. The neuropsychological mental status examination overlaps greatly with respect to questions concerning the assessee's consciousness, emotional state, thought content and clarity, memory, sensory perception, performance of action, language, speech, handwriting, and handedness. The mental status examination administered for the express purpose of evaluating neuropsychological functioning may delve more extensively into specific areas of interest. For example, during a routine mental status examination, the examiner might require the examinee to interpret the meaning of only one or two proverbs; on the neurological mental status examination, many proverbs may be presented to obtain a more comprehensive picture of the patient's capacity for abstract thought. Throughout the history taking and the mental status examination, the clinician will take note of gross and subtle observations pertinent to the evaluation. For example, the examiner will note the presence of involuntary movements (such as facial tics), locomotion difficulties, and other sensory and motor problems that may become apparent during the interview. The examiner may note, for example, that one corner of the mouth is slower to curl than the other when the patient smiles—a finding suggestive of damage to the seventh (facial) cranial nerve.

The Physical Examination

Most neuropsychologists do perform some kind of physical examination on patients, but the extent of this examination varies widely as a function of the expertise, competence, and confidence of the examiner. Some neuropsychologists have had, as part of their education, extensive training in performing physical examinations under the tutelage of neurologists in teaching hospitals. Such psychologists feel confident and competent in performing many of the same *noninvasive* procedures (procedures that do not involve any intrusion into the examinee's body) that neurologists perform as part of their neuropsychological examination. In the course of the following discussion, we list some of these noninvasive procedures. We precede this discussion with the caveat that it is the physician and not the neuropsychologist who is always the final arbiter of medical questions.

In addition to making observations about the examinee's appearance, the examiner may also physically examine the scalp and skull for any unusual enlargements or depressions. Muscles may be inspected for their tone (soft? rigid?), strength (weakness or tiredness?), and size relative to other muscles. With respect to the last point, the examiner might find, for example, that Ralph's right biceps are much larger than his left biceps. Such a finding could indicate muscular dystrophy in the left arm, but it also could be reflective of the fact that the patient has been working as a shoemaker for the last 40 years—a job in which he is constantly hammering with and building up the muscle in his right

Table 15-5
Sample Tests Used to Evaluate Muscle Coordination

Walking-running-skipping

If the examiner has not had a chance to watch the patient walk for any distance, he may ask the patient to do so as part of the examination. We tend to take walking for granted; but, neurologically speaking, it is a highly complex activity that involves proper integration of many varied components of the nervous system. Sometimes abnormalities in gait may be due to nonneurological causes; if, for example, a severe case of bunions is suspected as the cause of the difficulty, the examiner may ask the patient to remove his or her shoes and socks so that the feet may be physically inspected. Highly trained examiners are additionally sensitive to subtle abnormalities in, for example, arm movements while the patient walks, runs, or skips.

Standing-still (technically, the Romberg test)

The patient is asked to stand still with feet together, head erect, and eyes open. Whether patients have their arms extended straight out or at their sides and whether or not they are wearing shoes or other clothing will be a matter of the examiner's preference. Patients are next instructed to close their eyes. The critical variable is the amount of sway exhibited by the patient once the eyes are closed. Since normal persons may sway somewhat with their eyes closed, experience and training is required to determine when the amount of sway is indicative of pathology.

Nose-finger-nose

The patient's task here is to touch her nose with the tip of her index finger, then touch the examiner's finger, and then touch her own nose again. The sequence is repeated many times with each hand. This test, as well as many similar ones (such as the toe-finger test, the finger-nose test, the heel-knee test), are designed to assess, among other things, cerebellar functioning.

Finger wiggle

The examiner models finger wiggling (that is, playing an imaginary piano or typing), and then the patient is asked to wiggle his own fingers. Typically, the nondominant hand cannot be wiggled as quickly as the dominant hand, but it takes a trained eye to pick up a significant decrease in rate. The experienced examiner will also be looking for abnormalities in the precision of the movements and the rhythm of the movements, "mirror movements" (uncontrolled similar movements in the other hand when instructed to only wiggle one), and other abnormal involuntary movements. Like the nose-finger test, finger wiggling supplies information concerning the quality of involuntary movement and muscular coordination. A related task involves tongue wiggling.

---

arm. This patient's case serves to underscore the importance of careful history taking when evaluating physical findings. In addition to physical examination of the skull and the musculature, simple reflexes may be tested. *Reflexes* are involuntary motor responses to stimuli. Many reflexes have survival value for infants but then disappear as the child grows older. One such reflex is the mastication (chewing) reflex. Stroking the tongue or lips will elicit chewing behavior in the normal infant; however, if chewing is elicited in the older child or adult, it is indicative of neurological deficit. In addition to testing for the presence or absence of various reflexes, the examiner might examine muscle coordination by using tests such as those listed in Table 15-5.

A complete examination is designed to assess not only the functioning of the brain but aspects of the functioning of the nerves, muscles, and other organs and systems as well. Some procedures used to shed light on the adequacy and functioning of some of the 12 cranial nerves are summarized in Table 15-6. Needless to say, other more specific tests and procedures may be employed as the examiner sees fit. Additionally, medical practitioners have at their disposal a variety of sophisticated apparatuses and procedures to assist in the answering of diagnostic questions. Some of these diagnostic aids are illustrated in the *Close-up* for this chapter (see pages 578–579).

Table 15-6

Sample Tests Used by Neurologists to Assess the Intactness of Some of the 12 Cranial Nerves

Cranial Nerve	Test
I (olfactory nerve)	Closing one nostril with a finger, the examiner places some odiferous substance under the nostril being tested and asks whether the smell is perceived. Subjects who perceive it are next asked to identify it. Failure to perceive an odor when one is presented may be indicative of lesions of the olfactory nerve, a brain tumor, or other medical conditions. Of course, failure may be due to other factors, such as oppositional tendencies on the part of the patient or intranasal disease, and such factors must be ruled out as causal.
II (optic nerve)	Assessment of the intactness of the second cranial nerve is a highly complicated procedure, for this is a sensory nerve with functions related to visual acuity and peripheral vision. A Snellen eye chart will therefore be one of the tools used by the physician in assessing optic nerve function. If the subject at a distance of 20 feet from the chart is able to read the small numbers or letters in the line labeled line "20," then the subject is said to have 20/20 vision in the eye being tested. 20/20 vision is only a standard; and although many persons can read only the larger print at higher numbers on the chart (that is, a person who reads the letters on line "40" of the chart would be said to have a distant vision of 20/40), some persons have better than 20/20 vision. An individual who could read the line labeled "15" on the Snellen eye chart would be said to have 20/15 vision.
V (trigeminal nerve)	The trigeminal nerve supplies sensory information from the face, and it supplies motor information to and from the muscles involved in chewing. Information regarding the functioning of this nerve will be examined by the use of tests for facial pain (pinpricks will be made by the physician), facial sensitivity to different temperatures, and other sensations. Another part of the examination will entail having the subject clamp his jaw shut. The physician will then feel and inspect the facial muscles for weakness and other abnormalities.
VIII (acoustic nerve)	The acoustic nerve has functions related to the sense of hearing and the sense of balance. Hearing may be formally assessed by the use of an apparatus called the audiometer. More frequently, the routine assessment of hearing will involve the use of a "dollar watch." Provided the examination room is quiet, an individual with normal hearing should be able to hear a dollar watch ticking at a distance of about 40 inches from each ear (30 inches if the room is not very quiet). Other quick tests of hearing involve the placement of a vibrating tuning fork on various portions of the skull. Individuals who complain of dizziness, vertigo, disturbances in balance, and so forth may have their vestibular system examined by means of specific tests.

Neuropsychologists have at their disposal a wealth of psychological tests that may be valuable in assessing deficits, particularly deficits in the mild to moderate range. We now turn our attention to some of those instruments.

Neuropsychological Tests

Tests and assessment procedures have been created to assess virtually all conceivable aspects of neuropsychological functioning, including sundry aspects of perceptual, motor, verbal, memory, cognitive, and related functioning. Neuropsychological tests are used in screening for deficit and are also used as an adjunct to medical examinations, especially when the suspected deficit is mild or questionable in nature. Further, data derived from psychological testing are capable of providing information as to the site, progression, or regression of a

Medical Diagnostic Aids in Neuropsychological Examinations

Data from neuropsychological testing combined with data derived from various medical procedures can in some cases yield a thorough understanding of a neurological problem. For example, certain behavioral indices evident in neuropsychological testing may lead the neuropsychologist to recommend that a particular site in the brain be further explored for the presence of lesions—a suspicion that may be confirmed by a diagnostic procedure that yields cross-sectional pictures of the site.

The trained neuropsychologist has a working familiarity with the armamentarium of nonpsychological—medical—tests that may be brought to bear on neuropsychological problems. In this discussion, we describe a sampling of such tests and measurement procedures. We begin with a brief description of the medical procedure and apparatus that is perhaps most familiar to us all—whether from experience in a dentist's chair or elsewhere—the X ray.

To the radiologist, the X-ray photograph's varying shades convey information about the corresponding density of the tissue through which the X rays have been passed. With front, side, back, and other X-ray views of the brain and the spinal column, the diagnosis of tumors, lesions, infections, and other abnormalities can frequently be made. There are many different types of neuroradiologic procedures that can be employed. These range from the simple X ray of the skull to more complicated procedures involving the injection of some tracer element into the bloodstream (as is required for a cerebral angiogram).

Perhaps you have also heard or read about another X-ray-type of procedure, the "CAT (computerized axial tomography) scan" or "CT" scan (Figure 1). The *CT scan* is superior to traditional X rays because the structures in the brain may be represented in a systematic series of three-dimensional views, a feature that is extremely important in assessing conditions such as spinal anomalies. *PET* (positron emission tomography) scans are a tool of nuclear medicine particularly useful in diagnosing biochemical lesions in the brain. PET has also been used as a tool in evaluation research with schizophrenics and other psychiatric patients (Trimble, 1986). Conceptually related to the PET scan is *SPECT* (single photon emission computed tomography), a technology that records the course of a radioactive tracer fluid (iodine) producing exceptionally clear photographs of organs and tissues (Figure 2).

Also referred to as a "radioisotope scan," the *brain scan* procedure involves the introduction of radioactive materials into the brain through an injection. The cranial surface is then scanned with a special camera to track the flow of material. Alterations in blood supply to the brain are noted, including alterations that may be associated with disease such as tumors.

The *electroencephalograph* (EEG) is a machine that measures the electrical activity of the brain by means of electrodes pasted to the scalp. It is a relatively safe, painless procedure that can be of significant value in diagnosing and treating seizure and other disorders. The electroencephalographer is trained to distinguish normal from abnormal brain-wave activity. EEG activity will vary as a function of age, level of arousal (awake, drowsy, asleep), and other variables in addition to brain abnormalities. EEG technology has been used to study a wide variety of neuropsychological phenomena such as electrical activity of the brain in Alzheimer's disease (see, for example, Martin-Loeches et al., 1991).

The *electromyograph* (EMG) is a machine that records electrical activity of muscles by means of an electrode that is inserted directly into the muscle. Abnormalities found in the EMG can be used with other clinical and historical data as an aid in making a final diagnosis. The *echoencephalograph* is a machine that transforms electric energy into sound (sonic) energy. The sonic energy ("echoes") transversing the tissue area under study is then converted back into electric energy and displayed as a printout. This printout is used as an adjunct to other procedures in helping the neurologist to determine the nature and location of

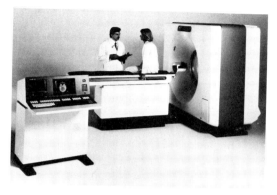

Figure 1

The CT scan is useful in pinpointing the location of tumors, cysts, degenerated tissue, or other abnormalities, and its use may eliminate the need for exploratory surgery or painful diagnostic procedures used in brain or spinal studies.

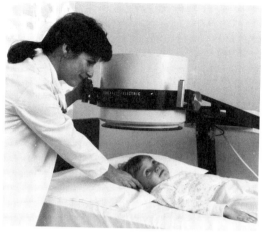

Figure 2

SPECT technology has been found to be of promising value in evaluating conditions such as cerebral vascular disease, Alzheimer's disease, and seizure disorders.

certain types of lesions in the brain. Radio waves in combination with a magnetic field can also be used to create detailed anatomical images—as illustrated in Figure 3.

Information about nerve damage and related abnormalities may be obtained by direct electrical stimulation of nerves and notation of movement or lack of movement in corresponding muscle tissue. Examination of the cerebrospinal fluid for blood and other abnormalities is an important diagnostic aid to the neurologist. A sample of the fluid is obtained by means of a medical procedure called a *lumbar puncture*—in everyday terminology, a spinal tap. This procedure entails the insertion of a special needle into the widest spinal interspace, after a local anesthetic has been applied. In addition to providing information concerning the chemical normality of the fluid, the test also provides the neurologist with the opportunity to gauge the normality of the intracranial pressure.

Laboratory analysis of blood, urine, and other cells will provide the physician with a wealth of leads concerning possible bases for suspected neurological difficulties. For example, a presenting problem of decreased sensation may be due to a number of different causes, such as diabetes mellitus (which could be diagnosed by a glucose tolerance test).

Figure 3

This magnetic resonance system utilizes a magnetic field and radio waves to create detailed images of the body. These and related imaging techniques may be employed not only in the study of neuropsychological functioning but in the study of abnormal behavior as well; see, for example, Kellner et al.'s (1991) study of obsessive-compulsive disorder.

neurological disease and can therefore be essential to accurate diagnosis and treatment (Pincus & Tucker, 1974). Additionally, neuropsychological tests can also be helpful in the assessment of

- change in mental status or other variables as a result of medication, surgery, or some disease process
- abnormalities in function before abnormalities in structure can be detected
- strengths and weaknesses of the neurologically impaired patient, thus facilitating the rehabilitation process
- the ability of an individual to stand trial (that is, the ability to understand the charges against him)
- changes in a disease process over the course of a longitudinal neurological study

A detailed review of the hundreds of available neuropsychological tests is beyond the scope of this brief overview. In the following sections, we review a sampling of techniques used by neuropsychologists in their in-depth evaluations and by clinicians and school psychologists in their neuropsychological screenings. Note that although we discuss these tests under certain headings, most of the tests yield information that overlaps into other areas; a test that is designed primarily to test for memory, for example, might well be capable of yielding a wealth of information about perceptual functioning.

Specialized Interviews and Rating Scales

A number of structured interviews and rating forms are available as aids in the neuropsychological screening and evaluation process. Neuropsychological screening devices point the way to further areas of inquiry with more extensive evaluation methods. Such devices can be used economically with members of varied populations who may be at risk for neuropsychological impairment, such as psychiatric patients, the elderly, and alcoholics (Berg et al., 1987; Errico et al., 1990; Goldstein, 1986; Yozawitz, 1986). Some of these measures, such as the Short Portable Mental Status Questionnaire (Pfeiffer, 1975), are completed by an assessor, and others, such as the Neuropsychological Impairment Scale (NIS) (O'Donnell & Reynolds, 1983; O'Donnell, DeSoto, DeSoto, & Reynolds, 1993), are self-report instruments. The revised NIS surveys complaints indicative of neuropsychological difficulties, correlates .70 with a more traditional measure of neuropsychological impairment, and has a median test-retest reliability over a three-month period of .84 (O'Donnell, DeSoto, & DeSoto, 1993). Research with another self-report-type neuropsychological instrument, the Patient's Assessment of Own Functioning (PAF), has not been encouraging. Studies suggest that when used with populations of general neuropsychological referrals and alcoholics, the PAF may yield a measure more reflective of affective state than actual neuropsychological impairment (Chelune et al., 1986; Shelton & Parsons, 1987).

In addition to some sort of questionnaire, an interview is a frequently used tool in neuropsychological evaluations. The Structured Interview for the Diagnosis of Dementia (SIDD), for example, can be used to detect cognitive impairment arising from Alzheimer's disease, strokes, and other medical causes. Conclusions drawn from this interview have been shown to correlate .89 to .93 with other such measures and are predictive of the diagnosis of dementia (Zaudig, 1992).

Intellectual Ability Tests in Neuropsychology

Tests of intellectual ability, particularly the Wechsler scales, occupy a prominent position among the diagnostic tools available to the neuropsychologist. In fact, a survey of members of the APA Division of Clinical Neuropsychology and members of the National Academy of Neuropsychologists indicated that of all psychological tests and test batteries, the Wechsler scales were far and away the most frequently used in practice by neuropsychologists; although many neuropsychologists use a variety of different techniques in their daily practice, one test virtually all of them use is a Wechsler intelligence test (Seretny et al., 1986).

The varied nature of the tasks on the Wechsler scales and the wide variety of responses required of the subject make it a good bet that if a neuropsychological deficit exists, some clue to the existence of the deficit will be brought to light. Thus, for example, difficulties in attention, concentration, or conceptualization might be noted during the administration of the Arithmetic items—a possible clue to a neurological deficit as opposed to a lack of arithmetic ability. Because certain patterns of test response are indicative of particular deficits, the examiner will look beyond performance on individual tests to a study of the pattern of test scores, a process referred to as *pattern analysis.* Thus, for example, extremely poor performance on the Block Design and other performance subtests in a record that contains relatively high scores on all the verbal subtests might, in combination with other data, lead the examiner to suspect damage in the right hemisphere. A number of researchers intent on developing a definitive sign of brain damage have devised various ratios and quotients based on patterns of subtest scores. David Wechsler himself referred to one such pattern called a "deterioration quotient" or "DQ" (also referred to by some as a "deterioration index"). However, neither Wechsler's DQ nor any other WAIS-based index has performed satisfactorily enough to be deemed a stand-alone measure of neuropsychological impairment. Fuld (1984) proposed that patients with Alzheimer's disease would present with WAIS-R profiles featuring high scores on Information and Vocabulary, low scores on Digit Symbol and Block Design, and middle-range scores on the Digit Symbol, Block Design, and Object Assembly subtests. However, independent research has not supported the predictive validity of this profile (Logstdon et al., 1989).

We have already noted the need to administer standardized tests in a manner that rigidly conforms to the instructions in the test manual. Yet because of the limited ability of the testtaker, such "by the book" test administrations are not always possible or desirable when testing members of the neurologically impaired population. Because of various problems or potential problems (such as the shortened attention span of some neurologically impaired individuals), the experienced examiner may find it necessary to modify the test administration in ways that will accommodate the testtaker yet yield clinically useful information. The examiner administering a Wechsler scale may deviate from the prescribed order of test administration when administering the test to an individual who becomes fatigued quickly; in such cases, the more taxing subtests will be administered early in the exam. In the interest of shortening the total test administration time, the trained examiner might judge it necessary to omit certain subtests that he or she suspects will not provide any information over and above that already obtained. Let us reiterate that such deviations in the administration of standardized tests such as the Wechsler scales can be made—and meaningfully interpreted—by trained and experienced neuropsychologists. For the rest of us, it's *by the book*!

Memory Tests

Memory is an important, multifaceted, cognitive function. The thorough neuropsychological evaluation of memory will include assessments of immediate memory, intermediate memory, and remote memory. A clinician may informally test for intermediate memory by mentioning something (for example, three states—Mississippi, Rhode Island, and Idaho) at the beginning of an examination; then, ten minutes or so later, the clinician asks the examinee to recall the states mentioned. Formal testing for memory may involve the use of instruments such as the Wechsler Memory Scale—Revised (WMS-R), a psychometrically sound instrument (Holden, 1988) that is appropriate for use with people from age 16 to 74 (D'Elia et al., 1989) and that has many potential applications (see, for example, O'Leary et al., 1991), including in the identification of individuals who are attempting to appear head-injured to make insurance claims (Mittenberg et al., 1993). In general, the task of the testtaker is to recall stories and other verbal stimuli, and the test yields composite scores for Verbal Memory, Visual Memory, General Memory (Verbal and Visual Memory), Attention/Concentration, and Delayed Recall (see Table 15–7 for a description of the subtests).

Verbal memory can also be assessed by any number of existing tests that involve the presentation of words, digits, nonsense syllables, sentences, or other such stimuli that must subsequently be recalled. Such tests include the Randt Memory Test (Randt & Brown, 1983), the Rey Auditory Verbal Learning Test, and the Selective Reminding Test. Nonverbal memory may be assessed by means of tests such as the Benton Test of Visual Retention—Revised and the Memory for Designs Test, two tests that provide a measure of the testtaker's ability to perceive and retain images of visually presented geometric figures.[3] Milner (1971) devised another nonverbal memory measure, this one employing twisted pieces of wire that are in essence "tactile nonsense figures." The exam-

---

3. A comparison of the effectiveness of these two instruments indicated that the Benton was preferable to the Memory for Designs Test in evaluating patients with mild to moderate brain damage (Marsh & Hirsch, 1982). Another study (Tamkin & Kunce, 1985) indicated that the Benton was a valid predictor of neuropsychological problems by itself, but that its predictive validity increased when used in combination with two other neuropsychological tests (the Hooper Visual Organization Test and the Weigl Color-Form Sorting Test).

Table 15-7
Subtests of the WMS-R

Index	Subtest	Description
Verbal Memory	Logical Memory I	Two stories are read to the examinee, who then retells them from memory.
	Verbal Paired Associates I	Eight word pairs are read to the examinee. Then the first word is read and the examinee supplies the second word from memory.
Visual Memory	Figural Memory	A set of abstract designs is shown to the examinee, who must identify them from a larger set.
	Visual Paired Associates I	The examinee identifies the color associated with each of six abstract designs.
	Visual Reproduction I	The examinee draws from memory geometric designs that are presented.

Delayed Recall (administered 30 minutes after original presentation)

Index	Subtest	Description
	Logical Memory II	Examinee retells the stories originally presented.
	Verbal Paired Associates II	Examinee recalls the second word from the eight word pairs originally presented.
	Visual Paired Associates II	Examinee identifies the colors associated with the previously presented designs.
	Visual Reproduction II	Examinee reproduces from memory the previously presented geometric designs.
Attention/ Concentration	Digit Span	Examinee repeats sequences of numbers in forward order (Part I) and in reverse order (Part II).
	Visual Memory Span	Examinee taps sequences of squares in forward order (Part I) and in reverse order (Part II).

inee's task is to match the figures using the right or left hand (Figure 15–4). Another tactile memory test involves an adaptation in the administration of the Seguin-Goddard Formboard. Although the formboard was initially designed to assess visuopractic ability, Halstead (1947a) suggested that it could be used to assess tactile memory if subjects were blindfolded during the test and a recall trial was added.

Are verbal and visual (or nonverbal) memory actually distinct from each other? Using a sample of neurologically impaired people as subjects, researchers administered a series of tests, including the WAIS-R and the WMS-R. They found that subtests of the WMS-R designed to assess visual memory and expected to load on a visual memory factor, instead loaded on several different factors, including one of general memory (Leonberger et al., 1992). Similarly, researchers conducting a factor analysis of test battery data obtained from a sample of people who were not neurologically impaired also identified a general memory factor on which both verbal and nonverbal subtests loaded (Smith et al., 1992). Taken together, these two studies suggest that traditional distinctions between verbal and nonverbal memory, so long taken virtually for granted, may require further study.

One effort to make memory tests more "real world" in nature is to substitute memory tasks that people must perform each day (for example, those

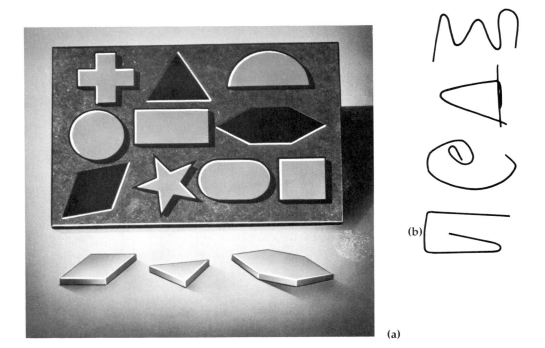

Figure 15–4
Two Tools Used in the Measurement of Tactile Memory

(a) *Shown here is one form of the Seguin-Goddard Formboard. Blindfolded examinees are in-structed to fit each of the 10 wooden blocks into the appropriate space in the formboard with each hand separately and then with both hands. Afterward, the examinee may be asked to draw the formboard from memory. All responses are timed and scored for accuracy.* **(b)** *Four pieces of wire bent into what are in essence "tactile nonsense figures" can be used in a tactile test of immediate memory. Examinees may be instructed to feel one of the figures with their right or left hand (or both hands) and then locate a matching figure.*

related to driving, meeting new people, remembering lists) for memory tasks that involve memorizing strings of numbers or words. In one 15-test comput-erized battery developed by Thomas Crook and described by Hostetler (1987), such "real world" tasks are incorporated in measures such as telephone dialing and name-face association. Crook's memory test battery is currently being used not for diagnostic purposes but for evaluating the effects of various drugs in the treatment of Alzheimer's disease.

Tests of Cognitive Functioning

Difficulty in thinking abstractly is a relatively common consequence of brain injury, regardless of the site of the injury. One popular measure of verbal-abstraction ability is the Wechsler Similarities subtest, isolated from the age-appropriate version of the Wechsler intelligence scale. The task is to identify how two objects (for instance, a ball and an orange) are alike. Proverb interpretation is another method used to assess ability to think abstractly. As an example, interpret the following proverb before reading on:

A stitch in time saves nine.

If your interpretation got across the idea that "haste makes waste," then you evidenced an ability to think abstractly. By contrast, some people with neurological deficits might have interpreted that proverb more concretely—with less abstraction. An interpretation such as "When sewing, take one stitch at a time—it'll save you from having to do it over nine times" might (or might not, depending on other factors) betray a deficit in abstraction ability. The Proverbs Test (Gorham, 1956) contains a number of proverbs along with standardized administration instructions and normative data. In one form of this test, the subject is instructed to write an explanation of the proverb. In another form of the test, this one multiple-choice, each proverb is followed by four choices, three of which may be either common misinterpretations or representative of a concrete-type response.

Nonverbal tests of abstraction include any of the various sorting tests—tests that require the respondent to sort objects in some logical way. Common to most of the sorting tests are instructions like "Group together all the ones that belong together," followed by questions such as "Why did you group those objects together?" Representative of such tests is the Object Sorting Test (refer back to Figure 15–3 on page 570), which contains familiar objects the subject is asked to sort according to various categories (such as color or use). Alternatively, the examiner may group a few of the objects together and ask the subject to determine why those objects go together or to select the object that does not belong with the rest. Another such sorting test is the Color-Form Sorting Test (also referred to as Weigl's Test), wherein the subject's task is to sort objects of different shapes and colors according to the directions of the examiner. The Wisconsin Card Sorting Test (WCST) requires the subject to sort a pack of 64 cards with different geometric figures of different colors according to rules that (1) must be inferred and (2) shift as the test progresses. WCST scores have been found to be elevated among people who are neurologically impaired. However, elevated WCST scores have also been found in nonneurologically impaired psychiatric populations. In one study, WCST data correctly classified 91% of neurologically impaired subjects, but it erroneously indicated the presence of neurological impairment in 73% of the people in the sample with schizophrenia, and 70% of the people in the sample with mood disorders (Heinrichs, 1990).

Brain damage may result in deficits with respect to organizing and planning abilities as well as ability to reason. One tool used in assessing ability to organize and plan is the Porteus Maze Test (see Figure 15–5). Here the subject's task is to trace a path through mazes, from start to finish without entering a blind alley. Porteus Maze Test scores may decline in older adults because of a reduction in prefrontal lobe functioning as part of normal aging (Daigneault et al., 1992). Insight into a subject's other reasoning abilities may be assessed

Figure 15–5
"Where do we go from here, Charly?"

A Porteus-mazelike task is being illustrated by the woman in the white coat to actor Cliff Robertson as "Charly" in the now-classic film of the same name.

by means of the Comprehension subtest on Wechsler intelligence tests or by Binet-type Verbal Absurdities or Picture Absurdities items (see item *a* in Figure 15–6). Wechsler subtests such as Digit Span, as well as numerous other tests, including the MMPI (Gass et al., 1990), may be useful in the assessment of other aspects of cognitive functioning, such as concentration.

Common to many types of neurological impairment are disorders of orientation—a lack of awareness of one's relationship to one's surroundings. Orientation difficulties usually become apparent during the mental status inter-

Figure 15–6
Sample Items from Some Tests That May Be Used in a Neuropsychological Examination ▶

(a) *"What's wrong or silly about this picture?"* This is the type of question asked in conjunction with picture absurdity–type items; **(b)** *the Mooney Closure Faces Test requires subjects to sort the faces—shaded to varying degrees of ambiguity—into piles labeled boy, girl, grown man, grown woman, old man, and old woman.* **(c)** *The task in a Field of Search items is to locate a match to a sample figure as quickly as possible;* **(d)** *the Trail Making Test is a connect-the-circles task that provides information about visual-conceptual and visual-motor tracking ability.*

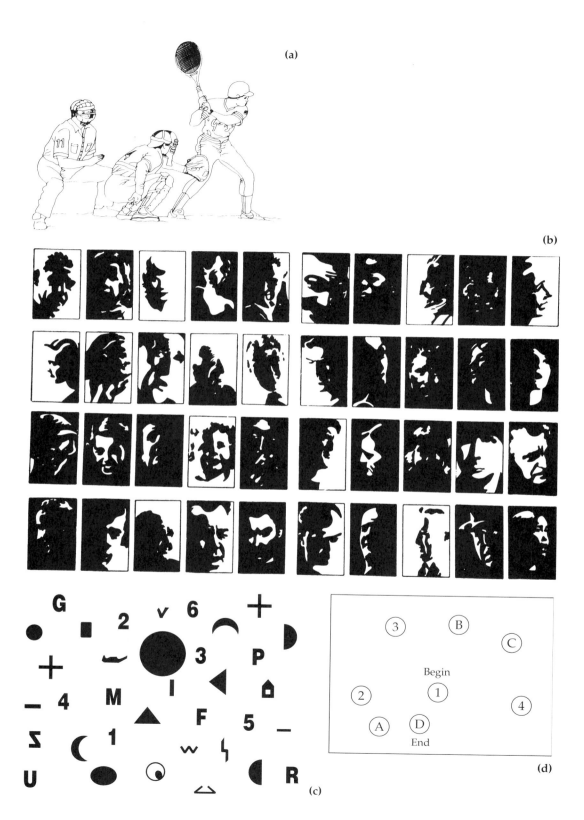

(a)

(b)

(c)

(d)

view. One formal, now-classic measure of personal orientation is Head's (1925) Eye, Hand and Ear Test. The examiner sits in front of the examinee and alternately points to his right and left eye, and right and left ear, while the patient's task is to imitate this movement on his or her own body. Noting that the examiner giving this test might model the desired movements to the examinee, Maloney, Ball, and Edgar (1970) modified and standardized the procedure by using large pictures of a person pointing to the right or left ear or eye with the right or left hand. Another aspect of spatial orientation can be assessed by the Standardized Road-map Test of Direction Sense (Money, 1976). On that test, the task of the assessee is to describe turns in a path the examiner traces on a grid.

Tests of Verbal Functioning

Aphasia, not to be confused with *aphagia*, refers to a loss of ability to express oneself and/or to understand spoken or written language because of some neurological deficit.[4] A number of batteries such as the Neurosensory Center Comprehensive Examination of Aphasia (NCCEA) have been designed to help identify the extent and nature of the communication deficit. The NCCEA (Spreen & Benton, 1969), for example, is composed of 24 subtests, 20 of which are designed to assess various aspects of auditory and visual comprehension and oral/written expression. The remaining four subtests address visual and tactile functioning, and these subtests are administered only when the examiner suspects a visual or tactile sensory deficit.

Verbal fluency and fluency in writing are sometimes affected by injury to the brain, and there are tests to assess the extent of the deficit in such skills. In the Controlled Word Association Test (formerly called the Verbal Associative Fluency Test), the examiner says a letter of the alphabet and it is the subject's task to say as many words as he or she can think of that begin with that letter. Each of three trials employing three different letters as a stimulus lasts one minute, and the testtaker's final score on the test reflects the total number of correct words produced weighted by factors such as the gender, age, and education of the testtaker. Controlled Word Association Test scores are related in the predicted direction to the ability of dementia patients to complete tasks of daily living, such as using the telephone or writing a check (Loewenstein et al., 1992). And although people with dementia tend to do poorly on the test as compared with controls, the differences observed have not been significant enough to justify the use of the test as an indicator of dementia (Nelson et al., 1993).

Aphasia is assessed more broadly with the Reitan-Indiana Aphasia Screening Test (AST) (Reitan, 1984a). Available in both a child and an adult form, this test contains a variety of items involving the use of language, including naming common objects, following verbal instructions, and writing familiar words. Factor analysis has suggested that these tasks load on two factors: language abilities and coordination involved in writing words or drawing objects (Williams

---

4. *Aphagia* refers to an inability to eat.

& Shane, 1986). Both forms of the test were designed to be screening devices that can be administered in 15 minutes or less. As with other neuropsychological screening tools, if any problems are observed, more extensive assessment would be in order. Used alone as a screening tool (Reitan, 1984a, 1984b; Reitan & Wolfson, 1992), or in combination with other tests (Tramontana & Boyd, 1986), the AST may be of value in distinguishing testtakers who have and do not have brain damage.

The Sequenced Inventory of Communication Development (SICD) is a test designed to assess the development of receptive and expressive communication in children aged 4 months to 4 years. The test contains a number of observation and test procedures designed to assess various aspects of the young child's awareness and understanding. In support of the test's construct validity are two studies that showed that chronic middle ear infections (otitis media) in young children produce a delay in language development as measured by the SICD (Friel-Patti & Finitzo, 1990; Wallace et al., 1988).

Perceptual, Motor, and Perceptual-Motor Tests

Brain injury can have a disruptive effect on perceptual, motor, and perceptual-motor functioning, and a number of tests designed to assess functioning in these areas exist (see Figure 15–6). Neurologically impaired individuals may exhibit difficulty in making sense out of fragmented or jumbled stimuli, and tests such as Mooney's Closure Faces Test are designed to assess the existence and extent of this deficit. People with right hemisphere lesions may exhibit deficits in visual scanning ability, and a test such as the Field of Search can be of value in discovering such deficits. Color blindness may be screened for using the Ishihara (1964) test, though more specialized instruments are available if rare forms of color perception deficit are suspected. Among the tests available for measuring deficit in auditory functioning is the Wepman Auditory Discrimination Test. This brief, easy-to-administer test requires that the examiner read a list of 40 pairs of monosyllabic meaningful words (such as "muss"/"much") pronounced with lips covered. The examinee's task is simply to determine if the two words just presented are the same or different. It's quite a straightforward test—provided that the examiner (1) isn't suffering from a speech defect, (2) has no heavy foreign accent, and (3) exhibits no proclivities toward muttering. The standardization sample for the test represented a broad range within the population, but there is little information available about the reliability and validity of the test. The test manual also fails to outline standardized administration conditions, which are particularly critical for the test, given the nature of the stimuli (Pannbacker & Middleton, 1992).

An example of a test designed to assess gross and fine motor skills is the Bruininks-Oseretsky Test of Motor Proficiency. Designed for use with children aged 4½ to 14½, this instrument includes subtests that assess running speed and agility, balance, strength, response speed, and dexterity. A sphere referred to by its manufacturer as a "Neuro Developmental Training Ball" (see Figure 15–7) may be used to assess balance and the vestibular sense. Performance on specified tasks with this tool of assessment has been shown to improve in response

Figure 15–7
Neuro Developmental Training Balls

to interventions designed to improve sensorimotor skills (Polatajko et al., 1991). Additional evidence for the validity of this measure comes from a correlational study that compared the performance of developmentally disabled individuals on it with the Papcsy-DePaepe test (a test that entails walking on beams of varying heights and widths). The correlation between the two measures was .64 (DePaepe & Ciccaglione, 1993). A measure of manual dexterity that was originally developed in the late 1940s as an aid in employee selection is the Purdue Pegboard Test (Figure 15–8). The object here is to insert pegs into holes using one hand, then the other hand, and then both hands. Each of these three segments of the test has a time limit of 30 seconds, and the score is equal to the number of pegs correctly placed. Normative data are available, and it is noteworthy that in a non-brain-injured population, women generally perform slightly better on this task than men. With brain-injured subjects, this test may be employed to help answer questions regarding the lateralization of a lesion.

A number of tests are designed to assess visual-motor integration. The Beery-Buktenica Development Test of Visual-Motor Integration is a test in which the examinee's task is to copy geometric forms arranged in increasing order of difficulty. In studies with subjects from a geriatric population, the test was found to correlate .64 to .70 with WAIS-R scores and .40 with ratings of adaptive functioning (Ferere et al., 1992). The Frostig Developmental Test of

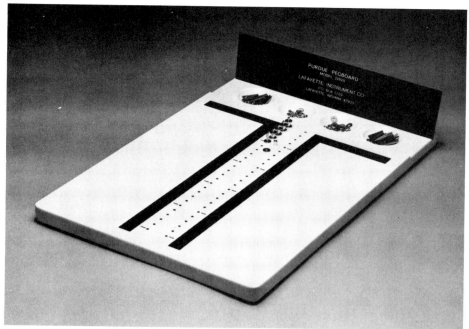

Figure 15–8
The Purdue Pegboard Test

Visual Perception measures some aspects of visual perception and eye-hand coordination by means of subtests that entail drawing lines between boundaries, finding embedded figures, distinguishing target shapes from other shapes, locating a rotated figure, and copying simple forms and patterns by joining dots. The test as a whole demonstrates moderate internal consistency (.72), with individual subtests demonstrating relatively low internal consistency reliability (.31 to .58). Item analysis suggested that more than half of the items are either passed or failed by a very large majority of testtakers—that is, some items are passed by almost all testtakers, and other items are failed by almost all testtakers—indicating that the items are poor sources of information about differences between testtakers (Brand, 1989).

One test widely used as a neuropsychological screening device is the Bender-Gestalt test. Interestingly, although the test enjoys widespread use by clinicians and school psychologists (Golden & Kupperman, 1980; Lubin et al., 1971), it is not particularly popular among neuropsychologists (Seretny et al., 1986), perhaps because they have more specialized instruments at their disposal.

The Bender Visual-Motor Gestalt Test   Usually referred to as the "Bender-Gestalt" or simply "the Bender," the test consists of nine cards, on each of which is printed one design. The designs had been used by psychologist Max Werthei-mer (1923) in his study of the perception of *gestalten* (German for "configura-tional wholes"). Lauretta Bender (see the box opposite) believed they could be used to assess perceptual maturation and neurological impairment. Bender (1938) proposed that a testtaker be shown each of the cards in turn and in-structed, "Copy it as best you can." There is no time limit for response, and usually all cards are copied in no more than five minutes. Unusually long or short administration times for this part of the test can be of diagnostic signifi-cance. After all nine designs have been copied, a fresh, blank piece of paper is placed before the testtaker with the instructions, "Now please draw all of the designs you can remember." Referred to as the *recall* phase of the test, this sec-ond phase was not an element of the original test. Gobetz (1953) proposed this procedure as a means of testing a hypothesis about differential performance on the Bender as a function of personality.[5] At the conclusion of the test, the test-taker may be asked to sign and date each sheet of paper. The examiner may draw an arrow on the back of the sheets to indicate the direction in which the paper was slanted. Related extra-test considerations, such as the handedness of the testtaker and distractions that may have occurred during administration, will also be noted on the reverse side of the sheets.

Bender (1938, 1970) intended the test to be scored by means of clinical judg-ment. Still, a number of quantitative scoring systems for this appealingly simple test soon became available for adult (Hutt, 1985; Pascal & Suttell, 1951; Watkins, 1976) and child (Koppitz, 1963, 1975) protocols. A sampling of scoring terms common to many of these systems is presented in Figure 15–9. In addition, the test has inspired the creation of various alternative versions, including the so-called BIP Bender (a Bender that employs a background interference procedure; Canter, 1963, 1966), a multiple-choice Bender (designed to better distinguish perceptual from motor problems; Labrentz et al., 1976), and procedures in-structing testtakers to verbalize associations to the designs (Hutt, 1977; Suczek & Klopfer, 1952). Like Halpern (1951) and others, Koppitz (1963, 1975) attrib-uted symbolic significance to errors in producing specific Bender designs (see Table 15–8).

Evidence in support of the use of the Bender-Gestalt as an instrument to assess personality is tenuous (Holmes et al., 1984). And although early reviews bearing on the Bender's validity as a neuropsychological screening tool tended to be quite favorable (e.g., Heaton et al., 1978; Spreen & Benton, 1965), the use of the test for neuropsychological screening purposes has also been called into question. It seems that many of the early validity studies contained method-ological deficiencies, including inappropriate subject selection procedures.

Bigler and Ehrenfurth (1980, 1981) noted a high rate of false negatives as-sociated with the use of the Bender; that is, the test yields no indication of or-ganic brain damage when such a deficit is indeed known to exist. These

---

5. Gobetz (1953) had hypothesized that, owing to the pressure of the unexpected second test, sub-jects diagnosed as neurotic would be able to recall fewer figures on the recall portion of the test than would normal subjects. The recall procedure is routinely used with the Bender today not to provide personality data but rather to provide additional neuropsychological data.

Lauretta Bender (1897–1987)

Born on August 9, 1897, to John Oscar Bender, an attorney, and Katherine Irvine Bender, Lauretta was the youngest of four children. Lauretta repeated first grade three times and was thought to be mentally retarded, in large part because of her tendency to reverse letters in reading and writing. However, by the time she completed grammar school, any concerns about mental retardation were quelled, since she had proved herself an able student.

The family moved often. Lauretta attended high school in Los Angeles, where she cultivated an interest in biological research. She earned her B.S. and M.A. degrees at the University of Chicago and while there pursued research that led to her first scientific publications—hematological studies on experimental tuberculosis of the guinea pig. Accepted at the State University of Iowa Medical School, she was granted a research and teaching assistantship and assigned to Dr. Samuel Orton in the department of neuropathology. In 1926 she earned her M.D. degree. This was followed by some study overseas, an internship at the University of Chicago, a residency at Boston Psychopathic Hospital, and a research appointment at the Henry Phipps Psychiatric Clinic of Johns Hopkins Hospital. White at Hopkins she met and wrote a publication with the Viennese psychoanalyst and contemporary of Freud's Paul Schilder, M.D., Ph.D. Although Schilder was married and eleven years her senior, Bender is said to have fallen in love with him and moved to New York with him in 1930 to work at Bellevue Hospital once Schilder had been offered and had accepted a position there. After Schilder's divorce, the two were married in November of 1936 and within the following four years the couple had three children. Tragedy struck shortly after the birth of their third child in 1940; leaving the hospital after visiting Lauretta and his newborn daughter, Paul was struck down and killed by a car. Lauretta did not marry again until she was 70 years old, this time to Henry B. Parkes, Ph.D., and was widowed again after only five years of marriage.

Lauretta Bender may be best remembered for her "Visual-Motor Gestalt Test" first published in 1938, though this prolific psychiatrist's writings have made contributions in a very wide range of areas. Bender served on the psychiatric staff at Bellevue Hospital from 1930 through 1956 and was appointed head of the Children's Psychiatric Division in 1934. Bender also held numerous other positions, including a professorship at New York University and the post of editorial advisor to Action Comics—the latter stemming in part from an article she wrote that focused on the role of comics in developing children's reading skills. Lauretta Bender's accomplishments have been acknowledged by numerous professional organizations, which have bestowed on her a variety of honors and awards. Even in retirement in Maryland, Bender served as a consultant to various organizations, including the Anne Arundel County Board of Education.

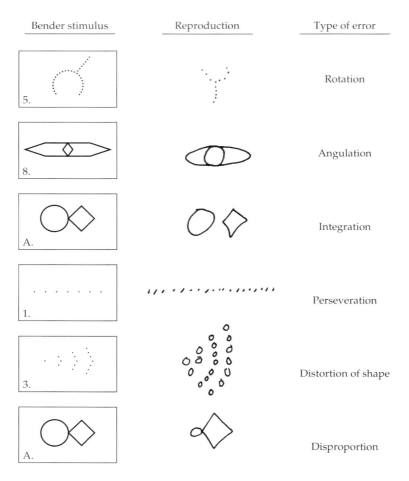

Bender stimulus	Reproduction	Type of error
5.		Rotation
8.		Angulation
A.		Integration
1.		Perseveration
3.		Distortion of shape
A.		Disproportion

Figure 15–9
Sample Errors on the Bender-Gestalt

These types of errors may be suggestive of organic impairment. Not all the illustrated errors are signs of organic impairment at all ages.

researchers provided numerous examples of satisfactory performance on the Bender in individuals with documented organic brain damage, and they estimated that the rate of false negatives obtained through the use of the test is "in the neighborhood of 40% or worse" (p. 567). The cost of false negatives can be high (Krug, 1971; Satz, 1966) and such considerations may give avid Bender users pause.

Another cause for hesitation comes in the form of research reports indicating that the Bender test may yield a high rate of false positives. Margolis et al. (1989) administered the Bender and a neuropsychological test battery to a group

Table 15–8
Emotional Indicators on the Bender

The following are the twelve Bender "emotional indicators" (EIs) enumerated by Koppitz (1963, 1975). Koppitz (1975, p. 92) cautioned that the "presence of three or more EIs on a Bender test protocol tends to reflect emotional difficulties that warrant further investigation."

1. *Confused order:* Associated with poor planning and inability to organize material.
2. *Wavy line on Figures 1 and 2:* Associated with poor motion coordination and/or emotional instability.
3. *Dashes substituted for circles on Figure 2:* Associated with impulsivity and lack of interest in young children.
4. *Increasing size on Figures 1, 2, or 3:* Associated with low frustration tolerance and explosiveness.
5. *Large size:* Associated with acting-out behavior in children.
6. *Small size:* Associated with anxiety, withdrawal, and timidity in children.
7. *Fine line:* Associated with timidity, shyness, and withdrawal in young children.
8. *Careless overwork or heavily reinforced lines:* Associated with impulsivity, aggressiveness, and acting-out behavior in children, although some researchers have found it to be related to high intelligence and good achievement.
9. *Second attempt:* Associated with impulsivity and anxiety.
10. *Expansion:* Associated with impulsivity and acting-out behavior in children.
11. *Box around design:* Associated with children who have weak inner control, they need and want limits and controls to function in school and at home.
12. *Spontaneous elaboration or additions to design:* Associated with children who are overwhelmed by fears and anxieties and are totally preoccupied with their own thoughts; they often have a tenuous hold on reality and may confuse fact and fantasy.

of elderly patients who were known to have or not have cognitive impairment. In addition to a high rate of false negatives, the researchers observed a high rate of false positives; that is, the test identified neuropsychological deficit in patients where none was known to exist. Presumably, some patients may have appeared to be neuropsychologically impaired owing to depression or other psychiatric disorders. The cost of false positives in a neuropsychological screening device can be counted not only in dollars (for professional time in what amounts to needless retesting with more extensive assessment procedures) but also in the raised anxiety levels generated in patients informed of the (false) positive findings.

Neuropsychological Test Batteries

The "Flexible" Battery

The tests we've listed only begin to illustrate the diversity that exists with respect to the numerous techniques and methods available to the clinician doing neuropsychological assessment. On the basis of the mental status examination, the physical examination, and the case history data, the neuropsychologist will typically administer a *flexible battery* of neuropsychological tests; specific tests will be chosen for some purpose relevant to the unique aspects of the patient and the presenting problem. This so-called flexible battery of tests hand-picked by the neuropsychologist stands in contrast to a standard or prepackaged battery of neuropsychological tests, wherein all examinees are administered the same subtests in the context of a standardized procedure.

The clinician who administers a flexible battery has not only the responsibility of selecting the tests to be used but also the burden of integrating all the findings from each of the individual tests—no simple task, since each test may have been normed on different populations. Another problem inherent in the use of a flexible battery is that the tests administered frequently overlap with respect to some of the functions tested, and the result is some waste in testing and scoring time. Regardless of these and other drawbacks attendant on the administration of a flexible battery, it is the preference of most highly trained neuropsychologists to tailor a battery of tests to the unique and specific demands of a particular testing situation.

The Prepackaged Battery

Prepackaged neuropsychological test batteries are designed to comprehensively sample the patient's neuropsychological functioning. The prepackaged battery is appealing to clinicians, especially clinicians who are relatively new to neuropsychological assessment, because it tends to be less demanding in many ways. Whereas a great deal of expertise and skill is required to fashion a flexible battery that will adequately answer the referral question, a prepackaged battery represents a non-tailor-made but comprehensive alternative. Various tests sampling various areas are included in the battery, and each is supplied with clear scoring methods. One major drawback of the prepackaged variety of tests, however, is that the specific disability of the patient may greatly—and adversely—influence performance on the test; thus, an individual with a visual impairment, for example, may perform poorly on many of the other subtests of a battery that require certain visual skills.

Keeping in mind that trained neuropsychologists may administer a prepackaged battery, may modify a prepackaged battery for the purposes of a particular case at hand, or administer their own hand-picked assortment of tests, we now look at some representative test batteries.

Halstead-Reitan Neuropsychological Battery Ward C. Halstead (1908–1969) was an experimental psychologist whose interest in the study of brain–behavior correlates led him to the establishment of a laboratory for that purpose at the University of Chicago in 1935—the first such laboratory of its kind in the world. During the course of 35 years of research, Halstead studied over 1,100 brain-damaged persons. From his observations, Halstead (1947a, 1947b) derived a series of 27 tests designed to assess the presence or absence of organic brain damage—the Halstead Neurological Test Battery. A student of Halstead's, Ralph M. Reitan, would subsequently elaborate on his mentor's findings. In 1955, Reitan published two papers that dealt with the differential intellectual effects of various brain lesion sites (Reitan, 1955a, 1955b). Fourteen years and much research later, Reitan (1969) would privately publish a book entitled *Manual for Administration of Neuropsychological Test Batteries for Adults and Children*—the forerunner of the Halstead-Reitan Neuropsychological Test Battery (H-R).

Table 15-9
Subtests of the Halstead-Reitan Battery

Category

This is a measure of abstracting ability in which stimulus figures of varying size, shape, number, intensity, color, and location are flashed on an opaque screen. Subjects must determine what principle ties the stimulus figures together (such as color) and indicate their answer among four choices by pressing the appropriate key on a simple keyboard. If the response is correct, a bell rings; if incorrect, a buzzer sounds. The test primarily taps frontal lobe functioning of the brain.

Tactual performance

Blindfolded examinees complete the Seguin-Goddard Formboard (see Figure 15-4) with their dominant and nondominant hands and then with both hands. Time taken to complete each of the tasks is recorded. The formboard is then removed, the blindfold is taken off, and the examinee is given a pencil and paper and asked to draw the formboard from memory. Two scores are computed from the drawing: the *memory* score, which includes the number of shapes reproduced with a fair amount of accuracy, and the *localization* score, which is the total number of blocks drawn in the proper relationship to the other blocks and the board. Interpretation of the data includes consideration of the total time to complete this task, the number of figures drawn from memory, and the number of blocks drawn in the proper relationship to the other blocks.

Rhythm

First published as a subtest of the Seashore Test of Musical Talent and subsequently included as a subtest in Halstead's (1947a) original battery, the subject's task here is to discriminate between like and unlike pairs of musical beats. Difficulty with this task has been associated with right temporal brain damage (Milner, 1971).

Speech sounds perception

This test consists of 60 nonsense words administered by means of an audiotape adjusted to the examinee's preferred volume. The task is to discriminate a spoken syllable, selecting from four alternatives presented on a printed form. Performance on this subtest is related to left hemisphere functioning.

Finger-tapping

Originally called the "finger oscillation test," this test of manual dexterity measures the tapping speed of the index finger of each hand on a tapping key. The number of taps from each hand is counted by an automatic counter. The number of taps from each hand is counted over five consecutive, 10-second trials with a brief rest period between trials. The total score on this subtest represents the average of the five trials for each hand. A typical, normal score is approximately 50 taps per 10-second period for the dominant hand and 45 taps for the nondominant hand (a 10 percent faster rate is expected for the dominant hand). Cortical lesions may differentially affect finger-tapping rate of the two hands.

Time sense

The examinee watches the hand of a clock sweep across the clock and then has the task of reproducing that movement from sight. This test taps visual motor skills as well as ability to estimate time span.

Other tests

Also included in the battery is the Trail Making Test (see Figure 15-6), in which the examinee's task is to correctly connect numbered and lettered circles. A strength-of-grip test is also included; strength of grip may be measured informally by a handshake grasp and more scientifically by an instrument called a dynamometer (see Figure 15-10).

To determine which eye is the preferred or dominant eye, the Miles ABC Test of Ocular Dominance is administered. Also recommended is the administration of a Wechsler intelligence test, the MMPI (useful in this context for shedding light on questions concerning the possible functional origin of abnormal behavior), and an aphasia screening test adapted from the work of Halstead and Wepman (1959).

Various other sensorimotor tests may also be included. A test called the "critical flicker fusion test" was also at one time part of this battery but has since been discontinued by most examiners. If you have ever been in a disco and watched the action of the "strobe" light, you can appreciate what is meant by a light that flickers. To administer the flicker fusion test, an apparatus that emits a flickering light at varying speeds is required, and the examinee is instructed to adjust the rate of the flicker until the light appears to be steady or fused.

Administration of the H-R requires a highly trained examiner conversant with the procedures necessary to administer the various subtests (see Table 15-9). Even with such an examiner, the test generally requires a full workday to complete. Subtest scores are interpreted not only with respect to what they mean by themselves but also by their relation to scores on other subtests.

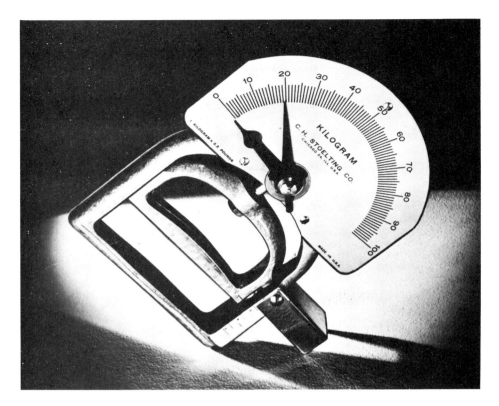

Figure 15–10
A Dynamometer of the Kind Used as Part of the Halstead-Reitan Battery to Measure Strength of Grip

The examinee is instructed to squeeze the grips as hard as possible, two trials with each hand. The score is recorded in number of pounds of pressure exerted.

Appropriate interpretation of the findings requires the eye of a trained neuro-psychologist, though H-R computer interpretation software—no substitute for clinical judgment but an aid to it—is available. Scoring yields a number referred to as the "Halstead Impairment Index," and an index of .5 or above, the cutoff point, is indicative of a neurologic problem; data on over 10,000 patients in the standardization sample were used to establish that cutoff point. Normative in-formation has also been published with respect to other populations, such as epileptics (Klove & Matthews, 1974), the retarded (Matthews, 1974), and neu-rologically intact, nonpsychiatric adults (Fromm-Auch & Yeudall, 1983). Leck-liter and Matarazzo (1989) have cautioned that H-R performance may be affected by factors such as age, education, IQ, and gender, and that there is a "critical need to use clinical judgment in the selection of appropriate reference norms" (p. 509).

Conducting test-retest reliability studies on the H-R is a prohibitive endeavor in light of the amount of time it may take to complete one administration of the battery, as well as other factors (such as practice effects and effects of memory). Still, as Matarazzo, Matarazzo, Wiens, Gallo, and Klonoff (1976) observed after their review of a number of reliability studies, "Despite the lack of comparability across the four samples on many dimensions, including age and test-retest intervals, the results again reveal a high degree of clinical as well as purely psychometric reliability for most of the tests in the neuropsychological battery" (pp. 348–349). A growing body of literature attests to the validity of the instrument in differentiating brain-damaged subjects from subjects without brain damage, and also for identifying the location of the brain damage (Reitan, 1994). One study that employed a children's version of the battery yielded findings supportive of the test's construct validity. The battery has also been used to identify neuropsychological impairment associated with learning disabilities (Batchelor et al., 1990; Batchelor et al., 1991), as well as cognitive, perceptual, motor, and behavioral deficits associated with particular neurological lesions. This battery is used as a standardized means of assessing neuropsychological capabilities (Dean, 1983; Guilmette & Faust, 1991; Guilmette et al., 1990; Whitworth, 1984).

A distinction has been made between tests that are theoretical and tests that are relatively atheoretical in approach (Kelly & Dean, 1990). The Halstead-Reitan battery lies at the atheoretical end of the spectrum. We now look at a battery that lies at the other end.

Luria-Nebraska Neuropsychological Battery   Based on the theoretical postulations of the Russian neuropsychologist Aleksandr Luria, the Luria-Nebraska Neuropsychological Battery (LNNB) is available in two forms for adults and adolescents and in one form for children. The first effort to organize Luria's neuropsychological testing procedures into a standardized testing procedure was made by Christensen (1975). Some of Christensen's items were incorporated into the development of Form 1 of the LNNB (Golden et al., 1980), as well as the second, somewhat longer form (Golden et al., 1985). In 1987, the LNNB-C, a version of the test designed for use with children ages 8 through 12, was published (see Hooper, 1992, for a review).

The LNNB has 11 clinical scales on Form 1 and 12 clinical scales on Form 2. Clinical scales are designed to assess cognitive processes and functions such as reading, writing, arithmetic, memory, motor functions, receptive and expressive speech, and concept formation. In Form 2, the additional scale is one designed to measure intermediate memory (the ability to recall information after the passage of several minutes). Combinations of the clinical scales called summary scales yield scores that purportedly identify areas of damage to the brain. Raw scores are converted to *T*-scores for ease of interpretation. High scores on three or more clinical scales are said to be indicative of neuropsychological impairment.

Inter-rater agreement regarding the determination of brain damage has been estimated to be in the high .90s (Kane et al., 1987). Test-retest reliability over a six-month interval was estimated to be .77 to .96 for individual clinical scales (Golden et al., 1985). Independent examination of the reliability of two of the scales over a seven-week period yielded coefficients of .69 and .83 (Moses & Maruish, 1990). Across the various clinical scales, internal consistency averages in the high .80s, an acceptable level (Bryant et al., 1984).

Many of the items are identical on Form 1 and Form 2. The clinical scales of the two forms correlate in the mid .80s, and the two forms yield similar means and standard deviations. Still, questions remain regarding the equivalence of the two forms (Moses & Maruish, 1990; Van Gorp, 1992), especially since the second form was undertaken to improve on, and therefore not be exactly parallel to, the first form in content. Garmoe et al. (1991) note that no data have been published concerning the equivalence of Form 1 and Form 2. The LNNB was normed on a relatively small group of people. Form 1 was normed on 50 subjects, Form 2 was normed on 73 subjects (Garmoe et al., 1991; Stambrook, 1983), and the LNNB-C was normed on 125 children (Hooper, 1992). The test has been criticized with reference to the relatively few people in its standardization sample, as well as on other grounds (see *Everyday Psychometrics*, pages 602–605).

As far as convenience is concerned, the LNNB is an appealing test because it typically takes about one-third the time taken to administer the H-R, is more portable than the H-R, and can be administered at bedside (whereas the H-R cannot because of the need for special equipment).[6] However, the psychometric soundness of this test has been called into question, being overdependent on language skills (Franzen, 1985) and for yielding a high rate of false-negative findings, especially with respect to aphasia (Crosson & Warren, 1982; Delis & Kaplan, 1982).

Other neuropsychological batteries   Among the other available neuropsychological batteries is the Montreal Neurological Institute Battery (Taylor, 1979), a test devised in large part as a result of intensive observation of neurosurgical patients. This battery contains many published tests, including the Wechsler intelligence tests, the Mooney Closure Faces Test, and the Wisconsin Card Sorting Test. The battery is particularly useful to trained neuropsychologists in locating specific kinds of lesions. The battery was administered preoperatively and postoperatively to hundreds of patients who underwent a surgical excision of a defined area of brain tissue as the method of treatment for a brain tumor or epilepsy. Since the research on the battery was executed primarily with individuals who had surgically induced focal lesions, it is understandable that the battery has more utility in cases involving focal as opposed to diffuse lesions.

Many published and unpublished neuropsychological test batteries are designed to probe deeply into one area of neuropsychological functioning instead of surveying for possible behavioral deficit in a variety of areas. Thus, test batteries exist that focus on visual, sensory, memory, and communication prob-

---

6. A portable and inexpensive version of the Halstead-Reitan Category Test that eliminates the need for a cumbersome projection box apparatus has been described by Slay (1984). A parts list for the "do-it-yourself" neuropsychological assessor is included in the article.

lems; indeed, batteries can focus on virtually any specific area of brain–behavior functioning. One such specialized battery is the Southern California Sensory Integration Tests. Designed to assess sensory-integrative and motor functioning in children 4 to 9 years of age, this battery consists of 18 standardized subtests. The Southern California is helpful not only in identifying children who are having sensorimotor problems but also in identifying the nature of those problems. A well-trained examiner is required to administer the tests and interpret the findings. The manual (Ayres, 1972) for this battery contains research bearing on the psychometric data of the individual tests and the battery as a whole as well as appropriate cautions regarding interpretations of test performance. Normative data provided in the test manual are sketchy, and some critics suspect that many of the functions assessed in this battery may be related more to intelligence than to the targeted functions. Another specialized neuropsychological battery is the Cognitive Behavioral Driver's Inventory, designed to help determine whether individuals with brain damage are capable of driving a motor vehicle (Engum et al., 1988; Lambert & Engum, 1992).

A neuropsychological battery called the Severe Impairment Battery (SIB; Saxton et al., 1990) is designed for use with severely impaired assessees who might otherwise perform at or near the floor of existing tests. The battery is divided into six subscales: Attention, Orientation, Language, Memory, Visuoperception, and Construction. Additionally, there are brief measures of responding to name, praxis, and social skills—the last abstracted from Holland's (1980) test of Communicative Abilities in Daily Living. Many of the tasks included in this battery—as well as the kinds of abilities measured by each of the tasks—will (or should) sound familiar to the reader completing this chapter. For example, some of the tasks include counting and repeating digits, naming photographs of everyday objects, and drawing and copying shapes. Experimenting with a relatively small sample of subjects (41), Saxton et al. (1990, p. 301) tentatively concluded that the SIB "successfully elicits a range of performance in a variety of cognitive domains in severely demented patients." Based on what you now know about assessing neurological deficit, what other kind of test(s) would you advise the authors of the SIB to add to their new test?

A Perspective

As we saw in this chapter's *Close-up,* medical diagnostic tools in the areas of neurological and neuropsychological assessment are technologically sophisticated. With increasing precision, these tools may soon be able to pinpoint areas of the nervous system that have in some way been damaged or compromised. Given this state of affairs, will the role of the neuropsychologist and the enterprise of neuropsychological assessment be obsolete in the years to come? Hardly. If anything, neuropsychological assessment is a growing and vital area. Beyond physically locating areas of damage or deficit, there is a great need to understand cognitive strengths and weaknesses (Mapou, 1988) and to put that understanding to work in prevention, treatment, and rehabilitation efforts.

Validity of the LNNB

The validity of the Luria-Nebraska Neuropsychological Battery (LNNB) has been a topic of controversy in psychometric circles almost since the test was published (Adams, 1985). Why? Let's look at some of the issues.

Construct Validity

Luria believed that specific behaviors are the product of several different functions of the brain and that damage to a brain area will affect behavior. Yet to localize through outward behavior an area of the brain that is not functioning properly can be a very complicated process. A proper examination requires evaluation of many different behaviors that are the product of partially overlapping brain functions (Stambrook, 1983). If a person with suspected brain damage is unable to follow a verbal instruction to pick up a pencil, for example, that inability may be the result of any of several singular or overlapping problems. The inability may be the result of deafness, the inability to comprehend language in general, or the inability to comprehend names of objects (such as "pencil"). The inability may be the result of paralysis or other difficulties associated with motor movement. The person's inability to respond might even be due to a memory deficit so severe that instructions cannot be remembered long enough to be followed. Of course, yet another alternative is that the testtaker is faking bad for some reason. To determine which one (or ones) of these possible problems is operative in a particular case, the examiner must administer several different tests. For example, the examiner may test for varied language-related abilities to rule out language-related hypotheses about the inability to follow instructions.

Like most other neuropsychologists, Luria routinely fitted the methods of assessment he used to the unique presenting problem of the case at hand. There was no set order to the types of tests he would administer; rather, the demands of the particular case dictated both the types of tests employed and the order in which the tests would be administered. In some ways, the work of the neuropsychological assessor is analogous to that of a detective attempting to solve a crime. Decisions about how to proceed with the investigation are made as information is gathered. In like fashion, the examiner administering the LNNB is viewed as an active participant in the assessment, ever making decisions about what direction the assessment should take (Golden et al., 1985).

Of course, given the nature of any standardized test, there are limits as to how flexible the examiner/detective can be. A standardized procedure typically requires a beginning, a middle, and an end, and any significant alteration in this sequence, or any addition or subtraction of procedures, is very much against the rules. And herein lies the LNNB controversy: although the test manual provides standardized instructions, it also encourages, in the tradition of Luria, flexibility in test administration (Adams, 1980b; Stambrook, 1983).

A casualty of this conflict between open-ended flexibility and standardization in test administration is the construct validity of the test. This is so because the construct the test was designed to measure is neuropsychological impairment as conceptualized (and assessed) by Luria. Yet by its very nature, no standardized test may be able to measure neuropsychological impairment in the manner of Luria. Assessment of neuropsychological deficit in the manner of Luria simply does not readily lend itself to assessment by standardized means (Adams, 1985).

Beyond academic debate regarding the viability of the foundation on which the LNNB was built, more practical concerns relate to data from factor analyses of the test's clinical scales. Contrary to the expectation that each of the clinical scales is unidimensional in nature, the scales have been shown to be multidimensional in nature. For all practical purposes, this means that each of the LNNB clinical scales is not simply measuring what its label would suggest it is measuring. Rather, each scale may be measuring a number of different constructs. Factor analysis across all 12 of the clinical scales yielded 50 factors (Golden et al., 1985). Findings such as these complicate the task of interpreting the meaning of high or low scores.

Criterion Validity

Is the LNNB capable of differentiating between people with and without neurological impairment? If so, can test data indicate where and how brain function is impaired?

Beginning with Christensen's (1975) items, Golden et al. used an empirical criterion-keying approach to select only those items on which a sample of 50 impaired individuals performed differently from a sample of 50 unimpaired individuals. Items were then placed into clinical scales using Christensen's organization. Several summary scales were created from individual test items and clinical scales, again using an empirical approach. A "pathognomic summary scale" was created from those items that most clearly discriminated between neurological and control groups. "Localization summary scales" were created from algebraic combinations of clinical scales found to discriminate between controls and people with damage to particular areas of the brain.

The procedures just described have been faulted on various grounds. Item selection was done on small groups of subjects with no cross-validation (Adams, 1980a, 1980b; Snow, 1992). Small numbers of subjects (in some cases nine, or even six) were used to create the summary scales that were intended to provide information about the location of brain damage, again with no cross-validation. As you may recall from the discussion of validity shrinkage in Chapter 7, validity generally declines somewhat when the test is cross-validated. Validity shrinkage may be considerable if the initial group of subjects used to select items or create scales was small. This is so because item selection based on small samples in essence magnifies chance differences between the groups. To understand why this magnification takes place with small samples, consider research designed to determine what the average New York City marathon runner is like on variables such as height, weight, general health, eating habits, pet ownership, educational level, and annual household income. If you compared only ten marathon runners with ten "couch potatoes" on a large number of these variables, you would likely find

(continued)

Validity of the LNNB *(continued)*

some differences between these small groups. If you then looked for those same differences between a new group of marathon runners and couch potatoes, you might well not find them. The original differences you identified may have simply been the result of chance and not a reflection of what people in the two groups are actually like. This problem would be reduced if you had started with large numbers of individuals in each of the two groups.

A second concern about criterion validity data obtained on the LNNB (and other neuropsychological tests as well) involves base rates (Adams, 1980a; Duncan & Snow, 1987). In this context, the *base rate* reflects the proportion of people who have a neuropsychological problem in the population from which the study subjects are drawn. For a test to be considered valid, the validity coefficient should be higher than the base rate (Meehl & Rosen, 1955). To understand why, consider the following example. If a neuropsychological test is applied in a setting in which 85% of the patients are neurologically impaired, the test should identify the presence or absence of impairment with more than 85% accuracy. That is because if no neuropsychological information whatsoever was available about the assessees, an apparently high level of accuracy could be achieved by placing everyone into the more common category. Classifying each person as having a neuropsychological problem would result in 85% accuracy in this case! A neuropsychological test must "beat" the base rate to be considered valid (Duncan & Snow, 1987).

A practical implication of this fact of psychometric life is that a test may be valid in one setting but not in

another. Settings with very high or very low base rates will require highly valid tests to increase accuracy rates above those that would be obtained by simply placing all assessees into the more common category (Duncan & Snow, 1987). In contrast, accuracy rates in settings with less extreme base rates may well be improved with tests having more moderate validity coefficients. Many researchers evaluate the validity of neuropsychological tests using an artificially constructed base rate of 50%, wherein half of the subjects are known to be neurologically impaired and half are known to be unimpaired. In that context, a test may be valid if 80% accuracy is obtained. That same test would not be valid in a setting having a base rate of 85%, because 85% accuracy could be obtained simply by classifying all subjects as neurologically impaired.

Despite the foregoing reservations, independent evaluations of the LNNB have generally been supportive of the test's ability to identify neuropsychological impairment (Van Gorp, 1992). The LNNB has been shown to accurately distinguish between impaired and nonimpaired subjects with an accuracy rate of about 75% to 90%, a rate that is approximately equal to that of the Halstead-Reitan battery (Adams, 1985; Garmoe et al., 1991; Kane et al., 1987; Stambrook, 1983).

Of course, the test user generally wants more from a neuropsychological battery than a present/absent indication concerning neurological impairment. Information about the type of impairment, including the area of the brain affected, is also important. One cross-validation study published by the test authors suggests that the LNNB can determine which hemisphere is damaged with 78% accuracy, and which particular location of the brain is affected with 75% accuracy. However, other research, reviewed by Stambrook (1983) and Van Gorp (1992), has been less supportive of the accuracy of the LNNB in determining the site of brain damage.

Independent evidence has also appeared concerning the criterion-related validity of specific clinical scales on the LNNB (Moses & Maruish, 1988). For example, the LNNB contains a clinical scale designed to measure intellectual skills. Correlations between this LNNB clinical scale and full-scale WAIS and WAIS-R IQs have been reported in the range of − .54 to − .86 (Bryant et al., 1984). (The correlations are negative because higher scores on the LNNB indicate more impairment.) The intelligence scales also correlate slightly less highly with other LNNB scales than they do with the Intellectual Processes scale, within a particular study, which is evidence for discriminative construct validity. For example, the Intellectual Processes scale correlated with WAIS IQ − .84, and the remaining LNNB scales correlated with WAIS IQ − .53 to − .80 (McKay et al., 1981). The LNNB also contains a memory scale, which correlates − .60 to − .82 with the Wechsler Memory Scale (Moses & Maruish, 1988). Thus, at least two of the clinical scales have criterion-related validity evidence to support them.

Content Validity

According to Spiers (1981), the use of Christensen's system to organize the test items has resulted in problems for the test's content validity. For example, the clinical scale designed to measure motor function includes 14 items that seem to assess motor functioning, along with 37 others that seem to assess very different functions, including the sense of one's body position in space and right-left orientation. Such weaknesses in content validity make difficult the task of interpreting clinical scale scores. For example, a high score on the expressive language clinical scale may mean that (1) one cannot express oneself, (2) one has poor reading skills, or (3) one has weaknesses in short-term memory.

Hutchinson (1984) has argued that any test that involves the assessment of specific brain functions through observing behavior will be subject to these kinds of criticisms. Hutchinson states that it is impossible to create "pure" test items, reflecting only memory or language skills, because behaviors are the product of several brain functions working together. Spiers (1984) agreed, but he argued that some of the LNNB scales do not even vaguely reflect the ability or skill they claim to assess.

We have reviewed only some of the questions that have been raised about the LNNB. We have not resolved—nor are we ambitious enough to think that we could resolve—the controversy surrounding the validity of this test. Despite the concerns that have been raised about the LNNB's validity, the test is viewed by many neuropsychologists as the principal (and less time-consuming) alternative to the H-R, a fact that will keep the test "in play" as researchers continue to consider its strengths and weaknesses.

16

The Assessment of People with Disabling Conditions

We are living in an era in which the special needs of our physically challenged citizens are being acknowledged more than they ever before have been. The effects of this ever increasing acknowledgment are visibly evident in things like special access ramps alongside flights of stairs; specially equipped buses designed to accommodate passengers in wheelchairs; large-print newspapers, books, and magazines for the visually impaired; captioned television programming for the hearing-impaired; and signing and pantomiming of important speeches for the hearing-impaired.[1] As medical technology continues to increase the chances that society's disabled citizenry will survive, so society has responded with environmental aids and legal protection for the exceptional individual.[2] In 1973, Congress passed the Rehabilitation Act, a law that has been referred to as "The Bill of Rights for Handicapped Citizens," since it addressed many of the special needs of people with disabilities and outlawed job discrimination on the basis of disability by agencies of the federal government and by entities receiving federal funds. This protection was extended to disabled people involved with private companies through the Americans with Disabilities Act of 1990 (Public Law 101-336). Similar protections have been extended to children as well. In 1975, Congress passed Public Law 94-142, the Education for All Handicapped Children Act, mandating appropriate educational assessment and programs to meet the needs of handicapped children aged 3 to 18.

---

1. Like the noun "mime," the verb *pantomime* has to do with communication by gesturing. As used in the context of psychological testing, pantomime is something that a test administrator might do with a deaf or hearing-impaired examinee to help convey the meaning of some instruction, question, or response.
2. In accordance with general usage of the word in educational contexts, the word "exceptional" is used here in its broadest sense; an *exceptional* individual is someone who differs from most other people with respect to some physical and/or mental ability. People with disabling conditions—as well as the gifted—may in this context be referred to as "exceptional."

This act was amended in 1986 (Public Law 99-457) to extend the age range covered by the law to birth. A 1990 amendment of the same act (Public Law 101-476) specified the broad range of conditions covered by the law: "mental retardation, hearing impairments including deafness, speech or language impairments, visual impairments including blindness, serious emotional disturbance, orthopedic impairments, autism, traumatic brain injury, other health impairments, or specific learning disabilities" (Section 101). Psychologists assessing individuals with such disabling conditions have a legal obligation to "use tests and other assessment materials which have been validated for the purposes for which they are being used" (Department of Health, Education, and Welfare, 1977a, 1977b)—this in the face of a paucity of psychological tests that have been standardized on disabled populations. Further, as O'Keeffe (1993) observed, as many as one in seven Americans has a disability that interferes with activities of daily living and that presumably may compromise the ability to take a psychological test and earn a meaningful score.

In this chapter, we survey some of the special considerations that must be taken into account in testing people who have sensory, motor, and/or cognitive deficits. We begin with a consideration of the factors that must be taken into account when testing blind or visually impaired people.

The Visually Impaired and the Blind

A three-category taxonomy of visual impairment useful in considerations related to testing and assessment was proposed by Bauman (1974). Included in the first category are people for whom vision is of no practical use in a testing or working assignment. The totally blind fall into this classification. Also included in this category are individuals who can differentiate between light and dark or even some who can distinguish shapes but can do so only when those shapes are held between the eyes and the source of light. The next category includes people for whom vision is of some assistance in handling large objects, locating test pieces in a work space, or following the hand movements of the examiner during a demonstration, but who cannot read even enlarged ink print effectively enough to be tested using such materials. Such individuals may be tested with materials that do not rely heavily on vision but, rather, require a combination of vision and touch. The third category includes people who read ink print efficiently, although they may need large type, may hold the page very close to their eyes, or may use a magnifier or some other special visual aid.

Issues in Test Administration and Interpretation

A valid assessment of a visually impaired or blind examinee requires an examiner who is attuned not only to the examinee's visual deficit but also to related deficits that may or may not be present in areas such as language development, socialization skills, and personality in general.[3] Sensitivity to these factors may be developed through experience with such a population and from reading about the experiences of various assessment specialists such as Bauman and Kropf (1979), Bradley-Johnson (1986), Bradley-Johnson and Harris (1990), Drinkwater (1976), Evans (1978), Tillman (1973), and Vander Kolk (1977).

Although the nature of the specific assessment procedures employed will, of course, vary with the particular objective of the assessment, in general, the examiner will proceed in much the same way as with a fully sighted person, except that special attention will be paid to the developmental nature of the deficit and its consequences. Background information collected in the course of a comprehensive assessment may include information about the circumstances of the mother's pregnancy; health in infancy; health in early childhood; adjustment; socialization history; full health history, including age of onset of visual deficit; complete diagnosis, including related deficits such as color recognition skills, prognosis (including the findings of all specialists who have treated the patient), treatments administered (including lens prescription if available); and records of previous testing and school attendance, as well as related records. The choice of the test instrument will, of course, depend on the specific purpose of the assessment, but the instrument should contain pictures, diagrams, and the like only to the extent that the examinee will be capable of seeing such visual materials. The following are some other commonsense guidelines in testing a visually impaired or blind person:

- Modify the amount of light in the room so that it is optimal for the person being tested. Some examinees may require more light, and all that may be required is an extra lamp on an adjacent desk. Other examinees may be disturbed by excessive light and glare.

- It is important under any testing conditions to have a quiet testing room that is free of distractions. However, this requirement takes on added importance in the testing of blind or visually impaired people, since these individuals may be more distracted by extraneous sounds than are the fully sighted.

- The work space should be relatively compact so that all equipment is within grasp of the examinee.

- If the test stimulus materials to be administered require some reading and the test is being administered to a partially seeing person, then it is advisable to retype the materials in large type if they are not already in large type. For the totally blind, an administration in braille may be appropriate; however, it is a fact that relatively few totally blind individuals read braille and relatively few of these people read it well.

---

3. The phenomenon whereby one problem (such as a physical disability) may cause other kinds of difficulties for a particular individual (for example, personality-related problems) is referred to informally by clinicians as a "ripple effect." Needless to say, our caveat here concerning test-user sensitivity with respect to how one problem in an examinee's life could have affected other areas of that person's life is applicable to the assessment of all people and not just the blind or visually impaired.

- For the partially seeing examinee, writing instruments and written materials should be appropriate for the task. Thus, for example, a black felt-tip pen or crayon in most instances will be more appropriate than a fine-point ballpoint pen. Similarly, special wide-lined paper may be in order.

- In general, persons with impaired vision require more time than do non-impaired individuals. It may take longer to dictate materials than for the examinees to read the materials themselves. When the partially sighted person is asked to use residual vision, test fatigue may set in, evidenced by behavior such as eye rubbing or other extraneous movements. Adequate time must be allowed for when testing the visually impaired, and speeded tests may be inappropriate (Nester, 1993).

- The use of multiple-choice questions, even when such questions are presented in braille, is frowned on by experts in this area, because this type of question places an extra burden of concentration on the visually impaired examinee.

- Introduction to the testing situation should include time for the examinee with a severe visual impairment to touch all the materials he or she will be working with during the test. During testing, more verbal information about what is going on may be required than with a sighted individual.

It is difficult, time-consuming, and expensive to develop norms applicable for use with the blind and the visually impaired; the number of cases is relatively small, and the group is quite varied in degree of sightedness and in related factors, including time of life in which vision became impaired or was lost, experience with respect to rehabilitative efforts, and other deficits compounding the effect of the visual impairment. Interpretation of standardized tests that have been modified for administration to blind or visually impaired people—like the interpretation of standardized tests that have been modified for administration to people with any other disabling conditions—is a matter of professional judgment; in many instances no relevant normative data will be available.

Available Instruments

The Verbal Scale of the Wechsler intelligence tests has been used frequently in assessing the intellectual functioning of blind and visually impaired people. The Verbal Scale is orally administered and does not include any visual stimuli, except in some portions of the Arithmetic subtest that can be easily modified. One study that compared the performance of sighted children with that of blind and visually impaired children suggested that norms specifically developed for the blind and visually impaired are necessary (Groenveld & Jan, 1992). Children who were blind or had severe visual impairment tended to perform about 1 standard deviation below the mean of sighted children on the Comprehension subtest, and their scores were close to the average for sighted children on the Information, Similarities, Vocabulary, and Arithmetic subtests.

The fourth edition of the Stanford-Binet contains two subtests (Memory for Sentences, Memory for Digits) that can be administered without modification to visually impaired individuals. The use of braille versions for other subtests has been recommended (Delaney & Hopkins, 1987), although interpretation of findings must be cautious because of the absence of relevant norms. An intelligence test specifically designed for use with the blind and the visually impaired is the Haptic Intelligence Scale (HIS). The word *haptic* refers to the sense of touch, and the HIS exclusively employs the sense of touch in its administration; partially sighted examinees must wear a blindfold when taking this test, for viewing the test materials would invalidate the findings. Some of the subtests are described in Figure 16-1.

A number of other tests of intellectual ability have been developed for use with the visually impaired. Some have been modeled after existing intelligence tests (such as the Interim Hayes-Binet and the Perkins Binet), whereas others are independent in rationale from existing tests (for example, the Vocational Intelligence Scale for the Adult Blind, the Tactile Progressive Matrices, the Tactile Reproduction Pegboard, and the Blind Learning Aptitude Test).

In the area of personality assessment, most existing methods available for use with the sighted (see Part 4 of this book) can be readily adapted for use with the visually impaired and the blind. Test materials that must be read can be reprinted in large type, read to the examinee, or prerecorded on tape. Even a test such as the Thematic Apperception Test can be administered to a blind person if the blind person hears a description of the card and then proceeds to tell a story about it. A specially developed TAT-like test for the blind is the Sound Test, which contains prerecorded sounds such as footsteps, running water, and music, combined in some instances with verbal interchanges; the examinee's task is to construct a story about such aural stimuli. Other specially devised personality tests include The Emotional Factors Inventory and the Adolescent Emotional Factors Inventory, two tests that include scales measuring the examinee's adjustment to blindness. The Maxfield-Bucholz Social Competency Scale for Blind Preschool Children is a measure of social competence and adaptive behavior designed for use with blind children from birth to age 6. The scale is administered to a third party such as the parent, guardian, or primary caregiver, and it is designed to explore areas such as the subject's physical development, ability with respect to self-care, and social competency.

Tests have also been developed to help the blind and the visually impaired with vocational guidance. Many of the available tests of finger and hand dexterity are used with this population. Available vocational interest inventories are administered to this population in large-print editions, braille, or other adaptations. One such test, the PRG Interest Inventory, was based entirely on the content of the types of jobs held by and the types of hobbies indulged in by blind respondents. In the test's instructions, examinees are advised to respond as if they have the visual capabilities to handle the description of the various jobs. The instructions were worded this way so that the test would yield a veritable measure of interest as opposed to perceived capability.

Visual impairment may affect the outcome of neuropsychological tests (Kempen et al., 1994), thus prompting a neurologically oriented neuropsychologist to look to the brain for answers about the poor test performance. However, as Kempen et al. (1994) have advised, a simple vision test may be all that is necessary in some cases to answer key questions about poor test performance.

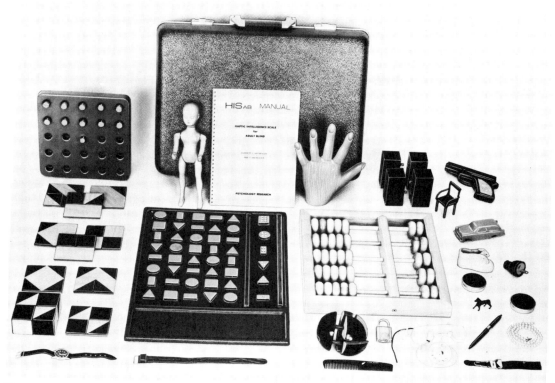

Figure 16–1
The Haptic Intelligence Scale

The Haptic Intelligence Scale (Shurrager & Shurrager, 1964) is an individually administered intelligence test designed for use with the adult blind. The test is composed of the following subtests:

Digit Symbol—Different patterns of raised dots (not braille) on sample geometric forms provide the code that the examinee uses to identify and "decode" like objects.

Block Design—Blocks with two rough sides and two sides diagonally bisected into half rough/half smooth sides are arranged in designs that reproduce a model design.

Object Assembly—As in the Wechsler test, jigsawlike pieces are assembled into objects (such as a hand, a ball, a human figure).

Object Completion—Modeled after the Wechsler Picture Completion subtests, this subtest asks the subject to identify the missing part of a familiar object through touching it.

Pattern Board—The testtaker's task on this subtest is to reproduce the pattern felt on a board that has rows of holes with pegs in them.

Bead Arithmetic—An abacus is used to solve arithmetic problems of varying difficulty.

The Hearing-Impaired and the Deaf

Hearing-impaired individuals differ with respect to variables such as magnitude of hearing loss, age of onset of loss, and consequential effects of the loss on language skills and social adjustment. Examiners who work with this population typically have access to a wealth of background information on each examinee (developmental, family, and school history; medical history, including audiological and speech evaluation; and so forth). Such background information will be useful not only in answering the particular assessment question asked but also in formulating meaningful recommendations for treatment or remediation. For example, the examinee whose history shows the onset of severe hearing loss before the development of speech and language will require a remedial program that will be quite different from an examinee who suffered the hearing loss after the development of speech, although the two examinees might have had the exact same test scores on some psychological tests.

Issues in Test Administration and Interpretation

Most psychologists do not have technical expertise in American Sign Language (ASL) or other languages that have been devised for communication with the deaf. It is also true that many of the deaf or hearing-impaired people to be examined with psychological tests are not proficient enough in lipreading for the examiner to be certain that all test-related communications have been received. If the hearing impairment is mild, amplification of the examiner's voice through the use of an electronic amplification apparatus (or a hearing aid worn by the examinee) may be all that is required to be able to administer the test. However, if the hearing problem is more severe, the communication problem may be solved by one or more of the following solutions: (1) presenting written instructions at a reading level appropriate to the examinee, (2) pantomiming instructions and questions, and (3) conducting the examination through the use of an "interpreter" who will sign and/or pantomime all communication to the examinee and translate the examinee's responses when necessary.

Essential as one or more of the solutions outlined are, there are drawbacks associated with each. For example, using written communication instead of spoken communication introduces another variable (reading proficiency) into the task where no such variable had existed before. Pantomiming instructions and cues in the absence of explicit directions for doing so in the test manual results in a situation where different pantomimists (that is, different test administrators) may well have different ideas about how to get a point across by gestures; hence, the standardization of the instructions to the examinee will suffer. The introduction of an interpreter into the situation may have the effect of diminishing the rapport between the examiner and the examinee. Further, a certain amount of error in expressive and receptive translations can also be expected. The interpreter's signing skills must be compatible with the assessee's receptive skills. It would be inappropriate, for example, for the interpreter to sign in Coded Sign English (a method of communication more closely linked to the written/verbal expression of people with no hearing impairment) if the assessee is more fluent in ASL. Verbal information, especially idioms and proverbs, is not readily amenable to translation into sign, and the assessor must carefully examine test materials in advance with that fact in mind—and appropriately modify the administration materials if need be. Sign language is, in fact, a different language from English, and translations of tests into sign language should be treated with as much care as any foreign-language translation (Nester, 1993).

In the interpretation of test findings, an important distinction arises between performance that is due to substandard English-language skills and performance that is due to lack of intelligence or psychopathology. Relatively few psychologists have a great deal of experience assessing the deaf (Gibbins, 1989), and to the inexperienced assessor, the communication style of a deaf person may seem fragmented or concrete, much like the communication style of schizophrenics or people with other disorders (Misaszek et al., 1985). An inexperienced assessor might readily see intellectual and/or personality deficits, whereas a more experienced assessor might see only speech and language difficulties along with a certain amount of immaturity that is typically associated with such difficulties (Chess & Fernandez, 1981; Sullivan & Vernon, 1979). Prevention of such problems can be fostered by supervised work in assessment settings for the deaf and the hearing-impaired under the aegis of an experienced assessor, and by familiarity with the relevant literature (see, for example, Cates & Lapham, 1991; Elliot et al., 1987; and Zieziula, 1982). Where appropriate, test findings should be supplemented with case history data, as well as information derived from behavioral observation and reports from caregivers such as parents or teachers.

Available Instruments

The Wechsler tests for testtakers in the appropriate age group are in popular use with the hearing-impaired and the deaf to assess intellectual functioning. Generally, just the Performance Scale of the age-appropriate Wechsler test is used, and that scale has been the most studied: one review of testing with this population turned up 102 studies that used the Performance Scale but only five studies that used the Verbal Scale (Braden, 1992). With regard to the WAIS-R Performance Scale, meta-analysis of nine studies indicated that the average performance for deaf and hearing-impaired testtakers was very similar to that of hearing testtakers. The mean full scale WAIS-R score for deaf and hearing-impaired adults was 102.84. A meta-analysis of 44 studies of the WISC-R with deaf and hearing-impaired children produced an average full scale score of 100.81 (Braden, 1992). Almost all of the studies in these meta-analyses used hearing norms to compute IQ scores. WISC-R norms have been developed for hearing-impaired children (Anderson & Sisco, 1977), thus allowing comparison of an individual's performance with that of similarly disabled and/or hearing peers. Ray (1979) developed an adapted WISC-R Performance Scale designed to minimize examiner-examinee communication through the use of supplemental and alternative instructions that make great use of examples. These sample items are unscored and are repeated until the task is understood by the examinee.

The Kaufman Assessment Battery for Children contains a nonverbal scale for children from age 4 through 12½. The subtests are administered in pantomime or gesture and require a nonverbal or motoric response. Nonverbal norms allow for comparison with similarly challenged and/or hearing peers. Validity studies with this scale have generally supported its use (Gibbins, 1988; Kennedy & Hiltonsmith, 1988; Phelps & Branyan, 1988).

A continuing source of controversy in the assessment of intelligence of the hearing-impaired and the deaf concerns the necessity of separate norms. Braden (1992) argued against separate norms on the grounds that the norms would likely be based on a much smaller sample of testtakers than existing norms for hearing individuals. Additionally, at least with respect to norms for certain scales of existing intelligence tests, Braden (1992) argued that the specially devised norms would end up being quite similar to norms for hearing people. As you may conclude for yourself while reading on, Braden's (1992) position on this matter is controversial.

Measures of academic achievement using tests such as the Metropolitan Achievement Test and the Stanford Achievement Tests can be useful, since both of these tests have been standardized with members of this population. In general, hearing-impaired and deaf children do not perform as well on such tests as do their hearing peers. This is due not only to their language impairment but also to the lack of curriculum methods developed specifically to meet the educational needs of the deaf. Only 5% of graduates from educational programs for the deaf attain a tenth-grade education; 41% achieve a seventh- or eighth-grade-level education, and 30% are functionally illiterate.

Experts in the area of the personality assessment of the deaf, especially children who have never had hearing, do not encourage such assessment by means of paper-and-pencil inventories. A reading level above sixth grade is rare among the prelingual deaf because of the great obstacles to language acquisition they face (Trybus, 1973). A modification of the 16 PF (Form E), expressly designed to be at a reading level between third and fifth grade, was once thought to have great promise for use with the prelingual deaf, but poor intratest reliability has plagued it (Jensema, 1975).

The Rorschach has been recommended for use with only those deaf people known to be above average in intelligence and able to sign fluently (Vernon & Brown, 1964), although clinicians experienced with this special population may be able to use it more routinely (Sachs, 1976). Other projective measures, such as those involving drawings (Johnson, 1989; Ouellette, 1988), the Bender Visual-Motor Gestalt Test used projectively (Gibbins, 1989), and the TAT (Vernon & Brown, 1964), may prove insightful. Cates and Lapham (1991) caution that although the TAT may be useful, deaf children and adolescents may concretely label the cards, then perseverate on themes in an effort to supply the "right" answer:

> A potential difficulty in administering apperception techniques to deaf children and adolescents is a tendency toward response perseveration. For example, if unfamiliar with the task, the deaf student may initially attempt to label the picture. If this response is corrected, the deaf student may then perceive the first story told as the correct response. If the first correct response is a story contain-

ing a violent theme, then the deaf client may assume that violence is desired or appropriate in the stories and perseverate on violent themes. The clinician must decide whether to allow the perseveration or restructure the response set of the child or adolescent. The authors generally noted the perseverative phenomenon, then restructured the response set, indicating that each picture may elicit differing themes. (p. 125)

Cates and Lapham (1991) also reported on concrete types of response that may be given on another projective measure, the Hand Test. They found that

deaf children and adolescents give a higher frequency of concrete responses to the Hand Test than do their hearing counterparts. For example, in response to the first card—a hand held up, palm outward—the deaf child may initially provide a description of the hand (e.g., "It's a hand, held up. Five fingers.") rather than describe the hand in some form of activity, as requested in the instructions. In the Hand Test scoring system, this type of descriptive response is considered indicative of severe disturbance. The clinician using the Hand Test, then, may wish to administer the test according to standardized procedure, followed by a testing-the-limits procedure, in which the deaf child is urged to provide more appropriate responses. Alternatively, following the first descriptive response, the clinician may wish to reemphasize the instructions, elicit a more appropriate response, and consider the initial response as training. The deaf subject may also benefit from an inclusion to the standard directions that the hands are not signing. (p. 122)

Behavior checklists and rating scales can prove to be valuable tools of assessment with the deaf (McCoy, 1972). The most extensively used checklist with deaf children and adolescents is the Meadow-Kendall Social-Emotional Assessment Inventory (Meadow et al., 1980), appropriate for use with individuals age 7 to 21 years old. Other such instruments, not necessarily designed especially for the deaf, include the Behavior Problem Checklist (Quay & Peterson, 1967, 1983), the Devereaux Adolescent Behavior Rating Scale (Spivack et al., 1967), the Devereaux Child Behavior Rating Scale (Spivak & Spotts, 1966), the Child Behavior Checklist (Achenbach, 1978), and the Walker Problem Behavior Identification Checklist (Walker, 1976).

A measure of general aptitude in common use with the deaf and the hearing-impaired is the Nebraska Test of Learning Aptitude developed by Marshall S. Hiskey (1966) and frequently referred to as "the Hiskey Nebraska." Another widely used measure of aptitude is the Arthur Adaptation of the Leiter International Performance Scale (Arthur, 1950). Vocational aptitude testing with this population may include tests of manual dexterity, mechanical aptitude, and spatial relations ability. Vocational interests tests designed for use with the hearing-impaired rely heavily on pictures as opposed to words (for example, The Geist Picture Interest Inventory).

The Deaf-Blind

In response to the rubella epidemic that spread across the United States from 1963 to 1965 and the resulting increase in multiply handicapped babies, Congress created ten Regional Centers for Deaf-Blind Youths and Adults in 1967. These centers were charged with the responsibility of identifying and assessing such children.

Although relatively few in number, the deaf-blind as a group are legally entitled by federal law to a free and appropriate public school education. Unfortunately, few school psychologists or other professional personnel in the schools have much training or experience in working with such multiply handicapped youngsters. The assessment of members of this population represents the "most difficult diagnosis task a psychologist can be asked to do" (Vernon et al., 1979, p. 291). The psychologist must be particularly wary of diagnostic errors that might lead to the placement of such children into programs for the mentally or emotionally impaired when, in fact, such programs would be inappropriate for the particular child.

Few standardized tests are appropriate for use with the deaf-blind. Standardized tests developed for and standardized on individuals with other disabling conditions do not adequately take into account the multiplicity and the pervasiveness of impairments of the deaf-blind. Psychological assessment of the deaf-blind most typically involves assessment of adaptive behavior (to be discussed later in greater detail) as well as interviews with caregivers and analysis of case history material. One of the few tests designed for use with, and standardized on, this population is the Callier-Azusa Scale (CAS).

The CAS is a behavior checklist that enables the examiner to compare the subject's development in a number of areas (motor, perceptual, language, daily living skills, and socialization) with typical development for deaf-blind children, from birth to 9 years, who have received appropriate interventions. The test is useful both in educational program planning and as a posttest to assess behavior change after a specific intervention. Stillman (1974) recommends that more than one rater assess the child's behavior both at home and at school for at least two weeks. Information is usually provided by a parent, the teacher, and/or some other person having extensive contact with the child. Adequate reliability has been reported with respect to the test's 16 subscales. The test authors also reported that the scale's reliability was not significantly influenced by the child's educational setting or the number of people rating the child (Bennett et al., 1979). Related to validity evidence, Diebold, Curtis, and Dubose (1978) have demonstrated the strong relationship for a sample of 6- to 13-year-old deaf-blind children between systematic observation of daily behavior measures and performance on CAS developmental scales. The 16 subscales of the CAS yield an age-equivalent score rather than IQ, but the conversion table is psychometrically unsound and therefore few professionals use it. Credit for particular items is awarded only if the behavior is "present fully and regularly." Behaviors that are just emerging are not credited. If the deaf-blind child has additional disabilities, such as a motor deficit, specific CAS items can be omitted.

Another standardized test that can be used with the deaf-blind is the Assessment of Development Levels by Observation (ADLO; Wolf-Schein, 1993). As its name implies, the ADLO entails systematic observation of behavior and classification of it by developmental level. Behavior is assessed and classified on variables related to self-help skills, fine and gross motor skills, receptive (listening and understanding) and expressive language, and relationships with adults. Typically, the test is conducted in a setting familiar to the child; an observer evaluates the child playing alone, interacting with familiar and unfamiliar adults, and working with a language specialist. Norms are available for children from birth to 8 years of age. Measured inter-rater reliability for this test is good (in the range of .86 to .92). Work remains to be done to establish the test's validity. The only available validity information is based on one study, which found that the ADLO and the Vineland Adaptive Behavior Scales (discussed later in this chapter) agree on developmental level of the assessee in 70% of cases (Wolf-Schein, 1993).

Motor Disabilities

Motor deficits come in many forms and from many varied causes, and may involve any muscle or muscle group in the body. Paralysis, tremors, involuntary movement, gait difficulties, and problems with volitional movement and speech are some of the many types of motor problems that may exist. The cause of the motor problem may be an inherited muscular or neurological difficulty or one acquired as a result of a trauma to the muscle, the brain, or the spinal cord. Other causal factors include the wide range of neuromuscular diseases. Cases of cerebral palsy, for example, are believed to occur at the rate of 1.6 to 5 per 1,000 in the under-21 population. The palsy may be caused by an endocrine imbalance, low blood sugar, anoxia, a high forceps delivery, or any of a variety of other factors before, during, or after birth.

Issues in Test Administration and Interpretation

Most of the tests used to assess intellectual functioning rely at least in part on the respondent's ability to manipulate some materials—be they cards, blocks, beads, or whatever; the test that does not contain such tasks would be criticized by experts as being too loaded on verbal as opposed to performance measures of intelligence. Examiners wishing to assess the intelligence of motor-handicapped people will attempt to select an existing test that does not need to be modified in any way for administration to the particular individual being assessed. If all available tests were to require modification, the test requiring the least modification would be selected. An example of a modification that might be employed when administering a block design task, for example, would require the examiner to physically turn the blocks until the examinee indicates that the rotation of the block is his or her response. The examinee might indicate this with a verbal response or, if there is a speech deficit, with some other response, such as a wink of the eye. On paper-and-pencil tasks that require fine motor coordination, such as tests that involve blackening tiny grids with number 2 pencils, the motor-handicapped individual might require a writer to enter the responses. The alternative (not to administer any motor tasks to the motor-handicapped examinee) is the approach taken by some examiners; the rationale

Attitudes Toward the Disabled

Besides assessment of the disabled, psychological tests may serve related purposes, such as increasing our understanding of attitudes existing toward the disabled. With this latter goal in mind, you may wish to try the following exercise. Make up a story with a beginning, a middle, and an end in response to the TAT-like picture that appeared on page 440. Now do the same thing in response to the picture below. Finally, analyze the content of your two stories with respect to any dif-ferences that emerge solely as a function of the pros-thetic device the man is wearing in the second picture. What do these differences tell you, if anything, about your own attitudes toward the disabled? You and your classmates may wish to try this exercise with a few people willing to serve as your research subjects—perhaps some who are disabled and some who are not—to get a sense of the nature of narrative specif-ics pertaining to the prosthetic device.

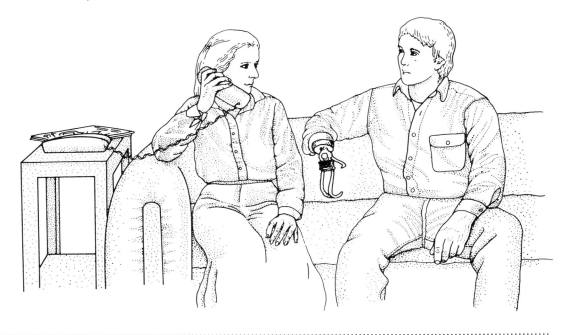

here is that a verbal test such as the Vocabulary subtest of a Wechsler examina-tion correlates highly with the rest of the examination and may therefore be used as a rough estimate of both verbal and nonverbal intelligence. However, such a procedure provides only a *rough estimate* and is never in good practice if used for placement decisions in the absence of other assessment data.

Available Instruments

Many existing instruments used to assess intelligence, personality, educational achievement, and the like are amenable to adaptation for use with motor-handicapped examinees. Sattler (1972) investigated the adaptation of selected Stanford-Binet (Form L-M) and WISC items for use with members of this population. Using "normal" and mentally retarded children and children with cerebral palsy, Sattler modified all subtests (between levels I and V) that involved a verbal or motor response. These modifications included changes in test stimuli and changes in the method of response (similar to the yes-no response discussed earlier). The tests that couldn't be modified were omitted and alternate tests were used. Overall, this modified form appeared to have an acceptable level of concurrent validity (Sattler, 1972). Perhaps the primary finding was that mentally retarded and cerebral-palsied children scored higher mean IQs on the modified form than on the original standard form. Sattler also continued with modifications at the upper levels (ages 9 to 12), particularly in memory subtests. The results at this age level were not as encouraging. Sattler believed that modification of the memory tests made them easier. Sattler also modified some of the WISC subtests (Digit Span, Block Design, and Coding) and concluded that there was a significant correlation between the modified and the standardized form and the modification would therefore be appropriate for use with handicapped children.

Katz (1955) also conducted studies with cerebral palsied and nonhandicapped children with the Standford-Binet (Form L). Again, response modifications such as pointing were used on certain subtests. His results suggested that at least for the levels of the questions he had employed in his study (levels II through VI), the Stanford-Binet was an appropriate tool for use in evaluating the intelligence of cerebral-palsied children. Other possible ways to modify existing instruments for use with members of this population include the "eye-pointing" method proposed by Reynell (1970) and the "halfstep" method introduced by Theye (1970). Theye administered the WISC Block Design and Picture Arrangement subtests using cues he called halfsteps to help the examinees complete the items. Conceivably, the notion of "halfsteps"—graduated cues to facilitate item completion—could be applied to various kinds of motor tasks administered to persons with motor deficits.

Psychologists and special educators who assess variables such as the severity of a motor deficit have a number of tests at their disposal for use. Four test batteries in current use are the Purdue Perceptual-Motor Survey, the Bruininks-Oseretsky Test of Motor Proficiency, the Frostig Movement Skills Test Battery, and the Southern California Sensory Integration Tests. The Purdue is a screening device that provides guidelines for assessing various gross and fine motor functions in children aged 6 to 10 years. The Bruininks-Oseretsky also tests gross and fine motor skills as well as general motor proficiency. It is a technically sound test but one that requires (1) a very well trained examiner to administer and interpret and (2) extensive space to administer (such as a playground or a specially equipped room). The Frostig is designed to assess sensorimotor development, gross and fine motor coordination, balance, strength, and flexibility in children aged 6 to 12 years. It is popular among many examiners because it is relatively simple to administer, contains a relatively wide range of motor skills sampled, and is easy to score. The Southern California is also a measure of sensory integrative functioning designed for use with children aged 4 to 9 years. However, this time-consuming test must be administered and interpreted by a highly trained examiner. (See Chapter 15 for more on the last three of these tests.) Other motor skills tests have been developed for use with elderly individuals, including the Physical Disability Index (PDI; Gerety et al., 1993). Designed specifically for "frail" elderly populations, the PDI assesses strength, balance, mobility, and range of motion. The test authors report good levels of inter-rater (.81 to .99) and test-retest (.97) reliability, and criterion-related validity coefficients ranging from .27 to .56.

Cognitive Disabilities

Throughout this text, we have discussed assessment considerations that are applicable in assessing people who are cognitively exceptional in some way. Particularly relevant, of course, are the chapters on the assessment of intelligence and personality. In Chapter 10 (Educational Assessment), we focused on the definition and assessment of learning disabilities, which also may be thought of as a cognitive exceptionality. In Chapter 14 (Clinical and Counseling Assessment), there was some discussion of people with thought disorders and psychoses, and those categories, too, might qualify for discussion as "cognitive disabilities." Here we focus our discussion on the mentally retarded. Keep in mind that many of the assessment techniques we present are applicable in the assessment of a variety of people. Thus, for example, although we discuss assessment of adaptive behavior with reference to the mentally retarded, it might also be appropriate to assess adaptive behavior of the psychotic, the neurologically impaired, the gifted, or other different kinds of individuals.

Developmental Disability

The most widely accepted definition of mental retardation is the one set forth in 1983 by the American Association of Mental Deficiency (AAMD): "Mental retardation refers to significantly subaverage general intellectual functioning existing concurrently with deficits in adaptive behavior, and manifested during the developmental period."

The deficits in adaptive behavior refer to deficits in adjusting to the demands of the environment, and the diagnosis of mental retardation is made not only on the basis of an individual intelligence test but also on the basis of an assessment of adaptive behavior. Table 16-1 (pages 622–623) describes levels of mental retardation. Most mentally retarded people can be classified according to the AAMD classification system as mildly retarded. The remaining 15 percent or so may be classified as moderate, severe, or profound in retardation.

Assessing Adaptive Behavior

The concept of "adaptive behavior" has a long history rooted not only in psychology but in anthropology and sociology as well. Lambert (1978) notes that references to concepts like adaptive behavior were being made by authorities in the field of mental retardation before 1850. In 1905, Alfred Binet made reference to a concept we would now recognize as "adaptive behavior" when he said "an individual is normal if he is able to conduct his affairs of life without having need of supervision of others, if he is able to work sufficiently remunerative to supply his own personal needs . . ." (Binet, quoted in Goddard, 1916). The concepts of intelligence and adaptive behavior are indeed very closely related—so closely related that at least in one introductory psychology textbook, intelligence tests were defined as "measures of an individual's adaptive behavior in meeting a particular set of environmental challenges" (Zimbardo & Ruch, 1975, p. 206). Although there is clearly overlap between the two concepts, adaptive behavior has been more traditionally viewed as synonymous with terms such as adjustment, social maturity (Doll, 1953), adaptive capacity (Fullan & Loubser, 1972), and personal and social competence (Cain et al., 1963). For our purposes, we will define *adaptive behavior* as the personal and social effectiveness and appropriateness of one's actions. As you might appreciate, this definition is wide-ranging and includes everything from the development of self-feeding skills to the ability of an adult to earn a living and be a productive member of society.

Tests of adaptive behavior are in structure more like interviews than they are "tests" per se. Typically, a third party familiar with the assessee is asked a series of questions about the assessee's behavior in a variety of situations. Exactly what situations are asked about will depend in part on the chronological age of the individual being assessed. For infants, the assessment of adaptive behavior might take the form of questioning whether the infant is able to stand up without assistance. For the preschooler, questions concerning personal hygiene and self-care will be asked. Through the school years and into adulthood, additional questions concerning self-care and personal hygiene will be asked as well as questions concerning interpersonal relations, finances, social awareness, and other areas.

The Vineland Adaptive Behavior Scales   The Vineland Social Maturity Scale was originally developed by Edgar A. Doll (1953), then the Director of Research at the Vineland Training School in Vineland, New Jersey. Three decades later, the test was revised and published as the Vineland Adaptive Behavior Scales (VABS; Sparrow et al., 1984). The revised test, like its predecessor, is usually referred to simply as "the Vineland." In the tradition of its predecessor, it emphasizes social competence, which Doll (1953, p. 2) conceived of as "a functional composite of human traits which subserves social usefulness as reflected in self-sufficiency and service to others." The primary use of the Vineland is to assess the adaptive behavior of developmentally disabled individuals.

The revised Vineland is available in three forms: the Survey Form of the

Table 16–1
Levels of Mental Retardation

Level	Preschool Age: Birth to 5 Years	School Age: 6 to 21 Years
Mild retardation	Can develop social and communication skills; minimal retardation in sensorimotor areas; rarely distinguished from normal until later age.	Can learn academic skills to approximately sixth-grade level by late teens. Cannot learn general high school subjects. Needs special education, particularly at secondary school age levels.
Moderate retardation	Can talk or learn to communicate; poor social awareness; fair motor development; may profit from self-help; can be managed with moderate supervision.	Can learn functional academic skills to approximately fourth-grade level by late teens if given special education.
Severe retardation	Poor motor development; speech is minimal; generally unable to profit from training in self-help; little or no communication skills.	Can talk or learn to communicate; can be trained in elemental health habits; cannot learn functional academic skills; profits from systematic habit training.
Profound retardation	Gross retardation; minimal capacity for functioning in sensorimotor areas; needs nursing care.	Some motor development present; cannot profit from training in self-help; needs total care.

Interview Edition, the Expanded Form of the Interview Edition, and the Classroom Edition. The two Interview Edition forms (Sparrow et al., 1984a, 1984b) were designed for use with individuals from birth to age 18, as well as with low-functioning adults. They are both structured interviews undertaken with a parent or some other informant who is very familiar with the assessee. The Survey Form contains 297 items and requires 20 to 60 minutes to administer. The Expanded Form is a more detailed version of the interview that contains 577 items (including the 297 items in the briefer form). It takes between 60 and 90 minutes to administer. The third form of the Vineland, the Classroom Edition (Sparrow et al., 1985), is a 244-item form completed by a teacher that focuses primarily on behavior in an academic context. It is designed for use with assessees ranging in age from 3 to 13 years old.

All three forms of the test tap the areas, or "domains," of daily living, socialization, motor function, and communication. In addition, the two Interview Edition forms contain items relevant to maladaptive behavior. In each domain, the informant is asked to provide information relative to actual behaviors. Skills are broken down into component behaviors so that the level of ability can be specified. For example, in the area of daily living skills, the informant is asked

Adult: Over 21 Years	Range in Standard Deviation Value	Approximate Mental Age at Adulthood	Percent in Population	Stanford-Binet 4th Edition IQ Range	Wechsler Scale IQ Range
Capable of social and vocational adequacy with proper education and training. Frequently needs guidance when under serious social or economic stress.	−2.01 to −3.00	8.3 to 10.9	0.8	67−52	69−55
Capable of self-maintenance in unskilled or semiskilled occupations; needs supervision and guidance when under mild social or economic stress.	−3.01 to −4.00	5.7 to 8.2	0.10	51−36	54−40
Can contribute partially to self-support under complete supervision; can develop self-protection skills to a minimal useful level in controlled environment.	−4.01 to −5.00	3.2 to 5.6	0.04	35−20	39−25
Some motor and speech development; totally incapable of self-maintenance; needs complete care and supervision.	< −5.00	<3.2	0.02	<20	<25

about the individual's ability to put on shoes, including the individual elements of this ability, such as lacing shoes and tying a bowknot. In the area of socialization skills, the informant may be asked about the assessee's table manners, and everything from using a napkin to requesting items on the table.

Normative data are available for all forms of the Vineland. For the Interview Edition, data were gathered on about 4,800 people without disabilities. For the Classroom Edition, approximately three thousand children and adolescents constituted the normative sample. All standardization data were gathered from normative groups that had been drawn nationally and were stratified according to the 1980 U.S. Census for sex, geographical region, size of community, parents' education, and race and ethnicity. Raw scores on the test are converted into standard scores with a mean of 100 and a standard deviation of 15. Scores are calculated separately for each domain. A total score, called the Adaptive Behavior Composite, incorporates evaluative data from each of the domains. More on psychometric aspects of this test is presented in *Everyday Psychometrics*.

The AAMD Adaptive Behavior Scales   Other commonly used tests of adaptive behavior are the Adaptive Behavior Scale (ABS) and the Adaptive Behavior Scale,

Psychometric Evaluation of the Vineland

Quick quiz before reading on: Based on what you have read about the Vineland to this point, what specific types of reliability and validity do you think are (or should be) available for this test? Check your answer against the discussion that follows.

The manuals for the Vineland provide information about the internal consistency reliability, test-retest reliability, and inter-rater reliability of the Survey Form of the Interview Edition (Sparrow et al., 1984b) as well as the Classroom Edition (Sparrow et al., 1985). Because no alternate forms of these editions exist, no measure of alternate-forms reliability can be obtained. Few reliability data are available for the Expanded Form (Sparrow et al., 1984a).

In evaluating the test's internal consistency, each domain is conceived of as a homogeneous unit, even though a wide variety of skills is assessed. Internal consistency of the Survey Form was estimated using a split-half procedure, and coefficient alpha was used to estimate the internal consistency of the Classroom Edition. Acceptably high levels of internal consistency were reported for the various domains of both the Survey Form and the Classroom Edition. Additionally, an acceptably high level of internal consistency was reported for the Maladaptive Behavior scale, which is part of the Survey Form only (see the following table). Note that the test authors did not report estimates of internal consistency for the Expanded Form.

The internal consistency of the Adaptive Behavior Composite, a combination of the test's various scales, was calculated to be .89 to .98 (median = .94) for the Survey Form and .96 to .98 (median = .98) for the Classroom Edition. These values are as high as or higher than the reliability estimates for the separate Vineland scales. From this observation, one might suspect that the various scales of the test overlap to measure the same construct or constructs. This hypothesis should be kept in mind when considering the construct validity of the test.

High coefficients of test-retest reliability are typically expected with regard to tests of adaptive func-

Internal Consistency of the Vineland

Area Assessed	Form	
	Survey form	Classroom form
Communication domain	.89	.93
Daily living skills domain	.90	.95
Socialization domain	.86	.94
Motor skills domain	.83	.80
Maladaptive behavior scale	.86	NA

tioning. This is so because the construct the test is measuring is presumed to be relatively stable over the short term. The test-retest reliability of the Survey Form was calculated over a two- to four-week retest interval. Over this period, the Adaptive Behavior Composite was found to range from .83 to .93, with a median test-retest reliability of .89. Median test-retest reliabilities for the specific domains also demonstrated stability. The test-retest reliability coefficients reported were .80 (Socialization), .81 (Motor Skills), .86 (Communication), and .85 (Daily Living Skills). The median Maladaptive Behavior test-retest reliability was .87. Test-retest reliability coefficients were not reported for either the Expanded Form or the Classroom Edition.

A third type of reliability relevant to a psychometric evaluation of the Vineland is inter-rater reliability. Although the test manual attempts to provide clear guidelines about how to score particular responses, some examiner judgment is necessary and might contribute to error in the test scores. For example, one of the items in the Communication domain asks whether the assessee "relates experiences in detail when asked" (Sparrow et al., 1984a, p. 270). A Socialization domain item asks whether the subject "imitates adult phrases heard on previous occasions" (Sparrow et al., 1984a, p. 296). Because of the lack of sufficiently detailed scoring guidelines, there is a danger that the individual judgment of the respondent, and not the quality of the assessee's behavior, will account for a great proportion of the scoring variance. What criterion is used to determine how much detail is sufficient to be scored as "relating experience in detail"? How good must the imitation of a phrase be to be scored satisfactorily on the item that lists imitation of adult phrases as a criterion? These unanswered questions may have the effect of giving interviewers and informants wide latitude in scoring protocols.

Inter-rater reliability data on the Survey Form were gathered through the use of two interviewers, with interviews separated by 1 to 14 days (the average interval of separation between the first and second interview was 8 days). Differences between the conclusions of the two interviewers may be due to differences between the interviewers themselves. Alternatively, differences between the conclusions of the two interviewers may reflect changes in the informant's responses (a finding that could be made as a result of a test-retest reliability study). Inter-rater reliability coefficients would therefore be expected to be smaller than the test-retest reliability coefficients; after all, not only is information being collected twice, but also more variance is being added to the data collection process (because of different interviewers). In fact, the inter-rater reliability coefficients were lower than the test-retest reliability coefficients. Reported inter-rater reliability estimates were .62 (Socialization domain), .72 (Daily Living Skills domain), .72 (Communication domain), and .78 (Motor Skills domain). An inter-rater reliability coefficient of .74 was reported for both the Adaptive Behavior Composite and the Maladaptive Behavior score. Inter-rater reliability was not assessed for the Expanded Form or the Classroom Edition.

Other inter-rater reliability-related questions with regard to a test such as the Vineland concern the reliability not of the interviewers but of the judges or informants. How reliable is a parent's report on the child from one day to the next? How consistent are reports on a particular child from one teacher to the next? The test's manual is silent on such questions,

decreasing the possibility of a comprehensive evaluation of the Vineland.

Although no quantitative evidence for the content validity of this test is presented, the authors make their case for the test's content validity on the basis of a rational analysis of the content areas surveyed by the items. Especially with regard to the items in the Expanded Form, efforts to tap the widest possible range of adaptive behaviors are described as having been made. And much like those of its expanded version, the items of the Survey Form were designed to sample broadly from various areas of adaptive behavior. The Classroom Edition was designed to contain items that reflect behavior primarily in the academic setting.

Data relative to the test's criterion-related validity are presented for both the Survey Form and the Classroom Edition, though no such data are presented for the test's Expanded Form. Correlations between the original Vineland and the revised Vineland Survey Form ranged from .55 to .97, according to Sparrow et al. (1984b). However, an independent study of the relationship between these two versions of the Vineland yielded a correlation of only .38 (Raggio & Massingale, 1990). Taken as a whole, these data cast doubt on the expectation that the two versions of the same test are indeed measuring the same thing.

Criterion-related validity evidence can also be gathered from examinations of the relationship between the Vineland and other adaptive behavior scales (some of which are discussed later in this chapter). These types of studies have yielded correlations between .40 and .70, according to Sparrow et al. (1984b). However, other researchers have observed higher correlations between the Vineland and other adaptive behavior measures. Correlations of between .50 and .95 were reported by Middleton et al. (1990), and correlations of approximately .90 were reported by Roberts et al. (1993). Reported correlations of the Vineland Survey Form with two other parent-report instruments of

(continued)

Psychometric Evaluation of the Vineland *(continued)*

problem behavior ranged from .46 to .71 (Pearson & Lachar, 1994). Correlations between the Vineland Classroom Edition and other adaptive behavior measures range from .18 to .51 and from .62 to .92 (Harrison, 1985).

Evidence offered in support of the Vineland's construct validity begins with the observation that in children, adaptive behavior increases with age. If Vineland scores also increased with age, this could be construed as evidence to support the notion that the Vineland is indeed measuring adaptive behavior. Both in the Survey Form and in the Classroom Edition, progressive increases are found in average raw scores for each age group in the standardization samples (Sparrow et al., 1984b, 1985). Another way to examine the construct validity of this test has to do with expected differences for special groups. Children with Down's syndrome tend to develop steadily for the first several years, after which development often slows dramatically. Evidence for the construct validity of the Vineland would be obtained by the observation that scores on the test paralleled this known developmental path. In one study, children with Down's syndrome did show age-related gains in raw score on the Vineland through age 6 or 7. After that, the average raw score no longer increased, and performance became more variable. This pattern of results indicated that some children continued to advance, some stayed the same, and others began to decline (Dykens et al., 1994). In general, the results were deemed supportive of the Vineland's construct validity.

Construct validity evidence may also come from relationships among a test's scales as indicated by factor analysis. Recall that the internal consistency reliability computations indicated that the Vineland, across domains, is internally consistent. Such consistency could be expected to correspond with substantial correlations among the various domain scales. Indeed, as reported by the test's authors, median correlations for pairs of domain scales range from .39 to .55 for the Survey Form and from .43 to .70 for the Classroom Edition. Factor analysis by the test's authors resulted in a single factor that accounts for 55–70% of the variance in each age group on the Survey Form. The same single factor was also found to account for 67–80% of the variance in each age group on the Classroom Edition. An independent assessment of the factor structure of the Survey Form produced similar findings, with a single factor explaining 75% of the variability in test scores (Roberts et al., 1993). These findings suggest that the Vineland is assessing a single underlying construct, which could be labeled "adaptive behavior." The findings may also be construed to support the use of the Adaptive Behavior Composite as an index of level of adaptive behavior.

Evidence concerning the convergent and discriminant validity of the Vineland is also reported in the test manuals. Consistent with the idea of discriminant validity, the Vineland correlates less well with measures of intelligence than it does with other measures of adaptive behavior. Stated another way, the Vineland seems to tap a construct that is somewhat distinct from intelligence. According to Sparrow et al. (1984b), correlations between children's scores on the Vineland's Survey Form Adaptive Behavior Composite and the Kaufman Assessment Battery for Children (K-ABC) Mental Processing Composite ranged from .13 to .41 (median = .22). Correlations between the Survey Form Adaptive Behavior Composite and the Peabody Picture Vocabulary Test, Revised (PPVT-R), ranged from .12 to .37 (median = .21). Somewhat higher correlations were observed between the Vineland Classroom Edition and the K-ABC Mental Processing Composite (range .31 to .53, median = .48), as well as the PPVT-R (.20 to .45, median = .31). Communication domain scores tend to correlate most highly with intelligence scales. The skills tapped in the Communication domain may more closely reflect cognitive skills than the other domains of the Vineland (Sparrow et al., 1985).

To demonstrate convergent and discriminant validity, the correlations between the Vineland and other adaptive behavior measures should be greater than the correlations between the Vineland and tests of intelligence. The wide range of discriminant validity coefficients obtained, coupled with the wide range of the criterion-related validity coefficients with which they might be compared, makes such comparisons difficult. For the purposes of clarification, discriminant and convergent validity coefficients within one particular study could be compared. When this is done with the Roberts et al. (1993) data, for instance, evidence of convergent validity (the two adaptive behavior measures correlate .90) and discriminant validity (intelligence correlates with the adaptive behavior measures .26 and .31) can be found.

Now return to the question raised at the very beginning—how did you do? If you were a test reviewer for a scholarly journal, what would you write about the Vineland? Evans and Bradley-Johnson (1988) did scholarly reviews of the Vineland and other adaptive behavior measures. They argue that the moderate levels of test-retest and internal consistency reliability achieved by the Vineland are not as high as they should be for a test of this type. Levels of inter-rater reliability are still lower and are conceptualized only in terms of the reliability of the interviewer. Informant reliability would seem to be an important issue, but it is not considered. Evans and Bradley-Johnson (1988) also conclude that insufficient reliability evidence is available. Only the Survey Form is thoroughly examined relative to reliability issues: no such information is available on the Expanded Form, and only limited reliability information is presented for the Classroom Edition.

Evans and Bradley-Johnson (1988) addressed the validity of the adaptive behavior measures they reviewed as well. They note that none of the measures has very complete information concerning validity, and we concur. Based on the test author's survey of the domains sampled, the test appears to be content-valid, but we would have appreciated some quantitative evidence to support that contention. As it is, our acceptance of the content validity of the test is based more on faith than anything else. Criterion-related validity evidence is so mixed that making relevant comparisons with discriminant validity coefficients is difficult. The range in the magnitude of reported validity coefficients yields a puzzling picture regarding the validity of the Vineland. The fact that the test is not highly correlated with its predecessor and namesake only adds to the mystery. There is some evidence, however, that clearly supports the construct validity of the test. Here we refer to the finding that a single factor underlies scores in the various domains, and that expected age-related changes occur for normal and Down's syndrome children.

Clearly, more thorough study of the Vineland is necessary (Evans & Bradley-Johnson, 1988). Until compelling reliability and validity data are published for all versions of the Vineland, the test should not be considered a solid foundation on which to base important decisions about the lives of disabled individuals.

School Edition (ABSSE), both published by the American Association of Mental Deficiency. The ABS is appropriate for ages 3 to 69, and the ABSSE is appropriate for ages 3 to 16. The ABS was developed as a result of detailed studies of deficient behaviors in the retarded. The instrument is designed to identify behaviors that need remediation. A description of the domains assessed in these scales (independent functioning, physical development, and so forth) appears in Table 16-2. The test yields raw scores that can then be converted to decile scores (though the manual labels them percentile scores). Graphic representations of scores can be made so that scores across behavioral domains can be compared.

The ABS was standardized on approximately four thousand persons aged 3 to 59 residing in 68 residential facilities for the mentally retarded throughout the United States. The ABSSE was standardized on approximately 6,500 people ranging in age from 3 to 16 in classes for the retarded and in normal classes in the states of California and Florida. The scales can be criticized for having unrepresentative standardization samples and for the lack of compelling reliability and validity data presented in the test manuals. Independent research has suggested that when mentally retarded adults in training settings are evaluated by their supervisors using the ABS, inter-rater reliability ranges from .45 to .93, depending on the particular domain being assessed (Salagaras & Nettelbeck, 1984). Some systematic differences between kinds of raters have been identified. In one study using parents and teachers as informants with respect to a child, it was found that parents tended to rate the child's level of adaptive behavior more favorably than did the teacher (Mealor & Richmond, 1980). In another study addressed to the validity of the ABS, performance on the scale was found to be related to productivity in a sheltered workshop setting (Cunningham & Presnall, 1978). Construct validity evidence includes the finding that ABS scores are higher among those who are more retarded and living relatively less independently. ABS scores are lower among retarded adults who are close to being moved from a training setting to a work setting (Salagaras & Nettelbeck, 1984). Factor-analytic studies of the items on the scales have consistently yielded factors labeled "Personal Independence," "Social Maladaption," and "Personal Maladaption" across ages (Nihira, 1969a, 1969b). Still, the content of the individual items is probably too vague in most instances for use in developing detailed intervention programs, and the ABS and ABSSE are probably best thought of as screening instruments, not to be used in important diagnostic or program placement decisions.

Other measures of adaptive behavior The Scales of Independent Behavior (SIB; Bruininks et al., 1985) is an adaptive behavior scale that measures motor, social, personal living, and community skills. Each of these areas is further divided into subareas so that specific strengths and weaknesses can be assessed. Scores in the 14 subareas can also be combined to produce a single "Broad Independence score." Although the SIB is most commonly used with children, norms exist for adults as well. The test is also used with older adults who have Alzheimer's disease or who have experienced a loss of cognitive function as a result of strokes (DeBettignies et al., 1993). The test is administered in the form of a

Table 16–2
Domains Assessed by the ABS and the ABSSE

Part 1 66 items on ABS; 56 on ABSSE
   I. Independent functioning
      A. Eating (use of utensils, table manners)
      B. Toilet use
      C. Cleanliness (bathing, menstruation)
      D. Appearance (posture)
      E. Care of clothing
      F. Dressing and undressing
      G. Travel (sense of direction and use of public transportation)
      H. Other independent functioning (telephone use)
  II. Physical development
      A. Sensory development (vision and hearing)
      B. Motor development (balance, ambulation, motor control)
  III. Economic activity
      A. Money handling (knowledge of money) and budgeting
      B. Shopping skills
  IV. Language development
      A. Expression (articulation, writing, word usage)
      B. Comprehension (understanding complex sentences and reading)
      C. Social language development (conversational language skills)
  V. Numbers and time
  VI. Vocational activity (performance of complex jobs safely and reliably)
  VII. Self-direction
      A. Initiative (initiation of activities and passivity)
      B. Perseverance (attention and persistence)
      C. Leisure time (free-time activities)
  VIII. Responsibility (care of personal belongings and general responsibility)
  IX. Socialization (appropriate and inappropriate behaviors)
  X. Domestic activity (ABS only; cleaning, food, and serving)

Part 2 44 items on ABS; 39 on ABSSE. For each of these ratings the subject responds either "occasionally" or "frequently"
  I. Rebelliousness (disobedience and insubordination)
  II. Antisocial vs. social behavior (teasing, bossing, disruptive behavior, inconsiderate behavior)
  III. Aggressiveness (personal property damage and temper tantrums)
  IV. Trustworthiness (lying, stealing)
  V. Withdrawal vs. involvement (inactivity, withdrawal, and stress)
  VI. Stereotyped behavior and odd mannerisms
  VII. Appropriateness or interpersonal manners
  VIII. Acceptability of vocal habits
  IX. Acceptability of habits (unacceptable or eccentric habits)
  X. Activity level (hyperactive tendencies)
  XI. Symptomatic behavior (possible emotional disturbance)
  XII. Use of psychoactive medications (for control of hyperactivity, seizures, etc.)
  XIII. Self-abusive behavior (ABS only)
  XIV. Sexually aberrant behavior (ABS only; masturbation, homosexuality, rape)

structured interview with an informant who knows the assessee. An adaptation has been developed for use with visually impaired children (Woo & Knowlton, 1992).

Construct validity evidence includes good convergent and discriminant validity evidence with regard to the Vineland Adaptive Behavior Scales. In one study of young children, the composite indices for the Vineland and the SIB were found to correlate .83, and the corresponding domain scores correlated .50 (for the two motor skills domain scores) to .95 (for the two personal living skills scores). Most of the discriminant validity coefficients are lower than the corresponding convergent validity coefficients. For example, the Vineland and SIB Communication domain scores correlate .92. This correlation is higher than correlations of either Communication score with other domains measured by the Vineland or the SIB, which range from .22 to .90 (with a median correlation of .72; Middleton et al., 1990). Others have also reported a high correlation (.90) between the Vineland and the SIB, and an appropriately low (.26) correlation between the SIB and a measure of intelligence (Roberts et al., 1993). Although SIB scores seem to be related to intelligence, the SIB is not measuring the same thing that is assessed by intelligence tests.

One instrument specifically designed for use in assessing the sexual knowledge and attitudes of the developmentally disabled is the Socio-Sexual Knowledge & Attitudes Test (Wish et al., 1980). Topic areas covered by the instrument include anatomy terminology, menstruation, masturbation, dating, marriage, intimacy, intercourse, pregnancy, childbirth, alcohol and drugs, homosexuality, and venereal disease (Figure 16–2). Since expressive language required by the examinee is minimal—most responses are made by pointing or indicating "yes" or "no"—the test is suitable for administration to those with limited language skills or ability. Though the test manual includes normative data on developmentally disabled individuals aged 18 to 42, the intent of the test authors is that the test be used in a criterion-referenced as opposed to a norm-referenced fashion, as a measure of what the individual testtaker knows, believes, or doesn't know. Using a testing-the-limits procedure, it is possible for the examiner to employ some of the pictorial stimuli to explore the examinee's understanding of diseases such as AIDS, and concepts such as sexual abuse and sexual harassment.

A Perspective

The disabled individual must be able to take the test the examiner wishes to administer; the examiner who wishes to administer, for example, the Wepman Auditory Discrimination Test to a totally deaf individual is engaging in an exercise in futility, since the examinee will be unable to hear the stimulus words. When working with the disabled individual, then, the examiner must either devise a new test designed for administration to people with the identified disability or modify an existing test so that it can be administered to the disabled person. If, for example, an existing test such as the WISC-III is administered

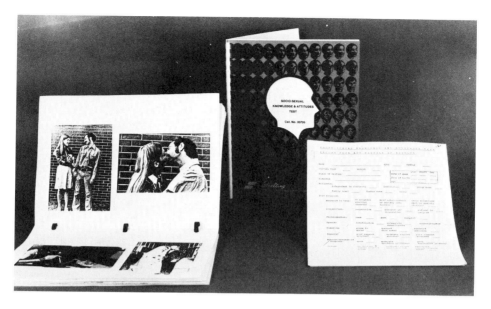

Figure 16–2
The Socio-Sexual Knowledge & Attitudes Test

with modifications to an individual with sensory deficits, the question arises "How relevant are these norms—based solely on the performance of nondisabled people—to the performance of people with disabling conditions who have the test administered to them in ways that deviate from the standardized guidelines?"

The problem of normative comparisons of the performance of disabled and nondisabled individuals is a thorny one, to be sure. It is incumbent on the examiner to keep in mind the question being asked in the assessment before relying on a particular set of norms. If the question asked in the assessment concerns how a disabled individual would perform in a mainstream classroom, a regular job situation, or any situation in which the disabled individual will be competing or working with nondisabled individuals, it is generally appropriate to judge the disabled individual with reference to norms gathered on nondisabled persons. If, however, the question being asked in the assessment concerns how the disabled individual compares with others with the same disability—for diagnostic purposes, placement in a sheltered workshop, or any other purpose that would necessitate evaluation of the disability per se—then norms developed on a population of people with that specific disability would be an appropriate reference source. When a standardized test in use with nondisabled people is modified for use with people with one or another deficit, there are in many instances no published norms that are directly applicable. The assessor in such an instance will then rely on the published norms applicable to nondisabled individuals but use caution in making interpretations with respect to the performance of a nonmember of the normative population who was administered a modified version of the test. All of this may sound unscientific and nonstandardized to the reader. It is. In practice, however, appropriate norms are not readily available for every type of modification that may be made in an existing standardized test so that it is amenable for administration to a person who is disabled in some way. In practice, the assessor of members of a disabled population may be compelled to improvise not only with respect to administration procedures but in making interpretations as well.

CHAPTER 17

Industrial/Organizational Assessment

Industrial psychology is defined as "the application of the methods, facts, and principles of psychology to people at work" (Schultz, 1982, p. 6). The subspecialty areas of organizational psychology, personnel psychology, and engineering psychology are all included within this definition. *Organizational psychology* focuses on the nature and quality of the structure of the organization (corporation, business, military, or other), including such variables as formal and informal lines of communication, management-staff relations, public relations, research and development, and related areas. Underscoring how closely related the areas of industrial and organizational psychology are is the fact that, in 1970, the division of the American Psychological Association then known as the Division of Industrial Psychology officially changed its name to the Division of Industrial and Organizational Psychology. *Personnel psychology* is that area of industrial/organizational (I/O) psychology that deals with matters related to the hiring, firing, promotion, and transfer of workers as well as issues of worker productivity, motivation, and job satisfaction. *Engineering psychology* is concerned with the study of human factors involved in the operation of mechanical things ranging from household gadgets to spacecraft.

I/O psychologists employ tools of assessment in a number of different ways. They measure the knowledge, skills, interest, and abilities of people contemplating various careers, the better to guide them into an occupational choice best suited to them. They analyze what the job requirements are for various employment positions, and then have a hand in hiring, transferring, or promoting applicants aspiring to hold that position. I/O psychologists measure current employees on sundry variables to identify areas in which further training or some other types of intervention may be necessary. In an effort to protect employers as well as others from loss, I/O psychologists have, with increasing frequency in recent years, become involved in drug testing and so-called integrity testing. I/O psychologists and engineering psychologists work to design instrumentation and equipment, as well as corporate and living environments.

In this chapter, we survey a sampling of the tools of assessment used by contemporary I/O psychologists. Many I/O psychologists are involved in the screening, selection, classification, and placement of personnel, and we begin with a look at the tools of measurement used in such endeavors. Keep in mind that although the perspective in much of this chapter is that of the I/O psychologist employed by an organization, I/O and other psychologists (such as counseling psychologists) may use many of the same tools to help guide students or clients with regard to career choices.

Screening, Selection, Classification, and Placement

A *career* may be defined as simply as "a sequence of positions occupied by a person during the course of a lifetime" (Super & Hall, 1978, p. 334). Cohen (1994, p. 400) defined an *occupation* as "a vocation, profession, or other activity that one regularly works at, keeps busy at, and/or earns one's livelihood through," and a *job* as "a task, an undertaking, or an activity performed for pay." Thus, for example, at one point in her or his career, an individual may be a plumber (occupation), performing tasks (jobs) such as repairing leaks and unclogging toilets. Of course, in everyday conversation, "job" is an exceptionally broad term used to refer to everything from one's role as student to whatever it is that a person does to earn money.

In contemplating career options, or focusing on one particular occupational choice, chances are you have wondered about the type of work for which you are best suited. You may have raised questions in your own mind about your abilities, aptitudes, and interests. You may have wondered about the type of work setting that would provide the best fit for your personality. You may have given some thought to the types of things you could do that would be personally satisfying. I/O psychologists have wondered about many of the same things, and they employ ability, aptitude, interest, and personality tests, among others, to help answer such questions. Some of the tests may be used for screening purposes, and others may be used for selection, classification, or placement.

In the context of I/O psychology, *screening* refers to a relatively superficial process of evaluation based on certain minimal requirements. For example, a municipal fire department may screen for certain minimal requirements for height, weight, physical health, and physical strength for admission to a training program for firefighters. The government may use a group-administered test of intelligence to screen out those unsuitable for military service or to identify highly intelligent recruits for special assignments.

Although the terms *selection, classification,* and *placement* are frequently used interchangeably, there are differences among them. It is appropriate to use the term *selection* only when each person considered will be either selected or rejected. The decision to hire or not and the decision to grant or deny admission are examples of situations that involve selection. By contrast, *classification* does not imply acceptance or rejection but, rather, a rating (or "pigeonholing") with respect to two or more criteria. A military draft board, for example, might *clas-*

sify registrants on the basis of criteria such as physical suitability for military service, marital status, age, and related variables. Like classification, *placement* carries no implication of acceptance or rejection. It is appropriate to use the term *placement* when a rating is being made on the basis of one criterion. If, for example, you took a college-level course when still in high school, the score you earned on the advanced placement test in that subject area may have been the sole criterion used to place you in an appropriate section of that college course upon your acceptance to college.

Businesses, schools, the military, and other organizations regularly screen, select, classify, and/or place individuals. The test user has a wide array of tests that could be used as aids to decision making. Measures of ability, aptitude, interest, and personality may all be of value, depending on the demands of the particular decision. For everyday employment situations, and especially at the preemployment stage, some of the most common tools of assessment in use include the letter of application and the résumé, the job application form, the letter of recommendation, and the interview.

The Résumé and the Letter of Application

There is no one standard résumé; résumés can be "as unique as the individuals they represent" (Cohen, 1994, p. 394). Typically, information related to one's work objectives, qualifications, education, and experience is included on a résumé. A companion cover letter to a résumé, called a letter of application, can provide a job applicant with the opportunity to demonstrate motivation, businesslike writing skills, and his or her unique personality. Neither a résumé nor a letter of application is likely to be the sole vehicle through which employment is secured. At best, both of these documents are stepping-stones to personal interviews or other evaluation situations on the way to getting hired. On the other hand, the employer, the personnel psychologist, or some other individual reading the applicant's résumé and cover letter may use these documents as a basis for rejecting an application. The cover letter and the résumé may be read and analyzed for details such as quality of written communication, perceived sincerity, and appropriateness of the applicant's objectives, education, motivation, and prior experience with regard to the available position. From the perspective of the evaluator, much the same is true of another common tool of assessment in employment settings, the application blank.

The Application Blank

Application blanks may be thought of as biographical sketches that supply employers with information pertinent to the acceptability of job candidates. In addition to demographic information (such as name, address, and telephone number), pertinent details about other areas, such as educational background, military service, and previous work experience, may be requested. As noted in Table 17–1, each item in an application blank should ideally be relevant to whether the employer should continue to consider the applicant for employment. The application blank is a highly useful tool for quick screening in numerous settings.

Table 17–1
Checklist for an Application Blank Item

1. Is the item necessary for identifying the applicant?
2. Is it necessary for screening out those who are ineligible under the company's basic hiring policies?
3. Does it help to decide whether the candidate is qualified?
4. Is it based on analysis of the job or jobs for which applicants will be selected?
5. Has it been pretested on the company's employees and found to correlate with success?
6. Will the information be used? How?
7. Is the application form the proper place to ask for it?
8. To what extent will answers duplicate information to be obtained at another step in the selection procedure—for example, through interviews, tests, or medical examinations?
9. Is the information needed for selection at all, or should it be obtained at induction or even later?
10. Is it probable that the applicants' replies will be reliable?
11. Does the question violate any applicable federal or state legislation?

Source: Ahern (1949)

Letters of Recommendation

Another useful tool in the preliminary screening of applicants is the letter of recommendation (Arvey, 1979; Glueck, 1978). Such letters may be a unique source of detailed information about how the applicant has performed in the past, the quality of the applicant's relationships with peers, and so forth. Of course, such letters are not without their drawbacks. It is no secret that applicants solicit letters from those individuals who they believe will say only positive things about them. Another possible drawback to letters of recommendation is the variance in the observational and writing skills of the letter writers. In research that employed application files for admission to graduate school in psychology, it was found that an applicant might variously be described as "analytically oriented, reserved, and highly motivated" or "free-spirited, imaginative, and outgoing" depending on the letter writer's perspective. As the authors of that study pointed out, "Although favorable recommendations may be intended in both cases, the details of and bases for such recommendations are varied" (Baxter et al., 1981, p. 300). Efforts to minimize the drawbacks inherent in the open-ended letter of recommendation have in some instances taken the form of "questionnaires of recommendation" wherein former employers, professors, and other letter writers respond to structured questions concerning the applicant's prior performance. Some such questionnaires employ a forced-choice format designed to force respondents to make negative as well as positive statements about the applicant.

Interviews

Interviews, be they individual or group in nature, provide an occasion for the face-to-face exchange of information between interviewers and interviewees. Like other interviews, the employment interview may fall anywhere on a continuum from highly structured, with uniform questions being asked to all, to highly unstructured, with the questions to be asked left largely to the interviewer's discretion. As with other interviews, too, the interviewer's biases and prejudices may creep into the evaluation and ultimately influence the outcome. Other factors, such as the order of interviewing, might also affect outcomes by reason of contrast effects. For example, an average applicant may appear better or less qualified depending on whether the preceding candidate was particularly poor or outstanding. Factors that may affect the outcome of an employment interview, according to Schmitt (1976), include the backgrounds, attitudes, motivations, perceptions, expectations, knowledge about the job, and interview behavior of both the interviewer and the interviewee. Situational factors, such as the nature of the job market, may also affect the outcome of the interview.

Portfolio Assessment

In the context of industrial/organizational assessment, *portfolio assessment* entails an evaluation of an individual's work sample for the purpose of making some screening, selection, classification, or placement decision. A video journalist applying for a position at a new television station may present a portfolio of video clips, including rehearsal footage and outtakes in support of a job application. An art director for a magazine may present a portfolio of art to a prospective employer, including material such as rough drafts and notes about how to solve a particular art-related problem. In cases in which portfolio assessment is undertaken, the assessor may have the opportunity to (1) evaluate many work samples created by the assessee, (2) obtain some understanding of the assessee's work-related thought processes and habits through an analysis of the materials from rough draft to finished form, and (3) question the assessee further regarding various aspects of his or her work-related thinking and habits. The result may be a more complete picture of the prospective employee at work in the new setting than might otherwise be available.

Performance Tests

As its name implies, a *performance test* requires assessees to demonstrate certain skills or abilities under a specified set of circumstances. The typical objective of such an exercise is to obtain a job-related performance sample. If you have ever taken a word processing test as a prerequisite for employment, you have had firsthand experience with performance tests. Sometimes the line between performance tests and achievement and aptitude tests is blurred, as when the work sample required takes the form of the completion of a standardized test of skill or ability. For example, the Seashore Bennett Stenographic Proficiency Test is a standardized measure of stenographic competence. The test materials include a recording in which a voice dictates a series of letters and manuscripts that the assessee must transcribe in shorthand and then type. The recorded directions provide a uniform clarity of voice and rate of dictation. Whether one views the test protocol as an achievement test, an aptitude test, or a performance sample is, in practice, up to the discretion of the test user.

One widely used instrument designed to measure clerical aptitude and skills is the Minnesota Clerical Test (MCT). The MCT comprises two subtests, Number Comparison and Name Comparison. Each subtest contains two hundred items, with each item consisting of either a pair of names or a pair of numbers (depending upon the subtest) to be compared. For each item, the assessee's task is to check whether the two names (or numbers) in the pair are the same or different. A score is obtained by simply subtracting the number of incorrect responses from the number of correct ones. Because speed and accuracy in clerical work is important to so many employers, this deceptively simple test has been used for decades as an effective screening tool in the workplace (Dorcus & Jones, 1950; Ghiselli, 1973; Selover, 1949). Not only can it be administered and scored quickly and easily, but also the pattern of the testtakers' errors or omissions on this timed test may suggest whether the testtaker values speed over accuracy or vice versa.

More sophisticated varieties of performance assessment are regularly employed in the field of aviation in the training and evaluation of pilots (Kennedy et al., 1982), air traffic controllers (Ackerman & Kanfer, 1993), and others (Retzlaff & Gibertini, 1988). Kennedy et al. (1982) lauded commercially available video games for the extent to which they compare favorably with more conventional tests of psychomotor skills and cognition. Ackerman and Kanfer (1993) noted that computer simulations permit assessors to evaluate assessees' response to a standardized set of air traffic control tasks and to precisely monitor the time of response.

Performance tests vary widely in the kind of special equipment necessary for their administration (see Figure 17–1). For example, during World War II, the assessment staff of the Office of Strategic Services (OSS) selected American secret agents, saboteurs, propaganda experts, and other personnel for overseas assignments. In addition to interviews, personality tests, and other paper-and-pencil tests, OSS administered situational performance tests. One such test was the "brook exercise," wherein a group of candidates, given only boards, rope, a pulley, and a barrel, had to transport a log and a rock across a stream. Today, the Israelis, among other military powers, use similar methods. Tziner and Eden

Figure 17–1
Games I/O Psychologists Play ▶

*Psychologists have long recognized the value of gamelike situations in the process of evaluating prospective personnel. During World War II, the Office of Strategic Services (OSS) assessed leadership ability and emotional stability by means of in-the-field performance tests. **(a)** Here, subjects were called on to rebuild a blown bridge, though they were not supplied with sufficient materials to do so. In some of the OSS exercises, "assistants"—actually confederates of the experimenters—acted in ways to further frustrate the efforts of the assessees (for example, by being sluggish or by being eager but incorrect). **(b)** A task referred to as the "Manufacturing Problem" was used as part of the AT&T Management Progress Study conducted in 1957. The assessee's task here is to collaborate with others in the buying of parts and the manufacture of a "product."*

(a)

(b)

(1985) described experiments with three-person military crews performing military tasks in a military field setting. Individuals were assigned to the crews on the basis of levels of ability and motivation, and assignment by all possible combinations of these levels was varied in an effort to determine the optimal composition of a crew.

A commonly used performance test in the assessment of business leadership ability is a leaderless group situation. Communication skills, problem-solving ability, the ability to cope with stress, and other skills can also economically be assessed by a group exercise in which the participants' task is to work together in the solution of some problem or the achievement of some goal. As group members interact, the assessors make judgments with respect to questions such as "Who is the leader?" and "What role do other members play in this group?" The answers to such questions will no doubt figure into decisions concerning the individual assessee's future position in the organization. Another performance test frequently used to assess leadership or managerial ability is the in-basket technique. This technique is an exercise that simulates the way a manager or an executive deals with his or her "in-basket" filled with mail, memos, announcements, and various other notices and directives. Assessees are instructed that they have only a limited amount of time, usually two or three hours, to deal with all the items in the "basket" (more commonly, a manila envelope). Through posttest interviews and an examination of the way that the assessee handled the materials, assessors can make judgments concerning variables such as organizing and planning, problem solving, decision making, creativity, leadership, and written communication skills.

The assessment center A widely used tool in selection, classification, and placement is the *assessment center*. Although it sounds as if it might be a place, the term actually denotes an organizationally standardized *procedure* involving multiple assessment techniques such as paper-and-pencil tests and situational performance tests. The assessment center concept had its origins in the writings of Henry Murray and his associates (1938). Assessment-center-like activities were pioneered by military organizations both in the United States and abroad (Thornton & Byham, 1982). In 1956, the first application of the idea in an industrial setting occurred with the initiation of the Management Progress Study (MPS) at American Telephone and Telegraph (Bray, 1964). MPS was to be a longitudinal study that would follow the lives of over four hundred telephone company management and nonmanagement personnel. Each participant would attend a 3½-day assessment center in which he or she would be interviewed for two hours, would take a number of paper-and-pencil tests designed to shed light on cognitive abilities and personality (for example, the School and College Ability Test and the Edwards Personal Preference Schedule), and would participate in individual and group situational exercises (such as the in-basket test and a leaderless group). Additionally, projective tests such as the Thematic Apperception Test and the Sentence Completion Test were administered. All the data on each of the assessees were integrated at a meeting of the assessors, at which judgments on a number of dimensions were made. The dimensions, grouped by area, are listed in Table 17–2.

Table 17–2
Original Management Progress Study Dimensions

Area	Dimension
Administrative skills	Organizing and planning—How effectively can this person organize work, and how well does he or she plan ahead?
	Decision making—How ready is this person to make decisions, and how good are the decisions made?
	Creativity—How likely is this person to solve a management problem in a novel way?
Interpersonal skills	Leadership skills—How effectively can this person lead a group to accomplish a task without arousing hostility?
	Oral communication skills—How well would this person present an oral report to a small conference group on a subject he or she knew well?
	Behavior flexibility—How readily can this person, when motivated, modify his or her behavior to reach a goal? How able is this person to change roles or style of behavior to accomplish objectives?
	Personal impact—How forceful and likable an early impression does this person make?
	Social objectivity—How free is this person from prejudices against racial, ethnic, socioeconomic, educational, and other social groups?
	Perceptions of threshold social cues—How readily does this person perceive minimal cues in the behavior of others?
Cognitive skills	General mental ability—How able is this person in the functions measured by tests of intelligence, scholastic aptitude, and learning ability?
	Range of interests—To what extent is this person interested in a variety of fields of activity such as science, politics, sports, music, art?
	Written communication skill—How well would this person compose a communicative and formally correct memorandum on a subject he or she knew well? How well written are memos and reports likely to be?
Stability of performance	Tolerance of uncertainty—To what extent will this person's work performance stand up under uncertain or unstructured conditions?
	Resistance to stress—To what extent will this person's work performance stand up in the face of personal stress?
Work motivation	Primacy of work—To what extent does this person find satisfactions from work more important than satisfactions from other areas of life?
	Inner work standards—To what extent will this person want to do a good job, even if a less good one is acceptable to the boss and others?
	Energy—How continuously can this person sustain a high level of work activity?
	Self-objectivity—How realistic a view does this person have of his or her own assets and liabilities, and how much insight into his or her own motives?
Career orientation	Need for advancement—To what extent does this person need to be promoted significantly earlier than his or her peers? To what extent are further promotions needed for career satisfaction?
	Need for security—How strongly does this person want a secure job?
	Ability to delay gratification—To what extent will this person be willing to wait patiently for advancement if confident advancement will come?
	Realism of expectations—To what extent do this person's expectations about his or her work life with the company conform to what is likely to be true?
	Bell System value orientation—To what extent has this person incorporated Bell System values such as service, friendliness, justice of company position on earnings, rates, wages?
Dependency	Need for superior approval—To what extent does this person need warmth and nurturant support from immediate supervisors?
	Need for peer approval—To what extent does this person need warmth and acceptance from peers and subordinates?
	Goal flexibility—To what extent is this person likely to reorient his or her life toward a different goal?

Source: Bray (1982)

The use of the assessment center method has mushroomed, with an estimated two thousand or more business organizations relying on some form of it for selection, classification, placement, promotion, career training, and early identification of leadership potential (Gaugler et al., 1987). The method has been subject to numerous studies concerning its validity, and a consensus is emerging that the method has much to recommend it (Cohen et al., 1977; Gaugler et al., 1987; Hunter & Hunter, 1984; McEvoy & Beatty, 1989; Schmitt et al., 1984). The question of the day seems to be not *if* the assessment center method is valid but *why* it is valid (Klimoski & Brickner, 1987).

Physical Tests

A lifeguard who is visually impaired is seriously compromised in his or her ability to perform the job. A wine taster with damaged tastebuds is of little value to a vintner. An aircraft pilot who has lost the use of his arms . . . the point is clear: physical requirements of a job must be taken into consideration when screening, selecting, classifying, and placing applicants. Depending on the specific requirements of the job, a number of physical subtests may be used. Thus, for example, for a job in which a number of components of vision are critical, a test of visual acuity might be administered along with tests of visual efficiency, stereopsis (distance/depth perception), and color blindness. General physical fitness is required in many jobs, such as in police work where successful candidates might one day have to chase a fleeing suspect on foot or defend themselves against a suspect resisting arrest. The tests used in assessing such fitness might include a complete physical examination, tests of physical strength, and a performance test that meets some determined criterion with respect to running speed and running agility. Tasks like vaulting some object, stepping through tires, and going through a window frame would be included to simulate running on difficult terrain.

In some instances, an employer's setting certain physical requirements for employment are so reasonable and so necessary that they would readily be upheld by any court if challenged. Other physical requirements for employment, however, may fall into a gray area. How reasonable is it, for example, for a municipal police or fire department to maintain height and weight standards or weight-lifting requirements? In general, the law favors physical standards that are both nondiscriminatory and job-related. As we will see in the discussion of legal/ethical issues later in this chapter, exceptions do exist to this general rule.

Also included under the heading of physical tests are tests of sensory intactness/impairment, including tests to measure color-blindness, visual acuity, visual depth perception, and auditory acuity. These types of tests are routinely employed in industrial settings in which the ability to perceive color or the possession of reasonably good eyesight or hearing is essential to the job. Additionally, physical techniques have been applied in the assessment of integrity and honesty, as is the case with the polygraph.

Assessment of Ability, Aptitude, Interest, and Personality

In some instances, dozens, hundreds, or even thousands of people are vying for the same position. If you asked a personnel psychologist who should be offered the job, the answer you would probably receive would go something like this: "the person whose ability, aptitude, interests, personality, and motivation are best suited to the particular position." But even knowing that, how does one determine who the best person is? The answer to that question is, in a word, "tests."

Measures of Ability and Aptitude

As we saw in Chapter 10, achievement, ability, and aptitude tests measure prior learning to some degree, but they differ in the uses to which the test data will be put. Beyond that, aptitude tests may tap a greater amount of informal learning than do achievement tests. Achievement tests may be more limited and focused in scope than aptitude tests.

Ability and aptitude measures vary widely in topics covered, specificity of coverage, and other variables. The Wonderlic Personnel Test measures mental ability in a general sense. This brief (12-minute) test includes items that assess spatial skill, abstract thought, and mathematical skill. The Bennet Mechanical Comprehension Test is a widely used, paper-and-pencil measure of a testtaker's ability to understand the relationship between physical forces and various tools (for example, pulleys and gears) as well as other common objects (carts, steps, and seesaws). Other mechanical tests, such as the Hand-Tool Dexterity Test, blur the lines between aptitude, achievement, and performance tests by requiring the testtaker to actually take apart, reassemble, or otherwise manipulate materials, usually in a prescribed sequence and within some prescribed time limit. If a job consists mainly of securing tiny transistors into the inner workings of an electronic appliance or game, then the employer's focus of interest might well be on prospective employees' perceptual-motor abilities, finger dexterity, and related variables. In such an instance, the test user might find a test such as the O'Connor Tweezer Dexterity Test to be the instrument of choice (see Figure 17–2). This test requires the examinee to insert brass pins into a metal plate using a pair of tweezers. Other tests designed to measure specific aptitudes exist for a wide variety of occupational fields. For the professions, a number of psychometrically sophisticated assessment programs are in place to screen and/or select applicants by means of aptitude tests. These programs include the Medical College Admissions Tests, the Law School Admission Test, the Dental Admission Testing Program, and the specialized tests that are part of the Graduate Record Examination, such as the specialty examination in psychology.

For a while, one of the most widely used of all aptitude tests was the General Aptitude Test Battery. A description of the test, as well as the controversy surrounding it, follows.

Figure 17–2
The O'Connor Tweezer Dexterity Test

The General Aptitude Test Battery   The United States Employment Service (USES) developed the General Aptitude Test Battery (GATB) and first put it into use in 1947 after extensive research and development. The GATB (pronounced like "Gatsby" without the *s*) is available for use by state employment services as well as other agencies and organizations (such as certain school districts and non-profit organizations that have obtained official permission from the government to administer the test). The GATB is a tool used to identify aptitudes for occupations, and it is a test just about anyone of working age can take. The test is administered regularly at local state offices (referred to by names such as the "Job Service," "Employment Security Commission," and "Labor Security Commission") to people who want the agency to help find them a job, to people who are unemployed and have been referred by a state office of unemployment, or to employees of a company that has requested such aptitude assessment. If you're curious about your own aptitude for work in fields as diverse as psychology, education, and plumbing, you may just want to visit your local state employment office. Be prepared to sit for an examination that will take about three hours if you take the entire test; the GATB consists of twelve timed tests that measure nine aptitudes that in turn can be divided into three composite aptitudes. About one-half the time will be spent on psychomotor tasks, and the other half of the time will be spent on paper-and-pencil tasks. In some instances, depending on factors such as the reason assessment is undertaken, only selected tests of the battery will be administered—this (referred to as a Special Aptitude Test Battery or SATB) as a means of measuring aptitude for a specific line of work. And even if you take the full GATB, various SATBs—aptitudes deemed necessary for specific occupations—can be isolated for study from the other test data.

In recent years, the GATB has evolved from a test with multiple cutoffs to one that employs regression and validity generalization for making recommendations based on test results. The rationale and process by which the GATB has made this evolution has been described by John E. Hunter (1980, 1986), Frank Schmidt, and their associates (Hunter & Schmidt, 1983; Hunter et al., 1982; Hunter & Hunter, 1984—the latter Hunter is more than an associate; she's John's wife), and validity generalization is the subject of our chapter *Close-up.* Briefly, recommendations with respect to aptitude for a particular job had in the past been made on the basis of GATB validity studies bearing on specific jobs; if, for example, there existed 500 job descriptions covering 500 jobs for which scores on the GATB were to be applied, there would be 500 individual validation studies with the GATB—one validation study for each individual job, typically with a relatively small sample size (many of these single studies containing an average of only 76 subjects). Further, there were no validation studies for the other 12,000-plus jobs that exist in the American economy according to the *Dictionary of Occupational Titles* published by the United States Department of Labor (1977). Using meta-analysis to cumulate results across a number of validation studies and statistically correct for error such as sampling error, Hunter demonstrated that all the jobs could be categorized within five families of jobs, those families based on what are called "worker function codes" of the *Dictionary of Occupational Titles.* The five families of jobs are (1) Setting Up, (2) Feeding and Off-Bearing, (3) Synthesizing and Coordinating, (4) Analyzing, Compiling, and Computing, and (5) Copying and Comparing. Regression equations for each of the families were then developed, and using these equations Hunter found that recommendations for individual testtakers could be generalized to various jobs.

In the late 1980s, the GATB became a center of controversy when it became public knowledge that the test had been race-normed. *Race-norming* refers to the process of adjusting scores to show an individual testtaker's standing within his or her own racial group. With the race-normed GATB, high-scorers within racial groups were recommended for employment. For example, among people being considered for a skilled job, a GATB raw score of 300 was "translated into percentile scores of 79, 62, and 38, respectively, for Blacks, Hispanics, and others" (Gottfredson, 1994, p. 966). Only percentile scores and not raw scores were reported to employers.

In an attempt to address the ensuing controversy, the U.S. Department of Labor asked the National Academy of Sciences (NAS) to conduct a study. The NAS issued a report (Hartigan & Wigdor, 1989) that was generally supportive of race-norming. The NAS noted that the GATB appeared to suffer from slope bias such that the test correlated more highly with criterion measures for White samples (.19) than for Black samples (.12). Intercept bias was also present, with the result that the performance of Blacks would be overpredicted relative to the

Validity Generalization and the GATB

Can a test validated for use in personnel selection for one occupation also be valid for use in personnel selection for another occupation? Must the validation of a test used in personnel selection be situation-specific? Stated more generally, can validity evidence for a test be meaningfully applied to situations other than those in which the evidence was obtained? These are the types of questions that are raised when the topic of *validity generalization* is discussed.

As applied to employment-related decision making on the basis of test scores achieved on the General Aptitude Test Battery (GATB), *validity generalization* refers to the fact that the same test-score data may be predictive of aptitude for all jobs; the implication is that if a test is validated for a few jobs selected from a much larger cluster of jobs—each requiring similar skills at approximately the same level of complexity—the test is valid for all jobs in that cluster. For example, if a validation study conclusively indicated that GATB scores are predictive of aptitude for (and ultimately proficiency in) the occupation of assembler in an aircraft assembly plant, an entirely new validation study may not be needed to apply such data to the occupation of assembler in a shipbuilding plant; if the type and level of skill required in the two occupations can be shown to be sufficiently similar, it may be that the same or similar procedures used to select aircraft assemblers can profitably be used to select assemblers of ships.

Validity generalization (VG) as applied to personnel selection using the GATB makes unnecessary the burden of conducting a separate validation study with the test for every one of the over 12,000 jobs that exist in the American economy. The application of VB to GATB scores also enables GATB users to supply employers with more precise information about testtakers. To understand why this is so, let's begin by consulting the "pie chart" (Figure 1).

Note that the inner circle of the chart lists the 12 tests in the General Aptitude Test Battery and that the next ring of the circle lists eight aptitudes derived

from the 12 tests. Not illustrated here is a ninth aptitude, General Learning Ability, which is derived from scores on the Vocabulary, Arithmetic Reasoning, and Three-Dimensional Space tests. A brief description of each of the nine aptitudes measured by the GATB follows:

General Learning Ability (also referred to as *intelligence*) (G)—"Catching on" and understanding instructions and principles as well as reasoning and judgment are tapped here. G is measured by Tests 3, 4, and 6 in the diagram.

Verbal Aptitude (V)—Understanding the meaning of words and relationships between them as well as using words effectively are some of the abilities tapped here. V is measured by Test 4.

Numerical Aptitude (N)—N is measured by tasks requiring the quick performance of arithmetic operations. It is measured by Tests 2 and 6.

Spatial Aptitude (S)—The ability to visualize and mentally manipulate geometric forms is tapped here. S is measured by Test 3.

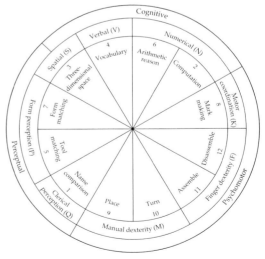

Figure 1
Aptitudes Measured by the General Aptitude Test Battery

Form Perception (P)—Attention to detail, including the ability to discriminate slight differences in shapes, shading, lengths, and widths, as well as ability to perceive pertinent detail is measured. P is measured by Tests 5 and 7.

Clerical Perception (Q)—Attention to detail in written or tabular material as well as the ability to proofread words and numbers and to avoid perceptual errors in arithmetic computation is tapped here. Q is measured by Test 1.

Motor Coordination (K)—This test taps the ability to quickly make precise movements that require eye-hand coordination. K is measured by Test 8.

Finger Dexterity (F)—This test taps the ability to quickly manipulate small objects with the fingers. F is measured by Tests 11 and 12.

Manual Dexterity (M)—The ability to work with one's hands in placing and turning motions is measured here. M is measured by Tests 9 and 10.

Referring back to the diagram and more specifically to the outermost ring, note that the three composite aptitudes can be derived from the nine specific aptitudes: a Cognitive composite, a Perceptual composite, and a Psychomotor composite. The nine aptitudes that compose the three composite aptitudes may be summarized as follows:

The Nine GATB Aptitudes	The Three Composite Scores
G General Learning Ability (also referred to as *intelligence*)	
V Verbal Aptitude	Cognitive
N Numerical Aptitude	
S Spatial Aptitude	
P Form Perception	Perceptual
Q Clerical Perception	
K Motor Coordination	
F Finger Dexterity	Psychomotor
M Manual Dexterity	

Traditionally—before the advent of VG—testtakers who sat for the GATB might subsequently receive counseling as to how they did in each of the nine aptitude areas. Further they might have been informed (1) how their own pattern of GATB scores compared with patterns of aptitude (referred to as Occupational Aptitude Patterns or OAPs) deemed necessary for proficiency in various occupations, and/or (2) how they performed with respect to any of the 467 constellations of a Special Aptitude Test Battery (SATB) that could potentially be extracted from a GATB protocol. Using VG makes possible additional information useful in advising prospective employers and counseling prospective employees. Such information includes more precise data concerning a testtaker's performance with respect to OAPs, as well as scores (usually expressed in percentiles) with respect to the five job families. Research (Hunter, 1982) has indicated that the three composite aptitudes can be used to validly predict to job proficiency for all jobs in the United States economy. All jobs may be categorized according to five job families, and the aptitude required for each of these families can be described with respect to various contributions of the three composite GATB scores. For example, Job Family 1 (Set-up Jobs) is 59% Cognitive, 30% Perceptual, and 11% Psychomotor in nature. GATB scoring is done by computer as is weighting of scores to determine suitability for employment in jobs in each of the five job families.

Proponents of VG as applied to use with the GATB list the following advantages:

1. *The decreased emphasis on multiple cutoffs as a selection strategy has advantages for both prospective employers and prospective employees.* In a multiple cutoff selection model, a prospective employee would have to achieve certain minimum GATB scores in each of the aptitudes deemed critical for proficiency in a given occupation; failure to meet the minimal cutting score in these aptitudes would mean elimination from the candidate pool for that occupation. Using VG, a potential benefit for the prospective employee is that the requirement of a

(continued)

Validity Generalization and the GATB *(continued)*

minimum cutting score on any specific aptitude is eliminated. For employers, VG encourages the use of a "top-down" hiring policy: one in which the best-qualified people (as measured by the GATB) are offered jobs first.

2. *Research has suggested that the relationship between aptitude test scores and job performance is linear (Waldman & Avolio, 1989), a relationship that is statistically better suited to VG than to the multiple cutoff selection model.* The nature of the relationship between scores on a valid test of aptitude and ratings of job performance is illustrated in Figure 2. Given that such a relationship exists, Hunter (1980, 1982) notes that from a technical standpoint, linear data are better suited to analysis using a VG model than using a model with multiple cutoffs.

3. *More precise information can be reported to employers regarding a testtaker's relative standing in the continuum of aptitude test scores.* Consider in this context Figure 3, and let's suppose that an established and validated cutoff score for selection in a particular occupation using this hypothetical test of aptitude is 155. Examinee *X* and Examinee *Y* both meet the cutoff requirement, but Examinee *Y* is probably better qualified for the job—we say "probably" because there may be exceptions to this general rule depending on variables such as the actual demands of the specific job. Although the score for Examinee *X* falls below the median score for all testtakers, the score for Examinee *Y* lies at the high end of the distribution of scores. All other factors being equal, which individual would you prefer to hire if you owned the company? Using a simple cutoff procedure, no distinction with respect to aptitude score would have been made between Examinee *X* and Examinee *Y* provided both scores met the cutoff criterion.

4. *VG better assists employers in their efforts to hire qualified employees.* Studies such as one conducted at the Philip Morris Company suggest that a significant increase in the rate of training success can be expected for employees hired using a selection procedure that uses VG as compared with employees hired by other means (Warmke, 1984).

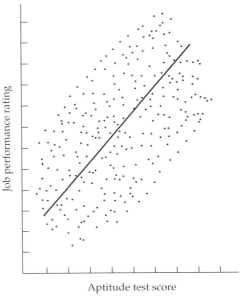

Figure 2
The Linear Relationship Between Aptitude Test Scores and Job Performance Ratings

Is VG "The Answer" to all personnel selection problems? Not at all. VG is, to put it simply and straightforwardly, one rationale for justifiably avoiding the time and expense of conducting a separate validation study for every single test with every possible group of testtakers under every possible set of circumstances—too often with too few subjects to achieve meaningful findings. It should be noted, however, that with the convenience of VG come many concerns about the efficacy of the procedures employed. And although we have devoted a fair amount of time to acquainting you with this important concept in the personnel selection literature, it is equally important for you to be aware that a number of technical issues with respect to VG are currently being debated in the professional literature.

You will recall that in the development of VG as applied to personnel selection, Hunter and his colleagues used a process called meta-analysis to cumulate findings across a number of studies. One important aspect of this work involved statistically correcting for the small sample sizes that occurred in the studies analyzed. The types of procedures used in such a process and the types of interpretations that can legitimately be made as a result have been the subject of a number of critical analyses of VG. The amount of unexplained variance that remains even after statistical corrections for differences in sample size have been made (Cascio, 1987), the unknown influence of a potential restriction-of-range problem with respect to subject self-selection (Cronbach, 1984), objections with respect to using employer ratings as a criterion (Burke, 1984), and the fact that alternative models may explain variation in validity coefficients as well as the cross-situational consistency model (James et al., 1986) are some of the technical issues that have been raised with respect to the use of VG (see also Zedeck & Cascio, 1984). With specific reference to VG as applied to use with the GATB, one might inquire further: What problems arise when over 12,000 occupations are grouped into five job families?

Is it really meaningful to place an occupation such as "truck driver" in the same job family as "secretary"?

Clearly, much remains to be learned about how VG can most effectively be brought to bear on problems related to personnel testing. Difficult questions—some psychometric in nature, others that relate more to societal values—will have to be addressed. Compounding the task of addressing such questions is a litany of variables that are neither psychometric in nature nor directly related to values; included here are variables such as the strength of the economy, the size of the available labor pool, the experience of the available labor pool, the general desirability of specific jobs, and the salaries being offered for various kinds of work. Whether one looks favorably or not at the government's experimentation with VG in personnel selection, it seems reasonable to assume that there is much to be learned in the process, and the field of personnel selection may ultimately profit from the experience.

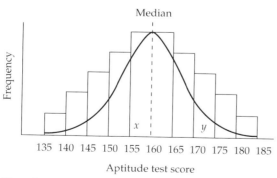

Figure 3
Results of a Hypothetical Aptitude Test

performance of Whites if the same regression line were used for both groups. The practice of race-norming amounted to using different regression lines, each with the accurate slope and intercept for the specific racial group. The NAS found race-norming to be a reasonable method for correcting for the bias of the test.

The NAS report also addressed more general issues concerning the utility of the GATB as a predictor of job performance. Using a database of 755 studies, the NAS noted the GATB correlated approximately .22 with criteria such as supervisory ratings. Others have estimated the test's validity to be .20 (Vevea et al., 1993) and .21 (Waldman & Avolio, 1989). These relatively small coefficients were viewed by the NAS as modest but acceptable. To understand why they were considered acceptable, recall from Chapter 6 that criterion validity is limited by the reliability of the measures. Although the GATB has adequate test-retest reliability (around .81), the likely poor reliability of supervisory ratings may depress the GATB's validity coefficient. Such depression of a validity coefficient could be expected to occur for any test designed to predict job performance that is validated against supervisors' ratings (Hartigan & Wigdor, 1989). Also, as noted in the discussion of Taylor-Russell tables in Chapter 6, even predictors with modest criterion validity can improve personnel selection decisions. Thus, despite the low criterion validity coefficients, the GATB is widely viewed as a valid means for selecting employees.

The NAS recommendation to continue the practice of race-norming the test may have done more to fan the flames of controversy than to quell them. In July of 1990, the Department of Labor proposed a two-year suspension in the use of the GATB, during which time the efficacy of the test and its scoring procedures would be further researched. The legality of the practice of race-norming had also become a heated topic of debate by that time (Baydoun & Neuman, 1992; Delahunty, 1988). The question of whether race-norming of the GATB should continue became moot after Congress passed the Civil Rights Act of 1991, a law that made the practice of race-norming illegal.

Today, the GATB is still in use by the U.S. Employment Service. However, reports to employers are no longer race-normed. The raw scores of people from all racial groups are now converted to interpretable standard scores using the same norms (Mowrey, 1994).

Measures of Interest

On the presumption that interest in one's work promotes better performance, greater productivity, and greater job satisfaction, both employers and prospective employees have much to gain from methods that can help individuals identify their interests and a job tailored to those interests. Using such methods, individuals can discover, for example, if their interests lie in being a starship captain and "seeking new worlds and exploring new civilizations" or in something more along the lines of dentistry (see Figure 17–3). Employers can use information about their employees' interest patterns in formulating job descriptions and attracting new personnel. For example, a company could design an employment campaign emphasizing that the position offers security if security

Figure 17–3
It's Not Just a Job, It's an Adventure!

Had Orin Scrivello, D.D.S. (Steve Martin) in the film Little Shop of Horrors *taken an interest survey, the results might have been quite bizarre. As a child, young Orin's interests leaned toward bashing the heads of pussycats, shooting puppies with a BB gun, and poisoning guppies. He was able to put what his mother described as his "natural tendencies" to use in gainful employment: he became a dentist.*

was found to be the chief interest of the successful workers currently holding the same job. Although many instruments designed to measure interests have been published, our discussion will focus on the one with the longest history of continuous use, the Strong Interest Inventory (SII).

Strong Interest Inventory   As early as 1907, psychologist G. Stanley Hall had developed a questionnaire to assess children's recreational interests. However, it was not until the early 1920s that Edward K. Strong, Jr., after attending a seminar on the measurement of interest, began a program of systematic investigation into the measurement of human interests. One product of this work was the 420-item Strong Vocational Interest Blank (SVIB) for men, published with a test manual by Stanford University Press in 1928 and revised in 1938. In 1935, a 410-item SVIB for women was published, along with a test manual. The women's SVIB was revised in 1946. Both the men's and the women's SVIB were again revised in the mid-1960s. Amid concern about the existence of sex-specific forms of the test in the late 1960s and early 1970s (McArthur, 1992), a merged form was published in 1974. Developed under the direction of David P. Campbell, the merged form was called the Strong-Campbell Interest Inventory (SCII). The test was revised and expanded in 1985 and is now known as the Strong Interest Inventory (SII) (Strong et al., 1985).

Strong's approach to test construction was empirical and straightforward: (1) select hundreds of items that might conceivably distinguish the interests of a person by that person's occupation, (2) administer this "rough cut" of the test to several hundred people selected so as to be representative of certain occupations or professions, (3) sort out which items seemed of interest to persons by occupational group and discard items with no discriminative ability, and (4) construct a final version of the test that would yield scores describing how an examinee's pattern of interest corresponded to that of people actually employed in various occupations and professions. With the availability of such a test, college students majoring in psychology could, for example, see how closely their pattern of interests paralleled that of working psychologists. Presumably, if your interests closely match those of psychologists (in contrast to the interests of, say, tow truck operators), you would probably enjoy the work of a psychologist.

The test as it exists today consists of a total of 325 items to which the examinee responds by blackening boxes on an answer sheet grid to indicate preference of some sort. Items 1 through 281 require respondents to indicate whether they "Like," "Dislike," or are "Indifferent" to various occupations, school subjects, activities, amusements, and types of people. For example, do you like or dislike, or are you indifferent to, the work of a bookkeeper? algebra? sewing? golf? people who live dangerously? For items 282 through 311, respondents indicate their preference between two activities (such as "taking a chance" and "playing it safe") or indicate that they cannot make up their mind. For items 312 through 325, respondents describe themselves by indicating "yes," "no," or uncertainty ("?") to statements like "win friends easily."

Men and women in the standardization sample for the test were all between the ages of 25 and 55. The sample was divided into members of a general reference group and an occupational reference group; members of the latter all had to like their work and have at least three years of experience at it to be included. The general reference group served as a kind of control group; its members were selected to represent men or women "in general."

The test protocols can be scored only by computer; not only would scoring by hand be inordinately difficult and time-consuming, but also the item weights and scoring algorithms are registered trade secrets of the copyright owner. Along with scoring (a Profile Report), a computer-prepared narrative description of the testtaker's pattern of scores (an Interpretive Report) is available to the test user. Also available with the 1985 Revised Edition of the test is an individualized, interactive video interpretation of the findings along with career counseling and exploration. Three types of general scales—General Occupational Themes, Basic Interest Scales, and Occupational Scales—are scored and interpreted with reference to six personality types distinguished by Holland (1973): enterprising, conventional, realistic, social, investigative, and artistic. The personality characteristics associated with each of Holland's types are included in each SII report. The General Occupational Theme score is a kind of summary statement of how similar the respondent is to each of Holland's occupational types. Scores on the Basic Interest Scales and Occupational Scales allow the interpreter of the test to see at a glance how similar or dissimilar the respondent's interests are to those of people holding a variety of jobs. In addition to these primary scales, scores on two "special scales" are reported. One of these is called the "Academic Comfort" scale, and it is designed to discriminate between students who might and might not feel comfortable in an academic setting. The other special scale is the IE (introversion-extraversion) scale; the higher the score on this scale, the more introverted the testtaker is presumed to be. Also on the answer sheet are two administrative indices ("Total Responses" and "Infrequent Responses"), there for the purpose of detecting carelessness, random responding to items, misunderstanding of directions, the presence of response sets, and possible errors in the computer scoring. Since there are 325 items, a Total Responses "score" of anything less than 325 may prompt further investigation. The "Infrequent Responses" index provides a measure of the number of rare or unusual responses to items made by the testtaker.

SII data may be used by counselors to assist in the counseling of students as well as others (such as job applicants, current employees, and prisoners) in making employment and career decisions. It is also true that a scored report with a narrative interpretation returned to a testtaker may require little or no interpretation by a counselor, since it comes with a very clear test guide for interpreting the findings. SII data can assist individuals in a particular line of work to better understand why they might not be happy with that line of work. The possible research applications of the test are many. A partial listing of the ways this test could potentially be used in research is as follows: studying characteristics of particular occupations, individuals, and groups; studying general societal trends and cross-cultural influences; and studying interpersonal relationships such as the interest patterns of friends, lovers, and happily married as opposed to divorced couples.

Voluminous data that had been compiled on the original, sex-specific forms of the SVIB became unusable when the two forms were merged (McArthur, 1989). The SII test authors report that the revised test has good test-retest reliability and concurrent validity. Median test-retest reliability coefficients were reported to be in the high .80s and low .90s for intervals ranging from two weeks to three years. Concurrent validity, defined as the ability of the scale to "discriminate between people of different occupations" (Campbell & Hansen, 1981, p. 67), was acceptably high. The SII has also been found to correlate with college major. One study found that 80.8% of college students had selected a major that was at least moderately related to their interests as indicated on the SII (Hansen & Tan, 1992). However, little psychometric data on the SII have been generated by independent researchers. The ability of the test to predict future behavior has not been examined in any depth. Another weakness in the development and validation of the entire Strong series of tests is the relative lack of information about how the protocols of people of color are to be interpreted (Carter & Swanson, 1990). At least with respect to the currency of occupational titles, it cannot be said that the SII does not keep up with the times. The latest (1985) edition included a variety of new scales, including one for Athletic Trainer.

In addition to the SII, many other interest inventories (e.g., Holland, 1985; Kuder, 1979) are now in widespread use by counseling psychologists (Watkins et al., 1994). The Minnesota Vocational Interest Inventory is an empirically keyed instrument designed to compare the respondents' interest patterns with those of persons employed in a variety of nonprofessional occupations (such as stock clerks, painters, printers, truck drivers). An instrument called the Career Decision Scale has been used to examine cognitive processes associated with general career indecision (see Osipow & Reed, 1985) as well as specialty indecision among people who have decided on a career (Savickas et al., 1985). A number of interest tests designed for use with people who do not read well uses drawings and other pictures in media such as slides and filmstrips (Elksnin & Elksnin, 1993).

How well do interest measures predict the kind of work in which individuals will be successful and happy? In considering this question, let's note the finding from one study that interest and aptitude measures correlated in the range of .40 to .72 (Lam et al., 1993). From this study, one might infer that people are interested in things that they do well and/or that they develop abilities in areas in which they are interested.

In one of the few studies examining the accuracy with which interest and aptitude tests predict future job performance and satisfaction, Bizot and Goldman (1993) identified people who had been tested in high school with measures of vocational interest and aptitude. Eight years later, these individuals reported on their satisfaction with their jobs. Further, they permitted the researchers to contact their employers for information about the quality of their work. The researchers found that when a good match existed between subjects' aptitudes in high school and the level of their current job, then their job performance was likely to be evaluated positively by the employer. When a poor match existed between the subjects' aptitude as measured in high school and the level of their current job, they would be more likely to be rated as poor in job performance by the employer. The extent to which employees were satisfied with their jobs was not related to aptitudes as measured in high school. As for the predictive validity of the interest tests administered in high school, the tests predicted neither job performance nor job satisfaction eight years later. The results of this study, as well as of related studies (e.g., Jagger et al., 1992), sound a caution to counselors regarding overreliance on interest inventories. Still, this genre of test seems to have value in bringing a dimension to vocational counseling that is not typically found in many other tests.

Personality Measures

Although ample research may be cited to cast doubt on the application of personality tests in various I/O contexts (e.g., Ghiselli, 1973; Ghiselli & Barthol, 1953; Guion & Gottier, 1965; Kinslinger, 1966; Schmitt et al., 1984), a trend seems to be toward a more charitable view of personality tests in I/O settings, especially when such tests are carefully selected for a particular study and used properly (Day & Silverman, 1989; Lord et al., 1986; Schneider, 1987; Weiss & Adler, 1984). In the past, methodological problems as well as theoretical inadequacies in research have plagued many I/O studies that employed personality measures (Hollenbeck & Whitener, 1988). Additionally, past studies deemphasized the specific role requirements of various jobs, and inappropriate personality tests may have been employed in the research. The role requirements of, say, an emergency medical technician are quite different from those of a computer programmer or a salesperson. Different personality traits are of greater or lesser importance in considering each of these occupations within the context of I/O psychology, and the same personality test might not be well suited for each of them. Cascio (1982) drew attention to the distinction between task-related and people-related aspects of an occupation and the differential role each of these variables might play in predicting overall success in an occupation or a particular job. Keeping this distinction in mind, as well as the caveat that personality measures must be job-relevant, it would appear that personality measures have an important place in I/O psychology (Bray et al., 1979; Day & Silverman, 1989; Grimsley & Jarrett, 1975; Hogan et al., 1985).

A personality test such as the MMPI-2, widely used in clinical settings, may have limited application in I/O contexts. Other personality tests, such as the Guilford-Zimmerman Temperament Survey and the Edwards Personal Preference Schedule may be preferred for use in I/O research, perhaps because the measurements they yield tend to be more related to the specific variables under study. One test that seems to be riding a wave of popularity for use in workplace-related measurements is the Myers-Briggs Type Indicator (MBTI). We have selected that test for a closer look here.

The Myers-Briggs Type Indicator Inspired by the theoretical typology of Carl Jung (1923), the Myers-Briggs Type Indicator (MBTI) was developed by Isabel Briggs Myers and her mother, Katharine Cook Briggs (Myers & Briggs, 1943/1962) (see the box on page 656). In the late 1950s, Educational Testing Service (ETS) marketed the MBTI as a research instrument while the company conducted its own research into the test's psychometric properties. After several years of evaluation, ETS elected to terminate its relationship with the test (Pittenger, 1993). In 1975, Consulting Psychologists Press, Inc. (CPP), published the test along with a wide range of ancillary materials, including interpretive guides and software to create psychological reports. Now available in a children's form, a research form, and a form for personal analysis, the test is represented to have application in contexts ranging from vocational guidance to marriage counseling (Consulting Psychologists Press, 1994).

Consistent with Jung's writings, the MBTI was designed to assess four bipolar dimensions of personality, each dimension believed to be a component of one's psychological type: introversion vs. extraversion (with respect to where one focuses one's energy), perceiving vs. judgment (with respect to responding to experience; not part of Jung's theory), sensing vs. intuition (with respect to perception), and thinking vs. feeling (with respect to making judgments).

The Origins of the MBTI

What makes one person different from another psychologically? How can those differences be classified?
These questions were important to Myers and Briggs.
Although neither woman had formal training in psychology, both read biographies with great interest and
studied people, attempting to gain a meaningful understanding of individual differences. Briggs's interest
in individual differences grew still further when, in
1915, her daughter introduced her future husband,
Clarence Myers—he was well liked but seemed different in some fundamental ways from members of the
Briggs family. Briggs developed her own category
system for psychological types in an effort to capture
some of those individual differences. In 1923, Briggs
learned of personality theorist Carl Jung's writings in
this area and eagerly studied them with her daughter.
Years later, Myers decided to put the ideas she had so
long discussed with her mother into test form. This
was partly a product of her experiences during World
War II; she felt that she was foolishly wasting her life
worrying about what bad events the future might
hold, and decided to do something productive. That
"something" grew out of her long-standing shared interests with her mother and eventually became the
Myers-Briggs Type Indicator, a project on which she
worked productively the rest of her life. (Source: Center for Applications of Psychological Type, Inc.,
Gainesville, Florida)

(a)

(b)

(a) *Isabel Briggs Myers (1897–1980) and* (b) *her mother,
Katharine Cook Briggs (1875–1968), authors of the Myers-
Briggs Type Indicator.*

According to Jung, people can be classified at the extremes of these bipolar dimensions. For example, people who usually make judgments on the basis of
feelings will seldom, if ever, make judgments on the basis of thought. This assumption regarding each of these bipolar dimensions is reflected in the way
MBTI test items are written (a forced-choice format reflective of opposite poles
of dimensions) as well as in the way the test responses are scored and interpreted.

The primary form of the test (Form G) contains a total of 126 forced-choice test items. Based on the testtaker's pattern of response to the items, numerical scores are tabulated. The scores are used to classify the testtaker in one or another of the extreme poles of each of the four dimensions. Ultimately, each testtaker is identified as one of sixteen personality types. There are two poles for each of four dimensions yielding 16 ($2 \times 2 \times 2 \times 2$) different possible types. A person may be identified, for example, as an extraverted-intuitive-perceiving-feeling type. In this chapter's *Everyday Psychometrics,* we take a closer look at the scoring and interpretation of the MBTI, as well as at related psychometric issues.

Assessment of Productivity, Motivation, and Attitude

Beyond their use in preemployment counseling and in the screening, selection, classification, and placement of personnel, tools of measurement are used to assess employee productivity, motivation, and job satisfaction, as well as sundry aspects of the work environment.

Productivity

"Productivity" is used here in the broadest sense to be meaningful with reference to workers in all occupations, including those who do not necessarily "produce" (such as service workers). If a business endeavor is to succeed, monitoring output with the ultimate goal of maximizing output is essential. Measures of productivity help to define not only where a business is but also what it needs to do to get where it wants to be. A manufacturer of television sets, for example, might find that the people who are manufacturing the wood casing for the sets are working at optimal efficiency but that the people responsible for installing the picture tubes in the cabinets are working at one-half the expected efficiency. A productivity evaluation can help identify the factors responsible for the sagging performance of the picture-tube people.

Using techniques such as supervisor ratings, interviews with employees, and the planting of undercover employees in the picture-tube workshop, management might determine what—or who in particular—is responsible for the unsatisfactory performance. Perhaps the most common method of evaluating worker productivity or performance is through the use of rating and ranking procedures by superiors in the organization. One type of ranking procedure used when large numbers of employees are being assessed is called the *forced distribution technique.* This procedure involves the distribution of a predetermined number or percentage of assessees into various categories that describe performance (such as Unsatisfactory, Poor, Fair, Average, Good, Superior). Another index of on-the-job performance is number of absences within a given period. It typically reflects more poorly on an employee if he or she is absent on, say, twenty separate occasions than on twenty consecutive dates as the result of a bout with illness. The *critical incidents* technique (Flanagan & Burns,

The Use of the Myers-Briggs Type Indicator in Academic and Preemployment Counseling

The Myers-Briggs Type Indicator (MBTI) is used as an aid in the selection of college major and in occupational choice. Its use is based on the notion that people with certain personality types will be most comfortable with one or another college major and occupation. What evidence exists to support this use of this test?

One answer to that question involves a look at the way the MBTI is scored. On the basis of their responses to the test items, testtakers are classified at one or the other end of the four bipolar dimensions. In practice, this means that testtakers may be classified as extraverted if (1) they demonstrate a very strong tendency to be extraverted or (2) they demonstrate a tendency to be extraverted that is judged to be just slightly stronger than the tendency they exhibit to be introverted (Harvey & Murry, 1994). One is either introverted or extraverted, either "thinking" or "feeling" in making judgments, and so forth. Note that there is no middle ground or gray area with regard to the scoring of the four personality dimensions of the MBTI, nor any room for situation-specific circumstances to alter that classification. This type of scoring has been criticized for both the systematic loss of information it may entail and its oversensitivity to responses to single items; a testtaker may be classified as an extravert if the extraversion score is slightly higher than the introversion score, whereas a different response to just one item could produce a slightly lower extraversion score and result in the person's being classified as an introvert (Lorr, 1991). To avoid such problems, an alternative scoring system that reflects each dimension in a continuous manner using latent-trait methods has been proposed (Harvey & Murry, 1994).

Published research also casts doubt on the bipolarity of the dimensions the test purports to measure. In one such study (Girelli & Stake, 1993), a modified MBTI was designed with separate rating scales for intuition, sensing, feeling, thinking, introversion, and extraversion. The judging/perceiving dimension was not included because it was not part of Jung's theory. If these dimensions were in fact bipolar, negative cor-

relations between characteristics assumed to be on opposite ends of the dimensions would be expected. But that was not the case. Thinking and feeling were positively, albeit weakly, correlated (.19). The same was true of sensing and intuition (.09). Introversion and extraversion were negatively correlated ($-.36$), but this correlation was so low that over 8% of subjects scored in the top one-third of the distribution on both dimensions (and thus were both "highly introverted" and "highly extraverted").

Another study that casts doubt on the bipolar nature of the MBTI dimensions focused on the distribution of the test scores underlying the classification of individuals into specific types. If the introversion vs. extraversion dimension was in fact bipolar, then one would expect a bimodal distribution of underlying scores. That is, testtakers should be either introverts or extraverts, with relatively few people being a mixture of the two. In actuality, the distributions underlying MBTI test scores are unimodal (Pittenger, 1993), with most people exhibiting a mixture of (1) introversion and extraversion, (2) thinking and feeling, and (3) sensing and intuition. These and related findings raise serious concerns about the construct validity of the MBTI dimensions.

The finding of a unimodal distribution of test scores also creates problems with regard to the reliability of the bipolar MBTI scales. A large proportion of subjects cluster within a standard error of measurement of the point used to divide the dimension. Even with a reasonably reliable underlying score, measurement error is likely to result in small changes in some subjects' scores upon retesting. Because so many subjects cluster around the point used to divide the distribution, a substantial proportion of individuals who are initially on one side, say "thinkers," may become "feelers" upon retesting. This creates an unstable situation with regard to one's MBTI personality type. Fully half of all testtakers have been found to change in classification of personality type over the course of only five weeks (Pittenger, 1993). The test scores underlying the placement of subjects on dimensions have been found to be more reliable than the type designations. Test-retest reliability for dimension has been estimated to be .56 to .90 over a one- to five-week retest interval (Girelli & Stake, 1993). Unfortunately, it is at the level of the personality type, and not the level of the dimension, that the test manual recommends interpretation of the findings (Pittenger, 1993).

Evidence of the test's validity can be found in the MBTI test manual and elsewhere (e.g., Davey et al., 1993; LaCorte & Risucci, 1993; Lowenthal, 1994). A typical study cited to support the validity of the MBTI demonstrates either that (1) people from varied occupational or educational groups were found to systematically differ in their MBTI personality type or that (2) people with different MBTI personality types behave differently in the workplace. One cross-cultural study compared Chinese and European managers by MBTI types and workplace behavior. For the Chinese managers, the researchers reported that introversion and perceiving were associated with poor management practices on a wide range of dimensions. For the European managers, it was found that thinking was associated with good management practices and judging was associated with poor management practices (Furnham & Stringfield, 1993). On its face, the study might be used to support the validity of MBTI, by providing evidence that different styles of managerial behavior could be predicted as a function of MBTI classification. Yet closer scrutiny of the study indicates that of the 224 correlations reported between manager behavior and MBTI scales, less than 25% were statistically significant. Further, none of the reported correlations exceeded .25 in magnitude (Furnham & Stringfield, 1993).

In general, a problem with many of the MBTI validity studies has been the small samples of people with which they are conducted. For that reason, the reported differences may not be reliable (Pittenger, 1993). It is also true that many studies simply do not yield compelling differences in occupational membership or interest as a function of MBTI type. For example, one study examined MBTI types for people selecting different concentrations within a Masters in Business Administration program. An attempt to predict which concentrations people would select on the basis of their MBTI scores achieved no greater accuracy than if the individuals had been assigned randomly to groups (Martin & Bartol, 1986).

In cases in which the MBTI type does accurately predict an individual's occupational choice or educational pursuit, the reason may have little to do with personality type. Sex differences on the MBTI have been repeatedly noted; some personality types are more common to men or women. Pittenger (1993) observed that the most common MBTI profiles for a particular occupation or education often predict or postdict the sex of the people who are most often employed in that profession. Primary and secondary teaching, for example, attract more women than men. The personality types described in the MBTI manual implicitly reflect that fact, listing personality types of the typical teacher that tend to be more common to women than men. Pittenger (1993) expressed concern that the MBTI may simply reinforce stereotypes about what "appropriate" occupations are for men and for women.

Factor-analytic studies do not support a four-factor structure for the MBTI; as many as six factors may be identified. In addition, test items from more than one dimension, such as judging vs. perceiving items and sensing vs. intuition items, may load on the same factor, indicating that the dimensions are not independent (Pittenger, 1993). Although some research has found MBTI dimensions to be measuring constructs (such as "introversion/extraversion") that are recognizable as such on other personality measures (MacDonald et al., 1994; McCrae & Costa, 1989), this has not always been the case (Zumbo & Taylor, 1993).

The 16 MBTI personality types have also been examined using a procedure called cluster analysis. In this application of cluster analysis, individuals are assigned to groups based on similarity of group members. If the 16 MBTI personality types are in fact distinct, cluster analysis should place individuals into 16 clusters. From a cluster analysis of the MBTI scores of two samples, each containing 100 men, only four to six clusters emerged. The only personality type to appear in both samples as a distinct cluster was the introverted-sensing-feeling-judging type. Other clusters were mixtures of various personality types (Lorr, 1991). Taken together, the factor-analytic and cluster-analytic findings indicate that the scales of the MBTI may not be as independent as they are represented to be. Viewing all of the literature on the MBTI with some perspective, we may well find that the test promises to deliver more than it actually does.

1955) involves the recording of positive and negative employee behaviors by the supervisor. The notations are catalogued according to various categories (for example, "dependability; initiative") for ready reference when an evaluation needs to be made. There is some evidence to suggest that a "honeymoon" period of about three months or so occurs when a new worker starts a job and that supervisory ratings will be more truly reflective of the worker at the conclusion of that period (see Helmreich et al., 1986).

Peer ratings or evaluations made by other workers of the same level have proved to be a valuable method of identifying talent among employees. Although peers have a tendency to rate their counterparts higher than these people would be rated by superiors, the information obtained from the ratings and rankings of peers can be highly predictive of future performance. For example, one study involved 117 inexperienced life insurance agents who attended a three-week training class. At the conclusion of the course, the budding insurance agents were asked to list the three best people in their class with respect to each of 12 situations. From these data, a composite score for each of the 117 agents was obtained. After one year, these peer ratings and three other variables were correlated with job tenure (number of weeks on the job) and with production (number of dollars of insurance sold). As can be seen from Table 17–3, peer ratings had the highest validity in all of the categories. By contrast, a near zero correlation was obtained between final course grade and all categories.

Of course, ratings are not perfect measures of productivity or potential. Error may result from different types of bias on the part of the raters, such as leniency and halo effects. Still, in one study, self-ratings and ratings by supervisors and peers correlated with one another, as well as with a detailed measure of job performance (Vance et al., 1988). Such intercorrelations in the predicted direction may be interpreted as evidence for the validity of the ratings.

Motivation

Why do some people skip lunch, work overtime, and take home work nightly, whereas others strive to do as little as possible and live a life of leisure at work? At a practical level, light may be shed on such questions using assessment instruments such as The Study of Values (see Chapter 14), which tap the values of the assessee. Dealing with a population of unskilled personnel may require specially devised techniques. Champagne (1969) responded to the challenge of knowing little about what might appeal to rural, unskilled people in attempts to attract them to work, so he devised a motivational questionnaire. As illustrated by the three items in Figure 17–4 (see page 662), the questionnaire used a paired comparison (forced-choice) format that required the subject to make choices relative to 12 factors used by companies to entice employment applications: fair pay, steady job, vacations and holidays with pay, job extras such as pensions and sick benefits, a fair boss, interesting work, good working conditions, chance for promotion, a job close to home, working with friends and neighbors, nice people to work with, and praise for good work. The job-seeking factor found to be most important in Champagne's sample of 349 male and fe-

Table 17–3

Peer Ratings and Performance of Life Insurance Salespeople

	Job tenure		Production	
	6 months	1 year	6 months	1 year
Peer rating	.18*	.29**	.29**	.30**
Age	.18*	.24**	.06	.09
Starting salary	.01	.03	.13	.26**
Final course grade	.02	.06	−.02	.02

*$p = .05$ (one-tailed test)
**$p = .01$ (one-tailed test)

Source: Mayfield (1972)

male, rural unskilled subjects was "steady job." The least important factor was found to be "working with friends and neighbors." "Praise for good work" was a close runner-up for being least in importance. In interpreting the findings, Champagne cautioned that "the factors reported here relate to the job-seeking behavior of the unskilled and are not measures of how to retain and motivate the unskilled once employed. . . . What prompts a person to accept a job is not necessarily the same as what prompts a person to retain a job or do well in it" (p. 268).

On a theoretical level, there exists an abundance of theories that seek to delineate the specific needs, attitudes, social influences, and other factors that might account for differences in motivation. For example, Vroom (1964) proposed an expectancy theory of motivation, which essentially holds that employees expend energy in ways designed to achieve the outcome they want; the greater the expectancy that an action will achieve a certain outcome, the more energy that will be expended to achieve that outcome. Maslow (1943, 1970) constructed a theoretical hierarchy of human needs (see Figure 17–5) and proposed that as one category of need is met, people move on to satisfy the next category of need. Employers who subscribe to Maslow's theory would seek to identify (1) the need "level" the job requires of the employee and (2) the need level the prospective employee is at. Alderfer (1972) proposed an alternative need theory of motivation, one that was not hierarchical in nature. Whereas Maslow saw the satisfaction of one need leading to the satisfaction of the next need in the hierarchy, Alderfer proposed that once a need was satisfied it was possible that the organism strove to satisfy it to an even greater degree. The Alderfer theory also provides that the frustration of one need might lead to the channeling of energy into the achievement of a need at another level.

In a widely cited program that undertook to define the characteristics of achievement motivation, McClelland (1961) used as his measure of that motivation stories written under special instructions about TAT and TAT-like pictures. McClelland described the individual with a high need for achievement as one who prefers a task that is not too simple or extremely difficult, something with moderate as opposed to extreme risks. A situation with little or no risk will not lead to feelings of accomplishment if the individual succeeds. On the other

Figure 17–4
Studying Values with the Unskilled

Champagne (1969) used test items such as those pictured in a recruitment study with a rural, unskilled population.

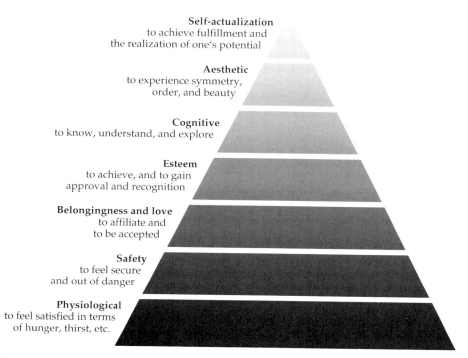

Figure 17–5
Maslow's Hierarchy of Needs (adapted from Maslow, 1970)

hand, an extremely high-risk situation may not lead to feelings of accomplishment because of the high probability of failure. Persons with high need for achievement enjoy taking responsibility for their actions because they desire the credit and recognition for their accomplishments. Such individuals also desire information about their performance to constantly improve their output. Other researchers also used TAT-like pictures and their own specially devised scoring systems to study related areas of human motivation such as the fear of failure (Birney et al., 1969; Cohen & Houston, 1975; Cohen & Parker, 1974; Cohen & Teevan, 1974, 1975; Cohen et al., 1975) and the fear of success (Horner, 1973).

Motivation may be conceptualized as stemming either from incentives that are primarily internal or from incentives that are primarily external in origin. Another way of stating this is to speak of *intrinsic motivation* (where the primary force driving the individual stems from things such as the individual's involvement in work or satisfaction with work products) as opposed to *extrinsic motivation* (where the primary force driving the individual stems from rewards, such as salary and bonuses, or from constraints, such as job loss). A scale designed to assess aspects of intrinsic and extrinsic motivation is the Work Preference Inventory (WPI; Amabile et al., 1994). The WPI contains 30 items rated on a four-point scale based on how much the testtaker believes the item to be self-descriptive. Factor analysis indicates that the test does appear to tap two distinct factors, intrinsic and extrinsic motivation. Each of these two factors may be divided into two subfactors. The intrinsic motivation factor may be divided into one subfactor that has to do with the challenge of the work tasks and another that has to do with the enjoyment of work. The extrinsic motivation factor may be divided into one subfactor that has to do with compensation for work and another that has to do with external influences (such as the recognition by others for one's work). The WPI correlates in the predicted direction with behavioral and other questionnaire measures of motivation, as well as with measures of vocational interest, personality, and creativity. The test is internally consistent (the reliability coefficient was .70 for the extrinsic scale and .75 for the intrinsic scale) and evidences good test-retest reliability (.80 for the extrinsic scale, .89 for the intrinsic scale over a six-month interval).

Worker productivity and motivation have long been thought to be related to various work-related attitudes. As we will see in what follows, attitudes toward one's job, toward one's co-workers, and even toward a corporate environment may all be of interest to the I/O psychologist.

Attitude

An *attitude* may be formally defined as a presumably learned disposition to react in some characteristic manner to a particular stimulus. The stimulus may be an object, a group, an institution—virtually anything. In the following chapter on assessment in consumer psychology, we will see how attitudes toward goods and services are measured. More immediately, however, we focus on workplace-related attitudes. Although attitudes do not necessarily predict behavior (Tittle & Hill, 1967; Wicker, 1969), I/O psychologists are very interested in measuring the attitudes of employers and employees toward each other, as well as toward numerous variables in the workplace. A great deal of research has been done, for example, on the subject of job satisfaction.

Job satisfaction Compared with dissatisfied workers, satisfied workers in the workplace are believed to be more productive (Petty et al., 1984), more consistent in work output (Locke, 1976), less likely to complain (Burke, 1970; Locke, 1976), and less likely to be absent from work or to be replaced (Herzberg et al., 1957; Vroom, 1964). Although these assumptions are somewhat controversial (Iaffaldano & Muchinsky, 1985) and should probably be considered on a case-by-case basis, employers, employees, researchers, and consultants have maintained a long-standing interest in the measurement of job satisfaction. Traditionally, *job satisfaction* has been defined as "a pleasurable or positive emotional state resulting from the appraisal of one's job or job experiences" (Locke, 1976, p. 300).

Contemporary measures of job satisfaction go well beyond the mere measurement of feeling states and may focus more on cognitive evaluations of specific facets of the job or one's supervisor (Organ & Near, 1985). Measures of job satisfaction may even focus on one's self-perception, including the perception of one's role in the organization and the degree of ambiguity and conflict that attends that role (Brown & Peterson, 1993). Other facets of job satisfaction as-

Table 17-4

Consequences of Organizational Commitment Level for Individual Employees and the Organization

	Level of organizational commitment		
	Low	Moderate	High
The Individual Employee	Potentially positive consequences for opportunity for expression of originality and innovation, but an overall negative effect on career advancement opportunities	Enhanced feeling of belongingness and security, along with doubts about the opportunity for advancement	Greater opportunity for advancement and compensation for efforts, along with less opportunity for personal growth and potential for stress in family relationships
The Organization	Absenteeism, tardiness, workforce turnover, and poor quality of work	As compared with low commitment, less absenteeism, tardiness, turnover, and better quality of work, as well as increased level of job satisfaction	Potential for high productivity, but sometimes accompanied by lack of critical/ethical review of employee behavior and by reduced organizational flexibility

sessed by various instruments run the gamut from the measurement of attitude toward the nature and extent of one's work, to the measurement of the attitudes of one's friends and family toward one's job (Cook et al., 1981). As with more traditional measures of attitude, job satisfaction measures typically employ a Likert-scale format. Some commonly used measures include the Job Descriptive Index, the Job Diagnostic Survey, the Job Characteristics Inventory, and the Job Discrimination Index (Smith et al., 1969). The last measure, for example, comprises five subscales designed to measure satisfaction with work, pay, coworkers, supervision, and promotions. The validity of a measure of job satisfaction is typically established by the demonstration of high correlations either with other measures of job satisfaction or with presumed correlates of job satisfaction.

Organizational commitment The concept of *organizational commitment* is defined in terms of the strength of one's loyalty to and involvement in an organization, as well as the degree to which one's value system is consistent with that of an organization and the degree to which one would exert a special effort on behalf of the organization (Porter et al., 1974; Steers, 1977). Measures of organizational commitment frequently employ many items tapping the above-listed areas through the use of five- or seven-point Likert rating scales (Gatewood & Perloff, 1990). Presumed correlates of high and low organizational commitment as observed by Randall (1987) are summarized in Table 17-4.

Organizational culture Much like different places at different times throughout history, organizations and corporations have developed distinctive cultures. There are values that tend to be held and enforced by the organization. There may be distinctive ceremonies, rights, or privileges—formal as well as informal—attached to advancement, as well as sanctions that are tied to failure. As noted by Trice and Beyer (1984), a corporate culture may have distinctive rites of passage, as well as its own methods of renewal, enhancement, and conflict reduction.

Although there are published tests designed to measure some aspects of the work environment (for example, a measure called the Work Environment Scale), a truly comprehensive assessment entails detailed study of several organizational characteristics. As summarized by Gatewood and Perloff (1990), these characteristics include a company's physical setting, its representations about itself to the outside world (in annual reports, brochures, and related documents), how it deals with strangers, how employees spend their time, and to what the company attributes its success. It is also essential to get a sense of the types of people who work at the company and to gather data from employees about "career paths, lengths of time in specific jobs, the content of messages, and the anecdotes and stories that are regularly discussed" (Gatewood & Perloff, 1990, p. 498).

Other Varieties of I/O Assessment

Since the beginnings of I/O psychology nearly one hundred years ago, the field has been evolving constantly. In addition to assessing attitudes, such as those related to corporate commitment and organizational culture, other relative newcomers to the list of variables that I/O psychologists have been called upon to measure include personal integrity and drug use. In engineering psychology, a subspecialty of I/O psychology, psychologists play a key role in the design of instrumentation and equipment, as well as environments. We briefly survey aspects of the use of tests and measurement in these areas.

Drug Testing and Tests of Integrity

Today, personnel and human resource managers are as concerned as ever that the people they hire, as well as current employees, have the knowledge and abilities necessary for successful job performance. Increasingly, however, employers are seeking some type of assurance that the people they will hire, or the people that they currently employ, are not prone to theft or drug use. To help obtain such assurance, they are turning more and more to the use of drug tests and tests of integrity.

Drug testing and its alternatives   The dollar amounts vary by source, but estimates of corporate losses in the workplace that are due, directly or indirectly, to employee drug or alcohol use run into the tens of billions of dollars. Revenue may be lost because of injury to people or animals, damage to products and the environment, or employee absenteeism, tardiness, or sick leave. And no dollar amount can be attached to the tragic loss of life that may result from a drug- or alcohol-related mishap. For those reasons, testing for drug use is a growing practice in corporate America. Today, 40–50% of companies use drug testing in some form (West & Ackerman, 1993), with large companies and industries more likely to test than small companies and service organizations. Companies that do drug testing most commonly test all applicants during the selection process and test actual employees only if drug use is suspected. Random drug testing is relatively unusual in private companies, although it is common in government agencies and in the military (Murphy & Thornton, 1992).

Methods of drug testing vary. One method, the Immunoassay Test, employs the subject's urine to determine the presence or absence of drugs in the body by identifying the metabolized by-products of the drug (*metabolites*). Although widely used in workplace settings, the test can be criticized for its inability to specify the precise amount of the drug that was taken, when it was taken, and which of several possible drugs in a particular category was taken. Further, there is no way to estimate the degree of impairment that occurred in response to the drug. The Gas Chromatography/Mass Spectrometry (GCMS) Test also examines metabolites in urine to determine the presence or absence of drugs, but it can more accurately specify which drug was used. GCMS technology cannot, however, pinpoint the time at which the drug was taken or the degree of impairment that occurred as a consequence.

Many employees object to drug testing as a condition of employment (Labig, 1992) and have argued that such testing violates their constitutional rights to privacy and freedom from unreasonable search and seizure. In the course of legal proceedings, a question that emerges frequently is the validity of drug testing. The consequences of *false positives* (an individual tests positively for drug use when in reality there has been no drug use) and *false negatives* (an individual tests negatively for drug use when in reality there has been drug use) in such cases can be momentous. A false positive in such a test may result in, among other things, the loss of one's livelihood. A false negative may result in the continuance of an impaired person in a position of responsibility that places others at risk.

Modern laboratory techniques tend to be relatively accurate in detecting tell-tale metabolites. Error rates are generally well under 2% (West & Ackerman, 1993). However, laboratory techniques may not always be used correctly. By one estimate, fully 93% of laboratories that do drug testing fail to meet standards designed to reduce human error (Comer, 1993). Error may also occur in the interpretation of results. Metabolites may be identified accurately, but whether their origin was in the abuse of some illicit drug or in some over-the-counter medication cannot always be determined. To help prevent such confusion, administrators of the urine test typically ask the subject to compile a list of any medications currently being taken. However, not all subjects are willing or able to remember all medications they may have taken. Further, some employees are reluctant to report some prescription medications they may have taken to treat conditions to which any possible social stigma may be attached, such as depression or epilepsy. Additionally, some foods may also produce metabolites that mimic the metabolites of some illegal drugs. For example, metabolites of opiates will be detected following the subject's ingestion of (perfectly legal) poppy seeds (West & Ackerman, 1993).

Another question related to the validity of drug tests concerns the degree to which drugs identified through testing actually affect job performance. Some drugs leave the body very slowly. For example, a person may test positive for marijuana use up to a month after the last exposure to it. Thus, the residue of the drug remains long after any discernible impairment from having taken the drug. By contrast, cocaine leaves the body in only three days. It is possible for a habitual cocaine user to be off the drug for three days, be highly impaired as a result of cocaine withdrawal, yet still test negative for drug use. Thus, neither a positive nor a negative finding with regard to a drug test necessarily means that behavior has or has not been impaired by drug use (Comer, 1993).

An alternative to drug testing involves directly examining impairment using performance tests. For example, sophisticated video-game-style tests of coordination, judgment, and reaction time are available to compare current performance with baseline performance as established on earlier tests. Advantages that these performance tests have over drug testing include a more direct assessment of impairment, fewer ethical concerns regarding invasion of privacy, and immediate information about impairment. The last advantage is particularly vital in preventing potentially impaired individuals from hurting themselves or others. Organizations using such electronic tests have reported benefits with regard to employee satisfaction and fewer accidents (Comer, 1993).

Tests of integrity   Integrity tests may serve to screen new employees as well as to "keep honest" those already hired. Paper-and-pencil screening instruments purporting to predict who will and will not be an honest employee—so-called *integrity tests*—have been around for many years. However, the use of such tests has increased dramatically with the passage of legislation prohibiting the use of polygraphs ("lie detectors") in most employment settings. In fact, it has been estimated that integrity testing has mushroomed into a thirty-million-dollar-a-year industry (Lawlor, 1990), with an estimated 15 million people taking such tests annually (Gavzer, 1990).

Sackett, Burris, and Callahan (1989) dichotomize existing instruments into what they term "overt integrity tests" (which may straightforwardly ask the examinee questions like "Do you always tell the truth?"), and "personality-based measures," which resemble in many ways objective personality inventories such as the MMPI. Items on the latter type of test may be far more subtle than on the former. Also, responses to items on the personality-based measures are less likely to be interpreted on the basis of the face validity of the item and more likely to be interpreted with reference to the responses of groups of people known to have, or lack, "integrity" as defined by the particular test.

Whether integrity tests measure what they purport to measure is debatable. Reviews of the validity of such measures have ranged from mixed (APA, 1991a; Sackett & Harris, 1984; Sackett et al., 1989) to positive (DePaulo, 1994; Honts, 1994; Sackett, 1994; Saxe, 1994). Perhaps the fairest conclusion from this literature is that when the test has been professionally developed, it stands an excellent chance of meeting acceptable standards of validity. *Model Guidelines for Preemployment Integrity Testing Programs* is a document developed by the Association of Personnel Test Publishers (APTP, 1990) that addresses many of the issues surrounding integrity tests, including issues relating to test development, administration, scoring, interpretation, confidentiality, public statements regarding the tests, and test-marketing practices. Specific guidelines in these areas are provided, and the responsibilities of test users and publishers are discussed (see Jones et al., 1990, for an overview).

Beyond issues regarding the validity of integrity tests lie broader questions that relate to various aspects of the use of such tests (Camara & Schneider, 1994). For example, is privacy being invaded when a prospective employee is asked to sit for such a test? Can such tests be used in support of discrimination practices? Should such tests be used alone or in combination with other measurement procedures as a basis for granting or denying employment? Interestingly, White (1984) suggests that preemployment honesty testing may induce negative work-related attitudes. Having to undergo such a test may be interpreted by prospective employees as evidence of high levels of employee theft—with the (paradoxical) result being a new and higher norm of stealing by employees.

Engineering Psychology

Employed by industry and organizations, as well as by academic institutions, engineering psychologists conduct what is variously referred to as ergonomic (work-related) or human factors research. Engineering psychologists employ a variety of measures, mostly custom-designed, to help develop the plans for everything from household items (Hsu & Peng, 1993) to components for automobiles (Chira-Chavala & Yoo, 1994) and aircraft (Begault, 1993). In some cases, standardized psychological tests, such as tests of personality, may be employed in attempts to understand a particular population or work environment—the better to design instrumentation, equipment, or a work environment.

A Perspective

Especially since the 1950s, the specialty area of industrial/organizational psychology has expanded in scope well beyond occupational testing. Along with this expansion has come a great deal of social change, and greater complexity in the tasks of test developers and the responsibilities of test users. For example, the utility of the traditional three-category taxonomy of validity—what Guion (1980) referred to as the "trinitarian" view—has been called into question. Citing claims made in workplace discrimination litigation in which content-related. criterion-related, and construct-related test validation strategies were challenged, Landy (1986) argued that a new, unitarian view of validity might be of greater efficacy than a view that categorizes types of validity evidence. Lawshe (1985) advanced a similar view when he argued that different kinds of validity do not exist; rather, different kinds of validity analysis strategies exist. A corollary to the view expressed by both Landy (1986) and Lawshe (1985) is that it is inappropriate to refer to the validity of a test; instead, one should refer only to the validity of inferences from test scores.

Beyond academic and psychometric-related controversies in the field of industrial/organizational assessment are numerous legal and ethical issues and controversies. Employers are often placed in a legal bind as they attempt to act within the confines of legislation that outlaws disparate impact (racial imbalance) in employee selection. As Gottfredson (1994) has observed, the use of valid and unbiased selection procedures often guarantees disparate impact because of racial disparities in job-related skills and abilities. She wrote that "the biggest contribution personnel psychologists can make in the long run may be to insist collectively and candidly that their measurement tools are neither the cause nor the cure for racial differences in job skills and consequent inequalities in employment" (Gottfredson, 1994, p. 963). Others have considered the merits of within-group norming and other forms of score adjustment (Sackett & Wilk, 1994), although the issues surrounding these and other affirmative action strategies are extremely complex (Crosby, 1994; Eberhardt & Fiske, 1994).

Another gray area in the law concerns legal mandates that any psychological or physical measure used as a condition of employment be both job-related and nondiscriminatory. Measures on which one sex or race performs better than another have been upheld by courts, however, in cases in which it has been clearly demonstrated that such standards are necessary for success in a particular job. In the case of *Hail v. White,* for example, a challenge was made to the height and weight standards applied to the hiring of police officers. The existing requirements mandated that applicants be at least 5 feet 7 inches tall and weigh at least 135 pounds. A suit alleging sex discrimination was brought on the grounds that these requirements excluded more women than men. The defendant police department showed that these same standards were routinely employed by other police departments and that the standards were necessary for police officers to deal with violent perpetrators. The court upheld the use of these physical standards in hiring, ruling that they were not unreasonable and that they were job-related. Focusing on the issue of tests of physical strength for physically demanding jobs, job applicants, especially women, may benefit greatly from test preparation in the form of physical training (Hogan & Quigley, 1994).

In *Callery v. New York City Parks and Recreation Department,* a preemployment condition for a position as a lifeguard was the same physical requirement for employment as in the case cited above (5 feet 7 inches tall, 135 pounds). Ruling that no compelling evidence had been presented to justify these requirements as job-related, the court found them to be discriminatory and unenforceable.

In the case of *United States v. New York,* the court ruled against the requirement that New York State troopers be able to aim a gun over a patrol vehicle. The court found this guideline to be a hidden height requirement that was racially discriminatory and was not clearly job-related. Similarly, in *Guardians Association v. Civil Service Commission,* a height standard for the position of police officer was found to constitute discrimination on the basis of race and national origin because 77.8% of White men, 80.9% of Black men, and only 45.9% of Hispanic-American men met the height standard of 5 feet 7 inches. The court ruled that the height requirement could not be used.

The argument that tests can be instruments that in effect violate one's right to privacy has been alive and well since the 1950s. Today, this argument finds what may be its most vigorous expression in cases involving drug testing in the workplace. In general, the courts have permitted drug testing, even random drug testing, when the testing is done with regard to an occupation in which impairment would place people at risk. Two 1989 Supreme Court decisions illustrate this concern for public safety. In one case (*National Treasury Employees Union v. Von Raab*), the position in question entailed carrying firearms and enforcing drug laws, and in the other case (*Skinner v. Railway Labor Executives' Association*), the position entailed the operation of a train.

Laws regarding the treatment of the disabled are sure to have an effect on the way that I/O testing and assessment is undertaken in the future. For example, the Americans with Disabilities Act of 1990 (PL 101-336) prohibits an employer from refusing to hire or promote someone on the basis of disability if the individual is qualified to perform the job. In effect as of July 26, 1992, for employers with 25 or more employees, and July 26, 1994, for employers with 15 to 24 employees, PL 101-336 covers most individuals with mental disabilities and all individuals with physical disabilities, including those in treatment for drug and alcohol abuse and those with AIDS or HIV infection. Employers are prohibited from asking a prospective employee whether he or she has been treated for mental health problems. The skills measured by any preemployment tests must be directly related to the skills necessary for successful performance of the job. Individuals who do not possess fine motor coordination skills sufficient to take a paper-and-pencil test might not be required to take such a test if the job does not require such skills. Visually impaired or blind individuals are to be provided with a recorded version of job applications. The hearing-impaired and the deaf have to be interviewed in such a way that they are not penalized for their disability. The law further requires employers to make reasonable accommodation for individuals with a disability if such accommodation will enable the individual to perform the job (Klimoski & Palmer, 1993).

We now turn from discussion of psychological testing and assessment in the workplace to a look at that enterprise in the consumer marketplace.

18

*Consumer Assessment**

onsumer psychology is that branch of social and industrial/organizational (I/O) psychology that deals primarily with the development, advertising, and marketing of products and services. As is true with almost all other specialty areas within psychology, some consumer psychologists work exclusively in academia, some work in applied settings, and many do both (Tybout & Artz, 1994). In both applied and research studies, consumer psychologists can be found working closely with professionals in fields such as marketing and advertising to help answer questions such as the following:

- Does a market exist for this new product?

- Does a market exist for this new use of an existing product?

- Exactly who, with respect to age, sex, race, social class, and other demographic variables, constitutes the market for this product?

- How can the targeted consumer population cost-effectively be made aware of this product?

- How can the targeted consumer population most cost-effectively be persuaded to purchase this product?

- What is the best way to package this product?[1]

---

*An earlier version of this chapter was written with the assistance of David W. Stewart.

1. Questions concerning packaging and how to make a product stand out on the shelf have been referred to as questions of "shelf-esteem" by consumer psychologists with a sense of humor.

An Overview

One area of interest shared by the consumer psychologist and psychologists in other specialty areas is the measurement of attitudes; for the consumer psychologist, however, the attitude of interest might be one toward a particular product or concept. We begin our survey of tests and measurement in consumer psychology with a brief look at the process of measuring attitudes.

The Measurement of Attitudes

Attitudes formed about products, services, or brand names are frequent foci of interest in consumer attitude research. Attitude is typically measured by self-report, using tests and questionnaires. A limitation of this approach is that people differ in their ability to be introspective and in their level of self-awareness. People also differ in the extent to which they are willing to be candid about their attitudes. In some instances, the use of an attitude measure may, in essence, create an attitude where none existed before; in such studies, the attitude being measured may be viewed as an artifact of the measurement procedure (Sandelands & Larson, 1985).

Questionnaires and other self-report instruments designed to measure consumer attitudes are developed in ways similar to those previously described for psychological tests in general (see Chapter 7). A more detailed description of the preparation of measures of attitude can be found in the now classic work *The Measurement of Attitude* (Thurstone & Chave, 1929). A monograph entitled "A Technique for the Measurement of Attitudes" (Likert, 1932) provided researchers in this area with a simple procedure for constructing an instrument for measuring attitudes. Essentially, this procedure consists of listing statements (either favorable or unfavorable) that reflect a particular attitude. These statements are then administered to a group of respondents whose responses are analyzed to identify the most discriminating statements—items that best discriminate people at different points on the hypothetical continuum—which are then included in the final scale. Each statement included in the final scale is accompanied by a five-point continuum of alternative responses that may range, for example, from "Strongly Agree" to "Strongly Disagree." Scoring is accomplished by assigning numerical weights of 1 through 5 to each category such that "5" represents the strongest favorable response and "1" reflects the least favorable response.

Measures of attitude found in the psychological literature run the gamut from instruments devised solely for research and testing of academic, theoretical formulations, to scales with wide-ranging, "real world" applications. In the latter context, we might find sophisticated industrial/organizational measures designed to gauge workers' attitudes toward their work, or scales designed to measure the general public's attitudes toward some politician or issue. Attitude scales with applied utility may also be found in the educational psychology literature—consider, for example, measures such as the Study Attitudes and

Methods Survey (a scale designed to assess study habits) and the Minnesota Teacher Attitude Survey (a scale designed to assess student-teacher relations). And given the title of this chapter, you may have already correctly assumed that attitude measurement is very much a part of consumer psychology.

The Tools of the Consumer Psychologist

To answer questions such as those posed at the beginning of this chapter (as well as others such as those concerned with the *positioning* of products—see Figure 18–1), consumer psychologists rely on a variety of methods, used individually or in combination with each other. Included here are surveys and polls, motivation research, behavioral observation, and a variety of other methods.

Surveys and polls   When the attitudes, opinions, or beliefs of large numbers of people need to be known, the measurement method of choice is a survey or a poll. Politicians frequently engage pollsters to obtain a sense of how their constituency is feeling about controversial issues (such as abortion, gun control, and surrogate motherhood). The consumer psychologist might use this tool to gauge the receptivity of consumers to a new product or a new use for an existing product. As we will see, survey or poll questions may be put to the consumer in a face-to-face interview, over the phone, or through the mail, and at least hypothetically, through other means as well (for example, through a computer terminal).

Occasions arise when research questions cannot be answered through a survey or a poll; consumers may be unable or unwilling to cooperate. As an example of an inability to cooperate, consider the hypothetical case of "Ralph," who smokes a hypothetical brand of cigarettes we will call "Cowboy." When asked why he chooses to smoke "Cowboy" brand cigarettes, Ralph might reply "taste." It may be the case, however, that Ralph began smoking "Cowboy" because the advertising for this brand appealed to Ralph's image of himself as an independent, macho type—even though Ralph is employed as a clerk for a dry cleaner. Consumers may also be unwilling or reluctant to respond to some survey or poll questions. Suppose, for example, that the manufacturers of Cowboy cigarettes wished to know where on the product's packaging the Surgeon General's warning could be placed so that it would be least likely to be read. How

Figure 18–1
Positioning a Product ▶

Positioning of a product in the marketplace generally refers to highlighting a particular benefit of a product. Thus, for example, one dishwashing detergent might be positioned as the "best cleaning," another as "gentlest to your hands," and another as "most economical." Sometimes products undergo radical changes in their positioning. For example, although Listerine is currently positioned in the marketplace as a plaque-killer and conqueror of gingivitis, it was at one time positioned not as a mouthwash but as a scalp rinse.

Scalp troubles?
Loose DANDRUFF?

Read letters below—

they tell much better than we could the amazing results accomplished by Listerine in treating scalp disorders.

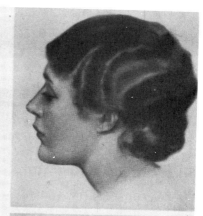

MEN and women are constantly writing us of the beneficial effects of using full strength Listerine on the scalp and hair, either as a part of the usual shampoo or independent of it. In many cases they report that Listerine brought relief from scalp troubles after other methods of treatment had failed.

The letters below, selected from many hundreds, show a number of uses to which Listerine has successfully been put. The value of this safe antiseptic lies primarily in its ability to destroy germs almost instantly, and therefore combat infection. At the same time it is soothing and healing to tissue. Lambert Pharmacal Co., St. Louis, Mo.

Relieved Itching Scalp

My husband and I can't find praise enough for Listerine. It sure is wonderful. For months he was troubled with dandruff and his scalp itched him terribly. He'd come home from work so grouchy, that you could hardly speak to him and he'd always say "How can I help it? My scalp itches so badly, that it nearly drives me crazy, and I have so much dandruff that I'm ashamed to be seen anywhere."

One of our friends advised him to try Listerine. At first he laughed, but I finally persuaded him to try it. He did and with such wonderful results the first time that he went right to the druggist's and purchased a large bottle. He has been using it regularly once a week and I can truthfully say that he hasn't a bit of dandruff, or noticed any itching of the scalp since he's been using it.

Yours truly,
MRS. VIRGIL HELBIG
Newport, Kentucky

Ended Baby's "Milk Crust"

When my infant daughter reached the age of four months, a fine film of "milk crust" commonly known as "cradle cap" formed on her scalp. I attempted to soften this film with olive oil, hoping thereby, to release it from the scalp but soon discovered that this treatment was ineffective as the "cap" had thoroughly imbedded itself in the scalp. Combing with a fine tooth comb helped somewhat but was not recommended as it tended to irritate the sensitive scalp and one had to be extremely careful of the soft opening at the top of the head. The scalp not only was unsightly but refused to respond to treatment.

Finally my husband suggested Listerine, two parts of Listerine to one part of warm water, and rinsing the baby's head with this solution.

Skeptical, I gave it a trial for a week, soaking baby's head thoroughly once daily with the diluted Listerine. At the end of the week I noticed that the "crust" had almost disappeared and that the remaining flakes were quite loose and could be combed out with gentle movements. I continued using the diluted Listerine for the two successive weeks and at the end of that time baby's scalp was clean. I noticed no irritation or discomfiture on her part, therefore was certain that Listerine was as harmless to infants' sensitive scalps as to adults' more hardened ones.

Sincerely yours,
MRS. MILDRED S. MACLEOD
Jamaica, L. I., N. Y.

Relieves Itching of Diabetic Patient

Early in our education as student nurses we are taught, among other important duties, the Nurse should not prescribe, and also, she should be seen and not heard.

But, as regards Listerine, and its valuable properties, I feel it is necessary that I be heard. If I may so express myself, I find Listerine to be the last word in securing a cooling, refreshing and permanent relief or cure from the annoyance of, not alone dandruff, but skin conditions, especially those of the scalp so often prevalent in diabetes.

A small piece of cotton dipped in Listerine and applied to the scalp, after parting the hair, not only relieves the itching, but refreshes the patient confined to bed (which automatically reacts on the general physical health and soothes them to sleep many times) and it entirely removes the large itching spots that occur on the scalp in the diabetic patient.

These spots often appear on the forehead, on the sides of the face and around back of the neck, bordering the hair and are visible, about the size of a quarter. They not only itch but are embarrassing; as skin desquamates and falls on the eyebrows finally rests on the chest and shoulders. These irritated spots, thanks to Listerine which I always apply to the infected area, are controlled, at the same time soothed, and ultimately obliterated.

Cordially yours,
MARY WILSON PATTON, R. N.
San Antonio, Texas

Got Rid of Dandruff

I would like to state just two of my reasons for recommending Listerine to our patients who have scalp diseases or irritations. One is that it is a permanent remover, and the other is that it is so pleasant to use, as it does not leave the unpleasant odor as do so many of the others, but leaves the hair with a soft, luxurious texture, and with a sweet fragrance. And as the scalp is, in most cases, very sensitive, we must use something that not only removes the dandruff, but that will also cool and soothe the irritations. After recommending Listerine, I find that innumerable people return to thank me for my suggestion. Personally I believe that Listerine is the only treatment for dandruff.

Sincerely yours,
ETHELWYNE D. AKER
Registered Certified Nurse
San Diego, California

Too Much Oil in Hair

I use Listerine exclusively to correct oily and dull hair. My method is simple. Every morning I set a water-wave in my hair with a mixture of Listerine and water, using a quarter cupful of each. I dip a small, clean hairbrush in this solution, and brush the hair with it until thoroughly wet. Then I set the wave and let it dry.

By washing the brush in soapy water after using, this process serves to clean the hair and remove the oil; thus doing away with the necessity of frequent shampoos, which only aggravate the oily condition.

As the hair comes back into condition, clear water may be substituted for the Listerine solution on alternate days, or oftener.

The improvement in my hair is remarkable; it is now soft, fluffy and a bright brown, with those much-desired "highlights"; instead of the forlorn, hair-colored mass of an earlier time. And I am always free of scalp troubles and dandruff.

Cordially,
MRS. CLAIRE B. BURCHETT
Derby, Colorado

LISTERINE *cleans, cools, soothes the scalp*

KILLS 200,000,000 GERMS IN 15 SECONDS

many consumers would be willing to entertain such a question? Indeed, what would even posing such a question do for the public image of the product? It can be seen that if this hypothetical company was interested in obtaining an answer to such a question, it would have to do so through means other than a survey or a poll.

Motivation research methods Motivation research is so named because it typically involves the analysis of motives for consumer behavior and attitudes. Motivation research methods include individual interviews and focus groups, and these methods are used to examine in depth the reactions of a representative group of consumers to whatever the focus of the study is—be it a concept for a new product, the packaging of a new product, a particular television or radio commercial, or an entire advertising campaign. Such research may be useful in determining what is appealing about a product that is in wide use and what is unappealing about a product that the public has rejected. For example, in the late 1940s it became evident that instant coffee, a revolutionary convenience item at that time, did not enjoy wide acceptance by the public. Polling indicated that people didn't buy instant coffee because they didn't like the flavor. However, a classic, in-depth, market research study suggested that the real reason people weren't buying it was that they might be perceived, either by themselves or by others, as lazy, extravagant, and shirking their household duties (Haire, 1950).

One variety of motivation research involves a technique called a *focus group,* so named because it involves a group of people whose members, with the aid of a group moderator, focus on some issues presented in the group. Another technique used in motivation research is the in-depth interview. Each of these techniques is discussed in greater detail later in this chapter.

Behavioral observation In October 1982, the sales of pain relievers such as aspirin, Bufferin, Anacin, and Excedrin rose sharply. Was this rise in sales due to the effectiveness of the advertising campaigns for these products? No. The sales rose sharply in 1982 when it was learned that seven people had died from Tylenol capsules that had been laced with cyanide. As Tylenol, the pain reliever with the largest share of the market, was withdrawn from the shelves of stores nationwide, there was a corresponding rise in the sale of alternative preparations. A similar phenomenon occurred in 1986. The point here is that if market researchers were to base their judgments concerning the effectiveness of an ad campaign on sales figures alone, the interpretation of the data would, no doubt, be spurious. Thus, it is not unusual for market researchers to station behavioral observers in stores as a technique for monitoring what really prompts a consumer to buy this or that product at the point of choice. Such an observer at a store selling pain relievers in October of 1982 might have observed, for example, a conversation with the clerk about what the best alternative to Tylenol would be. Behavioral observers in a supermarket who studied the purchasing habits of people buying breakfast cereal concluded that children accompanying the purchaser requested or demanded a specific brand of cereal (Atkin, 1978). Hence, it would be wise for breakfast cereal manufacturers to gear their advertising to children and not the adult consumer. Behavioral observation can also be used to study reactions to television advertising (see the box on pages 678–679).

Other methods   A number of other methods and tools may be brought to bear on marketing and advertising questions. Consumer psychologists at times have occasion to employ projective tests—existing as well as custom-designed—as an aid in answering the questions raised by their clients. As we will see, special instrumentation, including tachistoscopes and electroencephalographs, has also been used in efforts to uncover consumer motivation. Consumer participation through interviews and focus groups combined with special computer programs—as well as some creativity—may be used to derive brand names for new products. Thus, for example, when Honda wished to position a new line of its cars as "advanced precision automobiles," a company specializing in the naming of new products conducted a computer search of over 6,900 English-language morphemes to locate word roots that mean or imply "advanced precision." The applicable morphemes were then computer-combined in ways the phonetic rules of English would allow. From the resulting list, the best word (that is, one that has visibility among other printed words, one that will be recognizable as a brand name, and so forth) was then selected; in this case, that word was *Acura* (Brewer, 1987).

Finally, literature reviews represent another method available to consumer psychologists in their armamentarium of tools that can be brought to bear on clients' questions. A literature review might suggest, for example, that certain sounds or imagery in a particular brand tend to be more popular with consumers than other sounds or imagery (see Figure 18–2, page 681). Schloss (1981) observed that the sound of the letter *K* was represented better than six times more than would be expected by chance in the initial letters of two hundred top brandname products (such as Sanka, Quaker, Nabisco—and, we might add, Acura). Schloss went on to speculate about the ability of this as well as other sounds of words to elicit emotional as opposed to rational reactions.

Measurement with Surveys and Polls

Survey Techniques

Survey research attempts to obtain answers to relatively structured questions from a reasonably representative set of individuals. For example, one survey (Mittal, 1994) found that over one-half of subjects disliked television commercials, whereas only about one-fourth liked them. Reasons for the generally negative attitudes toward television advertising were also explored in the survey and included perceptions that TV commercials are often absurd or misleading and that they foster materialism. In conducting these kinds of surveys, most often the sample is large (several hundred at a minimum) so that statistical inferences may be drawn about the larger population that the survey respondents represent. Because survey research seeks to reach relatively large numbers of

But Is Anybody Watching?

A television commercial may cost $100,000 or more to develop and produce. The budget for airing the commercial may be ten times that amount. Add to that sum of money the cost of pre- and postresearch of the commercial's effectiveness and you have a very rough estimate of what it can cost to advertise on television. . . . But is anybody watching the commercials?

That question was addressed in a study by Nevid and Cohen (1987) that employed an at-home behavioral observation technique. An encased television camera and video recorder was installed on the living room television for the purpose of recording subjects' behavior as they watched television. All subjects were given a videotape that ran for approximately two hours. On the tape was (1) a movie that ran approximately 90 minutes, and (2) a pilot situation comedy that ran for 30 minutes, with order of presentation of program material randomly assigned to households. Different commercials varying in length (120 seconds, 60 seconds, 30 seconds, and 15 seconds) were interspersed in pods throughout the tape in a manner similar to the way they would usually be interspersed in a commercial television presentation. Subjects were given instructions to "watch television as you normally do." The video record of subjects' commercial-watching behavior was analyzed with respect to a

number of variables such as "fixed attention" and "absent from room." Additionally, about one hour after their viewing of the program, all subjects were called and asked a number of questions designed to determine which commercials they remembered viewing. These questions were classified as being of the "product category prompt" variety (such as "Do you remember seeing a commercial for a long-distance telephone company?") and as the "specific brand prompt" variety (such as "Do you remember seeing a commercial for MCI?").

The mounds of resulting behavioral data were analyzed for each commercial length by each response category. Suffice it to say that the results from this one study cannot be taken as very encouraging for television advertisers or their agencies. In general, a rather low level of attending to television commercials was observed. Focusing on the data for the seven 30-second commercials on the tape, it was found that about half the subjects watched them an average of less than one second; the median viewing time for these seven commercials ranged from a low of 0.4 second to a high of 7 seconds. Recall of commercials was also quite low; generally, only two or three of the 20 subjects in this study were able to recall 30-second commercials on the reel—and that was true even after a category or brand prompt.

people, it is not possible to obtain the depth and richness of information from any one individual that would be possible with individual interviews or focus groups. This loss of information is compensated for by the types of analyses and inferences that may be made from survey data. Survey research may be carried out by face-to-face personal interviews, telephone interviews, mail questionnaires, or some combination of these methods.

Face-to-face survey research   Personal interviews involve a face-to-face encounter with the respondent. The interviewer asks questions and records responses as they are given. This personal interaction helps ensure that questions are clearly understood and can provide such clarification as the parties desire. This

A video camera/recorder mounted directly on a television set in the home of subjects enabled the experimenters to observe and subsequently analyze subjects' behavior during the viewing of television commercials.

Generalization from this research must be made with extreme caution because of factors such as the limited sample size (ten married couples) and geographical location (all from Brooklyn, New York). Additionally, although subjects were instructed to watch television as they normally would, common sense dictates that the presence of a television camera recording behavior would alter it (to varying and unknown degrees). Further, it was deemed judicious to place the television camera recording subjects' behavior on top of televisions located in the living room of the home only. Although subjects typically had televisions in other rooms of their homes and presumably watched television in those rooms as well, placement of a television camera in rooms other than the living room could potentially have resulted in unique dilemmas regarding the analysis of the recorded behaviors.

face-to-face encounter may, however, introduce some bias into the responses of individuals. Respondents may seek to give answers they think the interviewer wants, or they may be reluctant to provide information on sensitive or potentially embarrassing topics.

Personal interviewing is a very common method of survey research, and it can be conducted almost anywhere—on a commuter bus or ferry, at a ball game, or in the vicinity of an election polling station. A common site for face-to-face survey research on consumer products is a shopping mall; "mall intercept studies" (as they are called) can be conducted by interviewers with clipboards who approach shoppers. The shopper may be asked to participate in a survey by answering some questions right then and there or may be led to a booth or room where a more extended interview takes place. Another face-to-face survey method, this one more popular with political pollsters, is the door-to-door approach; here an entire neighborhood may be polled by knocking on the door at individual households and soliciting responses to the questionnaire.

A unique advantage in face-to-face survey research is the ability to present respondents with stimuli (such as a product or a list of items from which to select) to which they may be asked to respond. The advantage of having an interviewer who can interact with the respondent creates a need for careful selection and training of the interviewer. Thus, since personal interviewing is labor-intensive, it is the most expensive and time-consuming method of survey research. The least expensive method of survey research, and the fastest method for obtaining information, is the telephone survey.

Telephone surveys Perhaps the most widely used form of survey research is the telephone survey. Since telephone interviews require less social interaction between the interviewer and the respondent than does the personal interview, the biases inherent in such interaction and the intensive training required for personal interviewing are reduced. In addition, it is easy to coordinate and monitor the performance of telephone interviewers, since telephoning can take place in a centralized location. And with new technology currently available to telephone survey researchers, subjects are called by a computer, called back if the subject isn't home, and interviewed by a pretaped voice—all without the necessity of a human interviewer. New technology in assessment is also available to interviewers, through the techniques of adaptive testing. Although more typically employed in other types of applications, adaptive testing techniques may be put to use not only to evaluate consumer usage patterns of a particular product but also to sell them on a particular product or service. This chapter's *Close-up* (page 682) provides a real-life case example.

One type of telephone poll in common use in consumer research is designed to obtain a measure of the memorability of advertising, most typically, a televi-

Figure 18–2
What's in a Name? ▶

"What's in a name? A rose by any other name would smell as sweet." Sentiments such as this may be touching to read and beautiful to behold when spoken by talented actors on Broadway. However, they wouldn't have taken William Shakespeare very far on Madison Avenue. The name given to a product is an important part of what is referred to as the "marketing mix": the way a product is positioned, marketed, and promoted in the marketplace. In the ad shown, reproduced from a 1927 magazine, the benefits of a toothbrush with the brand name Pro-phy-lac-tic are touted. The creator of this brand name no doubt wished to position this toothbrush as being particularly useful in preventing disease. However, the word prophylactic *(defined as "protective") became more identified in the public's mind with condoms, a fact that could not have helped the longevity of this brand of toothbrush in the marketplace. Today, researchers use a variety of methods, including word association, to create brand names.*

REACHES ALL
—Cleans All

PRO-PHY-LAC-TIC protects
every tooth in
your mouth

When you have found a tooth brush that reaches *all* your teeth, you have taken the most important step in keeping your teeth permanently sound and beautiful.

Study the picture of the Pro-phy-lac-tic Tooth Brush, shown here. Notice how the bristles are arranged. See how they form a curve ending in a large pyramidal tuft. You can see that this curve is sensibly shaped to fit snugly against the outside and inside profiles of *all* your teeth. The molars in the rear, so hard to get at with an ordinary tooth brush, are easily reached by this convenient end tuft.

The bent handle is the third feature which makes it easy to reach *all* thirty-two of your teeth. Nature aligned most of your teeth on a curve. It naturally follows that a curved handle accommodates itself to this formation more easily and more comfortably than a handle that is straight.

Sold in three sizes by all dealers in the United States, Canada, and all over the world. Prices in the United States and Canada are: Pro-phy-lac-tic Adult, 50c; Pro-phy-lac-tic Small, 40c; Pro-phy-lac-tic Baby, 25c. Made in three different bristle textures—hard, medium, and soft—and with white handles or colored transparent handles—red, green, or orange. *Always sold in the yellow box.* (A larger Pro-phy-lac-tic with four rows of bristles is priced 60 cents.) Pro-phy-lac-tic Brush Company, Florence, Massachusetts.

© 1927, P. B. Co.

Pro-phy-lac-tic Brush Company,
Dept. 210, Florence, Mass.

Please send me your instructive booklet on the care and preservation of the teeth.

Name ....
Address ....
City .... State ....

Are you sure you don't need a new tooth brush?

A Pro-phy-lac-tic Tooth Brush is made so well that it doesn't look worn out even when it should be replaced with a new one. The handle and even the bristles appear as good as ever. But the best bristle will after continued use lose its springiness and elasticity. Pro-phy-lac-tic bristles are the best that Nature provides, but three or four months of steady twice-daily use will take away their liveliness.

Don't try to wear out your Pro-phy-lac-tic Tooth Brush. Get a new one every three months. Keep several on hand. To present a Pro-phy-lac-tic in a yellow box to an overnight guest is a thoughtful courtesy.

FREE... an interesting booklet containing valuable information on the care of the teeth.

Adaptive Testing, Friends, and Family

*A*daptive testing refers to testing that is individually tailored to the testtaker. Other terms used to refer to adaptive testing include *tailored testing, sequential testing, branched testing,* and *response contingent testing.* As typically employed in tests of ability, adaptive testing might pose to a testtaker a question in the middle range of difficulty. If the testtaker responds correctly to the item, an item of greater difficulty is posed next. If the testtaker responds incorrectly to the item, an item of lesser difficulty is posed. Adaptive testing is, in essence, designed, as Wainer (1990, p. 10) put it, "to mimic automatically what a wise examiner would do." In many instances, adaptive testing serves to make the assessment experience shorter and more pleasant for the assessee. Items that the examinee would find to be too easy or too difficult have been eliminated from the test.

From a psychometric standpoint, a challenge associated with adaptive testing is that testtakers may wind up taking entirely different versions of the same test, including different numbers of items. Usually, the methods employed for developing adaptive or tailored tests provide that the more difficult the item, the more credit given. Statistically sophisticated methods for developing such scales are described by Wainer (1990).

Although best associated with tests of ability and personnel selection (Weiss, 1983), adaptive testing procedures may also be employed in behavioral assessment (Kratochwill et al., 1991), the measurement of personality (Jackson, 1991), and the measurement of attitudes and values (Balasubramanian & Kamakura, 1989; Bechtel, 1985; Kamakura & Srivastava, 1983; Singh et al., 1990). Bainsbridge (1991) described how adaptive testing could be used in consumer assessment and marketing. In this context, he noted how integral adaptive assessment techniques were to the development of a promotional program for MCI called *Friends and Family.* In that program, millions of MCI customers obtained discounts off their long-distance phone bills when they called other MCI customers who were part of their "calling circle." MCI contacted noncustomers listed in their customers' calling circles in an effort to convert them to MCI as their long-distance carrier. The use of techniques akin to adaptive testing with the consumer population of the United States, including flexible question formats and item sequencing, enabled MCI to successfully implement its *Friends and Family* program.

sion commercial. Thus, for example, the day after the airing of the Academy Awards on television, randomly selected households in selected communities might be telephoned and the interviewer might ask questions such as "Did you watch the Academy Awards last evening? . . . What commercials do you recall seeing on that show? . . . Do you recall seeing a commercial for Mermaid Brand Sardines?"

The telephone survey offers a number of advantages, but it does suffer from some limitations. Generally, the amount of information that can be obtained by telephone is less than that which can be obtained by personal interview or mail. It is not possible to show respondents visual stimuli over the phone. In addition, bias may be introduced if telephone directories are used for identifying respondents. As many as 40 percent of all telephones in some cities are not listed.

A partial solution to this last problem is random-digit dialing (see Glaser & Metzger, 1972), a procedure that randomly changes the last one or two digits of a telephone number taken from a directory. Use of this process generally yields contacts with households that have unlisted telephone numbers, as well as those with listed numbers. However, even with this procedure, it is necessary to exercise caution by calling at different times of the day and on different days of the week. Otherwise, households that have no one home at particular times will be missed (Bureau of the Census, 1973). One study indicated, for example, that the greater the number of attempts to reach a household, the greater the likelihood that the household reached would be in the higher income brackets (Lansing & Morgan, 1971).

Lest we stray too far from the subject of psychology in measurement, let us hasten to point out that although telephone surveys may be viewed with favor by members of the marketing community, they may be viewed in a less attractive light by interviewees; they may be viewed at best as an unwelcome annoyance and at worst as an unwarranted invasion of privacy.

Mail surveys A mail survey may be the most appropriate survey method when the survey questionnaire is particularly long and will require some time to complete. In general, mail surveys tend to be relatively low in cost, since they do not require the services of a trained interviewer and can provide large amounts of information. They are also well suited for obtaining information about which respondents may be sensitive or shy in a face-to-face or even a telephone situation. They are also well suited to posing questions that require the use of records or consultation with others (such as family members) for an answer. Note also that much of what we say about mail surveys also applies to "electronic mail surveys" or surveys conducted by means of fax machines.

The major disadvantages of mail questionnaires are (1) the possibility of no response at all from the intended recipient of the survey (for whatever reason—the survey was never delivered, or it was thrown out as "junk mail" as soon as it arrived), (2) the possibility of response from someone (perhaps a family member) who was not the intended recipient of the survey, and (3) the possibility of a late—and hence useless for tabulation purposes—response. If large numbers of people fail to respond to a mail questionnaire, it is impossible to determine whether those individuals who did respond are representative of those who did not. People may not respond to a mail questionnaire for many different reasons; and various techniques, ranging from incentives to follow-up mailings, have been suggested for dealing with various types of nonresponse (Furse & Stewart, 1984).

It is possible to combine the various survey methods to obtain the advantages of each. For example, the survey researcher might mail a lengthy questionnaire to potential respondents, then obtain responses by telephone. Alternatively, those individuals not returning their responses by mail might be contacted by telephone or in person.

Many commercial research firms maintain a list of a large number of people or families who have agreed to respond to questionnaires that are sent to them; the people who make up this list are referred to as a *consumer panel.* In return for their participation, panel members may receive incentives such as cash and free samples of all the products about which they are asked to respond in surveys. One special type of panel is called a *diary panel,* and here the respondents must keep detailed records of their behavior (for example, keeping a record of products they purchased, use of coupons, radio stations they listened to while driving to and from work, or what newspapers and magazines they read). Specialized panels exist that monitor general product or advertising awareness, attitudes, and opinions on social issues, as well as a variety of other variables.

As with any research, care must be exercised when interpreting the results of a survey. Both the quantity and the quality of the data may vary from survey to survey. Response rates may differ, questions may be asked in different forms, and data collection procedures may vary from one survey to another. Ultimately, the utility of any conclusions rests on the integrity of the data on which the conclusions are based.[2] More guidelines may be needed in survey research because of the differences that exist in the methodologies of various polling firms (Henry, 1984).

Designing Survey Research Questionnaires

Whether the survey will be conducted face to face or over the telephone, the questionnaire must be designed so that it will not take a substantial amount of a respondent's time. With a mail survey, the length of the questionnaire may be longer; respondents can complete the questionnaire at their convenience and can pace themselves in completing it. However, because the mail survey will be completed at home without the presence of an interviewer to clarify questions, the mail survey must be written very clearly lest the frustration of not understanding the intention of an item prompt the respondent to "forget the whole thing."

Some of the standard items on a survey (such as demographic information) will not require very much talent to prepare, whereas it may require considerable effort to word other questions to best reflect the objective of the question. Two broad approaches to the assessment of attitudes in surveys are referred to as *aggregate scaling* and *multidimensional scaling.* We review these approaches in the pages to follow. In addition, we look at the application of the semantic differential technique—discussed earlier in Part 4—in the field of consumer psychology.

Aggregate scaling methods Aggregate methods represent the average of some group of people on some measure. The measure may range from an opinion item (such as "Should the death penalty be abolished?") to a self-report of behavior (such as "How often do you eat in a fast-food restaurant each month?"). The federal government and large corporations are among the largest users of aggregate measures; they can be used to "take the pulse" of a given population on a given issue, determine who buys certain products or services, or assess

---

2. Further discussion of the evaluation of survey research may be found in Wheeler (1977) and in marketing research textbooks (such as Kinnear & Taylor, 1983; Lehmann, 1985).

what customers think of products and services. The user of an aggregate measure is typically keenly interested not only in a measure of central tendency but also in dispersion or variance about the mean; such dispersion will tell whether people tend to be heavily divided with respect to the issue assessed. Attitudes may be based on many factors. For example, consumers may judge an automobile on the basis of its styling, its power, its comfort, its fuel economy, its price, or any number of other attributes. When using aggregate scaling methods, the assumption is made that attitudes toward all these attributes can be combined into a single or composite score.

The simplest aggregative method is the *one-dimensional preference* scale, in which respondents are asked to provide an overall rating for an object, a person, or an institution rather than rating individual attributes. For example, respondents might be asked to use the following scale to rate, say, various brands of canned sardines:

Like	Like Somewhat	Neutral	Dislike Somewhat	Dislike
1	2	3	4	5

The numbers 1 through 5 are assigned to scale values, and ratings can be expressed in quantitative form.

A five-point preference scale, such as that used in this example, is an example of a Likert scale. Note that an assumption inherent in the use of such a technique is that respondents can sort out their opinions about the various attributes of the product in question and come up with a valid, overall reaction ranging from "like" to "neutral" to "dislike."

One shortcoming of this form of scaling is that the different ratings are not necessarily interval in nature and therefore the number of statistical manipulations that can legitimately be performed with such data is limited. A rating of 3 on the scale may not be equally different from ratings of 2 and 4. The scale is an *ordinal* one, and a rating of 3 may legitimately be viewed only as greater than 1. Another limitation inherent in such aggregative data is that there is no assurance that respondents have considered all relevant attributes in arriving at their conclusion. Additionally, the use of an overall rating obscures the possibility that respondents may, indeed, have quite different attitudes toward different attributes of the object being rated.

An alternative approach would be to rate each attribute separately and then sum the individual ratings to obtain an overall score. For example, let us assume that respondents are asked to rate a particular brand of sardines on four attributes—flavor, freshness, aroma, and appearance—using a Likert scale. And let's further assume that one respondent has rated a particular brand as follows:

Flavor	4
Freshness	2
Aroma	3
Appearance	5

The total rating for these sardines would be 14—obtained by summing the ratings of the individual attributes. This total rating can then be treated in a variety of statistical ways in making comparisons between brands.

Table 18–1
Individual Ratings
Combined with
Attribute Importance

Attributes	Brand Rating		Attribute Importance		Total
Flavor	4	×	5	=	20
Freshness	2	×	5	=	10
Aroma	3	×	4	=	12
Appearance	5	×	2	=	10
Total				=	52

Aside from questions about the level of measurement represented in the scaling device, this approach has one major limitation: namely, each attribute is treated as though it were equally important in arriving at an overall attitude toward the sardines. And although that may be true in some cases, it certainly cannot be presumed to be true all of the time. One way of avoiding this potential pitfall is by employing a variation of the Fishbein-Rosenberg method of scaling. In this approach, respondents are asked two sets of questions. First, they are asked to rate relevant attributes according to their importance. Then, individual objects are rated according to the extent to which they possess each of the attributes in question. Applying this approach to our example, we might find that the attribute of flavor is rated 5 in importance, freshness is also rated 5, and aroma and appearance are rated 4 and 2, respectively. We can now combine the rating of the individual attribute with the rating of attribute importance as shown in the matrix in Table 18–1. Through the procedure, each attribute rating is multiplied by the importance of the attribute to weight it properly. The weighted results can then be submitted to various statistical treatments for making comparisons between brands.

Another method of aggregate scaling designed to give greater weight to some attributes than to others is an adaptation of Guttman scaling (Guttman, 1944). The Guttman method employs an ordered set of statements about a stimulus object, such as a hypothetical brand of sardines called "Mermaid":

Mermaid Sardines taste good	Yes	No
Mermaid Sardines stay fresh	Yes	No
Mermaid Sardines have a nice aroma	Yes	No
Mermaid Sardines look appetizing	Yes	No

The statements are ordered according to their relative importance, with the first statement being most important and the last statement being the least important. The specific statements used and their order are usually determined by interviews with persons familiar with the stimulus object. Often, several orderings are investigated to find the most appropriate one. The global rating is computed by counting the "Yes" responses to the ordered questions. A "Yes" is counted as 1 and a "No" as 0. The preference score is determined by asking the questions in order and adding 1 to the total score for each "Yes" answer obtained. When a "No" is encountered, the process stops. The overall rating is a summation of the number of "Yes" responses.

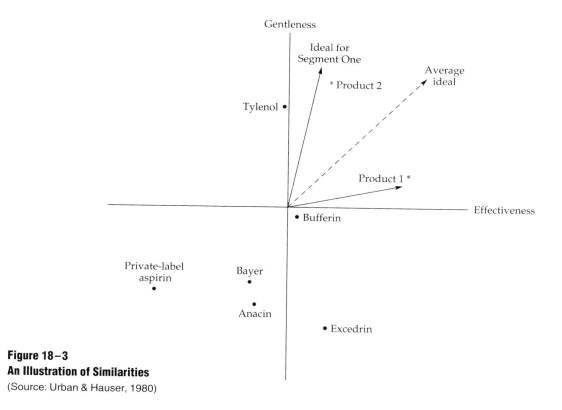

Figure 18–3
An Illustration of Similarities
(Source: Urban & Hauser, 1980)

A number of other aggregate scaling techniques may be used. Those shown have been introduced to clarify the nature of aggregate scaling and to point up one of the problems of summing attribute ratings—namely, that certain attributes are more important than others and must be weighted in some way to provide a valid rating.

Multidimensional scaling Multidimensional scaling (MDS) is a relatively recent development in psychometric research. Unlike aggregate scaling methods, MDS methods reject the notion that attitudes about a stimulus object can be combined into a single score. MDS attempts to locate objects within the framework of an "attribute space" based on perceptions of similarities and differences among the objects.

Figure 18–3 is an example of multidimensional scaling. Several points should be noted about this figure. First, consumer perceptions and preferences for pain relievers can be ordered in a two-dimensional space made up of the two attributes of gentleness and effectiveness. Second, each pain reliever can be located in this space in a position that represents a specific combination of these two attributes. Thus, Tylenol is perceived as very gentle compared with other pain relievers, but not so effective as Excedrin. Excedrin, on the other hand, is perceived as somewhat effective but not at all gentle. Third, different pain relievers may cluster according to their perceived similarity. Bayer, Anacin, and private-label aspirin are perceived as similar on both gentleness and effectiveness. Bufferin, Excedrin, and Tylenol tend to occupy unique positions within the space. The optimal combination of gentleness and effectiveness is represented by the line labeled "Average ideal." Note that different groups of consumers may, in fact, have different ideals. Tylenol is the product most similar to the ideal product for segment one. It is apparent that multidimensional scaling is a useful technique for identifying the position of products in a relevant product space and for relating existing products to the ideal product of consumers.

The construction of a product space through the use of multidimensional scaling is beyond the scope of this text. Essentially, however, it is a computer-based technique that locates products in a space of minimum dimensionality based on perceived similarities and differences. Since MDS is wholly a numerical procedure, it ignores the problem of axis labeling. It is not necessary, therefore, when employing the MDS technique, to specify the attributes on which objects are to be judged. One simply obtains judgments of similarity about the objects being studied in the hope that the most salient attributes will be identified by the ultimate structure obtained in the analysis. By examining the location of objects within the space that is generated, and by being familiar with the characteristics of the objects, the analyst is often able to identify the most salient features on which the data have been mathematically ordered. It is also possible to map attributes on to the derived space to facilitate interpretation of the axes.

Multidimensional scaling, using as input data the naive perceptions of consumers, appears to have promise as a systematic approach for ordering and analyzing perceptions and preferences (Schiffman et al., 1981). The technique has been used to study a wide variety of consumer (Johnson & Horne, 1992), industrial (DeSarbo & Hoffman, 1987), and corporate (Dowling, 1988) judgments.

The semantic differential technique   The semantic differential is one of the most widely used and versatile scaling techniques employed in marketing research. Originally developed as a clinical tool for defining the meaning of concepts and relating concepts to one another in a "semantic space," the basic technique has undergone modification in its adaptation to a wide range of purposes.

As initially conceived by Osgood, Suci, and Tannenbaum (1957), the semantic differential involved repeated judgments of a concept using a series of descriptive bipolar adjectives (such as good/bad or strong/weak) on a seven-point scale such as this one:

GOOD ____/ ____/ ____/ ____/ ____/ ____/ ____/ BAD

In the fields of consumer and social psychology, the semantic differential has been used to measure opinions of brands, products, companies, social programs, stores, product users, political candidates, and so forth. A number of modifications in the semantic differential as originally described by Osgood, Suci, and Tannenbaum (1957) are made when this technique is used in consumer-related studies (Mindak, 1961). For example, the bipolar adjective might be replaced by descriptive phrases (such as "something very special" versus "just another drink" with reference to a particular brand of beer).

The semantic differential is a very popular tool in consumer-related research because it provides a relatively simple, efficient way of collecting quantifiable data from large samples and can be used effectively as a "before-and-after" test (for example, before and after exposure to a commercial or an informational film). It is useful in obtaining an index of attitude that might be difficult to obtain through other approaches, and it can provide a quantifiable "benchmark" with which competing brands can be compared. Since it requires very little verbal skill, it is quite useful in measuring the attitudes of children and adult respondents who have limited language abilities. Data from the use of this technique also tend to be quite reliable.

Do consumer surveys predict consumer behavior? The validity of surveys purporting to measure consumer satisfaction has been questioned by researchers who argue that the context in which evaluation takes place may be more critical to the response obtained than whatever it is that is being evaluated (Peterson & Wilson, 1992). Still, survey responses predict behavior in the marketplace to varying degrees. One measure of attitudes toward purchasing imported products, called the Consumer Ethnocentric Tendencies Scale, can predict purchasing behavior to the extent that it explains about 30 percent of the variability in automobile purchases (Herche, 1992). Another study of the validity of survey data is cited in this chapter's *Everyday Psychometrics* feature.

Qualitative Assessment

A distinction can be made between *quantitative* research, which typically involves large numbers of subjects and elaborate statistical analyses, and *qualitative* research, which typically involves few respondents and little or no statistical analysis; the emphasis in the latter type of research is not on quantity (of subjects or of data) but on the qualities of whatever it is that is under study. Included under the heading of "qualitative assessment" are the motivation research techniques of one-on-one interviews, focus groups, and specially designed projective techniques.

There are many occasions when it is important to study in detail a small number of individuals. This may occur when one desires a great deal of information from each individual and when relatively little is known about the phenomenon of interest. Qualitative research often provides the opportunity to develop hypotheses about why consumers behave as they do. These hypotheses may then be tested with a larger number of consumers. Qualitative research also has diagnostic value. The best way to obtain highly detailed information about what a consumer likes and dislikes about a product, a store, or an advertisement is to use qualitative research. Qualitative research may help a government service agency determine how individuals will respond to new intervention programs or how to better deliver their services. Such research might also assist a compensation manager to assess reaction to compensation programs, benefits packages, or commission structures for sales personnel. It may also help detect problems that might otherwise be unidentified.

Brand Equity: Smile!

In the language of marketing and consumer psychology, *brand equity* refers to the value added to a product by the reputation of an established brand name. Consider for a moment whether you would be willing to pay a little more for a juice blend with the brand name Tropicana on it than for the same type of product of a brand unknown to you. For some people, paying a little more for a product with a brand name on it is a good investment, whereas other people might make purchases based solely on price. Brand equity is the amount of additional money that people are generally willing to pay to purchase a known brand over an unknown brand of equal quality. How might brand equity be measured?

Park and Srinivasan (1994) developed a mathematical model for studying brand equity and tested it on consumer purchases of toothpaste and mouthwash. These products were chosen precisely because their benefits to the consumers purchasing them are relatively difficult to assess. Some toothpastes and mouthwashes claim to reduce plaque, but in most cases, a consumer's belief about whether these products live up to that claim is probably based more on

faith than anything else. Some toothpastes position themselves in the marketplace as teeth whiteners, although the extent to which brushing with them actually whitens teeth is seldom obvious.

Simply determining whether consumers prefer a more expensive known brand over an unknown brand is not sufficient to determine the brand equity of a brand. The known brand may in fact be sufficiently superior to warrant the additional cost it involves. Park and Srinivasan (1994) proposed a comparison between two measurements: (1) an objective measure of the quality of the brands based on expert opinion and laboratory analysis and (2) a subjective measure of perceived value based on the opinion of the person in a household who held primary responsibility for household shopping. Four national brands of toothpaste (Aqua-fresh, Close-Up, Colgate, and Crest), five national brands of mouthwash (Close-Up, Colgate, Listerine, Plax, and Scope), and one local store brand of toothpaste and mouthwash (either Walgreen brand or Rite-Aid brand, depending on geographical area) were used in the study. The subjective evaluation of the products was carried out by means of a telephone

One-on-One Interviews

Individual interviews with consumers have the advantage of providing very rich information and avoiding the influence of others on the opinion of any one individual. However, individual interviews tend to be expensive and time-consuming. As a result, it is unlikely that large numbers of people will be interviewed for any one research project.

One type of individual interview is sometimes referred to as a "depth interview." A depth interview is a relatively unstructured interview that involves considerable probing of an individual consumer's beliefs and attitudes. The purpose of this type of interview is to get beyond surface or superficial reactions of a consumer to more fundamental processes underlying responses to some stimulus. Sometimes a depth interview may contain some structured questions relating to how the consumer chooses a particular product; what information is sought (for example, price? quality? brand name?) and how the information is survey conducted with two hundred consumers. Toothpaste and mouthwash users were asked to rate these products on a series of attributes, such as plaque-fighting ability and prevention of cavities. They were also asked which brand of toothpaste and/or mouthwash they had purchased most recently.

The objective evaluation of the products was done by a mail survey of dentists and by ratings reported in *Consumer Reports* magazine on relevant variables. About half of all dentists contacted by the researchers responded to the survey ($n = 120$), and their ratings were compared with the laboratory ratings reported in *Consumer Reports*. The researchers reported that the dentists' ratings closely corresponded to those in the magazine.

The experts' and consumers' ratings were then compared to provide the basis for evaluating brand equity. We'll focus here on their findings with regard to the brand equity of Crest as compared with the local store brand. In this specific comparison, after a technical analysis, brand equity was found to be 55 cents. This means that, after adjusting for any real differences in quality as rated by the experts between

Crest and the store brand, people were willing to pay 55 cents more for a tube of Crest toothpaste. (Note that all prices were for 6-ounce tubes of toothpastes.) It was determined that about 11 cents' worth of the difference in price consumers were willing to pay for Crest was attributed to consumer-perceived differences between Crest and the store brand. The remaining 44 cents' difference could not be readily explained given the actual and perceived differences between brands.

The study is useful in illustrating how research and measurement are used in consumer psychology. The perceptions of consumers, sometimes in relation to experts, are given great weight. Consumer psychologists are always on the lookout for new and more accurate ways to measure those perceptions. Also, because the purchase behavior of consumers is influenced by so many factors, analysis of consumer behavior may also, at times, be extremely complex—so complex, that even sophisticated mathematical models cannot account for 44 of 55 cents in one brand of toothpaste's brand equity.

evaluated and processed. And when it comes to the question "to buy or not to buy," what factors are primarily responsible for the choice?

The same factors that make for a good interview in other settings make for a good interview to assess social or economic phenomena. In fact, such interviews are often carried out by psychologists with clinical training or other experience in interviewing. As an exercise in depth interviewing, approach some (approachable) person you know who wears Coca-Cola clothing that prominently displays the company's symbol. Tell the person you are conducting a survey for one of your classes and your assignment is to determine what motivates people to buy such clothing. Next, conduct a depth interview. At some point in the interview, you may discover that your interviewee is—though it may not be fashionable to admit—quite patriotic; the Coca-Cola symbol may be seen as synonymous with "American," and sporting such clothing may be quite analogous to the blue-collar workers' wearing of American flag patches and lapel pins (Cohen, 1986).

Focus Groups

A *focus group* is a group interview led by a trained, independent moderator who, ideally, has a knowledge of group-discussion facilitation techniques and group dynamics.[3] As their name implies, "focus groups" are designed to focus group discussion on something—such as a particular commercial, a concept for a new product, or packaging for a new product. The range of possible foci of focus groups is limited only by the needs and imagination of the person commissioning them. Focus groups have examined everything from the choice to purchase organically grown rather than conventionally grown produce (Hammitt, 1990) to issues surrounding the purchase of condoms by college students (Mays et al., 1993).

Focus groups usually consist of from six to 12 participants who may have been recruited off the floor of a shopping mall or may have been selected in advance to meet some preset qualifications for participation in the group; the usual objective here is to have the members of the group be in some way representative of the population of targeted consumers for the product or service being focused on. Thus, for example, only beer drinkers (defined, for example, as males who drink at least two six-packs per week and females who drink at least one six-pack per week) might be solicited for participation in a focus group designed to explore one or various attributes of a new brand of beer—including such variables as its taste, its packaging, its advertising, and its "bar call," this last phrase being an industry term that refers to the ease with which one could order the brew in a bar. Because of the high costs associated with introducing a new product and advertising a new or established product, professionally executed focus groups complete with a representative sampling of the targeted consumer population are a valuable tool in market research.

Depending on the requirements of the moderator's client (usually an advertiser or an advertising agency), the group discussion can be relatively structured (with a number of points to be covered) or relatively unstructured (with few points to be covered exhaustively). After establishing a rapport with the group, the moderator may, for example, show some advertising or a product to the group and then pose a general question to the group (such as "What did you think of the beer commercial?") to be followed up by more specific kinds of questions (such as "Were the people in that commercial the kind of people *you* would like to have a beer with?"). The responses of the group members may build on those of other group members, and the result of the free-flowing discussion may be new information, new perspectives, or some previously overlooked problems with the advertising or product.

---

3. Focus-group moderators vary greatly in training and experience (McDonald, 1993). Ideally, a focus-group moderator should be independent so that he or she can dispassionately discuss the topics at hand with some distance and perspective. It is true, however, that some advertising agencies maintain an in-house focus-group moderator staff to test the advertising produced by the agency. Critics of the practice of using advertising agency employees to test advertising developed by the agency have likened the process to assigning wolves to guard the henhouse.

Focus groups typically last from one to two hours and are usually conducted in rooms (either conference rooms or living rooms) equipped with one-way mirrors (from which the client's staff may observe the proceedings) and audio or video equipment so that a record of the group session will be preserved. Aside from being an "active listener" and an individual who is careful not to suggest answers to questions or draw conclusions for the respondents, the focus-group moderator's duties include (1) following a discussion guide and keeping the discussion on the topic, (2) drawing out "silent" group members so that everyone is heard from, (3) limiting the response time of group members who might dominate the group discussion, and (4) writing a report that provides not only a summary of the group discussion but also psychological and / or marketing insights to the client. Recent years have witnessed experimentation with computer equipment in focus groups so that second-by-second reaction to stimulus materials such as commercials can be monitored. Cohen described the advantages (1985) and limitations (1987) of a technique whereby respondents watching television commercials pressed a calculatorlike keypad to indicate how positive or negative they were feeling on a moment-to-moment basis while watching television. The response could then be visually displayed as a graph and played back for the respondent, who could be asked about the reasons for the spontaneous response.

The focus group was a tool used by the publisher of the Strong Vocational Interest Blank (SVIB-SCII) when, in 1984, the profile was undergoing redesign in preparation for its 1985 revision. A group of counseling psychologists from a variety of work settings served as the respondents; an objective was to make the profile optimally responsive to the needs of users of the test. As a result, the new Strong Interest Inventory (SII) (1) is color-coded for easy reference to different scales, (2) reads from left to right by type of scale, (3) has a large, easily read type size, and (4) has a white background in which test users, counselors, and others can make notations.

Focus groups are widely employed in consumer research, and there is a growing literature on various aspects related to their potential (for example, Greenbaum, 1988; Langmaid & Ross, 1984; Schlackman, 1984; Skibbe, 1986). Among the uses of these groups are the following:

1. To generate hypotheses that can be further tested quantitatively
2. To generate information for designing or modifying consumer questionnaires
3. To provide general background information about a product category
4. To get impressions on new product concepts for which little information is available
5. To obtain new ideas about older products
6. To generate ideas for product development
7. To interpret the results of previously obtained quantitative results

In general, the focus group tends to be thought of as a highly useful technique for exploratory research, a technique that can provide a valuable springboard to more comprehensive quantitative studies. Because so few respondents are typically involved in such groups, the findings from them cannot automatically be thought of as representative of the larger population. Still, many a client (including advertising agency creative staff) has received inspiration from the words spoken by ordinary consumers on the other side of a one-way mirror.

Projective Techniques

Various projective techniques have been applied in consumer research. Word association techniques may be used to screen brand names for negative connotations or to help uncover consumers' feelings about new products. A study by the Governor's Advisory Committee on the Tourist Industry in Hawaii used word associations to obtain emotional reactions to words associated with the islands. Among the results was the finding that, although the word *Hawaii* had no negative associations, *Waikiki* gave rise to responses such as "cheap and gaudy," "crowded," "flashy," and "overpublicized" (Grossack, 1964).

A number of variations of the word association approach have been devised. Controlled word association is a variation in which respondents are asked to respond with a class of words. For example, a list of products may be read, one at a time, and the subjects are asked to respond with brand names. Chain or successive word association requires that the subject respond with a series of words rather than just a single word in response to the stimulus. There is some evidence that deeper levels of feeling may be reached through chain associations, since concealed resentments often do not appear until the third or fourth word in the chain (Grossack, 1964).

Another frequently used projective technique in consumer research is the sentence completion test. Like word association techniques, sentence completion techniques may be used in an effort to obtain information that for whatever reason may otherwise be inaccessible. Kassarjian and Cohen (1965) asked 179 smokers who thought cigarettes were a health hazard why they continued to smoke. The majority of the answers gave the impression that smokers were relatively happy with their lot and smoked because they enjoyed it or felt that moderate smoking was all right. When these same respondents were given the opportunity to finish the sentence "People who never smoke are _____," they responded with comments such as "happier," "smarter," "wiser," and so forth. For the sentence "Teenagers who smoke are _____," respondents completed the thought with comments such as "foolish," "crazy," "uninformed," "stupid," "showing off," and "immature." Clearly, the sentence completion test shows cigarette smokers to be more anxious, concerned, and dissatisfied with their habit than was revealed by the direct question.

Other projective techniques employed in consumer research include TAT-like pictures about which respondents are asked to construct stories. Still other projective techniques involve presentation of cartoonlike characters with "empty balloons" to be filled in by respondents; the cartoons depict situations relevant to the research question (see the box opposite).

Projective Stimuli in Consumer Research

In his overview of the use of projectives in consumer research, Levy (1985) described the use of the picture of "two boys buying hot dogs" (a). After being told that one of the boys purchased the brand his mother told him to get and the other bought the brand that he wanted, respondents were asked to make up stories about the pictures. The obedient boy tended to be seen as middle class and the purchaser of a national brand, whereas the other child was seen as purchasing a more frivolous-seeming brand and pocketing the change.

More ambiguous, TAT-like pictures have also been employed in research with consumers. Stories in response to the picture (b) served to differentiate two groups of consumers as a function of the brand of a particular product they used. For users of one brand, the stories tended to be relatively calm, peaceful, and accepting of the figure as relaxed, contemplative, idle—suggestive to Levy (1985) that this market segment was conventional, able to relax, and accepting of the moment. Stories in response to this picture from users of a competitive brand tended to be more "troubled," with more negative emotions and adverse events being described. Levy found this latter group to be "people who saw more complexity in life"—an outlook that was "compatible with a brand that represented a stronger sense of striving and achievement" (p. 76).

Cohen (1983b) used a projectivelike task to study corporate images as reflected in corporate logos. Respondents were told that they were participating in a "test of symbolism" and were asked to verbalize their immediate association to symbols such as the Post Office eagle, the Merrill-Lynch bull, and the Bell telephone. One of the more interesting findings was that the Bell logo conjured up associations to reliability and security but not high technology.

(a)

(b)

Other Techniques

Before leaving the realm of the perceptual to proceed to the realm of the psychophysiological, we should also mention the use of an instrument called a *tachistoscope* in consumer (as well as other) research. The tachistoscope is an apparatus used to present visual stimuli for extremely minute instants of time. The machine may be set for the desired length of presentation of a stimulus, usually in milliseconds (thousandths of a second). Traditionally used in perceptual and psychophysiological research, the tachistoscope has found application in consumer psychology, where researchers use it primarily to assess the effectiveness of trademarks, brand names, and corporate logograms. Often abbreviated to *logo*, a *logogram* is a symbol that represents an entire word, such as $ for "dollar(s)." Some examples of corporate logos are the specially designed letter *N* symbolizing the National Broadcasting Company, the *M*, representing McDonald's, and the distinctive *31* in a circle, symbolic of the 31 ice cream flavors offered each month by Baskin-Robbins. Consumer psychologists use the tachistoscope in research designed to test the ease of recognition and recall of corporate brand names and logos. Is the logo recalled amid other logos? Is the logo recognized when flashed for an instant? What does the subject recall about the logo after seeing it for a period of time so brief that it is just recognizable? These types of questions may be asked in assessing consumer response to various logos with a tachistoscope.

Other types of consumer assessment may entail situational testing; consumers are placed in hypothetical situations where the object is to determine what factors prevail in motivating them to buy one product rather than another. A number of situational as well as paper-and-pencil measures purport to measure constructs referred to as *purchase intent, brand loyalty,* and *involvement* in products (see Jacoby & Chestnut, 1978; Lilien & Kotler, 1983; Traylor & Joseph, 1984; Zaichowsky, 1985). A common situational approach in new-product research places the consumer in a simulated shopping situation where he or she has the opportunity to actually purchase the new product—even though the product may not be available in the "real world."

Psychophysiological Measures

In search of an uncontaminated and "pure" measure of consumer response to products and their promotion of same, some researchers in the fields of marketing and advertising have looked to psychophysiological measures for answers to their questions. Here we briefly describe and review a number of these measurement techniques, all of which have been employed in experimental situations where the subject watches a commercial or discusses a product while psychophysiological measurements are simultaneously taken.

Pupillary Response

Pupillary response first gained attention as a potential psychophysiological measure of consumer response in the early 1960s when research suggested that pupil size seemed to vary directly with the pleasurableness of observed stimuli (Hess & Polt, 1960). Subsequent study of the phenomenon has suggested that the interpretation of those initial findings was probably an oversimplification (Stewart & Furse, 1982). Although pupillary response may be related to affect, exactly how it is related and the nature of the physiological mechanism that is operating remain unclear. The best data available to date suggest that pupillary response appears to be related to the amount of information processing evoked by a stimulus and therefore may be viewed as a measure of attention and cognitive effort—not affect.

Electrodermal Response

The term *electrodermal response* refers to a measure of the degree to which a small electric current is conducted or resisted by the surface of the skin (a measure that is usually, but not always, gauged by taping an electrode to the palm or putting a ringlike monitor around a finger). There is evidence that electrodermal responses may be related to arousal, affect, and amount of information processing. However, these responses tend to be very unstable over time, and attempts to establish the reliability of this measurement technique have not proved to be successful. Further, some important methodological issues are as yet unresolved with respect to this method. For example, different results may be obtained depending on whether resistance (sometimes referred to as Galvanic Skin Response, or GSR) or conductance is the measured response; conductance and resistance are reciprocally related. Perhaps the primary complaint of those who have experimented with electrodermal response as a criterion measure is that although it may indicate an affective response, there is no way of discerning by means of the technique whether the response is favorable or unfavorable to the stimulus. Moreover, the specific mechanisms that give rise to electrodermal responses are not well understood.

Brain-Wave Measurement

Attempts have been made to gauge consumer response to stimuli such as commercials by having the consumer watch the commercials while an electroencephalograph (EEG) simultaneously monitors brain-wave activity (Price et al., 1986). Although it has been noted that brain-wave patterns do change in response to stimuli, the reasons for such change and even the meaning of such changes remain matters of controversy (Cacioppo & Petty, 1985; Nevid, 1984; Stewart, 1984; Stewart & Furse, 1982).

Other Measures

Numerous other psychophysiological measures have been experimented with in the search for the "pure" measure of consumer reaction. The electromyograph (EMG) measures minute movement in muscles, and it has been applied to facial muscles as subjects are exposed to various stimuli (Ekman et al., 1982). Voice-pitch analysis is another method that has been experimented with, the rationale here being that voice pitch is an involuntary consequence of muscular contractions of the larynx (Brickman, 1980; Nighswonger & Martin, 1981). However, it is not always clear what the factors responsible for a change in voice pitch may be. Factors such as time of day of the recordings, the method of recording, characteristics of the interviewer, and the general health of the respondent are all capable of influencing voice pitch. Perhaps most important, a discrepancy exists in the literature on voice-pitch analysis between reports of accuracy of vocal-auditory recognition and the lack of evidence for the acoustic differentiation of vocal expression (Scherer, 1986).

One measure shown to be of value in assessing consumer response to print advertising is eye-movement tracking equipment. In some of the older versions of this equipment, the subject is strapped into a harness and looks through lenses at slides of print ads while eye-movement recorders simultaneously record exactly where in the ad the gaze of the subject's eye is going. A newer version of the eye-tracking device features a tiny fiberoptic material embedded in a specially prepared pair of glasses that acts as a camera; virtually everywhere the subjects look as they go through specially constructed magazines or other test stimuli is recorded on videotape by this pinhead-size recording device.

In general, psychophysiological measures as applied to consumer research offer promise—but a promise that has yet to be fulfilled. Rather than the "pure" measures of attitude and/or affect their proponents had hoped they would be, psychophysiological measures can at best be thought of as indicating such factors as type and stage of information processing (Stewart & Furse, 1982).

Numerous, as-yet-unresolved, methodological issues regarding such measures exist. For example, the fact that some changes in psychophysiological measures are not independent of the baseline measures (a phenomenon referred to as the *law of initial values*) suggests that such dependence must be controlled by statistical means. Second, although there is a generalized response to similar stimuli that is common to all individuals (stimulus-response specificity), each individual has a unique response set (individual response stereotype) that must be controlled. Third, the use of a single physiological measure, which has been typical of many applications of these measures, fails to provide information concerning individual response sets and provides an incomplete picture of response. Current psychophysiological texts suggest the use of multiple measures; and the use of measurement from a number of different psychophysiological assessment devices requires that all the measures be converted to comparable scaling units. Fourth, numerous experimental controls are required to ensure that an individual is responding only to the intended stimulus and not to the experimental situation and/or extraneous events in the environment. Finally, there are a variety of issues related to instrumentation that must be considered when using psychophysiological measures; such characteristics as sensitivity, precision, and accuracy must be carefully examined when selecting instrumentation for use in psychophysiological studies.

A Perspective

The research literature in the area of consumer psychology, including consideration of measurement issues (see Figure 18–4) is growing. Every day, consumer

Figure 18–4
Assessment in Consumer Psychology

Specialized journals such as Psychology & Marketing *regularly contain articles dealing with aspects of consumer assessment. Examples include studies of cross-cultural influences on product evaluation (Alden et al., 1994; Hoyer, 1994), the impact of mood on consumer behaviors (Curren & Harich, 1994; Groenland & Schoormans, 1994), gender differences in Christmas-shopping activities (Fischer & Arnold, 1994), and the influence of foreign-sounding product names on American buyers (Harris et al., 1994). Articles pertaining to consumer assessment and related areas may also be found in many other journals, including* Journal of Advertising Research, Journal of Applied Communication Research, Journal of Consumer Research, Journal of Marketing, Journal of Marketing Research, *and the* Journal of Consumer Psychology.

psychologists are bringing the tools of behavioral research to bear on questions of great import for the well-being of producers and consumers alike. To the extent that the tools of psychological measurement are used ethically and professionally, it would appear that we all benefit.

Moving now from consumers to computers, we cap off our study of psychological testing and assessment with a look at some of the issues surrounding the invasion of automation in the field of measurement.

C H A P T E R

19

Computer-Assisted Psychological Assessment*

The use of machines to process psychological assessment data is not a recent innovation (Fowler, 1985). As early as 1930, electromechanical scoring for at least one psychological test, the Strong Vocational Interest Blank (SVIB), was available (Campbell, 1971). In 1946, thanks to the efforts of a Minneapolis engineer named Elmer Hankes, SVIB scoring and profiling had become mechanized. One year later, Hankes adopted the same technology to score and profile the MMPI (Dahlstrom et al., 1972). By the late 1950s, computers were being used not merely to score or develop profiles but also to interpret test data (Rome et al., 1965). And by 1965, the Roche Psychiatric Service Institute had initiated the first national, mail-in MMPI service: clinicians could administer the MMPI, mail in the protocol, and get back a computer-scored and computer-interpreted report.

Perhaps the greatest stimulus to the growth of the field of computer-assisted psychological assessment was the development of the desktop microcomputer. Affordably priced IBM-PCs, Macintosh, and other such hardware held out the promise of in-office, computerized test administration, combined with quick and accurate test data interpretation. Recent years have witnessed the development of a growing number of psychological and educational testing software packages, as well as the establishment of a number of new companies marketing various computer-related assessment services. Computerized tests to assess intelligence, personality (projectively as well as in other ways), neuropsychological functioning, adjustment, vocational aptitudes and interests, scholastic achievement, and sundry other variables either are currently on the market or soon will be.

---

*An earlier version of this chapter was written with the assistance of Kevin L. Moreland.

An Overview

The Process

Use of the term *computer-assisted assessment* in its broadest sense always implies that the assessor is somehow being assisted by a computer; it does *not* necessarily imply that the assessee is directly being assisted by a computer or even using a computer to enter data. The SAT and the GRE are examples of instruments of assessment that can be considered "computer-assisted," since they are designed for computer scoring. Yet until very recently, these instruments had not been administered on a computer terminal; the only "word processor" used in taking such tests was a number 2 pencil applied to sheets of paper with printed grids.

Increasingly, computer-assisted assessment entails computerized test administration: the individual testtaker sits before a computer video display and responds to prompts that appear on the screen (or prompts "spoken" by a speech simulator). The examinee's responses may be made by pressing keys on a keypad, by using a "light pen" and indicating a response by pointing to some area of the display, or by some other means. The nature of the interaction between the computer and the examinee will depend on how interactive the computer has been programmed to be. *Computerized adaptive testing* is the term used to denote an interactive process of testtaking; the directions and/or the test items administered to individual testtakers will vary as a function of the testtaker's response. As in traditional testing, the test might begin with some sample, practice items. However, the computer may not permit the testtaker to continue with the test until the practice items have been responded to in a satisfactory manner and the testtaker has provided evidence that he or she understands the test procedure. Computerized adaptive testing gets much more complicated than that. A test may be different for each testtaker, depending on individual performance on the items presented. Each item on an achievement test, for example, may have a known difficulty level and discrimination index. These data as well as other data (such as a statistical allowance for blind guessing) will be factored in when it comes time to derive a final score on the items administered—we deliberately don't say "final score on the test" because "the test" is ultimately different for different testtakers. Computer-adaptive testing has been found to reduce the number of test items that need to be administered by as much as 50% while simultaneously reducing measurement error by 50% (Weiss & Vale, 1987). The item statistics used in such tests must be very precise, so very large samples of respondents are needed to establish those statistics.

The Advantages

Butcher (1987) described the advantages of computer-assisted psychological assessment (CAPA) in terms of the objectivity, accuracy, reliability, and efficiency such techniques can offer. According to Jackson (1986, p. 5), the advantages, or at least what he called the "perceived advantages," of CAPA can be summarized as follows:

1. Economy of professional time
2. The possibility of employing trained assistants to monitor test administration at times when no psychologist is available
3. The negligible time lag between the administration of a test and its scoring and interpretation
4. The virtual elimination of scoring errors resulting from human lapses of attention or judgment
5. The capacity of a computer to combine data according to a rule more accurately than the capacities of humans
6. The standardization of interpretations by eliminating unreliability traceable to differing points of view in professional judgment
7. The potential for systematically gathering and accessing extensive normative databases that transcend the capacities of human test interpreters
8. The possibility of employing complex scoring and data combination strategies that are not otherwise practical
9. The application of computer-based assessment to special populations

As an example of the last advantage, Jackson cites the work of Wilson et al. (1982), who developed a dental plate activated by the tongue as the mechanism for test response to be used by testtakers who lacked the capacity for speech or control of their hands or limbs. The device permitted five distinct responses, depending on the area of the plate depressed by the tongue. As demonstrated by such apparatuses, CAPA would appear to offer a seemingly limitless number of potential applications.

On conventional, paper-and-pencil tests, testtakers are usually able to see all the test's items; they can preview items coming up or review items they have completed. For some testtakers, seeing the entire test at one time heightens test anxiety, leading to hurried responses, which may not have been adequately thought out. By contrast, items presented on a computer monitor are presented a few at a time, at most; the respondent typically has no way of knowing the total number of items on the test. Thus, in some cases, administration by computer might lead to more careful attention to items.

Computer programs designed to facilitate the construction of administration, scoring, and interpretation of assessor-made tests, such as teacher-made achievement tests, are proliferating in record numbers. These programs, some with names such as *Make-A-Test* (see Figure 19–1), *Create-A-Test, The Grand Inquisitor,* and *The First National Item Bank and Criterion-Referenced Scoring System,* typically make use of two advantages of computerized testing: the ability to store items in an "item bank" and the ability to individualize testing through a technique called "item branching."

Item banking   An *item bank* is a relatively large, easily accessible collection of test questions. Instructors who regularly teach a particular course sometimes create their own item bank of questions they have found to be useful on examinations. One of the many potential advantages of an item bank is accessibility

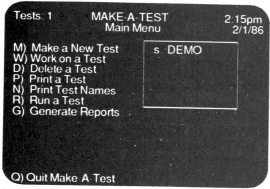

Manager Main Menu Screen: All program options are accessed through simple menu structures. Submenus and prompts help users know available options.

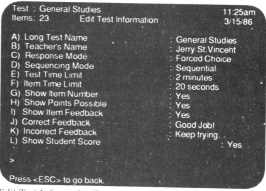

Edit Test Information Screen: Tests of up to 500 items may be given with one of several presentation options.

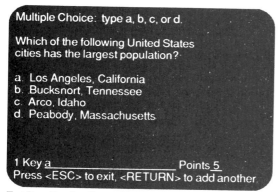

Test Item Creation Screen: Test items are created with a simple text editor. Editing is performed using the same word processing–style editor.

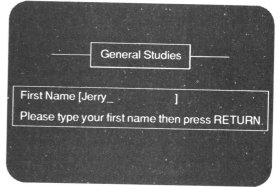

Run a Test Screen: The Run a Test option allows instructor preview of the test in student mode with timing and scoring.

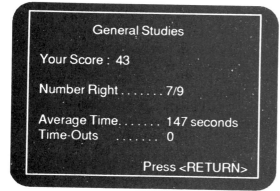

On-Line Test Completion Screen: At the end of a computer-administered test, immediate scoring results can be displayed to the student.

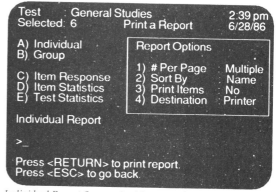

Individual Report Screen: A wide range of report types and styles can be ordered by the user. Reports can also be viewed on-line before printing.

Figure 19–1
Sample Display Screens from the WICAT Make-A-Test Program

to a large number of test items conveniently classified by subject area, item statistics, or other variables. And just as funds may be added to or withdrawn from a more traditional bank, so items may be added to, withdrawn from, and even modified in an item bank (see the *Close-up*, pages 706–709).

Item branching One of the major advantages of computer-based test administration is the capability of *item branching*—the ability of the computer to tailor the content and order of presentation of test items on the basis of responses to previous items. A computer may have a bank, for example, of achievement test items of different difficulty levels. The computer may be programmed (1) not to present an item of the next difficulty level until two consecutive items of the previous difficulty level are answered correctly and (2) to terminate the test when five consecutive items of a given level of difficulty have been answered incorrectly. Alternatively, the pattern of items to which the testtaker is exposed may be based not on the testtaker's response to preceding items but on a random drawing from the total pool of test items. Green (1984) commented on the advantage of such a procedure:

> Conventional tests can be compromised by theft of test forms, or by each of several applicants memorizing a few items for later mutual benefit. Future applicants can then be coached on specific item content, or even furnished with test answer keys. But when the computer selects items at random from its pool, each applicant gets a different test form, and such specific coaching is much less effective. In fact, if the item pool is sufficiently large and extensive, it can be published for all to see, on the grounds that anyone who can answer all these items, knows the material being tested.

Green went on to cite the case of a computer-administered driving-license test—the written portion—as an instance that might be particularly amenable to the administration of randomly drawn items. And given a large enough bank of items, it would even be possible to keep a record of the items administered to an applicant on a first administration of the test—an administration on which the applicant did not receive a passing score—and randomly draw from the remaining (unused) items in the bank for succeeding administrations to the same applicant.

Jackson (1986) mused about how item branching might be employed in a computer-administered personality test, the better to get a more accurate picture of the testtaker:

> If a respondent has already responded to four items in such a way as to deny visual hallucinations, it would be reasonable to conclude that this [is] a less fruitful avenue of investigation than that of depression, where three or four items have been endorsed. By selecting items to present to the respondent from the depression area, one might obtain a more complete and accurate picture of psychopathology in terms of such sub-dimensions as suicidal tendencies, despair over the future, fatigue and eating disorders. (p. 11)

Another potential application of item-branching technology in personality tests has to do with monitoring the purposefulness of examinees' responses. Should a profile of responses appear indicative of a situation wherein the examinee is responding in a nonpurposive or inconsistent fashion or in a manner indicative of faking, the computer may be programmed to respond in a pre-scribed way, such as by admonishing the respondent to be more careful and/or refusing to proceed until a purposive response is given. For example, on a computer-based true-false test, if the examinee responds "True" to an item such as "I spent Christmas in Beirut last year," there would be reason to suspect that the examinee is responding nonpurposively, randomly, or in some way other than genuinely. You might conclude at this point in our overview that automation has done for psychological assessment exactly what it has done in many other spheres of daily living—greatly enhanced the quality of life. Is that, in fact, the case?

As our overview continues, you will become acquainted with some of the problems and issues that the rush to computer technology has left in its wake. Subsequently, we'll examine some of the more technical pros and cons of, and issues associated with, CAPA.

The Disadvantages

The testtaker's perspective   From the perspective of a testtaker, particularly a testtaker who is not "computer savvy" or experienced, a computer-administered test may be in itself an intimidating experience. Testtakers may find themselves prevented from engaging in various testtaking strategies that have worked for them in the past, such as previewing or reviewing test materials and skipping around to answer only questions they are certain of first. Examinees whose practice it is to skim through and survey all the items on a test at the outset may not be able to do so during a computerized test administration. Typically, an answer is required to an item before the computer's cursor proceeds to the next. Having completed the test or any portion of it, testtakers may be electronically prohibited from reviewing previously entered answers. During the test, because an answer may be required before the next item is presented for response, the examinee is deprived of the option of purposefully omitting items. And because every item must be answered (and in many instances verified with a prompt from the computer, such as "You answered TRUE; if that is correct press RETURN"), the computer administration of a test may actually take longer for some testtakers than the administration of the same test with paper and pencil. Note, however, that computer administrations of tests typically take less time than conventional administrations for the average examinee (White et al., 1985). Such a time savings has been found with the computerized Differential Aptitude Test (Dimock & Cormier, 1991) and the computerized MMPI (Watson et al., 1992).

The test user's perspective   A great paradox of the computer era is that although such technology is designed to be time-saving, many long hours must frequently be invested reading tomes of documentation—perhaps even a number of ancillary books written as easy guides to the primary books—before the technology can be used. Once the obstacle of learning to use computer software and/or specially designed hardware is overcome, and the inevitable "bugs" have been worked out, other problems may arise.

Designing an Item Bank

Developing a bank of items for an item bank is typically no easy chore; many questions and issues relating to the development of such a bank and to the maintenance of a satisfactory pool of items will need to be resolved (Hiscox, 1983; Hiscox & Brzezinski, 1980). As an introduction to the many potential problems inherent in developing an item bank, consider the following: You are a testing consultant who has been asked by a national association of people who go to people's homes and exercise with them—we'll call this group "The Association of Personal Physical Trainers Who Make House Calls (APPTHC)"—to develop an item bank of questions. This item bank will be made up of questions that any physical trainer who makes house calls should reasonably be able to answer. APPTHC officials inform you that their ultimate objective will be to use this item bank to develop an APPTHC certification examination. How would you go about developing such an item bank? What questions would need to be asked?

Struggle with the APPTHC exercise before looking at the following table, as an APPTHC member in good standing might say, "No pain, no gain!"

Questions to Be Answered in Designing an Item Bank

I. Items

  A. *Acquisition and development*

    1. Develop/use your own item collection or use collections of others?

      a. If develop your own item collection, what development procedures will be followed?

      b. If use collections of others, will the items be leased or purchased; is the classification scheme sufficiently documented and are the item format specifications sufficiently compatible for easy transfer and use?

    2. What types of "items" will be permitted?

      a. Will open-ended (constructed response) items, opinion questions, instructional objectives, or descriptions of performance tasks be included in the bank?

      b. Will all the items be made to fit a common format (e.g., all multiple-choice with options *a, b, c,* and *d*)?

      c. Must the items be calibrated, be validated, or otherwise carry additional information?

    3. What will be the size of the item collection?

      a. How many items per objective/subtopic (collection depth)?

      b. How many different topics (collection breadth)?

    4. What review, tryout, and editing procedures will be used?

      a. Who will perform the review/editing?

      b. Will there be a field tryout, and if so, what statistics will be gathered, and what criteria will be used for inclusion in the bank?

  B. *Classification*

    1. How will the subject matter classifications be performed?

      a. Will the classification by subject matter use fixed categories, keywords, or some combination of the two?

      b. Who will be responsible for preparing, expanding, and refining the taxonomy?

      c. How detailed will the taxonomy be? Will it be hierarchically or nonhierarchically arranged?

      d. Who will assign classification indices to each item, and how will this assignment be verified?

    2. What other assigned information about the items will be stored in the item bank?

3. What measured information about the items will be stored in the bank? How will the item measures be calculated? *

C. *Management*

1. Will provision be made for updating the classification scheme and items? If so:

   a. Who will be permitted to make additions, deletions, and revisions?

   b. What review procedures will be followed?

   c. How will the changes be disseminated?

   d. How will duplicate (or near-duplicate) items be detected and eliminated?

   e. When will a revision of an item be trivial enough that item statistics from a previous version can be aggregated with revisions from the current version?

   f. Will item statistics be stored from each use, or from last use, or will they be aggregated across uses?

2. How will items that require pictures, graphs, special characters, or other types of enhanced printing be handled?

3. How will items that must accompany other items, such as a series of questions about the same reading passage, be handled?

II. Tests

A. *Assembly*

1. Must the test constructor specify the specific items to appear on the test, or will the items be selected by computer?

2. If the items are selected by computer:

   a. How will one item out of several that matches the search specification be selected (randomly, time since last usage, frequency of previous use)?

   b. What happens if no item meets the search specifications?

   c. Will a test constructor have the option to reject a selected item, and if so, what will be the mechanism for doing so?

   d. What precautions will be taken to ensure that examinees who are tested more than once do not receive the same items?

3. What item or test parameters can be specified for test assembly (item format restrictions, limits on difficulty levels, expected score distribution, expected test reliability, etc.)?

4. What assembly procedures will be available (options to multiple-choice items placed in random order, the test items placed in random order, different items on each test)?

5. Will the system print tests or just specify which items to use? If the former, how will the tests be printed or duplicated and where will the answers be displayed?

B. *Administration, scoring, and reporting*

1. Will the system be capable of on-line test administration? If so:

   a. How will access be managed?

   b. Will test administration be adaptive, and if so, using what procedures?

2. Will the system provide for test scoring? If so:

   a. What scoring formula will be used (rights only, correction for guessing, partial credit for

*This question is the subject of considerable controversy and discussion in the technical-measurement literature. For example, to obtain a latent-trait difficulty parameter, concern has been expressed about sample size, calibration procedure (Rasch, 3-parameter), linking models (major axis, least squares, maximum likelihood), and number of items common to the equating forms.

(continued)

Designing an Item Bank *(continued)*

some answers, weighting by discrimination values)?

b. How will constructed responses be evaluated (off-line by the instructor, on-line/off-line by examiners comparing their answers to a key, on-line by computer with/without employing a spelling algorithm)?

3. Will the system provide for test reporting? If so:

a. What records will be kept (the tests themselves, individual student item responses, individual student test scores, school or other group scores) and for how long? Will new scores for individuals and groups supplement or replace old scores?

b. What reporting options (content/format) will be available?

c. To whom will the reports be sent?

C. *Evaluation*

1. Will reliability and validity data be collected? If so, what data will be collected by whom, and how will they be used?

2. Will norms be made available and, if so, based on what norm-referenced measures?

III. System

A. *Acquisition and development*

1. Who will be responsible for acquisition/development, given what resources, and operating under what constraints?

2. Will the system be made transportable to others? What levels and what degree of documentation will be available?

B. *Software/hardware features*

1. What aspects of the system will be computer-assisted?

a. Where will the items be stored (computer, paper, card file)?

b. Will requests be filled using a batch, on-line, or manual mode?

2. Will a microcomputer be used and, if so, what

special limits does such a choice place on item text, item-bank size, and test development options?

3. Will items be stored as one large collection or will separate files be maintained for each user?

4. How will the item-banking system be constructed (from scratch; by piecing together word processing, database management, and other general-purpose programs; by adopting existing item-banking systems)?

5. What specific equipment will be needed (for storage, retrieval, interactions with the system, etc.)?

6. How user- and maintenance-friendly will the equipment and support programs be?

7. Who will be responsible for equipment maintenance?

C. *Monitoring and training*

1. What system features will be monitored (number of items per classification category, usage by user group, number of revisions until a user is satisfied, distribution of test lengths or other test characteristics, etc.)?

2. Who will monitor the system, train users, and give support (initially, ongoing)?

3. How will information about changes in system procedures be disseminated?

D. *Access and security*

1. Who will have access to the items and other information in the bank (authors/owners, teachers, students)? Who can request tests?

2. Will users have direct access to the system or must they go through an intermediary?

3. What procedures will be followed to secure the contents of the item bank (if they are to be secure)?

4. Where will the contents of the item bank be housed (centrally or will each user also have a copy)?

5. Who will have access to score reports?

IV. Use and Acceptance

  A. *General*

    1. Who decides to what uses the item bank will be put? And will these uses be the ones that the test users need and want?

    2. Who will develop the tests and who will be allowed to use the system? Will those people be acceptable to the examinees and recipients of the test information?

    3. Will the system be able to handle the expected demand for use?

    4. Is the output of the system likely to be used and used as intended?

    5. How will user acceptance and item-bank credibility be enhanced?

  B. *Instructional improvement.* If this is an intended use:

    1. Will the item bank be part of a larger instructional/decision-making system?

    2. Which textbooks, curriculum guidelines, and other materials, if any, will be keyed to the bank's items? Who will make that decision and how will the assignments be validated?

    3. Will items be available for drill and practice as well as for testing?

    4. Will information be available to users that will assist in the diagnosis of educational needs?

  C. *Adaptive testing.* If this is an option:

    1. How will the scheduling of the test administrations take place?

    2. How will the items be selected to ensure testing efficiency yet maintain content representation and avoid duplication between successive test administrations?

    3. What criteria will be used to terminate testing?

    4. What scoring procedures will be followed?

  D. *Certification of competence.* If this is an intended use:

    1. Will the item bank contain measures that cover all the important component skills of the competence being assessed?

    2. How many attempts at passing the test will be allowed; when? How will these attempts be monitored?

  E. *Program/curriculum evaluation.* If this is an intended use:

    1. Will it be possible to implement the system so as to provide reliable measures of student achievement in a large number of specific performance areas?

    2. Will the item bank contain measures that cover all the important stated objectives of the curriculum? That go beyond the stated objectives of the curriculum?

    3. Will the item bank yield commensurable data that permit valid comparisons over time?

  F. *Testing and reporting requirements imposed by external agencies.* If meeting these requirements is an intended use:

    1. Will the system be able to handle requirements for program evaluation, student selection for specially funded programs, assessing educational needs, and reporting?

    2. Will the system be able to accommodate minor modifications in the testing and reporting requirements?

V. Costs

  A. *Cost feasibility*

    1. What are the (fixed, variable) costs (financial, time, space, equipment, and supplies) to create and support the system?

    2. Are those costs affordable?

  B. *Cost comparisons*

    1. How do the item-banking system costs compare with the present or other testing systems that achieve the same goals?

    2. Do any expanded capabilities justify the extra cost? Are any restricted capabilities balanced by cost savings?

Source: Millman and Arter (1984).

In contrast to psychological tests administered by clinicians themselves, automated testing is typically designed for administration by a nonprofessional member of the clinician's staff or for self-administration by the assessee. Thus, in contrast to the clinician-administered test, an automated testing situation may provide diminished, if any, opportunity for the assessor to (1) establish a rapport with the assessee, (2) observe the assessee's testtaking behavior, and (3) note any unusual extra-test conditions that may have affected responses.

When computers are used to administer tests, they can be "tied up" for relatively long periods of time, and clinicians, as a result, can be deprived of their use. For example, although some testtakers can complete a computer-administered version of the MMPI-2 in as little as 45 minutes, others may take as long as two hours. Given that a clerk can key in all 567 MMPI-2 responses from an answer sheet in about five minutes or so, and given that an optical mark reader could process an answer sheet in less than five seconds, why should the computer be tied up for as long as two hours?

The age of computers has brought with it new kinds of crime: computer theft and computer mischief, the latter exemplified by computer "viruses" capable of altering or erasing a computer's memory. Just as clinicians have for decades protected the security of tests and test data with tools such as locked, steel filing cabinets, so clinicians who use CAPA technology have the obligation to protect these tests and test data. A significant obstacle modern clinicians face, however, is the time and expense entailed in keeping up with the latest and most effective means of electronic security.

Perhaps the most vexing concern of clinicians who use computerized assessment software, particularly software that provides automated interpretations of findings, is the paucity of studies documenting the validity of computer-generated interpretations of findings (Spielberger & Piotrowski, 1990). A related question has to do with the equivalence of data obtained from a computerized version of a test with data derived from the more traditional paper-and-pencil administration.

Despite these problems, CAPA is probably here to stay, so we now turn to gaining a better understanding of it. One way to conceptualize CAPA-related products and services is in terms of computer inputs and outputs—that is, what goes into and what comes out of the computer. Below we delve in detail into the intricacies of computer input and output as they relate to CAPA.

Computer Input

For purposes of discussion, let's dichotomize "computer input" into two categories: (1) the testtaker's input of responses directly into a computer—a process referred to as *on-line test administration*—and (2) the test user's input of assessees' responses into a computer for the purpose of scoring and/or interpretation.

On-line Test Administration

Most tests that are currently available for on-line administration were originally developed for conventional (that is, paper-and-pencil) administration. A primary concern of test users is how factors related to on-line test administration—factors that are irrelevant to the original design of the test—might influence testtaker performance. For example, in a computer-assisted administration of a test, testtakers typically must enter their responses through a keyboard. But what if the testtaker is woefully unfamiliar with it? In some tests, such as one in which the testtaker's task is to quickly list words (as in some tests of divergent thinking or creativity), testtakers unfamiliar with computer keyboards are penalized. Concerns have also been expressed regarding the applicability of published norms and of reliability and validity data; typically such data are obtained using conventional test administrations, and generalizing those data to a computer-assisted test administration is risky at best, and inappropriate at worst.

"Can scores on a conventionally administered test be considered equivalent to scores on a computer-assisted administration of the same test?" Ultimately, this question will have to be answered on an individual, test-by-test basis. In general, research into the equivalency of test scores as a function of method of administration has focused on, among other variables, the effects of item type, item content, and the testtaker's attitude. In some cases, equivalency between tests using traditional and computerized formats is not an issue, because the test can be administered only with a computer. A brief sampling of representative research in each of these areas follows.

Effects of item type   There is evidence that certain types of items may yield significantly different scores as a function of the mode of test administration. Significant differences in scores on speeded arithmetic tests as a function of whether the tests were conventionally administered or computer-administered have been found (Greaud & Green, 1986). By contrast, on tests involving mostly multiple-choice and true-false items, the two modes of test administration were deemed equivalent (Hoffman & Lundberg, 1976). A clear exception to the latter finding was matching-type items: the computer presentation of matching items resulted in significantly lower scores, different numbers of changed responses, and different patterns of changed responses, as compared with conventionally presented matching items.

On paper-and-pencil tests, a testtaker can, by design or omission, fail to respond to a particular item by not placing pencil to paper to respond to it. But in a mode of test administration whereby the computer will not proceed unless an item is responded to in some way, the testtaker who wishes not to respond is compelled, in some way, to enter this "nonresponse." This fact of life of computerized test administration has implications for the data obtained in many types of tests, including personality tests (Honaker, 1988). For example, when the Adjective Checklist is administered by computer, respondents must actively reject an adjective, rather than passively fail to endorse it—a fact that may lead to differences in scores (Allred & Harris, 1984).

Effects of item content   The content of items—whether, for example, they call for the respondent to reveal something very personal—may also be affected by mode of administration of the item. Writing decades ago, Smith (1963) mused that testtakers might prefer an impersonal computer to face-to-face contact when "confession-type" questions were being asked. This hypothesis has been explored in a number of studies, some of which have yielded conflicting findings. Skinner and Allen (1983) found no differences in respondents' willingness to describe their alcohol and illegal drug use when using a paper-and-pencil questionnaire or a computer, though such differences have been observed by others (Evan & Miller, 1969; Hart & Goldstein, 1985; Koson et al., 1970). Koson et al. (1970) found that females tended to be more honest than males on computerized tests. More pathological MMPI scores were found as a function of computerized as opposed to conventional test administration (Bresolin, 1984). Rezmovic (1977) found mode-of-administration effects most pronounced at the extreme ends of a distribution of test scores; computer administration caused extreme scorers to become even more extreme.

Although studies both support and fail to support the "honest confession to an impersonal computer" hypothesis, perhaps the most reasonable conclusion on the basis of the available literature is that nonequivalence as a function of mode of test administration is typically small enough to be of no practical consequence (Beaumont & French, 1987; Harrell & Lombardo, 1984; Holden & Hickman 1987; Honaker et al., 1988; Lukin et al., 1985).

Tests specifically designed for on-line administration   Not all computer-administered psychological tests have a paper-and-pencil predecessor. Some test developers have used the advantages of computerized assessment to design tests that simply would not work, or would not work as well, using more traditional formats. One example is a test developed in France called the *Examen Cognitif par Ordinateur* (ECO; Ritchie et al., 1993). Although this translates literally as the "Cognitive Test by Computer," the test is better known in the United States either by its French acronym (ECO) or as the Cognitive Examination of the Elderly. One part of the ECO involves identifying matching shapes. The shapes appear on the computer screen, and subjects respond by touching the "touch screen" of the computer. The procedure allows not only for a recording of the response but also for a very precise measure of response time. The computer also maintains a record of the types of errors made relative to particular locations on the screen. Adaptive testing procedures are built in, since responses to earlier items determine the sequence of later items.

The testtaker's attitude and emotional reaction   Most people have favorable attitudes regarding computerized test administration (Burke et al., 1987; French & Beaumont, 1987; Honaker, 1988; Llabre et al., 1987), even if a computer is initially more anxiety-provoking than paper-and-pencil questionnaires (Lushene et al., 1974). Indeed, many people even seem to prefer computer to conventional testing (Bresolin, 1984; Honaker, 1988; Rozensky et al., 1986). One study involving college students indicated that neither students' level of familiarity with computers nor the amount of anxiety experienced in response to using the computers was a factor in responding to a computerized format of the Verbal Reasoning subtest of the Differential Aptitude Test (Dimock & Cormier, 1991).

However, a minority of testtakers are uncomfortable with computerized testing. The elderly compose one demographic group who tend to be uncomfortable with keyboards, monitors, and other even more exotic instruments of assessment (Carr et al., 1982; Volans & Levy, 1982). Yet even college students in the 1990s may initially be overwhelmed by an ability test in computerized format—to the extent that their score on the test may be affected (Dimock & Cormier, 1991).

Inputting Data from Tests

Placing yourself in the shoes of a test user, consider some of your options with regard to having the tests you administer computer-scored and/or computer-interpreted: central processing, teleprocessing, and local processing.

Central processing   Central processing entails sending test protocols completed (usually using the traditional paper-and-pencil method) at one location to some other central location for processing—that is, for scoring and/or interpretation. The results may then be returned to the test user in an oral report by telephone or in a written report by mail, fax, or other delivery system. An example of central processing is the Roche Psychiatric Service Institute service for computerized scoring of MMPI protocols.

Because ownership of any expensive equipment is not required, the chief advantage of central processing is its low cost. Particularly when test results do not have to be "turned around" very quickly, and when there are large numbers of protocols to be processed, central processing offers the most economical test-scoring and interpretation alternative. Clinicians who test clients only on occasion, or companies, such as personnel selection firms testing large numbers of people, may find central processing to be best suited to their needs.

As the prices of technology such as microcomputers and optical mark readers continue to go down, and as mailing, shipping, and related costs rise, the cost-efficiency edge of central processing will dwindle. Another factor militating against widespread future use of central processing is the increasingly interactive nature of many tests. More and more computer-administered tests are designed to be individually tailored to the responses of the testtaker; that is, the sequence, even the total number, of items administered to a testtaker may depend on responses to previous questions. Users of central processing can administer tests with a fixed item sequence only.

Teleprocessing   The processing of test data at a remote location over telephone lines is referred to as *teleprocessing*. An interface between a personal computer and the central computer, called a *modem,* may be used to send the raw data in and receive the processed scores and/or interpretive data back. Test users pay a fee to the company offering teleprocessing services. The user must also pay for the telephone-time charges, which can be substantial if large numbers of tests are being processed. In general, teleprocessing represents an attractive alternative to central processing because test results are available in minutes.

Teleprocessing is also an attractive alternative to local processing (see below) because start-up costs are much lower. The only equipment needed for teleprocessing is a data communications terminal. Such a terminal, which does nothing but transmit, receive, and print data, can be purchased for a few hundred dollars. Alternatively, many relatively inexpensive microcomputers can be adapted for use as a data communications terminal. Further, such relatively inexpensive microcomputers purchased for the purpose of teleprocessing can "double" in some other capacity (such as a word processor, a computer bulletin board, or some other non-assessment-related application) during downtime.

Perhaps the chief disadvantage of teleprocessing is its inavailability for processing many different types of tests.

Local processing Local processing refers to on-site computer processing, whether by home microcomputer, optical mark reader, or some other automated technology. A microcomputer used for local test processing can also be used for teleprocessing, though the reverse isn't necessarily true; software used for local test processing is typically available only for the most popular microcomputers.

The two primary advantages of local processing for the test user are control and flexibility. By having the system entirely "in-house," the test user has total control over every facet of the processing of the tests, including factors such as hours of operation, when servicing of the system will take place, and quality control of the operation. And because the user of local processing typically has at least one powerful computer on the premises, the flexibility to use that computer for test-administration purposes—or some other non-assessment-related purpose—is another advantage.

Software for local test processing is plentiful; such software is not necessarily published by the test publisher and may be produced by any number of competing manufacturers. Most software for local test processing yields an interpretive report but seldom contains a program for administering the test or a scoring program. This is because of legal issues surrounding ownership of the items in the test and the system used to score the test. Test items and scoring information are owned by the test developer or publisher and cannot legally be copied into a computer without the owner's permission—permission that is seldom forthcoming. Central-processing and teleprocessing services that involve scoring are available legally only from the test publisher or licensees. By contrast, local processing involves the generation of interpretive findings (in various forms, such as a narrative report), based on scoring that was done either by hand or by owner-licensed computer software. Most test publishers offer only one "official" interpretive system for a given application of a particular test, though independent companies may offer a variety of test-interpretation software.

The costs of launching local-processing services, including the cost of purchasing computer hardware and software, and the time that must be invested to get the system running properly are the greatest potential disadvantages of such testing services.

Computer Output

Perhaps the most fundamental "output question" is "What does the computer put out when I use this product or service, and does whatever it puts out meet my needs and objectives?" To state this another way, the questions a prospective user might ask about a test-interpretation service or test-interpretation software product include: "What is the output? Will I get a simple scoring report such as a tally of scores? item analysis data? graphically drawn profiles? an interpretive report complete with a narrative summary? Is this computer output service appropriate and feasible for use with this client? Is it feasible for me as a user given cost and time considerations?"

Generally, two broad categories of computer output options exist: scoring reports and interpretive reports.

Scoring Reports

Simple scoring reports   With simple scoring reports, the name says it all—what you get are test scores. Some tests, such as vocational interest inventories that contain over a hundred scales, are much too cumbersome—if not impossible—to score by hand. The scores may be listed or drawn on a profile. Some tests can readily be scored by hand, but what if one had dozens of protocols to score? In such an instance, time considerations dictate that the most prudent approach would be automated scoring. The scoring of tests with as few as 20 scales, with each protocol costing approximately five dollars for a computer-generated simple scoring report, is typically less expensive and more accurate than having a trained clerk manually do the same job. And given the dollar value of a clinician's time, automated scoring represents a great advantage over hand scoring.

Extended scoring reports   A scoring report that also contains detailed statistical output but little or no case-specific narrative is referred to as an *extended scoring report* (Zachary, 1984). Extended scoring reports are particularly useful when it is important for the test user to know at a glance whether certain differences between subtest or scale scores are statistically significant or merely the result of measurement error. Extended scoring reports that provide key statistical information about the results, as well as the relationships between the various subtests or scales for intelligence tests, ability tests, neuropsychological test batteries, and vocational interest tests, can provide a great deal of information in a glance to the trained eye.

Interpretive Reports

When raw assessment data are fed into a computer, in many cases it is possible to get back output that goes much further than a mere reporting of scores, profiles, or statistics; it is possible to obtain a written interpretation of the findings, referred to as an *interpretive report*. The process of computer-assisted test interpretation (CATI) may yield one or another, or some combination, of the following types of interpretive reports: a descriptive report, a screening report, and a consultative report.

Descriptive reports "Description" in the term *descriptive report* refers to a comment—typically a most succinct and to-the-point comment—on each of the scales on the test. Such reports are especially helpful when a particular test contains scales reported in terms of different types of standard scores or different normative samples; such reports allow the test user to quickly identify the most important scores.

Screening reports Screening reports typically supply more information than descriptive reports; comments are not necessarily limited to one scale at a time, and interpretation of the relationship between different scales may be provided.

A computerized screening report may present the results of a dedicated screening instrument—that is, a self-contained test used solely for screening—or screening data regarding particular variables from some other test. In the latter context, various computerized screening reports based on an MMPI administration have been developed. One such "screener" (as it may be referred to in the vernacular of industry professionals) is The Minnesota Report: Personnel Screening System for the MMPI (University of Minnesota, 1984). Although this screening device is based on the MMPI, there is no direct correspondence between any scale on it and any one MMPI scale. Rather, a complex set of decision rules governs the scale values that will emerge on The Minnesota Report—and ultimately the interpretations that will be made. For example, for this screening report to spew out an interpretive comment (such as "The client may keep problems to himself too much"), the following conditions must be met:

- Lie and Correction scales are greater than the Infrequency scale, *and*
- the Infrequency scale is less than a *T*-score of 55, *and*
- the Depression, Paranoia, Psychasthenia, and Schizophrenia scales are less than a *T*-score of 65, *and*
- the Conversion Hysteria scale is greater than 69*T, or*
- the Need for Affection subscale is greater than 63*T, or*
- the Conversion Hysteria scale is greater than 64*T*, and the Denial of Social Anxiety subscale or Inhibition of Aggression subscale is greater than 59*T, or*
- the Repression scale is greater than 59*T, or*
- the Brooding subscale is greater than 59*T.*

Screening reports may prove useful in alerting test users to patterns of test findings that may require further investigation. Suppose you were a psychologist responsible for screening the mental health of applicants for state police positions in your state. And let's further suppose that you were using The Minnesota Report for that purpose. This instrument might interpret as "suspect" the mental health of a candidate whose test responses indicated that the applicant (1) is a thrill seeker who, among other things, enjoys driving fast cars and shooting guns, (2) is obsessive to the extent that the ability to act effectively in an emergency is impaired, and/or (3) may have a substance abuse problem.

Before denying employment with the state police to an applicant with such a pattern of test findings, you would have to investigate further. For example, it may well be that just about every current employee on your state police force scored high in thrill seeking on this instrument. Further, it may be the case that officers who have had long, satisfying, and successful careers in administrative and clerical state police positions scored high in obsessiveness. As for the finding of substance abuse, further investigation here might take the form of a blood test, a urinalysis, and/or research into other medical records. It would not be enough to merely suspect substance abuse on the basis of a screening report; before a momentous decision such as the denial of employment is made, you would have to *know* that such abuse was indeed taking place.

Consultative reports   A consultative report is one that provides a detailed analysis of test data in language appropriate for communication between testing professionals (Dahlstrom et al., 1972). Of the various types of computerized reports that are available, a consultative report is perhaps the one most readily associated with "computer-assisted test interpretation" in the minds of most psychologists. In a manner analogous to that of a professional consultation, a consultative report provides a test user with the expert opinion of an individual, or group of individuals, who may have devoted years of study to the interpretation of a particular instrument. The Roche Psychiatric Service Institute system for interpreting the MMPI was the first such system to produce consultative reports. Ideally, a consultative report generated by a computer is in many ways indistinguishable from a report written by a highly trained and knowledgeable testing professional.

Integrative Reports

Capitalizing on the computer's extraordinary capacity for memory and organization of data, as well as its ability to organize and integrate data from varied sources into readable graphics, is a new breed of evaluative report—one that is *integrative* in nature. As an example, consider a computerized report that integrates behavioral assessment data, data about medication and therapeutic activities, and related information. Envision that the output of such a computer program includes bar graphs indicating the effect on adaptive and maladaptive behavior of various types of intervention, including psychotherapy and medication. Unlike a consultative report, which is presumed to reflect expert opinion regarding the assessee, the integrative report simply integrates clinical and administrative data from various sources and presents it in graphic formats. The technology for producing such reports now exists, and it is described further in *Everyday Psychometrics.*

Issues in CAPA

In general, many of the issues that exist with regard to CAPA can be categorized as relating to (1) computer-assisted test administration, (2) computer-assisted test interpretation, (3) access to CAPA products, and (4) standards for CAPA products.

Computer-Assisted Behavioral Assessment

A number of systems have been developed, in theory and in practice, to apply the benefits of a digital computer to the enterprise of behavioral assessment (Farrell, 1986; Fitzpatrick, 1977; Flowers, 1982; Paul, 1987; Santoro et al., 1994). Santoro et al.'s (1994) Treatment/Evaluation Manager-2000, or TEM (pronounced like "team")-2000, is described here to illustrate some of the applications of the computer in this context.

TEM-2000

Designed for use by hospitals, day care centers, community mental health centers, prisons, and other institutions that provide mental health services, TEM-2000 is a software package that integrates components for behavioral assessment and other aspects of evaluation with functions having to do with psychological and medical treatment, as well as administrative work. Each client (referred to in some settings as patient, member, prisoner, etc.) is assigned a hard copy or electronic "clinical data recorder" (CDR) on which staff members record behavioral observations throughout the day. In turn, these behavioral records, along with other pertinent information, are stored in computer memory. The TEM-2000 program prompts the user to keep track of numerous evaluation- and treatment-related variables, including medication administered, a client's daily activities, the nature of dysfunctional behavior exhibited, if any, the nature of the staff's response to the dysfunctional behavior, and the effect of the staff's intervention on the dysfunctional behavior. In addition to guiding the collection and organization of clinical data, the program collects, organizes, and integrates administrative data (date of entry, projected date of discharge, etc.). The result is a detailed and comprehensive database that can readily be accessed to make treatment-related decisions.

Although 24-hour behavioral monitoring and recording does require extra effort on the part of the staff, the effort is rewarded by ready access to day-to-day records that describe in detail the client's progress and other essential clinical data. For example, consider a situation in which a client engages in dysfunctional behavior such as assaulting a staff member. How does the staff respond? And how does the staff on the next shift respond if the patient again engages in such dysfunctional behavior? What type of response would be in the best interest of both the institution and the client? Given the client's history, what is the best way to respond to such dysfunctional behavior? Instant access to the record of the client's behavioral history at the institution can assist the professional who must answer such critically important questions. The system will provide a record of the dates and conditions under which some form of staff intervention was required, as well as the outcome of the interventions employed. Use of such a feature can help ensure that effective interventions will be employed consistently by all staff on all shifts. Further, the information has application in the design and refinement of treatment strategies. In a similar vein, important information about the effectiveness of medication is also readily accessed (see Figure 1).

The Pros and Cons of Computer-Assisted Behavioral Assessment

The advantages of a computerized behavioral assessment system such as TEM-2000 can be summarized as follows:

- *Daily recording of behavioral observations provides an atheoretical, highly detailed, evaluative database that can be used in treatment decisions.* As compared with other varieties of assessment data, including clinical impressions, patient self-report, and psychological test reports, ongoing behavioral assessment (1) requires a lower level of inference regarding personality-related constructs; (2) need not be linked to any particular theory of personality; (3) helps identify environmental conditions that are acting to maintain certain behaviors; (4) provides behavioral baseline data with which other behavioral data, after

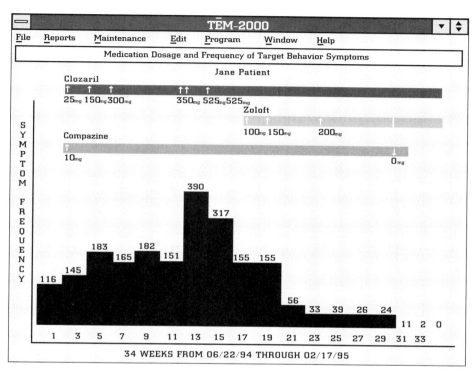

Figure 1
Change in Behavior as a Function of Medication

Daily behavioral recording makes available information and graphics relevant to the day-to-day effectiveness of medication. Staff and other interested parties are able to see a clear, sometimes dramatic picture of how changes in medication affect or fail to affect changes in behavior. This TEM-2000 *screen lists frequency of dysfunctional behaviors on the Y axis and time on the X axis. One possible interpretation is that the drug Clozaril is more effective in decreasing the frequency of dysfunctional behavior when paired with the drug Zoloft. What is another possible interpretation? What other types of information might be useful in coming to conclusions about the patient?*

intervention, may be compared; (5) provides a record of patients' behavioral strengths and weaknesses across a variety of situations; (6) helps target specific behavioral patterns for modification through interventions; (7) can be organized or graphically displayed in ways that may stimulate innovative or more effective treatment ap-

proaches; and (8) provides a ready means for standardizing evaluations in both the psychometric sense (for example, reporting inter-rater reliability on a behavioral observation measure) and the procedural sense (for example, the protocols used in the course of behavioral

(continued)

Computer-Assisted Behavioral Assessment *(continued)*

observation). Among third-party payers for mental health services (such as insurance companies), there have been increasing demands for uniformity and accountability in the reporting of assessment-related data. Behavior-based assessment systems are well suited to such an environment because client progress is gauged on the basis of documented behavioral events.

■ *A computerized system helps the contemporary clinician deal with all facets of clinical and administrative duties more efficiently.* The storage and organizational capabilities of computers have important time-saving advantages in completing forms required by government agencies, insurance companies, and other third-party payers for mental health services. Forms may require different varieties of detailed documentation for every phase of the service process from referral and preadmission through discharge and follow-up. And because one client's treatment may be paid for by more than one funding source, the time-consuming nature of the administrative work is multiplied yet again. Computerized systems that integrate behavioral and administrative data, and simplify the process of administrative paperwork, are welcomed by both clinicians and the agencies to which the clinicians are accountable.

■ *Institutional use of the system can unite staff into "team players."* On the basis of seven years of experience with TEM-2000 at an inpatient facility, the authors of the TEM-2000 system offer their subjective report that staff involvement in each client's treatment seems heightened as a result of the implementation of the system. Additionally, they report that the use of this system has a noticeably beneficial effect on staff morale. Paraprofessionals, who may once have performed only custodial duties, now feel involved personally in the evaluation and treatment process. Indeed, many staff members become involved in evaluation and treatment, since almost all of the staff may input behavioral data related to the clients.

Along with "pros" of virtually any assessment system, there are bound to be "cons." Some of the disadvantages of using a computerized behavioral assessment system are as follows:

■ *Full-time behavioral observation is not always economically feasible for the institution.* Some computer-assisted behavioral assessment systems, such as that conceptualized by Paul (1987), require highly trained personnel who do little but observe patients' behavior. Thus, in addition to the initial cost of setting up and maintaining a system such as that described by Paul (1987), financial outlays are necessary for the training and employment of dedicated behavioral observers. Although it is clearly desirable to have highly trained professionals whose job description includes little more than behavioral observation and rating, there is a real question as to whether such an employment position is economically feasible. Santoro et al. (1994) recommend that all of the staff of the facility employing a behavioral assessment system be trained to make such assessments and that they do so in the course of their routine activities.

■ *Inter-rater reliability of all the people responsible for behavioral observation must be acceptably high.* An important consideration in evaluating the utility of behavioral data gathered by two or more assessors is the degree to which inter-rater reliability between the assessors has been established. Clearly, the institution of such a program requires a commitment to training staff members who will be performing the assessments. In the case of the TEM-2000 program, Santoro et al. (1994) recommended that staff be given about 40 hours of in-service instruction and about 30 days of on-the-job training in the behavioral rating system. In a study of inter-rater reliability of the TEM-2000 system, Santoro et al. (1994) reported reliability coefficients ranging from a high of .98 on an "activity outcome rating" variable to a low of .77

on an "interventions" variable. Median inter-rater reliability across all observational categories was .87.

- *Staff concerns that behavior-rating tasks would diminish their effectiveness in other spheres of their work must be addressed.* Clinicians conducting individual or group therapy, as well as other staff members performing other duties, may view the minute or two it takes to complete a client's CDR as a distraction from their other duties. In such cases, practice with the system or the entering of data after the activity is completed will often allay such concerns.

- *Staff may be "computerphobic" or harbor otherwise negative attitudes toward the introduction of computers into their daily routine.* Many legitimate concerns about the use of computers in mental health settings have been expressed by both clinicians (Elliott, 1988; Hartman, 1986a, 1986b; Reimers et al., 1987; Skinner & Pakula, 1986; Witt & Elliott, 1985) and their clients (Romanczyk, 1986). In addition, certain mental health professionals, presumably like members of other occupations, are reluctant to trade in more traditional ways of working for a lifestyle that relies on computer hardware and software. The challenge here is to effectively address all legitimate concerns, while eradicating irrational "computerphobia," by exposure to the benefits of the computerized approach. In the case of TEM-2000, for example, it is possible for clients' CDRs to be completed in many ways, ranging from on-line data entry to paper-and-pencil entry in a booklet. In the latter case, all clients' booklets are submitted to clerical staff to encode the CDR entries.

The Future of Computer-Assisted Behavioral Assessment

Judging from a sampling of what has been written about the potential applications of computers in behavioral assessment to date (e.g., Flowers & Leger, 1982; Kratochwill & Sheridan, 1990; Kratochwill et al.,

1986; Reynolds et al., 1985; Romanczyk, 1984; Tombari et al., 1985), it would seem that the future of computers as tools in the process of behavioral assessment is bright. Computers can also be expected to play an increasingly greater role in the collection, organization, and management of indirect forms of behavioral assessment, including self-report measures, standardized checklists, and rating scales (Fowler et al., 1986).

An intriguing area for future research has to do with the creation of norms for data derived from a system such as TEM-2000. For example, data for patients by various demographics (including psychiatric diagnosis) at a given institution could be processed along with the behavioral data to help answer questions such as these:

- What types of activity, therapy programs, and other interventions work best for this client?

- What course of therapeutic progress could typically be expected from an individual in this type of facility receiving a particular course of treatment?

- How does the therapeutic progress of one patient with a particular diagnosis compare with that of other patients with the same diagnosis? What accounts for differences, if any, in therapeutic progress?

As with other computerized approaches to evaluation, perhaps the greatest challenge for computer-assisted behavioral assessment lies in demonstrating the validity of these methods for the contexts in which they were designed to be used. Also in common with other computerized approaches to evaluation, important issues regarding the use of such systems by unqualified personnel have yet to be resolved.

Table 19–1

Questions to Raise When Considering the Use of a Computer-Administered Version of a Conventional Test

1. Is the computer administration psychometrically equivalent to its traditional counterpart?
   a. Are there differences in the rank order of the scores? If so, data from the conventional version of the test cannot be used with the computerized version.
   b. Are there differences in the mean scores or in the shape of the distribution of scores? If so, data from the conventional version of the test can be used with the computerized version only if an equating formula has been used to adjust the computerized scores for these differences.
2. Has this particular program of a computerized version of the test been shown to be equivalent?
3. Will this computerized version be equivalent on my particular computer? Is my computer different, in some critical way, from the computers used to do the equivalency research?
4. For which of my clients will this computerized version be equivalent? Stated another way: for what types of clients has the program been demonstrated to be equivalent?
5. How will my clients react to the computerized test?

Source: Adapted from Hofer and Green (1985) and Honaker (1990)

Computer-Assisted Test Administration: Equivalency

A key issue regarding the computerized administration of tests that were originally developed for paper-and-pencil administration is that of equivalence. Of the relatively few studies that have been done to test the equivalence of traditional and computerized versions of a test, findings have ranged from major differences as a function of format (French & Beaumont, 1991) to relatively moderate ones (Kobak et al., 1993; Watson et al., 1992). It seems to be the case that some sort of difference emerges as a function of the format of the test administration. In one study, for example, subjects seemed to favor reporting various problems (fears, insomnia, depression, and other mental and physical symptoms) to a computer over reporting them to a clinician (Kobak et al., 1993).

Addressing the equivalence question in an article subtitled "Everything You Should Know About Computer Administration But Will Be Disappointed If You Ask," Honaker (1990) noted that

> in light of the large number of psychologists who use [computer-administered] tests . . . it is disheartening to know that there is not one . . . program available for which we know all the answers [to the questions listed in Table 19–1]. For most programs there is little or no research data which addresses whether or not the computer version is psychometrically equivalent to its traditional counterpart. When research is available, it is either incomplete or inconclusive . . . software developers should consider themselves lucky that the current *Guidelines for Computer-Based Tests and Interpretations* . . . are guidelines rather than standards. (pp. 3–4)

Honaker went on to caution that if a psychologist doubts the equivalency of a particular mode of test administration, the questionable test-administration method should not be used. Of course, as Honaker readily acknowledged, strict adherence to such a caution would render unusable most of the CAPA products currently on the market! Hofer and Green (1985, p. 832) took a somewhat more liberal position when they advised that "interpretation of computer-obtained scores with conventionally obtained data should be rejected if there are plausible reasons for expecting nonequivalence." Moreland (1987, p. 36) directed attention to the unique skills demanded by each of the many different ways a test can be administered when he wrote that "if a computerized administration procedure is comparable to a conventional one, comparable results will be obtained."

In summary, state-of-the-art computer-assisted test administration has not yet progressed to the point where there are more answers than questions regarding the equivalency of various modes of test administration. But research on the many variables involved (such as the work described previously in the On-line Test Administration section of this chapter) shows promise in helping us to understand better exactly why and how data derived from various modes of test administration may differ.

Computer-Assisted Test Interpretation: Validity

Perhaps the most thorny issue regarding computer-assisted test interpretation has to do with the validity of the growing number of such interpretation programs becoming available on the market (Butcher, 1994). "Is this system valid for administration to the people I test?" is the key question of interest for users of CAPA products. For test users in many settings, especially settings that differ markedly from the setting where the CAPA instrument was developed, the answer to this question is probably no.[1] Some of the reasons why that might be the case are touched on below. And as you will see, some of the problems are not confined to CAPA instruments.

A CAPA interpretation may be invalid for widespread use because the standardization sample on which the program was based was not representative of the general population with which the test might be used. Thus, for example, Goldstein and Shelly (1982) questioned the advisability of using an actuarial interpretation system for the Halstead-Reitan Neuropsychological Battery (Russell et al., 1970), developed in a United States armed forces veterans hospital, outside veterans hospitals.

Neuropsychological test data may be validated against "hard" evidence such as brain tumors (Adams et al., 1984). However, other instruments, such as personality inventories, are frequently validated against things like other tests or expert opinions (see, for example, Labeck et al., 1983; and Vale & Keller, 1987). Unfortunately, the standard of accuracy in such studies hinges on the reliability and the validity of the specific test(s) and/or clinician(s) used as a standard; it is possible for the CAPA instrument in question to be at variance with such standards, yet still be a useful tool (Graham, 1967).

Another potential problem in the validation of many CAPA personality inventories—as well as non-CAPA inventories—is the Barnum effect (see

---

1. For somewhat more technical material on why generalization from CAPA products may be difficult, see Mitchell (1986) and Payne and Wiggins (1968).

pages 557–562 for a complete description of this phenomenon). The concern here is that raters charged with the task of assessing the accuracy of computer-derived personality descriptions may rate such descriptions as accurate not because they are in fact individualized descriptions of the testtakers but because they contain generalities true of most people; such generalities cannot be dismissed as inaccurate, but they are probably not very useful.[2]

In his survey of available test-interpretation programs, Lanyon (1984, p. 690) opined that "lack of demonstrated program validity has now become the norm." Writing in 1978, Butcher observed what he called "misstatements of staggering proportions" in some test-interpretation programs—a situation that had only gotten worse as time went on and such programs proliferated (Butcher, 1987). Yet Butcher's ire was clearly tempered by his belief that as invalid as many actuarial interpretation programs might or might not be, they were still generally preferable to strictly clinical interpretations. He made this point in an article written with Raymond Fowler:

> Studies of clinician-generated "interpretations" have yielded unimpressive results. . . . Although the studies of the validity of computerized interpretations thus far reported in the literature leave much to be desired, they are more extensive by far than the studies of individually prepared clinical reports . . . in the two studies that have made a direct comparison, human test interpreters did not do much better than the computer. (Fowler & Butcher, 1986, pp. 94–95)

In recent years, organizations of professionals concerned with testing have published special guidelines for CAPA interpretation systems. Typically, such guidelines encourage the gathering and publication of information to ensure that the computerized interpretation does indeed mimic expert interpretation (see Bartram et al., 1987; and Moreland, 1987). For example, what follows are two of the American Psychological Association's *Guidelines for Computer-Based Tests and Interpretations* (1986) dealing, respectively, with reliability and validity:

23. Information should be provided to users of computerized interpretations concerning the [reliability of interpretive] classifications, including, for example, the number of classifications and the interpretive significance of changes from one classification to adjacent ones. (p. 21)
24. When predictions of particular outcomes or specific recommendations are based on quantitative research, information should be provided showing the . . . relationship between the classification and the probability of [the prediction or recommendation being accurate] in the validation group. (p. 22)

However, since the field of computer-assisted psychological assessment has preceded the development of these guidelines by at least 35 years, it can reasonably be expected that it will be some time before years of professional practice catch up with recent guidelines.

---

2. In recent years, several studies using various instruments have attempted to control for the Barnum effect. See, for example, Eyde, Kowal, and Fishburne (1990), Guastello and Rieke (1990), Jackson and Murray (1986), Moreland and Onstad (1985), Prince and Guastello (1990), Snyder and Hoover (1989), and Snyder, Lachar, and Wills (1988).

Standards for CAPA Products

Professional groups like the American Psychological Association develop guidelines and standards with regard to the use of CAPA products. Unfortunately, it is only APA members who can be held to adherence to such guidelines and standards. Many people who use tests do not belong to professional organizations and, indeed, may not even be members of a licensed profession.

Traditionally, quality control in test-related materials has been maintained by a combination of factors, including (1) efforts made by commercial publishers to publish only materials that pass muster with their professional reviewers and (2) a professional marketplace sufficiently knowledgeable about such products to embrace or reject them. But the computer era in testing is, in at least some respects, changing all of that. Mom-and-pop-type operations offering CAPA-related products are getting into the publishing game in record numbers; and just about anyone with a computer, something the person feels he or she has to offer professionals in the field, and an entrepreneurial bent can play. The phenomenon is due at least in part to the small amount of capital needed to start such a business, in comparison with the large investment that would be needed to found a more traditional publishing company. With a computer, many aspects of such a business—from accounting on spreadsheet programs to the design of advertising on desktop publishing programs—can be done rather cheaply in-house. The major cash outlay for the would-be publisher may be not for the development of or research into the product but, rather, for its advertising and marketing. The CAPA-related product itself, usually a piece of software, may be available in the form of a floppy disk that the publisher purchases blank for small change. Once the publisher's program has been copied onto the disk, that same disk might be sold for hundreds of dollars. Of course, the validity of the test-interpretation (or other) program that the publisher has copied onto the disk is an entirely different matter; it may well be worth hundreds of dollars, or it may not be worth the small change spent on the blank floppy disk.

Currently, no governmental regulation exists for CAPA-related publishing or traditional psychological test publishing. Opinion is divided as to whether such regulation should be introduced. Some have called for governmental regulation of psychological tests, in a manner akin to the way that the Food and Drug Administration oversees the pharmaceutical and cosmetics industries. Others believe that the hodgepodge of checks and balances currently in place for years with respect to traditional tests will also be sufficient for CAPA-related products; according to this view, the marketplace has sufficient sophistication to reject products lacking professional merit. It is probably reasonable to expect no governmental regulation of published psychological testing–related products until "solid" evidence of public harm comes as the result of some unscrupulous publisher.

Access to CAPA Products

The issue of access to CAPA-related products is perhaps the least controversial of the many issues facing test users; professionals tend to agree that only qualified professionals should have access to CAPA-related products. The problem, of course, is much the same as the one that has existed, and continues to exist, with regard to more traditional testing products; and that is the definition of a "qualified professional." Licensing laws help solve that problem in some, but not all, states, and even where licensing laws exist, there is often sufficient vagueness to allow just about anyone access to the use of psychological assessment–related products.

A fear on the part of many testing professionals is that the widespread availability of testing software increases the danger that test security will be breached. Further, as such software falls into the "wrong hands," the stage will be set for abuse of such tests, and public disenchantment with, if not rejection of, psychological tests altogether. As a result, special committees of concerned professional organizations have been formed to study the potential problems (see, for example, Eyde et al., 1988). To date, there is no research to confirm or disconfirm the gnawing suspicion of many testing professionals that CAPA products are being abused more than more conventional test–related products.

And while we are on the subject of the qualified user of psychological tests, we conclude by extending our best wishes to you, the reader, should *you* continue to pursue a career path that will make you a "qualified user." As you have seen in our survey of psychological testing and assessment, many challenging opportunities await individuals with psychometric expertise in a wide range of applied and academic areas in clinical counseling, or other specialties within psychology, business and industry, education and special education . . . the list goes on. And should you decide to pursue such a career, we hope you will think about some of the issues we have raised here as well as elsewhere throughout this book. Perhaps it will be *your* contribution and insights we will be citing in some future edition of *Psychological Testing and Assessment: An Introduction to Tests and Measurement.*

References

Abel, G. G., Blanchard, E. B., Murphy, W. D., Becker, J. V., & Djenderedjian, A. (1981). Two methods of measuring penile response. *Behavior Therapy, 12,* 320–328.

Abel, G. G., Rouleau, J., & Cunningham-Rathner, J. (1986). Sexually aggressive behavior. In W. J. Curran, A. L. McGarry, & S. Shah (Eds.), *Forensic psychiatry and psychology: Perspectives and standards for interdisciplinary practice* (pp. 289–314). Philadelphia: Davis.

Achenbach, T. M. (1978). *Child Behavior Profile.* Bethesda, MD: Laboratory of Developmental Psychology, National Institute of Mental Health.

Achenbach, T. M. (1981). A junior MMPI? *Journal of Personality Assessment, 45,* 332–333.

Achenbach, T. M. (1993). Implications of Multiaxial Empirically Based Assessment for behavior therapy with children. *Behavior Therapy, 24,* 91–116.

Achenbach, T. M., & Edelbrock, C. (1983). *Manual for the Child Behavior Checklist and Revised Child Behavior Profile.* Burlington, VT: University of Vermont, Department of Psychiatry.

Achenbach, T. M., & Edelbrock, C. (1986). *Manual for the Teacher's Report Form and Teacher Version of the Child Behavior Profile.* Burlington, VT: University of Vermont, Department of Psychiatry.

Achenbach, T. M., & Edelbrock, C. (1987). *Manual for the Youth Self-Report and Profile.* Burlington, VT: University of Vermont, Department of Psychiatry.

Achenbach, T. M., McConaughy, S. H., & Howell, C. T. (1987). Child/adolescent behavioral and emotional problems: Implications of cross-informant correlations for situational specificity. *Psychological Bulletin, 101,* 213–232.

Ackerman, M. (1987). Child sexual abuse: Bona fide or fabricated? *American Journal of Family Law, 2,* 181–185.

Ackerman, P. L., & Kanfer, R. (1993). Integrating laboratory and field study for improving selection: Development of a battery for predicting air traffic controller success. *Journal of Applied Psychology, 78,* 413–432.

Adams, K. M. (1980a). In search of Luria's battery: A false start. *Journal of Consulting and Clinical Psychology, 48,* 511–516.

Adams, K. M. (1980b). An end of innocence for behavioral neurology? Adams replies. *Journal of Consulting and Clinical Psychology, 48,* 522–524.

Adams, K. M. (1984). Luria left in the lurch: Unfulfilled promises are not valid tests. *Journal of Clinical Neuropsychology, 6,* 455–458.

Adams, K. M., Kvale, V. I., & Keegan, J. R. (1984). Relative accuracy of three automated systems for neuropsychological interpretation based on two representative tasks. *Journal of Clinical Neuropsychology, 6,* 413–431.

Adams, R. L. (1985). Review of the Luria-Nebraska Neuropsychological Battery. In J. V. Mitchell, Jr. (Ed.), *The ninth mental measurements yearbook.* Lincoln: The Buros Institute of Mental Measurements, University of Nebraska.

Adams-Tucker, C. (1982). Proximate effects of sexual abuse in childhood: A report on 28 children. *American Journal of Psychiatry, 139,* 1252–1256.

Addeo, R. R., Greene, A. F., & Geisser, M. E. (1994). Construct validity of the Robson Self-Esteem Questionnaire in a sample of college students. *Educational and Psychological Measurement, 54,* 439–446.

Adelman, S. A., Fletcher, K. E., Bahnassi, A., & Munetz, M. R. (1991). The Scale for Treatment Integration of the Dually Diagnosed (STIDD): An instrument for assessing intervention strategies in the pharmacotherapy of mentally ill substance abusers. *Drug and Alcohol Dependence, 27,* 35–42.

Adler, A. (1927/1965). *Understanding human nature.* Greenwich, CT: Fawcett.

Adler, A. (1933/1964). *Social interest: A challenge to mankind.* New York: Capricorn.

Adler, T. (1990). Does the 'new' MMPI beat the 'classic'? *APA Monitor, 20* (4), 18–19.

Adler, T. (1993, January). Separate gender norms on tests raise questions. *APA Monitor, 24,* 6.

Ahern, E. (1949). *Handbook of personnel forms and records.* New York: American Management Association.

Aikman, K. G., Belter, R. W., & Finch, A. J. (1992). Human figure drawings: Validity in assessing intellectual level and academic achievement. *Journal of Clinical Psychology, 48,* 114–120.

Airasian, P. W., Madaus, G. F., & Pedulla, J. J. (1979). *Minimal competency testing.* Englewood Cliffs, NJ: Educational Technology Publications.

Alden, D. L., Stayman, D. M., & Hoyer, W. D. (1994). Evaluation strategies of American and Thai consumers. *Psychology and Marketing, 11,* 145–161.

Alderfer, C. (1972). *Existence, relatedness and growth: Human needs in organizational settings.* New York: Free Press.

Alderson, J. C., Krahnke, K. J., & Stansfield, C. W. (1987). *Reviews of English language proficiency tests.* Washington, DC: TESOL.

Alexander, R. C., Surrell, J. A., & Cohle, S. D. (1987). Microwave oven burns in children: An unusual manifestation of child abuse. *Pediatrics, 79,* 255–260.

Algera, J. A., Jansen, P. G., Roe, R. A., & Vijn, O. (1984). Validity generalization: Some critical remarks on the Schmidt-Hunter procedure. *Journal of Occupational Psychology, 57,* 197–210.

Allen, M. J., & Yen, W. M. (1979). *Introduction to measurement theory.* Monterey, CA: Brooks/Cole.

Allison, D. B., Kalinsky, L. B., & Gorman, B. S. (1992). A comparison of the psychometric properties of three measures of dietary restraint. *Psychological Assessment, 4,* 391–398.

Allport, G. W. (1937). *Personality: A psychological interpretation.* New York: Holt.

Allport, G. W., & Odbert, H. S. (1936). Trait-names: A psycholexical study. *Psychological Monographs, 47* (Whole No. 211).

Allport, G. W., Vernon, P. E., & Lindzey, G. (1951). *Study of values* (Rev. ed.). Boston: Houghton Mifflin.

Allred, L. J., & Harris, W. G. (1984). *The nonequivalence of computerized and conventional administrations of the Adjective Checklist.* Unpublished manuscript, Johns Hopkins University.

Alpher, V. S., & Blanton, R. L. (1985). The accuracy of lie detection: Why lie tests based on the polygraph should not be admitted into evidence today. *Law & Psychology Review, 9,* 67–75.

Amabile, T. M., Hill, K. G., Hennessey, B. A., & Tighe, E. M. (1994). The Work Preference Inventory: Assessing intrinsic and extrinsic motivational orientations. *Journal of Personality and Social Psychology, 66,* 950–967.

Ambrosini, P. J., Metz, C., Bianchi, M. D., Rabinovich, H., & Undie, A. (1991). Concurrent validity and psychometric properties of the Beck Depression Inventory in outpatient adolescents. *Journal of the American Academy of Child and Adolescent Psychiatry, 30,* 51–57.

Amelang, M., & Borkenau, P. (1982). [On the factor structure and external validity of some questionnaire scales measuring dimensions of extraversion and neuroticism]. *Zeitschrift fur differentielle und diagnostische psychologie, 3,* 119–146.

American Association of Counseling and Development. (1988). *Ethical standards.* Washington, DC: Author.

American Board of Forensic Odontology, Inc. (1986). Guidelines for analysis of bite marks in forensic investigation. *Journal of the American Dental Association, 12,* 383–386.

American College Testing Program (1973). *Highlights of the ACT technical report.* Iowa City: American College Testing Program.

American College Testing Program. (1978). *The ACT assessment counselor's handbook.* Iowa City: American College Testing Program.

American Law Institute. (1956). *Model penal code.* Tentative Draft Number 4.

American Psychiatric Association. (1968). *Diagnostic and statistical manual of mental disorders* (2nd ed.). Washington, DC: Author.

American Psychiatric Association. (1980). *Diagnostic and statistical manual of mental disorders* (3rd ed.). Washington, DC: Author.

American Psychiatric Association. (1987). *Diagnostic and statistical manual of mental disorders* (3rd ed., rev.). Washington, DC: Author.

American Psychiatric Association. (1994). *Diagnostic and statistical manual of mental disorders* (4th ed.). Washington, DC: Author.

American Psychological Association. (1953). *Ethical standards of psychologists.* Washington, DC: Author.

American Psychological Association. (1954). *Technical recommendations for psychological tests and diagnostic techniques.* Washington, DC: Author.

American Psychological Association. (1966a). Automated test scoring and interpretation practices. In Proceedings of the American Psychological Association. *American Psychologist, 21,* 1141.

American Psychological Association. (1966b). *Standards for educational and psychological tests and manuals.* Washington, DC: Author.

American Psychological Association. (1967). *Casebook on ethical standards of psychologists.* Washington, DC: Author.

American Psychological Association. (1974). *Standards for educational and psychological tests and manuals.* Washington, DC: Author.

American Psychological Association. (1977). Standards for providers of psychological services. *American Psychologist, 32,* 495–505.

American Psychological Association. (1985). *Standards for educational and psychological testing.* Washington, DC: Author.

American Psychological Association, Division of Industrial and Organizational Psychology. (1980). *Principles for the validation and use of personnel selection procedures* (2nd ed.). Washington, DC: American Psychological Association.

American Psychological Association. (1981a). *Ethical standards of psychologists.* Washington, DC: Author.

American Psychological Association, Committee on Professional Standards. (1981b). Specialty guidelines for the delivery of services by clinical psychologists. *American Psychologist, 36,* 640–651.

American Psychological Association, Committee on Professional Standards. (1981c). Specialty guidelines for the delivery of services by counseling psychologists. *American Psychologist, 36,* 652–663.

American Psychological Association, Committee on Professional Standards. (1981d). Specialty guidelines for the delivery of services by industrial/organizational psychologists. *American Psychologist, 36,* 664–669.

American Psychological Association, Committee on Professional Standards. (1981e). Specialty guidelines for the delivery of services by school psychologists. *American Psychologist, 36,* 670–681.

American Psychological Association. (1981f). Ethical principles of psychologists. *American Psychologist, 36,* 633–638.

American Psychological Association, Committee on Professional Standards and Committee on Psychological Tests and Assessment. (1986). *Guide-*

lines for computer-based tests and interpretations. Washington, DC: Author.

American Psychological Association. (1987). *Casebook on ethical principles of psychologists*. Washington, DC: Author.

American Psychological Association. (1990). Ethical principles of psychologists (Amended June 2, 1989). *American Psychologist, 45*, 390–395.

American Psychological Association. (1991a). *Questionnaires used in the prediction of trustworthiness in pre-employment selection decisions: An APA Task Force Report*. Washington, DC: Author.

American Psychological Association. (1991b). Ethical principles revised. *APA Monitor, 21*(6), 28–32.

American Psychological Association. (1992). Ethical principles of psychologists and code of conduct. *American Psychologist, 47*, 1597–1611.

American Psychological Association. (1993, January). Call for book proposals for test instruments. *APA Monitor, 24*, 12.

American Psychological Association. (in press). *Standards for educational and psychological testing*. Washington, DC: Author.

Ames, L. B., Learned, J., Metraux, R. W., & Walker, R. N. (1952). *Child Rorschach responses*. New York: Paul B. Hoeber.

Ames, L. B., Metraux, R. W., Rodell, J. L., & Walker, R. N. (1974). *Child Rorschach responses: Developmental trends from two to ten years* (Rev. ed.). New York: Bruner/Mazel.

Ames, L. B., Metraux, R. W., & Walker, R. N. (1971). *Adolescent Rorschach responses: Developmental trends from ten to sixteen years*. New York: Bruner/Mazel.

Anastasi, A. (1968). *Psychological testing* (3rd ed.). New York: Macmillan.

Anderson, R. J., & Sisco, F. H. (1977). *Standardization of the WISC-R Performance Scale for deaf children*. Washington, DC: Office of Demographic Studies, Gallaudet College.

Andrew, G. (1953). The selection and appraisal of test pictures. In G. Andrew, S. W. Hartwell, M. L. Hutt, & R. E. Walton (Eds.), *The Michigan Picture Test* (No. 7-2144). Chicago: Science Research Associates.

Angoff, W. H. (1962). Scales with nonmeaningful origins and units of measurement. *Educational and Psychological Measurement, 22*, 27–34.

Angoff, W. H. (1964). Technical problems of obtaining equivalent scores on tests. *Educational and Psychological Measurement, 1*, 11–13.

Angoff, W. H. (1966). Can useful general-purpose equivalency tables be prepared for different college admissions tests? In A. Anastasi (Ed.), *Testing problems in perspective* (pp. 251–264). Washington, DC: American Council on Education.

Angoff, W. H. (1971). Scales, norms, and equivalent scores. In R. L. Thorndike (Ed.), *Educational measurement* (2nd ed.). Washington, DC: American Council on Education.

Anthony, L., LeResche, L., Niaz, U., et al. (1982). Lim-its of the "Mini-Mental State" as a screening test for dementia and delirium among hospital patients. *Psychological Medicine, 12*, 397–408.

Appollonio, I., Grafman, J., Clark, K., & Nichelli, P. (1994). Implicit and explicit memory in patients with Parkinson's disease with and without dementia. *Archives of Neurology, 51*, 359–367.

Archer, R. P. (1992). Review of the Minnesota Multiphasic Personality Inventory—2. In J. J. Kramer & J. C. Conoley (Eds.), *The eleventh mental measurements yearbook*. Lincoln: The Buros Institute of Mental Measurements, University of Nebraska.

Archer, R. P., & Jacobson, J. M. (1993). Are critical items "critical" for the MMPI-A? *Journal of Personality Assessment, 61*, 547–556.

Archer, R. P., Maruish, M., Imhof, E. A., & Piotrowski, C. (1991). Psychological test usage with adolescent clients: 1990 survey findings. *Professional Psychology: Research and Practice, 22*, 247–252.

Archer, R. P., Pancoase, D. L., & Gordon, R. A. (1994). The development of the MMPI-A Immaturity Scale: Findings for normal and clinical samples. *Journal of Personality Assessment, 62*, 145–156.

Arizmendi, T., Paulsen, K., & Domino, G. (1981). The Matching Familiar Figures Test: A primary, secondary, and tertiary evaluation. *Journal of Clinical Psychology, 37*, 812–818.

Arnetz, B. B., Wasserman, J., Petrini, B., et al. (1987). Immune function in unemployed women. *Psychosomatic Medicine, 19*, 3–12.

Arthur, G. (1950). The Arthur adaptation of the Leiter International Performance Scale. *Journal of Clinical Psychology, 5*, 345–349.

Arvey, R. D. (1979). *Fairness in selecting employees*. Reading, MA: Addison-Wesley.

Ary, D. D., Toobert, D., Wilson, W., & Glasgow, R. E. (1986). Patient perspectives on factors contributing to non-adherence to diabetes regimen. *Diabetes Care, 9*, 168–172.

Association of Personnel Test Publishers (APTP). (1990). Model guidelines for preemployment integrity testing programs. Washington, DC: APTP.

Atkin, C. K. (1978). Observation of parent-child interaction in supermarket decision-making. *Journal of Marketing, 42*, 41–45.

Atkinson, J. W. (Ed.). (1958). *Motives in fantasy, action, and society*. Princeton, NJ: Van Nostrand.

Atkinson, J. W. (1981). Studying personality in the context of an advanced motivational psychology. *American Psychologist, 36*, 117–128.

Atkinson, L., Bevc, I., Dickens, S., & Blackwell, J. (1992). Concurrent validities of the Stanford-Binet (Fourth Edition), Leiter, and Vineland with developmentally delayed children. *Journal of School Psychology, 30*, 165–173.

Atlas, J. A., & Miller, A. L. (1992). Human figure drawings as estimates of intelligence for adolescents in an inpatient psychiatric unit. *Perceptual and Motor Skills, 75*, 690.

Austin, J. J., (1970). *Educational and Developmental Profile*. Muskegon, MI: Research Concepts.

Ayres, A. J. (1972). *Southern California Sensory Integration Test.* Los Angeles: Western Psychological Services.

Ayres, R. R., & Cooley, E. J. (1986). Sequential versus simultaneous processing on the K-ABC: Validity in predicting learning success. *Journal of Psychoeducational Assessment, 4,* 211–220.

Bachman, J. G., Wallace, J. M., O'Malley, P. M., et al. (1991). Racial/ethnic differences in smoking, drinking, and illicit drug use among American high school seniors, 1976–1989. *American Journal of Public Health, 812,* 372–377.

Back, R., & Dana, R. H. (1977). Examiner sex bias and Wechsler Intelligence Scale for Children scores. *Journal of Consulting and Clinical Psychology, 45,* 500.

Bagby, R. M., Rogers, R., Buiis, T., & Kalemba, V. (1994). Malingered and defensive response styles on the MMPI-2: An examination of the validity scales. *Assessment, 1,* 31–38.

Bain, S. K. (1993). Sequential and simultaneous processing in children with learning disabilities: An attempted replication. *The Journal of Special Education, 27,* 235–246.

Bainsbridge, W. S. (1991). Computerized sociometric marketing: Advances and prospects. *Psychology & Marketing, 8,* 259–273.

Baker, E. L., O'Neill, H. F., & Linn, R. L. (1993). Policy and validity prospects for performance-based assessment. *American Psychologist, 48,* 1210–1218.

Baker, F. B. (1988). Computer technology in test construction and processing. In R. L. Linn (Ed.), *Educational measurement* (3rd ed.). New York: American Council on Education/Macmillan.

Balasubramanian, S. K., & Kamakura, W. A. (1989). Measuring consumer attitudes toward the marketplace with tailored interviews. *Journal of Marketing Research, 26,* 311–326.

Baldwin, A. L., Kalhorn, J., & Breese, F. H. (1945). Patterns of parent behavior. *Psychological Monographs, 58* (Whole No. 268).

Ball, J. D., Archer, R. P., Gordon, R. A., & French, J. (1991). Rorschach depression indices with children and adolescents: Concurrent validity findings. *Journal of Personality Assessment, 57,* 465–476.

Barbaree, H. E., & Marshall, W. L. (1989). Erectile responses among heterosexual child molesters, father-daughter incest offenders, and matched non-offenders: Five distinct age preference profiles. *Canadian Journal of Behavioral Science, 21,* 70–82.

Barbarin, O. A., & Chesler, M. (1986). The medical context of parental coping with childhood cancer. *American Journal of Community Psychology, 14,* 221–235.

Barclay, A., & Yater, A. (1969). A comparative study of the Wechsler Preschool and Primary Scale of Intelligence and the Stanford-Binet Intelligence Scale, Form L-M among culturally deprived children. *Journal of Consulting and Clinical Psychology, 33,* 257.

Bardis, P. D. (1975). The Borromean family. *Social Science, 50,* 144–158.

Bardos, A. N. (1993). Human figure drawings: Abusing the abused. *School Psychology Quarterly, 8,* 177–181.

Barends, A., Westen, D., Leigh, J., Silbert, D., & Byers, S. (1990). Assessing affect-tone of relationship paradigms from TAT and interview data. *Psychological Assessment: A Journal of Consulting & Clinical Psychology, 2,* 329–332.

Barker, R. (1963). On the nature of the environment. *Journal of Social Issues, 19,* 17–38.

Barko, N. (1993, August). What's your child's emotional IQ? *Working Mother, 16,* 33–35.

Baron, J., & Norman, M. F. (1992). SATs, achievement tests, and high-school class rank as predictors of college performance. *Educational and Psychological Measurement, 52,* 1047–1055.

Barrera, M. (1981). Preliminary development of a scale of social support. *American Journal of Community Psychology, 9,* 435–447.

Bartell, T. P., & Fremer, J. (1986). *Procedures for developing a code of fair testing in education.* Paper presented at the annual meeting of the American Psychological Association, Washington, DC.

Bartram, D., Beaumont, J. G., Cornford, T., & Dann, P. L. (1987). Recommendations for the design of software for computer based assessment: Summary statement. *Bulletin of the British Psychological Society, 40,* 86–87.

Bass, B. M. (1956). Development of a structured disguised personality test. *Journal of Applied Psychology, 40,* 393–397.

Bass, B. M. (1957). Validity studies of proverbs personality test. *Journal of Applied Psychology, 41,* 158–160.

Bass, B. M. (1958). Famous Sayings Test: General manual. *Psychological Reports, 4,* Monograph Number 6.

Batchelor, E. S., Gray, J. W., & Dean, R. S. (1990). Empirical testing of a cognitive model to account for neuropsychological functioning underlying arithmetic problem solving. *Journal of Learning Disabilities, 23*(1), 38–42.

Batchelor, E., Jr., Sowles, G., Dean, R. S., & Fischer, W. (1991). Construct validity of the Halstead-Reitan Neuropsychological Battery for children with learning disorders. *Journal of Psychoeducational Assessment, 9,* 16–31.

Batson, D. C. (1975). Attribution as a mediator of bias in helping. *Journal of Personality and Social Psychology, 32,* 455–466.

Baugh, V. S., & Carpenter, B. L. (1962). Comparison of delinquents and non-delinquents. *Journal of Social Psychology, 56,* 73–78.

Baughman, E. E., & Dahlstrom, W. B. (1968). *Negro and white children: A psychological study in the rural south.* New York: Academic Press.

Bauman, M. K. (1974). Blind and partially sighted. In M. V. Wisland, (Ed.), *Psychoeducational diagnosis of exceptional children* (pp. 159–189). Springfield, IL: Charles C. Thomas.

Bauman, M. K., & Kropf, C. A. (1979). Psychological tests used with blind and visually handicapped persons. *School Psychology Digest, 8,* 257–270.

Bavolek, S. J. (1984). *Handbook for the adult-adolescent parenting inventory.* Eau Claire, WI: Family Development Associates.

Baxter, J. C., Brock, B., Hill, P. C., & Rozelle, R. M. (1981). Letters of recommendation: A question of value. *Journal of Applied Psychology, 66,* 296–301.

Baydoun, R. B., & Neuman, G. A. (1992). The future of the General Aptitude Test Battery (GATB) for use in public and private testing. *Journal of Business and Psychology, 7,* 81–91.

Bayley, N. (1955). On the growth of intelligence. *American Psychologist, 10,* 805–818.

Bayley, N. (1959). Value and limitations of infant testing. *Children, 5,* 129–133.

Bayley, N. (1969). *Bayley Scales of Infant Development: Birth to two years.* New York: Psychological Corporation.

Bayley, N. (1993). *Bayley Scales of Infant Development (2nd Edition) manual.* San Antonio, TX: The Psychological Corporation.

Bear, D. M., & Fedio, P. (1977). Quantitative analysis of interictal behavior in temporal lobe epilepsy. *Archives of Neurology, 34,* 454–467.

Beaumont, J. G., & French, C. F. (1987). A clinical field study of eight automated psychometric procedures: The Leicester/DHSS Project. *International Journal of Man-Machine Studies, 26,* 311–320.

Beavers, R. (1985). *Manual of Beavers-Timberlawn Family Evaluation Scale and Family Style Evaluation.* Dallas, TX: Southwest Family Institute.

Bechtel, G. (1985). Generalizing the Rasch model for consumer rating scales. *Marketing Science, 4,* 62–73.

Beck, A. T. (1963). Thinking and depression: 1. Idiosyncratic content and cognitive distortions. *Archives of General Psychiatry, 9,* 324–333.

Beck, A. T. (1967). *Depression: Causes and treatments.* Philadelphia: University of Pennsylvania Press.

Beck, A. T. (1976). *Cognitive theory and emotional disorders.* New York: International Universities Press.

Beck, A. T. (1978). Depression Inventory. Philadelphia, PA: Center for Cognitive Therapy.

Beck, A. T., & Beamesderfer, A. (1974). Assessment of depression: The Depression Inventory. In P. Picket (Ed.), *Psychological measurements in psychopharmacology: Modern problems in pharmacopsychiatry* (Vol. 7; pp. 151–169). Basel, Switzerland: Kargel.

Beck, A. T., Rush, A. J., Shaw, B. F., & Emery, G. (1979). *Cognitive therapy for depression.* New York: Guilford Press.

Beck, A. T., & Steer, R. A. (1993). *Beck Depression Inventory manual.* San Antonio, TX: The Psychological Corporation.

Beck, A. T., Steer, R. A., Epstein, N., & Brown, G. (1990). Beck Self-Concept Test. *Psychological Assessment: A Journal of Consulting & Clinical Psychology, 2,* 191–197.

Beck, A. T., & Stein, D. (1961). Development of a Self-Concept test. Unpublished manuscript, University of Pennsylvania School of Medicine, Center for Cognitive Therapy, Philadelphia.

Beck, A. T., Ward, C. H., Mendelson, M., Mock, J., & Erbaugh, J. (1961). An inventory for measuring depression. *Archives of General Psychiatry, 4,* 561–571.

Beck, S. J. (1944). *Rorschach's test: Vol. 1. Basic processes.* New York: Grune & Stratton.

Beck, S. J. (1945). *Rorschach's test: Vol. 2. A variety of personality pictures.* New York: Grune & Stratton.

Beck, S. J. (1952). *Rorschach's test: Vol. 3. Advances in interpretation.* New York: Grune & Stratton.

Beck, S. J. (1960). *The Rorschach experiment.* New York: Grune & Stratton.

Becker, H. A., Needleman, H. L., & Kotelchuck, M. (1978). Child abuse and dentistry: Orificial trauma and its recognition by dentists. *Journal of the American Dental Association, 97*(1), 24–28.

Becker, R. E., & Heimberg, R. G. (1988). Assessment of social skills. In A. S. Bellack & M. Hersen (Eds.), *Behavioral assessment: A practical handbook* (3rd. ed.). New York: Pergamon Press.

Begault, D. R. (1993). Head-up auditory displays for traffic collision avoidance advisories: A preliminary investigation. *Human Factors, 35,* 707–717.

Beier, E. G., & Sternberg, D. P. (1977). Marital communication. *Journal of Communication, 27,* 92–100.

Bellack, A. S. (1983). Recurrent problems in the behavioral assessment of social skill. *Behaviour Research and Therapy, 21,* 29–42.

Bellack, A. S., & Hersen, M. (Eds.). (1988). *Behavioral assessment: A practical guide* (3rd ed.). Elmsford, NY: Pergamon Press.

Bellack, A. S., Hersen, M., & Lamparski, D. (1979). Role-play tests for assessing social skills: Are they valid? Are they useful? *Journal of Consulting and Clinical Psychology, 47,* 335–342.

Bellack, A. S., Morrison, R. L., Mueser, K. T., Wade, J. H., & Sayers, S. L. (1990). Role play for assessing the social competence of psychiatric patients. *Psychological Assessment: A Journal of Consulting and Clinical Psychology, 2,* 248–255.

Bellak, L. (1944). The concept of projection: An experimental investigation and study of the concept. *Psychiatry, 7,* 353–370.

Bellak, L. (1971). *The TAT and CAT in clinical use* (2nd ed.). New York: Grune & Stratton.

Bellak, L., & Bellak, S. (1965). *The CAT-H—A human modification.* Larchmont, NY: C.P.S.

Bellak, L., & Bellak, S. S. (1973). *Senior Apperception Technique.* New York: C.P.S.

Bellak, L., & Hurvich, M. (1966). A human modification of the Children's Apperception Test. *Journal of Projective Techniques, 30,* 228–242.

Belter, R. W., Lipovsky, J. A., & Finch, A. J., Jr. (1989). Rorschach egocentricity index and self concept in children and adolescents. *Journal of Personality Assessment, 53,* 783–789.

Bem, D. J., & Allen, A. (1974). On predicting some of the people some of the time: The search for cross-situational consistencies in behavior. *Psychological Review, 81,* 506–520.

Bem, D. J., & Funder, D. C. (1978). Predicting more of the people more of the time: Assessing the personality of situations. *Psychological Review, 85,* 485–501.

Bender, L. (1938). A visual-motor gestalt test and its clinical use. *American Orthopsychiatric Association Research Monographs,* No. 3.

Bender, L. (1970). The visual-motor gestalt test in the diagnosis of learning disabilities. *Journal of Special Education, 4,* 29–39.

Benedict, R. H., Schretlen, D., & Bobholz, J. H. (1992). Concurrent validity of three WAIS-R short forms in psychiatric inpatients. *Psychological Assessment, 4,* 322–328.

Benjamin, J. (1964). A method for distinguishing and evaluating formal thinking disorders in schizophrenia. In L. Kasanin (Ed.), *Language and thought in schizophrenia* (pp. 65–88). New York: Norton.

Bennett, F., Hughes, A., & Hughes, H. (1979). Assessment techniques for deaf-blind children. *Exceptional Children, 45,* 287–288.

Bennett, G., Seashore, H., & Wesman, A. (1974). *The fifth edition manual for the Differential Aptitude Tests—Forms S and T.* New York: Psychological Corporation.

Ben-Porath, Y. S., & Butcher, J. N. (1989). The comparability of MMPI and MMPI-2 scales and profiles. *Psychological Assessment: A Journal of Consulting and Clinical Psychology, 1,* 345–347.

Ben-Porath, Y. S., Hostetler, K., Butcher, J. N., & Graham, J. R. (1989). New sub-scales for the MMPI-2 social introversion (Si) scale. *Psychological Assessment: A Journal of Consulting and Clinical Psychology, 1,* 169–175.

Benton, A. L. (1994). Neuropsychological assessment. *Annual Review of Psychology, 45,* 1–25.

Berg, M. (1984). Expanding the parameters of psychological testing. *Bulletin of the Menninger Clinic, 48,* 10–24.

Berg, M. (1985). The feedback process in diagnostic psychological testing. *Bulletin of the Menninger Clinic, 49,* 52–69.

Berg, R., Franzen, M., & Wedding, D. (1987). *Screening for brain impairment: A manual for mental health practice.* New York: Springer.

Berk, R. A. (Ed.). (1982). *Handbook of methods for detecting test bias.* Baltimore: The Johns Hopkins University Press.

Berkeley, G. (1710). *A treatise concerning the principles of human knowledge.*

Bernardin, H. J. (1978). Effects of rater training on leniency and halo errors in student ratings of instructors. *Journal of Applied Psychology, 63,* 301–308.

Bernardin, H. J., & Buckley, M. R. (1981). Strategies in rater training. *Academy of Management Review, 6,* 205–212.

Bernhardt, G. R., Cole, D. J., & Ryan, C. W. (1993). Improving career decision making with adults: Use of portfolios. *Journal of Employment Counseling, 30,* 67–72.

Bernstein, L. (1956). The examiner as an inhibiting factor in clinical testing. *Journal of Consulting Psychology, 20,* 287–290.

Berry, J. W. (1976). *Human ecology and cognitive style: Comparative studies in cultural and psychological adaptation.* Beverly Hills: Sage.

Bersoff, D. N., & Hofer, P. (1988). Legal implications of computer-based test interpretation. In T. B. Gutkin & S. L. Wise (Eds.), *The computer as adjunct to the decision-making process.* Hillside, NJ: Erlbaum.

Besetsny, L. K., Ree, M. J., & Earles, J. A. (1993). Special test for computer programmers? Not needed: The predictive efficiency of the Electronic Data Processing Test for a sample of Air Force recruits. *Educational and Psychological Measurement, 53,* 507–511.

Besharov, D. J. (1985). "Doing something" about child abuse: The need to narrow the grounds for state intervention. *Harvard Journal of Law and Public Policy, 8,* 539–589.

Bienvenu, M. J., Sr. (1978). *A counselor's guide to accompany a Marital Communication Inventory.* Saluda, NC: Family Life.

Bigler, E. D., & Ehrenfurth, J. W. (1980). Critical limitations of the Bender-Gestalt test in clinical neuropsychology: Response to Lacks. *Clinical Neuropsychology, 2,* 88–90.

Bigler, E. D., & Ehrenfurth, J. W. (1981). The continued inappropriate singular use of the Bender Visual Motor Gestalt Test. *Professional Psychology, 12,* 562–569.

Billmire, M. G., & Myers, P. A. (1985). Serious head injury in infants: Accident or abuse? *Pediatrics, 75,* 34–342.

Binet, A., & Henri, V. (1895a). La psychologie individuelle. *L'Année Psychologique, 2,* 411–465.

Binet, A., & Henri, V. (1895b). La mémoire des mots. *L'Année Psychologique, 1,* 1–23.

Binet, A., & Henri, V. (1895c). La memoire des phrases. *L'Année Psychologique, 1,* 24–59.

Binet, A., & Simon, T. (1905). Méthodes nouvelles pour le diagnostic du niveau intellectuel des anormaux. *L'Année Psychologique, 11,* 191–244.

Bing, R., & Vischer, A. L. (1919, April 26). Some remarks on the psychology of internment, based on observations of prisoners of war in Switzerland. *Lancet,* 696–697.

Birch, H. G., & Diller, L. (1959). Rorschach signs of "organicity": A physiological basis for perceptual disturbances. *Journal of Projective Techniques, 23,* 184–197.

Birney, R. C., Burdick, H., & Teevan, R. C. (1969). *Fear of failure.* New York: Van Nostrand Reinhold.

Birren, J. E. (1968). Increments and decrements in the intellectual status of the aged. *Psychiatric Research Reports, 23,* 207–214.

Bizot, E. B., & Goldman, S. H. (1993). Prediction of satisfactoriness and satisfaction: An 8-year follow up. Special issue: The theory of work adjustment. *Journal of Vocational Behavior, 43,* 19–29.

Black, H. (1963). *They shall not pass.* New York: Morrow.

Black, H. C. (1979). *Black's law dictionary* (Rev. ed.). St. Paul: West Publishing.

Blader, J. C., & Marshall, W. L. (1984). The relationship between cognitive and erectile measures of sexual arousal in non-rapist males as a function of depicted aggression. *Behaviour Research and Therapy, 22,* 623–630.

Blain, G. H., Bergner, R. M., Lewis, M. L., & Goldstein, M. A. (1981). The use of objectively scorable House-Tree-Person indicators to establish child abuse. *Journal of Clinical Psychology, 37,* 667–673.

Blanchard, E. B., Kolb, L. C., & Prins, A. (1991). Psychophysiological responses in the diagnosis of posttraumatic stress disorder in Vietnam veterans. *The Journal of Nervous and Mental Disease, 179,* 97–101.

Blanchard, E. B., & Young, L. D. (1974). Clinical applications of biofeedback training: A review of evidence. *Archives of General Psychiatry, 30,* 573–589.

Blatt, S. J., Wein, S. J., Chevron, E., & Quinlan, D. M. (1979). Parental representations and depression in normal young adults. *Journal of Abnormal Psychology, 88,* 388–397.

Blazer, D. (1982). Social support and mortality in an elderly community population. *American Journal of Epidemiology, 115,* 684–694.

Block, J. (1961). *The q-sort method in personality assessment and psychiatric research.* Springfield, IL: Charles C. Thomas.

Block, J. (1965). *Challenge of response sets.* New York: Appleton-Century-Crofts.

Block, J., Block, J. H., & Harrington, D. M. (1974). Some misgivings about the Matching Family Figures Test as a measure of reflection-impulsivity. *Developmental Psychology, 10,* 611–632.

Bloom, A. S., Allard, A. M., Zelko, F. A. J., Brill, W. J., Topinka, C. W., & Pfohl, W. (1988). Differential validity of the K-ABC for lower functioning preschool children versus those of higher ability. *American Journal of Mental Retardation, 93*(3), 273–277.

Bloom, B. (1964). *Stability and change in human characteristics.* New York: Wiley.

Bloxom, B. M. (1978). Review of the 16 PF. In O. K. Buros (Ed.), *The eighth mental measurements yearbook.* Lincoln: The Buros Institute of Mental Measurements, University of Nebraska.

Blum, G. S. (1950). *The Blacky pictures: A technique for the exploration of personality dynamics.* New York: Psychological Corporation.

Blum, M. L., & Naylor, J. C. (1968). *Industrial psychology: Its theoretical and social foundations.* (Rev. ed.). New York: Harper & Row.

Bock, R. D., & Jones, L. V. (1968). *The measurement and prediction of judgment and choice.* San Francisco: Holden-Day.

Boivin, M. J., Green, S. D. R., Davies, A. G., et al. (1995). A preliminary evaluation of the cognitive and motor effects of pediatric HIV infection in Zairian children. *Health Psychology, 14,* 13–21.

Bond, G. G., Aiken, L. S., & Somerville, S. C. (1992). The health belief model and adolescents with insulin-dependent diabetes mellitus. *Health Psychology, 11,* 190–198.

Bonnie, R. J. (1983). The moral basis of the insanity defense. *American Bar Association Journal, 69,* 194–197.

Boone, D. E. (1991). Item-reduction vs. subtest-reduction short forms on the WAIS-R with psychiatric inpatients. *Journal of Clinical Psychology, 47,* 271–276.

Boone, D. E. (1994). Validity of the MMPI-2 Depression content scale with psychiatric inpatients. *Psychological Reports, 74,* 159–162.

Booth, A., & Edwards, J. (1983). Measuring marital instability. *Journal of Marriage and the Family, 45,* 387–393.

Booth-Kewley, S., & Friedman, H. S. (1987). Psychological predictors of heart disease: A quantitative review. *Psychological Bulletin, 101,* 343–362.

Boring, E. G. (1923, June 6). Intelligence as the tests test it. *The New Republic,* pp. 35–37.

Boring, E. G. (1950). *A history of experimental psychology* (Rev. ed.). New York: Appleton-Century-Crofts.

Borman, W. C., & Hallman, G. L. (1991). Observation accuracy for assessors of work-sample performance: Consistency across task and individual-differences correlates. *Journal of Applied Psychology, 76,* 11–18.

Boulton, B. F. (1978). Review of the 16 PF. In O. K. Buros (Ed.), *The eighth mental measurements yearbook.* Lincoln: The Buros Institute of Mental Measurements, University of Nebraska.

Boyle, J. P. (1987). Intelligence, reasoning, and language proficiency. *Modern Language Journal, 71,* 277–288.

Bracken, B. A. (1985). A critical review of the Kaufman Assessment Battery for Children (K-ABC). *School Psychology Review, 14,* 21–36.

Bracken, B. A. (1992). Review of the Wechsler Preschool and Primary Scale of Intelligence—Revised. In J. J. Kramer & J. C. Conoley (Eds.), *The eleventh mental measurements yearbook.* Lincoln: The Buros Institute of Mental Measurements, University of Nebraska.

Bracken, B. A., & McCallum, R. S. (1981). Comparison of the PPVT and PPVT-R for white and black preschool males and females. *Educational and Psychological Research, 1,* 79–85.

Bracken, B. A., & Prasse, D. P. (1982). Comparison of the PPVT, PPVT-R, and intelligence tests used for the placement of black, white, and Hispanic EMR students. *Journal of School Psychology, 19,* 304–311.

Bracken, B. A., Prasse, D. P., & McCallum, R. S. (1984). Peabody Picture Vocabulary Test—Revised. An appraisal and review. *School Psychology Review, 13,* 49–60.

Bracy-Nipper, D., Karmos, J. S., & Mouw, J. (1987). WISC-R vs. DCAT for predicting academic performance in a high school learning disabled population. *Journal of Instructional Psychology, 14,* 41–47.

Braden, J. P. (1990). Do deaf persons have a characteristic psychometric profile on the Wechsler Performance Scales? *Journal of Psychoeducational Assessment, 8,* 518–526.

Braden, J. P. (1992). Intellectual assessment of deaf and hard-of-hearing people: A quantitative and qualitative research synthesis. *School Psychology Review, 21*, 82–84.

Bradley, G. W., & Bradley, L. A. (1977). Experimenter prestige and feedback related to acceptance of genuine personality interpretations and self-attitude. *Journal of Personality Assessment, 41*, 178–185.

Bradley-Johnson, S. (1986). *Psychological assessment of visually impaired and blind students: Infancy through high school.* Austin, TX: Pro-Ed.

Bradley-Johnson, S., & Harris, S. (1990). Best practices in working with students with a visual loss. In A. Thomas & J. Grimes (Eds.), *Best practices in school psychology II* (pp. 871–885). Washington, DC: National Association of School Psychologists.

Bradway, K. P. (1945). Predictive values of Stanford-Binet preschool items. *Journal of Educational Psychology, 36*, 1–16.

Bradway, K. P., & Thompson, C. W. (1962). Intelligence at adulthood: A twenty-five-year follow-up. *Journal of Educational Psychology, 53*, 1–14.

Braginsky, B. M., Braginsky, D. D., & Ring, K. (1969). *Methods of madness.* New York: Holt, Rinehart & Winston.

Bramlett, R. K., Smith, B. L., & Edmonds, J. (1994). A comparison of nonreferred, learning-disabled, and mildly retarded students utilizing the Social Skills Rating System. *Psychology in the Schools, 31*, 13–19.

Brand, H. J. (1989). Reliability of the Frostig Test of Visual Perception in a South African sample. *Perceptual and Motor Skills, 69*, 273–274.

Brandt, P. A., & Weinert, C. (1981). The PRQ—A Social support measure. *Nursing Research, 30*, 277–280.

Brannigan, G. G., Ash, T., & Margolis, H. (1980). Impulsivity-reflectivity and children's intellectual performance. *Journal of Personality Assessment, 44*, 41–43.

Brassard, M., et al. (Eds.). (1986). *The psychological maltreatment of children and youth.* Elmsford, NY: Pergamon Press.

Braswell, J. (1978). The College Board Scholastic Aptitude Test: An overview of the mathematical portion. *Mathematics Teacher, 71*(3), 168–180.

Bray, D. W. (1964). The management progress study. *American Psychologist, 19*, 419–429.

Bray, D. W. (1982). The assessment center and the study of lives. *American Psychologist, 37*, 180–189.

Bray, D. W., Campbell, R. J., & Grant, D. L. (1979). *Formative years in business.* Huntington, NY: Krieger Publishing.

Bray, G. A. (1986). Effects of obesity on health and happiness. In K. D. Brownell & J. P. Foreyt (Eds.), *Handbook of eating disorders* (pp. 3–44). New York: Basic Books.

Breen, M. J. (1981). Comparison of the Wechsler Intelligence Scale for Children—Revised and the Peabody Picture Vocabulary Test—Revised for a referred population. *Psychological Reports, 49*, 717–718.

Bresolin, M. J., Jr. (1984). A comparative study of computer administration of the Minnesota Multiphasic Personality Inventory in an inpatient psychiatric setting. *Dissertation Abstracts International, 46*, 295B. (University Microfilms No. 85-06, 377)

Brewer, S. (1987, January 11). A perfect package, yes, but how 'bout the name? *Journal-News* (Rockland County, NY), pp. H-1, H-18.

Brickman, G. A. (1980, April). Uses of voice-pitch analysis. *Journal of Advertising Research, 20*, 69–73.

Bridgeman, B. (1992). A comparison of quantitative questions on open-ended and multiple-choice formats. *Journal of Educational Measurement, 29*, 253–271.

Bridgeman, B., & Rock, D. A. (1993). Relationships among multiple-choice and open-ended analytical questions. *Journal of Educational Measurement, 30*, 313–329.

Briggs, K. C., Myers, I. B., & Saunders, D. (1987). *Type Differentiation Indicator (Research Edition).* Palo Alto, CA: Consulting Psychologists Press.

Brim, D., Glass, D., Nevlinger, J., Firestone, I., & Lerner, S. (1969). *American beliefs and attitudes about intelligence.* New York: Russell Sage Foundation.

Bringle, R., Roach, S., Andler, C., & Evenbeck, S. (1979). Measuring the intensity of jealous reactions. *Catalogue of Selected Documents in Psychology, 9*, 23–24.

Brittain, H. L. (1907). A study in imagination. *The Pedagogical Seminary, 14*, 137–207.

Brody, D., Serby, M., Etienne, N., & Kalkstein, D. S. (1991). Olfactory identification deficits in HIV infection. *American Journal of Psychiatry, 148*, 248–250.

Brody, M. L., Walsh, B. T., & Devlin, M. J. (1994). Binge eating disorder: Reliability and validity of a new diagnostic category. *Journal of Consulting and Clinical Psychology, 62*, 381–386.

Brody, N. (1972). *Personality: Research and theory.* New York: Academic Press.

Brodzinsky, D. M., & Dein, P. (1976). Short-term stability of adult reflection-impulsivity. *Perceptual and Motor Skills, 43*, 1012–1014.

Brogden, H. E. (1946). On the interpretation of the correlation coefficient as a measure of predictive efficiency. *Journal of Educational Psychology, 37*, 65–76.

Brogden, H. E. (1949). When tests pay off. *Personnel Psychology, 2*, 171–183.

Brotemarkle, R. A. (1947). Clinical psychology, 1896–1946. *Journal of Consulting and Clinical Psychology, 11*, 1–4.

Brown, D. C. (1994). Subgroup norming: Legitimate testing practice or reverse discrimination. *American Psychologist, 49*, 927–928.

Brown, G., Nicassio, P. W., & Wallston, K. A. (1989). Pain coping strategies and depression in rheumatoid arthritis. *Journal of Consulting and Clinical Psychology, 57*, 652–657.

Brown, G. W. (1989). Life events and measurement. In G. W. Brown & T. Harris (Eds.), *Life events and illness.* New York: Guilford.

Brown, J. M. (1984). Imagery coping strategies in the treatment of migraine. *Pain, 18,* 157–167.

Brown, L. L., & Hammill, D. D. (1978). *The Behavior Rating Profile: An ecological approach to behavioral assessment.* Austin, TX: Pro-Ed.

Brown, R. D. (1972). The relationship of parental perceptions of university life and their characterizations of their college sons and daughters. *Educational and Psychological Measurement, 32,* 365–375.

Brown, S. P., & Peterson, R. A. (1993). Antecedents and consequences of salesperson job satisfaction: Meta-analysis and assessment of causal effects. *Journal of Marketing Research, 30,* 63–77.

Browning, D. L. (1987). Ego development, authoritarianism, and social status: An investigation of the incremental validity of Loevinger's Sentence Completion Test (Short Form). *Journal of Personality and Social Psychology, 53,* 113–118.

Bruch, H. (1962). Perceptual and conceptual disturbances in anorexia nervosa. *Psychosomatic Medicine, 24,* 187–194.

Bruininks, R. H., Woodcock, R. W., Hill, B. K., & Weatherman, R. F. (1985). *Scales of Independent Behavior.* Allen, TX: DLM Teaching Resources.

Bruininks, R. H., Woodcock, R. W., Weatherman, R. F., & Hill, B. K. (1984). *Scales of Independent Behavior.* Allen, TX: DLM Teaching Resources.

Bryant, E. T., Maruish, M. E., Sawicki, R. F., & Golden, C. J. (1984). Validity of the Luria-Nebraska Neuropsychological Battery. *Journal of Consulting and Clinical Psychology, 52,* 445–448.

Bryer, J. B., Martines, K. A., & Dignan, M. A. (1990). Millon Clinical Multiaxial Inventory Alcohol Abuse and Drug Abuse scales and the identification of substance-abuse patients. *Psychological Assessment: A Journal of Consulting and Clinical Psychology, 2,* 438–441.

Bucholz, K. K., Cadoret, R., Cloninger, C. R., & Dinwiddie, S. H. (1994). A new, semi-structured psychiatric interview for use in genetic linkage studies: A report on the reliability of the SSAGA. *Journal of Studies on Alcohol, 55,* 149–158.

Buck, J. N. (1948). The H-T-P technique: A qualitative and quantitative scoring manual. *Journal of Clinical Psychology, 4,* 317–396.

Buck, J. N. (1950). *Administration and interpretation of the H-T-P test: Proceedings of the H-T-P workshop at Veterans Administration Hospital, Richmond, Virginia.* Beverly Hills: Western Psychological Services.

Buckle, M. B., & Holt, N. F. (1951). Comparison of Rorschach and Behn Inkblots. (1951). *Journal of Projective Techniques, 15,* 486–493.

Bucofsky, D. (1971). Any learning skills taught in the high school? *Journal of Reading, 15*(3), 195–198.

Bukatman, B. A., Foy, J. L., & De Grazia, E. (1971). What is competency to stand trial? *American Journal of Psychiatry, 127,* 1225–1229.

Bureau of the Census. (1973). *Who's home when.* Washington, DC: U.S. Government Printing Office.

Burgess, A. W., McCausland, M. P., & Wolbert, W. A. (1981, February). Children's drawings as indicators of sexual trauma. *Perspectives in Psychiatric Care, 19,* 50–58.

Burisch, M. (1984a). Approaches to personality inventory construction: A comparison of merits. *American Psychologist, 39,* 214–227.

Burisch, M. (1984b). You don't always get what you pay for: Measuring depression with short and simple versus long and sophisticated scales. *Journal of Research in Personality, 18*(1), 81–98.

Burke, M. J. (1984). Validity generalization: A review and critique of the correlation model. *Personnel Psychology, 37,* 93–115.

Burke, M. J., Normand, J., & Raju, N. S. (1987). Examinee attitudes toward computer-administered ability testing. *Computers in Human Behavior, 3,* 95–107.

Burke, R. J. (1970). Occupational and life strains, satisfactions, and mental health. *Journal of Business Administration, 1,* 35–41.

Burns, A., Jacoby, R., & Levy, R. (1991). Progression of cognitive impairment in Alzheimer's disease. *Journal of the American Geriatrics Society, 39,* 39–45.

Burns, G. L., & Patterson, D. R. (1990). Conduct problem behaviors in a stratified sample of children and adolescents: New standardization data on the Eyberg Child Behavior Inventory. *Psychological Assessment: A Journal of Consulting and Clinical Psychology, 2,* 391–397.

Burns, R. C., & Kaufman, S. H. (1970). *Kinetic Family Drawings (K-F-D): An introduction to understanding through kinetic drawings.* New York: Brunner/Mazel.

Burns, R. C., & Kaufmann, S. H. (1972). *Actions, styles, and symbols in Kinetic Family Drawings (K-F-D).* New York: Brunner/Mazel.

Buros, O. K. (1938). *The 1938 mental measurements yearbook.* New Brunswick, NJ: Rutgers University Press.

Buros, O. K. (1974). *Tests in print II.* Highland Park, NJ: Gryphon Press.

Burstein, A. G. (1972). Review of the Wechsler Adult Intelligence Scale. In O. K. Buros (Ed.), *The seventh mental measurements yearbook* (pp. 786–788). Highland Park, NJ: Gryphon Press.

Burt, C. (1958). The inheritance of mental ability. *American Psychologist, 13,* 1–15.

Burwen, L. S., & Campbell, D. T. (1957). The generality of attitudes toward authority and nonauthority figures. *Journal of Abnormal and Social Psychology, 54,* 24–31.

Butcher, J. N. (1978). Computerized scoring and interpreting services [Re: Minnesota Multiphasic Personality Inventory]. In O. K. Buros (Ed.), *The eighth mental measurements yearbook* (Vol. 1, pp. 942–945, 947–956, 958, 960–962). Highland Park, NJ: Gryphon Press.

Butcher, J. N. (Ed.). (1979). *New developments in the use of the MMPI.* Minneapolis: University of Minnesota Press.

Butcher, J. N. (1987). The use of computers in psychological assessment: An overview of practices and issues. Available. In J. N. Butcher (Ed.), *Computerized psychological assessment: A practitioner's guide* (pp. 3–14). New York: Basic Books.

Butcher, J. N. (1990). *MMPI-2 in psychological treatment.* New York: Oxford University Press.

Butcher, J. N. (1994). Psychological assessment by computer: Potential gains and problems to avoid. *Psychiatric Annals, 24,* 20–24.

Butcher, J. N., Dahlstrom, W. G., Graham, J. R., Tellegen, A., & Kaemmer, B. (1989). *Minnesota Multiphasic Personality Inventory—2 (MMPI-2): Manual for administration and scoring.* Minneapolis: University of Minnesota Press.

Butcher, J. N., & Graham, J. R. (1989). *Topics in MMPI-2 Interpretation.* Minneapolis, MN: MMPI-2 Workshops and Symposia.

Butcher, J. N., Graham, J. R., Williams, C. L., & Ben-Porath, Y. (1989). *Development and use of the MMPI-2 Content Scales.* Minneapolis: University of Minnesota Press.

Butcher, J. N., & Pope, K. S. (1990). MMPI-2: A practical guide to psychometric, clinical, and ethical issues. *The Independent Practitioner, 10*(1), 33–40.

Butcher, J. N., & Tellegen, A. (1966). Objections to MMPI items. *Journal of Counseling Psychology, 30,* 527–534.

Byrne, D. (1974). *An introduction to personality* (2nd ed.). Englewood Cliffs, NJ: Prentice-Hall.

Cacioppo, J. T., & Petty, R. E. (1985). Physiological responses and advertising effects: Is the cup half full or half empty? *Psychology & Marketing, 2,* 115–126.

Cain, L. F., Levine, S., & Elsey, F. F. (1963). *Cain-Levine Social Competency Scale.* Palo Alto, CA: Consulting Psychologists Press.

Caliso, J. A., & Milner, J. S. (1994). Childhood physical abuse, childhood social support, and adult child abuse potential. *Journal of Interpersonal Violence, 9,* 27–44.

Callero, P. L. (1992). The meaning of self-in-role: A modified measure of role-identity. *Social Forces, 71,* 485–501.

Camara, W. J., & Schneider, D. L. (1994). Integrity tests: Facts and unresolved issues. *American Psychologist, 49,* 112–119.

Camilli, G., & Shepard, L. A. (1985). A computer program to aid the detection of biased test items. *Educational & Psychological Measurement, 45,* 595–600.

Campbell, D. P. (1968). The Strong Vocational Interest Blank: 1927–1967. In P. McReynolds (Ed.), *Advances in psychological assessment* (Vol. 1; pp. 105–130). Palo Alto, CA: Science and Behavior Books.

Campbell, D. P. (1971). *Handbook for the Strong Vocational Interest Blank.* Palo Alto, CA: Stanford University Press.

Campbell, D. P., & Hansen, J. C. (1981). *Manual for the SVIB-SCII—Third Edition.* Stanford, CA: Stanford University Press.

Campbell, D. T., & Fiske, D. W. (1959). Convergent and discriminant validation by the multitrait-multimethod matrix. *Psychological Bulletin, 56,* 81–105.

Campo, V., & Vilar, N. P. (1977). Clinical usefulness of the Draw-An-Animal Test. *British Journal of Projective Psychology and Personality Study, 22*(1), 1–7.

Cancro, R. (1969). Abstraction on proverbs in process-reactive schizophrenia. *Journal of Consulting and Clinical Psychology, 33,* 267–270.

Canter, A. (1963). A background interference procedure for grapho-motor tests in the study of deficit. *Perceptual and Motor Skills, 16,* 914.

Canter, A. (1966). A background interference procedure to increase the sensitivity of the Bender Gestalt Test to organic brain disorders. *Journal of Consulting Psychology, 30,* 91–97.

Carey, M. P., Faulstich, M. E., Gresham, F. M., Ruggerio, L., & Enyart, P. (1987). Children's Depression Inventory: Construct and discriminant validity across clinical and nonreferred (control) populations. *Journal of Consulting and Clinical Psychology, 55,* 755–761.

Carey, N. B. (1994). Computer predictors of mechanical job performance: Marine Corps findings. *Military Psychology, 6,* 1–30.

Carlson, L., & Reynolds, C. R. (1981). Factor structure and specific variance of the WPPSI subtests at six age levels. *Psychology in the Schools, 18,* 48–54.

Carmichael, L. (1927). A further study of the development of behavior in vertebrates experimentally removed from the influence of external stimulation. *Psychological Review, 34,* 34–47.

Carr, A. C., Wilson, S. L., Ghosh, A., Ancil, R. J., & Woods, R. T. (1982). Automated testing of geriatric patients using a microcomputer-based system. *International Journal of Man-Machine Studies, 17,* 297–300.

Carr, M. A., Sweet, J. J., & Rossini, E. (1986). Diagnostic validity of the Luria-Nebraska Neuropsychological Battery—Children's Revision. *Journal of Consulting and Clinical Psychology, 54,* 354–358.

Carr, R. (1994, April). Do you have what it takes? *Writer's Digest, 74,* 20–23.

Carroll, J. B. (1985, May). Domains of cognitive ability. Symposium: Current theories and findings on cognitive abilities. Los Angeles: AAAS.

Carson, K. P., & Gilliard, D. J. (1993). Construct validity of the Miner Sentence Completion Scale. *Journal of Occupational and Organizational Psychology, 66,* 171–175.

Carter, D. E., & Moran, J. J. (1991). Interscorer reliability for the Hand Test administered to children. *Perceptual and Motor Skills, 72,* 759–765.

Carter, R. T., & Swanson, J. L. (1990). The validity of the Strong Interest Inventory with Black Americans: A review of the literature. *Journal of Vocational Behavior, 36,* 195–209.

Carver, C. S., Scheier, M. F., & Pozo, C. (1991). Conceptualizing the process of coping with health problems. In H. Friedman (Ed.), *Hostility, coping, and health* (pp. 167–187). Washington, DC: American Psychological Association.

Carver, R. P. (1968–1969). Designing an aural aptitude test for Negroes: An experiment that failed. *College Board Review, 70,* 10–14.

Carver, R. P. (1969). Use of a recently developed listening comprehension test to investigate the effect of disadvantagement upon verbal proficiency. *American Educational Research Journal, 6,* 263–270.

Cascio, W. F. (1982). *Applied psychology in personnel*

management (2nd ed.). Reston, VA: Reston Publishing Company.

Cascio, W. F. (1987). *Applied psychology in personnel management* (3rd ed.). Englewood Cliffs, NJ: Prentice-Hall.

Cascio, W. F., Outtz, J., Zedeck, S., & Goldstein, I. L. (1991). Statistical implications of six methods of test score use in personnel selection. *Personnel Psychology, 4,* 233–264.

Cash, T. F., & Brown, T. A. (1987). Body image in anorexia nervosa and bulimia nervosa: A review of the literature. *Behavior Modification, 11,* 487–521.

Cassel, R. N. (1958). *The leadership q-sort test: A test of leadership values.* Murfreesboro, TN: Psychometric Affiliates.

Cassel, R. N. (1971). The group intelligence test IQ paradox. *College Student Journal, 5,* 31–33.

Castilla, L. M., & Klyczek, J. P. (1993). Comparison of the Kinetic Person Drawing Task of the Bay Area Functional Performance Evaluation with measures of functional performance. *Occupational Therapy in Mental Health, 12,* 27–38.

Cates, J. A., & Lapham, R. F. (1991). Personality assessment of the prelingual, profoundly deaf child or adolescent. *Journal of Personality Assessment, 56,* 118–129.

Cattell, H. E. P. (1993). Comment on Goldberg. *American Psychologist, 48,* 1302–1303.

Cattell, J. M. (1887). Experiments on the association of ideas. *Mind, 12,* 68–74.

Cattell, J. M., & Bryant, S. (1889). Mental association investigated by experiment. *Mind, 14,* 230–250.

Cattell, P. (1940) *Cattell Infant Intelligence Scale.* New York: Psychological Corporation.

Cattell, R. B. (1940). A culture free intelligence test, Part I. *Journal of Educational Psychology, 31,* 161–179.

Cattell, R. B. (1946). *The description and measurement of personality.* New York: Harcourt, Brace & World.

Cattell, R. B. (1947). Confirmation and clarification of the primary personality factors. *Psychometrika, 12,* 197–220.

Cattell, R. B. (1948a). The primary personality factors in the realm of objective tests. *Journal of Personality, 16,* 459–487.

Cattell, R. B. (1948b). The primary personality factors in women compared with those in men. *British Journal of Psychology, Statistical Section, 1,* 114–130.

Cattell, R. B. (1950). *Personality: A systematic theoretical and factual study.* New York: McGraw-Hill.

Cattell, R. B. (1957). *Personality and motivation, structure and measurement.* Yonkers, NY: World Book.

Cattell, R. B. (1965). *The scientific analysis of personality.* Baltimore: Penguin Books.

Cattell, R. B. (1971). *Abilities: Their structure, growth, and action.* Boston: Houghton Mifflin.

Cattell, R. B. (1978). *The scientific use of factor analysis in behavioral and life sciences.* New York: Plenum.

Cattell, R. B. (1986). The 16 PF personality structure and Dr. Eysenck. *Journal of Social Behavior and Personality, 1,* 153–160.

Cattell, R. B., Cattell, A. K. S., & Cattell, H. E. P. (1993). *16 PF, Fifth Edition.* Champaign, IL: Institute for Personality and Ability Testing.

Cattell, R. B., & Krug, S. E. (1986). The number of factors in the 16 PF: A review of the evidence with special emphasis on methodological problems. *Educational and Psychological Measurement, 46,* 509–522.

Cattell, R. B., & Luborsky, L. B. (1952). *IPAT humor test of personality: Manual.* Champaign, IL: Institute for Personality and Ability Testing.

Ceci, S. J., Ross, D. F., & Toglia, M. P. (1987). Suggestibility of children's memory: Psycholegal implications. *Journal of Experimental Psychology, 116,* 38–49.

Celis, W., III. (1994, December 16). Computer admissions test found to be ripe for abuse. *New York Times,* pp. A1, A32.

Cerney, M. S. (1984). One last response to the Rorschach test: A second chance to reveal oneself. *Journal of Personality Assessment, 48,* 338–344.

Champagne, J. E. (1969). Job recruitment of the unskilled. *Personnel Journal, 48,* 259–268.

Chan, D. W. (1994). The Chinese Ways of Coping Questionnaire: Assessing coping in secondary school teachers and students in Hong Kong. *Psychological Assessment, 6,* 108–116.

Chandler, L. A., Shermis, M. D., & Lampert, M. E. (1989). The need-threat analysis: A scoring system for the Children's Apperception Test. *Psychology in the Schools, 26,* 47–53.

Chantler, L., Pelco, L., & Mertin, P. (1993). The psychological evaluation of child sexual abuse using the Louisville Behavior Checklist and human figure drawing. *Child Abuse and Neglect, 17,* 271–279.

Chaplin, W. F., John, O. P., & Goldberg, L. R. (1988). Conceptions of state and traits: Dimensional attributes with ideals as prototypes. *Journal of Personality and Social Psychology, 54,* 541–557.

Chapman, L., & Chapman, J. (1967). Genesis of popular but erroneous psychodiagnostic observations. *Journal of Abnormal Psychology, 72,* 193–204.

Chattin, S. H., & Bracken, B. A. (1989). School psychologists' evaluation of the K-ABC, McCarthy Scales, Stanford-Binet IV, and WISC-R. *Journal of Psychoeducational Assessment, 7*(2), 112–130.

Chelune, G., Heaton, R., & Lehman, R. (1986). Neuropsychological and personality correlates of patients' complaints of disability. In G. Goldstein (Ed.), *Advances in clinical neuropsychology* (Vol. 3, pp. 95–126). New York: Plenum Press.

Chess, S., & Fernandez, P. (1981). Do deaf children have a typical personality? *Annual Progress in Child Psychiatry and Child Development,* 295–305.

Chess, S., & Thomas, A. (1973). Temperament in the normal infant. In J. C. Westman (Ed.), *Individual differences in children.* New York: Wiley.

Child denied IQ test because of her race. (1994, April 18). *Jet, 85,* 22.

Chinoy, E. (1967). *Society: An introduction to sociology.* New York: Random House.

Chira-Chavala, T., & Yoo, S. M. (1994). Potential safety benefits on intelligence cruise control systems. *Accident Analysis & Prevention, 26,* 135–146.

Chiu, C. (1989). A study of self-concept of Cambodian children in two Richmond Public schools. Paper presented at the Annual Meeting of the Eastern Educational Research Association, Savannah, GA. (ERIC Document Reproduction Service No. ED 303 559).

Choca, J., Bresolin, L., Okonek, A., & Ostrow, D. (1988). Validity of the Millon Clinical Multiaxial Inventory in the assessment of affective disorders. *Journal of Personality Assessment, 52,* 96–105.

Choca, J. P., Shanley, L. A., Peterson, C. A., & Van Denburg, E. (1990). Racial bias and the MCMI. *Journal of Personality Assessment, 54,* 479–490.

Christiansen, A. J., Weibe, J. S., Smith, T. W., & Turner, C. W. (1994). Predictors of survival among hemodialysis patients: Effects of perceived family support. *Health Psychology, 13,* 521–525.

Christensen, A. L. (1975). *Luria's neuropsychological investigation.* New York: Spectrum.

Christenson, S. L. (1990). Review of Child Behavior Checklist. In J. J. Kramer & J. C. Conoley (Eds.), *The supplement to the tenth mental measurements yearbook* (pp. 40–41). Lincoln: The Buros Institute of Mental Measurements of the University of Nebraska.

Christenson, S. L. (1991). Authentic assessment: Straw man or prescription for progress? *School Psychology Quarterly, 6,* 294–299.

Chun, K., Cobb, S., & French, J. R. P., Jr. (1975). *Measures for psychological assessment.* Ann Arbor, MI: Survey Research Center of the Institute for Social Research.

Church, A. T., & Burke, P. J. (1994). Exploratory and confirmatory tests of the Big Five and Tellegen's three- and four-dimensional models. *Journal of Personality and Social Psychology, 66,* 93–114.

Cicchetti, D., & Carlson, V. (Eds.). (1989). *Child maltreatment: Theory and research on the causes and consequences of child abuse and neglect.* New York: Cambridge University Press.

Cieutat, V. J. (1965). Examiner differences with the Stanford-Binet IQ. *Perceptual and Motor Skills, 20,* 317–318.

Clarizio, H. F. (1989). *Assessment and treatment of depression in children and adolescents.* Brandon, VT: Clinical Psychological Publishing.

Clark, B. (1979). *Growing up gifted.* Columbus, OH: Merrill.

Clark, B. (1988). *Growing up gifted.* (3rd ed.). Columbus, OH: Merrill.

Clark, M. E. (1994). Interpretive limitations of the MMPI-2 anger and cynicism content scales. *Journal of Personality Assessment, 63,* 89–96.

Cleckley, H. (1976). *The mask of sanity* (5th ed.). St. Louis, MO: Mosby.

Cliff, N. (1984). An improved internal consistency reliability estimate. *Journal of Educational Statistics, 9,* 151–161.

Clifford, C. (1992, Spring). What kind of intelligence do you have? *YM,* pp. 34–39.

Cloninger, C. R., Przybeck, T. R., & Svrakis, D. M. (1991). The Tridimensional Personality Questionnaire: U.S. normative data. *Psychological Reports, 69,* 1047–1057.

Coates, S. (1972). *Preschool Embedded Figures Test.* Palo Alto, CA: Consulting Psychologists Press.

Code of Fair Testing Practices in Education. (1988). Washington, DC: Joint Committee on Testing Practices.

Coffman, W. E. (1985). Review of the Kaufman Assessment Battery for Children. In J. V. Mitchell, Jr. (Ed.), *The ninth mental measurements yearbook* (Vol. 1). Lincoln: University of Nebraska Press.

Cohen, B. M., Moses, J. L., & Byham, W. C. (1977). *The validity of assessment centers: A literature review* (Rev. ed.; Monograph No. 2). Pittsburgh, PA: Development Dimensions Press.

Cohen, E. (1965). Examiner differences with individual intelligence tests. *Perceptual and Motor Skills, 20,* 1324.

Cohen, F., & Lazarus, R. S. (1973). Active coping processes, coping dispositions, and recovery from surgery. *Psychosomatic Medicine, 35,* 375–389.

Cohen, J. (1960). A coefficient of agreement for nominal scales. *Educational and Psychological Measurement, 20,* 37–46.

Cohen, R. J. (1977). Socially reinforced obsessing: A reply. *Journal of Consulting and Clinical Psychology, 45,* 1166–1171.

Cohen, R. J. (1979a). *Malpractice: A guide for mental health professionals.* New York: Free Press.

Cohen, R. J. (1979b). *Binge! It's not a state of hunger . . . It's a state of mind.* New York: Macmillan.

Cohen, R. J. (1983a). The professional liability of behavioral scientists: An overview. *Behavioral Science & the Law, 1*(1), 9–22.

Cohen, R. J. (1983b). *A study of the goodwill associated with the Bell Symbol.* Unpublished manuscript.

Cohen, R. J. (1985). Computer-enhanced qualitative research. *Journal of Advertising Research, 25*(3), 48–52.

Cohen, R. J. (1986). Patriotic chic (Editor's Note). *Psychology & Marketing, 3,* 239–241.

Cohen, R. J. (1987). Overview of emerging evaluative and diagnostic methods technologies. In *Proceedings of the fourth annual advertising research foundation workshop: Broadening the horizons of copy research.* New York: Advertising Research Foundation.

Cohen, R. J. (1988). *A student's guide to psychological testing.* Mountain View, CA: Mayfield.

Cohen, R. J. (1992). *65 exercises in psychological testing and assessment* (2nd ed.). Mountain View, CA: Mayfield.

Cohen, R. J. (1994). *Psychology & adjustment: Values, culture, and change.* Boston: Allyn and Bacon.

Cohen, R. J. (1996). *101 exercises in psychological testing and assessment.* Mountain View, CA: Mayfield.

Cohen, R. J., Becker, R. E., & Teevan, R. C. (1975). Perceived somatic reaction to stress and hostile press. *Psychological Reports, 37,* 676–678.

Cohen, R. J., & Houston, D. R. (1975). Fear of failure and rigidity in problem solving. *Perceptual and Motor Skills, 40,* 930.

Cohen, R. J., & Mariano, W. E. (1982). *Legal guidebook in mental health.* New York: Free Press.

Cohen, R. J., Montague, P., Nathonson, L. S., & Swerdlik, M. E. (1988). *Psychological testing: An introduction to tests and measurement.* Mountain View, CA: Mayfield.

Cohen, R. J., & Parker, C. (1974). Fear of failure and death. *Psychological Reports, 34,* 54.

Cohen, R. J., & Smith, F. J. (1976). Socially reinforced obsessing: Etiology of a disorder in a Christian Scientist. *Journal of Consulting and Clinical Psychology, 44,* 142–144.

Cohen, R. J., & Teevan, R. C. (1974). Fear of failure and impression management: An exploratory study. *Psychological Reports, 35,* 1332.

Cohen, R. J., & Teevan, R. C. (1975). Philosophies of human nature and hostile press. *Psychological Reports, 37,* 460–462.

Cohen, S., & Syme, S. L. (1985). *Social support and health.* San Francisco: Academic Press.

Colarusso, R. P., & Hammill, D. D. (1972). *Motor-Free Visual Perception Test.* San Rafael, CA: Academic Therapy.

Cole, S. T., & Hunter, M. (1971). Pattern analysis of WISC scores achieved by culturally disadvantaged children. *Psychological Reports, 20,* 191–194.

Coleman, L. (1989). Medical examination for sexual abuse: Are we being told the truth? *Family Law News, 12*(2).

Coleman, M. J., et al. (1993). The Thought Disorder Index: A reliability study. *Psychological Assessment, 5,* 336–342.

College Board Review, The (1990–91, Winter). Roundtable: The new SAT: Debating its implications. *The College Board Review, 158,* 22–27.

Colligan, R. C., Osborne, D., Swenson, W. M., & Offord, K. P. (1983). *The MMPI: A contemporary normative study.* New York: Praeger.

Colligan, R. C., Osborne, D., Swenson, W. M., & Offord, K. P. (1984). *Contemporary norms for the MMPI: Summarizing one year of clinical experience.* Paper presented at the 93rd annual meeting of the American Psychological Association, Toronto, Ontario, Canada.

Comer, D. R. (1993). Workplace drug testing reconsidered. *Journal of Managerial Issues, 5,* 517–531.

Committee on Ethical Guidelines for Forensic Psychologists. (1991). Guidelines for child custody evaluations in divorce proceedings. *American Psychologist, 15,* 655–665.

Commons, M. (1985, April). How novelty produces continuity in cognitive development within a domain and accounts for unequal development across domains. Toronto: SRCD, Ontario, Canada.

Comrey, A. L. (1992). *A first course in factor analysis.* Hillsdale, NJ: Erlbaum.

Comrey, A. L., Backer, T. E., & Glaser, E. M. (1973). *A sourcebook for mental health measures.* Los Angeles: Human Interaction Research Institute.

Comrey, A. L., & Duffy, K. E. (1968). Cattell and Eysenck factor scores related to Comrey personality factors. *Multivariate Behavioral Research, 4,* 379–392.

Comrey, A. L., & Marggraff, W. (1958). A factor analysis of items on the MMPI schizophrenia scale. *Educational and Psychological Measurement, 18,* 310–311.

Comrey, A. L., Michael, W. B., & Fruchter, B. (1988). J. P. Guilford (1897–1987). *American Psychologist, 43,* 1086–1087.

Cone, J. D., & Hawkins, R. P. (Eds.). (1977). *Behavioral assessment: New directions in clinical psychology.* New York: Brunner/Mazel.

Conger, A. J. (1985). Kappa reliabilities for continuing behaviors and events. *Educational and Psychological Measurement, 45,* 861–868.

Connolly, A. J., Nachtman, W., & Pritchett, E. W. (1976). *KeyMath Diagnostic Arithmetic Test Manual.* Circle Pines, MN: American Guidance Service.

Connolly, J. (1976). Life events before myocardial infarction. *Journal of Human Stress, 3,* 3–17.

Conoley, J. C., & Impara, J. C. (Eds.). (1994). *The supplement to the eleventh mental measurements yearbook.* Lincoln: The Buros Institute of Mental Measurements, University of Nebraska.

Consulting Psychologists Press, Inc. (1994). *1994 catalog.* Palo Alto, CA: Author.

Conte, H. R., & Plutchik, R. (1981). A circumplex model for interpersonal personality traits. *Journal of Personality and Social Psychology, 40,* 701–711.

Conte, H. R., Plutchik, R., Buck, L., Picard, S., & Karasu, T. B. (1991). Interrelations between ego functions and personality traits: Their relation to psychotherapy outcome. *American Journal of Psychotherapy, 45,* 69–77.

Cook, J. D., Hepworth, S. J., Wall, T. D., & Warr, P. B. (1981). *The experience of work.* New York: Academic Press.

Cooper, A. (1981). A basic TAT set for adolescent males. *Journal of Clinical Psychology, 37*(2), 411–414.

Cooper, D. H., & Shephard, K. (1992). Review of DIAL-R. *Learning Disabilities Research and Practice, 7,* 171–174.

Cooper, M. L. (1994). Motivations for alcohol use among adolescents: Development and validation of a four-factor model. *Psychological Assessment, 6,* 117–128.

Cooper, Z., Copper, P. J., & Fairburn, C. G. (1985). The specificity of the Eating Disorder Inventory. *British Journal of Clinical Psychology, 24,* 129–130.

Coopersmith, S. (1967). *The antecedents of self-esteem.* San Francisco: Freeman.

Corish, C. D., Richard, B., & Brown, S. (1989). Missed medication doses in rheumatoid arthritis patients: Intentional and unintentional reasons. *Arthritis Care and Research, 2,* 3–9.

Cornell, D. G. (1985). External validation of the Personality Inventory for Children—Comment on Lachar, Gdowski, and Snyder. *Journal of Consulting and Clinical Psychology, 53,* 273–274.

Corwin, D., Berlinger, L., Goodman, G., Goodwin, J., & White, S. (1987). Child sexual abuse and custody disputes: No easy answers. *Journal of Interpersonal Violence, 2,* 91–105.

Costa, P. T., Jr. (1991). Clinical use of the five-factor model: An introduction. *Journal of Personality Assessment, 57*, 393–398.

Costa, P. T., Jr., & McCrae, R. R. (1985). *The NEO Personality Inventory manual.* Odessa, FL: Psychological Assessment Resources.

Costa, P. T., Jr., & McCrae, R. R. (1988). From catalog to classification: Murray's needs and the five-factor model. *Journal of Personality and Social Psychology, 55*, 258–265.

Costa, P. T., Jr., & McCrae, R. R. (1989). *The NEO-PI/NEO-FFI manual supplement.* Odessa, FL: Psychological Assessment Resources, Inc.

Costa, P. T., Jr., & McCrae, R. R. (1992a). Four ways five factors are basic. *Personality and Individual Differences, 13*, 653–665.

Costa, P. T., Jr., & McCrae, R. R. (1992b). Reply to Eysenck. *Personality and Individual Differences, 13*, 861–865.

Costa, P. T., Jr., & McCrae, R. R. (1992c). *The NEO PI-R/NEO-FFI professional manual.* Odessa, FL: Psychological Assessment Resources, Inc.

Costantino, G., Malgady, R., & Rogler, L. H. (1988). *Tell-Me-A-Story—TEMAS—Manual.* Los Angeles: Western Psychological Services.

Cote, J. A., McCullough, J., & Reilly, M. (1985). Effects of unexpected situations on behavior-intention differences: A garbology analysis. *Journal of Consumer Research, 12*, 188–194.

Cotton, P. (1992). Women's health initiative leads way as research begins to fill gender gaps. *Journal of the American Medical Association, 267* (4), 469–470, 473.

Covetkovic, R. (1979). Conception and representation of space in human figure drawings by schizophrenic and normal subjects. *Journal of Personality Assessment, 43*(3), 247–256.

Coyne, J. C. (1976). The place of informed consent in ethical dilemmas. *Journal of Consulting and Clinical Psychology, 44*, 1015–1017.

Cozby, P. C., Worden, P. E., & Kee, D. W. (1989). *Research methods in human development.* Mountain View, CA: Mayfield.

Craig, R. J. (1990). Current utilization of psychological tests at diagnostic practicum sites. Paper presented at Annual Meeting of the Society for Personality Assessment, San Diego, CA.

Crevecoeur, M. G. St. J. de (1951). What is an American letter? In H. S. Commager (ed.), *Living ideas in America.* New York: Harper. (Originally published in *Letters from an American farmer,* 1762.)

Crocker, L., Llabre, M., & Miller, M. D. (1988). The generalizability of content validity ratings. *Journal of Educational Measurement, 25*, 287–299.

Cronbach, L. J. (1949). Statistical methods applied to Rorschach scores: A review. *Psychological Bulletin, 46*, 393–429.

Cronbach, L. J. (1951). Coefficient alpha and the internal structure of tests. *Psychometrika, 16*, 297–334.

Cronbach, L. J. (1970). *Essentials of psychological testing* (3rd ed.). New York: Harper & Row.

Cronbach, L. J. (1975). Five decades of public controversy over mental testing. *American Psychologist, 30*, 1–13.

Cronbach, L. J. (1984). *Essentials of psychological testing* (4th ed.). New York: Harper & Row.

Cronbach, L. J., & Gleser, G. C. (1965). *Psychological tests and personnel decisions* (2nd ed.). Urbana: University of Illinois Press.

Cronbach, L. J., Gleser, G. C., Nanda, H., & Rajaratnam, N. (1972). *The dependability of behavioral measurement: Theory of generalizability for scores and profiles.* New York: Wiley.

Cronbach, L. J., & Meehl, P. E. (1955). Construct validity in psychological tests. *Psychological Bulletin, 52*, 281–302.

Crosby, F. J. (1994). Understanding affirmative action. *Basic & Applied Social Psychology, 15*, 13–41.

Crosson, B., & Warren, R. L. (1982). Use of the Luria-Nebraska Neuropsychological Battery in aphasia: A conceptual critique. *Journal of Consulting and Clinical Psychology, 50*, 22–31.

Crowne, D. P., & Marlowe, D. (1964). *The approval motive: Studies in evaluative dependence.* New York: Wiley.

Cummings, J. A. (1981). An evaluation of Kinetic Family Drawings. Paper presented at the annual meeting of the American Psychological Association. Los Angeles, California.

Cummings, M. A., & Merrell, K. W. (1993). K-ABC score patterns of Sioux children: Mental processing styles, effects of school attendance, and relationship between raw scores and age. *Journal of Psychoeducational Assessment, 11*, 38–45.

Cundick, B. P. (1976). Measures of intelligence on Southwest Indian students. *Journal of Social Psychology, 81*, 151–156.

Cunningham, T., & Presnall, D. (1978). Relationship between dimensions of adaptive behavior and sheltered workshop productivity. *American Journal of Mental Deficiency, 82*, 386–393.

Cureton, E. E. (1957). The upper and lower twenty-seven per cent rule. *Psychometrika, 22*, 293–296.

Curren, M. T., & Harich, K. R. (1994). Consumers' mood states: The mitigating influence of personal relevance on product evaluations. *Psychology and Marketing, 11*, 91–107.

Dahlstrom, W. G. (1970). Personality. *Annual Review of Psychology, 21*, 1–48.

Dahlstrom, W. G., Brooks, J. D., & Peterson, C. D. (1990). The Beck Depression Inventory: Item order and the impact of response sets. *Journal of Personality Assessment, 55*, 224–233.

Dahlstrom, W. G., Lachar, D., & Dahlstrom, L. E. (Eds.). (1986). *MMPI patterns of American minorities.* Minneapolis: University of Minnesota Press.

Dahlstrom, W. G., Meehl, P. E., & Schofield, W. (1986). Obituary—Starke Rosecrans Hathaway (1903–1984). *American Psychologist, 41*, 834–835.

Dahlstrom, W. G., & Welsh, G. S. (1960). *An MMPI handbook: A guide to use in clinical practice and research.* Minneapolis: University of Minnesota Press.

Dahlstrom, W. G., Welsh, G. S., & Dahlstrom, L. E.

(1972). *An MMPI handbook. Volume 1, Clinical interpretation.* Minneapolis: University of Minnesota Press.

Daigneault, S., Braun, C. M. J., & Whitaker, H. A. (1992). Early effects of normal aging on perseverative and non-perseverative prefrontal measures. *Developmental Neuropsychology, 8,* 99–114.

Dana, R. H., & Cantrell, J. D. (1988). An update on the Millon Clinical Multiaxial Inventory (MCMI). *Journal of Clinical Psychology, 44,* 760–763.

Darlington, R. B., & Bishop, C. H. (1966). Increasing test validity by considering interitem correlation. *Journal of Applied Psychology, 50,* 322–330.

Darlington, R. B., & Stauffer, G. F. (1966). Use and evaluation of discrete test information in decision making. *Journal of Applied Psychology, 50,* 125–129.

Darwin, C. (1859). *On the origin of species by means of natural selection.* London: Murray.

Das, J. P. (1972). Patterns of cognitive ability in nonretarded and retarded children. *American Journal of Mental Deficiency, 77,* 6–12.

Das, J. P., Kirby, J., & Jarman, R. F. (1975). Simultaneous and successive synthesis: An alternative model for cognitive abilities. *Psychological Bulletin, 82,* 87–103.

Das, J. P., Kirby, J. R., & Jarman, R. F. (1979). *Simultaneous and successive cognitive processes.* New York: Academic Press.

Datel, W. E., & Gengerelli, J. A. (1955). Reliability of Rorschach interpretations. *Journal of Projective Techniques, 19,* 322–338.

Davey, J. A., Schell, B. H., & Morrison, K. (1993). The Myers-Briggs Personality Indicator and its usefulness for problem solving by mining industry personnel. *Group and Organization Management, 18,* 50–65.

Davidson, H. A. (1949). Malingered psychosis. *Bulletin of the Menninger Clinic, 13,* 157–163.

Davidson, T. N., Bowden, L., & Tholen, D. (1979). Social support as a moderator of burn rehabilitation. *Archives of Physical Medicine and Rehabilitation, 60,* 556.

Davies, P. L., & Gavin, W. J. (1994). Comparison of individual and group/consultation treatment methods for preschool children with developmental delays. *American Journal of Occupational Therapy, 48,* 155–161.

Davis, A. (1951). Socioeconomic influences upon children's learning. *Understanding the Child, 20,* 10–16.

Davis, G. A. (1989). Testing for creative potential. *Contemporary Educational Psychology, 14,* 257–274.

Davis, G. A., & Rimm, S. B. (1979). *GIFFI I and II: Group inventories for finding interests.* Watertown, WI: Educational Assessment Service.

Davis, G. A., & Rimm, S. B. (1982). Group Inventory for Finding Interests (GIFFI) I and II: Instruments for identifying creative potential in the junior and senior high school. *Journal of Creative Behavior, 16,* 50–57.

Davis, R., Butler, N., & Goldstein, H. (1972). *From birth to seven: A report of the National Child Development Study.* London: Longman.

Day, D. V., & Silverman, S. B. (1989). Personality and job performance: Evidence of incremental validity. *Personnel Psychology, 42,* 25–36.

Dean, A. (Ed.). (1985). *Depression in multidisciplinary perspective.* New York: Brunner/Mazel.

Dean, R. S. (1983). Neuropsychological assessment. In Staff College (Ed.), *Handbook of diagnostic and epidemiological instruments.* Washington, DC: National Institute of Mental Health.

Deaux, K. (1985). Sex and gender. *Annual Review of Psychology, 36,* 46–92.

Deaux, K., & Major, B. (1987). Putting gender into context: An interactive model of gender related behavior. *Psychological Review, 94,* 369–389.

DeBettignies, B. H., Mahurin, R. K., & Pirozzolo, F. J. (1993). Functional status in Alzheimer's disease and multi-infarct dementia: A comparison of patient performance and caregiver report. *Clinical Gerontologist, 12,* 31–49.

DeCato, C. M. (1994). Toward a training model for Rorschach scoring revisited: A follow-up study on a training system for interscorer agreement. *Perceptual and Motor Skills, 78,* 3–10.

DeDombal, F. T. (1979). Computers and the surgeon: A matter of decision. *The Surgeon, 39,* 57.

Delahunty, R. J. (1988). Perspectives on within-group scoring. *Journal of Vocational Behavior, 33,* 463–477.

Delaney, E. A., & Hopkins, T. F. (1987). *Examiner's handbook: An expanded guide for Fourth Edition users.* Chicago: Riverside Publishing Company.

D'Elia, L., Satz, P., & Schretlen, D. (1989). Wechsler Memory Scale: A critical appraisal of the normative studies. *Journal of Clinical and Experimental Neuropsychology, 11,* 551–568.

Delis, D. C., & Kaplan, E. (1982). The assessment of aphasia with the Luria Nebraska Neuropsychological Battery: A case critique. *Journal of Consulting and Clinical Psychology, 50,* 32–39.

Deloria, D. J. (1985). Review of the Miller Assessment for Preschoolers. In J. V. Mitchell, Jr. (Ed.), *The ninth mental measurements yearbook.* Lincoln: The Buros Institute of Mental Measurements, University of Nebraska.

Demo, D. H. (1985). The measurement of self-esteem: Refining our methods. *Journal of Personality and Social Psychology, 48,* 1490–1502.

Dennis, M., & Barnes, M. A. (1994). Neuropsychologic function in same-sex twins discordant for perinatal brain damage. *Journal of Developmental Behavioral Pediatrics, 15,* 124–130.

Dennis, W., & Dennis, M. G. (1940). The effect of cradling practice upon the onset of walking in Hopi children. *Journal of Genetic Psychology, 56,* 77–86.

Dennis, W., & Najarian, P. (1957). Infant development under environmental handicap. *Psychological Monographs, 71,* No. 7 (Whole No. 436).

DePaepe, J. L., & Ciccaglione, S. (1993). A dynamic balance measure for persons with severe and profound mental retardation. *Perceptual and Motor Skills, 76,* 619–627.

Department of Health, Education, and Welfare (1977a). Nondiscrimination on basis of handicap: Implementation of Section 504 of the Rehabilitation Act of 1973. *Federal Register, 42*(86), 22676–22702.

Department of Health, Education, and Welfare (1977b). Education of Handicapped Children: Implementation of Part B of the Education of the Handicapped Act. *Federal Register, 42*(163), 42474–42518.

DePaulo, B. M. (1994). Spotting lies: Can humans learn to do better? *Current Directions in Psychological Science, 3,* 83–86.

Derogatis, L. R., Abeloff, M. D., & Melisaratos, N. (1979). Psychological coping mechanisms and survival time in metastatic breast cancer. *Journal of the American Medical Association, 242,* 1504–1508.

Derrow, P. (1993, June). Are your habits healthy? *Weight Watchers Magazine, 26,* 18–20.

DeSarbo, W. S., & Hoffman, D. L. (1987). Constructing MDS joint spaces for binary choice data: A multidimensional unfolding threshold model for marketing research. *Journal of Marketing Research, 24,* 40–54.

DeStefano, L. Y., & Thompson, D. S. (1990). Adaptive behavior: The construct and its measurement. In C. R. Reynolds & R. W. Kamphaus (Eds.), *Handbook of psychological and educational assessment of children: Personality, behavior, & context* (pp. 445–469). New York: Guilford Press.

Detterman, D. K. (1986). Qualitative integration: The last word? In R. J. Sternberg & D. K. Detterman (Eds.), *What is intelligence?* (pp. 163–166). Norwood, NJ: Ablex.

DeWitt, K. (1991, March 29). Looking overseas for school exams. *New York Times,* p. B6.

Diabetes Control and Complications Trial Research Group. (1994). A screening algorithm to identify clinically significant changes in neuropsychological functions in the diabetes control and complications trial. *Journal of Clinical and Experimental Neuropsychology, 16,* 303–316.

DiClemente, C. C., & Hughes, S. O. (1990). Stages of change profiles in outpatient alcoholism treatment. *Journal of Substance Abuse, 2,* 217–235.

Diebold, M. H., Curtis, W. S., & DuBose, R. F. (1978). Developmental scales versus observational measures for deaf-blind children. *Exceptional Children, 44,* 275–278.

Digman, J. M. (1990). Personality structure: Emergence of the five-factor model. *Annual Review of Psychology, 41,* 417–440.

Digman, J. W., & Takemoto-Chock, N. K. (1981). Factors in the natural language of personality: Reanalysis, comparison, and interpretation of six major studies. *Multivariate Behavioral Research, 16,* 149–170.

DiMatteo, M. R., Hays, R. D., Grita, E. R., et al. (1993). Patient adherence to cancer control regimens: Scale development and initial validation. *Psychological Assessment, 5,* 102–112.

Dimock, P. H., & Cormier, P. (1991). The effects of format differences and computer experience on performance and anxiety on a computer-administered test. *Measurement and Evaluation in Counseling and Development, 24,* 119–126.

Distefano, M. K., Pryer, M. W., & Erffmeyer, R. C. (1983). Application of content validity methods to the development of a job-related performance rating criterion. *Personnel Psychology, 36,* 621–631.

Diven, K. (1937). Certain determinants in the conditioning of anxiety reactions. *Journal of Psychology, 3,* 291–308.

Dmitruk, V. M., Collins, R. W., & Clinger, D. I. (1973). The Barnum effect and acceptance of negative personal evaluation. *Journal of Consulting and Clinical Psychology, 41,* 192–194.

Dohrenwend, B. P., & Shrout, P. E. (1985). Hassles in the conceptualization and measurement of life stresses variables. American *Psychologist, 40,* 780–785.

Dokecki, P. R, Frede, M. C., & Gautney, D. B. (1969). The criterion, construct, and predictive validities of the WPPSI. *Proceedings of the Annual Convention of the American Psychological Association, 4,* 505–506.

Doll, E. (1965). *Vineland Social Maturity Scale.* Minneapolis: American Guidance Service.

Doll, E. A. (1917). A brief Binet-Simon scale. *Psychological Clinic, 11,* 197–211, 254–261.

Doll, E. A. (1953). *Measurement of social competence: A manual for the Vineland Social Maturity Scale.* Circle Pines, MN: American Guidance Service.

Donahue, E. M. (1994). Do children use the big five, too? Content and structural form in personality description. *Journal of Personality, 62,* 45–66.

Donahue, E. M., Robins, R. W., Roberts, B. W., & John, O. P. (1993). The divided self: Concurrent and longitudinal effects of psychological adjustment and social roles on self-concept differentiation. *Journal of Personality and Social Psychology, 64,* 834–846.

Donders, J. (1992). Validity of the Kaufman Assessment Battery for Children when employed with children with traumatic brain injury. *Journal of Clinical Psychology, 48,* 225–230.

Donlon, T. (Ed.). (1984). *The College Board technical handbook for the Scholastic Aptitude and Achievement tests.* New York: College Board Publications.

Dorcus, R. M., & Jones, M. H. (1950). *Handbook of employee selection.* New York: McGraw-Hill.

Doty, R. L., Shaman, P., & Dann, M. (1984). Development of the University of Pennsylvania Smell Identification Test: A standard microencapsulated test of olfactory dysfunction. *Physiological Behavior, 32,* 489–502.

Dowling, G. R. (1988). Measuring corporate images: A review of alternative approaches. *Journal of Business Research. Special Issue: Marketing Research, 17,* 27–34.

Dreger, R. M., & Miller, K. S. (1960). Comparative studies of Negroes and Whites in the U.S. *Psychological Bulletin, 51,* 361–402.

Drinkwater, M. J. (1976). Psychological evaluation of visually handicapped children. *Massachusetts School Psychologists Association Newsletter, 6.*

Drummond, R. J. (1984). Review of Edwards Personal Preference Schedule. In D. J. Keyser & R. C. Sweetland (Eds.), *Test critiques* (Vol. 1; pp. 252–258). Kansas, MO: Test Corporation of America.

Drummond, R. J., McIntire, W. G., & Skaggs, C. T. (1978). The relationship of work values to occupational level in young adult workers. *Journal of Employment Counseling, 15,* 117–121.

DuBois, P. H. (1966). A test-dominated society: China 1115 B.C.–1905 A.D. In A. Anastasi (Ed.), *Testing problems in perspective* (pp. 29–36). Washington, DC: American Council on Education.

DuBois, P. H. (1970). *A history of psychological testing.* Boston: Allyn and Bacon.

Dudek, S. (1954). An approach to fundamental compatibility in marital couples through the Rorschach. *Journal of Projective Techniques, 18,* 400.

Dudek, S., & Gottlieb, S. (1954). An approach to fundamental compatibility in marital couples through the Rorschach. *American Psychologist, 9,* 356.

Dudycha, G. J. (1936). An objective study of punctuality in relation to personality and achievement. *Archives of Psychology, 204,* 1–319.

Dugdale, R. (1877). *The Jukes: A study in crime, pauperism, disease, and heredity.* New York: Putnam.

Dunbar, J. (1990). Predictors of patient adherence: Patient characteristics. In S. A. Shumaker, E. B. Schron, & J. D. Ockene (Eds.), *The handbook of health behavior change* (pp. 348–360). New York: Springer.

Duncan, D., & Snow, W. G. (1987). Base rates in neuropsychology. *Professional Psychology: Research and Practice, 18,* 368–370.

Dunkel-Schetter, C., Feinstein, L. G., Taylor, S. E., & Falke, R. L. (1992). Patterns of coping with cancer. *Health Psychology, 11,* 79–87.

Dunn, L. M. (1959). *Peabody Picture Vocabulary Test.* Minneapolis: American Guidance Service.

Dunn, L. M., & Dunn, L. M. (1981). *Peabody Picture Vocabulary Test—Revised.* Circle Pines, MN: American Guidance Service.

Dunnette, M. D. (1963). A modified model for selection research. *Journal of Applied Psychology, 47,* 317–323.

Dunnette, M. D., & Borman, W. C. (1979). Personnel selection and classification systems. *Annual Review of Psychology, 30,* 477–525.

Dunphy, D. C. (1963). The social structure of urban adolescent peer groups. *Sociometry, 26,* 230–240.

Duran, R. P. (1986). *Purposes for a code of fair testing in education.* Paper presented at the annual meeting of the American Psychological Association, Washington, DC.

Duran, R. P. (1988). Testing of linguistic minorities. In R. L. Linn (Ed.), *Educational measurement* (3rd ed.). New York: American Council on Education/Macmillan.

Durrell, D. D., & Catterson, J. H. (1980). *Durrell Analysis of Reading Difficulty manual* (3rd. ed.). New York: Psychological Corporation.

Dworkin, G. (1974). Two views on IQs. *American Psychologist, 29,* 465–467.

Dyer, J. R. (1979). *Understanding and evaluating educational research.* Reading, MA: Addison-Wesley.

Dyer, P. (1994, June). Cited in T. DeAngelis, New tests allow takers to tackle real-life problems. *APA Monitor, 25,* 14.

Dykens, E. M., Hodapp, R. M., & Evans, D. W. (1994). Profiles and development of adaptive behavior in children with Down Syndrome. *American Journal on Mental Retardation, 98,* 580–587.

Dykes, L. (1986). The whiplash shaken infant syndrome: What has been learned? *Child Abuse and Neglect, 10,* 211.

Dysken, M. W., Chang, S. S., Cooper, R. C., et al. (1979). Barbiturate-facilitated interviewing. *Biological Psychiatry, 14,* 421–432.

Dysken, M. W., Kooser, J. A., Haraszti, J. S., et al. (1979). Clinical usefulness of sodium amytal interviewing. *Archives of General Psychiatry, 36,* 789–794.

Earles, J. A., & Ree, M. J. (1992). The predictive validity of the ASVAB for training grades. *Educational and Psychological Measurement, 52,* 721–725.

Earls, C. M., & Marshall, W. L. (1983). The current state of technology in the laboratory assessment of sexual arousal patterns. In J. G. Greer & I. R. Stuart (Eds.), *The sexual aggressor: Current perspectives on treatment* (pp. 336–362). New York: Van Nostrand Reinhold.

Earls, C. M., Quinsey, V. L., & Castonguay, L. G. (1987). A comparison of three methods of scoring penile circumference changes. *Archives of Sexual Behavior, 6,* 493–500.

Ebel, R. L. (1973). Evaluation and educational objectives. *Journal of Educational Measurement, 10,* 273–279.

Eberhardt, J. L., & Fiske, S. T. (1994). Affirmative action in theory and practice: Issues of power, ambiguity, and gender versus race. *Basic & Applied Social Psychology, 15,* 201–220.

Edelbrock, C. (1988). Informant reports. In E. S. Shapiro & T. R. Kratochwill (Eds.), *Behavioral assessment in schools* (pp. 351–383). New York: Guilford Press.

Educational Testing Service. (1977). *Graduate Record Examinations information bulletin: 1977–1978.* Princeton, NJ: Educational Testing Service.

Edwards, A. L. (1953). *Edwards Personal Preference Schedule.* New York: Psychological Corporation.

Edwards, A. L. (1957a). *Techniques of attitude scale construction.* New York: Appleton-Century-Crofts.

Edwards, A. L. (1957b). *The social desirability variable in personality assessment and research.* New York: Dryden.

Edwards, A. L. (1966). Relationship between probability of endorsement and social desirability scale value for a set of 2,824 personality statements. *Journal of Applied Psychology, 50,* 238–239.

Edwards, A. L., & Walsh, J. A. (1964). Response sets in

standard and experimental personality scales. *American Education Research Journal, 1,* 52–60.

Eichler, R. M. (1951). A comparison of the Rorschach and Behn-Rorschach inkblot tests. *Journal of Consulting Psychology, 15,* 185–189.

Einhorn, H. J. (1984). *Accepting error to make less error in prediction.* Paper presented at the 92nd annual meeting of the American Psychological Association, Toronto, Ontario, Canada.

Eisen, S. V., Dill, D. L., & Grob, M. C. (1994). Reliability and validity of a brief patient-report instrument for psychiatric outcome evaluation. *Hospital and Community Psychiatry, 45,* 242–247.

Ekman, W., Friesen, V., & Ellsworth, P. (1982). *Emotions in the human face.* New York: Pergamon Press.

Elbert, J. C. (1984). Training in child diagnostic assessment: A survey of clinical psychology graduate programs. *Journal of Clinical Child Psychology, 13,* 122–123.

Elksnin, L. K., & Elksnin, N. (1993). A review of picture interest inventories: Implications for vocational assessment of students with disabilities. *Journal of Psychoeducational Assessment, 11,* 323–336.

Ellerstein, N. S. (Ed.). (1981). *Child abuse and neglect: A medical reference.* New York: Wiley.

Elliot, H., Glass, L., & Evans, J. (Eds.). (1987). *Mental health assessment of deaf clients: A practical manual.* Boston: Little, Brown.

Elliott, A. N., O'Donohue, W. T., & Nickerson, M. A. (1993). The use of sexually anatomically detailed dolls in the assessment of sexual abuse. *Clinical Psychology Review, 13,* 207–221.

Elliott, C. D. (1990a). *The Differential Ability Scales.* San Antonio, TX: The Psychological Corporation.

Elliott, C. D. (1990b). *Technical Handbook: The Differential Ability Scales.* San Antonio, TX: The Psychological Corporation.

Elliott, S. N. (1988). Acceptability of behavioral treatments in educational settings. In J. C. Witt, S. N. Elliott, & F. M. Greshma (Eds.), *The handbook of behavior therapy in education* (pp. 121–150). New York: Plenum.

Endicott, J., & Spitzer, R. L. (1978). A diagnostic interview: The Schedule for Affective Disorders and Schizophrenia. *Archives of General Psychiatry, 35,* 837–844.

Engin, A., Wallbrown, F., & Brown, D. (1976). The dimensions of reading attitude for children in the intermediate grades. *Psychology in the Schools, 13*(3), 309–316.

Engum, E. S., Pendergrass, T. M., Cron, L., Lambert, E. W., & Hulse, C. K. (1988). The Cognitive Behavioral Driver's Inventory. *Cognitive Rehabilitation, 6,* 34–50.

Entwistle, N. J., & Ramsden, P. (1983). *Understanding student learning.* London: Croom Helm.

Epping-Jordan, J. E., Compas, B. E., & Howell, D. C. (1994). Predictors of cancer progression in young adult men and women: Avoidance, intrusive thoughts, and psychological symptoms. *Health Psychology, 13,* 539–547.

Epstein, J. L., & McPartland, J. M. (1978). *The Quality of School Life Scale administration and technical manual.* Boston: Houghton Mifflin.

Epstein, N., Baldwin, L., & Bishop, S. (1983). The McMaster Family Assessment Device. *Journal of Marital and Family Therapy, 9,* 171–180.

Epstein, Y. M., & Borduin, C. M. (1985). Could this happen? A game for children of divorce. *Psychotherapy, 22,* 770–773.

Erdelyi, M. H. (1974). A new look at the new look: Perceptual defense and vigilance. *Psychological Review, 81,* 1–25.

Erdelyi, M. H., & Goldberg, B. (1979). Let's not sweep repression under the rug: Toward a cognitive psychology of repression. In J. F. Kihlstrom & F. J. Evans (Ed.), *Functional disorders of memory.* Hillsdale, NJ: Erlbaum.

Erdelyi, M. H., & Kleinbard, J. (1978). Has Ebbinghaus decayed with time? The growth of recall (hypermnesia) over days. *Journal of Experimental Psychology: Human Learning and Memory, 4,* 275–289.

Erickson, M. L. (1976). *Assessment and management of developmental changes in children.* St. Louis, MO: Mosby.

Errico, A. L., Nixon, S. J., Parsons, O. A., & Tassey, J. (1990). Screening for neuropsychological impairment in alcoholics. *Psychological Assessment: A Journal of Consulting and Clinical Psychology, 2,* 45–50.

Ervin, S. J. (1965). Why Senate hearings on psychological tests in government. *American Psychologist, 20,* 879–880.

Evan, W. M., & Miller, J. R. (1969). Differential effects of response bias of computer vs. conventional administration of a social science questionnaire. *Behavioral Science, 14,* 216–227.

Evans, E. D. (1988). Review of Reynolds Adolescent Depression Scale. In D. J. Keyser & R. C. Sweetland (Eds.), *Test critiques* (Vol. 7; pp. 485–495). Kansas City, MO: Test Corporation of America.

Evans, L. D. (1993). Standard Score Comparison is 2.0: Second-generation learning disability regression software. *Behavior Research Methods, Instruments, and Computers, 25,* 199–202.

Evans, L. D., & Bradley-Johnson, S. (1988). A review of recently developed measures for adaptive behavior. *Psychology in the Schools, 25,* 276–287.

Evans, M. (1978). Unbiased assessment of locally low incidence handicapped children. *IRRC practitioners talk to practitioners.* Springfield, IL: Illinois Regional Resource Center.

Exner, J. E. (1962). A comparison of human figure drawings of psychoneurotics, character disturbances, normals, and subjects experiencing experimentally induced fears. *Journal of Projective Techniques, 26,* 292–317.

Exner, J. E. (1966). Variations in WISC performance as influenced by difference in pretest rapport. *Journal of General Psychology, 74,* 299–306.

Exner, J. E. (1969). *The Rorschach systems.* New York: Grune & Stratton.

Exner, J. E. (1974). *The Rorschach: A comprehensive system.* New York: Wiley.

Exner, J. E. (1978). *The Rorschach: A comprehensive system: Vol. 2. Current research and advanced interpretations.* New York: Wiley-Interscience.

Exner, J. E. (1983). Rorschach assessment. In I. B. Weiner (Ed.), *Methods in clinical psychology* (2nd ed.). New York: Wiley.

Exner, J. E. (1986). *The Rorschach: A comprehensive system: Vol. 1. Basic foundations* (2nd ed.). New York: Wiley.

Exner, J. E. (1990). *Workbook for the comprehensive system* (3rd ed.). Asheville, NC: Rorschach Workshops.

Exner, J. E., Jr. (1993). *The Rorschach: A comprehensive system. Vol. 1. Basic foundations* (3rd ed.). New York: Wiley.

Exner, J. E. (in press). *The Rorschach: A comprehensive system: Vol. 2. Current research and advanced interpretation* (2nd ed.). New York: Wiley.

Exner, J. E., Armbruster, G. L., & Viglione, D. (1978). The temporal stability of some Rorschach features. *Journal of Personality Assessment, 42,* 474–482.

Exner, J. E., & Weiner, I. B. (1982). *The Rorschach: A comprehensive system: Vol. 3. Assessment of children and adolescents.* New York: Wiley.

Eyberg, S. M., & Robinson, E. A. (1983). Conduct problem behavior: Standardization of a behavioral rating scale with adolescents. *Journal of Clinical Child Psychology, 12,* 347–357.

Eyberg, S. M., & Ross, A. W. (1978). Assessment of child behavior problems: The validation of a new inventory. *Journal of Clinical Child Psychology, 7,* 113–116.

Eyde, L. D. (Ed.). (1987). Computerized psychological testing (Special issue). *Applied Psychology: An International Review, 36*(3–4).

Eyde, L. D., Kowal, D. M., & Fishburne, F. J., Jr. (1990). The validity of computer-based test interpretations of the MMPI. In S. Wise & T. B. Gutkin (Eds.), *The computer as adjunct to the decision-making process.* Lincoln: Buros Institute of Mental Measurements, University of Nebraska.

Eyde, L. D., Moreland, K. L., Robertson, G. J., Primoff, E. S., & Most, R. B. (1988). Test user qualifications: A data-based approach to promoting good test use. *Issues in Scientific Psychology.* Report of the Test User Qualifications Working Group of the Joint Committee on Testing Practices. Washington, DC: American Psychological Association.

Eyde, L. D., & Primoff, E. S. (1986). Test purchaser qualifications: A proposed voluntary system based on test ethics. In Scientific Affairs Office, American Psychological Association (Ed.)., *Test purchaser qualifications: Present practice, professional needs, and a proposed system.* Washington, DC: American Psychological Association.

Eysenck, H. J. (1947). *Dimensions of personality.* New York: Praeger.

Eysenck, H. J. (1961). The effects of psychotherapy. In H. J. Eysenck (Ed.), *Handbook of abnormal psychology: An experimental approach* (pp. 697–725). New York: Basic Books.

Eysenck, H. J. (1967). Intelligence assessment: A theoretical and experimental approach. *British Journal of Educational Psychology, 37,* 81–98.

Eysenck, H. J. (1972). Primaries or second-order factors: A critical consideration of Cattell's 16PF battery. *British Journal of Social and Clinical Psychology, 11,* 265–269.

Eysenck, H. J. (1985). Can personality study ever be scientific? *Journal of Social Behavior and Personality, 1,* 3–19.

Eysenck, H. J. (1986). A reply to Dreger, Cattell, and Cummings. *Journal of Social Behavior and Personality, 1,* 309–314.

Eysenck, H. J. (1991). Dimensions of personality: 16, 5, or 3?—Criteria for a taxonomic paradigm. *Personality and Individual Differences, 12,* 773–790.

Eysenck, H. J. (1992a). Four ways five factors are *not* basic. *Personality and Individual Differences, 13,* 667–673.

Eysenck, H. J. (1992b). A reply to Costa and McCrae. P or A and C—The role of theory. *Personality and Individual Differences, 13,* 867–868.

Eysenck, H. J. (1993). Comment on Goldberg. *American Psychologist, 48,* 1299–1300.

Fagan, J., Broughton, E., Allen, M., Clark, B., and Emerson, P. (1969). Comparison of the Binet and WPPSI with lower class five year olds. *Journal of Consulting and Clinical Psychology, 33,* 607–609.

Faller, K. C. (1988). *Child sexual abuse.* New York: Columbia University Press.

Fantuzzo, J. W., & Moon, G. W. (1984). Competency mandate: A model for teaching skills in the administration of the WAIS-R. *Journal of Clinical Psychology, 40,* 1053–1059.

Farrall, F. R., & Card, R. D. (1988). Advancements in physiological evaluation of assessment and treatment of the sexual transgressor. In R. A. Prentky & V. L. Quinsey (Eds.), *Human sexual aggression: Current perspectives* (pp. 261–273). New York: Annals of the New York Academy of Sciences.

Farrell, A. D. (1986). The microcomputer as a tool for behavioral assessment. *The Behavior Therapist, 1,* 16–17.

Faust, D. S., & Hollingsworth, J. O. (1991). Concurrent validation of the Wechsler Preschool and Primary Scale of Intelligence—Revised (WPPSI-R) with two criteria of cognitive abilities. Special issue: Wechsler Preschool and Primary Scale of Intelligence (WPPSI-R). *Journal of Psychoeducational Assessment, 9,* 224–229.

Faust, D. S., & Ziskin, J. (1988a). The expert witness in psychology and psychiatry. *Science, 241,* 31–35.

Faust, D. S., & Ziskin, J. (1988b). Response to Fowler and Matarazzo. *Science,* 1143–1144.

Fee, A. F., Elkins, G. R., & Boyd, L. (1982). Testing and counseling psychologists: Current practices and implications for training. *Journal of Personality Assessment, 46,* 116–118.

Felton, B. J., & Revenson, T. A. (1987). Age differences in coping with chronic illness. *Psychology and Aging, 2,* 164–170.

Ferere, H., Burns, W. J., & Roth, L. (1992). Use of the Revised Developmental Test of Visual-Motor Integration with chronic mentally ill adult population. *Perceptual and Motor Skills, 74,* 287–290.

Ferguson, R. L., & Novick, M. R. (1973). Implementation of a Bayesian system for decision analysis in a program of individually prescribed instruction. *ACT Research Report,* Number 60.

Feshback, S. (1961). The influence of drive arousal and conflict. In J. Kagan & G. Lesser (Eds.), *Contemporary issues in thematic apperception methods.* Springfield, IL: Charles C Thomas.

Filsinger, E. (1983). A machine-aided marital observation technique. The Dyadic Interaction Scoring Code. *Journal of Marriage and the Family, 2,* 623–632.

Fingarette, H., & Hasse, A. F. (1979). *Mental disabilities and criminal responsibility.* Berkeley: University of California Press.

Finkel, N. J., Shaw, R., Bercaw, S., et al. (1985). Insanity defenses: From the jurors' perspective. *Law and Psychology Review, 9,* 77–92.

Finkelhor, D., & Dziuba-Leatherman, J. (1994). Victimization of children. *American Psychologist, 49,* 173–183.

Fischer, E., & Arnold, S. J. (1994). Sex, gender identity, gender role attributes, and consumer behavior. *Psychology & Marketing, 11,* 163–182.

Fiske, D. W. (1967). The subjects react to tests. *American Psychologist, 22,* 287–296.

Fitts, W. H. (1965). *Manual for the Tennessee Self-Concept Scale.* Nashville: Counselor Recordings and Tests.

Fitzgibbons, D. J., & Shearn, C. R. (1972). Concepts of schizophrenia among mental health professionals: A factor-analytic study. *Journal of Consulting and Clinical Psychology, 38,* 288–295.

Fitzpatrick, L. J. (1977). Automated data collection for observed events. *Behavior Research Methods and Instrumentation, 14,* 241–249.

Flanagan, D. P., & Alfonso, V. C. (1993a). Differences required for significance between Wechsler Verbal and Performance IQs and WIAT subtests and composites: The predicted-achievement method. *Psychology in the Schools, 30,* 125–132.

Flanagan, D. P., & Alfonso, V. C. (1993b). WIAT subtest and composites predicted-achievement values based on WISC-III Verbal and Performance IQs. *Psychology in the Schools, 30,* 310–320.

Flanagan, J. C. (1938). Review of Measuring Intelligence by Terman and Merrill. *Harvard Educational Review, 8,* 130–133.

Flanagan, J. C., & Burns, R. K. (1955). The employee business record: A new appraisal and development tool. *Harvard Business Review, 33*(5), 99–102.

Fleishman, J. A., & Foogel, B. (1994). Coping and depressive symptoms among people with AIDS. *Health Psychology, 13,* 156–169.

Flett, G. L., Blankstein, K. R., Pliner, P., & Bator, C. (1988). Impression management and self-deception components of appraised emotional experience. *British Journal of Social Psychology, 27,* 67–77.

Fliess, J. L. (1971). Measuring nominal scale agreement among many raters. *Psychological Bulletin, 76,* 378–382.

Flowers, J. H. (1982). Some simple Apple II software for the collection and analysis of observational data. *Behavior Research Methods and Instrumentation, 14,* 241–249.

Flowers, J. H., & Leger, D. W. (1982). Personal computers and behavior observation: An introduction. *Behavior Research Methods and Instrumentation, 14,* 227–230.

Flugel, J. C., & West, D. J. (1964). *A hundred years of psychology: 1833–1933.* New York: Basic Books.

Foerster, L. M., & Little Soldier, D. (1974). Open education and native American values. *Educational Leadership, 32,* 41–45.

Folstein, M. F., Folstein, S. E., & McHugh, P. R. (1975). "Mini-Mental State": A practical method for grading the cognitive state of patients for the clinician. *Journal of Psychiatric Research, 12,* 189–198.

Fontana, V. J., Donovan, D., & Wong, R. J. (1963, December 8). The maltreatment syndrome in children. *New England Journal of Medicine, 269,* 1389–1394.

Forbes, G. B. (1985). The Personality Inventory for Children (PIC) and hyperactivity: Clinical utility and problems of generalizability. *Journal of Pediatric Psychology, 10,* 141–149.

Ford, J. K., & Wroten, S. P. (1984). Introducing new methods for conducting training evaluation and for linking training evaluation to program design. *Personnel Psychology, 37,* 651–665.

Forer, B. R. (1949). The fallacy of personal validation: A classroom demonstration of gullibility. *Journal of Abnormal and Social Psychology, 44,* 118–123.

Foreyt, J. P. (1987). Issues in the assessment and treatment of obesity. *Journal of Consulting and Clinical Psychology, 55,* 677–684.

Forrest, D. W. (1974). *Francis Galton: The life and works of a Victorian genius.* New York: Taplinger.

Forrester, G., Encel, J., & Geffen, G. (1994). Measuring post-traumatic amnesia (PTA): An historical review. *Brain Injury, 8,* 175–184.

Forth, A. E., Hart, S. D., & Hare, R. D. (1990). Assessment of psychopathy in male young offenders. *Psychological Assessment: A Journal of Consulting and Clinical Psychology, 2,* 342–344.

Fourqurean, J. M. (1987). A K-ABC and WISC-R comparison for Latino learning-disabled children of limited English proficiency. *Journal of School Psychology, 25,* 15–21.

Fowler, D. R., Finkelstein, A., & Penk, W. (1986). *Measuring treatment responses by computer interview.* Paper presented at the 94th annual meeting of the American Psychological Association, Washington, DC.

Fowler, R. D. (1969). Automated interpretation of personality test data. In J. N. Butcher (Ed.), *MMPI: Research developments and clinical applications* (pp. 105–126). New York: McGraw-Hill.

Fowler, R. D., & Matarazzo, J. D. (1988). Psychologists and psychiatrists as expert witnesses. *Science, 241,* 1143.

Fraboni, M., & Saltstone, R. (1992). The WAIS-R number-of-factors quandary: A cluster-analytic approach to construct validation. *Educational and Psychological Measurement, 52,* 603–613.

Frank, L. K. (1939). Projective methods for the study of personality. *Journal of Psychology, 8,* 389–413.

Franklin, M. R., Duley, S. M., Rousseau, E. W., & Sabers, D. L. (1981). Construct validation of the Piers-Harris Children's Self-Concept Scale. *Educational and Psychological Measurement, 41,* 439–443.

Franzen, M. D. (1985). Review of Luria-Nebraska Neuropsychological Battery. In D. J. Keyser & R. C. Sweetland (Eds.), *Test critiques* (Vol. 3; pp. 402–414). Kansas City, MO: Test Corporation of America.

Franzen, M. D. (1986). Review of Luria-Nebraska Neuropsychological Battery, Form II. In D. J. Keyser & R. C. Sweetland (Eds.), *Test critiques* (Vol. 4; pp. 382–386). Kansas City, MO: Test Corporation of America.

Frederiksen, N., Saunders, D. R., & Wand, B. (1957). The in-basket test. *Psychological Monographs, 71*(9, Whole No. 438).

Fredman, N., & Sherman, R. (1987). *Handbook of measurements for marriage & family therapy.* New York: Brunner/Mazel.

Fredrickson, N. (1993). CRA: Has it had its day? *Educational and Child Psychology, 10,* 14–26.

French, C. C. & Beaumont, J. G. (1987). The reaction of psychiatric patients to computerized assessment. *British Journal of Clinical Psychology, 26,* 267–278.

French, C. C., & Beaumont, J. G. (1991). The Differential Aptitude Test (Language Usage and Spelling): A clinical study of a computerized form. *Current Psychology: Research and Reviews, 10,* 31–48.

French, J. L. (Ed.). (1964). *Educating the gifted.* New York: Holt, Rinehart & Winston.

French, J., Graves, P. A., & Levitt, E. E. (1983). Objective and projective testing of children. In C. E. Walker & M. C. Roberts (Eds.), *Handbook of clinical child psychology* (pp. 209–248). New York: Wiley.

Freud, S. (1913/1959). Further recommendations in the technique of psychoanalysis. In E. Jones (Ed.) and J. Riviere (Trans.), *Collected papers* (Vol. 2). New York: Basic Books.

Freud, S., Ferenczi, S., Abraham, K., Simmel, E., & Jones, E. (1921). *Psychoanalysis and the war neuroses.* New York: International Psychoanalytic Press.

Freund, K. (1963). A laboratory method for diagnosing predominance of homosexual and heterosexual erotic interest in the male. *Behavior Research and Therapy, 1,* 85–93.

Freund, K., Sedlacek, E., & Knob, K. (1965). A simple transducer for mechanical plethysmography of the male genital. *Journal of Experimental Analysis of Behavior, 8,* 169–170.

Friedman, H. S. (Ed.). (1990). *Personality and disease.* New York: Wiley.

Friedman, M., & Rosenman, R. H. (1974). *Type A behavior and your heart.* New York: Knopf.

Friedrich, W. M., Urquiza, A. J., & Beike, R. (1986). Behavioral problems in sexually abused young children. *Journal of Pediatric Psychiatry, 11,* 47–57.

Friel-Patti, S., & Finitzo, T. (1990). Language learning in a prospective study of otitis media with effusion in the first two years of life. *Journal of speech and Hearing Research, 33,* 188–194.

Frisch, M. B., Cornell, J., Villanueva, M., & Retzlaff, P. J. (1992). Clinical validation of the Quality of Life Inventory: A measure of life satisfaction for use in treatment planning and outcome assessment. *Psychological Assessment, 4,* 92–101.

Fromm-Auch, D., & Yeudall, L. T. (1983). Normative data for the Halstead-Reitan Neuropsychological Tests. *Journal of Clinical Neuropsychology, 5,* 221–238.

Frostig, M. (1966). *Frostig Developmental Test of Visual Perception.* Palo Alto, CA: Consulting Psychologists Press.

Fuld, P. A. (1984). Test profile of cholinergic dysfunction and of Alzheimer-type dementia. *Journal of Clinical Neuropsychology, 6,* 380–392.

Fullan, M., & Loubser, J. (1972). Education and adaptive capacity. *Sociology of Education, 45,* 271–287.

Funder, D. C., & Colvin, C. R. (1991). Some behaviors are more predictable than others. *The Score, 13*(4), 3–4.

Furnham, A., & Stringfield, P. (1993). Personality and occupational behavior: Myers-Briggs Type Indicator correlates of managerial practices in two cultures. *Human Relations, 46,* 827–848.

Furse, D. H., & Stewart, D. W. (1984). Manipulating dissonance to improve mail survey response. *Psychology & Marketing, 1,* 71–84.

Gakhar, S. C. (1986). Correlational research—individual differences in intelligence, aptitude, personality and achievement among science, commerce, and arts students. *Journal of Psychological Researches, 30,* 22–29.

Gallagher, J. J. (1966). *Research summary on gifted child education.* Springfield, IL: State Department of Public Instruction.

Gallucci, N. T. (1986). General and specific objections to the MMPI. *Educational and Psychological Measurement, 46,* 985–988.

Galton, F. (1869). *Hereditary genius.* London: Macmillan. (Macmillan edition published in 1892.)

Galton, F. (1874). *English men of science.* New York: Appleton.

Galton, F. (1879). Psychometric experiments. *Brain, 2,* 149–162.

Galton, F. (1883). *Inquiries into human faculty and its development.* London: Macmillan.

Gammon, J. A. (1981). Ophthalmic manifestations of child abuse. In N. S. Ellerstein (Ed.), *Child abuse and neglect: A medical reference* (pp. 121–139). New York: Wiley.

Garbarino, J., et al. (1987). *The psychologically battered child.* San Francisco: Jossey-Bass.

Gardner, R. A. (1971). *The boys and girls book about divorce.* New York: Bantam.

Gardner, R. A. (1982). *Family evaluation in child custody litigation.* Cresskill, NJ: Creative Therapeutics.

Gardner, R. W., Holzman, P. S., Klein, G. S., Linton, H. B., & Spence, D. F. (1959). Cognitive control: A study of individual consistencies in cognitive behavior. *Psychological Issues, 1,* (4).

Garfield, S., & Kurtz, R. M. (1973). Attitudes toward training in diagnostic testing. A survey of directors of internship training. *Journal of Consulting and Clinical Psychology, 40,* 350–355.

Garfield, S. L., & Eron, L. D. (1948). Interpreting mood and activity in TAT stories. *Journal of Abnormal and Social Psychology, 43,* 338–345.

Garmoe, W. S., Schefft, B. K., & Moses, J. A., Jr. (1991). Evaluation of the diagnostic validity of the Luria-Nebraska Neuropsychological Battery Form II. *International Journal of Neuroscience, 59,* 231–239.

Garner, D. M., & Garfinkel, P. E. (1981). Body image in anorexia nervosa: Measurement, theory, and clinical implications. *International Journal of Psychiatry in Medicine, 11,* 263–284.

Garner, D. M., Garfinkel, P. E., Stancer, H. C., & Moldofsky, H. (1976). Body image disturbances in anorexia nervosa and obesity. *Psychosomatic Medicine, 38,* 327–336.

Garrett, H. E., & Schneck, M. R. (1933). *Psychological tests, methods and results.* New York: Harper.

Gass, C. S., Russell, E. W., & Hamilton, R. A. (1990). Accuracy of MMPI-based inferences regarding memory and concentration in closed-head-trauma patients. *Psychological Assessment: A Journal of Consulting & Clinical Psychology, 2,* 175–178.

Gaston, L. (1991). Reliability and criterion-related validity of the California Psychotherapy Alliance Scales—Patient version. *Psychological Assessment: A Journal of Consulting and Clinical Psychology, 3,* 68–74.

Gatewood, R., & Perloff, R. (1990). Testing and industrial application. In G. Goldstein & M. Hersen (Eds.), *Handbook of psychological assessment* (pp. 486–501). New York: Pergamon Press.

Gaugler, B. B., Rosenthal, D. B., Thornton III, G. C., & Bentson, C. (1987). Meta-analysis of assessment center validity. *Journal of Applied Psychology, 72,* 493–511.

Gavzer, B. (1990, May 27). Should you tell all? *Parade Magazine,* pp. 4–7.

Geiger, M. A., Boyle, E. J., & Pinto, J. K. (1993). An examination of ipsative and normative versions of Kolb's Revised Learning Style Inventory. *Educational and Psychological Measurement, 53,* 717–726.

Gerety, M. B., Mulrow, C. D., Tuley, M. R., Hazuda, H. P., Lichtenstein, M. J., Bohannon, R., Kanten, D. N., O'Neil, M. B., & Gorton, A. (1993). Development and validation of a physical performance instrument for the functionally impaired elderly: The Physical Disability Index (PDI). *Journal of Gerontology: Medical Sciences, 48,* M33–M38.

Gerken, K. C. (1991). Assessment of preschool children with severe handicaps. In B. A. Bracken (Ed.), *The psychoeducational assessment of preschool children* (2nd ed.; pp. 392–429). Needham, MA: Allyn and Bacon.

Gerry, M. H. (1973). Cultural myopia: The need for a corrective lens. *Journal of School Psychology, 11,* 307–315.

Gerstle, R. M., Geary, D. C., Himelstein, P., & Reller-Geary, L. (1988). Rorschach predictors of therapeutic outcome for inpatient treatment of children: A proactive study. *Journal of Clinical Psychology, 44,* 277–280.

Gesell, A. (1945). *The embryology of behavior. The beginnings of the human mind.* New York: Harper.

Gesell, A. (1954). The ontogenesis of infant behavior. In L. Carmichael (Ed.), *Manual of child psychology.* New York: Wiley.

Gesell, A., & Amatruda, C. S. (1947). *Developmental diagnosis: Normal and abnormal child development* (2nd ed.). New York: Harper & Row.

Gesell, A., & Thompson, H. (1929). Learning and growth in identical twin infants. *Genetic Psychology Monographs, 6,* 1–124.

Gesell, A., et al. (1940). *The first five years of life.* New York: Harper.

Ghiselli, E. E. (1973). The variety of aptitude tests in personnel selection. *Personnel Psychology, 26,* 461–477.

Ghiselli, E. E., & Barthol, R. P. (1953). The validity of personality inventories in the selection of employees. *Journal of Applied Psychology, 38,* 18–20.

Ghiselli, E. E., Campbell, J. P., & Zedeck, S. (1981). *Measurement theory for the behavioral sciences.* San Francisco: Freeman.

Gibbons, S. (1988, April). *Use of the K-ABC and WISC-R with deaf children.* Paper presented at the Annual Meeting of the National Association of School Psychologists, Chicago.

Gibbins, S. (1989). The provision of school psychological assessment services for the hearing impaired: A national survey. *The Volta Review, 91,* 95–103.

Gill, W., & Hayes-Butler, K. (1989). *The effects of schoolwide discipline, role play, modeling and video utilization upon the self concept of elementary school children: A preliminary report.* Paper presented at the Society of School Librarians International Conference, San Antonio, TX. (ERIC Document Reproduction Service No. ED 305 888)

Gillingham, W. H. (1970). An investigation of examiner influence on Wechsler Intelligence Scale for Children scores (Doctoral dissertation, Michigan State University, 1970). *Dissertation Abstracts International, 31,* 2178-A. (University Microfilms No. Order 70-20, 458)

Girelli, S. A., & Stake, J. E. (1993). Bipolarity in Jungian type theory and the Myers-Briggs Type Indicator. *Journal of Personality Assessment, 60,* 290–301.

Glaser, G. J., & Metzger, G. D. (1972). Random digit dialing as a method of telephone sampling. *Journal of Marketing Research, 9,* 59–64.

Glaser, R. (1981). The future of testing: A research agenda for cognitive psychology and psychometrics. *American Psychologist, 36,* 923–936.

Glaser, R., & Nitko, A. J. (1971). Measurement in learning and instruction. In R. L. Thorndike (Ed.), *Educational measurement* (2nd ed.). Washington, DC: American Council on Education.

Gleghorn, A., Penner, L., Powers, P., & Schulman, R. (1987). The psychometric properties of several measures of body image. *Journal of Psychopathology and Behavioral Assessment, 9,* 203–218.

Gluck, M. R. (1955). The relationship between hostility in the TAT and behavioral hostility. *Journal of Projective Techniques, 19,* 21–26.

Glueck, W. F. (1978). *Personnel: A diagnostic approach.* Dallas, TX: Business Publications.

Glutting, J. J. (1989). Introduction to the structure and application of the Stanford-Binet Intelligence Scale—Fourth Edition. *Journal of School Psychology, 27,* 69–80.

Glutting, J. J., & McDermott, P. A. (1989). Using "teaching items" on ability tests: A nice idea, but does it work? *Educational and Psychological Measurement, 49,* 257–268.

Gobetz, W. A. (1953). Quantification, standardization, and validation of the Bender-Gestalt test on normal and neurotic adults. *Psychological Monographs, 67,* No. 6.

Goddard, H. H. (1908). The Binet and Simon tests of intellectual capacity. *Training School, 5,* 3–9.

Goddard, H. H. (1910). A measuring scale of intelligence. *Training School, 6,* 146–155.

Goddard, H. H. (1912). *The Kallikak family.* New York: Macmillan.

Goddard, H. H. (1913). The Binet tests in relation to immigration. *Journal of Psycho-Asthenics, 18,* 105–107.

Goddard, H. H. (1916). *Feeblemindedness.* New York: Macmillan.

Goddard, H. H. (1917). Mental tests and the immigrant, *Journal of Delinquency, 2,* 243–277.

Goffin, R. D. (1991). Personality, vocational interest, and cognitive predictors of managerial job performance and satisfaction. *Personality and Individual Differences, 12,* 221–231.

Goffman, E. (1959). *The presentaton of self in everyday life.* New York: Anchor.

Goffman, E. (1963). *Behavior in public places.* Glencoe, IL: Free Press.

Goh, D. S., & Cordonig, B. (1989). *Comparison of the Stanford-Binet Fourth Edition with WAIS-R in college learning disabled students.* Paper presented at the Annual Meeting of the National Association of School Psychologists, Boston.

Gokhale, D. V., & Kullback, S. (1978). *The information in contingency tables.* New York: Marcel Dekker.

Goldberg, J. O., Shaw, B. F., & Segal, Z. V. (1987). Concurrent validity of the Millon Clinical Multiaxial Inventory depression scales. *Journal of Consulting & Clinical Psychology, 55,* 785–787.

Goldberg, L. R. (1970). Man vs. model of man: A rationale, plus some evidence, for a method of improving on clinical inferences. *Psychological Bulletin, 73,* 422–432.

Goldberg, L. R. (1978). The reliability of reliability: The generality and correlates of intra-individual consistency in response to structured personality inventories. *Applied Psychological Measurement, 2,* 269–291.

Goldberg, L. R. (1981). Language and individual differences: The search for universals in personality lexicons. In L. Wheeler (Ed.), *Review of personality and social psychology* (Vol. 2; pp. 141–165). Beverly Hills: Sage.

Goldberg, L. R. (1992). The development of markers of the Big-Five factor structure. *Psychological Assessment, 4,* 26–42.

Goldberg, L. R. (1993). The structure of phenotypic personality traits. *American Psychologist, 48,* 26–34.

Goldberg, T. E., Gold, J. M. Greenberg, R., Griffin, S., Schulz, S. C., Pickar, D., Kleinman, J. E., & Weinberger, D. R. (1993). Contrasts between patients with affective disorders and patients with schizophrenia on a neuropsychological test battery. *American Journal of Psychiatry, 150,* 1355–1362.

Golden, C. J., Hammeke, T. A., & Purisch, A. D. (1980). *The Luria-Nebraska Neuropsychological Battery: Manual.* Los Angeles: Western Psychological Services.

Golden, C. J., et al. (1981). Cross validation of the Luria-Nebraska Neuropsychological Battery for the presence, lateralization, and localization of brain damage. *Journal of Consulting and Clinical Psychology, 49,* 491–507.

Golden, C. J., Purisch, A. D., & Hammeke, T. A. (1985). *Luria-Nebraska Neuropsychological Battery: Forms I and II, manual.* Los Angeles: Western Psychological Services.

Goldfarb, L. A., Dykens, E. M., & Gerrard, M. (1985). The Goldfarb Fear of Fat Scale. *Journal of Personality Assessment, 49,* 329–332.

Goldfried, M. R., & Davison, G. C. (1976). *Clinical behavior therapy.* New York: Holt, Rinehart, & Winston.

Goldfried, M. R., Stricker, G., & Weiner, I. B. (1971). *Rorschach handbook of clinical and research applications.* Englewood Cliffs, NJ: Prentice-Hall.

Goldfried, M., & Zax, M. (1965). The stimulus value of the TAT. *Journal of Projective Techniques, 29,* 46–57.

Golding, S. L. (1975). Flies in the ointment: Methodological problems in the analysis of the percentage of variance due to persons and situations. *Psychological Bulletin, 82,* 278–288.

Goldman, R., & Fristoe, M. (1972). *Goldman-Fristoe Test of Articulation.* Circle Pines, MN: American Guidance Service.

Goldman, R., Fristoe, M., & Woodcock, R. (1970). *Goldman-Fristoe-Woodcock Test of Auditory Discrimination.* Circle Pines, MN: American Guidance Service.

Goldstein, A. S. (1967). *The insanity defense.* New Haven, CN: Yale University Press.

Goldstein, G. (1986). The neuropsychology of schizophrenia. In I. Grant & K. M. Adams (Eds.), *Neuropsychological assessment of neuropsychiatric disorders* (pp. 146–171). New York: Oxford University Press.

Goldstein, G., & Shelly, C. (1982). A further attempt to cross-validate the Russell, Neuringer, and Goldstein neuropsychological keys. *Journal of Consulting and Clinical Psychology, 50,* 721–726.

Goldstein, K. (1927). Die lokalisation in her grosshim

rinde. *Handb. norm. pathol. psychiologie.* Berlin: J. Springer.

Goldstein, K. (1939). *The organism.* New York: American Book.

Goldstein, K. (1963a). *The organism.* Boston: Beacon.

Goldstein, K. (1963b). The modifications of behavior consequent to cerebral lesions. *Psychiatric Quarterly, 10,* 586–610.

Goldston, D. B., O'Hara, M. W., & Schartz, H. A. (1990). Reliability, validity, and preliminary normative data for the Inventory to Diagnose Depression in a college population. *Psychological Assessment: A Journal of Consulting & Clinical Psychology, 2,* 212–215.

Goldwater, B. C. (1972). Psychological significance of pupillary movements. *Psychological Bulletin, 77,* 340–355.

Good, R. H., Chowdhri, S., Katz, L., Vollman, M., & Creek, R. (1989, March). *Effect of matching instruction and simultaneous/sequential processing strength.* Paper presented at the Annual Meeting of the National Association of School Psychologists, Boston.

Good, R. H., & Lane, S. (1988). *Confirmatory factor analysis of the K-ABC and WISC-R: Hierarchical models.* Paper presented at the Annual Meeting of the American Psychological Association, Atlanta, GA.

Good, R. H., & Thornton, J. (1988). *Stanford-Binet Intelligence Scale, Fourth Edition regional database: Preliminary results.* Paper presented at the Annual Meeting of the National Association of School Psychologists, Chicago.

Good, R. H., Vollmer, M., Creek, R. J., & Katz, L. (1993). Treatment utility of the Kaufman Assessment Battery for Children: Effects of matching instruction and student processing strength. *School Psychology Review, 22,* 8–26.

Goodman, G. S., & Reed, R. S. (1986). Age differences in eyewitness testimony. *Law and Human Behavior, 10,* 317–332.

Goodwin, D. A. J., Boggs, S. R., & Grahm-Pole, J. (1994). Development and validation of the Pediatric Oncology Quality of Life Scale. *Psychological Assessment, 6,* 321–328.

Gorham, D. R. (1956). A Proverbs Test for clinical and experimental use. *Psychological Reports, Monograph Supplement, 2,* No. 1, 2–12.

Gorsuch, R. L. (1974). *Factor analysis.* Philadelphia: Saunders.

Gorsuch, R. L. (1983). *Factor analysis* (2nd ed.). Hillsdale, NJ: Erlbaum.

Gottfredson, L. S. (1988). Reconsidering fairness: A matter of social and ethical priorities. *Journal of Vocational Behavior, 33,* 293–319.

Gottfredson, L. S. (1994). The science and politics of race-norming. *American Psychologist, 49,* 955–963.

Gough, H. G. (1960). The Adjective Check List as a personality assessment research technique. *Psychological Reports, 6,* 107–122.

Gough, H. G., & Heilbrun, A. B., Jr. (1980). *The Adjective Checklist manual (Revised).* Palo Alto, CA: Consulting Psychologists Press.

Graf, M. H., & Hinton, R. N. (1994). A 3-year comparison study of WISC-R and WISC-III IQ scores for a sample of special education students. *Educational and Psychological Measurement, 54,* 128–133.

Graham, J. R. (1967). A Q-sort study of the accuracy of clinical descriptions based on the MMPI. *Journal of Psychiatric Research, 5,* 297–305.

Graham, J. R. (1977). *The MMPI: A practical guide.* New York: Oxford University Press.

Graham, J. R. (1990a). *MMPI-2: Assessing personality and psychopathology.* New York: Oxford University Press.

Graham, J. R. (1990b). Congruence between MMPI and MMPI-2 code types. *News and Profiles: A Newsletter of the MMPI-2 Workshops and Symposia, 1*(2), 1–2, 12.

Graham, J. R., & Butcher, J. N. (1988, March). *Differentiating schizophrenic and major affective disorders with the revised form of the MMPI.* Paper presented at the 23rd Annual Symposium on Recent Developments in the Use of the MMPI, St. Petersburg, FL.

Granat, D. (1990, September). What makes you so smart? *Washingtonian, 25,* 134–141.

Grayson, H. M., & Backer, T. E. (1972). Scoring accuracy of four automated MMPI interpretation report agencies. *Journal of Clinical Psychology, 28,* 366–370.

GRE 1993–94 guide to the use of the Graduate Record Examination program. (1993). Princeton, NJ: Educational Testing Service.

GRE 1994–95 bulletin. (1994). Princeton, NJ: Educational Testing Service.

GRE 1994–95 General Test descriptive booklet. (1994). Princeton, NJ: Educational Testing Service.

GRE technical manual. (1993). Princeton, NJ: Educational Testing Service.

Greaud, V. A., & Green, B. F. (1986). Equivalence of conventional and computer presentation of speed tests. *Applied Psychological Measurement, 10,* 23–34.

Green, A. (1986). True and false allegations of sexual abuse in child custody disputes. *Journal of the American Academy of Child Psychology, 25,* 449–456.

Green, B. F. (1984). *Computer-based ability testing.* Paper delivered at the 91st annual meeting of the American Psychological Association, Toronto, Ontario, Canada.

Green, P. E., Carmone, F. J., Jr., & Smith, S. M. (1989). *Multidimensional scaling: Concepts and applications.* Boston: Allyn and Bacon.

Greenbaum, T. L. (1988). *The practical handbook and guide to focus group research.* Lexington, MA: Heath.

Greene, R. L. (1985). New norms, old norms, what norms for the MMPI? *Journal of Personality Assessment, 49,* 108–110.

Greene, R. L. (1988). Assessment of malingering and defensiveness by objective personality measures. In R. Rogers (Ed.), *Clinical assessment of malingering and deception* (pp. 123–158). New York: Guilford Press.

Greenspoon, J. (1955). The reinforcing effect of two spoken sounds on the frequency of two responses. *American Journal of Psychology, 68,* 409–416.

Greenspoon, J., & Gersten, C. D. (1967). A new look at psychological testing: Psychological testing from the standpoint of a behaviorist. *American Psychologist, 22,* 848–853.

Gregg, N., & Hoy, C. (1985). A comparison of the WAIS-R and the Woodcock-Johnson Tests of Cognitive Ability with learning-disabled college students. *Journal of Psychoeducational Assessment, 3,* 267–274.

Gresham, F. M. (1989). Review of the Parenting Stress Index. In J. C. Conoley & J. J. Kramer (Eds.), *The tenth mental measurements yearbook.* Lincoln: The Buros Institute of Mental Measurements, University of Nebraska.

Gresham, F. M., & Elliott, S. M. (1990). *Social Skills Rating System.* Circle Pines, MN: American Guidance Service.

Grey, R. J., & Kipnis, D. (1976). Untangling the performance appraisal dilemma: The influence of perceived organizational context on evaluative processes. *Journal of Applied Psychology, 61,* 329–335.

Grimsley, G., & Jarrett, H. (1975). The relation of past managerial achievements to test measures obtained in the employment situation: Methodology and results—II. *Personnel Psychology, 28,* 215–231.

Grinker, R. R., & Spiegel, J. P. (1945). *Men under stress.* New York: Blakiston.

Groenland, E. A. G., & Schoormans, J. P. L. (1994). Comparing mood-induction and affective conditioning as mechanisms influencing product evaluation and product choice. *Psychology and Marketing, 11,* 183–197.

Groenveld, M., & Jan, J. E. (1992). Intelligence profiles of low vision and blind children. *Journal of Visual Impairment and Blindness, 86,* 68–71.

Gross, M. L. (1962). *The brain watchers.* New York: Random House.

Grossack, M. M. (1964). *Understanding consumer behavior.* Boston: Christopher.

Grossman, I., Mednitsky, S., Dennis, B., & Scharff, L. (1993). Validation of an "amazingly" short form of the WAIS-R for a clinically depressed sample. *Journal of Psychoeducational Assessment, 11,* 173–181.

Grunzke, N., Gunn, N., & Staufer, G. (1970). *Comparative performance of low-ability airmen* (Technical Report 70-4). Lackland AFB, TX: Air Force Human Resources Laboratory.

Guastello, S. J. (1993). A two-(and-a-half)-tiered trait taxonomy. *American Psychologist, 48,* 1298–1299.

Guastello, S. J., & Rieke, M. L. (1990). The Barnum Effect and the validity of computer-based test interpretations: The Human Resource Development Report. *Psychological Assessment, 2,* 186–190.

Guidelines for computer-based interpretation and assessment. (1985). Washington, DC: American Psychological Association.

Guidelines for computer-based tests and interpretations. (1986). Washington, DC: American Psychological Association.

Guilford, J. P. (1948). Some lessons from aviation psychology. *American Journal of Psychology, 3,* 3–11.

Guilford, J. P. (1954a). *Psychometric methods.* New York: McGraw-Hill.

Guilford, J. P. (1954b). A factor analytic study across the domains of reasoning, creativity, and evaluation. I. Hypothesis and description of tests. *Reports from the psychology laboratory.* Los Angeles: University of Southern California.

Guilford, J. P. (1959). *Personality.* New York: McGraw-Hill.

Guilford, J. P. (1967). *The nature of human intelligence.* New York: McGraw-Hill.

Guilford, J. P., et al. (1974). *Structure-of-Intellect Abilities.* Orange, CA: Sheridan Psychological Services.

Guilford, J. P. (1975). Factors and factors of personality. *Psychological Bulletin, 82,* 802–814.

Guilford, J. P. (1985). A sixty-year perspective on psychological measurement. *Applied Psychological Measurement, 9,* 341–349.

Guilmette, T. J., & Faust, D. (1991). Characteristics of neuropsychologists who prefer the Halstead-Reitan Battery or the Luria-Nebraska Neuropsychological Battery. *Professional Psychology: Research and Practice, 22*(1), 80–83.

Guilmette, T. J., Faust, D., Hart, K. & Arkes, H. R. (1990). A national survey of psychologists who offer neuropsychological services. *Archives of Clinical Neuropsychology, 5,* 373–392.

Guion, R. M. (1967). Personnel selection. *Annual Review of Psychology, 18,* 191–216.

Guion, R. M. (1980). On trinitarian doctrines of validity. *Professional Psychology, 11,* 385–398.

Guion, R. M., & Gottier, R. F. (1965). Validity of personality measures in personnel selection. *Personnel Psychology, 18,* 81–91.

Gulliksen, H. (1950). *Theory of mental tests.* New York: Wiley.

Gulliksen, H., & Messick, S. (Eds.). (1960). *Psychological scaling: Theory and applications.* New York: Wiley, 1960.

Gunnison, J. (1984). Developing educational interventions from assessments involving the K-ABC. *Journal of Special Education, 18,* 325–344.

Gur, R., & Sackheim, H. A. (1979). Self-deception: A concept in search of a phenomenon. *Journal of Personality and Social Psychology, 37,* 147–169.

Gustafson, J. E. (1985). Measuring and interpreting *g. The Behavioral and Brain Sciences, 8,* 231–232.

Gutkin, T. B., Reynolds, C. R., & Calvin, G. A. (1984). Factor analyses of the Wechsler Adult Intelligence Scale—Revised (WAIS-R): An examination of the standardization sample. *Journal of School Psychology, 22*(1), 83–93.

Gutkin, T. B., & Wise, S. L. (Eds.). (1988). *The computer as adjunct to the decision-making process.* Hillsdale, NJ: Erlbaum.

Guttman, L. (1944a). A basis for scaling qualitative data. *American Sociological Review, 9,* 139–150.

Guttman, L. A. (1944b). A basis for scaling qualitative data. *American Sociological Review, 9,* 179–190.

Guttman, L. (1947). The Cornell technique for scale and intensity analysis. *Educational and Psychological Measurement, 7,* 247–280.

Gwartney-Gibbs, P. A. (1986). The institutionalization of premarital cohabitation: Estimates from marriage license applications, 1970–1980. *Journal of Marriage and the Family, 48,* 423–434.

Gynther, M. D., & Gynther, R. A. (1976). Personality inventories. In I. B. Weiner (Ed.), *Clinical methods in psychology.* New York: Wiley.

Gyurke, J. S. (1991). The assessment of children with the Wechsler Preschool and Primary Scale of Intelligence—Revised. In B. A. Bracken (Ed.), *The psychoeducational assessment of preschool children* (2nd ed.; pp. 86–132). Needham Heights, MA: Allyn and Bacon.

Gyurke, J. S., Stone, B., & Beyer, M. (1990). A confirmatory factor analysis of the WPPSI-R. *Journal of Psychoeducational Assessment, 8*(1), 15–21.

Hackett, R. D., Bycio, P., & Hausdorf, P. A. (1994). Further assessment of Meyer and Allen's (1991) three component model of organizational commitment. *Journal of Applied Psychology, 79,* 15–23.

Hadaway, N., & Marek-Schroer, M. F. (1992). Multidimensional assessment of the gifted minority student. *Roeper Review, 15,* 73–77.

Haensly, P. A., & Torrance, E. P. (1990). Assessment of creativity in children and adolescents. In C. R. Reynolds & R. W. Kamphaus (Eds.), *Handbook of psychological and educational assessment of children: Intelligence & achievement* (pp. 697–722). New York: Guilford Press.

Hagender, H. (1967). *Influence of creative writing experiences on general creative development.* Master's research paper, University of Minnesota, Minneapolis.

Hahn, M. E. (1984). *The California Life Goals Evaluation Schedules manual.* Los Angeles: Western Psychological Services.

Hainsworth, P. K., & Siqueland, M. L. (1969). *Meeting Street School Screening Test.* Providence, RI: Crippled Children and Adults of Rhode Island.

Haire, M. (1950). Projective techniques in marketing research. *Journal of Marketing, 14,* 649–652.

Hall, C. S., & Lindzey, G. (1970). *Theories of personality.* New York: Wiley.

Halleck, S. L. (1976). Discussion of "Socially Reinforced Obsessing." *Journal of Consulting and Clinical Psychology, 44,* 146–147.

Halperin, K., Snyder, C. R., Shenkel, R. J., & Houston, B. K. (1976). Effects of source status and message favorability on acceptance of personality feedback. *Journal of Applied Psychology, 61,* 85–88.

Halpern, F. (1951). The Bender Visual Motor Test. In H. H. Anderson & G. Anderson (Eds.), *An introduction to projective techniques* (pp. 324–341). Englewood Cliffs, NJ: Prentice-Hall.

Halpern, F. (1958). Child case study. In E. F. Hammer (Ed.), *The clinical application of projective drawings* (pp. 113–129). Springfield, IL: Charles C Thomas.

Halstead, W. C. (1947a). *Brain and intelligence.* Chicago: University of Chicago Press.

Halstead, W. C. (1947b). *Brain and intelligence: A quantitative study of the frontal lobes.* Chicago: University of Chicago Press.

Halstead, W. C., & Wepman, J. M. (1959). The Halstead-Wepman Aphasia Screening Test. *Journal of Speech and Hearing Disorders, 14,* 9–15.

Hambleton, R. K. (1979). Latent trait models and their application. *New Directions in Testing and Measurement, 4,* 13–32.

Hambleton, R. K. (1988). Principles and applications of item response theory. In R. L. Linn (Ed.), *Educational measurement* (3rd ed.). New York: American Council on Education/Macmillan.

Hambleton, R. K., & Cook, L. L. (1977). Latent trait models and their use in the analysis of educational test data. *Journal of Educational Measurement, 14,* 75–96.

Hambleton, R. K., & Jurgensen, C. (1990). Criterion-referenced assessment of school achievement. In C. R. Reynolds & R. W. Kamphaus (Eds.), *Handbook of psychological and educational assessment of children: Intelligence & achievement* (pp. 456–476). New York: Guilford Press.

Hambleton, R. K., & Novick, M. R. (1973). Toward an integration of theory and method for criterion-referenced tests. *Journal of Educational Measurement, 10,* 159–170.

Hamburg, D., & Adams, J. E. (1967). A perspective on coping behavior: Seeking and utilizing information in major transitions. *Archives of General Psychiatry, 17,* 277–284.

Hammer, E. F. (1958). *The clinical application of projective drawings.* Springfield, IL: Charles C Thomas.

Hammer, E. F. (1981). Projective drawings. In A. I. Rabin (Ed.), *Assessment with projective techniques: A concise introduction* (pp. 151–185). New York: Springer.

Hammitt, J. K. (1990). Risk perceptions and food choice: An exploratory analysis of organic- versus conventional-produce buyers. *Risk Analysis, 10,* 367–374.

Hammond, K. R., & Allen, J. M. (1953). *Writing clinical reports.* New York: Prentice-Hall.

Hamsher, J. H., & Farina, A. (1967). "Openness" as a dimension of projective test responses. *Journal of Consulting Psychology, 31,* 525–528.

Haney, W. (1981). Validity, vaudeville, and values: A short history of social concerns over standardized testing. *American Psychologist, 36,* 1021–1034.

Haney, W., & Madaus, G. F. (1978). Making sense of the competency testing movement. *Harvard Educational Review, 48,* 462–484.

Hansen, J. C. (1986). *Strong-Hansen occupational guide.* Palo Alto, CA: Consulting Psychologists Press.

Hansen, J. C., & Tan, R. N. (1992). Concurrent validity of the 1985 Strong Interest Inventory for college major selection. *Measurement and Evaluation in Counseling and Development, 25,* 53–57.

Hanson, R. K., Hunsley, J., & Parker, K. C. H. (1988). The relationship between WAIS subtest reliability, "g" loadings, and meta-analytically derived validity estimates. *Journal of Clinical Psychology, 44,* 557–563.

Hare, R. D. (1980). A research scale for the assessment of psychopathy in criminal populations. *Personality and Individual Differences, 1,* 111–119.

Hare, R. D. (1985). *The Psychopathy Checklist.* Unpublished manuscript. University of British Columbia, Vancouver, Canada.

Hare, R. D., Harpur, A. R., Hakstian, A. R., Forth, A. E., Hart, S. D., & Newman, J. P. (1990). The Revised Psychopathy Checklist: Reliability and Factor Structure. *Psychological Assessment: A Journal of Consulting and Clinical Psychology, 2,* 338–341.

Hargadon, F. (1981). Tests and college admissions. *American Psychologist, 36,* 1112–1119.

Hargrave, G. E., Hiatt, D., Ogard, E. M., & Karr, C. (1994). Comparison of the MMPI and the MMPI-2 for a sample of peace officers. *Psychological Assessment, 6,* 27–32.

Harnett, R., & Feldmesser, D. (1980). College admissions testing and the myth of selectivity: Unresolved questions and needed research. *AAHE Bulletin, 32*(7).

Harrell, T. H., & Lombardo, T. A. (1984). Validation of an automated 16PF administration procedure. *Journal of Personality Assessment, 48,* 638–642.

Harrington, R. G. (1985a). Review of Scales of Independent Behavior. In D. J. Keyser & R. C. Sweetland (Eds.), *Test critiques* (Vol. 3). Kansas City, MO: Test Corporation of America.

Harrington, R. G. (1985b). Review of Battelle Developmental Inventory. In D. J. Keyser & R. C. Sweetland (Eds.), *Test critiques* (Vol. 2; pp. 72–82). Kansas City, MO: Test Corporation of America.

Harris, D. (1963). *Children's drawings as measures of intellectual maturity.* New York: Harcourt, Brace & Jovanovich.

Harris, D. B. (1978). A review of Kinetic Family Drawings. In O. K. Buros (Ed.), *The eighth mental measurements yearbook* (Vol. 1; pp. 884–885). Highland Park, NJ: Gryphon Press.

Harris, G. T., Rice, M. E., & Cormier, C. A. (1989). Violent recidivism among psychopaths and non-psychopaths treated in a therapeutic community. *Penetanguishene Mental Health Centre Research Report VI* (No. 181). Penetanguishene, Ontario, Canada: Penetanguishene Mental Health Centre.

Harris, P. M. (1994). Client management classification and prediction of probation outcome. *Crime and Delinquency, 40,* 154–174.

Harris, R. J., Garner-Earl, B., Sprick, S. J., & Carroll, C. (1994). Effects of foreign product names and country-of-origin attributions on advertisement evaluations. *Psychology and Marketing, 11,* 129–144.

Harrison, P. L. (1985). *Vineland Adaptive Behavior Scales, Classroom Edition: Manual.* Circle Pines, MN: American Guidance Service.

Harrison, P. L. (1990). *AGS Early Screening Profiles.* Circle Pines, MN: American Guidance Service.

Harrison, P. L., Kaufman, A. S., Hickman, J. A., &

Kaufman, N. L. (1988). A survey of tests used for adult assessments. *Journal of Psychoeducational Assessment, 6*(3), 188–198.

Hart, R. R., & Goldstein, M. A. (1985). Computer-assisted psychological assessment. *Computers in Human Services, 1,* 69–75.

Hart, R. R., Lutz, D. J., McNeill, J. W., & Adkins, T. G. (1986). Clinical comparability of the standard MMPI and the MMPI-168. *Professional Psychology: Research and Practice, 17,* 269–272.

Hart, S. D., Kropp, P. R., & Hare, R. D. (1988). Performance of male psychopaths following conditional release from prison. *Journal of Consulting and Clinical Psychology, 56,* 227–232.

Hart, S. N. (1989). Review of the Child Abuse Protection Inventory, Form IV. In J. C. Conoley & J. J. Kramer (Eds.), *The tenth mental measurements yearbook.* Lincoln: The Buros Institute of Mental Measurements, University of Nebraska.

Hart, V. (1992). Review of the Infant Mullen Scales of Early Development. In J. J. Kramer & J. C. Conoley (Eds.), *The eleventh mental measurements yearbook.* Lincoln: The Buros Institute of Mental Measurements, University of Nebraska.

Hartigan, J. A., & Wigdor, A. K. (1989). *Fairness in employment testing: Validity generalization, minority issues, and the General Aptitude Test Battery.* Washington, DC: National Academy Press.

Hartley, D. (1749). *Observations on man, his frame, his duty, and his expectations.*

Hartman, D. E. (1986a). On the use of clinical psychology software: Practical, legal, and ethical concerns. *Professional Psychology: Research and Practice, 17,* 462–465.

Hartman, D. E. (1986b). Artificial intelligence or artificial psychologist? Conceptual issues in clinical microcomputer use. *Professional Psychology: Research and Practice, 17,* 528–534.

Hartman, S., Griksby, D. W., Crino, M. D., & Chhokar, J. S. (1986). The measurement of job satisfaction by action tendencies. *Educational and Psychological Measurement, 46,* 317–329.

Hartmann, D. P. (1977). Considerations in the choice of inter-observer reliability estimates. *Journal of Applied Behavior Analysis, 10,* 103–116.

Hartmann, D. P., Roper, B. L., & Bradford, D. C. (1979). Some relationships between behavioral and traditional assessment. *Journal of Behavioral Assessment, 1,* 3–21.

Hartshorne, H., & May, M. A. (1928). *Studies in the nature of character. Vol. 1: Studies in deceit.* New York: Macmillan.

Harvey, R. J., & Murry, W. D. (1994). Scoring the Myers-Briggs Type Indicator: Empirical comparison of preference score versus latent-trait methods. *Journal of Personality Assessment, 62,* 116–129.

Hathaway, S. R., & McKinley, J. C. (1940). A multiphasic personality schedule (Minnesota): 1. Construction of the schedule. *Journal of Psychology, 10,* 249–254.

Hathaway, S. R., & McKinley, J. C. (1951). *The MMPI manual.* New York: Psychological Corporation.

Hathaway, S. R., & Meehl, P. E. (1951). *An atlas for the clinical use of the MMPI*. Minneapolis: University of Minnesota Press.

Hattrup, K., & Schmitt, N. (1990). Prediction of trades apprentices' performance on job sample criteria. *Personnel Psychology, 43,* 453–466.

Hayden, B. C. (1981). Rorschach cards IV and VII revisited. *Journal of Personality Assessment, 45,* 226–229.

Hayden, D. C., Frulong, M. J., & Linnemeyer, S. (1988). A comparison of the Kaufman Assessment Battery for Children and the Stanford-Binet IV for the assessment of gifted children. *Psychology in the Schools, 25,* 239–243.

Haynes, J. R., & Sells, S. G. (1963). Assessment of organic brain damage by psychological tests. *Psychological Bulletin, 60,* 316–325.

Haynes, R. B., Taylor, D. W., & Sackett, D. L. (Eds.). (1979). *Compliance in health care.* Baltimore: Johns Hopkins University Press.

Haywood, T. W., Grossman, L. S., & Cavanaugh, J. L. (1990). Subjective versus objective measurements of deviant sexual arousal in clinical evaluations of alleged child molesters. *Psychological Assessment: A Journal of Consulting & Clinical Psychology, 2,* 269–275.

Head, H. (1925). *Aphasia and kindred disorders of speech.* New York: Cambridge University Press.

Heath, C. P., & Obrzut, J. E. (1986). Adaptive behavior: Concurrent validity. *Journal of Psychoeducational Assessment, 4,* 53–59.

Heath, C. P., & Obrzut, J. E. (1988). An investigation of the K-ABC, WISC-R, and WJPB, Part Two, with Learning Disabled children. *Psychology in the Schools, 25,* 358–364.

Heathington, B. S., & Alexander, J. E. (1978). A child-based observation checklist to assess attitudes toward reading. *The Reading Teacher, 31,* 769–771.

Heaton, R. K., Baade, L. E., & John, K. L. (1978). Neuropsychological test results associated with psychiatric disorders in adults. *Psychological Bulletin, 85,* 141–162.

Hedges, C. (1994, September 8). It's Israel, where teenagers cram for the Army. *New York Times,* p. A4.

Heesacker, M. (1981). *A review of the history of field dependence.* Los Angeles, CA: Paper presented at the Annual Convention of the American Psychological Association. (ERIC Document Reproduction Service No. ED 211 888)

Heidrich, S. M., Forsthoff, C. A., & Ward, S. E. (1994). Psychological adjustment in adults with cancer: The self as mediator. *Health Psychology, 13,* 346–353.

Heilbrun, A. B., & Goodstein, L. D. (1961a). Social desirability response set: Error or predictor variable. *Journal of Psychology, 51,* 321–329.

Heilbrun, A. B., & Goodstein, L. D. (1961b). The relationship between individually defined and group defined social desirability and performance on the Edwards Personal Preference Schedule. *Journal of Consulting Psychology, 25,* 200–204.

Heilbrun, H. B., Jr. (1972). Edwards Personal Preference Schedule. In O. K. Buros (Ed.), *The seventh mental measurements yearbook* (Vol. 1). Highland Park, NJ: Gryphon Press, 1972.

Heinrichs, R. W. (1990). Variables associated with Wisconsin Card Sorting Test performance in neuropsychiatric patients referred for assessment. *Neuropsychiatry, Neuropsychology, and Behavioral Neurology, 3,* 107–112.

Heitzmann, C., & Kaplan, R. M. (1988). Assessment of methods for measuring social support. *Health Psychology, 7,* 75–109.

Helfer, R. E., & Kempe, R. S. (Eds.). (1988). *The battered child* (4th ed.). Chicago: University of Chicago Press.

Helmes, E., & McLaughlin, J. D. (1983). A comparison of three MMPI short forms: Limited clinical utility in classification. *Journal of Consulting and Clinical Psychology, 51,* 786–787.

Helmes, E., & Reddon, J. R. (1993). A perspective on developments in assessment psychopathology: A critical review of the MMPI and MMPI-2. *Psychological Bulletin, 113,* 453–471.

Helmreich, R. L., Sawin, L. L., & Carsrud, A. L. (1986). The honeymoon effect in job performance: Temporal increases in the predictive power of achievement motivation. *Journal of Applied Psychology, 71,* 185–188.

Helsel, W. J., & Matson, J. L. (1984). The assessment of depression in children: The internal structure of the Child Depression Inventory (CDI). *Behavior Research & Therapy, 22,* 289–298.

Helzel, M. F., & Rice, M. E. (1985). On the validity of social skills assessments: An analysis of role-playing and ward staff ratings of social behavior in a maximum security setting. *Canadian Journal of Behavioral Science, 17,* 400–411.

Henk, W. A. (1993). New directions in reading assessment. *Reading and Writing Quarterly: Overcoming Learning Difficulties, 9,* 103–120.

Henry, E. M., & Rotter, J. B. (1956). Situational influences on Rorschach responses. *Journal of Consulting Psychology, 20,* 457–462.

Henry, J. D. (1984). Syndicated public opinion polls: Some thoughts for consideration. *Journal of Advertising Research, 24,* I-5–I-8.

Henry, W. E. (1956). *The analysis of fantasy.* New York: Wiley.

Herbert, B. (1994, October 26). Throwing a curve (editorial). *New York Times,* p. A27.

Herche, J. (1992). A note on the predictive validity of the CETSCALE. *Journal of the Academy of Marketing Science, 20,* 261–264.

Herlihy, B. (1977). Watch out, IQ myth: Here comes another debunker. *Phi Delta Kappan, 59,* 298.

Hermann, B. P., & Whitman, S. (1984). Behavioral and personality correlates of epilepsy: A review, methodological critique, and conceptual model. *Psychological Bulletin, 95,* 451–497.

Herrnstein, R. J. (1971). IQ. *Atlantic Monthly, 228,* 43–64.

Herrnstein, R. J. (1982, August). IQ testing and the media. *Atlantic Monthly,* 68–74.

Herrnstein, R., & Murray, C. (1994). *The bell curve.* New York: The Free Press.

Hersen, M., & Bellack, A. S. (1988). *Dictionary of behavioral assessment techniques.* Elmsford, NY: Pergamon Press.

Herzberg, F., Mausner, B., Peterson, R. O., & Capwell, D. F. (1957). Job attitudes: Review of research and opinion. *Journal of Applied Psychology, 63,* 596–601.

Hess, A. K. (1992). Review of the NEO Personality Inventory. In J. J. Kramer & J. C. Conoley (Eds.), *The eleventh mental measurements yearbook.* Lincoln: The Buros Institute of Mental Measurements, University of Nebraska.

Hess, E. H. (1965). Attitude and pupil size. *Scientific American, 212,* 46–54.

Hess, E. H. (1972). Pupillometrics: A method of studying mental, emotional and sensory processes. In N. S. Greenfield & R. A. Sternbach (Eds.), *Handbook of psychophysiology* (pp. 491–531). New York: Holt, Rinehart & Winston.

Hess, E. H., & Polt, J. M. (1960). Pupil size as related to interest value of visual stimuli. *Science, 132,* 349–350.

Hess, E. H., & Polt, J. M. (1964). Pupil size in relation to mental activity during simple problem solving. *Science, 143,* 1190–1192.

Hess, E. H., & Polt, J. M. (1966). Changes in pupil size as a measure of taste difference. *Perceptual and Motor Skills, 23,* 451–455.

Hetherington, E. M., & Parke, R. D. (1993). *Child psychology: A contemporary viewpoint* (4th ed.). New York: McGraw-Hill.

Higgins, R. L., Alonso, R. R., & Pendleton, M. G. (1979). The validity of role-play assessments of assertiveness. *Behavior Therapy, 10,* 655–662.

Hills, D. A. (1985). Prediction of effectiveness in leaderless group discussions with the Adjective Check List. *Journal of Applied Social Psychology, 15,* 443–447.

Hinrichsen, J. J., & Bradley, L. A. (1974). Situational determinants of personal validation of general personality interpretations: A re-examination. *Journal of Personality Assessment, 38,* 530–534.

Hiscox, M. D. (1983). *A balance sheet for educational item banking.* Paper presented at the annual meeting of the National Council for Measurement in Education, Montreal, Canada.

Hiscox, M. D., & Brzezinski, E. (1980). *A guide to item banking in education.* Portland, OR: Northwest Regional Educational Laboratory, Assessment and Education Division.

Hiskey, M. S. (1966). *Hiskey-Nebraska Test of Learning Aptitude.* Lincoln, NE: Union College Press.

Hjemboe, S., & Butcher, J. N. (1990, June). *Analysis of MMPI-2 profiles of couples in marital counseling.* Paper presented at the 25th Annual Symposium on Recent Developments in the Use of the MMPI (MMPI-2), Minneapolis, MN.

Hofer, P. J., & Green, B. F. (1985). The challenge of competence and creativity in computerized psychological testing. *Journal of Consulting and Clinical Psychology, 53,* 826–838.

Hoffman, B. (1962). *The tyranny of testing.* New York: Crowell-Collier.

Hoffman, D. A. (1978). Field independence and intelligence: Their relationship to leadership and self-concept in sixth grade boys. *Journal of Educational Psychology, 70,* 827–832.

Hoffman, K. I., & Lundberg, G. D. (1976). A comparison of computer monitored group tests and paper-and-pencil tests. *Educational and Psychological Measurement, 36,* 791–809.

Hoffman, W. F. (1985). Hypnosis as a diagnostic tool. *American Journal of Psychiatry, 14,* 272–273.

Hogan, A. E., Quay, H. C., Vaughn, S., & Shapiro, S. K. (1989). Revised Behavior Problem Checklist: Stability, prevalence, and incidence of behavior problems in kindergarten and first-grade children. *Psychological Assessment: A Journal of Consulting and Clinical Psychology, 1,* 103–111.

Hogan, J., & Quigley, A. M. (1986). Physical standards for employment and the courts. *American Psychologist, 41,* 1193–1217.

Hogan, J., & Quigley, A. (1994). Effects of preparing for physical ability tests. *Public Personnel Management, 23,* 85–104.

Hogan, R., Carpenter, B., Briggs, S., & Hanson, R. (1985). Personality assessment and personnel selection. In H. J. Bernardin & D. A. Bownes (Eds.), *Personality assessment in organizations.* New York: Praeger.

Holden, R. H. (1988). Review of Wechsler Memory Scale—Revised. In D. J. Keyser & R. C. Sweetland (Eds.), *Test critiques Volume VII* (pp. 633–638). Kansas City, MO: Test Corporation of America.

Holden, R. R., & Hickman, D. (1987). Computerized versus standard administration of the Jenkins Activity Survey (Form T). *Journal of Human Stress, 13,* 175–179.

Holland, A. (1980). *Communicative abilities in daily living: A test of functional communication for aphasic adults.* Baltimore, MD: University Park.

Holland, J. L. (1973). *Making vocational choices.* Englewood Cliffs, NJ: Prentice-Hall.

Holland, W. R. (1960). Language barrier as an educational problem of Spanish speaking children. *Exceptional Children, 27,* 42–47.

Hollander, E. P., & Willis, R. H. (1967). Some current issues in the psychology of conformity and nonconformity. *Psychological Bulletin, 68,* 62–76.

Hollenbeck, J. R., & Whitener, E. M. (1988). Reclaiming personality traits for personal selection: Self-esteem as an illustrative case. *Journal of Management, 14,* 81–91.

Hollingshead, A. B., & Redlich, F. C. (1958). *Social class and mental illness: A community study.* New York: Wiley.

Hollon, S. D., & Kendall, P. C. (1980). Cognitive self-statements in depression: Development of an automatic thoughts questionnaire. *Cognitive Therapy and Research, 4,* 383–395.

Holmen, M., & Docter, R. (1972). *Educational and psychological testing.* New York: Russell Sage Foundation.

Holmes, C. B., Dungan, D. S., & Medlin, W. J. (1984). Reassessment of inferring personality traits from

Bender-Gestalt drawing styles. *Journal of Clinical Psychology, 40,* 1241–1243.

Holmes, D. S. (1974). The conscious control of thematic projection. *Journal of Consulting and Clinical Psychology, 42,* 323–329.

Holmstrom, R. W., Silber, D. E., & Karp, S. A. (1990). Development of the Apperceptive Personality Test. *Journal of Personality Assessment, 54,* 252–264.

Holt, R. R. (1968). Editor's foreword. In D. Rapaport, M. M. Gill, & R. Schafer, *Diagnostic psychological testing* (Rev. ed.). New York: International Universities Press.

Holt, R. R. (1971). *Assessing personality.* New York: Harcourt Brace Jovanovich.

Holtzman, W. H. (1993). An unjustified, sweeping indictment by Motta et al. of human figure drawings for assessing psychological functioning. *School Psychology Quarterly, 8,* 189–190.

Holzman, P. S. (1954). The relation of assimilation tendencies in visual, auditory, and kinesthetic time-error to cognitive attitudes of leveling and sharpening. *Journal of Personality, 22,* 375–394.

Holzman, P. S., & Gardner, R. W. (1960). Leveling-sharpening and memory organization. *Journal of Abnormal and Social Psychology, 61,* 176–180.

Holzman, P. S., & Klein, G. S. (1954). Cognitive system-principles of leveling and sharpening: Individual differences in assimilation effects in visual time-error. *Journal of Psychology, 37,* 105–122.

Honaker, L. M. (1988). The equivalency of computerized and conventional MMPI administration: A review. *Clinical Psychology Review, 8,* 561–577.

Honaker, L. M. (1990, August). Recommended guidelines for computer equivalency research (or everything you should know about computer administration but will be disappointed if you ask). In W. J. Camara (Chair), *The state of computer-based testing and interpretation: Consensus or chaos?* Symposium conducted at the Annual Convention of the American Psychological Association, Boston.

Honaker, L. M., Harrell, T. H., & Buffaloe, J. D. (1988). Equivalency of Microtest computer MMPI administration for standard and special scales. *Computers in Human Behavior, 4,* 323–337.

Honts, C. R. (1994). Psychophysiological detection of deception. *Current Directions in Psychological Science, 3,* 77–82.

Honzik, M. P. (1967). Environmental correlates of mental growth: Prediction from the family setting at 21 months. *Child Development, 38,* 337–364.

Hooper, S. R. (1992). Review of the LNNB Children's Revision. In J. J. Kramer & J. C. Conoley (Eds.), *The eleventh mental measurements yearbook.* Lincoln: The Buros Institute of Mental Measurements, University of Nebraska.

Hopkins, K. D., & Bracht, G. H. (1975). Ten years stability of verbal and nonverbal IQ scores. *American Educational Research Journal, 12,* 469–477.

Hopkins, K. D., & Glass, G. V. (1978). *Basic statistics for the behavioral sciences.* Englewood Cliffs, NJ: Prentice-Hall.

Horn, J. (1988). Thinking about human abilities. In J. R. Nesselroade & R. B. Cattell (eds.), *Handbook of multivariate psychology.* New York: Plenum.

Horn, J. L., & Cattell, R. B. (1966). Refinement and test of the theory of fluid and crystallized intelligence. *Journal of Educational Psychology, 57,* 253–270.

Horner, M. S. (1973). A psychological barrier to achievement in women: The motive to avoid success. In D. C. McClelland & R. S. Steele (Eds.), *Human motivation* (pp. 222–230). Morristown, NJ: General Learning Press.

Horner, T. M., Guyer, M. J., & Kalter, N. M. (1993). Clinical expertise and the assessment of child sexual abuse. *Journal of the American Academy of Child and Adolescent Psychiatry, 32,* 925–931.

Horowitz, R., & Murphy, L. B. (1938). Projective methods in the psychological study of children. *Journal of Experimental Education, 7,* 133–140.

Horst, P. (1953). Correcting the Kuder-Richardson reliability for dispersion of item difficulties. *Psychological Bulletin, 50,* 371–374.

Hostetler, A. J. (1987). Try to remember. *APA Monitor 18*(5), 18.

Houston, B. K., Fox, J. E., & Forbes, L. (1984). Trait anxiety and children's state anxiety, cognitive behaviors, and performance under stress. *Cognitive Therapy & Research, 8,* 631–641.

Howarth, E., & Browne, J. A. (1971). An item factor analysis of the 16 P-F. *Personality, 2,* 117–139.

Howes, R. J. (1981). The Rorschach: Does it have a future? *Journal of Personality Assessment, 45,* 339–351.

Hozier, A. (1959). On the breakdown of the sense of reality: A study of spatial perception in schizophrenia. *Journal of Consulting Psychology, 23,* 185–194.

Hsu, S-H, & Peng, Y. (1993). Control / display relationship of the four-burner stove: A re-examination. *Human Factors, 35,* 745–749.

Hudson, W. W. (1982). *The clinical measurement package: A field manual.* Chicago: Dorsey Press.

Huebner, E. S. (1994). Preliminary development and validation of a multidimensional life satisfaction scale for children. *Psychological Assessment, 6,* 149–158.

Hughes, H. M., & Pugh, R. (1984). The Behavior Rating Form—Revised: A parent-report measure of children's self-esteem. *Journal of Clinical Psychology, 40,* 1001–1005.

Hulse, W. G. (1951). The emotionally disturbed child draws his family. *Quarterly Journal of Child Behavior, 3,* 151–174.

Hulse, W. G. (1952). Childhood conflict expressed through family drawings. *Quarterly Journal of Child Behavior, 16,* 152–174.

Hume, D. (1739). *A treatise on human nature.*

Hunt, J. McV. (1961). *Intelligence and experience.* New York: Ronald Press.

Hunt, R. A. (1978). The effect of item weighting on the Locke-Wallace Marital Adjustment Scale. *Journal of Marriage and the Family, 40,* 249–256.

Hunter, J. E. (1980). *Validity generalization for 12,000 jobs: An application of synthetic validity and validity generalization to the General Aptitude Test Battery (GATB).* Washington, DC: U.S. Employment Service, U.S. Department of Labor.

Hunter, J. E. (1982). *The dimensionality of the General Aptitude Test Battery and the dominance of general factors over specific factors in the prediction of job performance.* Washington, DC: U.S. Employment Service, U.S. Department of Labor.

Hunter, J. E. (1986). Cognitive ability, cognitive aptitudes, job knowledge, and job performance. *Journal of Vocational Behavior, 29,* 340–362.

Hunter, J. E., & Hunter, R. (1984). Validity and utility of alternate predictors of job performance. *Psychological Bulletin, 96,* 72–98.

Hunter, J. E., & Schmidt, F. L. (1976). A critical analysis of the statistical and ethical implications of various definitions of "test bias." *Psychological Bulletin, 83,* 1053–1071.

Hunter, J. E., & Schmidt, F. L. (1981). Fitting people into jobs: The impact of personal selection on normal productivity. In M. D. Dunnette & E. A. Fleishman (Eds.), *Human performance and productivity: Vol. 1. Human capability assessment.* Hillsdale, NJ: Erlbaum.

Hunter, J. E., & Schmidt, F. L. (1983). Quantifying the effects of psychological interventions on employee job performance and work-force productivity. *American Psychologist, 38,* 473–478.

Hunter, J. E., & Schmidt, F. L. (1990). *Methods of meta-analysis.* Newbury Park, CA: Sage.

Hunter, J. E., Schmidt, F. L., & Jackson, G. B. (1982). *Meta-analysis: Cumulating research findings across studies.* Beverly Hills: Sage.

Hunter, M. S. (1992). The Women's Health Questionnaire: A measure of mid-aged women's perceptions of their emotional and physical health. *Psychology and Health, 7,* 45–54.

Hunter, N., & Kelley, C. K. (1986). Examination of the validity of the Adolescent Problems Inventory among incarcerated juvenile delinquents. *Journal of Consulting and Clinical Psychology, 54,* 301–302.

Hurt, S. W. (1986). Diagnostic Interview for Borderlines: Psychometric properties and validity. *Journal of Consulting and Clinical Psychology, 54,* 256–260.

Hutchinson, G. L. (1984). The Luria-Nebraska Neuropsychological Battery controversy: A reply to Spiers. *Journal of Consulting and Clinical Psychology, 52,* 539–545.

Hutt, M. L. (1977). *The Hutt adaptation of the Bender-Gestalt* (3rd ed.). New York: Grune & Stratton.

Hutt, M. L. (1985). *The Hutt adaptation of the Bender-Gestalt Test* (4th ed.). Orlando, FL: Grune & Stratton.

Hutton, J. B., Dubes, R., & Moir, S. (1992). Assessment practices of school psychologists: Ten years later. *School Psychology Review, 21,* 271–284.

Hysjulien, C., Wood, B., Benjamin, G., Andrew, H. (1994). Child custody evaluations: A review of methods used in litigation and alternative dispute resolution. *Family and Conciliation Courts Review, 32,* 466–489.

Iaffaldano, M. T., & Muchinsky, P. M. (1985). Job satisfaction and job performance: A meta-analysis. *Psychological Bulletin, 97,* 251–273.

Ilyin, D. (1976). *The Ilyin oral interview.* Rowley, MA: Newbury House.

Ingham, J. G., Kreitman, N. B., Miller, P. M., Sashidharan, S. P., & Surtees, P. G. (1986). Self-esteem, vulnerability, and psychiatric disorder in the community. *British Journal of Psychiatry, 148,* 375–385.

Ingram, R. E., Slater, M. A., Atkinson, J. H., & Scott, W. (1990). *Psychological Assessment: A Journal of Consulting & Clinical Psychology, 2,* 209–211.

Ingram, R. E., & Wisnicki, K. S. (1988). Assessment of positive automatic cognition. *Journal of Consulting & Clinical Psychology, 56,* 898–902.

Innocenti, M. S., Huh, K., & Boyce, G. C. (1992). Families of children with disabilities: Normative data and other considerations on parenting stress. *Topics in Early Childhood Special Education, 12,* 403–427.

Institute for Juvenile Research. (1937). *Child guidance procedures, methods and techniques employed at the Institute for Juvenile Research.* New York: Appleton-Century.

Iragui, V. J., Kalmijn, J., Thal, L. J., & Grant, I. (1994). Neurological dysfunction in asymptomatic HIV-1 infected men: Evidence from evoked potentials. *Electroencephalography and Clinical Neurophysiology: Evoked Potentials, 92,* 1–10.

Ironson, G. H., & Subkoviak, M. J. (1979). A comparison of several methods of assessing item bias. *Journal of Educational Measurement, 16,* 209–225.

Irwin, M. R., Patterson, T. L., Smith, T. L., et al. (1990). Reduction of immune function in life stress and depression. *Biological Psychiatry, 27,* 22–30.

Ishihara, S. (1964). *Tests for color blindness* (11th ed.). Tokyo: Kanehara Shuppan.

Ivancevich, J. M. (1983). Contrast effects in performance evaluation and reward practices. *Academy of Management Journal, 26,* 465–476.

Iwata, B. A., Pace, G. M., Kissel, R. C., Nau, P. A., & Farber, J. M. (1990). The Self-Injury Trauma (SIT) Scale: A method for quantifying surface tissue damage caused by self-injurious behavior. *Journal of Applied Behavior Analysis, 23,* 99–110.

Jackson, D. E., & Murray, B. S. (1986). Predicting accuracy and liking ratings for bogus and real personality feedback. *Journal of Psychology: Interdisciplinary and Applied, 119,* 495–503.

Jackson, D. E., O'Dell, J. W., & Olson, D. (1982). Acceptance of bogus personality interpretations: Face validity reconsidered. *Journal of Clinical Psychology, 38,* 588–592.

Jackson, D. N. (1964). Desirability judgments as a method of personality assessment. *Educational and Psychological Measurement, 24,* 223–238.

Jackson, D. N. (1970). A sequential system for personality scale development. In C. D. Spielberger (Ed.), *Current topics in clinical and community psychology.* New York: Academic Press.

Jackson, D. N. (1982). Some preconditions for valid person perception. In M. P. Zanna, E. T. Higgins,

& C. P. Herman (Eds.), *Consistency in social behavior: The Ontario Symposium* (Vol. 2; pp. 251–279). Hillsdale, NJ: Erlbaum.

Jackson, D. N. (1984a). *Personality Research Form manual.* Port Huron, MI: Research Psychologists Press.

Jackson, D. N. (1984b). *Jackson Vocational Interest Survey manual* (2nd ed.). Port Huron, MI: Research Psychologists Press.

Jackson, D. N. (1986). *Computer-based personality testing.* Washington, DC: Scientific Affairs Office, American Psychological Association.

Jackson, D. N. (1988). Computer-based assessment and interpretation: The dawn of discovery. In T. B. Gutkin & S. L. Wise (Eds.), *The computer as adjunct to the decision-making process.* Hillsdale, NJ: Erlbaum.

Jackson, D. N., & Messick, S. (1958). Content and style in personality assessment. *Psychological Bulletin, 55,* 243–252.

Jackson, D. N., & Messick, S. (1962). Response styles and the assessment of psychopathology. In S. Messick & J. Ross (Eds.), *Measurement in personality and cognition.* New York: Wiley.

Jacobs, J. (1970). Are we being misled by fifty years of research on our gifted children? *Gifted Child Quarterly, 14,* 120–123.

Jacoby, J., & Chestnut, R. (1978). *Brand loyalty: Measurement and management.* New York: Wiley.

Jaffe, A. J., & Kilby, M. M. (1994). The Cocaine Expectancy Questionnaire (CEQ): Construction and predictive utility. *Psychological Assessment, 6,* 18–26.

Jaffe, L. T., & Archer, R. P. (1987). The prediction of drug use among college students from the MMPI, MCMI, and Sensation Seeking scales. *Journal of Personality Assessment, 51,* 243–253.

Jagger, L., Neukrug, E., & McAuliffe, G. (1992). Congruence between personality traits and chosen occupation as a predictor of job satisfaction for people with disabilities. *Rehabilitation Counseling Bulletin, 36,* 53–60.

Jagim, R. D., Wittman, W. D., & Noll, J. O. (1978). Mental health professionals' attitudes towards confidentiality, privilege, and third-party disclosure. *Professional Psychology, 9,* 458–466.

Jahanshahi, M., & Philips, C. (1986). Validation of a new technique for the assessment of pain behavior. *Behavior Research and Therapy, 24,* 35–42.

James, L. R., Demaree, R. G., & Mulaik, S. A. (1986). A note on validity generalization procedures. *Journal of Applied Psychology, 71,* 440–450.

Janisse, M. P. (1973). Pupil size and affect: A critical review of the literature since 1960. *Canadian Psychologist, 14,* 311–329.

Janzen, H. L. (1981). Why use the Binet? *The Alberta School Psychologist, 2,* 25–38.

Jastak, J. F., & Jastak, S. (1984). *Wide Range Achievement Test—Revised.* Wilmington, DE: Jastak Associates.

Jay, S. M., Elliott, C. H., Ozolines, M., Olson, R., & Pruit, S. D. (1987). Behavioral management of children's distress during painful medical procedures. *Behavioral Research and Therapy, 23,* 513–520.

Jenkins, C. D., Zyzanski, S. J., & Rosenman, R. H. (1979). *Jenkins Activity Survey: Manual.* San Antonio, TX: Psychological Corporation.

Jensema, C. (1975). A statistical investigation of the 16PF Form E as applied to hearing impaired college students. *Journal of Rehabilitation of the Deaf, 9,* 21–29.

Jensen, A. R. (1962). The culturally disadvantaged: Psychological and educational aspects. *Educational Research, 10,* 4–20.

Jensen, A. R. (1967). The culturally disadvantaged: Psychological and educational aspects. *Educational Research, 10,* 4–20.

Jensen, A. R. (1969). How much can we boost IQ and scholastic achievement? *Harvard Educational Review, 39,* 1–123.

Jensen, A. R. (1974). The strange case of Dr. Jensen and Mr. Hyde. *American Psychologist, 29,* 467–468.

Jensen, A. R. (1980). *Bias in mental testing.* New York: Free Press.

Jensen, A. R. (1984). The black-white difference on the K-ABC: Implications for future tests. *Journal of Special Education, 18*(3), 377–408.

Johnson, G. S. (1989). Emotional indicators in the human figure drawings of hearing-impaired children: A small sample validation study. *American Annals of the Deaf, 134,* 205–208.

Johnson, J. A., & Ostendorf, F. (1993). Clarification of the five-factor model with the abridged big five dimensional circumplex. *Journal of Personality and Social Psychology, 65,* 563–576.

Johnson, L. J., Cook, M. J., & Kullman, A. J. (1992). An examination of the concurrent validity of the Battelle Developmental Inventory as compared with the Vineland Adaptive Scales and the Bayley Scales of Infant Development. *Journal of Early Intervention, 16,* 353–359.

Johnson, M. D., & Horne, D. A. (1992). An examination of the validity of direct product perceptions. *Psychology and Marketing, 9,* 221–235.

Johnson, O. G. (1976). *Tests and measurements in child development: Handbook II* (Vols. 1–2). San Francisco: Jossey Bass.

Johnson, R. C. (1963). Similarity in IQ of separated identical twins as related to length of time spent in same environment. *Child Development, 34,* 745–749.

Jolles, J. (1952). *A catalogue for the qualitative interpretation of the H-T-P.* Los Angeles: Western Psychological Services.

Jones, C., Rowan, M., & Taylor, H. (1977). An overview of the mathematics achievement tests offered in the admissions testing program of the College Entrance Examination Board. *Mathematics Teacher, 70*(3), 197–208.

Jones, D. P., & McGraw, J. M. (1987). Reliable and fictitious accounts of sexual abuse to children. *Journal of Interpersonal Violence, 2,* 27–45.

Jones, J. W., Arnold, D., & Harris, W. G. (1990). Introduction to the Model Guidelines for Preemployment Integrity Testing. *Journal of Business and Psychology, 4,* 525–532.

Jones, P., & Rodgers, B. (1993). Estimating premorbid IQ in schizophrenia. *British Journal of Psychiatry, 162,* 273–274.

Jung, C. G. (1910). The association method. *American Journal of Psychology, 21,* 219–269.

Jung, C. G. (1923). *Psychological types.* London: Rutledge & Kegan Paul.

Kagan, J. (1956). The measurement of overt aggression from fantasy. *Journal of Abnormal and Social Psychology, 52,* 390–393.

Kagan, J. (1965). Impulsive and reflective children: Significance of conceptual tempo. In J. D. Krumboltz (Ed.), *Learning and the educational process.* Chicago: Rand McNally.

Kagan, J., Pearson, L., & Welch, L. (1966). Modifiability of an impulsive tempo. *Journal of Educational Psychology, 57,* 359–365.

Kagan, J., Rossman, B. L., Day, D., Albert, J., & Phillips, W. (1964). Information processing in the child: Significance of analysis and reflective attitudes. *Psychological Monographs, 78,* 1–37.

Kahn, M., & Taft, G. (1983). The application of the standard of care doctrine to psychological testing. *Behavioral Sciences and the Law, 1,* 71–84.

Kaiser, H. F. (1958). A modified stanine scale. *Journal of Experimental Education, 26,* 261.

Kaiser, H. F., & Michael, W. B. (1975). Domain validity and generalizability. *Educational and Psychological Measurement, 35,* 31–35.

Kamakura, W. A., & Srivastava, R. K. (1983). Adaptive latent trait theory for attitude scaling. In W. R. Darden, K. B. Monroe, & W. R. Dillon (Eds.), *Procedures of the 1983 AMA Winter Educators' Conference: Research methods and casual modeling in marketing* (pp. 263–267). Chicago: American Marketing Association.

Kamin, L. J. (1974). *The science and politics of IQ.* New York: Wiley.

Kamiya, J. (1962). *Conditional discrimination of the EEG alpha rhythm in humans.* Paper presented at the annual meeting of the Western Psychological Association (April).

Kamiya, J. (1968). Conscious control of brain waves. *Psychology Today, 1*(11), 56–60.

Kamphaus, R. W., Benson, J., Hutchinson, S., & Platt, L. O. (1994). Identification of factor models for the WISC-III. *Educational and Psychological Measurement, 54,* 174–186.

Kamphaus, R. W., Kaufman, A. S., & Kaufman, N. L. (1982). *A cross-validation study of sequential-simultaneous processing at ages 2½–12½ using the Kaufman Assessment Battery for Children (K-ABC).* Paper presented at the Annual Meeting of the American Psychological Association, Washington, DC.

Kamphaus, R. W., & Pleiss, K. L. (1993). Comment on "The use and abuse of human figure drawings." *School Psychology Quarterly, 8,* 187–188.

Kamphaus, R. W., & Reynolds, C. R. (1984). Development and structure of the Kaufman Assessment Battery for Children. *Journal of Special Education, 18,* 213–218.

Kamphaus, R. W., & Reynolds, C. R. (1987). *Clinical and research applications of the K-ABC.* Circle Pines, MN: American Guidance Service.

Kane, J. S., & Lawler, E. E., III. (1978). Methods of peer assessment. *Psychological Bulletin, 85,* 555–586.

Kane, J. S., & Lawler, E. E., III. (1980). In defense of peer assessment: A rebuttal to Brief's critique. *Psychological Bulletin, 85,* 555–586.

Kane, R. L., Goldstein, G., & Parsons, O. A. (1989). A response to Mapou. *Journal of Clinical and Experimental Neuropsychology, 11,* 589–595.

Kane, R. L., Parsons, O. A., Goldstein, G., & Moses, J. A., Jr. (1987). Diagnostic accuracy of the Halstead-Reitan and Luria-Nebraska Neuropsychological Batteries: Performance of clinical raters. *Journal of Consulting and Clinical Psychology, 55,* 783–784.

Kaplan, B. J. (1990). Review of Reynolds Adolescent Depression Scale. In J. J. Kramer & J. C. Conoley (Eds.), *The supplement to the tenth mental measurements yearbook* (pp. 217–218). Lincoln: The Buros Institute of Mental Measurements of the University of Nebraska.

Kaplan, C. (1993). Predicting first-grade achievement from pre-kindergarten WPPSI-R scores. *Journal of Psychoeducational Assessment, 11,* 133–138.

Karp, S. A., Holmstrom, R. W., & Silber, D. E. (1990). *Apperceptive Personality Test Manual (Version 2.0).* Orland Park, IL: International Diagnostic Systems, Inc.

Karp, S. A., & Konstadt, N. (1963/1971). *Children's Embedded Figures Test.* Palo Alto, CA: Consulting Psychologists Press.

Karr, S. K., Carvajal, H. H., Elser, D., & Bays, K. (1993). Concurrent validity of the WPPSI-R and the McCarthy Scales of Children's Abilities. *Psychological Reports, 72,* 940–942.

Karson, S., & O'Dell, J. W. (1989). The 16 PF. In C. S. Newmark (Ed.), *Major psychological assessment instruments, Vol. II* (pp. 45–66). Needham Heights, MA: Allyn and Bacon.

Kassarjian, H. H., & Cohen, J. B. (1965). Cognitive dissonance and consumer behavior: Reaction to the Surgeon General's Report on Smoking and Health. *California Management Review, 8,* 55–64.

Katz, E. (1955). Success of Stanford-Binet Intelligence Scale test items of children with cerebral palsy as compared with nonhandicapped children. *Cerebral Palsy Review, 16,* 18–19.

Katz, R. C., Santman, J., & Lonero, P. (1994). Findings on the Revised Morally Debatable Behaviors Scale. *Journal of Psychology, 128,* 15–21.

Katz, W. F., Curtiss, S., & Tallal, P. (1992). Rapid automatized naming and gesture by normal and language-impaired children. *Brain and Language, 43,* 623–641.

Kaufman, A. S. (1971). Piaget and Gesell: A psychometric analysis of tests built from their tasks. *Child Development, 42,* 1341–1360.

Kaufman, A. S. (1973a). Comparison of the performance of matched groups of black children and white children on the Wechsler Preschool and Primary Scale of Intelligence. *Journal of Consulting and Clinical Psychology, 41,* 186–191.

Kaufman, A. S. (1973b). Comparison of the WPPSI, Stanford-Binet, and McCarthy Scales as predictors of first-grade achievement. *Perceptual and Motor Skills, 36,* 67–73.

Kaufman, A. S. (1975). Factor analysis of the WISC-R at eleven age levels between 6½ and 16½ years. *Journal of Consulting and Clinical Psychology, 43,* 135–147.

Kaufman, A. S. (1979). *Intelligent testing with the WISC-R.* New York: Wiley.

Kaufman, A. S. (1984). K-ABC and giftedness. *Roeper Review, 7*(2), 83–88.

Kaufman, A. S. (1990). *Assessing adolescent and adult intelligence.* Needham Heights, MA: Allyn and Bacon.

Kaufman, A. S. (1993). Joint exploratory factor analysis of the Kaufman Battery for Children and the Kaufman Adolescent and Adult Intelligence Test for 11- and 12-year olds. *Journal of Clinical Child Psychology, 22,* 355–364.

Kaufman, A. S., Ishkuma, T., & Kaufman-Packer, J. L. (1991). Amazingly short forms of the WAIS-R. *Journal of Psychoeducational Assessment, 9,* 4–15.

Kaufman, A. S., & Kamphaus, R. W. (1984). Factor analysis of the Kaufman Assessment Battery for Children (K-ABC) for ages 2½ through 12½ years. *Journal of Educational Psychology, 76*(4), 623–637.

Kaufman, A. S., & Kaufman, N. L. (1983). *Kaufman Assessment Battery for Children (K-ABC) Interpretative Manual.* Circle Pines, MN: American Guidance Service.

Kaufman, A. S., Kaufman, N. L., & Goldsmith, B. (1984). *Kaufman Sequential or Simultaneous (K-SOS).* Circle Pines, MN: American Guidance Service.

Kaufman, A. S., & McLean, J. E. (1986). K-ABC/WISC-R factor analysis for a learning disabled population. *Journal of Learning Disabilities, 19,* 145–153.

Kaufman, A. S., & McLean, J. E. (1987). Joint factor analysis of the K-ABC and WISC-R with normal children. *Journal of School Psychiatry, 25,* 105–118.

Kavan, M. G. (1990). Review of *Children's Depression Inventory.* In J. J. Kramer & J. C. Conoley (Eds.), *The supplement to the tenth mental measurements yearbook* (pp. 46–48). Lincoln: The Buros Institute of Mental Measurements, University of Nebraska.

Kazdin, A. E., Colbus, D., & Rodgers, A. (1986). Assessment of depression and diagnosis of depressive disorder among psychiatrically disturbed children. *Journal of Abnormal Child Psychology, 14,* 499–515.

Kazdin, A. E., Rodgers, A., & Colbus, D. (1986). The Hopelessness Scale for Children: Psychometric characteristics and concurrent validity. *Journal of Consulting and Clinical Psychology, 54,* 241–245.

Keane, T. M., Malloy, P. F., & Fairbank, J. A. (1984). Empirical development of an MMPI subscale for the assessment of combat-related posttraumatic stress disorder. *Journal of Consulting and Clinical Psychology, 52,* 881–891.

Keenan, P. A., & Lachar, D. (1988). Screening preschoolers with special problems: Use of the Personality Inventory for Children (PIC). *Journal of School Psychology, 26*(1), 1–11.

Keilitz, I. (1987). Researching and reforming the insanity defense. *Rutgers Law Review, 39,* 289–322.

Keith, T. Z. (1985). Questioning the K-ABC: What does it measure? *School Psychology Review, 1,* 21–36.

Keith, T. Z., Cool, V. A., Novak, C. G., White, L. J., & Pottebaum, S. M. (1988). Confirmatory factor analysis of the Stanford-Binet Fourth Edition: Testing the theory-test match. *Journal of School Psychology, 26*(3), 253–274.

Keith, T. Z., & Dunbar, S. B. (1984). Hierarchical factor analysis of the K-ABC: Testing alternate models. *Journal of Special Education, 18,* 367–375.

Keith, T. Z., Hood, C., Eberhart, S., & Pottebaum, S. M. (1985). *Factor structure of the K-ABC for referred school children.* Paper presented at the Annual Meeting of the National Association of School Psychologists, Las Vegas, NV.

Keith, T. Z., & Novak, C. G. (1987). Joint factor structure of the WISC-R and K-ABC for referred school children. *Journal of Psychoeducational Assessment, 5*(4), 370–386.

Keith, T. Z., & Reynolds, C. R. (1990). Measurement and design issues in child assessment research. In C. R. Reynolds & R. W. Kamphaus (Eds.), *Handbook of psychological and educational assessment of children: Intelligence & achievement* (pp. 29–61). New York: Guilford Press.

Keller, L. S., & Butcher, J. N. (1989, March). *Use of the MMPI-2 with chronic pain patients.* Paper presented at the 24th Annual Symposium on Recent Developments in the Use of the MMPI, Honolulu, HA.

Keller, S. W., Weiss, J. M., Schleifer, S. J., Miller, N. E., & Stein, M. (1981). Suppression of immunity by stress: Effect of graded series of stressors on lymphocyte proliferation. *Science, 213,* 1397–1400.

Kelley, S. J. (1985). Drawings: Critical communications for the sexually abused child. *Pediatric Nursing, 11,* 421–426.

Kelley, S. J. (1988). Physical abuse of children: Recognition and reporting. *Journal of Emergency Nursing, 14*(2), 82–90.

Kelley, T. L. (1939). The selection of upper and lower groups for the validation of test items. *Journal of Educational Psychology, 30,* 17–24.

Kelley, M., & Surbeck, E. (1983). History of preschool assessment. In K. Paget & B. Bracken (Eds.), *The psychoeducational assessment of preschool children* (pp. 1–16). New York: Grune & Stratton.

Kellner, C. H., Jolley, R. R., Holgate, R. C., Austin, L., Lydiard, R. B., Laraia, M., & Ballenger, J. C. (1991). Brain MRI in obsessive-compulsive disorder. *Psychiatry Research, 36,* 45–49.

Kelly, D. H. (1966). Measurement of anxiety by forearm blood flow. *British Journal of Psychiatry, 112,* 789–798.

Kelly, E. J. (1985). The personality of chessplayers. *Journal of Personality Assessment, 49,* 282–284.

Kelly, G. A. (1955). *The psychology of personal constructs.* New York: Norton.

Kelly, M. D., & Dean, R. S. (1990). Best practices in neuropsychology. In A. Thomas & J. Grimes (Eds.), *Best practices in school psychology-II.* Washington, DC: National Association of School Psychologists.

Kempen, J. H., Kritchevsky, M., & Feldman, S. T. (1994). Effect of visual impairment on neuropsychological test performance. *Journal of Clinical and Experimental Neuropsychology, 16,* 223–231.

Kendall, M. G. (1948). *Rank correlation methods.* London: Griffin.

Kendall, P. C., & Finch, A. J., Jr. (1978). A cognitive-behavioral treatment for impulsivity. A group comparison study. *Journal of Consulting and Clinical Study, 46,* 110–115.

Kennedy, M. H., & Hiltonsmith, R. W. (1988). Relationships among the K-ABC Nonverbal Scale, the Pictorial Test of Intelligence and the Hiskey-Nebraska Test of Learning Aptitude for speech- and language-disabled preschool children. *Journal of Psychoeducational Assessment, 6*(1), 49–54.

Kennedy, O. A. (1971). Pupillometrics as an aid in the assessment of motivation, impact of treatment, and prognosis of chronic alcoholics. *Dissertation Abstracts International, 32,* 1214B–1215B.

Kennedy, R. S., Bittner, A. C., Harbeson, M., & Jones, M. B. (1982). Television computer games: A "new look" in performance testing. *Aviation, Space and Environmental Medicine, 53,* 49–53.

Kent, G. H., & Rosanoff, A. J. (1910). A study of association in insanity. *American Journal of Insanity, 67,* 37–96, 317–390.

Kent, N., & Davis, D. R. (1957). Discipline in the home and intellectual development. *British Journal of Medical Psychology, 30,* 27–33.

Kerlinger, F. N. (1973). *Foundations of behavioral research* (2nd ed.). New York: Holt.

Kern, J. M., Miller, C., & Eggers, J. (1983). Enhancing the validity of role-play tests: A comparison of three role-play methodologies. *Behavior Therapy, 14,* 482–492.

Kerr, M. M., & Nelson, C. M. (1989). *Strategies for managing behavior problems in the classroom* (2nd ed.). Columbus, OH: Merrill.

Keyser, D. J., & Sweetland, R. C. (Eds.). (1984–1988). *Test Critiques* (Vols. I–VII). Kansas City, MO: Test Corporation of America.

Kiecolt-Glaser, J. K., & Glaser, R. (1988). Psychological influences on immunity: Implications for AIDS. *American Psychologist, 43,* 892–898.

Kiewra, K. A., & McShane, D. (1992). Review of the Style of Learning and Thinking. In J. J. Kramer & J. C. Conoley (Eds.), *The eleventh mental measurements yearbook.* Lincoln: The Buros Institute of Mental Measurements, University of Nebraska.

Kim, S. P., Siomopoulos, G., & Cohen, R. J. (1977). Verbal abstraction and culture: An exploratory study with proverbs. *Psychological Reports, 41,* 967–972.

King, B. M. (1959). *Predicting submarine school attrition from the Minnesota Multiphasic Personality Inventory.* USN Medical Research Laboratory Report, New London, CT: *18* (Whole No. 313).

King, M. A., & Yuille, J. C. (1987). Suggestibility and the child witness. In S. J. Ceci, M. P. Toglia, & D. F. Ross (Eds.), *Children's eyewitness testimony.* New York: Springer-Verlag.

Kinnear, T. C., & Taylor, J. A. (1983). *Marketing research.* New York: McGraw-Hill.

Kinslinger, H. J. (1966). Application of projective techniques in personnel psychology since 1940. *Psychological Bulletin, 66,* 134–149.

Kinston, W., Loader, P., & Miller, L. (1985). *Clinical assessment of family health.* London: Hospital for Sick Children, Family Studies Group.

Kirby, J. R., Moore, P. J., & Schofield, N. J. (1988). Verbal and visual learning styles. *Contemporary Educational Psychology, 13,* 169–184.

Kirchner, W. K. (1966). A note on the effect of privacy in taking typing tests. *Journal of Applied Psychology, 50,* 373–374.

Kirk, S. A., McCarthy, J. J., & Kirk, W. D. (1968). *Illinois Test of Psycholinguistic Abilities.* Urbana: University of Illinois Press.

Klanderman, J. W., Perney, J., & Kroeschell, Z. B. (1985). Comparison of the K-ABC and WISC-R for LD children. *Journal of Learning Disabilities, 18,* 524–527.

Klein, D. (1989). The Depressive Experiences Questionnaire: A further evaluation. *Journal of Psychological Assessment, 53,* 703–715.

Klein, G. S., & Holzman, P. S. (1950). The "schematizing process": Personality qualities and perceptual attitudes in sensitivity to change. *American Psychologist, 5,* 312.

Klimoski, R., & Brickner, M. (1987). Why do assessment centers work? The puzzle of assessment center validity. *Personnel Psychology, 40,* 243–259.

Klimoski, R., & Palmer, S. (1993). The ADA and the hiring process in organizations. *Consulting Psychology Journal, 45,* 10–36.

Kline, R. B., & Lachar, D. (1992). Evaluation of age, sex, and race bias in the Personality Inventory for Children (PIC). *Psychological Assessment, 4,* 333–339.

Kline, R. B., Lachar, D., & Boersma, D. C. (1993). Identification of special education needs with the Personality Inventory for Children (PIC): A hierarchical classification model. *Psychological Assessment, 5,* 307–316.

Kline, R. B., Lachar, D., & Gdowski, C. L. (1992). Clinical validity of a Personality Inventory for Children (PIC) profile typology. *Journal of Personality Assessment, 58,* 591–605.

Kline, R. B., Lachar, D., & Sprague, D. J. (1985). The Personality Inventory for Children (PIC): An unbiased predictor of cognitive and academic status. *Journal of Pediatric Psychology, 10,* 461–477.

Kline, R. B., Snyder, J., Guilmette, S., & Castellanos, M. (1993). External validity of the Profile Variability Index for the K-ABC, Stanford-Binet, and WISC-R: Another cul-de-sac. *Journal of Learning Disabilities, 26,* 557–567.

Klockars, A. J. (1978). Personality variables related to peer selection. *Educational and Psychological Measurement, 32,* 513–517.

Klopfer, B., Ainsworth, M., Klopfer, W., & Holt, R. R. (1954). *Developments in the Rorschach technique: Vol. 1. Technique and theory.* Yonkers-on-Hudson, NY: World.

Klopfer, B., & Davidson, H. (1962). *The Rorschach technique: An introductory manual.* New York: Harcourt.

Klopfer, W. G. (1984). Application of the consensus Rorschach to couples. *Journal of Personality Assessment, 48,* 422–440.

Klove, H., & Matthews, C. G. (1974). Neuropsychological studies of patients with epilepsy. In R. M. Reitan & L. A. Davidson (Eds.), *Clinical Neuropsychology: Current status and applications* (pp. 237–365). New York: Winston.

Knobloch, H., & Pasamanick, B. (1966). *Prediction from assessment of neuromotor and intellectual status in infancy.* Paper presented at the American Psychopathological Association Meeting (February), Washington, DC.

Knoff, H. M. (1989). Review of the Personality Inventory for Children, Revised Format. In J. C. Conoley & J. J. Kramer (Eds.), *The tenth mental measurements yearbook.* Lincoln: The Buros Institute of Mental Measurements, University of Nebraska.

Knoff, H. M. (1990a). Evaluation of projective drawings. In C. R. Reynolds and T. B. Gutkin (Eds.), *Handbook of school psychology* (2nd ed.; pp. 898–946). New York: Wiley.

Knoff, H. M. (1990b). Review of Children's Depression Inventory. In J. J. Kramer & J. C. Conoley (Eds.), *The supplement to the tenth mental measurements yearbook* (pp. 48–50). Lincoln: The Buros Institute of Mental Measurements, University of Nebraska.

Knoff, H. M., & Prout, H. T. (1985). *The Kinetic drawing system: Family and school.* Los Angeles: Western Psychological Services.

Kobak, K. A., Reynolds, W. M., & Greist, J. H. (1993). Development and validation of a computer-administered version of the Hamilton Anxiety Scale. *Psychological Assessment, 5,* 487–492.

Kolb, B., & Whishaw, I. Q. (1980). *Fundamentals of human neuropsychology.* San Francisco: Freeman.

Kolbe, K., Shemberg, K., & Leventhal, D. (1985). University training in psychodiagnostics and psychotherapy. *The Clinical Psychologist, 38*(3), 59–61.

Kolotkin, R. A., & Wielkiewicz, R. M. (1984). Effects of situational demand in the role-play assessment of assertive behavior. *Journal of Behavioral Assessment, 6,* 59–70.

Kopelman, M. D. (1975). The contrast effect in the selection interview. *British Journal of Educational Psychology, 45,* 333–336.

Koppitz, E. M. (1963). *The Bender-Gestalt Test for young children.* New York: Grune & Stratton.

Koppitz, E. M. (1975). *The Bender-Gestalt Test for young children* (Vol. 2). New York: Grune & Stratton.

Kordinak, S. T., Vingue, F. J., & Birney, S. D. (1968). Head Start: Who needs it? That is the question. *American Psychologist, 76,* 618.

Korner, I. N., & Westwood, D. (1955). Inter-rater agreement in judging student adjustment from projective tests. *Journal of Clinical Psychology, 11,* 167–170.

Koson, D., Kitchen, C., Kochen, M., & Stodolsky, D. (1970). Psychological testing by computer: Effect on response bias. *Educational and Psychological Measurement, 30,* 803–810.

Kotkov, B., & Goodman, M. (1953). The Draw-A-Person tests of obese women. *Journal of Clinical Psychology, 9,* 362–364.

Kovacs, M. (1977). *Children's Depression Inventory.* Pittsburgh: Western Psychiatric Institute and Clinic.

Kraepelin, E. (1892). *Uber die Beeinflussung einfacher psychischer Vorgange durch einige Arzneimittel.* Jena: Fischer.

Kraepelin, E. (1895). Der psychologische versuch in der psychiatrie. *Psychologische Arbeiten, 1,* 1–91.

Kraepelin, E. (1896). Der psychologische versuch in der psychiatrie. *Psychologische Arbeiten, 1,* 1–91.

Kramer, J. J., & Conoley, J. C. (Eds.). (1992). *The eleventh mental measurements yearbook.* Lincoln: The Buros Institute of Mental Measurements of the University of Nebraska.

Kratochwill, T. R., Doll, E. J., & Dickson, W. P. (1986). Microcomputers in behavioral assessment: Recent advances and remaining issues. *Computers in Human Behavior, 1,* 277–291.

Kratochwill, T. R., Doll, E. J., & Dickson, W. P. (1991). Use of computer technology in behavioral assessments. In T. B. Gutkin & S. L. Wise (Eds.), *The computer and the decision-making process* (pp. 125–154). Hillsdale, NJ: Erlbaum.

Kratochwill, T. R., & Sheridan, S. M. (1990). Advances in behavioral assessment. In C. R. Reynolds & T. B. Gutkin (Eds.), *Handbook of school psychology* (2nd ed.). New York: Wiley.

Kresel, J. J., & Lovejoy, F. H. (1981). Poisonings and child abuse. In N. S. Ellerstein (Ed.), *Child abuse and neglect: A medical reference* (pp. 307–313). New York: Wiley.

Kroger, R. O., & Wood, L. A. (1993). Reification, 'faking,' and the big five. *American Psychologist, 48,* 1297–1298.

Krohn, A., & Mayman, M. (1974). Object representations in dreams and projective tests. *Bulletin of the Menninger Clinic, 43,* 515–524.

Krohn, E. J., & Lamp, R. E. (1989). Concurrent validity of the K-ABC and Stanford-Binet—Fourth Edition for Head Start Children. *Journal of School Psychology, 27*(1), 59–67.

Krohn, E. J., Lamp, R. E., & Phelps, C. G. (1988). Validity of the K-ABC for a black preschool population. *Psychology in the Schools, 25,* 15–21.

Krug, R. S. (1971). Antecedent probabilities, cost efficiency, and differential prediction of patients with cerebral organic conditions or psychiatric disturbance by means of a short test for aphasia. *Journal of Clinical Psychology, 27,* 468–471.

Kruskal, J. B., & Wish, M. (1978). *Multidimensional scaling.* Beverly Hills: Sage.

Kuder, G. F. (1979). *Kuder Occupational Interest Survey, Revised: General manual.* Chicago: Science Research Associates.

Kuder, G. F., & Richardson, M. W. (1937). The theory of the estimation of reliability. *Psychometrika, 2,* 151–160.

Kuhlmann, F. (1912). A revision of the Binet-Simon system for measuring the intelligence of children. *Journal of Psycho-Asthenics Monograph Supplement, 1*(1), 1–41.

Kulka, R. A., Schlenger, W. E., Fairbank, J. A., Hough, R. L., Jordan, B. K., Marmar, C. R., & Weiss, D. S. (1988). *Contractual report of findings from the national Vietnam veterans readjustment study: Vol. 1. Executive summary, description of findings, and technical appendices.* Research Triangle Park, NC: Research Triangle Institute.

Kuncel, R. B., & Fiske, D. W. (1974). Stability of response process and response. *Educational and Psychological Measurement, 34,* 743–755.

Kundert, D. K. (1990). Review of Reynolds Adolescent Depression Scale. In J. J. Kramer & J. C. Conoley (Eds.), *The supplement to the tenth mental measurements yearbook* (pp. 218–219). Lincoln: The Buros Institute of Mental Measurements, University of Nebraska.

Labeck, L. J., Johnson, J. H., & Harris, W. G. (1983). Validity on an automated on-line MMPI interpretive system. *Journal of Clinical Psychology, 39,* 412–416.

Labig, C. E., Jr. (1992). Supervisor and nonsupervisory employee attitudes about drug testing. *Employee Responsibilities and Rights Journal, 5,* 131–141.

Labrentz, E., Linkenhoker, F., & Aaron, P. G. (1976). Recognition and reproduction of Bender-Gestalt figures: A developmental study of the lag between perception and performance. *Psychology in the Schools, 13,* 128–133.

Lachar, D. (1982). *Personality Inventory for Children (PIC): Revised format manual supplement.* Los Angeles: Western Psychological Services.

Lachar, D. (1987). Automated assessment of child and adolescent personality. In J. N. Butcher (Ed.), *Computerized psychological assessment: A practitioner's guide* (pp. 261–291). New York: Basic Books.

Lachar, D., & Gdowski, C. L. (1979a). Problem-behavior factor correlates of Personality Inventory for Children profiles scales. *Journal of Consulting and Clinical Psychology, 47,* 39–48.

Lachar, D., & Gdowski, C. L. (1979b). *Actuarial assessment of child and adolescent personality: An interpretive guide for the Personality Inventory for Children profile.* Los Angeles: Western Psychological Services.

Lachar, D., Gdowski, C. L., & Snyder, D. K. (1985).

Consistency of maternal report and the Personality Inventory for Children: Always useful and sometimes sufficient—Reply to Cornell. *Journal of Consulting and Clinical Psychology, 53,* 275–276.

Lachar, D., & Gruber, C. P. (1993). Development of the Personality Inventory for Youth: A self-report companion to the Personality Inventory for Children. *Journal of Personality Assessment, 61,* 81–98.

Lachar, D., Kline, R. B., & Boersma, D. C. (1986). The Personality Inventory for Children: Approaches to actuarial interpretation in clinic and school settings. In H. M. Knoff (Ed.), *The psychological assessment of child and adolescent personality* (pp. 273–308). New York: Guilford Press.

Lachar, D., & Wirt, R. D. (1981). A data-based analysis of the psychometric performance of the Personality Inventory for Children (PIC): An alternative to the Achenbach review. *Journal of Personality Assessment, 45,* 614–616.

Lachar, D., & Wrobel, T. A. (1979). Validating clinicians' hunches: Construction of a new MMPI critical item set. *Journal of Consulting and Clinical Psychology, 47,* 277–284.

LaCombe, J. A., Kline, R. B., Lachar, D., Butkus, M., & Hillman, S. B. (1991). Case history correlates of a Personality Inventory for Children (PIC) profile typology. *Psychological Assessment: A Journal of Consulting and Clinical Psychology, 3,* 678–687.

LaCorte, M. A., & Risucci, D. A. (1993). Personality, clinical performance, and knowledge in paediatric residents. *Medical Education, 27,* 165–169.

Lah, M. I. (1989a). Sentence completion tests. In C. S. Newmark (Ed.), *Major psychological assessment instruments* (Vol. 2; pp. 133–163). Needham Heights, MA: Allyn and Bacon.

Lah, M. I. (1989b). New validity, normative, and scoring data for the Rotter Incomplete Sentences Blank. *Journal of Personality Assessment, 53,* 607–620.

Lake, D. G., Miles, M. B., & Earle, R. B., Jr. (1973). *Measuring human behavior.* New York: Teachers College Press.

Lam, C. S., Chan, F., Hilburger, J., Heimburger, M., Hill, V., & Kaplan, S. (1993). Canonical relationships between vocational interests and aptitudes. *Vocational Evaluation and Work Adjustment Bulletin, 26,* 155–160.

Lamb, D. G., Berry, D. T. R., Wetter, M. W., & Baer, R. A. (1994). Effects of two types of information on malingering of closed head injury on the MMPI-2: An analog investigation. *Psychological Assessment, 6,* 8–13.

Lamb, M. E. (Ed.). (1981). *The role of the father in child development* (2nd ed.). New York: Wiley.

Lambert, E. W., & Engum, E. S. (1992). Construct validity of the Cognitive Behavioral Driver's Inventory: Age, diagnosis, and driving ability. *The Journal of Cognitive Rehabilitation, 10,* 32–45.

Lambert, N. M. (1978). The Adaptive Behavior Scale—Public School Version: An overview. In W. A. Coulter & H. W. Morrow (Eds.). *Adaptive behavior: Concepts and measurements.* New York: Grune & Stratton.

Lamp, R. E., & Krohn, E. J. (1990). Stability of the Stanford-Binet Fourth Edition and K-ABC for young black and white children from low income families. *Journal of Psychoeducational Assessment, 8,* 139–149.

Landers, S. (1986, December). Judge reiterates I.Q. test ban. *APA Monitor, 17,* 18.

Landrum, M. S., & Ward, S. B. (1993). Behavioral assessment of gifted learners. *Journal of Behavioral Education, 3,* 211–215.

Landry, M., & McKelvie, S. J. (1985). Validity of conventional and unbiased intelligence test items for groups differing in age and education. *Psychological Reports, 57,* 975–981.

Landy, F. J., & Farr, J. H. (1980). Performance rating. *Psychological Bulletin, 87,* 72–107.

Langer, E. J., & Abelson, R. P. (1974). A patient by any other name: Clinician group difference in labeling bias. *Journal of Consulting and Clinical Psychology, 42,* 4–9.

Langmaid, R., & Ross, B. (1984). Games respondents play: A look at the importance of game analysis as a technique for enriching the understanding of group discussions. *Journal of the Market Research Society, 26,* 221–229.

Lansing, J. B., & Morgan, J. N. (1971). *Economic survey methods.* Ann Arbor: University of Michigan Press.

Lansky, L. L., List, M. A., Lansky, S. B., Cohen, M. E., & Sinks, L. B. (1985). Toward the development of a play performance scale for children (PPSC). *Cancer, 56,* 1837–1840.

Lansky, S. B., List, M. A., Lansky, L. L., Ritter-Sterr, C., & Miller, D. A. (1987). The measurement of performance in childhood cancer patients. *Cancer, 62,* 1651–1656.

Lanyon, R. I. (1984). Personality assessment. *Annual Review of Psychology, 35,* 667–701.

Lanyon, R. I. (1986). Psychological assessment procedures in court-related settings. *Professional Psychology: Research and Practice, 17,* 260–268.

Lanyon, R. I. (1993). Assessment of truthfulness in accusations of child molestation. *American Journal of Forensic Psychology, 11,* 29–44.

Lanyon, R. I., & Goodstein, L. D. (1971). *Personality assessment.* New York: Wiley.

Lapoint, F. H. (1972). Who originated the term "psychology"? *Journal of the History of the Behavioral Sciences, 8,* 328–335.

Larzelere, R., & Huston, T. (1980). The Dyadic Trust Scale: Toward understanding interpersonal trust in close relationships. *Journal of Marriage and the Family, 43,* 595–604.

Lasee, M. J., & Smith, D. K. (1991). *Relationships between the K-ABC and the Early Screening Profiles.* Paper presented at the Annual Meeting of the National Association of School Psychologists, Dallas, TX.

Last, J. M. (1983). Comprehensive early memory scoring system manual. Unpublished manuscript.

Last, J. M., & Bruhn, A. R. (1983). The psychodiagnostic value of children's earliest memories. *Journal of Personality Assessment, 47,* 597–603.

Last, J. M., & Bruhn, A. R. (1985). Distinguishing child diagnostic types with early memories. *Journal of Personality Assessment, 49,* 187–192.

Latham, G. P., Wexley, K. N., & Pursell, E. D. (1975). Training managers to minimize rating errors in the observation of behavior. *Journal of Applied Psychology, 60,* 550–555.

LaTour, M. S., Pitts, R. E., & Snook-Luther, D. C. (1990). Female nudity, arousal, and ad response: An experimental investigation. *Journal of Advertising, 19,* 51–62.

Laurent, J., Swerdlik, M., & Ryburn, M. (1992). Review of validity research on the Stanford-Binet Intelligence Scale: Fourth Edition. *Psychological Assessment, 4,* 102–112.

Lavelle, E. (1993). Development and validation of an inventory to assess processes in college composition. *British Journal of Educational Psychology, 63,* 489–499.

Lavelle, T., Hammersley, R., & Forsyth, A. (1991). A short scale for predicting drug misuse using selected items from the MMPI. *British Journal of Addiction, 86,* 49–55.

Lawlor, J. (1990, September 27). Loopholes found in truth tests. *USA Today,* p. D-1.

Laws, D. R., & Osborne, C. A. (1983). How to build and operate a behavioral laboratory to evaluate and treat sexual deviance. In J. G. Greer & I. R. Stuart (Eds.), *The sexual aggressor: Current perspectives on treatment* (pp. 293–335). New York: Van Nostrand Reinhold.

Lawshe, C. H. (1975). A quantitative approach to content validity. *Personnel Psychology, 28,* 563–575.

Leahy, A. (1932). A study of certain selective factors influencing prediction of the mental status of adopted children or adopted children in nature-nurture research. *Journal of Genetic Psychology, 41,* 294–329.

Leahy, A. M. (1935). Nature-nurture and intelligence. *Genetic Psychology Monographs, 17,* 241–306.

Leckliter, I. N., & Matarazzo, J. D. (1989). The influence of age, education, IQ, gender, and alcohol abuse on Halstead-Reitan Neuropsychological Test Battery performance. *Journal of Clinical Psychology, 45,* 484–512.

Lee, S. D. (1968). *Social class bias in the diagnosis of mental illness.* Unpublished doctoral dissertation, University of Oklahoma.

Lee, S. W., & Piersel, W. C. (1989). Reliability and reactivity of self-recording by preschool children. *Psychological Reports, 64,* 747–754.

Lehmann, D. R. (1985). *Market research and analysis.* Homewood, IL: Richard D. Irwin.

Leichtman, S. R., Burnett, J. W., & Robinson, H. M., Jr. (1981). Body image concerns of psoriasis patients as reflected in human figure drawings. *Journal of Personality Assessment, 45,* 478–483.

Leigh, J., Westen, D., Barends, A., Mendel, M. J., & Byers, S. (1992). The assessment of complexity of representations of people using TAT and interview data. *Journal of Personality, 60,* 809–837.

Leming, J. S. (1978). Cheating behavior, situational influence, and moral development. *Journal of Educational Research, 71,* 214–217.

Lennon, R. T. (1978). Perspective on intelligence testing. *Measurement in Education, 9,* 1–2.

Leonberger, F. T., Nicks, S. D., Larrabee, G. J., & Goldfader, P. R. (1992). Factor structure of the Wechsler Memory Scale—Revised within a comprehensive neuropsychological battery. *Neuropsychology, 6,* 239–249.

Lerner, B. (1980). *Minimum competence, maximum choice: Second chance legislation.* New York: Irvington.

Lerner, B. (1981). The minimum competence testing movement: Social, scientific, and legal implications. *American Psychologist, 36,* 1056–1066.

Lerner, P. M. (1990). Rorschach assessment of primitive defenses: A review. *Journal of Personality Assessment, 54,* 30–46.

Lesser, G. S., Fifer, G., & Clark, D. H. (1965). Mental abilities of children from different social-class and cultural groups. *Monographs of the Society for Research in Child Development, 30* (Serial No. 102).

Levy, J., & Epstein, N. (1964). An application of the Rorschach test in family investigation. *Family Process, 3,* 344–376.

Levy, S. (1982). Use of the Peabody Picture Vocabulary Test with low functioning autistic children. *Psychology in the Schools, 19,* 24–27.

Levy, S. J. (1985). Dreams, fairy tales, animals and cars. *Psychology and Marketing, 2,* 67–81.

Lewis, C. (1986). Test theory and psychometrika: The past twenty-five years. *Psychometrika, 51,* 11–22.

Lewis, R., Turtletaub, J., Pohl, R., Rainey, J., & Rosenbaum, G. (1990). MMPI differentiation of panic disorder patients from other psychiatric outpatients. *Psychological Assessment: A Journal of Consulting and Clinical Psychology, 2,* 164–168.

Liaboe, G. P., & Guy, J. D. (1985). The Rorschach "Father" and "Mother" cards: An evaluation of the research. *Journal of Personality Assessment, 49,* 2–5.

Liang, M. H., Larson, M. G., Cullen, K. E., & Schwartz, J. A. (1988). Comparative measurement efficiency and sensitivity of five health status instruments in arthritis research. *Arthritis and Rheumatism, 28,* 542–547.

Libb, J. W., Murray, J., Thurstin, H., & Alarcon, R. D. (1992). Concordance of the MCMI-II, the MMPI, and Axis I discharge diagnosis in psychiatric inpatients. *Journal of Personality Assessment, 58,* 580–590.

Libb, J. W., Stankovic, S., Sokol, R., Freeman, A., Houck, C., & Switzer, P. (1990). Stability of the MCMI among depressed psychiatric outpatients. *Journal of Personality Assessment, 55,* 209–218.

Libby, W. (1908). The imagination of adolescents. *American Journal of Psychology, 19,* 249–252.

Lichtenstein, D., Dreger, R. M., & Cattell, R. B. (1986). Factor structure and standardization of the Preschool Personality Questionnaire. *Journal of Social Behavior and Personality, 1,* 165–181.

Lieberman, J. N. (1965). Playfulness and divergent thinking: An investigation of their relationship at the kindergarten level. *Journal of Genetic Psychology, 107,* 219–224.

Likert, R. (1932). A technique for the measurement of attitudes. *Archives of Psychology,* Number 140.

Lilien, G. L., & Kotler, P. (1983). *Marketing decision making: A model building approach.* New York: Harper & Row.

Lilly, R. S., Hoaglin, A., & Anderson-Kulman, R. (1989). *The use of factor analysis in published psychological research.* Paper presented at the Annual Meeting of the American Psychological Association, New Orleans, LA.

Lindemann, J. E., & Matarazzo, J. D. (1990). Assessment of adult intelligence. In G. Goldstein & M. Hersen (Eds.), *Handbook of psychological assessment* (2nd ed; pp. 79–101). New York: Pergamon Press.

Lindgren, B. (1983, August). N or N–1? [Letter to the editor]. *American Statistician,* p. 52.

Lindholm, L., & Wilson, G. T. (1988). Body image assessment in patients with bulimia nervosa and normal controls. *International Journal of Eating Disorders, 7,* 527–539.

Lindstrom, E., Wieselgren, I. M., & von Knorring, L. (1994). Interrater reliability of the Structured Clinical Interview for the Positive and Negative Syndrome Scale for schizophrenia. *Acta Psychiatrica Scandinavica, 89,* 192–195.

Lindzey, G. (1950). An experimental examination of the scapegoat theory of prejudice. *Journal of Abnormal and Social Psychology, 45,* 296–309.

Lipkus, I. M., Barefoot, J. C., Williams, R. B., & Siegler, I. C. (1994). Personality measures as predictors of smoking initiation and cessation in the UNC Alumni Heart Study. *Health Psychology, 13,* 149–155.

Lippmann, W. (1922, October). The mental age of Americans. *New Republic.*

Lipsitt, P. D., Lelos, D., & McGarry, A. L. (1971). Competency for trial: A screening instrument. *American Journal of Psychiatry, 128,* 105–109.

Lis, D. J., & Powers, J. E. (1979). Reliability and validity of the Group Embedded Figures Test for a grade school sample. *Perceptual and Motor Skills, 48,* 660–662.

Lisansky, E. S. (1956). The inter-examiner reliability of the Rorschach test. *Journal of Projective Techniques, 20,* 310–317.

Little, S. G. (1992). The WISC-III: Everything old is new again. *School Psychology Quarterly, 7,* 148–154.

Llabre, M. M., Clements, N. E., Fitzhugh, K. B., & Lancelotta, G. (1987). The effect of computer-administered testing on test anxiety and performance. *Journal of Educational Computing Research, 3,* 429–433.

Locke, E. A. (1976). The nature and causes of job satisfaction. In M. D. Dunnette (Ed.), *Handbook of industrial and organizational psychology.* Chicago: Rand McNally.

Locke, H. J., & Wallace, K. M. (1959). Short marital adjustment and prediction tests: Their reliability and validity. *Marriage and Family Living, 21,* 251–255.

Locke, J. (1690). *An essay concerning human understanding.*

Loevinger, J. (1957). Objective tests as instruments of psychological theory. *Psychological Reports, 3,* 635–694.

Loevinger, J. (1966). The meaning and measurement of ego development. *American Psychologist, 21,* 195–206.

Loevinger, J., & Ossorio, A. G. (1958). Evaluation of therapy by self-report: A paradox. *American Psychologist, 13,* 366.

Loevinger, J., Wessler, R., & Redmore, C. (1970). *Measuring ego development: Vol. 1. Construction and use of a sentence completion test. Vol. 2. Scoring manual for women and girls.* San Francisco: Jossey-Bass.

Loewenstein, D. A., Rubert, M. P., Berkowitz-Zimmer, N., Guterman, A., Morgan, R., & Hayden, S. (1992). Neuropsychological test performance and prediction of functional capacities in dementia. *Behavior, Health, and Aging, 2,* 149–158.

Loftus, E. F. (1979). *Eyewitness testimony.* Cambridge, MA: Harvard University Press.

Loftus, E. F., & Davies, G. M. (1984). Distortions in the memory of children. *Journal of Social Issues, 40,* 51–67.

Logstdon, R. G., Teri, L., Williams, D. E., Vitiello, M. V., & Prinz, P. N. (1989). The WAIS-R profile: A diagnostic tool for Alzheimer's Disease? *Journal of Clinical and Experimental Neuropsychology, 11,* 892–898.

Lohman, D. F. (1989). Human intelligence: An introduction to advances in theory and research. *Review of Educational Research, 59,* 333–373.

London, P. (1976). Psychotherapy for religious neuroses? Comments on Cohen and Smith. *Journal of Consulting and Clinical Psychology, 44,* 145–147.

Lord, F. M. (1978). *A prediction interval for scores on a parallel test form* (Research Bulletin RB-78-5). Princeton, NJ: Educational Testing Service.

Lord, F. M. (1980). *Applications of item response theory to practical testing problems.* Hillsdale, NJ: Erlbaum.

Lord, F. M., & Novick, M. R. (1968). *Statistical theories of mental test scores.* Menlo Park, CA: Addison-Wesley.

Lord, R. G., De Vader, C. L., & Alliger, G. M. (1986). A meta-analysis of the relation between personality traits and leadership perceptions: An application of validity generalization procedures. *Journal of Applied Psychology, 71,* 402–410.

Lorr, M. (1991). An empirical evaluation of the MBTI typology. *Personality and Individual Differences, 12,* 1141–1145.

Losak, J. (1978). What do the students say? *The College Board Review, 108,* 25–27.

Loveland, N., Wynne, L., & Singer, M. (1963). The Family Rorschach: A new method for studying family interaction. *Family Process, 2,* 187–215.

Lowenthal, W. (1994). Myers-Briggs Type Inventory preferences of pharmacy students and practitioners. *Evaluation and the Health Professions, 17,* 22–42.

Lowman, J. C. (1980). Measurement of family affective structure. *Journal of Personality Assessment, 44,* 130–141.

Loyd, B. H., & Abidin, R. R. (1985). Revision of the Parenting Stress Index. *Journal of Pediatric Psychology, 10,* 169–177.

Lubin, B. (1967). *Depression Adjective Check Lists: Manual.* San Diego, CA: Educational and Industrial Testing Service.

Lubin, B. (1981). Additional data on the reliability and validity of the brief lists of the Depression Adjective Check Lists. *Journal of Clinical Psychology, 37,* 809–811.

Lubin, B., Larsen, R. M., Matarazzo, J. D., & Seever, M. F. (1985). Psychological test usage patterns in five professional settings. *American Psychologist, 40,* 857–861.

Lubin, B., & Levitt, E. E. (1979). Norms for the Depression Adjective Check Lists: Age group and sex. *Journal of Consulting and Clinical Psychology, 47,* 192.

Lubin, B., & Lubin, A. W. (1972). Patterns of psychological services in the U.S.: 1959–1969. *Professional Psychology, 3,* 63–65.

Lubin, B., Wallis, R. R., & Paine, C. (1971). Patterns of psychological test usage in the United States: 1935–1969. *Professional Psychology, 2,* 70–74.

Luborsky, L. B., & Cattell, R. B. (1947). The validation of personality factors in humor. *Journal of Personality, 15,* 283–291.

Lucio, E., Reyes-Lagunes, I., & Scott, R. (1994). MMPI-2 for Mexico: Translation and adaptation. *Journal of Personality Assessment, 63,* 105–116.

Lukin, M. E., Dowd, E. T., Plake, B. S., & Kraft, R. G. (1985). Comparing computerized versus traditional psychological assessment. *Computers in Human Behavior, 1,* 49–58.

Lung, R. J., Miller, S. H., Davis, T. S., & Graham, W. P. (1977). Recognizing burn injuries as abuse. *American Family Physician, 15,* 134–135.

Luria, A. R. (1966a). *Human brain and psychological processes.* New York: Harper & Row.

Luria, A. R. (1966b). *Higher cortical functions in man.* New York: Basic Books.

Luria, A. R. (1970, March). The functional organization of the brain. *Scientific American, 222,* 66–78.

Luria, A. R. (1973). *The working brain: An introduction to neuropsychology.* New York: Basic Books.

Luria, A. R. (1980). *Higher cortical functions in man* (2nd ed.). New York: Basic Books.

Lushene, R. E., & Gilberstadt, H. (1972, March). *Validation of VA MMPI computer-generated reports.* Paper presented at the Veterans Administration Cooperative Studies Conference, St. Louis, MO.

Lushene, R. E., O'Neil, H. F., & Dunn, T. (1974). Equivalent validity of a completely computerized MMPI. *Journal of Personality Assessment, 38,* 353–361.

Lusk, E. J., & Wright, H. (1981). Differences in sex and curricula on learning in the Group Embedded Figures Test. *Perceptual and Motor Skills, 53,* 8–10.

Lutey, C., & Copeland, E. P. (1982). Cognitive assessment of the school-age child. In C. R. Reynolds & T. B. Gutkin (Eds.), *The handbook of school psychology.* New York: Wiley.

Lyman, H. B. (1972). Review of the Wechsler Adult Intelligence Scale. In O. K. Buros (Ed.), *The seventh mental measurements yearbook* (pp. 788–790). Highland Park, NJ: Gryphon Press.

Lynn, R., Hampson, S. L., & Magee, M. (1983). Determinants of educational achievement at 16+: Intelligence, personality, home background and school. *Personality and Individual Differences, 4,* 473–481.

Lynn, R., Hampson, S. L., & Magee, M. (1984). Home background, intelligence, personality and education as predictors of unemployment in young people. *Personality and Individual Differences, 5,* 549–557.

Lyons, J. A., Gerardi, R. J., Wolfe, J., & Keane, T. M. (1988). Multidimensional assessment of combat-related PTSD: Phenomenological, psychometric, and psychophysiological considerations. *Journal of Traumatic Stress, 1,* 373–394.

Maccoby, E. E., & Jacklin, C. N. (1974). *The psychology of sex differences.* Stanford, CA: United Press.

MacDonald, D. A., Anderson, P. E., Tsagarakis, C. I., & Holland, C. J. (1994). Examination of the relationship between the Myers-Briggs Type Indicator and the NEO Personality Inventory. *Psychological Reports, 74,* 339–344.

MacFarlene, K., & Krebs, S. (1986). Techniques for interviewing and evidence gathering. In K. MacFarlene et al. (Eds.), *Sexual abuse of young children.* New York: Guilford Press.

Machover, K. (1949). *Personality projection in the drawing of the human figure: A method of personality investigation.* Springfield, IL: Charles C. Thomas.

Macmillan, D. L., & Meyers, C. E. (1980). Larry P.: An education interpretation. *School Psychology Review, 9,* 136–148.

Magnello, M. E., & Spies, C. J. (1984). Francis Galton: Historical antecedents of the correlation calculus. In B. Laver (Chair), *History of mental measurement: Correlation, quantification, and institutionalization.* Paper session presented at the 92nd annual convention of the American Psychological Association, Toronto, Ontario, Canada.

Mahoney, T. A., & England, G. W. (1965). Efficiency and accuracy of employer decision rules. *Personnel Psychology, 18,* 361–377.

Malcolm, P. B., Davidson, P. R., & Marshall, W. L. (1985). Control of penile tumescence: The effects of arousal level and stimulus content. *Behaviour Research & Therapy, 23,* 273–280.

Malgady, R. G., Costantino, G., & Rogler, L. H. (1984). Development of a Thematic Apperception Test (TEMAS) for urban Hispanic children. *Journal of Consulting and Clinical Psychology, 52,* 986–996.

Malone, P. S., Brounstein, P. J., von Brock, A., & Shaywitz, S. S. (1991). Components of IQ scores across levels of measured ability. *Journal of Applied Social Psychology, 21,* 15–28.

Maloney, M. P., Ball, T. S., & Edgar, C. L. (1970). Analysis of the generalizability of sensory-motor training. *American Journal of Mental Deficiency, 74,* 458–469.

Maloney, M. P., & Ward, M. P. (1976). *Psychological assessment.* New York: Oxford University Press.

Mandell, C. J., & Fiscus, E. (1981). *Understanding exceptional people.* St. Paul, MN: West Publishing Company.

Mannarino, A. P., Cohen, J. A., & Berman, S. R. (1994). The Children's Attributions and Perceptions Scale: A new measure of sexual-abuse related factors. *Journal of Clinical Child Psychology, 23,* 204–211.

Manz, C. C., & Sims, H. P. (1984). Searching for the "unleader": Organizational member views on leading self-managed groups. *Human Relations, 37,* 409–424.

Mapou, R. L. (1988). Testing to detect brain damage: An alternative to what may no longer be useful. *Journal of Clinical and Experimental Neuropsychology, 10,* 271–278.

Maranell, G. M. (1974). *Scaling: A sourcebook for behavioral scientists.* Chicago: Aldine.

Marcoulides, G. A. (1994). Selecting weighting schemes in multivariate generalizability studies. *Educational and Psychological Measurement, 54,* 3–7.

Mardell-Czudnowski, C. D., & Goldenberg, D. S. (1983, 1990). *Developmental Indicators for the Assessment of Learning—Revised.* Circle Pines, MN: American Guidance Service.

Margolis, R. B., Williger, N. R., Greenlief, C. L., Dunn, E. J., & Gfeller, J. D. (1989). The sensitivity of the Bender-Gestalt Test as a screening instrument for neuropsychological impairment in older adults. *The Journal of Psychology, 123,* 179–186.

Marks, P. E., & Seeman, W. (1963). *The actuarial description of personality: An atlas for use with the MMPI.* Baltimore: Williams & Wilkins.

Marquette, B. W. (1976). *Limitations on the generalizability of adult competence across all situations.* Paper presented at the annual meeting of the Western Psychological Association, Los Angeles, CA.

Marsh, D. T., Stile, S. A., Stoughton, N. L., & Trout-Landen, B. L. (1988). Psychopathology of opiate addiction: Comparative data from the MMPI and MCMI. *American Journal of Drug and Alcohol Abuse, 14,* 17–21.

Marsh, G. G., & Hirsch, S. H. (1982). Effectiveness of two tests of visual retention. *Journal of Clinical Psychology, 38,* 115–116.

Marsh, H. W. (1990). Confirmatory factor analysis of multitrait-multimethod data: The construct validation of multidimensional self-concept responses. *Journal of Personality, 58,* 661–692.

Marsh, H. W., & Holmes, I. W. M. (1990). Multidimensional self-concepts: Construct validation of responses by children. *American Educational Research Journal, 27,* 89–117.

Marshall, G. N., Hays, R. D., Sherbourne, C. D., & Wells, K. B. (1993). The structure of patient satisfaction with outpatient medical care. *Psychological Assessment, 5,* 477–483.

Marshall, W. L., Barbaree, H. E., & Butt, J. (1988). Sexual offenders against male children: Sexual preferences. *Behavior Research and Therapy, 26,* 383–391.

Martin, D. C., & Bartol, K. M. (1986). Holland's Vocational Preference Inventory and the Myers-Briggs Type Indicator as predictors of vocational choice among Master's of Business Administration. *Journal of Vocational Behavior, 29,* 51–65.

Martin, R. P. (1986). Assessment of the social and emotional functioning of preschool children. *School Psychology Review, 15,* 216–232.

Martin, R. P. (1988). *Assessment of personality and behavior problems.* New York: Guilford Press.

Martin, R. P., Hooper, S., & Snow, J. (1986). Behavior rating scale approaches to personality assessment in children and adolescents. In H. M. Knoff (Ed.), *The assessment of child and adolescent personality* (pp. 309–351). New York: Guilford Press.

Martin-Loeches, M., Gil, P., Jimenez, F., Exposito, F. J., Miguel, F., Cacabelos, R., & Rubia, F. J. (1991). Topographic maps of brain electrical activity in primary degenerative dementia of the Alzheimer type and multiinfarct dementia. *Biological Psychiatry, 29,* 211–223.

Mash, E. J., & Terdal, L. G. (1988). *Behavioral assessment of childhood disorders* (2nd ed.). New York: Guilford Press.

Masling, J. (1959). The effects of warm and cold interaction on the administration and scoring of an intelligence test. *Journal of Consulting Psychology, 23,* 336–341.

Masling, J. (1960). The influence of situational and interpersonal variables in projective testing. *Psychological Bulletin, 57,* 65–85.

Masling, J. (1965). Differential indoctrination of examiners and Rorschach responses. *Journal of Consulting Psychology, 29,* 198–201.

Maslow, A. H. (1943). A theory of motivation. *Psychological Review, 50,* 370–396.

Maslow, A. H. (1970). *Motivation and personality* (2nd ed.). New York: Harper & Row.

Matarazzo, J. D. (1986). Response to Fowler and Butcher on Matarazzo. *American Psychologist, 41,* 96.

Matarazzo, J. D. (1990). Psychological assessment versus psychological testing: Validation from Binet to the school, clinic, and courtroom. *American Psychologist, 45,* 999–1017.

Matarazzo, J. D., Matarazzo, R. G., Wiens, A. N., Gallo, A. E., & Klonoff, H. (1976). Retest reliability of the Halstead Impairment Index in a normal, a schizophrenic and two samples of organic patients. *Journal of Clinical Psychology, 32,* 338–349.

Matarazzo, J. D., & Wiens, A. N. (1977). Black Intelligence Test of Cultural Homogeneity and Wechsler Adult Intelligence Scale scores of black and white police applicants. *Journal of Applied Psychology, 62,* 57–63.

Mather, N. (1991). *An instructional guide to the Woodcock-Johnson Psycho-Educational Battery— Revised.* Allen, TX: DLM Teaching Resources.

Matthews, C. G. (1974). Applications of neuropsychological test methods in mentally retarded subjects. In R. M. Reitan & L. A. Davison (Eds.), *Clinical neuropsychology: Current status and applications* (pp. 267–287). New York: Winston.

Mattison, R. E., Handford, A., Kales, H. C., Goodman, A. L., & McLaughlin, R. E. (1990). *Psychological Assessment: A Journal of Consulting & Clinical Psychology, 2,* 169–174.

Maurer, T. J., & Alexander, R. A. (1991). Contrast effects in behavioral measurement: An investigation of alternative process explanations. *Journal of Applied Psychology, 76,* 3–10.

Maxwell, J. K., & Wise, F. (1984). PPVT IQ validity in adults: A measure of vocabulary, not of intelligence. *Journal of Clinical Psychology, 40,* 1044–1048.

Mayfield, E. C. (1972). Value of peer nominations in predicting life insurance sales performance. *Journal of Applied Psychology, 56,* 319–323.

Mayman, M. (1968). Early memories and character structure. *Journal of Projective Techniques and Personality Assessment, 31,* 303–316.

Mayman, M., & Faris, M. (1960). Early memories as expressions of relationship paradigms. *American Journal of Orthopsychiatry, 30,* 507–520.

Mays, V. M., Cochran, S. D., Hamilton, E., & Miller, N. (1993). Just cover up: Barriers to heterosexual and gay young adults' use of condoms. *Health Values: The Journal of Health Behavior, Education, and Promotion, 17,* 41–47.

Mazzuca, S. A. (1982). Does patient education in chronic disease have therapeutic value? *Journal of Chronic Diseases, 35,* 521–529.

McArthur, C. (1989). The superiorities of Form M of the Strong Vocational Interest Blank. *Journal of Personality Assessment, 53,* 837–840.

McArthur, C. (1992). Rumblings of a distant drum. *Journal of Counseling and Development, 70,* 517–519.

McArthur, D. S., & Roberts, G. E. (1982). *Roberts Apperception Test for Children manual.* Los Angeles: Western Psychological Services.

McCall, W. A. (1922). *How to measure in education.* New York: Macmillan.

McCall, W. A. (1939). *Measurement.* New York: Macmillan.

McCallum, R. S., & Bracken, B. A. (1981). Alternate form reliability of the PPVT-R for white and black preschool children. *Psychology in the Schools, 18,* 422–425.

McCallum, R. S., & Karnes, F. A. (1987). Comparison of intelligence tests. *School Psychology International, 8,* 133–139.

McCallum, R. S., Karnes, F. A., & Edwards, R. P. (1984). The test of choice for assessment of gifted children: A comparison of the K-ABC, WISC-R, and Stanford-Binet. *Journal of Psychological Assessment, 2,* 57–64.

McCann, J. T. (1990). A multitrait-multimethod analysis of the MCMI-II clinical syndrome scales. *Journal of Personality Assessment, 55,* 465–476.

McCann, J. T. (1991). Convergent and discriminant validity of the MCMI-II and MMPI personality disorders scales. *Psychological Assessment: A Journal of Consulting and Clinical Psychology, 3*(1), 9–18.

McClelland, D. C. (1951). *Personality.* New York: Holt-Dryden.

McClelland, D. C. (1961). *The achieving society.* Princeton, NJ: Van Nostrand.

McClelland, D. C. (1980). Motive dispositions: The merits of operant and respondent measures. In L. Wheeler (Ed.), *Review of personality and social psychology* (Vol. 1, pp. 10–41). Beverly Hills, CA: Sage.

McClelland, D. C., & Atkinson, J. W. (1948). The projective expression of needs: I. The effect of different intensities of the hunger drive on perception. *Journal of Psychology, 25,* 205–222.

McCloskey, G. W. (1989, March). *The K-ABC sequential-simultaneous information processing model and classroom intervention: A report—the Dade County Classroom research study.* Paper presented at the Annual Meeting of the National Association of School Psychologists, Boston.

McClure-Butterfield, P. (1990). Issues in child custody evaluation and testimony. In C. R. Reynolds & R. W. Kamphaus (Eds.), *Handbook of psychological and educational assessment of children: Personality, behavior and context* (pp. 576–588). New York: Guilford Press.

McConaughty, S. H., & Achenbach, T. M. (1988). *Practical guide for the Child Behavior Checklist and related materials.* Burlington: University of Vermont, Department of Psychiatry.

McCormack, J. K., Barnett, R. W., & Wallbrown, F. H. (1989). Factor structure of the Millon Clinical Multiaxial Inventory (MCMI) with an offender sample. *Journal of Personality Assessment, 53*(3), 442–448.

McCoy, G. F. (1972). *Diagnostic evaluation and educational programming for hearing impaired children.* Springfield, IL: Office of the Illinois Superintendent of Public Instruction.

McCrae, R. R. (1991). The five-factor model and its assessment in clinical settings. *Journal of Personality Assessment, 57,* 399–414.

McCrae, R. R., & Costa, P. T., Jr. (1986). Personality, coping, and coping effectiveness in an adult sample. *Journal of Personality, 54,* 385–405.

McCrae, R. R., & Costa, P. T., Jr. (1987). Validation of the five-factor model across instruments and observers. *Journal of Personality and Social Psychology, 52,* 81–90.

McCrae, R. R., & Costa, P. T., Jr. (1989). Reinterpreting the Myers-Briggs Type Indicator from the perspective of the five factor model of personality. *Journal of Personality Assessment, 57,* 16–40.

McCrae, R. R., & Costa, P. T., Jr. (1991). Adding *liebe und arbeit:* The full five-factor model and well-being. *Personality and Social Psychology Bulletin, 17,* 227–232.

McCraw, R. K., & Pegg-McNabb, J. (1989). Rorschach comparisons of male juvenile sex offenders and nonsex offenders. *Journal of Personality Assessment, 53,* 546–553.

McCubbin, H., Larsen, A., & Olson, D. (1985). F-COPES: Family Crisis Oriented Personal Evaluation Scales. In D. H. Olson, H. I. McCubbin, H. L. Barnes, A. S. Larsen, M. Muxen, & M. Wilson (Eds.), *Family inventories* (Rev. ed.). St. Paul: Family Social Science, University of Minnesota.

McCubbin, H. I., Patterson, J. M., & Wilson, L. R. (1985). FILE: Family Inventory of Life Events and Changes. In D. H. Olson, H. I. McCubbin, H. L. Barnes, A. S. Larsen, M. Muxen, & M. Wilson (Eds.), *Family inventories* (Rev. ed.). St. Paul: Family Social Science, University of Minnesota.

McCubbin, J. A., Wilson, J. F., Bruehl, S., Brady, M., Clark, K., & Kort, E. (1991). Gender effects on blood pressures obtained during an on-campus screening. *Psychosomatic Medicine, 53,* 90–100.

McCullough, C. S. (1990). Best practices for utilizing technology. In A. Thomas & J. Grimes (Eds.), *Best practices in school psychology II* (pp. 773–786). Washington, DC: National Association of School Psychologists.

McDonald, W. J. (1993). Focus group research dynamics and reporting: An examination of research objectives and moderator influences. *Journal of the Academy of Marketing Science, 21,* 161–168.

McElrath, K. (1994). A comparison of two methods for examining inmates' self-reported drug use. *International Journal of the Addictions, 29,* 517–524.

McEvoy, G. M., & Beatty, R. W. (1989). Assessment centers and subordinate appraisals of managers: A seven-year examination of predictive validity. *Personnel Psychology, 42,* 37–52.

McFall, M. E., Smith, D. E., Mackay, P. W., & Tarver, D. J. (1990). Reliability and validity of Mississippi Scale for Combat-Related Posttraumatic Stress Disorder. *Psychological Assessment: A Journal of Consulting and Clinical Psychology, 2,* 114–121.

McGinnies, E. (1949). Emotionality and perceptual defense. *Psychological Review, 56,* 244–251.

McGuire, A. M. (1994). Helping behaviors in the natural environment: Dimensions and correlates of helping. *Personality and Social Psychology Bulletin, 20,* 45–56.

McGurk, F. J. (1975). Race differences—twenty years later. *Homo, 26,* 219–239.

McKay, S. E., Golden, C. J., Moses, J. A., Jr., Fishburne, F., & Wisniewski, A. (1981). A correlation of the Luria-Nebraska Neuropsychological Battery with WAIS. *Journal of Consulting and Clinical Psychology, 49,* 940–946.

McKeachie, W. J. (1986). *Teaching tips: A guidebook for the beginning college teacher* (8th ed.). Lexington, MA: D. C. Heath.

McKenna, T., & Butcher, J. N. (1987, March). *Use of the revised MMPI in the assessment of chemical dependency.* Paper presented at the 22nd Annual Symposium on Recent Developments in the use of the MMPI, Seattle, WA.

McKenzie, S. J., Klein, K. R., Epstein, L. H., & McCurley, J. (1993). Effects of setting and number of observations on generalizability of parent-child interactions in childhood obesity treatment. *Journal of Psychopathology and Behavioral Assessment, 15,* 129–139.

McKinley, J. C., & Hathaway, S. R. (1940). A multiphasic schedule (Minnesota): II. A differential study of hypochondriases. *Journal of Psychology, 10,* 255–268.

McLemore, C. W., & Court, J. H. (1977). Religion and psychotherapy—ethics, civil liberties, and clinical savvy: A critique. *Journal of Consulting and Clinical Psychology, 45,* 1172–1175.

McNamara, J. R., Porterfield, C., Miller, L. G. (1969). The relationship of the WPPSI with the Coloured Progressive Matrices and the Bender Gestalt test. *Journal of Clinical Psychology, 25,* 65–68.

McNaughton, M. E., Smith, L. W., Patterson, T. L., & Grant, I. (1990). Stress, social support, coping resources, and immune status in the elderly. *Journal of Nervous and Mental Disease, 178,* 460–461.

McNeish, T. J., & Naglieri, J. A. (1993). Identification of individuals with serious emotional disturbance using the Draw A Person: Screening Procedure for Emotional Disturbance. *The Journal of Special Education, 27,* 115–121.

McNemar, Q.(1964). Lost: Our intelligence. Why? *American Psychologist, 19,* 871–882.

McPhee, J. P., & Wegner, K. W. (1976). Kinetic-Family-Drawing styles and emotionally disturbed childhood behavior. *Journal of Personality Assessment, 40,* 487–491.

McReynolds, P. (1987). Lightner Witmer: Little-known founder of clinical psychology. *American Psychologist, 42,* 849–858.

McWatters, M. (1989). *The self-concept of the retarded reader and the achieving reader at the high school level.* Unpublished Master's thesis, Kean College, NJ. (ERIC Document Reproduction Service No. ED 313 681)

Meadow, K. P., Karchmer, M. A., Petersen, L. M., & Rudner, L. (1980). *Meadow-Kendall Social-Emotional Assessment Inventory.* Washington, DC: Gallaudet University.

Meadows, G., Turner, T., Campbell, L., Lewis, S. W., Reveley, M. A., & Murray, R. M. (1991). Assessing schizophrenia in adults with mental retardation: A comparative study. *British Journal of Psychiatry, 158,* 103–105.

Mealor, D. J., & Richmond, B. O. (1980). Adaptive behavior: Teachers and parents disagree. *Exceptional Children, 46,* 386–388.

Mednick, S. A. (1962). The associative basis of the creative process. *Psychological Review, 69,* 220–232.

Mednick, S. A., Higgins, J., & Kirschenbaum, J. (1975). *Psychology.* New York: Wiley.

Meehl, P. E. (1954). *Clinical versus statistical prediction: A theoretical analysis and a review of the evidence.* Minneapolis: University of Minnesota Press.

Meehl, P. E. (1956). Wanted: A good cookbook. *American Psychologist, 11,* 263–272.

Meehl, P. E. (1959). A comparison of clinicians with five statistical methods of identifying psychotic MMPI profiles. *Journal of Clinical Psychology, 6,* 102–109.

Meehl, P. E. (1965). Seer over sign: The first good example. *Journal of Experimental Research in Personality, 1,* 27–32.

Meehl, P. E. (1984). Clinical and statistical prediction: A retrospective and would-be integrative view. In R. K. Blashfield (Chair), *Clinical versus statistical prediction.* Symposium presented at the 92nd annual meeting of the American Psychological Association, Toronto, Ontario, Canada.

Meehl, P. E., & Rosen, A. (1955). Antecedent probability and the efficiency of psychometric signs, patterns or cutting scores. *Psychological Bulletin, 52,* 194–216.

Meeker, M., & Meeker, R. (1973). Strategies for assessing intellectual patterns in black, Anglo, and Mexican-American boys—or any other children—and implications for education. *Journal of School Psychology, 11,* 341–350.

Meenan, R. F., & Pincus, T. (1987). The status of patient status measures. *Journal of Rheumatology, 14,* 411–414.

Megargee, E. I. (1972). *The California Psychological Inventory handbook.* San Francisco: Jossey-Bass.

Mehrens, W. A., & Lehmann, I. J. (1991). *Measurement and evaluation in education and psychology* (4th ed.). Fort Worth: Harcourt Brace Jovanovich.

Meier, S. T. (1984). The construct validity of burnout. *Journal of Occupational Psychology, 57,* 211–219.

Meier, S. T. (1991). Tests of the construct validity of occupational stress measures with college students: Failure to support discriminant validity. *Journal of Counseling Psychology, 38,* 91–97.

Mellenbergh, G. J. (1994). Generalized linear item response theory. *Psychological Bulletin, 115,* 300–307.

Melton, G. B. (1989). Review of the Child Abuse Protection Inventory, Form VI. In J. C. Conoley & J. J. Kramer (Eds.), *The tenth mental measurements yearbook.* Lincoln: The Buros Institute of Mental Measurements, University of Nebraska.

Melton, G. B., & Limber, S. (1989). Psychologists' involvement in cases of child maltreatment. *American Psychologist, 44,* 1225–1233.

Melton, G. B., & Limber, S. (1991). Caution in child maltreatment cases. *American Psychologist, 46,* 80–81.

Melzack, R., & Wall, P. D. (1982). *The challenge of pain.* New York: Basic Books.

Meng, K., & Patty, D. (1991). Field dependence and contextual organizers. *The Journal of Educational Research, 84,* 183–189.

Menninger, K. A. (1953). *The human mind* (3rd ed.). New York: Knopf.

Mentality tests: A symposium. (1916). *Journal of Educational Measurement, 7,* 229–240, 278–286, 358–360.

Mercer, J. R. (1976). A system of multicultural pluralistic assessment (SOMPA). In *Proceedings: With bias toward none.* Lexington: Coordinating Office for Regional Resource Centers, University of Kentucky.

Merenda, P. F., & Fava, J. L. (1994). Role of behaviorally descriptive adjectives in description of personality. *Psychological Reports, 74,* 259–274.

Merrell, K. W., & Popinga, M. R. (1994). An alliance of adaptive behavior and social competence: An examination of relationships between the Scales of Independent Behavior and the Social Skills Rating System. *Research in Developmental Disabilities, 15,* 39–47.

Merrens, M. R., & Richards, W. S. (1970). Acceptance of generalized versus "bona fide" personality interpretation. *Psychological Reports, 27,* 691–694.

Merz, W. R. (1984). K-ABC critique. In D. J. Keyser & R. C. Sweetland (Eds.), *Test Critiques* (Vol. 1; pp. 393–405). Kansas City, MO: Test Corporation of America.

Meyers, C. E. (1975). *What I Like To Do—An inventory of students' interests.* Chicago: Science Research Associates.

Meyers, C. J. (1986). The legal perils of psychotherapeutic practice: The farther reaches of the duty to warn. In L. Everstine & D. S. Everstine (Eds.), *Psychotherapy and the law.* New York: Grune & Stratton.

Meyers, D. V. (1978). Toward an objective procedure evaluation of the Kinetic Family Drawings (KFD). *Journal of Personality Assessment, 42,* 358–365.

Miale, F. R., & Selzer, M. (1975). The *Nuremberg mind.* New York: Quadrangle Books.

Micceri, T. (1989). The unicorn, the normal curve and other improbable creatures. *Psychological Bulletin, 105,* 156–166.

Michael, W. B., Michael, J. J., & Zimmerman, W. S. (1980). *Study Attitudes and Methods Survey manual of instructions and interpretations.* San Diego, CA: Educational and Industrial Testing Service.

Michael, W., Young, L., Michael, J., Hooke, G., & Zimmerman, W. (1971). A partial redefinition of the factorial structure of the Study Attitudes and Methods Survey (SAMS) Test. *Educational and Psychological Measurement, 31,* 545–547.

Middleton, H. A., Keene, R. G., & Brown, G. W. (1990). Convergent and discriminant validities of the Scales of Independent Behavior and the Revised Vineland Adaptive Behavior Scales. *American Journal on Mental Retardation, 94,* 669–673.

Mikail, S. F., DuBreuil, S., & D'Eon, J. L. (1993). A comparative analysis of measures used in the assessment of chronic pain patients. *Psychological Assessment, 5,* 117–120.

Miller, C. K., Chansky, N. M., & Gredler, G. R. (1972). Rater agreement on WISC protocols. *Psychology in the Schools, 7,* 190–193.

Miller, G. A. (1962). *Psychology.* New York: Harper & Row.

Miller, H. R., & Streiner, D. L. (1986). Differences in MMPI profiles with the norms of Colligan et al. *Journal of Consulting and Clinical Psychology, 54,* 843–845.

Miller, I. W., Kabacoff, R. I., Epstein, N. B., & Bishop, D. S. (1994). The development of a clinical rating scale for the McMaster Model of Family Functioning. *Family Process, 33,* 53–69.

Miller, N. E. (1969). Learning of visceral and glandular responses. *Science, 163,* 434–445.

Miller, T. (1991). The psychotherapeutic utility of the five-factor model of personality: A clinician's experience. *Journal of Personality Assessment, 57,* 415–433.

Miller, W. R., Heather, N., & Hall, W. (1991). Calculating standard drink units: International comparisons. *British Journal of Addiction, 86,* 43–47.

Millman, J. (1974). Criterion-related measurement. In W. J. Popham (Ed.), *Evaluation and education.* Berkeley, CA: McCutchan.

Millman, J. (1979). Reliability and validity of criterion-referenced test scores. *New Directions in Testing and Measurement, 1*(4), 75–92.

Millman, J., & Arter, J. A. (1984). Issues in item banking. *Journal of Educational Measurement, 21,* 315–330.

Millon, T. (1969). *Modern psychopathology.* Philadelphia, PA: Saunders.

Millon, T. (1981). *Disorders of personality: DSM-III, Axis II.* New York: Wiley.

Millon, T. (1983). *Millon Clinical Multiaxial Inventory manual.* Minneapolis, MN: National Computer Systems.

Millon, T. (1986a). Personality prototypes and their diagnostic criteria. In T. Millon & G. L. Klerman (Eds.), *Contemporary directions in psychopathology: Toward the DSM-IV.* New York: Guilford Press.

Millon, T. (1986b). A theoretical derivation of pathological personalities. In T. Millon & G. L. Klerman (Eds.), *Contemporary directions in psychopathology: Toward the DSM-IV.* New York: Guilford Press.

Millon, T. (1987). *Millon Clinical Multiaxial Inventory II manual.* Minneapolis, MN: National Computer Systems.

Millon, T. (1994). *Millon Clinical Multiaxial Inventory III.* Minneapolis, MN: National Computer Systems.

Millon, T., & Green, C. (1989). Interpretive guide to the Millon Clinical Multiaxial Inventory (MCMI-II). In C. S. Newmark (Ed.), *Major psychological assessment instruments* (Vol. 2; pp. 5–43). Needham Heights, MA: Allyn and Bacon.

Millon, T., Green, C. J., & Meagher, R. B. (1982). *Millon Adolescent Personality Inventory.* Minneapolis, MN: National Computer Systems.

Millon, T., Millon, C., & Davis, R. (1993). *Millon Adolescent Clinical Inventory.* Minneapolis, MN: National Computer Systems.

Milner, B. (1971). Interhemispheric differences in the localization of psychological processes in man. *British Medical Bulletin, 27,* 272–277.

Milner, J. (1989). Additional cross-validation of the Child Abuse Potential Inventory. *Psychological Assessment: A Journal of Consulting and Clinical Psychology, 1,* 219–223.

Milner, J. S. (1989). Applications of the Child Abuse Potential Inventory. *Journal of Clinical Psychology, 45,* 450–454.

Milner, J. S. (1991). Additional issues in child abuse assessment. *American Psychologist, 46,* 82–84.

Milner, J. S., Gold, R. G., & Wimberley, R. C. (1986). Prediction and explanation of child abuse: Cross-validation of the Child Abuse Protection Inventory. *Journal of Consulting and Clinical Psychology, 54,* 865–866.

Mindak, W. A. (1961). Fitting the semantic differential to the marketing problem. *Journal of Marketing, 25,* 28–33.

Misaszek, J., Dooling, J., Gieseke, M., Melman, H., Misaszek, J. G., & Jorgensen, K. (1985). Diagnostic considerations in deaf patients. *Comprehensive Psychiatry, 26,* 513–521.

Mischel, W. (1966). Theory and research on the antecedents of self-imposed delay of reward. In B. A. Maher (Ed.), *Progress in experimental personality research* (Vol. 3; pp. 85–132). New York: Academic Press.

Mischel, W. (1968). *Personality and assessment.* New York: Wiley.

Mischel, W. (1973). Toward a cognitive social learning reconceptualization of personality. *Psychological Review, 80,* 252–283.

Mischel, W. (1977). On the future of personality measurement. *American Psychologist, 32,* 246–254.

Mischel, W. (1979). On the interface of cognition and personality: Beyond the person-situation debate. *American Psychologist, 34,* 740–754.

Mitchell, J. V., Jr. (Ed.). (1983). *Tests in print III.* Lincoln: University of Nebraska Press.

Mitchell, J. V., Jr. (Ed.). (1985). *The ninth mental measurements yearbook.* Lincoln: University of Nebraska Press.

Mitchell, J. V., Jr. (1986). Measurement in the larger context: Critical current issues. *Professional Psychology: Research and Practice, 17,* 544–550.

Mittal, B. (1994). Public assessment of TV advertising: Faint praise and harsh criticism. *Journal of Advertising Research, 34,* 35–53.

Mittenberg, W., Azrin, R., Millsaps, C., & Heilbronner, R. (1993). Identification of malingered head injury on the Wechsler Memory Scale—Revised. *Psychological Assessment, 5,* 34–40.

Moir, A., & Jessel, D. (1992, January). Discover your brain's sex. *Reader's Digest* (Canadian English Edition), *140,* 89–91.

Molloy, D. W., Alemayehu, E., & Roberts, R. (1991). Reliability of a standardized Mini-Mental State Examination compared with the traditional Mini-Mental State Examination. *American Journal of Psychiatry, 148,* 102–105.

Money, J. (1976). *The Standardized Road-map Test of Direction Sense: Manual.* San Rafael, CA: Academic Therapy Publications.

Mooney, C. M. (1957). Age in the development of closure ability in children. *Canadian Journal of Psychology, 11,* 219–226.

Mooney, K. C. (1984). Review of Child Behavior Checklist. In D. J. Keyser & R. C. Sweetland (Eds.), *Test critiques* (Vol. 1; pp. 168–184). Kansas City, MO: Test Corporation of America.

Mooney, R. L., & Gordon, L. V. (1950). *Mooney Problem Check Lists.* New York: Psychological Corporation.

Moos, R. H., & Moos, B. S. (1981). *Family Environment Scale manual.* Palo Alto, CA: Consulting Psychologists Press.

Moreland, K. L. (1983, April). *A comparison of the validity of the two MMPI interpretation systems: A preliminary report.* Paper presented at the 18th Annual Symposium on Recent Developments in the Use of the MMPI, Minneapolis, MN.

Moreland, K. L. (1985). Validation of computer-based test interpretations: Problems and prospects. *Journal of Consulting and Clinical Psychology, 53,* 816–825.

Moreland, K. L. (1986). An introduction to the problem of test user qualifications. In R. B. Most (Chair), *Test purchaser qualifications: Present practice, professional needs, and a proposed system.* Symposium presented at the 94th annual convention of the American Psychological Association, Washington, DC.

Moreland, K. L. (1987). Computerized psychological assessment: What's available. In J. N. Butcher (Ed.), *Computerized psychological assessment: A practitioner's guide* (pp. 26–49). New York: Basic Books.

Moreland, K. L. (1990). Some observations on computer-assisted psychological testing. *Journal of Personality Assessment, 55,* 820–823.

Moreland, K. L., & Onstad, J. A. (1985). *Validity of the Minnesota Report: 1. Mental health outpatients.* Paper presented at the 20th Annual Symposium on Recent Developments in the Use of MMPI, Honolulu, HI.

Morey, L. C., & LeVine, D. J. (1988). A multitrait-multimethod examination of the Minnesota Multiphasic Personality Inventory (MMPI) and Millon Clinical Multiaxial Inventory (MCMI). *Journal of Psychopathology and Behavioral Assessment, 10,* 333–344.

Morgan, C. D., & Murray, H. A. (1935). A method for investigating fantasies: The Thematic Apperception Test. *Archives of Neurology and Psychiatry, 34,* 289–306.

Morrow, G. R. (1984). The assessment of nausea and vomiting: Past problems, current issues, and suggestions for future research. *Cancer, 53,* 2267–2278.

Morrow, P. C. (1993). *The theory and measurement of work commitment.* Greenwich, CT: JAI Press.

Morse, S. J. (1985). Excusing the crazy: The insanity defense reconsidered. *Southern California Law Review, 58,* 777–836.

Moses, J. A., Jr., & Maruish, M. E. (1988). A critical review of the Luria-Nebraska Neuropsychological Battery literature. III. Concurrent validity. *International Journal of Clinical Neuropsychology, 10,* 12–19.

Moses, J. A., Jr., & Maruish, M. E. (1990). A critical review of the Luria-Nebraska Neuropsychological Battery literature. XII. New developments, 1987–1988. Part one. *International Journal of Clinical Neuropsychology, 12,* 191–205.

Moses, S. (1991). Major revision of SAT goes into effect in 1994. *APA Monitor, 22*(1), 35.

Mosier, C. I. (1947). A critical examination of the concepts of face validity. *Educational and Psychological Measurement, 7,* 191–206.

Mostkoff, D. L., & Lazarus, P. J. (1983). The Kinetic Family Drawing: The reliability of an objective scoring system. *Psychology in the Schools, 20*, 16–20.

Motta, R. W., Little, S. G., & Tobin, M. I. (1993a). The use and abuse of human figure drawings. *School Psychology Quarterly, 8*, 162–169.

Motta, R. W., Little, S. G., & Tobin, M. I. (1993b). A picture is worth less than a thousand words: Response to reviewers. *School Psychology Quarterly, 8*, 197–199.

Mount, M. K., Barrick, M. R., & Strauss, J. P. (1994). Validity of observer ratings of the big five personality factors. *Journal of Applied Psychology, 79*, 272–280.

Mowrey, C. Personal communication, September 23, 1994.

Mueller, C. G. (1949). Numerical transformations in the analysis of experimental data. *Psychological Bulletin, 46*, 198–223.

Mulvey, E. P., & Lidz, C. W. (1984). Clinical considerations in the prediction of dangerousness in mental patients. *Clinical Psychology Review, 4*, 379–401.

Mungas, D., Blunden, D., Bennington, K., Stone, A., & Palma, G. (1990). Reliability and validity of scales for assessing behavior in epilepsy. *Psychological Assessment: A Journal of Consulting and Clinical Psychology, 2*, 423–431.

Murden, R. A., McRae, T. D., Kaner, S. T., & Bucknam, M. E. (1991). Mini-Mental State Exam scores vary with education in blacks and whites. *Journal of the American Geriatric Society, 39*, 149–155.

Murphy, G. (1949). *Historical introduction to modern psychology* (Rev. ed.). New York: Harcourt, Brace, & World.

Murphy, G. E. (1984). The prediction of suicide: Why is it so difficult? *American Journal of Psychotherapy, 38*, 341–349.

Murphy, K. R., Balzer, W. K., Lockhart, M. C., & Eisenman, E. J. (1985). Effects of previous performance on evaluations of present performance. *Journal of Applied Psychology, 70*, 72–84.

Murphy, K. R., & Thornton, G. C., III (1992). Characteristics of employee drug testing policies. *Journal of Business and Psychology, 6*, 295–309.

Murphy-Berman, V. (1994). A conceptual framework for thinking about risk assessment and case management in child protective service. *Child Abuse and Neglect, 18*, 193–201.

Murray, H. A. (1940). What should psychologists do about psychoanalysis? *Journal of Abnormal and Social Psychology, 35*, 150–175.

Murray, H. A. (1943). *Thematic Apperception Test manual.* Cambridge, MA: Harvard University Press.

Murray, H. A. (1951). Uses of the TAT. *American Journal of Psychiatry, 1071*, 577–581.

Murray, H. A. (1959). Preparations for the scaffold of a comprehensive system. In S. Koch (Ed.), *Psychology: A study of science* (Vol. 3). New York: McGraw-Hill.

Murray, H. A., et al. (1938). *Explorations in personality.* Cambridge: Harvard University Press.

Murray, H. A., & Kluckhohn, C. (1953). Outline of a conception of personality. In C. Kluckholn, H. A. Murray, & D. Schneider (Eds.), *Personality in nature, society, and culture* (2nd ed.; pp. 3–52). New York: Knopf.

Murray, H. A., & MacKinnon, D. W. (1946). Assessment of OSS personnel. *Journal of Consulting Psychology, 10*, 76–80.

Murstein, B. J. (1961). Assumptions, adaptation level, and projective techniques. *Perceptual and Motor Skills, 12*, 107–125.

Murstein, B. J. (1963). *Theory and research in projective techniques.* New York: Wiley.

Mussen, P. H., & Krauss, S. R. (1952). An investigation of the diagnostic validity of the Szondi test. *Journal of Abnormal and Social Psychology, 47*, 399–405.

Mussen, P. H., & Naylor, H. K. (1954). The relationship between overt and fantasy aggression. *Journal of Abnormal and Social Psychology, 49*, 235–240.

Mussen, P. H., & Scodel, A. (1955). The effects of sexual stimulation under varying conditions on TAT sexual responsiveness. *Journal of Consulting and Clinical Psychology, 19*, 90.

Myers, I. B. (1962). *The Myers-Briggs Type Indicator: Manual.* Palo Alto, CA: Consulting Psychologists Press.

Myers, I. B., & Briggs, K. C. (1943/1962). *The Myers-Briggs Type Indicator.* Palo Alto, CA: Consulting Psychologists Press.

Myers, I. B., & McCaulley, M. H. (1985). *Manual for the Myers-Briggs Type Indicator: A guide to the development and use of the MBTI.* Palo Alto, CA: Consulting Psychologists Press.

Nagle, R. J., & Bell, N. L. (1993). Validation of Stanford-Binet Intelligence Scale: Fourth Edition Abbreviated Batteries with college students. *Psychology in the Schools, 30*, 227–231.

Naglieri, J. A. (1981). Concurrent validity of the Revised Peabody Picture Vocabulary Test. *Psychology in the Schools, 18*, 286–289.

Naglieri, J. A. (1985a). Use of the WISC-R and K-ABC with learning disabled, borderline mentally retarded, and normal children. *Psychology in the Schools, 22*, 133–141.

Naglieri, J. A. (1985b). Normal children's performance on the McCarthy Scales, Kaufman Assessment Battery and Peabody Individual Achievement Test. *Journal of Psychoeducational Assessment, 3*, 123–129.

Naglieri, J. A. (1989). A cognitive processing theory for the measurement of intelligence. *Educational Psychologist, 24*, 185–206.

Naglieri, J. A. (1990). *Das-Naglieri Cognitive Assessment System.* Paper presented at the conference "Intelligence: Theories and Practice," Memphis, TN.

Naglieri, J. A. (1993). Human figure drawings in perspective. *School Psychology Quarterly, 8*, 170–176.

Naglieri, J. A., & Anderson, D. F. (1985). Comparison of the WISC-R and K-ABC with gifted students. *Journal of Psychoeducational Assessment, 3*, 175–179.

Naglieri, J. A., Braden, J. P., & Gottling, S. H. (1993).

Confirmatory factor analysis of the Planning, Attention, Simultaneous, Successive (PASS) cognitive processing model for a kindergarten sample. *Journal of Psychoeducational Assessment, 11,* 259–269.

Naglieri, J. A., & Das, J. P. (1988). Planning-arousal-simultaneous-successive (PASS): A model for assessment. *Journal of School Psychology, 26,* 35–48.

Naglieri, J. A., & Harrison, P. L. (1978). Comparison of the McCarthy and Cognitive Indexes and Stanford-Binet for educable mentally retarded children. *Perceptual and Motor Skills, 48,* 1252–1254.

Naglieri, J. A., & Jensen, A. R. (1987). Comparison of black-white differences on the WISC-R and the K-ABC: Spearman's hypothesis. *Intelligence, 11,* 21–43.

Naglieri, J. A., McNeish, T. J., & Bardos, A. N. (1991). *Draw A Person: Screening Procedure for Emotional Disturbance—Examiner's manual.* Austin, TX: Pro-Ed.

Naglieri, J. A., & Naglieri, D. A. (1981). Comparison of the PPVT and PPVT-R for preschool children: Implications for the practitioner. *Psychology in the Schools, 18,* 434–436.

Naglieri, J. A., & Reardon, S. M. (1993). Traditional IQ is irrelevant to learning disabilities—Intelligence is not. *Journal of Learning Disabilities, 26,* 127–133.

Narens, L., & Luce, R. D. (1986). Measurement: The theory of numerical assignments. *Psychological Bulletin, 99,* 166–180.

Nathan, P. E. (1994). DSM-IV: Empirical, accessible, not yet ideal. *Journal of Clinical Psychology, 50,* 103–110.

National Association of School Psychologists. (1984). *Principles for professional ethics.* Washington, DC: Author.

National Association of School Psychologists. (1992). *Principles for professional ethics. Professional conduct manual,* pp. 1–23. Washington, DC: Author.

National Joint Committee on Learning Disabilities. (1985). *Learning disabilities and the preschool child: A position paper of the National Joint Committee on Learning Disabilities.* Baltimore, MD: Author.

Naylor, J. C., & Shine, L. C. (1965). A table for determining the increase in mean criterion score obtained by using a selection device. *Journal of Industrial Psychology, 3,* 33–42.

Neale, E. L., & Rosal, M. L. (1993). What can art therapists learn from projective drawing techniques for children? A review of the literature. *The Arts in Psychotherapy, 20,* 37–49.

Needham, J. (1959). *A history of embryology.* New York: Abelard-Schuman.

Neisser, U. (1979). The concept of intelligence. *Intelligence, 3,* 217–227.

Nellis, L. & Gridley, B. E. (1994). Review of the Bayley Scales of Infant Development—Second Edition. *Journal of School Psychology, 32,* 201–209.

Nelson, D. V., Harper, R. G., Kotik-Harper, D., & Kirby, H. B. (1993). Brief neuropsychologic differentiation of demented versus depressed elderly inpatients. *General Hospital Psychiatry, 15,* 409–416.

Nelson, W. J., & Birkimer, J. C. (1978). Role of self-instruction and self-reinforcement in the modification of impulsivity. *Journal of Consulting and Clinical Psychology, 46,* 143.

Nester, M. A. (1993). Psychometric testing and reasonable accommodation for persons with disabilities. *Rehabilitation Psychology, 38,* 75–85.

Nevid, J. S. (1984). Methodological considerations in the use of electroencephalographic techniques in advertising research. *Psychology & Marketing, 1*(2), 5–19.

Nevid, J. S., & Cohen, R. J. (1987). Watching people watch: But is anybody watching? In R. J. Cohen (Chair), *Aspects of the consumer experience.* Symposium presented at the 95th annual convention of the American Psychological Association, August 31, 1987, New York.

Newcomb, T. M. (1929). *Consistency of certain extrovert-introvert behavior patterns in 51 problem boys.* New York: Columbia University Bureau of Publications.

Newman, H. H., Freeman, F. N., & Holzinger, K. J. (1937). *Twins.* Chicago: University of Chicago Press.

Newstead, S. E. (1992). A study of two "quick-and-easy" methods of assessing individual differences in student learning. *British Journal of Educational Psychology, 62,* 299–312.

Nichols, D. S. (1992). Review of the Minnesota Multiphasic Personality Inventory—2. In J. J. Kramer & J. C. Conoley (Eds.), *The eleventh mental measurements yearbook.* Lincoln: The Buros Institute of Mental Measurements, University of Nebraska.

Nighswonger, N. J., & Martin, J. R. (1981). On using voice analysis in marketing research. *Journal of Marketing Research, 18,* 350–355.

Nihira, K. (1969a). Factorial dimensions of adaptive behavior in adult retardates. *American Journal of Mental Deficiency, 73,* 868–878.

Nihira, K. (1969b). Factorial dimensions of adaptive behavior in mentally retarded children and adolescents. *American Journal of Mental Deficiency, 74,* 130–141.

Nitko, A. J. (1988). Designing tests that are integrated with instructions. In R. L. Linn (Ed.), *Educational measurement* (3rd ed.). New York: American Council on Education/Macmillan.

Nolan, Y., Johnson, J. A., & Pincus, A. L. (1994). Personality and drunk driving: Identification of DUI types using the Hogan Personality Inventory. *Psychological Assessment, 6,* 33–40.

Noles, S. W., Cash, T. F., & WInstead, B. A. (1985). Body image, physical attractiveness, and depression. *Journal of Consulting and Clinical Psychology, 53,* 88–94.

Norbeck, J. S., Lindsey, A. M., & Carrieri, V. L. (1981). The development of an instrument to measure social support. *Nursing Research, 30,* 264–269.

Norman, W. T. (1963). Toward an adequate taxonomy of personality attributes: Replicated factor structure in peer nomination personality ratings. *Journal of Abnormal and Social Psychology, 66,* 574–583.

Notarius, C., & Markman, H. (1981). Couples Interaction Scoring System. In E. Filsinger & R. Lewis, (Eds.)., *Assessing marriage: New behavioral approaches.* Beverly Hills, CA: Sage.

Notarius, C. I., & Vanzetti, N. A. (1983). The Marital Agendas Protocol. In E. Filsinger (Ed.), *Marriage and family assessment: A sourcebook for family therapy.* Beverly Hills, CA: Sage.

Nottingham, E. J., IV, & Mattson, R. E. (1981). A validation study of the Competency Screening Test. *Law and Human Behavior, 5,* 329–335.

Novick, M. R. (1981). Federal guidelines and professional standards. *American Psychologist, 36,* 1035–1046.

Novick, M. R., & Lewis, C. (1967). Coefficient alpha and the reliability of composite measurements. *Psychometrika, 32,* 1–13.

Nunnally, J. C. (1978). *Psychometric theory* (2nd ed.). New York: McGraw-Hill.

Oakland, T. (1985). Review of the Slosson Intelligence Test. In J. V. Mitchell (Ed.), *The ninth mental measurements yearbook* (pp. 1401–1403). Lincoln: University of Nebraska Press.

Oakland, T., & Dowling, L. (1983). The *Draw-A-Person Test:* Validity properties for nonbiased assessment. *Learning Disability Quarterly, 6,* 526–534.

Obrzut, A., Nelson, R. B., & Obrzut, J. E. (1987). Construct validity of the Kaufman Assessment Battery for Children with mildly mentally retarded students. *American Journal of Mental Deficiency, 92*(1), 74–77.

Obrzut, J. E., & Bolick, C. A. (1986). Thematic approaches to personality assessment with children and adolescents. In H. M. Knoff (Ed.), *The assessment of child and adolescent personality* (pp. 173–198). New York: Guilford Press.

O'Donnell, W. E., DeSoto, C. B., & DeSoto, J. L. (1993). Validity and reliability of the Revised Neuropsychological Impairment Scales (NIS). *Journal of Clinical Psychology, 49,* 372–382.

O'Donnell, W. E., DeSoto, C. B., DeSoto, J. L., & Reynolds, D. M. (1993). *The Neuropsychological Impairment Scale (NIS) manual.* Los Angeles: Western Psychological Services.

O'Donnell, W. E., & Reynolds, D. McQ. (1983). *Neuropsychological Impairment Scale (NIS) manual.* Annapolis, MD: Annapolis Neuropsychological Services.

Ogdon, D. P. (1982). *Psychodiagnosis and personality assessment: A handbook.* Los Angeles: Western Psychological Services.

O'Hara, M. W., Hoffman, J. G., Phillips, L. H. C., & Wright, E. J. (1992). Adjustment in childbearing women: The Postpartum Adjustment Questionnaire. *Psychological Assessment, 4,* 160–169.

O'Keefe, T., & Argulewicz, E. N. (1979). Test-retest reliability of Matching Familiar Figures Test scores of female undergraduates. *Perceptual and Motor Skills, 49,* 698.

O'Keeffe, J. (1993). Disability, discrimination, and the Americans with Disabilities Act. *Consulting Psychology Journal, 45*(2), 3–9.

O'Leary, K. M., Brouwers, P., Gardner, D. L., & Cowdry, R. W. (1991). Neuropsychological testing of patients with borderline personality disorder. *American Journal of Psychiatry, 148,* 106–111.

O'Leary, M. R., Calsyn, D. A., & Fauria, T. (1980). The Group Embedded Figures Test: A measure of cognitive style or cognitive impairment. *Journal of Personality Assessment, 44,* 532–537.

Oliver, J. M., & Baumgart, E. P. (1985). The dysfunctional attitude scale: Psychometric properties and relation to depression in an unselected adult population. *Cognitive Therapy & Research, 9,* 161–167.

Ollendick, T. H. (1983). Reliability and validity of the Revised Fear Survey Schedule for Children (FSSC—R). *Behavior Research & Therapy, 21,* 685–692.

Olson, D. H., & Barnes, H. L. (1985). Quality of Life. In D. H. Olson, H. I. McCubbin, H. L. Barnes, A. S. Larsen, M. Muxen, & M. Wilson (Eds.), *Family inventories* (Rev. ed.). St. Paul: Family Social Science, University of Minnesota.

Olson, D. H., Larsen, A. S., & McCubbin, H. I. (1985). Family Strengths. In D. H. Olson, H. I. McCubbin, H. L. Barnes, A. S. Larsen, M. Muxen, & M. Wilson (Eds.), *Family inventories* (Rev. ed.). St. Paul: Family Social Science, University of Minnesota.

Oltman, P. K., Raskin, E., & Witkin, H. A. (1971). *Group Embedded Figures Test.* Palo Alto, CA: Consulting Psychologists Press.

Omizo, M. M., & Williams, R. E. (1981). Biofeedback training can calm the hyperactive child. *Academic Therapy, 17,* 43–46.

Organ, D. W., & Near, J. P. (1985). Cognition versus affect in measures of job satisfaction. *International Journal of Psychology, 20,* 241–253.

Ornstein, R. (1988). *Psychology: The study of human experience* (2nd ed.). San Diego, CA: Harcourt Brace Jovanovich.

Orr, D. B., & Graham, W. R. (1968). Development of a listening comprehension test to identify educational potential among disadvantaged junior high school students. *American Educational Researcher Journal, 5,* 167–180.

Orr, R. R., Cameron, S. J., Dobson, L. A., & Day, D. M. (1993). Age-related changes in stress experienced by families with a child who has developmental delays. *Mental Retardation, 31,* 171–176.

Osgood, C. E., Suci, G. J., & Tannenbaum, P. H. (1957). *The measurement of meaning.* Urbana: University of Illinois Press.

Osipow, S. H., & Reed, R. (1985). Decision making style and career indecision in college students. *Journal of Vocational Behavior, 27,* 368–373.

Osman, A., Gifford, J., Jones, T., et al. (1993). Psychometric evaluation of the Reasons for Living Inventory. *Psychological Assessment, 5,* 154–158.

OSS Assessment Staff. (1948). *Assessment of men: Selection of personnel for the Office of Strategic Service.* New York: Rinehart.

Otis, A., & Lennon, R. (1979). *Otis-Lennon School Ability Test.* New York: Psychological Corporation.

Ouellette, S. E. (1988). The use of projective drawing

techniques in the personality assessment of pre-lingually deafened young adults: A pilot study. *American Annals of the Deaf, 133,* 212–217.

Outtz, J. (1994, June). Cited in T. DeAngelis, New tests allow takers to tackle real-life problems. *APA Monitor, 25,* 14.

Overholser, J. C. (1990). Retest reliability of the Millon Clinical Multiaxial Inventory. *Journal of Personality Assessment, 55*(1 & 2), 202–208.

Ozer, D. J. (1985). Correlation and the coefficient of determination. *Psychological Bulletin, 97,* 307–315.

Ozer, D. J., & Reise, S. P. (1994). Personality assessment. *Annual Review of Psychology, 45,* 357–388.

Paget, K. D. (1985). Assessment in early childhood education. *Diagnostique, 10,* 76–87.

Palmore, E. (Ed.). (1970). *Normal aging.* Durham, NC: Duke University Press.

Panell, R. C., & Laabs, G. J. (1979). Construction of a criterion-referenced, diagnostic test for an individualized instruction program. *Journal of Applied Psychology, 64,* 255–261.

Pannbacker, M., & Middleton, G. (1992). Review of Wepman's Auditory Discrimination Test, Second Edition. In J. J. Kramer & J. C. Conoley (Eds.), *The eleventh mental measurements yearbook.* Lincoln: The Buros Institute of Mental Measurements, University of Nebraska.

Pantle, M. L., Evert, J. M., & Trenerry, M. R. (1990). The utility of the MAPI in the assessment of depression. *Journal of Personality Assessment, 55,* 673–682.

Paolo, A. M., & Ryan, J. J. (1991). Application of WAIS-R short forms to persons 75 years of age and older. *Journal of Psychoeducational Assessment, 9,* 345–352.

Park, C. S., & Srinivasan, V. (1994). A survey-based method for measuring and understanding brand equity and its extendibility. *Journal of Marketing Research, 31,* 271–288.

Parker, K. C. (1983). Factor analysis of the WAIS-R at nine age levels between 16 and 74 years. *Journal of Consulting and Clinical Psychology, 51,* 302–308.

Parker, K. C. H., Hanson, R. K., & Hunsley, J. (1988). MMPI, Rorschach, and WAIS: A meta-analytic comparison of reliability, stability, and validity. *Psychological Bulletin, 103,* 367–373.

Parron, D. C., Solomon, F., & Jenkins, C. D. (Eds.). (1982). *Behavior, health risks, and social disadvantage.* Washington, DC: National Academy Press.

Pascal, G. R., & Suttell, B. J. (1951). *The Bender-Gestalt Test: Quantification and validity for adults.* New York: Grune & Stratton.

Pasewark, R. A., Rardin, M. W., & Grice, J. E. (1971). Relationship of the WPPSI and the Stanford-Binet L-M in lower class children. *Journal of School Psychology, 9,* 45–50.

Pasewark, R. S., & Sawyer, R. N. (1979). Edwards Personal Preference Schedule scores of rural high school students. *Educational and Psychological Measurement, 39,* 81–84.

Paul, G. L. (1987). *The time-sample behavioral checklist: Observational assessment instrumentation for service and research.* Champaign, IL: Research Press.

Paulhus, D. L. (1984). Two-component models of socially desirable responding. *Journal of Personality and Social Psychology, 46,* 598–609.

Paulhus, D. L. (1986). Self-deception and impression management in test responses. In A. Angleitner & J. S. Wiggins (Eds.), *Personality assessment via questionnaire* (pp. 142–165). New York: Springer.

Paulhus, D. L. (1990). Measurement and control of response bias. In J. P. Robinson, P. R. Shaver, & L. Wrightsman (Eds.), *Measures of personality and social-psychological attitudes* (pp. 17–59). San Diego, CA: Academic Press.

Paulhus, D. L., & Levitt, K. (1987). Desirable response triggered by affect: Automatic egotism? *Journal of Personality and Social Psychology, 52,* 245–259.

Paulhus, D. L., & Reid, D. B. (1991). Enhancement and denial in socially desirable responding. *Journal of Personality and Social Psychology, 60,* 307–317.

Pavot, W., & Diener, E. (1993). Review of the Satisfaction with Life Scale. *Psychological Assessment, 5,* 164–172.

Payne, D. A. (1992). *Measuring and evaluating educational outcomes.* New York: Merrill.

Payne, F. D., & Wiggins, J. S. (1968). Effects of rule relaxation and system combination on classification rates in two MMPI "cookbook" systems. *Journal of Consulting and Clinical Psychology, 32,* 734–736.

Pearson, D. A., & Lachar, D. (1994). Using behavioral questionnaires to identify adaptive deficits in elementary school children. *Journal of School Psychology, 32,* 33–52.

Pearson, K., & Moul, M. (1925). The problem of alien immigration of Great Britain illustrated by an examination of Russian and Polish Jewish children. *Annals of Eugenics, 1,* 5–127.

Pedersen, D. M., Shinedling, M. M., & Johnson, D. L. (1968). Effects of sex of examiner and subject on children's quantitative test performance. *Journal of Personality and Social Psychology, 10,* 251–254.

Pellegrini, A., & Putnam, P. (1984). The amytal interview in the diagnosis of late onset psychosis with cultural features presenting as catatonic stupor. *Journal of Nervous & Mental Disease, 172,* 502–504.

Penner, L. A., Thompson, J. K., & Coovert, D. L. (1991). Size estimation among anorexics: Much ado about very little? *Journal of Abnormal Psychology, 100,* 90–93.

Perry, J. C., Jacobs, D. (1982). Overview: Clinical applications of the amytal interview in psychiatric emergency settings. *American Journal of Psychiatry, 139,* 552–559.

Peterson, N. S., & Novick, M. R. (1976). An evaluation of some models for culture-fair selection. *Journal of Educational Measurement, 13,* 3–29.

Peterson, R. A., & Wilson, W. R. (1992). Measuring customer satisfaction: Fact and artifact. *Journal of the Academy of Marketing Science, 20,* 61–71.

Petrie, K., & Chamberlain, K. (1985). The predictive validity of the Zung Index of Potential Suicide. *Journal of Personality Assessment, 49,* 100–102.

Petty, M. M., McGhee, G. W., & Cavender, J. W.

(1984). A meta-analysis of the relationships between individual job satisfaction and individual performance. *Academy of Management Review, 9,* 712–721.

Pfeiffer, E. (1975). A Short Portable Mental Status Questionnaire for the assessment of organic brain deficit in elderly patients. *Journal of the American Geriatric Society, 23,* 433–441.

Phelps, L., & Branyon, B. (1988). Correlations among the Hiskey, K-ABC Nonverbal Scale, Leiter, and WISC-R Performance Scale with public school deaf children. *Journal of Psychoeducational Assessment, 6,* 354–358.

Phillipson, H. (1955). *The object relations technique.* Glencoe, IL: Free Press.

Piaget, J. (1954). *The construction of reality on the child.* New York: Basic Books.

Piaget, J. (1971). *Biology and knowledge.* Chicago: University of Chicago Press.

Pichot, P. (1984). Centenary of the birth of Hermann Rorschach. (S. Rosenzweig & E. Schreiber, Trans.). *Journal of Personality Assessment, 48,* 591–596.

Piedmont, R. L., McCrae, R. R., & Costa, P. T., Jr. (1991). Adjective Check List scales and the five-factor model. *Journal of Personality and Social Psychology, 60,* 630–637.

Piedmont, R. L., McCrae, R. R., & Costa, P. T., Jr. (1992). An assessment of the Edwards Personal Preference Schedule from the perspective of the five-factor model. *Journal of Personality Assessment, 58,* 67–78.

Piedmont, R. L., & Weinstein, H. P. (1993). A psychometric evaluation of the new NEO-PIR facet scales for agreeableness and conscientiousness. *Journal of Personality Assessment, 60,* 302–318.

Piers, E. V. (1969). *Manual for the Piers-Harris Children's Self-Concept Scale.* Nashville, TN: Counselor Recordings and Tests.

Pilkonis, P. A., Heape, C. L., Ruddy, J., & Serrao, P. (1991). Validity in the diagnosis of personality disorders: The use of the LEAD standard. *Psychological Assessment: A Journal of Consulting and Clinical Psychology, 3,* 46–54.

Pincus, J. H., & Tucker, G. J. (1974). *Behavioral neurology.* New York: Oxford.

Pintner, R. (1931). *Intelligence testing.* New York: Holt.

Piotrowski, C., & Keller, J. (1991, March). *Psychological testing practices in applied settings: A literature review from 1980–1990.* Paper presented at the annual meeting of the Southeastern Psychological Association, New Orleans, LA.

Piotrowski, C., & Keller, J. W. (1989). Psychological testing in outpatient mental health facilities: A national study. *Professional Psychology: Research and Practice, 20*(4), 423–425.

Piotrowski, C., & Keller, J. W. (1992). Psychological testing in applied settings: A literature review from 1982–1992. *The Journal of Training and Practice in Professional Psychology, 6,* 74–82.

Piotrowski, C., & Lubin, B. (1990). Assessment practices of health psychologists: Survey of APA Division 38 clinicians. *Professional Psychology: Research and Practice, 21,* 99–106.

Piotrowski, C., Sherry, D., & Keller, J. W. (1985). Psychodiagnostic test usage: A survey of the Society for Personality Assessment. *Journal of Personality Assessment, 49,* 115–119.

Piotrowski, Z. (1957). *Perceptanalysis.* New York: Macmillan.

Pittenger, D. J. (1993). The utility of the Myers-Briggs Type Indicator. *Review of Educational Research, 63,* 467–488.

Plutchik, R., & Conte, H. R. (1989). Measuring emotions and the derivatives of emotions: Personality traits, ego defenses, and coping styles. In S. Wetzler & M. M. Katz (Eds.), *Contemporary approaches to psychological assessment.* New York: Brunner/Mazel.

Polatajko, H. J., Law, M., Miller, J., Schaffer, R., & Macnab, J. (1991). The effect of a sensory integration program on academic achievement, motor performance, and self-esteem in children identified as learning disabled. *The Occupational Therapy Journal of Research, 11,* 155–176.

Polyson, J., Norris, D., & Ott, E. (1985). The recent decline in TAT research. *Professional Psychology: Research and Practice, 16,* 26–28.

Ponterotto, J. G., Pace, T. M., & Kaven, M. G. (1989). A counselor's guide to the assessment of depression. *Journal of Counseling and Development, 67,* 301–309.

Popham, W. J. (1981). *Modern educational measurement.* Englewood Cliffs, NJ: Prentice-Hall.

Popham, W. J. (1993). Educational testing in America: What's right, what's wrong? *Educational Measurement: Issues and Practice, 12,* 11–14.

Porter, L., Steers, R. T., Mowday, R. T., & Boulian, P. V. (1974). Organizational commitment, job satisfaction and individual performance. *Journal of Applied Psychology, 59,* 603–609.

Porter, R. B., Cattell, R. B., et al. (1992). *Handbook for the Children's Personality Questionnaire.* Champaign, IL: Institute for Personality and Ability Testing.

Pound, E. J., & McChesney, S. R. (1982, March). *Relationship of the PPVT-R and WISC-R for children referred for evaluation.* Paper presented at the annual convention of the National Association of School Psychologists, Toronto, Ontario, Canada.

Prasse, D. P., & Bracken, B. A. (1981). Comparison of the PPVT-R and WISC-R with white and black urban Educable Mentally Retarded students. *Psychology in the Schools, 18,* 174–177.

Prater, G. F. (1957). Cited in Swenson, C. H., Jr. Empirical evaluations of human figure drawings. *Psychological Bulletin, 54,* 431–466.

Premack, S. L., & Wanous, J. P. (1985). A meta-analysis of realistic job preview experiments. *Journal of Applied Psychology, 70,* 706–719.

Preston, R. (1961). Improving the item validity of study habits inventories. *Educational and Psychological Measurement, 21,* 129–131.

Price, G., Dunn, R., & Dunn, K. (1982). *Productivity Environmental Survey manual.* Lawrence, KS: Price Systems.

Price, L., Rust, R., & Kumar, V. (1986). Brain-wave

analyses of consumer responses to advertising. In J. Olson & K. Sentis (Eds.), *Advertising and consumer psychology* (Vol. 3; pp. 17–34.). New York: Praeger.

Prince, R. J., & Guastello, S. J. (1990). The Barnum Effect in a computerized Rorschach interpretation system. *Journal of Psychology: Interdisciplinary and Applied, 124,* 217–222.

Procedures for evaluating specific learning disabilities. (1977). *Federal Register,* December 29, Part III.

Procidano, M. E., & Heller, K. (1983). Measures of perceived social support from friends and from family: Three validation studies. *American Journal of Community Psychology, 11,* 1–24.

Prosser, N., & Crawford, V. V. (1971). Relationship of scores on the WPPSI and the Stanford-Binet Intelligence Scale Form L-M. *Journal of School Psychology, 9,* 278–283.

Prout, H. T., & Phillips, P. D. (1974). A clinical note: The kinetic school drawing. *Psychology in the Schools, 11,* 303–396.

Psychological Corporation, The. (1991). *Wechsler Intelligence Scale for Children—Third Edition: An update.* San Antonio, TX: Author.

Psychological Corporation, The. (1992a). *Wechsler Individual Achievement Test.* San Antonio, TX: Author.

Psychological Corporation, The. (1992b). *Wechsler Individual Achievement Test manual.* San Antonio, TX: Author.

Pulakos, E. D. (1986). The development of training programs to increase accuracy with different rating tasks. *Organizational Behavior and Human Decision Processes, 38,* 76–91.

Q and A on balancing the SAT scores. (1994). New York: The College Board.

Quay, H. C., & Peterson, C. (1983). *Manual for the Revised Behavior Problem Checklist.* Coral Gables, FL: Authors.

Quay, H. C., & Peterson, D. R. (1967). *Behavior Problem Checklist.* Champaign: University of Illinois Press.

Quinsey, V. L. (1985). Men who have sex with children. In D. Weistubb (Ed.), *Law and mental health: International perspectives* (Vol. 2; pp. 84–121). New York: Pergamon Press.

Quinsey, V. L., Chaplin, T. C., & Upfold, D. (1984). Sexual arousal to nonsexual violence and sado-masochistic themes among rapists and non-sex-offenders. *Journal of Consulting and Clinical Psychology, 52,* 651–657.

Quinsey, V. L., Steinman, C. M., Bergersen, S. G., & Holmes, T. F. (1975). Penile circumference, skin conductance, and ranking responses of child molesters and "normals" to sexual and non-sexual visual stimuli. *Behavior Therapy, 6,* 213–219.

Radloff, L. (1977). The CES-D Scale: A self-report depression scale for research in the general population. *Applied Psychological Measurement, 1,* 385–401.

Raggio, D. J., & Massingale, T. W. (1990). Comparability of the Vineland Social Maturity Scale and the Vineland Adaptive Behavior Scale—Survey Form with infants evaluated for developmental delay. *Perceptual and Motor Skills, 71,* 415–418.

Raju, N. S., Drasgow, F., & Slinde, J. A. (1993). An empirical comparison of the area methods, Lord's chi-square test, and the Mantel-Haenszel technique for assessing differential item functioning. *Educational and Psychological Measurement, 53,* 301–314.

Rakowiski, W., Dube, C. E., Marcus, B. H., et al. (1992). Assessing elements of women's decisions about mammography. *Health Psychology, 11,* 111–118.

Ramseyer, G. C., & Cashen, V. M. (1971). The effect of practice sessions on the use of separate answer sheets by first and second graders. *Journal of Educational Measurement, 8,* 177–181.

Randall, D. M. (1987). Commitment and the organization: The organization man revisited. *Academy of Management Review, 12,* 460–471.

Randolph, C. Mohr, E., & Chase, T. N. (1993). Assessment of intellectual function in dementing disorders: Validity of WAIS-R short forms for patients with Alzheimer's, Huntington's, and Parkinson's disease. *Journal of Clinical and Experimental Neuropsychology, 15,* 743–753.

Randt, C. T., & Brown, E. R. (1983). *Randt Memory Test.* Bayport, NY: Life Science Associates.

Rankin, R. J., & Henderson, R. (1968). Standardized tests and the disadvantages. *American Psychologist, 76,* 618.

Ranseen, J. D., & Humphries, L. L. (1992). The intellectual functioning of eating disorder patients. *Journal of the American Academy of Child and Adolescent Psychiatry, 31,* 844–846.

Rapaport, D. (1946–1967). Principles underlying nonprojective tests of personality. In M. M. Gill (Ed.), *David Rapaport: Collected papers.* New York: Basic Books.

Rapaport, D., Gill, M. M., & Schafer, R. (1945–1946). *Diagnostic psychological testing.* (2 vols.). Chicago: Year Book Publishers.

Rapaport, D., Gill, M. M., & Schafer, R. (1968). *Diagnostic psychological testing* (Rev. ed.), R. R. Holt (Ed.). New York: International Universities Press.

Rappeport, J. R. (1982). Differences between forensic and general psychiatry. *American Journal of Psychiatry, 139,* 331–334.

Rasbury, W., McCoy, J. G., & Perry, N. W. (1977). Relations of scores on WPPSI and WISC-R at a one year interval. *Perceptual and Motor Skills, 44,* 695–698.

Raskin, D. C., & Yuille, J. C. (1987). Problems of evaluating interviews of children in sexual abuse cases. In S. J. Ceci, M. P. Toglia, & D. F. Ross (Eds.), *New perspectives on the child witness.* New York: Springer-Verlag.

Raskin, L. M., Bloom, A. S., Klee, S. H., & Reese, A. H. (1978). The assessment of developmentally disabled children with the WISC-R, Binet and other tests. *Journal of Clinical Psychology, 34,* 111–116.

Raulin, M. L., & Wee, J. L. (1984). The development and initial validation of a scale to measure social fear. *Journal of Clinical Psychology, 40,* 780–784.

Rawling, P. J., & Coffey, G. L. (1994). The Simulation Index: A single case study. *Australian Psychologist, 29,* 38–40.

Ray, S. (1979). *An adaptation of the Wechsler Intelligence Scale for Children—Revised for the deaf*. Natchitoches, LA: Steven Ray.

Razran, G. (1961). The observable unconscious and the inferable conscious in current Soviet psychophysiology: Introceptive conditioning, semantic conditioning, and the orienting reflex. *Psychological Review, 68*, 81–147.

Record, R. G., McKeown, T., & Edwards, J. H. (1969). The relationship of measured intelligence to birth order and maternal age. *Annals of Human Genetics, 33*, 61–69.

Ree, M. J., & Earles, J. A. (1990). *Differential validity of a differential aptitude test* (Rpt 89–59). Texas: Brooks Air Force Base.

Reece, R. N., & Groden, M. A. (1985). Recognition of non-accidental injury. *Pediatric Clinics of North America, 32*, 41–60.

Reed, H. B. C., Jr., Reitan, R. M., & Klove, H. (1965). Influence of cerebral lesions on psychological test performances of older children. *Journal of Consulting Psychology, 19*, 247–251.

Rees, D. W. (1985). Health beliefs and compliance with alcohol treatment. *Journal of Studies of Alcohol, 46*, 517–524.

Reidy, T. J., & Bolter, J. F. (1994). Neuropsychological toxicology of methylene diphenyl diisocyanate: A report of five cases. *Brain Injury, 8*, 285–294.

Reidy, T. J., & Carstens, C. (1990). Stability of the Millon Adolescent Personality Inventory in an incarcerated delinquent population. *Journal of Personality Assessment, 55*, 692–697.

Reimers, T. M., Wacker, D. P., & Koeppl, G. (1987). Acceptability of behavioral treatments: A review of the literature. *School Psychology Review, 16*, 212–227.

Reinehr, R. C. (1969). Therapist and patient perceptions of hospitalized alcoholics. *Journal of Clinical Psychology, 25*, 443–445.

Reitan, R. M. (1955a). An investigation of the validity of Halstead's measures of biological intelligence. *Archives of Neurology and Psychiatry, 73*, 28–35.

Reitan, R. M. (1955b). Certain differential effects of left and right cerebral lesions in human adults. *Journal of Comparative and Physiological Psychology, 48*, 474–477.

Reitan, R. M. (1969). *Manual for administration of neuropsychological test batteries for adults and children*. Indianapolis: Author.

Reitan, R. M. (1984a). *Aphasia and sensory-perceptual disorders in adults*. South Tucson, AZ: Neuropsychology Press.

Reitan, R. M. (1984b). *Aphasia and sensory-perceptual disorders in children*. South Tucson, AZ: Neuropsychology Press.

Reitan, R. M. (1994). Ward Halstead's contributions to neuropsychology and the Halstead-Reitan Neuropsychological Test Battery. *Journal of Clinical Psychology, 50*, 47–70.

Reitan, R. M., & Davison, L. A. (1974). *Clinical neuropsychology: Current status and applications*. New York: Winston/Wiley.

Reitan, R. M., & Wolfson, D. (1992). A short screening examination for impaired brain functions in early school-age children. *The Clinical Neuropsychologist, 6*, 287–294.

Remzy, I., & Pickard, P. M. (1949). A study in the reliability of scoring the Rorschach inkblot test. *Journal of General Psychology, 40*, 3–10.

Renzulli, J. S., & Smith, L. H. (1977). Two approaches to identification of gifted students. *Exceptional Children, 43*, 512–518.

Reschly, D. J. (1978). WISC-R factor structures among Anglos, Blacks, Chicanos, and Native-American Papagos. *Journal of Consulting and Clinical Psychology, 46*, 417–422.

Reschly, D. J. (1981). Psychological testing in educational classification and placement. *American Psychologist, 36*, 1094–1102.

Reschly, D. J. (1982). Assessing mild mental retardation: The influence of adaptive behavior, sociocultural status, and prospects for nonbiased assessment. In C. R. Reynolds & T. B. Gutkin (Eds.), *The handbook of school psychology*. New York: Wiley.

Reschly, D. J. (1990). Found: Our intelligences: What do they mean? *Journal of Psychoeducational Assessment, 8*, 259–267.

Reschly, D. J., & Grimes, J. P. (1990). Best practices in intellectual assessment. In A. Thomas & J. Grimes (Eds.), *Best practices in school psychology II* (pp. 425–439). Washington, DC: National Association of School Psychologists.

Resnick, P. J. (1988). Malingered psychosis. In R. Rogers (Ed.), *Clinical assessment of malingering and deception* (pp. 34–53). New York: Guilford Press.

Retzlaff, P. D., & Gibertini, M. (1988). Objective psychological testing of U.S. Air Force officers in pilot training. *Aviation, Space, and Environmental Medicine, 59*, 661–663.

Retzlaff, P. D., Sheehan, E. P., & Lorr, M. (1990). MCMI-II scoring: Weighted and unweighted algorithms. *Journal of Personality Assessment, 55*, 219–223.

Reynell, J. (1970). Children with physical handicaps. In P. Mittler (Ed.), *The psychological assessment of mental and physical handicaps* (pp. 443–469). London: Methuen.

Reynolds, C. E., & Brown, R. T. (Eds.). (1984). *Perspectives on bias in mental testing*. New York: Plenum.

Reynolds, C. R., & Clark, J. (1983). Assessment of cognitive abilities. In K. Paget & B. Bracken (Eds.), *The psychoeducational assessment of preschool children* (pp. 163–190). New York: Grune & Stratton.

Reynolds, C. R., Gutkin, T. B., Doppen, L., & Wright, D. (1979). Differential validity of the WISC-R for boys and girls referred for psychological services. *Perceptual and Motor Skills, 48*, 868–870.

Reynolds, C. R., & Kaiser, S. M. (1990a). Test bias in psychological assessment. In T. B. Gutkin & C. R. Reynolds (Eds.), *The handbook of school psychology* (2nd ed.; pp. 487–525). New York: Wiley.

Reynolds, C. R., & Kaiser, S. M. (1990b). Bias in assessment of aptitude. In C. R. Reynolds & R. W. Kamphaus (Eds.), *Handbook of psychological and educational assessment of children: Intelligence & achievement* (pp. 611–653). New York: Guilford Press.

Reynolds, C. R., McNamara, J. R., Marion, R. J., & To- bin, D. L. (1985). Computerized service delivery in clinical psychology. *Professional Psychology: Re- search and Practice, 16,* 339–353.

Reynolds, S. E. (1984). Battle of the experts revisited: 1983 Oregon legislation on the insanity defense. *Willamette Law Review, 20,* 303–317.

Reynolds, W. M. (1985). Review of the Slosson Intelli- gence Test. In J. V. Mitchell (Ed.), *The ninth mental measurements yearbook* (pp. 1403–1404). Lincoln: University of Nebraska Press.

Reynolds, W. M. (1987). *Reynolds Adolescent Depression Scale: Professional manual.* Odessa, FL: Psychologi- cal Assessment Resources.

Reynolds, W. M. (1988). Measurement of academic self-concept in college students. *Journal of Person- ality Assessment, 52*(2), 223–240.

Rezmovic, V. (1977). The effects of computerized ex- perimentation on response variance. *Behavior Re- search Methods and Instrumentation, 9,* 144–147.

Reznikoff, M., & Tomblen, D. (1956). The use of hu- man figure drawings in the diagnosis of organic pathology. *Journal of Consulting Psychology, 20,* 467–470.

Richards, J. T. (1969). The effectiveness of the WPPSI in the identification of mentally retarded chil- dren. *Dissertation Abstracts, 29,* 3880.

Richardson, M. W., & Kuder, G. F. (1939). The calcula- tion of test reliability based upon the method of rational equivalence. *Journal of Educational Psy- chology, 30,* 681–687.

Richmond, B. O., Rodrigo, G., & deRodrigo, M. (1988). Factor structure of a Spanish version of the Revised Children's Manifest Anxiety Scale in Uruguay. *Journal of Personality Assessment, 52,* 165–170.

Ridley, S. E. (1987). The high score approach to scoring two Rorschach measures of cognitive develop- ment. *Journal of Clinical Psychology, 43,* 390–394.

Rierdan, J., & Koff, E. (1981). Sexual ambiguity in chil- dren's human figure drawings. *Journal of Person- ality Assessment, 45,* 256–257.

Ritchie, K., Allard, M., Huppert, F. A., Nargeot, C., Pinek, B., & Ledesert, B. (1993). Computerized cognitive examination of the elderly: The devel- opment of a neuropsychological examination for clinic and population use. *International Journal of Geriatric Psychiatry, 8,* 899–914.

Ritson, B., & Forest, A. (1970). The simulation of psy- chosis: A contemporary presentation. *British Journal of Medical Psychology, 43,* 31–37.

Ritzler, B. A., Sharkey, K. J., & Chudy, J. F. (1980). A comprehensive projective alternative to the TAT. *Journal of Personality Assessment, 44,* 358–362.

Roach, R. J., Frazier, L. P., & Bowden, S. R. (1981). The Marital Satisfaction Scale: Development of a measure for intervention research. *Journal of Mar- riage and the Family, 21,* 251–255.

Roback, A. A. (1961). *History of psychology and psychia- try.* New York: Philosophical Library.

Roberts, C., McCoy, M., Reidy, D., & Crucitti, F. (1993). A comparison of methods of assessing adaptive behaviour in pre-school children with develop- mental disabilities. *Australia and New Zealand Journal of Developmental Disabilities, 18,* 261–272.

Roberts, R. E., Lewinsohn, P. M., & Seeley, J. R. (1991). Screening for adolescent depression: A compari- son of depression scales. *Journal of the American Academy of Child and Adolescent Psychiatry, 30,* 58–66.

Robertson, G. J. (1990). A practical model for test de- velopment. In C. R. Reynolds & R. W. Kamphaus (Eds.), *Handbook of psychological and educational assessment of children: Intelligence & achievement* (pp. 62–85). New York: Guilford Press.

Robin, A. L., & Foster, S. L. (1989). *Negotiating parent- adolescent conflict: A behavioral family systems ap- proach.* New York: Guilford Press.

Robin, A. L., Koepke, T., & Moye, A. (1990). Multidi- mensional assessment of parent-adolescent rela- tions. *Psychological Assessment: A Journal of Consulting and Clinical Psychology, 2,* 451–459.

Robinson, J. P., Shaver, P. R., & Wrightsman, L. S. (Eds.). (1991). *Measures of personality and social psychological attitudes.* San Diego: Academic Press.

Robson, P. J. (1988). Self-esteem: A psychiatric view. *British Journal of Psychiatry, 153,* 6–15.

Rocklin, T. (1987). *Student perceptions of differences among test items.* Poster presentation at the 1987 annual convention of the American Psychologi- cal Association, New York.

Rodin, E., & Schmaltz, S. (1984). The Bear-Fedio per- sonality inventory and temporal lobe epilepsy. *Neurology, 34,* 591–596.

Roesch, R., & Golding, S. L. (1980). *Competency to stand trial.* Urbana: University of Illinois Press.

Rogers, C. R. (1959). A theory of therapy, personality, and interpersonal relationships, as developed in the client-centered framework In S. Koch (Ed.), *Psychology: A study of a science* (Vol. 3; pp. 184– 256). New York: McGraw-Hill.

Rogers, L. S., Knauss, J., & Hammond, K. R. (1951). Predicting continuation in therapy by means of the Rorschach Test. *Journal of Consulting Psychol- ogy, 15,* 368–371.

Rogers, R. (1986). *Structured interview of reported symp- toms* (SIRS). Unpublished scale. Toronto: Clarke Institute of Psychiatry.

Rogers, R., & Cavanaugh, J. L. (1980). Differences in psychological variables between criminally re- sponsible and insane patients: A preliminary study. *American Journal of Forensic Psychiatry, 1,* 29–37.

Rogers, R., & Cavanaugh, J. L. (1981). Rogers Criminal Responsibility Assessment Scales. *Illinois Medical Journal, 160,* 164–169.

Rogers, R., Dolmetsch, R., & Cavanaugh, J. L. (1981). An empirical approach to insanity evaluations. *Journal of Clinical Psychology, 37,* 683–687.

Rogers, R., Seman, W., & Wasyliw, D. E. (1983). The RCRAS and legal insanity: A cross validation study. *Journal of Clinical Psychology, 39,* 554–559.

Rogers, R., Sewell, K. W., & Salekin, R. T. (1994). A meta-analysis of malingering on the MMPI-2. *Assessment, 1,* 227–237.

Rogers, R., Wasyliw, D. E., & Cavanaugh, J. L. (1984). Evaluating insanity: A study of construct validity. *Law & Human Behavior, 8,* 293–303.

Rokeach, M. (1973). *The nature of human values.* New York: Free Press.

Romanczyk, R. G. (1984). Micro-computers and behavior therapy: A powerful alliance. *Behavior Therapist, 7,* 59–64.

Romanczyk, R. G. (1986). *Clinical utilization of micro-computer technology.* New York: Pergamon Press.

Romano, J. (1994, November 7). Do drunken drivers get railroaded? *New York Times,* pp. NNJ1, NNJ19.

Rome, H. P., Mataya, P., Pearson, J. S., Swenson, W., & Brannick, T. L. (1965). Automatic personality assessment. In R. W. Stacey & B. Waxman (Eds.), *Computers in biomedical research* (Vol. 1; pp. 505–524). New York: Academic Press.

Rorer, L. G. (1965). The great response-style myth. *Psychological Bulletin, 63,* 129–156.

Rorer, L. G., Hoffman, P. J., LaForge, G. E., & Hsieh, K. (1966). Optimal cutting scores to discriminate groups of unequal size and variance. *Journal of Applied Psychology, 50,* 153–164.

Rorschach, H. (1921/1942). *Psycho-diagnostics: A diagnostic test based on perception* (P. Lemkau & B. Kronenburg, Trans.). Berne: Huber. (First German edition: 1921. Distributed in the United States by Grune & Stratton.)

Rosch, E. R. (1978). Human categorization. In N. Warren (Ed.), *Studies in cross-cultural psychology.* London: Academic Press.

Rosenman, R. H., Brand, R. J., Jenkins, C. D., Friedman, M., Straus, R., & Wurm, M. (1975). Coronary heart disease in the Western Collaborative Group Study: Final followup experience of 8½ years. *Journal of the American Medical Association, 233,* 872–877.

Roszkowski, M. J. (1984). Stability of IQs from group-administered tests: Some further data. *Psychological Reports, 54,* 482.

Rotter, J. B. (1966). Generalized expectancies for internal versus external control of reinforcement. *Psychological Monographs, 80* (Whole Number 609).

Rotter, J. B., & Rafferty, J. E. (1950). *The manual for the Rotter Incomplete Sentences Blank.* New York: Psychological Corporation.

Rotton, J., & Kelly, I. W. (1985). Much ado about the full moon: A meta-analysis of lunar-lunacy research. *Psychological Bulletin, 97,* 286–306.

Routh, D. K., & King, K. W. (1972). Social class bias in clinical judgment. *Journal of Consulting and Clinical Psychology, 38,* 202–207.

Rozensky, R. H., Honor, L. F., Rasinski, K., Tovian, S. M., & Herz, G. I. (1986). Paper-and-pencil versus computer administered MMPIs: A comparison of patients' attitudes. *Computers in Human Behavior, 2,* 111–116.

Rubin, L. S. (1974). The utilization of pupillometry in the differential diagnosis and treatment of psychotic and behavioral disorders. In M. P. Janisse (Ed.), *Pupillary dynamics and behavior* (pp. 75–134). New York: Plenum.

Rubin, S. (1964). A comparison of the Thematic Apperception Test stories of two IQ groups. *Journal of Projective Techniques, 28,* 81–85.

Ruff, G. A., & Barrios, B. A. (1986). Realistic assessment of body image. *Behavioral Assessment, 8,* 237–252.

Rulon, P. J. (1939). A simplified procedure for determining the reliability of a test by split-halves. *Harvard Educational Review, 9,* 99–103.

Ruschival, M. L., & Way, J. G. (1971). The WPPSI and the Stanford-Binet Form L-M: A validity and reliability study using gifted preschool children. *Journal of Consulting and Clinical Psychology, 37,* 163.

Russell, E. W., Neuringer, C., & Goldstein, G. (1970). *Assessment of brain damage: A neuropsychological key approach.* New York: Wiley.

Russell, J. S. (1984). A review of fair employment cases in the field of training. *Personnel Psychology, 37,* 261–276.

Russell, M., & Karol, D. (1994). *The 16PF fifth edition administrator's manual.* Champaign, IL: Institute for Personality and Ability Testing, Inc.

Rust, J., & Golombok, S. (1985). The Golombok-Rust Inventory of Sexual Satisfaction (GRISS). *British Journal of Clinical Psychology, 24,* 63–64.

Ryan, E. R., & Bell, M. D. (1984). Changes in object relations from psychosis to recovery. *Journal of Abnormal Psychology, 93,* 209–215.

Ryan, E. R., & Cicchetti, D. V. (1985). Predicting quality of alliance in the initial psychotherapy interview. *The Journal of Nervous and Mental Disease, 173,* 717–725.

Ryan, J. J., & Sattler, J. M. (1988). Wechsler Adult Intelligence Scale—Revised. In J. M. Sattler, *Assessment of children* (3rd ed.; pp. 219–244). San Diego, CA: J. M. Sattler.

Sabatelli, R. M. (1984). The Marital Comparison Level Index: A measure for assessing outcomes relative to expectations. *Journal of Marriage and the Family, 46,* 651–662.

Sacco, W. P., Levine, B., Reed, D. L., & Thompson, K. (1991). Attitudes about condom use as an AIDS-relevant behavior: Their factor structure and relation to condom use. *Psychological Assessment: A Journal of Consulting and Clinical Psychology, 3,* 311–326.

Sachs, B. B. (1976). Some views of a deaf Rorschacher on the personality of deaf individuals. *Hearing Rehabilitation Quarterly, 2,* 13–14.

Sackett, P. R. (1994). Integrity testing for personnel selection. *Current Directions in Psychological Science, 3,* 73–76.

Sackett, P. R., Burris, L. R., & Callahan, C. (1989). Integrity testing for personnel selection: An update. *Personnel Psychology, 42,* 491–529.

Sackett, P. R., & Harris, M. M. (1984). Honesty testing for personnel selection: A review and critique. *Personnel Psychology, 37,* 221–245.

Sackett, P. R., & Wilk, S. L. (1994). Within group norming and other forms of score adjustment in pre-employment testing. *American Psychologist, 49,* 929–954.

Sacks, E. (1952). Intelligence scores as a function of experimentally established social relationships between child and examiner. *Journal of Abnormal and Social Psychology, 47*, 354–358.

Salagaras, S., & Nettelbeck, T. (1984). Adaptive behavior of mentally retarded adults in work-preparation settings. *American Journal of Mental Deficiency, 88*, 437–441.

Salive, M. E. (1994). Evaluation of aging pilots: Evidence, policy, and future directions. *Military Medicine, 159*, 83–86.

Sallis, J. F., Grossman, R. M., Pinsky, R. B., et al. (1987). The development of scales to measure social support for diet and exercise behaviors. *Preventive Medicine, 16*, 825–836.

Sallis, J. F., Hovell, M. F., & Hofstetter, C. R. (1992). Predictors of adaptation and maintenance of vigorous physical activity in men and women. *Preventive Medicine, 21*, 237–251.

Salvia, J., & Hritcko, T. (1984). The K-ABC and ability training. *Journal of Special Education, 18*, 345–356.

Salvia, J., & Ysseldyke, J. E. (1981). *Assessment in special and remedial education* (4th ed.). Boston: Houghton Mifflin.

Salvia, J. A., & Ysseldyke, J. E. (1988). *Assessment in special and remedial education* (5th ed.). Boston: Houghton Mifflin.

Sampson, J. P., Jr. (1987). "Computer-assisted" or "computerized": What's in a name? *Journal of Counseling and Development, 66*, 116–118.

Samuda, R. J. (1982). *Psychological testing of American minorities: Issues and consequences.* New York: Harper & Row.

Samuel, W. (1977). Observed IQ as a function of test atmosphere, tester expectation, and race of tester: A replication for female subjects. *Journal of Educational Psychology, 69*, 593–604.

Sandoval, J., Sassenrath, J., & Penaloza, M. (1988). Similarity of WISC-R and WAIS-R scores at age 16. *Psychology in the Schools, 25*, 373–379.

Sandwith, P. (1994, January). Building quality into communications. *Training and Development, 48* (1), 55–59.

Sanfilippo, J., et al. (1986). Identifying the sexually molested preadolescent girl. *Pediatric Annals, 15*, 621–624.

Sanford, R. N. (1936). The effects of abstinence from food upon imaginal processes: A preliminary experiment. *Journal of Psychology, 2*, 129–136.

Santoro, J., Bergman, A. S., & Cohen, R. J. (1994). *TEM (Treatment/Evaluation Manager)—2000.* Brewster, NY: Supervised Lifestyles, Inc.

Sarason, I. G., Levine, H. M., Basham, R. B., & Sarason, B. R. (1983). Assessing social support: The Social Support Questionnaire. *Journal of Personality and Social Psychology, 44*, 127–139.

Sarnoff, D. (1982). Biofeedback: New uses in counseling. *Personnel and Guidance Journal, 60*, 357–360.

Satinsky, D., & Frerotti, A. (1981). Biofeedback treatment for headache: A two-year follow-up study. *American Journal of Clinical Biofeedback, 4*, 62–65.

Sattler, J. M. (1972). *Intelligence test modifications on handicapped and non-handicapped children.* Washington, DC: Department of Health, Education, and Welfare.

Sattler, J. M. (1982a). *Assessment of children's intelligence and special abilities.* Boston: Allyn and Bacon.

Sattler, J. M. (1982b). *Assessment of children's intelligence and special abilities* (Rev. ed.). Boston: Allyn and Bacon.

Sattler, J. M. (1988). *Assessment of children* (3rd ed.). San Diego, CA: Author.

Sattler, J. M. (1991). How good are federal judges in detecting differences in item difficulty on intelligence tests for ethnic groups? *Psychological Assessment: A Journal of Consulting and Clinical Psychology, 3*, 125–129.

Sattler, J. M. (1992). Assessment of children: WISC-III and WPPSI-R supplement. San Diego: Author.

Sattler, J. M., Andres, J. L., Squire, L. S., Wisely, R., & Maloy, C. F. (1978). Examiner scoring of ambiguous WISC-R responses. *Psychology in the Schools, 15*, 486–489.

Sattler, J. M., & Gwynne, J. (1982). White examiners generally do not impede the intelligence test performance of black children: To debunk a myth. *Journal of Consulting and Clinical Psychology, 50*, 196–208.

Sattler, J. M., & Ryan, J. J. (1988). Wechsler Adult Intelligence Scale—Revised. In J. M. Sattler, *Assessment of children* (3rd ed.; pp. 219–244). San Diego, CA: J. M. Sattler.

Sattler, J. M., Winget, B. M., & Roth, R. J. (1969). Scoring difficulty of WAIS and WISC Comprehension, Similarities and Vocabulary responses. *Journal of Clinical Psychology, 25*, 175–177.

Satz, P. (1966). A block rotation task: The application of multi-variant and decision theory analysis for the prediction of organic brain disorders. *Psychological Monographs, 80* (21, Whole No. 629).

Saunders, E. A. (1991). Rorschach indicators of chronic childhood sexual abuse in female borderline inpatients. *Bulletin of the Menninger Clinic, 55*, 48–65.

Saxe, L. (1994). Detection of deception: Polygraph and integrity tests. *Current Directions in Psychological Science, 3*, 69–73.

Saxton, J., McGonigle-Gibson, K. L., Swihart, A. A., Miller, V. J., & Boller, F. (1990). Assessment of the severely impaired patient: Description and validation of a new neuropsychological test battery. *Psychological Assessment: A Journal of Consulting and Clinical Psychology, 2*, 298–303.

Sayer, A. G., Willett, J. B., & Perrin, E. C. (1993). Measuring understanding of illness causality in healthy children and in children with chronic illness: a construct validation. *Journal of Applied Developmental Psychology, 14*, 11–36.

Saylor, C. F. (1984). Construct validity for measures of childhood depression: Application of multitrait-multimethod methodology. *Journal of Consulting and Clinical Psychology, 52*, 977–985.

Saylor, C. F., Finch, A. J., Spirito, A., & Bennett, B. (1984). The Children's Depression Inventory: A systematic evaluation of psychometric properties. *Journal of Consulting and Clinical Psychology, 52,* 955–967.

Scalise, J. J., Ginter, E. J., & Gerstein, L. H. (1984). A multidimensional loneliness measure: The Loneliness Rating Scale (LRS). *Journal of Personality Assessment, 48,* 525–530.

Schag, C. A., Heinrich, R. L., Aadland, R. L., & Ganz, P. A. (1990). Assessing problems of cancer patients: Psychometric properties of the cancer inventory of problem situations. *Health Psychology, 9,* 83–102.

Schaie, K. W. (1965). A general model for the study of development problems. *Psychological Bulletin, 64,* 92–107.

Schaie, K. W. (1973). Developmental processes and aging. In C. Eisdorfer & M. L. Lawton (Eds.), *The psychology of adult development and aging.* Washington, DC: American Psychological Association.

Schaie, K. W. (1974). Transactions in gerontology— From lab to life. *American Psychologist, 29,* 802–807.

Schaie, K. W. (1978). External validity in the assessment of intellectual development in adulthood. *Journal of Gerontology, 33,* 695–701.

Scheier, M., & Carver, C. (1987). Dispositional optimism and physical well-being: The influence of generalized outcome expectancies on health. *Journal of Personality, 55,* 169–210.

Scheier, M. F., & Carver, C. S. (1993). On the power of positive thinking: The benefits of being optimistic. *Current Directions in Psychological Science, 2,* 26–30.

Scherer, K. R. (1986). Vocal affect expression: A review and a model for future research. *Psychological Bulletin, 99,* 143–165.

Schiffman, S. S., Reynolds, M. L., & Young, F. W. (1981). *Introduction to multidimensional scaling: Theory, methods and applications.* New York: Academic Press.

Schlackman, W. A. (1984). A discussion of the use of sensitivity panels in market research: The use of trained respondents in qualitative studies. *Journal of the Market Research Society, 26,* 191–208.

Schloss, I. (1981). Chicken and pickles. *Journal of Advertising Research, 21,* 47–49.

Schmidt, F. L., & Hunter, J. E. (1974). Racial and ethnic bias in psychological tests: Divergent implications of two definitions of test bias. *American Psychologist, 29,* 1–8.

Schmidt, F. L., & Hunter, J. E. (1977). Development of a general solution to the problem of validity generalization. *Journal of Applied Psychology, 64,* 609–626.

Schmidt, F. L., & Hunter, J. E. (1984). A within setting empirical test of the situational specificity hypothesis in personnel selection. *Personnel Psychology, 37,* 317–326.

Schmidt, F. L., Hunter, J. E., McKenzie, R. C., & Muldrow, T. W. (1979). Impact of valid selection procedures on work force productivity. *Journal of Applied Psychology, 64,* 609–626.

Schmidt, F. L., Hunter, J. E., Outerbridge, A. N., & Trattner, M. H. (1986). The economic impact of job selection methods on size, productivity, and payroll costs of the federal work force: An empirically based demonstration. *Personnel Psychology, 39,* 1–29.

Schmidt, F. L., Hunter, J. E., & Pearlman, K. (1981). Task differences as moderators of aptitude test validity in selection: A red herring. *Journal of Applied Psychology, 66,* 166–185.

Schmitt, N. (1976). Social and situational determinants of interview decisions: Implications for the employment interview. *Personnel Psychology, 29,* 79–101.

Schmitt, N., Gooding, R., Noe, R., & Kirsch, M. (1984). Meta-analysis of validity studies published between 1964 and 1982 and the investigation of study characteristics. *Personnel Psychology, 37,* 407–422.

Schneider, B. (1987). The people make the place. *Personnel Psychology, 40,* 437–453.

Schneider, M. F. (1989). Children's Apperceptive Story-telling Test. Austin, TX: Pro-Ed.

Schneider, M. F., & Perney, J. (1990). Development of the Children's Apperceptive Story-Telling Test. *Psychological Assessment: A Journal of Consulting and Clinical Psychology, 2,* 179–185.

Schouten, P. G. W., & Kirkpatrick, L. A. (1993). Questions and concerns about the Miller Assessment for Preschoolers. *The Occupational Therapy Journal of Research, 13,* 7–28.

Schuerger, J. M., Zarrella, K. L., & Hotz, A. S. (1989). Factors that influence the temporal stability of personality by questionnaire. *Journal of Personality and Social Psychology, 56,* 777–783.

Schuh, A. J. (1978). Contrast effect in the interview. *Bulletin of the Psychonomic Society, 11,* 195–196.

Schultz, D. P. (1969). *A history of modern psychology.* New York: Academic Press.

Schultz, D. P. (1982). *Psychology and industry today* (3rd ed.). New York: Macmillan.

Schwartz, L. A. (1932). Social situation pictures in the psychiatric interview. *American Journal of Orthopsychiatry, 2,* 124–132.

Schwitzgebel, R. L., & Rugh, J. D. (1975). Of bread, circuses and alpha machines. *American Psychologist, 30,* 363–370.

Scott, L. H. (1981). Measuring intelligence with the Goodenough-Harris Drawing Test. *Psychological Bulletin, 89,* 483–505.

Sears, R. R. (1977). Sources of life satisfaction of the Terman gifted men. *American Psychologist, 32,* 119–281.

Seashore, C. E. (1938). *Psychology of music.* New York: McGraw-Hill.

Sebold, J. (1987). Indicators of child sexual abuse in males. *Social Casework, 68,* 75–80.

Select Committee on Equal Educational Opportunity in the United States Senate. (1972). *Environment, intelligence, and scholastic achievement.* Washington, DC: U.S. Government Printing Office.

Selover, R. B. (1949). Review of the Minnesota Clerical

Test. In O. K. Buros (Ed.), *The third mental measurements yearbook* (pp. 635–636). New Brunswick, NJ: Rutgers University Press.

Selzer, M. L. (1971). The Michigan Alcoholism Screening Test: The quest for a new instrument. *American Journal of Psychiatry, 127,* 1653–1659.

Semrud-Clikeman, M. (1990). Assessment of childhood depression. In C. R. Reynolds & R. W. Kamphaus (Eds.), *Handbook of psychological and educational assessment of children: Personality, behavior & context* (pp. 279–297). New York: Guilford Press.

Serby, M., Corwin, J., Conrad, P., et al. (1985). Olfactory dysfunction in Alzheimer's disease and Parkinson's disease. *American Journal of Psychiatry, 142,* 781–782.

Serby, M., Larson, P., & Kalkstein, D. (1991). The nature and course of olfactory deficits in Alzheimer's disease. *American Journal of Psychiatry, 148,* 357–360.

Seretny, M. L., Dean, R. S., Gray, J. W., & Hartlage, L. C. (1986). The practice of clinical neuropsychology in the United States. *Archives of Clinical Neuropsychology, 1,* 5–12.

Serin, R. C., Peters, R. DeV., & Barbaree, H. E. (1990). Predictors of psychopathy and release outcome in a criminal population. *Psychological Assessment: A Journal of Consulting and Clinical Psychology, 2,* 419–422.

Sewell, T. E. (1977). A comparison of the WPPSI and Stanford-Binet Intelligence Scale among lower SES black children. *Psychology in the Schools, 14,* 158–161.

Shah, S. A. (1969). Privileged communications, confidentiality, and privacy: Privileged communications. *Professional Psychology, 1,* 56–59.

Shapiro, E. S., & Eckert, T. L. (1993). Curriculum-based assessment among school psychologists: Knowledge, use, and attitudes. *Journal of School Psychology, 31,* 375–383.

Shapiro, E. S., & Kratochwill, T. R. (Eds.). (1988). *Behavioral assessment in schools: Conceptual foundation and practical application.* New York: Guilford Press.

Shapiro, E. S., & Skinner, C. H. (1990). Principles of behavior assessment. In C. R. Reynolds & R. W. Kamphaus (Eds.), *Handbook of psychological and educational assessment of children: Personality, behavior & context* (pp. 343–363). New York: Guilford Press.

Shavelson, R. J., & Webb, N. M. (1991). *Generalizability theory: A primer.* Newbury Park, CA: Sage.

Shavelson, R. J., Webb, N. M., & Rowley, G. L. (1989). Generalizability theory. *American Psychologist, 44,* 922–932.

Shelton, M. D., & Parsons, O. A. (1987). Alcoholics' self-assessment of their neuropsychology functioning in every day life. *Journal of Clinical Psychology, 43,* 395–403.

Shepard, L. A. (1983). The role of measurement in educational policy: Lessons from the identification of learning disabilities. *The Journal of Special Education, 14,* 79–91.

Sherman, L. J. (1958). The influence of artistic quality on judgments of patient and non-patient status from human figure drawings. *Journal of Projective Techniques, 22,* 338–340.

Shneidman, E. S. (1952). Manual for the Make a Picture Story Method. *Projective Techniques Monographs, 2.*

Shneidman, E. S. (1958). Some relationships between thematic and drawing materials. In E. F. Hammer (Ed.), *The clinical applications of projective drawings* (pp. 296–307). Springfield, IL: Charles C. Thomas.

Shockley, W. (1971). Models, mathematics, and the moral obligation to diagnose the origin of Negro IQ deficits. *Review of Educational Research, 41,* 369–377.

Shrout, P. E. (1993). Analyzing consensus in personality judgments: A variance components approach. *Journal of Personality, 61,* 769–788.

Shuey, A. M. (1966). *The testing of Negro intelligence* (2nd ed.). New York: Social Science Press.

Shurrager, H. C., & Shurrager, P. S. (1964). *Manual for the Haptic Intelligence Scale for Adult Blind.* Chicago: Psychology Research.

Siegel, L. J. (1986). Review of The Children's Depression Inventory. In D. J. Keyser & R. C. Sweetland (Eds.), *Test critiques* (Vol. 5). Kansas City, MO: Test Corporation of America.

Siegler, R. S., & Richards, D. (1980). The development of intelligence. In R. S. Sternberg (Chair), *People's conception of the nature of intelligence.* Symposium presented at the 88th annual convention of the American Psychological Association, Montreal, Canada.

Silverstein, A. B. (1969). An alternative factor analytic solution for Wechsler's Intelligence Scales. *Educational and Psychological Measurement, 29,* 763–767.

Silverstein, A. B. (1982). Factor structure of the Wechsler Adult Intelligence Scale—Revised. *Journal of Consulting and Clinical Psychology, 50,* 661–664.

Silverstein, A. B. (1990). Short forms of individual intelligence tests. *Psychological Assessment: A Journal of Consulting and Clinical Psychology, 2,* 3–11.

Silverstein, A. B., & Fisher, G. M. (1960). Reanalysis of sex differences in the standardization data of the Wechsler Adult Intelligence Scale. *Psychological Reports, 7,* 405–406.

Simon, R. J. (1967). *The jury and the defense of insanity.* Boston: Little, Brown.

Simon, R. J., & Aaronson, D. E. (1988). *The insanity defense.* New York: Praeger.

Simpson, R. (1970). Study of the comparability of the WISC and WAIS. *Journal of Consulting and Clinical Psychology, 2,* 156–158.

Sines, J. O. (1966). Actuarial methods in personality assessment. In B. Maher (Ed.), *Progress in experimental personality research* (Vol. 3; pp. 133–193). New York: Academic Press.

Sines, J. O. (1985). Review of the Roberts Apperception Test for Children. In J. V. Mitchell, Jr. (Ed.), *The ninth mental measurements yearbook* (pp. 1289–1291). Lincoln: The Buros Institute of Mental Measurements, University of Nebraska.

Singh, J., Howell, R. D., & Rhoads, G. K. (1990). Adaptive designs for Likert-type data: An approach for implementing marketing surveys. *Journal of Marketing Research, 27,* 304–321.

Sinnett, E. R., Rogg, K. L., Benton, S. L., & Downey, R. G. (1993). The Woodcock-Johnson Revised: Its factor structure. *Educational and Psychological Measurement, 53,* 763–769.

Sivik, H. J., Lynn, S. J., & Garske, J. P. (1994). The effect of somatoform disorders and paranoid psychotic role-related dissimulations as a response set on the MMPI-2. *Assessment, 1,* 69–81.

Sivik, T., & Hosterey, U. (1992). The Thematic Apperception Test as an aid in understanding the psychodynamics of development of chronic idiopathic pain syndrome. *Psychotherapy and Psychosomatics, 57,* 57–60.

Skibbe, A. (1986). Assessing campus needs with nominal groups. *Journal of Counseling and Development, 64,* 532–533.

Skinner, H. A., & Allen, B. A. (1983). Does the computer make a difference? Computerized versus face-to-face versus self-report assessment of alcohol, drug, and tobacco use. *Journal of Consulting and Clinical Psychology, 51,* 267–275.

Skinner, H. A., & Pakula, A. (1986). Challenge of computers in psychological assessment. *Professional Psychology: Research and Practice, 17,* 44–50.

Slade, P. D. (1985). A review of body-image studies in anorexia nervosa and bulimia nervosa. *Journal of Psychiatric Research, 19,* 255–265.

Slakter, M. J., Crehan, K. D., & Koehler, R. A. (1975). Longitudinal studies of risk taking on objective examinations. *Educational and Psychological Measurement, 35,* 97–105.

Slate, J. R., Jones, C. H., Murray, R. A., & Coulter, C. (1993). Evidence that practitioners err in administering and scoring the WAIS-R. *Measurement and Evaluation in Counseling and Development, 25,* 156–161.

Slate, N. M. (1983). Nonbiased assessment of adaptive behavior: Comparison of three instruments. *Exceptional Children, 1,* 67–70.

Slay, D. K. (1984). A portable Halstead-Reitan Category Test. *Journal of Clinical Psychology, 40,* 1023–1027.

Sloan, W., & Birch, J. W. (1955). A rationale for degrees of retardation. *American Journal of Mental Deficiency, 60,* 258–264.

Slobogin, C. (1985). The guilty but mentally ill verdict: An idea whose time should not have come. *George Washington Law Review, 53,* 494–527.

Slosson, R. L. (1963). *Slosson Intelligence Test (SIT) for children and adults.* New York: Slosson Educational Publications.

Slosson, R. L. (1991) *Slosson Intelligence Test (SIT-R).* East Aurora, NY: Slosson Educational Publications.

Smith, A. (1962). Ambiguities in concepts and studies of ''brain damage'' and ''organicity.'' *Journal of Nervous and Mental Disease, 135,* 311–326.

Smith, C. A., & Wallston, K. A. (1995). On babies and bathwater: Disease impact and negative affectivity in the self-reports of persons with rheumatoid arthritis. *Health Psychology, 14,* 64–73.

Smith, D. E. (1986). Training programs for performance appraisal: A review. *Academy of Management Review, 11,* 22–40.

Smith, D. K. (1985). *Test use and perceived competency: A survey of school psychologists.* Unpublished manuscript, University of Wisconsin-River Falls, School Psychology Program, River Falls, WI.

Smith, D. K., & Bauer, J. J. (1989). *Intelligence measures in a preschool sample: S-B:FE and K-ABC relationships.* Paper presented at the Annual Meeting of the American Psychological Association, New Orleans, LA. (ERIC Document Reproduction Service No. ED 316 574)

Smith, D. K., Bauer, J. J., & Lyon, M. A. (1987, April). *Young children's performance on three measures of ability.* Paper presented at the Annual Meeting of the American Educational Research Association, Washington, DC. (ERIC Document Reproduction Service No. ED 281 874)

Smith, D. K., Bolin, J. A., & Stovall, D. R. (1988). K-ABC stability in a preschool sample: A longitudinal study. *Journal of Psychoeducational Assessment, 6,* 396–403.

Smith, D. K., & Knudtson, L. S. (1990). *K-ABC and S-B:FE relationships in an at-risk preschool sample.* Paper presented at the Annual Meeting of the American Psychological Association, Boston.

Smith, D. K., Lasee, M. J., & McCloskey, G. M. (1990). *Test-retest reliability of the AGS Early Screening Profiles.* Paper presented at the Annual Meeting of the National Association of School Psychologists, San Francisco.

Smith, D. K., Lasee, M. J., Steenson, K. A., & Ouradnik, L. (1991). *The Early Screening Profiles: A stability study.* Paper presented at the Annual Meeting of the National Association of School Psychologists, Dallas, TX.

Smith, D. K., & Lyon, M. A. (1987). *Children with learning difficulties: Differences in ability patterns as a function of placement.* Paper presented at the Annual Meeting of the American Educational Research Association, Washington, DC. (ERIC Document Reproduction Service No. ED 285 317)

Smith, D. K., Lyon, M. A., Hunter, E., & Boyd, R. (1988). Relationships between the K-ABC and WISC-R for students referred for severe learning disabilities. *Journal of Learning Disabilities, 21,* 509–513.

Smith, D. K., St. Martin, M. E., & Lyon, M. A. (1989). A validity study of the Stanford-Binet Fourth Edition with students with learning disabilities. *Journal of Learning Disabilities, 22,* 260–261.

Smith, G. E., Malec, J. F., & Ivnik, R. J. (1992). Validity of the construct of nonverbal memory: A factor-analytic study in a normal elderly sample. *Journal of Clinical and Experimental Neuropsychology, 14,* 211–221.

Smith, G. M. (1985). The Collaborative Drawing Technique. *Journal of Personality Assessment, 49,* 582–585.

Smith, M. (1948). Cautions concerning the use of the

Taylor-Russell tables in employee selection. *Journal of Applied Psychology, 32,* 595–600.

Smith, M. H., May, W. T., & Lebovitz, L. (1966). Testing experience and Stanford-Binet scores. *Journal of Educational Measurement, 3,* 229–233.

Smith, R. E. (1963). Examination by computer. *Behavioral Science, 8,* 76–79.

Smith, S. R., & Meyer, R. G. (1987). *Law, behavior and mental health: Policy and practice.* New York: New York University Press.

Smither, J. W., Reilly, R. R., & Buda, R. (1988). Effect of prior performance information on ratings of present performance: Contrast versus assimilation revisited. *Journal of Applied Psychology, 73,* 487–496.

Smucker, M. R., Craighead, W. E., Craighead, L. W., & Green, B. J. (1986). Normative and reliability data for the Children's Depression Inventory. *Journal of Abnormal Child Psychology, 14,* 25–39.

Snow, J. H. (1992). Review of the Luria-Nebraska Neuropsychological Battery: Forms I and II. In J. J. Kramer & J. C. Conoley (Eds.), *The eleventh mental measurements yearbook.* Lincoln: The Buros Institute of Mental Measurements, University of Nebraska.

Snyder, C. R. (1974). Acceptance of personality interpretations as a function of assessment procedures. *Journal of Consulting and Clinical Psychology, 42,* 150.

Snyder, C. R., & Larson, G. R. (1972). A further look at student acceptance of general personality interpretations. *Journal of Consulting and Clinical Psychology, 38,* 384–388.

Snyder, C. R., & Newburg, C. L. (1981). The Barnum effect in a group setting. *Journal of Personality Assessment, 45,* 622–629.

Snyder, C. R., & Shenkel, R. J. (1976). Effects of "favorability," modality, and relevance on acceptance of general personality interpretations prior to and after receiving diagnostician feedback. *Journal of Consulting and Clinical Psychology, 44,* 34–41.

Snyder, C. R., Shenkel, R. J., & Lowery, C. R. (1977). Acceptance of personality interpretations: The "Barnum effect" and beyond. *Journal of Consulting and Clinical Psychology, 45,* 104–114.

Snyder, C. R., Shenkel, R. J., & Schmidt, A. (1976). Effect of role perspective and client psychiatric history on locus of problem. *Journal of Consulting and Clinical Psychology, 44,* 467–472.

Snyder, D. K. (1981). *Marital Satisfaction Inventory (MSI) manual.* Los Angeles: Western Psychological Services.

Snyder, D. K., & Hoover, D. W. (1989, August). *Validity of the computerized interpretive report for the Marital Satisfaction Inventory.* Paper presented at the Annual Convention of the American Psychological Association, New Orleans.

Snyder, D. K., Lachar, D., & Wills, R. M. (1988). Computer-based interpretation of the Marital Satisfaction Inventory: Use in treatment planning. *Journal of Marital and Family Therapy, 14,* 397–409.

Snyder, D. K., Widiger, T. A., & Hoover, D. W. (1990). Methodological considerations in validating computer-based test interpretations: Controlling for response bias. *Psychological Assessment, 2,* 470–477.

Snyder, P., Lawson, S., Thompson, B., Stricklin, S., & Sexton, D. (1993). Evaluating the psychometric integrity of instruments used in early intervention research: The Battelle Developmental Inventory. *Topics in Early Childhood Special Education, 32,* 273–280.

Sodowsky, G. R., Taffe, R. C., Gutkin, T. B., & Wise, S. L. (1994). Development of the Multicultural Counseling Inventory: A self-report measure of multicultural competencies. *Journal of Counseling Psychology, 41,* 137–140.

Sokal, M. M. (1991). Psyche Cattell (1893–1989). *American Psychologist, 46,* 72.

Solomon, I. L., & Starr, B. D. (1968). *The School Apperception Method.* New York: Springer.

Solovay, M. R., Shenton, M. E., Gasperetti, C., Coleman, M., Kestnbaum, E., Carpenter, J. T., & Holzman, P. S. (1986). Scoring Manual for the Thought Disorder Index (Rev. version). *Schizophrenia Bulletin, 12,* 483–496.

Sontag, L. W., Baker, C. T., & Nelson, V. L. (1958). Personality as a determinant of performance. *American Journal of Orthopsychiatry, 25,* 555–562.

Spanier, G. (1976). Measuring dyadic adjustment: New scales for assessing the quality of marriage and similar dyads. *Journal of Marriage and the Family, 38,* 15–28.

Spanier, G. B., & Filsinger, E. (1983). The Dyadic Adjustment Scale. In E. Filsinger (Ed.), *Marriage and family assessment.* Beverly Hills, CA: Sage.

Sparrow, S. S., Balla, D. A., & Cicchetti, D. V. (1984a). *Vineland Adaptive Behavior Scales, Interview Edition: Expanded form manual.* Circle Pines, MN: American Guidance Service.

Sparrow, S. S., Balla, D. A., & Cicchetti, D. V. (1984b). *Vineland Adaptive Behavior Scales, Interview Edition: Survey form manual.* Circle Pines, MN: American Guidance Service.

Sparrow, S. S., Balla, D. A., & Cicchetti, D. V. (1985). *Vineland Adaptive Behavior Scales, Classroom Edition manual.* Circle Pines, MN: American Guidance Service.

Spearman, C. (1927). *The abilities of man: Their nature and measurement.* New York: Macmillan.

Spearman, C. S. (1930–1936). Autobiography. In C. Murchison (Ed.), *A history of psychology in autobiography* (3 vols.). Worcester, MA: Clark University Press.

Spielberger, C. D., et al. (1980a). *Preliminary Manual for the State-Trait Anger Scale.* Center for Research in Community Psychology, University of South Florida, Tampa, FL.

Spielberger, C. D., et al. (1980b). *Test Anxiety Inventory-Research Edition.* Palo Alto, CA: Consulting Psychologists Press.

Spielberger, C. D., Edwards, C. D., Montuori, J., & Lushene, R. (1973). *State-Trait Anxiety Inventory for Children.* Palo Alto, CA: Consulting Psychologists Press.

Spielberger, C. D., Gorsuch, R. L., & Lushene, R. E.

(1970). *State-Trait Anxiety Inventory.* Palo Alto, CA: Consulting Psychologists Press.

Spielberger, C. D., & Piotrowski, C. (1990). Clinician's attitudes toward computer-based testing. *The Clinical Psychologist, 43,* 60–63.

Spiers, P. A. (1981). Have they come to praise Luria or to bury him? The Luria-Nebraska Battery controversy. *Journal of Consulting and Clinical Psychology, 49,* 331–341.

Spiers, P. A. (1984). What more can I say? In reply to Hutchinson, one last comment from Spiers. *Journal of Consulting and Clinical Psychology, 52,* 546–552.

Spitzer, R. L. (1983). Psychiatric diagnosis: Are clinicians still necessary? *Comprehensive psychiatry, 24,* 399–411.

Spitznagel, E. L., & Helzer, J. E. (1985). A proposed solution to the base rate problem in the kappa statistic. *Archives of General Psychiatry, 42,* 725–728.

Spivack, G., & Spotts, J. (1966). *Devereux Child Behavior Rating Scale Manual.* Devon, PA: Devereux Foundation.

Spivack, G., Spotts, J., & Haimes, P. E. (1967). *Devereux Adolescent Behavior Rating Scale.* Devon, PA: Devereux Foundation Press.

Spranger, E. (1928). *Types of men* (P. J. W. Pigors, Trans.). Halle: Niemeyer.

Spreen, O., & Benton, A. L. (1965). Comparative studies of some psychological tests for cerebral damage. *Journal of Nervous and Mental Disease, 140,* 323–333.

Spreen, O., & Benton, A. L. (1969). *Neurosensory Center Comprehensive Examination for Aphasia.* Victoria, Canada: University of Victoria.

Spruill, J. A. (1993). Secondary assessment: Structuring the transition process. *Learning Disabilities Research & Practice, 8,* 127–132.

Spruill, J., & May, J. (1988). The mentally retarded offender: Prevalence rates based on individual versus group intelligence tests. *Criminal Justice and Behavior, 15,* 484–491.

St. Lawrence, J. S., Reitman, D., Jefferson, K. W., et al. (1994). Factor structure and validation of an adolescent version of the Condom Attitude Scale: An instrument for measuring adolescents' attitudes toward condoms. *Psychological Assessment, 6,* 352–359.

Stambrook, M. (1983). The Luria-Nebraska Neuropsychological Battery: A promise that *may* be partly fulfilled. *Journal of Clinical Neuropsychology, 5,* 247–269.

Standing, L. G., & Keays, G. (1986). Computer assessment of personality: A demonstration of gullibility. *Social Behavior and Personality, 14,* 197–202.

Stanford Special Report, Number 9. (1992). Bias control. San Antonio, TX: The Psychological Corporation/Harcourt Brace Jovanovich.

Stanley, J. C. (1971). Reliability. In R. L. Thorndike (Ed.), *Educational Measurement* (2nd ed.). Washington, DC: American Council on Education.

Starch, D., & Elliot, E. C. (1912). Reliability of grading of high school work in English. *School Review, 20,* 442–457.

Stark-Adamec, C., & Adamec, R. E. (1986). Psychological methodology versus clinical impressions: Different perspectives on psychopathology and seizures. In B. K. Doane & K. E. Livingstone (Eds.), *The limbic system: Functional organization and clinical disorders* (pp. 217–227). New York: Raven Press.

Steers, R. M. (1977). *Organizational effectiveness: A behavioral view.* Santa Monica, CA: Goodyear.

Stehouwer, R. S. (1985). Review of Beck Depression Inventory. In D. J. Keyser & R. C. Sweetland (Eds.), *Test critiques* (Vol. 2; pp. 83–87). Kansas City, MO: Test Corporation of America.

Steinberg, M., Cicchetti, D., Buchanan, J., & Hall, P. (1993). Clinical assessment of dissociative symptoms and disorders: The Structured Clinical Interview for DSM-IV Dissociative Disorders (SCID-D). *Dissociation: Progress in Dissociative Disorders, 6,* 3–15.

Stephens, J. J. (1992). Assessing ethnic minorities. *SPA Exchange, 2*(1), 4–6.

Stephenson, W. (1953). *The study of behavior: Q-technique and its methodology.* Chicago: University of Chicago Press.

Stephenson, W. (1980). Newton's fifth rule and q-methodology: Application to educational psychology. *American Psychologist, 35,* 882–889.

Sternberg, R. J. (1981). The nature of intelligence. *New York Education Quarterly, 12*(3), 10–17.

Sternberg, R. J. (1982, April). Who's intelligent? *Psychology Today,* pp. 30–33, 35–36, 38–39.

Sternberg, R. J. (1985). *Beyond IQ: A triarchic theory of human intelligence.* Cambridge: Cambridge University Press.

Sternberg, R. J. (1986). Intelligence is mental self-government. In R. J. Sternberg & D. K. Detterman (Eds.), *What is intelligence?* (pp. 141–148). Norwood, NJ: Ablex.

Sternberg, R. J. (1987, September 23). Commentary: The uses and measures of intelligence testing. *Education Week,* pp. 22, 28.

Sternberg, R. J. (1992). Ability tests, measurements, and markets. *Journal of Educational Psychology, 84,* 134–140.

Sternberg, R. J. (1994). PRSVL: An integrative framework for understanding mind in context. In R. J. Sternberg & R. K. Wagner (Eds.), *Mind in context* (pp. 218–232). Cambridge: Cambridge University Press.

Sternberg, R. J., & Berg, C. A. (1986). Quantitative integration: Definitions of intelligence: A comparison of the 1921 and 1986 symposia. In R. J. Sternberg & D. K. Detterman (Eds.), *What is intelligence?* (pp. 155–162). Norwood, NJ: Ablex.

Sternberg, R. J., Conway, B. E., Ketron, J. L., & Bernstein, M. (1981). People's conceptions of intelligence. *Journal of Personality and Social Psychology, 41,* 37–55.

Sternberg, R. J., & Detterman, D. K. (Eds.). (1986). *What is intelligence?* Norwood, NJ: Ablex.

Stevens, G., & Gardner, S. (1982). *The women of psychology: Vol. 2. Expansion and refinement.* Cambridge, MA: Schenkman.

Stevens, M. R., & Reilley, R. R. (1980). MMPI short forms: A literature review. *Journal of Personality Assessment, 44,* 368–376.

Stewart, D. W. (1984). Physiological measurement of advertising effects: An unfulfilled promise. *Psychology & marketing, 1,* 43–48.

Stewart, D. W., & Furse, D. H. (1982). Applying psychophysiological measures to marketing and advertising research problems (pp. 1–38). *Current issues and research in advertising.* Ann Arbor: University of Michigan.

Stillman, R. (1974). *Assessment of deaf-blind children: The Callier-Azusa Scale.* Paper presented at the Intercom '74, Hyannis, MA.

Stinnett, T. A., Oehler-Stinnett, J., & Stout, L. J. (1989). Ability of the *Social Skills Rating System-Teacher* version to discriminate behavior disordered, emotionally disturbed, and nonhandicapped students. *School Psychology Review, 18,* 526–535.

Stokes, J. B. (1977). Comment on "Socially reinforced obsessing: Etiology of a disorder in a Christian Scientist." *Journal of Consulting and Clinical Psychology, 45,* 1164–1165.

Stone, A. A. (1986). Vermont adopts *Tarasoff:* A real barn-burner. *American Journal of Psychiatry, 143,* 352–355.

Stone, B. J. (1992). Prediction of achievement by Asian-American and White children. *Journal of School Psychology, 30,* 91–99.

Stone, M. H., Lewis, C. M., & Beck, A. P. (1994). The structure of Yalom's Curative Factors Scale. *International Journal of Group Psychotherapy, 44,* 239–245.

Strassberg, D. S., Tilley, D., Bristone, S., & Oei, T. P. S. (1992). The MMPI and chronic pain: A cross-cultural view. *Psychological Assessment, 4,* 493–497.

Straus, M. A. (1979). Measuring intrafamily conflict and violence: The Conflict Tactics (CT) Scales. *Journal of Marriage and the Family, 41,* 75–85.

Straus, M. A., & Brown, B. (1978). *Family measurement techniques: Abstracts of published instruments, 1935–1974.* Minneapolis: University of Minnesota Press.

Strauss, A. A., & Lehtinen, L. E. (1947). *Psychopathology and education of the brain injured child.* New York: Grune & Stratton.

Streiner, D. L., & Miller, H. R. (1989). The MCMI-II: How much better than the MCMI? *Journal of Personality Assessment, 53,* 81–84.

Stricker, G., & Healey, B. J. (1990). Projective assessment of object relations: A review of the empirical literature. *Psychological Assessment: A Journal of Consulting and Clinical Psychology, 2,* 219–230.

Stricker, L. J., Messick, S., & Jackson, D. N. (1968). Desirability judgments and self-reports as predictors of social behavior. *Journal of Experimental Research in Personality, 3,* 151–167.

Strong, E. K., Jr., Hansen, J. C., & Campbell, D. C. (1985). *Strong Vocational Interest Blank. Revised edition of Form T325, Strong-Campbell Interest Inventory.* Stanford, CA: Stanford University Press. (Distributed by Consulting Psychologists Press)

Subkoviak, M. J. (1980). The reliability of mastery classification decisions. In R. A. Burk (Ed.), *Criterion-referenced measurement: The state of the art.* Baltimore: Johns Hopkins University Press.

Suczek, R. F., & Klopfer, W. G. (1952). Interpretation of the Bender-Gestalt Test: The associative value of the figures. *American Journal of Orthopsychiatry, 22,* 62–75.

Suen, H. K., Lu, C-h, Neisworth, J. T., & Bagnato, S. J. (1993). Measurement of team decision-making through generalizability theory. *Journal of Psychoeducational Measurement, 11,* 120–132.

Sugarman, A. (1991). Where's the beef? Putting personality back into personality assessment. *Journal of Personality Assessment, 56,* 130–144.

Sullivan, H. S. (1953). *The interpersonal theory of psychiatry.* New York: Norton.

Sullivan, P. M, & Vernon, M. (1979). Psychological assessment of hearing impaired children. *School Psychology Digest, 8,* 271–287.

Suls, J., Wan, C. K., & Blanchard, E. B. (1994). A multi-level data-analytic approach for evaluation of relationships between daily life stressors and symptomatology: Patients with irritable bowel syndrome. *Health Psychology, 13,* 103–113.

Sundberg, N. D. (1955). The acceptability of "fake" versus "bona fide" personality test interpretations. *Journal of Abnormal and Social Psychology, 50,* 145–147.

Sundberg, N. D. (1992). Review of the Beck Depression Inventory, Revised. In J. J. Kramer & J. C. Conoley (Eds.), *The eleventh mental measurements yearbook.* Lincoln: The Buros Institute of Mental Measurements, University of Nebraska.

Sundberg, N. D., & Tyler, L. E. (1962). *Clinical psychology.* New York: Appleton-Century-Crofts.

Super, D. E. (1970). *Work Values Inventory.* Boston: Houghton Mifflin.

Super, D. E., & Hall, D. T. (1978). Career development: Exploration and planning. *Annual Review of Psychology, 29,* 333–372.

Sutker, P. B., Allain, A. N., Smith, C. J., & Cohen, G. H. (1978). Addict descriptions of therapeutic community, multimodality, and methadone maintenance treatment clients and staff. *Journal of Consulting and Clinical Psychology, 46,* 508–517.

Sutker, P. B., Bugg, F., & Allain, A. N. (1991). Psychometric prediction of PTSD among POW survivors. *Psychological Assessment: A Journal of Consulting and Clinical Psychology, 3,* 105–110.

Sutker, P. B., Winstead, D. K., Galina, Z. H., & Allain, A. N. (1990). Assessment of long-term psychosocial sequelae among POW survivors of the Korean Conflict. *Journal of Personality Assessment, 54,* 170–180.

Sweeney, J. A., Clarkin, J. F., & Fitzgibbon, M. L. (1987). Current practice of psychological assessment. *Professional Psychology: Research and Practice, 18,* 377–380.

Sweet, J. J., Moberg, P. J., & Tovian, S. M. (1990). Evaluation of Wechsler Adult Intelligence Scale—Revised premorbid IQ formulas in clinical populations. *Psychological Assessment, 2,* 41–44.

Sweetland, R., & Keyser, D. (Eds.). (1986). *Tests* (2nd ed.). Kansas City, MO: Test Corporation of America.

Swensen, C. H. (1968). Empirical evaluations of human figure drawings: 1957–1966. *Psychological Bulletin, 70,* 20–44.

Swenson, W. M., Pearson, J. S., & Osborne, D. (1973). *An MMPI source book: Basic item, scale, and pattern data on 50,000 medical patients.* Minneapolis: University of Minnesota Press.

Swerdlik, M. E. (1985). Review of Brigance Diagnostic Comprehensive Inventory of Basic Skills. In J. V. Mitchell, Jr. (Ed.), *The ninth mental measurements yearbook* (pp. 214–215). Lincoln: The Buros Institute of Mental Measurements, University of Nebraska.

Swerdlik, M. E. (1988). *A concurrent validity study of the Stanford-Binet Fourth Edition and three measures of classroom achievement.* Paper presented at the Annual Meeting of the National Association of School Psychologists, Chicago.

Swerdlik, M. E. (1991). Review of the Otis-Lennon School Ability Test. In J. J. Kramer & J. C. Conoley (Eds.), *The eleventh mental measurements yearbook.* Lincoln: The Buros Institute of Mental Measurements, University of Nebraska.

Swerdlik, M. E., & Dornback, F. (1988, April). *An interpretation guide to the fourth edition of the Stanford-Binet Intelligence Scale.* Paper presented at the annual meeting of the National Association of School Psychologists, Chicago.

Swift, J. W. (1944). Reliability of Rorschach scoring categories with pre-school children. *Child Development, 15,* 207–216.

Swoboda, J. S., Elwork, A., Sales, B. D., & Levine, D. (1978). Knowledge of and compliance with privileged communication and child-abuse-reporting laws. *Professional Psychology, 9,* 448–457.

Sylvester, R. H. (1913). Clinical psychology adversely criticized. *Psychological Clinic, 7,* 182–188.

Symonds, P. M. (1949). *Adolescent fantasy: An investigation of the picture-story method of personality study.* New York: Columbia University Press.

Tallent, N. (1958). On individualizing the psychologist's clinical evaluation. *Journal of Clinical Psychology, 114,* 243–244.

Tamkin, A. S., & Kunce, J. T. (1985). A comparison of three neuropsychological tests: The Weigl, Hooper and Benton. *Journal of Clinical Psychology, 41,* 660–664.

Tan, U. (1993). Normal distribution of hand preference and its bimodality. *International Journal of Neuroscience, 68,* 61–65.

Tasto, D. L. (1977). Self-report schedules and inventories. In A. R. Ciminero, K. S. Calhoun, & H. E. Adams (Eds.), *Handbook of behavioral assessment.* New York: Wiley.

Taylor, H. C., & Russell, J. T. (1939). The relationship of validity coefficients to the practical effectiveness of tests in selection. *Journal of Applied Psychology, 23,* 565–578.

Taylor, L. B. (1979). Psychological assessment of neurosurgical patients. In T. Rasmussen & R. Marino (Eds.), *Functional neurosurgery.* New York: Raven Press.

Teague, W. (State Superintendent of Education) (1983). *Basic competency education: Reading, language, mathematics specifications for the Alabama High School Graduation Examination* (Bulletin No. 4). Montgomery: Alabama State Department of Education.

Tellegen, A., Butcher, J. N., Hoeglund, T. (1993, March). *Are unisex norms for the MMPI-2 needed? Would they work?* Paper given at the 28th Annual Symposium on Recent Developments in the Use of the MMPI/MMPI-2/MMPI-A. St. Petersburg, Florida.

Tellegen, A., et al. (1969). Personality characteristics of members of a serpent-handling religious cult. In J. Butcher (Ed.), *MMPI: Research developments and clinical applications.* New York: McGraw-Hill.

Telzrow, C. F. (1985). Best practices in reducing learning disability qualification. In A. Thomas & J. Grimes (Eds.), *Best practices in school psychology.* Kent, OH: National Association of School Psychologists.

Terman, L. M. (1911). The Binet-Simon scale for measuring intelligence: Impressions gained by its application. *Psychological Clinic, 5,* 199–206.

Terman, L. M. (1916). *The measurement of intelligence.* Boston: Houghton Mifflin.

Terman, L. M., & Childs, H. G. (1912). A tentative revision and extension of the Binet-Simon Measuring Scale of Intelligence. *Journal of Educational Psychology, 3,* 61–74, 133–143, 198–208, 277–289.

Terman, L. M., et al. (1925). *The mental and physical traits of a thousand gifted children: Vol. 1. Genetic studies of genius.* Stanford, CA: Stanford University Press.

Terman, L. M., & Merrill, M. A. (1960). *Stanford-Binet Intelligence Scale Manual for the third revision, Form L-M.* Boston: Houghton Mifflin.

Terman, L. M., & Tyler, L. E. (1954). Psychological sex differences. In L. Carmichael (Ed.), *Manual of child psychology* (2nd ed.; pp. 1004–1114). New York: Wiley.

Terpylak, O., & Schuerger, J. M. (1994). Broad factor scales of the 16 PF fifth edition and Millon personality disorder scales: A replication. *Psychological Reports, 74,* 124–126.

Tharinger, D. J., & Stark, K. (1990). A qualitative versus quantitative approach to evaluating the Draw-A-Person and Kinetic Family Drawing: A study of mood- and anxiety-disorder children. *Psychological Assessment: A Journal of Consulting and Clinical Psychology, 2,* 365–375.

Theorell, T., Lind, E., & Folderus, B. (1975). The relationship of disturbing life changes and emotions to the early development of myocardial infarction and some other serious illnesses. *International Journal of Epidemiology, 4,* 281–293.

Theron, P. A. (1948). Peripheral vasomotor reactions as indices of basic emotional tension and lability. *Psychosomatic Medicine, 10,* 335–346.

Theye, F. W. (1970). Violation of standard procedure on the Wechsler Scales. *Journal of Clinical Psychology, 26,* 70–71.

Thomas, A. D., & Dudek, S. Z. (1985). Interpersonal affect in Thematic Apperception Test Responses: A scoring system. *Journal of Personality Assessment, 49,* 30–36.

Thompson, A. E. (1986). An object relational theory of affect maturity: Applications to the Thematic Apperception Test. In M. Kissen (Ed.), *Assessing object relations phenomena* (pp. 207–224). Madison, CT: International Universities Press.

Thompson, B., & Melancon, J. G. (1987). Measurement characteristics of the Group Embedded Figures Test. *Educational and Psychological Measurement, 47,* 765–772.

Thompson, C. (1949). The Thompson modification of the Thematic Apperception Test. *Journal of Projective Techniques, 13,* 469–478.

Thompson, J. K., (1990). *Body image disturbance: Assessment and treatment.* Elmsford, NY: Pergamon Press.

Thompson, J. K., & Spana, R. E. (1988). The adjustable light beam method for the assessment of size estimation accuracy: Description, psychometric, and normative data. *International Journal of Eating Disorders. 7,* 521–526.

Thompson, J. K. & Thompson, C. M. (1986). Body size distortion and self-esteem in asymptomatic, normal weight males and females. *International Journal of Eating Disorders, 5,* 1061–1068.

Thompson, J. M. & Sones, R. (1973). *The Education Apperception Test.* Los Angeles: Western Psychological Services.

Thompson, L. A., & Fagan, J. F. (1991). Longitudinal prediction of specific cognitive abilities from infant novelty preference. *Child Development, 62,* 530–538.

Thompson, R. J., & Curry, J. F. (1985). Missouri Children Behavior Checklist profiles with developmentally disabled children: Construct validity. *Journal of Clinical Psychology, 41,* 556–564.

Thompson, R. J., Gustafson, K. E., Meghdadpour, S., & Harrell, E. S. (1992). The role of biomedical and psychosocial processes in the intellectual and academic functioning of children and adolescents with cystic fibrosis. *Journal of Clinical Psychology, 48,* 3–10.

Thorndike, E. L., et al. (1921). Intelligence and its measurement: A symposium. *Journal of Educational Psychology, 12,* 123–147, 195–216.

Thorndike, E. L., Bregman, E. O., Cobb, M. V., Woodward, E., & the staff of the Division of Psychology of the Institute of Educational Research of Teachers College, Columbia University. (1927). *The measurement of intelligence.* New York: Bureau of Publications, Teachers College, Columbia University.

Thorndike, E. L., Lay, W., & Dean, P. R. (1909). The relation of accuracy in sensory discrimination to general intelligence. *American Journal of Psychology, 20,* 364–369.

Thorndike, R. L. (1971). Concepts of cultural fairness. *Journal of Educational Measurement, 8,* 63–70.

Thorndike, R. (1985). Reliability. *Journal of Counseling & Development, 63,* 528–530.

Thorndike, R. L., Hagen, E. P., & Sattler, J. P. (1986a).

Guide for administering and scoring the fourth edition of the Stanford-Binet Intelligence Scale. Chicago: Riverside Publishing.

Thorndike, R. L., Hagen, E. P., & Sattler, J. P. (1986b). *Technical manual for the Stanford-Binet Intelligence Scale, Fourth Edition.* Chicago: Riverside Publishing.

Thorndike, R. L., & Scott, J. (1986). Assessing the pattern and level of cognitive abilities with the fourth edition of the Stanford-Binet. In G. J. Robertson (Chair), *Perspectives on intelligence assessments: 1986.* Symposium presented at the 94th annual convention of the American Psychological Association, Washington, DC.

Thornton, G. C., & Byham, W. C. (1982). *Assessment centers and managerial performance.* New York: Academic Press.

Thurber, S., Snow, M., & Thurber, D. (1990). Psychometric properties of the Child Evaluation Inventory. *Psychological Assessment: A Journal of Consulting and Clinical Psychology, 2,* 206–208.

Thurstone, L. L. (1925). A method of scaling psychological and educational tests. *Journal of Educational Psychology, 16,* 433–451.

Thurstone, L. L. (1926). The mental age concept. *Psychological Review, 33,* 268–278.

Thurstone, L. L. (1927). A law of comparative judgment. *Psychological Review, 34,* 273–286.

Thurstone, L. L. (1929). Theory of attitude measurement. *Psychological Bulletin, 36,* 222–241.

Thurstone, L. L. (1938). Primary mental abilities. *Psychometric Monographs,* No. 1. Chicago: University of Chicago Press.

Thurstone, L. L. (1947). *Multiple factor analysis.* Chicago: University of Chicago Press.

Thurstone, L. L. (1959). *The measurement of values.* Chicago: University of Chicago Press.

Thurstone, L. L. & Chave, E. J. (1929). *The measurement of attitude.* Chicago: University of Chicago Press.

Tillman, M. H. (1973). Intelligence scale for the blind: A review with implications for research. *Journal of School Psychology, 11,* 80–87.

Timbrook, R. E., & Graham, J. R. (1994). Ethnic differences on the MMPI-2? *Psychological Assessment, 6,* 212–217.

Timbrook, R. E., Graham, J. R., Keiller, S. W., & Watts, D. (1993). Comparison of the Wiener-Harmon Subtle-Obvious Scales and the standard validity scales in detecting valid and invalid MMPH-2 profiles. *Psychological Assessment, 5,* 53–61.

Timex and VALS engineer product launch. (1984, September). *Ad Forum,* 12–14.

Tinsley, H. E., & Tinsley, D. J. (1987). Uses of factor analysis in counseling psychology research. *Journal of Counseling Psychology, 34,* 414–424.

Tombari, M. L., Fitzpatrick, S. J., & Childress, W. (1985). Using computers as contingency managers in self monitoring interventions: A case study. *Computers in Human Behavior, 1,* 75–82.

Torgerson, W. S. (1958). *Theory and methods of scaling.* New York: Wiley.

Torrance, E. P. (1966). *Torrance Tests of Creative Thinking.* Bensenville, IL: Scholastic Testing Service.

Torrance, E. P. (1974). *The Torrance Tests of Creative Thinking: Technical-norms manual.* Bensenville, IL: Scholastic Testing Service.

Torrance, E. P. (1987a). *Guidelines for administration and scoring/comments on using the Torrance Tests of Creative Thinking.* Bensenville, IL: Scholastic Testing Service.

Torrance, E. P. (1987b). Some evidence regarding development of cerebral lateralization. *Perceptual and Motor Skills, 64,* 261–262.

Torrance, E. P. (1987c). *Survey of the uses of the Torrance Tests of Creative Thinking.* Bensenville, IL: Scholastic Testing Service.

Torrance, E. P., Khatena, J., & Cunningham, B. F. (1973). *Thinking Creatively with Sounds and Words.* Bensenville, IL: Scholastic Testing Service.

Tramontana, M. G., & Boyd, T. A. (1986). Psychometric screening of neuropsychological abnormality in older children. *International Journal of Clinical Neuropsychology, 8,* 53–59.

Tramontana, M. G., Hooper, S. R., & Selzer, S. C. (1988). Research on the preschool prediction of later academic achievement: A review. *Development Review, 8,* 89–146.

Trautscholdt, M. (1883). Experimentelle Unterschungen uber die association der vorstellungen. *Philosophesche Studien, 1,* 213–250.

Travin, S., Cullen, K., & Melella, J. T. (1988). The use and abuse of erection measurements: A forensic perspective. *Bulletin of the American Academy of Psychiatry and Law, 16,* 235–250.

Traylor, M. B., & Joseph, W. B. (1984). Measuring consumer involvement in products: Developing a general scale. *Psychology & Marketing, 1,* 65–77.

Trice, H. M., & Beyer, J. M. (1984). Studying organizational cultures through rites and ceremonies. *Academy of Management Review, 9,* 653–669.

Trimble, M. R. (Ed.). (1986). *New brain imaging techniques and psychopharmacology.* Oxford: Oxford University Press.

Truscott, D. (1990). Assessment of overcontrolled hostility in adolescence. *Psychological Assessment: A Journal of Consulting & Clinical Psychology, 2,* 145–148.

Trybus, R. J. (1973). Personality assessment of entering hearing-impaired college students using the 16PF, Form E. *Journal of Rehabilitation of the Deaf, 116,* 427–434.

Tryon, R. C. (1957). Reliability and behavior domain validity: Reformulation and historical critique. *Psychological Bulletin, 54,* 229–249.

Tsudzuki, A., Hata, Y., & Kuze, T. (1957). A study of rapport between examiner and subject. *Japanese Journal of Psychology, 27,* 22–28.

Tsujimoto, R. N., Hamilton, M., & Berger, D. E. (1990). Averaging multiple judges to improve validity: Aid to planning cost-effective research. *Psychological Assessment: A Journal of Consulting & Clinical Psychology, 2,* 432–437.

Tuddenham, R. D. (1968). *Psychometricizing Piaget's méthode clinique.* Paper presented at the annual convention of the American Educational Research Association (February), Chicago, IL.

Tukey, J. W. (1977). *Exploratory data analysis.* Reading, MA: Addison-Wesley.

Tulchin, S. H. (1939). The clinical training of psychologists and allied specialists. *Journal of Consulting Psychology, 3,* 105–112.

Tupes, E. C., & Christal, R. E. (1961). Recurrent personality factors based on trait ratings (USAF ASD Tech. Rep. No. 61–97). Lackland Air Force Base, TX: Air Force.

Turk, D. C., & Rudy, T. E. (1986). Assessment of cognitive factors in pain: A worthwhile enterprise? *Journal of Consulting and Clinical Psychology, 54,* 760–768.

Turner, C. (1990). How much alcohol is in a "standard drink"? An analysis of 125 studies. *British Journal of Addiction, 85,* 1171–1175.

Turner, D. R. (1966). Predictive efficiency as a function of amount of information and level of professional experience. *Journal of Projective Techniques and Personality Assessment, 30,* 4–11.

Tuttle, F. B., & Becker, A. (1980). *Characteristics and identification of gifted and talented students.* Washington, DC: National Education Association.

Tybout, A. M., & Artz, N. (1994). Consumer psychology. *Annual Review of Psychology, 45,* 131–169.

Tyler, L. E. (1961). Research explorations in the realm of choice. *Journal of Counseling Psychology, 8,* 195–202.

Tyler, L. E. (1965). *The psychology of human differences* (3rd ed.). New York: Appleton-Century-Crofts.

Tyler, R. W. (1978). *The Florida Accountability program: An evaluation of its educational soundness and implementation.* Washington, DC: National Education Association.

Tziner, A., & Eden, D. (1985). Effects of crew composition on crew performance: Does the whole equal the sum of its parts? *Journal of Applied Psychology, 70,* 85–93.

Udry, J. R. (1981). Marital alternatives and marital disruption. *Journal of Marriage and the Family, 43,* 889–897.

Ulrich, R. E., Stachnik, T. J., & Stainton, N. R. (1963). Student acceptance of generalized personality interpretations. *Psychological Report, 13,* 831–834.

Umberger, F. G. (1985). Peabody Picture Vocabulary Test—Revised. In D. J. Keyser & R. C. Sweetland (Eds.), *Test Critiques* (Vol. 3). Kansas City, MO: Test Corporation of America.

Undergraduate admissions: The realities of institutional policies, practices and procedures. (1980). American Association of Collegiate Registrars and Admissions Officers and the College Board. New York: College Entrance Examination Board.

Uniform guidelines on employee selection procedures. (1978). *Federal Register, 43*(166), 38296–38309.

United States Department of Labor. (1977). *Dictionary of occupational titles.* Washington, DC: U.S. Government Printing Office.

University of Minnesota. (1984). *User's guide for the Minnesota Report: Personal Selection System.* Minneapolis: National Computer Systems.

Urban, G. L., & Hauser, J. R. (1980). *Design and market-*

ing of new products. Englewood Cliffs, NJ: Prentice-Hall.

Urbina, S., & Clayton, J. (1991). WPPSI/WISC-R: A comparative study. *Journal of Psychoeducational Assessment, 9,* 247–254.

U.S. Department of Labor. (1977). *Dictionary of occupational titles.* Washington, DC: U.S. Government Printing Office.

Ussher, J. M., & Wilding, J. M. (1991). Performance and state changes during the menstrual cycle, conceptualised within a broadband testing framework. *Social Science and Medicine, 32,* 525–534.

Vaidya, S., & Chansky, N. (1980). Cognitive development and cognitive style as factors in mathematics achievement. *Journal of Educational Psychology, 72,* 326–330.

Vale, C. D., & Keller, L. S. (1987). Developing expert computer systems to interpret psychological tests. In J. N. Butcher (Ed.), *Computerized psychological assessment: A practitioner's guide* (pp. 64–83). New York: Basic Books.

Vale, C. D., & Prestwood, J. S. (1988). *Manual for the Minnesota Clerical Assessment Battery.* St. Paul, MN: Assessment Systems Corporation.

Vance, R. J., MacCallum, R. C., Coovert, M. D., & Hedge, J. W. (1988). Construct validity of multiple job performance measures using confirmatory factor analysis. *Journal of Applied Psychology, 73,* 74–80.

Vander Kolk, C. J. (1977). Intelligence testing for visually impaired persons. *Journal of Visual Impairment & Blindness, 71,* 158–163.

Van der Merwe, A. B., & Theron, P. A. (1947). A new method of measuring emotional stability. *Journal of General Psychology, 37,* 109–124.

Van Gorp, W. G. (1992). Review of the Luria-Nebraska Neuropsychological Battery: Forms I and II. In J. J. Kramer & J. C. Conoley (Eds.), *The eleventh mental measurements yearbook.* Lincoln: The Buros Institute of Mental Measurements, University of Nebraska.

Van Hagen, J., & Kaufman, A. S. (1975). Factor analysis of the WISC-R for a group of mentally retarded children and adolescents. *Journal of Consulting and Clinical Psychology, 43,* 661–667.

Varon, E. J. (1936). Alfred Binet's concept of intelligence. *Psychological Review, 43,* 32–49.

Veldman, D. J., & Sheffield, J. R. (1979). The scaling of sociometric nominations. *Educational and Psychological Measurement, 39,* 99–106.

Venable, T. C. (1981). Declining SAT scores: Some unpopular hypotheses. *Phi Delta Kappan, 62,* 443–445.

Vernon, M., Blair, R., & Lotz, S. (1979). Psychological evaluation and testing of children who are deaf-blind. *School Psychology Digest, 8,* 291–295.

Vernon, M., & Brown, D. W. (1964) A guide to psychological tests and testing procedures in the evaluation of deaf and hard-of-hearing children. *Journal of Speech and Hearing Disorders, 29,* 414–423.

Vernon, P. E. (1950). *The structure of human abilities.* New York: Wiley.

Vernon, P. E. (1964). *Personality assessment: A critical survey.* New York: Wiley.

Vevea, J. L., Clements, N. C., & Hedges, L. V. (1993). Assess the effects of selection bias on validity data for the General Aptitude Test Battery. *Journal of Applied Psychology, 78,* 981–987.

Vitaliano, M. A., Maiuro, R. D., Russo, J., & Becker, J. (1987). Raw versus relative scores in the assessment of coping strategies. *Journal of Behavioral Medicine, 10,* 1–19.

Volans, P. J., & Levy, R. (1982). A re-evaluation of an automated tailored test of concept learning with elderly psychiatric patients. *British Journal of Psychology, 21,* 210–214.

von Knorring, L., & Lindstrom, E. (1992). The Swedish version of the Positive and Negative Syndrome Scale (PANSS) for schizophrenia: Construct validity and interrater reliability. *Acta Psychiatrica Scandinavica, 86,* 463–468.

Vroom, V. H. (1964). *Work and motivation.* New York: Wiley.

Wachspress, M., Berenberg, A. N., & Jacobson, A. (1953). Simulation of psychosis: A report of three cases. *Psychiatric Quarterly, 27,* 463–473.

Waddell, D. D. (1980). The Stanford-Binet: An evaluation of the technical data available since the 1972 restandardization. *Journal of School Psychology, 18,* 203–209.

Wade, T. C., & Baker, T. B. (1977). Opinions and uses of psychological tests: A survey of clinical psychologists. *American Psychologist, 32,* 874–882.

Wainer, H. (1990). *Computerized adaptive testing: A primer.* Hillsdale, NJ: Erlbaum.

Wald, A. (1947). *Sequential analysis.* New York: Wiley.

Wald, A. (1950). *Statistical decision function.* New York: Wiley.

Waldman, D. A., & Avolio, B. J. (1989). Homogeneity of test validity. *Journal of Applied Psychology, 74,* 371–374.

Walker, H. M. (1976). *Walker Problem Behavior Identification Checklist.* Los Angeles: Western Psychological Services.

Walker, H. M. (1983). *Walker Problem Behavior Identification Checklist.* Los Angeles: Western Psychological Services.

Walker, S., & Rosser, R. (Eds.). (1988). *Quality of life: Assessment and application.* London: MTP Press.

Wallace, I. F., Gravel, J. S., McCarton, C. M., & Ruben, R. J. (1988). Otitis media and language development at 1 year of age. *Journal of Speech and Hearing Disorders, 53,* 245–251.

Wallach, M. A., & Kogan, N. (1965). *Modes of thinking in young children.* New York: Holt, Rinehart & Winston.

Wallbrown, F., Brown, D., & Engin, A. (1978). A factor analysis of reading attitudes along with measures of reading achievement and scholastic aptitude. *Psychology in the Schools, 15,* 160–165.

Waller, N. G., & Waldman, I. D. (1990). A reexamination of the WAIS-R factor structure. *Psychological Assessment: A Journal of Consulting and Clinical Psychology, 2,* 139–144.

Waller, N. G., & Zavala, J. D. (1993). Evaluating the big five. *Psychological Inquiry, 4*, 131–135.

Wallston, K. A., Wallston, B. S., & DeVellis, R. (1978). Development of the Multidimensional Health Locus of Control (MHLC) Scales. *Health Education Monographs, 6*, 160–170.

Walsh, J. P., Weinberg, R. M., & Fairfield, M. L. (1987). The effects of gender on assessment center evaluations. *Journal of Occupational Psychology, 60*, 305–309.

Walsh, T. M (1966). Responses on the Famous Sayings Test of professional and nonprofessional personnel in a medical population. *Psychological Reports, 18*, 151–157.

Walters, G. D. (1991). Predicting the disciplinary adjustment of maximum and minimum security prison inmates using the Lifestyle Criminality Screening Form. *International Journal of Offender Therapy and Comparative Criminology.*

Walters, G. D., Revella, L., & Baltrusaitis, W. J., II. (1990). Predicting parole/probation outcome with the aid of the Lifestyle Criminality Screening Form. *Psychological Assessment: A Journal of Consulting and Clinical Psychology, 2*, 313–316.

Walters, G. D., & White, T. W. (1989). The thinking criminal: A cognitive model of lifestyle criminality. *Criminal Justice Research Bulletin, 4*(4), 1–10.

Walters, G. D., White, T. W., & Denney, D. (1991). The Lifestyle Criminality Screening Form: Preliminary data. *Criminal Justice and Behavior, 18*, 406–418.

Wanderer, Z. W. (1967). *The validity of diagnostic judgments based on "blind" Machover figure drawings.* Unpublished doctoral dissertation, Columbia University, New York.

Wanous, J. P. (1977). Organizational entry: Newcomers moving in from outside to inside. *Psychological Bulletin, 84*, 601–618.

Wantz, R. A. (1989). Review of the Parenting Stress Index. In J. C. Conoley & J. J. Kramer (Eds.), *The tenth mental measurements yearbook.* Lincoln: The Buros Institute of Mental Measurements, University of Nebraska.

Ward, L. C., & Dillon, E. A. (1990). Psychiatric symptom correlates of the Minnesota Multiphasic Personality Inventory (MMPI) Masculinity Femininity Scale. *Psychological Assessment: A Journal of Consulting & Clinical Psychology, 2*, 286–288.

Ward, P. B., McConaghy, N., & Catts, S. V. (1991). Word association and measures of psychosis proneness in university students. *Personality and Individual Differences, 12*, 473–480.

Waring, E. M., & Reddon, J. (1983). The measurement of intimacy in marriage: The Waring Questionnaire. *Journal of Clinical Psychology, 39*, 53–57.

Warmke, D. L. (1984). *Successful implementation of the "new" GATB in entry-level selection.* Presentation at the American Society for Personnel Administrators Region 4 Conference, October 15, 1984, Norfolk, VA.

Warren, J. M., & Akert, K. (1964). *The frontal granular cortex and behavior.* New York: McGraw-Hill.

Watkins, C. E., Jr. (1986). Validity and usefulness of WAIS-R, WISC-R, and WPPSI short forms. *Professional Psychology: Research and Practice, 17*, 36–43.

Watkins, C. E., Jr., & Campbell, V. L. (1989). Personality assessment and counseling psychology. *Journal of Personality Assessment, 53*, 296–307.

Watkins, C. E., Campbell, V. L., & Manus, M. (1990). Personality assessment training in counseling psychology programs. *Journal of Personality Assessment, 55*, 380–383.

Watkins, C. E., Jr., Campbell, V. L., & McGregor, P. (1988). Counseling psychologists' uses of and opinions about psychological tests: A contemporary perspective. *The Counseling Psychologist, 16*, 476–486.

Watkins, C. E., Jr., Campbell, V. L., & Nieberding, R. (1994). The practice of vocational assessment by counseling psychologists. *The Counseling Psychologist, 22*, 115–128.

Watkins, E. O. (1976). *Watkins Bender-Gestalt Scoring System.* Novato, CA: Academic Therapy Publications.

Watson, C. G. (1967). Relationship of distortion to DAP diagnostic accuracy among psychologists at three levels of sophistication. *Journal of Consulting Psychology, 31*, 142–146.

Watson, C. G. (1990). Psychometric posttraumatic stress disorder measurement techniques: A review. *Psychological Assessment: A Journal of Consulting and Clinical Psychology, 2*, 460–469.

Watson, C. G., Felling, J., & Maceacherr, D. G. (1967). Objective draw-a-person scales: An attempted cross-validation. *Journal of Clinical Psychology, 23*, 382–386.

Watson, C. G., Thomas, D., & Anderson, P. E. D. (1992). Do computer-administered Minnesota Multiphasic Personality Inventories underestimate booklet-based scores? *Journal of Clinical Psychology, 48*, 744–748.

Waxman, S. G., & Geschwind, N. (1975). The interictal behavior syndrome of temporal lobe epilepsy. *Archives of General Psychiatry, 32*, 1580–1586.

Webb, E. J., Campbell, D. T., Schwartz, R. D., & Sechrest, L. (1966). *Unobtrusive measures: Nonreactive research in the social sciences.* Chicago: Rand McNally.

Webb, J. T., Miller, M. L., & Fowler, R. D. (1970). Extending professional time: A computerized MMPI interpretation service. *Journal of Clinical Psychology, 26*, 210–214.

Webb, W. B., & Hilden, A. H. (1953). Verbal and intellectual ability as factors in projective test results. *Journal of Projective Techniques, 17*, 102–103.

Wechsler, D. (1939). *The measurement of adult intelligence.* Baltimore, MD: Williams & Wilkins.

Wechsler, D. (1944). *The measurement of adult intelligence* (3rd ed.). Baltimore: Williams & Wilkins.

Wechsler, D. (1955). *Manual for the Wechsler Adult Intelligence Scale.* New York: Psychological Corporation.

Wechsler, D. (1958). *The measurement and appraisal of adult intelligence* (4th ed.). Baltimore, MD: Williams & Wilkins.

Wechsler, D. (1967). *Manual for the Wechsler Preschool and Primary Scale of Intelligence.* New York: Psychological Corporation.

Wechsler, D. (1974). *Manual for the Wechsler Intelligence Scale for Children—Revised.* New York: Psychological Corporation.

Wechsler, D. (1975). Intelligence defined and undefined: A relativistic appraisal. *American Psychologist, 30,* 135–139.

Wechsler, D. (1981). *Manual for the Wechsler Adult Intelligence Scale—Revised.* New York: Psychological Corporation.

Wechsler, D. (1989). *Wechsler Preschool and Primary Scale of Intelligence—Revised.* San Antonio, TX: The Psychological Corporation.

Wechsler, D. (1991). *Manual for the Wechsler Intelligence Scale for Children—Third Edition.* San Antonio, TX: Psychological Corporation.

Weinberger, L. J., & Bradley, L. A. (1980). Effects of "favorability" and type of assessment device upon acceptance of general personality interpretations. *Journal of Personality Assessment, 44,* 44–47.

Weiner, B. A. (1980). Not guilty by reason of insanity: A sane approach. *Chicago Kent Law Review, 56,* 1057–1085.

Weiner, I. B. (1966). *Psychodiagnosis in schizophrenia.* New York: Wiley.

Weiner, I. B. (1991). Editor's note: Interscorer agreement in Rorschach research. *Journal of Personality Assessment, 56,* 1.

Weiss, B., Weisz, J. R., Politano, M., Carey, M., Nelson, W. M., & Finch, A. J. (1991). Developmental differences in the factor structure of the Children's Depression Inventory. *Psychological Assessment: A Journal of Consulting and Clinical Psychology, 3,* 38–45.

Weiss, D. J. (1983). *New horizons in testing: Latent trait test theory and computerized adaptive testing.* New York: Academic.

Weiss, D. J. (1985). Adaptive testing by computer. *Journal of Consulting and Clinical Psychology, 53,* 774–789.

Weiss, D. J., & Davison, M. L. (1981). Test theory and methods. *Annual Review of Psychology, 32,* 629–658.

Weiss, D. J., & Vale, C. D., (1987). Computerized adaptive testing for measuring abilities and other psychological variables. In J. N. Butcher (Ed.), *Computerized psychological assessment: A practitioner's guide* (pp. 325–343). New York: Basic Books.

Weiss, D. S., Zilberg, N. J., & Genevro, J. L. (1989). Psychometric properties of Loevinger's Sentence Completion Test in an adult psychiatric outpatient sample. *Journal of Personality Assessment, 53,* 478–486.

Weiss, H. M., & Adler, S. (1984). Personality and organizational behavior. In B. M. Straw & L. L. Cummings (Eds.), *Research in organizational behavior* (Vol. 6; pp. 1–50). Greenwich, CT: JAI.

Weiss, R., & Summers, K. (1983). Marital Interaction Coding System III. In E. Filsinger (Ed.), *Marriage and family assessment: A sourcebook of family therapy.* Beverly Hills, CA: Sage.

Weisskopf, E. A., & Dieppa, J. J. (1951). Experimentally inducted faking of TAT responses. *Journal of Consulting Psychology, 15,* 469–474.

Weissman, H. N. (1991). Forensic psychological examination of the child witness in cases of alleged sexual abuse. *American Journal of Orthopsychiatry, 6,* 48–58.

Weithorn, L. A. (Ed.). (1987). *Psychology and child custody determinations.* Lincoln: University of Nebraska Press.

Welcher, D., Mellitis, E. D., & Hardy, J. B. (1971). A multivariate analysis of factors affecting psychological performance. *The Johns Hopkins Medical Journal, 129,* 19–35.

Welsh, G. S. (1956). Factor dimensions A and R. In G. S. Welsh & W. G. Dahlstrom (Eds.), *Basic readings on the MMPI in psychology and medicine* (pp. 264–281). Minneapolis: University of Minnesota Press.

Welsh, G. S., & Dahlstrom, W. G. (Eds.). (1956). *Basic readings on the MMPI in psychology and medicine.* Minneapolis: University of Minnesota Press.

Welsh, J. R., Kucinkas, S. K., & Curran, L. T. (1990). *Armed Services Vocational Aptitude Battery (ASVAB): Integrative review of validity studies* (Rpt 90-22). San Antonio, TX: Operational Technologies Corp.

Wenar, C., & Curtis, K. M. (1991). The validity of the Rorschach for assessing cognitive and affective changes. *Journal of Personality Assessment, 57,* 291–308.

Wepman, J. M. (1978). *Wepman Auditory Discrimination Test.* Chicago: Language Research Associates.

Werner, H., & Strauss, A. A. (1941). Pathology of figure-background relation in the child. *Journal of Abnormal and Social Psychology, 36,* 236–248.

Wertheimer, M. (1923). Untersuchungen zur Lehre von der Gestalt. *Psychologische Forschung* [Studies in the theory of Gestalt Psychology. *Psychology for Schools,*] *4,* 301–303. Translated by Don Cantor in R. J. Herrnstein & E. G. Boring (1965), *A sourcebook in the history of psychology.* Cambridge, MA: Harvard University Press.

Wesman, A. G. (1949). Effect of speed on item-test correlation coefficients. *Educational and Psychological Measurement, 9,* 51–57.

Wesman, A. G. (1968). Intelligent testing. *American Psychologist, 23,* 267–274.

Wessberg, H. W., Mariotto, M. J., Conger, A. J., Conger, J. C., & Farrell, A. D. (1979). The ecological validity of role plays for assessing heterosocial anxiety and skill of male college students. *Journal of Consulting and Clinical Psychology, 47,* 525–535.

West, L. J., & Ackerman, D. L. (1993). The drug-testing controversy. *The Journal of Drug Issues, 23,* 579–595.

Westen, D., Barends, A., Leigh, J., Mendel, M., & Silbert, D. (1988). *Manual for coding dimensions of object relations and social cognition from interview data.* Unpublished manuscript. Ann Arbor: University of Michigan.

Westen, D., Silk, K. R., Lohr, N., & Kerber, K. (1985). *Object relations and social cognition: TAT scoring manual.* Unpublished manuscript. Ann Arbor: University of Michigan.

Wetter, M. W., Baer, R. A., Berry, D. T. R., & Reynolds, S. K. (1994). The effect of symptom information on faking on the MMPI-2. *Assessment, 1,* 199–207.

Wettstein, R. M., Mulvey, E. P., & Rogers, R. (1991). A prospective comparison of four insanity defense standards. *American Journal of Psychiatry, 148,* 21–27.

Wetzler, S. (1900). The Millon Clinical Multiaxial Inventory (MCMI): A review. *Journal of Personality Assessment, 55,* 445–464.

Wexley, K. N., Sanders, R. E., & Yukl, G. A. (1973). Training interviewers to eliminate contrast effects in employment interviews. *Journal of Applied Psychology, 57,* 233–236.

Wexley, K. N., Yukl, G. A., Kovacs, S. Z., & Sanders, R. E. (1972). Importance of contrast effects in employment interviews. *Journal of Applied Psychology, 56,* 45–48.

Wheeler, M. (1977). *Lies, damn lies, and statistics.* New York: Dell.

Whisman, M. A., Strosahl, K., Fruzzetti, A. E., Schmaling, K. B., Jacobson, N. S., & Miller, D. M. (1989). A structured interview version of the Hamilton Rating Scale for Depression: Reliability and validity. *Psychological Assessment: A Journal of Consulting and Clinical Psychology, 1,* 238–241.

White, B. L. (1971). *Human infants: Experience and psychological development.* Englewood Cliffs, NJ: Prentice-Hall.

White, D. M., Clements, C. B., & Fowler, R. D. (1985). A comparison of computer administration with standard administration of the MMPI. *Computers in Human Behavior, 1,* 153–162.

White, J. L., Moffitt, T. E., Caspi, A., Bartusch, D. J., Needles, D. J., & Stouthamer-Loeber, M. (1994). Measuring impulsivity and examining its relationship to delinquency. *Journal of Abnormal Psychology, 103,* 192–205.

White, L. T. (1984). Attitudinal consequences of the preemployment polygraph examination. *Journal of Applied Social Psychology, 14,* 364–374.

White, S., Santilli, G., & Quinn, K. (1988). Child evaluator's roles in child sexual abuse assessments. In E. B. Nicholson & J. Bulkley (Eds.), *Sexual abuse allegations in custody and visitation cases: A resource book for judges and court personnel* (pp. 94–105). Washington, DC: American Bar Association.

Whitehead, W. E. (1994). Assessing the effects of stress on physical symptoms. *Health Psychology, 13,* 99–102.

Whitmyre, J. W. (1953). The significance of artistic excellence in the judgment of adjustment inferred from human figure drawings. *Journal of Consulting Psychology, 17,* 421–424.

Whitworth, R. H. (1984). Review of Halstead-Reitan Neuropsychological Battery and allied proce-

dures. In D. J. Keyser & R. C. Sweetland (Eds.), *Test critiques* (Vol. 1; pp. 305–314). Kansas City, MO: Test Corporation of America.

Whitworth, R. H., & Unterbrink, C. (1994). Comparison of MMPI-2 clinical and content scales administered to Hispanic and Anglo-Americans. *Hispanic Journal of Behavioral Sciences, 16,* 255–264.

Wicker, A. W. (1969). Attitudes versus actions: The relationship of verbal and overt behavioral responses to attitude objects. *Journal of Social Issues, 25,* 41–78.

Wickes, T. A., Jr. (1956). Examiner influences in a testing situation. *Journal of Consulting Psychology, 20,* 23–26.

Wicklund, R. A., & Koller, M. (1991). Psychological antecedents of consistency in applying traits. *Journal of Research in Personality, 25,* 108–134.

Widiger, T. A. (1992). Review of the NEO Personality Inventory. In J. J. Kramer & J. C. Conoley (Eds.), *The eleventh mental measurements yearbook.* Lincoln: The Buros Institute of Mental Measurements, University of Nebraska.

Wiederanders, M. R., & Choate, P. A. (1994). Beyond recidivism: Community adjustments of conditionally released insanity acquittees. *Psychological Assessment, 6,* 61–66.

Wiegersma, S. (1951). Een onderzoek naar de gelddigheid van de Szonditest voor de psychologische praktijk. [Investigation of the validity of the Szondi Test for psychological practice.] *Psychological Abstracts, 25,* No. 372.

Wiggins, J. S. (1973). *Personality and prediction: Principles of personality assessment.* Reading, MA: Addison-Wesley.

Wiggins, W. (1966). Individual viewpoints on social desirability. *Psychological Bulletin, 66,* 68–77.

Wilcox, R., & Krasnoff, A. (1967). Influence of test-taking attitudes on personality inventory scores. *Journal of Consulting Psychology, 31,* 185–194.

Wilcox, V. L., Kasal, S. V., & Berkman, L. F. (1994). Social support and physical disability in older people after hospitalization: A prospective study. *Health Psychology, 13,* 170–179.

Williams, C. L., Ben-Porath, Y. S., Uchiyama, C., Weed, N. C., & Archer, R. P. (1990). External validity of the new Devereux Adolescent Behavioral Rating Scales. *Journal of Personality Assessment, 55,* 73–85.

Williams, J. M., & Shane, B. (1986). The Reitan-Indiana Aphasia Screening Test: Scoring and factor analysis. *Journal of Clinical Psychology, 42,* 156–160.

Williams, R. (1975). The BITCH-100: A Culture-specific test. *Journal of Afro-American Issues, 3,* 103–116.

Williams, S. K., Jr. (1978). The Vocational Card Sort: A tool for vocational exploration. *Vocational Guidance Quarterly, 26,* 237–243.

Willson, V. L., Reynolds, C. R., Chatman, S. P., & Kaufman, A. S. (1985). Confirmatory analysis of simultaneous, sequential and achievement factors on the K-ABC at 11 age levels ranging from 2½ to 12½ years. *Journal of School Psychology, 23,* 261–269.

Wilson, S. L., Thompson, J. A., & Wylie, G. (1982). Automated psychological testing for the severely physically handicapped. *International Journal of Man-Machine Studies, 17,* 291–296.

Winslade, W. J. (1986). After Tarasoff: Therapist liability and patient confidentiality. In L. Everstine & D. S. Everstine (Eds.), *Psychotherapy and the law.* Orlando, FL: Grune & Stratton.

Wirt, R. D., Lachar, D., Klinedinst, J. K., & Seat, P. D. (1977/1984). *Multidimensional description of child personality: A manual for the Personality Inventory for Children.* (1984 revision by David Lachar). Los Angeles: Western Psychological Services.

Wirtz, W. (1977). *On further examination: Report on the advisory panel on the Scholastic Aptitude Test score decline.* New York: College Entrance Examination Board.

Wish, J., McCombs, K. F., & Edmonson, B. (1980). *Socio-Sexual Knowledge & Attitudes Test.* Chicago: Stoelting.

Witkin, H. A., & Berry, J. W. (1975). Psychological differentiation in cross-cultural perspective. *Journal of Cross-Cultural Psychology, 6,* 4–87.

Witkin, H. A., Dyk, R. B., Faterson, H. F., Goodenough, D. R., & Karp, S. A. (1962). *Psychological differentiation.* New York: Wiley.

Witkin, H. A., & Goodenough, D. R., (1977). Field dependence and interpersonal behavior. *Psychological Bulletin, 84,* 661–689.

Witkin, H. A., & Goodenough, D. R. (1981). *Cognitive styles: Essence and origins* (Psychological Issues Monograph 51). New York: International Universities Press.

Witkin, H. A., Lewis, H. B., Hertzman, M., Machover, K., Meissner, P. B., & Wapner, S. (1954). *Personality through perception: An experimental and clinical study.* New York: Harper.

Witmer, L. (1902). *Analytical psychology: A practical manual for colleges and Normal schools.* Boston: Ginn.

Witmer, L. (1907). Clinical psychology. *Psychological Clinic, 1,* 1–9.

Witmer, L. (1911). *The special class for backward children.* Philadelphia: Psychological Clinic Press.

Witmer, L. (1913). *Progress in education of exceptional children in public schools during the year 1912–13.* Washington, DC: U.S. Bureau of Education.

Witt, J. C., & Elliott, S. N. (1985). Acceptability of classroom management strategies. In T. R. Kratochwill (Ed.), *Advances in school psychology* (Vol. 4; pp. 251–288). Hillsdale, NJ: Erlbaum.

Witt, J. C., Heffer, R. W., & Pfeiffer, J. (1990). Structural rating scales: A review of self-report and informant rating processes, procedures and issues. In C. R. Reynolds & R. W. Kamphaus (Eds.), *Handbook of psychological and educational assessment of children: Personality, behavior and context* (pp. 364–394). New York: Guilford Press.

Wittenborn, J. R., & Holzberg, J. D. (1951). The Rorschach and descriptive diagnosis. *Journal of Consulting Psychology, 15,* 460–463.

Wittgenstein, L. (1953). *Philosophical interventions.* New York: Basil Blackwell.

Witty, P. (1940). Some considerations in the education of gifted children. *Educational Administration and Supervision, 26,* 512–521.

Wohlfarth, H. (1982). *International Journal of Biosocial Research, 3,* 35–43.

Wolf, T. M. (1981). Measures of deviant behavior, activity level, and self-concept for educable mentally retarded-emotionally disturbed students. *Psychological Reports, 48,* 903–910.

Wolfe, J., Keane, T. M., Lyons, J. A., & Gerardi, R. J. (1987). Current trends and issues in the assessment of combat-related post-traumatic stress disorder. *Behavior Therapist, 10,* 27–32.

Wolff, C. (1732). *Psychologia empirica.*

Wolff, C. (1734). *Psychologia rationalis.*

Wolfner, G., Fause, D., & Dawes, R. M. (1993). The use of anatomically detailed dolls in sexual abuse evaluations: The state of the science. *Applied and Preventive Psychology, 2,* 1–11.

Wolfram, W. A. (1971). Social dialects from a linguistic perspective: Assumptions, current research, and future directions. In R. Shuy (Ed.), *Social dialects and interdisciplinary perspectives.* Washington, DC: Center for Applied Linguistics.

Wolf-Schein, E. G. (1993). Assessing the ''untestable'' client: ADLO. *Developmental Disabilities Bulletin, 21,* 52–70.

Wong, D. L. (1987). False allegations of child abuse: The other side of the tragedy. *Pediatric Nursing, 13,* 329–333.

Woo, I., & Knowlton, M. (1992). Developing a version of the Scales for Independent Behavior, adapted for students with visual impairments. *RE:view, 24,* 72–83.

Woodcock, R. W. (1990). Theoretical foundations of the WJ-R measures of cognitive ability. *Journal of Psychoeducational Assessment, 8,* 231–258.

Woodcock, R. W., & Johnson, M. B. (1989). *Woodcock-Johnson Psycho-Educational Battery—Revised.* Allen, TX: DLM Teaching Resources.

Woodcock, R. W., & Mather, N. (1989). *WJ-R Tests of Cognitive Ability—Standard and Supplemental Batteries: Examiner's Manual.* In R. W. Woodcock & M. B. Johnson, *Woodcock-Johnson Psychoeducational Battery—Revised.* Allen, TX: DLM Teaching Resources.

Woodcock, R. W., & Mather, N. (1989, 1990). *WJ-R Tests of Achievement: Examiner's Manual.* In R. W. Woodcock & M. B. Johnson, *Woodcock-Johnson Psychoeducational Battery—Revised.* Allen, TX: DLM Teaching Resources.

Woodworth, R. S. (1917). *Personal Data Sheet.* Chicago: Stoelting.

Woolfolk, J. M. (1992, Spring). Are you psychic? *YM,* pp. 60–64.

Woo-Sam, J. M., & Zimmerman, I. L. (1973). Research with the Wechsler Preschool and Primary Scale of Intelligence (WPPSI): The first five years. *School Psychology Monographs, 1,* 25–50.

Worchel, F. F., & Dupree, J. L. (1990). Projective storytelling techniques. In C. R. Reynolds & R. W. Kamphaus (Eds.), *Handbook of psychological and educational assessment of children: Personality, be-*

havior, & context (pp. 70–88). New York: Guilford Press.

Worlock, P., et al. (1986). Patterns of fractures in accidental and non-accidental injury in children. *British Medical Journal, 293*, 100–103.

Wright, B. D., & Stone, M. H. (1979). *Best test design: Rasch measurement*. Chicago: Mesa Press.

Wright, L., McCurdy, S., & Rogoll, G. (1992). The TUPA Scale: A self-report measure for the Type A subcomponent of time urgency and perpetual activation. *Psychological Assessment, 4*, 352–356.

Wright, M. W., Sister, G. C., & Chylinski, J. (1963). Personality factors in the selection of civilians for isolated northern stations. *Journal of Applied Psychology, 47*, 24–29.

Wylie, R. C. (1974). *The self-concept: 1. A review of the methodological considerations and measuring instruments* (Rev. ed.). Lincoln: University of Nebraska Press.

Wylie, R. C. (1979). *The self-concept: 2. Theory and research on selected topics* (Rev. ed.). Lincoln: University of Nebraska Press.

Yamamoto, J., & Seeman, W. (1960). A psychological study of castrated males. *Psychiatric Research Report, 12*, 97–103.

Yamamoto, K., & Frengel, B. A. (1966). An exploratory component analysis of the Minnesota tests of creative thinking. *California Journal of Educational Research, 17*, 220–229.

Yater, A. C., Barclay, A., & Leskosky, R. (1971). Goodenough-Harris Drawing Test and WPPSI performance of disadvantaged preschool children. *Perceptual and Motor Skills, 33*, 967–970.

Youth, R. (1986, June). Corporate use of polygraphs raises fairness questions. *The New York State Psychologists, 37*, 5, 32.

Yozawitz, A. (1986). Applied neuropsychology in a psychiatric center. In I. Grant & K. M. Adams (Eds.), *Neuropsychological assessment of neuropsychiatric disorders* (pp. 121–146). New York: Oxford University Press.

Ysseldyke, J. E. (1990). Goodness of fit of the Woodcock-Johnson Psycho-Educational Battery—Revised to the Horn Cattell Gf-Gc theory. *Journal of Psychoeducational Assessment, 8*(3), 268–275.

Yule, W., Berger, M., Butler, S., Newham, V., & Tizard, J. (1969). The WPPSI: An empirical evaluation with a British sample. *British Journal of Education Psychology, 39*, 1–13.

Yussen, S. R., & Kane, P. T. (1980). *Children's conception of intelligence*. Madison report for the project on studies of instructional programming for the individual student. University of Wisconsin, Technical Report #546.

Zachary, R. (1984, August). Computer-based test interpretations: Comments and discussion. In J. D. Matarazzo (Chair), *Computer-based test interpretation: Prospects and problems*. Symposium conducted at the Annual Convention of the American Psychological Association, Toronto.

Zaichowsky, J. L. (1985). Measuring the involvement construct. *Journal of Consumer Research, 12*, 281–300.

Zaudig, M. (1992). A new systematic method of measurement and diagnosis of "mild cognitive impairment" and dementia according to ICD-10 and DSM-III-R criteria. *International Psychogeriatrics, 4*, 203–219.

Zbaracki, J. U., Clark, S. G., & Wolins, L. (1985). Children's Interests Inventory, grades 4–6. *Educational and Psychological Measurement, 45*, 517–521.

Zedeck, S., & Cascio, W. F. (1984). Psychological issues in personnel decisions. *Annual Review of Psychology, 35*, 461–518.

Zeinder, M. (1994). Reactions of students and teachers towards key facets of classroom testing. *School Psychology International, 15*, 39–53.

Zeiss, R. A., & Dickman, H. R. (1989). PTSD 40 years later: Incidence and person-situation correlates in former POW's. *Journal of Clinical Psychology, 45*, 80–87.

Zeren, A. S., & Bradley, L. A. (1982). Effects of diagnostician prestige and sex upon subjects; acceptance of genuine personality feedback. *Journal of Personality Assessment, 46*, 169–174.

Zieziula, F. R. (Ed.). (1982). *Assessment of hearing-impaired people*. Washington, DC: Gallaudet College Press.

Zimbardo, P. G., & Ruch, F. L. (1975). *Psychology and life* (9th ed.). Glenview, IL: Scott, Foresman.

Zimmerman, I. L., & Woo-Sam, J. (1970). The utility of the WPPSI in the public school. *Journal of Clinical Psychology, 26*, 472.

Zimmerman, I. L., & Woo-Sam, J. M. (1978). Intelligence testing today: Relevance to the school age child. In L. Oettinger (Ed.), *Psychologists and the school age child with MBD/LD*. New York: Grune & Stratton.

Zimmerman, M., & Coryell, W. (1987). The Inventory to Diagnose Depression (IDD): A self-report scale to diagnose major depressive disorder. *Journal of Consulting and Clinical Psychology, 55*, 55–59.

Zimmerman, M., & Coryell, W. (1988). The validity of a self-report questionnaire for diagnosing major depressive disorder. *Archives of General Psychiatry, 45*, 738–740.

Zimmerman, M., & Coryell, W. (1994). Screening for major depressive disorder in the community: A comparison of measures. *Psychological Assessment, 6*, 71–74.

Zimmerman, M., Coryell, W., Corenthal, C., & Wilson, S. (1986). A self-report scale to diagnose major depressive disorder. *Archives of General Psychiatry, 43*, 1076–1081.

Zimmerman, W., Michael, J., & Michael, W. (1970). The factored dimensions of the Study Attitudes and Methods Survey test—Experimental form. *Educational and Psychological Measurement, 30*, 433–436.

Zimmerman, W., Parks, H., Gray, K., & Michael, W. (1977). The validity of traditional cognitive measures and of scales of the Study Attitudes and Methods Survey in the prediction of the academic success of Educational Opportunity Program students. *Educational and Psychological Measurement, 37*, 465–470.

Zubin, J., Eron, L. D., & Schumer, F. (1965). *An experimental approach to projective techniques*. New York: Wiley.

Zucker, S. (1985). *MSCA-K-ABC with high risk preschoolers*. Paper presented at the Annual Meeting of the National Association of School Psychologists, Las Vegas, NV.

Zucker, S., & Copeland, E. P. (1987). *K-ABC-McCarthy Scale performance among three groups of "at-risk" preschoolers*. Paper presented at the Annual Meeting of the National Association of School Psychologists, Las Vegas, NV.

Zuckerman, M. (1979). Traits, states, situations, and uncertainty. *Journal of Behavioral Assessment, 1,* 43–54.

Zuckerman, M. (1985). Review of the 16 PF Questionnaire. In J. V. Mitchell, Jr. (Ed.), *The ninth mental measurements yearbook*. Lincoln: The Buros Institute of Mental Measurements, University of Nebraska.

Zuckerman, M. (1990). Some dubious premises in research and theory on racial differences. *American Psychologist, 45,* 1297–1303.

Zuckerman, M. (1992). What is a basic factor and which factors are basic? Turtles all the way down. *Personality and Individual Differences, 13,* 675–681.

Zuckerman, M., Kuhlman, D. M., Joireman, J., Teta, P., & Kraft, M. (1993). A comparison of three structural models of personality: The big three, the big five, and the alternative five. *Journal of Personality and Social Psychology, 65,* 757–768.

Zuckerman, M., & Lubin, B. (1985). *Manual for the Multiple Affect Adjective Check List—Revised*. San Diego: Educational and Industrial Testing Service.

Zumbo, B. D., & Taylor, S. V. (1993). The construct validity of the Extraversion subscales of the Myers-Briggs Type Indicator. *Canadian Journal of Behavioural Science, 25,* 590–604.

Zybert, P., Stein, Z., & Belmont, L. (1978). Maternal age and children's ability. *Perceptual and Motor Skills, 47,* 815–818.

Name Index

Subject Index

American Psychological Association (*continued*)
  Division of Industrial and Organizational Psychology, 633
  professional and ethical standards, 25, 67–69, 71, 76, 176
  publications of, 67–68
  on test development, 24
  Testing Committee, 64
American Sign Language (ASL), 612–613
Americans with Disabilities Act of 1990, 62, 606, 671
Amnesia, 519
Analogue studies, 490, 492
Anatomically detailed dolls (ADDs), 552
Anchoring, 125
Anchor protocols, 314
Androgynous, 16
Anorexia nervosa, 14, 199
Anxiety
  factor analysis of, 207–208
  state-trait, 387
  test, 198
Anxiety proneness, 387
APA. *See* American Psychological Association
Aphagia, 588
Aphasia, 588, 600
Apperceptive Personality Test (APT), 449–450
Application blanks, 635–636
APT. *See* Apperceptive Personality Test
Aptitude tests, 351–360
  achievement tests vs., 351–353
  college level, 358–360
  elementary school level, 354–355
  General Aptitude Test Battery, 644–650
  for industrial/organizational assessment, 643–650
  predictive function of, 353–354
  secondary school level, 355–358
  See also specific aptitude tests by name
Arithmetic mean, 93–95
Armed Forces Qualification Test (AFQT), 329
Armed Services Vocational Aptitude Battery (ASVAB), 329–332
Arnett v. Ricketts, 66–67
Arthur Adaptation of the Leiter International Performance Scale, 615
ASL. *See* American Sign Language
Assessment
  assumptions in, 13, 15–24
  bias in, 22–23
  culture and, 53–60

defined, 6
error variance and, 21
ethical and legal considerations in, 60–81
testing vs., 4–6
tools for, 6–13, 14
See also specific types of assessment by name
Assessment center method, 640–642
Assessment of Development Levels by Observation (ADLO), 616–617
Assessment of Men (OSS), 6, 52
Assessment tools, 6–13, 14
  behavioral observation, 12
  case study, 11–12
  interviews, 9–10
  portfolios, 10–11
  tests, 6–8
Assimilation, 262
Association for Children and Adults with Learning Disabilities, 363
Association of Personnel Test Publishers, 668–669
AST. *See* Reitan-Indiana Aphasia Screening Test
ASVAB. *See* Armed Services Vocational Aptitude Battery
Asymptotic curve, 107
ATQ-N. *See* Automatic Thoughts Questionnaire
ATQ-P. *See* Positive Automatic Thoughts Questionnaire
At-risk preschool children, 338
Attitude measures
  Child's Attitude Toward Mother/Father Scale, 537
  Condom Attitude Scale—Adolescent Version, 556, 557
  in consumer assessment, 673–674
  in educational assessment, 379–380
  in industrial/organizational assessment, 664–666
  Likert scales, 223–224
  on people with disabling conditions, 618
  on sexual knowledge, 630, 631
Attribute rating, 686
Auditory functioning tests, 589
''Aunt Fanny'' effect, 558, 560
Authentic assessment, 377, 378–379
Automatic Thoughts Questionnaire (ATQ-N), 530
Average deviation, 101–103
A-V-L. *See* Allport-Vernon-Lindzey Study of Values

Banding, 217
Bar graph, 93, 94

Barnum effect, 557–558, 560–562, 723–724
Base rates, 80–81, 190, 301, 604
Basic English Skills Test (BEST), 348
Basic Inventory of Natural Language (BINL), 348
Battelle Developmental Inventory (BDI), 339
Batteries. *See* Test batteries
Bayley Scales for Infant Development, Second Edition (BSID-II), 160–161, 339
BDI. *See* Battelle Developmental Inventory; Beck Depression Inventory
Beavers-Timberlawn Family Evaluation Scale, 537
Beck Depression Inventory (BDI), 181, 528–529
Beck Self-Concept Test (BST), 465–466
Beery-Buktenica Development Test of Visual-Motor Integration, 590
Behavior
  adaptive, 621–630
  assessing problems with, 29
  functional analysis of, 490, 492
  giftedness and, 277, 278
  nervous system and, 564–569
  test-related predictions about, 22
  type A and type B, 408n
Behavioral assessment, 482–497
  analogue studies, 490, 492
  behavioral observation, 12, 487
  behavior rating scales, 277, 279, 466, 487–490, 498–499
  computer-assisted, 718–721
  issues in, 494–497
  overview of, 482–487
  psychophysiological methods of, 497–502
  role play, 493
  self-monitoring, 492
  third-party, 502–509
  traditional psychological assessment vs., 485
  unobtrusive measures, 493–494
Behavioral observation, 12, 487, 676–677
Behavior Problem Checklist, 466, 615
Behavior Rating Profile, 488
Behavior rating scales, 277, 279, 466, 487–490, 498–499
Behn-Rorschach Test, 430
Beier-Sternberg Discord Questionnaire, 537
Bell Adjustment Inventory, 501
Bell Curve: Intelligence and Class Structure in American Life, The (Herrnstein and Murray), 62, 282

Bell-shaped curve. *See* Normal curve
Bender Visual-Motor Gestalt test, 571n, 591–592, 594–595
  emotional indicators on, 595
  hearing impairments and, 614
  sample errors on, 594
Bennet Mechanical Comprehension Test, 643
Benton Test of Visual Retention—Revised, 582
BEST. *See* Basic English Skills Test
Bias, test, 200–201, 208–214
  assessment process and, 22–23
  culture and, 53–58, 288–294
  defined, 200
  fairness and, 212–214
  federal courts and, 211–212
  item analysis and, 243, 246
  race-norming and, 645, 650
  rating error and, 210–211
  rating scales and, 505–509
Bilingual Vocational Oral Proficiency Test (BVOPT), 348
Bimodal distribution, 96
Binet-Simon Scale, 296
BINL. *See* Basic Inventory of Natural Language
Biofeedback, 13, 497, 500
Biophysical definitions of personality, 383n
Biosocial definitions of personality, 383n
BITCH. *See* Black Intelligence Test of Cultural Homogeneity
Black English, 57–58
Black Intelligence Test of Cultural Homogeneity (BITCH), 290–291
Blacks. *See* African Americans
Blacky Pictures Test, 420, 448
Blind Learning Aptitude Test, 610
Blindness
  assessment process and, 607–611
  with deafness, 615–617
Body image tests, 14, 457–458
Body language, 58
Borderline personality disorder, 519
Boys and Girls Book About Divorce, The, 549
Braille tests, 610
Brain
  anatomy of, 564–569
  damage to, 568–569, 570, 571
  intelligence and, 264
Brain scans, 578
Brain Watchers, The (Gross), 61
Brain-wave measurement, 697
Branched testing, 301, 682
Brand equity, 690–691
Breathalyzer test, 166–167

Broad-band instruments, 488
Bruininks-Oseretsky Test of Motor Proficiency, 589, 619
BSID-II. *See* Bayley Scales for Infant Development, Second Edition
BST. *See* Beck Self-Concept Test
Bulimia nervosa, 14, 199
Burnout, 199n
Bureau of the Census, 683
Business assessment, 31–32
  See also Industrial/organizational assessment
Business letter format, 347
BVOPT. *See* Bilingual Vocational Oral Proficiency Test

California Achievement Tests, 340, 342–343
California Psychological Inventory (CPI), 418n
California Q-Sort, 468
California Test of Mental Maturity, 328
Callery v. New York City Parks and Recreation Department, 670
Callier-Azusa Scale (CAS), 616
Cannot Say scale, 404
CAP. *See* Child Abuse Potential Inventory
CAPA. *See* Computer-assisted psychological assessment
Career, defined, 634
Career Decision Scale, 654
Carl D. Perkins Vocational Act of 1984, 364
CAS. *See* Callier-Azusa Scale
Casebook on Ethical Principles of Psychologists (APA), 67
Case history, 11–12
  in clinical and counseling assessment, 11–12, 521–524
  giftedness assessment and, 277
CAST. *See* Children's Apperceptive Story-Telling Test
CAT. *See* Children's Apperception Test
Catalogues, test, 38
Categorical scaling, 225
CATI. *See* Computer-assisted test interpretation
CAT scan, 578, 579
CBA. *See* Curriculum-based assessment
CDI. *See* Children's Depression Inventory
CDR. *See* Clinical data recorder
Ceiling effect, 276
Ceiling level, 301
CELT. *See* Comprehensive English Language Test
Center for Epidemiological Studies (CES), 530

Central nervous system, 13, 564
Central processing, 713
Central tendency error, 210, 505
Cerebral palsy, 617, 619
Cerebral vascular disease, 579
CES-D (Center for Epidemiological Studies depression measure), 530
Character Education Inquiry, 472–473
Characteristic root, 207
Child abuse and neglect, 80–81, 550–554
  emotional and behavioral signs of, 552
  issues in reporting, 552–553
  physical signs of, 550–551
  risk assessment, 553–554
Child Abuse Potential Inventory (CAP), 80, 553–554
Child Behavior Checklist, 488, 490, 615
Children
  at-risk, 338
  cognitive style measures, 474, 476–482
  custody evaluations of, 548–550
  gifted, 275, 276
  measuring intelligence of, 270–271
  Personality Inventory for Children, 502–504
  physical abuse of, 80–81, 550–554
  Rorschach Inkblot Test and, 438, 440
  self-concept tests, 466–467
  situational performance measures, 472–473
Children's Apperception Test (CAT, CAT-H), 448, 549
Children's Apperceptive Story-Telling Test (CAST), 448–449
Children's Depression Inventory (CDI), 466, 529–530
Children's Embedded Figures Test, 477
Child's Attitude Toward Mother/Father Scale, 537
Chinese testing program, 41
Civil Rights Act
  of 1964, 63, 64
  of 1991, 215, 216
Classical test theory, 164, 480–481
Classification, employment, 634–635
Classroom tests, 253–254
CLEP. *See* College Level Examination Program
Clinical and counseling assessment, 30–31, 512–562
  case history, 11–12, 521–524
  child abuse and neglect, 550–554

Credits

Chapter 1—Figure 1-1: Photo by Karl Weatherly, © Tony Stone Worldwide. Page 9: Jim Estrin/NYT Pictures. Figure 1-2: AP/Wide World Photos. Figure 1-4: Mike Albans, AP/Wide World Photos. Figure 1-5: Courtesy National Archives. Page 34: From "Do You Have What It Takes?" by Robyn Carr, *Writer's Digest,* 1994. Reprinted by permission of the author.

Chapter 2—Figure 2-1: By Maynard Owen Williams. Copyright © 1927 National Geographic Society. Figure 2-2: Courtesy Staatsbibliothek, Bildarchiv, Berlin. Page 47: National Portrait Gallery, London. Used by permission. Page 48: Photo of James McKeen Cattell from the *Journal of Consulting Psychology,* Vol. 1, Number 1 (1937): In the public domain. Photo of Dr. Psyche Cattell courtesy of Hudson Cattell. Page 52: Courtesy Henry A. Murray. Page 55: Photo by Brown Brothers, *Life Magazine,* September 1990.

Chapter 4—Page 132: University College, London. Page 135: University College, London.

Chapter 5—Page 167: AP/Wide World Photos.

Chapter 6—Table 6-1: From Lawshe (1975). Copyright © 1974 Personnel Psychology, Inc. Reprinted by permission. Figure 6-1 and Table 6-2: From the Manual for the Differential Aptitude Tests. Copyright © 1973, 1974 by The Psychological Corporation. All rights reserved. Figure 6-2: *Test Service Bulletin,* "How Effective Are Your Tests?" Copyright © 1949 by The Psychological Corporation. Reproduced by permission. All rights reserved.

Chapter 7—Figures 7-3, 7-4: From *Introduction to Measurement Theory* by M. J. Allen and W. M. Yen. Copyright © 1979 by Wadsworth Inc. Reprinted by permission of Brooks/Cole Publishing Company, Pacific Grove, California. Figure 7-5: From *Measurement Theory for the Behavioral Sciences* by Ghiselli, Campbell, and Zedeck. Copyright © 1981 by W. H. Freeman and Company. Used with permission. Page 251: From Jackson (1970, p. 84). Reprinted by permission of the publisher. Copyright © 1970 Academic Press.

Chapter 8—Figure 8-2: Copyright © McGraw-Hill Book Company. Reproduced by permission. Figure 8-3: Reproduced by permission of the authors from Powell, *Assessment and Management of Developmental Changes and Problems in Children,* 2nd ed., 1981. Page 292: Sample test items from Cattell, R. B. (1940). A culture-free intelligence test, Part 1. *Journal of Educational Psychology,* 31, 161–179. In the public domain. Page 293: Copyright © 1977 by *Phi Delta Kappan* and reproduced by permission of the author and *Phi Delta Kappan.*

Chapter 9—Page 304: Courtesy Mrs. David Wechsler. Figure 9-1: Photo copyright © 1987 Sid Hecker. Figure 9-2: From *Children's Drawings as Measures of Intellectual Maturity.* Copyright © 1963 by The Psychological Corporation. Reproduced by permission. All rights re-

served. Pages 330–331: Permission to reprint granted by the Director of Testing, Headquarters, United States Military Entrance Processing Command, North Chicago, IL. Figure 9-3: Copyright © 1940 Meier Art Judgment Test. The University of Iowa, Iowa City, IA.

Chapter 10—Page 351: Model: Barbara Rich. Courtesy Richard Pavlo Photography and Insurance. Table 10-6: Reprinted from Kaufman, A. S., Kaufman, N. L., and Goldsmith, B. Z., Kaufman *Sequential or Simultaneous* (K-SOS) (1984) with modifications. Circle Pines, MN: American Guidance Service.

Chapter 11—Page 403: S. R. Hathaway quote from Mednick, Higgins, & Kirschenbaum (1975). Reprinted by permission of John Wiley & Sons. Photo, © 1987 Ronald Jay Cohen. All rights reserved. Page 407: Photos courtesy James Butcher, W. Grant Dahlstrom, and John R. Graham. Page 412: "Are Unisex Norms for the MMPI-2 Needed? Would They Work?" by Auke Tellegen, James Butcher, and Tawni Hoeglund, reprinted with permission from *MMPI-2 & MMPI-A News & Profiles,* 1993, *4* (1), 4–5.

Chapter 12—Page 427: Photo copyright © Hans Huber Publishers, Bern. Figure 12-4: Courtesy of Century Diagnostics Computer Interpreted Rorschach Report, Tempe, AZ. Page 431: From *Journal of Personality Assessment* 56:1, Reprinted by permission of Lawrence Erlbaum Associates, Inc. Page 439: Photo courtesy John E. Exner. Page 455: Illustrations from E. F. Hammer's "Projective Drawings," in A. L. Rabin's (ed.) *Assessment with Projective Techniques,* copyright © 1981 by Springer Publishing Company, Inc., New York. Used by permission.

Chapter 13—Page 475: Photo © 1988 by Ronald Jay Cohen. Used by permission. Figure 13-1: Tilting-room/tilting chair photo by David Linton, from *Scientific American,* February 1959. Figure 13-1 Modified and reproduced by special permission of the Publisher, Consulting Psychologists Press, Inc., Palo Alto, CA 94303, from *Group Embedded Figures Test* by Philip K. Oltman, Evelyn Raskin, and Herman Witkin. Copyright © 1971 by Consulting Psychologists Press, Inc. All rights reserved. Further reproduction is prohibited without the Publisher's written consent. Table 13-1: From "Differences between behavioral and traditional approaches to assessment," by D. B. Hartmann, B. L. Roper & D. C. Bradford in *Journal of Behavioral Assessment,* 1979. Reprinted by permission of Plenum Publishing Corporation. Figure 13-3: From B. A. Iwata, G. M. Pace, P. A. Nau, J. M. Farber, "The Self-Injury Trauma (SIT) Scale: A Method for Quantifying Surface Tissue Damage Caused by Self-Injurious Behavior," *Journal of Behavior Analysis,* 23.

Chapter 14—Page 526: Photo courtesy Dr. Elvira R. Strasser. Tables 14-1, 14-2, 14-3, 14-4: Copyright © 1971, the American Psychiatric Association. Reprinted with permission. Figure 14-1: left: CAT-H card reproduced by permission of the publisher, CPS, Inc., Larchmont, New York; right: reproduced by permission of Jason Aronson, Inc. Table 14-6: Condom Attitude Scale–Adolescent Version from "Attitudes About Condom Use as an AIDS-Relevant Behavior: Their Factor Structure and Relation to Condom Use" by W. P. Sacco, B. Levine, D. L. Reed, and K. Thompson, 1991, *Psychological Assessment: A Journal of Consulting and Clinical Psychology, 3,* 265–272. Copyright © 1991 by The American Psychological Association.

Chapter 15—Figure 15-3: Goldstein-Scheerer Color/Object Sorting and Color Form/Stick/Cube tests reproduced by permission of the Psychological Corporation, San Antonio, Texas. All rights reserved. Page 579: Photos courtesy General Electric Medical Systems. Figure 15-4: Seguin formboard photo courtesy of the C. H. Steolting Company, Chicago, Illinois. Tactile nonsense figures from Milner & Taylor (1972). Right hemisphere superiority in tactile pattern-recognition after cerebral commissurotomy. *Neuropsychologia, 10,* 1–15. Copyright © 1972 Pergamon Journals Ltd. Reprinted by permission. Figure 15-5: Photo courtesy of Cinerama Releasing Corporation. Page 587: Mooney Closure Faces Test from Mooney (1957). Copyright © 1957 Canadian Psychological Association. Reprinted with permission; Field of Search Item from Warren and Ekert, *Cortex and Behavior,* McGraw-Hill Book Company. Figure 15-7: Photo of Neuro Developmental Training Balls used by permission of Lafayette Instrument, a Bissell Healthcare Company. Figure 15-8: Photo of the Purdue Pegboard used by permission of the Lafayette Instrument Company, a Bissell Healthcare Company. Page 593: Photo

courtesy Dr. Peter Schilder; Lauretta Bender biographical material adapted from Stevens and Gardner (1982) with permission of the publisher, Schenkman Publishing. Figure 15-9: Test figures reproduced from the Bender Visual Motor Gestalt Test published by the American Orthopsychiatric Association, copyright © 1938. Figure 15-10: Courtesy the C. H. Stoelting Company, Chicago, Illinois.

Chapter 16—Figure 16-1: Photo courtesy of the C. H. Stoelting Company, Chicago, Illinois. Table 16-1: Reprinted with a change in notation by permission of the publisher. Copyright © 1955, American Association of Mental Deficiency. Figure 16-2: Photo courtesy of the C. H. Stoelting Company, Chicago, Illinois.

Chapter 17—Figure 17-1: "Manufacturing Problem" courtesy Dr. Douglas Bray. Used by permission; JET videogame copyright © 1985 Sublogic Corporation. Table 17-2: Copyright by the American Psychological Association. Reprinted by permission of the publisher and the author. Figure 17-2: Photo of the O'Connor Tweezer Dexterity Test by permission of the Lafayette Instrument Company, Lafayette, Indiana. Page 656: Photos of Katharine Briggs and Isabel Briggs Myers courtesy Center for Applications of Psychological Type, Inc. Figure 17-4: From J. E. Champaigne (1969). Job recruitment of the unskilled. *Personnel Journal, 48,* 259–268. Copyright 1968 by Personnel Journal, Inc.

Chapter 18—Figure 18-3: From Urban/Hauser, *Design and Marketing of New Products,* © 1980, p. 260. Adapted by permission of Prentice-Hall, Inc. Figure 18-4: Photo by Leo J. Kadehjian.

Chapter 19—Figure 19-1: Copyright © 1985, 1987 WICAT Systems, Inc. Reprinted with permission.